# Current Biography Yearbook® 2002

EDITOR
Clifford Thompson

SENIOR EDITOR
Miriam Helbok

PRODUCTION STAFF
Gray Young (Manager)
Steven C. Brown
Tia Brown
Richard J. Stein
Sandra Watson

ASSISTANT EDITORS
Jeremy K. Brown
Peter G. Herman

CONTRIBUTING EDITOR
Kieran Dugan

STAFF WRITERS
Karen E. Duda
Geoff Orens
Luke A. Stanton
Hope Tarullo
Cullen F. Thomas

CONTRIBUTING WRITERS
Dimitri Cavalli
Andrew I. Cavin
Kathleen A. D'Angelo
Josha Hill
Martha A. Hostetter
Patrick Kelly
Christopher Mari
Mari Rich
Kate Stern
Aaron Tassano

RESEARCHER
Verna J. Coleman

EDITORIAL ASSISTANT
Carolyn Ellis

THE H. W. WILSON COMPANY
NEW YORK DUBLIN

SIXTY-THIRD ANNUAL CUMULATION—2002

PRINTED IN THE UNITED STATES OF AMERICA

*International Standard Serial No. (0084-9499)*

*International Standard Book No. (0-8242-1026-3)*

*Library of Congress Catalog Card No. (40-27432)*

# Table of Contents

**Preface** . . . . . . . . . . . . . . . . . . . . . . . . . . . . . . . . . . . **v**

**List of Biographical Sketches** . . . . . . . . . . . . **vii**

**Biographical Sketches**. . . . . . . . . . . . . . . . . . . . . **1**

**Obituaries** . . . . . . . . . . . . . . . . . . . . . . . . . . . **603**

**Classification by Profession—2002**. . . . . . . . **662**

**2001–2002 Index** . . . . . . . . . . . . . . . . . . . . . . . . **666**

# PREFACE

The aim of *Current Biography Yearbook 2002*, like that of the preceding volumes in this series of annual dictionaries of contemporary biography, now in its seventh decade of publication, is to provide reference librarians, students, and researchers with objective, accurate, and well-documented biographical articles about living leaders in all fields of human accomplishment. Whenever feasible, obituary notices appear for persons whose biographies have been published in *Current Biography.*

*Current Biography Yearbook 2002* carries on the policy of including new and updated biographical profiles that supersede earlier articles. Profiles have been made as accurate and objective as possible through careful researching of newspapers, magazines, the World Wide Web, authoritative reference books, and news releases of both government and private agencies. Immediately after they are published in the 11 monthly issues, articles are submitted to biographees to give them an opportunity to suggest additions and corrections in time for publication of the *Current Biography Yearbook.* To take account of major changes in the careers of biographees, articles are revised before they are included in the yearbook.

*Classification by Profession—2002* and *2001–2002 Index* are at the end of this volume. *Current Biography Cumulated Index 1940–2000* cumulates and supersedes all previous indexes.

For their assistance in preparing *Current Biography Yearbook 2002*, I thank the staff of *Current Biography* and other members of The H. W. Wilson Company's General Reference Department, and also the staffs of the company's Computer and Manufacturing departments.

*Current Biography* welcomes comments and suggestions. Please send your comments to: The Editor, *Current Biography*, The H. W. Wilson Company, 950 University Ave., Bronx, NY 10452; fax: 718-590-4566; E-mail: cthompson@hwwilson.com.

Clifford Thompson

# List of Biographical Sketches

Yolanda Adams, *Gospel singer* .................... 1

Julie Aigner-Clark, *Creator of the Baby Einstein videos and books* .................... 3

Ken Alibek, *Microbiologist and biological-warfare expert* .................... 5

Don L. Anderson, *Geophysicist* .................... 8

Wes Anderson, *Screenwriter and film director* .................... 11

Kwame Anthony Appiah, *Writer and educator* .................... 14

María Celeste Arrarás, *Broadcast journalist* .................... 17

Scott Bakula, *Actor, director, and producer* .................... 20

Ashleigh Banfield, *Television newscaster and journalist* .................... 23

Etta Moten Barnett, *Singer and actress* .................... 25

Arnold O. Beckman, *Scientist, inventor, entrepreneur, and philanthropist* .................... 27

Bill Belichick, *Coach of the New England Patriots* .................... 29

Geoffrey C. Bible, *Businessman* .................... 32

Jack Black, *Actor and musician* .................... 35

blink-182, *Rock band* .................... 37

Michael R. Bloomberg, *Founder of Bloomberg L.P. and mayor of New York City* .................... 40

Andrea Bocelli, *Singer* .................... 46

Olga Borodina, *Opera singer* .................... 49

Mark Bowden, *Writer and journalist* .................... 50

Rick Bragg, *Journalist and memoirist* .................... 54

Bob Brenly, *Manager of the Arizona Diamondbacks* .................... 57

Bob Brier, *Egyptologist and professor of philosophy* .................... 60

Martin Brodeur, *Hockey player with the New Jersey Devils* .................... 63

Bob Broeg, *Sportswriter and sportscaster* .................... 65

Tom Brokaw, *Broadcast journalist and anchor of* NBC Nightly News .................... 67

Kwame Brown, *Basketball player for the Washington Wizards* .................... 72

Lee P. Brown, *Mayor of Houston* .................... 74

Ronald K. Brown, *Dancer and choreographer* .................... 77

Priscilla Buckley, *Former editor at the* National Review .................... 79

Mary-Ellis Bunim and Jonathan Murray, *Television producers and co-creators of* The Real World .................... 81

Vince Carter, *Basketball player with the Toronto Raptors* .................... 84

Richard B. Cheney, *Vice president of the United States* .................... 87

Hillary Rodham Clinton, *U.S. senator from New York and former First Lady of the U.S.* .................... 93

Daniel Clowes, *Comic-book artist and screenwriter* ........ 101
Thad Cochran, *U.S. senator from Mississippi* ........ 103
Rob Cohen, *Film director and producer* ........ 106
Linda Cohn, *Broadcast journalist* ........ 109
Sophia Collier, *Entrepreneur* ........ 111
Jennifer Connelly, *Actress* ........ 115
Craig Counsell, *Baseball player with the Arizona Diamondbacks* ........ 119
Creed, *Rock band* ........ 121
Nancy Currie, *Astronaut* ........ 124
Howard Dean, *Governor of Vermont* ........ 127
Nelson DeMille, *Writer* ........ 131
William Eddins, *Pianist and conductor* ........ 134
Jennifer Egan, *Writer* ........ 135
William Eggleston, *Photographer* ........ 137
Emerson String Quartet ........ 140
Eve Ensler, *Playwright, actress, and social activist* ........ 144
Oskar Eustis, *Artistic director of the Trinity Repertory Company* ........ 147
Etienne Gnassingbé Eyadéma, *President of the Republic of Togo* ........ 150
Sandra Faber, *Astronomer and astrophysicist* ........ 152
Jimmy Fallon, *Writer and actor on* Saturday Night Live ........ 154
Tina Fey, *Head writer for and actress on* Saturday Night Live ........ 156
The Flaming Lips, *Rock group* ........ 158
Jonathan Safran Foer, *Writer* ........ 162
Vernon Forrest, *Boxer* ........ 165
Shirley C. Franklin, *Mayor of Atlanta* ........ 167
Tommy R. Franks, *Commander in chief, United States Central Command* ........ 170
Bill Frist, *U.S. senator from Tennessee and surgeon* ........ 172
Fugazi, *Rock band* ........ 176
Ed Garza, *Mayor of San Antonio, Texas* ........ 179
Helene Gayle, *Epidemiologist and senior adviser for HIV/AIDS at the Bill and Melinda Gates Foundation* ........ 182
Michael Gerson, *Chief speechwriter for President George W. Bush* ........ 185
Charles Gibson, *Co-anchor of* Good Morning America ........ 186
Alberto R. Gonzales, *White House counsel* ........ 190
Franklin Graham, *Evangelist, CEO of the Billy Graham Evangelistic Association, and president of Samaritan's Purse* ........ 193
Richard Grasso, *Chairman and CEO of the New York Stock Exchange* ........ 197
Wilton D. Gregory, *President of the U.S. Conference of Catholic Bishops* ........ 200

Dave Grohl, *Singer, songwriter, and rock musician* .......... 202
David Grubin, *Documentary filmmaker* .......... 206
Hilary Hahn, *Violinist* .......... 210
Deidre Hall, *Star of the TV soap opera* Days of Our Lives .......... 213
William B. Harrison Jr., *CEO of J. P. Morgan Chase & Co.* .......... 215
Carolyn Hax, *Advice columnist* .......... 217
Donald A. Henderson, *Epidemiologist and director of the federal Office of Public Health Preparedness* .......... 219
Jacques Herzog and Pierre de Meuron, *Architects* .......... 223
Lleyton Hewitt, *Tennis player* .......... 226
Sylvia Ann Hewlett, *Economist, social activist, and writer* .......... 228
Chester Higgins Jr., *Photographer and writer* .......... 232
Grant Hill, *Basketball player with the Orlando Magic* .......... 234
Ian Holm, *Actor* .......... 237
Bernard Hopkins, *Boxer* .......... 241
Nancy Hopkins, *Molecular biologist, educator, and social activist* .......... 243
Jane Dee Hull, *Governor of Arizona* .......... 245
India.Arie, *Singer and songwriter* .......... 247
Juli Inkster, *Golfer* .......... 250
Ja Rule, *Rapper* .......... 253
Hal Jackson, *Radio personality and entrepreneur* .......... 255
Peter Jackson, *Film director, producer, and screenwriter* .......... 258
Edgerrin James, *Football player with the Indianapolis Colts* .......... 262
Jay-Z, *Rapper* .......... 264
Elizabeth A. Johnson, *Feminist theologian and educator* .......... 267
Bobby Jones, *Television host and gospel singer* .......... 268
Tom Joyner, *Radio personality* .......... 271
Jackie Judd, *Broadcast journalist* .......... 274
Dean Kamen, *Inventor and entrepreneur* .......... 276
Hamid Karzai, *President of Afghanistan* .......... 280
Leon R. Kass, *Bioethicist* .......... 283
Catherine Keener, *Actress* .......... 288
Randall Kennedy, *Writer and educator* .......... 290
Jason Kidd, *Basketball player with the New Jersey Nets* .......... 293
Junichiro Koizumi, *Prime minister of Japan* .......... 296
Anna Kournikova, *Tennis player* .......... 301
David W. Krause, *Paleontologist* .......... 303
Tony Kushner, *Playwright and director* .......... 307
La India, *Salsa singer* .......... 311

Ty Law, *Football player with the New England Patriots* ..... 313
Meave Leakey, *Paleontologist* ..... 315
Jeanette Lee, *Professional pool player* ..... 318
Al Leiter, *Pitcher with the New York Mets* ..... 320
David Letterman, *Television talk-show host, writer, and producer* ..... 323
Eugene Levy, *Actor, director, screenwriter, and producer* ..... 327
Abbey Lincoln, *Jazz singer, songwriter, and actress* ..... 329
Blanche Lambert Lincoln, *U.S. senator from Arkansas* ..... 332
Linkin Park, *Rock band* ..... 334
Charles Lloyd, *Jazz saxophonist* ..... 337
George Lucas, *Film director, producer, and screenwriter* ..... 339
Bernie Mac, *Comedian and actor* ..... 348
Tobey Maguire, *Actor* ..... 351
Emily Mann, *Playwright and theater director* ..... 354
Geoffrey W. Marcy and R. Paul Butler, *Astrophysicists* ..... 358
Doug Marlette, *Cartoonist and writer* ..... 362
Connie L. Matsui, *National president of Girl Scouts of the USA* ..... 365
Phillip McGraw, *Psychologist, writer, and television personality* ..... 366
Tim McGraw, *Country singer and guitarist* ..... 370
Alexander McQueen, *Fashion designer* ..... 373
Sam Mendes, *Film and stage director* ..... 376
Jean-Marie Messier, *Businessman* ..... 380
Debra Messing, *Actress* ..... 385
Ilir Meta, *Albanian politician* ..... 387
Edgar Meyer, *Bass player and composer* ..... 390
Nancy Meyers, *Filmmaker and screenwriter* ..... 394
Phil Mickelson, *Golfer* ..... 396
Dan Millman, *Writer and former champion gymnast* ..... 399
Robert Mirabal, *Flutist, percussionist, singer, and songwriter* ..... 402
Dean Mitchell, *Artist* ..... 404
T. S. Monk, *Jazz drummer* ..... 407
Gordon E. Moore, *Computer pioneer, chairman emeritus of Intel Corp., and philanthropist* ..... 409
Marc Morial, *Former mayor of New Orleans* ..... 413
Robert P. Moses, *Educator, civil rights activist, and founder and president of the Algebra Project* ..... 416
Anne M. Mulcahy, *Chair and CEO of Xerox* ..... 420
Ty Murray, *Rodeo performer* ..... 423
Richard B. Myers, *Chairman of the Joint Chiefs of Staff* ..... 425

Kathy Najimy, *Actress, director, producer, and playwright* .................... 430
Nelly, *Rapper* .................... 433
Michael J. Novacek, *Paleontologist and museum curator* .................... 435
Dirk Nowitzki, *Basketball player with the Dallas Mavericks* .................... 439
Jorma Ollila, *Chairman and CEO of Nokia* .................... 441
Sherry B. Ortner, *Anthropologist* .................... 444
Linda Sue Park, *Children's writer* .................... 447
Amy Pascal, *Chairwoman of Columbia Pictures* .................... 449
Peter Pau, *Cinematographer* .................... 451
Henry M. Paulson Jr., *Chairman and chief executive officer of the Goldman Sachs Group* .................... 453
Dave Pelzer, *Writer and self-help promoter* .................... 456
Paul Pierce, *Basketball player with the Boston Celtics* .................... 457
Harvey Pitt, *Former chairman of the U.S. Securities and Exchange Commission* .................... 459
Martha Plimpton, *Actress* .................... 463
Katha Pollitt, *Writer* .................... 466
Didier Queloz, *Astrophysicist* .................... 469
Sam Raimi, *Filmmaker* .................... 472
Ted Rall, *Editorial cartoonist and newspaper columnist* .................... 475
Manny Ramirez, *Baseball player with the Boston Red Sox* .................... 478
Charlotte Rampling, *Actress* .................... 481
Robert K. Ressler, *Criminologist and writer* .................... 484
Cruz Reynoso, *Vice chairman of the U.S. Commission on Civil Rights and former California Supreme Court justice* .................... 486
Gerhard Richter, *Artist* .................... 488
Terry Riley, *Composer and musician* .................... 491
Sylvia B. Rimm, *Educational psychologist* .................... 494
Skip Rimsza, *Mayor of Phoenix* .................... 496
Anthony Romero, *Executive director of the American Civil Liberties Union* .................... 498
Robert Ross, *Entrepreneur and medical-school founder* .................... 501
Donald H. Rumsfeld, *U.S. secretary of defense* .................... 503
John Sandford, *Crime novelist* .................... 510
José Saramago, *Nobel Prize–winning novelist, poet, and playwright* .................... 512
Jill Scott, *Singer and songwriter* .................... 516
Amy Sedaris, *Playwright and actress* .................... 518
Stephanie Seymour, *Fashion model* .................... 521
Tony Shalhoub, *Actor, director, and producer* .................... 522
Maggie Smith, *Actress* .................... 525

Olga Soffer, *Anthropologist and archaeologist* .......... 530
Susan Stroman, *Theatrical choreographer and director* .......... 533
Bert Randolph Sugar, *Sportswriter* .......... 537
Lawrence H. Summers, *President of Harvard University and former U.S. secretary of the treasury* .......... 539
Kiefer Sutherland, *Actor and film director* .......... 542
Ichiro Suzuki, *Baseball player with the Seattle Mariners* .......... 545
Koko Taylor, *Blues singer and songwriter* .......... 548
Tom Toles, *Editorial cartoonist* .......... 552
Mark Turner, *Jazz tenor saxophonist* .......... 554
Tweet, *Singer and songwriter* .......... 556
Nick Van Exel, *Basketball player with the Denver Nuggets* .......... 558
Meredith Vieira, *Television news journalist and co-host of* The View .......... 561
Mort Walker, *Creator of the* Beetle Bailey *comic strip* .......... 564
Valerie Wilson Wesley, *Mystery writer, novelist, and editor* .......... 566
Ken Wilber, *Writer and philosopher* .......... 568
Tyrone Willingham, *Head coach for the Notre Dame Fighting Irish football team* .......... 572
James Q. Wilson, *Political scientist and writer* .......... 575
Stan Winston, *Makeup artist and special-effects designer* .......... 579
Elijah Wood, *Actor* .......... 584
Jeffrey Wright, *Actor* .......... 587
Paula Zahn, *News anchor for CNN* .......... 589
Hans Zimmer, *Film composer* .......... 592
Anthony C. Zinni, *Special U.S. envoy to the Middle East* .......... 596
Jeff Zucker, *Head of NBC's entertainment division* .......... 599

# Current Biography Yearbook® 2002

# Current Biography Yearbook 2002

Steve Granitz/Retna Ltd.

## Adams, Yolanda

*Aug. 27, 1961– Gospel singer*

*Address: c/o Elektra Records, 75 Rockefeller Plaza, 15th Fl., New York, NY 10019*

Since the release of her first album, *Just As I Am*, in 1987, the gospel singer Yolanda Adams has found increasing success and visibility with each new enterprise. Believing that her jazz- and R&B–infused melodies would attract listeners beyond gospel's traditional fan base, she signed a contract with the mainstream label Elektra Records in 1999 and has since enjoyed brisk record sales. "I am making a conscious effort to not fit the mold," she told Lisa Collins for *Billboard* (July 8, 1995). "Sometimes you have to go out and do it differently. As a Christian, I'm not supposed to be like everybody else or follow what's going on. I am supposed to tread new ground." Adams has been praised by both the religious and secular music industries; she has won a number of Stellar Awards, honoring gospel music, as well as two Grammy Awards, five Image Awards from the National Association for the Advancement of Colored People (NAACP), two Soul Train Lady of Soul Awards, and an American Music Award. "I'm not out to change gospel music or anything like that," she told Joy Duckett Cain for *Essence* (July 2001). "I'm out to give God his just due, and my goal is to show people how really cool God is. . . . I know what I've been sent here for, and that's to make life easier for people as they go through their stuff."

The eldest of the six children of schoolteachers Major and Caroline Adams, Yolanda Yvette Adams was born on August 27, 1961 in Houston, Texas. Her family was tightly knit and religious, as she recalled to Shirley Henderson for the *Chicago Tribune* (December 24, 1995): "Our family was always in church. Our involvement kept us away from the negative elements." The family was also involved in musical endeavors; Adams's mother, who had been a music major in college, played the piano, and her father sang in the choir at Berean Baptist Church, where Adams joined him at age four. When she was 13 her father died of complications stemming from a car accident; Adams was suddenly thrust into the role of caretaker for her siblings and grieving mother. "At 13 I'm picking out flowers, a casket and making all the arrangements . . . ," she explained to Joy Duckett Cain. "[My mother] was 33, and the love of her life was gone. She was like: 'What am I going to do?'" Soon after her father's death, Adams was able to rededicate herself to music, when she joined the Southeast Inspirational Choir, a 25-member group of young professional singers drawn from Houston churches. After high school Adams attended Texas Southern University as a commuter student, living at home to help raise her younger siblings. Adams, who stood six-foot-one, "wanted to model," as she recalled to Henderson, but her grandfather "told me that as the oldest of six kids I should go to college and set an example." She graduated with a degree in radio and television communications and had hopes of becoming a television anchorwoman. After those plans failed to work out, she earned her teaching credentials and went to work in the Houston public schools.

While happily teaching second and third grades, Adams made time to continue singing with the Southeast Inspirational Choir. "I was teaching school during the week and singing on the weekends. So I had the best of everything," she explained in an interview for *Jet* (January 14, 2002). After a choir performance in 1986, she met the songwriter-producer Thomas Whitfield, who offered to produce a record for her. In 1987 they collaborated on her first album, *Just As I Am*, for the Sound of Gospel label. That good fortune was due largely to her membership in the Southeast Inspirational Choir, as she admitted to Geoffrey Himes for the *Washington Post* (February 11, 2000): "It was like everything was planned out for me. As a teenager, I was already making records and traveling all over the United States and Europe. I didn't have to record a demo; I didn't have to pound the pavement to get a deal, because I was already in one of the biggest choirs in the United States." She garnered a small following among gospel aficionados with *Just As I Am* and was offered a contract with Tribute/Verity Records, a gospel label, in 1990. Her first Tribute album, *Through the Storm*, was released in the following year. During this period she performed on the weekends as a solo act. Ultimately, as she told Himes, the dual career became overwhelming: "The engagements kept coming more and more, and I was making as much [money] on the weekends as I was during the week." In 1992 Adams left teaching to concentrate on music full-time, a risky venture for a gospel artist. "When I first started with Thomas Whitfield, my plan was to do the album during the summer on my time off from teaching," she explained to Lisa Collins in 1995. "I never dreamed of leaving the school system, and when I did it was a huge step, but I'm so glad I took that step on faith."

Adams's second Tribute album, *Save the World* (1993), quickly outpaced her previous recordings and spent more than a year on *Billboard*'s gospel chart. *Save the World* and one of its singles, "The Battle Is the Lord's," led to Adams's first honors at the Stellar Awards. She took home three 1994 Stellar Awards and won a legion of new fans, who appreciated the fact that her lyrics, while based on her religious faith, addressed difficult, painful subjects such as suicide ("Give It to Him") and loss. With *Save the World* still among the top-selling gospel albums, Adams returned to the studio to make *More than a Melody* (1995) for Verity. She won a Soul Train Lady of Soul Award and a Grammy Award nomination for *More than a Melody*, whose R&B elements widened her fan base. *Yolanda . . . Live in Washington*, a 1996 live recording, was showered with praise; Adams was honored with another Stellar Award and another Grammy nomination.

Having become one of gospel's best-selling artists, with sales averaging more than 200,000 units per album, Adams was highly sought-after when her contract with Tribute/Verity ended, upon the release of *Songs from the Heart* in 1998. She chose not to sign with another Christian label, she told Lisa Collins for *Billboard* (September 18, 1999, online), because she felt that her music had stretched past the boundaries of traditional gospel: "Musically, I had devolved, and my vision no longer fit. I thought maybe I needed to go where they can see the big picture." On the "Tour of Life" with Kirk Franklin and the Family, a hugely popular R&B/gospel group, she attracted the attention of Sylvia Rhone, the CEO of Elektra Records. Adams signed a contract with Elektra, to the dismay of some in the religious community, who felt that gospel music could not be properly packaged by a record company with a secular focus. Adams disagreed, as she told Collins: "People perceive that because I'm at a secular label I will be doing secular music, and that was never our motive. What it boiled down to was that Sylvia Rhone was the only one who could pull off what I wanted. She said, 'I love you; you don't have to change. I just want to expand where you are.'" Adams explained to Gwen Ifill for the PBS *Online NewsHour* (September 5, 2001): "I'm not trying to convert you and say, 'in the name of Jesus, do this.' That's not my job. . . . All I have to do is talk to you through my music, make you think, and then Sunday you'll go to church, you know, to someone's church, and then they'll speak the message that will speak to your heart again." Elektra provided Adams with access to top producers, such as Keith Thomas, Jimmy Jam, and Terry Lewis, as well as the network needed to distribute her singles for maximum radio play on R&B and urban music stations in addition to gospel stations. "I don't want to spend my life preaching to the choir," Adams told Barbranda Lumpkins Walls for *Heart & Soul* (May 2001, online). "The choir should already have it together. Young people need an avenue, an alternative to what's out there. That's why Christian rap is so popular right now. That's why Kirk Franklin and his hip-hop style are so popular. Young people [need a] cool alternative."

Adams's first Elektra album, *Mountain High . . . Valley Low*, was released in September 1999. "The project manages continuity and flow despite the diverse range of producers," Melanie Clark wrote in an undated review for *GospelFlava.com*. "A testimony to great production and Adams' broad ability and appeal, *Mountain High . . . Valley Low* manages to be a jack of all trades and master of them too." The album climbed to the top spot on *Billboard*'s gospel and contemporary Christian charts; its sales were outstanding by gospel standards, eventually surpassing platinum status (1 million copies) by more than 500,000. Listing *Mountain High . . . Valley Low* as one of *Amazon.com*'s Best of 1999, Mike McGonigal noted: "Not just updating black gospel music, [Adams] fearlessly revives it with contemporary music—and not in any hokey way, mind you—and a timeless, unassailably intense spirituality." The album earned Adams her first Grammy Award, for best contemporary gospel album; she also won five Stellar Awards, including those for artist of the year, female vocalist of the year, and CD of the year. In addition, *Mountain High . . . Valley Low* and its popular single "Open My Heart" (which spawned a frequently played music video) brought Adams four NAACP Image Awards and two Soul Train Lady of Soul Awards. "The great thing about ballads and songs that speak to the heart is that everybody has a heart . . . ," Adams explained to Barbranda Walls. "Music that comes from your heart speaks to someone else's heart." Also in 1999 Verity released a collection of some of Adams's more popular songs, on *Best of Yolanda Adams.*

In 2000 Adams toured with other top-selling gospel songstresses, such as Shirley Caesar and CeCe Winans, in the sold-out "Sisters in the Spirit" tour. "It's like an all-girl pajama party," Adams told C. Zawadi Morris in an interview posted on *BET.com* (November 1, 2000). "We're proving that there's a camaraderie with gospel women, not cat fights, because we represent something higher than us, that is so much greater that us." Her next release on Elektra was a 2000 holiday-season album, *Christmas with Yolanda Adams.* A live album released in March 2001, *The Experience,* offered her fans what *VH1.com* called "a career-defining live set." "The title states it, *The Experience,*" Adams told Andrea R. Williams in an interview posted on *Crosswalk.com.* "Many people have experienced all types of emotions, and all types of trials and tribulations in their lives." In February 2002 *The Experience* brought Adams her second Grammy Award, for best contemporary soul/gospel album. Adams did not tour in support of the album, having given birth to her first child, Taylor Ayanna, in January 2001. "I now have more awe for God because of the creation process," she admitted to Williams. "I have more faith now because of that. . . . Wow, I could have never imagined the beauty of motherhood the way that it really is." Taylor soon began to accompany Adams to her concerts, including a second round of the "Sisters in the Spirit" tour, which began in September 2001. Adams's fourth Elektra Records album, *Believe,* appeared in December 2001. Guest performers on the album include Mary Mary and Kevin Bond; among the album's songs are "Thank You," "Never Give Up," and "Darling Girl," which was inspired by Adams's baby daughter. *Believe* debuted at number one on the gospel charts and brought the singer a nomination for an American Music Award (AMA). In addition to performing at the AMA ceremony in January 2002, Adams was named favorite artist in the category of contemporary inspirational music.

Adams, who was married and divorced in the late 1980s, married the National Football League player turned stockbroker Tim Crawford, a childhood friend, in 1997. They live in Houston, where they enjoy playing golf and running in their free time. Much of Adams's charity work is focused on children; she plans to build a children's arts center in Houston. She had hoped to earn a master's degree from Howard University Divinity School in the late 1990s, but the demands of her "musical ministry" prevented her from doing so. — K.S.

Suggested Reading: *Chicago Tribune* II p13 Dec. 24, 1995, with photo; *Ebony* p42+ Aug. 2000, with photos; *Essence* p106+ July 2001, with photos; *Washington Post* N p8 Feb. 11, 2000

Selected Recordings: *Just As I Am,* 1987; *Through the Storm,* 1991; *Save the World,* 1993; *More than a Melody,* 1995; *Mountain High . . . Valley Low,* 1999; *The Experience,* 2001; *Believe,* 2001

---

## Aigner-Clark, Julie

*1966(?)– Entrepreneur; creator of Baby Einstein*

*Address: Baby Einstein Co., 9285 Teddy Ln., Suite 200, Lone Tree, CO 80124*

The entrepreneur Julie Aigner-Clark, founder of the Baby Einstein Co., has been focused on babies and their development since the mid-1990s, when she searched in vain for an age-appropriate way of introducing her infant daughter to the arts. "I started thinking, 'Am I the only mom who wants to develop the love of humanities and fine arts in her children?' So, the idea for Baby Einstein was born," she explained in an interview posted on *BlueSuitMom.com.* Weaving art, music, and language in a format that enthralls infants and toddlers, Baby Einstein videos, books, and toys have enjoyed runaway success since the first tapes went on sale, in 1997. In November 2001 the Baby Einstein Co. was acquired by the Walt Disney Co.

The daughter of an electrician and a secretary, Julie Aigner-Clark was born in about 1966 and raised in Grosse Pointe, Michigan, a suburb of Detroit. After attending Michigan State University, she became a middle-school and high-school teacher of English, art, and psychology. She married Bill Clark, an entrepreneur whose specialty is educational media (he founded the Optical Data Corp.); the couple later moved to Alpharetta, Georgia, a suburb of Atlanta.

Pregnant with her first child, Aigner-Clark was not planning to go back to work soon after giving birth. That was to change, however. Inspired by research indicating that children could learn foreign languages more easily if exposed to them as infants, she looked for products that would begin that process, but found nothing that satisfied her. "There were no videos out that addressed [this theory]," she told *Billboard* magazine (October 1998). After her first daughter, Aspen, was born, Aigner-Clark also found that art and music were lacking in products and television shows directed at babies. "[My daughter] started to become interested in things on TV," Aigner-Clark told Daisy Whitney for the *Denver Post* (May 30, 2001), "but with the exception of *Sesame Street* there wasn't anything good on TV. So I thought, wouldn't it be great if someone made something engaging and beautiful for kids to watch."

Courtesy of Disney Publishing Worldwide

*Julie Aigner-Clark*

With $18,000 in savings, she and her husband founded the Baby Einstein Co. In 1996, in their basement, they made a video that incorporated visual stimuli, language, and other sound. "It took forever," she recalled to Sharon Cotliar for *Time* (March 20, 2000). "It was all done at night, after my husband came home from work and Aspen went to bed." Shots of black-and-white patterns, stuffed animals, and a lava lamp were set to music. Finding several speakers of foreign languages at a language school and a local restaurant, Aigner-Clark hired the women to count, sing, and read poems while speaking in "motherese," a conversational, high-pitched tone; the resulting tape includes Hebrew, Spanish, Japanese, German, Russian, French, and English segments. "I wanted something that was not only entertaining but stimulating and engaging that would give [my daughter] exposure to things that were lovely," she told Nichole L. Torres for *Entrepreneur* (November 2000).

Baby Einstein planned to release its 30-minute, eponymous video in 1997. But with no marketing experience, Aigner-Clark felt unsure about how to proceed. In the end she attended the American International Toy Fair in New York City in February 1997 and sought out representatives from The Right Start, an upscale chain selling baby products. As she related to Nichole L. Torres: "I ran up to them [and said] 'You're going to love this video! You have to watch it! It's perfect for your store!'" Persuaded to offer the *Baby Einstein* video in about six of its 45 stores, The Right Start had sold more than $100,000 worth of videos by the end of 1997. "We didn't spend any money on marketing and advertising," Aigner-Clark recalled for *BlueSuitMom.com*. The Right Start's agreeing to sell the video, she said, was the "first big break. . . . The response was amazing. Parents loved the video and it flew off the shelves, really by word of mouth." The company also filled phone orders for the video with the help of a communications company that offered toll-free service. "When we made back all our money and produced another video, we started paying them," she explained to *Billboard*. "But they did it free for a whole year."

The "Baby Einstein phenomenon" appeared to take hold after *Parenting* magazine named *Baby Einstein* the best video of 1997. "That gave us a tremendous amount of credibility," Aigner-Clark noted on *BlueSuitMom.com*. *Baby Einstein* was followed by *Baby Mozart*—a second 30-minute video that had several elements in common with the original but was set to familiar compositions by Wolfgang Amadeus Mozart. *Baby Mozart*, selected by *Child* magazine as Video of the Year in 1998, coincidentally appeared just after the publication of Don G. Campbell's book *The Mozart Effect: Tapping the Power of Music to Heal the Body, Strengthen the Mind, and Unlock the Creative Spirit* (1997), which contends that listening to classical music offers a positive influence on intelligence and temperament. (*The Mozart Effect* set off debates in the academic community, still largely unresolved, regarding music's effect on babies and toddlers, Aigner-Clark's target audience. "It's wrong to say [the videos] will never make them smart," she explained to Nancy McAlister for the *Florida Times-Union* [October 16, 2000]. "We're all about engaging. I think a lot of parents have never themselves listened to Mozart. It's what people have e-mailed me about. They say, 'Thank you. It's given me a way to enjoy this as well as my baby.'") Relocated to Colorado in 1998, the Baby Einstein Co. expanded its product line to include books, toys, and more of its mainstay, videos: *Baby Bach* (1998), using familiar melodies from the composer; *Baby Shakespeare* (1999), with short recitations from Shakespeare's plays; and *Baby Van Gogh* (2000), using the famed artist's paintings to illustrate different colors, such as *Starry Night* for blue. More specialized offerings included *Baby Santa's Music Box* (2000), a holiday-themed video, *Baby Doolittle Neighborhood Animals* (2001), and *Baby Doolittle World Animals* (2001), the latter two of which were named *Parenting* magazine's Best Videos of 2001.

Sales of Baby Einstein products skyrocketed, totaling $4.5 million in 1999 and making more than $11 million in the last quarter of 2000, including Internet direct sales. Dismissing criticism that videos were supplanting parent-child bonding, Aigner-Clark explained to Eric Hubler for the *Denver Post* (March 12, 1999, on-line), "I'm not an advocate at all of sitting babies in front of the TV. We tell parents to use our videos like a video board book. A board book is a book that has pictures in it, no words, where you use the pictures to teach your baby concepts like up and down or where did it go. You're sitting with the baby and watching it together." In 2000 Baby Einstein products branched out from small, upscale retailers to share shelf space with merchandise at major discount stores, such as Target and Kmart. In the same year Aigner-Clark and the company moved to office space in Lone Tree, Colorado, marking the first time that she had worked outside of her home in her capacity as head of Baby Einstein.

In November 2001, several years after the birth of Aigner-Clark's second daughter, came the announcement that Walt Disney would acquire the Baby Einstein Co. for an undisclosed sum; Aigner-Clark and her husband were to stay on as consultants to Disney. "The sale will allow us to spend more time with our two little girls, who are growing up by the minute and remain the most important part of our lives," she wrote in a letter posted on the Baby Einstein Web site. "Like our children, Baby Einstein is growing up, too. Our collaboration with Disney, a company that has been bringing smiles to the faces of children for more than half a century, will allow us to take our little company to a whole new level." Among Disney's first priorities is to develop a line of "Little" products aimed at toddlers.

Aigner-Clark and her husband, Bill, live in Littleton, Colorado, with their two daughters, Aspen and Sierra. —K.S.

Suggested Reading: *Billboard* p72 Oct. 1998; *Denver Post* C p1 May 30, 2001; *Entrepreneur* (on-line) Nov. 2000; *People* p118 May 22, 2000, with photo

Selected Videos: *Baby Einstein*; *Baby Mozart*; *Baby Bach*; *Baby Shakespeare*; *Baby Van Gogh*; *Baby Santa's Music Box*; *Baby Doolittle Neighborhood Animals*; *Baby Doolittle World Animals*

Selected Books: *Poems for Little Ones*; *See and Spy Counting*; *Bard's Rhyme Time: A Lift-The-Flap Book*; *Jane's Animal Expedition*; *Language Nursery*; *Baby Santa's Christmas Joy!: A Celebration of the Holiday Spirit in Poetry, Photography, and Music*; *Dogs*; *Cats*; *Babies*; What Does Violet See? series: *Birds and Nests, Sand and Sea, Raindrops and Puddles, Snowflakes and Icicles*; *Puzzling Shapes: A Puzzle Book*; *Mirror Me: A Mirror Book*; *Baby Einstein: First Library*; *The ABCs of Art*

---

## Alibek, Ken

*1950– Microbiologist; biological-warfare expert; physician*

*Address: c/o Random House Publicity, 299 Park Ave., New York, NY 10171; c/o Hadron Inc., 5904 Richmond Hwy., Alexandria, VA 22303-1864*

Courtesy of Advanced Biosystems Inc.

The life story of the physician, microbiologist, and biological-warfare expert Ken Alibek reads like a spy novel. Raised in what was then the Soviet Union, Alibek became a skilled microbiological researcher and technician, developing some of the world's most powerful biological weapons. A staunch supporter of the Soviet government and a member of the Communist Party, he believed that the United States had its own flourishing biological-weapons program, for possible use in crippling the Soviet Union, and he thus felt that providing defensive weapons for his country was his duty. Alibek rose to powerful positions in the Soviet Army and in Biopreparat, a government institution created in 1973 to serve as a civilian/industrial shield for biological-weapons research. But as Soviet politics changed, Alibek's beliefs shifted. He became increasingly distressed by his awareness that his work, and that of thousands of others, violated the 1972 biological-weapons treaty (signed at that time by the Soviet Union, the United States, and Great Britain and, since then, by some 140 other nations) as well as by his belief that he had violated the oath he had taken when he became a doctor, one part of which states, "I will prevent disease whenever I can." "I always had a dream to do real work in the field of medical defense," he told Paula C. Squires for *Virginia Business* (December 2001, on-line). "It was not possible in the Soviet Union." In 1992 Alibek defected to the United States, where, for the past decade, he has worked to defend against the same organisms that, as a Soviet citizen, he had strived to turn into weapons of war.

He is the author of an autobiography, *Biohazard* (1999), which he wrote with Stephen Handelman. "Of course I feel guilty," Alibek told William J. Broad for the *New York Times* (June 27, 1999), regarding the Soviet stockpiles of biological weapons. "You know, if a solution of this problem would cost just my life, that's a pretty fair cost."

Ken Alibek was born Kanatjan Alibekov in 1950 in Kauchuk, in what was then the Kazakh Soviet Socialist Republic. Along with his brother, Bakhit, and sister, Saule, he was raised by his mother, Rosa, and father, Bayzak, a police officer, in Alma-Ata, the nation's capital. Ethnic Kazakhs, the Alibekov family descended from Tauke-Khan (1680–1718), who united the region and established a legal code; they also counted a Communist hero of the Russian Revolution among their forebears. With a strong military tradition in his family—Bayzak Alibekov, for example, served in World War II, during which he was wounded seven times—in 1973 Alibek entered the military half of the Tomsk Medical Institute, in Siberia, as a cadet intern. While taking a course in epidemiology, he did a research project on the 1942 Battle of Stalingrad and concluded that the Russian Army had attempted to use germ warfare against German soldiers but inadvertently—because of a shift in the wind—poisoned their own troops. His professor told him to abandon his conclusion, because, as he explained in *Biohazard*, "biological warfare was not the sort of thing you discussed openly." "But I was fascinated by this area of military medicine," he continued. "The romantic image of medics saving lives amidst the smoke and drama of a battlefield had appealed to me since I was a young boy. It struck me that military physicians were soldiers after their own fashion, waging a private war against an enemy that knew how to exploit every human weakness. The only weapons available to us were our skills in identifying symptoms and in applying the correct treatment." Alibek changed the focus of his studies to epidemiology and infectious disease rather than psychiatry, as he had originally planned. After he earned an M.D. degree, he was recruited to work for the Soviet government. He was told that his work would be under the aegis of the Council of Ministers, the highest governing body in the Soviet Union, and that the job was top secret; he was not permitted to tell even his parents where he had been assigned.

Commissioned as a junior lieutenant in the army, Alibek began his research career at the East European Scientific Branch of the Institute of Applied Biochemistry, located in Omutninsk, about 600 miles southeast of Moscow. He was trained to perform intricate laboratory procedures, which were to be applied to developing biological weapons for the Soviet Union. The same procedures were being used in the United States, he was told, despite the signing by both the USSR and the U.S. of the 1972 Biological and Toxin Weapons Convention, which banned the use of biological weapons and offensive research in germ warfare. "It was not difficult for me to believe that the United States would use any conceivable weapon against us, and that our own survival depended on matching their duplicity," Alibek recalled in *Biohazard*, which is subtitled "The Chilling True Story of the Largest Covert Biological Weapons Program in the World—Told from the Inside by the Man Who Ran It." During his first year of training, he occasionally wrestled with the ethics of using his skills to create weapons; at one point he even asked to be excused from the program. (The army's refusal to comply made Alibek think that he was vital to the defense ministry, and he felt flattered.) "Was it right for me to be involved in this business? I say no," he told Kirk Wolfinger for "Bioterror," the November 13, 2001 installment of the PBS television series *NOVA*, as transcribed for the PBS Web site. "Probably, I didn't have the right because of one important reason: Because I'm a physician. Somebody with no medical background—a chemist or biologist who didn't pledge not to cause harm—I cannot accuse this person of wrongdoing. But with my specific case, I was a physician. I tried to escape—I tried not to be involved in this business—but I was not able to do this."

In 1976, the year he married Lena Yemesheva, a foreign-language student, Alibek was transferred to the Siberian Branch of the Institute of Applied Biochemistry, in Berdsk. Charged to build a microbiology lab in that remote outpost, Alibek and others completed the task within four months and began working to propagate large amounts of *Brucella* bacteria, which causes brucellosis. A serious, highly contagious affliction among farm animals, brucellosis (also called Malta fever or undulant fever) can be transmitted to humans; usually nonfatal, it causes a severe fever and weakness and, if untreated, can persist for months. "After eight months of work, we presented our findings: our new growth medium produced a substantial yield of bacteria that could be weaponized," Alibek wrote in *Biohazard*. "Moscow headquarters was pleased. For me, it was a personal achievement—I had gone from being a pupil to a practitioner." The military and scientific paths of Alibek's professional life benefitted from this early success: he was promoted to a senior-scientist position at Berdsk and made a senior lieutenant in the army.

Alibek became an expert at mixing growth media and cultivating bacteria in large numbers. On orders from Biopreparat, he returned to Omutninsk with a new assignment: to lead a team that would create a strain of tularemia sturdy enough to survive a wide range of dispersal conditions. Also known as rabbit fever, tularemia has been prized in biowarfare because the organism that causes the disease is extremely hardy, infects its victims extremely easily, quickly multiplies and spreads to organs and lymph nodes, and results in fever and flu-like symptoms; without antibiotics, many victims develop pneumonia and other complications, and a small percentage of people die. (The Russian and German disease outbreaks during the Battle of

Stalingrad were caused by tularemia.) One night, while attending to what he thought was an air-pressure problem in a normally sealed compartment of his laboratory, Alibek found himself "standing in a puddle of liquid tularemia," as he recalled in *Biohazard.* "It was milky brown—the highest possible concentration. The puddle at my feet was only a few centimeters deep, but there was enough tularemia on the floor to infect the entire population of the Soviet Union." Two days later—although on the day of the accident he had been wearing a protective suit, had undergone disinfection after leaving the compartment, and had had no visible cuts or scratches—Alibek became ill with tularemia. (He believes that a tiny number of bacteria entered an imperceptible cut on his face when his protective mask brushed against his skin as he was removing it.) In order to prevent news of his illness from reaching his superiors, he treated himself with high doses of tetracycline while pretending that he simply had a bad cold.

For his achievement in turning huge quantities of tularemia into a powerful weapon of war, Alibek was awarded a Ph.D. in microbiology. Soon afterward he was reassigned to Stepnogorsk, a biological-research center in northern Kazakhstan, with the title of deputy director. Within weeks he was promoted to director of the facility, where nearly 1,000 people worked. His assignment there was to develop a "battle strain" of anthrax—"one that was reproducible in large quantities, of high virulence, and transportable," as he wrote in *Biohazard.* During the following years he and some of his employees produced a form of anthrax—dubbed Alibekov anthrax—that was four times as virulent as the natural bacterium. For that achievement, Alibek earned an honorary doctor of science degree in biotechnology, in 1988. "I was a little disappointed because the production facility . . . was not able to manufacture more than 300 tons of the anthrax during a 250-day period," Alibek told Kirk Wolfinger. "I was disappointed because I thought I would be able to reach something like 1,000 tons." "It's very difficult to say if I felt a sense of excitement over this," he told Richard Preston for the *New Yorker* (March 9, 1998), referring to his work with anthrax. "It's very difficult to say *what* I felt like. It wouldn't be true to say that I thought I was doing something wrong. I thought I had done something very important. The anthrax was one of my scientific results—my personal result."

Earlier, in 1987, Alibek was promoted to colonel and moved to Moscow as the new deputy chief of the Biopreparat's biosafety division. In this powerful position he approved experimentation with Venezuelan equine encephalitis (VEE), one or more forms of plague, and the smallpox and Marburg viruses at Vector (a facility in Koltsovo, Siberia). After his elevation to first deputy chief of Biopreparat, in 1988, he gained the ears of powerful military decision-makers. He gave the green light to scientists working to produce chimera viruses, which combine the DNA of two viruses to form new, more deadly organisms. "Russia has researched the generic alteration of smallpox," he told Richard Preston. "In 1990 and 1991, we engineered a smallpox at Vector. It was found that several areas of the smallpox genome can be used for the introduction of some foreign genetic material. The first development was smallpox and VEE."

Alibek's belief in the essential rightness of his work started to crumble in the late 1980s, after Mikhail Gorbachev, the president of the Soviet Union, launched his policies of *glasnost* (which created a more open society by permitting greater discussion of political and social issues among the citizenry) and *perestroika* (the restructuring of the Soviet government and economy). With Biopreparat no longer completely off-limits to foreigners, its officials struggled to hide evidence of biological-weapons activities from the American and British scientists and others who came to visit in early 1991. The visitors were shown areas that, unbeknownst to them, had been converted to civilian work; elsewhere, the production of offensive weapons-grade bacteria had continued steadily. Later that year, in a reciprocal move, Alibek and other Soviet scientists as well as Soviet government representatives visited American military and research sites. By that time Alibek had come close to accepting the American government's claim that U.S. research into offensive biological weapons had ceased in 1969. He has traced his inclination to believe it to a conversation in which he had asked two high-ranking Soviet military-intelligence officers for details about suspected American biological-weapons sites, and they had told him that they had no such information. Meanwhile, in late 1990 Alibek had accepted an additional post—that of director of Biomash, which designed and produced technical equipment used in biological-weapons development.

In August 1991, after some months of political unrest, the Gorbachev government lost control of the country for a few days. Despite its reinstallation, the president's power was undermined, and on December 24, 1991 Gorbachev resigned. Alibek has maintained that because many of his Biomash colleagues had not voiced their support for Gorbachev, he tendered his resignation, but the facility's director, Yury Kalinin, persuaded him to remain on staff. He resigned again, this time apparently without opposition, after Kalinin issued an official report stating (dishonestly, according to Alibek) that during their trip to the U.S., Alibek and his colleagues had found evidence that the U.S. was continuing to develop biological weapons, and that therefore Russia should do so, too. (By the time that report reached the Kremlin, the Soviet Union had splintered into 15 separate republics.)

Alibek took a job at a bank in Moscow, but after he discovered that he was being spied upon there, he went to Alma-Ata, where he interviewed successfully for the position of Kazakh minister of health. Then, by his own account, he learned that his main function would be to set up Kazakhstan's own biological-weapons program. Discouraged, he turned down the offer. "When I returned to Moscow, I felt trapped," he recalled in *Biohazard.* "There would be no Kazakh citizenship, and no medical or scientific career, unless I accepted the role that had been picked out for me. I couldn't even be sure I would be able to continue in private business. . . . I had burned my bridges in both Russia and Kazakhstan." In the fall of 1992, after making contacts with Americans he had met during his trip to the U.S., Alibek, his wife, and their three children defected to the United States.

Alibek spent much of his first year in the U.S. undergoing debriefing. Answering questions posed by U.S. military, intelligence, and other officials about Russia's biological-weapons program became virtually a full-time job for him. Many officials were shocked at the scale of the program at its peak. Moreover, as Alibek told Tim Weiner, he tried to warn them that the Russian facilities were "continu[ing] to do research to develop new biological agents; they conduct research and explain it as being for defensive purposes." Alibek has speculated that since his defection, Russian scientists have produced "Ebolapox," a chimera virus in which the smallpox and Ebola viruses—both of which are highly contagious—are joined. While some American scientists think Alibek may be right, others question the likelihood of that development. In any event, the Nobel Prize–winning American microbiologist Joshua Lederberg declared to Richard Preston, the fact that the Russians may be experimenting with Ebolapox does not "prove intent." "It's not even clear to me that adding Ebola genes to smallpox would make it more deadly," Lederberg told Preston. "What troubles me is that this kind of work is being done in a clandestine way. They are *not* telling us what is going on. To be doing such potentially evil research without telling us what is going on is a provocation." Alibek has also been alert to the possibilities that other countries have bioweapons technology; after his defection, he has said, several nations tried to recruit him to work on bioweaponry for them. Moreover, he believes that some of his former colleagues from the former Soviet Union may now be working on bioweapons technology in Iraq, Iran, India, North Korea, or other nations.

Now a U.S. citizen, Alibek is currently the president of Hadron Advanced Biosystems Inc., a Virginia biotechnology company. He supervises a team of 30 scientists who are trying to develop a universal shield to 70 known biological-warfare agents, including anthrax and smallpox. The shield would be a spray that heightens the immune system. Alibek is also a consultant to the U.S. government in his area of expertise, and in that capacity he was called upon in late 2001, when anthrax spores were being sent through the U.S. mail. His book, *Biohazard*, received mostly favorable reviews. "[American] government officials asked me not to [go public]," he told Broad. "For five years they tried to keep me silent," because, he contended, they feared that his life might be in danger. "Russia is angry" about the book, he told Broad. "It has denied what I am saying. But I will continue my disclosures. My final, ultimate objective is to have Russia as a partner—but after, just after, we know everything that is going on."

Ken and Lena Alibek live with their children in northern Virginia. A photo in *Biohazard* shows the couple with a daughter, Mira, and two sons, Alan and Timur. According to one source, the family now includes a fourth child. — K.S.

Suggested Reading: *New York Times* A p1+ Feb. 25, 1998, with photo; *New Yorker* p52+ Mar. 9, 1998; *Virginia Business* (on-line) Dec, 2001; *Washington Post* E p1 Oct. 29, 2001; Alibek, Ken, and Stephen Handelman. *Biohazard*, 1999

Selected Books: *Biohazard: The Chilling True Story of the Largest Covert Biological Weapons Program in the World—Told from Inside by the Man Who Ran It* (with Stephen Handelman), 1999

---

Courtesy of California Institute of Technology

## Anderson, Don L.

*Mar. 5, 1933– Geophysicist*

*Address: MS 252-2, California Institute of Technology, Pasadena, CA 91125*

"I've gotten to think of the earth as my research project," the geophysicist Don L. Anderson told Richard A. Kerr for *Science* (April 20, 1990). Anderson is known as a maverick in geophysics, a broad field that includes the study of Earth's composition and structure; the structural changes that have occurred during the planet's estimated 4.6-billion-year existence; and the processes responsible for those changes. A leading figure in "deep Earth" research—a phrase referring to the portions of the planet below the crust—Anderson has been credited with greatly advancing scientists' understanding of the makeup, configuration, and dynamics of planet Earth. "One of Don Anderson's major contributions has been forcing people to question their assumptions," Bradford H. Hager, a professor of Earth, atmospheric, and planetary sciences at the Massachusetts Institute of Technology, told Kerr. Anderson has helped develop sophisticated tools to learn about the composition of Earth's interior. These tools include seismic anisotropy (in which seismic waves—those produced by earthquakes or man-made explosions—are measured from different directions) and seismic tomography (which measures seismic waves to produce three-dimensional images of the internal structures of solid objects). Most recently he has developed a new theory of plate tectonics, called far-from-equilibrium self-organization. Anderson's honors indicate the breadth of his research: among them are awards from the American Geophysical Union (AGU), the National Aeronautics and Space Administration (NASA), the Royal Astronomical Society of Great Britain, and the Royal Swedish Academy of Sciences, the last of which recognized his achievements with the 1998 Crafoord Prize, which is considered equivalent to the Nobel Prize for basic research in such disciplines as mathematics, astronomy, ecology, and Earth science. In 1998 he received a National Medal of Science, the greatest honor the U.S. government bestows on scientists. "I jump around from seismology to petrology to planetary-type things," Anderson told Kerr. "There aren't many broad thinkers; that's why I get into trouble." Anderson has been a faculty member of the California Institute of Technology, in Pasadena, since he earned his doctorate, in 1962.

The son of Richard Anderson and Minola (Phares) Anderson, Don Lynn Anderson was born on March 5, 1933 in Frederick, Maryland. As a boy he enjoyed collecting rocks during field trips along the East Coast. He received a B.S. degree in geology and geophysics in 1955 from Rensselaer Polytechnic Institute, in Troy, New York. (Geophysics, in addition to being the study of the planet's structure, is concerned with Earth's atmosphere, magnetic field, volcanic activity, and oceans and other bodies of water, as well as properties of other planets and planetary satellites in the solar system. Geology, by contrast, focuses on rocks from the outermost layer of Earth, called the crust, and what they reveal about Earth's past. Geophysics also relies far more heavily on mathematical and physical principles than does geology.) As an undergraduate, Anderson joined the army ROTC (Reserve Officers' Training Corps). He then spent a year as an employee of the Chevron Oil Co., using man-made seismic waves to locate sources of oil in Montana, Wyoming, and California. For about two years beginning in 1956, he worked for a division of the Air Force Cambridge Research Center known as the Geophysics Directorate; his assignment involved investigating the properties of sea ice in northern Greenland. In 1958 he joined the Arctic Institute of North America, where he continued his sea-ice study, with the aim of determining areas strong enough to support the landing of airplanes. "The combination of my oil company experience and Air Force experience told me that not only can you use seismology to map underground structures, but also to map the physical properties and to determine things like how strong a material is, or what it's made out of, or what temperature it is," he explained to Bruce V. Bigelow for *ScienceWatch* (June 1994). He next entered the doctoral program in geophysics at the California Institute of Technology (Caltech), where he earned a master of science degree in 1959 and a Ph.D, in mathematics as well as geophysics, in 1962. The subject of his doctoral dissertation was seismic anisotropy, which he described to Bigelow as "just a fancy way of saying that the properties of a material depend on what way you look at it." (For example, measuring the velocities of seismic waves from different directions produces different results.) For the next year Anderson served as a research fellow at Caltech; he then became an assistant professor (1963–64), associate professor (1964–68), and professor (1968–89). Since 1989 he has held the title Eleanor and John R. McMillan Professor of Geophysics (with the addition of the word "emeritus" since his retirement, in January 2002).

By the time Anderson entered high school, in the late 1940s, scientists had determined that Earth's interior is composed of four concentric layers: the dense, solid inner core (consisting primarily of iron) surrounded by the liquid outer core (iron with some sulfur), which is covered with the mantle (which, being semi-solid and plastic-like, can flow and deform) and, above that, the relatively thin crust that supports all living things. During the next two decades, evidence accumulated for the validity of the theory of plate tectonics, according to which Earth's crust is made of huge, irregularly shaped, slowly moving slabs of rock (called plates) of varying dimensions. Scientists have identified about 28 plates, eight of which are far larger than the others; although the plates move at most a few inches per year, with the passage of millions of years, the distances covered become great. At any particular moment two plates may be moving apart; moving horizontally, in opposite directions, past each other; or colliding. With the acceptance of the plate-tectonics theory, geophysicists began to develop new explanations for such phenomena as mountain building, volcanic activity, earthquakes, and the existence of sea-floor rifts and subduction zones (some of which are continent-continent collision zones), the places where one colliding tectonic plate slides beneath the other and eventually moves beneath the crust.

In the early 1960s, along with others in his field, Anderson began to synthesize seismology and plate tectonics. Recordings and measurements of waves produced by two powerful earthquakes—one in Chile in 1960 and the other in Alaska in 1964—as well as what they revealed about Earth's interior greatly influenced his research. By the latter part of the decade, his work had led him to question the common wisdom that the mantle was uniform from top to bottom. To test the accuracy of that belief, he predicted how seismic waves from earthquakes would behave as they passed from the top of the mantle to the bottom, based on the assumption that the whole mantle was indeed composed of similar types of rocks in similar physical states and that these rocks resembled particular, available rocks of a type in which the behavior of seismic waves had already been recorded. (In forming this hypothesis, he drew upon the work of the Australian geochemist Ted Ringwood, who had offered a model for the mantle based on lavas from a volcanic eruption in Hawaii as well as other kinds of rocks squeezed up from the mantle in mountain belts, and had proposed that one type of rock formed the entire mantle.)

What Anderson found did not match his predictions. To explain his results, he theorized that the compositions of the upper part of the mantle (extending about 400 miles beneath the tectonic plates) and the lower part (extending a further 1,400 miles) are fundamentally different; in particular, he proposed that the mantle consists of two completely separate layers, the lower one richer in materials such as iron and silicon and thus denser than the upper one. According to Anderson's theory, no materials would pass from the lower mantle to the upper mantle, and the upper mantle would thus be the sole source of crustal rocks and volcanic hot spots; it would also be the repository for old oceanic tectonic plates. In a process of recycling, new oceanic crust and new plates emerge from the upper mantle. The deep mantle consists of dense material formed during Earth's violent creation. Anderson has theorized that boundaries in the mantle exist at depths of about 255, 400, and 625 miles.

Within the last several years there has been considerable debate among scientists as to the correctness of Anderson's mantle theory. Thomas H. Jordan, a former student of Anderson's who is now W. M. Keck Professor of Geophysics and the scientific director of the Southern California Earthquake Center at Southern California University, has proposed a different theory, according to which material in the mantle travels up and down, from the top of the mantle to the bottom. He came to that conclusion after he and his team of researchers used seismic waves generated by earthquakes to create images of oceanic plates sinking below the 400-mile barrier in the mantle. "The most robust constraints are from direct observation," Jordan told Kerr in 1990, referring to images produced from field studies. "I try not to use laboratory results to draw conclusions about the earth. Don is more confident about that. A lot of arguments for stratification of the mantle say you can't believe what you see." Anderson disagreed, claiming that the existence of layers in the mantle is supported by observations in the field as well as by laboratory research. Referring to those who dispute his two-layer theory, he told Kerr in 1990, "I can't think of many people with the whole story; I've got a counter to every one of their arguments. I think they'll eventually come around." But as images of slabs in the mantle (as deduced from seismic data) have become much more distinct, thanks to improvements in technology, an increasing number of scientists have come to believe that the mantle is a single layer and that tectonic plates have entered it. At the AGU's fall 1996 meeting, two teams of researchers presented independent evidence of plates' presence in the mantle. "There is no doubt—you see the slabs clearly penetrating all the way from the surface to the core-mantle boundary," the seismologist Michael Wysession of Washington University told Richard A. Kerr for *Science* (January 31, 1997). "In my opinion, this is the final argument. I'm convinced it's some form of whole-mantle circulation." But some scientists had doubts about the single-layer theory. "I guess I'm not convinced," Raymond Jeanloz, a professor of geology and geophysics at the University of California at Berkeley, told Kerr. "To what degree is what is inferred from the patterns in the eye of the beholder? I appreciate that the guys who are doing the hands-on data analysis feel the results just leap out at them . . . but how you link up these blobs of high velocity and whether you infer they represent slabs going straight through [to the bottom of the mantle] is not quite so obvious to me." Although Anderson did not accept the new findings as definitive proof of an unlayered mantle, he admitted that the images produced by the two groups of researchers impressed him. "The amazing thing to me is that their models agree so well even though they use completely different data and [analysis] techniques," he said to Kerr. (Since then, Rob van der Hilst, one of the researchers who produced such images, has argued that slabs do not sink to the core-mantle boundary and that the mantle contains layers.)

After the theory of plate tectonics was developed, scientists suggested that huge plumes of nearly molten rock from Earth's interior have risen to the surface in various places. They speculated that one such plume, located beneath the Pacific Ocean, raised the sea floor one hundred million years ago (during the Cretaceous period), pushing seawater onto land and starting a chain of reactions, among them a huge amount of volcanic activity, a great rise in temperature, and stabilization of Earth's magnetic field. A team of researchers studying flood basalts—the rocky evidence of the huge outpourings of lava that have covered large areas of the planet every few million years—found support for this theory when they discovered within the hundred-million-year-old remains of the lava large quantities of a form of helium that is believed to have originated near Earth's core. Anderson disputed that idea, on the grounds that the amount of primordial helium was unusually high only in comparison with the small amount of an isotope of helium created by the radioactive decay of uranium and thorium. His argument supports a view in which the part of the mantle that lies immediately below the crust is low in uranium and thorium, and cracking of the crust allows helium-rich bubbles to escape.

Anderson presented this argument at the AGU's December 1996 conference, as part of a new hypothesis regarding Earth's interior operations that he based in part on recently declassified satellite imagery. "It's becoming more and more clear that Earth is driven from above by motion of the lithosphere [Earth's crust, which is relatively cold] and cold 'fingers' sticking down under continents into the mantle," Anderson said in an interview prior to the conference, as quoted in a Caltech news release dated December 15, 1996. "So rather than Earth being like a pot on a stove that gets heated from below and boils, it's more like a glass of iced tea where ice cubes cause cold downwellings in the liquid beneath it from thermal convection, and cause cracking in the 'lid' that permits volcanism." The satellite-imagery maps, based on global satellite gravity data, show many hot-spot tracks (chains of volcanoes) located along preexisting cracks on the plate. Others lie where new cracks are forming as oceanic plates move under others. According to Anderson's analysis, there is compelling evidence that in five regions in the Pacific Ocean, hot spots of underwater volcanic activity are associated with new fractures in Earth's crust. Two of the hot regions are located a few hundred miles to the west of Chile; the third is near Samoa, the fourth near Easter Island; and the fifth near the Galápagos Islands.

In 1981 Anderson and Adam Dziewonski, currently the Frank B. Baird Jr. Professor of Science at Harvard University, established what is now the most widely accepted theory of the structure of Earth's interior, one that scientists use as a standard of comparison when new data appear. (In presenting this theory, Anderson's book, *Theory of the Earth* [1989], provides a synthesis of his broad and provocative research and focuses on the dynamics of Earth's interior.) Dziewonski developed new seismic techniques, while Anderson investigated differences in the velocities of seismic waves as functions of direction, depth, and frequency. Anderson's work in charting Earth's interior was groundbreaking in its use of shear waves and Rayleigh waves (a type of seismic wave produced by earthquakes) to map horizontal cross-sections of Earth at many depths, as well as vertical cross-sections encircling the planet at various latitudes. Although they had not worked together since the early 1980s, in 1998 Anderson and Dziewonski jointly received the $500,000 Crafoord Prize from the Royal Swedish Academy of Sciences. "I think it's very significant that deep-Earth geophysics is being honored by this award," Anderson told City News Service (April 29, 1998). "It is rare for our field to be acknowledged in this way." Later that year the White House announced that Anderson was among the winners of the 1998 National Medal of Science; he received that award from President Bill Clinton in April 1999.

Anderson directed the Seismological Laboratory at Caltech from 1967 to 1989, overseeing its development into an important center for earthquake studies in Southern California. From 1988 to 1990 he served as president of the AGU. He has published many articles in *Geology*, *Science*, *Physics Today*, and the *Proceedings of the National Academy of Sciences*, among other professional journals. He earned the 1966 James B. Macelwane Award and the 1991 William Bowie Medal from the AGU, the 1977 Distinguished Scientific Achievement Award from NASA, the 1986 Emil Wiechart Medal of the German Geophysical Society, the 1987 Arthur L. Day Gold Medal of the Geological Society of America, the 1988 Gold Medal of Great Britain's Astronomical Society, and a 1998 Guggenheim Foundation fellowship. He is a fellow of the American Academy of Arts and Sciences, the American Geophysical Union, the American Association for the Advancement of Science, the Geological Society of America, the National Academy of Sciences, the American Philosophical Society, and the Royal Astronomical Society of Great Britain.

Anderson has been married since 1956 to Nancy Lois Ruth Anderson, a professor of nursing at the University of California at Los Angeles who co-directs the Social Policy and Dissemination Core of the Center for Vulnerable Populations Research at that school. The couple have a daughter, Lynn Ellen; a son, Lee Weston; and four granddaughters. — K.E.D.

Suggested Reading: California Institute of Technology Web site; City News Service Apr. 29, 1998; *Rensselaer Alumni Magazine* Dec. 1998, with photo; *Science* p301+ Apr. 20, 1990, with photo, p613+ Jan. 31, 1997; *ScienceWatch* p3+ June 1994, with photo; *Who's Who in America 2001*

---

## Anderson, Wes

*1970– Screenwriter; director*

*Address: c/o United Talent Agency, 9560 Wilshire Blvd., Fifth Fl., Beverly Hills, CA 90212*

Guided by the singular, quirky vision that informs his three, critically acclaimed movies, Wes Anderson has carved out a successful place for himself as a screenwriter and director. "The appeal of [his movies] comes from the fact that Anderson has retained a boy's way of conceptualizing the world—

Armando Gallo/Retna Ltd.

*Wes Anderson*

but he conveys it with a sophistication that a boy could never articulate . . . ," Marshall Sella wrote for the *New York Times Magazine* (December 2, 2001). "He recreates the fun and cruelty of youth in a lexicon that real adults have forgotten and real children have yet to acquire." Anderson's first film, *Bottle Rocket* (1996), focuses on three aimless, sympathetic youths who embark on lives of petty crime; the next, *Rushmore* (1998), is an endearingly absurd tale about a precociously creative prep-school student; the most recent, *The Royal Tenenbaums* (2001), is about a family of troubled geniuses whose roguish absentee father tries to ingratiate himself back into their lives. A longtime movie lover who, as a filmmaker, pays meticulous attention to details, ranging from the costumes to the music, Anderson has cited the directors Joseph L. Mankiewicz, Martin Scorsese, John Cassavetes, Robert Altman, Hal Ashby, and Mike Nichols as influential in his professional development. Anjelica Huston, who played the role of the mother in *The Royal Tenenbaums*, told Sella, "Wes's process is as refined and evolved as it can be; he's relaxed and tremendously confident. He has a real voice, a real eye. It'd be an error to think that because he's young, he's not fully formed."

The second of three sons, Wes Anderson was born in Houston, Texas, in 1970. His father, Mel Anderson, an advertising executive, and his mother, Texas, an archaeologist turned real estate agent, divorced when he was eight. The split profoundly affected the young Anderson. He told Jan Stuart for the *Los Angeles Times* (November 11, 2001), "It was a real drag, a huge thing. . . . I was angry for years and years." Around the time of the divorce, he started writing plays for school—ambitious stage productions (akin to those that the schoolboy Max creates in *Rushmore*) such as a re-creation of the battle of the Alamo and an adaptation of George Lucas's 1977 movie, *Star Wars*. During this period his father, who was himself an aspiring writer and who always supported his son's creative inclinations, gave Anderson a Super 8mm movie camera. Anderson would script, cast, direct, and shoot his scenes in the neighborhood. His father recalled to Pamela Colloff for *Texas Monthly* (May 1998), "My wife and I would see snippets of his footage—kids staggering across the sand dunes by our beach house with fake blood on them. We didn't know quite what to make of it."

Anderson attended St. John's, a private preparatory school in Houston. (The school provided much inspiration for *Rushmore*, which Anderson filmed there.) After he graduated from St. John's, he enrolled at the University of Texas at Austin. In a playwriting class during his sophomore year, he met Owen C. Wilson, who became a good friend and his creative partner. Anderson cast Wilson in a play he wrote for the class; called *A Night in Tunisia*, it was an adaptation of Sam Shepard's well-known tragicomedy *True West*. After he earned a bachelor's degree, in philosophy, he shared living quarters in Houston with Owen and Owen's brother Luke. He got work at a local cable access station, where he shot short films and also acquired experience in editing.

Inspired by their kindred sense of humor and, in part, by their real-life mischief, Anderson and Owen co-wrote a full-length movie script about three inept young Texans who—for lack of anything better to do—try their hands at thievery. Anderson and Wilson had only enough money to shoot a less-than-15-minute short from the script; thanks to the writer and producer L. M. Kit Carson, a Wilson family friend, the short was shown at the Sundance Film Festival. Afterward, Carson helped Anderson and Wilson tighten the screenplay and then sent it to the producers Polly Platt and James L. Brooks at Gracie Films. Speaking of that screenplay, which grew into *Bottle Rocket*, Platt told Colloff, "Most scripts you read are pale imitations of films that have already been made, but I had never seen anything like their work. As a producer, you live for—pray for—finding that kind of writing. It was unique, unhomogenized, brilliant." Brooks persuaded Columbia Pictures to give Anderson and Wilson $5 million to make *Bottle Rocket* into a feature film. With that funding, Anderson and both Owen and Luke Wilson moved to Los Angeles, where they finished editing and polishing the movie. Released in 1996, *Bottle Rocket*, which stars Owen and Luke Wilson, grossed less than a million dollars, but it was a critical success and led many of those who saw it to become loyal fans of Anderson and the Wilsons. In a review for the Toronto *Globe and Mail* (February 27, 1996), the film critic Rick Groen wrote, "[*Bottle Rocket*] is a childlike source of ingenuous fun. . . . It's too fresh to be ignored." As quoted by Amy Wallace in *Los An-*

*geles Magazine* (December 2001), the *Los Angeles Times* film critic Kenneth Turan praised *Bottle Rocket* for having "an exact sense of itself." Anderson and the two Wilson brothers won a special award for "debut of the year" for 1996 from the Lone Star Film and Television Awards, which celebrate films and television programs made in Texas. In addition, the Los Angeles Film Critics Association gave Anderson its New Generation Award, and MTV hailed him as best new filmmaker. *Bottle Rocket* also helped launch the Wilson brothers' acting careers. (Each has appeared in more than a dozen movies since its release.)

In their next collaboration, Anderson and Owen Wilson wrote the script for *Rushmore*, about a nerdy 15-year-old prep-school student, Max, who gets involved in an unheard-of number of clubs and other extracurricular activities; he also becomes infatuated with a widowed first-grade teacher, for whose affections he viciously competes with a steel tycoon whom he has enlisted as a patron of his outlandish schemes. Anderson and Wilson made a deal with Joe Roth, the chairman of Walt Disney Studios, which provided them with a $10 million budget for the movie, and they recruited most of the crew from *Bottle Rocket* to work on it. Starring an 18-year-old neophyte—Jason Schwartzman, the son of the actress Talia Shire and a nephew of the director Francis Ford Coppola—as Max, and Bill Murray as the businessman, the relatively low-budget *Rushmore* fared well at the box office, bringing in more than $17 million, and received critical raves. After it premiered, in late 1998, *Rushmore* landed on a number of top-10 lists. *Spin* magazine called it "the best comedy of the year"; the New York *Daily News* critic Dave Kehr, as quoted on the *Internet Movie Data Base*, described *Rushmore* as "one of the freshest, richest, most original films to come out of Hollywood in a very long time"; Jeff Giles wrote for *Newsweek* (December 7, 1998), "[*Rushmore*] is a marvelous comedy from deep in left field—immaculately written, unexpectedly touching and pure of heart"; and the reviewer for *Interview* (February 1999, online) declared, "Not since the mid-to-late '80s . . . has there been a slice of post-modern Americana as funny, thoughtful, and downright weird as the unmissable *Rushmore*." For *Rushmore*, the Los Angeles Film Critics Association again honored Anderson with its New Generation Award, in 1998, and he won an Independent Spirit Award for best director the following year.

The music in *Rushmore*, mostly 1960s British-invasion rock (by the Kinks, the Rolling Stones, and Creation, among others), was a big part of the film's appeal. As with his other films, Anderson put together the soundtrack with great care. In an undated interview with Keith Phipps for the *Onion*, Anderson said, speaking in general of his choices of music, "The songs are . . . just always key stuff for me. Some of the ideas are kind of inspired by the songs, and I always want to use music to tell the story and give the movie a certain kind of mood. That's always essential to me." With regard to the way he and Owen Wilson write screenplays, Anderson has explained, as quoted by Joe O. in *Lost Armadillos in Heat* (on-line), "One of us will write a scene and hand it to the other, and they'll make marks and hand it back, act out things, add things. As it goes along we write more and more and we start to figure out if we need a scene. It sort of evolves that way, just the two of us hashing it out. The process starts with the way you want the movie to feel, the setting, the characters and the way they'll interact, and less the story."

Because of Wilson's busy acting schedule, Anderson devoted more time than his partner to the screenplay for their next project, *The Royal Tenenbaums* (though they shared the writing credits as equals). Having gone far toward establishing himself as a first-rate director, Anderson succeeded in getting a star-studded cast and a substantial budget—nearly $40 million—for his third film. Set in New York City as seen through a veil of nostalgia, *The Royal Tenenbaums* is about an estranged couple whose three children (portrayed by Ben Stiller, Gwyneth Paltrow, and Luke Wilson) have never fulfilled the potential they showed as child prodigies. The father (played by Gene Hackman, for whom Anderson and Wilson specifically wrote the part) is a selfish but charming rogue who tries to win back his family's affections after years of neglecting them. The cast also includes Bill Murray, Owen Wilson, Andrew Wilson (Owen and Luke's brother), and several other friends of the director's. In creating the screenplay, Anderson was inspired partly by J. D. Salinger's stories about the Glass family, which the director read when he was 15. "I always liked the idea of people who were really brilliant but troubled," he told Jill Bernstein for *Premiere* (January 2002).

Reactions to *The Royal Tenenbaums* among critics was mostly positive; some even touted it as a masterpiece. In his *Los Angeles Times* piece, Jan Stuart described *The Royal Tenenbaums* as "the most inventive and accomplished American comedy since, well, *Rushmore*." Roger Ebert, the reviewer for the *Chicago Sun-Times* (December 21, 2001), found the film "at heart profoundly silly, and loving." In *Maclean's* (December 31, 2001/January 7, 2002), Brian D. Johnson declared, "*The Royal Tenenbaums* juggles surreal whimsy and emotional truth more artfully than any movie this year." The film brought Anderson and Wilson best-screenplay nominations from the Writers Guild of America, the Online Film Critics Society, the Chicago Film Critics Association, and the British Academy of Film and Television Arts (BAFTA). Gene Hackman's acting in it earned him a Golden Globe Award and awards from both the National Society of Film and the American Film Institute.

Tall, thin, and bespectacled, Wes Anderson has been described as looking like a "bookish graduate student." Currently, he lives in New York City and is at work on a new filmscript. He told Joe O., "I like movies where there is real affection for the characters. In these movies I feel there aren't any bad guys. I think [the French filmmaker Jean] Renoir says something to the effect that everyone has their reasons. You have to make an effort to understand them." — C.F.T.

Suggested Reading: *Hollywood.com*; *Los Angeles Times* F p13 Nov. 11, 2001, with photo; *movieclub.com*; *New York Times Magazine* p80+ Dec. 2, 2001, with photo; *Premiere* p76+ Jan. 2002, with photo; *Texas Monthly* p112+ May 1998, with photo

Selected Films: *Bottle Rocket*, 1996; *Rushmore*, 1998; *The Royal Tenenbaums*, 2001

---

Courtesy of American Program Bureau Inc.

## Appiah, Kwame Anthony

(Ah-PEE-ah, KWAH-mee AN-thun-ee)

*May 8, 1954– Writer; educator*

*Address: University Center for Human Values, Louis Marx Hall, Princeton University, Princeton, NJ 08544*

"When people organize around their own separate groups," Kwame Anthony Appiah wrote for the *American Enterprise* (September/October 1995), "the result is not just difficulty in understanding across cultures but that we end up preferring our own kind. And if we prefer our own kind, it is easy enough to slip into preferring to vote for our own kind, to employ our own kind, and so on." A novelist and prominent member of what has been called the "New Black Intelligentsia," Appiah has been a professor of philosophy, African studies, and African-American studies at such elite universities as Cambridge, in England; Yale, in New Haven, Connecticut; Cornell, in Ithaca, New York; Duke, in Durham, North Carolina; and Harvard, in Cambridge, Massachusetts. In September 2002 he began teaching at Princeton University, in Princeton, New Jersey. Early in his career he focused on philosophy, particularly the philosophy of language, before moving on to African and African-American studies in later years. Working with his frequent collaborator Henry Louis Gates Jr., Appiah brought out two highly publicized reference books, *The Dictionary of Global Culture* (1996) and *Africana: The Encyclopedia of African and African American Experience* (1999), which sought to fill a perceived gap in information about the cultures and peoples of Africa. While he has often concentrated on the cultures of black people in the U.S. and abroad, Appiah has frequently contended that race is not a biological reality but a faulty construct based on superficial external characteristics. The concept of race, for Appiah, obscures the essential commonality among humans.

Kwame Anthony Appiah was born in London, England, on May 8, 1954 and was raised in Asante, the capital city of the Republic of Ghana. Appiah's father, Joe, was the president of the Ghana Bar Association and had worked alongside Kwame Nkrumah, Ghana's first prime minister and president, in helping to win his country's independence from Great Britain, in 1957. (Nkrumah later imprisoned Joe Appiah due to political differences.) Appiah's mother, Peggy, who is white and British, is the daughter of a British solicitor-general whose father was an English law lord (a member of the House of Lords qualified to perform its legal work). Appiah received his anglicized name, Anthony, from his revered paternal great uncle, Yao Anthony. He went to Sunday school at St. George's, a diverse church that welcomed Baptists, Copts, Catholics, Methodists, and Anglicans alike. He spent time with his family in England periodically and attended an English boarding school. "If my sisters and I were 'children of two worlds,'" Appiah wrote in his preface to his book *In My Father's House* (1992), as quoted on *PBS.org*, "no one bothered to tell us this; we lived in one world, in two 'extended' families divided by several thousand miles and an allegedly insuperable cultural distance that never, so far as I can recall, puzzled or perplexed us much." Appiah went to primary school at the Kwame Nkrumah University of Science and Technology, in Asante, and earned his B.A. and Ph.D. degrees in philosophy from Cambridge University.

Appiah's first teaching post was at the University of Ghana. His first published book, *Assertion and Conditionals* (1985), was a revised version of his doctoral dissertation, on semantics. This was followed by *For Truth in Semantics* (1986) and *Necessary Questions: An Introduction to Philosophy* (1989). In 1990 Appiah edited *Early African-American Classics*, which includes Frederick Douglass's *Narrative of the Life of Frederick Doug-*

*lass, An American Slave* (1845) and excerpts from W. E. B. Du Bois's *The Souls of Black Folk* (1903). Appiah's first novel, *Avenging Angel* (1991), was a murder mystery set in Cambridge. A reviewer for *Kirkus*, as quoted on *Amazon.com*, called it "aggressively literate and fawningly Anglophilic, though the storytelling is enervated and the detective a noble cipher."

In 1992 Appiah published *In My Father's House: Africa in the Philosophy of Culture*. In that book, as he explained in the preface, he drew "on the writings of . . . African and African-American thinkers to explore the possibilities and pitfalls of an African identity in the late twentieth century." In the opening chapters Appiah examined the roots of Pan-Africanism, an intellectual movement that attempts to establish a unifying identity for peoples of African descent—an effort of which Appiah is deeply suspicious. "The very invention of Africa (as something more than a geographical identity) must be understood, ultimately, as an outgrowth of European racialism," Appiah wrote, as quoted in the *New York Times* (June 21, 1992). "The notion of Pan-Africanism was founded on the notion of the African, which was, in turn, founded not on any genuine cultural commonality but . . . on the very European concept of the Negro. . . . The very category of the Negro is at root a European product: for the 'whites' invented the Negroes in order to dominate them." In subsequent essays Appiah explored African literature, the collision between modern African philosophy and traditional religion, and African politics. In *Africa Today* (1995) Nigel Gibson complained that "the realities of Africa's position in the world economy and 'real' life for the mass of Africans seem largely ignored [in *In My Father's House*]," but he nevertheless called the book a "wonderfully crafted collection of essays." In the *New York Times Book Review* (June 21, 1992), Charles Johnson wrote, "By applying precision of thought—indeed, the entire history of Western philosophy—throughout the interdisciplinary essays that constitute *In My Father's House*, Mr. Appiah delivers what may very well be one of the handful of theoretical works on race that will help preserve our humanity and guide us gracefully into the next century." *In My Father's House* won the Annisfield-Wolf Book Award and the 1993 Herskovits Award from the African Studies Association for the best work published in English on Africa.

In 1993 Appiah co-edited the Critical Perspectives Past and Present series, a collection of books of criticism and commentary about African-American literature. His collaborator was Henry Louis Gates Jr., whom Appiah had met as a graduate student at Cambridge and worked with at Yale, Cornell, and Duke before the two joined the faculty of Harvard University, in 1991. Authors whose works were analyzed in the series include Langston Hughes, Zora Neale Hurston, Gloria Naylor, Alice Walker, Richard Wright, and Toni Morrison. Reviewing the volume about Toni Morrison for *Melus* (Spring 1996), Kimberly Drake wrote, "[Appiah and Gates] have reconstructed this criticism so that it forms a conversation, a series of arguments; the essays speak to one another and to the reviews and interviews, offering multiple perspectives on various issues, so that readers can decide for themselves which analysis is more compelling—and can then turn to the interviews for Morrison's own opinion. The overlap encourages the reader to participate, to 'THINK,' something Morrison requires from readers of her fiction."

Appiah published his second novel, *Nobody Likes Letitia*, in 1994, and his third, *Another Death in Venice*, in 1995. Also in 1995 Gates and Appiah co-edited another book, *Identities*, a collection of 20 essays covering such topics as race, class, gender, postcolonialism, and globalization. In 1996 Appiah co-authored, with the Princeton professor Amy Gutman, *Color Conscious: The Political Morality of Race*, of which his essay "Race, Culture, Identity: Misunderstood Connections" makes up the first half. Just as Appiah had objected in *In My Father's House* to the misleading categorization implicit in Pan-Africanism, he took issue in "Race, Culture, Identity" with what he saw as the flawed concept of race as a biological category of humankind. Summarizing Appiah's argument, Jeremy Waldron wrote for the *London Review of Books* (March 19, 1998), "[Appiah] says that as a matter of biology, the underlying theory of race—that human beings can be divided into a fairly small number of groups whose members share a set of heritable moral and intellectual characteristics with one another that they do not share with members of any other race—is not slightly wrong, but wildly wrong." Furthermore, Appiah argued that race, though it certainly plays a role in forming people's identities, obscures the fact that people of a common race have more differences than similarities. "The identities we need," he wrote, as quoted by Todd Gitlin in *American Prospect* (March/April 1997), "will have to recognize both the centrality of difference within human identity and the fundamental moral unity of humanity." While Gitlin acknowledged that "the tricontinental philosopher [Appiah] brings to [*Color Conscious*] a valuable combination of tools, including the implements of analytic philosophy and a familiarity with historical and anthropological literatures from all over," he asserted that Appiah had failed to answer the "question of why identities feel so urgent these days" and "why should so many people today be striving to shore up such a fierce sense of group solidarity?" In *Choice* (April 1997) C. Taylor declared that "[Appiah's] argument, refuting scientific assumptions about race that grew out of the Enlightenment, is persuasive." *Color Conscious* won the Annual Book Award of the North American Society for Social Philosophy for the most significant contribution to social philosophy.

The year 1996 found Appiah and Gates collaborating once again, this time on a reference book, *The Dictionary of Global Culture*. That work contains entries relating to white cultural icons of Europe and North America but focuses more on documenting aspects of nonwhite cultures, in Asia, the Middle East, Africa, Latin America, and elsewhere. For instance, more space is given in the dictionary to the African-American jazz musician Charlie Parker than to the German classical composer Ludwig van Beethoven; and the former president of Zambia, Kenneth D. Kaunda, elicits a longer entry than does the British playwright William Shakespeare. Frank Kermode, in the *New York Review of Books* (February 6, 1997), asserted, "The true object of this dictionary is to question deep-rooted assumptions of European preeminence. . . . The concessions to Eurocentricity are tactical, and the true purpose is to establish a new and aggressive point of view." That point of view proved quite controversial. Those who were the most critical, such as Samuel McCracken, writing for *Commentary* (April 1997), accused Appiah and Gates of third-rate scholarship. "The myriad errors that disfigure [the work]," McCracken wrote, "reflect something more serious than sloppy editing; they reflect a truly alarming incomprehension. It is as if a small corps of uneducated undergraduates had been set to work reading other reference books and had then rendered in amateurish prose their imperfect grasp of the information gleaned thereby." Kermode, on the other hand, praised Appiah's and Gates's entries on non-Western and African-American culture, but questioned the efficacy of the dictionary as a truly "global" reference work. "It seems a pity that the dictionary . . . [couldn't] have avoided the temptation of globality," Kermode wrote, "and been designed as a dictionary of non-white cultures without constantly inviting disparaging or irrelevant comparisons, and wasting a lot of space." In the *New York Times* (February 2, 1997, on-line), James Shapiro applauded the dictionary for its accuracy, insight, and agenda. "No doubt a decade from now others will produce a new dictionary," Shapiro wrote, "one that will confront more directly the problems posed by hybrid identity and the homogenizing effects of mass culture. Any such work, though, will have to build on the pathbreaking achievement of *The Dictionary of Global Culture.*"

In 1999 Appiah and Gates compiled *Africana: The Encyclopedia of African and African American Experience*, acknowledging in their introduction their desire to carry on in the footsteps of the African-American scholar W. E. B. DuBois. DuBois had worked intermittently from 1909 until his death, in 1963, to realize his vision of an encyclopedia of African and African-related culture that he hoped might enjoy the status of the respected *Encyclopedia Britannica*; he never completed this task. Approximately 40 percent of *Africana*, which is more than 2,000 pages long, consists of entries about Africa, while the rest focuses on the Caribbean, Latin America, and the United States. The encyclopedia elicited mixed reviews. A critic for *Booklist* (February 15, 2000) stated, "Nearly all the articles fit the objective spirit expected of encyclopedias," while Julia Vitullo-Martin complained in *Commonweal* (February 25, 2000) that the encyclopedia was biased and inaccurate. "Granting an encyclopedia [the status of a *Britannica*] requires trust," Vitullo-Martin wrote: "Trust by the reader that the encyclopedia is thorough, meticulous, well researched, and—since the editors must make innumerable judgments—fair. *Africana* does not yet meet these standards." Similarly, John Thornton, in the *New York Times* (January 16, 2000, on-line), noted, "There are unfortunate errors [in *Africana*] even in the brief entries," but he nevertheless concluded that "*Africana* will be a very useful tool, and may even set new standards and change attitudes about the African and African-American experience. In so doing it should fulfill its authors' and even DuBois's goals." The encyclopedia was also released in 1999 in an expanded CD-ROM format, under the title *Encarta Africana*; that version consists of more than 2.5 million words and includes some 2,500 pictures, maps, graphs, sounds, and video clips.

Early in 2002 Appiah announced that he would be joining the faculty at Princeton University and leaving Harvard University, where he had been a professor of Afro-American studies and philosophy since 1991. The announcement came shortly after members of Harvard's Afro-American studies department, including Cornel West, questioned the commitment of Harvard's new president, Lawrence H. Summers, to the department and to affirmative action. Appiah told Jacques Steinberg for the *New York Times* (January 26, 2002) that he had simply grown tired of commuting to Cambridge from his home in New York City. He added, "I have no dissatisfaction with Larry Summers or anyone in the department at Harvard. I'm leaving because of personal and intellectual opportunities at Princeton." Appiah became Princeton's Lawrence S. Rockefeller university professor of philosophy in September 2002. He has recently been collaborating with his mother on a work with the tentative title "Bu Me Bé: Proverbs of the Akan," an annotated edition of 7,500 proverbs in the Twi language, spoken in Asante, Ghana. — P.G.H.

Suggested Reading: *Africa Today* p73+ no. 3 1995; *American Enterprise* p50 Sep./Oct. 1995; *American Prospect* p93+ Mar./Apr. 1997; *Black Issues in Higher Education* p14+ Jan. 17, 2002; *Commentary* p63+ Apr. 1997; *Commonweal* p26+ Feb. 25, 2000; *London Review of Books* p12+ Mar. 19, 1998; *Melus* p148+ Spring 1996; *New York Review of Books* p30+ Feb. 6, 1997; *New York Times* A p1+ Jan. 26, 2002, with photo; *New York Times* (on-line) Feb. 2, 1997, Jan. 16, 2000; *New York Times Book Review* p8 June 21, 1992; *Washington Times Book World* p3 June 14, 1992

Selected Books: as writer—*Assertion and Conditionals*, 1985; *For Truth in Semantics*, 1986; *Necessary Questions: An Introduction to*

*Philosophy*, 1989; *Avenging Angel*, 1991; *In My Father's House*, 1992; *Color Conscious: The Political Morality of Race* (with Amy Gutman), 1996; as editor—*Early African-American Classics*, 1990; as editor with Henry Louis Gates Jr.—*Alice Walker: Critical Perspectives Past and Present*, 1993; *Gloria Naylor: Critical Perspectives Past and Present*, 1993; *Langston Hughes: Critical Perspectives Past and Present*, 1993; *Richard Wright: Critical Perspectives Past and Present*, 1993; *Toni Morrison: Critical Perspectives Past and Present*, 1993; *Zora Neale Hurston: Critical Perspectives Past and Present*, 1993; *Identities*, 1995; *The Dictionary of Global Culture*, 1997; *Africana: The Encyclopedia of the African and African American Experience*, 1999

---

John Spellman/Retna ltd.

## Arrarás, María Celeste

*Sep. 27, 1961– Host of the television show* Al Rojo Vivo con María Celeste

*Address: Telemundo, 2290 West Eighth Ave., Hialeah, FL 33010*

"I've always been curious," the broadcast journalist María Celeste Arrarás told Yohana de la Torre for the *Miami Herald* (January 20, 2002). "Curious and hungry for the story, since my first day on the job." Often called the Katie Couric of Latin television, Arrarás has reported the news on Spanish-language television programs for more than a decade. She began anchoring newscasts for the Spanish-language network Univision in 1989; in early 2002 she moved to that station's rival, Telemundo, where she became the host of *Al Rojo Vivo con María Celeste*, her own news, features, and entertainment show. That same month NBC acquired Telemundo and arranged with Arrarás to make occasional contributions to NBC news programs. She will thus gain exposure to non–Spanish-speaking TV viewers, too.

María Celeste Arrarás was born in Mayaguez, Puerto Rico, on September 27, 1961. Her mother was a chemist. Her father, Jose Enrique Arrarás, was a university chancellor, newspaper publisher, and politician; he served as housing secretary for the Commonwealth of Puerto Rico and as minority leader in Puerto Rico's House of Representatives. Because of her father's involvement in politics, she told Judy Hevrdejs for the *Chicago Tribune* (April 17, 2002), "I grew up in the public eye and I hated it. We used to go out for dinners, whatever we would do, we would get interruptions constantly. I said I'll never do that and little did I know—I ended up doing the exact same thing." Her parents instilled in the young María the belief that she should stand out from the crowd. "My father would tell me, 'Don't bring a C to this house,'" she recalled to Mirta Ojito for the *New York Times* (May 5, 2002, on-line). "'You either get an A or an F, but never a C. You are either the best of the best or the worst of the worst.'" When she was 10, the Arrarás family moved to San Juan, the capital of Puerto Rico, where she attended an all-girls school, Colegio Puerto Riqueno de Ninas. (Her parents divorced in the same year.) Describing herself during that period to de la Torre, she said, "I've always been very tomboyish. I was never concerned with fashion and dolls. I was into accomplishing other things like volleyball, swimming and even fencing, and this made me challenge myself and learn competitiveness." In 1971 she won a gold medal in the backstroke at the swimming competition of the Central American Games, held in Cuba. She spent her junior year of high school at Pine Crest, an elite prep school in Fort Lauderdale, Florida. In 1976 she earned a spot on the Puerto Rican Olympic swim team, but she was unable to compete, because she fell ill with mononucleosis a week before the Games were to start.

Arrarás's first taste of journalism came at around that time, when her father asked her to write a column for young readers of the sports-oriented newspaper he owned. "It was like 'click.' A light went on," she recalled to Ojito of that experience. Arrarás attended Loyola University, in New Orleans, where she majored in communications. After she earned a bachelor's degree, in 1982, she returned to Puerto Rico and got a job as an advertising copywriter. Although she quickly won a promotion, she told Patricia Kitchen for *Newsday* (April 28, 2002), "I realized I was mediocre" at copywriting. "I didn't have passion" for that sort of work, she added. While attending an advertising awards luncheon, she met a media entrepreneur, who soon hired her to work for his new, 24-hour Caribbean television news channel. "This station had . . . trust in me," she told de la Torre. "I did everything and learned everything."

After a year with the station, Arrarás moved to New York City to anchor a local news program on Univision. Despite her solid skills, the station's news director asked her to relinquish her position, because she didn't look glamorous enough. "He said, 'I've handed you a bag of lemons. You can either get sour or make lemonade,'" she told Ojito. "I chose to stay and make lemonade." She continued working at Univision, and six months later she became the station's Los Angeles bureau chief. Not long afterward she moved to Miami, Florida, to anchor the network's weekend news program. In 1993, in what Univision told her would be a temporary placement, she became co-anchor of *Noticias y Mas* (News and More), a show (later renamed *Primer Impacto*, First Impact, or First Hit) that offers both entertainment and news. Her partner was Myrka Dellanos, an established broadcast journalist. Impressed by the chemistry between the two women, the show's producers made Arrarás's job permanent. Arrarás had altered her style for the program, making jokes and wearing more daring fashions, and she found that she could relax much more easily. "For the first time, I could smile on the air," she told Ojito. "It was refreshing and different, and it suited my personality better." *Primer Impacto* combines tabloid journalism—such as fantastical accounts of two-headed babies or of images of the Virgin Mary appearing in skillets, as well as a daily horoscope reading—with hard news. The program won an Edward R. Murrow Award in 1998 for an exposé of prison conditions in Venezuela, Panama, and El Salvador. Concurrently, Arrarás hosted the late-night Sunday series *Ver para Creer* (See to Believe). By the time she left Univision, in February 2002, hers had become a household name among Spanish-speakers in the U.S., and she enjoyed considerable popularity in the Spanish-language media; her portrait repeatedly graced the covers of Spanish-language magazines.

Arrarás gained a lot of publicity by landing an exclusive interview with Abraham Quintanilla, the father of the Tejano music superstar Selena Quintanilla Perez (known professionally as simply Selena), a few months after the singer's murder, in 1995; she also secured an interview with Yolanda Saldivar, the woman later convicted of the killing. Arrarás's book, *Selena's Secrets: The Revealing Story Behind Her Tragic Death* (1997), based on those interviews and other research, became a bestseller. "For some reason after doing my [initial] investigation, there were too many loose ends," she told de la Torre. "The book puts everything into perspective, always respecting Selena's memory." The book angered members of the young singer's family, however, because it portrayed Abraham Quintanilla as a controlling person who was more interested in money than his daughter's happiness, and it intimated that Selena may have been planning to leave her husband for another man and to abandon music in favor of a career in fashion. The book also describes Saldivar's life and includes Saldivar's account of Selena's death, which she claimed was accidental. That part of the book, too, angered Abraham Quintanilla; he complained to Robert Dominguez for the New York *Daily News* (March 12, 1997) that Arrarás was evidently "determined to slander [Selena's] image." With the proceeds from the book, Arrarás funded several scholarships, including one for students in the field of fashion.

On April 10, 2002 Arrarás announced her move to Telemundo, Univision's rival Spanish-language television network. That same day NBC received approval from the Federal Communications Commission to buy the network, which broadcasts to all major U.S. cities. Arrarás's hiring has been widely touted as NBC's first coup in the Latino media market. "She is a star, along the lines of talent like Diane Sawyer and Jane Pauley," Andrew Lack, the president of NBC, told Ojito. "I have confidence that she will bring her enormous talent to some of our programs in NBC." Her contract includes the option of contributing to such NBC programs as *Today* and *Dateline NBC*. "I hope it's a marriage made in heaven," Arrarás said at the April 10 news conference, as reported by Simon Applebaum for *Multichannel News* (April 15, 2002). "I feel that way." In terms of audience size, Telemundo has a long way to go to catch up to Univision, which, as Lisa de Moraes reported in the *Washington Post* (April 11, 2002), is the top Spanish-language station in the U.S. At the time of Arrarás's move, Univision was available in 93 percent of U.S. Hispanic households, and its prime-time audience averaged 3.4 million people; Telemundo, which was available in 88 percent of U.S. Hispanic households, drew an average of only 817,00 prime-time viewers. Arrarás believes that NBC's purchase of Telemundo will create new opportunities in the television industry for Hispanics and enable them to develop a greater presence in English-language programming. Currently, she said to Al Roker in an interview for the TV show *Today* (May 13, 2002), the 35 million Hispanics in the U.S. are "not really fairly represented" on English-language television.

*Al Rojo Vivo con María Celeste* (which, roughly, means "Red Hot with María Celeste"), her one-hour daily weekday show on Telemundo, offers a mixture of news, celebrity interviews, offbeat stories, advice, and segments on sports and health; according to Andrew Grossman in the *Hollywood Reporter* (May 15, 2002), Telemundo has referred to it as "a tabloid show on steroids." Arrarás herself has described the new program as a "news paella." In her conversation with Judy Hevrdejs, she said, "You get everything from health to entertainment to news, but angles that are more amazing and different. We're not going to get the presidential summit in Latin America, for example. But we'll get things that are more what people like to talk about at the table." Every installment of the show includes a segment about immigrant life and a "where-are-they-now" report on former newsmakers. "It's a mixture of . . . *Access Hollywood* with *Dateline*, with local news, with *Extra*," Arrarás told Al Roker, referring, respectively, to a celebrity-interview program on MSN, a news magazine on NBC, and a celebrity-saturated magazine on the WB Network. *Al Rojo Vivo* debuted on April 29, 2002, two months after Arrarás's departure from *Primer Impacto*; currently, it airs in the same time slot as *Primer Impacto*. Although she has remained friendly with Dellanos, Arrarás prizes the opportunity to go head-to-head with her former co-anchor. "When you go to war, you can't take any prisoners," she observed to Ojito. In its first week on the air, *Al Rojo Vivo* gained higher ratings than *Primer Impacto* in New York and Miami. Surpassing her former show consistently in the ratings is a tall order, however, as *Primer Impacto* has boasted an audience of 100 million in the U.S. and 15 Latin American countries. On the other hand, surveys conducted by Nielsen Media Research showed that *Primer Impacto* dropped an average of two to three ratings points after Arrarás's departure, while the debut of *Al Rojo Vivo* led to a 14 percent increase in Telemundo viewers during that time slot from one month to the next. Telemundo expects Arrarás's popularity in cities with large Latino populations to keep *Al Rojo Vivo*'s ratings high. The show is currently number one in its time slot in New York, beating all English-language programs and other Spanish-language offerings airing at the same time.

Arrarás has said that she wants her television audience to regard her as a real person. "I'm not the greatest anchor in the world, but what I lack in talent I make up with honesty," she told Ojito. "Viewers appreciate that. In my show, eventually, I want to tell my viewers that I'm not feeling well, that I have cold, that I lost my voice. I want them to see me as I am." While she reportedly welcomes opportunities to cross over into English-language television, she considers *Al Rojo Vivo* her top priority. "I'm not the kind of person who melts to be in English-language television," she told Ojito. "I'm quite comfortable with my audience, and Telemundo is my rice and beans."

Known for speaking her mind without hesitation, Arrarás is reportedly earning $1 million a year, an unprecedented figure for a Latina TV news figure. "I will be paying lots of taxes, but I'm making less than Katie Couric," she said at the April 10 news conference, as reported by Alex Veiga for the Associated Press (April 10, 2002, on-line). She has said that it was not the prospect of greater remuneration that motivated her to leave *Primer Impacto*, but rather the chance to have a show of her own, one that she could influence directly and strongly. "To me this was the key to the equation," she told Hevrdejs. "It wasn't the zeros at the end of the salary or anything like that. I've never been an on-camera talent that just goes there and reads. . . . I really like to get immersed in what goes into the concept of the show. I think that's a way of imprinting your style. I think the type of stories you choose reflects who you are. That's what's important to me. What we're doing with this show is we're basically offering a new version of a very successful concept in the Hispanic world. It's a format that has worked in the past, but in my opinion it needs to be revamped."

Arrarás often attends high-profile events in the Hispanic community. She hosted *People en Español*'s fifth anniversary celebration in New York on May 15, 2002; in 2001 she was on that magazine's list of "Most Beautiful [People] in Spanish News Programs" and was also named that year's most popular Spanish TV celebrity. She served as "godmother" of New York City's 2002 Puerto Rican Day Parade. She made a brief appearance as a newscaster in the film *Contact* (1997) and recently added her handprints to Mexico's Paseo de las Luminarias (Walk of the Luminaries). She made a guest appearance on two episodes of NBC's daytime drama *Passions* in late November; portraying herself, she was identified as a longtime friend of the character Pilar (Eva Tamargo Lemus), on a visit for a Latino version of a traditional Thanksgiving celebration. Arrarás was one of the 2002 honorees of the Hispanic Media 100. She has signed a contract with Random House to write a second book, scheduled to be published in May 2003.

A passionate supporter of animal rights, Arrarás is the first Latina celebrity spokesperson for the organization People for the Ethical Treatment of Animals (PETA). (During her childhood her father habitually rescued stray animals, as a result of which she had many pets while she was growing up.) She is currently working to outlaw the use of animals by circuses and other shows mounted in Puerto Rico. Arrarás has argued that while children may enjoy watching animals perform, they would be the first to condemn the treatment the creatures endure "behind closed doors" if they knew about it, as she put it to Magaly Morales for the Fort Lauderdale *Sun-Sentinel* (December 5, 2001). She is the only Hispanic reporter to receive the Genesis Award, with which the animal-protection organization Ark Trust honors "outstanding individuals in the major media and artistic community who have communicated animal-rights and animal-welfare issues with courage, artistry and integrity," according to the trust's Web site.

Arrarás also volunteers with the Aspira Association, a national organization devoted to the education and leadership training of Puerto Rican and other Latino young people, and Amor y Vida, an orphanage in Honduras that serves children infected with HIV. "I'm no Mother [Teresa], but I want people to realize that hard work and social involvement is a very positive drug," she told de la Torre. "It's like discovering the secret to happiness." Arrarás has denied that a conflict exists between the need for impartiality, which she must exercise as a reporter and news anchor, and her determination to speak out on issues close to her heart. "I'm a journalist first," she told Roker. "I never let one thing interfere with another. And I always . . . make a disclaimer when it has something to do with something that people do know I have a preference for."

The slender Arrarás has acknowledged undergoing breast-augmentation surgery in the mid-1990s. Her first marriage, to Guillermo Ramis, an advertising executive, ended in divorce. With her second husband, Manny Arbezu, a real-estate lawyer, she has three children under five: two sons, Julian and Adrian, and one daughter, Lara. The couple adopted Adrian, who was born in Russia, when he was 15 months old. Explaining the decision to adopt, she told de la Torre, "I decided to change somebody's world." In response to the criticism from some in the Latino community that she should have adopted a child from Latin America, she said that she had tried to do so but had been stymied by bureaucracy. Arrarás rises at 4:30 a.m. to prepare for her show, and despite her busy schedule, she has told interviewers, she strives to make sure that each of her children gets enough of her attention; she regularly prepares breakfast and lunch for them. "My kids are like mud," she told de la Torre. "I'm slowly and carefully molding them into my beautiful pieces of art." The family live near Miami with their two dogs. — K.E.D.

Suggested Reading: Associated Press (on-line) Apr. 10, 2002; *Chicago Tribune* Tempo p1 Apr. 17, 2002; (Fort Lauderdale, Florida) *Sun-Sentinel* E p4 Jun. 21, 2000, E p4 Dec. 5, 2001, with photo; *Hollywood Reporter* May 15, 2002; *Miami Herald* E p4 Jan. 20, 2002, with photo; *Multichannel News* p14 Apr. 15, 2002; (New York) *Daily News* Mar. 12, 1997; *New York Times* IX, p1 May 5, 2002, with photos; *Newsday* F p5 Apr. 28, 2002, with photo

Selected Books: *Selena's Secrets: The Revealing Story Behind Her Tragic Death*, 1997

---

Getty Images

## Bakula, Scott

(BAK-yew-luh)

*Oct. 9, 1954– Actor; director; producer*

*Address: 14431 Ventura Blvd., Suite 320, Sherman Oaks, CA 91423*

The actor Scott Bakula is best known for his portrayal of Sam Beckett on the popular television show *Quantum Leap*, which debuted on the NBC network in 1989. By the end of the program's four-year run, the series had developed a cult following and brought Bakula stardom and critical recognition: for his characterization of the amiable Beckett, he was nominated for four Emmy Awards and four Golden Globe Awards. In addition to his work on *Quantum Leap*, which included directing several episodes, Bakula has abundant other experience in show business. He has starred in more than a dozen films and more than 20 television shows during the past 15 years. He formed his own production company, Bakula Productions, in the mid-1990s, and has served as executive producer of four television programs, in which he also starred. As a stage actor Bakula was nominated for a Tony Award for his role in the 1988 Broadway production of *Romance, Romance*. In 2001 he landed the role of Captain Jonathan Archer in the highly anticipated *Star Trek: Enterprise*, the most recent spin-off of the late Gene Roddenberry's original *Star Trek* series. Bakula has received critical acclaim for his portrayal of Archer, whose brash personality and love for the unknown carry viewers to a future in which space travelers dare "to boldly go where no man has gone before."

Scott Stewart Bakula was born on October 9, 1954 in St. Louis, Missouri. He was the eldest of the three children of Sally and J. Stewart Bakula, the latter of whom was a lawyer and, at one time, the general counsel for the 7-Up beverage corporation. Bakula attended Keyser Grade School in the St. Louis suburb of Kirkwood, where his family—which included his sister, Linda, and his brother, Brad—lived. Bakula's father was an accomplished classical pianist, and Scott consequently took piano lessons. At Keyser he played keyboards in a rock band. He also displayed singing talent and a penchant for the dramatic. In 1967 he sang the title role in a St. Louis Symphony production of the Christmas-themed opera *Amahl and the Night Visitors*. Bakula attended Kirkwood High School, where he participated in extracurricular activities in music, theater, and sports. Clark Cole, a Kirkwood classmate of his, told Gail Pennington for the *St. Louis Post-Dispatch* (October 7, 1994), "He was so busy that he couldn't hang out as much as we'd have liked him to." Bakula lettered seven times in tennis and soccer, and he starred in several school productions of musicals, including *Fiddler on the Roof.* In the spring of his senior year, he secured the lead in *Godspell*, produced by the First Presbyterian Church of Kirkwood, where for some time he had sung in the choir.

After he graduated from high school, in 1973, Bakula enrolled at the University of Kansas at Lawrence. His plan was to follow in his father's footsteps and earn a law degree, but after two years he realized that law was not a career he wanted to pursue. He dropped out of school and joined a road production of *Godspell.* That job did not last long, and he returned to Kirkwood, becoming involved with local theater. He appeared in several musicals produced at nearby Jefferson College, including *The Man of La Mancha, Cabaret,* and *Joseph and the Amazing Technicolor Dreamcoat.*

Convinced that acting was his calling, Bakula moved to New York City in 1976. Three days after his arrival, he got a part in a touring production of the musical *Shenandoah.* After that, he acted in repertory and regional theater while living in New York, in "one of those gritty hotels where you feel little eyes following you down the corridor," as he told Edwin Kiester Jr. for *TV Guide* (December 23, 1989). In 1980, while performing in *The Baker's Wife* in Cincinnati, Ohio, Bakula met the actress Krista Neumann, whom he married a year later. The couple had a daughter, Chelsy, and a son, Cody, before their divorce, in 1996.

In 1983 Bakula got his first Broadway role, as the baseball legend Joe DiMaggio in *Marilyn: An American Fable.* Although it was an unremarkable production and had a brief run, the opportunity led to others, including roles in *It's Better with a Band* (1983) and *Three Guys Naked from the Waist Down* (1985). The next year, temporarily abandoning the stage, he went to Hollywood to try his hand at television acting. He was almost immediately offered a recurring role on the popular show *Designing Women*, as the chauvinistic ex-husband of the actress Annie Potts, one of the show's regulars. Also that year Bakula appeared in the short-lived TV show *My Sister Sam* and as the lead in the even shorter-lived *Gung Ho.* In 1988 Bakula took the role of the sleazy lawyer Bud Lutz Jr. in CBS's *Eisenhower and Lutz.* In a review for *USA Today* (March 14, 1988), Monica Collins wrote, "Bakula, comedy-cute though he may be, is not particularly strong as Lutz. The character is a weakling and a weak link." *Eisenhower and Lutz* did not survive the season. That same year Bakula returned to New York to star in the Broadway musical *Romance, Romance.* Unlike many of the shows in which he had appeared, the musical was extremely successful, both commercially and critically. For his work in *Romance, Romance*, he was nominated for a 1988 Tony Award.

In 1989 Bakula returned to Los Angeles and accepted the lead role in *Quantum Leap*, one of the few new television series that pleased critics at the time. Dorothy Swanson, president of Viewers for Quality Television, told Jess Cagle for *Entertainment Weekly* (March 29, 1991), "[*Quantum Leap*] appeals to the intellect and the emotion. It moves people." Although relatively few viewers tuned in to the seven episodes of its first season (it was ranked 72d in popularity among 111 shows), it was renewed for a second season and allotted 22 episodes. By the end of 1990 it had become a hit. *Quantum Leap* revolved around Sam Beckett, a scientist who became a reluctant time traveler because of a bungled physics experiment. In each episode Sam entered a different body and had to alter that individual's ill-fated course in order to continue on his own. The underlying premise was that if Sam was able to help enough unfortunates, he would eventually return to his former self permanently. Assisted by his best friend, Albert Calavacci (Dean Stockwell), and Ziggy, a semi-sentient supercomputer, Sam "quantum leaps" into any soul in need, ranging from a Chippendale dancer to an elderly black man in 1950s Mississippi to a 15-year-old female rape victim. In an interview with Daniel Cerone for the *Los Angeles Times* (July 15, 1990), Bakula described the role of Sam as "an acting tour de force." He later told David Martindale for the *Houston Chronicle* (March 14, 1999), "[*Quantum Leap*] was the ultimate opportunity for an actor. The format was just a thing of beauty."

During *Quantum Leap*'s run, Bakula was nominated for four Emmy Awards and four Golden Globes; he won a Golden Globe for best actor in a drama series in 1992. Don Bellisario, *Quantum Leap*'s creator and executive producer, told Cerone, "What most people don't realize, and what we take for granted, I guess, is Scott's genuine acting ability. Every week he plays a different character, a different role. And he plays each one with an arc, with its own subtle nuances." By the show's finale (entitled "The Leap Home," in which Sam was permanently reunited with himself), which aired in 1993, Sam had entered almost a hundred different bodies.

While starring in *Quantum Leap*, which often demanded seven-day-a-week shooting schedules, Bakula found time to make the transition to the big screen. His film debut—alongside Kirstie Alley in Carl Reiner's black comedy *Sibling Rivalry* (1990)—was not a success. Susan Wloszczyna quipped in *USA Today* (October 26, 1990), "As a black comedy, *Sibling Rivalry* is strictly gray slush." Audiences tended to agree; the film disappeared from theaters in a matter of weeks. Bakula next took the lead role in Stan Dragoti's football comedy *Necessary Roughness* (1991). Though this effort received mixed reviews, Bakula's performance—as a quarterback who returns to college at 34, 16 years after dropping out due to his father's death—captivated both critics and audiences. "The premise might sound gimmicky," Mick LaSalle wrote for the *San Francisco Chronicle* (September 27, 1991), "but it's realized honestly and specifically. . . . Bakula, playing Paul as humble and decent and quietly capable, becomes very easy to root for."

Before *Quantum Leap* drew to a close, Bakula was given a recurring role on the popular television series *Murphy Brown*, as the suave, adventurous news correspondent Peter Hunt, who emerges as a love interest of the show's title character (played by Candice Bergen). Commenting on his approach to playing such distinctly different characters as the charming Sam Beckett and the arrogant Peter Hunt, Bakula explained to Jefferson Graham for *USA Today* (September 20, 1993), "The producers [of *Murphy Brown*] wanted a nasty, yet likable guy. When I was on *Designing Women*, I played the nastiest, most chauvinistic guy on the show, yet people liked me. I like to play parts like this. It's nice to be different than Sam."

In 1994 Bakula played a small but important role opposite Bruce Willis and Jane March in Richard Rush's *Color of Night*, a film that disappointed many critics. When James Brady, writing for *Parade* (February 5, 1995), asked Bakula where he thought the film went wrong, the actor answered, "It was a movie I liked, but it went through a lot of changes in the script." Bakula also said, "I wanted to work with Richard Rush, and I also was curious about working with Bruce, because we both came from New York and from television."

In 1996, following his divorce from Krista Neumann, Bakula entered into a relationship with Chelsea Field, whom he had met in 1993 while acting opposite her in Rick King's *A Passion to Kill*. Shortly after she gave birth to Bakula's second son, Wil, Field was recruited for *The Bachelor's Baby* (1996), a made-for-TV movie produced by Bakula. The plot revolved around Jake (Bakula), a single man faced with fatherhood after a romantic fling with a woman named Jamie (Field). "There are certain aspects of this movie that do parallel our life together," Bakula admitted to Vicki Jo Radovsky for *Entertainment Weekly* (September 27, 1996).

In 1997 Bakula lent his baritone voice to the animated movie *Cats Don't Dance*. He next accepted the lead in *Major League: Back to the Minors* (1998), the third installment of a trilogy. Although the film did poorly at the box office, his performance as a washed-up pitcher who accepts a minor-league coaching position earned him some positive reviews. Among them was Mick LaSalle's, who wrote for the *San Francisco Chronicle* (April 18, 1998), "*Major League: Back to the Minors* is a pleasant way to spend 95 minutes. . . . Bakula is a large part of what holds the movie together."

Following a series of appearances on both television and screen—most notably as a gay man in Sam Mendes's Oscar-winning *American Beauty* (1999)—Bakula accepted the role of Captain Jonathan Archer in the much-anticipated TV series *Star Trek: Enterprise*. The new show, which airs on the UPN network, differs from its earlier counterparts in that its action takes place in the 22d century, a hundred years before the setting of the 1960s *Star Trek* series, which starred William Shatner as Captain James T. Kirk. Bakula plays the first captain of the *Enterprise*, the starship later commanded by Kirk. The show's executive producer, Rick Berman, who cast Bakula, explained to Bill Keveney for *USA Today* (July 20, 2001), "[Finding Bakula] was like a godsend, because we were looking for somebody with a little bit of Chuck Yeager and a little bit of Han Solo and someone who was charming. Scott fits the character perfectly." Bakula told Keveney that *Enterprise*'s premise was the ultimate enticement. "I don't believe I would have done the show if it had been the next version of [*Star Trek*:] *Voyager* 20 years later," he said. "But to be the first captain, that was a nice carrot to dangle out there." In its second week on television, *Enterprise* became the number-one-rated new drama with viewers ages 18 to 34. Dean Valentine, UPN's president and chief executive officer, told Bernard Weinraub for the *New York Times* (October 16, 2001), "It's a good show, it's an accessible show with a very broad appeal, and putting a TV star like Scott Bakula in it sent a signal that it was not just an insular [science-fiction] thing." Bakula's dedication to the program stems in part from his love of science fiction. As he explained to Keveney, "I guess the little kid in me is still hoping some of this stuff will happen while I can see it."

Bakula currently lives in the Los Angeles area with Chelsea Field. The couple's second child, Owen, was born in 1999. — J.H.

Suggested Reading: *Entertainment Weekly* p25+ Mar. 29, 1991, with photos, p61 Sep. 27, 1996, with photo; *Houston Chronicle* p5 Mar. 14, 1999, with photo; *Los Angeles Times* p2 July 15, 1990, with photos; *St. Louis Post-Dispatch* G p1 Oct. 7, 1994, with photos; *USA Today* E p5 July 20, 2001, with photo

Selected Films: as actor—*Sibling Rivalry*, 1990; *Necessary Roughness*, 1991; *Color of Night*, 1994; *A Passion to Kill*, 1994; *Cats Don't Dance*, 1997; *Major League: Back to the Minors*, 1998; *American Beauty*, 1999; as actor and producer—*The Bachelor's Baby*, 1996

Selected Theatrical Performances: *Amahl and the Night Visitors*, 1967; *Fiddler on the Roof*, 1973; *Godspell*, 1973; *Joseph and the Amazing Technicolor Dreamcoat*, 1973–76; *Cabaret*, 1976; *The Man of La Mancha*, 1976; *Shenandoah*, 1976; *The Baker's Wife*, 1980; *It's Better with a Band*, 1983; *Marilyn: An American Fable*, 1983; *Three Guys Naked from the Waist Down*, 1985; *Romance, Romance*, 1988

Selected Television Shows: as actor—*Designing Women*, 1986; *Gung Ho*, 1986; *My Sister Sam*, 1986; *Eisenhower and Lutz*, 1988; *Murphy Brown*, 1993–96; *Enterprise*, 2001– ; as actor and director—*Quantum Leap*, 1989–93; as actor and producer—*Mr. & Mrs. Smith*, 1996

Courtesy of MSNBC

## Banfield, Ashleigh

*Dec. 29, 1967– Television newscaster; journalist*

*Address: MSNBC TV, One MSNBC Plaza, Secaucus, NJ 07094*

In television news it sometimes happens that public crises catapult the reporters covering them to positions of international prominence. Ted Koppel's career, for example, peaked following his coverage of the 1979 Iran hostage crisis. Similarly, during the 1991 Persian Gulf War, Arthur Kent—a foreign correspondent then nicknamed the "Scud Stud"—rose to celebrity status. More recently, the Canadian-born news anchor Ashleigh Banfield has emerged as one of the leading faces in cable-television news, largely for her coverage of two critical news stories. The first was the controversial ballot re-count for the U.S. presidential election of 2000, when Banfield gained national attention for her energetic reporting and her trademark black-rimmed glasses, an accessory that prompted many viewers to dub her "the girl in the glasses." The second, in the next year, was the terrorist attacks of September 11, 2001, when Banfield led MSNBC's coverage and delivered what Marc Peyser, writing for *Newsweek* (September 24, 2001), called "some of the most powerful reporting" from Ground Zero. Just weeks into the U.S.–led war on terrorism, Banfield was sent to Central Asia to host her own news program, *A Region in Conflict*, which made headlines as the first nightly news show to anchor live from a war zone. (The program, later renamed *Ashleigh Banfield on Location*, was canceled in October 2002.) Banfield's manner, which is relaxed and spontaneous as well as confident, and her capable delivery have appealed to many viewers. As one of the hottest new faces in broadcast journalism, Banfield has become, in the words of Jim Rutenberg in the *New York Times* (October 29, 2001), "perhaps the most talked-about news personality since Sept. 11."

Ashleigh Banfield was born on December 29, 1967 in Winnipeg, in the central Canadian province of Manitoba. The youngest of the four children of John Banfield, an architect, and Suzie Banfield, the owner of a real-estate company, she exhibited a strong personality from childhood. "I was very precocious," she told Michael Granberry for the *Dallas Morning News* (July 4, 2001), "and . . . a naughty clown who was always getting into trouble. I always had an interest in performing or communicating or talking or debating or arguing." Banfield was educated largely at all-girls private schools, where she appeared in student productions of *Oliver Twist* and *Joseph and the Amazing Technicolor Dreamcoat*, among other theatricals, and often played male roles because of her relatively deep voice. With the goal of becoming a foreign correspondent, she attended Queen's University, in Kingston, Ontario. She graduated with a bachelor's degree in political studies and French in 1988.

In the same year Banfield accepted her first position in television news, working as a photographer/researcher/reporter at CJBN, in Kenora, Ontario. (She is the only member of her family to venture outside the field of business; her three siblings have careers as a commercial realtor, an owner of several Toronto hedge funds, and a mutual-fund manager for the Hong Kong Bank of Canada, respectively.) Soon afterward she returned to Winnipeg and took a job researching and reporting for CKY-TV's evening news. In 1989 she became a weekend news anchor for CFRN, in Edmonton, Alberta, a position she held until 1992. Upon leaving that job she lived briefly in Vancouver, Canada, having followed a boyfriend there. Her attempt to find work in Vancouver did not succeed. "There were comments made to me about my race," she told Granberry, "that suggested I was not particularly [in] need at that point. There was a very heavy Chinese concentration in Vancouver. I was told by a news director, 'We love your credentials, but unfortunately, your last name isn't Chung.'"

Banfield soon returned to Alberta, where she settled in Calgary. Before the end of 1992, she obtained a position as producer for CICT-TV. During the next three years, she earned several promotions at the station, becoming first a morning anchor and later an evening news anchor. For her series on the life of a homeless man, she won two Iris Awards (named for the "eye" of the camera, which lets in light), from the National Association of Television Program Executives; she earned the prizes, which honor excellence in local television, in the categories of best news documentary and best of festival. While in Calgary Banfield also freelanced as an associate producer for ABC's *World News Tonight*, covering such notable events as the 1991 summit meeting between U.S. president George Herbert

Walker Bush and Russian president Mikhail Gorbachev in Russia and the 1992 summit meeting between Bush and Gorbachev's successors, U.S. president Bill Clinton and Russian president Boris Yeltsin, in Vancouver.

Despite her apparent success at CICT-TV, in 1995 Banfield was asked to leave her position as a prime-time anchor and become a reporter for the station. "I suffered a very public demotion," she noted to Granberry. Amid rumors that colleagues of hers resented her ambition and that their feelings of rivalry had led to the station's request, Banfield decided to leave CICT-TV and seek employment outside Canada.

Within weeks Banfield had secured a morning anchor position at KDFW-TV (Channel 4), in Dallas, Texas. Speaking of her relocation, she recalled to Granberry, "It was wonderful and horrible all at the same time. My first year at Channel 4 was not an easy one. I had a very difficult time. I did not enjoy it. I had a difficult co-anchor. He was not very forgiving. He was not a supportive partner on the air, which is too bad, because, if anything, I needed the help." Despite her initial difficulties Banfield was promoted to co-anchor of KDFW's evening news broadcasts. She also earned public recognition of her competence as a journalist, garnering a regional Emmy Award as best news anchor for her story "Cadet Killers," about a local woman killed by two military-academy cadets. She was also a co-winner of a Texas Associated Press Broadcasters Award for a series called "To Serve and Survive."

While living in Dallas Banfield developed a persona outside the newsroom as a regular in the city's nightlife. She often appeared in clubs with the local rhythm-and-blues band Tommy Hyatt and the Haywires, belting out cover tunes, and she became part owner of a pool hall. Her late-night appearances sometimes landed Banfield in the gossip columns of the *Dallas Morning News*.

In 1999, amid contract negotiations with Fox News, which had purchased KDFW in 1997, Banfield made another job change. "Fox wasn't offering me enough money to stay, and they wanted a no-exit contract," she explained to Mark Donald for the *Dallas Observer* (February 8, 2001, on-line). "It was time to move on." Despite her love for Dallas, Banfield began sending résumé tapes to prospective employers around the country. Three weeks before her final broadcast, in October 1999, Banfield, who had never worn glasses in front of the camera, began wearing a pair with thick, black titanium frames that reportedly cost $400. While some observers suggested that she had started to wear glasses, and had chosen those particular frames, in a bid to appear serious to prospective employers, Banfield contended that she was squeamish about contact lenses and needed corrective lenses to see the TelePrompTer displaying her news copy.

In February 2000 Banfield joined the all-news cable channel MSNBC. She served first as host of an afternoon women's program entitled *HomePage* and, later, as a co-host with Lester Holt for the newsmagazine *Newsfront*. Later that year she contributed to MSNBC's election coverage by touring with then-Governor George W. Bush of Texas during his campaign for the presidency and with Bush's running mate, Richard B. Cheney. She also traveled to Sydney, Australia, to cover the 2000 Summer Olympic Games. Ten months into the job, Banfield found herself in the center of the story that brought her to new prominence: the counting of the ballots for the 2000 presidential election. On the morning after Election Day, results in Florida indicated a virtual tie between Bush and the Democratic presidential candidate, then–Vice President Al Gore. The count in that state was crucial, because the victor in Florida would win a majority of votes in the Electoral College and thus the presidency. There ensued 36 days of Democratic and Republican legal maneuvering, heated national debate, and media frenzy before Bush emerged as the winner. As officials undertook the task of trying to re-count thousands of ballots in several large Florida counties, members of the media grappled with the challenge of relating to the public the politically and legally complex turn of events. As the MSNBC news anchor Brian Williams explained to Granberry, "That was seat-of-the-pants television for all of us, during which Ashleigh managed to bring the arcane nature of electoral politics down to a conversational level. And she did so without dumbing it down. She smartened up our coverage by making it understandable." During the impasse, Banfield traveled through Texas and Florida, establishing her credentials as an astute reporter and delivering the story "with only a legal pad and her comic timing to work her way through the masses," as Mark Donald wrote. For Banfield, the assignment was "a dream story," as she described it to Shada Deziel for *Maclean's* (June 4, 2001). "The kind where journalists can showcase their talents without being salacious."

The following year Banfield again demonstrated her ability to work under pressure, in perhaps the gravest and most significant news story in a generation: the terrorist attacks of September 11, 2001. That morning, Banfield, who lives in New York City, was watching television when a plane hit the north tower of the World Trade Center. She rushed to the scene and was just blocks away when the tower collapsed. Banfield described her experience in an article for *TV Guide* (October 13, 2001): "As the debris cloud hit us from behind, I could feel my ears bending forward, and could feel sand, soot and crushed glass particles rushing past my face. When daylight returned . . . I dialed the office on my cell phone and finally got through, but I was sobbing: 'Don't let this call go [on-air], whatever you do! Oh, God! You have no idea what's just happened!'" Covered in ash and rubble, she reported live throughout the day, first by telephone and, after locating a small digital camera and a TV signal, via digital video. "The early reports were simply observations after surviving the debris blast," she recalled for *TV Guide*, "but soon I would realize the dimensions of this horror and would cry openly on the air, something I'd never done before. But then, America had never seen anything like this before." Banfield's candor and openly emotional style of reporting on that day resonated with viewers watching the continuous coverage. Throughout that day—and several days that followed—Banfield remained near Ground Zero, interviewing city residents, firefighters, and emergency workers and conveying some sense of the devastation.

Soon after the attacks Banfield became MSNBC's main foreign correspondent for the war on terrorism and took an assignment to host her own nightly news program, *A Region in Conflict*, from Central Asia. (She dyed her hair, which is blond, a darker color for the assignment, so that she would blend into her surroundings better. The move prompted a flurry of media attention, which she characterized as "despicable.") Debuting on September 24, 2001, *A Region in Conflict*—subsequently renamed *Ashleigh Banfield on Location*—was broadcast from a hotel rooftop in Islamabad, Pakistan; later, after Banfield arrived in Kabul, the capital of Afghanistan, her coverage provided a unique perspective on conditions inside the war-torn city. The technical challenges of producing this type of live programming proved difficult. "It's really been a very taxing effort to get this done," Banfield told Paul Farhi for the *Washington Post* (December 5, 2001), adding that getting the program on the air was a "logistical nightmare" for MSNBC technicians. In addition, Banfield and her crew had well-founded concerns about their own safety. In mid-November a broken satellite phone delayed a planned convoy of journalists traveling between the Afghan cities of Jalalabad and Kabul; if Banfield had taken this trip as planned, she would have been directly behind four journalists who were killed in an ambush. During the next year, Banfield continued to report on location throughout Central Asia and the Middle East; she also spent extended periods in the U.S.

Although some critics complained that Banfield lacked sufficient experience as a foreign correspondent, MSNBC officials strongly supported her. Erik Sorenson, the president of the network, told Farhi, "We've tried to pick people who speak and deliver the news in an authentic way, and Ashleigh does that." He also commended Banfield's ability to communicate effectively with younger audiences, who might be learning about the politics of places overseas for the first time. At its peak, *Ashleigh Banfield on Location* attracted more than half a million loyal viewers.

Because of low ratings, *Ashleigh Banfield on Location* was canceled in October 2002 and replaced with *MSNBC Investigates*, a news magazine for which Banfield and others alternate as anchor. She also appears regularly as a field news correspondence for both MSNBC and NBC News.

Banfield lives in Manhattan with her two dogs, Angus and Lilly. She is engaged to Drew Nederpelt, owner of a technology company; the couple plan to wed sometime in 2002. Banfield is reportedly writing a book about the proliferation of cable news services in the U.S. — K.A.D.

Suggested Reading: *Dallas Morning News* July 3, 2001; *Dallas Observer* (on-line) Feb. 8, 2001, with photo; *New York Times* C p1 Oct. 29, 2001; *People* p86 Mar. 12, 2001, with photo; *TV Guide* p56+ Oct. 13, 2001, with photo; *Washington Post* C p1 Dec. 5, 2001

---

Courtesy of Sue B. Ish

## Barnett, Etta Moten

*Nov. 5, 1901– Singer; actress; patron of the arts*

*Address: 3619 Martin Luther King Dr., Chicago, IL 60653*

The singer and actress Etta Moten Barnett has been called a living repository of African-American history. In the course of her long career, Barnett performed in venues around the world, met heads of state, served as an official representative of the U.S. abroad, and witnessed many of the profound social changes of the 20th century. In 1901, the year of her birth, racial discrimination and segregation were facts of life in the American South, and women had not yet received the right to vote; the abolitionist and orator Frederick Douglass had died only six years earlier; and the National Association for the Advancement of Colored People (NAACP), the nation's oldest civil rights organization, had not yet been founded. As she recently told Joy Bennett

Kinnon for *Ebony* (December 2001), Barnett has seen far greater progress for African-Americans than she ever expected. "Honey," she said, "I know I've seen so many changes. I know we're heading in the right direction—and I'm willing to wait."

Among her many other credits, Barnett appeared in George Gershwin's *Porgy and Bess* on Broadway in 1942 and performed with the composer Duke Ellington, the Chicago Symphony Orchestra, and the New York Philharmonic. In recognition of her achievements, she has received honorary degrees from Lincoln University, Northeastern Illinois University, Atlanta University, Spelman College, and the University of Illinois at Chicago. In 1979 she was inducted into the Black Filmmakers Hall of Fame.

The only child of the Reverend Freeman F. Moten and his wife, Ida Mae Norman, Barnett was born Etta Moten in Weimer, Texas, on November 5, 1901. Because of her father's frequent transfers from one pastorate to another, Barnett saw a lot of the United States from an early age. She attended school in Waco, Texas, and Los Angeles, California, before her family settled down for good, in Kansas City, Kansas. Her father served as a residing elder in a Kansas City church; her mother taught Sunday school. Barnett began singing in her church choir at age 10.

Barnett dropped out of school (and temporarily abandoned her plan to attend college) to marry Curtis Brooks, a schoolteacher and veteran of World War I. The couple moved to Oklahoma, where Brooks established a business while Barnett bore four children, one of whom died at birth. (Barnett's daughters from her first marriage are Sue Ish, Etta Traylor, and Gladys Brooks.) After six years the marriage ended. Barnett returned to Kansas City (her parents had offered to help care for the children) and, in a move highly unusual for a black American woman of that era, enrolled at the University of Kansas at Lawrence. She was one of only 150 African-Americans among the 6,000 students then attending the university; even more unusual for an undergraduate at that time, she was a single mother. Despite the obstacles she faced, Barnett took full advantage of the opportunities the university offered her. While studying voice and drama, she hosted her own radio show, called *I Remember When*, and in the summers she traveled and performed with the Jackson Jubilee Singers. Barnett's recitals slowly earned her a following, and in 1931, during her senior year, she received an invitation to join the Eva Jessye Choir in New York City. She accepted the offer, but not before she had completed her bachelor's degree and earned a teaching certificate.

On the advice of friends, en route to New York Barnett made a stop in Chicago, where she met Claude A. Barnett, the founder and first director of the Associated Negro Press. (The company supplied news and feature stories, opinion pieces, and reviews to black newspapers throughout the U.S.) She and Barnett, who had agreed to provide her with letters of introduction, were soon engaged, in spite of her initial insistence that she did not intend to remarry.

Two weeks after her arrival in New York, Barnett (known then as Etta Moten) successfully auditioned for a part in a Broadway production of *Fast and Furious*, by Fannie Hurst and Zora Neale Hurston. The play closed shortly after it opened. Barnett soon secured a leading role in *Zombie*, a musical set in Haiti, which did quite well. A national tour of *Zombie* provided Barnett with opportunities to visit Claude Barnett in Chicago and to try out for movie roles in Los Angeles. Her trip to Hollywood marked a watershed in Barnett's career. After dubbing songs for the actress Barbara Stanwyck in *Professional Sweetheart* (1933), she landed her first on-screen film role—an uncredited cameo appearance as a World War I widow lamenting her husband's death, in Busby Berkeley's *Gold Diggers of 1933*. Barnett became an instant heroine among African-Americans, in part because, unlike virtually every other black actress up to that time, she had portrayed an ordinary homemaker rather than a domestic servant and had performed a musical number that wasn't a spiritual. The black press immediately hailed her as a model of "the new Negro Woman."

In her next (and last) big-screen role, Barnett portrayed a Brazilian singer in *Flying Down to Rio* (1933), the first movie to pair Ginger Rogers and Fred Astaire. Barnett performed her number wearing fruit in her hair. (Several years later the Brazilian-born singer and movie actress Carmen Miranda became famous for her fruit-laden turbans.) Barnett's name appeared in *Flying Down to Rio*'s credits, and the song she performed, "The Carioca," was nominated for an Academy Award.

In 1934, during the first term of President Franklin Delano Roosevelt, Barnett became the first black woman to perform at the White House, when she sang "My Forgotten Man" (reportedly Roosevelt's favorite song) at a birthday party for the president. That same year she married Claude Barnett, in an unplanned ceremony in Virginia, where both of them happened to be on business. After the wedding she and her husband remained active in their respective careers. During the next few years, Etta Moten Barnett appeared in Broadway productions of *Sugar Hill* and *Lysistrata*.

Meanwhile, the composer George Gershwin, who was then working on his folk opera *Porgy and Bess*, had taken notice of Barnett's stage and screen performances. It has been said that Gershwin wrote the song "Summertime" with Barnett in mind. Although Barnett was a contralto, he wrote the part for soprano voice. When Gershwin approached Barnett and offered her the role of Bess, she asked him to transpose the character's songs to a lower key. He refused, and another singer, Ann Brown, played Bess when the opera premiered, in late 1935.

Over the next few years, Barnett experienced difficulty finding satisfying stage and film roles, as they were in short supply for black actresses. Consequently, when she was again offered the role of Bess, in 1942 (about five years after Gershwin's death), she accepted. That production of the opera was a hit with both critics and the general public, and after a year on Broadway, it toured the United States and Canada for two years. The strain of singing above her natural range for three years permanently damaged Barnett's vocal cords; although she performed from time to time during the 1950s and 1960s, *Porgy and Bess* essentially marked the end of her singing career. "I sang it too long," she told Joy Bennett Kinnon for *Ebony* (October 1997), "and it's really the reason I don't sing now."

Beginning in the late 1940s, Barnett and her husband began to travel extensively in Africa, promoting diplomatic and cultural exchanges, often as official representatives of the United States. The couple represented Presidents Dwight D. Eisenhower, John F. Kennedy, and Lyndon B. Johnson in the Ivory Coast, Tunisia, Libya, Ethiopia, Uganda, and Cameroon; served as goodwill ambassadors for the United States at the independence celebrations of Ghana, Nigeria, and Zambia; and, in 1960, attended the inauguration of Kwame Nkrumah, the first president of Ghana, whom they had befriended. In the course of their travels, they amassed one of the world's largest privately held collections of African art.

Barnett has played a prominent role as a civic leader and patron of the arts, especially in and around Chicago, where she makes her home. Among the organizations in which she has been active are the National Council of Negro Women, the Chicago Lyric Opera, the Field Museum, the DuSable Museum of African American History, the National Conference of Christians and Jews, the African American Institute, and the Alpha Kappa Alpha sorority.

Claude Barnett died in 1967, at the age of 78. On November 5, 2001 Barnett celebrated her 100th birthday. About 400 people, among them the singer Harry Belafonte, attended a birthday party for her, held at the Hyatt Regency Chicago. "She gave black people an opportunity to look at themselves on a big screen as something beautiful when all that was there before spoke to our degradation," Belafonte said during the event. "In her we found another dimension to being black in our time. She was a true shining star." Barnett has five grandchildren and six great-grandchildren. When asked about the secret to her longevity, she explained to Joy Bennett Kinnon for *Ebony* (December 2001) the benefits of eating sardines, then added: "You have to choose a good grandma and grandpa." — P.K.

Suggested Reading: *Ebony* p54+ Oct. 1997, with photos, p62+ Dec. 2001, with photos; *Jet* p34 Dec. 3, 2001, with photo; *Notable Black American Women*, 1992

Selected Films: *Professional Sweetheart*, 1933; *Gold Diggers of 1933*, 1933; *Flying Down to Rio*, 1933

Selected Operas: *Porgy and Bess*, 1942

Selected Musicals: *Zombie*; *Sugar Hill*

Selected Plays: *Fast and Furious*; *Lysistrata*

---

## Beckman, Arnold O.

*Apr. 10, 1900– Scientist; inventor; entrepreneur; philanthropist*

*Address: Beckman Institute, Caltech MC 139–74, Pasadena, CA 91125*

The inventions of the scientist Arnold O. Beckman—the pH meter and the DU spectrophotometer, among many other devices—have transformed medical research and the practice of clinical medicine; they have been credited with making possible our current understanding of human biology and thereby saving countless lives. Beckman has been compared to Galileo (1564–1642), the Italian astronomer and physicist whose construction of the first complete telescope and observations of the heavens transformed humankind's conception of the universe, and Antonie van Leeuwenhoek (1632–1723), the Dutch naturalist whose descriptions of the bacteria, protozoa, and other microorganisms that he viewed through microscopes of his own design revolutionized the science of biology. In 1935 Beckman founded what he later renamed Beckman Instruments Inc., which in time became a leading manufacturer of analytical equipment. In 1987 he was named to the National Inventors Hall of Fame, and in 1989 President George Herbert Walker Bush awarded him the National Medal of Science. Now nearly 102 years old, he is widely acknowledged as one of the most generous philanthropists in the country; to date he has given more than $400 million to American scientific institutions, many of them associated with universities.

Arnold Orville Beckman was born in Cullom, Illinois, a small farming community, on April 10, 1900 to a blacksmith and his wife. His interest in science was first aroused when, as a child, he read a chemistry textbook he found in the family's attic. Another source of inspiration was a series of books called *Fourteen Weeks in Science*, originally published in 1861; soon after reading them, young Arnold converted a toolshed his father had built for him into a makeshift chemistry lab.

Courtesy of Arnold and Mabel Beckman Foundation

*Arnold O. Beckman*

During World War I Beckman joined the United States Marines. He was stationed at the Brooklyn Navy Yard, in New York City, where, on Thanksgiving Day in 1918, he met his future wife, Mabel; a Brooklyn native and Red Cross volunteer, she was helping to prepare a holiday dinner for the servicemen at the shipyard. The pair corresponded for seven years and married in 1925.

Earlier, after his stint in the U.S. Marines, Beckman had enrolled at the University of Illinois. He earned money for his tuition by playing the piano at dances and in theaters showing silent movies. In 1922 he received a bachelor's degree in chemical engineering, and the following year he earned a master's degree in physical chemistry, also from the University of Illinois. Beckman was awarded a Ph.D. in photochemistry, in 1928, from the California Institute of Technology (commonly known as Caltech), in Pasadena; he and his wife had traveled to the West Coast in a Model T Ford so that he could attend. After he completed his doctorate, Caltech hired him as an instructor; the following year he was promoted to assistant professor.

In 1934, at the request of a friend who was working for the California Fruit Growers Exchange, Beckman invented the acidimeter—a device for measuring the acidity of lemon juice. The pH meter, as the invention came to be known, measures the relative acidity of a substance or its relative alkalinity (basicity) on a scale of 0 to 14; 7 is considered to be the pH of pure water, which is neither acidic nor basic. The pH meter soon became an indispensable tool in analytical chemistry; in medicine, it is vital in the diagnosis and treatment of many disorders, ranging from renal failure to chronic heartburn.

In 1935, while still teaching at Caltech, Beckman founded National Technical Laboratories and began producing pH meters for general sale. (The company was later christened Beckman Instruments Inc.) In 1940 he invented the DU spectrophotometer, a device that made chemical analysis of biological substances significantly faster and more accurate. Whereas before, a chemical analysis might take weeks, with a guaranteed accuracy of only 25 percent, the DU spectrophotometer produced results in minutes, with 99.9 percent accuracy. New models have been introduced in the last six decades, but hundreds, if not thousands, of the original instruments are still being used in laboratories around the world. Also in 1940 Beckman introduced a precision electrical-resistance device, similar to a radio volume control. Called the Helipot, the device became an essential component of the then-secret radar systems used in World War II. It is still used today in several products, including electronic games and home appliances.

Following the success of his inventions, Beckman left his teaching position at Caltech to devote himself to his company full-time. Numerous other inventions followed over the next six decades, among them an ultracentrifuge that breaks down compounds and measures molecular structures; an apparatus for recording concentrations of various gases in the atmosphere and thus indicating levels of air pollution; and a rock smasher used by the National Aeronautic and Space Administration (NASA).

During the 1980s Beckman Instruments merged briefly with the SmithKline Corp., a large pharmaceutical and health-care firm; it became independent again in 1989. In 1997 Beckman Instruments Inc. acquired the Coulter Corp., a Florida-based manufacturer of cellular-analysis systems, and the following year the concern was renamed Beckman Coulter Inc. Currently among the world's leading providers of laboratory systems and testing devices, Beckman Coulter employs 10,000 workers in 35 facilities worldwide.

In 1977 Beckman established the Arnold and Mabel Beckman Foundation, an independent, nonprofit agency dedicated to supporting scientific research in the fields of chemistry and the life sciences and to fostering the invention of new scientific methods, materials, and instruments. The foundation oversees the Beckman Scholars Program, which awards scholarships to outstanding undergraduate students of chemistry and biology at American universities, and funds "Young Investigator" prizes. According to Philip M. Boffey in the *New York Times* (November 5, 1985), in 1985 alone Beckman donated some $75.5 million to American scientific institutions. In 1998 the foundation instituted a program called Beckman@Science in California elementary schools. Meant to stimulate students' natural curiosity about science, the hands-on program will receive a total of almost $15 million in funding from the foundation. The foundation also provides ongoing support to five research facilities. They are located at Caltech; the University of Illinois at Urbana-Champaign; the City of Hope Hospital and Medical Center, the site of the Beckman Research Institute, in Duarte, California; Stanford University, in California; and the Beckman Laser Institute, in Irvine, California. "I accumulated my wealth by selling instruments to scientists," Beckman is quoted as saying on the official Beckman Coulter Web site. "So I thought it would be appropriate to make contributions to scientists, and that's been my number-one guideline for charity." Politically conservative, Beckman has also been known to make large contributions to the Republican Party.

Philip M. Boffey wrote that Simon Ramo, an engineer who was the chief scientist of the United States' intercontinental-ballistic-missile program during the 1950s and who identified himself as both a friend and colleague of Beckman's, described the inventor as "quiet, reserved, diffident, well-informed on a variety of subjects, very kindly and extremely ethical." Beckman is the founder of the Instrument Society of America, a professional organization. He is a member of the National Academy of Engineering and the American Chemical Society, and he is an honorary member of numerous other scientific and civic groups. In 1953 Beckman became the first Caltech alumnus to be elected to the school's board of trustees. He became chairman of the board in 1964 and chairman emeritus in 1974.

Among the several dozen awards that have recognized Beckman's scientific work and philanthropy are the 1998 Excellence in Entrepreneurship Hall of Fame Award, from Chapman University, in California, and the 1999 Public Welfare Medal, from the National Academy of Sciences. He holds honorary degrees from many colleges. A state-of-the-art secondary school currently under construction in Irvine, California, is to be named the Arnold O. Beckman High School.

Mabel Beckman, who devoted herself to the couple's son and daughter and to charitable activities, died in 1989. Arnold O. Beckman lives in southern California. "Although not as active as he was at 100 years of age, Dr. Beckman, who will turn 102 years old in April, continues to enjoy good health," Kathlene Williams, an assistant at the Beckman Foundation, told *Current Biography*. *Arnold O. Beckman: 100 Years of Excellence*, by Arnold Thackray, Minor Myers, and James D. Watson, was published by the Chemical Heritage Foundation in 2000. The book comes with a CD-ROM on which Beckman talks about his life and his ideas about invention, education, and philanthropy. — M.R.

Suggested Reading: Arnold and Mabel Beckman Foundation Web site; Beckman Coulter Web site; *Chemical & Engineering News* p17+ Apr. 10, 2000, with photo; *Chronicle of Higher Education* A p45+ Apr. 2 1999, with photo; *Forbes* p46+ Sep. 1, 1969, with photos; *Scientist* (on-line) Mar. 6, 2000, with photos; Stephens, Harrison. *Golden Past, Golden Future: The First Fifty Years of Beckman Instruments, Inc.*, 1985; Thackray, Arnold, Minor Myers, and James D. Watson. *Arnold O. Beckman: 100 Years of Excellence*, 2000

---

## Belichick, Bill

*Apr. 16, 1952– Coach of the New England Patriots*

*Address: New England Patriots, 60 Washington St., Foxboro, MA 02035*

"I am who I am," Bill Belichick, the head coach of the New England Patriots, told Jarrett Bell for *USA Today* (February 1, 2002, on-line). "In the end, I feel that what I'm accountable for is doing a good job as a football coach." Belichick, who eschews wearing dressy clothes, chatting at press conferences, and other such attention-getting methods, has seen his singular focus on his work pay off with three Super Bowl wins—two during his stint as the defensive coordinator for the New York Giants, in 1986 and 1990, and the third in 2002, in his second season as the head coach of the Patriots. He is as demanding of himself as he is of his players; as he explained to Peter King for *Sports Illustrated* (February 13, 2002), "The one thing I've figured out in this job is, when they put your name on the door with head coach on it, a lot of people in the building, not just players, will look to you for direction, and you'd better be ready to give it. I learn something new in this job every day, every week, every year. I'd better be a better coach than I was 10 years ago."

The only child of Steve and Jeanette Belichick, Bill Belichick was born on April 16, 1952 in Nashville, Tennessee. In the early 1950s Steve Belichick, who had played for the Detroit Lions in 1941, coached football at Vanderbilt University, in Nashville. In 1956 the family moved to Annapolis, Maryland, after he accepted a coaching position at the U.S. Naval Academy. Bill Belichick was named for his father's mentor, William M. "Bill" Edwards, the football coach at Western Reserve University (now part of Case Western Reserve University) from 1935 to 1941. Young Bill learned about football early, often accompanying his father on scouting trips. Because the practice of viewing game films to learn opponents' strategies was often prohibitively slow in the 1960s and 1970s (due to the relatively long time it took to receive the developed films), teams relied on advance scouts such as Steve Belichick. "One of the great learning experiences for me [was going] to some of the games with my father to scout," Belichick recalled to Peter

Robert Mora/Getty Images

*Bill Belichick*

King, "and what was important was seeing the game in person, being able to understand what was going on and bringing it back to the coaches so they knew what the latest information was. . . . Just watching him work during the game and understanding how he could see what all 11 players were doing on offense, defense and special teams was an education." When he was as young as eight or nine, Belichick reviewed films of the football team of the U.S. Naval Academy on weekday evenings. "When he was supposed to be studying," Steve Belichick told Robert Fachet for the *Washington Post* (February 7, 1991), "he'd be drawing up plays instead." Belichick attended Annapolis High School and the Philips Academy, in Andover, Massachusetts, before going to Wesleyan University, in Middletown, Connecticut. Throughout his school years he played football and, to a lesser extent, lacrosse and squash. On the football field he alternated between tight end and center, but at only five feet, 10 inches and 170 pounds, he had a size disadvantage. "He wasn't much of a player," Steve Belichick told Fachet, "but he was smarter than most and he'd know what some of the other players were going to do before they did."

Belichick majored in economics at Wesleyan and planned to go into business after graduation. But during his final semester, in 1975, he decided he wanted to try coaching football instead of pursuing a master's degree in business. Using his father's college-football connections, he tried in vain to find a graduate assistantship: in 1975 the National Collegiate Athletic Association (NCAA) reduced the number of jobs available, and since he had no experience, Belichick was deemed unqualified. He and his father then persuaded the staff of the Baltimore Colts, a National Football League (NFL) team, to create a graduate assistantship position. As an unpaid special assistant to the Colts' head coach, Ted Marchibroda, Belichick performed mostly unofficial duties. Partway through the season, after volunteering for an increasing number of assignments, he made the Colts' payroll, at $25 a week; by the end of the season, he was earning $50 a week. "It was a great opportunity for a guy with no coaching experience," he told Ron Borges for the *Boston Globe Magazine* (September 10, 2000, on-line). "I started breaking down film like I'd done with Dad, but they gave me more and more responsibility. I worked diligently, so they kept giving me more." During his crash course in football coaching and team management, he told Borges, "I didn't have a place to live, so I slept on a sofa. It was a 7-to-midnight shift every day. It was like a tutorial in coaching, listening to those guys. But Ted [Marchibroda] asked me what I thought. He treated me with the same respect as the others, even though I was 24."

Although the Colts won the 1975 American Football Conference (AFC) East title with a 10–4 record, before the 1976 season Belichick switched to the Detroit Lions, who had promised him a $15,000 annual salary and the use of a Ford Thunderbird. In Detroit he served as an assistant special-teams coach for one year and as a tight-end and receivers coach for one year after that. He then spent a year with the Denver Broncos, as the assistant special-teams coach and assistant to the defensive coordinator, but he felt unhappy in Denver and quit before securing a new job. In 1979, before the next season began, the New York Giants hired him as a defensive assistant and special-teams coach. Much of his responsibility in Detroit and Denver had revolved around analyzing game films, which had limited his interactions with players; with the Giants he had more responsibility. In 1980 he was promoted to linebackers coach, and in 1983, when Bill Parcells was named the head coach of the Giants, he took over some defensive-coordinating duties while continuing as a linebackers coach. Despite finishing with less-than-stellar records, the Giants made it to the NFL play-offs as wild cards in 1981, 1984, and 1985. Each of those years, the team won the Wild Card game but lost the NFC Divisional play-off game.

In 1985 Parcells appointed Belichick to the post of defensive coordinator. "To tell you the truth, working with the special teams was probably the most exciting job I've had," Belichick told Vinny DiTrani for the Bergen County, New Jersey, *Record* (January 21, 1987), "but they are just not involved in enough plays during the game. When I started helping out with the defense, I thought I was making more of a contribution." After Belichick's promotion, he and Parcells quickly began building a defensive empire. Imitating Parcells's bearish manner, Belichick had earned a reputation for being a tough coach, militaristic in his bearing and standoffish toward the press and, sometimes, his own players. But his defensive strategies were solid: in 1986 the New York Giants won the Super Bowl after compiling a 14–2 regular-season record. The Giants' defense was credited with creating excellent scoring opportunities for the offense and was named the second-best defense in the NFL. (It ranked first in defense against running plays.) The 1986 squad included the future Hall of Fame linebacker Lawrence Taylor, who was named the NFL's Most Valuable Player and led the league with 20.5 sacks that year. Each of the Giants' postseason victories was a rout: a 49–3 defeat of the San Francisco 49ers; a 17–0 defeat of the Redskins; and a 39–20 Super Bowl XXI win over the Denver Broncos.

After the Giants' magnificent 1986 season, rumors flew that Belichick might be offered a head-coaching position with the Tampa Bay Buccaneers, but an offer never materialized. The first three weeks of the 1987 season began with a strike, during which replacement players were used. Because of the altered lineups, Belichick and Parcells were forced to rethink their strategies. Injuries also hampered the team, as did fourth-quarter losses, and the 1986 Super Bowl champions finished the strike-shortened season with a 6–9 record. The Giants did not make the play-offs again until 1989, when they finished with a 12–4 record. They suffered an overtime defeat in the National Football Conference (NFC) Divisional play-off game, losing to the Los Angeles Rams, 19–13. In 1990 the Parcells-Belichick coaching duo took a fully rebuilt Giants to the play-offs again, after a 13–3 regular season. They went on to win the Super Bowl for the second time in five seasons.

Immediately after the Giants' victory in Super Bowl XXV, Parcells hinted at his intention to leave the team. His handpicked successor was Ray Handley—not, as many in football had expected, Belichick. In 1991 Belichick instead signed a five-year contract to be the head coach of the Cleveland Browns, becoming, at age 39, the youngest head coach in the NFL at that time. "I feel like I've been coaching for 30 years, starting at 8, around the films," he told Gerald Eskenazi for the *New York Times* (February 6, 1991) just after starting with the Browns. "I've done all the jobs in an organization: typing, going to the airport to meet guys, liming the field. In the last two years, since I had my first interview with Cleveland, I got to thinking like a head coach, how I would handle things." The Cleveland Browns had suffered through an awful 1990 season, limping to a 3–13 finish, a record that apparently did not faze Belichick. "I'm not worried about last year," he told Frank Litsky for the *New York Times* (August 8, 1991). "It didn't make any difference to me if they were 3–13 or 13–3. I wasn't here. At the Giants, whatever the record was the year before didn't have anything to do with the way we prepared." But unlike the Giants, who had boasted such players as Lawrence Taylor and Phil Simms, the Browns did not have a star. Despite his intensive efforts, Belichick could not produce a winning formula. In 1991 the Browns went 6–10; they posted a record of 7–9 in both 1992 and 1993. In 1993 Belichick had signed the free-agent quarterback Vinny Testaverde, whom he chose to use instead of the fan favorite Bernie Kosar; this move, coupled with his extremely guarded approach to the Cleveland press, had made him unpopular. His reputation for excellent defensive coaching was redeemed in 1994, when the Browns earned a play-off spot with an 11–5 record and set a team record for fewest points allowed (204) during the season. A losing record in 1995 (5–11) prompted the team's owner, Art Modell, to fire Belichick and move the team to Baltimore (where they became the Ravens; the Colts had moved to Indianapolis).

Instead of pursuing another head-coaching position, Belichick became the assistant of his mentor, Bill Parcells, who was the head coach of the New England Patriots. "Last season the timing was right, given the situation Bill was in and I was in," Belichick told Gerald Eskenazi for the *New York Times* (January 22, 1997). "The stars were in alignment for us to get back together again." In 1996, after an 11–5 regular season, the Patriots won their first two play-off games before falling to the Green Bay Packers in Super Bowl XXXI, 35–21. In 1997 Belichick and Parcells left the Patriots to become the assistant head coach and head coach, respectively, of the New York Jets. Three years of work with the Jets resulted in only one post-season appearance, in 1998, in which the 12–4 Jets were defeated in the AFC Conference Championship game.

Parcells quit the Jets after the 1999 season, thus vacating the head-coach position. Belichick accepted the post on January 3, 2000, but in a move that shocked the league, he resigned the following day; his departure triggered the rumor that he hoped to sign a contract to become head coach of the New England Patriots. (Belichick's lawyer claimed that Parcells had intimated that he would not fully withdraw from the Jets organization.) The NFL filed an antitrust suit against Belichick, and he was barred from entering negotiations with other teams. Several weeks later the Patriots and the Jets reached a complicated agreement, which released Belichick from his contract with the Jets; the Patriots promptly hired him as head coach. "I didn't resign [from the Jets] to get to this spot," Belichick declared at a news conference, according to Judy Battista in the *New York Times* (January 28, 2000). "I resigned because I wasn't comfortable with the situation with the Jets." Among other terms, the agreement required that the Patriots give the Jets a first-round draft pick. Following the dramatic off-season negotiations, the Patriots had a sub-par season in 2000, finishing with a record of 5–11. Belichick was hounded by the Boston-area press but calmly weathered the storm, remembering the rocky relationship that he had had with the press in Cleveland. "I watched what Bill [Parcells] did with the New York media when I was there, and maybe I tried to do some of those things," he told Steve Buckley for the *Boston Herald* (January

17, 2002, on-line). "And he was in a position where, honestly, he could get away with some things that other people can't get away with. And I don't think I really realized that."

The beginning of the 2001 season found the Patriots grappling with problems and misfortune: the wide receiver Terry Glenn was struggling with substance abuse; the quarterbacks coach, Dick Rehbein, died suddenly; and their star quarterback, Drew Bledsoe, sustained an early-season injury. In addition, the Patriots still felt the psychological effects of their poor showing of the previous season. In his usual way, Belichick refused to dwell on the past. "I knew at the beginning of training camp that we'd be better," he told Steve Buckley. Terry Glenn was ultimately traded, and Belichick decided that he would coach the quarterbacks himself. After a bumpy start, the Patriots finished the regular season at 11–5, behind excellent performances from Tom Brady, a young backup quarterback thrust into the limelight after Bledsoe's injury. (Belichick, pleased with Brady's play, did not reinstate Bledsoe when he recovered.) Belichick developed creative coaching methods, among them the holding of a mock funeral for a game ball after a dispiriting loss to Miami early in the season. Each week, at his direction, the team watched a film and, based on what they had seen, explored a particular theme; selections included basketball finals games, a horse race, and an IMAX movie about the Antarctic explorer Ernest Shackleton. "Your team gets tired of hearing you say the same thing day after day," Belichick explained to Jarrett Bell. "You have to find a different way to get the message across, so you come up with a different flavor." The Patriots performed well in every play-off game, with the help of clutch performances from the quarterbacks Brady and Bledsoe and the kicker Adam Vinatieri, who kicked two field goals—one to tie and one to win, 16–13, in overtime—during a snowy Division Championship play-off game against the Oakland Raiders. The Patriots won the AFC Conference championship, 24–17, against the Pittsburgh Steelers and overcame the St. Louis Rams, who boasted one of the strongest offenses in the NFL, to win Super Bowl XXXVI by a score of 20–17. Belichick told Peter King, "Of all the teams I've ever been around, these guys try so hard. They really try to do what you tell them." The Patriots' coaching received an A grade from the *Sporting News* (January 4, 2002), which noted, "[The] team is better than the sum of its parts. That's coaching."

Bill Belichick and the New England Patriots began the defense of their championship title by winning the first four games of the 2002 season. They then suffered four straight losses, thus making their participation in the play-offs uncertain.

In every city in which he has lived, Belichick has actively raised funds for local charities, including anti-gang groups and a women's homeless shelter. He has been married to Debby, his high-school sweetheart, since 1977. The couple have three children: Amanda, Stephen, and Brian. — K.S.

Suggested Reading: (Bergen County, New Jersey) *Record* FB p1 Jan. 21, 1987, with photo; *Sports Illustrated* p28+ Feb. 13, 2002, with photos; *USA Today* (on-line) Feb. 1, 2002; *Washington Post* D p1 Jan. 24, 1987, with photos, C p7 Feb. 7, 1991

---

## Bible, Geoffrey C.

*Aug. 12, 1937– Businessman*

*Address: Philip Morris Companies Inc., 120 Park Ave., New York, NY 10017*

Geoffrey C. Bible was named president and chief executive officer (CEO) of the New York–based Philip Morris Companies Inc. in June 1994. At that time the firm, which began as a tobacco concern and has expanded to many other areas, was suffering one of the worst periods in its more than 150-year history. In September 1992 the company's stock had peaked at over $86 a share, but by the beginning of Bible's tenure as CEO, the price had slipped to $50 a share, following the infamous "Marlboro Friday" of a year earlier—when the company had slashed the prices of its Marlboro cigarettes by 20 percent in an attempt to regain its market share, which had shrunk significantly. Philip Morris was also facing extensive litigation in several U.S. states, regarding its culpability in the medical expenses incurred by sufferers of tobacco-related diseases; the company was accused, along with others, of purposely misleading the public about the addictiveness of its cigarettes and of marketing to young people. By December 1994, however, when it was announced that Bible would assume the additional title and duties of chairman of the board (and relinquish the position of president), following the retirement of R. William Murray, Philip Morris had largely regained its position in the industry, thanks to several initiatives Bible had implemented. Following an aggressive campaign to alleviate stockholders' worries, the company had announced a plan to buy back as much as $6 billion of its stock over three years and had increased its yearly dividend by nearly 20 percent. At this news Philip Morris stock surged 16 percent and ended the year at $58, its highest price since April 1993.

Over the next seven years, Bible and the company experienced monumental struggles, which took place primarily in U.S. courtrooms. Although he initially rejected the idea of compromise, following the onslaught of lawsuits by 46 states, Bible was forced to capitulate to an overwhelmingly negative public opinion of his company's practices. In February 2000, as Wall Street experts awaited the outcome of a Florida class-action suit against Phil-

Hulton/Archive by Getty Images

*Geoffrey C. Bible*

ip Morris, the company's stock dipped to $19 a share. But Bible and the company vowed to overcome Philip Morris's troubles and to re-create the firm's image. In that spirit the company secured several key purchases, the largest being Nabisco, acquired in June 2000 for $14.9 billion. Like others among its subsidiaries, such as Kraft Foods and the Miller Brewing Co., Nabisco further diversified Philip Morris's offerings to consumers. By the end of the year, Philip Morris's enhanced portfolio boasted 91 brands that each generated more than $100 million in annual revenues, as well as 15 mega-brands that each brought in more than $1 billion a year. With the addition of Nabisco and its numerous products, Philip Morris became the largest supplier of packaged consumer goods in the world, with record operating revenues of more than $80 billion for the year 2000. The company's stock, in a year of immense volatility due to the presence of fledgling technology companies, was recognized as the year's best performer in the Dow Jones Industrial Average. Although the concern had lost several libel cases around the country, most notably in Florida, Texas, Mississippi, and Minnesota, those decisions are being appealed, while Philip Morris continues to thrive. In June 2001 the company issued its long-awaited initial public offering (IPO) of nearly 16 percent of its Kraft holdings, raising roughly $8.4 billion in revenue, which it plans to use to reduce its debt. Philip Morris still retains an 84 percent interest in Kraft shares, which has helped the firm to maintain its position as the second-largest food company in the world, despite surging competition. As of October 2001 Philip Morris's stock had again surpassed the $50-a-share mark.

At the company's most recent annual meeting with stockholders, held in Richmond, Virginia, on April 25, 2002, Bible announced that the company had met its 2001 performance goals of 8.9 percent growth in underlying, or actual, earnings per share; increased dividends by 9.4 percent, to an annualized rate of $2.32 per share; and repurchased $4 billion of Philip Morris common stock. Many industry insiders attributed Philip Morris's success in weathering its recent difficulties to Bible's creative policies. In April 2002 Bible stepped down from his position as CEO (the chief financial officer, Louis C. Camilleri, replaced him), and the following August, when he reached the company's mandatory retirement age of 65, he ended his tenure as chairman as well.

Geoffrey Cyril Bible was born on August 12, 1937 in Canberra, Australia, to Cyril Edward Bible and Dorothea Elizabeth (O'Brien) McGrath. He was trained as an accountant at the Institute of Chartered Accountants, in Australia, moving abroad in 1959 to accept a position as cost and management accountant and financial director for the United Nations for both Lebanon and Jordan. He held that post through 1964, then relocated to Switzerland, to perform the duties of budget manager for the Swiss-based International Labor Organization (ILO). On September 10, 1965 Bible married the former Sara Curtis Anderson-Emery. In the following year he became financial manager of the petrol giant Esso, also based in Switzerland.

In 1968 Bible received his first of many positions with Philip Morris, assuming the title of manager of corporate planning for Philip Morris Europe, headquartered in Switzerland. Except for the period from 1970 to 1976, during which he managed R.W. King & Yuill, an Australian stockbrokerage firm based in Geneva, Switzerland, Bible spent the following decades moving up through the ranks of Philip Morris. Although he served as Philip Morris Europe's director of corporate planning until 1978, Bible had moved to the company's headquarters in New York City two years earlier, when he had also assumed the title of vice president of Philip Morris International. Following a series of high-ranking positions in the company throughout the 1980s, both in the U.S. and Australia, Bible was named president and CEO of Philip Morris in June 1994, replacing Michael A. Miles, who had resigned after falling out of favor with the company's board of directors.

Along with Philip Morris's chairman, William Murray, and director, Rupert Murdoch—both fellow Australians—Bible completed the triumvirate often referred to in media circles as the "Kangaroo Mafia." Then, on February 1, 1995, Murray, having promised his family that he would retire upon his 60th birthday, stepped down from his post as chairman. The Smith Barney tobacco analyst Ronald Morrow, as quoted by Yumiko Ono for the *Wall Street Journal* (December 15, 1994), pointed out that Murray had briefly assumed the title of chairman "specifically to ease the transition" from

Miles to Bible, who was then given the position of chairman, retaining his title as CEO and vacating the company's presidency. One of Bible's first moves as chairman was to summon 350 stock-market analysts to a presentation in the Grand Ballroom of New York's Grand Hyatt hotel. His goal was to convince these industry insiders that Philip Morris's stock was on the rise. While the company's stock had already risen to more than $62 a share, Bible was not satisfied. As quoted by Richard Tomkins in the London *Financial Times* (March 9, 1995), he told those gathered, "Next to my wife and family, [Philip Morris's stock price] is the most important thing in my life." Investors, however, still feared substantial costs from imminent court battles. A day after Bible's impassioned presentation, the company's stock reflected this industry uneasiness, rising a mere 75 cents, to just over $63 a share. By the end of the year, though, as litigation threats were largely brushed aside, Philip Morris stock had risen more than 64 percent, outpacing the 38 percent gain in Standard & Poor's index of 500 stocks (S&P 500). For his part in the success of fiscal year 1995, Bible's base salary was increased by 32 percent, from $875,000 to $1.12 million. The chairman and CEO also received a bonus of $1.35 million, up from $1 million in 1994.

Bible used the success his company had enjoyed in the previous year as a platform from which to attack federal regulators and antismoking activists. He was quoted by Jay Mathews in the *Washington Post* (April 26, 1996) as proclaiming at the company's annual stockholders' meeting, "I pledge to you that we will continue to fight for our rights, for our freedoms and for our future on your behalf, as our stockholders." Bible further defended his company's practices, saying, "Cigarette manufacturing is a wonderful business. The industry creates jobs for more than 1.8 million Americans, from farmers and manufacturers to wholesalers and retailers. There are hard-working people in every state who raise families, pay taxes and vote in elections. Our activities alone generate more than $11 billion a year in taxes for federal, state and local governments here in the United States."

Still, by 1997 it had become clear to tobacco-industry leaders that threats of lawsuits would not disappear as they had in the past. Philip Morris and RJ Reynolds, which together were responsible for 72 percent of all U.S. cigarette sales that year, faced lawsuits from 46 states, each seeking to recover billions of dollars in Medicaid costs for patients suffering smoking-related illnesses. Before long, the media began to report a distinct shift in Bible's attitude; whereas the year before Bible's calls to "fight, fight, fight" seemed to quell stockholders' fears, he was now forced to acknowledge that the fight was lost, and as stock prices began to fall, the key phrase used by tobacco leaders—Bible among them—was "damage control." Philip Morris and four other tobacco companies reached settlements with the states that totaled an unprecedented $368.5 billion, payable over 25 years; Philip Morris, with almost half of the market share, was responsible for almost half of the settlement. While Philip Morris's attorneys appealed the decision, the company's stock continued to plummet.

In 1998 many states agreed to the tobacco companies' requests for the cessation of future legal action, in exchange for limits on cigarette advertising, especially ads that crossed into youth markets through television, live sports events, and popular magazines. But Minnesota, represented by attorney Michael Ciresi and others, refused to settle, which led to a series of highly publicized depositions. Minnesota attorneys held that Philip Morris and others had historically concealed the dangers and addictiveness of its cigarettes and had purposely marketed their products directly toward teenagers. Bible was the first tobacco executive called to testify in the case. Although he was able to sidestep many of Ciresi's questions, at one point he was presented with a letter he had written to shareholders in 1996, which stated, as quoted by Bill Dedman in the *New York Times* (March 3, 1998), "[Philip Morris's] one all-consuming ambition is to create wealth." Ciresi then asked the CEO if he valued profit over the health concerns of his customers. In response, Bible declared, "I don't think I'd set money above public health. I place them all at the highest ranking." Presented with additional documents suggesting that Philip Morris had actively marketed cigarettes to teenagers in the past, Bible responded, "We should not be marketing cigarettes to young people. It is certainly anomalous to the Philip Morris I know." Ciresi then countered, "If we keep seeing more anomalies, sooner or later it becomes usual, doesn't it?" Bible answered, "[Philip Morris is] a large company, and we sell a lot of products." At another point in his testimony, Bible stated, "I believe everyone in the world believes that smoking causes disease. I don't know [if it does]. There may be others who agree with me."

In the following year the $1.77 billion sought by Minnesota was granted by the court, contributing to a $254 billion agreement reached with 45 other states. While half of that figure would be the responsibility of Philip Morris, the sum was considerably less than the $368.5 billion originally sought—though the blanket immunity formerly agreed upon was now void. (Even the $254 billion total continues to be fought in appellate courts.) In response to negative press and uncertainties over the outcome of the lawsuits, by May 1998 Philip Morris's stock had dropped to $37 a share.

In October 1999 Bible moved closer to an admission of the direct links between cigarettes and disease. As part of a $100 million corporate image campaign to regain the trust of consumers, as quoted by Barry Meier in the *New York Times* (October 13, 1999), Philip Morris stated that there is an "overwhelming medical and scientific consensus that cigarette smoking causes" diseases such as cancer, emphysema, and heart disorders. Bible was also quoted as testifying that his company recognized that "under some definitions, cigarette smoking is addictive."

Despite the adverse effects of the past years' proceedings on the company's stock, Bible was highly praised within the industry for his role in negotiating the settlement between tobacco companies and U.S. states. He received a $3.5 million bonus from Philip Morris's compensation committee, in addition to his $1.5 million base salary. A statement from the committee, quoted by Constance L. Hays in the *New York Times* (March 16, 1999), read, "A primary factor in determining the size of the award was the committee's desire to reward Mr. Bible for his leadership in helping to obtain a nationwide settlement of health care cost recovery and other claims of the states against the company's domestic tobacco subsidiary."

The year 2000 proved to be a turning point in Philip Morris's recent woes, despite its stock's dropping below $20 a share early in the first quarter. With the purchase of Nabisco in June for $14.9 billion and Philip Morris's efforts to increase its hold on the international tobacco market, the company enjoyed record numbers. Commenting on the Nabisco purchase, Bible told Kenneth N. Gilpin for the *New York Times* (June 26, 2000), "Scale gives you great capability. The bigger you are, the better you are at delivering what the customer and the consumer want." Kraft subsidiaries include General Foods, Maxwell House, Post Cereals, Philadelphia Cream Cheese, Jell-O, Kool-Aid, and Tang, while the Nabisco purchase added Oreo cookies, Ritz Crackers, and Planters Nuts, thus allowing the parent company to retain its status as the world's number-two food company in terms of revenue, behind Nestlé. By the end of 2000, Philip Morris had become not only the largest but also the most profitable consumer-packaged-goods company in the world, with $8.5 billion in profits on $80.4 billion in revenues. Bible's Philip Morris stock options, which were worth $865,278 at the end of 1999, soared by the closing of the company's record year to $95.6 million.

At the April 25, 2002 annual Philip Morris stockholders' meeting, Bible stepped down from his position as CEO. The shareholders also voted at the meeting to change the name of the corporate parent company from Philip Morris Companies Inc. to Altria Group Inc. (The board of directors has not yet decided when the name change will go into effect.) Bible retained the title of chairman until he reached the company's mandatory retirement age, in August. He now works for Philip Morris as a consultant; the contract he negotiated includes such perks as access to company planes.

Bible has served on the board of directors of the New York Stock Exchange and Lincoln Center for the Performing Arts, both in New York City. A naturalized U.S. citizen, he lives in Greenwich, Connecticut, with his wife, Sara. The couple have three children: Mary, Tom, and Kim. — J.H.

Suggested Reading: *Financial Times* p23 Mar. 9, 1995, with photo; *Fortune* p62+ July 21, 1997, with photos, p142+ Apr. 16, 2001; *Mother Jones* p23 Sep./Oct. 1998; *New York Times* A p16 Mar. 3, 1998, A p15 Mar. 4, 1998, C p11 Mar. 16, 1999, A p1 Oct. 13, 1999, A p1 June 26, 2000, C p1 Mar. 15, 2001; *Time* p60 Apr. 28, 1997; *Wall Street Journal* B p4 Dec. 15, 1994; *Washington Post* F p3 June 22, 1994, F p1 Apr. 26, 1996, with photo, F p3 May 1, 1998, with photo; *Worldly Investor News* (on-line) Sep. 26, 2001

---

Armando Gallo/Retna Ltd.

## Black, Jack

*Apr. 7, 1969– Actor; musician*

*Address: c/o United Talent Agency, 9560 Wilshire Blvd., Beverly Hills, CA 90212*

After more than a decade of toiling in obscurity in the entertainment industry, Jack Black received a great deal of media attention for his performance in the film *High Fidelity* (2000); playing a record-store clerk and frustrated musician, Black was frequently described as a "scene-stealer." Having carved a niche for himself in Hollywood as a quirky sidekick, Black suddenly found himself in demand for darkly comic or slapstick films. He received his first leading role in the 2001 romantic comedy *Shallow Hal*. His first love remains music, however. Black is a member of the band Tenacious D, which combines heavy-metal music with bathroom humor. *Tenacious D*, the group's first album, was released in 2001. "There was a time when I really craved attention," Black revealed to Mark Olsen for the New York *Daily News* (November 4,

2001, on-line). "I can see now that's why I started acting—I needed the eyes to be on me. Now I find I want less attention—I want privacy. More and more, I'm freaked out by cameras and being in front of people."

Jack Black was born on April 7, 1969 in Los Angeles, California. "Jack Black" is a pseudonym; the actor has steadfastly refused to reveal his real name. He grew up in Hermosa Beach, California. His parents, both in their second marriages, divorced while he was a child. He has half-siblings from his parents' former marriages. Referring to his home life, he told Liz Braun for the *Toronto Sun* (February 4, 2001), as archived on the Jam! Showbiz Web site, "It was funny, and not funny 'ha-ha.' It was the '70s, and there was some crazy family synergy going on." At Culver City Junior High School, Black developed a taste for acid and other drugs. "I fell in with some rough dudes and did a lot of cocaine," he confessed to Guy Flatley for the New York *Daily News* (April 7, 2001, on-line). "Then I got taken out of the public school system and put into a private school for troubled youths." Acting provided an outlet for Black; he got his first job, in an Atari commercial, when he was 13. At Crossroads, a private high school with an arts focus located in Santa Monica, California, he performed regularly in school plays. In 1987 he enrolled at the University of California at Los Angeles as a theater major; after two years, he left. "I was an awful student and also, yeah, it was just a waste of time," he told Christy Lemire for the Associated Press, as published in the Albany, New York, *Times Union* (February 11, 2001). "It wasn't for me. I slept through everything." But, he added, "I did some stuff in there that I was proud of. I had some good plays."

Soon after leaving college Black joined Tim Robbins's Los Angeles–based theater troupe, the Actors' Gang. During the next several years, he had several well-reviewed turns in Actors' Gang productions of, among other works, the classic dramas *Peer Gynt*, *Woyzeck*, and *The Good Woman of Setzuan*. In 1989 he appeared in Robbins's play *Carnage* at the Edinburgh Theater Festival, in Scotland. He landed his first movie role in Robbins's directorial debut, the political satire *Bob Roberts* (1992). In Robbins's second directing project, the critical and popular success *Dead Man Walking* (1995), Black played the brother of the main character, a man on death row (played by Sean Penn). He also garnered a few guest spots on such television shows as *Touched by an Angel*, *The X-Files*, and *Picket Fences* and was cast in small parts in mostly forgettable films: *Demolition Man* and *Wasteland*, in 1993; *The NeverEnding Story III* and *Blind Justice*, in 1994; and *Waterworld*, in 1995. Those were followed by supporting roles in such motion pictures as *The Cable Guy* (1996), *Mars Attacks!* (1996), and *Enemy of the State* (1998), in which, for the most part, Black portrayed off-the-wall characters. In the Tim Robbins–directed *Cradle Will Rock* (1999), Black was cast as an untalented would-be ventriloquist.

Earlier, in 1994, Black had formed a musical duo with a fellow Actors' Gang member and guitarist, Kyle Gass. The pair called themselves Tenacious D, a term used by the sportscaster Marv Albert to refer to tough defensive action in basketball games. In the *Washington Post* (March 24, 1999), Richard Leiby resorted to fantasy to describe Tenacious D's idiosyncratic music: "If rock monsters Black Sabbath, Molly Hatchet and Iron Maiden had sex and produced a two-headed baby, it would be the world's greatest band. And this unholy spawn would be named . . . Tenacious D." Gass and Black play heavy-metal–inspired acoustic guitar and sing ironic, often bawdy lyrics; in their various Tenacious D incarnations (who go by such aliases as JB, Jables, KG, and Kage), they are equal parts musician and actor. This "mix of the Smothers Brothers, Cheech and Chong, Beavis and Butt-head and Spinal Tap," as Matthew Coltrin characterized the duo in the *Los Angeles Times* (April 1, 2000), has gained a tiny but fiercely loyal cult following. In 1997 Tenacious D had a series of 10-minute spots on HBO; their comedy series *Tenacious D: The Greatest Band on Earth* later ran briefly on the same cable channel. "I love Tenacious D," Black told Mark Olsen. "The main thing is Kyle and I write the stuff—everything we do, we are the masters of the puppet show. With the [stage and screen] acting, it's somebody else's brainchild, and I'm just sort of helping flesh it out. There's a special satisfaction to being the brains behind the operation."

One of Tenacious D's biggest fans is the actor John Cusack, who is a member of the Actors' Gang. "If you haven't had a chance to see Tenacious D play," Cusack told Matthew Coltrin, "it's one of the six or seven wonders of the world. Jack is great because somehow in his comedic aesthetic it's like he's the king of somewhere. It might not be on Earth, but it's definitely somewhere." Cusack, who helped adapt Nick Hornby's novel *High Fidelity* for the silver screen, thought that Black would be perfect as the character Barry, a sharp-tongued font of musical trivia who works in a record store. The film version of *High Fidelity* earned high marks for Cusack, who played the main character, while the part of Barry proved to be Black's breakout role. "Having already attained cult-hero status in HBO's delicious acoustic-metal satire, *Tenacious D*, Black added his own chapter to The Book of Scene-Stealing as a manic-sarcastic, frighteningly encyclopedic record-store clerk in *High Fidelity*," an *Entertainment Weekly* (December 22–29, 2000) critic wrote. The role of Barry, Black told Coltrin, was "definitely the best part I've had. It's the biggest, juiciest, funniest, best opportunity to get wild. I was intimidated by the part at first. They had to talk to me because I was afraid of failing. I'm really glad they did because if this movie was coming out with someone else in it I'd be freaking out."

Black's performance in *High Fidelity* captured the attention of casting agents and directors. He was soon cast in the director Dennis Dugan's *Sav-*

*ing Silverman* (2001), a comedy about two friends (Black and Steve Zahn) who are determined to prevent their best pal (Jason Biggs) from marrying a woman who doesn't like them. The movie's writing and direction failed to impress critics, but reviewers praised the humor in the performances of Black and Zahn. "Think of *Silverman* as a great screen test for the comedic talent of Steven Zahn and Jack Black," Desson Howe wrote for the *Washington Post* (February 9, 2001). "I mean, will someone please get some inspiration and write something funny for these two? They're great together, even in a bottom-of-the-barrel comedy like this. Save them from comedies like this."

After he appeared in *High Fidelity*, Black told Mark Olsen, "I was feeling my oats one day and told my agent, 'Alert the industry. I'm ready for my romantic lead. All-night shoots opposite Gwyneth Paltrow. She'll play my love interest.' I was spinning this ridiculous dream scenario once I'd had a little taste of success. I was joking—and then it . . . fell in my lap." Black co-starred as the title character opposite Paltrow in the Peter and Bobby Farrelly film *Shallow Hal* (2001). An average-looking guy who seeks physical perfection in potential mates, Hal pursues, and is routinely rejected by, beautiful women. After he is hypnotized by a self-help guru, he can see only inner beauty, and he promptly falls in love with Rosemary, a 300-pound blond played by Gwyneth Paltrow in a fat suit. Many fans of Farrelly brothers films thought the humor too subtle and the message too preachy, while other viewers were offended by jokes made at Rosemary's expense. Critics had varied reactions to Black's performance. One of the admirers was Roger Ebert, who wrote for the *Chicago Sun-Times* (November 9, 2001, on-line), "Black, in his first big-time starring role, struts through with the blissful confidence of a man who knows he was born for stardom, even though he doesn't look like your typical Gwyneth Paltrow boyfriend. He's not so thin either."

Speaking about his recently acquired celebrity, Black told Christy Lemire, "It can end at any time. I think it would be hard to go backwards. That's the weird thing that I'm a little bit scared about, is that if you're playing . . . character parts, smaller roles, supporting roles, you can maintain a thing like that for a whole career." The more than $1 million he earned per film in 2001 has also made him uneasy. "It was the magic number, but then after I got it, I wished that I'd gotten nine-ninety-nine instead. . . . It would have been way better to be just under that and not be newsworthy," he told Lemire. Perhaps to reassure himself about his future, Black focused anew on Tenacious D, working on an album for Epic Records. The highly rated debut album, *Tenacious D*, was released in mid-2001. When Mark Olsen asked him whether he would abandon acting or music, if compelled to drop one of them, he responded with a reference to the unbearable decision forced upon the character Sophie in William Styron's novel *Sophie's Choice*: "You want me to make Sophie's choice? That's what you're asking me to do, and it's not fair. You're asking me to choose between two children, the one that pays more and the one I secretly love more."

In 2002 Black appeared in Jake Kasdan's *Orange County*, playing Lance Brumder, the slacker brother of a high-school senior (played by Colin Hanks) who is desperate to gain acceptance to Stanford University. He also lent his voice to the animated film *Ice Age* and appeared in the independent film *Run Ronnie Run*.

Black lives in Los Angeles with his longtime girlfriend, Laura Kightlinger, a stand-up comedian, actress, and television comedy writer whose credits include *Saturday Night Live* and *Will & Grace*. Kightlinger's book of stories (in actuality, a thinly disguised memoir), *Quick Shots of False Hope: A Rejection Collection, Volume 1*, was published in 1999. "Being a two-career couple is good," Black told Liz Braun, "but we need an assistant. . . . We're both bringing home the bacon, so nobody wants to do the dishes." — K.S.

Suggested Reading: *Entertainment Weekly* p102+ Nov. 166 2001; *New York* p33+ Dec. 18–25, 2000; (New York) *Daily News* (on-line) Apr. 7, 2000, with photo, Nov. 4, 2001, with photo; *Premiere* p28+ Nov. 2001, with photo; *Toronto Sun* (on-line) Feb. 4, 2001; *Washington Post* C p 1 Mar. 24, 1999, with photo

Selected Films: *Bob Roberts*, 1992; *The Cable Guy*, 1996; *Mars Attacks!*, 1996; *Enemy of the State*, 1998; *Jesus' Son*, 1999; *High Fidelity*, 2000; *Saving Silverman*, 2001; *Shallow Hal*, 2001; *Orange County*, 2002; *Run, Ronnie, Run*, 2002

Selected Television Shows (as Tenacious D): *Mr. Show with Bob and David*, 1997; *Tenacious D*, 1999

Selected Albums: *Tenacious D*, 2001

---

## blink-182

*Rock band*

DeLonge, Tom
(de-LONG)
*Dec. 13, 1975– Guitarist; singer*

Hoppus, Mark
*Mar. 15, 1972– Bassist; singer*

Barker, Travis
*Nov. 14, 1975– Drummer*

*Address: c/o MCA Records, 2220 Colorado Ave., Santa Monica, CA 90404*

By mixing the driving, skate-punk rock associated with such bands as Agent Orange, the Adolescents,

Deverill Weekes/Retna Ltd.

*blink-182 (left to right): Tom DeLonge, Mark Hoppus, Travis Barker*

and Gang Green with lewd, scatological humor, blink-182 has earned a reputation as punk rock's merry pranksters. Whether running stark naked through suburban streets in their video for "What's My Age Again?" or bestowing double-entendre titles on such albums as *Take Off Your Pants and Jacket* (2001), the members of blink-182 have demonstrated that there is little they won't do to attract attention. However, along with their sophomoric hijinks, guitarist/singer Tom DeLonge, bassist Mark Hoppus, and drummer Travis Barker display excellent musicianship and strong songwriting skills. "There's a side of blink-182 where we get up onstage and just want to offend people," Hoppus told Lisa Russell for *People* (August 31, 2001). "And then there's the creative side, where we try to write great songs with some pretty serious themes." The group's 1999 album, *Enema of the State*, addresses such issues as teen suicide, unrequited love, and the anxiety of leaving home to go to college, while *Take Off Your Pants and Jacket* includes the song "Stay Together for the Kids," about the toll that divorce often takes on young children. Since the group achieved national stardom, in 1997, they have become favorites of the high-school set, primarily because, unlike many of their contemporaries, they are very much in touch with that age group. "You don't have to be at their level," Hoppus told David H. Freedman for *Inc.* (December 2000); "you just have to understand where they are and respect it. . . . The sad thing is, we all had expertise in relating to teens at one time, but we chose to grow up. I still consider myself a kid, and that's not true of most 28-year-olds." In addition to their careers in music, the members of blink-182 have undertaken various entrepreneurial pursuits. Hoppus and DeLonge own and operate a Web site, *loserkids.com*, that sells clothing, skates, and other items desirable to teenagers, while Barker owns Famous Stars and Straps, which sells belts and other accessories. In September 2001, with the help of Hoppus's sister, Anne, the group published a memoir, *Tales from Beneath Your Mom*. DeLonge told Russell, "We don't consider ourselves rock stars." Hoppus added, "We're just a bunch of normal dudes. We hang out with the same people we always hung out with."

Blink-182 originated in San Diego, California, when Mark Allan Hoppus (born on March 15, 1972 in Ridgecrest, California) met the guitarist Thomas Matthew DeLonge (born on December 13, 1975 in San Diego). Earlier, Hoppus, whose father was a U.S. Navy weapons engineer and whose mother was a travel coordinator, had received a bass and amp for helping his father paint a house. He began playing along with punk records by such groups as the Descendents and the Vandals, learning simple lines and songs. Soon he began to listen to college-rock groups, among them the Cure and the Replacements. During his junior year at California State University, in San Marcos, a mutual friend introduced him to DeLonge, a passionate punk fan and aspiring guitarist. DeLonge's parents, eager for their son to learn to play an instrument, had bought him a trumpet for Christmas when he was 11. " We . . . told him, 'When you get really good, you can wake us up with reveille,'" DeLonge's mother, Connie, told Gavin Edwards for *Rolling Stone* (August 3, 2000). "What we failed to emphasize was that we would decide when that day had come." Before long—exhibiting the prankishness that has marked his career—DeLonge began standing outside at five in the morning, waking his parents by blowing tonelessly into the instrument. When DeLonge was a teenager, a friend gave him a guitar that he had found at a dump. Shortly afterward DeLonge discovered such punk groups as Stiff Little Fingers, the Undertones, and Dinosaur Jr. while visiting another friend in Oregon.

Hoppus and DeLonge soon discovered their mutual interest in music and began writing songs together. After performing as a duo, they realized that, to replicate the sounds of the Vandals and other bands they admired, they needed a drummer. DeLonge knew someone in his school who fit the bill: 14-year-old Scott Raynor, a fan of heavy-metal music, who had become interested in drums while talking about forming a band with his friends, all of whom wanted to play other instruments.

With Raynor on board, the trio christened themselves Blink and began performing at all-age clubs in the San Diego area. Soon they developed a solid fan base among local skateboarders. Thanks to their growing reputation, the group came to the attention of the Vandals. The members of that band helped land Blink a deal with the small record label Grilled Cheese, through which they released a series of extended-play (EP) albums, including

*Lemmings* (1994) and *They Came to Conquer Uranus* (1995), and a demo entitled *Buddha* (1994). In 1995 they released their first full-length album, *Cheshire Cat.* Featuring such now-classic rock songs as "Fentoozler," "Romeo and Rebecca," and "Does My Breath Smell?," the album helped define their musical direction. The appearance of *Cheshire Cat* in record stores led to the threat of legal action from an Irish techno band also called Blink. To avoid a lawsuit, the American group added "182" to their name. Referring to that number, Hoppus told Gavin Edwards for *Rolling Stone* (January 20, 2000), "We just pulled it out of our ass. A lot of people think it's from [the 1985 movie] *Turk*, but why would we take the number from a terrible movie?"

Traveling in a decrepit old van, the newly christened blink-182 began touring in support of *Cheshire Cat.* As the tour progressed they saw their fan base expand. Record executives noticed this as well, and in 1996 the band accepted a joint contract with Cargo Music (a division of Grilled Cheese) and MCA Records. The following year brought the release of their first album for MCA, *Dude Ranch.* Its opening single, "Dammit (Growing Up)," a thundering, anthemic song about the frustration of losing one's girlfriend to another guy, got airplay on major radio stations and was featured prominently in the teen film *Can't Hardly Wait* (1998) and the popular television series *Dawson's Creek.* On the strength of that single, sales of *Dude Ranch* climbed to the platinum mark (selling one million copies), and blink-182 soon found that their popularity had spread nationwide. The group spent the remainder of 1997 and most of 1998 playing alongside such popular acts as Primus and the Aquabats at Sno-Core, a traveling music and snowboarding festival, and the Warped Festival, another touring concert, which was designed to appeal to young people who liked punk rock, ska, and skateboarding. During this time, while the band wrote new material for their next record, Raynor decided to leave the group. According to some sources, he left to go to college. Hoppus, however, told Gavin Edwards in January 2000, "Scott was kicked out of the band." When asked if the reason was related to his musicianship, Hoppus replied, "Well, it was what was going on outside of that, but it was affecting his performances." Blink-182 quickly recruited the Aquabats' drummer, Travis Barker, who had filled in for Raynor during his frequent absences. (Born on November 14, 1975 in Fontana, California, Barker began playing drums when he was four years old.)

In December 1998, with Barker in tow, blink-182 worked in the studio on their follow-up to *Dude Ranch.* Entitled *Enema of the State*, the album was released on June 1, 1999 and promptly landed in *Billboard*'s Top 10. A more accomplished record than any of its predecessors, *Enema of the State* features brighter melodies and catchier guitar hooks propelled by Barker's speedy, intricate drumming. Additionally, there are strong lyrics, in "All the Small Things" and other heartfelt love songs and in the haunting antisuicide ballad "Adam's Song."

On the strength of the first single on *Enema of the State*, "What's My Age Again?," whose video features the band streaking through Los Angeles suburbs, and of the video for "All the Small Things," in which the band parodied such teen pop stars as the Backstreet Boys and Britney Spears, sales for *Enema of the State* soon climbed to seven million. In addition, the album introduced a new generation to punk music, a genre that most teens had ignored of late. "The biggest compliment of all is a kid saying we opened his eyes to a new style of music," Hoppus told Edwards. "We're kind of like Fisher-Price: My First Punk Band."

To promote *Enema of the State*, blink-182 embarked on a major arena tour, performing in large venues for the first time. "This is the dream tour that everybody wishes they could do," DeLonge told Austin Scaggs for *Rolling Stone* (May 5, 2000). The band appeared on a special stage, designed to resemble a 1950s drive-in theater, complete with elaborate lighting and stock film footage from B-movies projected on a screen. Dubbed "The Mark, Tom and Travis Show," the tour was one of the most successful of 1999. To capitalize on its success, a limited-release live album, *The Mark, Tom and Travis Show (The Enema Strikes Back!)*, was rushed to stores in the fall of 2000. The album, which was available only until January 2001, contains live versions of songs from the band's earlier records as well as unreleased cuts and a new single, "Man Overboard."

After they completed the tour, the members of blink-182 tested new songs in small clubs and then headed into the studio to record them. "We tried to make [the next album] not as polished as *Enema of the State*," Hoppus told a reporter for *MTV.com.* "We tried to strip things down. . . . I just think the songs are stronger. I think the lyrics are a lot better. I think it's a heavier record." After toying with such titles as "If You See Kay" and "Genital Ben," blink-182 titled the album *Take Off Your Pants and Jacket*—a sly reference to the band's antics in the video for "What's My Age Again?" "I think the video is our nemesis," Hoppus told a reporter for *NYRock.com.* "Everybody always asks us to drop our pants again and if we're going to perform naked again or what. It's really bothersome, you know. So in a way the album title is our way of dealing with it, making some fun because we know the video will follow us until all eternity."

*Take Off Your Pants and Jacket* was released on June 12, 2001 and debuted at number one on the *Billboard* rock chart. Reviews of the album were mixed. "Blink-182 might never find themselves in danger of becoming respectable, committed as they are to three-chord kicks, bathroom-graffiti gags and staying quicker on the trou[ser]-dropping trigger than Britney Spears," Rob Sheffield wrote for *Rolling Stone* (July 5, 2001). "But as they plow in their relatively un-self-conscious way through the emotional hurdles of lust, terror, pain and rage, they reveal more about themselves and their audience than they even intend to, turning adolescent malaise into a friendly joke rather than a spiritual crisis." David Browne, by contrast, did not find any humor in the album, describing it in *Entertainment Weekly* (June 22, 2001) as "angrier and more teeth-gnashing than what you'd expect. The band work so hard at it, and the music is such processed-sounding mainstream rock played fast, that the album becomes a paradox: adolescent energy and rebellion made joyless." Nonetheless, *Take Off Your Pants and Jacket* was tremendously popular. Such singles as the Ramones-influenced "Rock Show" and the antidivorce anthem "Stay Together for the Kids" kept the album high on the charts for the remainder of the year and helped it go platinum. In April 2002 blink-182 embarked with the rock band Green Day on a tour dubbed "Pop Disaster," in which each group had equal time on stage.

In 2002 Barker and DeLonge, along with David Kennedy and Anthony Celestino, released *Boxcar Racer*, an album of punk music inspired by some of the members' favorite bands. "This record is directly influenced by the bands that mean the most to me," DeLonge explained on the Web site *boxcarracer.com*. "It's a tribute to the music that made me want to be in a band in the first place." In the fall of 2002, blink-182 embarked on a brief world tour.

Each member of blink-182 lives with his wife in a quiet suburb of San Diego. "We're very much suburbanites," DeLonge told Russell. "Going on tour is very much a culture shock." Hoppus and DeLonge enjoy fishing together. "We go eighty miles off the shore of San Diego, and we'll come back with a load of tuna," Hoppus told Jenny Eliscu for *Rolling Stone* (March 1, 2001). "It's great. You go out there and you're at total peace with yourself, just massacring helpless creatures." Barker owns a rehearsal studio and gives drum lessons in Riverside, California.

DeLonge's wedding to Jennifer Jenkins, an interior designer, in May 2001 was a traditional affair. "I'm not one of those dorks who goes, 'Yeah, I've gotta get married in, like, a tank top on the beach with my ripped-up Dickies,'" DeLonge told Elizabeth Kuster for *Cosmo Girl* (June/July 2001). "No, I want to have a nice wedding." Hoppus and his wife, Skye Everly, a former MTV production associate, became the parents of a son in August 2002. Barker's wife, Melissa Kennedy, is a student. "We know that our success will be short-lived," Hoppus told Edwards (August 3, 2001). "Well, not short-lived, but we'll only be able to do this for a finite amount of time. . . . But when the end does come, I'll just say, 'Thank God that I got a chance to do exactly what I love.'" — J.K.B.

Suggested Reading: *Inc.* p98+ Dec. 2000, with photos; *People* p124+ Aug. 13, 2001, with photos; *Rolling Stone* p33+ Jan. 20, 2000, with photos, p36+ Aug. 3, 2000, with photos

Selected Recordings: *Buddha*, 1994; *Cheshire Cat*, 1995; *Dude Ranch*, 1997; *Enema of the State*, 1999; *The Mark, Tom and Travis Show*, 2000; *Take Off Your Pants and Jacket*, 2001

---

## Bloomberg, Michael R.

*Feb. 14, 1942– Mayor of New York City (Republican); founder of Bloomberg L.P.*

*Address: City Hall, New York, NY 10007*

The multibillionaire Michael R. Bloomberg, founder of the Bloomberg financial empire, became one of the wealthiest men ever elected to political office when he won the mayorship of New York City, in November 2001. Two decades earlier Bloomberg, a onetime partner in the financial firm Salomon Brothers, had formed Bloomberg L.P., which sells computer systems that track the trading of securities; the systems can now be used to execute trades and keep abreast of the latest world and financial developments through Bloomberg News, which encompasses publications and programs in a variety of media. Bloomberg L.P. currently employs about 8,000 people in more than 100 offices around the world.

While he remains a shareholder of the company, Bloomberg relinquished the titles of chairman and chief executive officer prior to being sworn in as mayor of New York, on January 1, 2002. Although many did not believe that Bloomberg—who had never held elective office—was qualified to be mayor, he responded to such criticism by noting that he had successfully run a large corporation for two decades and had not only consistently turned large profits but built a reputation for staunch loyalty among his employees. He wrote during the campaign, as published in the *Gotham Gazette* (online), that becoming mayor of New York is "part accountability, the day to day running of a great organization with a quarter of a million dedicated employees and a 40 billion dollar budget. It is part enunciating a vision of where New York should go, and the practicality of getting us there. It is part innovation, and creativity, and an unwillingness to settle for the status quo. It is the service mentality of understanding who government should work for, and how to give people access and consideration. It is leadership, that intangible needed to motivate, inspire, and encourage others: To give confidence in the future, to convince people anything's possible if one works hard enough and collaborates with others, to encourage each of us to make the world better."

Mark Wilson/Newsmakers

*Michael R. Bloomberg*

Michael Rubens Bloomberg was born on February 14, 1942 in Boston, Massachusetts, one of the two children of William Henry Bloomberg and Charlotte Bloomberg. The family lived in Medford, a suburb of Boston. Bloomberg's father was the bookkeeper at a local dairy; his mother was a secretary. "I don't remember them ever beating me," he told Jim Hartz on May 20, 1997 for the *Real Bottom Line* (on-line). "I don't remember them ever doing anything bad. I don't even remember my parents ever fighting. If they ever had an argument, it was never done in front of my sister and I. . . . They were just your normal well-adjusted, lower-middle-class American family." He added, "I do remember them describing certain things, why we had an obligation to support certain charities. . . . I remember my father giving money to the NAACP, and I said to him, 'Why are you doing that?' And he said, 'Because if we don't help people who are being discriminated against, we will be discriminated against.'" Bloomberg learned from his father's example; he became so intent on helping others, his sister recalled to Dean E. Murphy for the *New York Times* (November 26, 2001), that their parents' friends would often request "to borrow Michael." He would also travel to a nearby town to perform chores for his aunt Ruth, who was retarded. "If he liked [doing something], he worked hard at it," Bloomberg's mother told Murphy. "But he had to find something he wanted to do."

Bloomberg attended public schools and joined the Boy Scouts, progressing all the way to Eagle Scout at the unusually young age of 12. In high school he joined the debate team and developed a fondness for horses. He spent his weekends attending lectures at a local museum and worked for a small electronics company during the summers. One of the few graduates from his high-school class to go on to college, he attended Johns Hopkins University, in Baltimore, Maryland, financing his education through loans and money he earned by parking cars. He joined a fraternity at the school and later recalled in an interview for the campus newspaper, as quoted by Dean E. Murphy, "We had a good time. We drank a lot of beer. We didn't study very much. I burned the candle at both ends." However, when he knew that few of his friends would notice, he would sneak off to work in the school's computer lab. His father died in 1963, a year before he graduated with a degree in electrical engineering. He earned a master's degree in business education from Harvard Business School, in Cambridge, Massachusetts, in 1966.

Bloomberg next joined the securities-brokerage firm of Salomon Brothers, in New York City. There, he rose to the position of general partner, heading departments in equity trading and sales as well as systems development. Linton Weeks, in the *Washington Post* (December 8, 1996), called his position "arguably the most macho job at what was then the most macho company in the world." Among his innovations at the company was the reprogramming of an old-fashioned stock machine known as a Quotron; he created, in effect, an updated tickertape, or early one-purpose computer, which was capable of performing some basic stock analyses and comparisons. By some accounts, Dean E. Murphy reported, at Salomon Bloomberg was "an insufferable know-it-all" who had difficult relationships with some of his fellow managers. When Salomon Brothers was purchased by the Phibro Corp., in 1981, Bloomberg found himself at odds with the new owners and was soon fired. "I read somewhere it was because I thought I could run the company better than they could, and that's probably a fair statement," Bloomberg recalled to Joe Holley for *Columbia Journalism Review* (May/June 1995). "Let's just say I disagreed with their accounting and hiring practices." Nonetheless, being fired was a devastating experience for him. "I remember being hurt in the sense that it was my company," he told Jim Hartz. "I had given 15 years of my life and I really believed that the name Salomon was my last name in every meaningful sense. . . . I built that firm as much as anybody else did. Not more, but I did my share. To be rejected was not a pleasurable thing."

Bloomberg left Salomon Brothers with shares in the firm worth $10 million. Instead of retiring, the 39-year-old founded Innovative Market Systems, which later became Bloomberg L.P. He had realized that computer technology could be used to compare past and present data on stocks and bonds; his company leased computers capable of such analysis—devices that became known popularly as "Bloombergs." Many, especially those in the bond market, found that this service represented a major improvement over the confusing handwritten system previously used. Bloomberg himself owned 70 percent of the new company, while the other 30 percent was owned by the financial firm Merrill Lynch—which was also the first customer of Bloomberg L.P., leasing 20 subscriptions to the service in 1982. The original price for one terminal was $1,500 a month. They are currently leased for $1,285 a month and hooked up to giant mainframes located in New York City and Princeton, New Jersey. By 1990 10,000 terminals had been installed. As of 1995 Bloomberg's company controlled roughly 17 percent of the $3.5 billion-a-year on-line business-information market, and was showing faster growth than its competitors. Bloomberg L.P. soon became known in the industry for both its perks and its supposed "sweatshop" atmosphere. Employees were situated (along with Bloomberg himself) in communal offices, had easy access to free snacks, and were given assistance in paying legal fees, health-care expenses, and other debts. At the same time, they received strong pressure to work 12-hour days, during which they were expected to stay mainly at their desks. Video cameras and electronic-card readers kept track of employees' comings and goings, and E-mail messages and phone calls were subject to surveillance. Employees who left were never allowed back. "We have a meritocracy where if you do more, you will be rewarded more," Bloomberg told Jim Hartz. "I cannot think of anything else that we could do that would be fair to everybody. And so nobody says you have to work as hard as Mike Bloomberg. But if you do, I just want to make sure that you get rewarded more than somebody that does not."

In 1989 Bloomberg expanded his operation to include a financial-news service, Bloomberg Business News (later Bloomberg News), which provided political and sports stories as well as business news to leading corporations, financial institutions, and newspapers throughout the world, via the "Bloomberg" machines. He chose Matthew Winkler, then a reporter for the *Wall Street Journal*, to organize and operate the service as editor in chief. As of 2001 Bloomberg News employed more than 1,200 reporters and editors in 82 bureaus worldwide. "Our mission is to provide everything that issuers of securities, investors and intermediaries need around the globe," Bloomberg told Barnaby J. Feder for the *New York Times* (March 29, 1991). "That includes news." Not long after Bloomberg Financial News was launched, the company began providing the officers of major newspapers with Bloomberg machines in exchange for installation fees. The move paid off: the company gained exposure and credibility when stories from the Bloomberg wire were cited or used in one of the papers. Offering reports in real time, Bloomberg news currently publishes approximately 4,000 stories a day. The Bloomberg operation moved into print in 1992 with the launch of the monthly magazine *Bloomberg*. The company also began printing *Bloomberg Personal*, a financial supplement that started as an insert in 18 metro dailies across the country before being sold by subscription. In 1994 *Bloomberg Personal* enjoyed the largest magazine launch ever, with six million copies of its first issue in circulation.

Meanwhile, in 1993 Bloomberg Radio began its broadcasts, which emphasized business stories and were soon syndicated to more than 200 radio stations across the United States. Among Bloomberg Radio's features are the Urban Business Report and Negocios Bloomberg, the first nationally syndicated radio reports to address the financial concerns of the African-American and Hispanic communities, respectively. In 1994 Bloomberg Television was launched; since that time it has been syndicated on 10 networks broadcasting in seven languages worldwide and is also seen on national and international cable and local network affiliates. Its first show, *Bloomberg Business News*, was produced by Maryland Public Television. Bloomberg's Web site, *Bloomberg.com*, went into operation in 1995 and quickly became one of the most popular finance sites on the Internet. In the following year the company established Bloomberg Tradebook, an electronic financial brokerage service, which currently has a daily trading average of more than 90 million over-the-counter and listed shares. In 2000 Bloomberg Tradebook set a volume record of more than 100 million shares in one day.

In 1997 the billionaire published his autobiography, *Bloomberg by Bloomberg*, written with Matthew Winkler. All proceeds from the book were donated to the Committee to Protect Journalists. Reviews were mixed. While noting the book's merits—which included some interesting anecdotes—Leah Nathans Spiro wrote for *Business Week* (May 5, 1997, on-line) that "*Bloomberg on Bloomberg* is an infomercial," adding, "His life story, or the semi-sanitized version we get in the book, isn't too interesting." David Whitford noted in his review for *Fortune* (May 12, 1997) that "getting at the nuggets involves wading through an awful pile of egotistical fluff." In 1998 Bloomberg L.P.'s first daily newspaper, *Bloomberg Money*, began publication. The company also announced that it would make news and data available through Skytel pagers. The following year the company started another magazine, *Bloomberg Wealth Manager*.

In July 2000 Bloomberg began to investigate the possibility of running for the mayorship of New York City. The mayor at that time, Rudolph W. Giuliani, a Republican, was nearing the end of his second term and was prohibited by city law from seeking a third. For the next several months, Bloomberg traveled in the five boroughs of New York on what he called a "listening tour." A lifelong Democrat, he switched to the Republican Party in November 2000, believing that he would have no chance as a party outsider of winning the Democratic nomination. Political observers and columnists were skeptical of his candidacy at first; many found it difficult to believe that a person with no political experience could convince voters that he could run a large metropolis. Bloomberg responded by maintaining that having run a multimillion-dollar corporation demonstrated his ability, and gave him the necessary experience, to run a large city government. He became increasingly serious about running for the office in early 2001 and denounced the city's campaign-finance reforms, saying that they amounted to an incumbent-protection program. He stated that if he ran for mayor he would avoid the system by using his own money. In addition, Bloomberg stepped down as chairman of the board of Bloomberg L.P., while staying on as the company's chief executive officer. He also expanded the board of directors, which included himself, from three to seven members. Analysts saw the move as a way to escape claims of a conflict of interest when the campaign began in earnest. On June 5, 2001 Bloomberg launched his first televison ads, and the following day he announced his candidacy in front of the press. He soon began to promote himself as the "education mayor" and came out in favor of yearly visits to students' homes by teachers and principals. He also stated that he supported abolishing the city's Board of Education to give principals more control over their schools. Bloomberg's other proposed education reforms included having all public-school students wear uniforms and instituting a voice-mail system that would provide parents with information about their children's grades and attendance and allow teachers to send messages to students. Bloomberg ran on a socially liberal but fiscally conservative platform, easing conservatives' minds by stating that he would not raise taxes while convincing some liberals that he did not share Giuliani's more hardline social views.

While the candidates for the Democratic Party's nomination for mayor faced a tight race and had to raise a great deal of money, Bloomberg maintained a comparably easy schedule for the first half of his campaign and managed to stay clear of the tough issues debated amongst the Democrats. He did face a brief controversy, however, in September 2001, when a pamphlet containing politically incorrect jokes supposedly written or spoken by Bloomberg—and given to him as a birthday present in 1990—was made public. To some, the episode raised the question of how well Bloomberg was able to work with others, since it had also come to light that he had been accused by employees of making comments about their co-workers' bodies. Three female staffers had sued him over the years for sexual discrimination, later dropping the suits or settling them out of court.

The face of the mayoral election changed drastically with the September 11, 2001 terrorist attacks in New York City; two airplanes crashed into and toppled the twin World Trade Center towers in Lower Manhattan. The attacks, which killed thousands and severely damaged the city's economy, also caused the primary elections, scheduled for that very day, to be postponed. In response to the crisis, Bloomberg wrote for the *Gotham Gazette* (on-line), "We will improve our public safety to the extent a civilized society can restrict and inhibit its daily lives. We will enhance our contingency plans to respond to future crises as yet unknown. We will catch and punish the guilty, not so much for retribution—although we all understand that instinct—but as a deterrent to anyone who contemplates another senseless barbaric attack. And we pledge the ultimate rebuke to this mindless savagery, the continuation of America's and New York's unparalleled democracy, civility and service to all humanity."

With the city in a state of emergency, the issues of the election suddenly shifted from education and housing to the rebuilding of the city's economy and financial district. Many observers felt that this shift helped Bloomberg. On September 25 the businessman easily won the Republican primary over former congressman Herman Badillo, 66 percent to 34 percent. In the general election, Bloomberg faced Mark Green, the city's public advocate. Green's candidacy had been damaged by a close primary election and the resulting run-off, which saw Democratic voters split largely down racial lines; nonetheless, with two weeks left in the race, polls showed Bloomberg facing a 16-point deficit. Bloomberg quickly closed in on Green, however. A late endorsement of Bloomberg by Mayor Giuliani, who was seen by many as a hero because of his efficient, compassionate leadership in the wake of the September 11 attacks, helped put Bloomberg on top. On November 6, 2001 Bloomberg, having spent an estimated $50 million of his own money in the most expensive mayoral race in U.S. history, narrowly defeated Green. "Tonight is not about Republicans or Democrats," Bloomberg said in his victory speech, as quoted by *New York 1* (on-line). "It's about New Yorkers. This is our victory, a victory for our vision and our faith in the future of the greatest city in the world."

After the election, Bloomberg traveled with others to Washington, D.C., seeking additional federal funds to help the city recover from the September 11 attacks. At the time the city was in the middle of its worst fiscal crisis since the 1970s. While the mission was ultimately unsuccessful, members of both parties of the New York delegation to Capitol Hill praised Bloomberg for his lobbying strength and compared him favorably in that regard with Giuliani. Bloomberg also impressed many by holding talks with both Democrats and members of the city's unions, which Giuliani had often refused to do. Acknowledging the more than 800,000 Puerto Ricans living in New York City, Bloomberg made a trip to Puerto Rico in November 2001 to meet with business and government leaders and assert his commitment to Puerto Rican concerns in New York City policy. Bloomberg later traveled to the Dominican Republic at the invitation of that nation's president, who also arranged for him to meet with some of the families of the victims of flight 587, which had crashed in Belle Harbor, New York, earlier that November en route to the Dominican Republic. Bloomberg stated that he would keep a lower profile than his predecessors and that he would continue to live in his Upper East Side townhouse rather than move into the mayor's mansion. He also announced that he would create a large, open office in City Hall, based on the central office at Bloomberg L.P. As he had at that company, he would sit amongst employees and use his private office mostly for ceremonial purposes. Regarding his role as chief executive of Bloomberg L.P., he stated that he would resign from that position but would continue to collect a share of his company's profits.

In December 2001 Bloomberg named his four deputy mayors, among them Patricia E. Harris (deputy mayor for administration), who had managed Bloomberg L.P.'s corporate communications department and philanthropic operations. Some Republican leaders later voiced their disappointment that no Republican Party member had been named a deputy mayor, corporation counsel, or leader of Bloomberg's transition team. Indeed, the only Republican Party member on Bloomberg's innermost staff was his press secretary, who had switched affiliation from Independent to Republican during the 2001 campaign. Bloomberg later named Carol A. Robles-Roman deputy mayor for legal affairs, a new position. In creating such an office and in other law-related appointments, Bloomberg hoped to drastically reduce the number of lawsuits brought against the city.

Bloomberg was sworn in on January 1, 2002 as the 108th mayor of New York City. He has since stated that the World Trade Center will be replaced by smaller structures and a memorial. Due to the city's financial crisis, he announced that he would cut his staff by 20 percent and encouraged other city officials to do the same. "Everybody has just got to understand we have to find a way to do as much as we can with less," he said, as quoted by the Associated Press (January 2, 2002). In a move unthinkable under Mayor Giuliani, he asked the police department to submit two lists of personnel cuts (with one having more extensive cuts than the other). Because of the city's budgetary problems, he came out against the Giuliani-approved plans for building new stadiums for both the New York Yankees and the New York Mets baseball teams.

In February 2002 Bloomberg presented his financial plan for the upcoming four years; the plan, which the City Council approved, called for drastic measures to end the city's $4.76 billion deficit, such as cuts to all of the city's agencies, including the police and fire departments, the school system, libraries, the city's cultural-affairs program (which gives money to various museums and cultural endeavors), and the suspension of much of the city's program of trash recycling. He also proposed raising the cigarette tax by $1.42, which he predicted would bring in an additional $250 million annually, and borrowing $1.5 billion. Bloomberg explained that the cuts were necessary to make up for the dramatic drop in tax revenues caused by the national recession and the September 11, 2001 destruction of the World Trade Center, and that he did not want to raise taxes for fear it would drive residents and businesses out of the city. "The budget that we're going to show you hurts everybody," Bloomberg said when he unveiled his proposals, according to Michael Cooper in the *New York Times* (February 14, 2002). "We don't think it hurts anybody fatally. But it is a spread-your-pain, no-sacred-cow kind of a solution to our problem." He insisted that despite the cuts, the city would still be able to keep its streets clean, repair crumbling school buildings, and prevent an increase in the crime rate.

During his first months in office, Bloomberg—as Giuliani had advocated—took steps to abolish the city's Board of Education and instead put himself (and mayors to come) in direct control of the city's school system. This was necessary, he maintained, because the Board of Education seemed more interested in retaining a bloated bureaucracy than in helping children learn. The New York State legislature approved Bloomberg's school proposal in June 2002. Soon afterward the mayor agreed to a new teachers' contract that called for an increase in salaries in return for a longer workweek. He also suggested that a voice-mail system be installed whereby parents of public-school pupils could check on their children's progress in class.

Bloomberg was careful not to criticize Giuliani's actions and approach to governing. He continued several of the former mayor's programs, but he also changed some policies significantly. For example, he eased procedures that affected welfare recipients with chronic social problems. He also returned to the so-called business-improvement districts powers that Giuliani had stripped away. In addition, he eliminated a mayoral office that, in handling new hires, had fostered patronage. In several cases he moved to settle class-action lawsuits hinging on social policy. In addition to his budget cuts, among the more controversial of his decisions was one to approve the housing of some homeless families in a former jail. He also aroused angry protests by proposing to ban smoking in all indoor public places. "The question before us is straightforward. Does your desire to smoke anywhere, at any time, trump the right of others to breathe clean air in the workplace? Common sense and common decency demand [that] . . . the need to breathe clean air is more important than the license to pollute it." Opponents of the ban (which, as of mid-November 2002, had not become law) have warned that it would dissuade tourists from coming to the city and might push some saloons out of business, thus hurting the city's economy. Bloomberg also said that he intended to look for ways to shave millions of dollars from the city's yearly cost of disposing of solid waste. "He is almost a classic turn-of-the-century reformer," Douglas Muzio, a professor of public affairs, told Jennifer Steinhauer for the *New York Times* (August 25, 2002). "He is not doing anything in a zealot way. I thought he was picking fights, but in fact I think it is just that he is such a believer in whatever he does."

On November 14, 2002, declaring a need for drastic measures to make up for a shortfall of $1.1 billion in the budget for the current fiscal year, which ends on July 1, 2003, and to forestall the feared $6.4 billion budget gap looming in the next fiscal year, Mayor Bloomberg called for huge tax increases, including a boost of 25 percent in property taxes and a tax on commuters—people who work in the city but live elsewhere—six times as large as the commuter tax that state legislators repealed in 1999. At the same time, he said, New York City residents' personal income taxes should be lowered. He also urged additional, drastic cuts in city services. Among other measures, he suggested closing eight firehouses; shrinking the police force by 1,600 through attrition; closing 30 senior-citizen centers and reducing the days of operation of the remaining 310 facilities; cutting 8,000 job slots from city government, through layoffs and attrition; and reducing to more modest proportions a planned expansion of day-care centers. Speaking without notes for one hour at a press conference, Bloomberg assured New Yorkers that the city's financial woes were not as dire as those that pushed the municipal government to the brink of bankruptcy in 1975. He also tried to ease concerns that his proposed actions would lead to a rise in crime and dirtier streets, declaring, "This city is not going to cut its expenses below where the quality of life would start to deteriorate." According to an editorial entitled "The Mayor's Real-World Budget" in the *New York Times* (November 15, 2002), Bloomberg "was performing a rare profile in courage by proposing such stunning tax hikes and inviting everyone to blame him for the pain." Noting that during his successful campaign for reelection in 2002, the governor of New York State, George Pataki, had insisted "that contrary to all available evidence, there would be no need for state tax increases next year," the editorial cncluded, "Mr. Pataki needs to acknowledge now that he has a responsibility to help raise revenue for communities that desperately need state help. And Mayor Bloomberg has earned the right to be first at the governor's door." Changes in the tax laws require approval by the state legislature; the mayor's other proposals cannot go into effect without the consent of the City Council.

In addition to his Upper East Side townhouse, Bloomberg has homes in Colorado; London; Bermuda; and Westchester County, New York. Although not very tall, he is known for being an imposing figure. Called by many a workaholic, Bloomberg told Jim Hartz, "I think I have always liked what I do. And when you like what you do, you do more of it because it gives you pleasure. When you do more of it, if you subscribe to 'the harder I work, the luckier I get' theory, the results will be better." He has continued to spend a great deal of time with his ex-wife and closest confidant, Susan Bloomberg (from whom he has been divorced since 1993), and his two daughters, Georgina and Emma Bloomberg. Michael Bloomberg has often appeared in the city's gossip columns in recent years for attending celebrity parties and dating prominent women. Famous for his short temper, he told Hartz, "I get it over instantly. I don't like to harbor grudges. If I have a disagreement with you, I will tell you. It may be at the top of my lungs and if you've got any guts, you'll tell me back at the top of your lungs." To relax, Bloomberg jogs, skis, and snowboards. An amateur pilot, he has walked away without major injuries from his crash landings of a helicopter and an airplane. He told Hartz that when he wants to figure things out, "I talk to myself. I go out and run. I think that's when I can work out my problems. That's when I talk to God. I've just always found counseling myself to be the best way for me. I'm not sure it's the best way for everybody, but it's been the best way for me." In a conversation with Elisabeth Bumiller for the *New York Times* (January 18, 2001), Bloomberg said, "Happiness for me has always been the thrill of the unknown, trying something that everyone says can't be done, feeling that gnawing pit in my stomach that says, 'Danger ahead.'"

Bloomberg is a trustee of the Jewish Museum, the Spence School, the Big Apple Circus, Prep for Prep, the High School of Economics and Finance, the Institute for Advanced Study, Lincoln Center for the Performing Arts, the New York Police & Fire Widows' and Children's Benefit Fund, the U.S. Chamber of Commerce, the S.L.E. Foundation, and the U.S. Ski Team Educational Foundation. He is a member of the board and co-chair of the individual gifts committee of the Central Park Conservancy. He has funded relief programs for victims of domestic violence in New York City and has volunteered with Bloomberg employees in painting public schools through the organization Publicolor; delivering meals to homebound elderly with City Meals-on-Wheels; and reading to children as part of Everybody Wins!, a literacy foundation. He is currently the chairman of Johns Hopkins University's board of trustees and chair of the Johns Hopkins Initiative, the university's Joint Trustee Committee on Development, and the Johns Hopkins Hospital and Health System. As chairman of the board of trustees, he led a fund-raising campaign that more than doubled the school's endowment and included his gift of $100 million, 30 percent of which was dedicated to financial aid for students. The hospital at the Johns Hopkins School of Hygiene and Public Health has been renamed the Bloomberg School of Public Health. — G.O.

Suggested Reading: *Columbia Journalism Review* p46+ May/June 1995; *Fortune* p96+ Apr. 1, 2002, with photos; *Gotham Gazette* (on-line); *New Republic* p18+ July 2, 2001; *New York* p20+ Apr. 15, 2002, with photos; *New York Times* D p4 Mar. 29, 1991, with photo, B p1 Jan. 18, 2001, p1+ Nov. 26, 2001, with photos, p1+ Feb. 14, 2002, with photos, A p1+ May 8, 2002, with photos; *New Yorker* p138+ Apr. 22–29, 2002; *Newsweek* p39+ Apr. 22, 2002, with photo, p50+ Sep. 9, 2002, with photo; *Real Bottom Line* (on-line); *Washington Post* H p1 Dec. 8, 1996, with photo; Bloomberg, Michael, with Matthew Winkler. *Bloomberg on Bloomberg*, 1997

---

Armando Gallo/Retna

## Bocelli, Andrea

(boh-CHEL-ee, ahn-DRAY-ah)

*Sep. 22, 1958– Singer*

*Address: c/o Universal Music Group, 825 Eighth Ave., New York, NY 10019-7416*

How many singers have performed for the Pope alongside Bob Dylan? How many have sung a Puccini aria at a rock concert, or performed before sold-out audiences in both opera halls and sports arenas? The Italian tenor Andrea Bocelli has done these things and more in his not-yet-decade-long professional singing career. Bocelli is that rare species in the music industry: a true crossover artist who moves effortlessly between the worlds of classical and popular music. Many have compared Bocelli's popularity to that of the "Three Tenors"—the singers Luciano Pavarotti, Placido Domingo, and José Carerras—who, in the early 1990s, broke through opera's traditional insularity to make best-selling albums and give rock-concert-like tours. Bocelli's career path is the reverse of theirs: in his first public appearances, he sang Tuscan street ballads in piano bars; later, he performed at rock concerts and made four highly successful pop albums—the last of which, *Romanza* (1997), vied for popularity with a Spice Girls album. Then, in 1999, he began recording his favorite arias and performing in operas. Currently, he is the best-selling classical artist in the world. "Depending on whom you talk to . . . either Andrea Bocelli is the greatest thing to happen to opera since the birth of bel canto"—a style of light, melodious singing—"or he's the harbinger of the art form's imminent apocalypse, the kiss of death to serious classical music," Brooks Peters wrote for *Opera News* (February 2000). To his fans, Bocelli's singing is lyrical, delicate, and passionate; to his detractors, his voice sounds untrained, weak, and artless. "Maybe in my voice there is something, I don't know," Bocelli told an *Entertainment Weekly* (December 25, 1998–January 1, 1999) reporter. "My secret is to sing with heart. Always. From the soul."

Andrea Bocelli was born on September 22, 1958 in Laiatico (sometimes spelled "Lajatico"), in the heart of Italy's Tuscany region and a stone's throw from the birthplace of Giacomo Puccini—one of Bocelli's favorite composers. His family owned a lucrative business (they sold agricultural machinery), and he grew up on a country estate amid vineyards and olive groves. Although his family was not particularly musical, he was given piano lessons, starting at age six, and later studied the saxophone and flute. Music, particularly opera, made a deep impression on him. "When I would get upset, the only thing that would calm me was the sound of a tenor or baritone voice," he told Lawrence B. Johnson in an interview for the *Detroit News* (October 20, 1999, on-line). "I was a very noisy little guy, so this was an important discovery for my mother. I was given a phonograph, and suddenly all my relatives were giving me opera records."

Bocelli was born with a rare condition called infantile glaucoma, and in childhood his vision was poor. At age 12 he lost his eyesight completely, as the result of an accident during a soccer game. "I don't want people to get too emotional about it. I took a knock on the head . . . and a few days later I was blind," James Scalzitti quoted him as saying in *Paninaro* (November 1997), archived on the Bocelli Network Web site. "I know what colors look like and I have an idea of the world," he told Celestine Bohlen for the *New York Times* (October 4, 1997). He added that, when performing in concert halls or opera houses, he relies on his childhood memories of such scenes. "I have been a spectator, so I know what it is like to be sitting in the audience, waiting for the curtain to rise."

After he graduated from high school, Bocelli moved to the nearby town of Pisa, where he studied law at the University of Pisa and earned a doctor of law degree. For a year he worked as a court-appointed defense lawyer. (He has since claimed to have been a "terrible" lawyer.) Convinced, as he has often said, that singing was his destiny, he made what he regarded as a make-or-break attempt to become a professional singer. Toward that end, he asked the great Italian tenor Franco Corelli to give him lessons. Although Corelli, whom Bocelli had admired since his boyhood, had retired, he agreed to provide musical guidance to the younger man. To earn the money to pay him, Bocelli began singing in piano bars and nightclubs.

In 1992 Bocelli heard that the Italian rock star Zucchero was holding auditions for tenors to record one of the parts on "Miserere," a song that he and Bono of the rock group U2 had co-written for Pavarotti. When Pavarotti heard Bocelli's demo tape, he reportedly demanded to learn the identity of this unknown singer with the amazing voice. "Let Andrea sing 'Miserere,'" the Bocelli Network Web site quotes Pavarotti as saying, "for there is no one finer."

Although Pavarotti rather than Bocelli eventually recorded the "Miserere" duet with Zucchero, he suggested that Bocelli go on tour with Zucchero and sing the tenor part. Thus it happened that, in 1993, Bocelli—an unknown singer of love ballads and arias—shared the stage with one of Europe's most popular rock stars. During the tour Bocelli regularly received standing ovations for his interpretation of "Nessun dorma" (No One Sleeps), the bittersweet tenor aria from Puccini's *Turandot*.

In the spring of 1994, Bocelli appeared at the San Remo Music Festival, a music competition that is broadcast live to more than 30 countries and is usually viewed by nearly a quarter of all Italians. His performance of "Il mare calmo della sera" (The Calm Evening Sea) earned the highest marks ever recorded for a new artist in the 40-year history of the festival. In September 1994 Bocelli and Pavarotti finally met, and they sang a duet together at Pavarotti's annual event for charity. Soon afterward Bocelli was introduced to Pope John Paul II, for whom he performed at a Christmas Eve concert that year, alongside the rock legend Bob Dylan. The next year he joined a group of singers and musicians, among them Al Jarreau, Bryan Ferry, and John Miles, for a touring concert called "Night of the Proms." This annual event features soloists performing contemporary and classical music, accompanied by a full symphony orchestra and 50-member choir. Bocelli sang to live audiences totaling 450,000 in Europe and reached a television audience estimated to number in the tens of millions. This massive exposure helped to push his first two albums, *Andrea Bocelli* and *Bocelli* (both released in 1995), to the tops of the charts throughout Europe.

A song from his second album, "Con te partiro" (Time to Say Goodbye), captured the interest of Sarah Brightman, a renowned English soprano. According to Clare Garner in the London *Independent* (May 19, 1997), Brightman was eating in a restaurant when she heard the song, and—echoing Pavarotti's words of a few years before—demanded to know who owned that beautiful voice. She tracked down Bocelli and invited him to sing the song with her as a prelude to a high-profile event: the retirement fight of the world light-heavyweight champion Henry Maske, in 1996. Wistful, romantic, and lush, the farewell song seemed perfect for the occasion; when it was sung, before the fight, "even Maske wept," Garner reported. Brightman and Bocelli's recording of the song in English, accompanied by the London Symphony Orchestra, became an international hit; in Germany, for example, the single was number one on the pop charts for 14 weeks. Later that same year Bocelli gave a concert in an historic town square in Pisa. The film of that performance, called *A Night in Tuscany*, was seen by millions worldwide (including viewers of public television in the U.S.), and it cemented the popular image of Bocelli as an old-fashioned, ruggedly handsome romantic with seemingly unlimited talent.

With his remarkable success, Bocelli could now pick and choose from an eclectic range of projects. For his third album, *Viaggio Italiano* (1996), he selected famous arias and traditional Neopolitan songs; the next, *Romanza* (1997), is a pop album that sold 14 million copies—more than the records of any other artist that year except for the Spice Girls. *The Opera Album* (1998), his first all-classical collection, contains arias from *Rigoletto*, *La Bohème*, *Tosca*, and *Carmen*. All the compositions on *Sogno* (1999) are entirely original; one of them, "The Prayer," a duet that Bocelli sang with Celine Dion, has become something of a secular hymn.

While clearly influenced by many musical styles, including sacred, pastoral, and contemporary forms, Bocelli has spoken often of his profound appreciation for classical music and, in particular, opera—the first music he remembers hearing as a child. "Pop music is easier. Everyone can listen and have some pleasure, but classical music can change you," he told Lawrence Johnson. "It can help you to grow up. This is even more important today than it was 100 years ago. . . . Our world is so noisy and confused, almost without values, and many people are troubled. Classical music, opera, can heal the spirit."

In the fall of 1999, in his first major operatic role, Bocelli played the title character in the French opera *Werther*, by Jules Massenet, at the Michigan Opera Theatre in Detroit. It was an appropriate role: Werther is a romantic poet and outsider in his society; Bocelli is a self-proclaimed romantic and an outsider in the exclusive world of opera. Portraying Werther presented him with new challenges. In addition to memorizing the music, he now had to memorize a set of gestures and expressions, so that he would appear to interact convincingly with the other singers. "A lot of people brought up the problem that I wouldn't be able to see the orchestral director and most people thought it would be impossible for me to act on stage," he told Jeremy Pound for *Classical Net* (1998, on-line) during rehearsals of *Werther*. "These two points have been blown away." He confessed to feeling nervous, however; he was used to large concert halls and auditoriums, but "in a theatre," he explained to Johnson, "all eyes and ears are on you. You feel the quiet." Midway through rehearsals, he began to feel more comfortable with his assignment. "When I began to study *Werther*, it was very difficult," he recalled to Johnson. "For one thing, it is in French. At first I thought, 'Oh, I can't do this.' Now everything is very clear. It is beautiful music and a powerful story."

Having first heard Bocelli perform on television, the opera critic Brooks Peters traveled to Detroit to hear how the superstar tenor would sound in person. What he heard at a dress rehearsal surprised and impressed him. "[Bocelli's] voice is purer and richer in person than in video or on CD," he reported in his *Opera News* article. "The timbre is warm and exotic. . . . There's a delicacy and poignancy to Bocelli's vibrato that is compelling. . . . The voice is not overwhelming, but I'd hesitate to call it small. . . . What he does exude is an acute intensity, a sense of seething emotions lying just at the surface. It's impossible not to watch him." Among those in his field, Peters's enthusiasm was rare; most other critics have dismissed Bocelli as a pop star who lacks the muscular voice and supple technique needed for live opera performance. *Entertainment Weekly* (April 23, 1999) critic J. D. Considine appreciated the lightness and beauty of Bocelli's voice but nonetheless lamented that the singer was "prone to artless phrasing and a muffled tone." Considine attributed Bocelli's recording success to his ability to take "the thrilling aspects of operatic vocabulary—the full-throated high notes, the intertwining vocal lines"—and translate them "into the pop vernacular." Bocelli will not become the "Fourth Tenor," he wrote, but will remain "a tenor for listeners who wouldn't dare spend a night at the opera."

Bocelli has become inured to this type of criticism. At the same time, he has readily admitted that he still has much to learn. "I pay attention only to those who notice the same weak points I hear myself in my performance," he told Ken Ringle for the *Washington Post* (April 26, 1998, on-line). "But I think I must also pay for the sin of being famous first for singing pop music." Of course, at one time, opera *was* pop music, and in recent years there have been efforts to make opera more accessible to the public, through the use of super-titles and amplification in some opera houses, for example. "If an art form like opera is to flourish," David DiChiera, the director of the Michigan Opera Theatre, told Peters, "it has to diversify and build new bridges." In 2000 Bocelli fulfilled a long-held dream when he recorded Puccini's rapturous *La Bohème*. The next year—to the delight of his fans and the dismay of his detractors—he joined some of the classical world's luminaries, including Renée Fleming and Olga Borodina, in recording Verdi's *Requiem*. Bocelli has expressed the hope that, through such recordings, he will attract more people to the music he loves. "I've never forgotten that opera is essentially about communication," he told Peters. He said to Bohlen, "I honestly don't know where [my career] will take me. But only a few people go to the opera, so I think it is right that those who have a voice dedicate it to the public."

Bocelli met his wife, Enrica, while singing in a piano bar in Pisa. The couple have two young sons, Amos and Matteo, and live in an old stone farmhouse in the Tuscan countryside. When he is not touring or practicing, Bocelli enjoys riding his Arabian horses on the beaches near his home or skiing in the Italian Alps. — M.A.H.

Suggested Reading: Bocelli Network Web site; Bocelli Online Web site; *Detroit News* (on-line) Oct. 20, 1999; *Entertainment Weekly* p60+ Apr. 23, 1999; *New York Times* B p8 Oct. 4, 1997; *Opera News* (on-line) Feb. 2000; *Washington Post* G p1 Apr. 26, 1998

Selected Recordings: *Andrea Bocelli*, 1995; *Bocelli*, 1995; *Viaggio Italiano*, 1996; *Romanza*, 1997; *The Opera Album*, 1998; *Sogno*, 1999; *La Bohème*, 2000; *Verdi Requiem*, 2001

Courtesy of San Francisco Opera

## Borodina, Olga

(boh-roh-dee-NAH)

*July 29, 1963– Opera singer*

*Address: Kirov Opera, Marinsky Theatre, 1 Teatralnaya Ploshchad, 190000 St. Petersburg, Russia*

In the decade or so since she first attracted the notice of opera lovers, the Russian mezzo-soprano Olga Borodina has emerged as one of the foremost singers of her generation. "Borodina . . . is one of the finest singers in the world," Jay Nordlinger wrote for the *National Review* (May 28, 2001). "She is also one of the finest singers . . . ever." "I was immediately amazed by the beauty of her voice, and by the total singer and musician she is," the legendary Spanish tenor Placido Domingo, who has performed with Borodina on several occasions, told Cori Ellison for the *New York Times* (April 22, 2001). "I'm full of admiration for the color of her voice, her effortless technique, her expression and her dedication. And she is the most beautiful human being you can imagine."

An only child, Borodina was born on July 29, 1963 and raised in Leningrad (now St. Petersburg), Russia. Her parents were amateur musicians and engineers in the Red October piano factory, an enterprise that, under czarist rule (when it was known as the Bekker piano factory), was famed for the quality of its instruments.

Influenced in part by her parents, Borodina took to music at an early age. "My parents both loved music and were active amateur musicians," she explained to Harlow Loomis Robinson for *Opera News* (November 1995). "As a girl, I asked Mama to put me into a children's chorus so I could sing. By then, I had decided I would be either a ballerina or a singer. But my physique and body type were obviously not quite right to be a ballerina. After singing in a children's choir for about six years, I finally entered the music school that operated under the auspices of the Leningrad Conservatory [now the St. Petersburg Conservatory]. I had to apply to this special school several times, because they wouldn't take me at first. They would say my voice wasn't right, or uninteresting. The same thing happened when I applied to enter the conservatory a few years later. They finally admitted me only the third time I tried. I was very insistent that this was what I wanted to do."

It was at the Leningrad Conservatory that Borodina took up opera in earnest. She regularly attended performances by the school's opera company, as well as those staged by the Kirov Opera (also known as the Maryinsky Opera) and the Maly Opera, two world-famous companies based in St. Petersburg. By 1987, during her third year of study, Borodina had perfected her craft to such an extent that she received an invitation to perform with the Kirov Opera. Even so, it was a few years before she came into her own at the Kirov. "[Yuri] Temirkanov [the Kirov's artistic director] didn't pay any special attention to me—he heard me but thought of me as a young, inexperienced singer," Borodina told Robinson. "I sang Siebel in Gounod's *Faust* and the small contralto role of Milovzor in Tchaikovsky's *Queen of Spades*. It was Valery Gergiev, who succeeded Temirkanov as artistic director at the Kirov, who really changed things for me. He made me work, and because he believed in me, he made me believe in myself."

Indeed, Borodina took her first major role, that of Marfa in Mussorgsky's *Khovanshchina*, at Gergiev's urging. Initially, "I resisted," she recalled to Robinson. "I really didn't think I could do Marfa—such a difficult, big role. I wasn't even graduated from the conservatory yet! But he made me do it. Once, the scheduled singer got sick, and I had only two hours of staging rehearsal. It was terrifying, but somehow I got through it. A while later, he even put me in the role of Marfa when the Kirov was televising the opera to Europe."

Under Gergiev's direction, the Kirov embarked on extensive tours of Western Europe in the early 1990s. During this period, Borodina performed with the company as Lyubasha in Rimsky-Korsakov's *The Tsar's Bride*; Salammbo in Mussorgsky's *Salammbo*; and Marina in that composer's *Boris Godunov*. Those roles, and the prominence she gained by winning the 1988 Rosa Ponselle International Vocal Competition and the 1989 Barcelona vocal competition, brought Borodina critical and popular recognition and established her reputation as one of opera's most promising young singers.

In 1992 Borodina made her debut at the Bastille Opera in Paris, performing once again in *Boris Godunov*. That same year, she ventured away from the Russian operatic tradition by appearing as Delilah, alongside Placido Domingo, in the French composer Saint-Saëns's *Samson and Delilah* at the Royal Opera House in London's Covent Garden. In the mid-1990s Borodina went on to perform across Europe as Amneris in Verdi's *Aida*; as Eboli, in that same composer's *Don Carlo*; and in the title role in Bizet's masterwork *Carmen*. In recent years, Borodina has become indelibly associated with her interpretations of Carmen and Delilah.

Borodina made her American debut performing the title role in a 1995 San Francisco Opera production of Rossini's *La Cenerentola*. She has since returned to San Francisco to perform in *Carmen*, *Samson and Delilah*, and *The Tsar's Bride*. In 1997 Borodina made her debut at New York's Metropolitan Opera in *Boris Godunov*, under the artistic direction of James Levine. More recently, she has performed in Verdi's *Requiem*, Ravel's *Sheherazade*, and Berlioz's *La mort de Cleopatre* in collaboration with Levine.

Although most critics stress her virtues as a live performer, Borodina has also recorded many of the works in her repertoire. Those works include *Khovanshchina*, *Boris Godunov*, *Samson and Delilah*, Prokofiev's *War and Peace*, Borodin's *Prince Igor*, Tchaikovsky's *Eugene Onegin* and *Pique Dame*, Rachmaninoff's *Vespers*, Stravinsky's *Pulcinella*, Berlioz's *Romeo et Juliette*, Verdi's *Requiem*, *Aida*, *Don Carlos*, and *La Forza del Destino*, and *Tchaikovsky Songs*, which was voted Best Debut Recording of 1994 by the jury of the Cannes Classical Music Awards.

Speaking with Cori Ellison for the *New York Times* (April 22, 2001), Borodina discussed her experience of singing as a type of catharsis. "Some people want to become stars, and others fulfill their mission from God. I go on the stage because I want to give people satisfaction and joy and purity in their soul. And this cleansing of their souls when they leave satisfies me. At the end of the performance, when I see all those eyes looking at me full of happiness, that is the best experience. It means that I was successful in doing what I wanted to. This doesn't happen each time, but it happens often enough."

Borodina remains close to her parents, who double as critics. "They often come to the theater when I'm performing," she told Robinson, "but not always. Just often enough to check up and see what sort of shape their daughter is in. Afterward, they give me their criticism. I can't say they're my unqualified fans. They come to make sure everything is all right. They tell me exactly what they think—you know, that dress really isn't right for you, it makes you look fat, and so on."

Borodina has been married twice. Her two children—Alyosha, from her first marriage, and Maksim, from the second—were born a dozen years apart. — P.K.

Suggested Reading: *National Review* p66+ May 28, 2001; *New York Times* 2p35 Apr. 22, 2001, with photos; *Opera News* p32+ Nov. 1995, p24+ Aug. 2001, with photos

Selected Recordings: *Khovanshchina*; *Boris Godunov*; *Samson et Dalila*; *War and Peace*; *Prince Igor*; *Eugene Onegin*; *Pique Dame*; *Vespers*; *Pulcinella*; *Romeo et Juliette*; Verdi *Requiem*; *Aida*; *Don Carlos*; *La Forza del Destino*; *The Tsar's Bride*; *Tchaikovsky Songs*

---

## Bowden, Mark

*1951– Writer; journalist*

*Address:* Philadelphia Inquirer, *400 N. Broad St., Philadelphia, PA 19101*

"I have always been drawn to the dramatic reporting and intensive interviewing of the New Journalism of the '60s . . . ," the writer Mark Bowden told Terry Conway for *Book* (May/June 2000, on-line). "I look for stories that have a strong dramatic center and will reveal things heretofore unknown." A professional journalist since 1973 and an investigative reporter for the *Philadelphia Inquirer* for more than 20 years, Bowden was a finalist for the Pulitzer Prize in journalism in 1997. Two years later he was a finalist for a National Book Award in nonfiction, for the third of his four books, *Black Hawk Dawn*, an account of the Battle of Mogadishu, fought in 1993, in which 18 American soldiers died on African soil. Bowden has also written many articles for *Men's Journal*, *Sports Illustrated*, *Playboy*, and *Rolling Stone*, among other magazines, and has won honors for pieces on subjects ranging from the breeding of cows to the plight of blacks in the United States. "Throughout my writing career, I have always made it a point to work on something that fully challenges me," he told Doug Childers for the *Wag* (May 2000, on-line), "even when that meant looking for freelance work when my newspaper editors weren't particularly interested in my projects."

The third of the eight children of Richard and Lois Bowden, Mark Bowden was born in 1951 in St. Louis, Missouri. He grew up in the suburbs of Chicago, New York City, and Baltimore, Maryland. Bowden took an early interest in reading (Bible stories, fairy tales and comic books were favorites) and started writing stories at the age of 10. Speaking with Monica Leal for the *Greyhound* (February 6, 2001), Bowden said that he was further encouraged by his paternal grandmother, who once taught correspondence courses in the art and craft of writing. "When I was a little kid, you know how your parents make you write letters to your grandparents thanking them for this thing or that? [My grandmother] would always write back and she would not just say thank you for your nice letter,

Heather Tyler/Courtesy of Grove Atlantic Inc.

*Mark Bowden*

she would always talk about the way the letter was written. I, as a result, as a little kid learned to think about writing, but also I thought I was really good at it because my grandmother told me I was."

After he graduated from high school, Bowden entered Loyola College, in Baltimore. Although, thanks to his good grade on an exam, he did not have to take an otherwise-required freshman course in composition, Bowden enrolled in the course at the urging of Tom Scheye, the instructor. Scheye (to whom he later dedicated his first book) encouraged Bowden to consider a career in writing. He also introduced Bowden to the works of the British writer George Orwell, which include journalism as well as essays and novels. In his sophomore year Bowden became the editor of the campus newspaper, a position that demanded writing on a regular basis. In his news stories Bowden sought to emulate the styles of such journalists and creative nonfiction writers as Tom Wolfe, Norman Mailer, Michael Herr, Peter Matthiessen, and John Hersey. Although he felt that "the nonfiction that the journalists were doing was more exciting than contemporary fiction," as he told *Current Biography*, he also drew inspiration from novelists, among them Thomas Pynchon, John Updike, and Saul Bellow.

After he earned a bachelor's degree in English, in 1973, Bowden, with Scheye's assistance, found a job with the *Baltimore News American*, a daily newspaper that has since ceased publication. (The last issue was printed on May 27, 1986.) "I wrote articles for a section of the paper called Young World," Bowden told Leal, "which was targeted toward teenagers, and I wrote searching exposes about acne, loneliness and braces, and [expletive] like that. But it was a good experience." Bowden next wrote features for the paper's Sunday magazine. "Working as a reporter does teach you diligence . . . ," he told *Current Biography*. "Frankly, I found that no matter how sappy the assignment, once you actually got out and met the people you were writing about, I really got into it." Nevertheless, after about two years on the job, Bowden quit the *News American* to explore other career opportunities.

After hitchhiking around the country for six months, Bowden returned to the *News American*. He was assigned to cover the Maryland state police. Because he regularly arrived at the office at four in the morning to call state police stations for news updates, he was often the only reporter on hand for stories that broke during the night. "I loved it," he told *Current Biography*. "I fell in love with reporting. . . . I ended up kind of being seduced by the fun of chasing breaking stories and . . . being out there." Moreover, because the *News American* had scant editorial resources, Bowden was given virtually free rein to write what he wanted. "I was experimenting . . . ," he told *Current Biography*. "I was writing stories in styles that I didn't see in any other newspaper, you know, imitating the writers that I admired, and for the most part, they would get in."

In 1979 Bowden left the *News American* to join the staff of the *Philadelphia Inquirer*. At the time, Bowden told Leal, the *Inquirer* was known "for allowing writers a lot of creative freedom in how they wrote their stories and giving reporters a lot of time and space for their stories." As a staff writer for the *Inquirer*, Bowden covered a variety of national and international issues. Especially memorable for him was a four-part 1982 series on the threatened extinction of the black rhino, an assignment that took him to Africa. "It made me think big," Bowden told *Current Biography*. "I learned to think that there was no story anywhere in the world that I couldn't get if I wanted to, and the *Inquirer* would back me." Another story, a three-part series about Joey Coyle, an unemployed Philadelphia longshoreman who found a sack containing $1.2 million by the side of a road, was later adapted into the 1993 movie *Money for Nothing*, starring John Cusack.

As Bowden tackled increasingly ambitious projects at the *Inquirer*, his articles grew correspondingly longer. He frequently produced multipart series, but by the mid-1980s, he had begun to feel that even that format was too limiting for some subjects. Bowden took the logical next step, which was to write a book-length story. In *Doctor Dealer*, published in 1987, Bowden recounted the activities of Lawrence W. Lavin, a Philadelphia-area dentist convicted of heading a multimillion-dollar drug operation. "I think the book captures a unique generational episode," Bowden told *Contemporary Authors* (2000), "the period roughly from 1978 to 1984 . . . when a large number of foolish, well-heeled young people bought the idea that cocaine was a harmless, recreational drug." Alison Knopf, reviewing *Doctor Dealer* for the *New York Times Book Review* (January 24, 1988), wrote, "[Bowden's] book is crammed with interesting details about dealing that can't be gleaned from *Miami Vice.*"

Bowden's second book, *Bringing the Heat: A Pro Football Team's Quest for Glory, Fame, Immortality, and a Bigger Piece of the Action* (1994), chronicles several years in the history of the Philadelphia Eagles football team. "I spent three years as the *Philadelphia Inquirer*'s beat reporter covering the Eagles, and I got to know all these characters, the players, the coaches, the owners," Bowden told Leal. "This book is just an opportunity for me to basically write, string together, profiles of about a dozen or so of these characters." Genevieve Stuttaford, in a review for *Publishers Weekly* cited by *Contemporary Authors*, wrote that *Bringing the Heat* "is as thorough an account of a sports franchise as any fan, even Eagles fanatics, could want." In the *New York Times Book Review* (October 16, 1994), Keith Dixon noted that *Bringing the Heat* "overflows with stories of pro football dreams, of bravery in the face of injury. Yet it also unflinchingly tells of the darker side of life in the National Football League: uncontrollable egos, ruined families, marital infidelity. Mr. Bowden makes no apologies for the defensemen's shortcomings; they only seem to deepen his admiration. And he employs a muscular, brazen writing style—a fitting approach for the defense he respects so deeply."

For his third book, *Black Hawk Down* (1999), Bowden tackled a more ambitious project: to describe the Battle of Mogadishu, the October 3, 1993 fight between U.S. troops and Somali militiamen in the streets of the capital of Somalia, in East Africa. The firefight, the largest involving American troops since the Vietnam War, resulted in the deaths of 18 American servicemen and more than 500 Somalis (not all of them combatants). It also had significant political repercussions, both in the United States and abroad. Television footage of exultant Somalis dragging the corpse of a U.S. soldier through the streets of Mogadishu had a profound effect on the American polity. The administration of President Bill Clinton responded by beating a hasty retreat from its doctrine of "assertive multilateralism" (a crucial provision of which was U.S. participation in and support for U.N. rapid-reaction operations). As a result, when Hutu extremists launched a campaign to exterminate the Tutsi minority in Rwanda, in east-central Africa, the following spring, the U.S. and other U.N. members, still mindful of the recent debacle in Somalia, refused to intervene. Even after the killing of an estimated 800,000 Rwandans, the shocking images from Mogadishu continued to influence U.S. foreign policy. As Bowden told Doug Childers for the *Wag* in 2000, "I think the extreme hesitance of the Clinton administration to intervene militarily anywhere for the last seven years stems directly from Mogadishu."

U.S. forces were first dispatched to Somalia in late 1992 by President George Herbert Walker Bush, in an effort to secure the distribution of relief supplies to regions of Somalia where drought and an ongoing civil war had caused widespread famine. Originally, Operation Restore Hope, as the mission was known, did not have an overt political objective. By early 1993, however, the scope of the mission had expanded to include the rehabilitation of Somali institutions—"nation-building," as some skeptics derisively called it—a project in which the Americans were to participate under U.N. auspices. This more ambitious plan stirred local resentment, particularly among factional leaders with political aspirations of their own, such as General Mohammed Farrah Aidid, the head of the Somali National Alliance and chief of the powerful Habr Gidr clan. By late spring tensions between U.N. forces and local militias had turned violent, and in June, after 24 Pakistani soldiers in the U.N. contingent were killed by fighters thought to be linked to Aidid, the U.N. Security Council issued a resolution calling for the arrest and prosecution of those responsible.

Jonathan Howe, a retired American admiral and the head of the U.N. mission in Somalia, eventually persuaded the Pentagon to dispatch an American force to capture Aidid. The group was to act under U.S., rather than U.N., command. At first, the Americans were successful: the first six missions to arrest various deputies and lieutenants of Aidid proceeded uneventfully. But on October 3, a mission to capture two lieutenants—which officials believed would take no longer than an hour—turned into a full-fledged battle after two American Black Hawk helicopters were shot down. U.S. forces on the ground, who had already apprehended the lieutenants, surrounded the crash sites to protect and recover the downed crews. Meanwhile, opposition on the ground turned "into something akin to a popular uprising," according to Bowden, as quoted by Brian Urquhart in the *New York Review of Books* (November 18, 1999). "It seemed like everybody in the city wanted suddenly to help kill Americans." Pinned down overnight, the Americans were forced to fight for their lives until their rescue the next morning by U.N. forces—who found the two lieutenants still in custody.

In researching the Battle of the Black Sea, as the Battle of Mogadishu is also known, Bowden conducted extensive interviews with surviving combatants from both sides of the conflict. He talked at length with U.S. soldiers who survived the battle and also met with the families of several men killed in Somalia. To speak with some of the surviving Somalis, he spent seven days in Mogadishu in 1997. "The country is basically an example of well-armed anarchy in full blossom," Bowden explained in an on-line chat for *talkcity.com* (April 19, 1999). "In order to travel and work safely, I had to hire armed guards to protect me. Basically, I attracted a great deal of commotion wherever I went.

I was delighted to have a chance to do my reporting there, but even more delighted when I got to leave. . . . I went thinking I was a guest of the Habr Gidr clan . . . only to find when I arrived that they were not expecting me, nor did they welcome me. I was ordered to leave the country, but I defied them and hired my own gunmen. That made for a very scary stay."

Bowden's account of the Battle of Mogadishu first appeared as a 29-part daily series in the *Philadelphia Inquirer* in late 1997. The series, which earned him the Overseas Press Club's Hal Boyle Award, was also posted on the Internet as part of an *Inquirer*-sponsored multimedia project that featured photos, maps, graphics, a video, and questions from readers. After publication of the series, Bowden continued to work on the story for most of 1998, expanding it into *Black Hawk Down.* The book, published in 1999, was a finalist for the National Book Award that year—a "wholly unexpected" honor, Bowden told Leal, "because the National Book Award is given to works of literature"—and became a *New York Times* best-seller. "Bowden has reconstructed this extremely violent episode with amazing vividness and detail," Brian Urquhart wrote. "The reader can visualize the action, smell the dust and sweat and the reek of explosives, and even enter into the exultation, fear, rage, pain, confusion, and exhaustion of the combatants. Bowden never loses sight of the human qualities and reactions that are, in the end, decisive in battle. Because he was able to interview survivors on both sides relatively soon after the action, Bowden's story has a vitality and freshness usually lacking in accounts of combat. He has written an extraordinary book. It is also a shocking one." "What [the] demotic, you-are-there prose lacks in literary finesse . . . it makes up in pure narrative drive," William Finnegan wrote for the *New York Times Book Review* (March 14, 1999). "Thankfully, Bowden provides useful glosses of the politics, both local and international, and the strategic reasoning (if that's the right term) that brought a humanitarian mission to such a bloody pass. Without this context, the battle itself would make no sense at all." *Black Hawk Down* also impressed many in the armed forces, so much so that the book is now required reading for Marine Corps officers. In addition, it has been adapted for the silver screen. Steve Zaillian, Stephen Gaghan, Ken Nolan, and three others co-wrote the screenplay; directed by Ridley Scott and produced by Jerry Bruckheimer, the film arrived in theaters in December 2001 to much critical acclaim. It earned over $100 million in domestic box-office receipts and won two Academy Awards (for editing and sound).

Meanwhile, Bowden continued to work as a *Philadelphia Inquirer* reporter. In 1997 he was named a Pulitzer Prize finalist in the category of spot reporting for his coverage of the armed confrontation between police and the multimillionaire John E. DuPont, an heir of the founder of the DuPont chemical company, after DuPont murdered an Olympic wrestler on his estate.

In his fourth and most recent book, *Killing Pablo: The Hunt for the Richest, Most Powerful Criminal in History* (2001), Bowden detailed the search for and killing of Pablo Escobar, the Colombian drug trafficker who built the Medellín drug cartel. It is believed by some that Escobar was murdered by an American Special Services operative as part of the U.S.-declared "war on drugs." "Bowden hits another home run with his chronicle of the manhunt for . . . Escobar . . . ," Mark Rotella wrote for *Publishers Weekly* (May 7, 2001). "While not ignoring the larger picture, e.g. the terrible drug-related murders that wracked the South American country in the late 1980s and early 1990s—Bowden never loses sight of the human story behind the search for Escobar, who was finally assassinated in 1993, and the terrible toll the hunt took on many of its main players." Will Self, in his review for the *New Statesman* (June 4, 2001), praised Bowden's thorough research but added, "Reading [*Killing Pablo*] is like watching *Jaws* without the shark. Apart from a couple of offhand remarks about wealthy Yanks wasting their money on marching powder, there is absolutely no cocaine in the book at all. If you came to this book without any background knowledge, . . . you'd be genuinely flummoxed as to what all the fuss was about. . . . This matters. Just as the futility of U.S. policy should, by rights, adumbrate the whole sorry story—yet is revealed only at the denouement—so the psychic and cultural reality of the drug itself is crucial."

In addition to the Pulitzer Prize and National Book Award nominations, Bowden has received many professional honors. They include the 1980 Science Writing Award from the American Association for the Advancement of Science; the 1985 and 1987 National Sunday Magazine Awards for best story; and the 1990 Associated Press Sports Editors Award for investigative reporting. A frequent lecturer, Bowden has spoken at CIA headquarters, the U.S. Army Command and General Staff College, the U.S. Army Central Command (headquartered at Florida's MacDill Air Force Base), the U.S. Military Academy at West Point, the Army War College, the White Sands Missile Range, Camp Pendleton, the Miramar Marine Air Base, and the Strategic Studies Institute at the Massachusetts Institute of Technology.

Bowden and his wife, the former Gail McLaughlin, have four sons and one daughter. Their oldest son, Aaron, is a reporter for the *Concord Monitor*, a New Hampshire newspaper; another son, B.J., is a corporal in the U.S. Marines. In an interview for the *Wag* (September 2001, online), Bowden told Woody Arbuckle that he had completed the text for an illustrated book about the Allied invasion of Normandy during World War II and was writing the script for the movie version of *Killing Pablo.* — P.K.

Suggested Reading: *New Statesman* p52 Jun. 4, 2001, with photo; *New York Review of Books* (on-line) Nov. 18, 1999; *New York Times Book Review* p7 Mar. 14, 1999; *Publishers Weekly* p230 May 7, 2001; *Wag* (on-line) May 2000, September 2001; *Contemporary Authors* new revision series vol. 90, 2000

Selected Books: *Doctor Dealer*, 1987; *Bringing the Heat: A Pro Football Team's Quest for Glory, Fame, Immortality, and a Bigger Piece of the Action*, 1994; *Black Hawk Down: A Story of Modern War*, 1999; *Killing Pablo: The Hunt for the Richest, Most Powerful Criminal in History*, 2001

---

Courtesy of the *New York Times*

## Bragg, Rick

*July 26, 1959– Journalist; memoirist*

*Address: c/o Knopf Publishing/Author Mail, 299 Park Ave., 4th Fl., New York, NY 10171*

The journalist and memoirist Rick Bragg has been hailed for his sympathetic portrayals of the lives of the poor and working class in the American South. Many of his fellow southerners have discovered in his books echoes of their own childhood struggles and an occasion to indulge in nostalgia for a way of life that has found few exponents in American letters. Readers elsewhere have been enchanted by his heartfelt stories, written in a style that Diane Roberts, in the *Atlanta Journal-Constitution* (September 14, 2001), called "unabashedly lyrical." A national correspondent for the *New York Times* since 1994, Bragg was awarded the Pulitzer Prize in 1996 for feature writing. His first book, *All Over but the Shoutin*' (1997), describes his penurious childhood in northeastern Alabama, the deep love he felt for his supportive, caring mother, and his steady rise as a journalist. The book became a best-seller and was named a *New York Times* notable book of the year. With *Ava's Man* (2001), Bragg reached farther back in time, to tell the story of Charlie Bundrum, his maternal grandfather, a rough-and-tumble southerner who made his own moonshine and grabbed whatever work he could to support his large family in the Depression-era Deep South. Some have compared *Ava's Man* to *Let Us Now Praise Famous Men*, the journalist James Agee's account of three tenant families during the Depression. "But where Agee approached their lives from the outside, Bragg writes from inside the culture," Robert Morgan wrote for the *New York Times Book Review* (September 2, 2001). "The family he tells us about is his own. Often he lets the people speak for themselves, and the authenticity of the voices and the setting grab you from the first sentence."

Ricky Edward Bragg was born on July 26, 1959 in Piedmont, Alabama. The second of three sons (a fourth died in infancy), he grew up in Possum Trot, a rural area of Alabama in the foothills of the Appalachian Mountains. Bragg and his brothers, Sam and Mark, were raised primarily by their mother, Margaret Marie Bragg. Their father was an alcoholic Korean War veteran; on the rare occasions when he was around, he often beat Margaret and neglected the children. The family had very little money, surviving on $50 a month from Social Security checks and the pittance Margaret earned from picking cotton and cleaning houses. After high school Bragg attended Jacksonville State University, in Alabama, where he wrote for the campus newspaper. Months before his freshman year ended, he had to drop out, because he ran out of money.

Soon afterward Bragg got a job with the *Anniston Star*, an Alabama newspaper, and began covering sports. In 1985 he became a reporter for the *Birmingham News*, also in Alabama, and in 1989 joined the *St. Petersburg Times*, a Florida daily. At the latter, he covered such events as the 1989 riots in Miami; Hurricane Andrew, in 1992; and the political unrest in Haiti. In 1992 he studied journalism for a year at Harvard University, in Cambridge, Massachusetts, on a prestigious Neiman Fellowship. Two years later Bragg was hired by the *New York Times*.

During the next few years, Bragg reported for the *New York Times* on such events as the 1994 landing in Haiti of U.S. troops, whose mission was to restore the ousted president Jean-Bertrand Aristide to power; the trial in South Carolina of Susan Smith, who was convicted in 1994 of drowning her two sons; the shootings by a 13-year-old boy and his 11-year-old cousin at a Jonesboro, Arkansas, middle school in 1994, which resulted in the deaths of four students and a teacher; and the bombing in 1995 of the Alfred P. Murrah Federal Building in Oklahoma City, Oklahoma, by Timothy J. McVeigh, which left 168 people dead. "The Oklahoma City bombing story was easy to write because I had no time," Bragg told Chip Scanlon in an interview for the Web site of the American Society of Newspaper Editors. "I went on automatic. . . . You don't have any time to think about it. You just try not to get in the way of it. I was so full of the emotion of what I had seen and from talking to people, that not only was it clear how awful it was through the quotes and some of the images and details, but you could almost see the horror of it between the lines."

Among many other subjects he covered for the *New York Times*, Bragg also wrote about a Mississippi laundress named Oseola McCarty, who saved from her meager earnings the astonishing sum of $150,000 and, in 1995, when she was 87, donated it to the University of Southern Mississippi to establish a scholarship fund for African-Americans. Another of his stories focused on elderly prisoners in an Alabama penitentiary. Talking about that article, titled "Where Alabama Inmates Fade into Old Age," Bragg told Chip Scanlon, "I'm not really smart enough to write a story where I have to rely on telling people what I see. I have to use images and details to show them. An old editor at the Birmingham (Ala.) News, Clarke Stallworth, told me once, 'Show me, don't tell me.' That's really all I tried to do in this story, and others, to give some scenery, almost a backdrop, for the characters. Another good lesson came years ago from an editor who said, 'You don't have to be ashamed to make the stories personal.' He didn't mean that my feelings necessarily had to show, but that it was all right to make it as though the reader were wading through the story, to give images and details and, I hate to say, color—to care about it one way or the other. . . . I do like it when people come up later and say, 'I felt like I was there.'"

In 1996 Bragg was awarded the Pulitzer Prize for "his elegantly written stories about contemporary America," as stated on the Pulitzer Prize Web site. Bragg brought his mother to the awards ceremony, and for the occasion she bought herself a new dress—her first in 18 years. Bragg later told Susan Larson for the New Orleans, Louisiana, *Times-Picayune* (August 21, 2001) that one of his happiest moments was "having my mama go with me to [receive] the Pulitzer, and walking off the dais and handing it to my mama. It was just a natural thing to do. It's not in [my] house. It hangs in her living room, and when you walk in the house, it's the first thing you see."

Bragg's first book, *All Over but the Shoutin'*, was largely a tribute to his mother's selflessness. In it he recorded an early childhood memory, of how Margaret used to drag him along rows of cotton on a burlap sack while she worked long days in the fields. "It would have been easy for me," he wrote, as quoted by Richard H. Weiss in the *St. Louis Post-Dispatch* (October 20, 1998), "to just accept the facade of blind sacrifice that has always cloaked her, to believe my momma never minded the back-breaking work and the physical pain as she dragged me up and down a thousand miles of clay. . . . I would like to believe she didn't even notice how her own life was running through her hands like water. But the truth is she did know, and she did think about it in the nighttime when her children were put to bed and there was no one left to keep her company except her blind faith in God and her own regret." Diane Roberts noted, "When Bragg writes about his mother, worn down from poverty and pain, self-sacrificing and self-effacing, he will flat make you cry."

The book also reveals Bragg's bristling anger—toward his father for abusing Margaret and forsaking his children, toward those who looked down on his family because they were poor, and toward editors who discounted him for his lack of a college degree. Roberts wrote, "Bragg attacks the American class system like one of those little banty roosters who'll try to fight an elephant. It is rare—and welcome—to find a writer who knows that America's national boast of classlessness is a crippling lie." A critic for *Kirkus Reviews* (July 1, 1997) wrote that Bragg "has a strong voice and a sweeping style that, like his approach to newspaper writing, is rich, empathetic, and compelling. His memoir is a model of humility combined with pride in one's accomplishments." Francine Prose, in *People* (September 15, 1997), felt that "occasionally, Bragg's folksy tone ('The people who know about books call it a memoir, but that is much too fancy a word for me . . .') seems like an affectation," but nevertheless viewed the book as "a testament to a mother's grace and determination, to Bragg's courage and resilience, and to the kindness of the neighbors, relatives and strangers who helped a poor family survive and a determined young man succeed."

In conjunction with the appearance of the book, his publisher, Pantheon, sent Bragg on a national reading and book-signing tour. The large audiences he attracted were impressed by his sincerity and distinctive southern drawl, an accent he described to Alix Madrigal for the *San Francisco Chronicle* (September 9, 2001) as "more pool hall than syrupy Southern." "We knew our best weapon [in selling the book] would be to use Rick Bragg himself," Janice Goldklang, Pantheon's vice president and publishing director, told Steven M. Zeitchik for *Publishers Weekly* (February 2, 1998). "When we first met him we were just bowled over. He immediately started telling us stories." Bragg enjoyed the tour; as he recalled to Zeitchik, "It was as though every book signing became a front-porch tale-telling session."

Sixty-five of Bragg's press pieces are gathered in his book *Somebody Told Me: The Newspaper Stories of Rick Bragg* (2000). Most were culled from the *New York Times*; five are from the *St. Petersburg Times* and one from the *Birmingham News*. The title of the volume reportedly derives from the answer Bragg has given when people ask him how he comes up with his remarkable tales. Telling Susan Larson that he regarded the collection as a good representation of his work, he compared it to the rooftops that his maternal grandfather built: "We'll go out around town, riding in the car, mama in the jump seat, and she'll say, 'Your granddaddy roofed that house.' And some of those old shingles are still on there. Even when some of those old barns are falling apart, you still see nails that he drove. He built houses that are still standing. And with *Somebody Told Me*, now, if I ever have a kid, I can show you: I never built a house, but I did this. That's what I did over a 10-year period of my life. I'm proud of it. I'm really proud of it."

The subject of Bragg's next book, *Ava's Man*, is his mother's father, Charlie Bundrum. Charlie was a roofer, a carpenter, a whiskey-maker, and a fisherman—a rough but tender patriarch who labored during the Depression years to provide for his wife and seven children. (An eighth died in infancy.) Even at times when the family had scarcely enough to eat, he shared what little they had with anyone who came to their door. He was also a drinker and a fighter who had his share of run-ins with the law. Charlie distilled moonshine; "He never sold a sip—not one sip—that he did not test with his own liver," Bragg wrote, as quoted by Jonelle Bonta in the *Atlanta Journal-Constitution* (August 29, 2001). Unlike many others, Charlie did not become violent after drinking heavily; rather, he liked to sing and play the banjo. But when angered he could be brutal; he once beat a man nearly to death for throwing a snake at one of his sons. He was almost universally loved and admired, and at his funeral cars from all over the county lined the blacktop for more than a mile.

Since Bragg never knew his grandfather—he died the year before Bragg was born—he gathered information for *Ada's Man* from talks with his mother and other relatives, who still so missed Charlie that their stories were often interrupted by tears. For Bragg, researching the lives of family members was more difficult than inquiring about those of strangers. "While you try to be conscientious with everybody, with your family you're walking on gilded splinters all the time," he explained to Alix Madrigal. "You don't want to hurt them, and you're not going to put the book out if it makes them unhappy. So there's always that fear, because you could not streamline or homogenize the man [his grandfather]. If you didn't use his foibles, his flaws and his sometimes out-and-out destructive nature, it wouldn't have rung true." Bragg also felt an obligation to his grandfather to not sugarcoat his story. "The one thing I am dead sure of," Bragg wrote in the book, as quoted by Bonta, "is that his ghost, conjured in a hundred stories, would have haunted me forever if I had whitewashed him. . . . A man like that, surely, would want a legacy with pepper on it."

*Ava's Man* quickly climbed the best-seller lists. Robert Morgan described the book as "a kind of sublime testimonial." "Bragg gets the combination of sentiment and independence and fear in this culture just right," he declared. Michael Kenney, in the *Boston Globe* (October 2, 2001), wrote, "It is a book that works on many levels—as an anecdotal social history of rural poverty, as the highly personalized sociology of a family, as an engaging compilation of regional folklore, and perhaps above all as just grand storytelling." A reviewer for *Publishers Weekly* (August 6, 2001) judged the work to be "a soulful, poignant portrait of working-class Southern life. . . . Bragg delivers, with deep affection, fierce familial pride, and keen, vivid prose that's as sharp and bone-bright as a butcher knife. In this pungent paean to his grandfather, Bragg also chronicles a vanished South that—like the once-wild Coosa River Charlie liked to ply in homemade boats—is becoming too tamed to accommodate those who would carve out a proud if hardscrabble living on its margins."

Bragg, who lives in New Orleans, has twice received the American Society of Newspaper Editors Distinguished Writing Award, and has also earned more than 50 other writing honors. He has taught writing at Harvard University; the Poynter Institute for Media Studies, in St. Petersburg, Florida; Boston University, in Massachusetts; and the University of South Florida. Bragg—who wrote in *All Over but the Shoutin'*, "I love writing the way some men love women"—divorced after a few years of marriage in the 1980s. In 1996 he bought a house for his mother. When Chris Rose for the *Times-Picayune* (September 18, 2001) asked him what his greatest extravagance had been after his first book landed on best-seller lists, Bragg replied, "Truthfully, all the money from the books goes to my mom, my family, but I did buy a jacket—I call it my author's jacket, which I wear to book signings—for $67." — A.I.C.

Suggested Reading: *Atlanta Journal-Constitution* L p10 Sep. 14, 1997, C p2 Aug. 29, 2001; *Boston Globe* F p2 Oct. 2, 2001; *Kirkus Reviews* p995 July 1, 1997; (New Orleans, Louisiana) *Times-Picayune* F p1 Aug. 21, 2001; *New York Times* VII p9 Sep. 2, 2001; *People* p42 Sep. 15, 1997, with photo; *Publishers Weekly* p34 Feb. 2, 1998, p74 Aug. 6, 2001; *San Francisco Chronicle* Sep. 9, 2001, with photo; *St. Louis Post-Dispatch* D p1 Oct. 20, 1998, with photo; *Tallahassee Democrat* D p4 Oct. 4, 2002

Selected Books: *All Over but the Shoutin'*, 1997; *Somebody Told Me: The Newspaper Stories of Rick Bragg*, 2000; *Ava's Man*, 2001

Courtesy of the Arizona Diamondbacks

## Brenly, Bob

*Feb. 25, 1954– Manager of the Arizona Diamondbacks*

*Address: Arizona Diamondbacks, Bank One Ballpark, 401 E. Jefferson St., Phoenix, AZ 85001*

The career of Bob Brenly, manager of the Arizona Diamondbacks, encompasses almost every facet of professional baseball. A skilled player in high school and college, Brenly became a free agent in 1976. In all but 48 of the games he played as a professional, he was associated with the San Francisco Giants system; after rising through the minor leagues on San Francisco farm teams, Brenly made his debut with the Giants, in 1981. A catcher and infielder for the Giants for nine seasons, he was known for his leadership and warm demeanor in the clubhouse. In 1990, feeling unsure about his future as a player, Brenly left the team and secured work as a baseball commentator for radio. But he missed the ballfield, so he returned to the Giants in 1992 and spent the next four years as a coach. He then tried his hand at television broadcasting, as a commentator for Fox, and next, in 1998, became the color commentator for a new expansion team, the Arizona Diamondbacks. Late in 2000 the Diamondbacks' owner, Jerry Colangelo, named Brenly manager. Despite his inexperience in that capacity, Brenly took the team all the way to the 2001 World Series, where they upset the reigning world champions, the New York Yankees.

Robert Earl Brenly was born on February 25, 1954 in Coshocton, a small town in an agricultural part of Ohio. A member of an athletic family, Brenly earned varsity letters in both baseball and basketball at Coshocton High School. "If I had been a little taller, I probably would have played basketball," he told Jack Magruder for the *Arizona Daily Star* (February 25, 2001). "I loved basketball." The six-foot two-inch Brenly was recruited to play baseball at Ohio University at Athens; he enrolled there at the urging of Bob Wren, who had coached the school's team, the Bobcats, to the College World Series in 1970. By the time Brenly had matriculated, in 1972, Wren had retired, but Brenly willingly put in four years as a Bobcat third baseman and catcher. In 1976 he was an All-American; additionally, he tied the school single-season home-run record—10—set earlier by the future Hall of Fame third baseman Mike Schmidt. He graduated in 1976 (some sources say 1977), with a B.S. degree in health education.

Despite Brenly's outstanding senior season at Ohio, no major-league baseball team drafted him out of college. "Bob was a big, strong, exceptional athlete who really understood the game, so we were all shocked when he didn't get drafted," Brenly's college baseball coach, Jerry France, told the Ohio University *News & Information* (November 5, 2001, on-line). Undaunted, Brenly threw his hat into the ring as a free agent and was picked up by the San Francisco Giants. In the minor leagues he played for an A-ball Giants-affiliated team in Cedar Rapids, Iowa, in 1977 and 1978 and for the AA Shreveport (Louisiana) Swamp Dragons (where he was team captain) in 1979 and 1980. In 1979 he served as a utility player until the Swamp Dragons' two catchers were injured in the first game of a doubleheader; as catcher in the second game, Brenly threw out two runners at second and tagged an out at the plate. His performance guaranteed his spot as a catcher during his remaining time in Shreveport.

Brenly got his big break in 1981; while playing for the Giants' Triple-A affiliate in Phoenix, Arizona, he unwittingly auditioned for San Francisco's management, which was touring the minor leagues during a major-league players' strike. He "had what he called the week of his life during their visit," Jack Magruder wrote. "He was immediately promoted to the big leagues when the strike ended in August." Brenly's major-league career had an auspicious debut: in 45 at-bats in 19 games in the last weeks of the 1981 season, his batting average was .333, with one home run, four runs batted in (RBIs), six walks, and only four strikeouts.

During his first full season as a San Francisco Giant, in 1982, Brenly was a utility player, filling in as a backup catcher, outfielder, or first or third baseman. Limited to only 180 at-bats in 65 games, he achieved a batting average of .283. He played in about two-thirds of Giant games in 1983, nearly always behind the plate, and contributed seven home runs and 34 RBIs while his batting average fell to .224. Brenly had his best offensive season in 1984, when he hit .291 with 20 home runs and 70 RBIs, all career-high numbers. He was named a National League representative to the 1984 All-Star Game, which was played in the Giants' Candlestick Park. The Giants did little to match the unusually fine performance of their catcher that season, losing 96 games. "You can lose and still play good," Brenly said to David Bush for the *San Francisco Chronicle* (March 2, 1985). "But we didn't. After a while you play so bad it's obvious you're just stinking up the joint." That season Brenly had played in 145 games, half of them with nagging knee injuries. "The doctors told me they could operate then or wait until the end of the year, and since I was hitting about .340 I wanted to wait," he explained to Bush. By the season's end he felt exhausted. "It had been a long time since I'd played a full season," he told Bush. "The last week I started swinging a lighter bat, but I should have done that sooner. At the end I couldn't swing a wiffle bat." Later, his injuries were corrected surgically.

Brenly arrived at spring training in 1985 with the intention of being firmer with the Giants' young pitching staff. "Probably my biggest fault was that I was too good a friend to the pitchers," he explained to David Bush. "I suffered along with them and stuck with them probably longer than I should have. This year if I think they're losing it, I'm going to tell [the Giants' manager, Jim] Davenport. Even though I like them, the team comes first." Nevertheless, neither the Giants nor Brenly had a good season: Brenly's batting average dropped to .220, with 19 home runs and 56 RBIs, and the Giants lost 100 games for the first time in franchise history.

The Giants showed marked improvement in the 1986 season. The team finished third in the National League West, with 83 wins and 79 losses. In 149 games Brenly compiled a .246 batting average, hit 16 home runs and 62 RBIs, and walked a career-high 74 times. One of the most memorable games of Brenly's career took place on September 14, 1986 at Candlestick Park, in a meeting with the Atlanta Braves. The Giants' third-baseman Chris Brown was injured, and Brenly was tapped to substitute. In the top of one inning (the fourth), Brenly made four defensive errors, something no major-league player had done since September 13, 1942 (when the Chicago Cubs shortstop Lennie Merullo made four errors while facing the Boston Braves). He thereby let Atlanta score four unearned runs. Between innings, the humiliated Brenly tried to collect himself. "I told the guys, 'I owe you four runs. I'll make 'em up somehow," he recalled to Bruce Jenkins for the *San Francisco Chronicle* (September 15, 1986). Three years later he told Jenkins, again for the *San Francisco Chronicle* (September 15, 1989), "I went into the dugout with every intention of firing a helmet, kicking a trash can, breaking the bat rack, something to blow off a little steam. Then I went by [the new] manager, Roger [Clark], and I could tell by the look in his eye that this would be a project for him. Somehow, he'd have me turn the day around." Brenly bounced back with a fifth-inning solo home run. In the seventh inning he unleashed a two-RBI single. In the area of defense, he was helped by being returned to the catcher's spot, his natural position. With two out at the bottom of the ninth, no one on base, and the score tied 6–6, Brenly was called up to bat. On a count of three balls and two strikes, he hit a home run. "Watching Brenly that day was like going through a 10-year period with an old friend, the guy who loses his job, then his wife, hits the skids for a while, then winds up being president of his company," Bruce Jenkins declared in 1989. The Giants pitcher Mike Krukow, too, marveled at what had occurred; as he said in a postgame interview, as quoted by Jenkins in 1986, "It wasn't a ballgame. It was a novel."

In 1987 the Giants won the National League West division with a win–loss record of 90–72. Brenly's batting average reached .267 during the regular season, but dropped to .235 by the end of the postseason National League Championship Series (NLCS), against the St. Louis Cardinals, which St. Louis won in seven games. Although Brenly had always been a leader in the clubhouse, in 1988 manager Roger Clark limited his playing time, while giving more opportunities to the up-and-coming infielder Bob Melvin. "With a different club, I'd probably be spouting off, saying some things that I shouldn't say," Brenly confided to Ray Ratto for the *San Francisco Chronicle* (April 18, 1988). "But being 34, being on a team that has a chance to win it all, I just want to contribute where I can, when I can." Brenly played in fewer than half the Giants games in 1988 and finished the season with a .189 batting average.

After waiting in vain for the Giants to renew his contract, Brenly signed with the Toronto Blue Jays, who assigned him to the positions of backup catcher and designated hitter when left-handed pitchers were on the mound. He found the move to Toronto and the American League difficult. "I never imagined playing for anybody else [but the Giants]," he told David Bush for the *San Francisco Chronicle* (May 2, 1989). "Even when the decision was made and I'd signed with Toronto . . . I was still in shock." Moreover, wearing a uniform other than the Giants' made him uncomfortable; as he told Bush, "I just can't get used to the blue shoes."

American League pitchers' penchant for off-speed throws did not suit Brenly; his batting average stood at about .170 when, in late July, after he had been up to bat only 88 times, the Blue Jays released him. He quickly signed a minor-league contract with the Giants. He played for a month with the Triple-A Phoenix Firebirds before being added to the Giants' roster in September. His batting average for the 12 games in which he played was below .200, and he was not included on the play-off roster. Brenly cheered from the sidelines when the Giants won the NLCS over the Chicago Cubs in five games. (In the 1989 World Series, San Francisco lost to the Oakland A's.)

Three teams, among them the Giants, invited Brenly to 1990 spring training, with the understanding that he was not guaranteed a spot. "I thought about it," Brenly told Bruce Jenkins for the

*San Francisco Chronicle* (March 27, 1990), "but I figured, why not go out on a high note, playing for a winner? I didn't want my last memory to be 'released from [the spring training facilities at] Indian Bend Park.'" He officially retired and then served, that year and the next, as a color commentator for Chicago Cubs games on WGN-AM radio, alongside Thom Brennaman and Harry Caray. In 1992 he returned to the San Francisco clubhouse as a coach. He worked for one year as the first-base coach and then, for three years, as the bullpen coach. He also hosted the less-than-half-hour-long *Bob Brenly Show*, a frank, occasionally caustic postgame program on KNBR radio, making observations that sometimes led to friction between him and Roger Clark. (Dusty Baker, who had played for the Giants with Brenly in 1984, succeeded Clark as the Giants' manager in 1993.) In 1996 Brenly left the Giants for the last time, accepting a position as a television baseball analyst for the Fox Network, where he was reunited with Thom Brennaman for the Fox game-of-the-week and World Series coverage. Two years later he became the Diamondbacks' color commentator and moved to Arizona with his family. One appeal of broadcasting for Brenly was that he felt virtually no stress from the job. "After a broadcast, the team won, lost, tied—it made no difference," he explained to Josh Elliott for *Sports Illustrated* (November 7, 2001). "You sign off the air and go home and really don't have to worry about the next game."

In October 2000, in a move that surprised many, the owner of the fledgling Arizona Diamondbacks, Jerry Colangelo, invited Brenly to become the team's new manager. Brenly had begun to miss being a coach, as he explained to Josh Elliott: "There's nothing like standing on the foul line, banging fists with guys you tried to put in a situation where they could succeed and then they did. That's a great feeling." The Diamondbacks, an expansion team staffed with veteran players, had begun competing in the major leagues in 1998. Only one year later the team earned the National League West division title, after winning 100 games. That victory notwithstanding, the players rebelled against the micromanagement style of manager Buck Showalter. One striking manifestation of his approach was the lengthy guide he had written, *The Diamondback Way*, which set rules governing many aspects of players' lives, off the playing field as well as on. To add to the players' dissatisfaction, several key members of the team had been injured during the 2000 season, and the ace pitcher Randy Johnson, who had turned 37, feared being driven too hard.

Showalter was fired after the 2000 season, and Colangelo interviewed more than a half-dozen potential replacements. "When I interviewed for the job, [Colangelo] asked me what I would do differently," Brenly told Josh Elliott for *Sports Illustrated* (March 26, 2001). "I focused on two things: giving the regulars more days off during the year and limiting the pitch counts of the starters." Brenly, who had never managed a team, cited his radio and television experience as simulated managing. "Part of my job as an analyst was to play manager and anticipate matchups and strategy," he explained to Tom Verducci for *Sports Illustrated* (February 26, 2001). Signing a three-year contract worth $2 million, Brenly became the Diamondbacks' manager.

The players immediately noticed a change. "The first thing he did in spring training was pull out our 80-page rule book and throw it on the ground," the veteran outfielder Luis Gonzalez told Chuck Johnson for *USA Today* (October 15, 2001, on-line). "Then he pulled a cocktail napkin out of his pocket and said these are the only rules he has: 'Be on time, play hard and give me everything you got.'" "Given the team I had to work with, that's the only way I could do it," Brenly told Johnson. "We've got a team full of guys that's played 8, 10, 12 years in the big leagues. These guys know what to do. I was very fortunate to walk into a situation and have professionals that don't need babysitting. They just need a little push in the right direction from time to time."

Brenly quickly became known for trusting his players as well as his hunches. "I don't have a crystal ball," he told Jack Magruder during spring training, "but I like to believe in my heart that this is a very motivated, veteran ball club. For a first-year manager, this is a best-possible situation. We have guys who know how to play the game and are comfortable playing with each other in this ballpark and have a common goal, to win a [World Series] ring. I think I'm in an ideal situation." Whenever possible, Brenly tried to restrict the pitching assignments of Randy Johnson and Curt Schilling, the top two pitchers in the league in terms of both number of innings pitched and strikeouts. (Johnson later won the 2001 Cy Young Award for the National League.)

The Diamondbacks, whose starting lineup featured a host of players over 30 years of age, finished the 2001 season with the best record in the National League West: 92–70. Arizona won the National League Division Series in a hotly contested five-game battle with the St. Louis Cardinals before handily defeating the National League East champion Atlanta Braves in the NLCS. In the World Series the Diamondbacks faced the New York Yankees, who were pursuing their fourth straight World Series Championship. In a hard-fought, dramatic series that spanned seven games and three times zones, the Arizona Diamondbacks emerged victorious in stunning, come-from-behind fashion, upsetting the Yankees' usually dominant closer Mariano Rivera. Brenly became only the fourth manager—and the first in 40 years—to win a World Series in his rookie season. He modestly gave credit for the team's success to the players. "They keep doing the things that I've asked them to do," he explained in a press conference after his team won the first World Series game, as reported by Josh Elliott, "and if I look smart because of it, it's only because they've succeeded."

In 2002 the Arizona Diamondbacks won the highly competitive National League West pennant race with an impressive record of 98 wins and 64 losses. In the ensuing National League Division Series, the St. Louis Cardinals swept to victory in three straight games, thus depriving the Diamondbacks of the chance to defend their World Series Championship.

Brenly and his wife, Joan, live in Scottsdale, Arizona, with their daughter, Lacey, and son, Michael. — K.S.

Suggested Reading: *San Francisco Chronicle* p41 Mar. 2, 1985, with photo, p61 Sep. 15, 1986, D p1 Sep. 15, 1989; *Sports Illustrated* p44+ Sep. 3, 1984, with photo, p44+ July 30, 2001, with photos, p52+ Nov. 7, 2001, with photos; *USA Today* (on-line) Oct. 15, 2001

---

Courtesy of Bob Brier

## Brier, Bob

*Dec. 13, 1943– Egyptologist; educator*

*Address: Dept. of Philosophy, C. W. Post Campus, Long Island University, 720 Northern Blvd., Brookville, NY 11548-1300*

"Mummies are little encyclopedias," the Egyptologist Bob Brier told Bryn Nelson for *Newsday* (December 19, 2000). "You've just got to know how to read them." In 1994, in an attempt to replicate the process of embalming devised by the ancient Egyptians, Brier mummified a human cadaver at the University of Maryland School of Medicine. The mummification—possibly the first to be performed in two millennia—attracted wide attention and, to date, remains a success: the preserved corpse shows no signs of decay. Brier, whose work has been featured in *Mr. Mummy* and other *National Geographic* television specials and who has hosted *The Great Egyptians* and other miniseries on the Learning Channel, is self-taught in Egyptology. Indeed, he began his professional life in the field of philosophy, specializing in symbolic logic and the philosophy of science. He has been a member of the Department of Philosophy at C. W. Post College, a division of Long Island University, in New York, since 1970. His books include *Egyptian Mummies: Unraveling the Secrets of an Ancient Art*; *The Encyclopedia of Mummies*; *The Murder of Tutankhamen: A True Story*; and *Daily Life of the Ancient Egyptians*, co-written by Hoyt Hobbs.

Robert Brier was born on December 13, 1943. He received a B.A. degree from Hunter College, which is now a division of the City University of New York, in the mid-1960s. While enrolled in a graduate program in philosophy at the University of North Carolina at Chapel Hill, he met Joseph Banks Rhine, a professor at Duke University and pioneer in parapsychology and psychical research; with Rhine, he co-edited the book *Parapsychology Today* (1968). In 1970, the year he earned his Ph.D. degree in philosophy, Brier began teaching in that subject at the C. W. Post division of Long Island University; currently, he holds the title of professor there. For some years he has taught courses in Egyptology as well as philosophy at the college. His book *Precognition and the Philosophy of Science: An Essay on Backward Causation* was published in 1974. With the C. W. Post English professor Joan Digby, he edited the book *Permutations: Readings in Science and Literature* (1985).

Earlier, in 1969, at the age of 25, Brier had become interested in ancient Egyptian culture while recuperating from severe injuries to both knees suffered in a basketball game. During his months of recovery, which found him in casts extending from his ankles to his hips, a friend lent him Alan Henderson Gardiner's textbook *Egyptian Grammar* (1957), about Egyptian hieroglyphics—the pictograms that constituted the ancient Egyptians' written language. Eager for a diversion, Brier studied the text for eight hours daily, and in time he became an expert in hieroglyphics. He also became fascinated with Egyptology, the study of all aspects of approximately 3,800 years of Egyptian civilization, beginning in about 3100 B.C. and ending in about 640 A.D., during the Arab conquest of the country. Intrigued by descriptions of mummies, in the mid-1970s Brier made the first of his many trips to Egypt to examine ancient tombs. He also took courses in a medical school to learn about anatomy and other subjects pertinent to the preservation of the dead. His book *Ancient Egyptian Magic: Spells, Incantations, Potions, Stories, and Rituals* was published in 1980. In 1990 he supervised the construction of a replica of an ancient Egyptian tomb at Long Island University. Two years later he curated the exhibition *Egyptomania* at the Hillwood Art Museum, on the C. W. Post campus, and wrote the catalog that accompanied the show.

Despite the wealth of knowledge available about ancient Egypt, as of the early 1990s a great deal still remained unknown. In *Archaeology* (January/February 2001), Brier listed some unanswered questions about mummification: "Did the embalmers drain the blood? How do you remove a brain through the nose? What kind of tools did the embalmers use? . . . What surgical procedures were performed?" He did not know, either, precisely how the mummifiers had used natron, a naturally occurring, water-absorbing salt. To satisfy his curiosity about these unknowns, he became determined to try to mummify a present-day human cadaver. "There are certain things you can only learn by doing it yourself," he told Chris Colin for *Salon.com* (May 4, 2001). For more than a year, he planned his experiment and assembled the material necessary to replicate as accurately as possible the way the ancient Egyptians preserved the bodies of the dead. No detailed description in hieroglyphics of the procedure has ever been found; instead, Brier relied primarily on an account written by the great fifth-century-B.C. Greek historian Herodotus, who witnessed a mummification in Egypt. Guided by Herodotus's report, Brier traveled to Wadi Natrun, a swampy area near the Nile Delta in northeastern Egypt, where he gathered hundreds of pounds of natron. He ordered palm wine shipped from Nigeria to Cairo, Egypt's capital city, and purchased such spices as frankincense and myrrh at a Cairo market. Back in the U.S., he hired craftspeople to make the same types of obsidian, bronze, and copper knives the Egyptians had used in the mummifying procedure. He even specified that the bronze contain the same percentages of copper and tin as the Egyptians' bronze tools. In addition, he commissioned the fashioning of exact replicas of ceramic jars, ankh symbols made of wood, and an embalming board, among other objects. To obtain a cadaver and permission to carry out the mummification process, Brier successfully solicited the help of Ronald S. Wade, director of the Anatomical Services Division of the Maryland State Anatomy Board, which ensures "the proper distribution of cadavers to qualified hospitals, medical schools, and other agencies engaged in medical education and research," according to the Maryland State Archives Web site.

After considering the cadavers of several people who had made it known that they wished to donate their bodies to science, Wade and Brier chose that of a Caucasian man who had died in his 70s of a stroke. The man's identity was not revealed to Brier, and the precise fate of the body was not divulged to the donor's family. Brier and Wade brought the remains to the University of Maryland's School of Medicine, in Baltimore, where, with the help of two morticians, among others, the mummification took place in 1994.

Brier and Wade began by trying to figure out how to remove the brain. According to Herodotus, the Egyptians had used a hooked metal tool, but that method did not work with the brains of two heads Brier and Wade had obtained from other body donors; as Brier explained to Wendy Marston for *Discover* (March 2000), the gray matter would not "adhere to the tool," because it was too gelatinous and slippery. Instead, they used the tool as a whisk to liquefy their cadaver's brain, then propped the body upright to let the resulting fluid drain through the nose. Since the ancient Egyptians did not know the function of the brain and considered the organ unimportant, Brier and Wade discarded it. They then cleansed and dried the inside of the skull (using the same tool, this time with linen strips wound around the hook to form a sort of sponge) and packed it with frankincense-treated linen. Next, Brier and Wade made the prescribed 3.5-inch slit in the cadaver's belly and proceeded to remove each organ through the cut. "Imagine sticking your hand inside a dark, crowded closet and untangling the clothes," Wade told Marston. "You can't see anything. You have to feel your way through." Like the ancient Egyptians, who believed that after death people were resurrected rather than reincarnated, Brier and Wade tried to mar the skin as little as possible. The liver, however, proved to be too large to pull through the small opening, so they extended the slit slightly. They did not remove the heart, which the Egyptians considered the location of the intellect and the soul. After Brier and Wade removed the organs and placed them in containers filled with natron, they inserted 29 linen packets of natron into the body cavity and then covered the whole cadaver with the salt, so as to dry it thoroughly. Then, to simulate conditions found in tombs in Egypt's Valley of the Kings, they left their subject in a room with an air temperature of 105 degrees Fahrenheit and 30 percent humidity.

After 35 days (half the length of time that Egyptians were required to abstain from worldly pleasure after a pharaoh died), Brier and Wade removed the natron surrounding the body—a difficult task, since some of it had solidified. Then they removed the natron packets, also with difficulty: since the interior and exterior natron had absorbed about 103 pounds of fluids, the cadaver had shrunk markedly, and the incision had tightened; the packets, meanwhile, with their liquid cargoes, had swelled. Brier noted with great interest that the shade of the mummy's skin—dark brown—now resembled that of ancient mummies, evidence that the drying process and not simply the passage of millennia had caused the change in color; as he explained in *Archaeology*, "As the tissue and blood dehydrates, various elements, like iron, become more concentrated." In the last step in this part of the experiment, Brier and Wade completed what Brier described as a "preliminary wrapping" of the body (a light draping with loosely arranged linen). They then left the mummy untouched for another four months. At the end of that period, using linen strips that had been soaked in oil containing frankincense, myrrh, and other ingredients, Brier and Wade rubbed the skin and then tightly wrapped the whole body. As Brier recited the requisite prayers, they wrapped each finger, toe, and limb separately. When they tried to cross the arms over the chest, in the ancient Egyptian style, they could not, because the arms had become totally rigid and, with pressure applied to them, would have broken. Judging by that unforeseen discovery, Brier theorized that the Egyptians had removed natron from their subjects before dessication had reached an advanced state. "When the body is totally dehydrated it can't be positioned for wrapping," he explained in *Archaeology*. "The goal of the embalmers was to remove as much fluid as necessary to prevent decay, but to leave just enough so the arms and other parts could be placed as desired." Brier described the mummification process in his book *Egyptian Mummies: Unraveling the Secrets of an Ancient Art* (1994). Five years later, he reported in his *Archaeology* article, the mummy, which rested at room temperature at the site of the Maryland State Anatomy Board, showed no signs of decay. Brier has speculated that his work on the mummy could help researchers understand why it has been difficult to replicate lengthy DNA sequences found in ancient mummies. He apparently does not believe that such replication is impossible. "DNA studies in mummies may also hold the answers to many Egyptological questions," he said, according to Colin. "We may be able to establish the origins of the Egyptians, and we may also be able to identify unknown royal mummies." In his 1998 book, *The Encyclopedia of Mummies*, Brier included a description of the entire mummification process. (That book offers information on mummies formed by natural means—for example, through burial in an extremely dry environment—as well as those preserved by people.)

In another of his projects, in which he worked with Gerald A. Irwin, the medical director of C. W. Post's Radiologic Technology Department, Brier examined videotaped X-rays of the mummified remains of the Egyptian pharaoh Tutankhamen (informally referred to in modern times as King Tut), who was born in about 1370 B.C. and died at the age of about 19. Based on what they found, he speculated that Tutankhamen was killed by a blow to the back of his head dealt by his elderly prime minister and closest adviser, Aye (or Ay). Although Brier pointed out that other researchers had already offered the same theory and that, in light of the lack of solid evidence, no contemporary jury would find Aye guilty "beyond a reasonable doubt," his account of the young pharaoh's death, made public in 1996, received much attention. In his book *The Murder of Tutankhamen: A True Story* (1998), he described clues that included an indication on the X-ray of a calcified blood clot at the base of Tutankhamen's skull; the contents of a missive, carved in hieroglyphics on a stone tablet, written by Tutankhamen's widow; and evidence of political intrigue. A reviewer for the *School Library Journal* (October 1998) described *The Murder of Tutankhamen* as an "engrossing tale that moves along at the pace of a well-crafted whodunit." "You may or may not be convinced by [Brier's] argument that Tutankhamen's death was a murder most foul . . . ," Richard Bernstein wrote in his critique of the book for the *New York Times* (May 6, 1998). "But you will find that Dr. Brier has made a persuasive case. More important, by the time you finish his intrigue-filled reconstruction of Tutankhamen's world—which includes such elements as teen-age love, religious heresy, the Orwellian rewriting of history and the desperate pleas of a terrified queen—you risk coming to care a good deal about the young Pharaoh's fate."

Brier's current projects include research on disease in ancient Egypt. "If you can figure out the . . . history of a disease, you have a better shot at predicting the future . . . of the disease," he said to Bryn Nelson. "So the more we learn about disease in the ancient world, the better off we are." He has also collaborated with scientists who are studying the remarkably well-preserved, frozen remains of three Inca youngsters, found in the Andes Mountains of Argentina about 500 years after they were sacrificed in a religious ritual.

In 2000 Brier became one of the first two C. W. Post professors to be named Faculty Fellows of the college's Teaching and Learning Initiative, whose aim is the sharing of ideas about teaching and learning among the faculty. He won the school's David Newton Award for Teaching Excellence in 1989 and the Long Island University Trustees Award for Scholarly Achievement in 2001. A two-time Fulbright Scholar, he directed the National Endowment for the Humanities student program "Egyptology Today" one summer.

Brier lives in the Riverdale section of the New York City borough of the Bronx. In his home, as well as in his C. W. Post office, he displays what he has termed "mummyobilia"—a mummy-shaped stapler and a mummy-decaled mug, among many other such items. "The kitschier, the better," he told Bryn Nelson. — G.O.

Suggested Reading: *Archaeology* p44+ May/June 1999, p44+ Jan./Feb 2001, with photos; *Chicago Tribune* C p1 Feb. 20, 1994; *Discover* p70+ Mar. 2000, with photos; *Newsday* C p3+ Dec. 19, 2000; *Salon.com* May 4, 2001

Selected Books: *Ancient Egyptian Magic: Spells, Incantations, Potions, Stories, and Rituals*, 1980; *Egyptian Mummies: Unraveling the Secrets of an Ancient Art*, 1994; *The Encyclopedia of Mummies*, 1998; *Daily Life of the Ancient Egyptians* (with Hoyt Hobbs), 1999

Courtesy of the New Jersey Devils

## Brodeur, Martin

(broh-DOOHR, mar-TAN)

*May 6, 1972– Hockey player*

*Address: New Jersey Devils, 50 Rt. 120 N., Continental Airlines Arena, East Ruther-ford, NJ 07073*

At age 30, Martin Brodeur of the New Jersey Devils is one of the best goalies in the National Hockey League (NHL). With his lightning-quick reflexes and ability to block shots by some of the league's best scorers, Brodeur helped lead the Devils to seven postseason appearances in eight years and to two Stanley Cup championships, in 1995 and 2000. In 2002 Brodeur helped to win a gold medal at the Winter Olympics, as the Canadian men's hockey team scored an impressive victory over the United States. For Brodeur, the victory had special significance, since his father, Denis, had won a bronze medal as part of the Canadian hockey team in the 1956 Winter Olympics. "Every time I saw [my father in the stands], I saw it in his eyes," Martin Brodeur told a writer for the *Sporting News* (February 24, 2002, on-line). "He was really enjoying his time here, living it up. It means a lot to be able to do this with him."

Martin Brodeur was born on May 6, 1972 in Montreal, Canada. His father, after years of playing amateur hockey, became a sports photographer, working for a local newspaper and then for the Montreal Canadiens hockey team and the Montreal Expos baseball team. When Martin was about three years old, his father took him to see his first hockey game, at the Montreal Forum, the old home of the Canadiens; when he was a little older, Martin went to the Forum often with his father, who took photographs at the games. "My dad would talk to players like Claude Lemieux and Stephane Richer and tell them one day his son was going to play in the NHL," Brodeur told Michael Farber, a contributor to *Sports Illustrated* (October 6, 1997).

Brodeur grew up idolizing goalies such as Patrick Roy, who played for the Canadiens and then the Colorado Avalanche, and Ron Hextall of the Philadelphia Flyers; their photographs adorned his room. During visits to the Forum, Brodeur often met Roy. "Questions, questions, questions," Roy told Larry Wigge, a writer for the *Sporting News* (June 4, 2001, on-line). "That's all I ever heard from Marty when he was growing up. His thirst to learn was incredible. He's always had a great mind for the position—and it shows in what he has done for the Devils." Brodeur attended the École de Hockey Co-Jean (Co-Jean Hockey School), north of Montreal, where, at age 16, he studied goaltending under François Allaire. He began playing for Montreal-Bourassa, an amateur team, in 1988. Appearing in 27 games, he posted 13 wins and 12 losses. The following season, 1989–90, he played for the St. Hyacinthe Lasers in the professional Quebec Major Junior Hockey League (QMJHL). In 42 games, Brodeur did well, collecting 23 wins, 13 losses, and two ties. His goal-against-average (GAA), however, was a relatively high 4.01. In 12 postseason games, Brodeur had five wins and seven losses. His skills attracted the attention of many U.S. colleges, some of which offered him scholarships. Brodeur told William N. Wallace, a reporter for the *New York Times* (May 25, 1994), that he planned to accept one of the offers if he was not picked by an NHL team in the first two rounds of the draft. In 1990 Brodeur was the New Jersey Devils' first draft choice and the 20th pick overall. Since the Devils already had three goalies on their roster at the time, the team sent Brodeur back to the Lasers to give him more experience. At one point, Brodeur got tired of playing hockey and considered quitting. However, his brother, Claude, who was a coach in the QMJHL, urged him to keep playing. Brodeur told Wallace that without his brother's encouragement he might have given up hockey.

In his second season with the Lasers, 1990–91, Brodeur's GAA fell to 3.30. (Despite that, the Lasers lost all four of their postseason games.) Brodeur enjoyed a solid year in 1991–92, with 27 wins and 16 losses and a 3.39 GAA. In addition to being named to the QMJHL All-Star second team, Brodeur was called up by the Devils in March 1992 to fill in for the team's injured goalies, Chris Terreri and Craig Billington. In his first NHL start, against the Boston Bruins on March 26, 1992, Brodeur blocked 24 shots and surrendered two goals in the Devils' 4–2 victory. The young goaltender told Herb Zurkowsky for the Montreal *Gazette* (March 27, 1992) about playing in the big leagues, "I'm watching and living a dream." Brodeur played in only three other regular-season games with the Devils as well as one postseason game, which the team lost.

After spending the 1992–93 season with the Devils' minor-league team (not affiliated with the QMJHL) in Utica, New York, Brodeur joined the Devils the following year. Brodeur, who shared the team's goal-tending duties with Chris Terreri, enjoyed a successful season, recording 27 wins, 11 losses, and eight ties. Brodeur blocked 1,238 shots, and his GAA was a solid 2.40. Brodeur told Robert Lipsyte for the *New York Times* (October 19, 1995) that during a game he tries "not to think too much, not to invent what will happen before it happens, not to get nervous by thinking, 'If they score now, it's tied, and then they'll score again and beat us.' So, I just go with the game, take what it gives me, and try to give it back." In the postseason Brodeur started most of the Devils' games. Brodeur and the Devils fought hard, defeating the Buffalo Sabres in seven games in the first round of the play-offs and the Boston Bruins in six games in the second round. The Devils faced their archrivals, the New York Rangers, in the NHL Eastern Conference finals. The series, which went to seven games, ended in dramatic fashion. In the second overtime of the final game, with the score tied, Brodeur surrendered a goal to the Rangers' Stéphane Matteau for the loss. (The Rangers went on to win the Stanley Cup.) After the season Brodeur was awarded the Calder Trophy, which honors the NHL's rookie of the year. Brodeur also signed a three-year contract with the Devils worth $5.3 million.

A lockout by the team owners delayed the start of the 1994–95 season by several months. When the season finally began, in January 1995, Brodeur was the Devils' full-time goalie. Over the course of 40 games, he recorded 19 victories, 11 losses, and six ties and had a 2.45 GAA. Brodeur also established himself as an aggressive goalie in the tradition of Ron Hextall, who was not afraid to leave the net to help out his defensemen. "Every puck that comes to me, I shoot it," Brodeur explained to Paul Hunter, a reporter for the *Toronto Star* (June 7, 2001). "If I make a save I take the puck and shoot it back or pass it back to a player. If you want to play the puck, you have to be strong. Because you sometimes have to overpower people to get it through." In the postseason Brodeur posted 16 wins and only four losses and managed an excellent 1.67 GAA. The Devils overcame the Bruins, the Pittsburgh Penguins, and the Philadelphia Flyers to advance to the Stanley Cup finals for the first time in the team's history. In the finals, the Devils won their first Stanley Cup, by sweeping the Detroit Redwings in four games as Brodeur made 73 saves and allowed only seven goals.

The Devils had a mediocre 1995–96 season and failed to make the play-offs. Over 77 games, Brodeur's record was 34–30 with a 2.34 GAA and a career-high 1,954 saves. The Devils improved in 1996–97. Although his record was 14–13, Brodeur recorded a league-leading 10 shutouts, and his GAA dropped to 1.88, which also led the league. In the postseason he played against his hometown team, the Canadiens, in the Eastern Conference quarterfinals. Brodeur scored a goal against the Canadiens in the first game of the series, which the Devils won in five games. They were then eliminated from the play-offs by the Rangers. That year Brodeur was named to the NHL All-Star team for the first time. He and Mike Dunham, the backup goalie, shared the William M. Jennings Trophy, which is presented to the goalie (who plays in at least 25 games) whose team surrenders the fewest goals.

Brodeur enjoyed one of his best seasons in 1997–98. Appearing in 70 games, he posted a career-high 43 wins and only 17 losses. Brodeur's GAA was at 1.89, and he made 1,569 saves and gave up only 130 goals. The Devils were nonetheless eliminated in the first round of the play-offs by the Ottawa Senators. That year he won his second William M. Jennings Trophy. Brodeur was also a member of Canada's hockey team in the 1998 Winter Olympic Games, in Nagano, Japan. (He sat on the sidelines while Patrick Roy guarded the net. Canada, which finished fourth, was eliminated in the medal rounds by Finland.) In 1998–99 Brodeur's GAA increased to 2.29, and his wins declined to 39. The Penguins eliminated the Devils from the play-offs in the first round that year, winning the series four games to three. Brodeur gave up four goals in the last game.

In 1999–2000, during the regular season, Brodeur won 43 games and blocked 1,797 shots. The postseason saw the Devils defeat the Florida Panthers, the Toronto Maple Leafs, and the Flyers to go to the Stanley Cup finals for the first time in five years. In the Eastern Conference finals, against the Flyers, the Devils won the first game but lost the next three, with Brodeur giving up 11 goals. Facing elimination, Brodeur limited the Flyers to one goal in each of the next three games, all of which the Devils won. In the Stanley Cup finals the Devils battled the Dallas Stars, who had won the cup the previous season. Leading the series three games to one, the Devils lost the fifth game in triple overtime when Brodeur surrendered a goal—marking his seventh straight play-off loss in overtime. However, in Game Six, Brodeur gave a masterful performance, as the Devils won 2–1 in double overtime to capture the Stanley Cup. "There were some bumps along the way, but I'm so happy it's over, and I'm glad we're on the good side of it," Brodeur told Alex Yannis for the *New York Times* (June 12, 2000). "It was a great feeling that it took us five years to get back to where we were supposed to be. Winning the cup every five years is not so bad." Yannis observed that Brodeur, with 59 combined wins in the regular season and the play-offs, tied the record set by Bernie Parent, the Flyers' goalie in 1973–74, for most wins in a single season. Brodeur told Yannis that he would always treasure that statistic.

Brodeur won 43 games and had a 2.32 GAA in 2000–01. The Devils returned to the Stanley Cup finals, in which they faced the Colorado Avalanche. Brodeur also got the chance to play against his boyhood idol, Patrick Roy, the Avalanche's goalie. After the Devils led the series, three games to two, the Avalanche scored seven goals against Brodeur in the last two games. With the Devils's offense scoring only one goal, the Avalanche won the two games and the Stanley Cup.

The NHL took a break in February 2002 to allow its players to represent their respective nations in the Winter Olympics, in Salt Lake City, Utah. Brodeur joined the Canadian team, which sought to win the nation's first Olympic gold medal in men's hockey in 50 years. Curtis Joseph, the goaltender for the Maple Leafs, started the first game, which Canada lost to Sweden, 5–2. Pat Quinn, the coach of the Canadian team, then replaced Joseph with Brodeur, who held Germany to two goals for a Canadian victory in the second game. Canada tied the Czech Republic in the third game and then avenged its loss to Finland four years earlier with a 2–1 win in the quarterfinals. After easily defeating Belarus 7–1 in the semifinals, Canada faced the U.S. In addition to a gold medal, the victor in that game could claim the unofficial distinction of producing the better hockey players in the NHL. Brodeur made 31 saves in the game, as Canada stunned the Americans with an easy 5–2 victory. "As an athlete, you want to be part of great things for your country, but you've also got the motivation of family," Martin Brodeur told a writer for the *Sporting News* (February 24, 2002, on-line). "We did a lot of great things today, and I can't imagine anything better."

Brodeur and the Devils played well during the 2001–02 season. The goaltender posted 38 wins; while his losses increased to 26, his GAA fell to 2.15, his lowest in four seasons. In the postseason the Carolina Hurricanes eliminated the Devils in the first round of the play-offs, in six games.

Martin Brodeur is married and has four children. He and his family live in North Caldwell, New Jersey, and spend their summers in Montreal.— D.C.

Suggested Reading: (Montreal) *Gazette* C p3 Mar. 27, 1992; New Jersey Devils Web site; *New York Times* VIII p2 Sep. 28, 1993, B p15+ May 25, 1994, with photos, B p12+ Oct. 19, 1995, with photos, D p9 June 12, 2000; *Sporting News* (online) June 4, 2001, Feb. 24, 2002; *Sports Illustrated* p72+ Oct. 6, 1997, with photos; *Toronto Star* Sports p2 June 7, 2001; *National Hockey League Official Guide & Record Book 2001*, 2001

---

## Broeg, Bob

(brayg)

*Mar. 18, 1918– Sports journalist; nonfiction writer*

*Address: c/o Pulitzer Publishing Co., 900 N. Tucker Blvd., St. Louis, MO 63101-1069*

In a career that has spanned more than a half a century, almost all of it in St. Louis, Missouri, the sportswriter Bob Broeg has covered hundreds of games of college football, for the University of Missouri Tigers; pro football, for the St. Louis Cardinals and the St. Louis Rams; and baseball, for the St. Louis Cardinals. For many years, until recently, he was the only person eligible to vote in the elections for the halls of fame of not only college and pro football but baseball as well. (His eligibility derived from his membership in the Baseball Writers' Association of America, the College Football Hall of Fame, and the board of selectors of the Pro Football Hall of Fame.) Regarded as more knowledgeable than anyone else about the history of sports in St. Louis, he has written or co-written 18 books, many of which deal with St. Louis sports teams and their heroes and, thanks to Broeg's longevity, contain eyewitness accounts dating from the 1940s. His books include *Stan Musial: "The Man's" Own Story* (1964); *Ol' Mizzou: A Story of Missouri Football* (1974); *Football Greats* (1977), written with Weeb Ewbank and Jack Buck; *Bob Broeg's Redbirds: A Century of Cardinals' Baseball* (1981); *Baseball from a Different Angle* (1988), co-written by William J. Miller Jr.; and *100 Great Moments in St. Louis Sports* (2000). Now in his ninth decade, Broeg wrote for the *St. Louis Post-Dispatch* from 1945 until 2001. He was the first sportswriter to be honored with the University of Missouri's journalism medal, in 1971. He was inducted into

National Baseball Hall of Fame Library

the National Baseball Hall of Fame's writing wing in the same year and into the National Sportscasters and Sportswriters' Hall of Fame, in Salisbury, North Carolina, in 1997.

The sportswriter was born Robert William Broeg on March 18, 1918 in St. Louis, Missouri, to Robert Michael Broeg and Alice (Wiley) Broeg. (Because many people mistakenly think his surname rhymes with "rogue," he wanted to entitle his 1995 autobiography "Broeg as in Plague," but his publisher rejected that idea, settling instead on *Bob Broeg: Memories of a Hall of Fame Sportswriter.*) He grew up in the Mount Pleasant section of St. Louis, where he attended elementary school. The summer after he turned eight, the St. Louis Cardinals baseball team won both their first National League pennant and the World Series. Broeg promptly fell in love with baseball and the Cardinals, and he became an avid reader of the sports sections of the four newspapers published daily in St. Louis at that time. (Currently, there is only one.) After he graduated from Cleveland High School, in St. Louis, he enrolled at the School of Journalism of the University of Missouri–Columbia (UMC, known informally as Mizzou), where he became a fan of the campus football team, the Tigers. In 1940, as a college senior, he worked for the National Semipro Baseball Congress (now the National Baseball Congress), a league based in Wichita, Kansas, under the leadership of its founder, Raymond "Hap" Dumont. "I learned so many things from—and about—Hap Dumont back in 1940 that rank high in my memories, my pleasant memories," Broeg was quoted as saying in the *Wichita Eagle* (July 22, 1998, on-line), after his election to the National Baseball Congress Hall of Fame. (Broeg's book about Dumont, *Baseball's Barnum*, was published in 1989.)

Shortly before he earned a bachelor's degree in journalism, in 1941, Broeg got two job offers: one from the Associated Press, to work as a correspondent, and the other from the University of Missouri, to fill the position of director of sports information. Taking to heart advice he had gotten earlier from the legendary J. G. Taylor Spink, who published the *Sporting News* from 1914 to 1962, he decided against a career in promotion. Broeg worked for the Associated Press in Jefferson City, Missouri, in 1941 and then in Boston, Massachusetts, in 1941–42.

Later in 1942 Broeg briefly reported for the *St. Louis Star-Times*. Then, in the same year, he joined the U.S. Marines. After he completed his military service, in 1945, he began working for the *St. Louis Post-Dispatch* as a sportswriter. Covering such events in baseball as the 1946 World Series, in which the Cardinals defeated the Boston Red Sox in seven games, and University of Missouri football games, he became "well-known to local sports fans for the convoluted style of his articles and columns," according to an on-line press release from the Western Historical Manuscripts Collection (WHMC) of the University of Missouri–St. Louis. (Broeg has donated the manuscripts of his books and other personal papers to the collection.) His first book, co-written with Bob Burrill, was published in 1946; entitled *Don't Bring THAT Up! Skeletons in the Sports Closet*, it describes mistakes on the playing field, among them the notorious blunder that cost the California Golden Bears the Rose Bowl in 1929: while running with the ball, Roy "Wrong Way" Riegels, a center for the Golden Bears, became disoriented and sprinted 70 yards toward his own team's end zone before a teammate managed to stop him.

In 1958 Broeg was named sports editor of the *St. Louis Post-Dispatch*; he succeeded J. Roy Stockton, who had been with the newspaper since 1918 and who, according to the WHMC press release, was Broeg's boyhood idol. Broeg remained sports editor until 1985, when his title became contributing sports editor. Concurrently, from 1977 to 1985, he served as assistant to the publisher. All the while, he continued to write for the sports pages. Broeg's columns were distinguished by his passionately written prose and the distinctive angles from which he presented his stories. "The art of it," he explained, as quoted by Steve Gietschier in the *Sporting News* (June 12, 1995), "is to be able to write with the integrity and skill that will enable you to retain a rapport with athletes and management without giving either the feeling that you're pro-boss or pro-player." Never denying that he was a hero-worshipper, he wrote in *Bob Broeg: Memories of a Hall of Fame Sportswriter* that the typical reader of the sports pages "wants to be entertained more than informed and informed more than infuriated," as quoted by Gietschier.

While the Cardinals were often contenders in the 1940s and 1950s, they did not win another pennant until 1964. Nonetheless, thanks in part to his close relationships with the players and coaches, Broeg harvested abundant material about the members of the club and their activities, much of which found its way into his columns and books. He detailed for *St. Louis Post-Dispatch* readers the exciting events of the 1960s, during which the team won three pennants and two World Series with the help of the pitcher Bob Gibson, and the 1980s, when, led by manager Whitey Herzog, the Cardinals again won three pennants and two World Series. More recently he described how the team, under manager Tony LaRussa, has become a contender again, winning three division titles. Broeg produced on-the-scene accounts of the triumphant 1998 season of the Cardinals' Mark McGwire, who broke the single-season home-run record (61, set by Roger Maris in 1961) by hitting 70 homers. While St. Louis football teams were far less successful, in 2000 the Rams won the first Super Bowl ever for the city; articles by Broeg about this unexpected win are included in *Eleven Men Believed: The Story of How the St. Louis Rams Rose from the Cellar to the Super Bowl, One Play at a Time* (2000), a compilation of pieces from the *St. Louis Post-Dispatch*.

Broeg's books about baseball include *Stan Musial: "The Man's" Own Story* (1964) and *The Man, Stan: Musial, Then and Now* (1977), both of which he wrote in collaboration with the great left-handed Cardinals slugger Stan Musial; *Superstars of Baseball: Their Lives, Their Loves, Their Laughs, Their Laments* (1971, updated in 1994); *We Saw Stars* (1976), profiles of baseball greats written with Stan Musial and the longtime St. Louis baseball radio commentator Jack Buck; *The Pilot Light and the Gas House Gang* (1980), about the Hall of Famer Frankie Frisch, a Cardinals manager and outstanding switch-hitter whose fiery personality, competitiveness, and sense of fun became team characteristics during the 1930s and led sportswriters to dub the Cardinals "The Gas House Gang"; *Bob Broeg's Redbirds: A Century of Cardinals' Baseball* (1981, updated in 1987 and 1992); *My Baseball Scrapbook* (1983); and *The St. Louis Cardinals Encyclopedia* (1998), written with Jerry Vickery, which Alfred Fleishman, in a review for the *St. Louis Business Journal* (October 19, 1998), described as "really an inside story . . . about ownership and management as well as the players who have never been written about before."

Broeg's most recent book is *100 Greatest Moments in St. Louis Sports*, a collection of vignettes that he wrote for KFNS radio in St. Louis as part of a series read by the sportscaster Bob Costas. Among those moments, in addition to McGwire's 70 home runs and the Rams' 2000 triumph, in Broeg's view, are the first forward pass in football, thrown in 1906 by St. Louis University's team; the day in July 1923 when a Cardinals rookie, Johnny "Stud" Stuart, pitched two complete games against Boston and won both of them; the extraordinary Lou Thesz's overpowering of Everett Marshall on December 29, 1937 to win the new American Wrestling Association belt; and the unexpected defeat of England's soccer team at the 1950 World Cup by the U.S. National Team, which included five natives of St. Louis.

Semiretired since 1985, Broeg retired fully from radio and print journalism in 2001, after suffering a stroke. He has continued to appear frequently as a guest on St. Louis television and radio programs.

In 1958 Broeg served as the president of the Baseball Writers Association of America. For three decades, beginning in 1972, he was a member of the Veterans Committee of the Baseball Hall of Fame. Among other honors, he received the 1980 Baseball Hall of Fame's writing award, called the J. G. Taylor Spink Award, and he is a five-time winner of the Missouri division of the National Sportscasters and Sportswriters Award (1962–65 and 1967). The St. Louis Chapter of the Society of American Baseball Research is named for him. In 2001 the Missouri Sports Hall of Fame honored him as a Missouri Sports Legend (a title bestowed earlier on such sports greats as Stan Musial and the golfer Payne Stewart).

Broeg's first wife, the former Dorothy Carr, whom he married in 1943, died in 1975. He and his second wife, the former Lynette A. Emmenegger, have been married since 1977. The couple live in St. Louis. Broeg's entry in *Who's Who in America 2001* includes the following statement: "As a newspaperman, I seek as an epitaph only: 'He was fair.' Hopefully 'fair' as in 'just,' not as in 'mediocre.'" — G.O.

Suggested Reading: Society of American Baseball Research Web site; *Sporting News* p8 June 12, 1995; *Wichita [Kansas] Eagle* (on-line) July 22, 1998; Broeg, Bob. *Bob Broeg: Memories of a Hall of Fame Sportswriter*, 1995; *Dictionary of Literary Biography* vol. 171, 1996; *Who's Who in America 2001*

Selected Books: as author—*Don't Bring That Up*, 1946; *Stan Musial: "The Man's" Own Story*, 1964; *Superstars of Baseball*, 1971; *Ol' Mizzou: A Story of Missouri Football*, 1974; *We Saw Stars*, 1976; *The Man, Stan: Musial, Then and Now*, 1977; *Football Greats*, 1977; *The Pilot Light and the Gas House Gang*, 1980; *Bob Broeg's Redbirds*, 1981; *My Baseball Scrapbook*, 1983; *Front Page*, 1984; *Baseball from a Different Angle*, 1988; *Baseball's Barnum*, 1989; *Ol' Mizzou, A Century of Tiger Football*, 1990; *Bob Broeg's Redbirds: A Century of Cardinals Baseball*, 1992; *Superstars of Baseball No. 2*, 1993; *Bob Broeg, Memories of a Hall of Fame Sportswriter*, 1995; as co-author—*That's a Winner, Jack Buck*, 1997; *St. Louis Cardinals' Encyclopedia*, 1998; *100 Greatest Moments in St. Louis Sports*, 2000

---

## Brokaw, Tom

*Feb. 6, 1940– Broadcast journalist*

*Address:* NBC Nightly News, *30 Rockefeller Plaza, New York, NY 10021*

Despite the emergence in recent years of 24-hour cable-news channels, the *NBC Nightly News* remains a powerhouse in the world of broadcast journalism; its success is due in no small part to Tom Brokaw, who has served as the program's anchor since 1982 and is perhaps the most-watched among the news anchors of the "Big Three" networks, having often topped Peter Jennings of ABC and Dan Rather of CBS in the ratings since the late 1990s. Brokaw began his career in the early 1960s, as a TV news reporter for a number of local NBC-affiliate stations; in 1973 he became the network's White House correspondent, and for six years beginning in 1976 he was the host of NBC's early-morning program, *Today*. Over the course of his career, in his signature straightforward manner, he has interviewed U.S. presidents and other world leaders and reported on historic events, from the assassination of Senator Robert F. Kennedy, in 1968, to the dismantling of the Berlin Wall, in

Spencer Platt/Newsmakers/Getty Images

*Tom Brokaw*

1989, to the terrorist attacks on the U.S. in 2001—a time when many viewers turned to him as a source of information and reassurance. Though he will yield the NBC anchor's chair to Brian Williams after the 2004 presidential elections, Brokaw will very likely continue to be a major presence at NBC News, contributing to magazine-style programs and specials. In addition, Brokaw is the best-selling author of three books on the generation who came of age during World War II.

Thomas John Brokaw was born in Webster, South Dakota, on February 6, 1940 to Anthony Orville Brokaw, a foreman on a United States Army Corps of Engineers dam, and Eugenia (Conley) Brokaw. Raised in Yankton, South Dakota, where he attended the local public schools, Brokaw developed an interest in politics and world affairs at an early age. "One of the advantages of a South Dakota childhood is that there is so little around you intellectually that you reach out for broader sources of material," he explained to Betty White in an interview for the *Saturday Evening Post* (May/June 1978). "I was always aware of what was going on in New York, or other power centers. . . . I was known as the town talker. I was always involved in whatever arguments were going, agitating things constantly, always had an opinion on everything." For a time Brokaw intended to become a lawyer, but his growing admiration for Chet Huntley and David Brinkley, who co-anchored NBC's award-winning nightly newscast the *Huntley-Brinkley Report* in the late 1950s and 1960s, prompted him to shift his attention to broadcast journalism. By the time he was 15, he had found an after-school job as an announcer at KYNT, a Yankton radio station.

Following his graduation from high school, in 1958, Brokaw enrolled at the University of South Dakota. He paid for his college education by working as a roving reporter for several radio stations in the university area. After earning a B.A. degree in political science, in 1962, Brokaw signed on as newscaster and morning news editor at KMTV, the NBC-affiliate television station in Omaha, Nebraska. There, he covered a wide variety of stories, ranging from murder trials to sanitation strikes to natural disasters. Because the station had such a small staff, he learned all phases of news broadcasting. He shot and edited his own film, wrote his own scripts, and even put on his own makeup before going on the air. In 1965 he joined WSB-TV in Atlanta, Georgia, as editor and anchorman of the 11:00 p.m. nightly news broadcast. Since NBC did not then have a network-staffed bureau in the South, he also contributed occasional reports on the burgeoning civil rights movement to the *Huntley-Brinkley Report.*

The following year Brokaw moved to the West Coast to become a reporter for and, later, anchorman of the late-night newscasts at KNBC-TV, the network-owned and -operated station in Los Angeles, California. Among the stories he covered during his tenure there were the assassination of Senator Robert F. Kennedy, the 1971 earthquake, and the gubernatorial campaigns of Ronald Reagan and Edmund G. "Jerry" Brown Jr. His cool, straightforward delivery so impressed network news executives that in April 1971 they chose him to anchor an edition of *First Tuesday*, NBC's monthly prime-time news magazine.

A self-described "political junkie," Brokaw jumped at the chance to become, in 1973, NBC's White House correspondent, even though it meant taking a sizable pay cut. At first scorned by veterans in the Washington press corps as an inexperienced lightweight, Brokaw quickly established himself as a combative and persistent reporter. As Ann Compton, the White House correspondent for ABC News, explained to Michael Ryan and Sally Bedell in an interview for *TV Guide* (May 14, 1977), "Tom always asked good questions at briefings. He always had a good angle on something that everybody else had missed." By the summer of 1974, Brokaw was making significant inroads into the popularity of his CBS counterpart, Dan Rather, and after Rather's reassignment later that year, he was widely regarded as the most dynamic reporter on the White House beat.

During his first 15 months as a White House correspondent, Brokaw devoted much of his time to the Watergate scandal, which followed a break-in at the Democratic Party's national headquarters and its subsequent cover-up—and which led to the resignation and disgrace of the Republican president Richard M. Nixon. Looking back on the news media's coverage of that extraordinary period, Brokaw told Arthur Unger, who interviewed him for the *Christian Science Monitor* (September 3, 1976), "They called it adversary journalism, but adversary is too weak a word. It reached the heights of hostility, and I'm not sure that either side—the press or the President—was well served." Still, he maintained that if the reporters had erred, "it was on the side of caution."

Special events relating to the presidency continued to command Brokaw's attention in the months following Nixon's resignation. In January 1975, for instance, he and John Chancellor conducted an exclusive one-hour live interview with President Gerald R. Ford. With his characteristic forthrightness, Brokaw bluntly asked the president about the widespread public conception that he was not intelligent enough for his job. While assigned to the White House, Brokaw also covered the 1974 off-year gubernatorial elections, anchored the Saturday evening edition of the *NBC Nightly News* and the 1973 sports documentary *The Long Winter of Henry Aaron*, and served as an on-camera reporter for the three-hour prime-time NBC News special *New World—Hard Choices: American Foreign Policy, 1976*, which was broadcast on January 5, 1976. During the summer of 1976, he was one of NBC's floor reporters at both the Democratic and Republican National Conventions. Working on the convention floor was "something I've always wanted to do," he told one interviewer, "like a kid wanting to grow up and play second base for the Yankees."

Meanwhile, in the summer of 1974, Brokaw's tenure at the White House nearly ended following his weeklong tryout as co-host, with Barbara Walters, of NBC's early-morning *Today* show. NBC executives, who were looking for a successor to Frank McGee, Walters's former co-host, were impressed by Brokaw's intelligence, poise, and humor as well as his journalistic experience, but Richard Wald, the president of NBC News, preferred to keep the correspondent in Washington. Partly because of Brokaw's lucid White House reports to the *NBC Nightly News*, that newscast was, for the first time in years, seriously challenging the ratings dominance of the *CBS News with Walter Cronkite*. For his part, Brokaw steadfastly refused to read commercials, a condition for the *Today* assignment. "I find doing commercials repulsive," he explained, as quoted in *Time* (July 15, 1974). "If that is a job requirement, it would not be negotiable with me." Moreover, he was unwilling to give up the fast-breaking Watergate story, so he let the opportunity pass, despite the prospect of a reported $225,000 annual salary increase, a considerable sum even for a leading broadcast journalist at the time. "I've never done anything purely for the money," he explained to Gary Deeb, the television reporter for the *Chicago Tribune* (January 12, 1977).

After Barbara Walters's celebrated defection to ABC News, in April 1976, NBC officials again asked Brokaw to join the *Today* show, this time as its sole host. Steadily losing ground in the early morning ratings race to ABC's slick new entry, *Good Morning America*, the program needed a boost, and since it was such a huge moneymaker, network executives were not prepared to take any chances. After the network dropped the requirement that the reporters do commercials, Brokaw agreed, in May 1976, to take over as host of *Today*, succeeding Jim Hartz.

Assuming his new post on August 30, 1976, Brokaw quickly won critical approval for his intelligent and informed interviewing technique and his relaxed and personable manner. His adroitness and poise served him well, since as host his responsibilities included—in addition to interviewing newsmakers—carefully monitoring the clock to maintain the smooth flow of the program's precisely timed segments and ad-libbing with the other regulars, among them Gene Shalit, the resident arts critic; news reader Floyd Kalber; Lew Wood, the weatherman and features reporter; and, beginning in October 1976, co-host Jane Pauley. Brokaw himself eventually read the morning news bulletins. Otherwise, unlike his predecessors, he worked without a script, relying instead on the information passed to him by reporters and researchers and on his own journalistic instincts.

To insure that *Today* continued to offer information instead of froth—the show had been accused of dealing in the latter to compete with *Good Morning America*—Brokaw insisted on taking an active part in the behind-the-scenes long-range planning discussions and in the daily production and story conferences. He frequently suggested topics for feature segments on such subjects as the economy, environmental protection, the social aspects of increased leisure, and special-interest political groups. In his first few months as host, for example, he reported on the widespread use of marijuana, the high prices of homes in Southern California, and the causes and effects of the mid-1970s oil crisis. He also managed to slip useful bits of information into entertainment features, as when he added to a fashion segment news on the rising consumer prices of ready-to-wear clothing. In addition, he went to Vienna to cover the signing of the SALT II accord and to Panama to discuss the canal treaties with the country's then-leader, Brigadier General Omar Torrijos Herrera. As *Today*'s principal interviewer, Brokaw earned his colleagues' respect for eliciting enlightening answers from even the most recalcitrant guests and being tough with people who, as he put it, "seem to be avoiding the issue or trying to peddle something that is not made of whole cloth." Among the wide variety of individuals Brokaw interviewed as the host of the *Today* show were Vice President Walter F. Mondale; Studs Terkel, the author and oral historian; journalist Richard Reeves; Governor James R. Thompson of Illinois; and Chicago Symphony Orchestra conductor Sir Georg Solti.

In July 1981 Brokaw signed a multiyear contract with NBC, which tapped him to co-anchor the *Nightly News* with Roger Mudd beginning in April 1982. The decision to have co-anchors for the evening news came as a compromise between then-NBC president Herb Schlosser and Bill Small, who was in charge of NBC News at the time. The *NBC*

*Nightly News*, anchored by John Chancellor, was coming in third in the ratings among the Big Three networks' nightly newscasts, and Schlosser and Small both believed it was time for a change. Schlosser wanted to bring in Tom Snyder to replace Chancellor; Small wanted Roger Mudd, who had just lost out to Dan Rather for the anchor position on the *CBS Evening News*. Brokaw, meanwhile, had been contemplating a move to ABC News, but he readily accepted NBC's offer. Within a year the new NBC president, Reuven Frank, decided that the "dual format was a bust, as was Mudd," as Verne Gay phrased it in *Newsday* (December 6, 2000)—and Brokaw became the sole anchor.

Though Brokaw was generally praised for his work as NBC's anchor, especially for his insightful questions for both interviewees and at-the-scene reporters, the *NBC Nightly News* struggled in the ratings for the better part of the next decade. Between 1983, when Brokaw took his place as the program's single anchor, and 1993, *NBC Nightly News* finished third behind the *CBS Evening News* and ABC's *World News Tonight*. Brokaw's ratings, as well as those for CBS and ABC, saw a decline in part because of shifting demographics; while older Americans tended to watch the network news broadcasts, many younger people turned elsewhere for news. Another factor was the explosion of 24-hour cable-news channels, which allowed viewers to receive information from a variety of sources. NBC was perhaps also hurt by its many experiments with its news format, which included tinkering with *Nightly News* itself as well as the introduction of news-magazine programs such as the short-lived *Now* (featuring Brokaw and Katie Couric)—and which alienated viewers looking for stability.

Nonetheless, during that decade Brokaw often covered major news stories in advance of his counterparts at ABC and CBS. In 1987 he scored one of the first U.S. interviews with Premier Mikhail Gorbachev of the Soviet Union. Two years later, in November 1989, he was the only American news anchor present when the Berlin Wall began to come down, heralding the nearly worldwide collapse of communism. A year later he returned to Berlin to mark the reunification of Germany, which had divided into Communist East Germany and non-Communist West Germany in 1945. In 1991 he covered the fall of the Soviet Union, and in December of the following year, he reported from Mogadishu, Somalia, during the landing of U.S. troops there on a humanitarian mission to insure that starving Somalis received food and medicine before local warlords hoarded them.

In the early to mid-1990s, *NBC Nightly News* began to see its viewership increase, often besting the *CBS Evening News* or ABC's *World News Tonight* to take second place among the Big Three. The ratings increase came as Brokaw, as managing editor (with responsibility for overseeing the content of the news), and executive producer Steve Friedman adopted a so-called populist approach and began focusing on U.S. domestic issues, related to such topics as the American family, health and medicine, drugs, and government waste. By 1995 NBC had begun making periodic jumps into first place; by 1997 it was consistently ranking number one in the ratings. The *Nightly News* also got a boost in the mid- and late 1990s from sensational news stories that received prominent coverage, including the O. J. Simpson murder trial and President Bill Clinton's affair with the former White House intern Monica Lewinsky.

It was during this period that critics began noting the move by evening news programs on all three networks away from "hard" news coverage, particularly that of foreign affairs and developments in Washington, D.C., and toward a pop-culture angle. Others characterized news coverage by the Big Three as increasingly sensationalistic, a charge Brokaw has denied. During an interview with Richard Zoglin for *Time* (February 17, 1997), Brokaw defended his choices, saying, "Washington has become disconnected from the rest of the nation. . . . We have to stay relevant to people." In his position as managing editor for NBC News, Brokaw helped the network to finally create a successful news-magazine program—in the form of *Dateline NBC*, which airs three times weekly. In July 1997 he signed a five-year contract with NBC, guaranteeing him $7 million a year through 2002.

In December 1998 Brokaw published *The Greatest Generation*, an assortment of recollections by men and women who came of age during World War II and helped to shape postwar America in a variety of ways. The idea for the book sprouted when he visited Normandy, France, in 1984 and 1994, to prepare documentaries on the 40th and 50th anniversaries of D-Day (June 6, 1944, which marked the beginning of the massive Allied invasion of Europe that led, in May 1945, to the surrender of Nazi Germany). In Normandy, Brokaw wrote in his introduction to the book, "I underwent a life-changing experience. As I walked the beaches with the American veterans who had returned for [the 40th] anniversary, . . . I was deeply moved and profoundly grateful for all they had done." He wrote the book, he explained, to pay tribute "in some small way . . . to those men and women who have given us the lives we have today." For *The Greatest Generation*, which he termed an "American family portrait album," Brokaw interviewed many people—both the famous and the uncelebrated—and then wrote their stories. Reviewing the book for *Biography Magazine* (February 1999), Marjorie Rosen cheered: "With his keen newsman's eye, Brokaw captures key details of each life he recounts. He also gives voice to blacks, Asians, Jews, and women, all of whom suffered discrimination in the armed forces and whose wartime participation has heretofore been downplayed. Written deftly, with deceptive simplicity and the same economy of emotion he embraces on TV, Brokaw paints a picture of an America that may have vanished—and of a generation that believed its obligations extended beyond its easy chairs and stock portfolios." Within two months of its publication, *The Greatest Generation* had sold more than two million copies. Brokaw followed it with two equally successful sequels: *The Greatest Generation Speaks* (1999) and *An Album of Memories: Personal Histories from the Greatest Generation* (2001).

On Election Night 2000 Brokaw and other news anchors, along with their networks, suffered a huge embarrassment when, before the polls closed in Florida, five of the six cooperative members of the Voter News Service—NBC, ABC, CBS, CNN, and Fox—announced that the Democratic candidate for president, Al Gore, had captured Florida. (The Voter News Service conducts exit polls at voting places nationwide, analyzes the results, and then passes that information to the networks and the Associated Press for interpretation.) At that point in the nationwide vote count, Florida's electoral votes were sufficient to give either Gore or the Republican candidate, George W. Bush, a majority in the Electoral College, so that whoever won Florida would win the presidential election. Within hours of the networks' announcement, it appeared that Bush, not Gore, had captured Florida, whereupon the networks declared Bush the winner of the election. Soon afterward it became evident that the vote in Florida was too close to call. (There followed five weeks of recounts and legal skirmishes in the state, which ended when the U.S. Supreme Court, by a 5–4 vote, decided, in effect, that the winner was Bush.)

Then came September 11, 2001, when hijackers connected to the Al Qaeda terrorist network crashed airplanes into the twin towers of the World Trade Center, in New York City, and the Pentagon, outside Washington, D.C.—destroying the towers, severely damaging the Pentagon, and killing more than 3,000 people. For the next four days, the Big Three networks threw out their commercials, losing upwards of $35 million in revenue daily, to cover those stunning events. Brokaw was on the air for 16-hour stretches, reporting on the crisis throughout the day as well as on *Nightly News* and the early-morning *Today* show. This remarkable, unprecedented coverage helped not only NBC, but also ABC and CBS, recover some of the public's trust, which had been compromised after the networks' premature announcements regarding the winner of the 2000 presidential election.

In October 2001 Brokaw became part of the news himself, when an unknown person mailed a letter containing anthrax spores to his office at Rockefeller Center, in New York City. While Brokaw himself was not infected, his assistant Erin O'Connor was, and the entire news staff at NBC had to take antibiotics. The letter sent to Brokaw was one of a host of anthrax-contaminated letters mailed that fall, with others going to the offices of ABC News, the *New York Post*, American Media Inc., and Senate Majority Leader Tom Daschle; several people died as a result of the mailings. In an interview with Stone Phillips for *Dateline* shortly after the attack, Brokaw remarked, as quoted by the *Washington Post* (October 18, 2001), "I'm mostly very angry. Look, the people I work with are very professional. They're dealing with this in a mature way. . . . Our employee's going to make a full recovery. There are a lot of people who are hurting in this city and in this country, and we think about them all the time as well."

At the end of May 2002, NBC announced that Tom Brokaw would be stepping down as anchor at the end of 2004 and would be succeeded by Brian Williams, long seen as Brokaw's heir apparent. Brokaw will continue to work on major news projects for the network after that time. While some pundits have predicted that Brokaw's departure will mean the end of NBC's dominance as a news leader, Brokaw has dismissed such talk. "When Dan [Rather] took over, when Peter [Jennings] took over, and when I took over, these same questions were raised about whether we were worthy successors," Brokaw said during a press conference, as quoted in the *New York Times* (May 29, 2002). "We're still a very important, indeed, viable component in the news and information sector."

Tom Brokaw has been married to the former Meredith Lynn Auld since August 17, 1962. Meredith Brokaw has written or co-written a series of books (among them *The Penny Whistle Lunch Box Book* and *The Penny Whistle Any Day Is a Holiday Book*) that offer suggestions for parents and children. The Brokaws have three daughters: Jennifer Jean, Andrea Brooks, and Sarah Auld. The couple live in New York City and also maintain a large ranch in Montana, where Tom Brokaw pursues a variety of outdoor activities. His memoir, *A Long Way from Home: Growing Up in the American Heartland*, was published in late 2002. — C.M.

Suggested Reading: *Biography Magazine* p98+ Feb. 1999; *Chicago Tribune* p61 Dec. 12 1976; *Columbia Journalism Review* p52+ Mar./Apr. 2002; *Electronic Media* p6+ Sep. 17, 2001, p16+ Apr. 8, 2002; *Los Angeles Times* IV p15 Nov. 8, 1977, with photo; (New York) *Daily News* p91 Aug. 20 1976, with photo; *New York Times* C p1 Nov. 5, 2001; *People* p91+ Jan. 18, 1999; *Saturday Evening Post* p78+ May/June 1978, with photos; *Time* p76+ Feb. 17, 1997; *USA Today* D p1+ Oct. 1, 1990; *Washington Post* B p1+ July 22, 1981, with photo; *Who's Who in America, 2001*

Selected Books: *The Greatest Generation*, 1998; *The Greatest Generation Speaks*, 1999; *An Album of Memories: Personal Histories from the Greatest Generation*, 2001; *A Long Way from Home: Growing Up in the American Heartland*, 2002

AP/Michael Dwyer

## Brown, Kwame

(KWAH-mee)

*Mar. 10, 1982– Basketball player*

*Address: Washington Wizards, MCI Center, 601 F St., N.W, Washington, DC 20004*

"If I got the chance to stand before God and say give me this and this and that in a player, and if I knew that he was going to give it to me, I would make it easy on him," Dan Moore, a basketball coach at the Glynn Academy, in Brunswick, Georgia, told Jeff Sentell for the *Savannah Morning News* (November 22, 2000 on-line). "I'd save him the trouble of putting all that together for me. I'd just tell him to give me Kwame." With a combination of height, power, ability, speed, and strength, Kwame Brown became a superstar at the high-school level. In June 2001 he became the first high-school player ever to be the first pick in a National Basketball Association (NBA) draft. Chosen by the Washington Wizards, for which the legendary Michael Jordan was then serving as head of basketball operations, Brown led many fans to hope that the long-mediocre Wizards would now improve. Although used sparingly in his first season as a professional, Brown has already been the focus of much media frenzy, and, by his own account, he has had to garner inner strength in order to cope. "If you're [playing basketball] for the money," he told Rachel Alexander Nichols for the *Washington Post* (October 11, 2001, on-line), "the mental stress is absolutely not worth it—you'd be much better off being a regular Tom, Dick or Joe."

The second youngest of the eight children of Willie Brown, a truck driver, and Joyce Brown, Kwame Brown was born on March 10, 1982 in Charleston, South Carolina. His father repeatedly abused Kwame and his siblings; as Brown recalled to a writer for *Sports Illustrated* (July 16, 2001), "He would tell us, 'I gave my life to the devil.' We couldn't say anything about God, about church—nothing. He would pick up whatever he could find and beat you and spank you. The next day he would come from work with a gift for you. I don't know why. I guess that was how he would try to buy your friendship." When Kwame was seven years old, his parents divorced. The following year Willie Brown received a sentence of life imprisonment without parole for murdering his girlfriend. Meanwhile, Joyce Brown had moved with her children to the small town of Brunswick, Georgia. There, she worked as a cleaning woman at a local hotel despite suffering from high blood pressure and back trouble and losing a kidney to disease. "My mom never asked me to do anything but my best," Brown told Michael Bradley for *Slam* (on-line). "If I got a C in school, she didn't spank me, she just asked if that was the best I could do. If it wasn't, she just told me to do better."

Despite his mother's standards and the positive example she set, Brown's behavior took a turn for the worse. "I grew up around a bunch of violent people," he told *Sports Illustrated*, "and if anybody did something wrong to me, I would hit the person. The payback for anything was physical abuse." His life changed when, as a sophomore at the Glynn Academy, a public high school, he befriended a local minister, John Williams. Williams saw that, despite his lack of direction, violent tendencies, and poor grades, Brown had the intelligence, height, and talent to play college basketball. Soon, Williams became a mentor to Brown. "I don't treat Kwame any different from any other kids I mentor, and he can't fire me, because he never hired me," Williams told Rachel Alexander Nichols. "Our relationship is based on telling each other the truth." With Williams's encouragement, Brown studied and practiced basketball diligently and before long had become the star of Glynn Academy's basketball team, the Red Terrors. He set several school records, among them number of career rebounds (1,235) and single-season boards (425). As a senior he averaged 20.1 points, 13.3 rebounds, and 5.8 blocked shots a game. In 2001 he was named high-school player of the year in the state of Georgia, the *Savannah Morning News*'s 2000–01 All-Coastal Empire player of the year, and McDonald's All-American. Asked by Ken Bikoff for *Basketball News* (on-line) about the criticism that he didn't make as much effort on the court in high school as he could have, Brown responded, "I would say that [those critics] are right. I didn't have to work hard. Why do all that when you can play at 10 or 15% and kill everybody? I mean, I wasn't pushed as hard as everybody else, but that doesn't mean I can't play harder." In his final game as a Red Terror, he scored 37 points and made 15 rebounds and five blocks in an 81–78 loss to the Berkmar Patriots in the state Class AAAAA semifinals. During four games in the state tournament, he scored 104 points and had 50 rebounds and 18 blocks, all despite reaggravating a partially healed sprained ankle.

After graduating from high school, Brown signed a national letter of intent to attend the University of Florida, having been asked by the school's basketball coach, Billy Donovan, to play for the campus team, the Gators. But he had a change of heart after he was told by insiders that if he put himself in the NBA draft, he might be among the top five picks. Brown sought advice from the former NBA all-star Larry Bird, among others. Rejecting the recommendation of many of his friends and neighbors that he attend college, Brown opted for the draft, confident in his abilities and hopeful that he could bring financial security to his family. "There are those who would say that the transition from high school to the NBA will be a difficult one," he told Joanne Korth for the *St. Petersburg Times* (May 13, 2001, on-line). "To those people, I say that difficult transitions are not new to my family and me. In fact, adversities have made my family stronger." Drafted by the Washington Wizards after telling Michael Jordan, "I promise you if you draft me you will never regret it," Brown signed a three-year, $11.9 million contract, $3.7 million of which was allotted for his rookie year. "I've never been so overwhelmed and nervous in my life," Brown admitted, as quoted by a reporter for *Time for Kids* (June 28, 2001, on-line). "I'm now the representative of all high school seniors, and I have to show it wasn't a mistake." With the signing of Brown, many fans began to hope that the long-failing franchise would turn around. As of 2001 the Wizards had not won a play-off game in 13 years (they had last won under their previous name, the Bullets). In the 2000–01 season, the Wizards had won only 19 games while losing 63.

As soon as Brown signed, he was barraged by attention from the press and fans. Their interest excited him at first, but he soon found it suffocating. One day, at a grocery store, other customers lined up just to see what kind of cereal he would choose. The reactions of friends and family to his newfound wealth presented him with other difficulties. "People see me as a ticket now . . . ," he told Rachel Alexander Nichols. "You want to help people, but you have 40-50 people calling you, and you can't help everybody. You try to make the right decisions, and then you have to let them know in a way so they don't get mad at you and think that just because you don't help them, you're not their friend anymore." With all the pressure and scrutiny placed upon him, he was relieved when he learned that Michael Jordan was coming out of retirement to play for the Wizards. "I'm hoping everyone will want to talk to Michael," Brown told Nichols, "and maybe I can just sneak out the back."

Brown impressed many in the summer league, which is composed of NBA rookies and young free agents. In his first summer-league game, he scored a team-high 15 points with six rebounds; over the course of the league season, he averaged 17 points and 7.4 rebounds per game. However, Brown's recurring back pain began to worsen, and familial obligations often kept him from practice. At one point the team's coach, Doug Collins, noted that Brown was out of shape and three months behind in his conditioning. Both Collins and Jordan demanded that he devote more time to practice. Brown began feeling increasingly pressured, and during one late-summer practice session, he suddenly left the court for the showers. Collins thereupon gave the young rookie advice that helped him, as Brown has acknowledged. "He told me I have to relax, that it's not a race, it's a marathon," Brown told Nichols. Jordan's tactic of intimidating his teammates through sharp play also benefited Brown; as Jordan had apparently intended, Brown learned from watching the older man. "Kwame is getting better every day," Collins told Nichols. "He's understanding what it is he has to do. He's going to be a terrific player. He's so quick. He's lighting quick off the dribble. He can come to a stop and drop the ball off, and that's a tremendous asset. When he's thinking out there, the skill is taken away."

Wearing number five, Brown played forward in his first regular-season game, against the New York Knicks on October 30, 2001. He scored two points (in the fourth quarter) and had three blocks. Then, with five and a half minutes left in the game, he sprained his ankle. After missing the next several games, he returned to the court in mid-November. Brown was used sparingly during the first half of the season; he saw more playing time toward the end of the season. In 57 games he averaged only 14.3 minutes of playing time. He also averaged 4.5 points, 3.5 rebounds, and 0.46 blocks per game. Nine times during the season, Brown scored at least 10 points, while the Wizards, who suffered the loss of Michael Jordan to a knee injury, slumped to a record of 37 wins and 45 losses. Although observers noted that Brown was making mistakes, he also showed a good deal of drive.

Brown is six feet, 11 inches tall and weighs 255 pounds. He recently bought a house in Gainesville, Florida, where he lives in the off-season. During the season he lives in Alexandria, Virginia. He has also bought a new house in Brunswick for his mother, who has not worked since 1994 because of a degenerative spinal disc. Described as charming, Brown is now known for his easygoing manner. "I know God wouldn't have given me all this pressure and attention if I couldn't handle it," he told Nichols, "but sometimes I second-guess him, say 'What are you doing, man?' Then I think about Michael [Jordan]. He's been through all of this, but a hundred times. Hopefully, he'll show me the way." — G.O.

Suggested Reading: *Basketball News* (on-line) June 12, 2001; *Savannah* [Georgia] *Morning News* (on-line) Nov. 22, 2000; *Slam* (on-line); *Sports Illustrated* p46+ July 16, 2001; *St. Petersburg* [Florida] *Times* (on-line) May 13, 2001; *Time for Kids* (on-line) June 28, 2001; *Washington Post* (on-line) D p1+ Oct. 11, 2001

Courtesy of Mayor Brown's office

## Brown, Lee P.

*Oct. 4, 1937– Mayor of Houston (Democrat); former director of the Office of National Drug Control Policy*

*Address: City Hall, 901 Bagby, Houston, TX 77002-2526*

"This is a city I love," Lee P. Brown, the Democratic mayor of Houston, Texas, told *Jet* magazine (December 17, 2001). "I want to make sure I do everything I can to see it progress." Brown, who began his first term on January 2, 1998 and has won reelection twice, is the first African-American to head the government of Houston, currently the fourth-largest city in the United States. (Houston mayoral elections are nonpartisan.) His résumé also includes his service, from 1993 to 1996, as the nation's drug czar—formally, the director of the Office of National Drug Control Policy. He has more than 30 years of law-enforcement experience as well, as a patrolman and then as head of the police departments of Atlanta, Georgia (1978–82), Houston (1982–90), and New York City (1990–92). Soon after he became Houston's chief of police, Brown introduced to his department the concept of community policing, which, among other goals, emphasizes building "a cooperative and mutually beneficial relationship . . . between the police and the community" and "encourages *active* citizen involvement in policing efforts," as Brown wrote for *Perspectives on Policing* (September 1989). Nearly two-thirds of police departments nationwide have since adopted community policing. As Houston's mayor Brown has strived to improve neighborhood leaders' access to city government officials, expand existing programs for children and launch new ones, and further develop the city's growing economy. In 2001 Houston was named Best City for African Americans by *Black Enterprise* magazine. "My job is to make a difference," Brown told Kevin Chappell for *Ebony* (January 1999). "I don't want to come to work and leave after my term is up and say, 'Lee Brown served.' I want to make a difference in the lives of the people in this city." Because of term limits, Brown's current term as mayor will be his last.

One of the seven children (six sons and one daughter) of Andrew and Zelma (Edwards) Brown, both of whom were farm workers, Lee Patrick Brown was born in Wewoka, Oklahoma, on October 4, 1937. When he was five his family loaded their belongings in a pickup truck and moved to a grape farm located in Fowler, in the San Joaquin Valley of central California. "We ended up with our first house in an old barn, where we used an old sheet to separate the [Browns'] side of the barn from others," he told Chappell. Later, the family moved to a one-bedroom house without running water or indoor plumbing. Brown has recalled that beginning in their grade-school years, he and his siblings picked cotton and grapes and mowed lawns to earn extra money.

As a child, Brown told Chappell, he "used to run around all the time" holding a book. "My friends used to tease me, and point their finger at me and call me a bookworm," he recalled. Heeding his mother's words about the importance of a good education, Brown attended Fresno State University on a football scholarship, earning a B.A. in criminology in 1960. After his graduation he took a job as a patrolman in San Jose, California. Referring to the difficulties of earning respect as a black law-enforcement officer at that time—the early years of the civil rights movement—he told Chappell, "I knew I had to do certain things above and beyond what the average person had to do if I wanted to achieve the same goals." In 1964 Brown earned an M.A. degree in sociology from San Jose State University. He received a second master's degree, this one an M.S. in criminology, from the University of California at Berkeley in 1968. That same year he left San Jose to join the faculty of Portland State University, in Oregon. Building on a law-enforcement certificate program there, he helped set up the university's Department of Administration of Justice. In 1972, two years after he earned a Ph.D. in criminology from the University of California at Berkeley, he took on three jobs at Howard University, in Washington, D.C.: associate director of the Institute of Urban Affairs and Research, director of criminal-justice programs, and professor of public policy. In 1975 he returned to the Portland area to serve as sheriff and then as director of Department of Justice Services in Multnomah County. He held the latter position from 1976 until 1978, when Mayor Maynard Jackson of Atlanta recruited him for the post of that city's chief of police.

Brown gained national attention during the two-year effort to solve what became known as the Atlanta Child Murders—a series of homicides that took the lives of at least 28 black children and young men. Beginning in the summer of 1979, after two of the bodies were discovered, investigations by the Atlanta police, and, later, FBI agents led to the conviction of Wayne B. Williams in two of the killings. Sharing the widely held belief that Williams was responsible for many of the other murders as well, Brown closed most of those cases after Williams was sentenced to two consecutive life terms in prison. Nevertheless, questions about Williams's guilt in some or all of the deaths have remained in some quarters.

In his next career move, in 1982 Brown became Houston's chief of police. During his eight years in that post, he was widely credited with easing racial tensions in the police department and fostering a better relationship between the police and residents, by instituting community policing—also called neighborhood-oriented policing—as both a set of programs and a philosophy. As a research fellow in the Program in Criminal Justice Policy and Management at the John F. Kennedy School of Government at Harvard University, in Cambridge, Massachusetts, Brown described that approach to law enforcement in such papers as "Community Policing: A Practical Guide for Police Officials," published in *Perspectives on Policing* (September 1989). He has also written a large number of other articles and book chapters on that and related subjects.

From 1990 to 1992 Brown served as the police commissioner of New York City. A major crisis erupted in August 1991, when a car driven by a member of the Lubavitcher Hasidim, a sect of ultra-orthodox Jews, jumped a curb in the Crown Heights section of the borough of Brooklyn while leading an entourage of other Lubavitchers, killing a young black boy of Guyanese parentage. The accident inflamed already-existing tensions among Crown Heights' blacks and Jews, and in the riots that ensued, a Hasidic rabbinical student from Australia was stabbed to death. As quoted by John Gizzi in *Human Events* (October 31, 1997), a 1992 report about the Crown Heights disturbances by Richard H. Girgenti, New York State's director of criminal justice, criticized Brown for failing to realize the seriousness of the growing hostilities in the neighborhood, and added, "The police commissioner did not effectively fulfill his ultimate responsibility for managing the department's activities to suppress rioting and preserve the public peace. He did not closely oversee the police response to the disturbance . . . the commissioner's leadership and performance were inadequate." According to the report Brown didn't realize how badly the situation had deteriorated until August 21, when he accompanied Mayor David Dinkins to Crown Heights and had to call for backup when demonstrators pelted their car with stones. Later, on other fronts, he received praise for his attempts to institute community policing in New York City and for helping to lower the city's crime rate. "Anyone who's honest will tell you that crime is going down because of the foundation I laid," he told Sam Howe Verhovek for the *New York Times* (September 23, 1997) during his first race for Houston's mayoralty. "[New York mayor Rudolph Giuliani is] benefitting from the groundwork that David Dinkins and I laid there in New York."

In 1992 Brown returned to Houston to take care of his wife of 34 years, the former Yvonne Streets, who was suffering from cancer; she died shortly thereafter. In April 1993, while he was serving as a professor and director of the Black Male Initiative program at Texas Southern University and also as a law-enforcement consultant, President Bill Clinton tapped him to direct the Office of National Drug Control Policy. Although the U.S. Senate confirmed him unanimously and he was the first drug czar to hold Cabinet-level rank, Brown's tenure was far from trouble-free, not least because of huge decreases in federal outlays for drug-control programs. While Brown blamed Congress for the cuts, which included a reduction in his staff of more than 80 percent, from about 150 to 25, in reality President Clinton had requested less funding for the office of drug control than the legislators ultimately approved.

In an interview with Clifford D. May for the *Denver Rocky Mountain News* (August 17, 1994), Brown described his drug-control strategy as "very balanced." "Previous strategies focused on interdiction," he explained. "We place a greater emphasis on reducing the demand for drugs, prevention, education and treatment. And we want to focus on the source countries before the drugs are exported." He also advocated the strengthening of treatment programs. In a speech to the 1995 American Cities Against Drugs conference, as reported in *Vital Speeches of the Day* (August 1, 1995), he said, "As one who has served in law enforcement for over thirty years, there is one thing that I am sure of and that is the impossibility of solely arresting our way to a solution to crime and drugs. We definitely need strong law enforcement measures, but that alone is not the answer." He also advocated programs that offered leniency to first-time, nonviolent offenders and opposed mandatory minimum sentencing in federal drug cases, on the grounds that it led to prison overcrowding and that it unfairly targeted minorities by requiring stiffer sentences for use of drugs favored by minorities than for use of those popular among whites. In addition, he suggested abandoning the "war on drugs" metaphor. "It implies someone wins, declares victory and goes home," he told Maudlyne Ihejirika for the *Chicago Sun-Times* (December 23, 1993). "It also is declaring war on your own people. Our goal is treatment on demand. If we can reduce the number of people using drugs, we can reduce the crime plaguing our society." Brown vehemently opposed drug legalization as a way to reduce the violence that often attends drug smuggling and illegal sales.

"Legalization is not an idea whose time has come," he said at the American Cities Against Drugs conference. "It is nothing more than a surrender to the forces that would poison our children and our communities. . . . I do not think it is an exaggeration to say that legalizing drugs would be the moral equivalent of genocide. Making addictive, mind altering drugs legal is an invitation to disaster for our communities that are already under siege. How could we as a nation even consider the possibility of helping more human beings destroy themselves—not to mention what they do to their families and neighborhoods? As leaders and policymakers, we have a solemn obligation to our citizens to propose and enact policies for the common good." Brown was lauded for the creation of High Intensity Drug Trafficking Area task forces. The work of the Miami area task force led to a series of major cases against factions of the Cali drug cartel and culminated in the indictment of the alleged drug kingpins Gilberto and Miguel Rodriguez Orejuela and Jose Santacruz Londono. Several former U.S. prosecutors who had represented cartel interests were also arrested during Brown's tenure as drug czar.

Brown resigned from the drug-control office in December 1995. In an assessment of his performance as drug czar, Pierre Thomas and Jim McGee wrote for the *Washington Post* (December 13, 1995), "Low-key in demeanor, Brown emerged as a second-tier administration cop, overshadowed by Attorney General Janet Reno and FBI Director Louis J. Freeh." Arnold Trebach, an activist in the drug-legalization movement, told Thomas and McGee, "If you look at the past drug czars, [Brown] is the most decent human being, the man with the greatest compassion for those struggling with drugs. He's a straight talking guy, who really tried. He had an impossible job . . . a job of no real power." After his departure from Washington, Brown spent a year at Rice University, in Houston, as a member of the Sociology Department.

In 1997 Brown made his first bid for the mayoralty of Houston. He ran on a platform that emphasized "neighborhood-oriented government" and sensitivity to the needs of a diverse public. (The population of Houston, which grew nearly 20 percent between 1990 and 2000, to more than 1.9 million people, is about 37 percent Hispanic, 31 percent white, 25 percent African-American, and 7 percent Native American, Asian, and other groups.) In 1997 Brown spent $2.7 million to defeat Robert Mosbacher, a businessman, with 53 percent of the vote in a runoff election; he also benefitted from the support of President Clinton, Vice President Al Gore, and the Reverend Jesse L. Jackson. In 1999 Brown cruised to a reelection victory, spending far less ($166,000) to win over 66 percent of the vote; he defeated "Jailbird" Jack Terence, the publisher of the weekly *Houstonian* (who earned 23 percent of the vote), and Outlaw Josey Wales IV, a regional wrestling-league promoter (close to 10 percent). In 2001, in the runoff election that followed a six-candidate competition, Brown narrowly defeated Orlando Sanchez, a construction-industry consultant and City Council member, with 52 percent of the vote. (While the mayoral contest in Houston is ostensibly nonpartisan, Brown has drawn mainly Democratic support in all three of his runs for mayor.) His current term will end in January 2004. A term-limits law will prevent him from running again.

Brown has said that five goals have shaped his leadership of the city: neighborhood-oriented government, opportunities for youth, better transportation and infrastructure, economic development and international trade, and continuous improvement in management. To encourage citizens to become involved in identifying and solving local problems, he has championed Super Neighborhood Councils, forums where neighborhood residents can discuss issues and ways to handle them. He has tried to remain accessible to everyone through such programs as "Mayor's Night In" (evenings when residents can discuss their concerns with him in his office), the Youth City Council (made up of youthful advisers), and regularly scheduled town-hall meetings. In the areas of transportation and infrastructure, the Brown administration launched a five-year, $4.3 billion capital-improvement plan to fix roads, modernize Houston's three airports, build new fire stations, expand the city's fire and police academies, and enhance the city's library and park systems. Brown has also begun implementing the 2000 Strategic Transportation Plan, which includes the city's first light-rail project, an attempt to ease the city's legendary traffic gridlock. He has worked hard to make technology available to all Houston residents: he pushed for SimHouston, a program—launched in 2001—that provides Internet access, document storage space, and E-mail accounts to all citizens at no cost via public libraries.

With the safety and well-being of Houston's children among his priorities, Brown has increased city resources devoted to after-school, reading, and sports programs. In three years he increased the library budget by nearly 25 percent. "I know that in the past, when the city went through a difficult time, one of the first agencies to suffer was the library," he told Norman Oder for *Library Journal* (September 15, 1999). "I don't see libraries as a throwaway. I see them as just as important as any agency in city government." With Brown's support, in one year the Houston Public Library system doubled the number of juvenile library cardholders, to 200,000. "I want [kids] to understand that there's nothing wrong with being smart, nothing wrong with reading," Brown told Oder. He has also created the Adopt-a-School program, through which the city's public employees tutor and mentor elementary, junior-high, and high-school students.

During Brown's terms in office, the downtown Houston area has been transformed, with $3.3 billion in construction projects recently completed or ongoing as of April 2002. In 2004 Houston will host Super Bowl XXXVIII, which is expected to generate $303 million. Houston recently built a new baseball stadium and is currently erecting a facility for basketball and hockey as well as a football stadium. (The Houston Oilers left the city for Tennessee in 1997; a new National Football League franchise, the Houston Texans, debuted in the fall of 2002.)

On June 8 and 9, 2001 Houston was hit hard by Tropical Storm Allison; the worst natural disaster in the city's 165-year history, the storm resulted in 22 deaths and left 7,000 people temporarily homeless and more than 40,000 homes seriously damaged. A disaster of another sort hit the city in December 2002, when Enron, once one of the world's leading energy, commodities, and services companies, filed for bankruptcy; amid widespread allegations of financial mismanagement, Enron laid off thousands of workers, causing a surge in Houston's unemployment rate. Nevertheless, the city has fared significantly better than much of the rest of the U.S. during the current economic downturn, with a net gain of 7,500 jobs in 2001 and another 15,000 expected in the second half of 2002.

In October 2002 Brown led a delegation of business executives on a trip to Saudi Arabia, the United Arab Emirates, and Qatar, with the goal of increasing both the number of Houston-based companies trading with those Middle Eastern countries and the volume of goods traded. While there, he met with government officials and signed an agreement entering Houston into a sister-city relationship with Abu Dhabi, the capital of the United Arab Emirates.

Brown's many honors include the Peace and Justice Award from the Martin Luther King, Jr. Center for Non-Violent Change (1981); the August Vollmer Award from the American Society of Criminology (1988); *Library Journal*'s Politician of the Year Award (1999); and the International Leadership Award from B'nai B'rith. He was named Father of the Year by the National Father's Day Committee (1991) and was inducted into the Gallup Hall of Fame (1993). In September 2002 he received a Special Achievement Award from the National Council for Public-Private Partnerships for his leadership in the Houston Area Water Corp. and his efforts to redevelop the city's downtown area. Brown is a co-author of the book *Police and Society: An Environment for Collaboration and Confrontation* (1981) and has served as president of the International Association of Chiefs of Police. From his first marriage, Brown has four grown children—Patrick, Torri, Robyn, and Jenna—and 10 grandchildren. He has been married to Frances Young, a Houston schoolteacher, since 1996. —K.E.D.

Suggested Reading: *American Spectator* Feb. 1994; *Ebony* p96+ Jan. 1999, with photos; *Library Journal* p44+ Sep. 15, 1999; *New York Times* A p1 Sep. 23, 1997, with photo; *Texas Monthly* p9+ July 1998; *Washington Post* A p27 Dec. 13, 1995, with photo

Rose Eichenbaum

## Brown, Ronald K.

*July 18, 1966– Dancer; choreographer*

*Address: P.O. Box 20389, London Terrace Station, New York, NY 10011-0004*

The dancer Ronald K. Brown has been hailed as one of the most talented choreographers of his generation. Brown began creating dances in 1985, the year he founded his own company, Evidence; his works combine such disparate elements as modern dance, African dance, and street dance and reflect a strong social conscience. "I want society to get better," he declared to Valerie Gladstone for the *New York Times* (September 26, 1999). "I want to move things forward." "Like rich African batik, Brown's choreography offers vibrant colors, complex patterns and powerful images," Rose Eichenbaum wrote for *Dance Magazine* (January 2000). "His dancers speak through explosive jumps, layouts, gestures and distinctive body formations. Bursts of physical energy hang in the air long after the performers have moved into new space." "His dances have a marvelous gravity (in the spiritual sense) and weight to them that seems redolent of African tribal dances," Clive Barnes wrote for the *New York Post* (October 1, 1999), "but his choreography is equally infused with contemporary American, so disco and hip-hop keep peeking out from disconcerting corners."

Brown's company has performed at many venues in the United States and abroad, including the Joyce Theater (New York City), the Kennedy Center (Washington, D.C.), Aaron Davis Hall (New York City), the National Black Arts Festival (Atlanta, Georgia), the American Dance Festival (Durham, North Carolina), Biennale de la Danse (Lyon,

France), and the Queer Up North Festival (Manchester, England). As a choreographer, Brown has created dances for numerous companies in addition to his own, among them the Alvin Ailey Repertory Ensemble, the Alvin Ailey American Dance Theater, the Dayton Contemporary Dance Company, Philadanco, and the Cleo Parker Robinson Dance Ensemble. He has received grants from the National Endowment for the Arts, the New York Foundation for the Arts, and the Guggenheim Foundation, and in 1998 won a Bessie Award (known formally as a New York Dance and Performance Award).

Ronald K. Brown was born on July 18, 1966 in the New York City borough of Brooklyn. Speaking with Joseph Carman for *New York Blade News* (October 23, 1998), he characterized himself as "one of those kids who was always dancing around the house." He also participated in dance-related activities sponsored by the Police Athletic League, among them demonstrations by a dancer who performed in the Broadway musical *The Wiz*. Brown's goal of becoming a dancer was temporarily sidetracked when his mother, a visual artist, went into labor with his younger brother on the day he had been scheduled to audition at Dance Theater of Harlem. Brown decided to become a "manly big brother," as he told Valerie Gladstone, and consequently abandoned the "sissy" pursuit of dancing.

For several years thereafter, Brown, who loved to read and write, set his vocational sights on journalism. He began to reconsider a career in dance in the summer of 1983, just after graduating from high school. That summer, with the help of a scholarship, he took classes at the Mary Anthony Dance Studio (run by the legendary modern dancer Mary Anthony), in Manhattan. "The minute Ron walked into the studio," Anthony recalled to Eichenbaum, "I recognized that he had a powerful, powerful energy inside of him. I knew almost immediately, here was a young man with incredible talent." By the end of the summer, Brown had decided to postpone his academic studies in order to devote himself fully to dance. He stayed at Anthony's academy for two years, studying modern dance and ballet technique as well as composition and the art of teaching. Throughout that time, Anthony encouraged him to create his own work. "I saw that Ron would eventually need to speak about his blackness and his heritage," she told Eichenbaum. "I understood that this was calling out to him and that he would need to find his own voice in the dance world." By the end of his studies with Anthony, Brown came to recognize those needs in himself. "I knew I had a perspective on things, subjects I needed to talk about, and a certain way I wanted to move," he told Eichenbaum. "I felt I could tell stories and inspire awareness through the language of dance. I came to believe I could create a dance folklore for the Afro-American community."

In 1985 Brown began studying and performing with The Works, a New York City–based dance company under the artistic direction of the choreographer Jennifer Muller. That same year he founded Evidence. Discussing with Rose Eichenbaum his motivations for doing so, he said, "I asked a friend if he thought I should create my own dance company and he said, 'You have to. Who else is going to tell your grandmother's stories?'" During the four years that he performed with Muller, Brown choreographed and staged his own performances in New York City. "My beginning work had to do with AIDS, men loving men, and dances to poetic text," he told Carman. (Brown has been openly gay since his teenage years.) From 1987 to 1989 he studied choreography with the master teacher Bessie Schonberg (for whom the Bessie Award is named). "She was tough," he recalled to Valerie Gladstone. "She'd ask: 'What do you want? What did you expect me to see?' If I was silent, she'd say, 'Speak up for yourself.'" Under her tutelage, he grew increasingly confident.

In 1990 Brown was accepted by the Young Choreographers and Composers in Residence program at the American Dance Festival (ADF) in Durham, North Carolina. (The descendant of the Bennington School of Dance, founded in Bennington, Vermont, in the 1930s, the ADF has occupied its present location since 1978. An important educational and artistic institution in the world of American modern dance, the ADF now operates affiliates around the world.) In 1991 Brown was invited back to ADF to teach; he has been a regular at the festival ever since.

Meanwhile, Brown continued to develop his own choreography. "First I tried to capture gesture," he told Eichenbaum. "Then I found I wanted to be as physical as I could, bringing in explosive flips and leaps. Then I felt it was important to add words to my work to give the dances context. By 1994, things started to jell. The integration of text with large, powerful movement and gesture, and the fusion of traditional Western African dance with modern dance, began to feel right." Tamara L. Brown reported in the *Washington Post* (February 15, 1992) that Brown "often gets ideas for his dances while riding the subway, dreaming or listening to the news." In a statement included in the Evidence media kit, Brown explained, "I use rhythm and time as a way to convey emotion. Drama and ritual use time as a way to get in touch with emotions, so I use rhythms that feel appropriate to the emotional point of a particular piece. There's a pretty consistent theme of folks walking slowly in my work. It's a metaphor for walking in peace and working with a clear vision. All the explosive dancing and rhythm lead to the ideal: being able to walk steadily with calm and resolve."

Because it incorporates elements of African dance, Brown's choreography has often been compared to the work of both Katherine Dunham, the dancer, choreographer, and anthropologist who in the 1930s and 1940s fused modern dance with Caribbean and African dance forms, and Alvin Ailey, the dancer and choreographer who combined elements of jazz and modern and African dance.

While he acknowledges their influence, Brown has stressed that he has drawn inspiration from other sources as well. "Both Dunham and Ailey were trying to be themselves, to be their Africa-descended selves and create work from all the information that had come into them," he told Thomas Connors for the *Chicago Tribune* (April 30, 2001). "And on one level, of course, I had to come from what they did. But I've worked with Mary Anthony, danced with Jennifer Muller, made work downtown, so there's a postmodern 'whatever' in there too. And because I've made a work about men loving men and AIDS, I think established, traditional black dance companies saw me as out there, that my work was kind of risky in terms of the content."

Nearly all of Brown's work is informed by a sense of social commitment; the Evidence dance company aims, among other things, "to offer cultural exchanges in the United States and abroad with a specific focus on developing African contemporary dance, and discussing issues of race, class, gender and assimilation" and "to examine societal conditioning, raise a wide range of cultural perspectives in select communities, and to engage and educate the community at large," according to the troupe's mission statement. "I want audiences to understand my stories and messages," Brown told Eichenbaum. "I want to share something that is specific. If you stir an audience, move them and inspire them, that shifts them to feel warm with each other and share a sense of community. Whatever they come away with ultimately has to do with where they're coming from. But I want to free the soul and physicality of each person. I want people to experience the desire to have their spirits lifted. I'm interested in sharing perspectives through modern dance, theater and kinetic storytelling. I want the work we do to be evidence of these perspectives. This is, in fact, why I named my company Evidence." Brown told Valerie Gladstone, "Choreography has to be about what can't be written or painted or sung. Ultimately, it has to be its own thing. I don't want to tell you what I'm feeling; I want you to see what I'm feeling."

Brown's dances dating from the late 1980s and early 1990s include *The Cove* (1991), which begins and ends with evocations of the security of the womb and includes what Tamara L. Brown described as an investigation of "incest, rape and molestation"; *Next* (1992), a tribute to victims of AIDS set to music by Stevie Wonder; and *Combat* (1992), a declaration of support for abortion rights. His more recent works include *Incidents* (1998), an exploration of the ways in which African-American women have been affected by the legacy of slavery, based in part on the autobiographical *Incidents in the Life of a Slave Girl* (1861), by Linda Brent (the pseudonym of Harriet A. Jacobs); *Water* (1999), a ritual purification of violence that incorporates the gestures of washing clothing, Senegalese dance, and text by the Trinidadian poet Cheryl Boyce Taylor; *Ebony Magazine* (1999), a critical commentary on the values of African-American glossy magazines, with music by Wunmi Olaiya; *Better Days* (1999), an examination of gay culture; *Upside Down* (1999), set to a score by the Malian singer Oumou Sangare and the Nigerian composer Fela Anikulapo Kuti; *High Life* (2001), a history and evocation of the African diaspora; and *Walking Out the Dark* (2002), a meditation on the idea of spiritual transformation that draws upon Cuban and African ceremonial dances for the dead.

In 2001 Brown co-curated, with Cheryl Boyce Taylor, "Toenails of Steel and Ruby Red Text," a series of works by lesbian and gay choreographers and writers, performed at the Thelma Hill Performing Arts Center, which is housed in a Brooklyn YMCA. He is a member of the executive committee of the International Association of Blacks in Dance and the board of trustees of Dance USA and a former board member of Black Pride NYC.

Brown makes his home in Brooklyn, in the vicinity of much of his extended family. To support himself, he teaches dance in the mornings; his afternoons are dedicated to rehearsing with the dozen or so members of Evidence. "I think about time all the time," Brown said, as quoted in the material from his media kit. "I always feel rushed. It is rare that I have the time to be social. I have a tremendous sense of obligation, so I am often torn. . . . I must pace myself, because the path before me is very long." — P.K.

Suggested Reading: *Chicago Tribune* V p3 Apr. 30, 2001, with photo; *Dance Magazine* p96 July 1995, p64+ Jan. 2000; *New York Times* II p8 Sep. 26, 1999, with photo

Selected Dances: *Evidence*, 1985; *Incidents*, 1998; *Water*, 1999; *Ebony Magazine*, 1999; *Better Days*, 1999; *Upside Down*, 1999; *High Life*, 2001; *Walking Out the Dark*, 2002

---

## Buckley, Priscilla L.

*Oct. 17, 1921– Editor; writer*

*Address: c/o* National Review, *215 Lexington Ave., Fourth Fl., New York, NY 10016*

For decades Priscilla L. Buckley was seen by many as the guiding light of, and organizing strength behind, the conservative magazine *National Review*. Although her brother William F. Buckley Jr. often received more attention in his position as editor in chief, Priscilla Buckley's work with the magazine met with applause from many important people on the right of the American political spectrum. During the more than 40 years that she worked as an editor for *National Review*, she edited pieces by numerous highly regarded conservatives, among them George Will, Gary Wills, Paul Gigot, David Brooks, Joan Didion, and Mona Charen. George Will said in a public tribute to her, as quoted by Ruth Bayard Smith in the *New York Times Book Review* (May 13, 2001), "She is the flute in our con-

Courtesy of Priscilla Buckley

*Priscilla Buckley*

servative orchestra, who taught, by example, the compatibility of political commitment and generosity of spirit." Former president Ronald Reagan said of Buckley, as noted by a reporter for UPI (May 3, 2001, on-line), that she had "a reputation unchallenged for journalistic skill and professionalism, as well as the sweetest disposition on the Eastern Seaboard." In 2001 Buckley, who is now semiretired, published *String of Pearls: On the News Beat in New York and Paris*, a memoir of her days as a reporter for United Press. The book, which received accolades from many reviewers, sheds light on her groundbreaking role as one of the few female reporters in the 1940s and 1950s.

Priscilla Langford Buckley was born in New York City on October 17, 1921, the daughter of William Frank Buckley Sr. and Aloise Steiner Buckley. Investments in Latin American oil companies turned her father into a multimillionaire; when he died, in 1958, he was worth an estimated $110 million. Patricia Buckley grew up on an estate in Sharon, Connecticut, with her 10 siblings; they included William F. Buckley Jr., the founder and editor in chief of *National Review*, host of the public television series *Firing Line*, and best-selling and sometimes controversial columnist and novelist who is considered one of the founders of the modern American conservative movement. Another brother, James L. Buckley, served as a Republican U.S. senator from New York from 1971 to 1977. Priscilla Buckley spent much of her childhood at exclusive schools abroad. She went to primary school at Cours Fenelon in Paris, France, before being sent to St. Mary's Convent in South Ascot, England. Returning to the U.S., she attended high school at the Nightingale-Bamford School, in New York City. After graduating she enrolled at Smith College, in Northampton, Massachusetts, where she was managing editor of the school's newspaper. She received her bachelor's degree in 1943. The following year she turned down a $35-a-week job at *The Book of Knowledge* to work for $18.50 a week as a copy girl at the United Press (UP) office in New York City. "With gay abandon," she wrote in *String of Pearls*, as quoted by the UPI reporter, "I tossed aside *The Book of Knowledge*'s security and a living salary, and opted for UP, starvation wages, and a wonderful life. Rich I did not become from the labor of my brow, but neither have I ever been bored." Although it had been rare for women to find such jobs, many employers desperately needed help at that time—the middle of World War II, when millions of American men were in the armed services. Buckley worked diligently and was soon promoted to a position at UP's Radio Sports Desk and then the UP Radio Desk, where incoming news stories from around the globe were rewritten for radio stations across the country and sent out by teletype. Buckley wrote the news broadcast for United Press Radio that announced the end of World War II. "You had to have an ear, good news sense, and an excellent memory, so that you could absorb the news that was bombarding you from all quarters and reshape it in your mind into a coherent story," she wrote in *String of Pearls*, as quoted by Jonathan Yardley in the *Washington Post* (April 19, 2001).

In 1949 Buckley left New York to become news editor of radio station WACA in Camden, South Carolina, a position she would hold until the following year. In 1951 she began working for the Central Intelligence Agency (CIA) in Washington, D.C., as a reports officer, a job she has referred to as "paperpushing." She left the CIA in 1953 to become a correspondent for the United Press in Paris. There, she worked at the American desk, where she and her co-workers gathered all the incoming news from France and then translated and rewrote it for the international English-language wire. The turnover in the overseas bureau was high, as the reporters had to work six days a week for little pay. Eventually, Buckley was permitted to write her own articles; she became known for covering all types of stories and lending a personal touch to them. All her articles were signed P. L. Buckley, so that the UP's European manager and others who did not approve of hiring women for such jobs would not know the gender of the person writing the pieces. In 1954, in one of her many adventures as a reporter in Paris, she and a colleague—after making an educated guess about what was being said "between the lines" on French wire reports—beat UP's chief rival, the Associated Press, by 15 minutes with the announcement that the Vietnamese city of Dien Bien Phu had fallen to Communist forces (the Viet Minh), thus putting an end to French colonial rule in Indochina.

In 1956 Buckley was persuaded by her younger brother William F. Buckley to leave the United Press for a job as assistant editor at the conservative magazine *National Review.* "I have no inkling," she recalled in *String of Pearls*, as quoted by Ruth Bayard Smith, "as I read the first issue of what a reader would later call 'a blue-bordered haven in the desert of slanted news,' that I will spend the next 35 years . . . helping make *National Review* a major player in America's turn to the right, the Reagan election and the end of the cold war." In 1959 she was promoted to managing editor of *National Review*, a position she held until 1986. "Any magazine, any collection of writers, is bound to have a generous share of marginal personalities," Jeffrey Hart wrote for *National Review* (April 16, 2001). "Priscilla, with her buoyant soul, optimism that never fractured, and strong common sense, kept the ship plowing through the waves." In 1986 Buckley was made senior editor of the magazine. While in that role she edited her brother William F. Buckley's *The Joys of National Review* (1995). In 1996 a book of her own, *The Light-hearted Years: Early Recollections at Home and Abroad*, was published. Three years later she retired from her position as senior editor but continued to work for *National Review* as a contributing editor.

Buckley's most publicized work of prose, *String of Pearls*, was published in 2001. The book encapsulates many of the experiences she had as a reporter for the United Press in New York and Paris in the 1940s and 1950s, relating anecdotes about the colorful characters she encountered in and out of the newsroom. "Its prose is energized by intelligence and concreteness," Jeffrey Hart wrote for the *National Review* (April 16, 2001). Hart added, "It is wonderfully evocative of a time and place." William F. Gavin noted for the *Washington Times* (June 11, 2001) that the book "is a funny, charming, light-hearted look at American journalism as it was practiced during and immediately after World War II." Ruth Bayard Smith agreed with the many positive reviews, but also noted that Buckley's confessions of uncertainty about names and dates "go beyond the subjectivity of a memoir and make one wish for more research or reporting."

Priscilla Buckley lives in Sharon, Connecticut. Her articles, book reviews, and travel pieces have appeared in the *New York Times Book Review*, *Harper's Bazaar*, *Chronicles*, *Cosmopolitan*, the *American Spectator*, *Shooting Sportsman*, *Rally*, *Human Life Review*, and the *National Review*, among other publications. From 1976 to 1980 she wrote a column, "One Woman's Voice," for Princeton Features. She has served as a trustee of the Sharon Hospital; Big Bothers of New York; Church Homes; the Hotchkiss Library in Sharon, Connecticut; and the Maplebrook School in Amenia, New York. Buckley has also been governor of the Sharon Country Club and twice served as president of the club (she was the first woman to fill that position). She is the author of *The Sharon Country Club, Its History* (1995). In addition, from 1984 to 1991 she was a member of the U.S. Advisory Commission on Public Diplomacy. In her spare time she enjoys painting, bird shooting, golfing, skiing, and ballooning. Her nickname is Pitts. "Get [a reader's] attention right away, something that grabs the eye" is her advice to aspiring journalists, as quoted by Jenny Chavez in the *Clackamas Print* (on-line). "A natural writer uses instinct and rhythm; write a piece you can speak as well as read." — G.O.

Suggested Reading: *National Review* p55+ Apr. 16, 2001, p38+ Jan. 20, 1992, with photos; *Washington Post* C p2 Apr. 19, 2001; Buckley, Priscilla L. *The Light-hearted Years: Early Recollections at Home and Abroad*, 1996, *Strings of Pearls: On the News Beat in New York and Paris*, 2001

Selected Books: *The Light-hearted Years: Early Recollections at Home and Abroad*, 1996; *String of Pearls: On the News Beat in New York and Paris*, 2001

---

## Bunim, Mary-Ellis, and Murray, Jonathan

Bunim, Mary-Ellis
*July 9, 1946– Television producer*

Murray, Jonathan
*1955– Television producer*

*Address: Bunim/Murray Productions, 6007 Sepulveda Blvd., Van Nuys, CA 91411*

"This is the true story of seven strangers, picked to live in a house and have their lives taped, to find out what happens when people stop being polite and start getting real." So goes the voiceover narration in the opening montage of *The Real World*, now in its 12th season on the MTV cable network. "We knew from the first 15 minutes of shooting the pilot that voyeuristic TV was in our future," Mary-Ellis Bunim, the veteran television producer and co-creator of *The Real World*, told Daniel Roth for *Fortune* (August 14, 2000). "Who knew it would spawn a growth industry years later? And what took so long?" Bunim and her business partner and fellow producer, Jonathan Murray, envisioned *The Real World* as a cross between a soap opera and a documentary and as a way of supplying MTV with a television program for only one-third the cost of a comedy or drama with professional actors. The handpicked cast was young, hip, attractive, and diverse; the initial location (downtown Manhattan) was fixed, but little else was—there was no script, and the show's drama unfolded over time, with multiple cameras capturing every fight, nasty comment, and facial expression. "The idea for *The Real World* was simple: real life can be as fascinating as something that's scripted if the story is well told and well edited," Murray explained to Bernard Weinraub for the *New York Times* (February 21, 2001).

*Jonathan Murray and Mary-Ellis Bunim* Courtesy of Bunim/Murray Productions

*The Real World* spawned a television schedule full of "reality" shows and imitators, some of them created by Bunim/Murray Productions: *Road Rules*, an MTV show (the first installment of which aired in 1995) featuring young, diverse personalities traveling in a Winnebago trailer and completing physical and mental challenges with the promise of a "handsome reward" at the end of a 10-week journey; *Making the Band* (launched in 2000), an ABC series about the fashioning of the pop-music band O-Town, from tryouts to first tour, by the music manager and record-label owner Lou Pearlman, who helped propel the bands 'N Sync and the Backstreet Boys to fame; and *Love Cruise* (which premiered in 2001), a Fox reality series in which 16 young singles compete to be the final man and woman standing—after voting during a 15-day Caribbean cruise eliminates the 14 other contestants. Other popular reality series, such as the CBS hit show *Survivor* and the ABC program *The Mole*, owe their existence to the groundbreaking methods of *The Real World*. As Andy Denhart explained in an article on *Salon.com* (July 3, 2001), "It all seems so familiar now—even more so with all the other reality shows on TV—but it's important to remember that *The Real World* actually invented an entire genre of television. By putting real people in an artificial context (a beautiful apartment stocked with cute, well-groomed roommates), producers Mary-Ellis Bunim and Jonathan Murray figured out a way to combine documentary and drama in a sort of soap opera that we'd never seen before. *The Real World* was so ahead of its trend that the rest of television took nine years to catch up." MTV, which gambled by putting *The Real World* on the air in 1992, has profited handsomely from the reality-programming revolution; during the 1999 and 2000 seasons, the show was consistently number one among 12- to 34-year-olds for basic cable in its time slot, drawing an average audience of 3.1 million people. Discussing the show's popularity, Bunim told Bernard Weinraub, "We have to credit MTV for stepping off the cliff with us."

The daughter of Frank and Roslyn (LaMontagne) Paxton, Bunim was born Mary-Ellis Paxton on July 9, 1946 in Northampton, Massachusetts. As a child, she recalled to Joey Bartolomeo and Laurel Naversen for *Harper's Bazaar* (March 2001), "I always watched the soaps. I was addicted to *The Secret Storm* and *General Hospital*." As an adult, Bunim worked on several daytime television series, logging more than 2,500 hours of supervisory experience as a producer for *Search for Tomorrow* (1976–81), *As the World Turns* (1981–84), and *Santa Barbara* (1984–86).

Jonathan Murray was born in 1955 in upstate New York to David and Paula Murray. A 1973 graduate of Fayetteville-Manlius High School, close to Rochester, New York, he went on to pursue a career in broadcast journalism; he served as a local news anchor in Green Bay, Wisconsin, and Atlanta, Georgia, before becoming the station manager at WOKR-TV in Rochester in the early 1980s. He had his sights set on becoming a network programmer.

Bunim and Murray first met in 1987 in Los Angeles, at the suggestion of their mutual talent agent. Murray had developed a script for a daily detective show on which actors reenacted real-life crimes, and Bunim was interested in producing the program. Though the project never got off the ground, the pair discovered that they worked well together, and they founded Bunim/Murray Productions in 1988. Both had been captivated by the 12-part PBS documentary *An American Family*, which aired in

1973. (*An American Family* was a true-life, uncensored look at the day-to-day existence of a Santa Barbara, California, family, the Louds, during seven consecutive months. "By today's standards, the show looks as if it was filmed on a bad convenience-store security camera," Robert Sullivan wrote for *Vogue* [June 2001], "but it is still eerily riveting. The parents split up; the kids fight, and a son comes out of the closet to all of America.") Jonathan Murray told Sullivan, "I remembered watching it and being totally amazed that they were capturing this family's life and that it was unfolding like drama and America was captivated, and Mary-Ellis had had the same reaction." At a 1988 television convention in New Orleans, Louisiana, Bunim and Murray were serendipitously seated next to Delilah Loud, one of the five Loud children, who had a job in television syndication. "We just . . . pumped her for information about the whole experience," Murray recalled to Sullivan. Bunim added: "We didn't know where this was going. We were just fascinated by the effect of that experience on real people." Bunim and Murray produced a six-episode series about families in crisis, called "American Families," for Fox Broadcasting. The series has never aired.

Around 1990 MTV executives came to Bunim seeking development of an arresting—but inexpensive—show to attract new viewers. Bunim initially proposed a soap opera, but such a show was thought to be too expensive to produce. Bunim and Murray then pitched the idea of a documentary and soap opera combined—a show that would dispense with scripts, professional actors, and much of the expense of a traditional television program. In his conversation with Robert Sullivan, Murray described the proposal to MTV: "What if we were to do an unscripted soap; what if we were to do sort of a rock-'n'-roll *American Family*, a group of young people living in New York for the first time in their lives, and making their own decisions and, potentially, mistakes?" MTV agreed to develop the pilot, and Bunim and Murray worked furiously to assemble a cast. "We started with just the two of us, working around the clock," Bunim told Marc Peyser for *Newsweek* (July 2, 2001). A loft in the SoHo neighborhood of New York City was outfitted for six young people to live in, rent-free and with a small stipend, for three months; the only catch was that their actions would be videotaped at all times and they would be required to spend time each week in a video "confessional," during which they could speak freely about any topic. (If a cast member chose to leave the show during filming, he or she could do so, but only after explaining the decision on camera.) After interviewing about 1,000 people in New York, Austin, Texas, and Birmingham, Alabama, Bunim and Murray chose seven participants instead of six, all of them young, attractive aspiring artists in various areas—such as poetry, acting, or rap music. "We didn't start with the idea of having all young 'artists,'" Murray told Daniel Cerone for the *Los Angeles Times* (May 28, 1992). "We interviewed a broad spectrum of people, but the people who were attracted to this project were generally these more open-minded, artistic people. The stockbroker, the telephone operator—they didn't pound down our doors. And those who did frankly weren't that interesting."

The first season of *The Real World* was taped over a three-month period, during which the director was stationed behind one of the loft walls, making decisions with story editors about which taped scenes to shape into story lines. For each of the 13 episodes, 30 to 50 hours of tape were whittled down to half an hour. Race and sexuality were two hot-button issues, prompting arguments and providing continuing drama for story lines. "We set up the situation purposefully so there would be conflict and sexual tension," Murray told Daniel Cerone. "The loft was a real pressure cooker. I mean, there are times in these episodes where people are literally in each other's face screaming at the top of their lungs." Bunim added: "Of course, critics might say, 'Oh, this is contrived.' We say, 'Well, of course it's contrived.' We designed the backdrop. We designed this family. And then we put them together to see what might happen, hoping for a dramatic effect. And that's what we got."

MTV's intended audience of people in their teens and 20s responded positively to the show, tuning in each week to follow the lives of the seven friends, enemies, and bedfellows. For the show's second season, Bunim/Murray Productions took a new cast to a house in Los Angeles. Tough issues were faced head-on, as one of the cast members had an abortion, announcing that decision and facing the aftermath on camera, and another was voted out of the house because of what was seen as his sexual aggression toward his female housemates. The third season of *The Real World* (shot in San Francisco), which had grown to encompass 20 episodes taped over a five-month period, remains one of the best-known. That year's episodes followed Pedro Zamora, a 22-year-old gay Latino man, as he lived with AIDS. After the filming ended for the season, Zamora, an educator and AIDS activist, returned to his home in Miami; he died a few months later, as the season's installments were being broadcast on MTV, and his story had so gripped the public that then-president Bill Clinton called Zamora's parents to offer condolences. Other story lines of the third season were heated with sex, politics, and roommate strife. A cast member named Puck was voted out of the house in the middle of the season for his rude behavior. "We weren't anxious either season to have somebody kicked out," Murray explained to Tom Green for *USA Today* (June 23, 1994). "But we have no choice. We go with what happens."

A decade after its debut, *The Real World* has not slowed down. The setting and cast change every year, but the core audience continues to tune in—and to apply for the spots on the show themselves. More than 35,000 audition videotapes arrive at the Bunim/Murray offices for each season, which now runs from 22 to 24 episodes. The voyeuristic look into the lives of young people has taken varied approaches—from having the participants work together at a community center in Boston (season six) to having them serve as interns for Arista Records in New York (season 10)—and explored different topics, including alcohol abuse (season eight, set in Hawaii) and sex and religion (season nine, set in New Orleans). Bunim and Murray have weathered criticism from both television professionals and cast members, who claim that the casting process is invasive and tantamount to typecasting and that the footage is manipulated to create drama at the expense of unvarnished truth. Murray told Marc Peyser that with the number of applications, diversity is virtually assured, but that "it ultimately comes down to who are the seven best people. All of the story has to come from the cast. If you don't have people with layers that are going to be peeled off throughout the season, you're not going to get your 24 episodes of series television." Bunim admitted to selecting one particular type of participant every season, telling Katherine Marsh for *Rolling Stone* (June 22, 2000), "We try to get at least one very down-to-earth, relatable kid. Someone who doesn't have that much life experience—a touchstone kid."

In August 2002 Bunim and Murray produced *The Real World Movie: The Lost Season*, a fictional made-for-television movie about a deranged fan who kidnaps the cast of *The Real World*. The film earned high ratings for the network. The following month marked the debut of *The Real World: Las Vegas*, the series' 12th edition.

*The Real World* led to other assignments for Bunim/Murray Productions, including the show *Road Rules*, a road-trip version of *The Real World* involving such activities as skydiving, bungee jumping, and living in the close quarters of a mobile home. With the rising tide of reality television, even though Bunim and Murray continued to work mostly for MTV, they were courted by bigger networks. In 1966, for NBC, they produced *Class Reunion*, which threw classmates from a 10-year high-school reunion together for a few days in a *Real World*–type setting. For ABC, Bunim/Murray Productions followed the creation and growth of the band O-Town, providing a glimpse into the lives of young, not-yet-famous pop musicians. *Making the Band* is currently taping installments for its third season. Bunim and Murray also produced the Fox show *Love Cruise*, a matchmaking and elimination game set on a ship, and are frequently in discussions to produce new shows or television movies. But of all Bunim/Murray shows, *The Real World* continues to generate the highest ratings. "There have been some very positive lessons [to] come out of the show," Murray explained to a television critic for the New Orleans *Times-Picayune* (April 16, 2001). "We've really found that our audience has connected with those issues. First and foremost, it's about entertaining, but there is this other side for many . . . [teenagers] who watch it. For them, they're learning real-life lessons. When they go off to college, perhaps they'll be more worldly, more prepared."

Both Bunim, who is divorced and has a daughter, and Murray live in southern California.—K.S.

Suggested Reading: *New York Times* E p1 Feb. 21, 2001, with photo; *Newsweek* July 2, 2001, with photo; *Rolling Stone* p71+ June 22, 2000; *USA Today* D p3 June 23, 1994; *Vogue* p191+ June 2001, with photos

Selected Television Series: *The Real World*, 1991– ; *Road Rules*, 1995– ; *Making the Band*, 2000– ; *Love Cruise*, 2001–

Selected Television Specials: *Class Reunion*, 1996

---

Reuters/Peter Jones

## Carter, Vince

*Jan. 26, 1977– Basketball player*

*Address: Toronto Raptors, Air Canada Centre, 40 Bay St., Suite 400, Toronto, Ontario, Canada, M5J 2X2*

When Vince Carter first entered the National Basketball Association (NBA), in 1998, he was known primarily for his formidable dunking ability. But after three-and-a-half seasons of playing guard with the Toronto Raptors, he has also gained recognition for his potent, if somewhat streaky, jump shot, his solid defense, and most notably, his ability to take over a game and lead his team to victory. Carter's athletic, six-foot seven-inch frame, his acrobatic play, and his engaging personality have evoked the inevitable comparisons to Michael Jordan that so many other promising young players have endured—but, along with the Los Angeles Lakers' Kobe Bryant, he has so far done more than perhaps any other player to justify those comparisons. Earning Rookie-of-the-Year honors in the 1998–99 season, he helped turn his lowly, fledgling Raptors into legitimate contenders in the NBA. His exciting style of play quickly made him a favorite with fans, who, because of his 41-inch vertical leap, began to refer to him as Air Canada (a play on the name of the Canadian airline and Michael Jordan's nickname, Air Jordan).

Born in Orlando, Florida, on January 26, 1977, Vincent Lamar Carter grew up in Daytona Beach, on Florida's east coast. Moments after little Vince came home from the hospital, his father, Vince Sr., and his older brother, Oliver, stood over his crib, passing a basketball back and forth. He was two when his brother took him to a basketball court to shoot his first ball. Carter joined his first basketball team at age seven, and by the time he was in seventh grade, he could dunk the ball, even though, at five feet, eight inches, he was far from reaching his adult height.

Carter's parents divorced when he was seven, and Vince Sr. largely dropped out of his life. Carter's mother, Michelle, got remarried, to Harry Robinson, a teacher at Daytona Beach's Mainland High School, which Carter would later attend. At Mainland High Carter participated in many extracurricular activities, particularly the band, which his stepfather led. He played saxophone, was a drum major, and helped write the school's homecoming song; he showed such skill as a musician that in his senior year, Bethune-Cookman College, in Daytona Beach, offered him a music scholarship. (He turned it down.) Carter also played football, ran track, and played basketball, the last of which had become his main sport by the time he entered high school. After his parents divorced, Carter had sometimes found family life trying, and basketball provided some solace for him; he referred to it as his "Old Faithful," as he told S. L. Price for *Sports Illustrated* (January 29, 2001). "When things are going badly, I go to the gym and shoot—and shoot and shoot," Carter explained. "All the frustrations, I let them go. Even when I miss, they're going away. That's helped my jump shot. Working out those frustrations: just shooting, shooting, shooting, and after two or three hours I feel fine."

In 1995 Carter entered the University of North Carolina (UNC) at Chapel Hill (Michael Jordan's alma mater). He played in 31 of the UNC Tar Heels' 32 games during the 1995–96 season. In his team's Atlantic Coast Conference (ACC) opener, against North Carolina State, Carter immediately made his presence felt by scoring 18 points. He scored in double figures 10 times during his freshman year and hit nearly 50 percent of his shot attempts. He improved on those numbers in the 1996–97 season, averaging 13 points per game and 52.5 percent shooting. With his help, the Tar Heels won the ACC title and advanced to the Final Four of the National Collegiate Athletic Association (NCAA) basketball tournament, a feat that the team repeated at the end of the 1997–98 season. Carter led the ACC that season with a .591 field-goal percentage, and his performance earned him First Team All-ACC honors.

After completing his junior year, Carter left college to join the NBA. He was drafted fifth overall (one place behind his former Tar Heels teammate Antawn Jamison) by the Golden State Warriors, who immediately traded him to the Toronto Raptors in exchange for Jamison. Though Carter had been an outstanding player in college, he debuted in the pros during the 1998–99 season with an authority few could have foreseen. In his very first NBA game, he scored 16 points to lead the Raptors to victory over the Boston Celtics. On March 17, 1999, in the fourth quarter of a contest with the Detroit Pistons, he scored 17 points, including the game-winning basket, for a total of 28. He carried the Raptors to an 88–87 victory over the Indiana Pacers on April 1, 1999 by hauling in 11 rebounds and scoring 31 points, including the Raptors' final six of the game. The Raptors' Canadian television ratings increased by 30 percent over the previous year, as fans got wind of the incredible dunks Carter was executing in nearly every game. Canadian sports stores found it impossible to keep in stock NBA replica jerseys bearing Carter's name. "I didn't plan for it to be this way," Carter told Michael Farber for *Sports Illustrated* (April 19, 1999). "My goal was to fit in, gradually work my way to being an impact player. My whole scheme fell through from Day One, but Butch [Carter, the Raptors' coach] is doing his best to keep me grounded." No one, however, could keep Carter literally grounded, particularly opponents, who had trouble preventing his high-flying dunks. Averaging 18.3 points per game and 5.7 rebounds per game, Carter was a runaway winner of the NBA's Rookie of the Year award and a unanimous selection for the All-Rookie First Team.

Carter continued to blossom during the 1999–2000 season. On February 27, 2000 he topped the 50-point mark by a point in a Raptors' victory over the Phoenix Suns, 103–102. His points-per-game average in the season was 25.7, fourth-best in the NBA. His consistently high-caliber play helped lead the young Raptors to their first play-offs trip, where the team was dispatched in the first round by the New York Knicks. Carter was voted to the NBA All-Star Team as a starter; the nearly two million votes he received from fans for the All-Star Game was the second-highest total ever, just behind Michael Jordan's total in 1997. In the All-Star Game Carter proved the fans right by scoring 12 points in 28 minutes and turning in one of the most extraordinary performances in the history of the NBA Slam Dunk Contest. For his first dunk of five, he jumped, spun 360 degrees in the air, and stuffed the ball authoritatively through the basket. The five judges all scored it a perfect 10, giving him a total score of 50. For his first dunk of the final round, he jumped so high that he seemed about to follow the ball through the net; his right arm plunged through the hoop up to his elbow, and he hung on the rim for a moment by the crook of his arm. That shot received a score of 50. In another impressive dunk, he leapt, caught a bounce pass on his way up, passed the ball through his legs, and jammed it in. That feat earned him another perfect 50. (His other two dunks earned scores of 49 and 48, respectively.) After Carter's performance, the Los Angeles Lakers center Shaquille O'Neal described him as "half man, half amazing," as quoted by Price. The basketball legends Julius "Dr. J" Irving and Earvin "Magic" Johnson went to the locker room after the contest to express their admiration for him.

Another factor that added to Carter's prestige in 2000 was his performance with the U.S. men's basketball team in the 2000 Olympics, held in Sydney, Australia. Carter had made the team only after Tom Gugliotta was forced to withdraw due to a knee injury; on the court he displayed aggressive play (he led the team in scoring, with an average of 14.8 points per game) and an uncharacteristically brash attitude (he taunted opposing players and strutted around after making big plays). In the team's successful encounter with the French squad, Carter delivered what some have called the most incredible dunk ever: driving to the basket against Frederic Weis, France's seven-foot two-inch center, Carter literally jumped over his opponent (who ducked his head slightly to avoid contact), and drove the ball home. The play was dubbed "the dunk seen round the world." "The turning point in the game [against France] was when Vince Carter dunked the ball [over Weis]," Carter's Olympic teammate Jason Kidd told a reporter for the U.S.A. basketball team's official Web site (September 25, 2000). "I think everybody was in awe, and nobody thought he was going to attempt that, but to me that was probably the greatest play in basketball I've ever seen."

Describing Carter's uncharacteristic cockiness during the Olympics, Price wrote, "He was a bully. He was an ass. He was an arrogant American set loose upon the world, doing that arrogant American thing. Strutting. Finger-pointing. Talking trash." Some attributed his behavior to the difficult times he had been having both professionally and off the court. In February 2000 Carter's agent, William Black, was charged with stealing money from his clients, including $300,000 from Carter. The next month Michael Jordan stated to the media that Kobe Bryant was a better all-around player than Carter, because of his defensive play, an assessment that cut Carter to the quick. In June 2000 Butch Carter, the Raptors' coach and Vince Carter's mentor, was fired, and in August Tracy McGrady, a teammate, friend, and distant relative of Carter's, left the Raptors; comments made publicly by McGrady implied that he had become tired of playing in Carter's shadow. Then, a week before Carter left for the Olympics, his mother told him that she and Harry Robinson were getting divorced. Many surmised that Carter's unseemly behavior at the Olympics simply reflected the accumulated stress he might have been experiencing.

For some, however, Carter's impassioned, if at times overexuberant, play in the international arena was a welcome change from his usual, more subdued court demeanor. A common criticism leveled at Carter throughout his career has been that he is too nice and lacks the competitive fervor that most champions possess. "Vince needs to find something that's going to motivate him to be as aggressive as he is when he's mad," Carter's fellow Raptor Antonio Davis told Price. "Because when he's not, he's a totally different player." Davis added, "[Carter's] edge is the excitement. His edge is the highlights, dunking, the oohs and aahs. But it's hard for that to be the motivation. Your motivation should be that you want to win."

During the 2000–01 season Carter provided plenty of evidence that he did indeed want to win. He led the Raptors in scoring in all but eight games and was ranked fifth in the NBA in scoring average, with 27.6 points per game. Once again he was the leading vote-getter for the All-Star Game, in which he scored 16 points. Moreover, he took his team further into the play-offs than ever before. As in the previous year, the Raptors faced the favored New York Knicks in the first round of the play-offs. After Carter played poorly and the Raptors fell behind in the series, two games to one, Carter's teammate Charles Oakley publicly challenged him to sharpen his game. The media became critical of Carter as well. He responded early in game four, when he scored on a dunk that appeared to spark his confidence. He proceeded to rack up 32 points, seven rebounds, and four assists, to lead the Raptors into game five. In that game he continued his tenacious play, scoring 27 points, with six rebounds and three assists, and perhaps most importantly, grabbing both an offensive rebound and a loose ball at the end of the game to seal a 93–89 victory and send his team to the next round—against Allen Iverson and the Philadelphia 76ers. Carter excelled in the series, proving that he could play at the level of Allen Iverson, one of the league's most respected players. After Iverson scored 54 points to even the series in game two, Carter bounced back in game three, scoring 50 points, with six rebounds, seven assists, and four blocked shots. Philadelphia won games four and five to gain the lead in the series, 3–2; then Carter made a 39-point showing in game six to even the series. On the morning of the final game, Carter caused an uproar by attending his UNC graduation ceremony (he had taken summer classes to earn his degree). Critics who warned that the graduation would harm his concentration got some ammunition for that charge when Carter missed a potential game-winning shot at the end of the game and the 76ers won, 88–87. "It all came down to one shot," Carter told Chris Broussard for the *New York Times* (May

21, 2001). "It was going to be a great day or a terrible day. It was almost a wonderful day."

As Carter neared the final year of his contract with the Raptors, many assumed he would sign with a more high-profile team. Speculation ended on August 1, 2001, when the Raptors announced that Carter had signed a six-year contract extension worth a reported $94 million. Meanwhile, Toronto's mayor, Mel Lastman, had declared the day "Vince Carter Day." "It would have been tough to go elsewhere when he made it my day," Carter told a reporter for the Associated Press (August 1, 2001, on-line).

Carter began strongly in the 2001–02 season, ranking first after 50 games in total number of baskets made (467). He was once again voted to the All-Star Team but was forced to sit it out due to damage to his quadriceps. Carter apparently failed to recover fully from the injury; he was noticeably hampered when he returned to the starting line-up. The Raptors went into a slump but, thanks to a late-season surge, finished the regular season with 42 wins and 40 losses. That record qualified them to face the Detroit Pistons in the first round of the play-offs; they lost the best-of-five series in five games.

Carter has contributed a portion of his earnings to Embassy of Hope, which he and his family founded in 1998; Carter's mother is its executive director. The activities of that nonprofit foundation have included a "Believing in Christmas" party for disadvantaged Florida children, at which the youngsters received gifts from their wish lists; the creation of a children's park in Daytona Beach; celebrity golf tournaments and softball fund-raisers; and participation in "Read Across America" events, in which Carter spoke to kids about the importance of education. In September 2002 Carter donated $2.5 million to his high-school alma mater, Mainland High, to help fund a new gymnasium, which will be named the Vince Carter Athletic Center. — P.G.H.

Suggested Reading: *Ebony* p108 Apr. 2000; *Maclean's* p46+ Apr. 26, 1999, p79 May 21, 2001; *Sporting News* p41 May 14, 2001; *Sports Illustrated* p90 Apr. 19, 1999, with photo, p36+ Feb. 28, 2000, p67+ Jan. 29, 2001, with photos

---

## Cheney, Richard B.

(CHAY-nee)

*Jan. 30, 1941– Vice president of the United States*

*Address: The White House, 1600 Pennsylvania Ave., Washington, DC 20500*

Courtesy of Executive Office of the President

Before July 25, 2000, when George W. Bush chose him as his running mate in that year's presidential race, Richard B. "Dick" Cheney may have been unknown to many Americans, partly as a result of his preference for exerting influence in low-key fashion behind the scenes. Less casual observers, however, had long seen him as a formidable presence on the political landscape. A staunch conservative and consummate Washington insider who had spent almost his entire career in the federal government, Cheney joined the staff of President Richard Nixon at the age of 29 and, when he was 34, became White House chief of staff—the youngest ever to hold that position—under President Gerald R. Ford. In 1978 he won election to the first of six terms as at-large congressman from his home state of Wyoming, and within a decade he had advanced through the ranks to become the Republican whip, his party's second-ranking post in the House. Cheney was next chosen by George W. Bush's father, President George Herbert Walker Bush, to head the Department of Defense, a post he occupied during the Persian Gulf War of 1991. Following a period spent in the private sector, Cheney provided the 2000 Republican presidential ticket with the heft that many thought was needed to compensate for the younger Bush's relative inexperience. Bush's election paved the way for Cheney's role as arguably the most influential vice president in U.S. history—a position made even more important by the attacks on the U.S. on September 11, 2001.

The son of Richard Herbert Cheney, a soil-conservation agent with the United States Department of Agriculture, and Marjorie Lauraine (Dickey) Cheney, Richard Bruce Cheney was born on

January 30, 1941 in Lincoln, Nebraska. In his early childhood he moved with his parents to Casper, Wyoming, where his chief interests were hunting, fishing, and playing football and baseball. At Natrona County High School, Dick Cheney, as he prefers to be called, was co-captain of the football team. In his senior year he was voted class president.

Following his graduation from high school, in 1959, Cheney enrolled at Yale University, in New Haven, Connecticut, on a full scholarship, only to drop out after just four semesters. "I wasn't a serious student," he told Jeanette Smyth for the *Washington Post* (April 4, 1976). "I never buckled down." Returning to the West, Cheney spent the next two years working on power lines in Colorado, Arizona, and Wyoming. In 1963 he resumed his education, at the University of Wyoming. During his time there, he participated in a nationwide contest, submitting an essay to the National Center for Education in Politics at New York University that one official at the center has since described as "by far the best among fifty papers, almost of dissertation quality." In his senior year of college, Cheney obtained an internship in the Wyoming state legislature, which required a 100-mile-a-day commute between the campus, in Laramie, and the state capitol, in Cheyenne.

The University of Wyoming awarded Cheney a B.A. degree in political science in 1965 and an M.A. degree in the same discipline a year later. Selected for an internship by the National Center for Education in Politics, Cheney then moved to Madison, Wisconsin, to work on the staff of Governor Warren Knowles. While he was living in Madison, Cheney also began work toward a Ph.D. degree at the University of Wisconsin, but in 1968 he left the program without completing his dissertation in order to accept an American Political Science Association congressional fellowship on the staff of Congressman William Steiger. Steiger, a Wisconsin Republican, later called Cheney "one of the brightest, most perceptive, most sensitive people I've ever had the chance to work with." In a conversation with Nicholas Lemann for the *New Yorker* (May 7, 2001), Cheney explained his decision to abandon academia for politics. His years as a graduate student at the University of Wisconsin coincided with widespread protests, on college campuses and elsewhere, over the Vietnam War; during this period, he was allowed to attend meetings of the university's senior faculty. Cheney told Lemann, "What happened in this meeting was a lot of complaints about the administration, the management of the university, oftentimes about the students. . . . There were days when the National Guard was out with its tear gas trying to control the protesters. [The faculty] were unhappy with what was happening, but in all the times I'd been in Wisconsin not one of these folks had ever stood up and been counted on either side of the debate. They were totally disengaged. . . . When I was given a choice between returning to academia or staying in the political arena, it really wasn't a close call."

In 1969 Steiger temporarily loaned Cheney to the staff of Donald Rumsfeld, a former congressman who had recently become the director of the Office of Economic Opportunity in the new administration of President Richard Nixon. Impressed by the young man, Rumsfeld appointed Cheney to the position of special assistant. When Rumsfeld became a White House counselor, in 1970, he asked his young protégé to become his deputy, and when he took on the additional job of director of the Cost of Living Council a year later, he named Cheney assistant director for operations. The two men parted company in February 1973, after Nixon appointed Rumsfeld ambassador to NATO (North Atlantic Treaty Organization), and Cheney chose not to accompany him to Brussels, Belgium, deciding instead to accept a vice presidency at Bradley, Woods and Co., a Washington-based investment firm that advised private industry on legislative issues. When Gerald Ford succeeded to the presidency following Nixon's resignation, in August 1974, he appointed Rumsfeld head of his transition team. Rumsfeld immediately recruited Cheney to serve as his deputy. A month later, Ford named Rumsfeld assistant to the president and Cheney deputy assistant.

In all but title, Rumsfeld was White House chief of staff, and Cheney was his alter ego. According to Paul Healy, writing for the New York *Daily News* (July 3, 1975), Rumsfeld and Cheney—who checked with one another continually throughout the day—were "as intuitive to one another as some identical twins." Often called upon to appease journalists and bureaucrats put off by Rumsfeld's abrasive manner, Cheney also regularly substituted for Rumsfeld at senior staff meetings and in briefings with the president. "Dick speaks for me—or the president . . . ," Rumsfeld told Healy in 1975. "Dick has natural good judgment and instincts. There's a nice tempo in his manner, he's very easy for people to get along with."

On November 5, 1975, after Rumsfeld had been named secretary of defense, Cheney became Ford's chief of staff. Determined to keep a low profile, Cheney refused Ford's offer to upgrade the chief-of-staff position to Cabinet status, and he continued to commute daily from his suburban home to the White House in a 10-year-old Volkswagen rather than in a chauffeured government car. Working an average of 15 hours a day, he supervised a White House staff of almost 500, arranged the president's schedule, approved appointments to top-level federal jobs, oversaw the flow of memos to and from the president, and frequently consulted with him.

After Gerald Ford lost the 1976 presidential election to Jimmy Carter, the Democratic candidate, Cheney returned to Casper, Wyoming, where he worked briefly in banking before deciding to seek election in 1978 as his sparsely populated state's sole member of the U.S. House of Representatives. During the Republican primary campaign, Cheney survived a mild heart attack and an attempt by one of his opponents, Ed Witzenburger, the popular state treasurer, to portray him as a carpetbagger; Cheney won his party's nomination by 7,705 votes. In the general election, Cheney easily defeated the Democratic nominee, Bill Bagley, winning 59 percent of the vote. He was subsequently returned to office by large margins in the elections of 1980, 1982, 1984, 1986, and 1988.

Cheney found serving in the House more to his liking than working on the president's staff. "The White House staff jobs give you a broader opportunity to influence a variety of events, but you're ultimately a hired gun," he told Martin Tolchin for the *New York Times* (April 6, 1982). "When you serve in the House, you may cast only one of 435 votes, but it's your decision to make." Early in his second term, Cheney scored a stunning victory over Congresswoman Marjorie S. Holt of Maryland, a five-term veteran, to become head of the Republican Policy Committee, the fourth-highest GOP post in the House.

With a few exceptions, Cheney strongly supported the domestic and foreign-policy programs of President Ronald Reagan in the 1980s, consistently receiving high approval ratings from such conservative organizations as the American Conservative Union and Americans for Constitutional Action. He was an especially staunch advocate of Reagan administration efforts to strengthen defense capabilities. Although he favored the Soviet-American treaty banning medium-range nuclear missiles, he approved funding for the development of the multibillion-dollar Strategic Defense Initiative, popularly known as "Star Wars," the deployment of the MX missile, and the production of new chemical weapons. A supporter of continued military aid to the Nicaraguan Contras and to the insurgents in Angola, he voted against a proposal—made in the wake of the Iran-Contra scandal—for requiring the president to notify Congress within 48 hours of the start of any secret intelligence operation. The "nay" vote was consistent with Cheney's belief that the president's ability to implement foreign policy had been hampered by repeated congressional attempts to impose restrictions on the White House.

Cheney's record on domestic issues was equally conservative. In 1986, for example, he sided with the House's so-called conservative coalition of Republicans and southern Democrats on every one of the 50 votes on which the two groups joined forces. Among other things, he opposed the Equal Rights Amendment, the practice of busing to achieve racial desegregation in public schools, and abortion rights, and supported prayer in the public schools and a constitutional amendment requiring a balanced federal budget. Cheney's only major difference with President Reagan on domestic policy was his opposition to the administration's effort to cut corporate and capital-gains taxes.

With regard to issues of immediate relevance to his constituents, Cheney, as a member of the House Committee on Interior and Insular Affairs, resisted efforts by fellow committee members to raise the fees charged to ranchers for the right to graze livestock on public lands. In the debate over the development of wilderness areas, he took a middle course. Initially supportive of Interior Secretary James Watt's efforts to open up such areas to oil and gas leasing, he changed his position in 1982, after learning about several pending leases for land in northwestern Wyoming, near Yellowstone National Park. Cheney subsequently introduced legislation that banned oil and gas leasing in Wyoming wilderness areas and added more than 650,000 wilderness acres to the state.

On June 4, 1987 Cheney became chairman of the Republican Conference, the third-highest post in the House Republican hierarchy. A month earlier he had been named vice chairman of the House committee investigating the Iran-Contra scandal. On August 4, following three months of hearings, Cheney delivered his closing statement. Although he conceded that the Reagan administration had made mistakes, he contended that there were "some mitigating factors . . . which, while they don't justify administration mistakes, go a long way to helping explain and make them understandable." Based on his examination of the facts, Cheney concluded: "There is no evidence that the president had any knowledge of the diversion of profits from the [sale of arms to Iran] to the Nicaraguan democratic resistance. . . . There is also no evidence of any effort by the president or his senior advisers to cover up these events." With his election, on December 5, 1988, as party whip, Cheney advanced to the number-two Republican position in the House.

On March 9, 1989 the Senate, in a vote of 53 to 47, rejected President George H. W. Bush's first choice for secretary of defense, former Texas senator John G. Tower. The following day Bush nominated Cheney, a man with no previous defense-related experience, to head the department. Questioned by reporters about his health, Cheney, who had now suffered three mild heart attacks and undergone a quadruple coronary bypass in August 1988, said that his cardiologist had assured him that there was no medical reason why he could not fulfill the duties of the office. The nominee deftly deflected queries about his lack of direct experience in defense matters, pointing out that, as President Ford's chief of staff, he had attended all meetings of the National Security Council and that he was currently the senior Republican on the Budget Subcommittee of the House Intelligence Committee. Hailed by congressional leaders from both parties, Cheney sailed through his confirmation hearing, and, on March 17, 1989, he was unanimously approved by the Senate. He entered the office of defense secretary four days later.

Only a few weeks after assuming office, Cheney was faced with the unpleasant task of trimming $10 billion from the defense budget for fiscal year 1990—a chore necessitated by Bush's decision to reject the defense budget he had inherited from Ronald Reagan, which called for annual defense increases of 2 percent above inflation for the next five years. To meet the Bush target of zero percent real growth for 1990, in April 1989 Cheney outlined for the House Armed Services Committee the "very, very painful" cuts that he said represented "a fundamental shift in direction." His most controversial proposal was to halt the planned production, at a projected cost of $22.6 billion, of the Marine Corps's new V22 Osprey aircraft, a combination helicopter and plane.

While budget constraints and the resulting cutbacks in military spending required much of Cheney's attention, his tenure as secretary of defense was ultimately defined by a series of international crises. In November 1989 President Corazon Aquino of the Philippines, faced with the threat of a coup by her country's military, turned to the U.S. for assistance. President Bush and Cheney together approved the use of U.S. jets stationed at Clark Air Base on the Philippine island of Luzon; the jets performed warning flyovers near rebel bases and were authorized to fire upon planes attempting to take off. The coup did not materialize. Meanwhile, in Panama, General Manuel Noriega ousted the democratically elected Guillermo Endara from the Panamanian presidency. (A U.S. grand jury had entered an indictment against Noriega in February 1988 for drug trafficking.) Events came to a head with the December 1989 shooting death of a U.S. serviceman stationed in Panama at the hands of Noriega's defense forces. In the same month the U.S. Department of Defense, led by Cheney, sent 12,000 troops to join the 12,000 already stationed in Panama, where within a few days the U.S. had driven Noriega from power and officially recognized Endara's presidency. (Noriega was later imprisoned on racketeering and drug-trafficking charges.)

The biggest challenge Cheney faced as defense secretary was the Persian Gulf War. On August 1, 1990 President Saddam Hussein of Iraq sent invading forces into Kuwait, a small but oil-rich country bordering Iraq to the south. Having seized control of Kuwait City, Hussein placed his 140,000-strong army along the Saudi Arabia–Kuwait border, signaling further aggression. Cheney publicly characterized Iraq's actions as threatening to U.S. interests in the region, and President Bush sent his secretary of defense to Saudi Arabia to ask King Fahd for permission to bring U.S. troops into that country. In a television interview on PBS's *Frontline* (on-line), Cheney later described his meetings with King Fahd. "From a military standpoint," he explained, "if we could not get into Saudi Arabia it was going to be very hard for us to do anything. . . . I told King Fahd that the Iraqis were amassed on his border and we briefed him on the intelligence in terms of the size of the force that the Iraqis had already used in Kuwait. Pointed out that it was very hard for us to be able to help [the Saudis] unless we could get plenty of advance time [because] it takes a long time to move heavy forces half way around the world and that timing was of the essence. That they did not have the luxury of waiting until Saddam began an invasion of Saudi Arabia and then ask for help because then it would be too late." The U.S. request was granted. In November the United Nations passed Resolution 678, demanding that Iraq withdraw its forces from Kuwait by January 15, 1991 or face military assault by the U.S. and its allies. Saddam Hussein refused to comply, and on January 17 the first phase of Operation Desert Storm began. The U.S. and its allies carried out an intensive air campaign against Iraq for five weeks before sending in ground troops on the morning of February 24 to drive Iraqi forces out of Kuwait—a mission accomplished in four days. President Bush, after consulting with Cheney and other members of his national-security team, declared a suspension of hostilities effective on midnight of February 27. A formal truce was then signed with Iraq on March 3, followed by a permanent ceasefire on April 6.

While then–Joint Chiefs of Staff chairman Colin L. Powell and General H. Norman Schwarzkopf, the leader of the Allied troops, were considered essential to the success of the campaign, many experts gave most of the credit to Cheney, who had been instrumental in the development of battle plans and their application. William J. Crowe, who served as chairman of the Joint Chiefs from 1985 to 1989, was quoted by James Rosen for *Talk* (May 2001) as proclaiming, "[The coalition] won the war, and from a political standpoint that's the bottom line. . . . [Cheney] can take full credit for that." On July 3, 1991 President Bush awarded Cheney the Presidential Medal of Freedom, the highest honor bestowed upon a U.S. civilian, for his leadership in the Gulf War.

After Bush was defeated in his 1992 reelection bid by Bill Clinton, Cheney entered the private sector, accepting a position as a senior fellow at the American Enterprise Institute, a conservative think tank in Washington, D.C. In addition, he joined the boards of directors of several companies, including the telecommunications firm U.S. West Inc. and the railroad conglomerate Union Pacific Corp. During the next two years, as the 1996 presidential election drew nearer, Cheney was mentioned in the press as a possible Republican Party nominee. Indeed, Cheney seemed poised to seek his party's nomination, as he set up a political-action committee, raised money, made speeches for various Republican politicians, and visited 47 states over the course of about a year and a half. In January 1995, however, he officially pulled out of the running. Political pundits offered numerous explanations for his decision, including concern over the public perception of Cheney's younger daughter, Mary, who was thought to be a lesbian. (As he has ever since, Cheney refused to discuss his daughter's sexual orientation.) Others mentioned his inability to raise enough money, coming from a state as small as Wyoming, as well as his lack of charisma on the campaign trail.

Cheney next accepted the post of chairman and chief executive officer of the Dallas, Texas–based Halliburton Corp., one of the world's leading engineering and construction firms, operating primarily in the oil industry. While his decision to take the job removed him to a great extent from the public spotlight, it also, over the course of the next five years, proved highly profitable, for both him and the company. Several key acquisitions during Cheney's reign at Halliburton—most notably the 1998, $8 billion purchase of its longtime rival Dresser Industries Inc., for which George H. W. Bush had once worked—catapulted the company from its marginal status in the business world to its position as the world's largest provider of oil-drilling, engineering, and construction services. In 1999, Cheney's last full year on the job, Halliburton's revenues reached a reported $14.9 billion.

The first months of 2000 saw much speculation over possible running mates for the presumed Republican presidential nominee, George W. Bush; the list included then–Pennsylvania governor Tom Ridge, New York governor George Pataki, and U.S. senators Fred Thompson of Tennessee, John C. Danforth of Missouri, and John S. McCain of Arizona. Cheney was hired by the Bush campaign to help manage the selection process. Because of his longstanding connection to the White House, however, as well as his alliance with the Bush family, Cheney himself emerged as the Republican hopeful's natural choice. In addition, it was thought that Cheney's wealth of foreign-policy expertise would reassure voters who were worried about Bush's lack of experience in that area. On July 25, 2000 Cheney retired from Halliburton after Bush officially named the former defense secretary as his vice-presidential running mate. At his retirement from Halliburton, Cheney's net worth was estimated at $40 million.

The choice of Cheney drew criticism from some corners. His reported $20 million retirement package from Halliburton led to doubts over his ability to remain unbiased toward the energy industry. His capacity to inspire voters was also questioned. Matt Bai wrote for *Newsweek* (October 2, 2000), "Cheney has an obvious decency about him but can be strangely impersonal." In his own defense, Cheney explained to Bai, "I have never been somebody who demonstrated a lot of emotion. It's just not who I am. But I still think there's room in the arena for somebody who's interested in substantive issues—a calm presentation, if you will, of the arguments. I think a lot of people appreciate that." Throughout the campaign Cheney steered clear of the spotlight as much as possible, which many Republicans viewed positively. Virginia governor James S. Gilmore III told Sean Scully for the *Washington Times* (August 1, 2000, on-line), "There's no aloofness or shyness about [Cheney]. I think at this point he doesn't need to get out and speak at length—his record speaks for itself. He continues to be in a supporting role to the candidate. The candidate is George W. Bush." Indeed, as pointed out by Bill Turque and Mark Hosenball in *Newsweek* (August 7, 2000), "Indiscretion and self-promotion are high crimes in Cheney's world." Perhaps the biggest concern over a prospective Cheney vice presidency was his health. Indeed, in late 2000, after the uncertain results of the presidential election led to vote recounts in Florida and elsewhere, Cheney was hospitalized with a fourth, mild heart attack. Doctors described his chronic heart condition as coronary artery disease. Asked by Bernard Shaw for *CNN* (November 29, 2000, on-line) if he worried about his condition, Cheney replied, "I've lived with this, Bernie, for over 20 years, since I was 37 years old. I've had, I think, a fairly successful career in government and in the private sector after the onset of coronary artery disease. I learned to live with it a long time ago." When Shaw asked if he feared another heart attack, Cheney responded, "I don't operate that way."

When election results were finalized in December 2000, after a lengthy court battle between the Bush campaign and that of the Democratic nominee, Vice President Al Gore, Bush emerged victorious. He and Cheney took the oath of office on January 20, 2001. On March 5 Cheney was again hospitalized. Doctors later reported that the 60-year-old vice president was suffering from a partially blocked artery, but assured the public that coronary artery disease, which affects more than five million Americans each year, was not life-threatening if one maintained a strict diet and exercise regimen. In addition to making lifestyle changes, Cheney had a pacemaker installed to regulate his heart rhythms, which were found to be abnormally fast at times.

Health issues aside, Cheney has often been described as the most powerful U.S. vice president ever. Nicholas Lemann noted in the *New Yorker* article, "It used to be that the sine qua non of Vice-Presidential power was a weekly private lunch with the President. Cheney has that, but for him it's almost an afterthought. He meets with the President early every morning and then several more times during a typical day. . . . If there is a meeting on any sensitive international matter in the Situation Room, Cheney attends." Lemann reported that Cheney also has regular meetings with Secretary of State Colin L. Powell, Secretary of Defense Donald Rumsfeld, and Condoleezza Rice, the national security adviser, among other top officials in the Bush administration.

The perception of Cheney as wielding influence unprecedented for a vice president was reinforced on September 11, 2001, when the nation suffered its worst attack ever at the hands of terrorists. When two hijacked airplanes crashed into the World Trade Center towers, in New York City, and a third struck the Pentagon, outside Washington, D.C., Cheney stood firmly at the nation's helm. President Bush, who had been visiting a school in Florida, was immediately taken to secure locations, first in Louisiana, then in Nebraska, leaving Cheney in charge at the White House to direct the government's initial response. On the vice president's orders, the U.S. Capitol was evacuated and congressional leaders were taken elsewhere in helicopters. Cheney kept in constant contact with the president as well as members of the House and Senate. He later said, as reported by Mike Allen for the *Washington Post* (September 17, 2001), that during the first hours of the crisis, his role and the president's "were sort of reversed." The article also quoted an unnamed congressional aide as having said, "[White House officials are] constantly having to show examples of Bush's gravitas—that he can handle it and that he's in charge. The fact that Dick Cheney is there reassures people."

In 2002 Cheney played a central role in garnering popular support for a military attack against Iraq and President Saddam Hussein. As an outgrowth of its post-September 11 security policy, the Bush administration vowed to take preemptive military action against any country or regime that threatened the safety and well-being of the United States. In his January 2002 State of the Union address, President Bush categorized Iraq, Iran, and North Korea as an "axis of evil" that posed such a threat; in particular, he accused Hussein of developing weapons of mass destruction, and it soon became clear that the administration was considering launching a military campaign to oust Hussein from power. Cheney strongly supported his removal, arguing that Iraq's disarmament was impossible as long as Hussein remained in power. In the spring Cheney traveled to England and the Middle East on what many analysts viewed as a mission to rally support for military action against Iraq. Although he failed to win Arab backing, he persuaded Egypt to pressure Iraq to allow U.N. weapons inspectors to return. On August 26, 2002, as the debate over Iraq intensified and both Democrats and Republicans urged Bush to proceed with caution, Cheney issued the most forceful and unequivocal rationale to date for an attack against Hussein. In a speech to a gathering of Veterans of Foreign Wars in Nashville, Tennessee, he warned, as reported in the *New York Times* (August 27, 2002), that Iraq would soon have nuclear weapons and that Hussein would "seek domination of the entire Middle East, take control of a great portion of the world's energy supplies, directly threaten America's friends throughout the region and subject the United States or any other nation to nuclear blackmail."

On other fronts, over the past year Cheney has been dogged by allegations that Halliburton Corp. carried out fraudulent accounting practices while he was chairman and CEO. In May 2002 the Securities and Exchange Commission began to investigate Halliburton's accounting methods, which were adopted in 1998. Two months later the private, nonprofit organization Judicial Watch, whose aim is to decrease corruption and strengthen ethics in government, filed a lawsuit against Cheney and Halliburton, claiming the two had deceived investors by engaging in practices that led to the overvaluation of the company's shares. Both Cheney and Halliburton have denied any wrongdoing. In addition, early in 2002 Congress began to investigate how the collapsed energy firm Enron, which lied about its profits and tried to conceal debts, might have influenced the Bush administration's energy policy; Enron executives had met with Cheney and his energy task force several times to discuss the energy plan that the White House announced later. After the vice president refused to relinquish to congressional committees documents detailing the talks he had held with Enron representatives, Congress tried legal means to force Cheney and other White House officials to turn over the documents. As of mid-November 2002, all congressional attempts to get hold of those records had proved fruitless.

Cheney and his wife, the former Lynne Anne Vincent, have been married since August 29, 1964. They have two daughters, Elizabeth and Mary, and three granddaughters. Lynne Cheney formerly taught English at George Washington University and served as chairwoman of the National Endowment for the Humanities from 1986 to 1993. Since then she has worked as a senior fellow at the American Enterprise Institute. She has written several books of fiction and nonfiction and a best-selling children's alphabet book. She and the vice president are the authors of *Kings of the Hill* (1983), an account of eight Speakers of the House of Representatives and their impact on American history. Dick Cheney's religious affiliation is Methodist. —J.H.

Suggested Reading: *American Spectator* p24+ July/Aug. 2001, with photo; *CNN* (on-line) Nov. 29, 2000; *Forbes* p162+ Jan. 11, 1999, with photos; *Frontline* (on-line); (New York) *Daily News* p64 July 3, 1975, with photo; *New York Times* A p20 Nov. 5, 1975, with photo, A p10 Mar. 11, 1989, A p34 Mar. 12, 1989, with photo, p2 Sep. 17, 2001, with photo, p1+ May 13, 2001; *New Yorker* p56+ May 7, 2001, with photos; *Newsweek* p28+ Aug. 7, 2000, p28 Oct. 2, 2000; *Wall Street Journal* B p4 July 26, 2000; *Washington Post* A p3 Nov. 6, 1975, with photo, G p1+ Apr. 4, 1976, with photos, A p9 Mar. 11, 1989, with photo, A p13 Sep. 17, 2001; *Washington Times* (on-line) Aug. 1, 2000

Selected Books: *Kings of the Hill* (with Lynne V. Cheney), 1983

John Spellman/Retna

## Clinton, Hillary Rodham

*Oct. 26, 1947– Democratic U.S. senator from New York*

*Address: 476 Russell Senate Office Bldg., Washington, DC 20510*

Over the course of her eight years as First Lady of the United States, Hillary Rodham Clinton aroused more controversy than any of her predecessors. While her detractors argued that the First Lady had no business in politics, the former lawyer was appointed by her husband, President Bill Clinton, to oversee a radical reform of the health-care system in the United States. Though she was ultimately unsuccessful in that goal, Hillary Clinton continued to an unprecedented degree to offer her opinions publicly and lobby for legislation in various areas on the part of the administration. The First Lady also found herself the object of a great deal of unwanted attention, in the form of the Whitewater investigation, which focused on her and her husband's past business dealings—and which cast a shadow over much of Bill Clinton's presidency. Although her honesty and legal ethics were put in question by the lengthy probe, Hillary Clinton preserved her public image sufficiently to win election in 2000 as United States senator from New York. Sworn in on January 3, 2001, and thus becoming the only First Lady in U.S. history to hold elective office, she surprised many by not immediately taking on issues of national significance. Instead, she concentrated initially on areas of direct concern to her adopted state. Still, by the end of 2001, she had begun to make bold statements on such subjects as health care, education, and energy, which are of concern to most Americans.

Clinton was born Hillary Diane Rodham on October 26, 1947 in Chicago, Illinois, the oldest child and only daughter of Hugh E. Rodham, who owned a drapery-making business, and Dorothy Howell Rodham, a full-time homemaker. Hillary and her brothers, Hugh and Tony, grew up in Park Ridge, Illinois, a middle-class suburb of Chicago to which the Rodhams moved when Hillary was four years old. As the new kid on the block, Hillary was often attacked by a girl named Suzy, the neighborhood bully. After running home in tears one time too often for her mother to countenance, Hillary was told to fight back the next time she was hit. She did, and from then on her natural leadership abilities attracted lots of friends—both boys and girls—at Eugene Field Elementary School, Emerson Junior High, Maine East High School, and the newly built Maine South High School, to which she was transferred in her senior year as a result of redistricting.

An outstanding student, Clinton excelled in nearly every endeavor she undertook. She maintained good grades, earned Girl Scout merit badges and DAR (Daughters of the American Revolution) community-service awards, played the piano, took ballet lessons, and engaged in competitive sports. A highly skilled member of the debating team and a participant in the student government in high school, she was a National Merit Scholarship finalist and a member of the National Honor Society. During the summers she worked as a lifeguard at a municipal swimming pool. Even as a teenager, she displayed a predilection for social activism. Spurred by the Reverend Don Jones, her youth minister at the First United Methodist Church, she organized baby-sitting services for local migrant workers. Taking his white, middle-class charges into Chicago's inner-city neighborhoods, Jones introduced them to black and Hispanic youths in an effort to eradicate prejudice among his pupils. On one occasion, the two groups of young people discussed the relevance of Picasso's painting *Guernica* to their own lives; on another day, in 1962, Jones took the teenagers to listen to a speech by the civil rights leader Martin Luther King Jr., to whom Jones introduced the group backstage. Sensing Clinton's insatiable intellectual curiosity, Jones lent her books by the theologians Dietrich Bonhoeffer, Reinhold Niebuhr, and Paul Tillich as well as J. D. Salinger's novel *The Catcher in the Rye*.

Despite her association with children from less-privileged backgrounds and her exposure to a variety of philosophies, Clinton remained, like her parents, staunchly Republican, supporting Barry Goldwater in the presidential campaign of 1964. After graduating in 1965 from Maine South High School in the top 5 percent of her class, which voted her the student most likely to succeed, Clinton enrolled at the all-female Wellesley College, near Boston, Massachusetts, where she promptly became head of the local chapter of the Young Republicans. It was not long, however, before the turbulence of the late 1960s reinforced the teachings of her youth minister and led her slowly leftward in her politics. The assassinations of Malcolm X in 1965 and of Martin Luther King Jr. and Robert F. Kennedy in 1968, coupled with the violence she witnessed at the Democratic National Convention in Chicago in the summer of 1968, dovetailed with her keen sense of social justice to convert her wholeheartedly to the Democratic Party. She campaigned for Eugene McCarthy for president in 1968, worked to enroll more black students at Wellesley, organized the school's first teach-ins on the Vietnam War (which turned into antiwar protests), and wrote her senior thesis on poverty and community development.

In 1969 Clinton graduated from Wellesley with a bachelor's degree in political science. As president of the student government, she was selected by her classmates to deliver the school's first student commencement address, immediately following a speech by Senator Edward W. Brooke, a liberal Republican from Massachusetts. After shocking her audience by castigating Brooke for the irrelevance of his remarks, she spoke about the attitudes and future of her graduating class. "We are, all of us, exploring a world that none of us understands and attempting to create within that uncertainty," she told her fellow graduating seniors. "But there are some things we feel, feelings that our prevailing, acquisitive, and competitive corporate life, including, tragically, the universities, is not the way of life for us. We're searching for more immediate, ecstatic, and penetrating modes of living." Clinton's words and her photograph were published in *Life* magazine. The national publicity she received through the article and through her victories as a contestant on the television quiz show *College Bowl* enhanced her already impressive résumé and helped to ensure that she would have her pick of the best law schools.

Clinton enrolled at Yale Law School, in New Haven, Connecticut, after a Harvard University professor told her that his school did not need any more female students. At Yale she served on the editorial board of the now-defunct *Yale Review of Law and Social Action* and presided over a mass meeting that was called in the spring of 1970 to formulate a response to the trials of the Black Panthers Ericka Huggins and Bobby Seale, which were then underway at a courthouse near the university. Recalling the campus atmosphere at the time in a speech to other Yale alumni in October 1992, she said, "There was a great amount of ferment and confusion about what was and wasn't the proper role of law school education. We would have great arguments about whether we were selling out because we were getting a law degree, whether in fact we should be doing something else, not often defined clearly but certainly passionately argued. That we should somehow be 'out there,' wherever 'there' was, trying to help solve the problems that took up so much of our time in argument and discussion."

The answer to Clinton's question—how to combine social activism and a legal career—presented itself in the figure of the civil rights lawyer and Yale alumna Marian Wright Edelman, the first black woman to pass the bar exam in Mississippi. After Edelman gave a speech at Yale in the spring of 1970 about her work in behalf of the poor and children's rights, Clinton volunteered to work for Edelman's Washington Research Project, the congressional lobbying and advocacy group that later became the Children's Defense Fund. Edelman could not afford to pay her for her services, so Clinton applied for a Law Student Civil Rights Research Council grant, obtained a stipend, and spent the summer of 1970 in Washington, D.C., interviewing the families of migrant laborers and reporting her findings to a Senate subcommittee headed by Walter F. Mondale of Minnesota. Back at Yale, she augmented her knowledge of the nascent children's rights field with classes on child psychology and family law. Scheduled to graduate in 1972, she prolonged her education for a year in order to work at Yale's Child Study Center, where she helped research a book by Anna Freud, Joseph Goldstein, and Albert Solnit entitled *Beyond the Best Interests of the Child* (1973). During her final year at Yale, Clinton also performed legal research for the Carnegie Council on Children, specializing in the rights of children to education and medical care.

Meanwhile, in her second year at Yale, Hillary Clinton had met her future husband, Bill Clinton, at the law library. According to the often-repeated story of their first meeting, the two stared at each other from opposite ends of a long corridor in the library until Hillary approached Bill and said, "Look, if you're going to keep staring at me, and I'm going to keep staring back, I think we should at least know each other. I'm Hillary Rodham. What's your name?" From then on, Hillary and Bill were inseparable. Well matched temperamentally as well as intellectually, they were equally dedicated to public service. Having spent the previous year in Oxford, England, on a Rhodes scholarship, Bill Clinton was then in his first year of law school. The couple spent the summer of 1972 in San Antonio, Texas, where Bill had run George S. McGovern's presidential campaign and Hillary had registered Hispanic voters. They graduated, in the same class, in 1973.

For several months after her graduation, Hillary worked as a staff attorney for the Children's Defense Fund in Cambridge, Massachusetts, while Bill taught at the University of Arkansas School of Law in Fayetteville. They kept in touch by telephone and occasional visits. In January 1974 Hillary Clinton moved to Washington, D.C., at the behest of John Doar, the special counsel to the House Judiciary Committee, who was in charge of the committee's inquiry into the possible impeachment of President Richard Nixon. One of only three women on the staff of 43 lawyers, Clinton was put in charge of legal procedures. She impressed her peers with her objectivity and her ability to distinguish advocacy from judicial guidance. Her colleagues found her to be energetic, emotionally supportive, and cooperative. When the impeachment staff was disbanded following Nixon's resignation, on August 8, 1974, Clinton was deluged with offers of high-paying jobs at prestigious law firms on the East Coast and also received an invitation to return to her post at the Children's Defense Fund. To the dismay of her friends and family, she instead joined Bill Clinton on the faculty of the University of Arkansas School of Law in Fayetteville in September 1974.

In the summer of 1974, Bill Clinton had launched a bid for a seat in the U.S. House of Representatives from Arkansas's Third Congressional District, a Republican stronghold. After demonstrating her remarkable organizing skills, Hillary became his unofficial campaign manager. Although Bill Clinton lost the election to the Republican incumbent, John Paul Hammerschmidt, by four percentage points, he came closer to defeating Hammerschmidt than any Democrat before or since. Over the course of the campaign, Hillary had made extensive contacts throughout the state; during this period she also discovered that she enjoyed teaching criminal law, running a legal-services clinic, and doing prison projects and advocacy work in Fayetteville, a quiet college town in the Ozark Mountains. Visits to friends and family in Illinois and to the East Coast in the summer of 1975 confirmed for Hillary that she was not missing anything by remaining in Arkansas. Upon her return to Fayetteville in August, Bill surprised her with a house and a proposal of marriage. When they were wed, on October 11, 1975, Hillary retained her maiden name, a decision that would surface as a controversial issue in her husband's subsequent political campaigns.

After Bill Clinton was elected state attorney general, in 1976, he and Hillary moved to Little Rock, where she taught law as an adjunct professor at the University of Arkansas and directed the school's legal-aid clinic. Earlier that year she had impressed Jimmy Carter with her work on his presidential campaign, which Bill had directed in Arkansas. In 1977 President Carter appointed her to the board of directors of the Legal Services Corp., a Washington-based organization that provides federal funds to legal-aid bureaus throughout the United States. In the same year she founded and presided over the Arkansas Advocates for Children and Families, a nonprofit legal advocacy group whose mandate was to identify the problems facing low-income children, and she was among the first female associates hired by Rose Law Firm, where her salary enabled her and Bill to buy a house in the upper-middle-class suburb of Hillcrest.

In 1978 Hillary campaigned for Bill in his first run for governor, in which he defeated his Republican opponent, A. Lynn Lowe, by a margin of almost two to one. Hillary, who had recently been named to the board of directors of the Children's Defense Fund, continued to work at Rose Law Firm after the election, giving Arkansas something it had never had: a working First Lady. After moving into the governor's mansion, Bill appointed Hillary chairperson of the Rural Health Advisory Committee, whose members tackled the problems involved with providing health care in isolated areas. Neither Hillary's retention of her last name nor her assumption of official duties engendered much controversy at that time. In early 1980 she was made a partner at Rose Law Firm and gave birth to Chelsea Victoria Clinton, who was named for Joni Mitchell's song "Chelsea Morning."

In announcing the birth of a daughter to Bill Clinton and Hillary Rodham, the governor offended some of his more traditional constituents, who began to carp that something must be wrong with his marriage if his wife would not take his name. Compounding his problems in 1980 (the year Ronald Reagan would sweep Republicans into office in a nationwide landslide) was President Carter's decision to intern 18,000 Cuban refugees at Fort Chaffee, Arkansas. After some of them rioted that summer, Bill Clinton's Republican opponent, Frank White, played on racist sentiments in his campaign and unseated Clinton, who fell into a period of despair. He traveled the state apologizing for his mistakes—among them, raising the tax on gasoline and hiking automobile licensing fees in order to finance a highway improvement program—and asking voters to forgive him. They did so, by returning him to office in 1982. After Hillary took her husband's last name, Arkansans also forgave Hillary for her "brash" independence. She changed in other ways, too: as part of a comprehensive image makeover, she traded in her thick glasses for contact lenses, lightened and tamed her hair, lost 15 pounds, and dressed more fashionably.

Over the following decade Hillary Clinton honed her campaigning skills as her husband was reelected governor in 1984, 1986, 1988, and 1990. She learned many valuable lessons—in dealing with the press, gaining popularity, and fending off attacks on her husband's character and the quality of their marriage—that would serve her well in 1992. In the meantime, she pursued a fulfilling career with the imprimatur of voters, legislators, and Governor Clinton himself, who, early in his career, signaled the depth of his confidence in her abilities by appointing her to top-priority posts. In 1983, as head of the Arkansas Education Standards Committee, Hillary Clinton set out to improve the quality of public education, in which Arkansas ranked 49th in the nation in per-pupil expenditures. Her most controversial recommendation was the establishment of teacher competency testing. She ultimately prevailed, and the state passed a law, instituted in 1985, allowing the dismissal of teachers who failed to demonstrate adequate reading, writing, and math skills. For her educational reforms, Hillary Clinton received the Arkansas Press Association's first headliner-of-the-year award, in 1984.

Throughout her years in the governor's mansion, Hillary Clinton exerted considerable influence through positions of public service. She provided disadvantaged families with access to an already existing program called HIPPY, which stood for Home Instruction Program for Preschool Youngsters; served on the board of directors of the Arkansas Children's Hospital; worked for the Southern Governors' Association Task Force on Infant Mortality; organized the state's first neonatal care unit and a helicopter service, called Angel One, that would bring emergency care to people living in outlying rural areas; and served on the American Bar Association's Commission on Women in the Profession. She served on the boards of directors of the retail giant Wal-Mart, TCBY (a yogurt company), and LaFarge, resigning from them all in May 1992. In 1988 and 1991 she was listed among the most influential lawyers in the United States by the *National Law Journal*, and in 1989 she was ranked among the best business-litigation attorneys in Arkansas.

Bill Clinton had been expected to run for president of the United States long before he actually threw his hat into the ring in 1991. He surprised many by taking the lead in some early polls, only to be hit with a barrage of unfavorable publicity stemming from the allegation by Gennifer Flowers, a former lounge singer, that she and Clinton had engaged in a 12-year-long affair. Unspecific reports of the governor's rumored infidelities had been published for years in the Arkansas press, and people in the Clinton camp feared that Flowers's charges might fatally derail his presidential campaign. Hillary Clinton, however, insisted on meeting the issue head-on. At her urging, the Clintons were interviewed by the CBS News correspondent Steve Kroft on the television news magazine *60 Minutes* on Super Bowl Sunday in January 1992. That extraordinary event constituted most Americans' introduction to Hillary Clinton. Grilled about whether he had betrayed his wife, Bill admitted that he had "caused pain" in their marriage but refused to be more specific. Hillary put an end to that line of questioning when she said that the public should respect the "zone of privacy" that surrounds the way any two people deal with their marital problems. "We've gone further [in discussing an issue of this nature] than anybody we know of, and that's all we're going to say," she declared. When it was reported that Flowers had been paid for her story, the Clintons went on the offensive, transforming the issue from a near-certain liability into an attack on the failure of the press to enforce the standards of responsible journalism.

Subjected to more intense scrutiny than any previous presidential candidate's wife, Hillary Clinton learned the danger of providing the media with sound bites that could easily be taken out of context. When Jerry Brown, who was seeking the Democratic nomination, attacked her professional record, she said, "Well, I suppose I could have stayed home and baked cookies and had teas, but what I decided to do was pursue my profession, which I entered before my husband was in public life." Although she went on to praise all the choices available to women, including staying home, the quote was widely interpreted as an indication of arrogance. Not long afterward, Clinton made another gaffe while talking to Gail Sheehy, who profiled her for *Vanity Fair* (May 1992): she complained that the public and the press were following a double standard in not investigating the alleged infidelities of President George Herbert Walker Bush, who would be Clinton's Republican opponent in the 1992 presidential election. In both instances, Hillary rescued her image—and the candidacy of her husband—by apologizing for her mistakes, which had made headlines that referred to the "Hillary Problem" and the "Hillary Factor." On Election Day 1992 Bill Clinton won the presidency, defeating both Bush and the independent multimillionaire Ross Perot.

Most of the negative publicity that Hillary Clinton attracted derived from anxiety about how much power she would wield if her husband were elected president of the United States, and how she would transform the role of First Lady. Early in the campaign, Bill Clinton had boasted that he and his wife represented a "buy one, get one free" package deal. Shortly after he became president, he named her to the unofficial post of leader of his Task Force on National Health Care Reform, whose 34 working groups and 500 employees worked in secrecy from January 25 to May 30, 1993 to come up with a viable way to tame the costs of the nation's $800 billion health-care industry while expanding services and coverage. After Bill Clinton unveiled his health-care package in a well-received speech to Congress, on September 22, 1993, Hillary Clinton, in an unprecedented demonstration of political clout for a First Lady, drummed up support for the legislation in testimony before two House committees. In defending the president's health plan, which he made the cornerstone of his domestic policy, she thoroughly impressed members of both parties with her command of detail, her poise, and, by combining flattery with persuasion at every turn, her public-relations expertise. The Clintons' bold reform plan, which was debated for months after its unveiling, would have provided health insurance to all Americans, including the 37 million who were uninsured and the 22 million who were considered to be "underinsured" at that time. The Clintons argued that by cutting wasteful spending through government regulation, raising taxes on alcohol and tobacco, and injecting "managed competition" into the health-insurance market, their plan to overhaul the nation's health-care system, which represented 14 percent of the United States economy, was superior to alternative proposals. However, the plan attracted strong criticism from several sides, including those who resented the fact that Hillary Clinton, who did not hold public office, was placed in charge of putting forth the package. It also worried many Americans when President

Clinton's secretary of health and human services, Donna E. Shalala, testified before the Senate Finance Committee that 40 percent of then-insured Americans would be charged more for their insurance under the plan. Furthermore, small-business organizations objected to the fact that the new legislation would require all employers to pay 80 percent of their employees' health-care premiums. Support for the plan petered out, and many Democrats blamed its lack of success on the methodology the Clintons had used in presenting and advocating the bill. Hillary Clinton eventually placed most of the blame on herself. "I think I was naive and dumb, because my view was results speak for themselves," she told Marian Burros of the *New York Times* Service, as quoted by the Toronto *Globe and Mail* (January 11, 1995). "I regret very much that the efforts on health care were badly misunderstood, taken out of context and used politically against the administration. I take responsibility for that, and I'm sorry for that."

Following the defeat of the Clintons' health-care reform package, Hillary Clinton attempted to withdraw to a degree from media scrutiny. She soon became embroiled, however, in several investigations that would plague the Clintons for the rest of Bill Clinton's tenure in office. The first, comparatively minor scandal was the so-called Travelgate affair, in which seven White House Travel Office employees were fired in May 1993 on the grounds that they had financially mismanaged the office for years. The validity of that charge was later challenged by reports in the media, which speculated that Hillary Clinton had pressured White House lawyers into firing the staff and then had the FBI investigate them so that Clinton associates could take over the positions. In a written response submitted to Congress in March 1996, Hillary Clinton stated, as quoted by a reporter for *ABC News.com* (June 22, 2000), that she "had no personal knowledge of, or direct involvement with that office," and had only "expressed my concern that if there were real problems in the travel office they should be addressed promptly." In June 2000 Independent Counsel Robert Ray cleared the Clintons of any wrongdoing regarding the incident. Ray noted, however, that while there was no evidence that Hillary Clinton had done anything illegal, it seemed clear that she had played a role in the firings and that she had given testimony that was inaccurate.

Of much greater consequence was the complex and far-reaching legal case known as Whitewater, so-called because it centered on the commodity and real-estate investments the Clintons had made in the 1970s and 1980s that were related to the Whitewater Development Corp., which the Clintons had formed in 1979 with their friends James and Susan McDougal The issue first surfaced during the 1992 presidential campaign, when the *New York Times* published a story suggesting that the McDougals had heavily financed the Clintons in the Whitewater Development Corp.'s investment of river real estate, in what was supposedly a 50-50 partnership. The article also stated that the Clintons had claimed tax deductions for interest payments on Whitewater, when those payments came from the Whitewater Corp. itself. The Clinton campaign responded by producing a report showing that the Clintons had made large investments in Whitewater with their own capital and had lost tens of thousands of dollars as a result. The controversy only continued, however. In 1993, after Bill Clinton had been sworn in as president, the deputy White House counsel and Clinton legal associate Vincent Foster committed suicide, following the eruption of the Travelgate affair; some wondered if he had been murdered (a theory that was later disproved) and whether or not legal documents regarding the Whitewater business had been removed before investigators appeared on the scene. (Foster had recently filed three years of tax returns for the Whitewater investment on the Clintons' behalf.) Reporters also uncovered the fact that Hillary Clinton had made a $1,000 commodities investment in 1978 that had returned an unheard-of $100,000 within 10 months. In the face of growing concern over Whitewater legal matters, Hillary Clinton held a press conference on April 22, 1994, in which she stated that she alone had been responsible for the trades that had earned her $100,000. However, she later admitted that Jim Blair—a friend and the chief attorney for the poultry producer Tyson Foods, which is headquartered in Arkansas—had advised her. She also denied having anything to do with Castle Grande, a fraudulent deal that was made by the Madison Guaranty Savings & Loan, run by James McDougal, and that ultimately cost the public $4 million. She stated at the time that one of her associates at the Rose legal offices had handled most of the work with Madison. This could not be independently verified, however, as her billing records had mysteriously disappeared.

As the investigations continued, the Madison savings-and-loan operation was revealed to have been used largely by high-ranking Arkansas politicians for ill-advised and fraudulent loans. The independent counsel assigned to the case by U.S. attorney general Janet Reno, Robert B. Fiske Jr., investigated the possibility that in the mid-1980s Hillary Clinton, acting as a lawyer for Madison, had won approval of an abnormal stock offering to keep the bank afloat. The First Lady continued to deny that she had done any substantial work for the bank or that the work she did for the savings and loan amounted to a conflict of interest (since her husband was governor of Arkansas at the time). It was later revealed, however, that in 1985 and 1986 Hillary Clinton represented the bank before state regulators appointed by Bill Clinton and that one of the regulators later approved the particular stock sale that helped the bank. While a report (costing $4 million) that the Resolution Trust Corp. issued from the law firm of Pillsbury, Madison & Sutro in 1995 concluded that there were no grounds for suing the Clintons over their Whitewater dealings, several Republicans in Congress alleged that the report was tainted by coverups and obstruction of justice, a claim backed up by testimony from investigators from the firm. In May 1995 the U.S. Senate opened its own investigation of the Whitewater affair.

In January 1996 Hillary Clinton's legal billing records suddenly surfaced, casting doubt upon her veracity, as they showed that she had put in 60 hours of legal work for Madison over a 15-month period. In June 1996, after 13 months of investigation, the Senate Whitewater panel concluded its probe but issued reports whose contradictions occurred along party lines. The Republicans on the committee accused Hillary Clinton and several high-ranking Clinton administration officials of obstructing justice, declaring their belief that Hillary Clinton was responsible for the withholding of her Whitewater billing records. That report concluded that the First Lady had been aware of the Castle Grande scheme, having held 22 conversations related to Castle Grande during her work with Madison. The report also alleged that she was responsible for the removal of incriminating evidence from Vincent Foster's office and had instructed aides to thwart an official search. The Democrats on the Whitewater panel, however, stated that there was no evidence of any wrongdoing on the part of the Clintons and denounced the Republicans' report as the product of a politically inspired witch hunt. In September of that year, a Federal Deposit Insurance Corp. inspector general's report concluded that Hillary Clinton had drafted a real-estate document used by Madison to con federal regulators in 1986. The document valued a piece of the Whitewater property at $400,000; six years later the federal government received only $38,000 following the collapse of the Madison bank. It was concluded that Madison had used the document to deceive bank examiners about hundreds of thousands of dollars in commissions paid to a prominent Arkansas businessman. But on September 20, 2000 Robert Ray, the third independent counsel for the Whitewater investigation, noted in his final report, as quoted by *CNN.com* (September 20, 2000, on-line), "This office has determined that the evidence was insufficient to prove to a jury beyond a reasonable doubt that either President or Mrs. Clinton knowingly participated in any criminal conduct . . . or knew of such conduct."

Meanwhile, a further source of difficulty for the First Lady was the Monica Lewinsky scandal, which was connected tangentially to the Whitewater investigation. The independent counsel Kenneth Starr, who had replaced Fiske on the Whitewater case, decided to investigate the possibility that Bill Clinton had had a sexual relationship with Monica Lewinsky, a former White House intern, and had later urged her to lie about the affair in her affidavit for the Paula Jones case. (Paula Jones, a former Arkansas state employee, had brought suit against Bill Clinton, whom she accused of sexual harassment.) On January 17, 1998 President Clinton gave his deposition in the Jones case, during which he denied that he had had an affair with Lewinsky. On January 21 the *Washington Post,* among other publications, broke the story and revealed the existence of secretly recorded audiotapes on which Lewinsky gave details of the alleged affair. While Bill Clinton continued making denials to the media and his Cabinet, Hillary Clinton appeared on several talk shows, declaring that the allegations were the product of a "right-wing conspiracy" to topple the administration. On February 11, 1998, as reported by *CNN.com* (February 11, 1998, on-line), she predicted that the charge would "slowly dissipate over time under the weight of its own insubstantiality." On August 17, 1998, however, after months of investigation, President Clinton testified before a grand jury that, while he had not engaged in witness tampering, he had been involved in a sexual relationship with Lewinsky; he repeated the admission in a televised address to the nation. On December 19, 1998 Clinton was impeached by the U.S. House of Representatives on charges of perjury and obstruction of justice (thus becoming only the second president, after Andrew Johnson in 1868, to be impeached); he was acquitted by the United States Senate the following February. In *Talk* magazine, according to *BBC* (August 1, 1999, on-line), Hillary Clinton defended her husband, noting, "Everyone has some dysfunction in their families. You don't walk away if you love someone. You help the person." According to the First Lady, her husband was guilty of a "sin of weakness, not a sin of malice."

Despite the distraction of the scandals, Hillary Clinton continued to be the most politically active First Lady in the history of the United States. In May 1995 she persuaded President Clinton to appoint an advisory committee on Persian Gulf War–related illnesses; taking her advice, the president extended the investigation after the panel supported the military's controversial findings, which blamed an undiagnosed illness as well as stress for veterans' memory losses, nervous-system disorders, headaches, joint pains, and feelings of chronic fatigue As quoted on her official U.S. Senate Web site, she said that the experience of trying to reform health care convinced her of the need to work in small steps, noting that "we must continue to make progress. It's still important that we increase access to quality health care for working families." To these ends, in 1997 she played leading roles in two White House conferences on child care. The first, the White House Conference on Early Childhood Development and Learning, focused on new scientific findings showing that children's experiences during their first years were of enormous importance to their future health and development. The second, the White House Conference on Child Care, represented an attempt to find ways to provide affordable and reliable child care for working families. Hillary Clinton's most prominent policy effort since 1993, the conference played a major role in the development of the president's Children's Health Insurance Program. The First Lady was also active in other health-related projects, such as helping to pass the Family and Medical Leave Act and the Adoption and Safe Family Act of 1997, which made for easier transitions for foster children moving to permanent homes and increased the number of adoptions.

Beginning in 1995 Hillary Clinton wrote a weekly syndicated newspaper column, "Talking It Over," in which she shared the observations she had made while meeting people of various nationalities in her capacity as First Lady. The popular column appeared in roughly 100 newspapers nationwide. The year 1996 saw the publication of Clinton's first book, *It Takes a Village and Other Lessons Children Teach Us*, the proceeds from which went to children's hospitals. A best-seller, *It Takes a Village* focuses on the role that society can play in raising children. Clinton noted that while parents bear the primary responsibility for their children, support from the larger society is also crucial to young people's well-being.

The negative publicity Hillary Clinton received during the Whitewater investigation was largely offset by the Lewinsky scandal, by the end of which many Americans had come to view her sympathetically as the wronged wife who had nonetheless stood by her husband. In the summer of 1999, after U.S. senator Daniel Patrick Moynihan of New York announced that he would not run for another term, Hillary Clinton began to set in motion her campaign to succeed him. Many observers predicted that she would be unable to rise above her own scandal-tainted past, the fact that she was not from New York State, or the popularity of her likely opponent, New York City mayor Rudolph Giuliani. Indeed, at the beginning of her run, she encountered tough personal questions and made a series of awkward comments in a seeming attempt to please opposing groups of voters simultaneously. Over the course of her campaign, she made some headlines by breaking with the Clinton administration's policy on several issues. While the administration officially stated that the sovereignty of the city of Jerusalem, which is claimed by both Israelis and Arabs, should be determined in peace talks, Hillary Clinton declared in July 1999 that Jerusalem was the "eternal and indivisible capital of Israel" and came out in favor of moving the U.S. embassy to that city from Tel Aviv, Israel, as soon as possible. (Many commentators saw this stance as being intended to make up for a March 1999 speech in which she expressed support for establishing a permanent Palestinian state.) In December 1999 she publicly criticized the administration's "don't ask, don't tell, don't pursue" policy, which applied to gays in the military. The First Lady characterized the policy as a political compromise that had proven ineffective, as the number of gays discharged from the service because of their sexual orientation had risen under the new rules. She announced that if elected she would attempt to change the law so that openly gay men and women would be allowed to serve in the military. Meanwhile, she embarked on an extensive tour of New York State, during which she listened to voters' concerns and fielded questions.

In early January 2000 Hillary Clinton moved into a $1.7 million house in Chappaqua, located in Westchester County, New York, to meet the residency requirements for running for office from New York State. On February 6 she officially announced her candidacy for the U.S. Senate, marking the first time a First Lady had run for office. "I'm a new Democrat," she said, as quoted by *CNN.com* (February 6, 2000, on-line). "I don't believe government is the source of all our problems or the solution to them, but I do believe that when people live up to their responsibilities, we ought to live up to ours." She made education a major issue of her campaign, stating that she supported more accountability in public schools, greater investment in teachers, an increased effort to hire top-notch teachers, school construction and modernization, smaller class sizes, and efforts to increase school safety. She also supported budgetary increases in after-school programs and arts and music education. On a different front, she promised legislation that would help boost the economy in upstate New York. On May 16, 2000 she accepted the nomination of the New York State Democratic Party for United States senator.

The tone of the campaign shifted drastically only a couple of days later, when Mayor Giuliani dropped out of the race to focus on his treatment for prostate cancer. In his absence, New York congressman Rick Lazio emerged as the Republican Senate nominee. Though Lazio initially lagged far behind Clinton in the polls, he soon gained momentum, and the two ran neck and neck for some time—until Lazio's constant attacks on the First Lady's character began to backfire. On Election Day 2000 Clinton prevailed, with 55 percent of the vote, compared with 43 percent for Lazio. To great fanfare, she was sworn in as senator in early January 2001.

Many expected Clinton to cause an immediate stir by proposing legislation of national significance. Instead, the former First Lady spent the first few months of her Senate career focusing primarily on New York State issues and deferring to ranking senators on more prominent topics. Nonetheless, she soon found herself in the media spotlight for her $8 million memoir contract with Simon & Schuster and the scandals that plagued the Clintons as they left the White House in early 2001. Among other developments, U.S. attorney Mary Jo White investigated Bill Clinton's full pardon of the fugitive commodities trader Marc Rich during the last hours of his presidency; White then expanded her probe to the granting of clemency to four Hasidic Jews who were convicted of defrauding the government of millions of dollars in 1999—and who lived in a small community that voted unanimously for Hillary Clinton in 2000. As a result of such issues, Hillary Clinton's statewide approval rating dropped from 59 percent to around 38 percent. (As of late September 2002, it hovered at 53 percent.)

On February 13, 2001 Hillary Clinton made her first address from the floor of the Senate, offering several moderate health-care initiatives. By mid-April she had introduced 10 bills, most of them part of an economic package for upstate New York. Surprising many, she avoided appearing on the Sunday-morning talk shows and rarely gave interviews. In June 2001 she took her first stance on a major issue when she introduced legislation to ban the practice of racial profiling in routine police investigations and to end arrest quotas. "It's a balancing issue," Clinton told Jonathan Alter for *Newsweek* (June 25, 2001). "There's a nearly unanimous belief that racial profiling is fundamentally wrong. On the other hand, we don't want to do anything to undermine legitimate law enforcement." In September 2001, along with Senator Joseph Lieberman of Connecticut, Hillary Clinton proposed the Media Marketing Accountability Act, which would make it illegal to market or promote adult-rated rap and rock-and-roll albums to children under 17 and would authorize the Federal Trade Commission to choose which R-rated films could be marketed to minors. In July 2001 Clinton was among the leaders to successfully challenge President George W. Bush's decision to reappoint Mary Gall to head the Consumer Product Safety Commission. By the end of 2001 she had introduced 70 pieces of legislation. Among them were bills to create a nursing corps, reduce arsenic levels in drinking water, and help people injured by landmines. A *Congressional Quarterly* report ranked her third-most-liberal among U.S. senators.

After the terrorist attacks on the United States on September 11, 2001, Hillary Clinton stated on the Senate floor, as quoted on her official Web page, "We will . . . stand united behind our President as he and his advisors plan the necessary actions to demonstrate America's resolve and commitment. Not only to seek out and exact punishment on the perpetrators, but to make very clear that not only those who harbor terrorists, but those who in any way aid or comfort them whatsoever will now face the wrath of our country." Along with New York's senior senator, Charles E. Schumer, she led the fight for the allocation of millions of dollars in federal disaster aid for New York City. While the state did not receive the amount informally promised by the White House, Clinton and Schumer pushed through Congress a sizable relief package.

On October 11, 2002 Clinton voted for the Senate resolution that gave President George W. Bush the authority to order U.S. armed forces to attack Iraq when he determined that such action was necessary. Although 22 other Democratic senators also approved the resolution, the vote aroused heated controversy regarding its constitutionality and its affect on international relations. In a speech on the floor of the U.S. Senate, as transcribed on her official government Web site, Clinton cited the problems of attacking Iraq unilaterally rather than with the approval of the members of the United Nations, which she described as "an organization that is still growing and maturing." "A vote for the resolution best serves the security of our nation," she declared. "If we were to defeat this resolution or pass it with only a few Democrats, I am concerned that those who want to pretend this problem [Iraq's weapons arsenal] will go way with delay will oppose any UN resolution calling for unrestricted inspections. This is a very difficult vote. This is probably the hardest decision I have ever had to make—any vote that may lead to war should be hard—but I cast it with conviction. My vote is not, however, a vote for any new doctrine of preemption, or for unilateralism, or for the arrogance of American power or purpose—all of which carry grave dangers for our nation, for the rule of international law and for the peace and security of people throughout the world."

Senator Clinton serves on the Senate Budget Committee, the Senate Environment and Public Works Committee, and the Senate Health, Education, Labor and Pensions Committee. In addition, she serves on the Subcommittees on Aging; Public Health; Clean Air, Wetlands, Public Property and Nuclear Safety; Fisheries, Wildlife and Water; and Superfund, Waste Control, and Risk Assessment. She has raised substantial sums for other Democratic Party candidates, with the goal, according to some observers, of setting the groundwork for a possible run for the presidency in 2004 or 2008. "I think she is doing everything that someone who wants to be a national candidate has to do," the political strategist Paul Friedman told Raymond Hernandez for the *New York Times* (January 24, 2002). "She is learning the ropes in the Senate. She is doing her constituency work in New York, and at the same time, she is putting a tremendous amount of work into raising money and contributing it to colleagues who are unlikely to forget the favor."

In keeping with her longstanding commitment to a healthful lifestyle, the blond, blue-eyed Hillary Rodham Clinton exercised regularly at YMCA facilities before moving to the White House, where she banned smoking. She currently stays in her house near Embassy Row in Washington, D.C., during the week, and usually spends her free time engaging in correspondence and reading reports on current issues and legislation. She spends her weekends at the home she shares with Bill Clinton in Chappaqua, New York. She loves art and sculpture and is a devout Methodist. Her second book, the lavishly illustrated *An Invitation to the White House: At Home with History*, co-written with Carl Sferrazza Anthony, was published in 2000. The Clintons' daughter, Chelsea, graduated from Stanford University and is currently studying in England, at Oxford University. — G.O.

Suggested Reading: *BBC News* (on-line) Oct. 25, 2000; *CNN.com* (on-line); *New York Times* B p5 June 3, 1999, B p1 July 9, 1999, B p1 May 17, 2000, B p1 Jan. 24, 2002, with photos; *Newsweek* p34 June 25, 2001; *Time* (on-line) Aug. 8, 2001; *Washington Post* A p1 Dec. 10, 1999, A p4 Feb. 13, 2001; Guernsey, JoAnn Bren. *Hillary Rodham Clinton: A New Kind of First Lady*, 1993; King, Norman. *Hillary: Her True Story*, 1993; Radcliffe, Donnie. *Hillary Rodham Clinton: A First Lady for Our Time*, 1993; Sherrow, Victoria. *Hillary Rodham Clinton*, 1993; Warner, Judith. *Hillary Clinton: The Inside Story*, 1993

---

Courtesy of Eric Reynolds

## Clowes, Daniel

(clowz)

*Apr. 14, 1961– Comic-book artist; screenwriter*

*Address: c/o Fantagraphics, 7563 Lake City Way NE, Seattle, WA 98115*

The work of the "alternative" cartoonist Daniel Clowes has more in common with J. D. Salinger's novel *The Catcher in the Rye* or the offbeat films of David Lynch than with the superhero adventures and animal fables for which the comic-book genre is typically known. "Clowes's stories are dreamlike and disturbing," Tad Friend wrote for the *New Yorker* (July 30, 2001), "set in Hopperesque bars and motels where lonely men are haunted by nightmares, rumors of the Apocalypse, and unslaked sexual desires." Inspired by the likes of R. Crumb, the cartoonist generally credited with inventing underground comics in the 1960s, and utilizing an eclectic mix of pop-culture references and surrealist oddities, Clowes is one of a handful of cartoonists who seem bent on demonstrating that the comic book can hold its own with film and print as a medium for serious artistic expression.

Over the course of his career, Clowes has garnered eight Harvey Awards (the comics industry's equivalent of an Oscar or an Emmy), including awards for best writer, best continuing series, and best single issue; published seven graphic novels, in addition to the series *Eightball*; become the first cartoonist ever featured in *Esquire*'s annual fiction issue; and co-written the screenplay for the live-action feature film *Ghost World*, based on his graphic novel of the same name. His work has appeared in *Details*, the *New Yorker*, *Blab!*, *Cracked*, *World Art*, and the *Village Voice*.

The second of the two sons of an auto-mechanic mother and a steel-mill-worker father, Daniel Clowes was born in Chicago, Illinois, on April 14, 1961. His parents were divorced about one year after he was born; soon thereafter, his mother remarried and opened an auto-repair shop on Chicago's South Side. Before his father remarried, when Clowes was a teenager, he assembled an airplane in the spare room of his apartment. Speaking of his parents' divorce, Clowes told Carina Chocano for *Salon.com* (December 5, 2000), "I remember never having got what had happened, and never having a sense of my parents' ever having been together. It was just this big mystery; nobody ever talked about it." Clowes's stepfather, a stock-car racer, was killed in a racing accident when Clowes was about two years old.

After the death of her second husband, Clowes's mother would often leave her young son with his grandparents every few days. (His grandfather, James Cate, was a professor of medieval history at the University of Chicago.) "Neither of my parents made much money, but my grandparents did okay, so we weren't really poor," he recalled to Kristine McKenna for the *LA Weekly* (July 20–26, 2001). "I lived in three separate houses throughout my childhood—my mother's, my father's and my grandparents'—and my grandparents' was the closest thing to a home for me."

The time Clowes spent with his grandparents would later exert a powerful influence on his artwork. "I spent summers with them at a lake in Michigan where there weren't any other kids," he said to McKenna, "and I was so isolated that I developed my own taste. I think having a good memory and an eye for detail is just part of being a lonely, sensitive kid. You really focus on minutiae when you grow up that way." "I'd be playing with sticks and rocks," he explained to Chocano, "pretending they were my friends—so if you want to turn your child into a cartoonist, lock him in a room with a bunch of sticks and rocks." Clowes has recalled that his grandparents "bought all of their stuff right after the war, down to the canned food and Perry Como records, and basically never bought new stuff," as he told Sarah Van Boven for

*Newsweek* (April 27, 1998). "I felt like I was living in the past my whole life." (Indeed, a number of reviewers have pointed out the resemblances between Clowes's aesthetic and that of 1950s-era noir films.)

Meanwhile, Clowes had discovered the comics collected by his older brother, James. Having convinced himself that the stack of old issues his brother had left behind contained a coded message meant for him, he spent hours poring over the stories in an effort to piece that message together. "I remember feeling like he was trying to tell me something," Clowes told Chocano, "as if by selecting these particular issues to buy, he was illustrating some psychological state. I was just picking this up intuitively. I always thought about it when I grew up. The comics all had these really specific images running through them that really haunted me." He admitted to Friend, "I took the one where Superman becomes evil and has an evil, sickly grin and I hid it under a box for years."

While still in high school, Clowes decided to become a comic-book artist, and upon graduating he enrolled at the Pratt Institute, in the New York City borough of Brooklyn. Although he earned a bachelor of fine arts degree from Pratt, in 1984, Clowes has said that he learned little there that was useful for creating comics. "You go [to art school] expecting that once you come out you'll be a really competent illustrator," he told Austin English for *Indy Magazine* (on-line). "Y'know, somebody who can draw cars, things like that, and can easily get work. Not necessarily that you can just walk right in and get work, but that you'd be trained in some kind of art, and you really are not. You're trained to do bad abstract paintings that nobody cares about anymore. 'Cause that's what all the teachers do." Indeed, as a cartoonist Clowes considers himself to be largely self-taught. "I didn't learn anything," he told Chocano, "but my worst fears about art were confirmed—that it was all about who you know and had a lot to do with having the gift of gab and being able to talk yourself into getting a gallery show and all that. I knew I didn't have that. So I trained myself to do what I wanted, which was to do comics."

After Pratt, Clowes scraped by with odd illustration jobs, including a stint with *Cracked*, the humor magazine modeled on *Mad*. "I was sort of a starving artist," Clowes told Keith Phipps for the *Onion A.V. Club* (on-line), "and, by some miracle, this ex-roommate of mine who owed me a lot of money got a job as the editor in chief of *Cracked*. He pretty much just walked in off the street and a month later was the editor of the thing. . . . I did a series called 'The Ugly Family' that was sort of a rip-off of the Addams Family, except they were far more grotesque; they were like nuclear mutations." For the most part, though, Clowes found freelancing to be quite frustrating. "I felt like I had a set of talents that were of absolutely no use to the world," he told McKenna. "It was as if I were a great blacksmith or something. I was always leaving my portfolio with publications, trying to get work as an illustrator, and most of the time they'd return it without even having opened it. I'd get home from my morning portfolio rounds at about noon, and my two choices were to drink myself into a stupor—and I'd started to drink very heavily during the period because I was really unhappy—or to actually try to work on something."

"I finally thought, to hell with it," he continued, "I might as well do something I enjoy, so I started working on a comic called *Lloyd Llewellyn* just for fun." A retro-noir private-eye parody, *Llewellyn* was picked up by the Seattle-based Fantagraphics Books and first published in 1985. It ran for six issues before Fantagraphics dropped it. "When *Lloyd Llewellyn* was canceled," Clowes told Chocano, "I thought, 'Oh well, there goes my career.'" He then began work on *Eightball*, a series that Ken Lieck, in the *Austin Chronicle* (September 8, 2000), characterized as an anthology of "cheap *Archie*-like gag pages, autobiographical meanderings, tales of twisted adventure, . . . [that] dips into a number of other genres." "I thought, 'Well, here's my chance to do whatever I want, and nobody will buy it, but at least I'll do a couple of issues,'" Clowes told Chocano. *Eightball* was also picked up by Fantagraphics, and first published in 1989; hugely successful, it remains in print today.

The first story to span several issues of *Eightball* (and the first to be reissued as a single-volume graphic novel) was *Like a Velvet Glove Cast in Iron*, the account of a young man's divagations through a surreal urban wasteland. (In the course of *Like a Velvet Glove*, the protagonist, Clay, encounters a potato-headed mutant, a headless dog with no orifices, a three-eyed prostitute, and a man having his eye sockets cleansed by "rare Asiatic sea crustaceans.") Packed with dark sexual humor and Pynchonesque conspiracies, *Like a Velvet Glove* has often been compared to the *Twilight Zone* TV show and David Lynch's miniseries *Twin Peaks*.

Looking back, Clowes has said that *Like a Velvet Glove* was in many ways about the collapse of his first marriage, which began in 1987 and ended in 1991. "When I read my comics years after having done them," he told McKenna, "they often seem like maps of what was going on in my subconscious. And when I reread *Velvet Glove* a few years ago, it was obvious to me it was about that marriage." Indeed, Clowes has stressed the importance to his work of unconscious fears and desires that provoke strong ambivalence. "Things often bob to the surface of my subconscious that I have intensely mixed feelings about, and with almost all the stuff in *Velvet Glove*, my initial thought was, 'My God, I can't draw this!' That's the most important stuff to put down, though, and I just sort of let it all go on the page."

Clowes's next long narrative, *Ghost World*, was likewise published serially in *Eightball* before it was rereleased, in 1998, as a graphic novel. Called "a masterpiece in comic form" by Matt Groening, the creator of *The Simpsons*, and "perhaps the keenest and most affecting portrayal of adolescence since *The Catcher in the Rye*" by Tad Friend, *Ghost World* is the coming-of-age story of Enid and Becky, two disaffected young women just out of high school. Like *Velvet Glove*, *Ghost World* offers a fictional world of ill-defined yet ubiquitous malaise; but *Ghost World* achieves this effect through more subtle means. "There has always been a feeling of jittery unease underscoring Clowes' work," Chocano wrote, "but in *Ghost World* the sense of dread and horror emanates more from the real world than from the supernatural one. The creepy disquiet of *Ghost World* is nourished by television, suburbia, and the soul-sucking banality of both. The serial's panels are cast in the eerie blue light of the television—which is always on, always talking, never saying anything."

*David Boring*, which Clowes completed in the spring of 2000, concerns the obsessions—romantic and otherwise—of a desolate 19-year-old security guard with an expressionless face. From time to time rumors of an ongoing apocalyptic war impinge upon the eerily calm narrative, which also explores themes such as the nature of artistic and literary paternity (specifically, comics' roots in the superhero adventure) and the literary potential of comic art. "*Boring*," Andrew D. Arnold wrote for *Time* (April 24, 2000), "with its concluding issue, has proved itself a work that captures the feeling of being young and filled with ennui and living in America at the end of the 20th century."

For his most recent project, Clowes collaborated with director Terry Zwigoff (whose 1995 documentary *Crumb* focused on the life of R. Crumb) to create a full-length feature film based on *Ghost World*. With Zwigoff's assistance, he adapted the original comic into a screenplay—a process that entailed considerable revision. "Basically, you have to throw away everything you have and start over again, and just sort of start with the same framework," Clowes explained to Phipps. "'Cause [screenwriting is] a completely different process, and it took me about a year before I figured that out. I tried to transcribe [the comic] into script form, and it wasn't working at all. . . . You have to really learn the mechanics of film storytelling, so I just watched a million films and read a million screenplays and sort of got the rudiments of it. I started from scratch with the same basic idea I had in the comics, but the characters are fairly true to what they were in the comics. But the story is much more fleshed out, much more. . . . You see a lot more of the world."

*Ghost World*, starring Thora Birch, Scarlett Johansson, and Steve Buscemi, was released in the summer of 2001. A hit at art-house theaters, the movie generally garnered raves from the critics. A.O. Scott, for example, wrote in the *New York Times* (July 20, 2001) that *Ghost World* is "surely the best depiction of teenage eccentricity since *Rushmore*, and its incisive satire of the boredom and conformity that rule our thrill-seeking, individualistic land, and also its question-mark ending, reminded me of *The Graduate*. With all due respect to Mike Nichols, Simon and Garfunkel, and Mrs. Robinson, I like *Ghost World* better." *Ghost World* "takes . . . a risky journey and never steps wrong," Roger Ebert wrote for the *Chicago Sun-Times* (August 3, 2001). "It creates specific, original, believable, lovable characters, and meanders with them through their inconsolable days, never losing its sense of humor."

Although the proceeds from *Ghost World* provided Clowes with enough money for a down payment on his Oakland, California, house, he has expressed ambivalence about undertaking other Hollywood projects. "I'm tempted to just sell these studios all my stuff," he told Friend. "But then I'd have to move to an island." In any event, he plans to continue working chiefly in the medium of comics—which, in his view, allows for greater artistic control. "In the end, I'm glad comics are beneath the radar," he continued. "I'm only interested in reaching those few people who can appreciate the subtleties of what I'm trying to do. But it's a very sad life."

Clowes's second wife, Erika, is a doctoral student in English at the University of California at Berkeley; she is currently working on a thesis on anality in modernism. The couple have two guinea pigs, Hotdog and Snoppy (not to be confused with Snoopy). — P.K.

Suggested Reading: *LA Weekly* (on-line) July 20–26, 2001, with photos; *Newsweek* p70 Apr 27, 1998; *Onion A.V. Club* (on-line) 2001; *Reason* p48+ May 2001; *Salon.com* (on-line) Dec 5, 2001, with photos

Selected Comics Collections: *Lout Rampage!*, 1992; *The Manly World of Lloyd Llewellyn*, 1994; *#$@&!: The Official Lloyd Llewellyn Collection*, 1995; *Pussey!*, 1995; *Orgy Bound*, 1996; *Like a Velvet Glove Cast in Iron*, 1998; *Ghost World*, 1998; *David Boring*, 2000; *Caricature: Nine Stories*, 2002

Selected Films: *Ghost World*, 2001

---

## Cochran, Thad

*Dec. 7, 1937– U.S. senator from Mississippi (Republican)*

*Address: 326 Russell Senate Office Bldg., Washington, DC 20501-2402*

Thad Cochran might be called Mississippi's "other" senator. In contrast to the high-profile, fiery Senate majority leader, Trent Lott, who hails from the same state, Cochran has a "courtly, soft-spoken manner" that "stands out as old-fashioned in the contemporary Senate," as a writer for *Politics in America 2000* put it. While their personal characteristics may differ, Cochran is just as conservative regarding many issues as his fellow Mississippian,

Courtesy of the U.S. Senate

*Thad Cochran*

having proven, for example, a staunch advocate of missile defense. At the same time, he does not blindly follow the Republican Party line, as evidenced by his support for campaign-finance reform and protection of the wilderness, among other positions. On November 5, 2002 Cochran won a fifth term in the Senate, roundly defeating the Reform Party's candidate, Shawn O'Hara, by a margin of more than five to one.

Thad Cochran was born on December 7, 1937 in Pontotoc, Mississippi, the older of the two sons of William Holmes Cochran, the principal of the school in the Beckham community, where the family then lived, and Emma Grace Cochran, a teacher. The Cochrans later moved, first to the Hurricane community in Pontotoc County and then to Tippah County. In the latter locale Thad Cochran started school, in the town of Walnut. The family moved again in 1946, this time to the Byram community, near Jackson, Mississippi.

Cochran was an active boy, joining the Boy Scouts, in which he progressed to Eagle Scout, and earning varsity letters in football, basketball, baseball, and tennis in high school. In addition, he enjoyed music; he performed a piano-and-voice recital in his senior year. An all-around student, Cochran became valedictorian of his high-school class. Among his other activities, he was a member of Daniel Memorial Baptist Church and the local 4-H Club, and he helped to found a Boy Scout troop at a nearby church, becoming its first junior assistant scoutmaster.

In 1955 Cochran enrolled at the College of Liberal Arts at the University of Mississippi, popularly known as Ole Miss, where he earned a B.A. degree in psychology, with a minor in political science, in 1959. During his undergraduate years he was voted head cheerleader, a role that brought with it enormous clout; he parlayed that success into election as vice president of the student government. He also served as president of his fraternity, Pi Kappa Alpha, and company commander of the school's navy ROTC, and was a member of the national honorary leadership fraternity Omicron Delta Kappa. Upon finishing college Cochran was commissioned as an ensign in the U.S. Naval Reserve. When his ship, the *U.S.S. Macon*, was decommissioned, in January 1961, he was assigned to a naval district in New Orleans, Louisiana, to complete his two years of active service. He then enrolled in the School of Law at the University of Mississippi, where he won the Frederick Hamel Memorial Award for highest scholastic average in the first-year class. He was also awarded a Rotary Foundation Graduate Fellowship and studied jurisprudence and international law at Trinity College at the University of Dublin, in Ireland. During his summer vacations in the years that he attended law school, Cochran returned to active duty in the U.S. Navy and taught military law and naval orientation at the Officer Candidate School in Newport, Rhode Island. He was eventually promoted to lieutenant in the naval reserve. After obtaining his law degree, Cochran worked for the prestigious firm of Watkins & Eager, in Jackson, becoming a partner there within three years.

Cochran's first foray into national politics came in 1968, when he served as executive director of Mississippi Citizens for Nixon-Agnew during the Republican Richard Nixon's ultimately successful campaign for the presidency that year. Four years later, when the retirement of Democratic representative Charles R. Griffin left an open seat in the state's Fourth Congressional District (comprising 12 counties in southwestern Mississippi), Cochran ran for the spot. He won a narrow victory. In each of his reelection campaigns, in 1974 and 1976, however, Cochran took more than 70 percent of the vote. In his second term as a congressional representative, *U.S. News & World Report* (November 3, 1975) quoted Cochran as stating, "Criticism of Congress is well earned in my opinion. Decision-making is hampered by partisan considerations in too many instances. . . . Energy problems and economic problems as complex as ours deserve the unselfish, thoughtful consideration of sincere and dedicated men and women. My impression during my short tenure here is that we have too many party loyalists and not enough statesmen." The votes he cast during his years as a representative included those in favor of arms sales to Chile, natural-gas deregulation, and the development of nuclear carriers and against cutting aid to South Korea's military and delaying production of the B-1 bomber.

In 1978 Cochran ran for the U.S. Senate seat being vacated by the Democrat James O. Eastland, who was retiring after 36 years as a senator. Running against the Independent Charles Evers, then the mayor of Fayette, Mississippi, and the Democratic nominee, attorney Maurice Dantin, Cochran won a plurality with 45 percent of the vote, becoming the first Republican elected to the Senate from Mississippi in a century. His earlier plea for bipartisanship notwithstanding, by the time of his election, according to *Time* (November 20, 1978), Cochran had earned a 95 percent voting-approval rating from the American Conservative Union and a rating of zero from the liberal Americans for Democratic Action.

As a junior senator Cochran was active on behalf of farmers, helping to secure marketing loans, or price supports, for growers of cotton and rice. (He would also contribute key elements to farm bills in 1985, 1990, and 1996.) In his first Senate term, Cochran voted in favor of retaining the marketing loans for tobacco, amending the Constitution to require a balanced budget, and subsidizing home-mortgage rates and against cutting funds for the B-1 bomber, cutting $1.2 billion from the fund for public-works jobs, and increasing the gas tax by five cents per gallon. In 1984 he ran for reelection against William F. Winter, Mississippi's popular governor. Winter had won praise for his passage of a landmark education bill aimed at improving the quality of the state's public schools. Winter was hampered, however, by his own indecision over whether to run; during the campaign Cochran outspent Winter by a three-to-one ratio on the way to garnering 61 percent of the vote. In 1990 Cochran ran unopposed. Seeking a fourth term in 1996, Cochran won over 70 percent of the vote against his Democratic challenger, the retired farmer James W. "Bootie" Hunt.

While Cochran has for the most part maintained sterling conservative credentials, he has also occasionally been active on traditionally Democratic fronts. He authored the Mississippi Wilderness Act, which was the first federal legislation ever passed for continued protection of land in Mississippi, and has helped develop and maintain the Natchez Trace Parkway, the Natchez Historical Park, the Vicksburg National Military Park, and the Gulf Islands National Seashore. In addition, he has worked to secure funds for historically black colleges and for vocational training for the disabled. In 1996, forming an alliance with Democrats, Cochran succeeded in maintaining subsidies and price-support programs for southern farm crops, including cotton, rice, peanuts, and sugar. (In 1998, in one failed attempt to direct funds to Mississippi—one of the poorest states in the union—Cochran and his fellow Mississippi senator Trent Lott joined forces to add a provision to a spending bill that would have given Russian businesses more than $300 million in agricultural credits to buy frozen chickens from a group of states that included Mississippi.)

In 1996, when Bob Dole gave up his post as Senate majority leader in his unsuccessful bid for the presidency, Cochran and Lott—who had followed a similar road to the Senate, having attended Ole Miss shortly after Cochran—competed to fill the position. By that time Cochran had become chairman of the Republican Conference, the number-three position in the Senate leadership. Meanwhile, Lott, first elected to the Senate a decade after Cochran, had bypassed his fellow Mississippian and defeated Alan K. Simpson in 1994 for the number-two position of Republican whip. On June 12, 1996 the Republican caucus handed Lott a resounding victory, choosing him over Cochran in a vote of 44–8. (With Vermont senator James Jeffords's defection from the Republican Party in 2001, Lott became Senate minority leader; the election of the following year returned him to the majority-leader post.)

In 1999, after Defense Secretary William Cohen announced a substantial increase in the Pentagon's budget for a national missile-defense program, Cochran quickly reintroduced a measure that would authorize national missile-defense deployment "as soon as technologically feasible." He had tried twice the year before to win Senate endorsement of the same measure, but the Cochran bill, as it was known, which needed 60 votes in the Senate even to be discussed, fell short by one. With a change of heart on the part of Nebraska Democrat Bob Kerrey, however, the bill passed. To gather further support for the bill before it was sent to President Bill Clinton, Cochran proposed an amendment that would call for yearly authorization of the costs connected with the project. Democrats embraced the provision, and the amendment was adopted by a unanimous vote. President Clinton signed the National Missile Defense Act into law on July 22, 1999.

Meanwhile, in February of that year, Cochran had cast two votes of "guilty" in the impeachment trial of President Clinton, who stood accused of perjury and obstruction of justice in connection with his affair with Monica Lewinsky, a White House intern. Among his other positions in the 106th Congress (1999–2001), Cochran voted in support of phasing out the estate tax, banning so-called partial-birth abortions, and establishing permanent trade relations with China; he opposed mandatory background checks for gun shows, the broadening of the list of felonies covered under the category of hate crimes, and a ban on nuclear testing.

In 2001 Cochran joined the Republican Arizona senator John McCain's movement for campaign-finance reform. The aim of the McCain-Feingold bill (co-sponsored by Senator Russell D. Feingold, a Wisconsin Democrat) was an end to unlimited contributions to political parties by corporations and wealthy individuals. Cochran's support was seen as crucial to the success of the bill. Scott Harshbarger, the president of Common Cause—which describes itself as "a nonprofit, nonpartisan citizen's lobbying organization promoting open, honest and accountable government"—stated on January 4, 2001, as quoted on the organization's Web site, "On behalf of the members of Common Cause and reform supporters everywhere, I thank Senator

Cochran for lending his support for this effort. Everyone knows that campaign finance reform has powerful opponents, and it takes a measure of courage to stand up in defiance of the Washington culture of money, access, and influence." McCain himself, quoted on Feingold's Web site, also praised Cochran, saying, "I'm very pleased that Thad Cochran is supporting campaign reform legislation. Thad's endorsement dramatically increases the Senate's chances of passing meaningful campaign reform in the wake of the explosion of independent attack ads and the record-shattering level of soft money that infiltrated campaigns [in 2000]." Thanks in part to Cochran's support, the bill passed in the Senate in April 2001. As quoted on his Web site, Cochran predicted that passage of the measure would "make the [election] process more transparent, and candidates will have a better chance of controlling their own campaigns. And, I think the confidence of the American people in the political process will be restored." The bill was ready to face a vote in the House of Representatives, but the vote was blocked by opponents of the bill, led by Trent Lott. (The House approved a similar measure, the Shays-Meehan bill, in mid-February 2002.)

After South Carolina's legislature voted in 2000 to remove the Confederate battle flag from atop the state capitol, and Georgia made a similar decision, Mississippi—the only state whose flag still incorporates the Confederate emblem, considered by many to be a symbol of racial bigotry—came under pressure to change its flag. The state held a public referendum and, on April 17, 2001, decided by a nearly two-to-one vote in favor of keeping the flag as it was. Though the controversy put Mississippi in the national spotlight, neither Cochran nor Lott expressed a position on the issue.

In May 2001 Cochran helped secure $3,785,000 for the acquisition of Deer Island. The funds were also to be used to create a state-operated recreational and scenic preserve.

Thad Cochran has served on the board of visitors of the Air Force Academy and as chairman of the board at the Military Academy at West Point. He is now a member of the board of the U.S. Naval Academy. He serves on the Senate Agriculture, Nutrition and Forestry Committee, the Appropriations Committee, the Government Affairs Committee, and the Rules and Administration Committee and on various subcommittees of those groups. He holds honorary degrees from Kentucky Wesleyan College, Mississippi College, Blue Mountain College, and the University of Richmond and is a member of the board of regents of the Smithsonian Institution and the board of the Museum of American History. On June 6, 1964 he married Rose Clayton. The couple have two children, Clayton and Kate. — A.T.

Suggested Reading: *Los Angeles Times* M p4+ Jan. 7, 2001; (New Orleans) *Times-Picayune* A p1+ Mar. 15, 1999, with photos; *New York Times* A p21+ Nov. 13, 1978, with photos, A p1 May 17, 1996, with photos, A p12+ Apr. 4, 2001, with photos; *Washington Post* A p1+ Nov. 17, 1994, C p3 Dec 5, 2000

---

## Cohen, Rob

*Mar. 12, 1949– Film director; film producer*

*Address: c/o William Morris Agency, One William Morris Pl., Beverly Hills, CA 90212*

A longtime producer of Hollywood films that have featured such stars as Diana Ross, Arnold Schwarzenegger, Michael J. Fox, and Mel Gibson, Rob Cohen has recently received much attention as the director of two exceptionally profitable action movies: *The Fast and the Furious* (2001) and *XXX* (2002). Those fast-paced films, both of which star Vin Diesel, contain what many critics have ranked among the most memorable action sequences in motion-picture history. Cohen traveled a long road to reach success. His first four years of producing ended with the box-office bomb *The Wiz* (1978). During the next half-dozen years, he directed two now-forgotten pictures. In the 1990s, after returning to producing for several years and also gaining more experience as a director, through television projects, Cohen directed two audience pleasers—*Dragon: The Bruce Lee Story* (1993) and *Dragonheart* (1996)—as well as several duds. With *The Fast and the Furious* and *XXX*, Cohen has joined the ranks of successful Hollywood directors. "Of all the movies I've done, I'm most proud of [*XXX*] because of how effective a roller coaster ride it is," Cohen told Martin A. Grove for *VinXperience* (online). "It has attitude, that's for sure."

Robert Cohen was born on March 12, 1949 in Cornwall-on-Hudson, New York. By the time he was in junior high school, he knew he wanted a career in filmmaking. Cohen attended Amherst College, in Amherst, Massachusetts, before transferring to Harvard University, in Cambridge, Massachusetts, where he studied anthropology. While at Harvard he shot a recruiting film for the school's admissions office and also took advantage of an opportunity to help Daniel Petrie direct the television film *Silent Night, Lonely Night* (1969), starring Lloyd Bridges and Shirley Jones. After Cohen graduated from Harvard, in 1971, he moved to Los Angeles, California, where he got a job with a film producer. Not long after his arrival, the producer went broke, and Cohen found himself out of work. After a stint as a janitor at a local animal hospital, he became a script reader for Mike Medavoy, the vice president in charge of the motion-picture department at the International Famous Agency. Cohen attracted notice by recommending to Medavoy the

Franck Prevel/AP Photo

*Rob Cohen*

filmscript for *The Sting*, written by David S. Ward; directed by George Roy Hill, *The Sting* (1973) won Academy Awards for best original screenplay, best picture, and best director and was a huge box-office success. Cohen left Medavoy to take a job as director of made-for-TV movies for 20th Century-Fox Television. Under his leadership the division made the TV pictures *Mrs. Sundance* (1974) and *Stowaway to the Moon* (1975).

The year 1973 had not yet ended when Berry Gordy, the head of the record label Motown, hired Cohen as executive vice president of Motown's new motion-picture division. Cohen's first assignment in his new position was to a find and produce a suitable filmscript for the Motown star Diana Ross. He complied by buying the script for *Mahogany*, written by Toni Ambler, John Byrum, and Bob Merrill, about a young woman (Ross) from an urban ghetto who puts herself through fashion school. The film, released in 1975, made a profit for Motown. During that period Cohen also produced the picture *The Bingo Long Traveling All-Stars & Motor Kings* (1976), a comedy about Negro League baseball in the 1930s; the television film *Scott Joplin* (1977), about the famous pianist and composer of ragtime music; the disco comedy *Thank God It's Friday* (1978), whose soundtrack includes the Academy Award–winning song "Last Dance," recorded by Donna Summer; the high-school comedy *Almost Summer* (1978); and the television film *Amateur Night at the Dixie Bar and Grill* (1979). Most prominently, he produced the movie musical *The Wiz* (1978); directed by Sidney Lumet, *The Wiz* has an all–African-American cast, with Diana Ross as Dorothy, Michael Jackson as the Scarecrow, Nipsey Russell as the Tin Man, Ted Ross as the Lion, and Richard Pryor as the Wiz. Adapted from the immensely popular 1939 film *The Wizard of Oz* (which in turn was based on L. Frank Baum's classic 1900 fantasy novel, *The Wonderful Wizard of Oz*), *The Wiz* cost $24 million to make. Its creators, Cohen told Jack Egan for the *Washington Post* (October 25, 1978), ignored the Hollywood convention that "a black picture with an all-black cast should not cost over a certain amount of money," as well as the belief that, in his words, "a large musical is a bad investment because of a limited foreign market, which has become more and more important as movies become more and more expensive." Moreover, Cohen noted, "We also took an American classic and reinterpreted it for the '70s. That's always a chancy thing, when the original work gets enshrined in people's memory. All movies are risky. It's only a question of to what degree. We just pushed it to the nth degree." Cohen earned the NAACP (National Association for the Advancement of Colored People) Image Award for best producer for his work on *The Wiz*. Hurt by mostly negative reviews—and, according to some observers, by its G rating, which gave prospective audiences the idea that it was uncool—*The Wiz* grossed only $13 million at the box office. (It later became something of a cult classic.)

Soon after *The Wiz* reached theaters, Cohen quit Motown, because the firm prohibited him from sharing in any profits from the movies he had worked on. He then signed a multi-picture, independent-producer's contract with United Artists. "After *The Wiz*, I could no longer be an employee of someone else's company," Cohen told a writer for *Forbes* (November 13, 1978). Rather than producing films at United Artists, as he had intended, he found himself in the director's chair. Cohen's directorial debut came with *A Small Circle of Friends* (1980), about three students (portrayed by Brad Davis, Karen Allen, and Jameson Parker) at Harvard University in the 1960s. Neither that film nor his next directorial effort, *Scandalous* (1984)—a comedy-mystery co-written by Cohen and John Byrum and starring Sir John Gielgud—attracted many moviegoers. Before long Cohen returned to producing, this time as head of the Taft-Barish Co. During the remainder of the 1980s, he produced several star-studded films, among them an adaptation of W. Somerset Maugham's novel *The Razor's Edge* (1984), with Bill Murray; *Light of Day* (1987), the first dramatic picture in which Michael J. Fox appeared; the hugely successful *The Witches of Eastwick* (1987), starring Jack Nicholson, Cher, Susan Sarandon, and Michelle Pfeiffer; and *The Running Man* (1987), with Arnold Schwarzenegger. Cohen also directed episodes of such top-rated television shows as *Miami Vice*, *thirtysomething*, and *Hooperman*.

In about 1987 Cohen left Taft-Barish and, along with the director and producer John Badham, set up an independent production company called the Badham/Cohen Group. The company was responsible for the romantic comedy cum adventure movie *Bird on a Wire* (1990), featuring Mel Gibson and Goldie Hawn, and *The Hard Way* (1991), a comedy with James Woods and Michael J. Fox in the leading roles. For both films Cohen served as the second-unit director—that is, the director of a separate production crew that shoots sequences not involving the principal actors. Serving in that role for *The Hard Way*, he filmed the action sequences.

In 1992 Cohen parted ways with Badham and again turned to directing. In that capacity he guided the making of *Dragon: The Bruce Lee Story* (1993), about the celebrated martial-arts star; he also wrote *Dragon*'s filmscript, based on a book by Robert Clouse and Linda Lee Cadwell. *Dragon* grossed over $35 million at the box office and garnered several good reviews. Among them was Richard Harrington's for the *Washington Post* (May 7, 1993, on-line), in which he wrote that Cohen "moves the story along briskly but smoothly" and described the film as "rousing entertainment with many faces—martial arts thrills, romance, mystery, comedy—and a double dose of poignancy." "I think that *Dragon* was ahead of its time in terms of interest in Asian-American subjects," Cohen told a writer for *About.com*. Cohen's next film was *Dragonheart* (1996), a fantasy in which the last living dragon, named Draco, forms a bond with a dragon slayer to defeat an evil king. Draco, who speaks with the voice of Sean Connery, was the first film character whose animation was accomplished entirely through digital technology. While the movie grossed over $51 million at the box office, critics disagreed about its merits. *Dragonheart* struck Kenneth Turan of the *Los Angeles Times* (May 31, 1996, on-line) as "a frustrating combination of the magical and the mundane"; to Janet Maslin of the *New York Times* (May 31, 1996, on-line), the movie seemed "unreasonably flat" even "while trying every sure-fire gambit it [could] borrow." By contrast, the *Chicago Sun-Times* (on-line) critic Roger Ebert wrote, "While no reasonable person over the age of 12 would presumably be able to take it seriously, it nevertheless has a lighthearted joy, a cheerfulness, an insouciance, that recalls the days when movies were content to be fun. Add that to the impressive technical achievement that went into creating the dragon, and you have something to acknowledge here."

Trying his hand at the action/thriller/disaster genre, Cohen directed *Daylight* (1996), with Sylvester Stallone as a disgraced former emergency-medical-services chief who tries to save survivors of an explosion in a tunnel connecting New York City and New Jersey before their air supply runs out or the Hudson River engulfs them. The film grossed over $32 million in the United States but received mostly negative reviews. Kenneth Turan, writing for the *Los Angeles Times* (December 6, 1996, on-line), described *Daylight* as "persuasive in its action moments but puny in terms of character and dialogue." Cohen next directed *The Rat Pack* (1998), a docudrama for TV about the exploits of five entertainers—Frank Sinatra (played by Ray Liotta), Dean Martin (Joe Mantegna), Sammy Davis Jr. (Don Cheadle), Peter Lawford (Angus MacFadyen), and Joey Bishop (Bobby Slayton)—in the late 1950s and early 1960s, including their involvement with John F. Kennedy, his brother Robert, and organized-crime figures. *The Rat Pack*, which premiered on HBO, earned several Emmy Awards and brought Cohen a Director's Guild nomination. Cohen's next feature film was *The Skulls* (2000), about a working-class undergraduate who joins an elite, unnaturally powerful secret society that has lots to hide. The film grossed $35 million in the domestic market but took a critical drubbing. In *Salon* (March 31, 2000, on-line), Andrew O'Hehir wrote that *The Skulls* "is such a generic, automatic-pilot movie—seemingly stitched together out of disconnected outtakes from the USA Network archives—that seeing it doesn't help you understand it any better." O'Hehir also complained that Cohen "seem[ed] to have little idea of what he want[ed]; the movie is chaste when it should be randy, boring when it should be mysterious and rambling when it should be tightly plotted."

Cohen's first big hit as a director, *The Fast and the Furious* (2001), focuses on street gangs who drag race high-speed Japanese cars late at night. The movie grossed over $144 million in the United States alone and helped make a star out of its lead actor, Vin Diesel. "I never expected it to be a blockbuster as it wasn't made to be one," Cohen told James Mottram for the BBC (on-line). "Until the first test-screening I didn't have any inkling it would have that potential. I knew that I was working in a worn-out genre, that had been overstepped by mega-budget production. . . . But I believed in the new sub-culture of illegal street racing, with its multi-ethnicity, and with this young cast, with a story that had character depth and soulfulness, as opposed to cars, cars, cars, we were approaching it differently." In addition, he said, "I looked at the other movies, and thought 'They're not fast!' *The Fast and the Furious* has a real representation of speed and that's what I set out to do." In order to experience the feeling of speed, Cohen hired a drag racer to drive him down a city street in a car specially modified for street racing. The car's speedometer hit 171 miles an hour during the brief drive. "The thing that I realized . . . was that there was no way to get that speed on film technically through traditional methods. . . . So, I began to look into the world of visual effects," Cohen told the writer for *About.com*. "I said, 'I think there's a way to get speed if we use the new techniques of frame dropping and frame blending.'"

In 2002, in the spy film *XXX*, Cohen once again directed Vin Diesel. In *XXX*, Diesel played an adrenaline junkie with a bad attitude; the U.S. government recruits him to uncover information about an organization that may to be plotting the destruction of the world. In choosing to direct *XXX*, Cohen told John Horn for *Newsweek* (August 5, 2002), "I just embraced the kid in me who loved the movies, instead of trying to be an intellectual guy from Harvard who was going to get the respect of the critics." After only two weeks in theaters, the film had grossed over $83 million. Within 11 weeks it had grossed over $141 million. In a representative positive review, Stephanie Zacharek wrote for *Salon* (August 9, 2002, on-line) that Cohen "knows what we want to see in an action movie, and *XXX* is suitably packed with thrills. . . . He loves all the action-movie conventions as much as we do, from sexy villains with extra-thick Russian accents . . . to the sight of fabulously expensive and beautiful cars being run into the ground by too many sharp turns and crazy skids. But you also feel Cohen pumping fresh air into *XXX* at regular intervals. With only a few exceptions, his action sequences are cleanly shot and move fast. Cohen allows his characters to be cartoons, but they're cartoons with great individuality." The *Los Angeles Times* (August 9, 2002, on-line) reviewer Kenneth Turan disagreed; he felt the movie was "more busy than exciting, more frantic than involving, more chaotic than entertaining." Cohen plans to direct the sequel to *XXX*, with the goal of having it released in 2004.

Cohen created and was the executive producer of *Vanishing Son* (1994), a series of movies that aired on the UPN television network. The series is about two young brothers who are forced to leave their native China for the U.S. after participating in a protest for political freedom. In the U.S. one brother focuses on music while the other becomes involved in organized crime. The movies became popular enough to lead to a syndicated television series (in which Cohen is not involved), also on UPN.

Currently unmarried, Cohen has one son, Kyle, who as a nine-year-old appeared in a bit part in *Dragonheart*. — G.O.

Suggested Reading: *About.com* (on-line); BBC (on-line); *Forbes* p216 Nov. 13, 1970, with photo; *Newsweek* p56+ Aug. 5, 2002; *Washington Post* D p1+ Oct. 25, 1978, with photo

Selected Films: as director—*A Small Circle of Friends*, 1980; *Scandalous*, 1984; *Dragon: The Bruce Lee Story*, 1993; *Dragonheart*, 1996; *Daylight*, 1996; *The Rat Pack*, 1998; *The Skulls*, 2000; *The Fast and the Furious*, 2001; *XXX*, 2002; as producer—*Mahogany*, 1975; *The Bingo Long Traveling All-Stars & Motor Kings*, 1976; *Scott Joplin*, 1977; *Thank God It's Friday*, 1978; *Almost Summer*, 1978; *The Wiz*, 1978; *The Razor's Edge*, 1984; *Light of Day*, 1987; *The Witches of Eastwick*, 1987; *The Running Man*, 1987; *Bird on a Wire*, 1990; *The Hard Way*, 1991

---

## Cohn, Linda

*Nov. 10, 1959– Broadcast journalist*

*Address: ESPN Television, ESPN Plaza, Bristol, CT 06010*

One of the anchors of *SportsCenter*, on the all-sports cable network ESPN, Linda Cohn works at what she calls her "dream job," as she told Jolie A. H. Apicella for the *Mount Holyoke News* (February 11, 1999, on-line). A lifelong sports fan, Cohn became the first female full-time sports anchor on a national radio network when she joined ABC Radio in 1987. Although she has faced some opposition from her co-hosts in the overwhelmingly male world of sports broadcasting, she explained to Apicella, "Being around guys has helped me. But I'm careful not to share all of my sports knowledge. I don't want to turn them off. I'd rather prove it to them on the air." Her success as a sports anchor is attributable in part to the low-key and friendly demeanor that she learned from the New York City sports anchors she admired when she was growing up. As she told an interviewer for *JournalismJobs* (on-line), there was "a guy named Len Berman, who just sort of talked to you when he did sports. He just talked to you, not scream at you, not do stupid phrases, talked to you like you're buddies and neighbors. And that's what I got from that."

Courtesy of ESPN

Linda Cohn was born on November 10, 1959 and grew up on Long Island, New York. She recalled to the interviewer for *JournalismJobs*, "My father is a huge sports fan, and that's why I became a sports fan." As a girl she became an avid follower of the

New York Rangers hockey team. (She considers the moment when the Rangers won the 1994 Stanley Cup to be equal in importance to her wedding day and the times she gave birth, she has joked.) While she enjoyed playing tennis and basketball as a girl, her favorite sports activity was pitching in softball games. In that role she became, as she told Apicella, "the center of attention." Cohn attended Newfield High School, where she tried out for the boys' hockey team, at first unsuccessfully. "[But] I opened up their eyes," Cohn told Apicella. "It was kinda cool." In her senior year she tried again, this time making the cut. She served as goalie in eight games, starting in six.

Cohn attended the State University of New York at Oswego, where she worked at the campus television and radio stations and on the student newspaper. She graduated in 1981 with a bachelor's degree in communications. Cohn found her first job that year, as a news anchor for WALK-AM/FM in Patchogue, New York. She recalled to the interviewer for *JournalismJobs* that viewers and listeners would tell her, "My goodness, when you get to the sports in your news report you just totally perk up and you're like so informative and you know what the heck you're talking about." Cohn volunteered to cover the New York Islander hockey games for WALK. She told the interviewer for *JournalismJobs* that she "brought a little tape recorder and put myself in position to show off what I know and also to have other people see me. It's kind of like putting yourself into a situation to get a break and that's what I did." In 1984 she left her job at WALK to work concurrently at three New York City radio stations—WGBB-AM (until 1985), WCBS-FM (until 1987), and WCBS NewsRadio 88 (until 1987). She recalled to the interviewer for *JournalismJobs*, "The great thing about radio is it's so just off the cuff. You can totally, always adlib. . . . You're just kind of speaking what's on your mind and it's ok. It's kind of cool to have the freedom to do that. I love that about radio." In 1985 she was hired by WLIG-TV on Long Island, where she worked part-time as an anchor, news director, and chief correspondent for *Long Island News Tonight*, a nightly news program. She remained at the station until 1986. In 1987 she worked briefly at WFAN-AM in New York, providing sports updates and commentary.

During the same year Cohn became the first full-time female sports anchor on a national radio network when she joined ABC Radio Network at WABC TalkRadio. Starting in the following year, she also served as a sports reporter for the cable television network Sports Channel America and for News 12 on Long Island. In 1988 Cohn left her jobs in New York and moved to Seattle, where she joined KIRO-TV as a reporter and weekend sports anchor. In that capacity she covered the games of three Seattle clubs—the Mariners baseball team, the Seahawks football team, and the Supersonics basketball team—as well as those of the Washington Huskies college teams; in addition, she reported on the 1990 Goodwill Games and the 1991 NCAA Basketball West regional series.

In 1992 Cohn joined ESPN. She told the interviewer for *JournalismJobs* that one of the reasons ESPN has a loyal following among sports fans is that its anchors and reporters often relate obscure information to viewers. In addition, the network's anchors write their own material. "People love that our personalities come out and that we're real people. We're not like heads reading prompters." She remarked in the same interview, "It's like a college campus here. We know what each other is doing; we all get along and stuff. It's definitely fun. I mean without the mascots roaming around it's fun. It's like stand up comedy—we crack jokes and have fun." Cohn currently hosts *SportsCenter* as well as LPGA tournament coverage on ESPN and ESPN2; she has also hosted *Baseball Tonight* and *National Hockey Night* as well as ESPN2's *NHL 2Night* and *RPM 2Night*. In 1998 she became one of the three alternating hosts for ESPN Radio's Sunday-long coverage of National Football League (NFL) games. In addition, she has contributed to ESPN's NFL Draft coverage, Major League Baseball play-off coverage, the ESPYs (the ESPN awards show), and Sunday NFL Countdown.

Cohn has noted that as a woman sportscaster she is put under intense scrutiny by male fans, many of whom, she has said, watch her because of her looks or wait for her to make mistakes. Nonetheless, she refuses to put excessive pressure on herself. "I can't be perfect," she told Apicella. "You'll drive yourself crazy. You can't win everyone over." While Cohn has acknowledged the increase in the number of women in the sports industry since her arrival, she has also noted that it is generally harder for a woman in the field to be recognized than it is for her male counterpart. If men "have to do somersaults" to win appreciation, she quipped to Apicella, "women have to do handstands on a balance beam and look good while doing them and then do it over and over."

Cohn and her husband, who married in the mid-1980s, have a daughter, born in 1991, and a son, born about five years later. Her husband, a market researcher, "works from home, does most of the cooking and tucks the kids into bed at night," as Cohn told Jennifer Barrett for *MSNBC-Newsweek* (June 6, 2002, on-line). As *SportsCenter* broadcasts live at 2:00 a.m., she usually arrives home at 4:00 a.m. and then sleeps till 10:00 a.m. "When Barry Bonds broke the home-run record, I didn't leave the studio until 6 a.m.," she recalled to Barrett. "That was a record for me." She is able to maintain such a hectic schedule in part because, as she told Apicella, she is what her friends call an "adrenaline junkie"; more important, as she explained to Barrett, "You can't get to where I am without a support mechanism. For me, it's my husband."

"The greatest compliment I ever get is from men who say to me, 'I never took sports from a woman, until you came along . . . ,' " Cohn told Barrett. "I love my job. You never know what's going to happen. There's always so much going on. It's the next best thing to being there [at sporting events]. I just want to keep doing things that keep me challenged—things that have people saying, 'Whoa, that's pretty cool.'" Cohn received the 1995 Women's Sports Journalism Award, presented by the Women's Sports Foundation. — G.O.

Suggested Reading: *JournalismJobs* (on-line) May 2001; *Mount Holyoke News* (on-line) Feb. 11, 1999; *MSNBC-Newsweek* (on-line) June 6, 2002, with photo

---

Courtesy of Northpoint Technology, Ltd.

## Collier, Sophia

(soh-FYE-uh)

*1956– CEO of Northpoint Technology Ltd.*

*Address: Northpoint Technology Ltd., 444 N. Capitol St., Suite 645, Washington, DC 20001*

For the president of a technology company, Sophia Collier has an unusual pedigree. A former member of the Divine Light Mission, a group that practiced yogic meditation, she spent much of her youth immersed in the hippie lifestyle, which included living in a commune and starting a natural-food store. She also ventured into traditionally male territory, starting a construction business in Maine, and spent time living on an Indian reservation—all before publishing her autobiography at the age of 21. Since then, Collier has started a soda company, which she later sold for $15 million, and founded Citizens Fund, one of the first mutual funds begun with an eye toward social consciousness. She is currently CEO of Northpoint Technology Ltd., a company attempting to compete with satellite and cable firms to provide TV and Internet service in the U.S. "So much of being a success is perseverance as much as ideas . . . ," Collier told Martine Costello for *CNN Money* (October 29, 1999, online). "I've always been interested in trying to get involved in things." Collier is known for her tenacity, political savvy, and marketing ability, all of which she will need to get her latest venture off the ground.

Sophia Whitridge Collier was born in 1956 in New York City. Her father, Oscar Collier, is a literary agent (he has co-written two books, *How to Write and Sell Your First Novel* and *How to Write and Sell Your First Nonfiction Book*); her mother won championships in duplicate bridge. Collier grew up in Easthampton, a prosperous town on Long Island, New York, where the Abstract Expressionist painter Jackson Pollock, who died the year of her birth, had been among the artists in her family's circle of friends. A precocious child, she read the Indian activist Mohandas K. Gandhi's autobiography before her 10th birthday, and at 11 she announced that she was becoming a vegetarian. "Even as a young person, she was canny about competition," her father recalled to Mike Dorning for the *Chicago Tribune* (July 4, 1993). Oscar Collier, according to Dorning, "remembers asking Sophia as a child how she was able so consistently to win the swimming races she entered. 'Well, I scout out the opposition. If I think there's anyone who would beat me, I don't enter,' was her response." Collier was kicked out of her Quaker high school for several infractions of school rules, such as wearing sneakers and bringing a yo-yo to class; she earned her high-school diploma at a boarding school in Sedona, Arizona, by age 16. Among the people who inspired her life's pursuits was one of her grandmothers, an unconventional woman who went to Paris in 1905, when she was just 16, to study at the Sorbonne. "My grandmother was quite an intrepid woman," Collier told Costello. "She was somebody I admired a great deal, who took an interest in me and encouraged me to be all I could be and get out in the world."

After high school Collier moved to Maine, where she started a small construction business as well as a cooperative natural-food store. Her autobiography, *Soul Rush: The Odyssey of a Young Woman of the '70s* (1978), was published by William Morrow when she was 21. The book recounts her experiences using marijuana and LSD; meeting the antiwar and social activist Abbie Hoffman; living on a Hopi Indian reservation and fixing boats in Arizona; her sexual assault by a man who picked her up while she was hitchhiking; and her move to a commune at 16. For a few years beginning when she was 17, she lived at a Divine Light Mission ashram, whose members followed the teachings of Guru Maharaj Ji. To this day she practices the meditation techniques she learned there. "At the ashram, we did things like staying up all night and meditating, things that taught us how to focus our minds," she told Ron Lieber for *Fast Company* (May 2001, on-line). "Those skills never leave you, and they're something that I still feel very connected to. There are times in my current work—and certainly in the past—when I've been involved in stressful business situations. Drawing on those experiences has definitely helped me maintain perspective."

On a hot day in August 1977, not long after Collier had left the ashram and moved to the New York City borough of Brooklyn, she and her roommate Constance Best, a childhood friend of hers, conducted an experiment for fun—mixing seltzer, juice, fruit, and several other ingredients in their kitchen sink. Thinking that the resulting beverage was a potential money-maker, they began bottling it and selling it under the name Soho Natural Soda, using $10,000 of Collier's book royalties to start the company. The sodas were made without caffeine, preservatives, or cane sugar and were packaged in bottles with a distinctive checkerboard design. "One of the most exciting things about a soda company was the opportunity to be involved with the product itself," Collier told Lieber. "We loved seeking new tastes and experimenting with all kinds of wonderful fruits and spices. . . . We could create the ultimate quality soda without hurting our ability to have a profitable product. The truth is, it's easy to make great soda. Most companies just choose not to do it because they think the public can't tell the difference between good and bad." The experience taught Collier valuable marketing skills. First, she and Best set out to persuade local retailers to carry the fledgling brand. "The key thing is not to insult the manager," she told Lieber. "A lot of the stores were owned by immigrants who were very recent arrivals. The manager was sometimes 14 years old. So I'd ask for the manager, look him in the eye, then open the cap on a cold soda, and just give it to him to try. Almost no one can resist an open soda."

It was while marketing her product in this way that Collier met members of the famous Rockefeller family, who were introduced to her as possible investors in the company. "I brought the cold sodas and the business plan" to the initial meeting with the Rockefellers, she told Lieber. Although she was unsure of how her sales pitch would be received, the Rockefellers were quite impressed and, along with others, funded the company—which was named American Natural Beverage—with about $1.3 million. Over the course of the 1980s, Soho Natural Soda developed a loyal customer base in many cities and on college campuses. (In the mid-1980s American Natural Beverage sued the Anheuser-Busch Co., which Collier accused of stealing her formula and customer lists from a manufacturer in Maryland before introducing a similar soft drink with similar packaging. American Natural Beverage won the suit, and Collier celebrated by buying the 1987 Mercedes 560 sedan she still drives.) Collier and Best built the business to the point at which it earned approximately $25 million in sales. In 1989 they sold the brand to Joseph E. Seagram & Sons for approximately $15 million. (The brand did not fare well under the Seagram's label and was purchased by other investors in 1992.)

After selling Soho Natural Soda, Collier purchased a 30-acre farm near Portsmouth, New Hampshire, where she retreated to relax and ponder her next venture. She spent her time sewing, doing organic gardening, dabbling in philanthropic endeavors, and serving, for seven months, as town treasurer of Durham, New Hampshire (a post to which she was appointed by the town council)—all the while reflecting on what had made Soho prosper. "You wonder if it was a fluke or a unique circumstance that allowed you to become successful," she told Lieber. She also spent time educating herself about possible future business ventures. "Because I didn't go to college, I've always been involved in trying to learn more things," she explained. Among other possibilities, she looked into starting a software company and investing in a local bank before deciding to pursue a project on a national scale.

Collier soon found the right avenue to combine her interests in good marketing and social responsibility. In 1991, at a time before socially responsible investing had caught on among the general public, Collier and a few investors purchased a money-market fund from Working Assets in San Francisco for $3.4 million, calling the new company Citizens Funds. (A money-market fund is a type of mutual fund, which consists of pooled money from many individuals, businesses, organizations, schools, or other groups, all of whom have similar, or "mutual," investment goals; the money is managed so as to generate income through investments in stocks, bonds, and other financial instruments.) The Citizens Core Growth Fund, a collection of about 300 large-cap stocks that have been screened for the quality of their effects on society, was launched in 1995 and soon became the company's best-known product. Citizens avoids Big Tobacco firms and firearms manufacturers as well as companies that have poor labor practices, use animals in research, have a negative impact on the environment, or get a large portion of their income from military contracts. The presence of women or racial minorities in high-level positions in a given company, on the other hand, would be regarded favorably. As the basis of the Citizens Index Fund, Collier created the Citizens Index of 300 large-cap companies, among them Microsoft, Cisco Systems, Intel, and MCI WorldCom. The company's other funds are Citizens Emerging Growth Fund, Global Equity Fund, Income Fund, Citizens Funds Value Fund, and the Working Assets Money Market Fund. "With the soda company, I tried to make a product that was very delicious, using high-quality ingredients, with packaging that was visually rich and aesthetically pleasing," Collier told Costello. "In some sense, creating a mutual fund is a similar activity. You're trying to create a product that has wonderful ingredients in an individual sense but form them into a portfolio where they make an improved whole." She told Costello that investing based on factors other than profits can be a good business practice. "We find socially responsible companies in every sector and virtually every industry. It seems such a natural way to invest. . . . Why buy into liabilities and hidden risks that are created by poor practices? It's a good way to assess companies." In 2001 Morningstar Inc., an investment-research firm, ranked Citizens Funds Value Fund first among large-cap value funds. As of mid-May 2002, Citizens Funds was managing $1.5 billion and was worth at least 10 times what Collier and her investors paid for the first money-market fund. Morningstar has placed the fund in the top 10 percent in its category. "We would never attempt to excuse poor financial performance by saying 'well, we did it in a socially responsible way,'" Collier told Vic Roberts for the *Christian Science Monitor* (April 3, 2000, on-line). Instead, she wanted to prove that socially responsible investors don't have to sacrifice large financial rewards. "What socially responsible investing [needs] . . . to have credibility is a strong financial record. Otherwise it's just another form of philanthropy, and one that's not very effective." She wanted an investor to be able, for example, to buy a house or have a comfortable retirement. "My master is my shareholder. . . . I don't see myself as a social crusader," she told Roberts.

"This fund carries a good message," Mark Groesbeck, a certified financial planner at Stanford Group Co. in Houston, told Costello. "You don't have to give up good returns to invest on a socially responsible basis." Citizens Funds is widely credited with bringing socially responsible investing to the mainstream. Although it experienced a few setbacks, the company built an excellent record, despite Collier's lack of experience in the mutual-funds industry. "I was amazed, frankly," John Shields, the CEO whom Collier hired to replace her when she stepped down, in 1999, told Lieber. "I had worked in the industry for 27 years, and I'd seen plenty of people with lots of experience who did not do as good a job as she did. Before I got here, I would not have thought that would have even been possible."

Collier left her position as CEO of Citizens Funds (she remains on the board of directors) to become CEO of a new company, Northpoint Technology, with which she has been involved since 1996. The tiny company, a wireless TV and Internet firm that has yet to begin providing service, has only 10 employees, a minuscule number compared with the staffs of its competitors. The origins of Northpoint can be traced to Saleem and Carmen Tawil, a Texas couple who developed the technology to use ground-based transmitters for television broadcasts. One of the drawbacks of almost all direct-broadcast satellite (DBS) services is that customers cannot receive local television channels, a problem that Northpoint's technology solves. Northpoint has patented a digital wireless system that would use ground-based transmitters and satellite dishes pointed north (existing DBS companies use dishes pointed south) to get more use from the digital spectrum. Because of the limited size of the electromagnetic spectrum that comprises all radio and television frequencies, only a limited number of pay-TV services can make use of it. If the new system developed by the Tawils—named Broadwave USA—works, twice as many pay-TV services could broadcast. In order to use the new technology, Northpoint had to first obtain a license from the Federal Communications Commission (FCC), which regulates space on the spectrum. The Tawils turned to the venture capitalist Chula Reynolds for assistance with this process, and she suggested that they consult Collier. As treasurer of the New Hampshire Democratic Party, Collier knew her way around the regulatory world of Washington, D.C. Northpoint proposed competing with DBS companies by offering a package of cable-television channels and high-speed Internet access at a steep discount, only $20 a month for almost 100 channels, or $40 a month for both Internet access and TV. (By contrast, EchoStar Communications and DirecTV typically charge $80 to $90 a month for the Internet-TV combination.) Northpoint's service could be offered at a low cost because it would not require launching satellites or laying cable. When word of the new company's plans spread, however, larger, established companies were quick to try to block the deal. EchoStar and DirecTV charged that the system would cause signal interference on their customers' DBS systems, causing poor reception.

Collier is not cowed by the size or tactics of the competition, though she realizes that those companies are formidable forces. "When I began this project, I believed the technology would solve some really tough problems," she told Kathy Chen for the *Wall Street Journal* (June 2, 2000, on-line). "What I've realized as time passes is: The power of incumbents is truly profound and very hard to overcome." Collier has enlisted many politically connected people to lobby on Northpoint's behalf, including former congressman Bob Livingston; the brother of President Bill Clinton's chief of staff; the wife of President George W. Bush's campaign manager; and the actress Lily Tomlin. Dozens of House and Senate members urged the FCC to approve Northpoint's bid to offer service nationwide, and in November 2000 the agency decided to allow new TV and Internet services to share part of the spectrum. Executives at DBS companies as well as the Satellite Broadcasting and Communications Association (SBCA) have claimed that the FCC gave Northpoint preferential treatment. "The FCC is cutting corners in this process," Steve Parry, a lobbyist for the SBCA, told Chen. "I think this FCC has been susceptible to political considerations." Chuck Hewitt, the president of SBCA, was also stunned at the decision. "It's incomprehensible that the FCC would allow sharing of the direct broadcast satellite frequency band [by land-based wireless companies]," he said, as quoted by Becky Yerak in *USA Today* (December 1, 2000, on-line). "There's already spectrum available for these types of technology." Merrill Spiegel, vice president for governmental affairs at DirecTV, believes that Northpoint's executives are unprepared to launch the service they propose. "They are spending a fortune lobbying and yet they have no infrastructure to build anything," he told Stephen Labaton for the *New York Times* (April 8, 2001). "When they go to Capitol Hill and say they will serve underserved places like Wyoming and Montana, it's very appealing. But the majority of people who have studied this issue say there is no way they will do it. There are technical impediments. And there aren't enough potential subscribers in Montana and Wyoming." For their part, Collier and others at Northpoint have said that the company can build a large network of local transmitters within two years of obtaining a license.

The question remains as to whether Northpoint will have to bid for use of the spectrum at auction, which could cause financial difficulties for the company. While independent local partners have pledged to pay the $1.5 billion cost of applying the wireless technology in their markets, the company has said that it cannot afford to spend millions of dollars for the right to use the spectrum, and that it shouldn't have to. (Northpoint has already spent more than $10 million in lobbying and legal costs.) "We don't support the concept of an auction," Collier said, as reported by Robert M. Cook in *Foster's Sunday Citizen* (January 13, 2001, on-line). "We think it is very unfair and will definitely delay the introduction of the new service." She added that because Northpoint patented the technology for spectrum-sharing between terrestrial and satellite broadcasts, it should be able to use the airwaves without bidding for them at auction. The firm's lawyers have also claimed that a law enacted in 2000 prohibits the auction of the satellite spectrum band. DBS firms argue that the law applies only to actual satellite services. Some DBS companies and lawmakers say it would be unfair to let Northpoint use the spectrum for free when wireless companies have paid billions of dollars to share it. Northpoint executive vice president Toni Cook Bush counters that DirecTV, the largest satellite company, "did not pay the U.S. Treasury one penny" for using the spectrum. Collier is equally quick to point out what she sees as the hypocrisy of the satellite companies' position. "Isn't it amazing that the largest telecommunications companies should be granted the spectrum . . . and those same parties advocate that small start-ups with new technology should be subjected to an auction?" she said, as reported by Yerak.

In an effort to avoid an auction, in March 2002 Northpoint announced that it would enhance its antenna-based wireless TV and Internet service with satellites. Under this plan, the company would use satellites to provide 300 national TV channels and would use its land-based antennas to supply local channels and high-speed Internet service. On April 23, however, the FCC rejected Northpoint's request for a spectrum license. Although the FCC authorized terrestrial use of the spectrum, Northpoint and other companies hoping to use it will have to bid for it at auction. In the past, Northpoint executives had said that if the company had to bid for licenses at auction, it would abandon its plans but retain its patents, thereby prohibiting other companies from receiving licenses to broadcast using a combination of ground-based transmitters and satellite dishes. But in a press release issued by Broadwave USA on April 23, Collier stated that Northpoint was considering an appeal of the FCC decision. "This is the first time the FCC has ever found that terrestrial operations can co-exist ubiquitously with satellites, so it is a real technical milestone," she was quoted as saying in the press release. She went on to express disappointment that the application of Northpoint's Broadwave affiliate system had been dismissed. "Granting the Broadwave applications would have more than tripled the participation of women and minority owners of video broadcasting properties in the United States. The Broadwave affiliates deserved approval, just as much as the large satellite companies who share the same spectrum. Last week, the FCC announced it would license them without auction. This disparate treatment of applicants that share the same spectrum is a poor public policy. It is also surprising that at a time when cable rates are rising at 7.5% a year and the industry is consolidating at an unprecedented pace the FCC would decide to dismiss, rather than accept, qualified applications of a new competitor with a proven technology." If Northpoint is forced to bid for rights to the spectrum, it is doubtful that the company could offer the low-cost service it proposes. With that in mind, in June 2002 Northpoint asked the Washington, D.C., Circuit Court of Appeals to reverse the FCC dismissal of the company's license applications. On September 10, 2002 Senator Mary Landrieu, a Louisiana Democrat, and Senator Conrad Burns, a Montana Republican, introduced legislation in Congress that, if passed, would facilitate deployment of terrestrial systems such as Northpoint.

Although it has been eight years since Northpoint first applied for a license from the FCC, those who know Collier don't believe that the company she helms is down for the count. "She has a reputation as a tenacious negotiator, willing to draw out talks to unusual lengths to gain concession," Dorning wrote. In the same article, he quoted a source who had faced Collier at the negotiating table as saying, "Dealing with her is something like having a close encounter with a steam roller."

In addition to serving as treasurer of the New Hampshire Democratic Party, Collier, who routinely works 12-hour days, is incorporator of the New Hampshire Charitable Fund and trustee of the New England Circle, a branch of the nonprofit group

Global Citizens Circle, which provides world leaders and social activists a forum to engage in civil discourse with people from around the world. She received an honorary doctor of laws degree from New Hampshire College in 1992 and was a guest of President Clinton on Air Force One in the mid-1990s. — K.E.D.

Suggested Reading: *Broadcasting & Cable* p80 June 11, 2001; *Chicago Tribune* VII p1 July 4, 1993; *Christian Science Monitor* (on-line) Apr. 3, 2000; *CNN Money* (on-line) Oct. 29, 1999; *Fast Company* (on-line) May and June 2001; *Foster's Sunday Citizen* (on-line) Jan. 13, 2002; *Money* B p3 Nov. 8, 2001; *New York Times* III p1 Apr. 8, 2001; *USA Today* (on-line) Dec. 1, 2000; *Wall Street Journal* (on-line) June 2, 2000

---

Armando Gallo/Retna

## Connelly, Jennifer

*Dec. 12, 1970– Actress*

*Address: c/o International Creative Management, 8942 Wilshire Blvd., Beverly Hills, CA 90211*

"With Jennifer, the irony is that it is her honesty and simplicity that achieve her great mystery and depth and that special ethereal quality," the film director Keith Gordon told Andrew Marton for the *Fort Worth Star-Telegram* (May 27, 2000). "We just aren't used to seeing that kind of simplified, open-hearted honesty on screen. Today it's more about seeing actors put on faces, put on sexiness. But Jennifer is seductive or mysterious by not putting on seductive or mysterious airs." Connelly's career in film began nearly 20 years ago, with several teen comedies. Until recently, she was often cast as sultry characters in adult dramas that, at best, might be described as mediocre. Thanks to her harrowing and critically acclaimed performance in *Requiem for a Dream* and her Oscar-winning performance opposite Russell Crowe in *A Beautiful Mind*, she has gained recognition as one of the most talented and versatile young actresses in American films today. "There was a period where I felt like I wasn't quite being considered for the projects that I wanted to work on because maybe people were thinking, 'I'm not going to cast the girl who was in that movie for this adult project'. . . ," Connelly told Fred Topel for *Beer.com* (December 26, 2001, online). "I've felt for a long time that this is what I want to do so I'm happy at this point to just take my time and work on projects that I feel really strongly about and the rest of the time just live my life."

The only child of Gerard Connelly, a clothing manufacturer, and Eileen Connelly (some sources spell her name "Ilene"), an antique dealer, Jennifer Connelly was born in a Catskill Mountains town, in New York State, on December 12, 1970. (According to the *International Motion Picture Almanac 2002*, she was born in New York City.) Until she was about seven, the Connellys lived in New York City's Brooklyn Heights neighborhood, across the East River from Manhattan. When she was in second grade, the family moved to Woodstock, New York. "It was great. . . . I basically remember climbing a lot of trees," Connelly recalled to David Wise for *Rolling Stone* (August 8, 1991). Four years later the family returned to Brooklyn, where Connelly attended the Saint Ann's School. No longer affiliated with a church by that time, the school was noted for its progressive approach to education and its rich arts and theater programs. "It was kind of one of those schools where everybody performed for each other all the time in school assemblies," Connelly told James Ryan for *BPI Entertainment News Wire* (on-line). At the suggestion of a family friend, when Connelly was 10 her parents sent her photo to the prestigious Ford modeling agency. Ford soon added her to its roster, and she began modeling for print ads and, later, for television commercials as well; her image also appeared on packaging for Danskin tights, among other products. Despite her busy work schedule, which included assignments in Europe, she never thought of modeling as a potential career; as she told Anna David for *People* (April 21, 1997), "I was so shy and I didn't like getting my picture taken." Instead, she dreamed of becoming a veterinarian.

In 1982 a casting director who had noticed Connelly's work set up an audition for her with the film director Sergio Leone, who was looking to cast a young girl to dance in one scene of his gangster epic *Once Upon a Time in America* (1984). "Not being a dancer, I had no idea what to do and I can only imagine how silly it must have looked, whatever it was I did," Connelly recalled to David Eimer for *Empire* (September 1996), as quoted on the *Jen-*

*nifer Connelly Center* Web site. Connelly won the role of Deborah, reportedly because the shape of her nose matched that of the actress Elizabeth McGovern, who played the adult Deborah. At around the same time, Connelly appeared in an episode of the British television series *Tales of the Unexpected* and in the video for the Duran Duran single "Union of the Snake"; a slew of other roles followed. "Before I knew it, [acting] became what I did. It was a very peculiar way to grow up, combined with my personality," she told Lauren Waterman for *Vogue* (November 2000). "I was so shy, and I wanted to make people happy, so I wound up being superficially mature but quite stagnated internally." In 1985 she starred as Jennifer Corvino, a girl who is able to communicate with insects, in Dario Argento's gory horror film *Phenomena.* In the same year she played the lead in another little-noticed movie, *Seven Minutes in Heaven.*

In a role that made Connelly a celebrity among teenagers, she starred as Sarah, opposite David Bowie (the Goblin King), in *Labyrinth*, Jim Henson's 1986 fantasy about growing up. A lover of fairy tales who resents having to babysit Toby, her little stepbrother, Sarah wishes that the Goblin King would spirit the boy away. After her wish comes true, she journeys to the Labyrinth to rescue Toby before the Goblin King turns him into a goblin. Other than Connelly, Bowie, and the toddler who played Toby, the cast consisted of muppets created by Henson and his staff. "I was at a stage where it was just kind of fun to be making movies," Connelly told Ian Spelling for *Starlog* (September 1997), as quoted on the *Jennifer Connelly Center.* "I was trying to do everything OK and trying to be grown up. I had the responsibility of doing this big movie and I was 14. . . . I remember it being really fun and loving Jim Henson. I had a great time running around a lot, sweating and playing with things. The movie sets were like this huge playground, this imaginative, fantastical world to play in. To me, it wasn't about my performance, which was fine at the time. I look back now, though, and say 'My God, what was I thinking?'"

Within the next few years Connelly appeared in a video for the Roy Orbison single "I Drove All Night" and in television commercials in Japan. In Japan she also released a single of her own, "Monologue of Love," which she sang in Japanese. In what she described to David Wise as "a phase that came early and went fast," she also embraced the New York club scene. In 1988 she appeared in Michael Hoffman's *Some Girls*, about an eccentric Canadian family. Recalling such efforts from her teens, she told David Eimer, "I hate to watch them, but every once in a while it'll be like a family thing and grandpa really wants to pop in an old video. And friends think it's really funny. 'Let's all rent this and have a good laugh at Jen.'"

After she graduated from high school, in about 1988, Connelly spent two years in college, first at Yale University, in New Haven, Connecticut, as an English major, and then at Stanford University, in Stanford, California, where she studied drama. She resumed her career with a featured role in *The Hot Spot* (1990), a steamy film noir directed by Dennis Hopper from an adaptation of Charles Williams's novel *Hell Hath No Fury.* Connelly's character, Gloria Harper, falls in love with a rootless loner (played by Don Johnson) who comes to work at the car dealership where she is an accountant. Roger Ebert, who judged the film to be a "superior work in an old tradition," wrote for the *Chicago Sun-Times* (October 26, 1990, on-line) that Connelly was "perfectly cast" as "the good girl who has been bruised by an uncaring world." *The Hot Spot* marked the first time the actress appeared topless in front of the camera. "The nudity was hard for me and something I thought about," she told Stephen Schaefer for *USA Today* (October 24, 1990), "but it's not in a sleazy context."

Connelly's next film was *Career Opportunities* (1991), seen by many as a professional low point for the actress. In that picture, directed by Bryan Gordon from a screenplay by John Hughes, she was cast as Josie McClellan, the unhappy daughter of the town's wealthiest businessman. Josie falls asleep in a dressing room at a Target department store and awakes to find that she is locked in with the overnight janitor (Frank Whaley). After a prickly start she and the janitor begin to fall in love. The plot thickens when they discover two petty crooks in the store, trying to carry out a heist. Much of the footage, as well as ads for the film, dwelled on Connelly's voluptuous figure. The movie received scathing reviews. "You don't want to get rid of your experiences, because they're your experiences—good or bad—and you need them," Connelly told Rory Evans for *Premiere* (December 2001, on-line). "But it would be great if they weren't on the video shelf." In a better role, Connelly starred as Jenny Blake in Disney's *The Rocketeer* (directed by Joe Johnston), a throwback to 1930s Hollywood adventure films. The story concerns a young pilot, Cliff Secord (Bill Campbell), whose discovery of a top-secret rocket pack leads to a confrontation with Nazis, among other villains. Roger Ebert, writing for the *Chicago-Sun Times* (June 21, 1991, on-line), noted that Connelly was "sweet and sexy as [Secord's] girlfriend, and projects the same innocent sensuality of the classic B-movie sexpots—an ability to seem totally unaware, for example, that she is wearing a low-cut dress." Although expectations that *The Rocketeer* would be a blockbuster were not borne out, Connelly appreciated its modest success, which far outweighed that of any of her earlier films. "I'm just excited to be in a movie that will be around theaters long enough that when I tell my friends to see my movie, they actually have the option of waiting till the end of the weekend it opens," she told David Wise in 1991. "Some of my movies, you blinked and you missed them." Six years later she recalled to Ian Spelling, "I had a hard time finding my niche in that movie because there was so much going on visually, and because it was so much about the story. The characters were kind of secondary to just telling the story. That was a strange place for me to be in." During shooting Connelly and Bill Campbell became romantically involved; after five years of on-again, off-again dating, the couple broke up.

Connelly followed *The Rocketeer* with the television film *Heart of Justice* (1992), directed by Bruno Barreto, in which she played a mysterious young woman from an eccentric, wealthy family. Her next film was the poorly received *Of Love and Shadows* (1994), based on a novel by the Chilean-born Isabel Allende, in which she portrayed a Chilean aristocrat who awakens both politically and romantically after she meets a photojournalist who has joined the resistance to their nation's military dictatorship. Somewhat more successful was John Singleton's *Higher Learning* (1995), in which a diverse group of students on the campus of the fictional Columbus University grapple with issues of race, sexuality, and identity. Connelly played Taryn, the lesbian head of a feminist student group.

Connelly next appeared in the small but central role of the sultry, promiscuous Allison Pond in *Mulholland Falls* (1996). Allison's murder leads a brutal Los Angeles anti-gangster police unit to uncover her sexual links to several prominent figures, including the married head of the anti-gangster squad (played by Nick Nolte). The film included several sex scenes in which Connelly was naked. "It kind of shocked everyone who knows me that I wound up doing this movie, because I had always been so careful about nudity," Connelly told Mark Green for *USA Today* (May 1, 1996). However, she explained, the sex "was very much a part of this character, and I couldn't be coy or guarded or self-conscious—otherwise it wouldn't work. It was sort of a challenge I wanted to take on, I guess." After a part in John Huddles's little-noticed independent film *Far Harbor* (1996), Connelly portrayed Eleanor Abbott, the "bad" sister, in *Inventing the Abbotts* (1997). Based on a short story by Sue Miller and directed by Pat O'Connor, *Inventing the Abbotts* focuses on two brothers and their romantic adventures with three sisters in 1957. Connelly's work in that film impressed the director, producer, and actor Ron Howard. "She not only was beautiful and seductive but gave some difficult psychological moments in the film a lot of depth and complexity," Howard told Barry Koltnow for the *Orange County Register* (January 2, 2002), as quoted on the *Jennifer Connelly Center*. "She had an extraordinary combination of talent and beauty, and I guess I stored that information in the back of my brain." In mid-1997 Connelly gave birth to a son. Her next role, a small one, was in the writer-director Alex Proyas's complicated thriller *Dark City* (1998), set in a surrealistic future society run by beings with telekinetic powers.

In 2000 Connelly demonstrated her acting skills—and sex appeal—in major roles in two movies: Keith Gordon's *Waking the Dead*, based on a novel by Scott Spencer, and Darren Aronofsky's *Requiem for a Dream*, for which Hubert Selby Jr. adapted one of his own novels. In *Waking the Dead* Connelly played Sarah, the supposedly deceased lover of a senatorial candidate (Billy Crudup) who starts catching glimpses of her again. A fervent left-wing activist, Sarah had reportedly been killed in a political car-bombing a decade earlier. "This was a very collaborative shoot," Connelly told Rick Leider for *Black Cat Media* (on-line). "We improvised more and more as the film progressed. As the relationships started to take on a life of their own, we kind of fell into a pattern [in which] the characters started to feel like they had their own lives and space, so it just happened." In his review of *Waking the Dead* for the *New York Times* (March 24, 2000, on-line), Stephen Holden noted that Connelly "captures a burning ethereality and willfulness that are very much of the period."

*Requiem for a Dream*, set in the Coney Island section of Brooklyn, is a harrowing depiction of drug addiction among three young friends—Marion Silver (Connelly); Harry Goldfarb (Jared Leto), Marion's boyfriend; and Tyrone Love (Marlon Wayans), Harry's best friend—and Sara Goldfarb, Harry's widowed mother (Ellen Burstyn). Small-time junkies who hope to amass a small fortune, the three friends succeed only in descending further into drug dependency and degradation. Under Harry's influence, for example, Marion has sex with her therapist and then begins to sell herself at stag parties. In her interview with *Black Cat Media*, Connelly recalled, "I personally approached the role by getting a separate apartment in my building and living like Marion would to get the feeling of isolation. I would go there and do everything that she would do because her life was so very separate from my own and it was difficult to balance the two to live for my own space and be her, so I would go to this apartment and paint and make clothes and listen to the music that she would listen to and spend a lot of time thinking about addiction and the origin of it for her and what that place was in myself. That kind of journey was very uncomfortable. It was a really crazy time for me. I had great compassion for my character. It was hard to be her all day and come home to my son and fingerpaint with him." Connelly also prepared for the part by hanging around addicts and attending Narcotics Anonymous meetings with a friend of hers who was recovering from drug addiction. In a review of *Requiem of a Dream* for the *New York Times* (October 6, 2000, on-line), Elvis Mitchell wrote, "It's [Connelly's] performance that gives the movie weight, since her fall is the most precipitous. By the end, when she curls into a happy fetal ball with a furtive smile on her face, she has come to love her debasement. . . . Her dank realization is more disturbing than anything in the novel, and Ms. Connelly has never before done anything to prepare us for how good she is here." The actress was also cast in a third film in 2000: *Pollock*, Ed Harris's rendition of the rise to fame and subsequent self-destruction of the American abstract painter Jackson Pollock, in which she appeared briefly as Ruth Kligman, the artist's last lover.

In 2001 Connelly starred as Alicia Nash, the wife of mathematical games theorist John Nash (played by Russell Crowe), in *A Beautiful Mind*. The movie relates the story of John Nash's career and battle with paranoid schizophrenia. A graduate student when the two meet, Alicia is attracted to Nash's genius and lonely demeanor. As her husband's psychological problems worsen, she is torn between her feelings of love for him and unhappiness about the debilitating effect of his illness on her life. "I thought they would never cast me," Connelly told Carla Meyer for the *San Francisco Chronicle* (December 16, 2001). "You come across a script like this every few years, and every actress is going to want it." In a review of *A Beautiful Mind* for the *Los Angeles Times* (December 21, 2000, on-line), Kenneth Turan described Connelly's work in it as "her most confident and impressive . . . ever." "There's an intelligence and a tartness to her performance," he wrote, "an ability to be energized rather than fazed or intimidated by her co-star's powers, that leads to a noticeable on-screen sizzle between them." Although highly critical of the film, Charles Taylor wrote in *Salon* (December 21, 2000, on-line), "Connelly has a knack for responding to a moment with all her emotions while retaining some semblance of composure . . . and that contrast provides the only honest emotion in the movie. It takes a great deal of talent to seem real in a movie as fundamentally dishonest as this one." For her performance in the film, Connelly won the 2002 Academy Award for best actress in a supporting role. She also won BAFTA (British Academy of Film and Television Arts) and Golden Globe Awards in the same category.

In 2001 Connelly appeared in the short-lived television series *The $treet*, having accepted the role—that of Catharine Miller, a tough new brokerage supervisor at a Wall Street firm—in part because the show was filmed near her home. In 2003 she is slated to appear as Betty Ross in *The Hulk*, directed by Ang Lee. "I've never seen an uninteresting female character in any of Ang's films," she told Nancy Mills for the New York *Daily News* (December 16, 2001). "He wants to make a psychodrama and Greek tragedy in the form of a comic book. I think it's going to be pretty collaborative. There's nothing more frustrating than when your opinions aren't wanted. When you feel a project going down the road of mediocrity, it's frightening and nauseating. I haven't done one of those in a while, and I'm immensely grateful." The actress has been cast as Kathy Nicolo, one of the main characters, in the film *House of Sand and Fog*, based on a novel by Andre Dubus III.

Connelly has expressed a desire to act on stage, but, as she told the interviewer for *Black Cat Media*, "I haven't felt that it was my time to do it. Every time I see a play now, being in New York and having so much theater available to me, I think that that's what I would like to do, but I would like to be in a little theater company and do plays. I would love that." "In terms of the work I do," she told Ian Spelling, "I'm happy with the way it's going. I've learned a few things, especially in the last couple of years. . . . For the last few years I've grown more and changed more, and things just feel different now. I'm still working and I have a lot to do, I have a lot I want to accomplish. That's just in terms of the integrity of my work, and not about how people perceive me or if I'm famous. I'm happy where I am."

Connelly speaks fluent Italian and French and enjoys such outdoor activities as hiking, camping, swimming, and bike riding. By her own account, she is also interested in quantum physics and philosophy. She lives with her son, Kai, in the West Village neighborhood of New York City; Kai's father, the photographer David Dugan (or "Dougan," as some sources spell it), lives elsewhere but is an active presence in the boy's life. Connelly also spends a great deal of time in a house in the Hamptons, on Long Island, New York. She has been dating the actor Josh Charles for some time. "The last few years, my biggest challenge was having Kai, and the period since then has had the most effect on me and my work," Connelly told Bob Ivry for the *Bergen Record* (March 21, 2000), according to the *Jennifer Connelly Center*. "Kai has been a huge catalyst for change and growth. I'd re-chosen this work way before he was born and decided that this is what I wanted to do. But now the choices I make have powerful reverberations. I have to be careful how I choose to spend my time. Kai is like a bell of mindfulness sounding throughout the day." —G.O.

Suggested Reading: *Beer.com*; *Black Cat Media* (on-line); *Jennifer Connelly Center* (on-line); *Newsweek* p50+ Jan. 21, 2002, with photo; *People* p47+ July 15, 1991, with photos, p73+ Feb. 4, 2002, with photos; *Premiere* p76+ Dec. 2001, with photo; *Rolling Stone* p59+ Aug. 8, 1991, with photos; *Vogue* p346+ Nov. 2000, with photo

Selected Films: *Phenomena*, 1985; *Seven Minutes in Heaven*, 1985; *Labyrinth*, 1986; *Ballet*, 1988; *Some Girls*, 1988; *The Hot Spot*, 1990; *Career Opportunities*, 1991; *The Rocketeer*, 1991; *Heart of Justice*, 1992; *Of Love and Shadows*, 1994; *Higher Learning*, 1995; *Mulholland Falls*, 1996; *Far Harbor*, 1996; *Inventing the Abbotts*, 1997; *Dark City*, 1998; *Waking the Dead*, 2000; *Pollock*, 2000; *Requiem for a Dream*, 2000; *A Beautiful Mind*, 2001

Selected Television Shows: *The $treet*, 2000

Courtesy of Arizona Diamondbacks

## Counsell, Craig

*Aug. 21, 1970– Baseball player*

*Address: Arizona Diamondbacks, Bank One Ballpark, 401 E. Jefferson St., Phoenix, AZ 85001*

"I love to play baseball," Craig Counsell, an infielder with the Arizona Diamondbacks, told Ken Rosenthal for the *Sporting News* (October 29, 2001). "You've got to believe that you're a good baseball player, that you can play in the big leagues, that you can have success. Despite obstacles, hurdles or bad luck, you've got to keep on busting." A professional baseball player since 1992, Counsell played in the minor leagues for five seasons before becoming a journeyman infielder in the majors. Shuttling among four teams in his six seasons in the major leagues, the injury-plagued Counsell has not emerged as a star player in the usual sense; he has, however, contributed excellent defense to the teams he has played for. "If you look at him from afar," Bob Brenly, the manager of the Diamondbacks, told Tyler Kepner for the *New York Times* (October 29, 2001), "he doesn't really do a lot of things that knock your eyes out. He's one of those players you have to see over a period of time and see the way he does things the way they're supposed to be done." And while he may not stand out on a regular basis, he has shown a remarkable ability to come through when needed: he has made clutch offensive contributions during postseason play, scoring the winning run in Game Seven of the World Series for the 1997 Florida Marlins and more than pulling his weight as a member of the 2001 World Champion Arizona Diamondbacks. One of the Diamondbacks' star starting pitchers, Curt Schilling, told Kepner, "He's just been incredible. . . . He finds a way to be in the middle of every important situation, whether he is at the plate or in the field."

A son of John and Jan Counsell, Craig John Counsell was born on August 21, 1970 in South Bend, Indiana. He grew up in Milwaukee, Wisconsin, where John Counsell worked for the Milwaukee Brewers baseball organization. Always welcome in the Brewers clubhouse, as a boy Craig Counsell spent time there with the baseball greats Paul Molitor and Robin Yount, both of whom had long, outstanding careers. "I was [at County Stadium] all the time, especially when I was little . . . ," Counsell told Tom Haudricourt for the *Milwaukee Journal Sentinel* (October 14, 1997, online). "I was around those guys a lot.

Not just at the park, but away from the field. I saw how they carried themselves. Guys like Molitor and Yount, there's no better example of how to approach the game and carry yourself than those two guys." Counsell graduated from Whitefish Bay High School in Milwaukee and enrolled at the University of Notre Dame, in Notre Dame, Indiana, where his father had been an outfielder and baseball team captain in the 1960s. Counsell spent four seasons as an infielder at Notre Dame, while majoring in accounting. Upon his graduation, in 1992, the Colorado Rockies—an expansion team—picked him in the 11th round of the draft as a shortstop/second base prospect.

Counsell went to work as an infielder in the Rockies farm system. His stints on the double-A team in Binghamton, New York, and the triple-A team in Colorado Springs, Colorado, though solid, were memorable less for his playing than for his multiple injuries. Over the course of several minor-league seasons, he fractured his right foot three times; as a left-handed batter he was particularly susceptible to that injury. "Three times, I broke a bone fouling a ball off my foot," he explained to Ken Rosenthal. "Foot, ankle, leg—it seemed like it never would end. But you've got to just keep at it, you know?" In July 1994, after playing shortstop steadily for almost three months after recovering from a broken foot, he broke his nose. During the 1995 season he played well at Colorado Springs, which won the Pacific Coast League title that year. Counsell was called up in September 1995 to join the expanded roster of the Colorado Rockies but played in only three games, as a shortstop, and had only one major-league at-bat. (He walked.) Sent back to Colorado Springs in the spring of 1996, he broke his right shin less than a month into the season. By the middle of the summer, he had recovered, only to injure his leg after three games; he played in only 25 games during the 1996 season.

Counsell's long-awaited major-league career began in earnest during the 1997 season. Having compiled a .335 batting average over 96 games for the triple-A Colorado Springs SkySox, he was called up to play for the Rockies in July. After only a week at second base for the Rockies, he was traded to the Florida Marlins, where he saw regular action as a second baseman, committing only three fielding errors and hitting .299 in his rookie season. "It was a good trade for me, a good opportunity," he told Tom Haudricourt, in part because the then–20-year-old Neifi Perez was seeking the role of a young, indispensable infielder for the Rockies. (Half a dozen years older than Perez, Counsell would have had less opportunity to play and less chance of securing a long-term contract.) "I had a lot of friends in Colorado, but I have no regrets because this has been a better opportunity. Sometimes you have to wait a long time for good things to happen, then it all happens at once." Although only a rookie, Counsell was with the Marlins as they marched into the 1997 play-offs as the National League wild-card team. Defeating the San Francisco Giants in a three-game sweep of the National League Division Series (NLDS), the Marlins faced the Atlanta Braves for the National League title. In a surprise development, Counsell performed brilliantly at the plate, batting .400 over the course of the National League Championship Series (NLCS), which the Marlins won, four games to two. He was eager to face the Cleveland Indians in the World Series, despite the frosty weather—which included snow—that awaited the Marlins in Ohio. "I can't wait to go out and play in it, to be honest with you," he said to Mike Lurie for *CBS SportsLine* (October 23, 1997). "To me growing up, this is always what the World Series was played in, [cold] weather. . . . It's the World Series, I don't care what the weather is going to be like. . . . If you let it affect you, you're crazy." In back-and-forth fashion, the World Series stretched to seven games, with the Marlins taking Games One, Three, and Five before winning Game Seven—and the championship—in Miami in the bottom of the 11th inning. Counsell tied the game at 2–2 in the bottom of the ninth by hitting a sacrifice fly; in the 11th, after reaching base on a Cleveland fielding error, he scored the World Series' winning run when he came home on a single by Edgar Renteria. Counsell's game-winning plays were recorded in the Baseball Hall of Fame.

Counsell struggled in the 1998 season, batting only .251 over 104 games. In August he was hit in the face by a fastball unleashed by Houston pitcher C. J. Nitowski. His jaw was broken and required surgery; he was out for the remainder of the 1998 season while his jaw was wired shut in order to heal. Counsell received letters and good wishes from all over the country while recuperating. Early in 1999 it appeared that he might lose his positions as second baseman and leadoff hitter to the speedy, switch-hitting Luis Castillo. "It's going to be that way every year for me because of the kind of player I am," he explained in an Associated Press interview (March 14, 1999) during spring training. "I'm not going to steal a lot of bases or hit a lot of home runs." Counsell played in 37 Marlins games in 1999 before he was released; his contract was picked up by the Los Angeles Dodgers, for whom he played 50 games at second base or shortstop.

Released by the Dodgers during 2000 spring training, Counsell was quickly picked up by the Arizona Diamondbacks, a team in its third year of existence. He was signed to a minor-league contract and began the 2000 season with the Diamondbacks' triple-A Tucson affiliate, the Sidewinders. After batting .348 in 50 games for the Sidewinders, Counsell was called up to the Diamondbacks at the end of May. As a utility infielder he divided his time among shortstop, second base, and third base, and he amassed a .316 batting average. In the 2001 season Counsell shared second-base responsibilities with Jay Bell, took over for the injured Matt Williams at third base, filled in for Tony Womack at shortstop, and even played a couple of games at first base; his batting average for the year stood at .275. The Diamondbacks entered the 2001 play-offs perched atop the National League West. In the NLDS, Arizona defeated the St. Louis Cardinals in a five-game series; Counsell knocked in a three-run homer in Game Three off a pitch by Mike Matthews, his first-ever home run against a left-handed pitcher. In a six-game NLCS win opposite the Atlanta Braves, Counsell continued his career-long streak of hitting Atlanta pitches well, batting .381 for the series with a four-RBI night (including two doubles) in Game Five. He picked up the NLCS Most Valuable Player award for his performance. "Any time you can help your team win, you are going to enjoy it," he told Tyler Kepner. "It's nothing more than that. I'm not trying to grab the spotlight or anything. I'm trying to help my team win." Facing the New York Yankees in the World Series, Counsell delivered a home run in the bottom of the first inning of Game One, which tied the game and opened the floodgates for Arizona hitters. Though he did not score again in the World Series, his game contributions helped to carry the team, including key pitcher Curt Schilling, through that game and several others. After exhausting, hard-fought games, the Arizona Diamondbacks eked out a win in the bottom of the ninth inning in Game Seven, handing the Yankees their first postseason series loss since 1997. "Oddly enough, I think this has been a lot more fun for me," Counsell told Henry Schulman for the *San Francisco Chronicle* (October 22, 2001). "I think when I was a rookie, you have those blinders on where you're just happy to be there. I thought it was easy. I went all the way through the play-offs and won a World Series, and I had two months in the big leagues. Four years later, you realize how hard this is to do." Valued for his defensive flexibility and easygoing manner at last, in January 2002 Counsell signed a three-year contract with Arizona, with options for 2005 and 2006.

In the 2002 season Counsell spent more than 90 games at third base in place of Matt Williams (who broke his leg in spring training) before moving back to his regular spots at second base or shortstop. By the end of the season, he had made 123 hits and 51 RBIs and earned a batting average of .282. The Diamondbacks advanced to the post-season, where they were defeated in three games by the St. Louis Cardinals.

Counsell, who is married, is listed as being six feet tall. His build is so slight that his own teammates have often pronounced him to be several inches shorter. (Curt Schilling, talking with Tyler Kepner, said that Counsell "has a presence about him that belies his 5-foot—what is he, 5-5, 5-6?") Counsell is known for his highly unusual batting stance, in which the bat is held high off his left shoulder and his legs are straight and planted far apart. "It makes me relax and puts me in a position where I feel I can see the ball well and can take a good swing at it," he told Chuck Johnson for *USA Today* (October 29, 2001). "It might look strange, but that's just where it feels comfortable for me." — K.S.

Suggested Reading: CBS *SportsLine* (on-line) Oct. 23, 1997, with photo ; *Milwaukee Journal Sentinel* (on-line) Oct. 13, 1997; *New York Times* D p8 Oct. 29, 2001, with photo; *Sporting News* p14+ Oct. 29, 2001, with photo

---

## Creed

*Rock band*

Phillips, Scott
*Feb. 22, 1973–*

Stapp, Scott
*Aug. 8, 1973–*

Tremonti, Mark
*Apr. 18, 1974–*

*Address: c/o Wind-up Records, 72 Madison Ave., New York, NY 10016*

Combining the hard-rock fury of grunge bands such as Pearl Jam with lyrics that address issues of spirituality and morality, Creed has emerged as one of the most popular rock bands in the United States. Their first two albums, *My Own Person* (1997) and *Human Clay* (1999), sold a total of more than 15 million copies, and the band was twice named *Billboard*'s rock artist of the year. While Creed has often been called a Christian band because of the topics of its songs, the members of the group take exception to that label. "We are not a Christian band," Creed's lead singer and lyricist, Scott Stapp, told Kevin A. Miller for *Christianity Today* (January 8, 2001). "A Christian band has an agenda to lead others to believe in their specific, religious beliefs. We have no agenda!" Unlike many other "alternative" rock bands, the group refuses to write songs about reveling in pain and anger. Stapp explained to Larry Flick for *Billboard* (November 10, 2001), "When I'm dealing with a heavy issue or something that stirs my anger, I don't want to stay there. I want to get out. I need to believe that there's eventual relief from the pain." The band often expounds on its optimistic outlook during its stage shows, which feature ample pyrotechnics and theatrics. Reviewing one of those shows for the *New York Times* (September 2, 2000), Ann Powers noted that Stapp "made so many heroic moves, it seemed as if this was his qualifying routine for the frontman olympics. He pranced and crouched and swept his arms heavenward, straining his enormous baritone, a foghorn warning all contenders to watch out for his wake." Though Creed's earnestness in tackling issues of spiritual growth—and their relentlessly upbeat attitude—have made them the object of jokes and derision among other rock groups and journalists, the band remains undeterred. Their album *Weathered* appeared in 2001. "You either love us or you hate us," guitarist Mark Tremonti told Chris Heath for *Rolling Stone* (February 28, 2002). "We haven't really done anything to anybody—we've always just had a positive message. There's just people who don't want anything positive to come out of this world." "The words I write, I write for myself," Stapp told Flick. "The idea of those words connecting with people who are also searching for light at the end of the tunnel is gratifying. This band has seen a whole lot of the country over the past few years, and it's been sad to feel the tension and anger among kids. If one of our songs can help break or relieve some of that tension, that's a staggering, truly humbling gift." Stapp is the founder and president of the Arms Wide Open Foundation, which tries to help low-income families during domestic crises.

One of the three children of Lynda Stapp and an ex-Marine who started a printing company, Scott Stapp was born Anthony Scott Flippen on August 8, 1973 in Orlando, Florida. Much of Stapp's early life was spent on the farm of his great aunt and great uncle and on the Cherokee Indian reservation in North Carolina, where one of his grandfathers lived. (Stapp's ancestors include Cherokee Indians.) Stapp's father and mother divorced when he was in preschool. Lynda Stapp told Steve Dougherty and Linda Trischitta for *People* (March 26, 2001) that as a child, her son was "very sensitive and intuitive. I never put him down for showing emotion, and I think that fuels his artistry." When Stapp was about 10, his mother married Steven Stapp, a dentist with two daughters of his own. The new, larger family lived near Orlando. While Stapp's mother had introduced a degree of religious and moral strictness in her household, Steven Stapp went further. "Our lives started revolving around religion," Scott Stapp told Chris Heath. "We started going to church on Wednesday nights, youth meetings on Friday, Sunday in the morning, Sunday at night. Every night or in the morning he'd do . . . devotionals—read something out of the Bible, and he would explain the moral behind it." Rock music was banned in the Stapp house. Punishment for failing to follow the household rules included having to write out long passages from the Bible. Although Stapp learned a great deal from his stepfather and enjoyed debating the meaning of biblical

Tammie Arroyo/Retna Ltd.

*The members of Creed (left to right): Scott Stapp, Scott Phillips, touring bass player Brett Hestla, Mark Tremonti*

passages with him, he could not bear the strictness of Christianity as it was taught in his home, and at age 17 he moved in with a friend's family. For a time he did not speak to his stepfather. "He had made the determination that I didn't have Christ in my life," he told Chris Heath. Still, the conflict with his stepfather did not change Stapp's feelings for him. "I love him," Stapp said of his stepfather to Steve Dougherty and Linda Trischitta. "He's a strong man for coming into a situation where a woman had three kids." Since that time, Stapp has continued to reevaluate his beliefs. "I am haunted by my past," he revealed to Kevin A. Miller. "I'm haunted by God. . . . I believe in God because it's what I've been told my entire life. So there's a conflict in me . . . I'm not preaching; I'm not trying to get people to believe in Christianity. And a lot of the songs are me trying to figure out if I believe at all."

After leaving home, Stapp worked as a janitor at his high school. Meanwhile, he began drinking and using assorted drugs. He attended Lee University, a Christian college in Cleveland, Tennessee, intending to become a lawyer, but he was expelled when he admitted to having used marijuana. By that time a college girlfriend of his has gotten him interested in music and introduced him to what became his favorite group—the Doors. Not wanting to return home, Stapp moved to Tallahassee, Florida, in 1994, after hearing that his idol, the late Jim Morrison—lead singer of the Doors—had lived there. In Tallahassee he reunited with his high-school acquaintance Mark Tremonti, who was born on April 18, 1974 in Detroit, Michigan. Tremonti had grown up in Detroit and moved with his family to Orlando during his freshman year in high school. He had begun playing guitar when he was about 11 years old. After reconnecting with Tremonti, Stapp began to write words to his friend's music, often doing so in his car, where he also slept. "I've learned how to write and got the poetic mind from Psalms and Proverbs," he told Kevin A. Miller. "And that's where a lot of my songwriting references come from—so when I'm trying to relate a point to someone, when I'm trying to paint a picture with words, it's biblical although I'm not even thinking about it."

Stapp and Tremonti formed Creed with the drummer Scott Phillips (born Thomas Phillips on February 22, 1973 in Madison, Florida). Originally the band's rhythm guitarist, Phillips proved so inept at playing that instrument that he switched to drums. The group initially called itself Naked Toddler and started out by playing mostly versions of other bands' songs, occasionally throwing in one of their own. The musicians changed their band name—and their bass guitar player—several times before deciding on the name Creed and the bass guitarist Brian Marshall, who was born on April 24, 1974 in Florida. The songwriting, however, was from the beginning a collaboration between Stapp and Tremonti. "Mark's like my brother," Stapp told Larry Flick for *Billboard* (November 10, 1992). "We have this unexplainable connection. I can be fearless and free in front of him in a way that I'm not able to be with almost anyone else in my life." Stapp also told Flick that he and Tremonti share the same priorities: "God, family, and Creed—nothing has or will ever come before that, and nothing will ever come between Mark and me. We're as tight as two people can be." "We don't aim for anything," Tremonti told John Wiederhorn for

*Guitar.com* (on-line), "but if there was a sound we'd all wanna go for it would be good old classic rock—stripped-down guitar, drums and vocals. No samples just a rockin' Led Zeppelin kind of sound."

In February 1997 Creed released their first album, *My Own Prison*, on their own label. Recorded for only $6,000, the album was later remixed by the producer Ron Saint-Germain of Soundgarden (a heavy-grunge band) after Creed signed to Wind-Up Records, the world's largest independent label. Since its re-release, in August 1997, the record has sold more than five million copies. With the songs "My Own Prison," "Torn," "What's This Life For," and "One," Creed also became the first band to have four number-one rock radio hits on its debut album. "With *My Own Prison*, I knew we had the talent to get a radio deal and I knew we had songs good enough to get played on the radio, but I never had any expectations of reaching this many people," Stapp was quoted as saying on the official Creed Web site. Reviewing the album for *All Music Guide* (on-line), Stephen Thomas Erlewine noted that the band "doesn't have an original or distinctive sound . . . but they work well within their boundaries. At their best, they are a solid post-grunge band, grinding their riffs out with muscle; at their worst, they are simply faceless." Creed was named rock artist of the year at *Billboard*'s 1998 Music Awards, and *My Own Prison* became the number-one-selling hard-rock album for that year on the hard-music chart compiled by SoundScan (a company that tracks retail music sales). Some of the lyrics on the album reflected Stapp's changing perceptions of his life. "I realized that I could not continue to blame others for why I was in the situations I had placed myself in," he told Kevin A. Miller. "I was blaming my parents, God, and anyone I could find, when really the only blame rested with me."

Creed's sophomore album, *Human Clay*, came out in 1999. At the time of its release, *My Own Prison* was still among the Top 100 albums in the United States. *Human Clay* debuted at number one on the album charts, and its first single, "Higher," a song about finding refuge from the difficulties of day-to-day life, spent a record 18 weeks at the number-one position on the mainstream rock airplay charts. "We had no gimmick," Tremonti told Chris Heath. "It was all about the music. Looking back, we did it perfectly." *Human Clay* sold more than six million copies and, a year after its release, became a Top 10 album once more, following Creed's extensive summer tour in 2000. "We're the type of band that functions really well under pressure," Stapp was quoted as saying on the official Creed Web site, "and there was definitely a pressure to try to top ourselves this time. Not so much what we sell, because we don't really care about that. We wanted to make a really great record. The band's goal has always been to make records that are solid from start to finish; records that take you through an entire range of emotions."

Reviewing *Human Clay* for *All Music Guide* (on-line), Stephen Thomas Erlewine stated, "It may not be the kind of thing that knocks out critics or grunge purists, but it does deliver for anyone looking for direct, grunge-flavored hard rock." "Despite the fact that the band perform well, have a good solid sound and . . . sometimes reveal a talent for a good tune," Valiere Potter noted for the British magazine *Q* (December 1999, on-line), "the album ultimately leaves the nagging feeling of having heard it all too often before." Among the album's hits on the radio was the anthemic "With Arms Wide Open," which Stapp wrote about becoming a father for the first time. "I think my songwriting is very direct and understandable," he said for the Creed Web site. "People can relate to that, so that's something I didn't want to move away from. At the same time, we're a little bit older and more mature now and we've been through a lot in the past two years, so we were looking to put things across in a way that reflected that." At *Billboard*'s 1999 Music Awards, Creed was again named rock artist of the year. In 2000 Brian Marshall left the group to pursue other interests. He was replaced by Brett Hestla for Creed's tour. That tour was a fulfilling experience for the band members. "We were out on tour for a long time, and wherever we went, there were people telling me how much certain songs meant to them and how they felt so close to them," Stapp said for the group's Web site. "That means more to me than any other kind of attention. It's important to feel as if you're doing something worthwhile, and in this band, I feel like I am."

Creed waited until after their two-year *Human Clay* tour before writing or recording any new material. This allowed the band, as Stapp told Larry Flick, to "breathe and think and evaluate the lives [we've] been leading. I'm proud of the fact that we've previously been able to write good music while traveling from one city to the next. There's a very specific, special energy going into the songs when you do that. But I honestly prefer to be able to concentrate on nothing more than the ideas at hand without outside distraction." Creed released their third record, *Weathered*, in 2001. The album was recorded without a new bass player; Tremonti played all the bass parts himself. *Weathered* debuted at number one, and its first single, "My Sacrifice," a song about the human need for connection, stayed on the Top 10 hard-rock airplay chart for eight weeks. Within two months the album had sold roughly four million copies. *Weathered* found Creed expanding their musical horizons; one track from the album was recorded with the Tennessee Boys Choir, and another, "Who's Got My Back," incorporated a Cherokee Indian prayer. "Every time I heard the intro to the song, I envisioned a tribal Indian chant," Stapp told Larry Flick for *Billboard* (November 10, 2001). "That sent me on a mission to get more information on my background and reconnect with that part of my history." Stephen Thomas Erlewine noted in his review for *All Music Guide* (on-line) that on *Weathered*, the group "simply works very earnestly within a tradition without ever expanding it, without ever adding humor or even cracking a smile." Stapp disagreed with such criticism. "Everything about this record is turned up a few extra notches," he told Flick. "The uptempo songs rock harder than anything we've imagined doing, and the softer, chilled songs have more depth, more complexity. We went for broke on this album—no boundaries, no limits." In *Rolling Stone* (January 17, 2001), James Hunter wrote that *Weathered* "is rock of unusual focus and arrest, a beautifully distressed dance of sustained style and unapologetic emotion. . . . Where other bands might have lightened up their tone by their third album, Creed keep exploring the intricacies of their own heavy-rock calibrations." In January 2002 Creed began a world tour; the trip was temporarily postponed after Stapp was reportedly injured in a car accident..

In addition to selling millions of albums, Creed has formed the With Arms Wide Open Foundation, funded with proceeds from Creed CD sales and concerts. The foundation assists homeless families in finding affordable housing and pays the deposit and the first two months' rent on each home. Recently the band have added a pager to their Web site, which allows fans to communicate with the band directly via on-line postings and E-mail. "That's the best part of doing this: having a direct line to the fans," Stapp told Flick. "Having the chance to hear their thoughts and address them in a personal way that's validating for everyone involved—especially the band." While the band are known as intense hard rockers, their habits differ from those of many such groups. The members of Creed try not to swear or indulge in excessive amounts of sex and drugs. "There is no rule that says if you're a rock star you have to have sex with as many groupies as you can," Stapp told Steve Dougherty and Linda Trischitta. "There is no rule number two that says take as much drugs as you can so you can die at 27." Stapp was married to an aspiring model, Hilaree Burns, for 16 months; they divorced in 1999. An attempted reconciliation failed, and Burns currently lives in a house near Stapp's in Orlando, Florida. "I think in her heart she would like a man who's home every day," Stapp told Dougherty and Trischitta about Burns. "I'm in a rock band and I'm gone a lot. I'll always love her. She gave me one of the greatest gifts in my life, my son." The birth of his son, Jagger, Stapp wrote in an on-line chat for *VH1.com*, "changed my outlook towards my father completely. It has helped me understand why he did what he did. Whether I feel like it is right or wrong, he did it to protect, teach and guard my heart. It's moved the band down on my priority list." Scott Phillips married his long-time girlfriend, April, in 2001

"I don't think it's our job to spread a message or to preach," Tremonti told Gabriella for *NY Rock* (December 1999, on-line). "We're not much different from the people who listen to our music. We even look like them. We don't have all the answers. So why should we pretend we have them? We wrote the lyrics because they meant something to us and, of course, it's a great bonus if they help somebody else. But we don't want to influence the way people think, or force our opinions and thoughts on them." — G.O.

Suggested Reading: *Billboard* p5 Nov. 10, 1992; *Christianity Today* p90+ Jan, 8, 2001, with photo; *People* p113+ Mar. 26, 2001, with photos; *Rolling Stone* p34+ Feb. 28, 2001, with photos

Selected Recordings: *My Own Prison*, 1997; *Human Clay*, 1999; *Weathered*, 2001

---

Courtesy of *www.spaceflight.nasa.gov*

## Currie, Nancy

*Dec. 29, 1958– Astronaut; industrial engineer*

*Address: Lyndon B. Johnson Space Center, Houston, TX 77058*

"I just dreamed about flying probably from the time I could walk," Nancy Currie told Don Montoya for *ArmyLink News* (on-line). In the 1980s Currie, who currently holds the rank of lieutenant colonel, became a master aviator with the United States Army, accumulating nearly 4,000 hours of flight experience. Then, in 1991, taking her dream to the ultimate frontier, she became an astronaut with the National Aeronautics and Space Administration (NASA). Since then Currie, who has a doctoral degree in industrial engineering, has flown on four missions in space, including one, in 1998, aboard the space shuttle *Endeavour*, during which she helped to assemble the work-in-progress known as the International Space Station, and another, in

2002, aboard the *Columbia*, during which she played a crucial role in boosting the capabilities of the Hubble Space Telescope. On a typical 12-day mission, she told Miles O'Brien, space correspondent for CNN (March 6, 2002, on-line), "you're doing an ascent, you're doing a rendezvous, you're doing five consecutive days of EVA [extravehicular activity, or spacewalking]—possibly a sixth—getting ready to come home and then doing a landing. It doesn't get any better than that."

Currie was born Nancy Jane Decker on December 29, 1958 in Wilmington, Delaware, to Warren and Shirley Decker. She attended Troy High School, in Troy, Ohio, which she considers her hometown. After completing high school, in 1977, she entered Ohio State University (OSU), in Columbus. While on campus she participated in the Army Reserve Officers' Training Corps (ROTC) program. (ROTC, an elective course available at many colleges, offers students management and leadership training, hands-on experience in a variety of fields, and scholarships. Each branch of the U.S. military has an ROTC program.) When, after 21 years in the military, Currie talked to Pam Frost Gorder for the OSU Web site, she said, "I'd have to say that starting out in the Army ROTC at Ohio State made a significant impact on me." Currie earned a B.A. degree in biological science, with honors, from OSU in 1980. She was elected to Phi Beta Kappa, and at her graduation the university honored her with an Arts and Sciences Award for Scholarship. "The saddest day in my life was the day I graduated," she told Gorder. "I loved my experience at Ohio State." After college she worked briefly as a neuropathology research assistant at OSU's College of Medicine.

In July 1981 Currie earned the rank of second lieutenant in the Army Air Defense Artillery. Later in 1981 she enrolled in the air-defense officer course at the Army Aviation School in Fort Rucker, Alabama, where, that same year, she graduated with distinction. She was an honor graduate of both the army rotary-wing aviator course, in 1982, and the army aviation-officer advanced course, in 1986. She also completed the fixed-wing multiengine qualification course and attended the Combined Arms and Services Staff School in Fort Leavenworth, Kansas, which trains people in the military to function as army staff officers in the field. During her time at the Army Aviation School in Fort Rucker, Currie held the position of helicopter instructor pilot and served as a section leader, platoon leader, and brigade flight-standardization officer. She was also an instructor pilot for all phases of rotary-wing flight, including combat skills and night-vision goggle operations.

One day during her training at the Army Aviation School, Currie witnessed a terrible accident. Instead of flying in her usual aircraft, as she recalled to Erin O'Briant for *IIE Solutions* (June 1999), a publication of the Institute of Industrial Engineers, she flew in another plane, taking the place of an ill student. As both planes were coming in to land, on parallel runways, the airplane in which she would normally have flown crashed, killing everyone on board. "It was a fluke that I wasn't there," she said to O'Briant, adding, "In the business that we're in, whether it be flying airplanes or helicopters or shuttles, if somebody makes a mistake on the ground or in the air it can have devastating results. So you don't go through life with a morbid outlook, but you have a realistic outlook. This is a job in which attention to detail and safety are paramount." In part because of that brush with death, Currie later studied safety engineering at the University of Southern California, at Los Angeles, earning an M.S. degree in that field in 1985. On January 28 of the following year, the space shuttle *Challenger* exploded moments after takeoff; millions of television viewers witnessed the tragedy, which left the shuttle's eight crew members dead. The *Challenger* disaster reinforced Currie's strong ideas about aeronautical safety precautions.

In 1987 the army assigned Currie to the Lyndon B. Johnson Space Center, run by NASA in Houston, Texas, to serve as a flight-simulation engineer on the shuttle training aircraft. Because the space shuttle is both a spaceship and an airplane, an astronaut pilot must know how to fly it in both space and Earth's atmosphere. A modified Grumman Gulfstream II, the training aircraft is used to simulate the actual shuttle's handling capabilities, cockpit motion, and landing. Currie's responsibilities included developing and directing the engineering flight tests. For her work, Currie earned a NASA Flight Simulation Engineering Award in 1988. During this period she also developed her determination to become an astronaut. "One of the astronauts came to the military installation where I was assigned because he knew I was interested in the space program," she recalled to O'Briant. "And as he told all the stories about flying in space, and what it was like to do a space walk, from that point on there was no question in my mind that this was what I wanted to do."

In 1991 Currie was accepted into NASA's astronaut program, becoming a member of the Army Space Command's Astronaut Detachment, based at the Johnson Space Center. Two years later she was named a mission specialist and flight engineer aboard the shuttle *Endeavour* on space flight STS-57, whose primary mission was to retrieve the European Retrievable Carrier Satellite (EURECA), which had been launched in 1992 and had been used in solar observations, material-technology investigations, and microgravity studies. The *Endeavour* was launched from the Kennedy Space Center, in Florida, on June 21, 1993. During the 239 hours of the flight (almost 10 full days), Currie (whose surname at that time was Sherlock) and the other crew members—the commander, pilot, payload commander, and two other mission specialists—traveled more than four million miles and orbited Earth 155 times. STS-57 also featured the first flight of Spacehab, a pressurized laboratory for conducting scientific experiments, both for the space program and for commercial interests; on that mission, those experiments included microgravity research; investigations of ways to improve water recycling in space-station environments; and investigations into the effects of space on human biotechnology (pharmaceuticals, for example).

Currie was aboard the space shuttle *Discovery* on her second space flight, STS-70, which lasted from July 13 to July 22, 1995. The main purpose of the mission was to deploy the last component of NASA's orbiting communication-satellite system, the Tracking and Data Relay Satellite, which provides continuous global monitoring of Earth-orbiting satellites. The STS-70 team also conducted a number of biomedical and remote-sensing experiments. The shuttle completed 143 orbits of Earth and traveled a total of 3.7 million miles. Because of fog and poor visibility at the ocean landing site on the day the mission had been scheduled to end, the shuttle splashed down the following day. "Despite the fact that we train for every possible malfunction we can encounter, certainly almost every mission something happens that we didn't quite plan for, so it's really up to the crew member to look at every conceivable training scenario in preparation for each mission," Currie told Marco Morales for the Defense Technical Information Center (on-line), a U.S. Department of Defense Web site.

With more than 400 hours in space under her belt, Currie returned to school, this time to the University of Houston, where she studied industrial engineering and earned a Ph.D. in that discipline in 1997. "As an astronaut, Nancy's [industrial engineering] skills have been invaluable," Bob Cabana, commander of the next space mission in which Currie participated, told O'Briant. "For anything we do in the space program, her engineering background is a great benefit." At about this time Currie was named chief of robotics at NASA's Astronaut Office, an arm of the Flight Crew Operations Directorate at the Johnson Space Center. In that position she was responsible for keeping track of all the robotics devices being constructed for the International Space Station (ISS), which, when completed, will serve as an orbiting complex of six solar-fueled laboratories for research on zero-gravity effects and other space-related phenomena. The ISS is a joint project of the United States, Canada, Brazil, Japan, Russia, and the 11 nations of the European Space Agency. Building the space station will require an estimated 45 missions, at a total cost of at least $96 billion.

Currie served as flight engineer on the spaceship *Endeavour* on STS-88, her third mission in space and one that marked a major step in the construction of the ISS. To prepare for the flight, she and her fellow crew members trained for more than two years. Speaking of the role of flight engineer, she told Don Montoya, "Some people refer to us as 'quarterback,' but it's my job as a flight engineer to recognize any malfunctions, to diagnose them, to send this off in an appropriate corrective action, and also keep track of where we are on . . . the nominal or normal steps. I'm kind of quarterbacking to make sure that everybody's in the right procedure, on the right page, adjusting or helping with any switch throws as necessary." During the dangerous and delicate mission, which began on December 4, 1998, Currie and the rest of the crew—in the first-ever delivery of hardware from the space shuttle to the incipient space station—connected the American-made module Unity, which will serve as a connecting passageway, and the Russian-made module Zarya, which contains power and propulsion systems. Currie operated the *Endeavour*'s 50-foot robotic arm to raise Unity in the spaceship's cargo bay and grab the 44,000-pound Zarya, which had been launched months earlier and was orbiting Earth on its own. Then the *Endeavour*'s thrusters were used to push the two large, cylindrical modules together. Unable to see the large objects she was grabbing and positioning, Currie accomplished the "blind" docking by using a computerized vision system and camera images—the first feat of this kind in the history of the space program. She told O'Briant, "When we got inside the highest element of the station, we made the call: 'Houston, this is the international space station.' Even we paused and had huge smiles on our faces because we knew what that meant to the thousands of engineers down here who had worked so long. There were people who had spent 15 years working on this program, never seeing anything in orbit before then. [We astronauts are] very fortunate in that we're a very visible part, but we're probably the most minor part of this whole program in terms of what it took to build something like the space station. We really felt like we were representing all those thousands of engineers." Currie also said to O'Briant, "There's rarely going to be another opportunity to do something like to literally be the first human being on board the international space station." Since that mission ISS has become the largest, most sophisticated, and most powerful spacecraft in history. Beginning in November 2000 the ISS has hosted a permanent human presence in space, with astronauts, mostly from the U.S., Russia, and the European Union, living for months at a time aboard the station.

In March 2002 Currie served as the flight engineer on STS-109, an 11-day mission during which the crew of the space shuttle *Columbia* made repairs and improvements to the Hubble Space Telescope, one of NASA's "crown jewels." Launched in 1990, Hubble orbits 375 miles above Earth; it has captured stunning pictures of the solar system and other parts of the universe, a function that is beyond the capabilities of other satellites or telescopes on the ground. STS-109 was the fourth mission to service Hubble, which was designed so that it could be maintained, repaired, and modernized by spacewalking astronauts. "[To be] one of the senior astronauts at this point—and to have all those duties—is really very challenging," Currie told the CNN correspondent Miles O'Brien. "And that's what makes this one more fun in particular. . . . Never in my wildest dreams did I think I'd be on a mission to service Hubble. . . . Hubble has always been this icon in terms of a mission assignment." In what *Communications Today* (March 14, 2002) described as "the most intricate and challenging Hubble servicing mission to date," the crew of the *Columbia* were charged with adding to Hubble a more powerful camera, a smaller, more powerful set of solar arrays, a fresh power-control unit, and an experimental cooling system. Operating the craft's 50-foot robotic arm, at the end of which is a workstation, Currie grabbed the telescope; then, during five spacewalks performed by others, she moved the astronauts into position for various tasks. In an article for CNN (on-line), she said, "I think pilots make good arm operators, because you're used to manipulating an aircraft and sort of always knowing where you are." In an interview for United Press International (March 9, 2002), Preston Burch, the Hubble program manager, described the telescope after that servicing as "a far better machine than when it was first launched."

Currie's honors include a Defense Superior Service Medal (1993); the Silver Order of St. Michael, Army Aviation Award (1997); and a NASA Space Flight Medal for each of her four space flights. She became a member of the Ohio Veterans' Hall of Fame in 1994, the Troy, Ohio, Hall of Fame in 1996, and the Ohio State University Army ROTC Hall of Fame, also in 1996. Currently single, she has one daughter, Stephanie Marie, from her marriage to David W. Currie. "Short-term, my goal is to put more pieces on the [international] space station . . . ," she told Erin O'Briant. "In terms of longer career aspirations, one of the reasons I got my Ph.D. was because I really wanted to go back and teach, and inspire students to come do jobs like this—really exciting engineering jobs. And I think after a few more years of doing this I'll feel like it's time to step aside and let somebody younger come experience the same great things that I've been able to experience." — C.F.T.

Suggested Reading: *ArmyLink News* (on-line); CNN (on-line) Mar. 6, 2002; *IIE Solutions* p18+ June 1999, with photos; Kennedy Space Center Web site; Lyndon B. Johnson Space Center Web site; Ohio State University Web site; *Super Science* p8+ Mar. 1999, with photo; U.S. Army Space and Missile Defense Command Web site

---

## Dean, Howard

*Nov. 17, 1948– Governor of Vermont (Democrat)*

*Address: Office of the Governor, Pavilion State Office Bldg., 109 State St., Montpelier, VT 05609*

Alex Wong/Getty Images

"Once in a generation an issue comes along where there can be no compromise when you either have to figure out, do I stand up for the principles I believe in or am I simply keeping this seat warm?" Howard Dean, the Democratic governor of Vermont, said in a speech to members of the Human Rights Campaign, as quoted by Tracy Schmaler in the *Rutland Herald* (January 27, 2002, on-line). "When the ball comes into your court . . . if you don't rise to that occasion then you have wasted your career in public service." The issue to which Dean referred was Vermont's civil-unions legislation; state law since July 2000, it offers eligible same-sex couples all the benefits available to married couples. The groundbreaking measure provoked much controversy and resulted in one of the most hotly contested gubernatorial elections in Vermont history. Dean won that election—and his fifth two-year term as governor—by a margin of only four-tenths of a percent.

Dean, who has served longer as his state's top administrator than any other incumbent Democratic governor in the U.S., worked as a physician before he won his first elective position, that of Vermont state representative, in 1981. He was serving as lieutenant governor when, in 1991, Vermont's governor, Richard Snelling, suddenly died. Dean succeeded him, and in 1992 he won the office in his own right. When Dean took over the reins of government, Vermont's budget deficit totaled $60 million. He has since overseen a considerable improvement in the state's financial situation: Vermont now has the best credit rating among the New England states. Also under his leadership, Vermont has instituted almost universal health insurance for children and has made significant reforms in the state's welfare system. But, as *Politics in America 2000* pointed out, "Dean is not a believer in giveaway programs": the state health-insurance plans call for co-payments to physicians, and the welfare formula includes work requirements and time limits. "Many of the principles I have about fiscal management are more akin to Republican than Democrat, no question about that," Dean told Tracy Schmaler for the *Barre-Montpelier Times Argus* (June 24, 2001, on-line). Nevertheless, he said, "I would never be comfortable in the Republican Party. The far right is just too awful. If you look at the extreme of both parties, I think the extreme right has no compassion whatsoever and the extreme left, while I strongly disagree with their methods and their financial views, has a core of compassion. What they're trying to do is help people who need a hand. But the extreme right simply wants to dictate personal choices to everybody, and they couldn't really care less if people needed a hand or not."

Dean has described himself as a firm centrist with no patience for ideologues. "My politics has been aimed at the middle . . . ," he told Robert Dreyfuss for the *American Prospect* (July 15, 2002, on-line). "I'm not an old-fashioned, 1960s liberal." For example, while he opposes such restrictions on abortion as parental-consent laws, his positions on gun control have earned him an A rating from the National Rifle Association, and he has taken a tough stance on crime. "Who are the biggest victims of crime? It's women, children and poor people, the people who can least defend themselves," he said in a July 2001 interview with Vermont Public Radio. "So to think that you're doing somebody a favor by letting criminals off with an easy sentence so they can go out and do it again, that's not being a liberal, that's being a fool."

Dean chose not to run for a sixth term as governor in 2002; he will relinquish his post in January 2003, when the next governor is sworn in. For some months he has been actively seeking the Democratic nomination for the U.S. presidency in the 2004 election. Described by Jonathan Cohn in the *New Republic* (July 1, 2002) as "a gifted communicator: passionate, intelligent, and brutally candid in an appealing sort of way," he has been likened to the straight-talking senator John S. McCain of Arizona. "I am who I am," Dean told Lisa Wangsness for the *Concord Monitor* (December 28, 2001, on-line). "I think America needs the vision of a fiscal conservative and a social progressive. And there's no point in my changing myself to accommodate. I think when this country gets in trouble, it's because they choose people who accommodate their views to whatever people want to hear in order to get elected."

The eldest of the four sons of Howard Bush Dean, a stockbroker, and Andrea (Maitland) Dean, an art appraiser, Howard Dean was born on November 17, 1948 in New York City. He grew up in East Hampton, a town on Long Island, New York, and on Manhattan's Upper East Side, and attended elite private schools. When he was an undergraduate at Yale University, in New Haven, Connecticut, he has said, three of his roommates—two African-Americans from the U.S. South and a student from rural Pennsylvania—raised his awareness of the experiences of minorities and the poor. After he graduated from Yale, in 1971, with a bachelor's degree in political science, he became a stockbroker in New York City. Two years later he quit his job. After traveling around a bit, he spent a year in Aspen, Colorado, as a self-described "ski bum." He then returned to New York City, where he volunteered in the emergency room at St. Vincent's Hospital and took pre-med courses at Columbia University. He earned an M.D. degree from the Albert Einstein College of Medicine, in the New York City borough of the Bronx, in 1978 and completed a residency in internal medicine four years later, at the Medical Center Hospital of Vermont. He then opened a practice in internal medicine in Shelburne, Vermont, in partnership with his wife, Judith Steinberg, who is also a physician.

Dean's involvement in politics began in 1980, when he volunteered in President Jimmy Carter's unsuccessful reelection campaign. He served in Vermont's House of Representatives for two terms, from 1982 to 1986, and held the post of assistant minority leader during his last year in the legislature. In 1986 he won election as Vermont's lieutenant governor. (In Vermont, candidates for governor and lieutenant governor run independently.) All the while, he continued to practice medicine; in Vermont, the positions of state representative and lieutenant governor are part-time. During his terms as a state legislator, he founded the Vermont Youth Conservation Corps and fought for protection of the state's 250-mile Long Trail. As lieutenant governor he created the Lieutenant Governor's Conference on Affordable Housing.

On August 14, 1991, while examining a patient, Dean got a call informing him that Vermont's governor, Richard Snelling, a Republican, had died of a heart attack; Dean completed his patient's physical and then drove to the state capital, Montpelier, to be sworn in as governor. His effectiveness in handling the state's finances made him very popular, and he was reelected by wide margins in the next three elections: 75 percent of the vote in 1992, 69 percent in 1994, and 71 percent in 1996. He had more forceful opposition in 1998 and 2000 from a formerly little-known Republican legislator, Ruth Dwyer, who earned 41 percent of the vote to Dean's 56 percent in 1998 and 38 percent to Dean's 50 percent in 2000.

With 9, 614 square miles, Vermont is the sixth-smallest state in area, and with 613,000 residents, it has the second-smallest population (behind Wyoming). Roughly two-thirds of Vermonters live in rural areas and almost 97 percent are white. The mountainous New England state is known for its good skiing and maple syrup; the leading industries (other than farming) are manufacturing and tourism. When Dean entered the governor's office, in 1991, Vermont was experiencing its worst economic recession since World War II, with a budget deficit of more than $60 million and a poor credit rating. The many Democrats who expected their new governor to loosen the tight budget soon learned that they were mistaken. As the Vermont political activist and writer Peter Freyne said to Alexandra Marks for the *Christian Science Monitor* (May 22, 2002, on-line), paraphrasing remarks by Dean, the governor told Democrats that "they'd never be successful as a party because the people did not trust them with their money." "He was right," Freyne continued: "He was the strict school teacher who taught the liberal Democrats in this state to be fiscal conservatives, and to be proud of it." Dean made budget cuts deeper than his predecessor had planned; he also cut state income taxes, removed the sales tax on most clothing, decreased the state workforce by about 6 percent, paid off the multimillion-dollar deficit, and worked with lawmakers to build fiscal reserves to help Vermont through future economic slumps.

Dean avidly supports universal health care, and in 1992 he introduced a plan to make it a reality in Vermont. After his proposal failed to become law, he presented a series of smaller pieces of health-care legislation. In that way he achieved many of his goals, ending up with a health-insurance plan for children that was more comprehensive than any other state's. At present, 96 percent of children in Vermont have health insurance, provided by the state or another source; Vermont is ranked second in the nation in the percentage of children with health-care coverage and first in percentage of children who have been immunized against such diseases as polio and measles. In addition, 92 percent of adults are covered by a state health-insurance plan or private insurance. Dean also expanded programs to help seniors pay for prescription drugs and signed into law a bill that provides unusually strong protections for consumers who claim that their health maintenance organizations (HMOs) have denied them necessary treatment or prevented them from getting adequate treatment. More recently, he has confronted pharmaceutical companies about the high cost of prescription drugs. "There was a time when I had no problem with the pharmacy companies," Dean told Tracy Schmaler. "I was one of those people who was willing to stand up for them . . . because I know how they work and I know how important their products are. But they are so arrogant and high-handed. They totally lack compassion."

Dean's accomplishments as governor also include the launching of the Success by Six program, through which the state offers the mothers of all newborns one home visit by a social worker. (Nearly 90 percent of mothers have accepted.) The program has been credited with bringing about a 50 percent drop in instances of abuse of children under the age of six. Other state programs, along with changes in welfare regulations, helped to reduce the rate of teenage pregnancy by 20 percent from 1993 to 1997. "It takes very little money to do these things and the results can be dramatic," Dean told Carey Goldberg for the *New York Times* (December 12, 1997). "And the real payoff—and the reason I did it—is so that 20 years from now we wouldn't have to be building so many prison beds."

In the area of conservation, Dean has used state funds (with the approval of the legislature) as well as private and federal monies to safeguard several hundred thousand acres of forest and farmland against development. In addition, he has backed the creation of bikeways and led an effort to restore commuter rail service in the state. Since he entered the governor's office, 76 of the state's leaking landfills have been closed, and measures were passed to reduce the emission of pollutants from power plants. "The most important [environmental issue] for me is land conservation," Dean told Richard Andrews and Timothy McQuiston for *Vermont Business Magazine* (January 1998). "We need to keep Vermont and its working farms and forests, which are largely responsible for our quality of life, intact and [resist] the pressure to suburbanize Vermont, which is intense." He has also proposed using state tax credits to encourage Vermonters to buy electric cars.

Many environmental groups do not consider Dean a strong advocate for their causes, however, primarily because, on environmental issues, he has preferred to compromise with businesses rather than alienate them by presenting nonnegotiable demands. Flexibility, he believes, is needed to attract and retain employers, particularly manufacturers. "Manufacturing is the key in Vermont, in addition to things like financial services, to turning around the economy and finding better wages, because we just can't do it by sitting back and letting the service sector create all the new jobs . . . ," he told Andrews and McQuiston. "I would like a higher percentage of financial service jobs and manufacturing jobs, because those are better paying than service jobs." Dean persuaded other states to join the Northeast Dairy Compact, which aimed to save the region's remaining dairy farms by setting a minimum price for milk sold within New England. (Congressional authorization for the compact has since expired.) Under Dean's watch, 41,000 new jobs have been created; the state's minimum wage has increased twice (it is currently $6.25 per hour, $1.10 higher than the federal minimum wage); incentive programs have expanded to help downtown areas attract new businesses; and tax incentives have been created to attract companies to the state and keep them there.

Vermont was the first state in the 1990s to reform welfare statewide. Dean's plan provides health care, child care, and job training for working parents; it also requires recipients to work 20 hours a week and limits how long they can receive assistance. According to the Web site of the Robert Wood Johnson Foundation, which is dedicated to improving health care, the state's welfare caseload dropped by 16 percent between 1998 and 2000, and the number of parents on welfare who also worked rose 37 percent. Dean was sharply critical of the welfare plan proposed by congressional Republicans in 1995 (and signed into law by President Bill Clinton in 1996); in particular, he opposed the replacement of federal programs with cash grants to the states, thus giving states control over their own welfare systems with little direction from the federal government. "I think some of [the Republicans] think they've got a mandate to starve children, and they don't," he told Dan Balz for the *Washington Post* (January 9, 1995).

Two of Dean's most controversial actions came in response to Vermont Supreme Court decisions. In the first, the so-called Brigham decision, the court ruled in the winter of 1996–97 that educational opportunities for all students in Vermont must be equal, and therefore that the existing system of funding schools was unconstitutional. That was so because the money for school systems came from property taxes, and taxes collected in affluent towns amounted to significantly more than those from poor communities. The legislature responded by passing the Equal Educational Opportunity Act, familiarly known as Act 60, in June 1997. Phased in over the next four years, the act levied a statewide property tax to provide each school district with $5,010 per student (currently, several hundred dollars more) and limited property taxes to 2 percent of income for those earning under $75,000. School districts wanting to spend more money could do so by raising additional funds, from which they had to donate a percentage to a pool shared by all districts in the state.

Act 60's many opponents complained that it raised taxes, diminished districts' control over their schools, and would lessen the quality of better schools while improving weaker schools only marginally. In an undated open letter to the press available on *www.act60.org*, the novelist John Irving, one of the law's most vociferous opponents, condemned what he described as "the deliberate, mean-spirited deterioration of education" and charged, "Act 60 is only superficially about education. It is a tax measure, not an educational one." Dean has said that he was not completely satisfied with the new system but regarded it as an improvement over the previous one. "The basic goal of equality of opportunity is there," he told Lisa Wangsness. While he admitted that Act 60 had "done a disservice to about 30 towns," he said that it had done "a very good service to 150."

In the second Supreme Court case, the justices ruled in December 1999 that, under the Vermont constitution, same-sex couples are entitled to virtually all the rights and privileges of marriage. On April 26, 2000 Dean made history by signing the nation's first law granting gay and lesbian couples who form civil unions the rights of married couples in such areas as taxation, inheritance, insurance coverage, family leave, and medical decision-making. The law went into effect on July 1, 2000. Referring to his signing of the bill, Dean told Mubarak Dahir for the *Advocate* (May 23, 2000, online), "This is not a vote that is about politics. This is a vote that is about principle, and that principle is respect for everyone. . . . That's a principle that is incredibly important to the success of this country, and it's not a principle that I have any regrets about supporting." The civil-unions law does not refer to the alliances as "marriages"; Dean had expressed his discomfort with applying the term "marriage" to committed gay or lesbian couples, because, as he pointed out, in legal terms marriage is the union of a man and a woman.

Not unexpectedly, Dean was attacked by people angered by the state government's legal recognition of gay couples. "You get the same old tired nonsense that we are going to be teaching homosexuality in the schools and that I am personally in favor of child abuse," Dean told Dahir. "That kind of talk is obviously, ridiculously irresponsible." Some gay- and lesbian-rights groups also criticized him, charging that the measure did not go far enough because it avoided endorsing the right to same-sex marriage. According to the Gay Vote Web site, "During debate of the bill, Dean was instrumental in moving the legislature away from opening marriage to same-sex couples. . . . Had marriage been redefined as allowing same-sex couples, the other States in the Union and the Federal government would have had an interesting constitutional fight on their hands. As [the law is] written, many of those issues have been sidelined." But most gay- and lesbian-rights organizations lauded Dean's courage in supporting the legislation, acknowledging that a bill explicitly allowing homosexual couples to marry had little chance of passage.

Dean's stances on Act 60 and the civil-unions law nearly cost him his job. His Republican opponent in the 2000 election was Ruth Dwyer, who attacked him for supporting both pieces of legislation. Indeed, many polls showed that a majority of Vermont residents agreed with Dwyer, who made opposition to the legalization of civil unions a central issue of her campaign. Complicating matters for Dean, a third major candidate—the self-described grassroots organizer Anthony Pollina, representing the Progressive Party—threatened to draw liberal votes away from him. Under Vermont law, the winner of the gubernatorial election must secure a majority of the votes; if none of the candidates does so, the state legislature chooses the winner. With Republicans certain to take control of the Vermont Senate and House of Representatives—in no small part because of the passage of the civil-unions law—Dean had to secure more than half the vote to retain the governorship. On Election Day, November 7, 2000, the ballot totals came to 50.4 percent for Dean, 38 percent for Dwyer, and 10 percent for Pollina, with a small percentage for other candidates. "I realized I could stand up and take the heat after the civil-unions election," Dean told Alexandra Marks six months later. "And I found that taking the heat wasn't so bad when you thought you were doing the right thing."

In early September 2001 Dean announced his decision not to run for governor in 2002. Two months later he formed a political-action committee, the Fund for a Healthy America, "to support the principles of fiscal stability, universal health insurance, better environmental protection, and equality for all Americans," according to the organization's Web site. He revealed his presidential ambitions publicly on May 30, 2002, when he filed with the Federal Election Commission to establish Dean for America, his campaign committee.

Dean has criticized the administration of President George W. Bush for intruding upon the rights of state governments, by imposing, for example, grade-school testing requirements in the January 2002 reauthorization of the Elementary and Secondary Education Act (also known as the "No Child Left Behind Act"). He also criticized sections of the Temporary Assistance for Needy Families reauthorization bill and the $3.3 trillion, 10-year tax cut. "This country is going in fundamentally the wrong direction in almost every area," Dean said to Marks. "This president is going to spend the country into oblivion. I want this country to start making decisions over the long-term—not, like this president does, in two- and four-year election cycles." He said to Wangsness, "I don't think tax cuts are responsible if you can't afford them, any more than spending money on programs is responsible if you can't afford them. This country could not afford the tax cut that President Bush ran through in his first months in office, and now we're going to live with the consequences."

Political observers regard the governor as a dark horse, and even friends of Dean's view his quest for the presidency as a long shot. "It's amazing to me that someone sets out to climb that mountain, particularly as far out on the plains as he is," William Sorrell, Vermont's attorney general, told Robert Dreyfuss for the *American Prospect* (July 15, 2002, on-line). "He's got a long walk even before he reaches the foothills." Others believe that Dean's mix of fiscal conservatism and social liberalism, particularly his work on expanding access to health care, could resonate with voters. "He's got a complete leg up on what is going to be the number-one issue of 2004, which is health care," James Carville, the Democratic consultant who helped make possible Bill Clinton's ascent from Arkansas governor to president, told Dreyfuss. "If he could raise money, he'd be dangerous." Dean has acknowledged that fund raising will be a problem, as he is not well known outside Vermont and, because of the new, shortened Democratic primary season, he has little time to accumulate a war chest and increase his recognition among voters. "The one thing he has in his favor is tremendous backbone," Peter Freyne told Marks. "I learned years ago, he's a man who should never be underestimated."

Dean has named George Washington and Mikhail Gorbachev, the former president of the Soviet Union, as the politicians he most admires, because both "ceded power voluntarily and, as a result, changed the course of history for their countries," as he told the *Praxis Post*. "If you look at what is going on worldwide, the weakest and most troublesome states are those in which individuals have made the decision to hang onto power whatever the cost to their country. Washington and Gorbachev made the opposite decision. Their country came first, and when changes had to be made, they were willing to make them in spite of what it might cost them personally." He believes that he himself, as he told the *Praxis Post*, has "a lot in common" with Harry S. Truman, a U.S. senator from Missouri who later became vice president and then occupied the White House, from April 1945 to January 1953. "I have a low tolerance for BS. And I move right along and basically govern by my instincts, i.e., what I internally think is right."

Dean is a member of the National Governor's Association's Executive Committee and served as that group's chair in 1994–95; during that time he initiated the Governors' Campaign for Children, which concentrated on efforts to improve health care, education, and social-service programs for children. He chaired the Democratic Governors' Association in 1997 and currently serves on its executive committee. He also currently chairs the Coalition of Northeastern Governors and has served on the National Education Goals Panel.

Dean and his wife live in Burlington, Vermont, with their two teenage children, Anne and Paul. The five-foot, nine-inch governor's favorite leisure activities include swimming, canoeing, sailing, and hiking.— K.E.D.

Suggested Reading: *American Prospect* (on-line) July 15, 2002; *Barre-Montpelier Times Argus* (on-line) June 24, 2001; *Christian Science Monitor* (on-line) Dec. 28, 2001, May 22, 2002, with photo; *New Republic* (on-line) July 1, 2002; *Praxis Post* (on-line) Aug. 9, 2000, with photo

---

## DeMille, Nelson

*Aug. 23, 1943– Writer*

*Address: c/o Author Mail, Warner Books, 1271 Ave. of the Americas, New York, NY 10020*

According to the *New York Times* (June 15, 1997), Nelson DeMille feels that compared with a movie or television writer, a novelist "has a higher responsibility to the consumer, because he or she has just spent 25 bucks and is about to invest 16 hours." A description of one of his books, in *Publishers Weekly* (August 22, 1994), might be applied

Ginny DeMille/Courtesy of Warner Books

*Nelson DeMille*

to his work in its entirety: "The pacing is expert: there is plenty of time for leisurely scenes, but the narrative tension never flags." DeMille's novels are often described as intelligent, dark thrillers; each combines elements of sex, violence, humor, and intrigue to form an entertaining whole. In the *Washington Post* (December 13, 1994), David Morrell observed, "DeMille is . . . skilled at depicting the romantic relationship between the hero and the heroine. Most writers who try to mix action and romance fail in the latter category, but DeMille has no difficulty in switching modes and making the reader enjoy the quiet moments." DeMille is the best-selling author of more than 10 novels, including *By the Rivers of Babylon* (1978), *Cathedral* (1981), *The Talbot Odyssey* (1984), *Word of Honor* (1985), *The Charm School* (1989), *The Gold Coast* (1990), *The General's Daughter* (1992), *Spencerville* (1994), *Plum Island* (1997), *The Lion's Game* (2000), and *Up Country* (2002). He co-authored *Mayday* (1981) with Thomas Block.

Nelson Richard DeMille was born in New York City on August 23, 1943 to Huron and Antonia (Panzera) DeMille. The family moved to Long Island, New York, in the early 1950s. During that time Long Island underwent rapid development, but according to *LIHistory.com* DeMille and his family "thought of it as a move to the country. We were surrounded by potato farms, and there was a woods nearby, a dairy farm and an old-fashioned general store. There were no shopping centers. But within five years there were supermarkets, a bowling alley and a strip mall." Linda Richards pointed out in her profile of DeMille for *January Magazine* (March 2000, on-line) that the novelist "is New York born and the place has left a mark on the author's speech and perhaps even on the way in which he views the world." In a piece he wrote for the *New York Times* (November 15, 1998), DeMille noted that he had "become known in some publishing circles as 'The Long Island Author,'" because several of his novels are set in that locale.

DeMille received a bachelor's degree in political science from Hofstra University, in Hempstead, Long Island, in 1970, but not before interrupting his studies to join the army. He served in Vietnam as a first lieutenant in the 1st Cavalry Division (the unit depicted in the movie *Apocalypse Now*) and received a Bronze Star, an Air Medal, an Infantryman's Badge, and the Vietnamese Cross of Gallantry. DeMille told *CNN.com/books* (February 17, 2000) that his military experience inspired him to become an author: "I went through a war and I was a combat infantry officer, so I said, 'I'm going to write the great American war novel.' That got me to the typewriter. I didn't get the novel published, but it got me into the process." During the early 1970s DeMille held various jobs, among them house painter, carpenter, stable boy, deck hand, salesperson for men's clothing, and insurance investigator. He told Linda Richards that through his investigations of insurance fraud, he learned the art of interviewing, which has proved valuable to him as a novelist.

In the early 1970s DeMille began writing crime novels under the pseudonym Jack Cannon; those books, which are currently out of print, include *Hammer of God* and *Sniper* (both published in 1974) and *The Cannibal* and *Smack Man* (both 1975). Under other pseudonyms he wrote three books that were published in 1976: the biography *The Five Million Dollar Woman: Barbara Walters*, a World War II novel called *Hitler's Children*, and a nonfiction book called *Killer Sharks: The Real Story*.

The first novel published under DeMille's real name, *By the Rivers of Babylon* (1978), is set in the Middle East and tells the story of an Israeli commando force's attempt to rescue hostages. The action in *Cathedral* (1981) takes place in New York City, where a group of terrorists take over St. Patrick's Cathedral. In addition to their fast pace, DeMille's novels are known for conveying a strong sense of place. In *The Talbot Odyssey* (1984), for example, DeMille set the story—about a Russian plot to disrupt the U.S. communications system—at a turn-of-the-century Glen Clove, Long Island, mansion called Killenworth. In reality, according to Sidney C. Schaer in *Newsday* (June 11, 1984), this mansion was the weekend retreat of the Soviet Union's diplomatic mission, which made it inaccessible for the purposes of DeMille's research. Instead, the author studied historical records to create an atmosphere sufficiently believable to ground the novel's wild, briskly moving plot. In an interview with Robert Dahlin for *Publishers Weekly* (October 4, 1985), DeMille discussed the ease with which he wrote *Word of Honor* (1985), a novel recalling his years in the army during the Vietnam

War. "This book wasn't concocted. It was the easiest and quickest book I've ever done. I just told the story of my own experiences, basically. It was a straight linear plot, and all I wanted to do was bring out the officers' side of the war. Officers had the worst time of it in many respects."

DeMille based his next novel, *The Charm School* (1989), on the widespread rumor that the Soviets ran a spy school to teach KGB agents how to fit perfectly into American society. Possibly DeMille's most critically acclaimed work to date is his 1990 novel, *The Gold Coast*, which has appeared on college reading lists along with F. Scott Fitzgerald's 1925 classic, *The Great Gatsby*, whose Long Island setting it shares. Writing for the *Washington Post Book World* (April 29, 1990), Consuelo Saah Baehr described the novel as a "captivating cautionary tale of soul-selling by a Wall Street lawyer seeking release from the stupefying boredom and compromise of upper-crust life."

DeMille's military experience has been a source of inspiration for several works by the author. Of these, arguably his most famous is *The General's Daughter* (1992), which deals with the issue of women in the military and was made into a movie of the same name. In his interview with *January Magazine*, he described the experience of seeing his work adapted to the screen: "I think the most amazing thing is when you go out to the set you realize that you sat there and wrote a novel. Which took a while but didn't cost you anything, really. It just cost some time and some paper. Then you see a 70 million dollar production rolling with hundreds of people standing around doing nothing and other people working and airplanes and helicopters. . . ." As for the actual book, Louise Titchener wrote in the *Washington Post* (November 9, 1992), "It's a pleasure to read a novel that speaks about important issues while holding us in thrall. Nelson DeMille is an intelligent and accomplished storyteller who's written a good book."

The events in *Spencerville* (1994), DeMille's next work, take place in rural Ohio. There, a retired CIA agent, Keith Landry, returns to his boyhood home and seeks out his high-school sweetheart, Annie Baxter, who has married the sadistic sheriff of the town. What follows is an "intense, absorbing, suspenseful read," in the words of a writer for the *Washington Post* (December 13, 1994). In *Plum Island* (1997), whose title refers to a real place located in Long Island Sound, the author "uses local myths to create an intriguing environment for the murder of two young, attractive modern-day scientists," as Lorraine Kreahling wrote for the *New York Times* (June 15, 1997). In *The Lion's Game* (2000), a New York City detective named John Corey is a member of the antiterrorist task force that must track down a Libyan terrorist. As in others of his books, DeMille's sense of humor pervades many aspects of the narrative, including the writer's depiction of the terrorist/antagonist Asad Khalil. The novel, DeMille explained during his interview with *January Magazine*, "could have been very dark. And most writers who are writing thrillers write dark thrillers. But people are funny. And cops are funny. Not only does the funny come from John Corey, but it also comes from Asad Khalil, unintentionally. He's making observations about American life through his eyes. He comes to America, he's been trained by the KGB and he's gotten information about America from KGB agents and also through his own observation. And some of his observations are funny. And probably right on. You have to lighten it a little bit otherwise people aren't going to stay with you that long. It's a long book." DeMille's latest novel, *Up Country* (2002), is a murder mystery set in Vietnam. In an interview with the *New York Times* (January 27, 2002), DeMille revealed that for this novel, he relied on his own experience instead of research. The result, he said, is the most personal of his 12 novels.

Nelson DeMille resides in Garden City, Long Island. From his first marriage, which ended in divorce, he has two children: Alexander and Lauren. According to *twbookmark.com*, while a sophomore at Columbia, Lauren collaborated with her father on "Revenge and Rebellion," a short story available in the Pocket Books anthology *Mary Higgins Clark Presents: The Plot Thickens*. Since 1988 he has been married to Ginny Cental Withe. He has received honorary doctorate degrees from Long Island University, Dowling College, and Hofstra University, where he was also the recipient of the Eastbrook Award. He is a member of the Mystery Writers of America; the Authors Guild; Mensa; the Garden City Historical Society; the Hofstra University Veterans Alumni Chapter; 1st Cavalry Division Association; Veterans of Foreign Wars; and the American Legion. He is an associate Fellow at Berkeley College at Yale University, a trustee for the Walt Whitman Birthplace association, and a judge for the Book-of-the-Month Club.

As with many authors, Nelson DeMille's relationship with his native region is a source of both creative inspiration and internal conflict. In the article he wrote for the *New York Times* (June 15, 1998), he explained, "There are times I think about breaking away. If I want crowds and expensive living, I can live in Paris, London, or Rome. If I want tranquility, I can live in New Hampshire or Utah. I can live like a nobleman in rural Spain or Portugal, I can live like an emperor in any third-world country. I can live next door to Marlon Brando in Tahiti. So what keeps me here? Maybe I like the overcrowding, traffic congestion, high cost of living, and attitude. Maybe I don't. I've traveled a good deal of the world, and I'm pretty adaptable, and I've seen a lot of places where I could live, and people are nice all over the world, so it's not a fear of the unknown that keeps me here. The fact is, I prefer Long Island." — L.A.S.

Suggested Reading: *January Magazine* (on-line) Mar. 2000; *New York Times* XIII p8 June 15, 1997, XIII p13 Jan. 27, 2002; *People* p95+ July 28, 1997; *Publishers Weekly* p28 Nov 23, 1992

Selected Books: *By the Rivers of Babylon*, 1978; *Cathedral*, 1981; *The Talbot Odyssey*, 1984; *Word of Honor*, 1985; *The Charm School*, 1989; *The Gold Coast*, 1990; *Spencerville*, 1994; *The Lion's Game*, 2000; *Up Country*, 2002

---

Courtesy of Omicron Artist Management

## Eddins, William

*Dec. 1964– Resident conductor of the Chicago Symphony Orchestra; pianist*

*Address: Chicago Symphony Orchestra, 220 S. Michigan Ave., Chicago, IL 60605; c/o Omicron Artist Management, 23 Gilbert St., Waltham, MA 02453*

William Eddins has been a piano virtuoso since elementary school, a professional pianist since his teens, and a conductor since his early 20s. Exceptional among conductors of symphony orchestras because of his race—African-American—as well as his youth, Eddins has sought to convey his enthusiasm for music in all of his performances. "I'm interested in exciting music trends wherever I find them," he told Janet Neiman for *Crain's Chicago Business* (November 6, 2000, on-line). "There's no difference between a hot show of the Fifth Symphony of Mr. Beethoven and a hot show by [the British rock group] The Who." Eddins has been associated with the Chicago Symphony Orchestra since 1995—first as assistant conductor and then as associate conductor—and in 1999 was appointed resident conductor, the first such position in the 111-year history of that orchestra. He has served as a guest conductor and pianist with orchestras nation- and worldwide, among them the New York Philharmonic and the St. Louis Symphony Orchestra, in the U.S.; the Berlin Staatskapelle, in Germany; the Barcelona Symphony Orchestra, in Spain; the Natal Philharmonic, in South Africa; and the Adelaide Symphony Orchestra, in Australia. A champion of contemporary classical music, he has commissioned and conducted the premieres of many new orchestral works. In March 2000 Eddins received the Seaver/NEA Conducting Award, a $50,000 triennial grant given to gifted young American conductors. In a conversation with Janelle Gelfand for the *Cincinnati Enquirer* (October 21, 1999, on-line), he said that he often thought of something the renowned pianist Rudolf Serkin once told him: "I'm still learning." "This was *Serkin*, who had played everything with everybody," Eddins said. "I didn't realize what he meant, but the more I do this, the more I know exactly what he was talking about. I'll wake up in the middle of the night with music running through my brain, trying to get a handle on what I do."

William Frederick Eddins was born in December 1964 in Buffalo, New York. His mother, Essie Eddins, was a medical sociologist, and his father, Berkley Eddins, was a professor of philosophy at the University of Buffalo. Eddins began taking piano lessons at age five, practicing on a Wurlitzer grand that had been purchased at a garage sale and had once belonged to the composer Sigmund Romberg. Immediately demonstrating prodigious talent and a knack for performing, Eddins was enrolled at the Calasanctius Preparatory School, in Buffalo, a facility for gifted children. (It has since closed.) He graduated from Calasanctius in 1979, at the age of 14, and was accepted to the prestigious Eastman School of Music, in Rochester, New York. Because Eddins was still a young teenager, his parents made the move to Rochester with him, to provide him with support in dealing with his college-age peers.

At the Eastman School Eddins majored in piano performance and also studied conducting with David Effron. When he graduated, at 18, he became the youngest student ever to complete an undergraduate degree there. His decision to study conducting at the graduate level came during a guest appearance he made with the New World Symphony, an orchestra founded by Michael Tilson Thomas as a training ground for music-conservatory graduates. A guest conductor who was leading the orchestra seemed to Eddins to be insensitive to the needs of musicians. "My part was up and down on the keyboard," he explained to Janelle Gelfand. "I remember looking up. When a musician in an orchestra looks up, the only thing they're really interested in is, . . . Where is the one [beat]? This guy was conducting wind through the trees and sunlight on the flowers, and I just wanted to know where the damn beat was." Confident that he himself could do better, Eddins began graduate work at Indiana University, in Bloomington, studying piano performance and conducting; he also studied conducting with Daniel Lewis at the University of Southern California at Los Angeles. At around this time Eddins gained conducting experience through various guest spots and through his work with some of the biggest names in conducting, among them Seiji Ozawa, of the Boston Symphony Orchestra. He also became the principal keyboardist with the New World Symphony.

In 1992 Eddins took an associate-conductor position with the Minnesota Orchestra. At Hamline University, in St. Paul, Minnesota, he founded a chamber-music group, the Prospect Park Players. He has since served as artistic director and host of the five concerts given by the ensemble each year; he plays the piano at the performances as well. In 1995 he became an assistant conductor with the Chicago Symphony Orchestra, under the direction of Daniel Barenboim. (Eddins had previously performed with the Chicago Symphony Orchestra as an apprentice conductor.) Three years later he was promoted to associate conductor of the group. He also continued to lead orchestras around the world as a guest conductor and to perform at the piano with both orchestras and chamber-music groups. His repertoire includes the Concerto in F and Rhapsody in Blue, by George Gershwin, and Beethoven's Triple Concerto.

As the 1990s came to a close, Eddins contemplated stretching his talents elsewhere. But Barenboim did not want the Chicago Symphony to lose him, so he created the position of resident conductor for Eddins. Entitled through his new position to create his own series of subscription concerts and to exert greater artistic control, Eddins has used the opportunity to promote his favorite pieces and composers. Sometimes he has been criticized for the frequency of his performances of works by American composers, especially such contemporary composers as Steve Reich and Aaron Jay Kernis. In response to such complaints, he told Gelfand, "We simply must take advantage of the fact that in this country we have 100 years of brilliant music. There is no reason why we should be ignoring it." During the 2002–03 season, he will conduct the Chicago Symphony Orchestra in the premiere of a work for piano and orchestra by another contemporary American composer, Daron Hagen, that Eddins commissioned.

Eddins has also used his influence to challenge stereotypes about African-Americans, in particular their supposed lack of interest in classical music. In 1992 he directed a special concert of the Los Angeles Philharmonic in South-Central Los Angeles, a poor section of the city that had been the site of violent riots in the same year. "Anyone who tells me that people of that socio-economic echelon aren't going to enjoy classical music should have seen the reception we got," he told K. Robert Schwarz for the *New York Times* (October 11, 1992). "Those people are hungry for any kind of art and culture, and just a sign of acceptance from our society. They are dying for it." Despite his appearance in South Central Los Angeles, Eddins hopes to diminish the need for special outreach programs. "The emphasis is to bring everyone to the hall," he explained to Gelfand. "You can't say, hey, it's African-American week. That's ridiculous. What you do is to make everyone feel welcome, to aggressively program interesting music which reflects all segments of society." "We [conductors] are first and foremost entertainers," he added. "If you are going to entertain people, you have to be able to connect with an audience."

In 1996 Eddins collaborated with the Minnesota Orchestra as the host and conductor for the video *On the Day You Were Born*; based on the children's book of the same name by Debra Frasier, the work was composed by Steve Heitzeg for narrator and orchestra. Proficient at playing rock keyboard and bass, Eddins has a long-standing interest in rock music and has penned an album's worth of it since the mid-1980s. When he can find the time, he hopes to record his compositions in a studio. He is also a skilled amateur chef and regards cooking as a potential backup career. "The second I walk offstage and realize I haven't had fun doing what I like to do, I [will] come home," he told Gelfand. "In my desk, is a completely filled out application to the Culinary Institute of America. The only thing I have to do is drop it in the mail and I will never walk onstage again." In September 2002 Eddins became the principal guest conductor of the National Symphony Orchestra of Ireland. — K.S.

Suggested Reading: *Buffalo* [New York] *News* G p3 Feb. 7, 1993, with photo; Chicago Symphony Orchestra Web site; *Cincinnati* [Ohio] *Enquirer* (on-line) Oct. 21, 1999; *Crain's Chicago Business* (on-line) Nov. 6, 2000, with photo; *New York Times* II p1 Oct. 11, 1992

Selected Videos: *On the Day You Were Born* (with the Minnesota Orchestra), 1996

---

## Egan, Jennifer

*Sep. 7, 1962– Novelist; journalist; short-story writer*

*Address: c/o Nan A. Talese, 1540 Broadway, 18th Fl., New York, NY 10036*

Jennifer Egan has intrigued critics and audiences alike with the clarity of her prose, the relevance of her themes, and her honest depictions of young heroines struggling to understand themselves and their worlds. Her first novel, *The Invisible Circus* (1995), is about a teenage girl who is trying to come to terms with her older sister's death. In 1996 Egan published a collection of her short fiction, *Emerald City and Other Stories*, which includes such tales as "Why China?" and "Sacred Heart." Her most recent book, the novel *Look at Me* (2001), is an ambitious examination of the troubled lives of individuals adrift in the contemporary, media-saturated culture of the United States; that widely discussed work earned a nomination for the 2001 National

Brennan Photography

*Jennifer Egan*

Book Award. Egan has published short fiction in prominent periodicals that include the *New Yorker*, *Harper's*, and *Ploughshares*. Her journalism has appeared in the *New York Times Magazine*, where she has written about modeling, self-mutilation, and gay teenagers' use of the Internet, among other issues.

The daughter of Donald Egan, a lawyer, and Kay Kimpton, an art dealer, Jennifer Egan was born in Chicago, Illinois, on September 7, 1962. She was raised in San Francisco, California. Eager to travel before attending college, she worked as a model for six months after her high-school graduation with the aim of saving for her trip. As she later told Michael Kenney for the *Boston Globe* (February 28, 1996), despite having the right height—five feet, nine inches—and "the basic bone structure," she was ill-suited for modeling. "I felt a desire to vanish and to speak—the two things you can't ever do as a model," she explained to Kenney. When she had saved enough money, she purchased a backpack and caught a flight to London, England. From there she traveled widely in Europe, her perambulations providing material that she would later develop in *The Invisible Circus*. Upon her return to the United States, she enrolled at the University of Pennsylvania, in Philadelphia, where she majored in English and began writing seriously. She graduated from the university with a B.A. in English in 1985. Following graduate study at St. John's College, in Cambridge, England, where she earned an M.A. degree in English literature in 1987, Egan embarked on a series of travels to China and other regions of central Asia. "Why China?," a short story published in the *New Yorker* on April 24, 1995 and later included in *Emerald City and Other Stories*, grew out of her experiences during that period.

Egan's debut novel, *The Invisible Circus*, is a coming-of-age story about a young girl who treks across Europe, hoping to gain insight into her elder sister's life and mysterious, untimely death. It opens in 1978 in San Francisco, where 18-year-old Phoebe is living with her widowed mother. It has been eight years since her sister, Faith, fell to her death from a cliff along the coast of Italy. Faith had been a 1960s flower child—reckless, adventurous, and carefree. Following the death of their father, Faith had run off to Europe with a boyfriend, sending postcards from the places she visited. One day the postcards had stopped coming, and the family had learned that she had died. Phoebe, who grew up in the shadow of these events, is convinced that life has already passed her by. After her high-school graduation and some troubling incidents at home, Phoebe makes an impromptu decision to go to Europe. Once there she follows the trail indicated by her sister's postcards, and in the process pieces together the events leading to Faith's death. Along the way she encounters the remnants of the once-lively 1960s scene and has some psychedelic experiences of her own; she also uncovers disturbing truths about her sister's past.

*The Invisible Circus* was well received by critics. Jesse Lee Kercheval, writing for *Ploughshares* (Spring 1995), called it a "marvelous first novel" and declared, "Only rarely does Egan's deft touch at integrating history into her characters' lives fail. . . . But for every occasional weak spot, there are a dozen luminous evocations of the period. To read *The Invisible Circus* is to see the sixties again in all its glimmering and illusive promise." Erica Abeel, in a review for *New York Newsday* (January 1, 1995), noted that Egan displayed "a sure command of narrative tension impressive in a first novelist." In 2001 the novel was made into a little-noticed movie starring Jordana Brewster as Phoebe, Cameron Diaz as Faith, Blythe Danner as the girls' mother, and Christopher Eccleston as Faith's boyfriend, Wolf.

The characters in Egan's next work, the collection *Emerald City and Other Stories*, are reminiscent of Dorothy, the heroine of L. Frank Baum's *The Wonderful Wizard of Oz*: in various ways they are struggling to cope with the trauma of disillusionment. In the story "Sacred Heart," a young Catholic-school girl named Sarah nurses an obsession with a mysterious new classmate, Amanda, who, in Egan's words, "wore silver bracelets embedded with chunks of turquoise" and "would cross her legs and stare into space in a way that suggested she lived a dark and troubled life," as quoted by Ginia Bellafante in *Time* (January 15, 1996). Sarah soon discovers that, in reality, Amanda is less mysterious than she seems. In the tale "Why China?"—which Susan Wood, in the *Houston Chronicle* (March 31, 1996), considered to be "perhaps the collection's most remarkable story"—a businessman takes his family on an outing to China, hoping to find release from his work and an escape from recent allegations of fraud. In Kunming he encounters a man who once conned him out of $25,000, and decides to accompany the swindler on a trip to some Buddhist caves. "Emerald City" focuses on Stacey, an aspiring model who has moved to New York City from Cincinnati, Ohio, to pursue her dream. She suffers a blow when a photographer tells her that her classic good looks are no longer in style. "Beauty today is ugly beauty," he tells her, as quoted by Linda Simon in *New York Newsday* (February 25, 1996). "Look at those girls, they're monsters—gorgeous, mythical monsters." Rory, a photographer's assistant, is in love with Stacey; he comes to the realization that New York City is "a place that glittered from a distance even when you reached it," as quoted by Jodee Stanley in *Ploughshares* (Spring 1996). As the story ends, Stacey and Rory are setting their sights in search of new horizons. In a review of *Emerald City and Other Stories* for *People* (February 26, 1996), Louisa Ermelino wrote that Egan "displays a gift for cool, clean, wrenching prose. [She] has modern life down pat, and in this smartly crafted collection, she hands it over." Linda Simon wrote that despite the despair evoked in some of the tales, Egan "sees a glimmer of happiness, even of deliverance, for her bewildered characters. She tempers cynicism with compassion; she believes in hope."

*Look at Me*, Egan's second novel, has generated a lot of interest, both critically and commercially. The book alternates between two narratives, each about a protagonist named Charlotte. Charlotte Swenson, a fashion model living in New York City, is recovering from a car crash in which she suffered multiple fractures of her facial bones. Charlotte Hauser, a teenager growing up in Rockford, Illinois, is leading a double life. An ordinary student by day, the young Charlotte begins an affair with her enigmatic math teacher. She is also being tutored by her uncle, Moose Metcalf, a mentally troubled cultural-studies professor with an obsessive interest in the Industrial Revolution. (Moose had been a rising academic star before he nearly blew up part of the Yale University campus while carrying out an experiment.) While taking walks with Charlotte in Rockford, Moose discourses on the unsettling effects of the Industrial Age, with the hope that his niece will be taken with the vision that has come to dominate his life. Charlotte increasingly retreats into the worlds of the two older men, thereby isolating herself from her friends and family. Charlotte Swenson, meanwhile, gets involved in a reality-based Web site that turns people's real lives into a form of entertainment.

In an interview posted on the Web site of the publisher Nan A. Talese (a division of Random House), Egan admitted that she had intentionally made the connection between the two Charlottes obscure. "After writing *The Invisible Circus*," she said, "in which the action of the novel is rather fully explained psychologically, I wanted to write a book whose connections were felt rather than understood, a book that was more deeply mysterious." She also said, in commenting on the shifting boundaries between reality and fantasy in contemporary American life, "I think that our culture's image saturation has resulted in a kind of media hangover—a longing for experience that is unmediated, or 'authentic.' . . . [Reality] has been fetishized into a style: a simulacrum of authenticity that appears to satisfy the viewer's genuine longing for it, but, in fact, leaves him empty. And the media respond to that emptiness with ever greater contortions of simulated reality, which is what I wanted to explore in *Look at Me*." Reviews of the book have tended to be mixed but appreciative. For example, in his assessment for the *Washington Post* (November 4, 2001), David Mulcahey wrote, "Ambitious as Egan is, she lets her narrative bloat. Subplot after subplot comes along . . . leaving the reader to wonder whether they add to the whole." "Nonetheless," he concluded, "Egan has created some compelling characters and written provocative meditations on our times." Katherine Dieckmann offered a similar assessment in the *New York Times Book Review* (September 23, 2001): "Just as Charlotte [Swenson]'s new face is held together with 80 titanium screws, a set of fragile pieces forever threatening to become dismantled, Egan's book is a tenuous assembly that manages to compel despite its occasionally confounding construction."

Egan has received fellowships from the National Endowment for the Arts and the Guggenheim Foundation. In 1992 she won the *Cosmopolitan*/Perrier Short Story Award for "Sacred Heart." She lives in the New York City borough of Brooklyn with her husband, David Herskovits, a director for theater, and their son. — A.I.C.

Suggested Reading: *Boston Globe* p73 Feb. 28, 1996; *Los Angeles Times* p2 Mar. 5, 1995; *Nation* p42+ Nov. 26, 2001; *New York Newsday* p33 Jan. 1, 1995, Feb. 25, 1996; *New York Times Book Review* p22 Sep. 23, 2001; *People* p32 Feb. 26, 1996; *Ploughshares* p193+ Spring 1995, p205+ Spring 1996; *Time* p72 Jan. 15, 1996; *Washington Post* T p6 Nov. 4, 2001

Selected Books: *The Invisible Circus*, 1995; *Emerald City and Other Stories*, 1996; *Look at Me*, 2001

---

## Eggleston, William

*1939– Photographer*

*Address: c/o Twin Palms Publishing, 54½ E. San Francisco St., Santa Fe, NM 87501*

When the photographer William Eggleston made his professional debut, with a one-man show at the Museum of Modern Art (MoMA) in New York City in the spring of 1976, he was hailed by some as a pioneer and dismissed by others as "boring" and "banal." While a number of critics and art lovers

Murray Riss

*William Eggleston*

saw an aesthetic breakthrough in Eggleston's photos, which focus on everyday moments and objects, others claimed they would be hard-pressed to differentiate between one of his prints and an ordinary color snapshot. In part, the negative response to the MoMA exhibit was a reaction to Eggleston's emphatically low-key subject matter: his casual, often mundane images from the American South included those of white plastic jugs spilled along an empty stretch of dirt road; a battered tricycle parked before a row of aging suburban homes; the stained green tiles of a much-used shower; a deserted swimming pool toward dusk; and a bleary-gazed businessman holding a drink while seated on the edge of a motel bed. For those who arrived at the MoMA show expecting a more overt romanticism, such images were disappointing. Some visitors to the museum even felt as if they had been had; among them was an indignant critic who dubbed Eggleston's aesthetic "cracker-chic."

Adding to the controversy was the fact that at that time, color photography was still regarded with considerable suspicion by the "fine-art" establishment. The Eggleston exhibition was only MoMA's second to feature color photography; as late as 1959 Walker Evans, then one of the world's foremost art photographers, had declared color photography to be "vulgar." While the first commercially viable process for producing color photographs was introduced in 1907, until the 1970s color photography was chiefly associated with commercial publishing, advertising, and the common snapshot; the few color photographs that aspired to art were, for the most part, pale imitations of abstract-expressionist painting. (Peeling walls were a favorite subject.) "The conspicuous successes of color photography are not many," John Szarkowski, then head of MoMA's department of photography, wrote in his preface to *William Eggleston's Guide* (1976), a selection of prints from the exhibition, "and most of these have depended on a high degree of prior control over the material photographed. . . . Outside the studio, where such control has been impossible, color has induced timidity and an avoidance of those varieties of meaning that are not in the narrowest sense aesthetic. Most color photography, in short, has been either formless or pretty."

Today, Eggleston is widely credited with changing that state of affairs. He accomplished this, according to the most common reading, by appropriating the subject matter of the typical snapshot—the ephemeral, the ordinary, the seemingly insignificant—and subtly intensifying it through the artful use of color. "He emphasizes hues that soak the scene or resonate in a critical way," Sean Callahan wrote for *New York* (June 28, 1976), "virtually creating effects of sound, silence, smell, temperature, pressure—sensations that black-and-white photography has yet to evoke." In a similar vein, Janet Malcolm, writing for the *New Yorker* (October 10, 1977), described an Eggleston print of "a lean older woman sitting in the center of a dilapidated outdoor chaise on a day at the end of summer. It is a color picture about color photography. The woman is sitting on and against cushions printed with a riotous pattern of yellow and orange and green flowers; her dress is another bold floral print, in magenta, blue, and red; above her head is a pattern of sun-dappled green leaves seen through the grid of a white lattice; and, finally, at her feet is yet another pattern, of dead leaves on flagstone. In black-and-white, these patterns—and, so to speak, the woman, the chaise, the leaves, the flagstone—would cease to exist."

But Eggleston's achievement goes beyond that of a technical innovator. While it is true that early commentators emphasized the more formal aspects of his work—in particular, his success in establishing color photography as a medium for "serious" artistic expression—more-recent reviewers have focused on the narrative qualities of his pictures. (All along, Eggleston has repeatedly characterized his work as "parts of a novel I'm doing.") Indeed, he has increasingly been recognized as a mythologist of day-to-day life in the American South, and has been compared by some, not unfavorably, to the novelist William Faulkner. "Like Faulkner," Richard B. Woodward wrote for *Vanity Fair* (October 1991), "he has shot holes in the fine plaster walls of the Old South, and documented a land of shopping centers and suburban tract homes that many of his neighbors would rather ignore. He has a shared history with the people and sites he portrays. And Eggleston's eye, without losing sight of the grotesque, forgives; he finds amazing harmonies in the most unlikely places." "Eggleston's pictures are enigmatic fragments of some vast novel of class, race and power in America," Jonathan Jones wrote for the London *Guardian* (March 22, 2001), "and we probably don't want to know how it ends."

In recognition of his achievements, Eggleston received the 1998 Erna and Victor Hasselblad Foundation International Award in Photography, awarded annually to "an individual who has made a pioneering achievement in photography, who has had a decisive impact on one or more younger generations of photographers or who has implemented one or more internationally significant photographic projects," according to the Hasselblad Foundation Web site. (Other recipients of the award include Henri Cartier-Bresson, Ansel Adams, Robert Frank, and Cindy Sherman.) In addition, Eggleston has received grants from the Guggenheim Foundation, the National Endowment for the Arts, and the Arts Survey.

William Eggleston was born into a wealthy southern family in Memphis, Tennessee, in 1939, and grew up on a family plantation in Sumner, Mississippi. His father, who was trained as an engineer at Rice University and later ran the plantation, died in 1965, according to some sources. (Others report that the photographer's father was killed in the Pacific theater during World War II.) Eggleston characterized his father to Woodward as "a particularly good-natured man." Eggleston's mother, the daughter of a judge, is "very much a lady," Walter Hopps, a longtime friend of the photographer's, told Woodward. "But she also looks as if she could have led a regiment of the Confederate Army."

Speaking with Woodward, Eggleston's mother recalled that as a child, her son was "very brilliant, very strange, separate from his confreres." He dabbled in photography as a boy, after acquiring two cameras that had belonged to his maternal grandfather. Eggleston received his primary education in the Sumner public schools, then attended the Webb School—a military-style boarding academy for the sons of the southern gentry—in Bell Buckle, Tennessee. (It has since become coeducational.) "It had a kind of Spartan routine to 'build character,'" Eggleston told Woodward. "I never have known what that was supposed to mean. It was so callous and dumb. It was the kind of place where it was considered effeminate to like music or painting."

After high school, Eggleston sporadically attended Vanderbilt University, in Nashville, Tennessee; Delta State College, in Cleveland, Mississippi; and the University of Mississippi at Oxford. Although he spent a total of about six years at those schools, he never earned a degree. "I went to class," he told Woodward, "but I never saw the point in taking a test." While at the University of Mississippi, where he took classes in art, Eggleston became serious about photography. In around 1962 he discovered and began emulating the French photographer Henri Cartier-Bresson, known especially for his influence on documentary photography and photojournalism. "A photographer friend of mine bought a book of Magnum work with some Cartier-Bresson pictures that were real art, period," Eggleston told Stanley Booth for *Salon.com* (September 7, 1999), referring to a famous photographers' cooperative that was founded in 1947. "You didn't think a camera made the picture. Sure didn't think of somebody taking a picture at a certain speed with a certain speed film. I couldn't imagine anybody doing anything more than making a perfect Cartier-Bresson. Which I could do, finally." Tom Young, a New York painter and friend of Eggleston's, recalled to Woodward that the photographer "was doing interesting imitations of Cartier-Bresson" at the time, "but I told him he was missing what was around him. And he said, 'I don't particularly *like* what's around me.' I said that could be a good reason to take pictures. And he said, 'You know, that's not a bad idea.' Bill doesn't always have a great respect for things, so he can see them for what they are."

Soon thereafter, Eggleston began experimenting with color. "What I set out to do was produce some color pictures that were completely satisfying, that had everything, starting with composition," he told Booth. "My first tries were ridiculous. . . . I'd assumed I could do in color what I could do in black and white, and I got a swift, harsh lesson. All bones bared. But it had to be. Then one night I stayed up figuring out what I was gonna do the next day, which was go to Montesi's, the big supermarket on Madison Avenue in Memphis. It seemed a good place to try things out. I had this new exposure system in mind, of overexposing the film so all the colors would be there. And by God, it all worked. Just overnight. The first frame, I remember, was a guy pushing grocery carts. Some kind of pimply, freckle-faced guy in the late sunlight. Pretty fine pictures, actually."

In around 1969 Eggleston showed up at MoMA with a suitcase full of color slides and introduced himself to John Szarkowski—"absolutely out of the blue," as Szarkowski recalled to Woodward. Szarkowski was deeply impressed with the young man's work, which struck him as, in his words, "a wholly successful use of color photography," but he was unable to convey his enthusiasm to the museum's Photography Committee. The museum purchased one Eggleston print in 1969; another seven years passed before the committee agreed to exhibit the photographer's work. *William Eggleston's Guide*, his first book, was published to accompany his 1976 MoMA exhibition. It contains an essay by Szarkowski.

Despite the breakthrough occasioned by his MoMA debut, Eggleston seemed for many years to regard the fine-art establishment—and his standing in it—with indifference. He remained actively engaged in photography and even accepted a number of commissions, including a 1976 documentary about Plains, Georgia, the hometown of President Jimmy Carter, and a 1983 documentary about Graceland, Elvis Presley's Memphis, Tennessee, home; but he did not publish another book of photographs until 1989, when *The Democratic Forest* (which has an introduction by Eudora Welty) came out, and did not mount a second MoMA exhibition until 1991. Since then he has exhibited with greater frequency and has issued several books, most of which feature photos selected from a reportedly sizable fund of unpublished work. Among his recent titles are *Faulkner's Mississippi* (1990), with text by Willie Morris; *Ancient and Modern* (1992); *Horses and Dogs* (1994); *William Eggleston: The Hasselblad Award* (1998); and *2¼* (1999).

An idiosyncratic man, Eggleston has received nearly as much press for his lifestyle as he has for his photographs. Rumors of alcohol and substance abuse have persistently dogged him, and Eggleston admitted to Woodward to having been jailed a dozen times. In his spare time, he reportedly relaxes by playing the piano dressed as a Gestapo officer or by firing shotguns from his porch. He has had many other interests as well; as Stanley Booth wrote, "When I first knew Eggleston, one occasionally heard the word 'dilettante' used to describe him, simply because one man isn't supposed to know about music, firearms, sound systems, television set construction and art." Eggleston has been married to the former Rosa Dosset for nearly 40 years. The couple have two sons, William and Winston, and a daughter, Andra. The sons are well-known designers of high-quality loudspeakers; they named one of their models the Andra. — P.K.

Suggested Reading: (London) *Guardian* p31 Mar. 5, 1992, with photo; *New York* p75 Jun. 28, 1976; *New Yorker* p107+ Oct. 10, 1977; *Salon.com* Sep. 7, 1999; *Vanity Fair* p215+ Oct. 1999, with photos

Selected Books: *William Eggleston's Guide*, 1976; *The Democratic Forest*, 1989; *Faulkner's Mississippi* (with Willie Morris), 1990; *Ancient and Modern*, 1992; *Horses and Dogs*, 1994; *William Eggleston: The Hasselblad Award*, 1998; *2¼*, 1999

---

## Emerson String Quartet

Drucker, Eugene
*May 17, 1952– Violinist*

Dutton, Lawrence
*May 9, 1954– Violist*

Finckel, David
*Dec. 6, 1951– Cellist; record producer*

Setzer, Philip
*Mar. 12, 1951– Violinist*

*Address: c/o Kirshbaum Demler & Associates, Inc., 711 West End Ave., Suite 5KN, New York, NY 10025*

Founded in the 1970s, the Emerson String Quartet has become an icon among chamber-music ensembles. The group's singular achievement lies not in its commercial successes, which include the sales of hundreds of thousands of records, or in industry accolades, among which are six Grammy Awards, but in its character. The quartet is famously balanced, both in terms of its repertoire—the group seamlessly performs works by 18th-century composers along with those of 20th-century artists—and the division of its duties: since its inception, violinists Philip Setzer and Eugene Drucker have divided the responsibilities, and accompanying prestige, of playing first violin. The Emerson String Quartet also has the distinction of having maintained the same roster for more than 20 years, a highly unusual feat in the often ego-driven world of classical music. In addition to Setzer and Drucker, who met at the Juilliard School, in New York City, the quartet includes the violist Lawrence Dutton, who joined in 1977, less than a year after the violinists decided that the ensemble should perform professionally, and the cellist David Finckel, who came on board in 1979.

"Our beginnings are not easily definable to a single year," Drucker told John Henken for the *Los Angeles Times* (October 13, 1996). The quartet's origins can be traced, however, to the student ensemble that Setzer and Drucker formed at the Juilliard School, in the early 1970s. The group signed with professional management in 1976, the year of the American bicentennial, and chose the name Emerson "because that was an American name associated with culture," as Drucker explained to Henken. Lawrence Dutton became the group's violist the following summer, replacing Guillermo Figueroa; the original cellist, Eric Wilson, left for a teaching position and was replaced by David Finckel in 1979. The foursome has remained intact ever since.

Philip Setzer, who alternates between first and second violin, was born on March 12, 1951 and grew up in the Cleveland, Ohio, suburb of South Euclid. Both his parents were violinists in the Cleveland Orchestra, and Setzer, who began to play violin at age four, was taught first by his father and later by the concertmasters of the Cleveland Orchestra. As he explained to Kenneth Herman for the *Los Angeles Times* (October 9, 1991), music was his constant companion at home, particularly after his father formed a string quartet. "I remember secretly listening to his quartet rehearsals in our home. After my mother put me to bed, I would sneak to the top of the stairs and crouch just out of sight in order to listen to the quartet music." Although George Szell, the conductor of the Cleveland Orchestra, recommended when Setzer was 15 that he begin training for a solo career, Setzer chose not to attend a music conservatory immediately; instead, he remained in his hometown, where he attended a public high school, played on the

Andrew Eccles/Courtesy of Kirshbaum Demler & Associates Inc.

*The Emerson String Quartet (left to right): David Finckel, cellist; Eugene Drucker, violinist; Philip Setzer, violinist; Lawrence Dutton, violist*

school football team, and toyed with the idea of becoming a surgeon. He was drawn back to a music education after hearing the violinist Oscar Shumsky perform a piece by Bach. "The power of Shumsky's Bach was phenomenal," he told Charles Michener for the *New York Times Magazine* (March 28, 1993). "I knew he was the teacher for me."

In Shumsky's violin class at Juilliard, Setzer met Eugene Drucker. The son of Ernest Drucker, a first violinist for the Metropolitan Opera Orchestra and, for a time, the second violinist in the Busch Quartet, Eugene Drucker was born on May 17, 1952. He began piano lessons at age five and switched to violin three years later. A native New Yorker, he became a private student of Shumsky's at only 13 years of age; later he decided that he was not interested in being a soloist. After hearing the Guarneri Quartet perform when he was a teenager, he aspired to be a string-quartet violinist.

An only child in a musical family, David Finckel was born on December 6, 1951 and grew up near Allentown, Pennsylvania. His father, Edwin Finckel, was a jazz pianist, composer, and conductor; in 1963 he founded Point Counterpoint, a chamber-music summer camp, with his wife, Helen. David Finckel began to play cello as a child, and at age 13 "fell in love" with a recording of the Saint-Saëns cello concerto, with Mstislav Rostropovich as soloist. As he explained to Charles Michener, "This was so beyond anything I'd ever heard. It was more emotional, more sensitive, more connected to the music." He was enthralled by Rostropovich's performances and cultivated a friendship with him; Rostropovich gave Finckel cello lessons, free of charge, for 10 years. Finckel spent a year at the Manhattan School of Music, in New York City, before becoming a freelance cellist.

Lawrence Dutton, known as Larry, was born on May 9, 1954 and raised in Wantagh, on Long Island, New York. Neither of his parents was musical; his father worked in a bank, and his mother was a secretary. Dutton nonetheless began playing the violin when he was eight years old. "I had been extremely shy, but with the violin I found a way of expressing myself—of making friends," he told Charles Michener. Persuaded by his teacher to switch to the viola at age 12, Dutton studied at the Eastman School of Music, in Rochester, New York, and then at Juilliard.

The Emerson String Quartet coalesced around Setzer and Drucker, the violinists. Joined by violist Figueroa and cellist Wilson, they hoped to win the Walter M. Naumburg Chamber Music Competition, to help launch their careers. But Figueroa left the group almost immediately. The remaining Emersonians, as they have sometimes been dubbed, auditioned 11 violists to fill the spot, which was won by Dutton, who described himself to Charles Michener as "a raw 22-year-old" at the time. With Dutton as a member, the quartet won the 1978 Naumburg Competition; as part of their prize, the Naumburg Foundation made arrangements for a number of concerts for them. They later went on more extended tours. An early tour of four concerts in far-flung parts of the U.S. netted them each only $50, but they soon won fervent supporters in the music world. They played a wide variety of classical music, from the first string quartets of the Austrian composer Franz Josef Haydn to works by the German composer Ludwig van Beethoven, the Russian composer Dmitry Shostakovich, and contemporary artists. Noted for their willingness to tackle new music, the Emerson String Quartet had the opportunity to give world premieres for modern compositions. Drucker told Charles Passy for *Ovation* (July 1988), "The music we play is of universal significance, even if it comes from specific folk roots or cultural trends. Naturally, you have to learn the elements of each style and each period, and try to incorporate them and not play everything the same way. And, at the same time, the way you approach everything *will* sound like you because it has the stamp of your individual personality on it."

While the quartet was slowly gaining a foothold, they endured a brief setback in 1979, when Wilson left the group. Setzer, Drucker, and Dutton knew whom they wanted to become their cellist—David Finckel, whom they knew from his work with New Jersey's Colonial Symphony, which Shumsky conducted. "When they lost their cellist, Phil came over with a bottle of Scotch, got me plastered and I agreed to audition," Finckel recalled for Michener, "even though I didn't know how I was going to put up with three brothers. When I sat down to play with Phil, Eugene and Larry, it was magic. I couldn't believe anything could sound so good." With Finckel officially installed as a member, the quartet succeeded relatively quickly in carving out its niche in the music world. For a time in the late 1970s, individual members often took gigs elsewhere to make ends meet. "The real turning point was the season in which we were totally self-sufficient," Setzer told Charles Passy. They were lauded for a March 1981 performance of all six quartets of the 20th-century Hungarian composer Béla Bartók, which turned out to be a career-defining set. (The group did not record those quartets until 1988.) While engaging in round-the-world tours, the group slowly built a discography, recording the quartets of Romantic composers, among them Johannes Brahms, Claude Debussy, and Maurice Ravel, in a four-volume set for Book-of-the-Month Records in 1984, as well as works of lesser-known modern composers for New World and Composers Recordings Inc. In 1987 the Emerson String Quartet signed a contract with the elite European label Deutsche Grammophon; the first release on that label contained the Beethoven Quartet in F Minor and Franz Schubert's Quartet no. 14 in D Minor, known as *Death and the Maiden*.

The quartet earned a reputation worldwide for its top-flight playing. They attracted attention from the beginning for their practice of having Setzer and Drucker alternate at the first-violin spot, an arrangement that Drucker had casually suggested while the two were still Juilliard students. "The clear [precedent] is for not switching," Setzer told Kenneth Herman, "especially in Europe, where there is still a tradition to name the group after the first violinist." Both violinists had the virtuosity to handle first-violin parts, and they generally shared first-violin duties. Equally important, Setzer explained to Charles Michener, is each violinist's willingness to play second fiddle—literally. " "We're credited for having two violinists who can play first violin, but we're not credited enough that there are two of us who can play second violin—who know when and how to get out of the way." In a conversation with Richard Dyer for the *Boston Globe* (January 20, 2002), Drucker revealed the practical side of having two first violinists: "Most quartet players would agree that the first violin part in most of the literature is more exposed than the others and requires some extra margin of practicing. It is a practical benefit that we can split that extra responsibility, and it is one reason why we can carry such a large repertoire."

The Emerson String Quartet established a pattern of performing about 45 pieces of music each year, with four to six of them new additions to their repertoire. Rehearsals and music selection were conducted cooperatively. "We don't have fundamental personal or musical disagreements," Finckel told Erica Jeal for the *Guardian* (May 3, 2000). "In our rehearsals there's a lot of debate, but when we listen back to our tapes and hear ourselves play we always agree on whether it was good or bad. I can't imagine how it would work if you worshipped at different temples musically." The group's tasks were parceled out fairly as well: Setzer was placed in charge of programming, Dutton began keeping the books, Finckel became the audio engineer, and Drucker set about writing program notes and taking care of other chores. "It's not really a democracy, because in a democracy you vote and the majority wins. It's more like a jury, because we have to agree unanimously," Setzer pointed out to Charles Passy.

The group kept busy on tour and in the studio. Their 1988 recording of the six Bartók quartets for Deutsche Grammophon won Grammy Awards in 1989 for best classical album and best chamber-music album. Recording was difficult for the quartet members, who tend to be perfectionists. Being in the studio, Dutton told Charles Passy, was "an incredible confrontation with yourself and your inadequacies." Nevertheless, the quartet won a 1993 Grammy for best chamber-music performance for their recording of string quartets by the American composers Samuel Barber and Charles Ives. In 1998 they won their fourth Grammy, for best chamber-music recording, for an album of all of Beethoven's string quartets, and in 2001 the group won their second "double" Grammy, for both best classical album and best chamber-music performance, for their renditions of the 15 string quartets of Shostakovich. The Emerson String Quartet's other albums include recordings of Prokofiev's two string quartets; a Schubert quartet and cello quintet, for which they were joined by Rostropovich; the clarinet quintets of Mozart and Brahms, with the clarinetist David Shifrin as their guest; quartets by Antonin Dvorák, Pyotr Ilich Tchaikovsky, and Aleksandr Borodin; works for string quartet by Anton von Webern; and, in the disk *Fifty Years of*

*American Music 1919–1969*, music by Henry Cowell, Arthur Shepherd, Roy Harris, Gunther Schuller, and Andrew Welsh Imbrie. The group's exclusive contract with Deutsche Grammophon has been extended to 2007. The quartet was named *Musical America*'s Ensemble of the Year in 2000.

The Emerson String Quartet has longstanding relationships with a number of institutions. For many years the group was the quartet in residence at the Hartt School of the University of Hartford, in West Hartford, Connecticut, and since 1981 it has been the quartet in residence at the Smithsonian Institution. In the fall of 2002, the group became the quartet in residence at the State University of New York at Stony Brook. The Emerson String Quartet performs in several benefit concerts over the course of a season, raising money to combat such problems as AIDS, hunger, and juvenile diabetes. The group's musicians pursue other projects during breaks in their schedules. Finckel and his wife, the pianist Wu Han, often perform and record duos together; in 1997 they created the record label ArtistLed, a small venture that allows musicians complete creative control. "In many ways for us, it's a very personal thing," Finckel explained to Theodore P. Mahne of the New Orleans *Times-Picayune* (January 21, 2001). "We don't have to give a second thought that some record company is going to delete our records from the catalogue. We don't have to worry about whether something is really going to sell or is right for the market. We just don't deal with those things. It's a shame that any artist has to." Drucker and his wife, the cellist Roberta Cooper, frequently perform together at chamber-music festivals; Drucker's only condition is that he will not play in another string quartet. "It seems redundant to engage in that activity," he told David Ramsey for the Syracuse, New York, *Post-Standard* (August 7, 2001). Dutton has performed with the Diamarel Trio, which includes his wife, the violinist Elizabeth Lim-Dutton. Setzer has an interest in stage performance—his wife, Linda, is an actress as well as a calligrapher—and he helped develop Shostakovich's 15th string quartet into a 90-minute performance piece, *The Noise of Time*, for the Emerson String Quartet and four actors. (The piece was conceived by the actor and theater director Simon McBurney.) *The Noise of Time*, which premiered in 2000, is an intimate look at the life of Shostakovich, leading up to a performance of the string quartet that he wrote the year before his death. "The movements of the remarkable musicians . . . and their shadows, the four actors, have been choreographed with stately precision in ways that seem both surprising and inevitable," Ben Brantley wrote in a review for the *New York Times* (March 4, 2000). "*Noise* builds a beautiful and enlightening bridge into one artist's sensibility. But it never mistakes the bridge for what it is leading us to. The production respectfully and wisely lets the music itself, so magnificently performed by the Emerson group, have the last word. Its ultimate and most valuable achievement is that it has successfully asked us to hear music with newly attuned ears."

To celebrate the quartet's 25th anniversary, the musicians co-wrote a book, *Converging Lines: The Extraordinary Story of the Emerson String Quartet's First 25 Years* (2001), published by Risk Books. The book contains detailed biographies of the musicians, a comprehensive timeline, and many photos, among other features. Proceeds from sales of the book were earmarked for the Risk Waters World Trade Center Foundation, in New York City.

The members of the Emerson String Quartet maintain the principles that have enabled them to stay at the top in their niche in American chamber music for 20 years. Despite their enormous stature among contemporary string quartets, they have retained their concern for keeping their approach fresh, as Setzer told Charles Passy during the quartet's 11th season: "I'm concerned about becoming too much a part of the establishment. I hope to hold on to some of that excitement about the Emerson Quartet when we first started out." Moreover, the musicians' determination to maintain their excellent rapport is as strong as their devotion to perfection in their music-making. The quartet, who travel for many of their more than 100 yearly concerts, "know how to give each other distance," Drucker told Richard Dyer. "We do not always fly on the same plane, and seldom sit together when we do, and we don't like to stay in adjacent hotel rooms." "I think we've been really fortunate," Dutton told Kyle MacMillan for the *Denver Post* (December 2, 2001). "We still really get along after all these years. We still have a lot of fun. And there's still much that we want to do in terms of recording and pieces to learn and projects."

The members of the Emerson String Quartet, which is based in New York City, all live in the New York metropolitan area with their wives and children. — K.S.

Suggested Reading: *Boston Globe* L p4 Jan. 20, 2002, with photo; *Denver Post* F p1 Dec. 2, 2001, with photo; *High Fidelity* Musical America edition MA p6+ Mar. 1984; *Los Angeles Times* p59 Oct. 13, 1996, with photo; *New York Times* VI p45 Mar. 28, 1993, with photo; *New York Times Magazine* p45+ Mar. 28, 1993, with photos; *Ovation* p10+ July 1988, with photos; *Converging Lines: The Extraordinary Story of the Emerson String Quartet's First 25 Years*, 2001

Selected Recordings: *Bartók: 6 String Quartets*, 1989; *Beethoven: The String Quartets*, 1997; *Shostakovich: The String Quartets*, 2000; *The Hayden Project*, 2001

Richard Stonehouse/CameraPress

## Ensler, Eve

*May 25, 1953– Playwright; actress; social activist*

*Address: c/o Villard Books, 201 E. 50th St., New York, NY*

"You can put anthrax or smallpox on the cover of a newspaper and no one seems disturbed but the word vagina sends people over the edge," Eve Ensler wrote during a live chat on the *Washington Post* Web site on January 22, 2001. "I'm now convinced that the reason people find the word so scary is because vagina is equal to life and truly living in an intimate, connected and vulnerable way and [is] far more terrifying than dying." Ensler has had plenty of opportunities to gauge people's reactions to the word. The playwright of *The Vagina Monologues* estimates that she has said it onstage more than 20,000 times since she began performing the show in 1996. Originating as a one-woman play in a tiny theater in New York City's SoHo district, *The Vagina Monologues* has become a major theatrical success. It consists of a series of monologues in which women of various ages, races, and backgrounds present first-person stories ranging from funny to thought-provoking to tragic. Productions of the piece, which has transformed into a three-woman play and often features big-name entertainers, have been mounted in most major cities in the U.S., in more than 40 other countries, and on more than 800 college campuses. In 1997, inspired to activism by the stories women told her after seeing the show, Ensler founded V-Day, a nonprofit organization working against the mistreatment of women. To raise funds, the group has organized benefit performances of Ensler's most famous work on February 14 for the past several years. Among the issues addressed by V-Day are women's rights in Afghanistan, female genital mutilation in Africa, and rape and domestic violence in the U.S. While Ensler has become known as "the vagina lady," despite the fact that she has written many other plays, the label doesn't bother her. "I'm perfectly happy to be defined by the *Vagina Monologues* . . . ," she wrote in the on-line chat. "I try not to worry about how other people define me but focus more on the work at hand."

The second of three children, Eve Ensler was born in New York City on May 25, 1953 and grew up in Scarsdale, New York. She has said that her father, a food-industry executive, mistreated her when she was young, in ways that included sexual abuse. While the instances of rape stopped when Ensler was 10, her father continued to abuse her physically, thrashing her with a belt or throwing her against a wall. (Her mother was unaware of the sexual molestation.) Ensler later suppressed the memories of the abuse, which resurfaced when she was in her late 30s. "I think when people have suffered for a long time, they learn how to cope, manage, and contain. It is only later, when kindness or safety comes, that they are able to experience their suffering," she wrote in a piece for *Awakened Woman* (January 1, 2002, on-line). During her childhood the abuse led her to "act out." "I was very sad, very angry, very defiant," she told William Plummer and Lynda Wright for *People* (February 12, 2001). "I was the girl with the dirty hair. I didn't fit anywhere." As a teenager she regularly ran away from home, staying with friends for weeks at a time. She also kept a journal. "I wrote down every single thing that happened to me," she told Plummer and Wright. "Writing saved me."

In 1975 Ensler earned a degree in English literature from Middlebury College, in Middlebury, Vermont, where she was known as a militant feminist. She has recalled that during that period, she suffered from a deep self-loathing. When she was in her early 20s, her drug and alcohol problems—which had begun in her teen years—intensified, and she became involved in several abusive relationships. One night she met a bartender, Richard McDermott, at the tavern where he worked in New York City; he offered her a place to stay and persuaded her to enter drug rehabilitation. She returned the favor by helping him get sober, and the two married in 1978. Ensler adopted her husband's son, the actor Dylan McDermott, who was 19 at the time and is less than eight years her junior. The two remain close, and Dylan McDermott appeared in the Off-Broadway run of Ensler's play *Scooncat* in 1987. "Eve's nurturing and support has meant the world to me," McDermott, now the star of the TV drama *The Practice*, told Plummer and Wright. Ensler, in turn, has credited her adopted son for teaching her "how to be a loving human being."

Following the near-catastrophe at the Three Mile Island nuclear plant, in Pennsylvania, in March 1979, Ensler co-founded Anonymous Women for Peace and CANDU (Chelsea Against Nuclear

Destruction United). She spent the next few years waitressing, protesting, and writing. "By writing I created an alternative persona that I could pretend I was, and she could hold all this info and feelings and thoughts for the future that I couldn't hold in me," she stated for the CNN Web site. "I had to write. I still feel that way. I have to write. Like it's the way I keep my sanity." One of her earliest pieces to be produced was *The Depot*, a one-woman play about nuclear disarmament directed by Joanne Woodward (whom Ensler had met through Dylan McDermott) and starring Shirley Knight (who has frequently appeared in her plays). *The Depot* premiered in the mid-1980s; during a two-year tour, it was presented at a nuclear test site in Nevada, among other places. In 1989 Ensler's *Ladies*, a series of monologues about homeless women living in a shelter, was produced at the Theatre of St. Clement's, in New York City. Featuring nine actresses, *Ladies* was based on conversations and interviews with more than 50 women Ensler had met while volunteering at a New York City shelter. "Writing about the homeless is very tricky, because everybody already has an image of what homeless women are or they have no image and don't want one," she told William Harris for the *New York Times* (April 2, 1989). "We're living in a world in which the most tragic things are completely invisible to most of us all of the time. We've all taught ourselves how to make reality invisible. I hope the play makes reality visible." Other plays produced Off-Broadway by Ensler at around this time addressed different social and political issues. *Conviction* is about two sisters, one of whom has been in prison; *Borrowed Light* is based on the writings of female prisoners at the Bedford Hills Correctional Facility; and *Extraordinary Measures* deals with the death of one of Ensler's friends from AIDS. *Lemonade* centers on a man who murders his family and takes on a new identity, and *Floating Rhonda and the Glue Man* is a tale of the search for love and the struggle between the sexes.

In 1996 Ensler wrote and starred in the one-woman play *The Vagina Monologues* in a 100-seat, Off-Off-Broadway theater. At that time the play consisted of roughly one dozen sketches based on 200 interviews Ensler conducted with women of various ages, races, and socioeconomic backgrounds. "I was having a conversation with this woman about menopause, and we stumbled on the subject of her vagina," she related to Andrea Lewis for the *Progressive* (March 2001). "She started saying things about her vagina that really surprised me—that she had enormous contempt for it, and it was all dried up and finished and done. She was a very forward-thinking woman and a feminist, and I thought, 'Wow! How odd. Is this what women think about their vaginas?'" In the course of her research, she found that many women were eager to talk about their bodies and their sexuality. "They had no context or place where they could do that," she told Melissa Giannini for the Detroit *Metro Times* (January 23, 2001). "And . . . by talking about [their vaginas], they made themselves more real, more present and more legitimate. I have no idea what people are talking about when they say [it's a vulgar word]." Getting the play staged proved to be difficult. "People were like, 'Change the title. Are you out of your mind? You can't talk about vaginas,'" she told CNN. She admitted that she herself initially hesitated to say the word out loud, but after pronouncing it 128 times per show for hundreds of performances, she has overcome her discomfort. "It makes everyone squirm, until they pass through the window," she told Megan Rosenfeld for the *Washington Post* (February 11, 2001). "It's like flying through the sound barrier. It's almost unbearable to go through the taboo, but then you discover this unbelievable grace, power, joy and sexuality that isn't tainted. You know that if you just go there it will be okay. It's a place we haven't been before. It's what it will look like when women are in power." Some remain uncomfortable with the play's title and terminology. "In Oklahoma City the newspaper refused to run advertisements for the show," Ensler told Rosenfeld. "In some places they would sell out the theater but couldn't print the name of the show on the tickets." Though Ensler originally performed the play as a one-woman show, it is now usually staged with a cast of three. There are no sets or costumes; in most productions the actresses sit on chairs and refer to the script while impersonating different kinds of women. Ensler has added several monologues to expand the piece to 90 minutes. The play's subjects include pubic hair, body scents, masturbation, sex, orgasm, menstruation, gynecological exams, birth, mutilation, and rape. The monologues include humorous stories as well as harrowing ones. David Stone, the producer of *The Vagina Monologues*, has said that humor makes the show—and feminism—more accessible. "What Eve brought back to feminism was she made it fun," he told Mark Peyser for *Newsweek* (February 18, 2002). "It almost sounds frivolous, but feminism became a burden, something that had to be talked about in a strident and passionate way. This is not only funny, it's fun. That's liberating." Since the play became a hit, Off-Broadway, the list of famous women who have performed *The Vagina Monologues* reads like a virtual Who's Who of the entertainment industry; the casts have included Jane Fonda, Melissa Etheridge, Oprah Winfrey, Whoopi Goldberg, Kate Winslet, Gillian Anderson, Brooke Shields, Susan Sarandon, Lily Tomlin, Rita Moreno, Alanis Morissette, Claire Danes, Marlo Thomas, Queen Latifah, Kelly McGillis, Teri Garr, Linda Ellerbee, Robin Givens, Winona Ryder, Kirstie Alley, Marisa Tomei, Melanie Griffith, Nell Carter, Cate Blanchett, Salma Hayek, Lynn Whitfield, Kathy Najimy, and Margaret Cho. A minor controversy erupted when New York mayor Rudolph Giuliani's estranged wife, Donna Hanover, performed in the play for several weeks. "Part of Ensler's brilliance is knowing how to tap into the celebrity guilt of good liberal actresses who are not doing theater anymore but are rich and famous from television and movies," Rosenfeld wrote. "By doing two weeks in *The Vagina Monologues* for scale wages they can rejoin the sisterhood and have fun doing live theater."

Most reviews of the play have been positive. "The jokes are great, there's no self-pity and the politics emerge subtly from the material. . . . Whether the evening is raw or not depends on the delicacy of your sensibilities, but it certainly has a bracing Rabelaisian lewdness," Lloyd Rose wrote for the *Washington Post* (December 1, 1998). Later in the review he stated, "The most remarkable and refreshing thing about *The Vagina Monologues* is the extent to which, without painting a sunshiny post-feminist picture, it isn't about suffering. . . . Fundamentally, Ensler appears to have been interested in female physical pleasure and inquired into it with a frankness that has its own erotic edge." Not everyone has been charmed by the show's candidness. In the *New Statesman* (May 28, 2001), for example, Dorothy Gallagher called the play "twaddle" and criticized its effort at audience participation, in which the actresses urge attendees to shout the word "vagina" with them. Finding Ensler "irritating" and self-important, she wrote, "There seems to be an assumption, shared by Ensler and her audience, that sexual pleasure was something unknown to women until Ensler pointed out the exact location of the vagina, its accoutrements and the best uses for the equipment." Several critics, including Camille Paglia, have called the play "anti-male." Actresses who have appeared in the show disagree with that assessment. Mercedes Ruehl, for one, told Rosenfeld that *The Vagina Monologues* is "ruefully good-natured towards men," and Ensler herself has said that she wasn't thinking about men at all when she wrote it. "I don't understand men," she confessed to Rosenfeld. "I love men, I live with a man. But I'm interested in writing for women. If they empower themselves and their vaginas, the world will be a better place." The New York production of *The Vagina Monologues* won an Obie Award in 1996 and was nominated for a Drama Desk Award. In addition, the Washington production was nominated for a Helen Hayes Award, and the London staging was nominated for an Olivier Award. (Ensler did not appear in those productions.) The play was made into a movie that aired on HBO in 2001.

In 1997 Ensler founded V-Day, a nonprofit, grassroots, global campaign to stop violence against women. "After every show, women lined up afterward to tell me how they'd been beaten or raped. And they felt such a desperate need to tell their stories that I started to feel insane," she told CNN. "I felt the way a war photographer feels, that you're taking photos of these terrible incidents, but you're not intervening on people's behalves. And I said either I was going to stop doing *The Vagina Monologues* or we would use *The Vagina Monologues* to do something about violence against women." To date V-Day has raised more than $7 million, which it has distributed to organizations fighting to protect the rights of women in Afghanistan, to stop genital mutilation in Kenya and other African countries, to establish rape-crisis centers in Bosnia, Croatia, and Chechnya, and to combat rape and other abuse against women in the U.S. Most of the funding for these projects is raised through performances of *The Vagina Monologues* on or around "V-Day," February 14. Through the V-Day movement, the play has been performed in more than 40 countries, including China, South Africa, Cameroon, Zaire, the Philippines, Brazil, Venezuela, Canada, England, Sweden, Greece, Norway, Germany, Croatia, Serbia, Turkey, Mexico, and Israel, as well as in Antarctica, and has been translated into more than 20 languages. V-Day events have taken place on more than 800 college campuses, with casts made up of students and faculty. In 2001 an all-star cast performed the play before 18,000 people at Madison Square Garden, in New York City, raising $2 million, as well as in many other venues across the country and internationally. V-Day events for 2002 took place at 533 U.S. college campuses and in 252 cities around the world. Many celebrities who have appeared in *The Vagina Monologues* have become passionate supporters of V-Day. "You don't just hook up with Eve," the actress Glenn Close said, as quoted on the Random House Web site. "You become part of her crusade. There's a core of us who are Eve's army."

Ensler has traveled around the world to witness first-hand the conditions under which women live. She visited Afghanistan toward the end of the Taliban's brutal control of that country, and Kenya, to meet with members of Tasura Ntomonok (Safe Motherhood Initiative), who are proposing a new coming-of-age ritual to take the place of female circumcision. Despite her awareness of the pervasiveness of rape, female genital mutilation, eating disorders, and other hardships women face, Ensler is confident that V-Day and other organizations can bring about a profound change. "We've reached critical mass," she told Simone Stein for the *San Francisco Metropolitan* (October 5–18, 1998, online). "Things are so terrible, so many atrocities are committed in such a mundane way, that it's got to change. I think that's why *The Vagina Monologues* is having such a good life. Women are furious, sad and they want things to change."

In addition to her work for V-Day, Ensler has continued to write plays. Most of her works consist of series of monologues addressing a central theme, which she researches by conducting interviews with hundreds of subjects. "The lives of people, the actual lives, are far more interesting than anything you could invent. . . . I mean the stories that I have heard and the stories I continue to hear, who could make these up?" she said to CNN. "When I do the interview, I take notes. But it's more just letting that person come into me so then I can write the character." *Necessary Targets*, which opened Off-Broadway in New York in February 2002, was drawn from the accounts of Bosnian rape victims she interviewed in 1994. "It started with a photograph I saw on the cover of *Newsday* of six young girls who had just been returned from a rape camp in Bosnia," she told Pamela Grossman for *Salon* (April 19, 2000, on-line). "I couldn't believe there were rape camps in the middle of Europe in 1993. . . . So I just knew I had to go there, had to go and see what it was." The play focuses on the ways in which two fictional Americans are affected by a trip to the troubled nation. Ensler is currently working on *The Good Body*, a play and book about liposuction, breast implants, and other methods women use to change their appearances to meet societal standards. She proudly calls herself a feminist, despite her awareness that for many the word has gone from being associated with equal rights, sexual liberation, and the joy of expressing oneself to suggesting humorlessness and hatred of males. "I feel honored to be called a feminist," she told Molly Ivins for *Time* (September 17, 2001). "I would hope young women really examine what the word means. To throw out the word itself would be to dishonor all the women who have gone before us. We need to reclaim, invigorate and update the word. If I have learned anything from all the great feminists before me, it's that this is a chain and we just keep widening the circle."

Ensler received the Guggenheim Fellowship in Playwriting in 1999 and the Amnesty International Media Spotlight Award for Leadership in 2002, and was named best feminist in America by *Time* magazine in 2001. She has also received the Berrilla-Kerr Award for Playwriting, the Elliot Norton Award for Outstanding Solo Performance, the Jury Award for Theater at the U.S. Comedy Arts Festival, and the Matrix Award from the Association for Women in Communication. Ensler, a petite woman who wears her dark hair in a blunt bob, has often been described as warm, outgoing, and funny. She and Richard McDermott divorced in 1988; since 1990 she has lived with Ariel Orr Jordan, an Israeli-born psychotherapist, in Manhattan's Chelsea neighborhood. A Buddhist, Ensler has recently begun to restore her relationship with her mother, whom she long blamed for not intervening to stop her father's abuse. (Her father died in the early 1990s.) "I've really come to love my mother," she told Plummer and Wright. "My desire for her to rise up and protect me was very strong. But when I look back I see that she had three kids and no place to go. What was she going to do? Part of what I'm learning now is forgiveness." — K.E.D.

Suggested Reading: *Awakened Woman* (on-line) Dec. 6, 2001; CNN Web Site; *Metro Times* (on-line) Jan. 23, 2001 (with photo); *New Statesman* p42+ May 28, 2001 (with photos); *New York Times* II p5 Apr. 2, 1989 (with photos); *Newsweek* p66+ Feb. 18, 2002 (with photo), *People* p69+ Feb. 12, 2001 (with photos), *Progressive* p39+ Mar. 2001; *Salon* (on-line) Apr. 19, 2000; *San Francisco Metropolitan* (on-line) Oct. 5–18, 1998, with photo; *Time* p68+ Sep. 17, 2001, with photos; *Washington Post* C p1 Dec. 1, 1998, with photo, G p1 Feb. 11, 2001; *Washington Post* (on-line) Jan. 22, 2001, with photo

Selected Works: *The Depot*; *Scooncat*, 1987; *Cinderella/Cendrillon*; *Ladies*, 1989; *Extraordinary Measures*; *Floating Rhoda and the Glue Man*; *The Vagina Monologues*, 1996; *Necessary Targets*, 2002

---

Courtesy of the Trinity Repertory Company

## Eustis, Oskar

*July 31, 1958– Artistic director of the Trinity Repertory Company*

*Address: Trinity Repertory Company, 201 Washington St., Providence, RI 02903*

Oskar Eustis, artistic director of the Trinity Repertory Company, in Providence, Rhode Island, since 1994, sees himself first and foremost as the leader of an institution. "I wasn't a very good actor," he told William K. Gale in an interview for the *Rhode Islander Magazine* (November 6, 1994), explaining how he found his calling, "and I couldn't think of living the life of an actor, of being in a position where you are dependent on someone else for what you do. And I'm a good director but not a great one. But what I can do is bring people together and make an institution work." Before coming to Trinity, which he has transformed from a financially struggling theater company into a thriving one, Eustis served as artistic director and dramaturg at several other regional companies, including the Eureka Theater Company, in San Francisco, and the Mark Taper Forum, in Los Angeles. Throughout his career, he has avidly sought out new works to develop; most notably, he commissioned Tony Kushner's Tony and Pulitzer Prize–winning play *Angels in America, Part I: Millennium Approaches*, a work whose 1991 world premiere Eustis directed at the Eureka. Several other plays Eustis helped create have also won national acclaim; Emily Mann's *Execution of Justice* and Anna Deavere Smith's *Twilight: Los Angeles, 1992*, for example, were both later mounted on Broadway. The former received a Helen Hayes Award and a Drama Desk nomination, the latter an Obie Award and two Tony nominations. More recently Eustis served as dramaturg for Kushner's *Homebody/Kabul*, which opened Off-Broadway, at the New York Theater Workshop, in December 2001; Eustis also directed a Trinity production of the play in March 2002 and has continued to work with Kushner on textual revisions. Since he took over the Trinity, he has been instrumental in renewing the mission of the company and, by extension, of regional theaters everywhere: to serve the emotional and spiritual needs of the public. "What makes him so right," Trinity actress Anne Scurria told Vicki Sanders for the *Boston Globe Magazine* (February 26, 1995), "is that Oskar knows this is not a personal journey, it's a community journey."

Paul Jefferson Eustis, nicknamed Oskar, was born on July 31, 1958 and spent his early years in Rochester, Minnesota. His mother, Doris, was a homemaker and sometime teacher; his father, Warren, a law partner of future vice president Walter F. Mondale, had political ambitions as well as a drinking problem. In 1964 President Lyndon B. Johnson nominated Warren Eustis to head the Small Business Administration; the night before his confirmation hearing was supposed to take place, he drank so much scotch that he was unable to attend it. Over the next six or seven years, Eustis's father was in and out of institutions for treatment of his alcoholism. In 1968 Eustis's parents divorced. (His mother remarried and later earned a doctoral degree.). Although Warren Eustis eventually quit drinking and founded a chemical-dependency program in Minnesota, Oskar Eustis was deeply affected by what happened to his father. "It made me want a world of knowledge," he told Gale; "it made me want to know everything, as if that would protect me. Even now, when I'm so tired I can't talk, I can still read for an hour."

As a youngster Eustis began acting in small theaters around Minneapolis. As he recalled to Gale, "Even as a little boy, I felt at home in the theater. It was the first and remains kind of the only place where I can feel complete—where all of the different parts of me belong." At 15 he graduated from high school as a National Merit Scholar. He spent the next year driving around the country and participating in theater festivals. He then settled in New York City, where he enrolled at New York University (he soon dropped out); he also became involved in the downtown theater scene. In 1976, at the age of 17, he founded the Red Wing Theater; two years later he was hired to co-direct Das Labor, an experimental extension of the Schauspielhaus, one of the largest theaters in Switzerland, located in Zurich. As he recalled to Gale, "I was nineteen and didn't know what I was doing. I didn't speak a word of German, I was being paid more money than God, and I was scared, tense, and driven. Some people took that for charisma."

In 1981 Eustis left Zurich and settled in San Francisco. That same year he began working as resident director and dramaturg of Eureka Theater Company. In 1986 he was promoted to artistic director. It was during this time that Eustis helped conceive the idea for Tony Kushner's play *Angels in America*, which was to be one of the major theatrical events of the following decade. In 1987 Eustis directed Kushner's first play, *A Bright Room Called Day*. The playwright then began talking with Eustis about writing a play on homosexuality and its political implications. Kushner wanted one of the characters to be Roy M. Cohn, the real-life conservative power broker and chief counsel for the anti-Communist "witch hunters" of the 1950s, led by Senator Joseph R. McCarthy; Cohn died of AIDS in 1986. As Eustis recalled to Richard Stayton for the *Los Angeles Times* (May 13, 1990), "I'll never forget this phone call that Tony and I had when we first started talking about this play. We talked about Cohn and how, at the heart of [his] right-wing ideology is the idea that, if you look into your heart, look into the soul of man, it is raging bestial chaos." In 1989 Eustis commissioned the play from Kushner; the director also co-wrote the grant application through which they gained funding for the play from the National Endowment for the Arts. Throughout the development of the play, Eustis acted as dramaturg, a role he described in an interview with Bill Rodriguez for the *Phoenix* (May 20, 2002, on-line): "What I am constantly trying to do is bring out the basic narrative and the basic action of the play and to make sure that the events of the play, the story the play is telling, is actually carrying the themes that Tony wants to write about." Kushner told Gale, "The play would absolutely not exist without Oskar. He called it into being, and shepherded it every step of the way."

*Angels in America* evolved into a six-hour, six-act play presented in two parts, *Millennium Approaches* and *Perestroika*. In 1989 Eustis left the Eureka and became the associate artistic director of the Mark Taper Forum, in Los Angeles. There, he mounted a workshop production of *Angels*, which received six Los Angeles Drama Critics Circle Awards; meanwhile, *Millennium Approaches* had its official premiere in 1991 at the Eureka. When *Millennium Approaches* moved to Broadway, Eustis was replaced by George C. Wolfe, due to differences in opinion between the director and Kushner. As Eustis explained to Vicki Sanders, "We each had a different vision of what the show should look like. It was a constant source of friction between us . . . about a week before *Angels* opened in Los Angeles, we realized [our views] weren't reconcilable. I backed out. *It was not fun.*" (The Broadway version of *Millennium Approaches* won the 1993 Pulitzer Prize for Drama, and both it and *Perestroika* won Tony Awards for best play, in 1993 and 1994, respectively.)

In 1994 Eustis was offered the position of artistic director of the financially troubled Trinity Repertory Company, in Providence, where, four years earlier, he had staged a production of *Julius Caesar.* As Eustis explained to Kevin Kelly in the *Boston Globe* (February 16, 1994), "I was not job hunting. Not looking. No intention of leaving the Mark Taper where I've been very happy. . . . When Trinity called, I was reluctant even to look at first. As soon as I started looking, there was an inexorable pull I just couldn't get away from." At the time, the Tony Award–winning theater had a $1.2 million deficit—over a third of its $3.4 million annual operating budget—and had lost a significant portion of its audience due to the poor direction of one of Eustis's predecessors. Eustis took the position with two goals in mind: to rebuild the company financially, and to turn it into a major center for American theater. To achieve the first goal, the director turned to local donors for support. In addition, he hired a literary manager (traditionally, that post entails recruiting and encouraging new talent) and started a program to commission and develop new work. As Eustis told Vicki Sanders, "I'm genuinely interested in other people's work, and it makes me feel good to provide a forum for that work."

Within months of becoming artistic director, Eustis won a $100,000 grant from Theatre Communications Group/Pugh Charitable Foundations to bring David Henry Hwang, who had written the celebrated play *M. Butterfly,* to Trinity as artist-in-residence. Since then, the company has produced several of Hwang's works, including his adaptation of Henrik Ibsen's *Peer Gynt,* which premiered in 1998, and *Largo,* a musical about the roots of American music, which is scheduled to open in 2003. In 2002 the Trinity received a $50,000 National Endowment for the Arts grant to stage the world premiere of Hwang's play *Savage in Paradise,* about the 19th-century French artist Paul Gauguin.

To those familiar with Eustis, his interest in the Asian-American playwright came as no surprise; the plays Eustis has developed over the years have come from a variety of ethnic and cultural voices. He told Bill Gale that because he often felt alone as a boy, "I felt marginalized myself, and that's why I'm interested in marginalized people now." In 1980 he commissioned Emily Mann to write *Execution of Justice,* about the real-life murder of the openly gay San Francisco politician Harvey Milk; four years later he directed its world premiere at the Actors Theatre of Louisville, in Kentucky. While at the Mark Taper Forum, Eustis helped create the Cuban-born playwright and filmmaker Eduardo Machado's *Floating Islands,* about the journey of four generations of Cubans from their homeland to California, and Anna Deavere Smith's one-woman show *Twilight: Los Angeles, 1992,* about the riots in that city that erupted after a jury acquitted four white police officers of beating Rodney King, an African-American. *Floating Islands* debuted at the Taper in 1993; *Twilight Los Angeles, 1992,* directed by Eustis, premiered there in 1994. All three plays went on to receive national acclaim. *Execution of Justice,* which opened on Broadway in March 1986, garnered many prizes, including the HBO New Plays USA Award, the Helen Hayes Award, and the Bay Area Critics Award; it was a co-winner of the Great American Play Contest and was nominated for a Drama Desk Award. *Floating Islands* has been produced in regional theaters across the U.S. *Twilight Los Angeles, 1992* has been mounted both on and off Broadway; it earned two Tony Award nominations, an Obie Award, a Drama Desk Award, and two theater awards from the National Association for the Advancement of Colored People (NAACP).

In bringing diverse voices to the theater, Eustis has attempted to present different perspectives on life in contemporary America. "What we try to do in the theater," he said during a talk with the writers and editors of the *Providence Journal,* as quoted on *gold.projo.com,* "is find stories that tell the truth. And telling the truth is complicated. Telling the truth does not just have to do with telling the facts. What you really want to do, in my business, is find a story whose arc or whose movement tells something true about life, that reveals something, which seems to be true, that uncovers a basic contradiction."

Eustis has reached his first goal: the Trinity Repertory Company is now the largest arts organization in Rhode Island, operating on a budget over twice the size that it was when Eustis started. The company's finances have been running in the black since 1996, and Trinity has begun constructing a third theater in a building recently donated to the company by Citizens Bank. Eustis has also succeeded in bringing a great deal of new work to the theater; during the 1996-97 season he inaugurated the annual Providence New Play Festival, which invites playwrights from around the country to present their work. In May 2001 Trinity and Brown University announced the creation of the Brown/Trinity Consortium, chaired by Eustis, which grants master's and doctorate degrees in theater. The new consortium played a role in Eustis's decision to turn down an offer that same year to become the dean of Yale Drama School and artistic director of Yale Repertory Theatre. Although the positions are, respectively, among the most prestigious in regional theater and in academia, Eustis chose to stay in Providence because, as he explained, he had not finished what he started out to do. "I've found that I'm deeply entrepreneurial. I really, really like building things, and Yale is built," he told William K. Gale in an interview for the *Providence Journal* (January 23, 2001). Most recently, Trinity has begun to expand beyond its home base of Rhode Island: in May 2002 the company presented its production of Keith Glover's *Thunder Knocking at the Door* at the Minetta Lane Theater in New York; the Manhattan production is part of Eustis's plan to achieve his second goal at the Trinity, creating a world-class theater.

In addition to his duties at Trinity, Eustis serves on Rhode Island's Governor's Task Force for Literacy in the Arts, the board of Theatre Communications Group Inc., and the RI Film Commission; in the past he served on a National Endowment for the Arts panel. He is a professor of theater, speech, and dance at Brown University, in Providence, and an adjunct professor at Rhode Island College; both institutions have granted him honorary doctorates. He and his wife, Laurie, live in Providence with their son, John, and Laurie's daughter, Kyle, whom Eustis has adopted.

Eustis believes it is his responsibility to help keep regional theater alive. "By no means is it a God-given reality that theater will exist in the future," he told William K. Gale in 1994. "If it does, it is up to us to make a theater that our own communities can't imagine existing without. The country may well be saying, We *are* willing to allow our theaters to fold. It falls to us to make a case compelling enough not to let that happen." — H.T.

Suggested Reading: *Boston Globe Magazine* p14+ Feb. 26, 1995, with photos; *Los Angeles Times* Calender p45+ May 13, 1990, with photo; *Providence Journal* A p1+ Jan. 23, 2001, with photo; *Providence Journal* (on-line) May 19, 1999; *Rhode Islander Magazine* p8+ Nov. 6, 1994, with photos

Selected Plays: *A Bright Room Called Day*; *Execution of Justice*; *Twilight: Los Angeles, 1992*; *Floating Islands*; *Angels in America, Part 1: Millennium Approaches*; *Julius Caesar*; *Peer Gynt*; *Homebody/Kabul*

---

AP/Diether Endlicher

## Eyadéma, Etienne Gnassingbé

*Dec. 26, 1937– President of the Republic of Togo*

*Address: c/o Palais Présidentiel, avenue de la Marina, Lomé, Togo*

Since 1967 the military general Etienne Gnassingbé Eyadéma, president of the West African nation of Togo and the continent's longest-standing head of state, has ruled his country's five million people with a strong hand. While his official biography calls Eyadéma a "force of nature," and the Togo media, according to the *Economist* (September 5, 1992), has often referred to him as "the Great Helmsman," he is in the view of others a dictator who has crushed dissent, refused to allow democratic reform, and served only the interests of himself, his loyal soldiers, and his tribe.

Eyadéma was born on December 26, 1937 into the Kabye tribe (sometimes spelled "Kabre" or "Kabiye") in Pya, in the Kara region of northern Togo, then under French rule. He was given the French name Etienne at birth but in 1974 added the African Gnassingbé, in a show of anticolonialism. When he was 16 Eyadéma, with some of his fellow tribesmen, crossed into Dahomey (now Benin), which borders Togo to the east, and joined the French army. He fought for a year and a half in French Indochina (which encompassed what is now Vietnam, Laos, and Cambodia), where France was struggling to hold onto its colonial interests. In 1956 Eyadéma was transferred to Algeria, also a French colony, which was then fighting for its independence. He remained there until 1961, when, still in uniform, he returned to West Africa to serve in Dahomey and Niger. Also in that year Eyadéma left the French army; for his military service in it during the 1950s, Eyadéma was named Grand Officier de l'Orde National du Mono and a Chevalier de la Légion d'Honneur and was honored with a military cross for valor. He then sought to join the national guard in Togo, which had gained its full independence from France in the previous year. Togo's first elected president, Sylvanus Olympio, refused to admit him or to sponsor Eyadéma after he was accepted into a military school in France. Instead, Eyadéma became an assistant, or adjutant, in the Togo army.

In early 1963 Eyadéma led a group of Togolese soldiers, who were angry over the conditions they faced after their discharge from the French army, in a rebellion against Olympio. The president was shot and killed as he tried to enter the U.S. Embassy in Togo to gain asylum. While the details of the assassination are not entirely clear, it is believed that Eyadéma himself fired the shots that killed Olympio. Owing to the reputation he earned as the leader of the rebellion and to the Kabye tribe's domination of the Togo army, Eyadéma advanced to the rank of captain in 1963, major a year later, and lieutenant-colonel in 1965.

In 1967 Eyadéma overthrew President Nicholas Grunitzky in a bloodless coup and banned all political parties. Norimitsu Onishi later described the incident for the *New York Times* (June 22, 1999) as "post-colonial Africa's first military coup." In the first of many assurances that would not be borne out, Eyadéma said that military control of the government would be temporary. On April 14 of the same year, Eyadéma declared himself Togo's president and minister of defense. In 1969, in an attempt to legitimize his power, he created the Assembly of the Togolese People (Rassemblement du Peuple Togolese, or RPT), a solitary national political party with himself as leader. In *Who's Who in Africa: Leaders for the 1990s* (1992), Alan Rake wrote that Eyadéma modeled the RPT after the political party of his close friend and ally Mobuto Sese Seko, the dictator and president of Zaire, who, before his overthrow in 1998, had been the longest-serving leader in Africa. In 1972 a national referendum authorized a seven-year presidential term for Eyadéma, who had run unopposed. William Borders wrote for the *New York Times* (October 7, 1970), "In the three and a half years since power was seized by Lieut. Col. Etienne Eyadéma, the tough young commander of the small army, a few tentative signs of well-being have begun appearing in a generally impoverished country." In the 1970s Togo's economy flourished, due mainly to its phosphate resources. But there were a number of attempted coups and mass protests by students and workers against Eyadéma's rule during that decade. In 1979 a new constitution was drawn up, and Eyadéma, again the sole candidate, was re-elected to a new seven-year term with more than 99 percent of the vote; another election took place, with the same result, in 1986.

Although he had had a relatively austere and modest lifestyle earlier on, Eyadéma was now accused of gross extravagance and corruption. Gilchrist Olympio, the son of the assassinated former president Sylvanus Olympio and the spokesman for the Movement for Togolese Democracy, was quoted by Bernard D. Nossiter in the *New York Times* (June 8, 1980) as saying, "We are being held captive by another Idi Amin," the notorious military ruler of Uganda who killed hundreds of thousands of opponents in the 1970s. "[Eyadéma] rules by fiat. He has bankrupted the country. He has got himself immensely rich and indulges in the most basic violation of human rights—arbitrary arrests, political assassination, collective punishment . . ." Eyadéma was also accused of fostering a cult of personality around himself. Olympio told Nossiter that Eyadéma had ordered children and civil servants to spend two hours a day dancing while literally singing his praises and that on the evening television news in Togo, Eyadéma appeared with angel wings on his shoulders. Eyadéma has kept Togo's media under tight control.

In the 1980s Togo's economy suffered from a drop in phosphate prices, and the country fell into substantial debt. There were bomb attacks and coup attempts against Eyadéma's government late in the decade, but the opposition was put down each time. According to Rake, Amnesty International and official French observers accused the government of torturing political prisoners. Eyadéma made concessions in 1987, holding a meeting with members of the long-inactive opposition political parties and setting up a national Human Rights Commission. The early 1990s saw more mass protests and demonstrations against Eyadéma's rule. A Reuters article that appeared in the *New York Times* (March 17, 1991) reported, "The growing opposition is demanding immediate multi-party rule, amnesty for dissidents abroad and a conference on the country's political future." The southern Ewe and Mina tribes, who together with Eyadéma's own Kabye tribe make up 99 percent of Togo's population, felt excluded from positions of power. As quoted by Kenneth B. Noble in the *New York Times* (July 25, 1991), Makau Matua, director of the Africa project for the New York–based Lawyers' Committee for Human Rights, said, "Eyadéma is truly among the last of Africa's old-line dictators."

In 1991 Eyadéma agreed to hold a national conference and to abide by its decisions, but when the opposition delegates suspended the constitution, elected a transitional prime minister, and stripped Eyadéma of most of his power while openly accusing him of horrible crimes, Eyadéma tried to suspend the conference. He eventually agreed to step down, but instead army troops attacked Eyadéma's political opponents and the house of the new interim prime minister, Koku Koffigoh, placing him in detention. Eyadéma forced the interim government to dissolve and quickly reasserted control of the country. A new, more democratic constitution was created and a multi-party election promised for 1993. The integrity of the elections in both 1993 and 1998, however, was seriously compromised. Citing alleged voting irregularities and human-rights violations, the European Union, the International Monetary Fund, and the World Bank suspended aid to Togo after the 1993 election, which was boycotted by the opposition parties; that aid has not resumed. Only France maintained high-level diplomatic relations with Togo. Following the election in 1998, the results of which were also disputed because of alleged voting irregularities, Amnesty International wrote a report accusing the

Togo government of killing hundreds of political opponents. As quoted by Onishi, the U.S. State Department also presented a human-rights report regarding the 1998 Togo election, which stated, "Security forces were responsible for extrajudicial killings, beatings and arbitrary arrests and detentions." In 2000 the United Nations and the Organisation of African Unity (OAU) created a joint panel to investigate Amnesty International's allegations against Eyadéma and his government for the killings of several hundred people during the 1998 elections. A second United Nations panel was arranged to investigate allegations that Eyadéma had breached official U.N. sanctions by helping the rebel leader Jonas Savimbi to wage civil war against the Angolan government. It was also in 2000, however, that Eyadéma assumed the rotating chairmanship of the OAU, a body set up in 1963 to promote unity and solidarity among African nations. (Of Africa's 54 countries, only Morocco is not a member of the group.) In response to Eyadéma's becoming chairman, Paul Japheth Sunwabe wrote for the *Perspective* (September 5, 2001, on-line), "The buffoons congratulated Eyadéma for thirty years of thievery, grotesque corruption," and applied to him such complimentary descriptions as "the chief arbiter of disputes in Africa, the African democratic icon and an apostle of peace."

"[African democracy] moves along at its own pace and in its own way," Eyadéma declared in his address as chairman to the opening session of the OAU, as quoted by Virginia Gidley-Kitchin for BBC News (July 12, 2000, on-line). In response to both internal and international pressure, Eyadéma has stated that he will not run in Togo's national election in 2003. — C.F.T.

Suggested Reading: BBC News (on-line) July 12, 2000; *africaonline.com*; *Christian Science Monitor* p5 June 4, 1990, with photos; *New York Times* III p33 Feb. 4, 1973, with photo, A p6 July 25, 1991; *International Who's Who 1997-98*; Rake, Alan. *Who's Who in Africa: Leaders for the 1990s* (1992)

---

## Faber, Sandra

*Dec. 28, 1944– Astronomer; astrophysicist*

*Address: Kerr 470, UCO/Lick Observatory, University of California, Santa Cruz, CA 95064*

Courtesy of *www.ucolick.org*

Sandra Faber has been recognized as one of the world's leading cosmologists. An astronomer and astrophysicist associated with the Lick Observatory, in California, Faber has made major contributions to the study of the structure and formation of elliptical galaxies, helped chart the streaming motions of many galaxies, assisted in the development of the Hubble Space Telescope and the Keck Observatory, in Hawaii, and been instrumental in the development of the concept of "cold dark matter." Elected in 1985 to the National Academy of Sciences and in 1989 to the American Academy of Arts and Sciences, Faber holds the title of University Professor at the University of California (UC) at Santa Cruz, the highest honor for faculty in the UC system. In 1984 *Science Digest* named her one of the 100 best American scientists under 40, and in 1986 she earned the Heineman Prize, from the American Astronomical Society.

Faber was born Sandra Moore in Boston, Massachusetts, on December 28, 1944 and grew up in Cleveland, Ohio. Her father, Donald Edwin Moore, was a civil engineer who had attained the rank of colonel in the army; her mother, Elizabeth (Borwick) Moore, like many women of that generation, sacrificed a career of her own to devote herself to homemaking and parenting. Her mother and father both retained keen memories of the Great Depression, and thus raised their daughter to believe that "nothing came free in life, but hard work would be rewarded," as Faber recalled to Alan Dressler, author of *Voyage to the Great Attractor: Exploring Intergalactic Space* (1994). "Education was the key to move upward," Faber continued; consequently, "I was doted on intellectually but not spoiled monetarily."

Even as a young child, Faber found herself dissatisfied with the social roles traditionally assigned to women. "I admired men," she told Dressler, "because they were active and in control of their destinies. Women seemed to me passive and weak, and their activities like housework and baby-tending were so much more boring than men's work out in the 'real world.' I had a lot of pride and did not relish the thought of spending my life waiting on other people's needs, which is what every woman in my world did."

For a while, Faber was something of a tomboy: she enjoyed playing sports with neighborhood boys or listening to her father trade stories with his buddies. As she grew older she found it increasingly difficult to ignore the social pressure to conform to a traditional gender role. In particular, she remembers being excluded from a Little League baseball team because she was female. Fortunately, she discovered "a way to fight back," as she explained to Dressler: "I saw that learning and studying could take me to faraway places that few of my peers could even dream of. I read incessantly, mostly about science, any kind of science. I had a rock collection; I learned how to identify every tree in the neighborhood; I spent hours reading about and watching spiders; I tracked the weather. I had a wonderful time escaping from people into the natural world. And I took delicious pleasure, I have to be honest, in acing academically the same boys who wouldn't let me play on the Little League team."

As an undergraduate, Faber attended Swarthmore College, in Swarthmore, Pennsylvania. She earned a bachelor's degree with high honors in physics in 1966. (She minored in mathematics and astronomy.) At Swarthmore, Faber never felt that her gender was an issue. "I never felt I was struggling against the odds," she told Dressler. "On the contrary, the educational establishment seemed to me to be working actively on my behalf. I am an example of *how the system is supposed to work*, and for that I feel extremely lucky."

For graduate study, Faber attended Harvard University, in Cambridge, Massachusetts. (Faber has written that while Harvard was less well known than Caltech for optical observational astronomy, her specialty, she chose the former school because it was closer to Swarthmore, where her future husband, Andrew Faber, was still working toward his undergraduate degree.) In 1972 Faber earned a Ph.D. in astronomy; her doctoral thesis formulated a "scaling law" for the relationship between the size and emission spectra of elliptical galaxies.

That same year Faber accepted a post as assistant professor at the Lick Observatory, a facility situated about 20 miles east of San Jose, California, and operated by the University of California at Santa Cruz. That development was a fortunate one, since Andrew Faber, whom she had married in 1967, had just been admitted to Stanford Law School, which is only about an hour's drive north of Santa Cruz.

On her very first day on the job at Lick, Faber discovered that she was pregnant. Because her position was tenured, Faber was not forced to choose between motherhood and her career as an astronomer, and she even managed, in the first three years after her daughter Robin was born, to broaden her knowledge of astronomy through part-time teaching in subjects she did not know thoroughly. Although she was the first female staff member at Lick in the observatory's 100-year history, Faber has written that she did not sense even "a trace" of discrimination there.

In 1976 Faber published a paper in the *Astrophysical Journal* about research she had done in collaboration with Robert Jackson, one of her graduate students. In the paper, the two described a new scaling law that established a relationship between the brightness of elliptical galaxies and the orbital velocities of the stars within them. The law, now known as the "Faber-Jackson relation," represented a major advance in the study of elliptical galaxies and galaxy formation.

Over the next few years, Faber wrote or co-authored a number of papers that linked extragalactic astronomy (the study of objects beyond the Milky Way, the galaxy that contains the solar system) with both cosmology (the study of the origin and ultimate fate of the observable universe) and particle physics. A paper about the masses of galaxies, written in collaboration with Jay Gallagher, "was very influential in convincing astronomers that galaxies were surrounded by massive, invisible dark halos—the so-called 'dark matter' in the universe," as Faber wrote in an autobiographical sketch posted in "Contributions of 20th Century Women to Science" on the Web site of the UC Los Angeles Department of Physics. (The existence of dark matter can be inferred only from its gravitational effects on other, directly observable objects. While the precise nature of dark matter remains a mystery, most astronomers believe that it constitutes as much as 90 percent of the mass of the universe.) That Faber-Gallagher paper was followed by two others, one of which she co-wrote with two other researchers, on the formation of galaxies from "quantum fluctuations" or "quantum seeds" in the aftermath of the Big Bang, the primordial explosion thought to have given rise to the present universe. In an outline of modern cosmology that she presented at a 1994 symposium sponsored by the Center for Particle Astrophysics at UC Berkeley, Faber explained, "These fluctuations exist in space at all eras but normally are harmless, dying away as quickly as they come. But, during inflation"—a phase of rapid outward expansion hypothesized to have taken place $10^{-35}$ seconds after the Big Bang—"they were seized by the rapidly expanding Universe and blown up to macroscopic size before they could die out. It is a staggering thought that our entire Milky Way Galaxy is really nothing but a microscopic quantum fluctuation preserved and magnified by inflation." While Faber wrote in her autobiographical statement that her ideas on galaxy formation were "probably wrong in certain details," they remain, in her words, "basically unchanged as the current working paradigm for structure formation in the Universe."

In the late 1980s the "Seven Samurai," as Faber's research group was nicknamed, stumbled upon a method of determining the distance from the Milky Way to other individual galaxies. That in turn led to the surprising discovery that the observable velocities of most nearby galaxies (relative to the Milky Way) did not accord with astronomers' predictions. Ever since the Big Bang, the universe has been expanding outward, with the result that galaxies have been spreading apart from each other like raisins in rising bread dough. Faber and her colleagues discovered that, in addition to that movement, galaxies possess a "peculiar motion" relative to one another, as if the raisins were also moving *within* the rising dough. Eventually, Faber and her colleagues were able to account for the peculiar motion of the Milky Way and thousands of other nearby galaxies: drawn by gravity, all are streaming toward a massive "supercluster" of galaxies dubbed the Great Attractor, located about 150 million light-years from Earth in the direction of the constellation Hydra-Centaurus.

Faber has taken an active role in the development and operation of the two most powerful instruments available to optical astronomers: the Hubble Space Telescope and the W. M. Keck Observatory. As a member of the Hubble Wide Field Planetary Camera Team (1985–97), Faber helped design the equipment that has captured some of the most striking images relayed to Earth via the Hubble Space Telescope; she also helped to diagnose and correct the flaw in the telescope's mirror that was detected soon after it was put into orbit. As co-chair of the Keck Observatory's Science Steering Committee (1991–93), Faber assisted in the construction of the facility that now houses the world's largest optical and infrared telescope. She played a major managerial role in the building of both the Hubble and the Keck telescopes. In addition, she helped persuade the larger scientific community of the usefulness and need for large optical telescopes.

Faber's current research focuses on the evolution and structure of distant galaxies, especially insofar as those galaxies, which date from early in the history of the universe, differ from nearby galaxies. She is also involved in the development of adaptive optics, a technology for improving the resolution of ground-based telescopes such as the Keck.

Faber has received honorary doctorates from Williams College and Swarthmore College. She and her husband, who practices law in San Jose, make their home in Los Gatos, California. The couple have two daughters, Robin and Holly. — P.K.

Suggested Reading: *Discover* p20+ Nov. 1989; *New York Times* Cp3 Apr. 28, 1987, with photo; *New York Times* Cp10 Jul. 20, 1993, with photo; *Omni* p62+ July 1990, with photo; Dressler, Alan. *Voyage to the Great Attractor: Exploring Intergalactic Space*, 1994; Oakes, Elizabeth H. *Encyclopedia of World Scientists*, 2001, *International Encyclopedia of Women Scientists*, 2002; Yount, Lisa. *A to Z of Women in Science*, 1999

Fabrice Trombert/Retna Ltd.

## Fallon, Jimmy

*Sep. 19, 1974– Comedian; actor*

*Address:* Saturday Night Live, *30 Rockefeller Plaza, New York, NY 10112*

"The people who pop first on this show are the ones who you believe you can see right into their hearts," Lorne Michaels, *Saturday Night Live*'s executive producer, told Ariel Levy for *New York* (October 18, 1999). "It was true of Gilda [Radner], it was true of John Belushi, and it's true of Jimmy. You just feel you know them." An engagingly absurd and animated comedian, Jimmy Fallon is *Saturday Night Live*'s latest breakout star. At 28, he is almost the same age as the show, which was created by Michaels in 1975 and has launched the careers of many well-known actor/comedians, among them Bill Murray and Eddie Murphy as well as Belushi and Radner. Fallon's youth and exuberance have helped revitalize *SNL*, particularly its "Weekend Update" segment, which parodies the news, as have his spoofs of songs and dead-on impersonations of such celebrities as Jerry Seinfeld, Adam Sandler, John Lennon, Howard Stern, and Chris Rock, some of whom are former *SNL* stars. For Fallon, starring on the long-running comedy show is a dream come true. "All he ever wanted was to be on *Saturday Night Live*," Fallon's former manager Randi Siegel told Jonathan Durbin for *Paper* (November 2001, on-line). "The first time I spoke with him on the phone, he told me how, growing up, he and his sister would practice *SNL* sketches in their living room. He's so genuinely in awe of everyone who was on the show before him. That's what's so endearing about him. His impressions aren't mean-spirited—they're a tribute to the people he grew up admiring."

The son of Jim and Gloria Fallon, James Fallon was born in the New York City borough of Brooklyn on September 19, 1974. His father served in the Vietnam War and, as a youth, performed with a doo-wop group; his mother lived briefly in a convent before deciding that a nun's life was not for her. During Fallon's early childhood his family, which included his older sister, Gloria, moved to Saugerties, a town near Woodstock, New York. Fallon began doing impressions when he was two years old; his first was of the actor James Cagney. His earliest memories of watching *Saturday Night Live* begin when he was about eight. "It used to make my parents laugh, and that meant a lot to me at the time . . . what is it that's making them laugh?" he told Dan Craft for the Bloomington, Illinois, *Pantagraph* (April 25, 2002). His parents would allow him to view only the "clean" parts of the show, and he soon began imitating many of *SNL*'s recurring characters. "Ever since I was 8, I used to do King Tut and the Wild and Crazy Guys," he recalled in an interview for *Jane* (on-line). "And then I started doing impressions, hard-core. I had a great Pee-wee Herman. My senior year in high school, I entered this impression contest in Poughkeepsie, and I closed with Pee-wee. And I won the contest. Then I went to college, and I added the guitar where I did songs and stuff about this troll doll." While attending the College of Saint Rose, in Albany, New York, where he majored in computer science, Fallon maintained his habit of watching *Saturday Night Live* and studying the techniques of the performers. Eager to become a member of its cast, Fallon dropped out of college in his senior year, just 15 credits short of earning his bachelor's degree. He relocated to Los Angeles and took acting lessons with the Groundlings Theater Company, which had launched the careers of Paul Reubens (a.k.a. Pee-wee Herman), Lisa Kudrow, and Will Ferrell, among others. After two years at Groundlings, he went to an open audition for *Saturday Night Live*, held at a club in New York City. "I did three minutes, and I couldn't get the audience," he recalled to Dan Craft. "It wasn't a good showcase for me. . . . So I didn't get it." Dispirited, he returned to Groundlings. A year later he received an invitation to perform for Michaels, this time at the *SNL* stage in Rockefeller Center. "I did like 10 impressions . . . , and I didn't want to name who because I figured if I was good enough, they'd know who I was doing," he recalled to Jonathan Durbin. "The whole afternoon, people had been telling me, 'Lorne doesn't laugh—he's seen it all, so don't think he doesn't think you're funny if he doesn't laugh.' It just went on and on, a huge psych-out. Anyway, I finished the audition with [Adam] Sandler . . . and Lorne turned his face away, but I could see that he'd cracked up. It was such a surreal and cool moment."

On September 26, 1998 Fallon began working as a featured player on *SNL*. In his first season he distinguished himself with his hilarious Halloween carols. (He has also performed songs about Valentine's Day, Christmas, and spring break.) His impressions of such diverse people as Alanis Morissette, Eminem, Jerry Seinfeld, and Adam Sandler attracted a large following of fans. On October 2, 1999 he was promoted to full cast member. He soon perfected signature characters, among them Nick Burns, a corporate employee who ridicules his co-workers while fixing their computers, and Sully, a teenager from Boston who runs a public-access cable show with his girlfriend and compulsively displays his affection for her in public. His repertoire has since expanded to include such subjects as David Bowie, Harry Connick Jr., Alan Dershowitz, John Lennon, Gilbert Gottfried, Chris Rock, Howard Stern, Richard Simmons, and Steven Tyler, among others.

For the 2000–01 season, Fallon and the *SNL* performer Tina Fey (who is also the show's head writer) were selected to co-anchor the long-running "Weekend Update" segment. (Their predecessor, Colin Quinn, left *SNL* to star in his own television sitcom.) Fallon and Fey spiced up "Weekend Update," cramming its segments with off-color bits and funny asides. "Fallon and Fey (as they're billed, like an old vaudeville team) have turned a dead-air segment of *SNL* into don't-touch-that-remote television," Joyce Millman wrote for *Salon.com*. "In Fallon and Fey's hands, 'Weekend Update' surges with fearless topical satire. It reverberates with the sweet thwack of jokes hit out of the park. . . . Watching Fallon and Fey is like hanging out in a cafe, perusing the *New York Times* with two intelligent, funny people who find the news as maddening and absurd as you do."

In addition to his work on *Saturday Night Live*, Fallon has made cameo appearances in such films as *Almost Famous* (2000) and *Band of Brothers*, an HBO television miniseries about an elite army unit in World War II. He was the co-host, with the actress Kirsten Dunst, of the 2001 MTV Music Awards and has performed stand-up routines at universities around the country as well as at noted clubs, among them the Improv, in Los Angeles, and Caroline's Comedy Club, in New York City. He has been cast in an upcoming Woody Allen movie, which is scheduled to be filmed in the summer of 2002. *I Hate This Place: A Pessimist's Guide to Life*, which Fallon wrote with his sister, Gloria, was published in 1999. In the fall of 2002, he released his first comedy album, *The Bathroom Wall*.

"Maybe the most surprising thing about Fallon—although not to the people who know him—is he has held on to his sense of wonder," Mark McGuire wrote after interviewing Fallon for the Albany, New York, *Times Union* (September 24, 1999). "He still feels gratitude, whereas too many in his business are overwhelmed by entitlement. You notice it in talking to him, the way he hangs out with other cast members—busting chops and taking abuse—and the way he dresses for comfort rather than statement. Fallon is a regular guy, a sincerely nice guy. It's no act." Fallon is unmarried and lives in New York City. — C.M.

Suggested Reading: *Interview* p83+ May 2002; *New York* p40+ Oct. 10, 1999; *Paper* (on-line) Nov. 2001; *TV Guide* p5 Mar. 6–12, 1999; *Washington Post* C p1 Oct. 1, 2001

Selected Books: *I Hate This Place: A Pessimist's Guide to Life*, 1999

Selected Recordings: *The Bathroom Wall*, 2002

---

Courtesy of NBC

## Fey, Tina

*May 18, 1970– Actress; writer*

*Address:* Saturday Night Live, *NBC-TV, 30 Rockefeller Plaza, New York, NY 10012*

The first female head writer for NBC's popular, long-running sketch-comedy series *Saturday Night Live*, Tina Fey is better known for her role as co-anchor of the show's "Weekend Update" segment, in which she and the comedian Jimmy Fallon satirize the latest news headlines. A writer for *Entertainment Weekly* (March 2, 2001, on-line) praised Fey for her "poison-filled jokes written in long, precisely parsed sentences unprecedented in 'Update' history," delivered with "a bright, sunny countenance [that] makes her all the more devilishly delightful." *Saturday Night Live* producer Lorne Michaels told Ellen Gray for the Philadelphia *Daily News* (December 15, 2000, on-line) that Fey's writing is distinguished by "intelligence and attack on the idea, an attitude. . . . There's something for you to enjoy after you've finished laughing." In her anchoring role, the writer and performer has become something of a sex symbol, a label Fey—sometimes described as shy—finds surprising. "It seems funny that anyone would call me a sex symbol," she told Michael Freidson for *Time Out New York* (September 27, 2001, on-line). "It feels like an elaborate prank." Thanks in part to her writing and her role on "Weekend Update," *Saturday Night Live* has risen in the ratings during the last three seasons. While the show's writing staff is still dominated by men, Fey sees room for progress. "I don't doubt that women have had a hard time here in the past," she told Gary Levin for *USA Today* (February 8, 2001, on-line), "but people here are pretty evolved at this point. It's not that we're not outnumbered; there's still a lot more men than women on the writing staff. Things change slowly."

Tina Fey was born on May 18, 1970 in Upper Darby, Pennsylvania, where she grew up in a predominantly Greek neighborhood. Her father was a grant writer for the University of Pennsylvania; her mother worked for a brokerage firm. She has an older brother, who currently works as a screenwriter. Fey's interest in comedy was inspired by such shows as *Monty Python's Flying Circus*, *The Honeymooners*, and *Saturday Night Live*. When she had to go to bed early on Saturday night, her brother would act out *Saturday Night Live* in its entirety for her the next day at breakfast. She acted and sang in productions in her high school and participated in other extracurricular activities as well, including writing for the school paper, playing varsity tennis, and working on the staff of the school yearbook. "I was sort of like an active nerd," she recalled to Ellen Gray. "I had friends and was in a lot of activities. I didn't really date or anything, but I had a pretty good time." Fey also worked at the box office and handled publicity duties for Upper Darby's Summer Stage, where she would spend two summers as a director during her college years.

Fey enrolled at the University of Virginia at Charlottesville, intending to major in English. She changed her mind quickly, however. "They were too snooty-pants in the English department," she told Alex Witchel for the *New York Times* News Service (November 29, 2001). "So I got sucked into drama, which of course was a much easier major, since it's the only one that's graded on effort." In addition to acting, Fey wrote a short comic play that was performed at the college. "I remember . . . sitting in the back of the theater . . . watching people laugh," she told Jason Gay for the *New York Observer* (March 5, 2001, on-line). "I was like, 'Oh my God, this is really cool.'" Fey graduated in 1992 and applied successfully to the graduate theater program at DePaul University, in Chicago, Illinois, but decided not to attend. "I just got this feeling like it wasn't going to work out . . . [that] they were going to take my money and then cut me loose from the program," she told Ellen Gray. Fey nonetheless moved to Chicago, where she worked folding towels at a YMCA while she took classes and performed in a local improvisational comedy troupe. She then studied comedy at the training center of Chicago's esteemed Second City troupe.

Second City produced the current *Saturday Night Live* cast members Rachel Dratch and Horatio Sanz as well as past stars of the show, including John Belushi, Chris Farley, and Bill Murray. "It was a weird mix in that all the guys were kind of these rebellious guys," she told Ellen Gray, "and most of the women were sort of honor students, college students, went to good schools, kind of good girls who somehow ended up in comedy." After two years in training, she became an understudy in Second City's touring company, where she met Jeff Richmond, one of the group's directors and a composer. They were married in the summer of 2001.

About four years earlier, Fey had moved up from the touring company to perform on Second City's main stage. In 1997 she sent samples of sketches she had written to Adam McKay, a former Second City colleague who worked at *Saturday Night Live.* McKay liked what he saw and arranged an interview with Lorne Michaels, the *Saturday Night* producer. Within five days of her first interview, Fey was hired as a writer for the show. Although Fey initially struggled in her new job, her first sketch, featuring Chris Farley as a gigantic baby on Sally Jessy Raphael's talk show, aired after several weeks. Hitting her stride, Fey penned a series of well-received parodies of the ABC talk show *The View.* Some of her other sketches starred Jimmy Fallon and Rachel Dratch as Sully and Denise, two stereotypical, working-class Boston teens.

Fey has tended to avoid writing sketches that have a single, repeated joke (a characteristic of many other *Saturday Night Live* skits over the years), instead aiming for more subtle humor. A typical week begins on Monday, when the group decide which of the week's news events to satirize in the opening sketch and meet with the guest host to talk about ideas for the show. The entire show is written on Tuesday, with scripts due the next day. Rewrites, which can take up to 12 hours to complete, are done on Thursday. On Friday the cast and crew run through blocking; during rehearsals on Saturday, each writer sits next to Lorne Michaels during his or her sketch, while Michaels makes notes for changes that must be implemented. Before the show starts the cast and crew decide which sketches will air. Because writers participate as extras in the show, Fey appeared in a number of sketches during the first two years that she worked as a writer.

In 1999 Fey was named writing supervisor of *Saturday Night Live,* becoming the first female head writer in the history of the show, which first aired in 1975. Initially, the job proved to be a difficult one for Fey. "It was hard to supervise people who were there longer than me and all older and a foot and a half taller," she told Michael Freidson. "The first year was very stressful. I micromanaged everything. With comedy writers, that's like micromanaging a bag of cats. They're gonna do what they want to do." Fey also served as head writer for the Emmy Award–winning special *Saturday Night Live—The 25th Anniversary.* For the 2000–01 season she was chosen along with cast member Jimmy Fallon to host the "Weekend Update" segment after cast member Colin Quinn, the former "Update" anchor, left the show. Fey has somewhat facetiously attributed the decision to put her in the role in part to her dieting, which resulted in her losing 30 pounds. She made her on-air debut as anchor in October 2000. The new anchor duo were almost immediately popular with the show's audience and helped revive a part of the program that many had found wanting. Fey's biting humor often succeeds in being caustic without crossing the line into offensiveness. "I try not to be off-putting," she told Michael Freidson. "I have to remember that it's not just like reading *Us Weekly* and ragging on somebody with your friends. It's on TV, and these people might hear it and get their feelings hurt, so you try to evaluate whether it's worth doing or not." For the 2000–01 season, the show was nominated for five Emmy Awards, including one for Fey and her writing staff.

Fey, who wears contact lenses off-screen, has received a great deal of attention for the large pair of glasses she wears during the "Weekend Update" sketches. (Those spectacles are a prop.) "One time I didn't wear them because I was going to be in a sketch, so I had put in contacts. The Internet did *not* like that," she joked to Jason Gay. "The four teenagers on the Internet wanted me to put my glasses back on." In addition to her performances on *Saturday Night Live,* Fey appeared with Rachel Dratch in the sketch-comedy show *Dratch & Fey,* which was performed at the Upright Citizens Brigade Theater, in New York City, in the summer of 2000. *Time Out New York,* as quoted on *NBC.com* (on-line), called *Dratch and Fey* "the funniest thing to be found on any New York comedy stage this summer." *Dratch & Fey* was directed by Fey's husband, Jeff Richmond. Most recently, in an SNL Studios and Paramount Pictures project, Fey has been at work adapting for the silver screen Rosalind Wiseman's book, *Queen Bees and Wannabes: Helping Your Daughter Survive Cliques, Gossip, Boyfriends, and Other Realities of Adolescence.* Because of her "Weekend Update" duties, Fey now shares the head-writing credit on *Saturday Night Live* with Dennis McNichols. She maintains a grueling schedule, sometimes working until daylight. — G.O.

Suggested Reading: *New York Observer* (on-line) Mar. 5. 2001; (Philadelphia) *Daily News* Dec. 15, 2000; *Time Out New York* (on-line) Sep. 27, 2001

Selected Shows: *Saturday Night Live,* 2000–

Selected Plays: as author and performer—*Dratch & Fey*

## Flaming Lips

*Rock group*

Coyne, Wayne
*Jan. 13, 1961– Guitarist; singer; songwriter*

Ivins, Michael
*Mar. 7, 1963– Bassist*

Drozd, Steven
*June 11, 1969– Drummer; guitarist; keyboardist*

*Address: c/o Warner Bros. Records, 3300 Warner Blvd., Burbank, CA 91505*

In an era of cookie-cutter teen bands and hybrid rap-metal poseurs who scream about their angst while collecting million-dollar paychecks, the Flaming Lips—Wayne Coyne, Michael Ivins, and Steven Drozd—have been quietly plotting a musical revolution. On the evidence of their newest album, *Yoshimi Battles the Pink Robots* (2002), they may succeed. The record, released in July 2002, has earned a warm reception from the public and critics, some of whom detect glimmers of the future of rock in the group's quirky, heartfelt music. During their nearly 20-year career, the Oklahoma City–based band has traveled a winding route, making music ranging from feedback-drenched pop anthems to grand, orchestral compositions such as *Zaireeka* (1997), a work comprising four CDs designed to be played simultaneously. Along the way, they also enjoyed a taste of mainstream stardom when their single "She Don't Use Jelly" found its way onto the alternative-music charts in 1994. During that year the band was seen on such TV shows as *Beverly Hills 90210* and *Late Show with David Letterman.* Following that commercial success, the band set about trying to chart new musical landscapes. While such albums as *Zaireeka* and *Clouds Taste Metallic* (1995) were lauded by critics, they went mostly unnoticed by the record-buying public. "We have failed more than we've succeeded," Coyne, the group's leader, told *Current Biography.* "We've really gotten lucky to still be able to do what we do. I wouldn't advise anyone to be like us." In 1999 they released *The Soft Bulletin,* which features songs about Superman, insects, and scientists trying to save the world, among other topics, performed with lush, orchestral stylings reminiscent of the Beach Boys' 1967 album *Pet Sounds. Yoshimi* continued in a similar vein, blending acoustic pop songs with electronic backings and towering soundscapes. Both albums have sold well, especially among the rock-music cognoscenti, and have been hailed by critics as masterpieces, while Coyne has found himself compared to the music giants Brian Wilson and Phil Spector. "I didn't create music," Coyne told *Current Biography.* "And I didn't really create even the ideas of what The Flaming Lips do. It really is [that] music is such a powerful entity, a powerful force. It has the power to move people, and me being attached to it makes it look like Wayne or The Flaming Lips is doing it."

The official origin of the Flaming Lips has been traced to 1983, when Coyne allegedly stole some musical instruments from a church hall. However, the seeds had been planted long before then. Wayne Coyne was born on January 13, 1961 in Pittsburgh, Pennsylvania, and grew up in a middle-class family in a suburb of Oklahoma City, Oklahoma, the second-youngest of six siblings. As children, Coyne and his brothers entertained themselves by staging boxing matches in their backyard. "It was endlessly entertaining, watching people beat each other up," Coyne told Peter Bochan in a 1995 interview for the Warner Bros. Records Web site. "All the little kids in the neighborhood would come and watch . . . and then we'd beat them up as well." Coyne's brothers and their friends also introduced him to music, teaching him to play guitar and exposing him to the work of different artists. "People always came around to see my brothers, and I'd inadvertently hang out," he told Chuck Dean for *Rolling Stone* (March 9, 1995). "There were all these loser guys who could play the latest Jeff Beck tune or whatever. I didn't know they were guitar lessons at the time. But there was always someone showing me a cool way to play 'Stairway to Heaven.'" Coyne was fascinated by all kinds of music and was greatly influenced by bands on the creative frontier. "My older brothers would take a lot of drugs and we'd sit around and listen to records—the Beatles' White Album, John and Yoko's experimental stuff," he told Bochan. "We never knew it was freaky or weird; we thought that was music that everyone listened to."

During the 1980s Coyne, who had opted not to attend college and was working at a Long John Silver's restaurant, began to put together a band, enlisting his brother Mark as the vocalist and long-time friend Michael Ivins (born on March 7, 1963 in Omaha, Nebraska) on bass. The trio, with Coyne on guitar, christened themselves the Flaming Lips, a name for which no definitive explanation has been given. "It's such a dumb name that it's so arbitrary that it doesn't matter," Coyne told Dean. "There are some great band names out there, like Fugazi, where you get an idea what it's about, but it's still mysterious enough to make you wonder. But the Flaming Lips? It's just [expletive] silly." They began performing around Oklahoma City with an ever-changing roster of drummers. Their first paying gig was at a transvestite club called the Blue Note.

After settling on percussionist Richard English, the band released its debut album, *The Flaming Lips* (1985), on their own record label, Lovely Sorts of Death. For Coyne, making an album had been the primary motivation from the time the group was begun. "I never thought of myself as, 'I'm a singer and guitar player, and we'll make records because I love to sing and play guitar,'" he told *Current Biography.* "I've really come at it from the opposite. I love making records, but quickly realized I don't sing or play guitar very good. So I've found other ways to do things that are interesting to me."

J. Michelle Martin/Courtesy of Hellfire Management

*The Flaming Lips (left to right): Steven Drozd, Wayne Coyne, Michael Ivins*

Beginning to garner attention, the group opened for such notable bands as Black Flag and Husker Du. During this period their musical tendencies shifted away from grinding punk rock to accommodate more melodic and classic-rock influences. Not long after the Flaming Lips' reputation began to build, Mark Coyne departed the band to get married. Pressing on, Wayne Coyne largely assumed creative control of the group. When the Flaming Lips played a series of dates in California with the Jesus and Mary Chain, a representative from Restless Records, a small label, attended one of the shows and offered the group a contract. The band released *Hear It Is* under the label in 1986 and *Oh My Gawd!!! . . . The Flaming Lips* a year later. The latter album contains the song "One Billionth of a Millisecond on a Sunday Morning," an ethereal anthem that comes in at nearly 10 minutes. The track became popular on underground radio and inspired comparisons to such art-rocker heavyweights as Pink Floyd and Procol Harum.

While touring for *Oh My Gawd!!! . . .* , Coyne met the concert promoter and guitarist Jon Donahue. The two struck up a friendship after a late-night jam session, and Donahue, who was also playing in the group Mercury Rev, agreed to work with the Lips as a sound technician. Around this time the group returned to the studio to record their third album for Restless, *Telepathic Surgery* (1989). Halfway through the recording sessions, English left the band and was replaced by drummer Nathan Roberts. Donahue also joined the band, under the stage name Dingus, as a guitar player. This lineup appeared on the group's fifth album, *In A Priest Driven Ambulance* (1990). A collection of songs structured loosely around the theme of religion, the album is noted by fans as a creative turning point for the band. According to Jim DeRogatis in *Penthouse* (Summer 2000), the record "took the familiar influences of the Stooges, the Velvet Underground, and Pink Floyd and distorted them as if in a funhouse mirror." In the *All Music Guide* (on-line), Jason Ankeny wrote, "*In a Priest Driven Ambulance* ranks as the first truly brilliant Flaming Lips album."

*In a Priest Driven Ambulance* was played frequently on college radio stations, and the Flaming Lips were on the verge of stardom in alternative-music circles. Two weeks after the album was released, however, Restless Records went out of business; the band, which was slated to tour with the Soup Dragons, suddenly had no label to generate publicity, and as a result the Flaming Lips found themselves playing to startlingly small audiences. They returned to Oklahoma to figure out their next move. The band members, who shared a house, realized that they needed a telephone if the act were to survive, but they now had no way to pay the bill. "So we knew if we could get a phone, we could abuse it for a good month and a half before they shut us off," Coyne told Jaan Uhelzski for the Web site *Addicted to Noise*. In that way they made contact with Roberta Peterson of Warner Bros. Records. "She came to see our show . . . and we decided what we'd do was try to burn the club down," Coyne told Uhelzski. "You know, like a Butthole Surfers thing, where you get the cymbal and pour alcohol in it and light it on fire. From the first song, the fire was going, . . . and the whole side of the stage and the PA was on fire, and she just thought it was a great show."

Peterson signed the group, which made its first album on Warner Bros., *Hit to Death in the Future Head*, in 1992. A more pop-driven record than they had previously done, *Hit to Death* represented the band's first, not very successful bid for mainstream attention. Undeterred, they released *Transmissions from the Satellite Heart*, featuring their new guitarist, Ronald Jones, and a new drummer, Steven Drozd, the following year. (Drozd was born on June 11, 1969 in Houston, Texas.) With three-chord sing-alongs ("Turn It On") alongside lush sonic tapestries ("Oh My Pregnant Head"), the album was seen by critics as the group's most cohesive effort up to that time. The group toured in support of *Transmissions* for a year before the record began to gather steam; they received a boost when a deejay in Oklahoma began playing "She Don't Use Jelly" at a local station. The song, with its catchy riffs and cheerfully nonsensical lyrics, soon began appearing on various playlists around the country. Before long the Flaming Lips found their video for "She Don't Use Jelly" (made for $12,000) in the cable channel MTV's "Buzz Bin" (a rotating list of the most popular videos). Additionally, they performed on *Late Show with David Letterman*, were featured on the second stage during the 1994 Lollapalooza tour, and, in a seemingly incongruous development, appeared on the TV teen drama *Beverly Hills 90210*. The success of "She Don't Use Jelly" convinced Warner Bros. Records that the band was a viable commodity, a fact the company had begun to doubt.

The group's next album for Warner Bros., *Clouds Taste Metallic* (1995), received good notices from critics. Writing in *Rolling Stone* (1995, on-line), Al Weisel noted, "Wayne Coyne is still singing about spaceships and animals in his weepy Neil Young-ish voice, backed by Beach Boys harmonies, fuzz guitar and sound effects. But determined to be more than just a Dr. Demento staple, the Lips have included some songs that even manage to be strangely touching." *Clouds Taste Metallic* included the song "Bad Days," which was also featured on the soundtrack to the 1995 movie *Batman Forever.* Nonetheless, the record sold only 50,000 copies, and the band returned to cult-favorite status.

Nineteen ninety-six proved a difficult year for the band. Drozd suffered a spider bite that became infected, nearly resulting in the loss of his hand. Jones left the group, reportedly to embark on a spiritual odyssey, and Ivins was nearly killed in a car accident involving a wheel that came off another car and pinned him inside his own. At the same time, the group was audited—without result, as it turned out—by the Internal Revenue Service. Those various bumps in the road led Coyne to reevaluate what the band was doing, and he began searching for new musical avenues to explore. He thus gathered 30 people from his hometown in a parking garage and provided them with specially designed cassette tapes to play in their cars. Directing the cars into position, Coyne stood in front of them and had the occupant of each car play his or her cassette on cue. Describing the result on the Web site *janecek.com*, a reporter wrote, "Soon sounds appear at one end of the garage, then slowly, it jumps around and the cacophony begins. . . . Every tape is unique, but made in relation to the others. As you wander around, from one end of the cars to the other, you realize that there is a song, a *composition*, [emanating] from the cars." Coyne conducted three of these Parking Lot Experiments, as they came to be known, in Oklahoma before he and Drozd staged one in Austin, Texas, in March 1997. The event was expected to draw only a few hundred people, but more than 1,000 showed up. "[The Parking Lot Experiments] truly were an experiment to us, even though they were entertaining to other people," Coyne told *Current Biography*. "We were sort of seeing what this collision of different compositions would be like. And the only way we could do it would be to get all these [cars] together. And it became more intriguing when we had an audience there responding to these things that we did. So it kind of looked like a grand kind of performance art thing that we were doing, but it really wasn't."

Working on the Parking Lot Experiments gave Coyne the inspiration for the Flaming Lips' next album. Entitled *Zaireeka* (the title came from the blending of "Zaire" with "Eureka," which Coyne intended to represent the fusion of anarchy and genius), the album comprised four CDs that could be properly played only at the same time. On a given song, for example, the drum track might be on the first disc, the bass on the second, the piano on the third, and the vocals on the fourth. The result was a work that yielded different sounds with each playing, because of the unlikelihood of pushing all four "play" buttons at exactly the same moment every time and because no two CD players produce sounds at precisely the same speed. Flaming Lips' CD "quartet" could be somewhat disorienting for the listener (in fact, one of the songs on the record came with such a warning). *Zaireeka* was hailed by critics as a bold rock experiment. "By the time *Zaireeka* envelops you in all of its feedback and regal horns, all of its barking dogs and disintegrating moths, you no longer care whether the whole equals the sum of its parts," John Kun wrote for *Rolling Stone* (December 11, 1997). "As one song puts it, 'The only thing that mattered were the pieces that prevailed.'" Creating the record was an enlightening experience for Coyne, confirming for him that it was more important to do what one enjoys than to try to break new ground. "Only through doing stuff like *Zaireeka* did I discover that the idea of creating some new form of music that's never been done before is always futile," he told *Current Biography*.

After releasing *Zaireeka*, the band put out *A Collection of Songs Representing an Enthusiasm for Recording . . . By Amateurs* (1998). Subtitled *The Flaming Lips: 1984-1990*, the album was a selection of songs from the band's years on Restless Records. Meanwhile, having created *Zaireeka*, Coyne realized that he could now reproduce music exactly the way he heard it in his head. "*Zaireeka* made us accept more sounds and raised our level of tolerance," Coyne told Cox, "as if we were runners who did five miles a day and suddenly found we were able to do 20." This revelation, along with lessons learned from the personal and professional upheavals the group had endured, resulted in what many consider to be their finest album. Retreating to a recording studio in Cassadaga, New York, Coyne, Ivins, and Drozd found themselves immersed in a feeling of hopelessness. "Not necessarily hopelessness in our lives," Coyne told Gil Kaufman for *Addicted to Noise*, "but when your art and your lives are so connected and your art feels so hopeless, you can't help but sometimes think that things are hopeless. I think that when we were making this music, we unknowingly fused it with an exaggerated amount of hope. If two people were stranded out in the ocean waiting for help or stranded in outer space, when they would talk to each other, they probably would want to just talk optimistically. Like, 'You know we're gonna be rescued here, things are gonna work out.' And even though they may not believe it, they say it over and over again so they don't have to hear that this is really beyond hope."

This sense of optimism in the face of gloom pervaded the group's 10th album of original material, *The Soft Bulletin* (1999), for which they abandoned the heavy bass-, guitar-, and drum-based sound that had marked their other recordings in favor of more orchestral tones, punctuated by harps, strings, and brass. The result drew comparisons to Phil Spector's famous "Wall of Sound" production style, as well as the Beach Boys' work of the late 1960s. The tracks on *The Soft Bulletin* deal with science, mortality, and the saving power of love. Such songs as "Race for the Prize" and "Waitin' for a Superman" tell stories of ordinary people facing extraordinary, seemingly life-altering situations, while "Feeling Yourself Disintegrate," even as it asserts that each of us is dying every day, points to the hope offered by love. Many of these ruminations on life, death, and pervasive hope were inspired by the death of Coyne's father, from cancer, in 1997.

*The Soft Bulletin* was hailed by many critics as the best album of the year. "*The Soft Bulletin* is The Flaming Lips' bravest, most philosophical statement yet," Cox wrote. "What makes the Lips unique is that over a decade into their career, ideas are still cascading from Coyne's head . . . ," a writer for the *New Music Express* (1999, on-line) observed. "He's determined to make music in different and ever more interesting ways, and on this album he succeeds triumphantly. The combination of the emotional and experimental is more touching and wonderful than it's ever been on any Flaming Lips record in the past. It's some achievement."

While Coyne was pleased with the reception of *The Soft Bulletin*, he also avoided falling prey to the trappings of the rock lifestyle that often follow such success. "If I was younger, I might have gotten caught up in that," he told *Current Biography*, "but I see how it's so arbitrary. It doesn't mean that it's not important to people. But that's really their own doing. The analogy I use is like this, if you came to my house and I cooked you a baked potato . . . and you said, 'Damn, Wayne, that's the best baked potato I ever had,' I'd say, 'Well that may be true, but the bottom line is, the potato does most of the work.'"

In 2000, while on tour in Europe, Coyne received a series of E-mail messages regarding a Japanese woman who was friendly with the band. "The e-mails were poorly translated to English from Japanese—so the message, unfortunately, was not easily understood," Coyne wrote in a 2002 press release. "But as the days went by we were able to, little by little, decipher the horrible news being transmitted—our friend [the Japanese woman] had become ill—a heart ailment of some kind—and suddenly and sadly had died." The news came as a shock to the band members and weighed heavily on Coyne's mind as the group put together a remixed single of "Race for the Prize." Needing a B-side for the song, Coyne decided to write a new song about the death of his friend. The song, about the healing effect summer can have on people, became the first in a series of numbers about the celebration of being alive, even in the face of death. The resulting album was titled *Yoshimi Battles the Pink Robots*. The title was inspired by a track on the album featuring the Japanese singer Yoshimi P-we. "I had this recording of her doing some screaming, and I thought, 'You know, it really sounds like she's in some kind of fight or something,'" Coyne told Andrew Dansby for *Rolling Stone* (April 12, 2002, on-line). "So I just thought, 'OK, I'll call it 'Yoshimi Battles the Pink Robots,' and that'll be that." Coyne then decided to use that title for the entire collection. "Once I had this title it really loosened the whole feel of what we were doing," he told Dansby. "A lot of times we get into these things that are philosophical and heavy, but there was a little bit of relief when we could just say, 'Why does everything have to be death-oriented or existential?'" On such songs as "Do You Realize?," "In the Morning of the Magicians," and "It's Summertime" (the song Coyne wrote about his friend's death), *Yoshimi* explores the vagaries of life and the inevitability of death, all through a sunny, Lewis Carrollesque prism. The album also continues *The Soft Bulletin*'s theme of the kinship of science and art, an idea in which Coyne firmly believes. "I try to speak of art and science in the same vein a lot," he told Sarah Vowell for *GQ* (December 1999). "Because when people look at art, especially the kind that I do, they think of drug-damaged, wacko, insane guys [as if they're] the only creative people out there. Where has this notion that only insane people make the great art come from? . . . Your *sewer systems* are based on creative ideas; rocket science is based on creative ideas."

Released on July 16, 2002, *Yoshimi Battles the Pink Robots* was received even more enthusiastically than its predecessor. "The long-reigning kings of big-sky psychedelia emerge from their Oklahoma City bunker to ask this musical question: If the Powerpuff Girls took on Black Sabbath's 'Iron Man,' who would win?" Greg Kot wrote for *Rolling Stone* (July 25, 2002). "The answer, in this case, is the listener." John Mulvey, reviewing the record for *Uncut* (July 2002), observed that *Yoshimi* "is fearlessly grand and sentimental music, music that understands the glib and the profound are sometimes interchangeable. That, heard in a certain frame of mind, a Broadway musical can say as much about the human condition as a philosophical treatise."

In August 2002 the singer Beck asked the Flaming Lips to be his backing band on his upcoming tour. "I think he just got the idea that we're a lot alike in the way that we think and do things," Coyne told *Current Biography*. Excited about the prospect of working with Beck, he added, "I do support people who will go do the weird idea. Sometimes I think a lot more people would do strange stuff if they felt as though there was an atmosphere that would encourage it." Drozd also felt that the offer presented many finet opportunities. "We thought it'd make a great story, great publicity," he told *Current Biography*, "and we'd get a chance to play to a lot of people we wouldn't [ordinarily] play to." Performing as Beck's backing band presented such challenges as learning almost the entire repertoire of another artist. "Musically, it was interesting, because we had to learn the songs, and then rebuild [them]," Drozd told *Current Biography*. "It was kind of tough, especially because we were trying to learn a good 25 songs in two weeks." The tour, which began in October 2002, has enjoyed a warm critical reception. Andrew Watson, writing for *Popmatters.com* (October 30, 2002), described the show as "high art minus the stale, pretentious air that typically worms its way into gigs like this. . . . The evening was an over-the-top success—a well conceived and tightly performed moment of hip-pop history in the making."

When he is not making music, Coyne keeps busy by working on a film, *Christmas on Mars*, which he is shooting in the backyard of his home in Classen Ten Penn, Oklahoma. The film, about a group of astronauts who celebrate the Christmas holidays with a Martian on a broken-down space station, stars Ivins, Drozd, and Steve Burns, the former host of the children's show *Blue's Clues*. Coyne, who plays the Martian in the film, has said that his love of the Christmas season inspired him to make the movie, which is slated to be released on video and DVD during the 2003 holiday season. "[Christmas] amounts to something," he told Jason Cohen for *New Music Monthly* (July 2002). "It's got great music, it's got a great idea behind it and it truly does work. . . . So I thought, I would love to have a movie that contributes to that. . . . At this point it really does seem doable, so let's hope we get a movie out of it." Coyne has downplayed the importance of the Flaming Lips' music in the larger scheme of life. "If there was nothing else ever invented, we would be fine," he told *Current Biography*. "Life is grand, no one needs to walk in and say '[Forget] all this, we need something else,' because I already think the world is a great, marvelous place. It would be arrogant for me to think, 'Oh it needs something else that I did to it.' I like the idea of doing things that are new to me." — J.K.B.

Suggested Reading: *Billboard* p11 Aug. 3, 2002, with photo; *GQ* p133+ Dec. 1999, with photos; *Los Angeles Times* p1+ June 23, 2002, with photos; *New Music Monthly* p33+ July 2002, with photos; *Rolling Stone* p26 Mar. 9, 1995, with photos; *Spin* p96+ Aug. 2002, with photos; *Washington Post* C p5 July 17, 2002

Selected Recordings: *The Flaming Lips*, 1985; *Hear It Is*, 1986; *Oh My Gawd!!! . . . The Flaming Lips*, 1987; *Telepathic Surgery*, 1989; *In a Priest Driven Ambulance*, 1990; *Hit to Death in the Future Head*, 1992; *Transmissions from the Satellite Heart*, 1993; *Clouds Taste Metallic*, 1995; *Zaireeka*, 1997; *A Collection of Songs Representing an Enthusiasm for Recording . . . By Amateurs*, 1998; *The Soft Bulletin*, 1999; *Yoshimi Battles the Pink Robots*, 2002

---

## Foer, Jonathan Safran

(fore)

*1977– Writer*

*Address: c/o Houghton Mifflin Co., Trade Division, Adult Editorial, 8th Fl., 222 Berkeley St., Boston, MA 02116-3764*

Even before Jonathan Safran Foer's first novel was published, the 25-year-old writer was designated a "genius" and a "wunderkind": his book, *Everything Is Illuminated* (2002), elicited almost universal advance praise and counted the novelists Joyce Carol Oates and Russell Banks, both former writing professors of Foer's, among its boosters. "*Everything Is Illuminated* pretends to be about a young man's search for the Ukranian woman who saved his grandfather from the Nazis but is really about pretty much everything else: love, history, memory, narrative, and death—and that's just for starters," Daniel Mendelsohn wrote for *New York* (April 22, 2002). By turns funny, bawdy, and puzzling, the book was inspired by Foer's real-life, unsuccessful search for the woman who rescued his grandfather during World War II. The author has credited his own book with giving his life direction. "I realized rather late in the game that writing presents itself as a kind of answer to that question, 'What should I be doing?'" he told Joyce Wadler for the *New York Times* (April 24, 2002). "What I realized is that the question is the final answer. That

Marion Ettlinger/Courtesy of Houghton Mifflin Co.
*Jonathan Safran Foer*

what I wanted to do with my life is figure out what I wanted to do with my life."

The second of three sons, Jonathan Safran Foer was born in 1977 in Washington, D.C. His mother, Esther Foer, is the executive vice president of the Hawthorn Group, an international public-relations firm; his father, Albert A. "Bert" Foer, an attorney, entrepreneur, and educator, currently heads the American Antitrust Institute, a think tank he founded in 1998. "My parents are creative in the way I most admire," Jonathan Safran Foer told Sarah Bernard for *New York* (April 15, 2002), "which has nothing to do with the outside world. It has everything to do with what they think is fun." His older brother, Franklin, is an associate editor at the *New Republic*; his younger brother, Joshua, writes for the on-line magazine *Slate*. Jonathan Safran Foer attended the private Georgetown Day School, where he was a good student but, by his own account, not especially creative. "I wasn't somebody who was writing or making things, and I wasn't even reading really," he explained to Peter Terzian for *Newsday* (May 30, 2002). "I was just sort of doing kid stuff . . . playing Atari and eating sugar cereals and watching a lot of TV." His Jewish upbringing was "a formality," he told Susan Josephs for the *Jewish Week* (December 20, 2001). "I had no interest in Hebrew school. They were like weekly doctor's appointments and everyone I knew felt the exact same way."

In the fall of 1995, Foer enrolled at Princeton University, in Princeton, New Jersey, where he majored in philosophy. During his freshman year he had a revelation in a sculpture class, after he was introduced to the work of the assemblage artist Joseph Cornell. Cornell, well known for his intricate dioramas, "is the most important person ever to enter my life," Foer told Peter Terzian. "His work just opened up a world to me, a world of having physical examples of things that you believe in." In an interview with Louis Jacobson for the *Princeton Alumni Weekly* (May 15, 2002, on-line), Foer elaborated on Cornell's impact on his life. "What captured my attention," he said, "was the way my attention was captured. I was in love with the way that I loved his art. I loved the way that it inspired me to go to the art library and look at all the images of his works, or to read his biography when it came out. It was something no one had done for me before." Combining his interest in Cornell's art with a newly uncovered passion for creative writing—nurtured by Joyce Carol Oates and others among his professors—he solicited fiction and poetry from other writers inspired by Cornell's work and collected the pieces in a single volume, *A Convergence of Birds*, which was printed in 2001 by Distributed Art Publishers. (The title refers to a frequent subject in Cornell's work.)

The summer after his sophomore year at Princeton, Foer took a brief trip to the Ukraine in pursuit of knowledge about his family's history. Although he had heard that his maternal grandfather, who had died when Foer was very young, had been saved from the Nazis by a woman in the town of Trachimbrod, discussion of the Holocaust was generally taboo in the family. Foer went to Trachimbrod in search of information and of anyone who might have known his grandfather. But he found that the town is "no longer extant," as he told Louis Jacobson. "It's just a field with a stone marker in the middle of it." He described his experience to Julia Llewellyn Smith for the London *Daily Telegraph* (May 31, 2002): "I went for three days and I did have this photograph of my grandfather—all we knew of him was that he had survived the destruction of this village in what used to be in Poland. But I was completely unprepared. I did no research, so I more or less jeopardised the trip before I had even started." Nonetheless, in an interview with Soledad O'Brien for NBC's *Saturday Today* (May 11, 2002), Foer described the trip as a turning point for him: "There was nothing in it in the sense that I didn't find the person I was looking for and I didn't find anything resembling what I thought I was looking for, which is to say, an explicit connection to somebody I had never met, my grandfather. But, what I did find was this great hole to replace."

From the Ukraine, Foer retreated to Prague, Czech Republic, where he spent 10 weeks furiously writing what would become *Everything Is Illuminated*. The novel's characters include a young American Jew named Jonathan Safran Foer who goes on a trip to find the woman who saved his grandfather. "But then the book quickly moves into fiction, and becomes very imaginative," Foer told Soledad O'Brien. "I tried to use other names [for the protagonist]," he explained to Susannah Meadows for *Newsweek* (June 17, 2002). "Even at the end I did one of those search-and-replaces, [but] it didn't feel genuine. This is how I am honest, by beginning with the life of my circumstances. You learn all these things you never could have known. My God, I was interested in Jewish things? I had no idea! Here's a piece of evidence of what I actually was. It's like looking at a picture of yourself and realizing you were pudgier than you thought." Among the novel's other characters are a Ukranian university student, Alex, who acts as a guide and translator for the Foer character, mangling one English idiom after another; Alex's melancholy and possibly blind grandfather, who is Foer's driver; and the grandfather's flatulent Seeing Eye dog, Sammy Davis Junior Junior.

The narrative of *Everything Is Illuminated* has three sections. One tells the story of Foer's visit to Trachimbrod; one comprises Alex's correspondence with him, after Foer's departure; and a third section—written in the magical-realist style—traces the fictional history of Trachimbrod, from the late 18th century through the beginnings of World War II. Foer did no research on the real town of Trachimbrod, as he told Peter Terzian: "I sort of went out of my way to be ignorant about a lot of stuff I was writing about just so I'd have more imaginative latitude."

Although Foer wrote his opus in a single summer, he spent more than two years editing and refining it. "It was excruciating," he admitted to Edward Guthmann for the *San Francisco Chronicle* (June 8, 2002). "It was like the greatest act of will I've ever committed in the sense that I didn't really want to do it." The editing of the book "changed it completely," he told Louis Jacobson—in spite of his having tried to remain true to the original spirit of the work. "What I was trying with the book was to create this sort of document of my 20-year-old self. Which is why, when I look back at it and I see things that are embarrassing, that I would change, I don't want to change them because then I would be making the book that I should make now," he explained to Guthmann.

After graduating from Princeton, in 1999, Foer held a variety of low-paying jobs, including tutoring, ghostwriting, and working as a receptionist at a public-relations firm. He spent his free time editing his book, writing other pieces, and cultivating relationships with a wide range of artists and writers. He also collected and framed blank sheets of paper from well-known writers, whom he had asked to give him the sheets they would have written on next. Foer explained the origins of his offbeat project to Joyce Wadler: "When [Isaac Bashevis] Singer's archivists entered what was his apartment, they found this incredibly old typewriter and next to it a stack of paper—paper with carbon between each sheet. . . . It had no obvious archival use, so my friend sent it to me. I loved this. I became obsessed with it. I found it moving in so many ways. . . . It hadn't been realized yet. Because it was an artifact of his life. Because it was waiting for him. It felt to me heavy with potential."

As for his novel, Foer did not have specific plans for it until a friend persuaded him to find an agent. After signing with Nicole Aragi, he found his manuscript the object of a bidding war; more than a dozen publishing houses competed for the rights to *Everything Is Illuminated.* Houghton Mifflin won out and proffered an advance reported to be between $400,000 and $500,000. (HarperCollins purchased the paperback rights for more than $900,000, and the actor Liev Schreiber bought the film rights and is working on a screen version.) "Surprised is not even the right kind of word," Foer told Clark Collis for the London *Observer* (June 2, 2002) about those developments. "I was a receptionist at a PR firm when I sold the book. I was just the guy who picked up the phone, making $11,000 a year. I always had this number of $20,000 floating in my head. I thought that if I made that then I could go away to Spain for a couple of months. . . . But then . . . it became a different story." In the midst of all the excitement over his book, Foer appeared to remain calm, staying at his receptionist job for another two months and opting not to move from his shared apartment in the New York City borough of Queens. "It's frustrating that a lot of people are so concerned with [the amount of the advance]," he said in an interview with *CNN.com* (June 17, 2002, on-line). "I'm extremely grateful . . . but other than that, it's no big deal." He did admit, however, to one new indulgence. "I have dessert all the time," he told Peter Terzian, "ice cream, cookies and brownies and all of that. I never bought it before because I filed it into 'luxury items that we're not going to do.' But now, I'll go to the big grocery store, and half of my cart will be ice cream."

The reviews of *Everything Is Illuminated*, which was published in April 2002, were mostly positive. (A brief portion of the book appeared in the *New Yorker* before its publication.) "Under it all there's a funny, moving, unsteady, deeply felt novel about the dangers of confronting the past and the redemption that comes with laughing at it, even when that seems all but impossible," Lev Grossman wrote for *Time* (April 29, 2002). "This is a brilliant but occasionally exasperating book . . . ," Janet Maslin wrote for the *New York Times* (April 22, 2002). "*Everything Is Illuminated* is a complex, ambitious undertaking, especially as its characters and events begin to run together in keeping with the author's ultimate plan. Mr. Foer works hard on these effects, and sometimes you will, too. But the payoff is extraordinary: a fearless, acrobatic, ultimately haunting effort to combine inspired mischief with a grasp of the unthinkable."

Foer went on a brief tour to promote the book, which led to another curatorial project: at each stop on the tour, he handed out index cards and envelopes, asking fans to create self-portraits and send them to him. "I couldn't help feeling that I—I owed them something," he explained to Soledad O'Brien. "And also I wanted the experience, this exchange of a book, to continue. Not to continue past the covers, to continue past this hour we get to spend with each other in a bookstore and to have a chance to communicate further. Which is what it's been. It's been more wonderful than I could have ever imagined." Foer lives in Queens. He recently completed a draft of his second novel, which is set partly in a museum and, like *Everything Is Illuminated*, features a character named Jonathan Safran Foer. — K.S.

Suggested Reading: *Book* p31+ Jan./Feb. 2002; *Entertainment Weekly* p108+ Apr. 26, 2002, with photo; (London) *Times* Features June 5, 2002; *New York* p34+ Apr. 15, 2002, with photo; *New York Times* B p2 Apr. 24, 2002, with photo; *Newsday* B p8 May 30, 2002, with photo

Selected Books: *Everything Is Illuminated*, 2002; as editor—*A Convergence of Birds*, 2001

---

Suzanne Plunkett/AP

## Forrest, Vernon

*Feb. 12, 1971– Boxer*

*Address: Destiny's Child Inc., 2221 Peachtree Rd. N.E., #D621, Atlanta, GA 30309-1148*

Vernon Forrest might be said to be three people. One is a religious man with a humanitarian spirit; another is an ambitious businessman; and then there is the professional boxer, nicknamed "The Viper," a champion with a formidable right hand and a 35–0 record. As an amateur, Forrest competed on the U.S. Olympic boxing team in 1992; as a pro, he has proven himself time and again to be a skilled and disciplined athlete. He won his first professional title in 1995, becoming the International Boxing Council (IBC) junior welterweight champion, before capturing the North American Boxing Federation (NABF) welterweight championship by defeating Adrian Stone in August 1998. In May 2001 he won a unanimous decision over Raul Frank to take the International Boxing Federation (IBF) welterweight belt, and in his highest-profile fight to date, the underdog Forrest beat "Sugar" Shane Mosley on January 26, 2002 to become the World Boxing Council (WBC) welterweight champ. Despite his impressive boxing skills, his titles, and the fact that he was unbeaten, Forest had fought in relative obscurity before his upset win over Mosley earned him the attention he had long been denied. In an article posted on the *Eastside Boxing* Web site the day after the fight, Cliff Clark wrote, "After a ten-year wait, the undefeated and unheralded Vernon Forrest has arrived. He showed the world what a great fighter is all about. He complimented Mosley profusely and promised him a rematch. This is how champions who are class acts conduct themselves." Retaining his WBC title, Forrest won a unanimous 12-round decision over Mosley in a rematch on July 20, 2002.

The sixth of eight children, Vernon Forrest was born on February 12, 1971 in Augusta, Georgia. Like many boys with brothers, he gained experience in fighting at an early age. He began his amateur boxing career when he was just nine years old and competed throughout his teenage years, compiling an impressive 225–16 record. Forrest won the U.S. junior welterweight national title in 1991 and the junior welterweight world amateur championship in the following year. (Boxers are divided by weight into different divisions. The upper limit for the welterweight class, in which Forrest currently fights, is 147 pounds.) Forrest received a scholarship to Northern Michigan University, in Marquette, where he studied business administration and trained under Al Mitchell, then the head coach of the U.S. National Boxing Team. He left school before graduating to pursue a spot on the U.S. Olympic Boxing Team, which would compete in the 1992 Olympic Games, in Barcelona, Spain. During the Olympic trials, Forrest fought Shane Mosley in the light-welterweight semifinals, prevailing on points, 24–15. In a November 4, 2000 interview with HBO that appeared on the *Talk City* Web site, Forrest said that making the Olympic team in 1992 and getting the chance to represent the United States was the greatest experience he had had up to that point in his boxing career. Forrest was considered the gold-medal favorite heading into the Olympic boxing tournament, but he lost his first-round fight, having suffered a bout of food poisoning the day before.

After the Olympics Forrest turned professional and moved from his hometown of Augusta to Atlanta, Georgia. He began his professional career by earning a technical knockout against Charles Hawkins, then proceeded to defeat four of his next five opponents by technical knockout before the end of the second round. Forrest averaged roughly three to five fights a year over the next eight years, except for the years 1994, 2000, and 2001, during each of which he fought only two bouts, and 1995, when he fought seven times. Although Forrest beat every challenger he faced, he was not the kind of offensively explosive or overwhelmingly powerful fighter who excited a lot of interest and demand; as a result, he did not get matches with the big names of his division, such as Felix Trinidad and Oscar de la Hoya, which would have resulted in much greater media attention, televised bouts, and larger paydays. Max Kellerman wrote of Forrest's plight in an article posted on the ESPN Web site (January 29, 2002): "Denied a crack at the best fighters and the accompanying paydays, fighters like Forrest and [Bernard] Hopkins are forced to fight the second-tier guys. They are simply not able to blow those second-tier guys away in the fashion that the spectacular offensive fighters do. . . . Here's the rub: The Vernon Forrests and Bernard Hopkinses are only able to show their complete selves when matched against other great fighters. Their greatness lies not in their ability to destroy overmatched opponents, but rather in their ability to outthink, outmaneuver, and outbox whoever is in front of them."

While Forrest was unknown to much of the general public for many years, boxing insiders definitely knew who he was. In an article dated January 29, 2002 that appeared on the *Max Boxing* Web site, Fiona Manning reported that Roger "Black Mamba" Mayweather—one of the most respected trainers in the sport and the uncle of "Pretty Boy" Floyd Mayweather, who is the top-ranked fighter in the junior-lightweight division—had called Forrest a consummate boxer and the most disciplined fighter with whom he had ever worked. Forrest is known to train hard for his fights and to study his opponents' styles exhaustively before bouts. At six feet, Forrest is blessed with a long arm reach of 73 inches, which means he can land punches from farther away than shorter opponents, a distinct advantage. He packs a strong right hand and is known as a smart fighter. In the interview with HBO, Forrest said, "Boxing is a science, there's an art to boxing, you don't just get in there and throw punches, there is a technique to it. If the media would take the time to educate the general public about the sport more, they would have a better understanding of what is going on when a fighter is fighting."

Forrest won his first title in 1995, becoming the IBC junior welterweight champion. Two years later he captured his second title, when he won a unanimous decision in a 12-round match against Ray Oliveira to become the WBC Continental Americas welterweight champion. Forrest relinquished his WBC title so that he could fight Adrian Stone for the North American Boxing Federation welterweight title. (Professional boxing has many different governing bodies; there are rules regarding fighting outside the governing body in which one holds a title.) Forrest defeated Stone by technical knockout in the 11th round to take the champion's belt. In an article for the *Herald News* that appeared on the *New Jersey* Web site, Stone himself, after having lost to Forrest, wrote, "Vernon Forrest . . . is an all-around good fighter. He's smart, he's got good movement, he's a good boxer. He's got that long jab that can keep you away from him and he's got that good right hand." In August 2000 Forrest took on Raul Frank for the IBF welterweight championship. In the third round of the fight, the two boxers bumped heads inadvertently. Frank's head began to bleed, and the referee stopped the fight, ruling it a no-contest. The much-anticipated rematch came in May 2001 at Madison Square Garden, in New York City. Forrest again displayed his savvy in the ring and won a unanimous 12-round decision over Frank, becoming the new IBF welterweight champion.

In addition to his longtime trainers Ronnie Shields, who is a former junior welterweight contender, and Al Mitchell, the former U.S. Olympic and National Team coach, the team around Forrest came to include his longtime friend Charles Watson, the renowned concert promoter Al Haymon, who helps guide Forrest's business decisions, and the respected boxing attorney Milt Chwasky. Forrest's victory over Frank for the IBF crown had given him world-champion status and a higher profile. In August 2001 he successfully defended his IBF title against Edgar Ruiz in a match that was the main event on the ESPN network's *Friday Night Fights* series. Forrest won in impressive fashion, knocking out Ruiz in the fourth round.

Forrest's January 26, 2002 fight at Madison Square Garden against Mosley was the most important of his career to date. He gave up his IBF title belt for the chance to fight Mosley for the WBC welterweight title. After his defeat at Forrest's hands in the 1992 Olympic trials, when they were both amateurs, Mosley had gone on to a brilliant professional career of 38 straight victories, including 35 knockouts. Known as "Sugar" Shane Mosley, he is considered one of the best "pound-for-pound" fighters in the world—"pound-for-pound" meaning that the boxer is judged according to his skills, technique, and power relative to others in his weight class. Despite being undefeated as a professional, just like Mosley, and despite having beaten the other man as an amateur, Forrest was a seven-to-one underdog going into the fight. In an article posted on the *Boxing Talk* Web site in the period leading up to the bout, Jeff Young wrote, "My problem is that Forrest has not shown me one thing that he does that indicates he can beat Mosley at the pro level. He is not that quick, and his resume does not set the world on fire. And let's remember that it took him 11 rounds to KO Adrian Stone. . . . Another problem I have is that he is putting too much emphasis on his win over Mosley in the amateurs." When Mosley and Forrest went before the media to discuss their upcoming fight, Forrest spoke of some of the stereotypes associated with boxing, telling Dan Rafael for *USA Today* (January 24,

2002, on-line), "It's a shame that you got to do crazy stuff and be unprofessional to get the attention. If I would have picked up a chair and busted [Mosley] across the head, we'd be on CNN. But just because I'm cordial with him and he's cordial with me, nobody wants to put it on Headline News. It's a shame it has to be like that. People see [Mike Tyson] and they think all boxers are barbarians. It's not like that."

Mosley won the first round of the fight. But in the second—during which the two boxers accidentally knocked heads—Forrest sent Mosley to the canvas twice, marking the first time Mosley had ever been knocked down in a professional fight. Forrest dominated most of the rest of the bout, knocking Mosley down again in the 10th round, before winning a unanimous decision—and the WBC welterweight title—after the 12th and final round. After the fight, Mosley told John Gregg for the *Boxing Times* (on-line), "[Forrest is] a terrific fighter, he's tall and rangy. I think early on in the [second] round the head butt got me. I think I got a little dizzy the first part, then he caught me with a right hand after the head butt." Forest told Dan Rafael for *USA Today* (January 27, 2002, on-line), "If [Mosley] is the best boxer in the world, the Michael Jordan of boxing, does that make me the Michael Jordan of boxing now? He was pound-for-pound the best, and I just beat the best. What does that make me?" Beating Mosley has landed Forrest on many people's "pound-for-pound" best-boxers lists. For the match Forrest earned a career-high $1.2 million, while Mosley took home $2.3 million. For his victory in the July 2002 rematch against Mosley, in Indianapolis, Indiana, Forrest earned $3 million, and his win–loss ratio rose to 35–0, with 26 knockouts. After that fight, Damon Hack wrote for the *New York Times* (July 21, 2002), "Forrest left [the arena] floating away on a cloud toward a future of big-money bouts against other members of the sport's elite."

Along with his girlfriend and her mother, Forrest, who is a religious man, established Destiny's Child Inc., which is dedicated to providing housing and assistance to mentally disabled adults in Atlanta, Georgia. Forrest is known to spend a good deal of time with the residents of the group home his organization runs. For a biography of the boxer posted on *SportsLine*, a CBS Web site, Forrest, speaking of those he helps, told the writer, "At first, you think they need you; but after a while, you realize you need them too."

Forrest has appeared in a number of independent films made in and around Atlanta. In addition to pursuing acting, he has plans to launch his own record label and manage music groups from Atlanta and Houston. Forrest continues to train in Houston. As is common with successful boxers, he aims to increase his weight so that he can move up to the higher weight divisions, with the goal of winning more titles.— C.F.T.

Suggested Reading: *Boxing Talk* (on-line); *Boxing Times* (on-line); *Eastside Boxing* (on-line); *Max Boxing* (on-line); *SportsLine* (on-line); *Talk City* (on-line); *USA Today* (on-line) Jan. 24, 2002, Jan. 27, 2002

---

## Franklin, Shirley C.

*May 10, 1945– Mayor of Atlanta (Democrat)*

*Address: Office of the Mayor, 55 Trinity Ave., Suite 2400, Atlanta, GA 30335*

Known for friendliness and for her love of her adopted city, Shirley Clarke Franklin was elected as the first female mayor of Atlanta, Georgia, on November 6, 2001. Although she had worked in and with the city's government for more than 20 years, Franklin had never sought an elective position herself. "I had an advantage in that I had never run for office," she explained to Patrik Jonsson for the *Christian Science Monitor* (January 6, 2002). "I didn't fall into that trap that some groups of people would vote for me, and some people wouldn't." Drawing from her experience under two different Atlanta mayors, as a community-government relations consultant and as part of the organizing committee for the 1996 Olympic Games, held in Atlanta, Franklin cast her net wide and appealed to a broad spectrum of voters; a Democrat, she won the post in a nonpartisan election. In less than a year on the job, she has helped to restore the public's confidence in the mayor's office while professing astonishment at her popularity. "I am still surprised to see that kids are doing reports on famous African-Americans and I am that person," she told Ernie Suggs for the *Atlanta Journal-Constitution* (April 17, 2002). "I am surprised that people come up to me and say they didn't want their taxes raised but knew I had no choice. I am surprised at how tough this job is. I am surprised that my stamina has stayed. I am surprised that I have been able to keep my sense of humor. And I have learned that [I] still have a lot to learn about this job and this city."

The daughter of Eugene Clarke, a judge, and Ruth White, a teacher, Shirley Clarke Franklin was born in Philadelphia, Pennsylvania, on May 10, 1945. "I was raised with a very strong sense of self," she told Angela Couloumbis for the *Philadelphia Inquirer* (March 28, 2002). "My mother always encouraged me to be exactly who I wanted to be—and no one else. And growing up, that was very encouraging, very nurturing for me." She grew up in a mostly black neighborhood in West Philadelphia and attended Dunlap Elementary School and Sayre Junior High School. She also par-

Erik S. Lesser/Getty Images

*Shirley C. Franklin*

ticipated in activities for young people organized by the National Association for the Advancement of Colored People (NAACP) and by Jack and Jill, a group founded to establish positive relationships among black children. "Clubs can be a way of identifying with people who are like you or that you aspire to be like," Franklin told Patricia Reid-Merritt for the book *Sister Power: How Phenomenal Black Women Are Rising to the Top* (1997). "I had access to a church [the Saint Thomas African Methodist Episcopal Church] that I felt had the right perspective that interested me." Her parents divorced when she was 10, and her relationship with her father was strained, due in part to his alcoholism. Still, her father "always encouraged me not to be bound by limitations," Franklin told Couloumbis. Growing up, Franklin was passionate about the arts. She studied ballet at the Cuyjet School of Dance and made the Philadelphia Museum of Art a regular stop on her route home from high school. An outstanding student, she was recruited to attend the minimally integrated Girls High, a public magnet school for gifted young women.

From Philadelphia, Franklin made her way to Howard University, a predominantly black school in Washington, D.C., where she earned good grades and became a student activist. Civil rights issues of concern both in the United States and abroad—particularly the system of racial apartheid in South Africa—had caught her attention in high school, and she pursued those causes as a student. "I wanted to see beyond the here and now of my life," she explained to Patricia Reid-Merritt. "I wanted to look at the world in a way that you could turn it upside down. I specifically wanted to be part of the group that overthrew the South African government." She told Angela Couloumbis, "Politics was in my blood." While still in college, she worked on political campaigns, including the victorious 1968 congressional campaign of Shirley Chisholm, who became the first African-American woman to serve as a member of the House of Representatives. As an undergraduate, Franklin also worked from 1966 to 1968 at the Department of Labor as a contract compliance officer. She graduated from Howard University in 1968 with a degree in sociology, to which she added a double minor in African studies and psychology. She earned a master's degree in sociology in 1969 from the University of Pennsylvania, whose graduate program she found "fairly racist in its orientation," as she told Reid-Merritt, explaining her belief that too many courses were taught solely from a white, male perspective.

In 1969 Franklin moved to the southern United States, having concluded that "there was so much going on there politically," as she recalled to Angela Couloumbis. She became a lecturer in political science and sociology at Talledega College, a predominantly black institution in Talledega, Alabama, teaching there until 1971. She then moved to Atlanta, where she married David Franklin, a lawyer, in 1972. Edging back into politics, she worked as a volunteer on the congressional campaigns of Andrew Young, who was elected in 1972 and reelected in 1974 and 1976. She also volunteered as a campaign worker for Maynard Jackson, who was elected mayor of Atlanta in 1973 and reelected in 1977. In 1978 Franklin, by then the mother of two daughters and a son, took her first job with the city of Atlanta, becoming a member of the Department of Cultural Affairs under Mayor Jackson. In time she was promoted to commissioner of cultural affairs, an assignment that combined her love of the arts with her deepening skill at public administration. "In public life you have to have a thick skin," she told Marilyn Milloy in an interview for *Essence* (June 1988). "It also takes intellectual aggressiveness. You have to be able to think new things and see old things in new ways."

When Andrew Young took office as mayor of Atlanta in 1982, he appointed Franklin as his chief administrative officer. In that job she oversaw the day-to-day running of the city; by her account, she faced both overt and subtle sexism in attending to her tasks. "More than resentment," she explained to Marilyn Milloy, "there was an assumption, particularly in the beginning, that there must be some man telling me what to do." She elaborated to Patricia Reid-Merritt: "I remember a prominent black businessman invited me to a meeting with some other black businesspeople. When he introduced me, he said, 'I've invited Shirley because [Mayor Young] appointed her to this important position. I don't know why she is not staying home with her children.' He thought that was a warm introduction." Franklin pressed on, however, working under Young for both of his terms in office, and managing a budget of close to $300 million and more than 7,000 city workers. Ineligible to run for mayor again in 1990, Young pursued the Democratic nomination for the Georgia governorship; Franklin worked for his campaign, which was ultimately unsuccessful. (Young lost the nomination, in a runoff, to Zell Miller, who was elected governor in 1990 and U.S. senator from Georgia in 1998.) From 1990 to 1991 Franklin served as Atlanta's executive officer for operations.

In 1991, after Atlanta had been selected to host the 1996 Summer Olympic Games, Franklin joined the Atlanta Committee for the Olympic Games (ACOG), working in community relations and local government operations. She left ACOG in 1993, when she was appointed president of the nonprofit Corporation for Olympic Development in Atlanta (CODA). CODA relied on Franklin to develop locations for Olympic venues, a job that required her to smooth the way for improvements in poor or underserved neighborhoods. After only a few months at CODA, Franklin returned to ACOG for the prestigious position of senior policy adviser on government relations. She helped establish policies for ACOG and insured its commitment to diversity; thanks both to her efforts and the contacts she had made as a government employee with business leaders and minority and women's organizations, about one-third of construction and improvement contracts for Atlanta handled by ACOG were awarded to minority-run firms. "The whole idea of the Games is to bring people together in peaceful competition, and we did that in our contract services as well as on the playing fields," former mayor Young told Kevin Sack for the *New York Times* (June 10, 1996).

After the 1996 Olympic Games, Franklin turned to consulting. She was affiliated with Amanda Brown-Olmstead and Associates before establishing Shirley Franklin & Associates in 1997 and focusing on community relations for businesses. In 1998 she became a majority partner of Urban Environmental Solutions, LLC, which was involved in creating urban planning solutions to problems involving water treatment and other issues. After the election of Roy Barnes as governor, in 1998, Franklin was selected to serve on his three-person transition team; Barnes then appointed her to the Georgia Regional Transportation Authority, where her peers elected her to the post of vice chair.

In May 2000 Franklin announced her candidacy for mayor of Atlanta, which was to hold nonpartisan elections in November 2001. Two years earlier she had told Maria Saporta for the *Atlanta Journal-Constitution* (August 7, 1998), "I never thought about running for mayor until I was approached by a number of people from all walks of life." She added, "It is a decision for me and my life. I'm a very private person. Obviously, I love this city, and I am drawn to public life. I have lots of opportunities open to me." In 2000, however, she felt that the time had come for a new administration—and for a woman to lead the city. "Yes, I wanted to show that a woman could do it," she admitted to Angela Couloumbis. "But [I] also strongly felt that the city needed new leadership." (Mayor Bill Campbell, who had led the city since 1994, had an embattled second term, which included calls for ethics investigations by the City Council.) After spending over two decades in public service, she was able to raise more money than any of her opponents, and she campaigned hard to unite many segments of Atlanta's increasingly diverse population, which had grown to encompass large pockets of Hispanic voters, gay voters, and others. "I knew I would appeal to the majority of people who are not anxious at all to return to the time when people didn't get along," she told Patrik Jonsson. "I don't think there's a move away from race, but a move toward inclusiveness." Franklin shared the spotlight with two other candidates, City Council president Rob Pitts and the economist and former city councilwoman Gloria Bromell-Tinubu. "I'm the only candidate running who has actually run city government, who actually knows how to lead in the public sector," Franklin told Rob Gurwitt for *Governing* (December 2001). "If you owned a $1 billion corporation with 7,000 employees, you would look for someone who had management and leadership experience." Many agreed with Franklin's assessment of her capabilities; she received endorsements from many powerful Atlanta groups, such as the Atlanta Labor Council, which represents 72 labor unions, as well as former mayors Jackson and Young and Georgia congressman John Lewis. Commanding 50.24 percent of the ballots on Election Day, November 6, 2001, Franklin barely escaped a runoff, which would have been required if none of the candidates had won at least 50 percent of the vote. Pitts placed second, with 33 percent; his camp proposed a recount, but Pitts himself eventually allowed Franklin's 200-vote margin of victory to stand. Franklin took office on January 7, 2002, at an event that she called the "People's Inauguration," which included performances by the rap acts Ludacris and Outkast, the violinist Tom Ford, and the rhythm-and-blues group 920.

As mayor, Franklin faced immediate challenges. Atlanta had a $90 million budget shortfall; the city's streets and sewers were in disrepair; and an unwieldy staff remained from Mayor Campbell's administration. Franklin promised to address all of the city's problems, explaining to Ernie Suggs for the *Atlanta Journal-Constitution* (January 13, 2002), "I am very laid back. . . . But I am going to get what needs to be done, done." Less than two weeks into her term, she personally filled a pothole on an Atlanta street, in a gesture that symbolized her administration's commitment to fixing the thousands that existed. By mid-April 2002 she had balanced the budget, trimmed more than 60 employees from the city payroll, approved the expansion of Atlanta's Hartsfield Airport, and persuaded the City Council to approve the new post of ethics officer. She also set about fulfilling her campaign promise to have an outside firm evaluate the effectiveness and efficiency of various city operations, including the contract-awarding process; money from 19 corporate donors rather than the public coffers paid for that review. "For some reason, people were skeptical," she told Suggs for the *Atlanta Journal-Constitution* (April 17, 2002). "When I talked about [the review audits] during the campaign, people glazed over and said, 'There she goes again. Her answer for everything is, "I'm going to study it."' They doubted that I could do the review audits. Not only are we doing it, but we raised $2 million from the private sector to do it." Many Atlantans had fallen under the spell of Franklin's personal appeal, during her "sleepovers" on the campaign trail—intimate weeknight gatherings for around 30 people at private homes—and during the Mayor's Night In, when she opened her office to individual citizens (71 the first time) for private meetings of five to 10 minutes. "I came in promising to stay accessible to the public, to build new partnerships and new relationships," she explained to Suggs for a February 7, 2002 *Atlanta Journal-Constitution* article. "If I had not been able to develop coalitions, I would not have won that election. That's what I do in my life. I reach out to people," she told D. L. Bennett for the *Atlanta Journal-Constitution* (January 6, 2002). "You just have to work hard and be honest. Folks will understand. They may not always agree with you, but they will understand."

Franklin and her husband, the parents of three grown children, divorced in 1986. Franklin is currently single and resides in southwest Atlanta with her three dogs. She enjoys music and movies and has a particular fondness for gardening, raising both vegetables and flowers in her spare time. —K.S.

Suggested Reading: *Atlanta Journal-Constitution* C p3 Aug. 7, 1998, with photo, A p1 Jan. 6, 2002, with photo; *Christian Science Monitor* p3 Jan. 16, 2002; *Essence* p26 June 1988, with photo; *Philadelphia Inquirer* (on-line) Mar. 28, 2002

---

Manny Ceneta/Getty Images

## Franks, Tommy R.

*June 17, 1945– Commander in chief, United States Central Command*

*Address: Headquarters United States Central Command, Public Affairs Office, MacDill AFB, Florida 33621*

As commander in chief of United States Central Command, General Tommy R. Franks is responsible for directing the day-to-day combat operations of the American-led antiterrorism campaign in Afghanistan, which began after the September 11, 2001 attacks on the U.S. Together with President George W. Bush, Defense Secretary Donald Rumsfeld, and the chairman of the Joint Chiefs of Staff, General Richard Myers, Franks is one of the four military and government officials charged with leading the military portion of the campaign.

U.S. Central Command, or "Centcom," as it is known in military parlance, is one of nine U.S. combatant commands (some located overseas) that answer directly to the defense secretary and the president. Centcom's territory encompasses 25 countries in Africa, Central Asia, and the Middle East, including Iran, Iraq, Pakistan, the Gulf states, the former Soviet Central Asian republics, and Afghanistan. (During the Persian Gulf War of 1991, Centcom was commanded by General H. Norman Schwarzkopf.) In ordinary times, the commander of Centcom oversees between 18,000 and 25,000 personnel.

On October 25, 2000, in his testimony before the Senate Armed Services Committee (quoted on *usinfo.state.gov*), Franks stated that Centcom's mission is "to promote and protect U.S. interests and almost 200,000 American citizens in the region; to deter aggression and stand ready to respond to attacks on our forces, our allies, our interests, and generally to conduct military operations; to ensure uninterrupted access to regional resources and markets; to assist regional friends in providing for their own security and regional stability; to promote the attainment of a just and lasting Middle East Peace; to counter the proliferation of weapons of mass destruction and other transnational threats; and to rapidly deploy joint and combined forces to support the full range of military operations." Centcom headquarters is located at MacDill Air Force Base, in Tampa, Florida. Franks, a Texan, has served in Vietnam, West Germany, Korea, Iraq (during the Persian Gulf War), and the

Pentagon during his more than 34 years in the military.

Tommy Ray Franks was born in Wynnewood, Oklahoma, on June 17, 1945. Shortly thereafter, his family relocated to Midland, Texas. A lanky young man who played on his high-school football team, Franks, it appears, escaped the notice of many of his teachers and classmates. "Franks wasn't an individual who could be accused of hitting his peak in high school," a reporter for the *Midland Reporter-Telegram* concluded after searching unsuccessfully for someone who could remember the future general, as cited by Jim Henderson for the *Houston Chronicle* (October 31, 2001). Henderson, who was more successful in similar investigative efforts, uncovered two former classmates who independently characterized Franks as "a real nice guy."

Upon graduating from Midland's Lee High School, in 1963, Franks enrolled at the University of Texas at Austin. In 1965, during his sophomore year, he dropped out of school to enlist in the army. Two years later he entered active military duty as a second lieutenant, after having graduated from the Artillery Officer Candidate School in Fort Sill, Oklahoma. Following a brief tour of duty at Fort Sill, Franks was assigned to a division operating in Vietnam, where he served as a forward observer and a fire-support officer. He was wounded three times. In 1968 Franks returned to Fort Sill, and after commanding a cannon battery for one year, he was chosen to take part in the army's "Boot Strap Degree Completion Program." That program allowed Franks to attend the University of Texas, Arlington, where he earned a bachelor's degree in business administration in 1971.

In the 1970s and early 1980s, Franks served additional tours of duty in West Germany and at the Pentagon. In 1984 he enrolled concurrently at the Army War College, in Carlisle, Pennsylvania, and at Shippensburg University, in Shippensburg, Pennsylvania. Franks received a master's degree in public administration from the latter institution in 1985. Meanwhile, he continued to rise through the military ranks: during Operation Desert Storm, in the 1991 Gulf War—the U.S. response to Iraq's invasion of Kuwait—Franks served as assistant division commander of the First Cavalry Division. In the mid-1990s he commanded an infantry division stationed in Korea.

Franks was promoted to four-star general and selected to lead Centcom in June 2000 by then–president Bill Clinton. The suicide attack on the destroyer USS *Cole* in the Yemeni port of Aden on October 12 of that year, in which 17 American crew members were killed, prompted Franks to designate terrorism as one of the most significant threats in the region. Indeed, comments he made before the House Armed Services Committee in April 2001, as cited by Jim Garamore for the *American Forces Press Services* (April 13, 2001), were prescient of the September 11, 2001 attacks on New York and Washington, D.C. "In addition to the use of unconventional weapons," Franks stated, "the potential for terrorists to regard unconventional targets (civilians and civilian infrastructure) as practical options for attack seems likely. As terrorist networks improve their ability to operate within the global communications environment, we see increased capability to support recruitment, conduct fund-raising, and direct sub-elements worldwide. The complex terrorist threat we face today is less predictable and potentially much more dangerous than we have seen in the past."

As commander in chief of Centcom, Franks, in contrast to his predecessor H. Norman Schwarzkopf, has appeared reluctant to engage the media. While Schwarzkopf appeared on camera almost daily during the Gulf War, Franks had held only a handful of news conferences in the month and a half following October 7, when the United States launched its military campaign (called Operation Enduring Freedom) against Taliban and Al Qaeda terrorist forces in Afghanistan. Moreover, on those occasions when he did appear, his statements—as a number of journalists complained—were often thick with military jargon, and were sometimes so vague as to be virtually meaningless. During an October 24 press conference in Bahrain, for example, Franks told journalists, as cited by Bob Franken for *cnn.com* (October 24, 2001), "The operations that we undertake go on 24 hours a day. They go on from the air, they go on day, they go on night and as you have seen I think in some of the media we have had elements on the ground in Afghanistan. The efforts that we're about with regard to what we're after for this objective are going very, very well, and I'll leave it at that at this point." When asked about the infrequency of his press conferences, Franks responded that the day-to-day planning of military operations left him little time to address the media. "The secretary and our president have asked me to do a job," Franks stated, as cited by Eric Schmitt for the *New York Times* (November 9, 2001). "What I have found up to this point is not a shyness for media; it very simply is an insufficient amount of time to be able to do, sir, what you have suggested."

Early in the campaign, Franks encountered criticism from those who wanted a more rapid deployment of ground forces in Afghanistan. The general defended himself against such charges by countering that his critics were impatient. "It is only those who believe that all of this should be done in two weeks' time or in one month or perhaps two months who are disappointed," he said at a November 9 press conference, according to Duncan Campbell in the London *Guardian* (November 17, 2001). But after the rapid collapse of Taliban power in the second week of November, most of those who had pressed for more ground troops conceded the effectiveness of the strategy devised by the president, the Defense Department, and the U.S. military. Operation Enduring Freedom had succeeded in routing the Taliban and destroying the safe havens and terrorist training camps of Osama bin Laden and his followers inside Afghanistan. In

March 2002, as the American military operation in Afghanistan wound down, Frank Pellegrini wrote for *Time* (March 8, 2002), "For being the commander—the man quietly placing and arranging American combat boots on the ground in Afghanistan with a mission to herd, trap and finish off thousands of hardened Al-Qaeda fighters—Army Gen. Tommy Franks is *Time.com's* Person of the Week. . . . Franks has been exactly what this war effort has required: Insistently realistic, never gloating, understated about victory and reassuringly honest about its inevitable costs. Throw in a touch of folksiness, some of the aw-shucks collar-tugging of an old artillery man blinking in the spotlight's white glare, and you have a fine war hero indeed."

Franks is reported to enjoy the personal support of President George W. Bush, who, according to Janie Dettmer in *Insight on the News* (December 24, 2001), often consults the general by telephone and has sided with him in behind-the-scenes disputes. Dettmer further reported that Franks has expressed to the president his views on two debates within the administration: first, he opposes extensive "nation building" in Afghanistan after the military action ends there (although he does support military protection of humanitarian aid efforts); and second, he feels the United States should not take military action against Iraq while still fighting in Afghanistan. (According to Dettmer, "There is no split within the administration about going after Saddam, only whether it should involve air strikes and covert action or a full-scale ground operation against Baghdad.")

Franks's military distinctions include the Defense Distinguished Service Medal; the Distinguished Service Medal; the Legion of Merit with three oak-leaf clusters; the Bronze Star Medal with four oak-leaf clusters and V device (the latter of which recognizes acts of heroism during fighting with an armed enemy); the Purple Heart with two oak-leaf clusters; an Air Medal; an Army Commendation Medal with V device; and a number of U.S. and foreign service awards. (Once, when asked about the medals and ribbons adorning his uniform, Franks reportedly replied, as quoted by Henderson, "That is a very embarrassing question. If you stay in the armed forces long enough, you will gain a lot of medals.")

Franks has been married to the former Cathryn Carley since 1969. The couple have one daughter, Jacqueline Franks Matlock. According to Duncan Campbell, Franks's grandchildren know him as General Pooh.— P.K.

Suggested Reading: *Esquire* p114+ Aug. 2002, with photo; *Houston Chronicle* p17 Oct 31, 2001, with photo; (London) *Guardian* p7 Nov 17, 2001, with photo; (London) *Guardian* (on-line) Nov 9, 2001; *Los Angeles Times* A p4 Nov 9, 2001; *New York Times* B p3 Nov 9, 2001, with photo; *People* p81+ Oct. 29, 2001, with photo; *Time* p35 Mar. 4, 2002, with photo

Philip Bermingham Photography/Courtesy of Bill Frist's office

## Frist, Bill

*Feb. 22, 1952– U.S. senator from Tennessee (Republican)*

*Address: United States Senate, 416 Russell Senate Office Bldg., Washington, DC 20510-4205*

Bill Frist of Tennessee, a heart- and lung-transplant surgeon, is currently the only physician in the United States Senate and is the first physician since 1928 to serve as a senator. A proponent of the idea of the citizen legislator, which holds that men and women with established careers outside politics can make valuable contributions as public servants, Frist won election to the Senate in 1994 and is now serving his second term, which will end in 2006. "The motivation for politics is very similar to medicine," Frist said in an interview posted on the *Physician's Practice Digest* Web site (September 1996). "As a physician, your goal is the health of the individual patient. As a United States Senator, it's the health of the nation." One difference between the two fields, as Frist explained to Renee Blankenau for *Hospitals & Health Network* (January 20, 1995), is that through politics he has a means of "contributing broadly to millions of people instead of [through] the one on one" relationships to which the practice of medicine is normally limited. He has been an important contributor to the government's ongoing debate regarding the future of Medicare and the health-care industry in the U.S. Frist, who founded the Vanderbilt University Transplant Center, in Nashville, Tennessee, in 1986, has performed more than 200 organ transplants; written three books—among them *Transplant: A Heart Surgeon's Account of the Life-*

*and-Death Dramas of the New Medicine* (1989) and *Tennessee Senators 1911–2001* (1999)—and edited a fourth; and authored or co-authored more than 100 scientific papers.

The youngest of the five children of Thomas Frist Sr., a physician, and Dorothy Frist, the senator was born William H. Frist in Nashville on February 22, 1952. He is a fourth-generation Tennessean; one of his great-great-grandfathers was among the 53 settlers of Chattanooga, Tennessee. Frist's father founded the Hospital Corp. of America (HCA), which merged with Columbia Hospital Corp. in 1994 to become the Columbia/HCA Healthcare Corp., the nation's largest chain of for-profit hospitals. A cardiologist and an internist, Thomas Frist Sr. practiced medicine for more than 50 years in the Nashville area and attended to the health of seven Tennessee governors before his death, in 1998. Frist's brother, Thomas Frist Jr., also a doctor, has served as chairman of the board of Columbia/HCA.

At Princeton University, in Princeton, New Jersey, Frist attended the Woodrow Wilson School of Public Policy and International Affairs, where he specialized in health-care policy. He was honored by the school as a Wilson Scholar and received the Harold Willis Dodds Award for outstanding leadership, along with his bachelor's degree, in 1974. While in college he spent a summer working for the Democratic congressman Joe Evans of Tennessee in Washington, D.C. Evans advised Frist to pursue what he really loved, and achieve success in it for 20 years, before looking to serve in public office. In 1978 Frist earned an M.D. degree, with honors, from Harvard University, in Cambridge, Massachusetts. He spent the next seven years as a surgical trainee at Massachusetts General Hospital, in Boston; Southampton General Hospital, in England; and the Stanford University Medical Center, in Stanford, California. He achieved board certification in the fields of general surgery and heart surgery. In 1985 Frist became a faculty member of the Vanderbilt University Medical Center, in Nashville. The following year he founded the highly regarded Vanderbilt University Multi-Organ Transplant Center and served as the director of the center's Heart and Lung Transplantation Program. From 1985 to 1994, when he went on leave following his election to the Senate, he was an assistant professor of cardiac and thoracic surgery at the Vanderbilt University School of Medicine, and he was a surgeon on the staff of the Nashville Veterans Administration Hospital from 1986 to 1993. Frist has performed more than 200 heart- and lung-transplant procedures, including the first combined heart-lung transplant ever attempted in the South. Jan Muirhead, a heart-transplant nurse coordinator who has worked with Frist at Vanderbilt University Hospital, told Renee Blankenau, "[Frist] has a knack for getting people involved and making the work interesting to everyone on the team."

Frist entered public service relatively late in life—when he was 40. According to Blankenau, the senator has admitted that he did not even register to vote until he was 34 years old. "I didn't realize until about [1992] how significant the impact of an individual could be by participating in the political process," he told Blankenau. "That involvement can stem from participating in a campaign, whether it's local, regional, national, or could include contributing money, putting on home events; there's a whole range." He said in the same interview, "My message is that individuals can make a difference." In 1992 the governor of Tennessee, Ned McWherter, appointed Frist the head of a task force on Medicaid reform. Frist backed the state administration's Medicaid-reform proposal, called TennCare, and led a statewide campaign to link organ-donation cards with Tennessee residents' driver's licenses.

On November 8, 1994, as part of the Republican sweep of the congressional elections that year, Frist defeated the three-term Democratic senator from Tennessee, Jim Sasser, by a 14-point margin (and with 56 percent of the vote) to win a seat in the U.S. Senate. Frist was the only challenger in that year's national elections to defeat a full-term incumbent senator. In his first year in the Senate, Frist introduced health-related legislation, including bills to establish medical savings accounts for citizens, protect patient confidentiality, and reform the Food and Drug Administration. In 1996 then–Senate Majority Leader Bob Dole named Frist chairman of the Senate Republican Medicare Working Group. In addition, Frist served on the National Bipartisan Commission on the Future of Medicare from 1998 to 1999. (According to the U.S. government's official Medicare Web site, Medicare, which covers more than 40 million Americans, most of whom are 65 years of age or older, is the country's largest health-insurance program. Most citizens receive hospital insurance through the program when they turn 65; the costs of the care are covered by Medicare taxes, which the federal government imposes on every working citizen. Medicare recipients must pay a monthly premium for the program's additional benefits, which involve medical insurance for health care that occurs outside hospitals.) At the start of his second year in the Senate, Frist introduced the Citizen Congress Act, a bill calling for the elimination of perquisites and privileges for members of Congress as a way of restoring the public's faith in elected leaders.

Frist has been a member of the Commerce, Science, and Transportation Committee and its subcommittees on Aviation, Communications, Manufacturing and Competitiveness, Surface Transportation and Merchant Marine, and Science, Technology, and Space, the last of which he has served as chairman. He has also sat on the Foreign Relations Committee and its subcommittees on International Operations and Terrorism, International Economic Policy, Export, and Trade Promotion, and African Affairs, of which he has been chairman; the Health, Education, Labor, and Pensions Committee and its subcommittees on Children and Families and Public Health and Safety, the latter of which he has chaired; the Budget Committee; the Labor and Human Resources Committee; and the Small Business Committee. He is the founder and co-chairman of the Senate Science and Technology Caucus.

After a Scottish research team announced in February 1997 that it had successfully cloned a sheep, named Dolly, thus bringing into the international spotlight questions regarding the very real prospect of human cloning, Senator Frist, as chairman of the Subcommittee on Public Health and Safety, held a well-attended forum to air his views on the weighty matter. (Other members of Congress did the same.) While he voted in early 1998 in favor of a law banning human cloning, Frist stressed the importance of understanding the potential benefits of cloning and recalled that before the idea of heart transplants became accepted and practiced, many people were alarmed by the thought of such procedures, just as many in contemporary times are alarmed by the idea of cloning.

In 1999 Senator Frist, along with Democratic senator John Breaux of Louisiana, introduced to the Senate the Medicare Preservation and Improvement Act of 1999 (often referred to as Breaux-Frist I). Under the bill, prescription-drug coverage would be subsidized by Medicare on a sliding scale based on each patient's income. (One of the most criticized aspects of Medicare, which in the mid- to late 1990s became the focus of heated debate in the media and the public arena, is that under the current plan prescription-drug costs—which can be very high—are not adequately covered.) In *Modern Healthcare* (March 5, 2001), Jonathan Gardner described the Medicare Preservation and Improvement Act of 1999 as a bill that "aims to change Medicare from a giant bill-payer to a system that pays most, but not all, of seniors' premiums for joining private-sector health plans." Those private-sector health plans could compete for senior clients; ideally, this competition would result in high-quality and affordable medicine for seniors. Frist and Breaux introduced a revised version of their 1999 bill the following year. The new proposal—alternately referred to as Breaux-Frist II, Breaux-Frist 2000, or the Medicare Prescription Drug and Modernization Act—would establish an independent Medicare agency to oversee all competing health-care plans; it would also ensure that health plans offer, at the very least, the current core benefits provided by Medicare, along with new prescription-drug coverage. In drafting the bill, Frist and Breaux envisioned a health-care system modeled on the Federal Employees' Health Benefit Plan, through which the government's Office of Personnel Management provides the members of Congress and millions of other federal employees a choice of a range of health-care plans. To date none of these bills has been passed into law.

Also in the late 1990s, Frist, as a member of the Budget Committee, played a part in creating the first balanced-budget plan passed by Congress in nearly 30 years. He was named deputy Republican whip of the Senate in 1999. The following year Frist was named Senate liaison to then-presidential candidate George W. Bush, and after Bush's election victory, Frist was named an adviser to the Transition Team of the President-Elect. Frist himself won a second six-year term in the Senate in 2000, beating Democratic Tennessean Jeff Clark, a professor, by the largest margin ever in a statewide election in the history of Tennessee. In 2001 Frist became the chairman of the National Republican Senatorial Committee, which raises money and works to ensure the election of Republican senators. In the same year he was named one of two congressional representatives to the United Nations General Assembly.

Before he won the presidential election, Bush asked Frist to work with him in drafting a patients' bill of rights. After years of discussion, in Congress and in the media, most lawmakers have agreed that there is a pressing need for a patients' bill of rights, but there is serious disagreement as to what such a bill should stipulate. As the only physician in the U.S. Senate, and one with knowledge of both the business and the practice of medicine, Frist is at the center of the most contentious area of debate regarding a patients' bill of rights—namely, the question of a patient's right to sue an employer or a health maintenance organization (HMO) and the liability of HMOs. "Health care is so complicated, in terms of the realities of what's going on. If you make it simplistic politically, the ramifications are not to the benefit of patients," Frist was quoted as saying by Mary Agnes Carey in *Congressional Quarterly* (March 24, 2001). "Part of my role here very much . . . is explaining the realities." Along with Senator Jim Jeffords of Vermont (who is now an Independent), Frist and Breaux introduced to Congress the Bipartisan Patients' Bill of Rights Act of 2001. (It is sometimes referred to as the Frist-Breaux-Jeffords Bill). "This legislation will help Americans get the care they need and deserve, without unnecessarily driving up consumers' health care costs, threatening employers with expensive and unnecessary lawsuits, or adding significant bureaucratic red-tape to the private health care system," Frist stated, as quoted in a summary of the bill on the U.S. Senate Web site. The legislation, which is supported by President Bush, would allow injured patients to sue HMOs in federal courts only and to collect damage awards for lost earnings, medical expenses, and related costs. Compensation for nonmonetary damages, such as pain and suffering, however, would be capped at $500,000, and punitive damages, which are usually largest, would be prohibited. Frist and those in favor of his proposal argued that a cap on damages and restrictions on a patient's right to bring lawsuits are necessary, because without those safeguards health plans would be open to frivolous lawsuits and massive legal costs, which in turn would force them to raise the monthly premiums. Many employers and individuals would then drop their coverage, advocates of the Frist legislation say, leaving millions of Americans without health insurance. In an interview with *Time.com* (June 20, 2001), Frist asserted that he wanted a "strong, enforceable Patients' Bill of Rights that will put doctors and patients back in charge of medical decisions and gets patients the care they need when they need it."

The Frist-Breaux-Jeffords patients' rights bill has been attacked for various reasons by senators in both parties as well as health-insurance companies and the American Medical Association (AMA). "The feeling is that [Frist] is not backing things that are important for patients and physicians," Thomas R. Reardon, a former president of the AMA, told Mary Agnes Carey. "As a physician, you have a marvelous opportunity to speak up for patients. . . . We hope he does that rather than furthering his own political situation." Other skeptics have argued that because he is tied so closely to his family's company, Columbia/HCA Healthcare Corp.—owning, according to Robert Dryfuss for *Mother Jones* (May/June 1997), more than $13 million of personal stock in the hospital chain—Frist is failing to represent the interests of patients, or, worse, is representing his own interests. "HCA isn't an HMO, the groups that are most directly affected by the bills now being debated in Congress," Howard Fineman, *Newsweek's* chief political correspondent, wrote for the MSNBC Web site. "But [Frist's] family's business is all too aware of what the courts can do for, or to, companies in the health care field." Some have derisively referred to Frist as "Senator HMO," because they see his proposal as protecting the rights of HMOs rather than patients. Many Democrats in Congress support an alternative patients' rights bill introduced by Democratic senators John Edwards of North Carolina and Edward M. Kennedy of Massachusetts. (Their proposed legislation, which has also been sponsored by Republican senators John McCain of Arizona and Greg Ganske of Iowa, is sometimes referred to as the Kennedy-Edwards Bill or the McCain-Kennedy-Ganske legislation.) Compared with the Frist-Breaux-Jeffords Bill, their version would give individuals a much broader right to sue HMOs, insurance companies, group health plans, and anyone who served as an agent of a health plan, with no limit on damages for pain and suffering. Advocates of this legislation say that the threat of large damage awards alone would cause health-insurance companies to treat patients with greater care.

With Senator Kennedy, Frist co-sponsored a bill authorizing grant programs for research in children's health, and he sponsored legislation to create a Center for Research on Minority Health at the National Institutes of Health. Senator Frist has also introduced or supported bills for investment in medical research and development, math and science education, and tax credits for private-sector research. In addition, he co-sponsored a bill to give state and local authorities more control over $11 billion of federal education money. He told Blankenau, "The federal government is not the best use of public resources, meaning tax dollars, because it is unable to identify the peculiar needs of individual communities. So that responsibility will fall to the local communities and require more rather than less community leadership."

Frist has been involved in several dramatic occurrences in Washington, D.C., over the years. In 1995 he sprinted to the side of the Reverend Graeme Sieber, who had suffered a heart attack on the fifth floor of the Dirksen Senate Office Building. Frist performed cardiopulmonary resuscitation (CPR) on Sieber, then restored the normal rhythm of Sieber's heart using medical equipment from the nearby Capitol physician's office. Sieber survived. According to *Congressional Quarterly*, Frist also helped to save the lives of several tourists and the life of Russell E. Weston Jr., who is accused of killing two Capitol guards before being shot himself, in 1998. (That case is still pending.)

Senator Frist is the author of three books: *Transplant: A Heart Surgeon's Account of the Life-and-Death Dramas of the New Medicine* (1989); *Tennessee Senators 1911–2001: Portraits of Leadership in a Century of Change* (1999), written with J. Lee Annis Jr.; and *When Every Moment Counts: What You Need to Know about Bioterrorism from the Senate's Only Doctor* (2002). In addition, he edited *Grand Rounds in Transplantation* (1995). In an article found of the Web site *Tennesseesenators.com*, First explained that the inspiration for *Tennessee Senators* came in the early 1990s, when he found himself "contemplating how to spend a period of my life in public service," which led him to "study the lives of public servants who had devoted a period of their lives to the U.S. Senate."

Frist lives in northwest Washington, D.C., with his wife, Karyn. They have three children: Harrison, Jonathan, and Bryan. The senator is a dedicated runner who has regularly participated in the Nike and Marine Marathons, among other races, and is a licensed commercial pilot. He was an alumnus trustee of his alma mater, Princeton University, from 1974 to 1978, and has been a charter trustee of the school since 1991. He has said that he will not seek reelection to the Senate in 2006, but will instead return to the full-time practice of medicine. — C.F.T.

Suggested Reading: *Congressional Quarterly* p642+ Mar. 24, 2001, with photos; *Hospitals & Health Network* (on-line) p46+ Jan. 20, 1995; *Medicare.gov*; *Mother Jones* p57 May/June 1997; *MSNBC.com*; *New York Times* I p26 May 6, 2001, A p18 May 16, 2001; *Senate.gov*; *Tennesseesenators.com*

Selected Books: *Transplant: A Heart Surgeon's Account of the Life-and-Death Dramas of the New Medicine*, 1989; *Tennessee Senators 1911–*

*2001: Portraits of Leadership in a Century of Change* (with J. Lee Annis Jr.), 1999; *When Every Moment Counts: What You Need to Know About Bioterrorism from the Senate's Only Doctor*, 2002; as editor—*Grand Rounds in Transplantation, 1995*

---

## Fugazi

(foo-GAH-zee)

*Rock band*

Canty, Brendan
*Mar. 9, 1966– Drummer*

Lally, Joe
*Dec. 3, 1963– Bassist*

MacKaye, Ian
*Apr. 16, 1962– Singer and guitarist*

Picciotto, Guy
*Sep. 17, 1965– Singer and guitarist*

*Address: c/o Dischord Records, 3819 Beecher St., N.W., Washington, DC 20007-1802*

"To many," Andy Kellman wrote for the *All Music Guide* (on-line), "Fugazi meant as much to them as Bob Dylan did to their parents." One of the most respected and influential rock acts performing today, the group Fugazi has risen to worldwide popularity despite the fact that they rarely promote their albums or give interviews in mass-media publications and have never appeared on MTV. Uninterested in achieving mainstream success, they have never recorded a music video or sold band-related merchandise, and tickets to their shows have continued to sell for around $5. One of the group's guitarists/vocalists, Ian MacKaye, was also the co-founder of the influential hardcore punk act Minor Threat in the early 1980s and is the co-founder of Dischord Records, the independent label on which Fugazi records. Like the band, Dischord has maintained a reputation for integrity in its 20-plus years of existence, recording only Washington, D.C., artists, putting ads mostly in small fan magazines, and charging only $10 per compact disc. The label has given rise to such well-regarded acts as Jawbox and Make Up. Ironically, the attention paid to Fugazi's and Dischord's avoidance of hype has often overshadowed the group's music, which has moved increasingly away from the groove-laden punk style of their earlier days to a more eclectic sound, utilizing varied tempos and instruments considered unusual for a punk group. Their lyrics, which have become more abstract over the years, range from social and political commentaries to introspective portraits. "Whatever we do as a band," the guitarist and vocalist Guy Picciotto told Tunde Oyewole for *Issues* (Spring 1995), "we try to maintain a sense of honesty—we try not to put ourselves in a position where we need to articulate it or justify it, but we insist on only doing what we're comfortable with, and what we can wake up and do everyday."

Ian MacKaye was born on April 16, 1962 in Washington, D.C. He grew up listening to such classic rock acts as Jimi Hendrix, Queen, and the Beatles; while attending Wilson High School, he became interested in punk music. A response to the heavily produced and intricately arranged rock music of the 1970s, punk music often offers a raw, unproduced sound; a fast tempo; antiestablishment lyrics; and only three or four chords. "When I came across this counterculture world in 1978," MacKaye told Peter Brandt for *Salon* (January 8, 2001, on-line), "it just made me so happy, because this is where I wanted to be. I've always felt really dedicated to the idea of continuing to support that area." At age 18, while still in high school, MacKaye formed his first punk band, the Teen Idles, and played bass guitar for the group. The Teen Idles released one, eponymous EP, which is given credit in many circles for starting the Washington, D.C., hardcore punk scene. The disc was pressed and distributed by Dischord Records, formed by MacKaye and Teen Idles drummer Jeff Nelson. Not wanting to spend years of his life at any sort of academic institution—or owing thousands of dollars in student loans—MacKaye decided not to attend college. Instead, in 1980, with Jeff Nelson, he formed the band Minor Threat, for which MacKaye played guitar. Combining extremely fast tempos and intense guitar lines with lyrics that focused on antiestablishment politics and self-actualizing, the group quickly became one of the more popular acts in the U.S. punk underground. In 1980 Dischord released Minor Threat's singles "Minor Threat" and "Straight Edge," the latter of which supplied the name for a movement of punk rockers who swore off alcohol and drugs. "It was just the title of a song that I wrote," MacKaye told Billy Bob Hargus for *Perfect Sound Forever* (April 1997, on-line). "I guess I coined the phrase but certainly never intended to start a movement." Over the next couple of years, Minor Threat toured extensively on the East Coast, releasing several singles, two EPs, and the album *Out of Step* (1982), which became so popular in the underground that the group began to be seen as stars. Not wanting that to happen, MacKaye broke up the band in 1983. Two years later he formed Embrace, which was one of the first bands dubbed by some as "emocore"; such bands wrote punk music with unconventional song structures and dynamics and highly personal lyrics. Embrace released one album, on Dischord Records, in 1987.

Another seminal emocore group was a fellow Dischord act, Rites of Spring, formed by the guitarist Guy Picciotto (born on September 17, 1965 in Washington, D.C.) and the drummer Brendan Canty (born on March 9, 1966, in Teaneck, New Jersey). Picciotto had discovered punk rock at age 15 and was inspired by such groups as the Cramps,

Shawn Scallen/Courtesy of Dischord Records

*The members of Fugazi (left to right): Joe Lally, Guy Picciotto, Brendan Canty, Ian MacKaye*

the Chumps, and the Urban Verbs. As a young teenager he saw those three groups play at a local radio-station benefit, and the experience changed his life. "It wasn't until I saw local bands and started seeing young people playing and people that I recognized from the street that I realized you could do it yourself. . . . I realized that you could be in music to create community, as opposed to being in music just to create music," he told Oyewole. "It was like joining a secret society," Picciotto recalled in an interview for *Current Biography*, discussing the Washington, D.C., music scene of the early and mid-1980s. "It was an amazing time, the witnessing of the birth of a scene; there was just an explosion of young kids forming bands. I went from feeling that the creation of music was something relegated to untouchable super beings to feeling that it was a personal imperative. Hanging out with your friends meant practicing, writing songs, playing shows. The music was just an extension of the friendships . . . and since we were all like 15, 16, 17, the time when your friendships are the most intense, the music was pretty intense as well." Rites of Spring became well known for their frenzied live shows, in which Picciotto would often leap around on, or jump off, the stage. The group released their debut album, *End on End*, in 1985. They followed with an EP, *All Through a Life* (1987), before breaking up. Picciotto and Canty then formed Happy Go Licky.

MacKaye formed Fugazi in 1987 with the bassist Joe Lally (born on December 3, 1963, in Rockville, Maryland) and Canty. Although it was begun with no special ambitions, the band soon grew in scope. MacKaye told Eric Brace for the *Washington Post* (August 1, 1993) that Fugazi "is just a word that I came across in a book called *Nam* with Vietnam veterans' recollections. It was their slang for [Expletive] Up Situation. I thought that was something we could agree on about the way the world is." Picciotto, meanwhile, worked with the group as a roadie and occasional singer; after the first few shows, he joined the band full-time. "When we started touring," he told Oyewole, "I knew I wanted to go out with them; so I was kind of going out to see what it was like and it just never stopped. . . . It was very different from any group I've been in, just because it was kind of an organic progression." Fugazi soon became known for its exciting live performances, and toward the end of 1988, they released their first EP, *Fugazi*. The band, in which MacKaye and Picciotto alternated as singers, explored various dynamics, from fast-paced punk numbers to slower songs with dub-like grooves. Among the EP's highlights were the anthemic "Waiting Room"; "Glue Man," a song written from the perspective of a drug addict; and "Suggestion," which was written from a female perspective and addressed the nature of sexual objectification: "Why can't I walk down a street free of suggestion? / Is my body my only trait in the eyes of man?" "We've had some very tense live moments when we've played that song," Picciotto told Oyewole. "People have come up to us and just been like, where . . . do you get off singing this song. It's a powerful thing, and that's what makes it so important. It generates ideas and it generates dialogue." The band followed with the EP *Margin Walker* in 1989. The two EPs were later combined on one CD, *13 Songs*, in 1990. In the *All Music Guide* (on-line), Andy Kellman wrote that *13 Songs* "is usually amongst the first records that springs to mind when defining alternative rock. Furious, intelligent, artful, and entirely musical, it's a baker's dozen of cannon shots to the gut—not just a batch of emotionally visceral and defiant songs recorded by angry young men, but something greater."

After the EP *Three Songs* (1990), Fugazi returned in the same year with the ferociously political *Repeater*. The record's title track, a fast-paced number with a ska-like groove that preached against labeling and conformity, became one of the band's best-known songs. "Once upon a time I had a name and a way / But to you I'm nothing but a number," MacKaye declared. Although criticized in some circles for exhibiting a holier-than-thou attitude, *Repeater* was also hailed as a hardcore punk masterpiece. According to Mark Kemp, writing about *Repeater* for *Rolling Stone* (on-line), "The D.C. quartet reinvented the sound of American hardcore. They wailed their emotionally charged political diatribes in between sturdy, lurching rhythms, Zeppelin-style changes in tempo and dynamics, and dissonant, distorted guitar textures." The album *Steady Diet of Nothing* (1991) found the group pushing in new directions, introducing more varied tempos, and occasionally toning down the guitars while the lyrics became a bit more abstract. "It was an attempt at learning," Picciotto told Oyewole. As for the lyrics, Picciotto told *Current Biography*, "It's kind of like you burn through the ideas that are closest to the surface when you're younger and if you continue you have to dig a bit deeper to find new ways to say things and new things to say." Despite the fact that the band did not promote their records with mainstream interviews or advertisements, *Steady Diet of Nothing* made it to number 65 on the British charts.

The year 1991 saw punk rock become part of mainstream culture, helped along by such bands as Nirvana and Pearl Jam. Although Fugazi's popularity continued to rise, they shunned a number of offers from major labels. As MacKaye told Hargus, "No amount of money is worth losing control of our music." The nature of Fugazi's shows dramatically changed with the rise of MTV-popularized punk music. "Suddenly, we were being inundated with kids who were going through with, what I thought was, ritualistically violent behavior," MacKaye told John Davis for *HeldLikeSound* (on-line). "They thought that's what they were supposed to do." Unhappy that some fans were making shows uncomfortable and dangerous for others, Fugazi soon became known for their anti-moshing and anti–crowd-surfing policies, which often caused confrontations between the group and the audience, as the band would stop playing until audience members complied with their wishes.

In 1993 Fugazi released *In on the Killtaker*, which contains some of the band's most aggressive and experimental work up to that point, including the feedback-drenched "23 Beats Off," about a military man infected with the AIDS virus, and "Smallpox Champion," a galloping number that ruminates on the near-decimation of the American Indian population: "This is the frontier with winters so cold / Greed informs action where action makes bold / To take all the cotton that's cut from the stalk / Weave the disease that's gonna take you right out." Although the band originally recorded the album with the producer Steve Albini, they were unhappy with the outcome and decided to reproduce it themselves. Matt Diehl, writing for *Rolling Stone* (on-line), noted that the album "explores almost every aspect of Fugazi's roots, serving as a virtual encyclopedia of punk-derived musical styles." The record hit number 153 on the *Billboard* Top 200 album charts; in England it reached number one on both the *Melody Maker* and *NME* independent charts and number 24 on the mainstream album charts. Two years later the group released *Red Medicine*, which contains several uptempo punk numbers but also found the group experimenting with samples, slower tempos, unorthodox melody lines, and new instruments. On "Version" the band did away with guitars altogether and instead focused on Picciotto's clarinet playing. "Instead of cramming angry diatribes down your throat, the group pulls back on several tunes, gently whispering its tales of the apocalypse through wavering sound effects," Mark Kemp wrote for *Rolling Stone* (July 13, 1995, on-line). "It's not really an experimental album—we just wanted to feel free to do whatever . . . we wanted," Picciotto explained to Fritz for *(Waiting for the) Ghost Train* (on-line). "Basically, that's always been the process, but I think on this . . . record it was highlighted a little more just because we'd had the time off and everyone else was exploring other things."

On the following tour MacKaye developed a severe case of pneumonia in Australia and was hospitalized for a couple of weeks. One of his lungs collapsed in the hospital and required surgery. Meanwhile, Lally got married, and Canty, who had married, became a father. These developments slowed down the band's recording schedule, but they found more time to work out the live formats of their songs. They returned in 1998 with *End Hits*, which continues the band's experimentation with twisting song structures and different uses of instruments as well as its general shift away from uptempo guitar tracks. Among the songs' topics are what the group saw as the evils of globalization and the lack of morals in mass media. In the following year the film *Instrument*, directed by Jem Cohen, was released. A documentary about Fugazi, *Instrument* was culled from Cohen's footage of performances dating back to the group's inception; it also features rare interviews and scenes of the band's life on the road. Made with the band's input and assistance, the film was followed by a Fugazi record, also called *Instrument*, filled with outtakes, demos, and instrumentals. "Making the *Instrument* video was one of the hardest projects we've ever done," Picciotto told Nathalie Claeys for *KindaMuszik* (on-line). "It involved 10 years of shooting, 3 years of editing and a lot of serious discussion between us and the director . . . about how we wanted to proceed with it. . . . We really wanted to make a film that would offer perspective on the band without just becoming some kind of glorious advertisement."

The band next made *The Argument* (2001) and an EP, *Furniture + 2*. For the full-length record, Fugazi virtually abandoned any semblance of their previous sound; with very few straightforward guitar tracks, the album is composed mostly of slower songs with heavy grooves and pop hooks. "I felt like we tried a lot of different ideas and didn't back down till we got things the way we wanted them," Picciotto told *Current Biography*. "It was the first time where we brought in other people to play on the tape—with extra drums and percussion, cello and other voices—so it's got an expanded sound to it." "Being both ear shattering and spine tingling at once, this is Fugazi at their 'musical' best," Chris True wrote for *All Music Guide* (on-line). "Incorporating melody with texture and their signature angular approach, the band has raised the bar for themselves and others once again." While many point out that the band's music has become more experimental, Fugazi's members feel that their work should be viewed in its historical context. "Not only have we changed quite a bit in this last decade, but so has the world," MacKaye told Chris Nelson for *Addicted to Noise* (May 1998, on-line). "The context has changed. People who are just getting into us today or over the last couple years really have no idea of how different it was when we started playing. Every record we put out, people are like, 'It's so weird, or so obtuse, or so challenging, or it's so experimental-sounding.' But you have to understand that when we put our first record out with 'Waiting Room' on it, people thought that was just outrageously weird and experimental within the context of what was going on at the time." The band's move away from their original sound has brought them much praise but also derision from some of their fans who feel the band has lost touch with their punk roots. "I don't think you can fault the listener because ultimately it's just a matter of taste," Picciotto said to *Current Biography*. "Certainly, the shifts in our sound haven't been as wildly dramatic as the Beatles', but we have always tried to push ourselves and not get too locked into comfortable formulas. . . . It's not like we've destroyed the past—we just don't want to be beholden to it."

Over the course of their 15-year existence, the band has played in cities and towns around the world, including some that are not known for having large rock scenes, such as Tromoso, Norway; Kuala Lumpur, Malaysia; and small towns in Brazil. "We've always had really good responses," Picciotto told *Current Biography*. "Almost everywhere at this point there are usually at least some people who have an inkling of who we are but it's also been cool to play to people who are really just there out of curiosity. Probably the show where we played to people who knew us the least was here in D.C., ironically enough, when we did a concert in the Lorton Correctional Facility. That was a tough one but even there we got a few people dancing."

Dischord continues to thrive as a recording label; it has released nearly 125 records since it was formed and now has subsidiary labels, run by Picciotto and Lally. Canty, meanwhile, has done soundtrack work for the Discovery channel. Picciotto and Lally currently live in Washington, D.C. MacKaye lives in nearby Arlington, Virginia, while Canty lives in Seattle, Washington. In Washington, D.C., the band plays only free concerts or benefits, often in collaboration with Positive Force, a Washington-based group advocating radical social change. Fugazi have raised over $100,000 for groups including Washington Peace Center, the Free Clinic, and ACT-Up. "Everything we've done—whether it's how we release our records or control ticket prices—has always been centered around making the most comfortable environment to play our music," MacKaye told Tim McMahan for *Lazy Eye* (on-line). "It should be that way for all bands." — G.O.

Suggested Reading: *Addicted to Noise* (on-line) May 1998; *HeldLikeSound* (on-line); *Issues* (on-line) Spring 1995; *Lazy Eye* (on-line); *Perfect Sound Forever* (on-line) Apr. 1997; *Salon* (on-line) Jan. 8, 2001; *(Waiting for) The Ghost Train* (on-line); *Washington Post* G p1 Aug. 1, 1993

Selected Recordings: *13 Songs*, 1990; *Repeater*, 1990; *Steady Diet of Nothing*, 1991; *In on the Killtaker*, 1993; *Red Medicine*, 1995; *End Hits*, 1998; *Instrument*, 1999; *The Argument*, 2001; as Embrace—*Embrace*, 1987; as Minor Threat—*Complete Discography*, 1988; as Rites of Spring—*End on End*, 1985

---

## Garza, Ed

*Jan. 30, 1969– Mayor of San Antonio, Texas (Democrat)*

*Address: Office of the Mayor, P.O. Box 839966, San Antonio, TX 78283-3966*

On June 1, 2001 Ed Garza, a 32-year-old, third-generation Mexican-American, was sworn in as mayor of San Antonio, Texas, his hometown. A Democrat who had served two terms on the San Antonio City Council, Garza won the city's nonpartisan mayoral election by capturing twice as many votes as his nearest rival, a popular Anglo councilman, in an 11-way race. Garza is the second Hispanic to serve as San Antonio's mayor in modern times; when he was inaugurated, he became the only Mexican-American mayor of a major U.S. city. (With a population of 1.144 million in 2000, San Antonio is the ninth-largest city in the United States and, after Houston and Dallas, the third-largest city in Texas.) Currently, he is one of only a few Hispanic mayors in the U.S. Trained in landscape architecture and urban planning, Garza has

Courtesy of the City of San Antonio

*Ed Garza*

an impressive array of professional and political experience, and he is known for his consensus-building leadership style. His youth, ethnicity, and prominence as mayor of a large American city have brought him national attention from the media—reporters for CNN and the *New York Times*, for example, interviewed him after the mayoral election—and from the Democratic National Committee, which hailed his victory in a press release. Garza has often been compared to Henry B. Gonzalez, a champion of civil rights who became the first Latino from Texas to be elected to Congress (and won reelection 17 times), and Henry G. Cisneros, who, in 1981, became the first Hispanic mayor of San Antonio since 1842 and who later, during President Bill Clinton's first term, served as secretary of the U.S. Department of Housing and Urban Development. By his own account, such comparisons do not faze Garza; as he told Jan Jarboe Russell for *Texas Monthly* (July 2001), "I don't feel any pressure to be extraordinary. Unlike my father, I'm not the first in my family to graduate from college. Unlike Henry Cisneros, I'm not the first Mexican American mayor of San Antonio. I'm free to be myself."

Ed Garza was born on January 30, 1969 in San Antonio. His father, Martin Garza, ran a house-painting business; his mother, Evangelina Garza, was a "civic dynamo," as Jim Yardley described her in the *New York Times* (June 2, 2001); the *San Antonio Express-News*, Yardley reported, named her one of the city's 10 outstanding women. Garza's parents were certain that assimilation was the key to their children's success. This conviction was inspired in part by the ideas and examples of Henry B. Gonzalez and Henry G. Cisneros, both of whom came from San Antonio's predominantly Hispanic West Side. Garza's mother and father encouraged Garza and his older brother, Martin, to speak English, with the result that Garza is fluent in English but not in Spanish. By the time Ed was born, his parents had moved from the city's West Side to a house they had bought just northwest of the city's downtown, in the middle-class, mainly white neighborhood of Jefferson, where they were among the first Mexican-American families on their block. His mother and father, Garza recalled to Russell, "were part of that generation that wanted more for their children: a better neighborhood and a better education." The young Ed felt comfortable with both his Latino and his Anglo neighbors. As Yardley wrote, "The elderly woman across the street became a surrogate grandmother" to the boy, and "another neighbor taught him to play the piano."

As a youngster Garza joined his parents in neighborhood political activities. "I was a seasoned block-walker at the age of eight," he recalled to Russell. At nine he ran unsuccessfully for president of the student council of the Woodlawn Elementary School, in a campaign that he has referred to as the first in his political career. He was 12 when, in 1981, his parents took him downtown to celebrate Henry Cisneros's extraordinary victory in that year's mayoral election in San Antonio. In becoming the first Hispanic to lead one of the country's 10 largest cities, Cisneros had opened a door for Garza and other Hispanics. Garza realized the significance of the moment, and in later years he tried to model himself after Cisneros. Garza attended Thomas Jefferson High School, a formerly all-white school that was becoming more racially and ethnically diverse, reflecting changes in San Antonio as a whole. "It was huge to go to Jefferson," he recalled to Belle Zars for the *Texas Observer* (September 9, 2001, on-line). "To be Hispanic and say you are going to Jefferson, that was an honor." He was elected president of his class in both his junior and senior years. While still in high school, he organized public opposition to a City Council member's plans to alter the Jefferson neighborhood. When Garza was 18 his mother died of cancer, at the age of 46. Her death taught him, as he told Yardley, to "focus on what you can do today and not put it off until tomorrow."

After his high-school graduation, in 1988, Garza entered the University of Texas at Austin, where he studied business administration. After two years he transferred to Texas A&M University, Cisneros's alma mater. When asked by Zars about any experiences of discrimination, Garza replied, "I don't think that in the scope of things that what I have seen comes anywhere close to what my grandparents or many other people have seen firsthand. I think I've felt some subtle discrimination—certainly going from a predominantly Hispanic high school to an Anglo college. . . . I was accepted [at Texas A&M] because I was different . . . but reminded that I was different." Garza earned a bachelor's degree in landscape architecture in 1992 and a master's degree in urban planning, also from Texas A&M, in 1994, at which time he received the school's Outstanding Graduate Award in Land Development. Noting some of the courses he took as an undergraduate or graduate student—among them land planning, design, architecture, social work, real-estate finance, and housing and community development—some observers believe that at heart Garza is an urban planner, and that his political ideology has grown out of his ideas about the built environment.

In 1997 Garza won a seat on the San Antonio City Council, becoming, at the age of 28, one of its youngest members ever. People immediately drew comparisons between Garza and Cisneros, who, in 1975, at 27, had become the youngest member of the City Council, and Gonzalez, who served two terms in the council during the 1950s. As the representative of Council District 7, Garza distinguished himself with his respectful and businesslike negotiating style and his ability to pull the council's contentious parties together. He served on many of the council's committees, including Affirmative Action, Federal and State Initiatives, International Relations, Municipal Court, Street Maintenance, Transportation and Water Policy, and Planning, as well as such groups as the Bexar County Housing Finance Corp., the Health Facility Development Corp., the San Antonio Industrial Development Authority, and the Urban Renewal Agency, among others. In 1999 Garza won reelection to the council. During his second term he led a campaign to fluoridate the city's water supply. Garza counts San Antonio voters' approval of the fluoridation measure among his biggest successes as a councilman.

In 2001 Garza ran for mayor of San Antonio. Although San Antonio is now nearly 60 percent Hispanic, no Hispanic candidate since Cisneros had won election as mayor. Heywood Sanders, professor of public administration at the University of Texas at San Antonio, told Belle Zars, "San Antonio's electorate is very divided in racial and ethnic terms. Anglo districts vote for Anglos; Hispanics vote for Hispanics." It has been speculated that after Cisneros left office, some Hispanic mayoral candidates alienated many in the Hispanic community by distancing themselves from that group's causes, while others failed to capture enough of the Anglo vote because they were too forceful in their support of the Hispanic community. Since a greater percentage of Anglos than Hispanics are registered voters, and a greater percentage of Anglo voters than Hispanic voters go to the polls, an Hispanic candidate must capture a substantial portion of the Anglo vote in order to win a mayoral election in San Antonio. Garza attracted strong support among not only Hispanics but also Anglo voters, as well as among Democrats and women. He did so, according to Jan Jarboe Russell, by "focusing on suburban issues: streets, parks, drainage projects, reducing airport noise, and solving traffic problems"—issues involving things that "make a city livable." Russell also wrote, "Garza's style is non-threatening to Anglos. He is tall, handsome, wears dark business suits and red ties, and speaks impeccable English." Russell reported that Garza raised more than $800,000 for his campaign, much of it coming from strong neighborhood associations and established business leaders, many of them white. During the campaign the incumbent mayor, Howard Peak, a Republican (who could not run again because of San Antonio's term-limit law), threw his support behind Garza, and Cisneros's mother walked the streets in the Hispanic West Side to encourage people to vote for him. Garza's chief rival among the 10 other mayoral candidates was the well-known, well-funded city councilman Tim Bannwolf.

On the day of the election, May 5, 2001, Garza won eight of San Antonio's 10 districts, capturing a total of 59 percent of the vote to Bannwolf's 29 percent. Amazingly, he even outpolled Bannwolf by five percentage points in the city's three traditionally white northern districts—a feat that "made Garza the first Hispanic in Texas to blur ethnic lines so completely," as Russell wrote. (Even Cisneros did not win those three districts—though he made a strong showing in them—when he beat the Anglo businessman John Steen in the San Antonio mayoral election of 1981.) Garza even came close to beating Bannwolf in the latter's home district. Part of the reason for Garza's success in the northern districts, according to various observers, is that their Hispanic populations are growing and now account for as much as a third of the North Side's total population. Cisneros, who had known both Garza and Bannwolf for several years, did not publicly favor either man, but after the election, he was quoted in a CNN article (September 5, 2001, on-line) as saying that Garza has the skills and character "to go a long way in American politics."

Garza was sworn in as mayor on June 1, 2001. In his inaugural address, as transcribed on the *San Antonio Community Portal* (on-line), he identified the four top items on his agenda as human development, neighborhood development, metropolitan development, and model governance. The last-named element, he explained, would include steps toward increasing accountability in the city's government and exploring, and then implementing, other ways to improve its functioning; toward that end, he announced, he intended to form a Citizens Charter and Governance Commission. The cornerstone of Garza's agenda is "growth from within," by which he means revitalizing the city's older neighborhoods (both to conserve them and to prevent the creation of more suburban-type sprawl) and using San Antonio's existing resources wisely, ever-mindful of long-term effects. As Belle Zars wrote, Garza "thinks about legacy and what the city will look like 20, 30, even 50 years from now."

Mayor Garza worked effectively with the City Council to pass the city's $1.3 billion 2001–02 budget. He has formed alliances with business and religious leaders and successfully fought for the passage of the Better Jobs Initiative presented jointly by Communities Organized for Public Service (COPS) and Metro Alliance, local organizations that build support for programs to help middle- and low-income San Antonians. Toward the goal of model governance, in November 2001 San Antonio voters, with Garza's encouragement, approved three changes to the city charter that made public officials more accountable. Two of the changes shifted the authority of certain nonelected officials to the City Council (whose members are elected); the third eliminated civil-service protection for such licensed professional employees as doctors and lawyers. Although only a little over 4 percent of voters expressed their opinions on the charter revisions, Garza interpreted the wide margins by which the propositions passed as evidence that San Antonians would be willing to agree to other, broader reforms. "Our citizens are ready for change," he declared, as quoted by William Pack in the *San Antonio Express-News* (November 6, 2001, on-line). Garza has also been collaborating closely with Nelson Wolff, the judge who heads the commission that governs Bexar County, which consists of San Antonio and a few suburbs. In addressing problems connected with the public-health, transportation, and water systems, among other issues, Garza and Wolff have pledged "to repair a city-county relationship that was strained in recent years," as John W. Gonzalez wrote for the *Houston Chronicle* (May 14, 2001).

In the wake of the terrorist attacks on the United States on September 11, 2001, Mayor Garza also helped to create the comprehensive City-County Emergency Preparedness Plans for San Antonio. In addition, he assisted in setting up the Mayor's Blue Ribbon Commission on the Economy, which has made recommendations for sustaining growth in the city's economy, and United San Antonio, a community-based commission dedicated to accentuating and building upon the strengths of San Antonio's multicultural citizenry and history.

Garza is the president of the Greystone Planning and Development Co. and serves as the vice president for land planning and development of the International Waterfront Group. Through the years he has also worked for other firms specializing in land planning and development, real-estate finance, and landscape architecture. He is an adjunct professor at St. Mary's University in San Antonio and has been involved with many professional, civic, and community organizations, among them the American Society of Landscape Architects, the International Council for Shopping Centers, and San Antonio Trees. Garza has served as a board member and president of the Jefferson and Woodlawn Neighborhood Associations. He is a 1996 graduate of the San Antonio Hispanic Chamber of Commerce leadership-development program. Also in 1996, the *San Antonio Business Journal* named him one of the city's "40 Under 40 Rising Stars." In 1998 Garza was chosen to serve on the board of directors of the Hispanic Elected Local Officials (HELO), an arm of the National League of Cities (NLC). Two years later he was selected to serve on the NLC's board of directors.

Garza married the former Anna Laura Gonzales, a bilingual-education teacher, in October 2001. His wife has been tutoring him in Spanish. He will be up for reelection in May 2003. — C.F.T.

Suggested Reading: *Aggie Network* (on-line); *Houston Chronicle* A p17 May 14, 2001, with photo; *New York Times* A p8 June 2, 2001, with photo; *San Antonio Community Portal* (on-line); *San Antonio Express-News* (on-line) Nov. 6, 2001; *Texas Monthly* p30+ July 2001, with photo; *Texas Observer* (on-line) Sep. 9, 2001; *Who's Who in American Politics 2001–2002*

---

Courtesy of Bill and Melinda Gates Foundation

## Gayle, Helene

*Aug. 16, 1955– Epidemiologist; senior adviser for HIV/AIDS at the Bill and Melinda Gates Foundation*

*Address: Bill & Melinda Gates Foundation, P.O. Box 23350, Seattle, WA 98102*

"HIV and AIDS is so much broader than just discussing a particular virus," the epidemiologist Helene Gayle explained to Rhonda Smith in July 2000, for the African American AIDS Policy and Training Institute Web site. "It is the paradigm for public health issues because it involves addressing so many other issues—poverty, gender, race, homophobia—that have broad ramifications." The human immunodeficiency virus (HIV), which causes acquired immune deficiency syndrome (AIDS), was a new, only partially understood pathogen when Gayle began her specialized epidemiological training at the U.S. Centers for Disease Control (CDC) in Atlanta, Georgia, in 1984. The virus had been identified and tracked in 1981, and was at first mistakenly linked only to gay men; as Linda Villarosa wrote for the *New York Times* (August 28, 2001), "No one knew for sure how [the disease] was caused or transmitted or even what to call it, much less how to stop it." But Gayle quickly attained expertise in the ways that the disease was acquired and spread, learned how to prevent it, and, as the CDC's chief of international AIDS research, became a voice for the United States on the world stage. The author or co-author of 15 papers on HIV and AIDS, she was selected to head the CDC National Center for HIV, Sexually Transmitted Disease and Tuberculosis Prevention upon its creation in 1995. Six years later, through an arrangement with the CDC, she accepted a two-year assignment as the senior adviser for HIV/AIDS at the Bill and Melinda Gates Foundation. Gayle has been called a "soldier" and a "warrior" in the worldwide battle to prevent, treat, and cure AIDS, and, accordingly, she was sworn in as an assistant surgeon general and rear admiral in the Commissioned Corps of the United States Public Health Service in 1997.

The third of five children, Helene Doris Gayle was born on August 16, 1955 in Buffalo, New York. Her father, Jacob Gayle Sr., was an entrepreneur, and her mother, Marietta, was a psychiatric social worker. Despite being hit by a car when she was 12 and confined by a body cast for months afterward, she had an active youth, leading the black student group at her local school. She majored in psychology at Barnard College, in New York City, graduated with honors in 1976, and enrolled at the University of Pennsylvania medical school. Gayle also attended Johns Hopkins University, in Baltimore Maryland, where she received a master's degree in public health, having been inspired by the worldwide effort to eradicate smallpox. In an interview with Renée D. Turner for *Ebony* (November 1991), she noted that her schooling "gave me an opportunity to be involved in the social and political aspects of medicine." She had been influenced by her parents, she explained to Turner: "Both my parents felt strongly that to make a contribution to the world around us is one of the greatest things you can do."

With M.D. and M.P.H. degrees in hand, Gayle went to Washington, D.C., to serve as an intern and resident in pediatrics at the Children's Hospital National Medical Center. She further refined her focus when she secured a place in the Epidemic Intelligence Service, the epidemiological training program at the CDC. "When I came to the CDC in 1984, AIDS was just beginning," she told Rhonda Smith. "It was a relatively new issue. It was an issue that seemed to be in the center of public health." Gayle completed a residency in preventive medicine at the CDC before becoming a staff epidemiologist there, in 1987. Researching the spread of HIV, she focused particularly on women, children, minority groups, and international rates of infection. She ran studies on mother-to-child transmission and partner infection, presenting her findings to the 1988 International AIDS Conference in Stockholm, Sweden, which was the first international colloquium on the disease. "At the beginning, once we figured out what we were dealing with, we focused on doing a general prevention campaign," Gayle explained to Linda Villarosa. "We tried to get as much information to as many people as possible. And to some extent it worked because nearly every adult can tell you what AIDS is and how it is spread." Over a period that ranges from a few months to more than a decade, AIDS reduces the efficacy of an infected individual's immune system, making the person increasingly susceptible to other illnesses. HIV is transmitted by an exchange of body fluids during sexual intercourse (via semen or vaginal fluids); by the use of contaminated intravenous drug paraphernalia (via blood); or to the baby of an infected mother, during pregnancy, birth, or breastfeeding (via blood, vaginal fluids, or breast milk).

As early as the late 1980s, Gayle had noted that some minority groups, such as African-Americans, showed disproportional rates of HIV infection. "Sometimes it gets to me," she admitted to *Black Enterprise* magazine (October 1988), speaking of the personal toll of her work. "The demands are great because the disease is overwhelming. The virus is so difficult to prevent that is gets frustrating. But we have to keep working." Her efforts to boost public safety, such as encouraging sexually active people to wear condoms and engage in other safer-sex practices and discouraging intravenous drug users from sharing needles, often failed because of "personal behaviors, which are culturally influenced and which societies are not very comfortable in facing," as she explained to Renée Turner. Internationally, Gayle attempted to develop and introduce AIDS-prevention methods for women, such as vaginal virucides, in countries "where women are more often affected but have less control over sexual interaction," as she told Turner.

Gayle has long been at the forefront of AIDS research, and her ideas have often been prescient. "We are going to see young people dying all around us as the disease spreads," she told *Black Enterprise* in 1988. "AIDS presents a challenge to deal with problems we've been twiddling our thumbs over. We haven't talked about important issues like sexually transmitted diseases, teenage pregnancy and drug abuse in recent years." During her tenure at the CDC, Gayle saw rates of infection slow as prevention campaigns took effect, only to rise sharply as a new generation matured. "Of the new HIV infections, 50 percent of those are among African Americans, keeping in mind that African Americans only make up 13 percent of our population. . . . 30 percent of new HIV infections are occurring among women," she told Jim Lehrer on the PBS program *NewsHour* (August 31, 1999, online). "We know that the fact that this was characterized initially as a white gay disease lulled the African American community into a sense of false security," Gayle continued, explaining why the infection rates among African-Americans had remained high for over a decade. But infection rates among gays had recently jumped as well, she told Lehrer: "We know that among the older white gay men who were part of the first wave of the epidemic, if you will, there was a lot of mobilization for HIV prevention and behaviors did change and rates did come down. But we are starting to see a resurgence in high risk behaviors in younger gay men, including younger white gay men. . . . And we are starting to see increases not only in HIV but also in other sexually transmitted diseases. But the impact even among gay men is still disproportionally high among African American and Hispanic young gay men, young men under the ages of 25, under the ages of 22."

Entering its third decade, HIV/AIDS "still qualifies for an epidemic," Gayle told Jim Lehrer. "It is diversifying, affecting different populations . . . [it is] a pandemic. In [the U.S.] we have higher rates of HIV infection and other sexually transmitted diseases than any other industrialized nation." With HIV "raging out of control" in Africa and Asia, as she explained to Lehrer, she has redoubled her efforts to prevent the spread of HIV and to treat those who have contracted AIDS. She has championed the use of newly developed drugs to slow the virus, although she has also warned of the virus's mutation and resistence to the drugs. Especially tragic, in her view, is the fact that many people with HIV do not know they are infected and therefore cannot take advantage of medications or other therapies; additionally, those unknowingly infected may pass along the virus to their sexual partners. Nevertheless, Gayle remained wary of the proposed federal HIV Partner Protection Act, which would have required the registration of HIV-positive people with state health authorities, allowing public access to names of HIV-positive individuals. "The Act departs from the CDC Guidelines and science-based public health practice by mandating reporting of all HIV-positive tests, by client name, without any provision to support the continuation of anonymous testing," Gayle stated in her testimony on September 29, 1998 before the Subcommittee on Health and Environment of the House Committee on Commerce. "The resulting effect will be to discourage and drastically reduce anonymous testing opportunities. Anonymous testing has been strongly encouraged by CDC Guidelines and is integral to public health practice because it has been proven to bring people for testing earlier in the course of infection. . . . CDC currently recommends that people who test positive in anonymous settings be linked with medical care so they can receive life-prolonging clinical services. It is also through this medical delivery system that clients develop the trusting relationships that facilitate the identification of exposed partners not revealed with the initial inquiry." While the HIV Partner Protection Act never reached the floor of the House for a vote, two-thirds of U.S. states have now passed legislation requiring HIV-positive individuals to be listed publicly by name.

As troubling to Gayle as the disease itself is the seeming complacency of the American public toward HIV infection, an attitude corresponding to a leveling-off of the numbers of people developing and dying from AIDS in the late 1990s, following a sharp drop in infections in the mid-1990s. She told Jim Lehrer, "With the advent of these powerful new therapies, I think people have relaxed a lot. People felt, well, you know, we now have this great treatment. HIV is not such a bad disease. It's not so serious. If you get it, you take some pills and it's not so bad. . . . We can't be lulled into a sense of complacency. But I think we have been." At the 2000 International AIDS Conference, Gayle gave a speech in which she urged the worldwide community to step up its assault on HIV infection. "While HIV prevention has reduced the level of risk and infection for many," she said, "it would appear that some at-risk communities have not been reached successfully, some have not been reached repeatedly, and some have become bored with HIV prevention." In her speech, she also attempted to combat the stereotypes that have hampered prevention of the disease since the beginning: "Unfortunately, many heterosexuals at risk have interpreted low risk to mean no risk, and we continue to see clusters of HIV infection among young people who believed that HIV could not touch their lives."

After 17 years of working at the CDC, six of those at the helm of the National Center for HIV, Sexually Transmitted Disease and Tuberculosis Prevention, where she launched coordinated worldwide efforts against syphilis and tuberculosis in addition to HIV/AIDS, Gayle accepted a two-year assignment with the Bill and Melinda Gates Foundation, which began on September 1, 2001. (Bill Gates, the founder of Microsoft, is also a prominent philanthropist.) As the senior adviser for HIV/AIDS, a newly created position, she will have an endowment of over $300 million to forge public and private partnerships in the effort to prevent and treat AIDS internationally.

Gayle has received several commendations for her service in the field of public health, including the University Medal of Excellence from Columbia University and the Meritorious Service Medal, the Outstanding Service Medal, and the Poindexter Award from the United States Public Health Service. In June 1997 she was made an assistant surgeon general, with the rank of rear admiral, in the Commissioned Corps of the United States Public Health Service.

Gayle, who is single, currently lives in Seattle. Although her career has kept her extremely busy, she has always made time to practice aerobics, dine with friends, and listen to music, including jazz and performances by African and Caribbean ensembles. — K.S.

Suggested Reading: *Black Enterprise* p62 Oct. 1988, with photo; *Ebony* p38+ Nov. 1991, with photos; *New York Times* F p6 Aug. 28, 2001, with photo; *Who's Who Among African-Americans, 1998–99*

---

Tim Dillon/*USA Today*

## Gerson, Michael

*1964– Chief speechwriter for President George W. Bush*

*Address: The White House, 1600 Pennsylvania Ave., N.W., Washington, DC 20500*

Neither President George W. Bush nor his father is "a naturally articulate man," an anonymous White House official remarked to Ryan Lizza for the *New Republic* (May 21, 2001). "The elder Bush responded to his inarticulateness by denigrating the importance of words. The son has responded to it by treating words with added respect." For George W. Bush—the author of such neologisms as "proculation," "subliminable," and "Hispanically"—treating words with added respect has included hiring Michael Gerson as his chief speechwriter. The choice was a wise one: even the president's political opponents have acknowledged Gerson's eloquence. Hendrik Hertzberg, for example, a former speechwriter for President Jimmy Carter and a sharp critic of George W. Bush, wrote for the *New Yorker* (February 5, 2001) that Bush's inaugural address, "taken as a whole and judged purely as a piece of writing, was shockingly good. . . . It was tightly constructed. Its rhythms flowed pleasingly. Its sentences were sculpted. Its sentiments, however familiar, were expressed in language that was consistently fresh, at once elevated and unpretentious, and almost entirely free of bombast, cliché, or sloganeering." Similarly, Eli Attie, the chief speechwriter for the 2000 Democratic presidential nominee, Vice President Al Gore, told Frank Bruni for the *New York Times* (April 3, 2001), "I don't agree with what [Gerson's] speeches say, but they're beautifully written."

Indeed, the most common criticism of Gerson's work is that it is sometimes too eloquent for the plainspoken Bush, and that the speechwriter's sonorous phrases sometimes ring hollow issuing from the president's lips. Wayne Fields, a professor of English at Washington University and author of *Union of Words: A History of Presidential Eloquence*, explained to Sandra Sobieraj for the Albany, New York *Times Union* (July 22, 2001), "The ill fit undermines the message, emphasizes the distance between the crafting of words and the speaking of them. The disjunctions, breaks and gaps make it even more difficult for Bush to build credibility as someone who is sure of himself and belongs there in the White House." Mark McKinnon, a Bush campaign adviser cited by Bruni, acknowledged that during the presidential race, Gerson "kind of wrote above the president on occasion"; but, he added, White House counselor Karen Hughes "kind of helped in that regard to pull it down to Bush-speak."

Michael Gerson was born in 1964 in New Jersey; he grew up near St. Louis, Missouri. His father, Michael, who died in 1992, was a dairy scientist and maker of ice-cream flavors; his mother, Betty, is an artist. Teachers at his high school, the Westminster Christian Academy in Creve Coeur, Missouri, have characterized the teenage Gerson as a bright student with a fascination for history, government, and politics. Michael Hearne, his 11th-grade American history teacher, told Brian Carlson for the *St. Louis Post-Dispatch* (February 27, 2001) that Gerson "was a particularly good student, right on top of the heap, one of the all-time best." Hearne also remembers Gerson, an evangelical Christian, as a deeply religious young man. "He was the sort of person who was very aware of his religious beliefs and integrated them into his life," Hearne said. "He had some real depth in what he did." "Michael recognized that how you act should reflect what you believe, and there should be a connection," Sherry Blough, Gerson's former guidance counselor, recalled to Carlson. "He acted upon more than just what was pragmatic. He had a well-articulated and thought-out philosophy of life."

Upon graduating from Westminster, in 1982, Gerson enrolled at Wheaton College, near Chicago, as a theology student. There, his efforts to reconcile libertarianism with Catholic social thought—the two intellectual traditions he considers most vital to modern conservatism—led him to embrace an early version of "compassionate conservatism," the philosophy espoused by President Bush. (To this day, Gerson characterizes himself as a compassionate conservative. "While he didn't coin the phrase," Lizza wrote, "he has thought through the oft-derided term more clearly than anyone else, including the president.") Gerson has named John F. Kennedy, Robert F. Kennedy, Lyndon B. Johnson, and Martin Luther King Jr. as speakers who have inspired him. "The great stories of our time," he told D. T. Max for the *New York Times Magazine* (October 7, 2001), "are moral stories and moral commitments: the civil rights movement, the War on Poverty."

Gerson received his first job offer while still at Wheaton, after someone sent Charles W. Colson, the founder of Prison Fellowship Ministries, a copy of a newspaper column that Gerson had written about Mother Teresa. On the strength of the article, Colson (a former special counsel to President Richard Nixon who spent seven months in federal prison for his involvement in the Watergate scandal) asked Gerson to help him write a book. Gerson went to work for Colson (whose nearly four dozen books center on Christianity) after he graduated from Wheaton, in 1986. Later, he served as a policy strategist and speechwriter for U.S. senator Daniel R. Coats, an Indiana Republican and an early standard bearer for compassionate conservatism. "He has an almost uncanny quality, an ability to sit and talk and think aloud with you," Coats told Gregg Zoroya for *USA Today* (April 11, 2001). "And translate your thoughts and conclusions and recommendations into a document that seems to express it even better than you expressed it." While working for Coats, Gerson also served as a policy adviser for Jack Kemp (a Republican former congressman from New York and later secretary of the Department of Housing and Urban Development) and occasionally wrote speeches for Senator Bob Dole of Kansas when Dole was running for president in 1996.

After Dole's electoral defeat Gerson worked for about two years as a journalist with the weekly magazine *U.S. News & World Report.* He left that position in 1999, after George W. Bush, who remembered Gerson's speechwriting during the 1996 presidential race, offered him a job with his 2000 presidential campaign. Gerson immediately set to work assembling a team of assistant speechwriters. Since then he has been recognized as the principal author of all of Bush's most important speeches: his acceptance speech at the 2000 Republican National Convention, his inaugural address, his February 2001 budget address to Congress, and his address before Congress in the wake of the September 11, 2001 terrorist attacks against New York City and the Pentagon. (The text of a typical presidential address is also scrutinized and edited by other members of the White House staff and the president himself prior to delivery.)

Reported to be one of President Bush's most trusted advisers, Gerson is said to wield unusual influence for a man in his position. In part that is because President Bush takes a more limited role in the creation of speeches than many of his predecessors in the White House. Whereas Bill Clinton, for example, often wrote his own material, Bush prefers to edit and rework drafts provided by Gerson and his staff. At the same time, Gerson is said to play an especially active role in the determination of administration policy—a function from which speechwriters have usually been excluded, at least since the administration of Lyndon B. Johnson. In particular, he sits in on meetings of the president's policy staff as well as his communication staff.

When asked by Zoroya to characterize his job, Gerson replied, "On most days in most circumstances, you are writing for the next day's headlines. In a few moments, you are writing for American history. And that's a tremendous honor. And then there may come a time, once or twice, when you are writing for the angels. For some great and decisive moment."

Gerson and his wife, the former Dawn Miller, have two young sons, Bucky and Nicholas. — P.K.

Suggested Reading: (Albany, New York) *Times Union* A p5 July 22, 2001; *New Republic* p14+ May 21, 2001; *New York Times* A p16 Apr. 3, 2001, with photo; *New York Times Magazine* p32+ Oct. 7, 2001, with photos; *St. Louis Post-Dispatch* A p6 Feb. 27, 2001

Selected Speeches: *Address to the Republican National Convention: Compassionate Conservatism,* in *Vital Speeches of the Day* p642+ Aug 15, 2000; *Inaugural address: Civility, courage, compassion and character* in *Vital Speeches of the Day* p226+ Feb 1, 2001; *The spirit of respect and cooperation: Changing the tone in the nation's capital* in *Vital Speeches of the Day* p322+ Mar 15, 2001; *Address by George W. Bush, president of the United States delivered to a joint session of Congress and the American people, Washington, D.C., September 20, 2001* in *Vital Speeches of the Day* p760+ Oct 1, 2001

---

## Gibson, Charles

*Mar. 9, 1943– Co-anchor of* Good Morning America *and* PrimeTime Thursday

*Address:* Good Morning America, *147 Columbus Ave., New York, NY 10023*

ABC's choice of Charles Gibson, a specialist in hard news and political coverage, as co-anchor of the network's news program *Good Morning America* (*GMA*) in 1987 surprised many observers. Initially faulted for his stiff manner while interviewing celebrities on *GMA*, Gibson proved his worth and remained with the show for 11 years, with Joan Lunden as his co-anchor for nearly all of that time. After an absence from *GMA* of less than a year, during which he held various jobs at ABC, he again

Debra L. Rothenberg/Retna Ltd.

*Charles Gibson*

took the anchor's seat, this time with Diane Sawyer as his partner, in what ABC executives announced as an interim measure until permanent replacements could be found. Gibson and Sawyer's short-term appointment with *GMA* has stretched to more than three years. After Gibson's return, *GMA*'s sagging ratings improved.

Born on March 9, 1943 in Evanston, Illinois, to Burdett and Georgiana (Law) Gibson, Charles DeWolf Gibson grew up in Washington, D.C. The illustrator Charles Dana Gibson, creator of the very popular Gibson Girl (an idealized image of a young 1890s woman), was one of his great-uncles. Gibson's father worked in the coal-mining-machinery business and later for the U.S. Department of Commerce; his mother was an interior decorator in Georgetown, an upscale section of the nation's capital. "Mother was an organizer, while Dad was very involved with each of the kids," Gibson recalled to Dotson Rader for *Parade* (February 7, 1988). Gibson attended a prep school, and then, with the help of a friend of his father's, gained admission to Princeton University, in Princeton, New Jersey, where he majored in history. "I'd never get into Princeton today," he told Rader. "I limped through with mediocre grades. I enjoyed Princeton enormously, but I didn't excel there, although it wasn't for lack of trying." For a while in college, he was the news director of the campus radio station. After earning an A.B. degree, in 1965, he served in the Marine Reserves. While in the military he considered applying to Yale Law School, but he chose to pursue a career in news broadcasting instead. "My father and I had watched the news together every night, from the time we got a television set, when I was 12," he told Rader. "We'd talk at the dinner table about what we'd seen, about politics. It seemed to me that television was the future of news. You felt you were at [congressional] hearings or in the hall[s of Congress]. I decided I would get to a network by the time I was 33. When I got out of the Marine Reserves, I gave myself 10 years."

Gibson started his professional life in 1966, as a producer for the RKO Radio Network in Washington, D.C. The next year he moved to the position of news director at WLVA-TV and Radio in Lynchburg, a small city in central Virginia. Although Lynchburg is only 170 miles from Washington, he found it light-years away in terms of racial attitudes. "To have grown up with a keen awareness of civil rights, which my parents would talk about, and to go down to Lynchburg, where the local newspaper didn't publish stories about blacks unless they'd committed a crime—that was surprising to me," he told Rader. "And I just assumed that my co-workers at the station would also find it strange." He and his colleagues in the news department complained about the fact that the station covered the football games of the white high school but not those of the black high school. The station agreed to cover the black high-school team, but to Gibson's dismay, they referred to the players only by their jersey numbers, not their names. "That's what the times were like," Gibson told Rader. "The paper called us Socialists and criticized us harshly." After a dispute with the station manager, he quit the job. As he was preparing to leave Lynchburg, he discovered that the tires of his car had been slashed. He also experienced difficulties in his next position, that of anchor and reporter for WMAL-TV (later WJLA), an ABC affiliate in Washington, whose staff he joined in 1970. His problems there stemmed from his personal opposition to the Vietnam War. (He and his wife, Arlene, whom he married in 1968, participated in demonstrations against the war in the 1960s and early 1970s.) Once, after images of antiwar demonstrations had aired, he stated on camera that people should be allowed to exercise their right to lawful assembly. "There were around 300 calls after the show"—all but two critical of him, he told Roderick Townley for *TV Guide* (December 5, 1987). In 1973, when WMAL's management told him that they considered him too "preppy" to be on TV and that they intended to transfer him to radio, he handed in his resignation notice. During the following year, with the aid of a National Endowment for the Humanities fellowship, he studied government policy as a national journalism fellow at the University of Michigan. He enjoyed his break from the world of broadcasting and again considered going to law school, but he ultimately decided against it. "Within three or four months" of his arrival at the university, he told Rader, "I knew I was going back to journalism. I was far more interested in the human story of a law case than in the points of law."

In 1974 Gibson joined Television News Inc. (TVN), a syndicated news service, for which he reported on the Watergate scandal, which began when men hired by the committee to reelect President Richard M. Nixon were caught in the act of burglarizing the Democratic Party's national headquarters; he also reported on a major consequence of the scandal: Nixon's resignation. In 1975 Gibson joined ABC News, where he was assigned to the White House during the administration of Gerald Ford. After Jimmy Carter's election as president, in 1976, Gibson became a general correspondent for ABC News. In 1981 he began covering the U.S. House of Representatives. While working his way up the ABC ladder, he sometimes handled unglamorous tasks. For use on Election Night in 1980, for example, he prepared one-minute reports on 30 key House and Senate races, a task that required an enormous amount of research. (None of the capsule accounts was broadcast.) Among his more satisfying jobs, he served as a reporter for *World News Tonight with Peter Jennings*, an occasional substitute for Ted Koppel on *Nightline*, and a substitute anchor on *World News This Morning*. He also sat in for the host of *Good Morning America*, David Hartman, about two dozen times. Despite his appearances on these shows and his solid reporting skills, many industry observers expressed surprise when, in 1987, ABC announced that the relatively little-known Gibson would replace Hartman, who for years had enjoyed great popularity. In *New York Newsday* (February 2, 1987), Marvin Kitman called Gibson "a total nobody. . . . What's the square root of zero? That's Charles Gibson's Q-rating"— a measure of how recognizable and popular celebrities are. "He's basically unknown, except to his immediate family." Gibson wasn't offended by such remarks. "Certainly no one knew who the hell I am," he told Jacqueline Trescott for the *Washington Post* (May 12, 1987) after he had hosted *GMA* for three months. "I think you can make a case that a good section of the country still doesn't. And that's fine."

Gibson began co-hosting *Good Morning America* with Joan Lunden on January 29, 1987. Although viewers seemed to take to him immediately, judging by the rise in ratings soon after his arrival, some media critics evaluated him harshly. In the *Chicago Tribune* (March 17, 1989), Clifford Terry lambasted Gibson's performance: "Gibson . . . is so relaxed he seems alternately bored and goofy. Decidedly, he is the most gauche and slipshod of all the [morning show] hosts." Even some ABC executives complained about his manner; one, for instance, described him as coming across as overly sophisticated and ill at ease when interviewing pop-culture celebrities. Gibson admitted that making the transition from hard news to a softer approach (as well as having to arise before 4:00 a.m. to prepare for each broadcast) was difficult. "You can ask the questions, you've just got to be more conversational than confrontational," he told Kathryn Baker for the *Chicago Tribune* (August 1, 1987). "And . . . that's taking some getting used to. So sometimes I think I'm pulling a punch or two.'" But others praised Gibson's skill in talking about a variety of topics, ranging from complex political issues to breezy anecdotes. "[Gibson] has the capacity, which not every broadcast correspondent has, to do the light as well as the heavy stories," George Henry Watson, then ABC's Washington-bureau chief, told Jacqueline Trescott. "On things as routine as the Christmas tree lighting he could bring a sparkle that gave him an extra dimension." As for his co-anchor, Lunden described Gibson to Roderick Townley as "a terrific team player. From the moment we were first on air together, there was rapport."

As co-anchor of *GMA*, Gibson found himself subjected to far more media scrutiny than he had encountered in his previous jobs. "That has come as a real surprise and I don't particularly like it," he told Trescott. "But it goes with the territory." He also concluded that many viewers feel significantly more personally connected to morning-news anchors than they do to anchors of news shows that air later in the day. That is because the morning, as he explained to Terence Smith for the PBS *Online NewsHour* (October 29, 1999), is "the most informal time of day. The beds aren't made. The dishes aren't done. Kids are running around like banshees, and then there we are, asking you to bring us into your home when you wouldn't have your best friends into the home at that hour of the day." He also said that he and his co-anchor "spend 95 percent of our time concentrating on the content of the broadcast. What is counter-intuitive to me is that 95 percent of the reaction to the show is to us as individuals, and I think that is because of the time of day."

In 1989 *GMA* reached the top of the ratings for its time slot. It held that rank until 1994, when NBC's *Today Show* surpassed it. *GMA*'s problems became more serious in 1995, when responsibility for the show moved from ABC's news division to its entertainment division. During the three years following that change, *GMA*'s audience shrank by 25 percent, and profits dropped by over half. As J. Max Robins wrote for *TV Guide* (February 6, 1999), "In just a few short years, the show that had been a viewer habit as strong as black coffee had become (in the words of one longtime insider) 'a case story in how to destroy a franchise.' Once one of the most profitable shows in the industry, and one that had virtually reinvented its genre, *GMA* was undone by executive indecision and a vast misreading of audience tastes." In 1997, after 17 years as co-host, Joan Lunden left the show—at ABC's request, according to some sources. Gibson, reportedly eager for a change, said farewell on May 1, 1998, during a special two-hour *GMA* tribute to him that included reminiscences and comments "from individuals as disparate as Joan Lunden and Kermit the Frog," as John Anderson wrote for *Newsday* (May 4, 1998). During the next eight months, Gibson continued to work for ABC News, hosting *20/20* once a week and reporting for others among the network's news programs.

Neither Lunden's successor, Lisa McRee, nor Gibson's, Kevin Newman, won an enthusiastic response from viewers. With *GMA*'s ratings in a free fall, in late 1998 ABC took drastic measures, asking Gibson to return and pairing him with an ABC star—Diane Sawyer, one of the best-known women in prime-time news. In the first three months after Gibson and Sawyer took over, on January 18, 1999, ratings surged 23 percent. Gibson blamed the program's earlier decline on what Howard Kurtz, writing for the *Washington Post* (April 13, 1999), described as "some very bad management decisions"—particularly, an attempt to appeal to a younger audience; as Gibson put it to Kurtz, the network ordered that *GMA* be "dumbed down." Gibson and Sawyer placed more emphasis on hard news and made the program more focused, too, partly by adopting a more predictable format and also by reducing topic-hopping. In another change, designed to attract a live audience on the streets of New York, as the *Today Show* (located at Rockefeller Center) was doing, ABC moved *GMA* to a street-level studio in Times Square. It also devoted additional news-division resources to the program, after Gibson told ABC News president David Westin "that the show needed to go back to what it had been," as Gibson recalled to Robins. "The audience had rejected New Coke, and it was time to go back to Coke Classic." He added that he was referring to the structure and content of the show, not the on-air talent; as he said to Robins, "Kevin and Lisa were done a terrible disservice. The audience never had a chance to acclimate itself to them, and they were under enormous pressure. It showed up as this slightly dysfunctional relationship on the air." Gibson and Sawyer have emphasized coverage of front-page news on *GMA*.

Gibson's interview subjects have included such politicians as Boris Yeltsin, Nelson Mandela, Yasir Arafat, Ronald Reagan, Richard M. Nixon, Margaret Thatcher, and Mikhail Gorbachev; the baseball player Cal Ripkin Jr.; the *Washington Post*'s publisher Katharine Graham; and the evangelist Billy Graham. A great lover of the arts, Gibson has also interviewed the novelists John Irving, James Michener, Sue Miller, John Updike, and Salman Rushdie; the poet Maya Angelou; the playwright Edward Albee; the composer and lyricist Stephen Sondheim; and the trumpeter, composer, and conductor Wynton Marsalis. In November 1995, in one among what are widely considered his finest professional moments, Gibson interviewed Leah Rabin hours after the funeral of her husband, the assassinated Israeli prime minister Yitzhak Rabin; in another, during a week of live broadcasts from Saudi Arabia in 1990, shortly before the start of the Persian Gulf War, he celebrated Thanksgiving with U.S. troops. He was also praised for his reporting on the Oklahoma City bombing, in 1995, and its aftermath. In 1997 he covered the Academy Awards ceremony, held in Los Angeles, and interviewed the Oscar winners Billy Bob Thornton and Juliette Binoche. He earned plaudits for his June 1999 interview on the subject of gun control with President Bill Clinton, which took place about a month after two students shot to death 13 others and themselves in Columbine High School, in Littleton, Colorado. During the interview he grilled the president on what he indicated was Clinton's lack of leadership on gun-control legislation; in the heated exchange that ensued, Clinton revealed the intense frustration he had felt in trying to deal with the complicated, highly politicized issue of gun control. "Charlie Gibson is a phenomenal interviewer," Shelley Ross, *GMA*'s executive producer, said to Steven A. Holmes for the *New York Times* (June 5, 1999) soon after that broadcast. "He didn't want to go over the same old gun-control debate. The intention was to be provocative, insightful and in-depth. He opened things up and we could see how deeply the President feels on this issue."

In his conversation with Terence Smith, Gibson noted that people seek more television news than they did several decades ago. *GMA*, he pointed out, is "the first news for about an eight-hour period [of each day]. People keep up now more than they used to on what's going on during the day. The old days when we sat down with [the television news anchors] Frank Reynolds or Walter Cronkite or Huntley/Brinkley at 6:30 [p.m.], and that was our first exposure, those are gone." When many people wake up, he continued, "they want to know that Cleveland didn't blow up overnight, that essentially your rice bowl is safe, and then we give you sort of the daily rundown of news, of what you need to know for the day." While reporters and anchors specializing in hard news once dismissed the morning news shows as lightweight, television executives now allocate more resources to them than ever before. That is undoubtedly because on every network morning news shows generate more ad revenue than evening news or prime-time news magazines. In 2001 *GMA* earned $395 million in ad revenues for ABC, nearly as much as the *Today Show* ($405 million) and far more than CBS's *The Early Show* ($177 million). "There's no question that there's been a tremendous change of emphasis in the attention of the news department," Gibson told Mike McDaniel for the *Houston Chronicle* (May 2, 2002). "[Years ago] we would normally do rehashes of stories that ran the night before. Now, you go to [ABC's] *World News* [*Tonight*] meeting at 10 o'clock in the morning, and there's at least a mention of one or two stories that were on *Good Morning America*. It's a fact that *GMA* sets the agenda for the news day." Gibson, for his part, has gotten more comfortable with mixing hard news and entertainment. *GMA* is "a much more spontaneous broadcast" than it was when he started, he told Terence Smith. "It is off-script. It's basically what's going through your head at the moment, and what interests you, what do you find intellectually intriguing in the morning."

During the week of June 3–7, 2002, the *Today Show* ranked first in number of viewers (6.12 million), *GMA* second, with 4.32 million, and

CBS's *The Early Show* a distant third, with 2.42 million. Gibson has claimed that he doesn't pay much attention to the ratings, because he doesn't want considerations of viewers' opinions to affect decisions about whether particular stories should run or how they should be presented. "You really have to say, 'What's the broadcast we ought to be doing?' And try to do it," he told Smith.

Since 1999, with Diane Sawyer, Gibson has co-anchored *PrimeTime Thursday*, which offers a mixture of news and features. He has also participated in *GMA* regional bus tours around the country, where his favorite stops have been college campuses. He has engaged in occasional projects not connected with ABC-TV, such as hosting a 1990 PBS documentary, *Lucky Numbers*, about compulsive gambling, and two "American Agenda" specials for the ABC Radio Network. Gibson is generally well-regarded by those in the broadcast news business and the political establishment. Colleagues of his have told reporters that he rarely displays the fierce competitiveness that often plagues the industry, and that he shows more interest in ensuring the quality of the stories that air than in making a scoop himself. He is known on Capitol Hill as a fair and unbiased reporter.

Gibson and his wife, Arlene Joy Gibson, headmistress of the Spence School, in New York City, live in New Jersey. The couple have two grown daughters, Jessica and Katherine. Gibson's leisure activities include skiing and playing tennis. He has served as a member of the Michigan Journalism Fellows board of directors since 1988. In 1992 he earned the John Maclean Fellowship, awarded until recently to Princeton alumni "who have made a major contribution to American society." — K.E.D.

Suggested Reading: *Chicago Tribune* I p14 Aug. 1, 1987, V p1 Mar. 17, 1989; *Houston Chronicle* (on-line) May 2, 2002; *New York Newsday* II p9 Feb. 2, 1987; *New York Times* A p11 June 5, 1999; *Online NewsHour* Oct. 29, 1999; *Parade* p20 Feb. 7, 1988; *TV Guide* p37+ Dec. 5, 1987, with photo, p36+ Feb. 6, 1999, with photos; *Washington Post* D p9 May 12, 1987, C p1 Apr. 13, 1999; *Who's Who in America, 2001*

---

## Gonzales, Alberto R.

*Aug. 4, 1955– White House counsel*

*Address: The White House, 1600 Pennsylvania Ave., N.W., Washington, DC 20500*

Alberto R. Gonzales was one of the top Hispanic lawyers in Texas when, in 1995, George W. Bush, who was then governor of Texas, recruited him to join his staff as general counselor. In Gonzales, Bush felt that he had found a capable lawyer whose political outlook resembled his own and whose presence in the state capitol would show Hispanics that they were represented in their government. Over the next six years, Governor Bush named Gonzales to two other positions—Texas secretary of state and then Texas Supreme Court justice. After Bush became president-elect of the United States, in December 2000, he chose Gonzales to serve as White House counsel. In that post Gonzales is effectively the White House ethics officer—a job of particular importance in light of all the ethical problems that dogged the previous president, Bill Clinton, during his administrations. "There's an ethical component to what I have to do," Gonzales told Gregory Rodriguez for the *Los Angeles Times* (March 25, 2001). He added, "My charge is to make sure that we don't even approach the line of what some could consider unethical. . . . There will be some instances where something is very important to the president's agenda, and my job is to try and find a way to do it in a way that's legal."

Gonzales knows that what Chitra Ragavan, in *U.S. News & World Report* (March 12, 2001), termed his "meteoric rise" since 1994 can be attributed in part to his ancestry. "I know that I've been helped because of my ethnicity," he told Rodriguez. "But the bottom line . . . is that Hispanics should expect nothing more than an equal opportunity. For us to now say that we should be given an opportunity because of our ethnicity, irrespective of our competence, means that we'll be discriminating against someone else who doesn't happen to be Hispanic, which is the very thing that we've been screaming about for decades. . . . Per-

Reuters/Larry Downing

sonally, I'm not offended that race is a factor. But it should never be the overriding factor or the most important factor." Many political observers believe that Gonzales has a good chance of being nominated to fill a seat on the U.S. Supreme Court if a vacancy occurs during the Bush presidency.

Alberto R. Gonzales was born on August 4, 1955 in San Antonio, Texas. The second of the eight children of Pablo and Maria Gonzales, he grew up in Houston, Texas, in a two-bedroom house that lacked both hot water and a telephone. To support his large family, Pablo Gonzales worked two jobs. Alberto Gonzales has credited his father with teaching him the importance of what he has termed "self-responsibility." His father "never asked for help or a handout except from his brothers and sisters," he told Chitra Ragavan. Gonzales attended Houston public schools. After he graduated from high school, where he was an honor student, he served for two years in the U.S. Air Force. Thinking that he wanted to make flying his career, he then enrolled at the U.S. Air Force Academy, in Colorado Springs, Colorado. After two years there, he decided to pursue a career in law instead. He transferred to Rice University, in Houston, where he received a bachelor's degree in political science in 1979. He then attended Harvard Law School, in Cambridge, Massachusetts, where he earned a J.D. degree in 1982. That same year he moved back to Houston and became an associate at Vinson & Elkins, arguably the most powerful law firm in Texas.

While building a reputation as an outstanding lawyer, Gonzales also taught law for some years as an adjunct professor at the University of Houston Law Center. From 1985 to 1991 he sat on the board of directors of Big Brothers Big Sisters in Houston, and from 1989 to 1993 on the board of Catholic Charities in Houston. In 1990 he was elected president of both the Houston Hispanic Bar Association and the Houston Hispanic Forum. That year President George Herbert Walker Bush asked Gonzales to work with him, but the lawyer turned down the offer, "focusing instead on making partner in his law firm," according to Chitra Ragavan. Gonzales became the first member of a minority group to become a partner at Vinson & Elkins.

In 1995, the year the younger Bush began his first term as governor of Texas, he appointed Gonzales his general counselor. Gonzales told Chitra Ragavan that when he asked George W. Bush why he had chosen him for the position, the governor told him, "You first got on my radar screen back . . . when you turned down my old man for a job." As general counselor Gonzales advised Bush on a variety of matters, including the state's controversial application of the death penalty. Gonzales's successful efforts to get Bush excused from jury duty in 1996 also aroused controversy during the 2000 presidential race. When it was disclosed during the last week of the campaign that Bush had been arrested in 1976 for drunk driving, some in the media pointed out that, had he fulfilled his jury duty, Bush would have been forced to disclose his arrest at that time.

In 1997 Governor Bush appointed Gonzales secretary of state of Texas. In that job Gonzales helped conduct the state's dealings with Mexico and served as Texas's chief election official. In 1998 he launched a campaign to end the decline in voter turnout, by asking students to urge their parents to cast ballots. In the more than 80 Texas schools that Gonzales and members of his staff visited, they also informed students that lawmakers and others were making decisions that would affect students' own lives, and that although they were not yet old enough to vote, they could express their opinions on current issues by writing to legislators.

In 1998 Governor Bush was reelected. The following year he appointed Gonzales to the Texas Supreme Court. Gonzales knew that his ethnicity had been a factor in his selection, but he had no complaints, because he had no doubt that he was capable of handling the job and had not been chosen merely because he was Hispanic. Indeed, he thought the choice of a Latino was a wise one. "In a state so heavily Hispanic," he explained to Gregory Rodriguez, "it is important to have at the highest levels of government people who look like the citizens who are being served by that government, that have some affinity to the leadership of government. . . . People have confidence when they see people of their own color making decisions, particularly from the bench."

In his short stint on the Texas high court, Gonzales was generally perceived as a moderate conservative. "He was a very workmanlike judge who was not likely to rule on either extreme," a top legal conservative who is acquainted with Gonzales told Ryan Lizza for the *New Republic* (May 27, 2002). "The only philosophy of judging you can extract from his opinions is he's the quintessential judge who goes in and tries to figure out the law and applies it." At work, he took care to keep to himself his opinions as an individual. "If I do my job right as a judge," he told Rodriguez, "people should not be able to tell how I feel about an issue personally. Because what I'm supposed to do is try to discern, try to find out what the legislature intended when it passed that law and to apply that law irrespective of my own personal feelings about that law." His vote with the majority of the court to allow minors to have abortions without notifying their parents in some instances outraged many conservatives. Speaking of his views on abortion, he told Chitra Ragavan, "All I'll say about it is, how I feel about it personally may differ with how I feel about it legally. . . . [The right to an abortion is] the law of the land." He also voted with the majority in overturning a lower-court ruling allowing class-action lawsuits against the Ford Motor Co. to proceed. That decision upset liberals who felt that the court was placing the desires of political contributors above consumers' legal rights. Moreover, the organization Texans for Public Justice charged that the Texas Auto Dealers Association had made large political contributions to Gonzales (who planned to run for election to keep his seat on the court) and other Supreme Court justices after the case opened. During his tenure on the Texas Supreme Court, Gonzales voted with the majority 47 times in decisions that favored individuals over businesses and 38 times with the majority in opinions that ruled for businesses over individuals. In a case that encouraged many plaintiffs' attorneys, he opposed the court's more conservative members in siding with an injured motorist who successfully sued the Texas Department of Transportation.

In 2000 Gonzales was elected to his seat unopposed. Several weeks later the U.S. Supreme Court, after recounts of votes in Florida, ruled that George W. Bush had won the U.S. presidency. Soon afterward Bush announced his selection of Gonzales as White House counsel. "I understand how important it is to have a person who I can trust and whose judgment I trust to serve as the White House Counsel," Bush was quoted as saying by *ABCNews.com* (December 20, 2000, on-line). "[Gonzales] is a man who has only one standard in mind when it comes to ethics, and that is the highest of high standards." Texans for Public Justice objected to Bush's choice, one reason being that Gonzales, like other Texas Supreme Court justices, had accepted large contributions from the Halliburton Co., which Vice President–elect Richard B. Cheney had headed since 1995; Gonzales had then ruled in favor of the company in cases that came before the court. According to Texans for Public Justice, Halliburton had contributed a total of over $79,000 to the justices during the previous three election cycles. From 1993 to 2000, in five cases involving Halliburton, the Texas Supreme Court had either ruled in favor of the company or refused to hear an appeal of a lower court's favorable verdict for Halliburton. The organization also noted that Halliburton had been a client of Vinson & Elkins and that Gonzales had worked in the section of the firm that handled Halliburton's legal business. Despite the ethical questions raised by those facts, the naming of Gonzales as White House counsel aroused little controversy. In accepting the job, Gonzales became the first Hispanic-American to serve in that position.

Gonzales's duties include selecting and vetting judicial appointees, among them, possibly, nominees to the U.S. Supreme Court; advising on ethical matters; and interpreting the law for members of the executive branch. His legal team includes members of the conservative Federalist Society and attorneys who worked for Kenneth Starr when Starr served as the U.S. independent counsel who investigated the scandal involving President Clinton and the onetime White House intern Monica Lewinsky. "If we get into a fight," Gonzales told Chitra Ragavan, "I need someone who can go into battle with me, and protect this president and protect this White House. That's my job." Ever since Gonzales's White House appointment, many have speculated that Bush will nominate him to fill the next seat that becomes vacant on the U.S. Supreme Court. For his part, Gonzales told Ragavan that he doesn't "plan on being a candidate" for Supreme Court justice.

In early 2001 Bush and Gonzales came under fire from liberal groups protesting Bush's decision to end the American Bar Association's longtime semiofficial vetting of potential candidates for federal judgeships. "No outside group should have a quasi-official, preferential role in the nomination process," Gonzales told Gregory Rodriguez. In December 2001 the president and his counsel again angered liberals, as well as many members of Congress, by invoking executive privilege in turning down a congressional request for various Justice Department documents. The documents pertained to matters ranging from the FBI's handling of informants in Boston in the 1960s to investigations into possibly illegal fund-raising by former president Bill Clinton. "Disclosure to Congress of confidential advice to the attorney general regarding the appointment of a special counsel and confidential recommendations to Department of Justice officials regarding whether to bring criminal charges would inhibit the candor necessary to the effectiveness of the deliberative process by which the department makes prosecutorial decisions," Bush said in a statement drafted with the help of Gonzales. Republican representative Dan Burton of Indiana, the chairman of the House Committee on Government Reform and Oversight, condemned the White House's refusal to turn over requested documents, declaring, as quoted by the Associated Press (December 13, 2001) and transcribed by *Truthout* (on-line), "This is not a monarchy. The legislative branch has oversight responsibility to make sure there is no corruption in the executive branch."

Acting on the advice of Gonzales, Vice President Cheney invoked executive privilege in an attempt to withhold from the General Accounting Office (GAO), an arm of Congress, information related to meetings of the Cheney-headed energy task force that was convened by the White House early in the Bush presidency. The identities of those who participated in those meetings, and the nature of the discussions that took place, became of particular interest in the wake of the bankruptcy of the huge energy company Enron Corp., representatives of which had met with Cheney half a dozen times in connection with the task force, which developed the administration's energy policy. (Parts of the administration's energy policy explicitly reflected requests made by Enron, whose chairman at that time, Kenneth Lay, had contributed hundreds of thousands of dollars to Bush's presidential campaign.) On January 30, 2002 the GAO announced that it was suing the White House for access to the documents. In response to that action, which marked the first time in its 80-year existence that the GAO filed suit against the executive branch, White House spokesperson Ari Fleischer said, "The president will stand on principle and for the right of presidents and this president to receive candid advice without it being turned into a news release." Gonazles wrote and publicly defended President Bush's controversial executive order that placed the fate of suspected terrorists who were not U.S. citizens at the hands of military tribunals. In another case that was greeted with much criticism overseas as well as domestically, he advised Bush to refuse to grant prisoner-of-war status to Al Qaeda prisoners held at the U.S. military base at Guantanamo Bay, in Cuba.

Alberto Gonzales, called Al by those close to him and nicknamed "the Judge," is known to be cordial and unassuming. Among his many honors and awards are a 1997 Presidential Citation from the State Bar of Texas for his dedication to addressing the legal needs of the indigent. He was chosen as one of five Outstanding Young Texans by the Texas Jaycees in 1994 and as the Outstanding Young Lawyer of Texas in 1992. In 1993 he was given the Commitment to Leadership Award by the United Way. He was recognized as the 1999 Latino Lawyer of the Year by the Hispanic National Bar Association and was named one of the 100 most influential Hispanics in 1999 by *Hispanic Business.* Gonzales is an elected member of the American Law Institute; he served as a board trustee of the Texas Bar Foundation from 1996 to 1999, board director for the State Bar of Texas from 1991 to 1994, and president of the Houston Hispanic Bar Association from 1990 to 1991. From 1993 to 1994 he served as both a board director of the United Way of the Texas Gulf Coast and president of Leadership Houston, the latter of which, according to its Web site, identifies "emerging and existing leaders" with the goal of "enhancing the quality of life in the greater Houston area." Gonzales and his wife have three children. — G.O.

Suggested Reading: *ABCNews.com* Dec. 20, 2000; *Los Angeles Times* M p3 Mar. 25, 2001; *New Republic* p16+ May 27, 2002, with photos; *U.S. News & World Report* (on-line) Mar. 12, 2001

---

Courtesy of *billygraham.org*

## Graham, Franklin

*July 14, 1952– Evangelist; CEO of the Billy Graham Evangelistic Association; president of Samaritan's Purse*

*Address: Samaritan's Purse, 801 Bamboo Rd., Boone, NC 28607-8721*

On January 20, 2001 thousands of spectators and millions of television viewers around the globe watched as the evangelist William Franklin Graham III, known as Franklin, presented the invocation at the inauguration of George W. Bush as president of the United States on the steps of the Capitol. His father, Billy Graham, who had been selected for that honor—and had served in that capacity at eight earlier presidential inaugurations—had bowed out because of ill health. Two months earlier Franklin Graham had succeeded his ailing father as the chief executive officer of the half-century-old Billy Graham Evangelistic Association, one of the largest Christian organizations in the United States. Franklin Graham has also headed, since 1979, Samaritan's Purse, a human-welfare organization that distributes millions of dollars in aid in dozens of countries annually while spreading the gospel of Jesus Christ as conveyed in the New Testament. While Franklin Graham practices the same vocation as his father and even bears a striking physical resemblance to him, friends and critics alike emphasize that he is his own man.

"Ever since the Colonial era," Gustav Niebuhr and Laurie Goodson wrote for the *New York Times* (January 1, 1999), "America has had a pre-eminent preacher who played an unofficial role as national evangelist, preaching a simple message of repentance and salvation and drawing vast crowds in the process. For the last 50 years, that role has been filled by the Rev. Billy Graham." Starting in the late 1940s, Billy Graham brought respectability to an evangelical movement many had written off as being irrational and out of touch with modern life. With his charismatic presence and Bible-thumping, finger-jabbing preaching style, Billy Graham achieved the sort of popularity typically associated with actors and singers. Over the years Billy Graham has preached to more than 200 million people around the world; indeed, he wields such influence that he has sometimes been referred to as the "Protestant Pope." At the same time, he has managed to project a dignity and moral authority shared by few of his brethren: while he has consorted with a number of senators and every president since Harry S. Truman, his public image, in comparison with that of other politically prominent evangelical Christians (Jerry Falwell and Pat Robertson, for example), is surprisingly nonpartisan; his religious views tend toward the ecumenical (he has appeared alongside popes, rabbis, Buddhists, and African tribal leaders, among others); and in terms of behavior, he has remained squeaky clean, avoiding the sort of scandal that sullied the reputations of the televangelists Jimmy Swaggart and Jim Bakker.

In short, as his father's elder son and namesake, William Franklin Graham III had a lot to live up to, and since his birth in Asheville, North Carolina, on July 14, 1952, he has been held to high expectations. The fourth of his parents' five children, he has three sisters and a younger brother. His sisters Virginia, now Gigi Tchividjian, and Ruth "Bunny" Bell Graham McIntyre, have written books (the latter under her maiden name); they have also been "active in ministries of their own," as Wendy Murray Zoba wrote for *Christianity Today* (April 5, 1999). His sister Anne Graham Lotz, who also writes, founded AnGel Ministries in 1988 and has preached worldwide. The youngest sibling, Nelson, called Ned, is the president of East Gates International, an evangelistic/humanitarian organization that focuses on China.

Franklin Graham grew up with his siblings in Montreat, a northwestern North Carolina community, in a house custom-built by his parents on their 200-acre spread. (A biography posted on the Billy Graham Web site reports that Franklin was "raised in a log home in the Appalachian Mountains outside Asheville.") For more than two decades after his birth, Franklin Graham's struggle with his father's legacy took the form of rebellion. "Just because my father was Billy Graham," he told Jeffery L. Sheler for *U.S. News & World Report* (May 3, 1993), "I wasn't going to live the life everybody expected me to live." His willful streak emerged early, despite the efforts of his mother, the former Ruth Bell, to discipline him. He preferred hunting and riding his dirt bike to attending church services, and he started smoking as a child, puffing on discarded butts. His mother once tried to break that habit by forcing him to smoke a whole pack in a single sitting, but the boy persisted: as Graham wrote in *Rebel with a Cause: Finally Comfortable Being Graham* (1995), his autobiography, as quoted by David Van Biema in *Time* (May 13, 1996), "By the time I finished all 20, I must have vomited five or six times . . . but it gave me great satisfaction not to give in." By his teens Graham had acquired a taste for hard liquor and motorcycles, too. At the Christian boarding school on Long Island, New York, at which his parents enrolled him, he habitually defied authority; as he recalled to Van Biema, "Whatever was expected of the student body, I wanted to do the opposite. I got a kick out of staying one step ahead of the 'law.'" At age 19 he was expelled from a small technical college in Texas for keeping his date out overnight. (Graham, who had taken flying lessons, had piloted a small plane for the outing and then had gotten grounded by fog.)

Speaking of his rebelliousness, Graham told Laurie Goodstein for the *New York Times* (January 20, 2001), "I pretended to be a Christian. But Christ wasn't in my heart. I was interested in living for myself, doing things in my life that would bring pleasure to me." He told Van Biema, "I was afraid if I surrendered my life to Christ I'd have, like, spiritual handcuffs on me. I had this picture of this God in heaven who had, like, a big stick, and if I surrendered my life, he'd just wait for me to go to the left or right and clobber me." Still, Graham continued, "something was missing. There was that emptiness you can't explain. There wasn't that joy; there wasn't that fulfillment."

Graham spent his 22d birthday in Switzerland, at a conference attended by both of his parents. While taking a walk with him there, his father and mother confronted him about his wastrel behavior. "Your mother and I sense there is a struggle for the soul of your life," his father said, as Graham recalled to Elizabeth Kaye for *George* (June 1999). "You're going to have to accept Jesus Christ or reject him. We love you. Our home will always be open to you. But you have to decide. We pray that you'll make the right choice." Although Graham tried to shrug off the conversation, he found that he couldn't put it out of his mind. A short while later, in a hotel room during a trip to Jerusalem, he opened a Bible and his eyes landed on a passage from I Corinthians: "God is faithful. He will not let you be tempted beyond your strength, but with the temptation will also provide the way of escape, that you may be able to endure it." (Van Biema cited as the pivotal lines these from Romans: "There is therefore now no condemnation for those who are in Jesus Christ.") Experiencing an epiphany, Graham dropped to his knees. "God, I've sinned against you," he prayed, according to Kaye, "and I'm sorry. I'll give you my life. But you'll have to make something clean of it." Graham has said that he was born again that night through his unconditional surrender to God's will: "I had no idea what God would do with my life. And I didn't really care." (Although he has reformed, and no longer smokes or drinks, Graham's wild streak has flared up occasionally. In 1987, for example, neighbors called the local sheriff after Graham felled a tree with a machine gun; when a *New York Times* [July 12, 1998] reporter asked him how he had felt about using a gun for that purpose, Graham responded, "Oh, it's fun. But it's not the most economical way to do it. It took 720 rounds and each round was about 20 cents apiece. You could buy a good chain saw for that.") Also in 1974 he earned an associate's degree from Montreat College and, in the same year, got married. In 1978 he received a B.A. degree from Appalachian State University, in Boone, North Carolina.

Earlier, in 1975, not long after his religious awakening in Switzerland, Graham embarked on a two-month evangelical tour of China, Indonesia, and India with Bob Pierce, a family friend who directed Samaritan's Purse, a Christian aid organization. Harnessing his native derring-do for evangelical purposes, Graham accompanied Pierce to various global hot spots, where they delivered food, medicine, and spiritual counsel. According to the Samaritan's Purse Web site, "Franklin saw the poverty of pagan religions and the utter despair of the people they enslave. God had captured his heart for missions." In 1979, about a year and a half after Pierce's death, Graham assumed the leadership of Samaritan's Purse. The mission of the organization, according to its Web site, is to "help meet needs of people who are victims of war, poverty, natural disasters, disease, and famine with the purpose of sharing God's love through His Son, Jesus Christ." In one recent year, Samaritan's Purse distributed nearly $130 million in federal aid and private donations in more than 115 countries.

The combination of religious and humanitarian activities carried out by Samaritan's Purse in El Salvador after earthquakes struck there in January 2001 led David Gonzalez, writing for the *New York Times* (March 5, 2001), to question whether the organization's use of federal funds was breaching the wall between church and state. Samaritan's Purse responded by issuing a press release stating that "federal funds accounted for less than 3 percent of its budget [in 2000] and are never used to fund direct Christian ministry," as paraphrased by *Christianity Today* (April 23, 2001), a magazine published by the Billy Graham Evangelistic Association (BGEA). Nevertheless, as David Gonzalez reported in the *New York Times* (March 8, 2001), the U.S. Agency for International Development (USAID), an independent U.S. federal agency that had allocated money to Samaritan's Purse, warned the organization to avoid even the appearance that government funds were being used for religious purposes.

Although Franklin Graham unhesitatingly ministered to victims of disasters of one kind or another in many parts of the world, sometimes piloting a small plane over dangerous terrain, for years he was hesitant to step up to the pulpit and preach, despite the suggestion of his father and several of his father's colleagues that he had inherited a gift for evangelism. As he told Kaye, he long held the attitude that "God called my father to the world's big stadiums and called me to its ditches." Then, in November 1983, John Wesley White, an associate evangelist with BGEA, persuaded Graham to lead a small revival in Saskatoon, Saskatchewan. Graham's attempt to do so failed abysmally: when he came to the "invitation," the point in a revival at which the preacher asks members of the audience to step forward and accept Jesus, not a single person responded. "You can't be tentative and feeble and be an evangelist," White explained to Van Biema. "He gave the invitation. And there was nothing. I mean nothing." "Don't you *ever* ask me to do *that* again," Franklin told White afterwards. "I'm *not* Billy Graham!" After that experience, Graham stayed clear of the pulpit for several years. The next time he ventured in front of a crowd was at a 1989 revival in Juneau, Alaska—doing so once again at White's prompting. This time, Graham's preaching succeeded. On the second night, White recalled to Van Biema, "they packed the place, drunks and divorcés and prostitutes. He gave the invitation, and they poured down. It was a miracle, and he knew it." Thereafter, Franklin began allotting a 10th of his time to preaching. (He continued to devote the greater part of his energies to relief work.)

Meanwhile, questions about who would succeed Billy Graham as the head of the Billy Graham Evangelical Association persisted, especially after it was revealed that the aging Billy Graham suffered from Parkinson's disease. Although Franklin Graham was an obvious choice, both Franklin and Billy Graham have maintained that they never discussed the topic until 1995. As Franklin recalled to Van Biema, it was he who approached his father. "I said, 'Daddy, at some point you and I have to have a conversation about the future, because if you want me involved, you need to tell me. If you don't want me involved, then I need to know that too.' He just kind of nodded like, 'Well, yeah, maybe.'" Billy Graham's ambivalence may have been due to some BGEA board members' opposition to giving Franklin the reins of the organization. As William Martin, a biographer of Billy Graham, explained to Van Biema in 1996, "If someone had asked me several years ago if Franklin was the man to take over, honestly I would have said, 'Good luck!' I think there was some question as to whether someone without much crusade experience was going to be able to just step in as the embodiment of the organization that for close to 50 years had the No. 1 crusade evangelist."

In the summer of 1995, the issue of succession came to a head. One night before Billy Graham was scheduled to begin a crusade in Toronto, he collapsed and was hospitalized with a bleeding colon. Franklin was asked to step in, but his opponents in the BGEA vociferously objected and quickly located another evangelist to do the job. After Billy Graham recovered, he realized he could no longer skirt the issue. As Kaye reported, Billy Graham said to his son, "I don't have plans to step down, but if something were to happen to me . . . Will you accept the leadership if the board of directors okay it?" Franklin answered that he would, and on November 7, 1995, with his father's support, the board of directors named him first vice chairman, the second-highest rank in the organization. He succeeded his father as CEO and chairman of BGEA five years later.

In contrast to his father, who almost always appears in public in well-tailored suits, Franklin Graham often wears jeans, a leather jacket, and leather boots in an effort to appeal to younger generations, a large proportion of whom are more likely than their elders to associate informality with authenticity. (As Christine J. Gardner noted for *Christianity Today* [June 15, 1998], about 55 percent of those who "made decisions for Christ" in a recent crusade were under 18 years of age.) Franklin Graham's preaching style also differs from that of his father: whereas Billy Graham was known for prowling about the stage, pantherlike, Franklin Graham tends to be low-keyed and restrained, often remaining in one spot. While critics and even some friends have suggested that Franklin does not possess the same intellectual curiosity as his father, others point out that he may be better suited than the older man to a culture dominated by television and Hollywood.

Some commentators have observed that Franklin and Billy Graham diverge on more substantive points as well. Although Billy Graham told Gardner, "Franklin and I preach the same gospel, we approach it a little bit differently," Wendy Murray Zoba pointed out that Franklin Graham "seems to be communicating an understanding of the Christian life that is rooted in behavior and harks back to the belligerent fundamentalism that his father and his 'new evangelical' cohorts eschewed."

Although Franklin has refused to align himself officially with either the Democratic or the Republican Party, he is known to hold conservative Republican views on many issues, and he is a close friend of the Bush family. Franklin spoke at the 2000 Republican National Convention (according to Laurie Goodstein in the *New York Times* [January 20, 2001], he said that he would have addressed the Democratic Convention as well but was not asked). Graham's invocation at the 2001 presidential inauguration was conspicuous in that, in a departure from previous inaugural prayers, it explicitly invoked the name of Jesus. His concluding words ("We pray this in the name of the Father, and of the Son, the Lord Jesus Christ, and of the Holy Spirit. Amen.") and those of Kirbyjon Caldwell, the Methodist clergyman who gave the benediction ("We respectfully submit this humble prayer in the name that's above all other names, Jesus the Christ. Let all who agree say, 'Amen.'"), as well as the absence of representatives of any non-Protestant religions at the microphones, elicited concern in some quarters about religious exclusion. "The recent presidential inauguration . . . is an unfortunate example of how the links between politics and religion have become increasingly controversial and divisive even at a solemn national occasion supposedly shared by all Americans, not just Protestant Christians," A. James Rudin, the senior interreligious adviser for the American Jewish Committee, wrote for the Albany, New York, *Times Union* (February 3, 2001). "The sermons at the Capitol certainly excluded the godless in America," a *New Republic* (February 5, 2001) correspondent wrote. "'Now, O Lord, we dedicate this presidential inaugural ceremony to you,' Graham intoned. Who, precisely, is 'we'? Surely we—that is, the citizenry of the United States—dedicate this presidential inaugural ceremony, and every other one, to liberty, to equality, to democracy, to justice: not to beings but to principles." Graham also gave a 15-minute sermon at the inaugural prayer service held at the National Cathedral, in Washington, D.C., on January 21, 2001.

Controversy again surfaced around Graham in the wake of the September 11, 2001 terrorist attacks in New York City and Washington, D.C. In October, as reported by the *Christian Century* (December 12, 2001), a public-affairs publication not associated with BGEA, Graham described Islam as "wicked, violent and not of the same God" and as not "this wonderful, peaceful religion. When you read the Qur'an and you read the verses from the Qur'an, it instructs the killing of the infidel for those who are non-Muslim." When questioned in November by NBC, according to the same article, Graham declared, "It wasn't Methodists flying into those buildings, and it wasn't Lutherans. It was an attack on this country by people of the Islamic faith." Two days later he said, as quoted in the *Christian Century*, "It is not my primary calling to analyze Islam or any other religions, though I recognize that all religions have differences. In the past, I have expressed my concerns about the teachings of Islam regarding the treatment of women and the killing of non-Muslims, or 'infidels.' I do not intend to comment further." In response to Graham's stance, an editorial in the *Charlotte [North Carolina] Observer* (November 20, 2001) noted the many cruelties perpetrated through the centuries by followers of Christianity, and then declared, "Given the intolerant, aggressive, bloody history of people acting in Christ's name, you'd hope Christians would think twice before calling somebody else's religion 'wicked.'" Graham, for his part, pointed out that thousands of the millions of gift-filled shoe boxes that Samaritan's Purse would be sending overseas as part of Operation Christmas Child were destined for Afghanistan.

Graham angered Muslims and others again in August 2002, when he told an interviewer for WBT-AM radio, in Charlotte, North Carolina, that Muslims had not yet adequately apologized for the attacks, and that they should help compensate the victims' families. He has also criticized Islam in his latest book, *The Name* (2002), in which he wrote, as reported by the *Macon [Georgia] Telegraph* (August 15, 2002, on-line), "Islam—unlike Christianity—has among its basic teachings a deep intolerance for those who follow other faiths."

Graham's other books, in addition to his autobiography, include *Miracle in a Shoe Box* (1995) and *Kids Praying for Kids* (1998), about Operation Christmas Child; *Living Beyond the Limits: A Life in Sync with God* (1998); and, with Jeanette Lockerbie, *Bob Pierce: This One Thing I Do* (1983).

Graham lives in Boone, North Carolina, with his wife, the former Jane Austin Cunningham, and their youngest child, Jane Austin (called Cissie). They also have three grown sons—William Franklin IV (called Will), Roy, and Edward—and one grandchild. — P.K.

Suggested Reading: *Boston Globe* p17+ Feb. 11, 2001, with photo; *Christianity Today* p50+ Apr. 5, 1999; *George* p94+ June 1999, with photos; *New York Times* A p8 Jan. 20, 2001, with photo; *Time* p66+ May 13, 1996, with photos

Selected Books: *Bob Pierce: This One Thing I Do*, 1983; *Rebel with a Cause: Finally Comfortable Being Graham*, 1995; *Miracle in a Shoe Box*, 1995; *Kids Praying for Kids*, 1998; *Living Beyond the Limits: A Life in Sync with God*, 1998; *The Name*, 2002

---

Mario Tama/Getty Images

## Grasso, Richard

*1946(?)– Chairman and CEO of the New York Stock Exchange*

*Address: New York Stock Exchange, 11 Wall St., New York, NY 10005*

When Fred Vogelstein of *Fortune* (April 15, 2002) asked Richard Grasso how he approaches his job as chairman and chief executive officer of the New York Stock Exchange (NYSE), Grasso alluded to attributes some might associate with major players in the financial world. "In case you haven't gotten it, I don't have the face, I don't have the height, I don't have the blood," he told Vogelstein. "I don't have any of the right things, okay? So I'd better at least want to win." In 1968 Grasso began working at the NYSE—an open market where shares of ownership in corporations are bought and sold—as an assistant listings clerk. His election as chairman of the NYSE, in 1995, marked the first time in the 210- year history of the institution that a staff member had ever risen through the ranks to attain the top position. At the time he was elected, the NYSE, the oldest and most prestigious stock exchange in the world, was facing unprecedented competition from the Nasdaq stock market, the Internet, and electronic communications networks, and many felt that the exchange, with its antiquated floor-trading system, simply could not remain relevant. But through a series of initiatives and changes, Grasso has not only kept the NYSE competitive; he has enabled it to restake its claim as the premier stock exchange. So much of the NYSE's turnaround is attributed to Grasso that the abovementioned issue of *Fortune* dubbed him "The Man Who Saved the New York Stock Exchange." Grasso has attributed the exchange's continued success—and, by extension, his own—to the faith of the investors. "At the end of the day," Grasso told Ferdinand Protzman for the Hoechst Internet Forum (on-line), "a person's word is his bond. There has to be absolute trust in the integrity and openness of the market and we will do everything to maintain that. Trust is the cornerstone of our franchise."

Richard Grasso was born in about 1946 in Jackson Heights, in the New York City borough of Queens. His father left the family when Grasso was an infant, and thereafter his mother and three aunts raised him. Grasso's background was decidedly working-class; he has often joked, as reported by Keith Damsell in the *National Post* (June 8, 2000), that his family drew its wealth from "the oil, the rubber and airline industries," since they operated an Exxon filling station near New York's LaGuardia Airport. As a teenager Grasso worked part-time in a Queens pharmacy; next door was a brokerage office, where his boss, an enthusiastic stock-market investor, would follow his investments. As Grasso recalled to Protzman, "The pharmacist bought shares in companies he understood and he understood pharmaceuticals and basic infrastructure companies involved in things such as transportation. I learned about the market by sitting with him in that broker's office, watching the ticker tape and that is where I bought my first stock." That stock consisted of $1,000 worth of shares in an airline company bought with the savings from the 13-year-old's job. In 1966 Grasso enlisted in the U.S. Army; for two years he served as a personnel-management specialist. The year he was discharged, the 21-year-old Grasso enrolled in the accounting program at Pace University, in New York, which he left after three years. Also at 21 he accepted what he thought was a temporary job as an assistant listings clerk at the New York Stock Exchange, a position at the bottom of the exchange's organizational structure. Grasso told Protzman, "I always wanted to come to Wall Street. I actually always wanted to trade." (According to Vogelstien, Grasso—with his mother's encouragement—had set out to be a police officer, but he had failed the vision test.)

At the NYSE Grasso's enthusiasm quickly distinguished him from his peers. When he first joined the exchange, very few companies went public with new listings on the NYSE; in fact, all but three companies were listed on other exchanges before moving to the Big Board, as the NYSE is sometimes called. Seeing the need for a change, Grasso aggressively sought out initial public offerings (IPOs) to add to the exchange's roster. His initiative caught the attention of John J. Phelan, a 13-year veteran and future CEO of the NYSE. The two discovered that they had similar philosophies about the exchange and formed a professional bond. One of the first important projects in which Phelan included Grasso was a trading-policy compromise. In 1971 a federal panel had called for the merger of all exchanges. In response, Phelan and Grasso worked out an agreement with the other exchanges and brokerage houses in which their trading policies were made uniform, thus ensuring that trades were as fair and efficient as possible. As a result, the Securities and Exchange Commission (SEC) did not insist on a megamerger, instead establishing the National Market System. In 1973, in the midst of negotiations, Grasso was promoted to director of listings and marketing at the NYSE.

Another major change in which Grasso was involved was the implementation of the designated order turnaround (DOT) system, which enabled the exchange to handle the increase in trading volume that began in the 1970s. Through the DOT system, small trade orders were routed electronically, and floor brokers and specialists could be avoided altogether, thus saving time. Not surprisingly, those two groups vehemently opposed the new system. Grasso and Phelan convinced them that the change was necessary for the survival of the exchange, and that more orders, regardless of what route they took, translated into more work for them. Robert Birnbaum, a former president of the NYSE, told Jack Willoughby for *Institutional Investor* (November 1998) that without the efforts of Grasso and Phelan, the brokers and specialists "never would have accepted DOT. Phelan and Grasso both understand the marketplace and why orders go where they do. Most guys who run these exchanges don't understand the systems." By 1977 the DOT system was in place. That same year Grasso was promoted to vice president of corporate services. In 1980 Phelan was elected president and chief operating officer of the New York Stock Exchange, and in 1984, chairman and CEO. A year after becoming president, Phelan promoted Grasso to senior vice president of corporate services, thus marking his entrance into the upper echelons of the exchange's organizational hierarchy. A former senior NYSE executive told Willoughby, "I think what impressed [Phelan] was Grasso's amazing aptitude for public speaking. He could speak lucidly without preparation on pretty well any aspect of exchange policy or trading and come away remembering names and faces . . . he's on a first-name basis with literally everyone."

With the CEO of the NYSE for an ally, Grasso saw his career move forward quickly. In 1986 he became executive vice president of capital markets, and in 1988 president and chief operating officer (COO). When Phelan stepped down from his position as chairman, in 1990, Grasso seemed to many the obvious choice as his successor. Yet in spite of his marketing skills, vast knowledge of the exchange system, and powerful allies, Grasso was passed over in favor of William Donaldson. Donaldson's pedigree was impeccable: he had been the first dean of Yale University's graduate school of management, an undersecretary of state and special counsel in the administration of president Gerald R. Ford, and a founding member of the investment firm Donaldson, Lufkin & Jenrette. Many of the exchange's voting members felt that Grasso, a career exchange employee, lacked the breadth of experience required for the position. Nevertheless, he continued to rise through the ranks; in 1991, while continuing in his capacity as president and COO, Grasso took on the additional title of executive vice chairman of the exchange. Finally, in 1995, he was elected chairman and CEO. That occasion was the first in the history of the NYSE in which an exchange staff member had risen to the top position.

Grasso became CEO in the middle of one of the greatest bull markets—or economic booms—ever. On October 28, 1997 trading volume topped one billion shares for the first time in the history of the NYSE, and on March 16, 1999 the Dow Jones Industrial Average (DJIA) topped 10,000 for the first time. (The DJIA is an average calculated by computers, second by second, by adding the prices of 30 representative industrial stocks and dividing that sum not by 30 but by a figure adjusted to account for such factors as stock splits.) Yet the 1990s were also marked by increasing competition from the Internet, which allowed investors to buy and sell stock with no intermediaries or through other exchanges. The Nasdaq stock market became the NYSE's chief rival for new companies. The Nasdaq is home to many technology stocks, such as Microsoft, Dell, and Intel; during the Internet mania of that decade, when technology and dot-com stocks were outperforming those in more traditional sectors, the Nasdaq's place in the American and global economy became increasingly important; the NYSE competitor began advertising itself as "the stock market for the next one hundred years." In addition, all of the stocks listed on the Nasdaq were traded electronically, either through electronic communication systems (ECNs) or through market makers sitting at computers. The NYSE, by contrast, was the only exchange in the world that still relied on the floor-trading system, and all transactions were recorded on paper. Compared with the Nasdaq, the New York Stock Exchange seemed positively archaic. This perception had a direct impact on the marketplace: between 1996 and 2000, about 3,000 new companies listed on the Nasdaq; the Big Board added far fewer. Some exchange members, such as Merrill Lynch, began starting their own electronic markets, and some urged the NYSE to shut its floor down entirely.

Grasso knew that the NYSE needed to do things differently. As he remarked in a December 6, 1999 letter to the exchange's investors and listed companies, as quoted on *nyse.com*, "For the Exchange to remain at the center of the capital marketplace and, most importantly, to serve the investing public, reinvention is not an option, it is essential." The chairman was intent on maintaining the NYSE as an enterprise involving face-to-face contact on the trading floor, while also employing the latest technology. "A blending of human and technology in terms of providing services to customers, that's what this is about," he said, as reported by Alex Berenson in the *New York Times* (October 12, 2001). "Our model works. No alternative model works." In 2000 he instituted Network NYSE; under this new system, investors could either place orders the old way, via specialists and brokers, or electronically, sending orders directly to the Big Board. In addition, trades were now recorded via computer software rather than on paper, thus allowing orders to be processed faster. Grasso also facilitated the exchange's transition from a fractional to a decimal pricing system. Under the old system, prices were measured in units of one 16th of a dollar; buyers and sellers could thus trade in units no smaller than 6.25 cents. Under the new system, prices were measured in one-cent units, resulting in 100 possible trading increments rather than 16. In undertaking such a change, the exchange sought to make the prices of stocks more comprehensible to individual investors, to reduce the so-called bid-ask spread (the difference between the price a buyer is willing to pay for a share and the price the seller is asking for it), and to conform to international trading norms. Decimalization was first approved by the NYSE's board of directors in June 1997 and was fully implemented by January 2001. The changes initiated under Grasso's tenure paid off: in the 12 months beginning in mid-April 2000, the number of shares traded on the exchange increased by 19 percent, while those traded on the Nasdaq decreased by 6 percent, according to the *Industry Standard* (April 23, 2001).

Grasso changed not only the way the New York Stock Exchange did business, but also whom it did business with. While he continued to pursue large companies, he also actively courted individual investors. As he said in a 1998 speech at the Economic Club of Washington (an organization of business and professional leaders), as quoted on the club's Web site, "There is a common denominator that traces the Exchange's founding. If the smallest investor has been treated fairly and had the same opportunity to capture a transaction as the largest institutional user of our market, the NYSE mission has been achieved, and the public's confidence in the marketplace in the United States has been reinforced." One tactic in his efforts to reach small investors was to invite the public onto the trading floor. Starting in the mid-1990s, Grasso allowed television stations to broadcast from the floor every day; today 22 TV and radio stations regularly broadcast from the exchange. He also invited various celebrities and dignitaries to ring the NYSE's bell, thus turning the daily opening and closing of the market into a media event. Never before had the New York Stock Exchange been so much a part of American popular culture.

On September 11, 2001, when two hijacked airplanes crashed into the twin towers of the World Trade Center, in New York, trading on the New York Stock Exchange came to a halt. Although the exchange's headquarters and computers were unscathed, the communication networks used by the entire financial district suffered damage. Almost immediately following the attack, Grasso began insisting that the markets reopen as quickly as possible. In so doing, he hoped to send out two messages. The first, directed at the American people, was that the free-market system had not been crippled by the attacks. The second, aimed at the terrorists responsible for the attacks, was that they had not succeeded in shutting down the U.S. economy. In the days that followed the attacks, Grasso worked around the clock to get the markets up and running. "One of the things you must do is restore people's confidence," Grasso told Walter Hamilton for the *Los Angeles Times* (September 19, 2001). "As heinous a crime as this was, it's not going to stop America's way of life, and you want to remind people of that." Grasso emerged as a public figure in the days following the attacks and was applauded for his display of optimism, strength, and courage. "His performance demonstrated that he's the best chairman we've ever had," Michael LaBranche, the CEO of a New York trading firm, told Hamilton. On Monday, September 17, just six days after the attacks, the NYSE opened. "Welcome back to the greatest market in the world," Grasso said as he opened the floor for trading, as reported by Frank Pellegrini in *Time* (September 18, 2001, on-line).

On August 2, 2002 Grasso announced proposed changes in the NYSE's standards for companies listed with the exchange. The changes, which require the approval of the SEC, came in the wake of the corporate scandals that had unfolded in the first half of the year and the resulting blow to investor confidence in corporate America. The new rules specify that a majority of board members of companies listed on the exchange must have no financial connections to those firms.

Grasso has received several honorary degrees, including doctor of law degrees from the Fordham University School of Law and Pepperdine University's Graziadio School of Business, and doctor of commercial science degrees from New York University and Pace University. He is vice chairman of the National Italian American Foundation, chairman of the Economic Club of New York, and a member of numerous civic organizations, including the Yale School of Management advisory board, the Baruch College School of Business Advisory Council, and the National Advisory Board of the Leon and Sylvia Panetta Institute for Public Policy. He also serves as a trustee for the Centurion Foundation, the New York City Police Foundation, and the Stony Brook Foundation. He has helped to raise money for the Tomorrows Children's Fund, which supports research to find cures for cancers that strike young people. In February 2002 the *Wall Street Letter* awarded Grasso its Enterprise, Leadership and Achievement of Note Award, and Boston College recently honored him with the institution's President's Medal for Excellence. When asked by Ferdinand Protzman how it felt to have worked at the same place throughout his adult life, Gross replied, "You can't call this work, that's a fractious use of the word."

Grasso and his wife have four children—three daughters and a son. The couple live on Long Island, New York. — H.T.

Suggested Reading: *archive.hoechst.com*; *Economist* p60 July 31, 1999; *Financial Times* p10+ Aug. 5, 2002; *Forbes* p274+ Nov. 13, 2000; *Fortune* p168+ Apr. 15, 2002, with photos; *Institutional Investor* p40+ Nov. 1998, p42+ Jan. 2000; *Los Angeles Times* III p5 Sep. 19, 2001, with photos; *National Review* (on-line) Mar. 13, 2002; *New York Times* A p1+ Sep. 17, 2001, with photos

---

Courtesy of the Catholic Diocese of Belleville

## Gregory, Wilton D.

*Dec. 7, 1947– President of the U.S. Conference of Catholic Bishops*

*Address: Chancery Office, 222 S. Third St., Belleville, IL 62220*

On November 13, 2001 Bishop Wilton D. Gregory was elected by an overwhelming margin to a three-year term as president of the United States Conference of Catholic Bishops, thus becoming the first African-American to lead the nation's 285 active Catholic bishops. The election was widely hailed as a milestone for African-American Catholics, a population estimated at between 2 million and 3.5 million. (Nationwide, there are about 64 million Catholics of all ethnicities.) Gregory's election "means that the church, the body of bishops, recognizes the qualities and talents that are within the African-American community and are willing to use those talents and qualities for the betterment of the church," J. Terry Steib, the bishop of Memphis, Tennessee, told the Religion News Service, as quoted by Cathy Lynn Grossman in *USA Today* (November 14, 2001). "For African-American Catholics it [is] almost equivalent to having an African-American president of the United States . . . ," Diana Hayes, a black Catholic and Georgetown University theologian, said shortly before Gregory's election, as quoted by the Associated Press (October 4, 2001). "It will mean recognition of the authenticity of their presence."

Thus far Gregory's presidency has been dominated by the sex-abuse scandal that rocked the Catholic Church in 2002. As scores of people have come forth claiming to have been abused by priests, and as church officials have admitted to covering up the crimes of the abusers, Gregory has drawn high praise for dealing with the crisis openly and honestly. He was one of the first clergymen to publicly call abuse a crime instead of a moral weakness that might be cured through prayer and religious counseling. He was also among the first to issue a public apology to the victims of abuse and to the laity. In dealing with the uproar, he has made his first priority the safety of children rather than the protection of the reputations of fellow clergymen or the maintaining of Catholic traditions. "Child abuse is a very devastating part of society, and so it's unpleasant to face this crisis," Gregory told Pat McCloskey for the *St. Anthony Messenger* (November 2002, on-line). "But it is such an important issue and so many people have been harmed as children and then carry those scars with them that, as a Church, we must shine light on these situations."

Shortly after his election, Gregory told reporters, as quoted in the *Christian Century* (November 21, 2001), "The Catholic Church, because we are a universal church, is no stranger to cultural, racial or language diversity. What may be new is the proportion and the number and the nations from which they are coming." The bishop is known for promoting the view that racism is a sin that is as bad as other, traditionally recognized sins. He has named racial profiling and white flight from urban schools as two of the nation's most pressing social ills, and has written that "all baptized Catholics have an obligation to move toward the elimination of racism," according to the Associated Press (October 4, 2001). In addition, Gregory is known for his extensive writings expressing opposition to euthanasia, physician-assisted suicide, and the death penalty.

The son of Wilton Gregory, a computer technician, and his wife, Ethel, Wilton D. Gregory was born on December 7, 1947 in Chicago, Illinois. Both of his parents were Protestants. Gregory told reporters that he first considered a vocation in the church at the age of 11, when, as a student in a Catholic school on Chicago's South Side, he was deeply influenced by two parish priests. By age 12 Gregory had decided to follow in the older men's footsteps, and in 1959 he was baptized as a Catholic at a parish Easter Vigil Mass. He received further education at the Quigley Preparatory Seminary South and Niles College of Loyola (now St. Joseph's Seminary), both in Chicago, and St. Mary of the Lake Seminary, in Mundelein, Illinois. In 1973 Gregory earned a master's degree in pastoral theology from the last-named institution; on May 9 of that year, he was ordained a priest of the Archdiocese of Chicago.

For the next three years, Gregory served as a parish priest in Glenview, Illinois, outside Chicago. In 1976 he began studies at the Pontifical Liturgical Institute of San Anselmo, in Rome; four years later he received a doctorate in sacred liturgy there. He then returned to St. Mary of the Lake as a seminary professor.

On December 13, 1983 Gregory was ordained a bishop; at 36, he was the youngest Catholic bishop in the United States. For about 10 years he served under Joseph Cardinal Bernardin as auxiliary bishop of Chicago. Then, in February 1994, Pope John Paul II installed him as the bishop of Belleville, a diocese in southern Illinois with about 105,000 parishioners.

In November 1998 Gregory was elected vice president of the National Conference of Catholic Bishops (NCCB). (On July 1, 2001 the NCCB was combined with another ecclesiastical organization, the United States Catholic Conference, to form the United States Conference of Catholic Bishops.) His election marked the first time that an African-American prelate was chosen to fill one of the organization's top two administrative posts. Bernard Cardinal Law, the archbishop of Boston, told Gustav Niebuhr for the *New York Times* (November 18, 1998) that Gregory "was elected on his own merit, but given that he is an African-American, it's a wonderful moment in the history of the church." "I hope it's a sign of the church's honest and sincere desire to include African-Americans at all levels of leadership and at all levels of the church," Gregory told reporters, as quoted by Niebuhr. After three years as vice president, Gregory won the presidency of the conference.

Gregory is currently grappling with what has been described as the worst crisis in the history of the Catholic Church: the sex-abuse scandal involving priests and young parishioners. In March 2002, in one of the most widely publicized cases, John Geoghan, a priest from the greater Boston area, was convicted of sexually abusing a young boy in 1991. Documents showed that Boston's archdiocese had known that Geoghan sexually abused children for more than three decades, yet he was not defrocked until 1998. Prior to that, church authorities had moved him from parish to parish, where over 200 people have accused him of abusing them sexually. Public outrage prompted Cardinal Bernard Law, the archbishop of Boston, to issue an apology and turn over to prosecutors the names of 90 priests who had been accused of molesting children over the past 50 years. As a result, many other dioceses across the nation were forced to admit that they, too, had covered up allegations of sexual abuse by moving priests from one parish to another. Gregory himself has called the scandal the worst crisis in the Church's history, because, as he explained to Marguerite Michaels for *Time* (June 17, 2002, online), "it cuts at the heart of the very fabric of the church. That is a fiduciary relationship. . . . To lose the trust of your people is to lose perhaps your most valuable ministerial tool. How can you witness the mystery of Jesus in his church to people who don't believe you? And they don't believe you because you violated the trust they had with you—that you wouldn't harm their children."

In April 2002 Gregory and Bishop William S. Skylstad, vice president of the U.S. Conference of Catholic Bishops, met with the Pope and other Vatican officials in Rome to discuss the escalating crisis. Gregory and Skylstad talked about the gravity of the situation and the need for a swift response. After returning to the States, Gregory gave a press conference in which he answered questions about the issue publicly, marking the first time since the scandal had erupted that an official had done so. It was also the first time an official had admitted that the Catholic Church had not handled some of the sexual-abuse cases well. Gregory said that the Vatican was leaving the abuse issue to the American Church to handle. Within 48 hours, however, Vatican authorities reversed their position and summoned all 13 U.S. cardinals and the leaders of the American bishops to Rome to discuss the situation, thereby acknowledging its seriousness. At the meeting, the Vatican issued a set of proposals for handling the sexual abuse cases, but they were unclear and left much to be decided at the annual meeting of the Conference of Bishops, which was to be held in June.

At that meeting, Gregory laid the blame for the abuse not on those who had perpetrated the crimes, but on the bishops themselves. "We are the ones, whether through ignorance or lack of vigilance or, God forbid, with knowledge, who allowed priest abusers to remain in ministry and reassigned them to communities where they continued to abuse," he told the bishops, as quoted by Laurie Goodstein in the *New York Times* (June 14, 2002). The bishops at the conference adopted a zero-tolerance policy, meaning that any priest who sexually abused a minor or was found to have done so in the past would be barred from ministerial duties. They also agreed to inform civil authorities of any alleged abuse. "From this day forward no one known to have sexually abused a child will work in the Catholic Church in the United States," Gregory said, according to the *New York Times* (June 15, 2002). "We bishops apologize to anyone harmed by one of our priests, and for our tragically slow response in recognizing the horror of sexual abuse." (In October 2002 the Vatican rejected the policy that had been proposed by the bishops the previous June and demanded that they rewrite parts of it so as to comply with Church laws.) Although had he acknowledged his role in helping to steer the Church through a period of change, Gregory has rejected the idea that he is a reformer. "The church is always going through some type of reform, and if I can be of assistance, then I'm pleased," he told Jeffrey L. Sheler for *U.S. News & World Report* (October 14, 2002). "But to say a 'reformer' like I have a plan? No."

Gregory's résumé includes service as chairman of the Bishops' Committee on the Liturgy and as a member of the Committee on Doctrine, the Ad Hoc Committee on Sexual Abuse, and the Committee on International Policy.

Gregory's parishioners and fellow clergy have characterized him as humble and approachable and as a gifted public speaker. According to Thomas Reese, the editor of the Jesuit magazine *America*, he is "very personable." "He knows how to build coalitions and how to count votes, even on a hot seat like the liturgy committee," Reese told Grossman. "He's the kind of man who may be the first black cardinal from the U.S. some day." — P.K.

Suggested Reading: *Christian Century* p14 Nov. 21, 2001, with photo; *Houston Chronicle* p4+ Nov. 14, 2001, with photo; *Jet* p35 Dec. 3, 2001, with photo; *St. Louis Post-Dispatch* A p2 Nov. 14, 2001, with photo; *USA Today* D p10 Nov. 14, 2001, with photo

---

## Grohl, Dave

*Jan. 14, 1969– Singer; songwriter; musician*

*Address: c/o Nasty Little Man Public Relations, 136 Church St., Third Fl., New York, NY 10007*

"Rarely in the history of rock has a musician switched bands and instruments simultaneously with such a high degree of success as Dave Grohl," Greg Prato declared in a brief profile of Grohl for the *All Music Guide* (on-line). For more than three years, beginning when he was 21, the singer, songwriter, and instrumentalist played drums for one of the most celebrated bands of the 1990s: the Seattle, Washington–based rock phenomenon Nirvana. With its new sound, dubbed "grunge"—a mixture of punk rock and heavy metal—Nirvana was widely credited with transforming the world of popular music. After the suicide of Kurt Cobain, the band's lead singer and songwriter, in 1994, Nirvana broke up. Less than a year later, driven by his passion for music and his determination to "keep moving," in his words, Grohl formed his own rock group, Foo Fighters. Whereas with Nirvana he had been a drummer exclusively, with Foo Fighters Grohl has served as lead vocalist, songwriter, and guitarist. Of Foo Fighters' original members, only Grohl and the guitarist Nate Mendel remain. Currently, their bandmates are the drummer Taylor Hawkins (who succeeded William Goldsmith in the Foo Fighter roster) and the bass guitarist Chris Shiflett (who replaced Franz Stahl, who came after Pat Smear departed). The turnover notwithstanding, Foo Fighters has enjoyed much critical and popular success. Each of the band's three albums—*Foo Fighters, The Colour and the Shape*, and *There Is Nothing Left to Lose*—has sold more than a million copies, and *There Is Nothing Left to Lose* won a Grammy Award for best rock album in 2000. The band's video "Learn to Fly" also won a Grammy Award, in the same year. A number of Foo Fighter singles, too, have been Top 10 hits, among them "Big Me," "Monkey Wrench," "Everlong," "Learn to Fly," and "My Hero." "Essentially," Adam Howorth wrote for the London *Times* (December 19, 2000), after attending a concert by the group in England,

M. B. Charles/Retna Ltd.

"[Foo Fighters'] secret is to take the misery out of the Nirvana formula and put a Disney face on it." The band maintains a busy concert schedule and has often appeared on television on the *Late Show with David Letterman*. Writing in 2000, Adam Howorth declared, "Foo Fighters are the greatest rock band on the planet." Using another superlative, Wendy Case wrote for the *Detroit News* (November 3, 2000), "Witty, talented and instantly likeable, Foo Fighters frontman Dave Grohl is the coolest guy in rock 'n' roll at a time when rock 'n' roll is having a hard time being cool at all."

Born on January 14, 1969 in Warren, Ohio, David Eric Grohl grew up with his sister in Springfield, Virginia, a suburb of Washington, D.C. His parents divorced when he was seven; afterward, Chris Mundy wrote for *Rolling Stone* (October 5, 1995), he remained on good terms with both his father and his mother, who lived near each other. At age 10 he was given a guitar and began teaching himself to play by ear. "Sitting on the couch watching TV," Grohl recalled to Eric Brace for the *Washington Post* (September 28, 1997), "I'd always have [my guitar] in my hands, and my mom was like, 'Put down that guitar and do your homework!'" Using a portable phonograph that his mother, a teacher, would borrow from her school, Grohl would "play along with records," as he told Brace, accompanying music by such heavy-metal groups as Led Zeppelin and Black Sabbath and such punk bands as Black Flag and the Stooges. He began training himself in drumming, too, by setting up pillows on his bed and pounding away at them with a pair of oversized marching-band drumsticks. He told Brace, "That's where I learned to hit so hard, beating on the pillows with those huge sticks." Soon after he acquired his first drum kit, when he was about 15, he began playing drums in several local punk-rock bands, among them Freakbaby, Mission Impossible, and Dain Bramage. His performances with Mission Impossible impressed Dante Ferrando, a Washington, D.C., nightclub owner and drummer; as Ferrando said of Grohl to Brace, "He was pretty young, and the stuff he was playing was simple, but he did it with so much power and precision. I remember someone telling me he'd only been playing live about eight months, and could I believe it? I was envious because I'd been playing for years and couldn't play like that." One day when Grohl was 17 and a senior in high school, he learned from a flier in a local record shop that Scream, his favorite band, was looking for a new drummer. After telling the Scream front man, Pete Stahl, that he was 20, Grohl secured an audition. He expected nothing more than bragging rights for having "jammed" with his idols, but Stahl and his bandmates offered Grohl the job. Unwilling to forgo the opportunity of accompanying Scream on its upcoming tours, Grohl dropped out of school.

While Scream never landed a major record deal, the four years that Grohl spent with the band benefitted him greatly. As he told Eric Brace, "When Pete found out my real age and that he was 10 years older than me, he became my father figure. We'd be on the road for months in a van, and he'd be teaching me how to behave on the road, how to survive without burning out, how to have fun, when to be serious." In mid-1990 Scream's bassist, Skeeter, quit in the middle of a nationwide tour, leaving the three other band members stranded in Los Angeles without any money to get home. While wondering what to do, Grohl received a phone call from Nirvana—then a little-known Seattle, Washington–based band—which was in dire need of a drummer (five had come and gone in the three years since its debut). Nirvana's two founding members, Kurt Cobain and Krist Novoselic (his first name appears as "Chris" on some recordings), had hoped to recruit Grohl after hearing him play at a Scream concert sometime earlier. In August 1990 Grohl flew to Seattle and joined Nirvana. For a short time afterward, Nirvana toured England with the all-female band L7.

In 1991, with Grohl at the drums, Nirvana released *Nevermind*, its second album (and first on a major label—Geffen Records). Within about a month *Nevermind* had reached number 35 on *Billboard*'s Top 200 album chart; by January 1992 it had knocked the pop king Michael Jackson's *Dangerous* from the top of the charts. To date, more than 10 million copies of *Nevermind* have been sold. Many observers believe that the album triggered a sea change in popular music. "There was definitely a pre-*Nevermind* and post-*Nevermind* music industry," Carrie Borzillo, the author of *Nirvana: The Day-by-Day Eyewitness Chronicle* (2000), told Renee Graham for the *Boston Globe* (September 30, 2000). "After the album came out and exploded, record companies weren't just scrambling to go into Seattle, but any other little scene where they thought they would find the next Nirvana. . . . And [*Nevermind*] completely changed radio. You never had these grungy-sounding, low-fi bands on commercial, mainstream pop radio. Suddenly, alternative radio formats really blossomed, and became more important than ever." Thanks to the album's success, Grohl and his bandmates became rich. "I went from having no money at all . . . to being set up for the rest of my life," Grohl told David Fricke for *Rolling Stone* (September 13, 2001). And whereas before *Nevermind* Nirvana had played to crowds of a hundred at bars and nightclubs, the band now performed in front of thousands. Soon it was filling stadiums overseas as well as in the U.S. and touring virtually nonstop. "One of the greatest feelings about 1991," Grohl told Chris Mundy, was that "we had no idea what was going to happen. The *Nevermind* tour just felt like everything was going to pop. I'd have numerous panic attacks every day. I mean, sweating, heart-pounding, have-to-sit-down panic attacks. It was so cool to be that close to going insane yet somehow not. I really thought every time I sat down on the drum stool that it would be the night where I fainted onstage. It was all so hilarious. It wasn't supposed to happen, but it did. One of the saddest things is that it can never happen again, but the greatest thing is that it did."

Nirvana's next recording, *Incesticide* (1992), offers what a reviewer for *CD Now* (on-line) described as "B-sides, one-offs and hard-to-find singles." It was followed by *In Utero* (1993), which contains the popular tracks "Heart-Shaped Box" and "All Apologies." The words and music for all but one of *In Utero*'s songs were composed by Cobain alone (the exception, "Scentless Apprentice," is credited to Novoselic and Grohl as well as Cobain). Grohl himself had been working on his own songs for several years; his cassette tape *Pocketwatch*, released in 1991 on the Simple Machine Records label, consists of songs he recorded in the basement studio of his friend Barrett Jones, a producer, toward the end of his association with Scream, and songs recorded with Geoff Turner, at WGNS Studios in Arlington, Virginia. Nevertheless, Grohl was relegated to a supporting role in Nirvana. By his own account, he sometimes felt frustrated, but he told Fricke in 2001 that not being "the focus of all the attention" was "one of the good things about being the drummer in Nirvana"; as he explained, "I got to sit back and discover what the pitfalls were, because none of them happened to me." Grohl was the featured drummer on the soundtrack of Iain Softley's film *Backbeat* (1993), about the Beatles' pre-stardom experiences in Hamburg, Germany.

In March 1994 Cobain attempted to take his own life, by swallowing a mixture of tranquilizers and alcohol. The next month, after disappearing from the recovery center to which he had been admitted, he killed himself with a gunshot to the head. In the deluge of media questioning that ensued, Grohl remained tight-lipped. As he explained to Chris Mundy, "I understand that people want to know [about Cobain's suicide], but there has to be a line drawn because the day after your friend dies and *American Journal* wants to talk to you and Diane Sawyer wants to do an interview. . . . It made me so [expletive] angry. It made me so angry that nothing was sacred anymore. No one could just stop not even for a day or a year or the rest of our lives, and just shut the [expletive] up. So I decided that I was just going to be the person to shut the [expletive] up."

Grohl also told Mundy, "I think about Kurt every day, and I miss him. . . . But at the same time things keep going, and I've got to make sure that things keep moving for me. . . . I have to feel like I'm moving forward." Grohl spent part of the latter half of 1994 touring with the singer/songwriter Tom Petty and his band, the Heartbreakers. He seriously considered Petty's offer of a full-time position with the band. "I was this close to joining," he told Mundy. "It was so much fun. . . . But I figured that I was 26 years old and didn't want to become a drummer for hire at the age of 26." Instead, Grohl began working in a professional studio with Barrett Jones, recording on tape cassette 15 of the many songs Grohl had written over the course of the previous six years. "It was just something I decided to go in and do because it was time to finally do something . . . ," he explained to Mundy. "I saw it as an exercise or a release to see what I can accomplish on my own." Except for a single guitar refrain provided by Greg Dulli of the Afghan Whigs, Grohl played every instrument used for the recording and sang every vocal track. Grohl completed the tape within one week in October 1994. The tape "became the object of a fierce record company bidding war," as Stephen Thomas Erlewine wrote for the *All Music Guide* (on-line).

Rather than release the tape as a solo album, Grohl decided to present it to the public as a group effort. With that in mind, he recruited the bassist Nate Mendel and the drummer William Goldsmith from the Seattle band Sunny Day Real Estate, as well as the guitarist Pat Smear, who had become the fourth member of Nirvana shortly before its demise. Thus the first incarnation of Foo Fighters came into being. (The expression "foo fighters" refers to the mysterious fireballs that a number of fighter pilots—some flying for the Allies and others for the Axis powers—reported seeing occasionally in the skies over Europe during World War II. "Foo," some sources suggest, is a distorted pronunciation of the French word for fire, "feu.") The band performed publicly for the first time in February 1995, at the Jambalaya Club in Arcata, California. Its debut album, called *Foo Fighters* (even though none of the members of the band except Grohl was represented on it), was released in the summer of 1995 on Grohl's own newly created label, Roswell Records, licensed to Capital Records in Los Angeles. The album earned critical praise, much of which, to Grohl's satisfaction, included admiring comparisons to the work of Nirvana. "Of course [Cobain] was an influence," Grohl told Eric Brace. "Everyone I've ever played with is an influence." Even before the appearance of the album, Foo Fighters had begun touring extensively, and after it came out, they continued to perform, in Europe, Australia, Japan, and North America. By 1997 *Foo Fighters* had sold more than a million copies. Sales were boosted when the music cable channel MTV aired the associated video "Big Me," which included all the members of Foo Fighters. A parody of a Mentos candy commercial, it earned the 1996 MTV Video Award for video of the year.

In early 1997 Goldsmith left Foo Fighters, due to artistic differences with the band. He was succeeded by the drummer Taylor Hawkins, who had previously played for the singer/songwriter Alanis Morissette. Foo Fighters' second album, *The Colour and the Shape*, was released in May 1997. "None of us were blind to the fact that people wanted to pay attention to us [because of Nirvana]," Grohl told Wendy Case in 2000. "That's why we didn't take too much time before the first and second records. We didn't want people to think it was a side project. It took a few years, but I think, finally, people see us as a legitimate rock force." According to a *New Music Express* (on-line) reviewer of *The Colour and the Shape*, "Grohl has the knack of slamming out a perfect, naggingly insidious tune every bit as good as any" written by his "illustrious predecessors," among them the Beatles, the Beach Boys, the Pixies, and, of course, Nirvana. "Grohl sounds blazingly optimistic . . . ," the *New Music Express* critic wrote. "*Foo Fighters* is not the sound of mourning, it is of liberation, of an almost obscenely talented man at last gaining the confidence and wherewithal to seize control of his own artistic destiny. Great bands are rare enough. Great spin-offs of great bands are scarcer still. Foo Fighters are one really worth celebrating." Soon afterward Pat Smear quit the band, reportedly because he found the group's tour schedule too exhausting; Grohl replaced him with the former Scream guitarist Franz Stahl. (During the same period Grohl composed the soundtrack for Paul Schrader's film *Touch.*) *The Colour and the Shape* had reached the Top 10 on both sides of the Atlantic by the time Foo Fighters launched their next world tour, in September 1997. The following month they opened for the Rolling Stones at two concerts.

In 1999 Grohl moved to Virginia from Los Angeles, where he had settled half a dozen years earlier. "I've always been very close to my family and friends, and that's where they all are," he explained to Mark Jenkins for the *Washington Post* (July 7, 2000). Grohl recorded Foo Fighters' third album, *There Is Nothing Left to Lose*, in a studio he had had built in his Virginia home. The disk, released in the fall of 1999, was made without Stahl, who had left the band shortly before Grohl's relocation. In a review of *There Is Nothing Left to Lose* for *Rolling Stone* (November 15, 2000), Matt Hendrickson described the album as "the Foos' best and most cohesive to date, a breezy collection of gnarly rockers and warm ballads." A reviewer for *The Rough Guide to Rock* wrote of the album, as quoted on *Amazon.com*, "Grohl and his two cohorts prove themselves to be tectonic giants in their own right. . . . The album throbs with confidence and maturity, with catchy numbers like 'Learn to Fly' and 'Gimme Stitches' standing out in a way that Foo Fighters' songs never have before. With effortless control, these compositions chop and snarl, gliding from anthemic grunge to country ballad. There are no surprises, but who needs surprises when the familiar is this refined?" Writing for *Amazon.com*, Adem Tepedelen, too, labeled the album "refined," and reported that he had found Grohl's vocals "increasingly sugar-sweet"; he concluded, "Even though the Foo Fighters' latest is seductively sweet in sound, there are just enough rough edges and lyrical angst to keep things interesting." Stahl's replacement, the guitarist Chris Shifflet, performed with the band on the tour that followed the release of *There Is Nothing Left to Lose*. In mid-December 1999 the album was certified platinum (one million copies sold). *There Is Nothing Left to Lose* won the 2000 Grammy Award for best rock album, and "Learn to Fly" earned the 2000 Grammy for best video, short form.

Grohl gives his attention to a variety of other musical projects in addition to Foo Fighters. In 2001 he initiated Probot, a collaborative project that sprang from his long-standing love of heavy metal. Somewhat to his surprise, some famous heavy-metal artists accepted his invitation to join him on the project. "I consider myself such a stupid, middle-of-the-road, alternative-rock idiot, I thought most of these people would be like, 'No, he's a dork' or 'No, he's a jerk,'" Grohl told Joe D'Angelo for *MTV.com* (January 29, 2001). "But they all agreed to do it." As of late October 2002, the completed album had not yet been released. Also in 2001, after speaking with favor about the heavy-metal band Queens of the Stone Age, Grohl contributed to the band's third album, *Songs for the Deaf* (2002), and toured with them as well.

On October 22, 2002 Foo Fighters released their fourth record, *One by One*. In *Entertainment Weekly* (October 23, 2002, on-line), after noting that *One by One* is "densely packed with glum song titles ('Tired of You'. . . , 'Disenchanted Lullaby'), grinding beats, and moaned vocals," David Browne wrote, "The result? Unexpected exhilaration."

Foo Fighters have contributed to the soundtracks to *Scream 2* (1997), *Godzilla* (1998), *X-Files Movie* (1998), *Mission: Impossible 2* (2000), and *Me, Myself, and Irene* (2000), among other films. In 2002 the band performed at a concert to raise funds for the Musicians' Assistance Program (MAP), which helps musicians fight their addictions to drugs or alcohol. (Taylor Hawkins is among those who have benefitted from MAP's programs.) The band's other public-service activities include attempts to increase awareness of alternative treatments for AIDS-related illnesses.

"So many bands get caught up in looking cool," Grohl told Richard L. Eldredge for the *Atlanta Constitution* (June 7, 2000). "That's definitely not [Foo Fighters]. I like demystifying the whole rock-star thing. We're just your normal next-door barbecuing neighborhood geeks. I know I'm cool, and that's enough." Referring to interviews, videos, and other extra-musical distractions, Grohl told Wendy Case, "We don't take all of the external stuff very seriously. We take our music very seriously. But . . . any of the stuff that's outside the music-making process we just kinda laugh at. We're really lucky to have the success that we do, but rock music is not the most important thing in the world. There's a lot more to life than this." Grohl's honors include induction into the Washington, D.C., Area Music Hall of Fame, in February 2002. His three-year marriage to the former Jennifer Youngblood, a photographer, ended in divorce in 1997. — J.H.

Suggested Reading: *Boston Globe* K p1 Sep. 30, 2001, with photos; *Detroit News* C p1 Nov. 3, 2000; Foo Fighters Web site; New Music Express Web site; *Rolling Stone* p40 Oct. 5, 1995, p75+ Sep. 13, 2001, with photos; *Washington Post* G p1 Sep. 28, 1997, with photos, WW p13 July 7, 2000

Selected Albums: *Foo Fighters*, 1995; *The Colour and the Shape*, 1997; *There Is Nothing Left to Lose*, 1999; *One by One*, 2002

---

## Grubin, David

*Jan. 26, 1944– Documentary filmmaker; producer; screenwriter*

*Address: David Grubin Productions, 125 W. 94th St., New York, NY 10025-7016*

"There's nothing like a documentary for bringing the past alive and making you feel that you're there," David Grubin has said. As his eight Emmy Awards, three George Foster Peabody Awards, three Writers Guild Documentary Awards, and many other honors attest, Grubin has brought the past alive for huge numbers of television viewers with the more than 100 documentaries that he has produced, filmed, and/or directed, alone or with others. He is perhaps best known for his four films about U.S. presidents—Theodore Roosevelt, Franklin Delano Roosevelt, Harry S. Truman, and Lyndon Baines Johnson—and his dual portrait of President Abraham Lincoln and his wife, Mary Todd Lincoln, all of which aired on the PBS series *The American Experience.* In collaborations with the television journalist Bill Moyers, Grubin has directed and produced documentaries about such subjects as the banker and philanthropist David Rockefeller; the poet and memoirist Maya Angelou; the city of Florence, Italy; poetry and poets; psychological, emotional, and spiritual aspects of physical healing; and, for the series *Walk Through the 20th Century with Bill Moyers*, advances in weaponry, the evolution of public relations, and World War II propaganda, among other topics. Grubin and Moyers also worked together on *The Power of the Word* (1989) and *The Language of Life* (1995), about poets and poetry. Other Grubin films include *The Promise of the Land* (1987), about agriculture in the U.S.; *American Dream at Groton* (1988), about the Groton School, in Massachusetts, and its changing student body; *The Great Air Race of 1924* (1991), about an around-the-world race organized by the U.S. Army; and *America 1900* (1998), which focuses on aspects of the U.S. at the turn of the 19th–20th centuries. "What we're doing is taking the facts of a story and working with them with our imaginations, just as a novelist might," Grubin said during a conversation on July 10, 1997 with another of his collaborators, the historian Geoffrey C. Ward, as recorded by the Writers Guild of America East. "So finding the structure and the theme comes out of trying to find what is important and then dramatizing it, making it come alive." "Deciding what is most important," he continued, "really has to do with who you are and how you empathize with your subject. As you begin to feel your way into a story, there's some part of it that begins to touch you, and that's the part that in the end drives the narrative. And that is what you're finally telling."

The son of a physician and his wife, David Grubin was born on January 26, 1944 in New Jersey. He grew up in two New Jersey towns—Hillside and then Short Hills. He earned a bachelor's degree in English from Hamilton College, in Clinton, New York, in 1965, and an M.A. degree in teaching from Harvard University, in Cambridge, Massachusetts, in 1966. By that time, as he recalled to Ted Loos for the *New York Times* (November 5, 2000), he had fallen in love with cinema verité and the work of such masters of the genre as Albert and David Maysles, whose many movies include *Gimme Shelter* (1970), and Richard Leacock, whose credits include, as cinematographer, *Louisiana Story* (1948) and, as director, *A Stravinsky Portrait* (1965). Grubin has also cited as pivotal in his career choice his viewing of a documentary about the U.S. presidential campaign of 1960, in which Democratic U.S. senator John F. Kennedy ran against the Republican Richard Nixon, who was then the vice president of the U.S. Eager to enter the film business "on the technical side" rather than as a writer or researcher, Grubin found work as an assistant cameraman; as he told Geoffrey C. Ward, "I thought in order to understand how you told the story on film you really had to understand how the cameraman was getting those pictures. . . . It was the era when the cameraman was really the director. The editor had to make sense of what the cameraman was seeing." As an assistant cameraman Grubin worked on a wide variety of films and also gained experience in filming for TV, for such programs as *60 Minutes*.

In time Grubin became a cameraman in his own right; later, he began wearing the hats of producer and director, mostly for projects for television. With Robert Young, he directed *The Maze* (1971), about the Canadian artist William Kurelek, whose paintings reflected his mental illness. In 1983 Grubin produced and directed *The Arming of the Earth*; one of the earliest of the many documentaries on which he has worked with Bill Moyers, the film shows how the airplane, the submarine, and the machine gun and other weapons both revolutionized warfare and greatly increased the toll of war on civilians. In 1984 he produced *The Image Makers*, about the emergence of public relations as a specialty in the early 20th century and the many ways it has since been used to disguise the truth. That same year, in collaborations with Moyers, Grubin produced and directed *Marshall, Texas*, about Moyers's hometown and the benefits and detriments of living in a place whose population is only 25,000; *The Reel World of News*, which focuses on newsreels, an important source of news for millions of movie-going Americans before the advent of television; and *World War II: The Propaganda Battle*. For the last-named picture, Grubin interviewed the German filmmaker Fritz Hippler, who served as the chief of the film department in the Nazi government's Propaganda Ministry; Hip-

Jo Ann Williams, courtesy of David Grubin Productions

*David Grubin*

pler's 1937 film, *The Eternal Jews*—which compared Jews to rats and interspersed footage of rats with images of Jews—was widely disseminated in Germany with the aim of persuading the German people that the extermination of Jews was vital. Also for *The Propaganda Battle*, Moyers interviewed the American filmmaker Frank Capra, who created the seven-film series "Why We Fight" for the U.S. War Department; these films were shown to every person entering the armed forces during World War II and in movie theaters nationwide.

Grubin produced, directed, co-wrote (with David McCullough), and served as cinematographer for *The Wyeths: A Father and His Family*, about the celebrated American painter N. C. Wyeth and his descendants (among them his son Andrew Wyeth and grandson Jamie Wyeth, both of whom have achieved great success as painters). *The Wyeths* aired on the television series *Smithsonian World* in 1986. In *American Heritage* (September 1991), Geoffrey C. Ward wrote that in *The Wyeths*, Grubin and McCullough had "deftly uncovered the complexity roiling just beneath the too tranquil surface of an outwardly happy family," and he described the picture as "one of the ten or fifteen best film biographies ever made." In *A Portrait of Maya Angelou* (1989), which Grubin produced and directed, Moyers and the African-American poet, memoirist, and actress visited her hometown and discussed the ways that growing up in a segregated community influenced her as a writer. Also in 1989 Grubin produced and directed *Garbage: Another Way of Seeing*, in which Moyers talked to an artist and an anthropologist, among others, in whose work trash played a crucial role. In 1990 he directed *The Power of the Past with Bill Moyers: Florence*, a survey of the art and architecture of that Italian city, punctuated by interviews with art historians and Florentine citizens. For that film Grubin earned an Emmy Award nomination for "outstanding individual achievement—informational programming."

Grubin's first documentary on a United States president, *LBJ*, is a four-hour film that chronicles the life of Lyndon Baines Johnson, who took the oath of office as the country's commander in chief on November 22, 1963, the day his predecessor, John F. Kennedy, was assassinated. "When I started *LBJ*, I didn't like [Johnson]," Grubin told Patricia Brennan for the *Washington Post* (October 5, 1997). "But in making the film, I began to appreciate him, and I was more sympathetic to Johnson." *LBJ* aired on the PBS television series *The American Experience* in 1991. In his *American Heritage* article, which is actually a review of *LBJ*, Geoffrey C. Ward labeled the film "a triumph . . . unblinking but evenhanded, and fascinating from first reel to last." He continued, "The Lyndon Johnson whom Grubin shows us is complex, contradictory, greatly gifted, and hugely capable, driven by decent instincts and great dreams for himself and his country. . . . He is also heedless, deceitful, venal, unscrupulous, egomaniacal, and . . . sometimes frighteningly close to paranoid. . . . It is the special strength of this program that LBJ, the human being, remains always at center stage. . . . Johnson's rise and fall is a tragedy in the classic sense, and in David Grubin's sure hands, even the most inveterate Johnson hater will be moved by this television version of it." *LBJ* was named one of the best documentaries of the year by the *New York Times*, the *Boston Globe*, *Newsday*, and *People*, and it earned the Alfred I. DuPont/Columbia University Journalism Award and a Writers Guild Award.

In 1993 Grubin wrote, directed, and filmed the documentary *Degenerate Art,* based on the exhibit "Degenerate Art: The Fate of the Avant-Garde in Nazi Germany," mounted at the Los Angeles County Museum of Art (LACMA) in 1991. The film focuses on an enormous show of modernist paintings, drawings, prints, and sculpture—650 pieces by 112 artists—exhibited in Munich, Germany, by the Nazis in 1937 with the expressed purpose of denouncing such art as dangerous and subversive. Subsequently, for four years, the exhibit—called "*Entartete Kunst,*" which means "Degenerate Art"—toured Austria and Germany, where three million people saw it, "making it the most popular art exhibit before or since," as Morrie Warshawski wrote for the *Jewish Bulletin* (April 9, 1993). Grubin's documentary includes interviews with people who attended the exhibit, among them the son of a painter who had burnt as much of his work as he could for fear of Nazi reprisals. It also offers images of a concurrent German show devoted to bland artwork (including paintings by the Nazi dictator Adolf Hitler) that the Nazis hailed as "wholesome." Grubin's documentary pointed out that the Nazis extended their notions of degeneracy to human beings; in the late 1930s and first half of the 1940s, they proceeded to imprison and kill people who did not meet their definition of "wholesome." "Although the PBS special might seem a bit rudimentary to those who fully engaged the LACMA exhibition," Christopher Knight wrote for the *Los Angeles Times* (April 10, 1993), "it is thorough and often moving as an introduction to the events of 1937. It's also a potent and timely reminder that those events have latent consequences, which linger to this day."

As executive producer, Grubin collaborated with Bill Moyers on the five-part series *Healing and the Mind,* broadcast on PBS in 1993. That documentary presents interviews with traditional doctors, practitioners of holistic or alternative medicine, various types of therapists, researchers, and patients and explores such phenomena as the connections among thoughts, emotions, wellness, and disease; the notion of chi, the "universal life force," as conceived by Asian philosophers; and the art of healing. *Healing and the Mind* won a 1993 Emmy Award for best information series, the American Television Award, and an award from the American Psychological Association. Grubin served as executive editor of the series' companion book, which remained on the *New York Times* best-seller list for 32 weeks, at one point reaching the number-one position.

Using as sources books by Geoffrey C. Ward and the historian Doris Kearns Goodwin and voluminous additional material, Grubin wrote and produced *FDR,* his four-and-a-half-hour film about Franklin Delano Roosevelt, the 32d president of the United States and the only one to be elected four times (in 1932, 1936, 1940, and 1944). The documentary aired on *The American Experience* in 1994. Talking about *FDR* in his conversation with Ward, Grubin said, "We're not just trying to find and assemble the facts of a life, but to tell a story, and through the story, interpret a life. Why was FDR important? What was it about him that made him able to do what he did?" During their talk, Ward gave an example of the "very powerful" manner in which Grubin showed Roosevelt dealing with the paralysis that affected his legs after his bout with polio, at age 39: "I have to say, if I wanted people to get a feel for what Roosevelt's struggle with polio meant to him, I would have them watch the twelve minutes of David's film that deals with the whole business of polio before suggesting they read my book [*A First-Class Temperament: The Emergence of Franklin Roosevelt*]. . . . FDR developed a technique for imitating walking that was meant to reassure the public. We found two and a half seconds of amateur film that showed him gripping his son's arm, holding a cane, and throwing his legs forward from the waist. David showed it over and over again in slow motion, and you can see for yourself the enormous effort he made." *FDR* won a bevy of prizes, among them the George Foster Peabody Award; the Alfred I. Dupont/Columbia University Journalism Award—the Silver Baton; the John O'Connor Award; and awards from the American Historical Association, the International Documentary Association, and the National Education Association.

Grubin's film *TR: The Story of Theodore Roosevelt* (1996), which brought Grubin and Ward Emmy Awards for their writing, documents the life of the 26th president of the United States. "What I wanted to do in *TR* was to get beyond the stereotypical image we have of him as the man with the glasses charging up San Juan Hill, teeth flashing, crying 'Bully!,'" Grubin told an interviewer for the *American Experience* Web site. In particular, Grubin wanted to show the "energetic, optimistic, spirited" sides of Roosevelt as well as the darker, melancholy side, the latter of which has been traced to his years of childhood struggle with illness and weakness, the early death of his father, and the deaths of his mother and his first wife within hours of each other, two days after the birth of his first child. To make vivid both Roosevelt's attempts to keep sadness at bay and his heroism at San Juan Hill during the Spanish American War (which was not recorded by any photographer), Grubin "used a visual metaphor," as he said during his talk with Ward. "It was a horse moving in both slow and pixelated motion. You see the hooves, you see the mane with the sun glinting off it, and you feel Theodore Roosevelt's presence. . . . You start thinking about the man's incredible energy, and you also remember [one of Roosevelt's aphorisms,] 'Black care rarely sits behind a rider whose pace is fast enough.' All of that is embodied in this image of a horse, which is also telling the story of the charge up San Juan Hill."

Grubin's four-and-a-half-hour film *Truman*, about Harry S. Truman, the 33d president of the U.S., debuted on *The American Experience* in 1997. Trying to bring the character of Truman to life was extremely difficult, he told Patricia Brennan. "We work very hard to make [the progression of events] seem inevitable. In this film, there were certain scenes I cut 20 times—more than any other film [I've made]. I try to dramatize the story, not just describe it. Each scene is constructed to have a conflict in it. In the center of the conflict is Truman. If it's not dramatic, you're not going to really understand the man at the center, so every story has a dramatic conflict involved." As with his experience with *LBJ*, the process of making *Truman* changed Grubin's opinion of the president. "You begin to see how hard it is to be president," he told Brennan. "He really had it tough. By the end, you really appreciate what he did. People didn't think he could do it, and he did do it. I think he was a good man. He accomplishes some things brilliantly; some things he fails at . . . it's a mixed record." Reflecting on his series of documentaries about the presidents, of which *Truman* was his last, Grubin told Lawrie Mifflin for the *New York Times* (October 8, 1997), "It's like one long story because they keep appearing in each other's stories. T.R. is in F.D.R's story, and F.D.R. in T.R.'s story, of course, because T.R. was Franklin Roosevelt's big hero. And L.B J.'s great hero was F.D.R., and Truman had to follow F.D.R., had to deal with following directly after the great man." *Truman* won an award from the Writer's Guild.

Grubin next wrote, directed, and produced *Napoleon* (2000), a documentary about the rise and fall of the brilliant early-19th-century French military leader and tyrannical emperor Napoleon Bonaparte. Grubin told an interviewer for the PBS Web site, "I was interested in the challenge of trying to tell a story before the invention of photography, and I think that's one of the reasons that I was interested in telling this story at this point in my filmmaking career." Describing Napoleon as "the first modern propagandist," Grubin noted to Loos that Napoleon surrounded himself with fine artists who made a visual record of his appearance and exploits. Grubin used images of more than 500 paintings, drawings, and prints, by such masters as David, Goya, and Ingres, in his documentary. Moreover, because Napoleon (unlike Theodore Roosevelt) spent most of his time at war, Grubin made re-creations of battles a prominent part of the film. "I would say that shooting the battle recreations were probably the high and low points at the same time," he told the PBS interviewer. The difficulties arose because rather than hire ordinary extras, he engaged 200 reenactors (people for whom the reenactment of battles is a serious hobby); the reenactors, as he explained, "liked imagining that they were part of a military organization, so if I wanted to have a private move five paces to get a better camera angle, I had to ask him by going through his sergeant. I couldn't ask him directly as you might an extra. . . . They got so into their roles that they sometimes wouldn't do the things that I needed them to do." In a review for the *Los Angeles Times* (November 8, 2000), Howard Rosenberg wrote that *Napoleon* is "as intoxicating as history on television gets. . . . Another superb work from David Grubin, *Napoleon* sets a standard for historical documentaries. Smart and accessible to the masses, it's a rich, pulsating account of a seminal figure rising vibrantly to life through scholarly words, gorgeous pictures, stunning reenactments and splendid narration . . . without being pretentious. . . . The greatest compliment you can give *Napoleon* is that it induces you to pick up a book." *Napoleon* won a George Foster Peabody Award; a Remi Grand Award for best TV production, at the Houston International Film Festival (called WorldFest); and the Edgar Dale Award for screenwriting (called a Chris Award), at the Columbus, Ohio, International Film and Video Festival.

For his next film, *Abraham and Mary Lincoln: A House Divided* (2001), Grubin, with the help of Geoffrey Ward, focused on the complex relationship between one of the United States' greatest leaders and his wife. "Although there are more books about [Lincoln] than any other President," he told Lawrie Mifflin, "[Mary Todd Lincoln] is always an auxiliary figure. I don't know even one book that takes both fully into the same story, and yet they really shed light on each other. When you see the role she played in his life, you understand him better." In examining the couple's courtship and marriage, the film illuminates the suffering and frequent depressions of each and suggests that their differences mirrored the division that existed in the nation during the Civil War. "I don't really think you can understand a man until you understand who he loves, and why he loves," Grubin told an interviewer for the *American Experience* Web site. "I think the challenge in doing a dual biography is to keep both characters center stage and to not feel that when one character's on the stage that you've forgotten all about the other one. And to make one scene, which may be about one character, link to the next scene, which may be about the other character. And then bring them together." The script grew from a planned four hours to six, but despite the need to raise more funds to make a longer film, those who read the script agreed that it should not be cut. As he worked on the documentary, Grubin acknowledged for the *American Experience* Web site, the "affection for [Lincoln] that I began with turned into some kind of deep and profound love. . . . I have to say he wasn't only a great president, he was a great man and you feel that about him. But somehow as you work with him, you're captured by him. He has a deep soul." *Abraham and Mary Lincoln* earned a Distinguished Achievement Award from the International Documentary Association.

David Grubin Productions, the filmmaker's independent, New York City–based company, coproduced, with Channel Thirteen/WNET New York, *The Secret Life of the Brain*, a five-part series that debuted on PBS in 2002. Grubin worked on the documentary, his first to tackle a scientific subject, for about six years. Explaining his choice of the human brain as a subject, he told Verne Gay for *Newsday* (January 22, 2002), "I want to know what makes people tick. If you're a biographer, you have to ask why we do the things we do, why we feel the way we do. . . . I've always wanted to look [at history] from a scientist's point of view. What better way than to understand the brain?" Through interviews with experts, animation, and segments about people grappling with potential or actual brain disorders, the film explored a new model of brain development that postulates that the brain retains its plasticity throughout life, though to what extent it can develop as people approach old age remains unknown. Arranging the series chronologically, with segments on the brain in infancy, childhood, adolescence, adulthood, and old age, Grubin strived to "give people a sense of excitement about brain resarch without promising too much," as he told Sandra Blakeslee for the *New York Times* (January 20, 2002). "The story of the brain is the ultimate human story," Grubin said, according to the Channel Thirteen Web site. "It has all the real-life drama of a biography, the scope of a great novel, and the thrills of a swashbuckler. Even with all the gains of the past ten years, we stand on the verge of a great age of discovery." Verne Gay judged *The Secret Life of the Brain* to be "provocative, and a triumph."

Grubin's most recent film, *Young Dr. Freud*, scheduled for release in late 2002, traces the life of Sigmund Freud, the founder of psychoanalysis, from his birth, in 1856, to the publication of his book *The Interpretation of Dreams*, in 1900. "I've always had a fascination with psychology and people," Grubin has said, according to the Web site for the documentary. Produced in cooperation with PBS and Deviller Donegan Enterprises, the two-hour *Young Dr. Freud* was filmed in Europe and contains, in addition to interviews and historical photographs, impressionistic re-creations of dreams and memories, to help show how Freud's theories related to his own inner life.

Grubin lives in New York City with his wife, the artist Joan Grubin, and their three children. — G.O.

Suggested Reading: *American Experience* Web site; *New York Times* E p8 Oct. 8, 1997; *Washington Post* Y p6 Oct. 5, 1997

Selected Films: as director, writer, and producer—*The Great Air Race of 1924, 1989; LBJ*, 1992; *Healing and the Mind*, 1993; *FDR*, 1994; *TR: The Story of Theodore Roosevelt*, 1996; *Truman*, 1997; *Young Doctor Freud*, 2002; as director, co-writer, and producer—*Abraham and Mary Lincoln: A House Divided*, 2001; as producer and director—*The World of David Rockefeller*, 1980; *A Portrait of Maya Angelou*, 1989; *The Power of the Past with Bill Moyers: Florence*, 1990; *The Language of Life with Bill Moyers*, 1995; *America 1900*, 1998

---

## Hahn, Hilary

*Nov. 27, 1979– Violinist*

*Address: c/o Sony Classical, 550 Madison Ave., New York, NY 10022-3211*

The 23-year-old violinist Hilary Hahn has long equated giving a musical performance with having a good time. "My first teacher told me to think of [performance] as giving a gift to the audience—as though you're inviting them in for a party," she told Michael Church for the London *Sunday Express* (September 3, 2000). In a 2001 interview for the PBS series *Great Performances*, Hahn said, "There is something about being on stage when I am well prepared, performing with other musicians for an attentive audience, that I have found incredibly satisfying ever since I was a child. The satisfaction, of course, depends on a fair amount of prior work, but communicating to people is something that I feel very lucky to be able to do." Hahn, who began violin lessons shortly before she turned four, made her professional debut with a major symphony orchestra during her adolescence and earned a bachelor's degree in music at 19. She has given solo performances all over the world and earned praise for both her dazzling technical abilities and her deeply felt, thoughtful, distinctive interpretations. Eager to introduce classical music to a wider audience, she has made herself unusually accessible to the public: after performances she often chats with those in attendance, for example, and she communicates with schoolchildren through a frequently updated on-line journal. The four albums that she has released so far, on the Sony Classical label, offer her renditions of standards of the repertoire, such as the notoriously difficult Brahms Violin Concerto, and such contemporary compositions as Leonard Bernstein's Serenade and Edgar Meyer's Violin Concerto. After a concert she gave when she was 18, Tim Page, referring to her youth, wrote for the *Washington Post* (October 23, 1998), "To her eternal credit, she plays that way. She does not pretend to be an old master; she has nothing of the diva in her manner; she is not merely another manufactured pocket superstar blazing her way through music that is beyond her comprehension." Speaking of Hahn, Fred Rogers, the writer, host, and producer of *Mister Rogers' Neighborhood*, a children's television pro-

Nana Watanabe/Courtesy of Sony Music

*Hilary Hahn*

gram on which she has appeared, told Terry Teachout for *Time* (July 9, 2001), "She can play a very complicated, unaccompanied piece by Bach, and then two minutes later play 'Tree, Tree, Tree,' which is one of the most simple songs in the world. But when Hilary plays them, she makes them both sound as if she has invested her whole self in the music." In 2001 *Time* magazine named Hahn the best young classical musician in the United States.

The only child of Steve Hahn and his wife, Anne, Hilary Hahn was born on November 27, 1979, in Lexington, Virginia. When she was three years old, the Hahns moved to Baltimore, Maryland, where her father's jobs included college librarian and journalist; her mother worked for the Baltimore Gas and Electric Co. and later became the assistant treasurer of its parent company, the Constellation Energy Group. While out for a walk one day, Hahn and her father saw a sign in a window advertising music lessons for four-year-olds at Peabody Preparatory, which is part of Peabody Institute, a prestigious music school that is a division of Johns Hopkins University. She and her father were invited to attend a lesson and "watched this little boy play 'Twinkle, Twinkle' on a tiny violin," as Hahn told Michael Goldfarb for National Public Radio's *Weekend Sunday* (September 28, 1997). "And I loved it, so I wanted to try it." In the fall of 1983, a few weeks shy of her fourth birthday, she began taking violin lessons in a Suzuki course. (Suzuki is a method of teaching violin to very young children. Developed by the Japanese music educator Shinichi Suzuki, it relies on mimicry of sound rather than sight-reading of notes and emphasizes the importance of parental involvement.) "I didn't start on the violin," Hahn recalled to Julia Zautinsky for *Strings* (August/September 1999). "I started on a book wrapped in wrapping paper with a ruler sticking out of it. I held that under my chin and just stood while a cassette played."

At age five, after about a year in the Suzuki class, Hahn began to study at Peabody Preparatory with Klara Berkovich, a Russian émigré who had taught violin for 25 years at the Leningrad School for the Musically Gifted. "She taught me how to draw my bow, how to play double stops, vibrato, pizzicato—basically everything you need to know to play the violin," she told Zautinsky. "She also taught me the basics of phrasing, so I knew what to do with a phrase and how to make something interesting." Berkovich, who also taught her to read music, advised her, "You only have to practice on the days you eat," as Hahn told Terry Teachout. Hahn also took piano lessons, with a different teacher.

Hahn gave her first full-length violin recital at age 10. She played a Handel sonata, parts of a Bach sonata, and several other pieces in a performance that lasted over one hour. At about this time Berkovich advised her to look for a new, more expert teacher. Meanwhile, Hahn, who had been practicing a Viotti concerto in preparation for a violin competition, performed the same concerto at an audition at another prestigious conservatory—the Curtis Institute of Music, in Philadelphia, Pennsylvania. (Berkovich's brother played in the institute's orchestra.) "I went to the audition entirely for the performance experience, and I didn't expect much to come of it," Hahn told Julia Zautinsky. "But a couple of weeks later, Gary Graffman, the director of Curtis, told me that I had been accepted and that I would be studying with Jascha Brodsky. Since you can't pick your teachers at Curtis—they pick you—I was extraordinarily lucky." Jascha Brodsky, who was then in his early 80s, was an illustrious violinist and teacher who had studied with two legendary violinists: Eugène Ysaÿe, in Paris in the 1920s, and Efrem Zimbalist, at Curtis in the 1930s. For the next two years, Hahn traveled twice weekly to Philadelphia for violin lessons with Brodsky; in Baltimore, she was home-schooled and took ballet classes. Referring to those years, Hahn told Justin Davidson for *Newsday* (October 23, 1997), "I've had a very balanced life. It just happened that I was more interested in the violin than other kids. There were kids who concentrated on sports. I focused on the violin."

At 11 Hahn won a Concerto Soloists of Philadelphia competition. The following year she made her debut with a major orchestra, playing one of Saint-Saëns's violin concertos with the Baltimore Symphony. Also in 1991 she moved with her father to Philadelphia to become a full-time Curtis student. (Her father later became a part-time administrator at the Philadelphia Chamber Music Society.) Father and daughter spent most weekends in Baltimore. While continuing her individual lessons with Brodsky and practicing violin for several hours daily, Hahn began preparing for her undergraduate degree in music, simultaneously fulfilling the requirements for a high-school diploma. Being the youngest student at Curtis did not faze her, she told EJ Johnson in a Barnes & Noble on-line chat (November 4, 2001), because "it really felt like a big family. There are students from all over the world who go to Curtis. And so you have people that are really different from each other coming together, playing in the orchestra, going to class, studying different things, spending time together, playing chamber music with one another. It's a perfect experience." Distributing chocolate-chip and oatmeal cookies that she baked increased her popularity among her fellow students.

Working with Brodsky until his death, when she was 17, Hahn steadily increased her repertoire to include more than two dozen concertos, caprices, partitas, and other pieces. "[Brodsky] gave me a thorough technical training and, like Mrs. Berkovich, wouldn't let me go on to the next thing until what I was working on was absolutely right," Hahn told Julia Zautinsky. "He had a kind of musical hierarchy that he wanted me to work through, with [the] Beethoven and Brahms [violin concertos] at the end." Because she "wanted so badly to be able to work on Beethoven and Brahms," she "put a lot of time and effort into the other pieces and moved fairly quickly through the repertoire," she told Zautinsky.

Taking the advice of Brodsky, David Zinman (the artistic director of the Baltimore Symphony), and others, Hahn strictly limited her concert engagements. "I've gone with the flow of it, but it's all coming at the right speed," she explained to Justin Davidson in 1997, when she was 17. "Some people have paced their careers in different ways, and gone on the prodigy circuit. I've tried to avoid that. I still want to stay in school. That way, I have a little time to think. I get the feeling that people who go really fast don't have time to get their bearings." For some time she performed about once a month, generally within easy driving distance of her home in Baltimore or Philadelphia, at such places as senior-citizen residences and community halls. "The whole idea was to let Hilary be a kid," Miryam Yardumian, the artistic administrator of the Baltimore Symphony Orchestra, told Linell Smith for the *Baltimore Sun* (February 20, 2000). "To get her the performances she needed to grow, but to not let her fall into the trap of only performing in major venues." Occasionally, however, she did perform in such prominent environments. At 13, for example, she was the featured soloist at a New Year's Eve concert with the Utah Symphony in Salt Lake City. She made her European debut at 15, playing the Beethoven Violin Concerto with the Bavarian Radio Symphony Orchestra in Munich, Germany. She went on a European tour that same year with the same orchestra, under the direction of Lorin Maazel. Her later experiences on concert tours enabled her "to see how a soloist's career would work for me," as she told Martin Kettle for the London *Guardian* (August 25, 2000).

By May 1996 Hahn had completed Curtis's graduation requirements, among them classes in harmony, the keyboard, and music history in addition to a liberal-arts curriculum, which, in Hahn's case, included years of German and many literature courses. But she remained at Curtis, because, as she explained to Julia Zautinsky, "I loved the school so much. . . . Once you leave you can't come back, so I decided to stay as long as I could. There were a lot of classes that interested me that I hadn't taken yet"—among them classes in literature and creative writing. Nevertheless, she signed a contract with IMG Artists, a management concern, and an exclusive contract with Sony Classical. Since Brodsky's death she has occasionally sought instruction and advice from the violinist Jaime Laredo and her longtime mentor David Zinman.

Hahn's debut album, titled *Hilary Hahn Plays Bach*, for which she performed the composer's Partitas nos. 2 and 3 and Violin Sonata no. 3, was released in October 1997. In a representative review, Daniel Cariaga wrote for the *Los Angeles Times* (November 9, 1997), "The 17-year-old violinist seems incapable of producing an unmusical reading or of misspeaking the composer's idiom. With time and repetition, her pristine playing may also blossom and mellow. For now, these performances resemble the blueprint of a room, handsomely designed yet incomplete, uncolored." In the *Washington Post* (November 9, 1997), Joseph McClellan wrote, "There is more in this music than Hilary Hahn, 17 years old, can find and bring out. In fact, there is more than [the master violinists] Jascha Heifetz, Itzhak Perlman or even Joseph Szigeti could present to their audiences—more than can be revealed in any one performance. But on the level of pure technical facility—the challenging chords and counterpoint—her performance is amazing. . . . I can hardly wait to hear her in music more suited to her age." A *Stereo Review* pick of the month, *Hilary Hahn Plays Bach* won the 1998 Diapason d'Or, a French award for young recording artists, and appeared for several weeks as a best-seller on *Billboard*'s classical-albums chart. "I like to record. It's very intense . . . ," Hahn explained to Peat O'Neil for the *Washington Post* (August 26, 1999). "But it's very educational—the one time you get to listen to yourself."

Hahn's second CD, released in 1999, contains an unusual pairing—Beethoven's Violin Concerto and Leonard Bernstein's concerto-like Serenade—played with the Baltimore Symphony under David Zinman. "For my first orchestral CD, I really wanted to play the Beethoven Concerto because I've played it more than any other concerto and I feel most comfortable with it," Hahn told Julia Zautinsky. She chose to couple it with Bernstein, she added, because "it made sense to me. [Beethoven and Bernstein] were both 36 when they wrote their concertos. They were both pianists and conductors, as well as composers. Both pieces are very large-scale, though they are almost complete opposites in form." The disk earned her a second Diapason d'Or and a Grammy nomination for best instrumental soloist (with orchestra).

Hahn's third album, in which she accompanied the St. Paul Chamber Orchestra under Hugh Wolff, came out in 2000. It offers works by two Americans: Samuel Barber's Violin Concerto, written in 1939, and Edgar Meyer's bluegrass-tinged violin concerto, commissioned by Sony and written in 1999 by the cellist and composer specifically for Hahn. When Meyer first heard Hahn play his concerto, according to Michael Church, he said, "She captured the essence of it. I don't imagine it'll ever be played better." Her most recent album, released in November 2001, contains the violin concertos of Brahms and Stravinsky, with Neville Marriner conducting the Academy of St. Martin in the Fields. Hahn wrote the liner notes for each of the four CDs she has released to date.

Hahn's hectic concert schedule keeps her on the road for about three-quarters of the year; her father remains her traveling companion and assistant, for tasks involving such necessities as having her laundry done. She performs annually at the Skaneateles Music Festival, in upstate New York, and at the Marlboro Chamber Music Festival, in Vermont. She regularly gives presentations at elementary schools, playing various pieces and talking about the violin and her life as a performer. From 1996 to 1999 she participated in a musical-outreach program for children in New York City schools, organized by the Lincoln Center Chamber Music Society. Hahn was among the musicians interviewed for Bruno Monsaingeon's documentary *The Art of Violin* (2001), which offers archival footage of the world's great 19th- and 20th-century violinists. The film aired on PBS in 2001. Hahn was also one of those interviewed by Dan G. Tripps for his book *Heart of Success: Conversations with Notable* Achievers (2000) and one of 11 musicians interviewed for the second volume of *Violin Virtuosos* (2000), a *Strings* magazine publication.

Hahn pursues her interests in photography and writing in part through her on-line *Hilary's Journal: Postcards from the Road*, which grew out of her promise to a third-grade class to send postcards from the cities where she would be performing in 1998. In the journal (early segments of which are located on Sony Classical's Web site, and more recent portions of which appear on her own Web site), Hahn describes her everyday life as a concert violinist and answers questions sent to her by students from two schools in New York City and one in Los Angeles. Every week or so she also writes a new note, describing everything "from Carnegie Hall to a dog that I met in upstate New York," in her words; she also includes photos that she has taken. So far the site contains about 150 entries and more than 2,500 photos.

"The most difficult aspect of being a soloist is getting enough sleep," Hahn told the interviewer for *Great Performances*. The violinist has been described as being unpretentious and poised and as having a porcelain complexion, blue-green eyes, and luxuriant, curly auburn hair. She maintains a residence in Philadelphia. In her leisure time she enjoys seeing movies, writing poetry as well as prose, and playing the mandolin, among other activities. — K.S.

Suggested Reading: Hilary Hahn's Web site; *Newsday* B p6 Oct. 23, 1997, with photos; Sony Classical Web site; *Strings* (on-line) Aug./Sep. 1999, with photo; *Time* p82 July 9, 2001, with photo; *USA Today* D p2 Apr. 6, 1999, with photo; *Washington Post* V p16 Aug. 26, 1999, with photo

Selected Recordings: *Hilary Hahn Plays Bach*, 1997; *Beethoven: Violin Concerto/Bernstein: Serenade*, 1999; *Barber, Meyer: Violin Concertos*, 2000; *Brahms, Stravinsky: Violin Concertos*, 2001

---

Jeff Katz/Getty Images

## Hall, Deidre

*Oct. 31, 1947– Actress; writer; producer*

*Address: c/o Shapira & Associates, 15301 Ventura Blvd., Suite 345, Sherman Oaks, CA 91403-3129*

The actress Deidre Hall has won her way into the hearts of countless television viewers as the character Marlena Evans on the long-running NBC daytime soap opera *Days of Our Lives*. She has been honored with *Soap Opera Digest*'s best-actress award six times and has received three Emmy Award nominations (1980, 1984, 1985) for her portrayal of Marlena, an embattled, sophisticated, and strong professional woman. In monthly reader polls conducted by *Daytime Television* magazine, Hall has been named favorite daytime actress 108 times. In her more than 30-year career, she has established herself as one of the most durable and beloved of television actresses.

The third of John and Jean Hall's five children, Deidre Hall was born in Milwaukee, Wisconsin, on October 31, 1947. Her twin sister, Andrea Hall Lovell, is also an actress. During Deidre Hall's childhood her father, a postal worker, and mother, a high-school secretary, moved the family to Lake Worth, Florida. In a conversation with Jill Pearlman and Michael Alexander for *People* (December 14, 1987), Hall described Lake Worth as a "cozy, comfortable, safe town where nothing rippled the water." When she was 12 years old, she won a beauty contest and was named Junior Orange Bowl Queen. She attended a local junior college before moving to Los Angeles, California, in the late 1960s, to try modeling and acting. She secured an agent, who helped her get assignments in television commercials, among other small acting jobs. "I liked the work of acting, studying people, repeating emotions," Hall recalled to Jerry Buck for the Associated Press (August 24, 1986). "I kept thinking I would act until I had a serious career in psychology. I woke up one day and found I had a serious career, but it was in acting." In 1972 she won the role of Sally Lewis, a nurse, on the television series *Emergency!*, which centered on a fire-department crew and a paramedic team. From 1973 to 1975 she appeared as Barbara Anderson on the daytime soap opera *The Young and the Restless*. During the next two years, she played Electra Woman on the Saturday-morning children's show *Electra Woman and Dyna Girl*. She told Jill Pearlman and Michael Alexander, "I meet men who say, 'I used to watch [*Electra Woman and Dyna Girl*] because of your costume.' It was all latex and rubber and hip boots."

From 1976 to 1987, and since 1991, Hall has played the role of the psychiatrist Marlena Evans on the enormously popular NBC daytime soap opera *Days of Our Lives*. (When Hall left the show in 1987, to focus on her role in the prime-time television series *Our House*, the *Days* writers had Marlena disappear in a plane crash, an unresolved plot development that left open the possibility of her return.) Over the years the elegant, stylish, strong-willed, compassionate, and troubled Marlena has been kidnapped by a gangster, confined to a psychiatric ward, locked in a dungeon, and possessed by the devil, among many other melodramatic situations. During the 1982 season, when her character was kidnapped and apparently killed by the so-called Salem Strangler (Salem is the fictional town in which the show's characters live), more than a thousand fans called the NBC studios to mourn and/or protest the death of their beloved Marlena, and several dozen picketed outside NBC's Burbank, California, studios. Attempting to console them, Hall spoke to hundreds of fans on the phone. "I am astonished," Hall said at the time to Jerry Buck for an Associated Press article (May 26, 1982). "I knew this character was popular, but to hear people crying and weeping for Marlena is something. They were so attached to her." To the great relief of the character's devotees, it was not Marlena who had been murdered but her twin sister, Samantha (played by Andrea Hall Lovell, who had made several appearances on the show between 1977 and 1980). In some ways a loyal wife to her husband, Roman, Marlena was also passionately in love with John, with whom she conceived a child. Marlena steadily became one of the best-loved characters on television, with Marlena fan clubs springing up in nearly every state in the U.S. Guided by the conviction that such adoration deserves something in return, in 1982 Hall took to organizing and hosting a yearly event in Los Angeles called Deidre Hall's Lunchbreak, during which the star greets and spends time with her fans. Roughly 2,500 people attended the 1984 event, which was captured on video. "Say [fans] run into me at Gelson's [Market] and want to talk," Hall told Pearlman and Alexander. "For me to say 'Do you mind? I'm trying to get to the margarine' is unforgivable. To ask for love and trust on the screen and then not be responsive in life is wrong."

Eager to experience acting on a prime-time television show, Hall took the role of Jessie Witherspoon, a widowed mother of three, on the weekly family drama *Our House*, which co-starred Wilfred Brimley as her curmudgeonly father-in-law and Shannen Doherty as one of her daughters. On *Days of Our Lives*, the actress told Jerry Buck, "I had learned a tremendous amount about the craft of television. Daytime has the least amount of time for rehearsals, for lighting, for preparation. You work under a handicap. I wanted to have the experience of trying what I do on a bigger canvas." In 1986 Hall worked on both shows, keeping her job with *Days of Our Lives* in case *Our House* did not survive its first season. "I'm doing two shows with great delight," she commented to Buck. "We have a schedule that permits me to work on *Our House* five days a week and to tape *Days of Our Lives* on Saturdays." Hall became the first actress ever to star simultaneously on both a daytime and a prime-time television series. When Larry Jordan, for the *Midwest Today* Web site, asked her about the different levels of respect that television viewers and critics accord to daytime and nighttime shows, Hall responded, "The fact is that daytime television is less valued than nighttime, and it's partly because of the product that we produce. We do a one-hour [*Days of Our Lives* episode] in 12 hours. Nighttime produces a one-hour show in seven to nine days. . . . So [the soap opera] doesn't look as completed, as finished, as 'tight' perhaps." *Our House* was the first television series honored with a seal of approval from the organization Viewers for Quality Television; for her role on the show, Hall was twice nominated for a People's Choice Award. In 1987 Hall left *Days of Our Lives* to concentrate on *Our House*; that show was canceled in 1988, after its second season.

The ABC television movie *Never Say Never: The Deidre Hall Story* (1995) depicted the actress's 20-year struggle to give birth to a child. It was written by her third husband, Steve Sohmer, and produced by Hall, who also played herself in the movie. The actress tried to become pregnant through artificial insemination six times. Later, she underwent exploratory surgery before attempting in-vitro fertilization; that, too, failed. Finally, in the early 1990s, she and Sohmer went to the Center for Surrogate Parenting in Beverly Hills, California, where Robin B., a divorced mother of three, agreed to serve as a surrogate mother. Artificially inseminated with Sohmer's sperm, Robin B.—she has declined to disclose her last name—gave birth to Hall's first son, David Atticus, in 1992 and her second son, Tully, in 1995.

Hall has appeared on various television shows, including *Hot Pursuit*, *Columbo*, *Wiseguy*, *Perry Mason*, *Hunter*, and *Murder, She Wrote*, among others. She also starred in the television movies *A Reason to Live* (1985) and *And the Sea Will Tell* (1991). The former was a family drama, co-starring Peter Fonda and Rick Schroder, in which the husband of Hall's character becomes suicidal after she tells him that she wants a divorce; the latter, based on a book by Vincent Bugliosi and Bruce B. Henderson, was a murder mystery and courtroom drama based on true events. In 1993 Hall made her stage debut in A. R. Gurney's play *Love Letters*.

According to the Web site *soapcentral.com*, during the 1990s Hall became an active supporter of the organizations Habitat for Humanity and PATH (People Assisting the Homeless). She received PATH's Family Support Award in 2000. Her honors also include two nominations for best actress by Viewers for Quality Television and the prestigious American Women in Radio and Television Award in 1994. *TV Guide* once selected her as one of the 10 most beautiful people in the U.S. and twice named her best-dressed woman. Her image has appeared on the covers of many magazines, among them *People*, *Woman*, *TV Guide*, *McCall's*, *Family Circle*, and *Shape*.

In 1977, after seven years of marriage, Hall divorced her first husband, Keith Barbour, a singer/songwriter. Her second marriage, to Michael Dubelko, the former president of Cannell Studios, lasted two years before ending in divorce, in 1989. The strain placed upon that marriage by the couple's unsuccessful attempts to have a child together was a major factor in the divorce. In 1991 Hall married her third husband, Steve Sohmer, a novelist and television producer to whom she had been engaged for a while before her second marriage. They live with their two sons in Los Angeles. In her leisure time the actress enjoys traveling and being with her family. Along with Mary Hart of *Entertainment Tonight*, she is a co-owner of the video company Custom's Last Stand.

Hall recently signed a two-year contract that will keep her on *Days of Our Lives* at least through August 2004. When Larry Jordan asked her about the differences between her and Marlena, Hall replied, "I don't think there are many dissimilarities. I play her from myself. We both have the same devotion to our families. We both love our careers. We enjoy our great women friends. I can't even think what the difference would be." — C.F.T.

Suggested Reading: *Days of Our Lives* Web site; *International Movie Database* (on-line); *McCall's* p140+ Feb. 1988, with photos; *Midwest Today* (on-line) Oct. 14, 1994, with photo; *People* p65+ Dec. 14, 1987, with photos, p68+ Sep. 28, 1992, with photos; *soapcity.com*; *soapdigest.com*; *TV Guide* p24+ Mar. 13–19, 1993, with photos, p30+ Dec. 9–15, 1995, with photos

Selected Television Shows: *Days of Our Lives*, 1976–87, 1991–

---

Courtesy of J. P. Morgan Chase & Co.

## Harrison, William B. Jr.

*Aug. 12, 1943– CEO of J. P. Morgan Chase & Co.; philanthropist*

*Address: J. P. Morgan Chase & Co., 270 Park Ave., 37th Fl., New York, NY 10017*

William B. Harrison Jr. has made a relatively quiet yet steady climb to the top of the banking and finance world. While not known as a particularly charismatic leader, Harrison has distinguished himself through a philosophy of team-building that has led to a series of big-business triumphs. In the year 2000 he successfully engineered one of the largest mergers in banking history, bringing together Chase Manhattan Corp. and J. P. Morgan to form the third-largest financial institution in the world;

retaining the positions he had held with Chase Bank, he is the president and chief executive officer (CEO) of the newly formed financial powerhouse J. P. Morgan Chase & Co. In 2001 the Executive Compensation Advisory Services listed Harrison as the third-highest-paid CEO in New York, one of the financial capitals of the world, with personal total earnings of close to $50 million a year. Harrison's friend Erskine Bowles, a former White House chief of staff, told a writer for *American Banker*, as quoted on *newyorkmetro.com*, "You have to lead, follow or stand aside. There's not much stand-aside in Bill Harrison. He's constantly challenging himself. And he's used to winning."

For Harrison, banking is a family affair. His grandfather ran a bank in Rocky Mount, North Carolina, where Harrison was born on August 12, 1943, the son of William Burrell Harrison Sr. and the former Katherine Spruill. Harrison's father worked at the bank full-time, as did Harrison himself during the summers when he was growing up. Also like his father before him, the younger Harrison attended the University of North Carolina at Chapel Hill, about a hundred miles west of his hometown. Before graduating, in 1966, with an A.B. degree in economics, the tall, lanky young man played basketball for the legendary North Carolina coach Dean Smith, whom Harrison has credited with teaching him some management skills. In 1967 Harrison took a job with Chemical Bank, which was founded in 1824 as an offshoot of a chemical-manufacturing company; he has remained with the bank ever since, staying on and advancing each time the company acquired another business, underwent a merger, or changed its name.

Harrison spent most of his first decade with the bank in its Mid-South and West Coast offices. In 1976 he became the district head of Chemical's Western Region, based in San Francisco, California. It was there that Harrison distinguished himself in the eyes of Walter V. Shipley, who became Harrison's mentor and, later, the bank's chairman; Shipley selected Harrison in 1978 to head the bank's London branch. Harrison became a senior vice president and divisional head for Europe in the early 1980s, after graduating from Harvard Business School's International Senior Management Program in Vevey, Switzerland, in 1979. During his time in Europe, Harrison met Douglas A. Warner III, who would become his longtime friend and the chairman of J. P. Morgan. In that capacity Warner would help oversee the successful merger with Harrison's Chase Bank two decades later.

Upon returning to the United States, Harrison was placed in charge of Chemical's corporate banking division. In the early 1990s he was promoted to vice chairman and worked with Shipley on Chemical's merger with the New York bank Manufacturer's Hanover. In 1996 they expanded the bank even further when they bought Chase Manhattan Bank for an estimated $10 billion, creating what was then the largest bank in the country, with assets nearing $300 billion. Though Chemical was the larger of the two banks, the company opted to take Chase's name, as it was older and better known (the famous Rockefeller family had been the driving force behind it). Harrison was praised during this period for his effective management style and his ability to integrate two large and complex companies. David Leonhardt wrote for the *New York Times* (September 14, 2000), "Mr. Harrison might not be the most charismatic leader, friends and associates said, but few other executives have his experience in overseeing complicated mergers." Leonhardt quoted Ronald Mandle, an analyst at the money-managing firm Sanford C. Bernstein & Co., as saying of Shipley and Harrison, "When they've done mergers, they've done them in a very collegial way." Paraphrasing James McCormick, the president of the First Manhattan Consulting Group, Leonhardt noted that Harrison's "experience handling bank mergers is unparalleled, particularly as it relates to not upsetting the large corporate clients of either bank."

In a speech given in Japan at the Nikkei Global Management Forum on October 30, 2001, as quoted on Nikkei's official Web site, Harrison spoke of his business philosophy, saying, "When mergers fail it's because people have remained at cross-purposes even though the strategic vision that inspired the merger was both clear and compelling. Now how do you avoid that problem? Speaking only from my own experience . . . I believe you should go into a major merger or acquisition with a mindset of equality and inclusiveness—a mindset of a merger of equals." He continued, "Equally important, you need to communicate, starting with a vision that unites your organization in carrying through the full course of the merger. People want to be informed, they want to belong to and feel part of a larger purpose, that larger vision. The only way to get at this is constant communication. It is communication that breaks down barriers and builds trust, which is the essence of teamwork and partnership, which is the essence of making these mergers work in my opinion." Many in the industry feel that Harrison, known for being a good listener and for having a gentle demeanor, learned his management style from Shipley, who is regarded as one of the most influential and important bankers of the 20th century.

Under the guidance of Shipley and Harrison, the new Chase Bank had higher profits in 1998 than any of its rivals. The next year Shipley announced that he would step down and that Harrison would replace him as the company's chief executive. On the occasion, Timothy L. O'Brien wrote for the *New York Times* (March, 25, 1999), "Mr. Shipley . . . made note yesterday of Mr. Harrison's talent for managing diverse personalities. Mr. Shipley said that was one of the leading factors in Mr. Harrison's favor when he began asking Chase's board to anoint his successor about six months ago." O'Brien quoted Shipley as saying, "Bill is the architect of what now represents about two-thirds of the bank's earnings."

Over the next couple of years, Harrison, now as CEO, made a concerted effort to improve the bank's existing technological capabilities. To that end, he introduced many of the bank's top executives to Bill Gates, the chairman of Microsoft, and Scott McNealy, the leader of Sun Microsystems. He then bought the San Francisco–based information-technology company Hambrecht & Quist. As he told Mary Kelleher for Reuters, in an interview that appeared in *Global Treasury News* (February 21, 2001, on-line), "I do believe in the Internet revolution, I do believe it is sustainable and real and I do believe it will have major, major impact on our business and our future. When I became CEO in June, 1999, I launched a full-court press on the Internet, to develop a greater understanding and a sense of urgency around it. . . . After we announced this company-wide focus on the Internet, we announced steps to reinforce the process of becoming a more Internet-driven company. It started with the creation of Chase.com, which is our focal point for Internet-based expansion at Chase. . . . If you don't adapt, you could really lose out."

Harrison followed those improvements with several relatively small acquisitions in order to put Chase in a position to merge with another large bank—a move necessitated by the highly competitive market, and one that highlighted the general trend of consolidation in the finance industry. In 2000, in a blockbuster deal estimated at more than $35 billion, Chase acquired the respected firm of J. P. Morgan, which was founded in 1861 by J. Pierpont Morgan, a towering figure in the world of banking and finance. The deal created J. P. Morgan Chase & Co., with assets of more than $650 billion, making it the third-largest financial-services company in the nation, behind only Citigroup and Bank of America. J. P. Morgan has been a leading and respected manager of money for companies and wealthy individuals, while Chase is best known for its large customer base and commercial banks. Harrison, speaking of the combination of strengths, was quoted by Kathleen Day in the *Washington Post* (September 14, 2000) as saying, "This is a situation where I am convinced one plus one will significantly exceed two."

In early January 2001 Harrison celebrated the merger by ringing the closing bell at the New York Stock Exchange. Harrison, whose titles of president and chief executive officer carried over to the new institution, was named Banker of the Year for 2000 by *American Banker*, a daily source of financial news and information. Another acknowledgment of Harrison's achievement came when J. P. Morgan was named Bank of the Year by the International Financing Review, a multimedia provider of information, in recognition of the bank's performance in 2000. As quoted on J. P. Morgan's company Web site, the review stated, in awarding the prize, "The rigours of mega-mergers, particularly those with cultural differences to bridge, are usually sufficient to distract most banks for at least a year. So to remain focused on the business in year one is striking in itself. To do it against a backdrop of market volatility and a severe industry downturn is remarkable." By the middle of 2001, however, with Wall Street in a considerable downturn, many financial-industry analysts, with the benefit of hindsight, expressed the opinion that J. P. Morgan and Chase had merged at an unfortunate time. In addition, J. P. Morgan Chase & Co. received bad publicity later in 2001 with revelations of the company's large loans to Enron, a huge energy trading corporation that went bankrupt amid high-profile scandals involving executive-level fraud, money laundering, and other criminal activities. J. P. Morgan Chase's stock dropped in value and the company's profits declined in 2001. Banking experts predicted that the company might not be able to recover until the climate of investment banking and other financial-service markets improved.

Harrison is involved with a number of charitable foundations and organizations, sitting on the boards of the United Negro College Fund, the Sloan-Kettering Cancer Center, the Central Park Conservancy, Carnegie Hall, and the New York City Partnership, which is dedicated to improving businesses in the city. In addition, he is a member of the Business Roundtable, the Business Council, the Group of Thirty, a nonprofit organization that explores matters of business practice and public policy, and the Committee to Encourage Corporate Philanthropy, a forum of CEOs focused on corporate charity. Harrison is also a director of the pharmaceutical firm Merck & Co. and the New York Stock Exchange. In 1985 he married Anne MacDonald Stephens. The couple have two daughters, Katherine and Anne, and homes in New York, Connecticut, and Maine, where Harrison enjoys a variety of physical activities, from horseshoes to badminton. — C.F.T.

Suggested Reading: *New York Times* III p10 Sep. 14, 2000, with photo; *Washington Post* V p1 Sep. 14, 2000; *Who's Who in America, 2001*

---

## Hax, Carolyn

*Dec. 5, 1966– Advice columnist*

*Address:* Washington Post, *Style Plus, 1150 15th St., N.W., Washington, DC 20071*

"The column was intended from the start to be the kind of advice you'd get from a friend if that friend were relatively stable and brutally honest and had possibly gotten up on the wrong side of the bed that year," Carolyn Hax wrote in the *Washington Post* (May 30, 1999) regarding her popular advice column, "Tell Me About It." First syndicated by the *Washington Post* Writers Group in early 1998, "Tell Me About It" now appears in more than 200 newspapers nationwide. Responding to readers' questions on subjects ranging from divorce and

Courtesy of Washington Post Writers Group
*Carolyn Hax*

death to pets and co-workers to love and heartache, Hax has earned high praise and built a loyal following with her bracing, no-nonsense, witty advice. The column, which is published three times a week, is billed on the *Washington Post Writers Group* Web site as "advice with attitude and a grounded set of values, geared toward the under-30 crowd." Hax's first book, *Tell Me About It: Lying, Sulking, Getting Fat . . . and 56 Other Things NOT to Do While Looking for Love*, was published by Hyperion in 2001.

The youngest of four daughters, Carolyn Hax was born in Bridgeport, Connecticut, on December 5, 1966. She grew up in nearby Trumbull. Her father is a corporate planner, and her mother is a secretary. After graduating from Harvard University, in Cambridge, Massachusetts, with a bachelor's degree in American history and literature, Hax went to work for the *Washington Post* in 1992. Before starting "Tell Me About It," Hax served the paper as a copy editor, news editor, and freelance reporter. Among other subjects, she wrote about crime in the Washington, D.C., area, teenage drinking, and abortion. Regarding the origins of her column, Hax explained in a *Washington Post* article (May 30, 1999) that in the spring of 1997, she approached an editor at the paper and suggested the idea of starting an advice column. In another version of how Hax got started, Tamala Edwards reported for *Time* (September 17, 2001) that in 1997 "an editor lamented to Hax that she was being forced to take on an advice column. I could do that, Hax replied, and banged out a few sample columns that won over her bosses."

Hax has said that her advice is based on her acceptance of her own flaws and deficiencies. "It occurred to me recently that I've been preparing for this job from birth," she told a writer for the *Washington Post* Writers Group Web site. "When you grow up the too-little-to-do-anything youngest kid in a big family, you spend year after year just watching. And learning. And itching, just once, to tell everyone else what to do." Hax continued, "In this expert-happy age, Tell Me offers people under 30 advice based on the experiences of someone who's been there . . . really, really recently. My 'expertise,' therefore, is in bad dates, school pressures, strict parents, dubious decisions, new marriages and combination skin. My specialty? Stupid teen-age stunts (though I prefer the term 'learning experiences')." Hax also credits her family as a strong influence: "[My family] tried, with varying success, to impart to me life's greatest gift: perspective. To make it out of the Hax house unscathed, we had to take our work seriously but never, ever ourselves. Pretense got us mercilessly teased. Still, we never doubted we were loved, and the unique chemistry of our home propelled all four of us to reasonably well-adjusted adulthoods. . . . Every week in my column, I try to duplicate that chemistry: supportive, demanding, maddening, funny, serious when it counts and virtually bromide-free."

When asked by Tamala Edwards what is most surprising about the letters she receives, Hax answered, "The things that people do to each other, the amount of pain that people can tolerate, the amount of kindness they can show." To a young man who wrote Hax explaining that he did not feel ready to be friends with his ex-girlfriend, Hax, as quoted by Edwards, wrote in response, "You don't have to hang out with anyone you don't want to hang out with, not until you acquire co-workers, in-laws or prison time." In another response that Edwards quoted, Hax wrote to an inquirer, "Sometimes a guy prefers a couchful of football to spending the day out with you. Is that always so wrong?" In a February 2002 "Tell Me About It" column, Hax told a recovering alcoholic worried that she was unworthy of being in a romantic relationship that she should accept her past and forgive herself: "Read your own letter. You're 'not proud,' not 'normal,' possibly not datable. Wow. You just kicked an addiction, pulled Excalibur out of the rock, and you're not good enough to date? Time to make up more excuses so you can go to Flogmyselfaholics Anonymous." Hax, who claims never to read self-help books, has said that she would never recommend an action that she herself would not take. Concerning the question of why people write to a newspaper instead of seeking the advice of friends or family, Hax wrote in her column (May 30, 1999), "I like to think those who solicit my opinion are good, wise, thoughtful people in need of disinterested counsel. Or maybe they're all just freaks. Either way, [they] gain a distinct advantage: Privacy. You laugh, but would you rather send a letter to me with no return address and signed 'Frilly in Fresno,' or look your best buddy in the eye and say, 'I'm wearing women's underwear. Is that so wrong?' It's the old stranger-on-the-train phenomenon; it's easier to confess to someone you'll never have to face again." Possessing no professional qualifications in counseling or psychiatry, Hax is sometimes asked how professionals in those fields respond to the advice she offers her readers. "The response from the pros—doctors, social workers, ministers, even—has been almost universally friendly," she wrote in her May 30, 1999 column. "I can't say the same for the nonprofessional public: Some people out there hate the column, and really, really hate me, and probably hate my dog. I have a special name for these critics, though: 'Readers.'"

Regarding her craft, Hax told Edwards, "I write at all hours and in all kinds of circumstances: office, home office, parents' couch, friend's kitchen table, beach—distractions don't distract me somehow—and I usually use my first draft." In July 2002, in response to popular demand, Hax began writing a third weekly installment of "Tell Me About It." The column, with accompanying cartoons by her former husband, Nick Galifianakis, now appears on Wednesdays as well as Fridays and Sundays. Readers, fans, and advice-seekers can also participate in chat-room discussions with Hax at noon on Fridays on the *Washington Post* Web site.

Hax noticed that many of those seeking advice from her regarding their troubled romantic relationships were making the same mistakes—"a virtual catalogue of the most counterproductive ways to interact with other human beings," in her words, as quoted by Pamela C. Patterson in *January Magazine* (September 2001, on-line). Hax began compiling a list of the most egregious and common blunders, which then became the material for her first book, *Tell Me About It: Lying, Sulking, Getting Fat . . . and 56 Other Things NOT to Do While Looking for Love* (2001). Among Hax's exhortations in the book are her cautions against having sex too early in a relationship; creating "intimacy imbalances," or revealing too much about oneself too quickly; and "training to date." In her review of *Tell Me About It*, Patterson wrote, "Brutal honesty has its merits. . . . I must admit that I laughed out loud numerous times while reading this book. Consider the following one-liners: On Scanning the Room for Better Prospects While We're Trying to Talk to You: 'If there's someplace you'd rather be, we'd like you to go there.' On Pining Silently for Your 'Friend': 'If you are pining, you are not "friends."' . . . Clearly, the woman does not suffer fools gladly. And neither should you, seems to be the message of *Tell Me About It*. If you feel like you're looking for love in all the wrong places, take a look inside this book. You might actually be enlightened—or at the very least, you'll learn to lighten up." "The book isn't a compilation of [Hax's] columns but covers similar topics," William O'Sullivan wrote for the *Washingtonian* (on-line), in his less positive review of *Tell Me About It*. "While I admire Hax's effort to write an original work when she could have faxed in her greatest hits, I missed the column's spontaneity and in some cases its brevity. Her trademark scathing yet humane take on relationships is often buried here in hard-to-navigate prose, with one-liners elbowing each other out of the way." He added: "Beneath all that, however, is an unerringly sensible mind."

Hax has lived in the Washington, D.C., area since 1988. She still collaborates with her former spouse, Nick Galifianakis, on her column and the accompanying cartoons. On the *Washington Post* Writers Group Web site, she described Galifianakis as a "mad-artist . . . with a quick laugh and bad allergies who freely contributes his opinions on every issue I address that has even a tangential connection to anything male. Sometimes, I even let him believe he's right." — C.F.T.

Suggested Reading: *postwritersgroup.com*; *Washington Post* F p1 May 30, 1999; *Washington Post* (on-line)

Selected Books: *Tell Me About It: Lying, Sulking, Getting Fat . . . and 56 Other Things NOT to Do While Looking for Love*, 2001

---

## Henderson, Donald A.

*Sep. 7, 1928– Epidemiologist; director of the federal Office of Public Health Preparedness*

*Address: U.S. Department of Health and Human Services, Hubert H. Humphrey Bldg., Rm. 636, 200 Independence Ave., Washington, DC 20201*

One of the world's foremost experts on virus eradication, vaccination, and infectious disease, the epidemiologist Donald A. Henderson has traveled the globe in his efforts to stamp out smallpox, polio, and other diseases and to change attitudes toward health care. He explained to Richard Rhodes for *Rolling Stone* (October 31, 1991), "The world doesn't really have a health-care system; it has a sickness-care system. People come into the system who are sick, and the system attempts to cure them. If you're really concerned about the *health* of the community, you have to have measurements of where the diseases are. Once you begin collecting those data and begin using them, then you're concerned about the health of a community." Although much of his career has focused on the threat of naturally occurring diseases, in the past decade Henderson has turned his attention to the potential use of viral agents as large-scale biological weapons. Following the September 11, 2001 terrorist attacks against the U.S. and the events of October–November 2001, when representatives of the U.S. government and the media were targets of anthrax-tainted letters that killed six, the U.S. secretary of Health and Human Services, Tommy Thompson, appointed Henderson as the director of

Courtesy of D. A. Henderson

*Donald A. Henderson*

the newly created Office of Public Health Preparedness. In that capacity, Henderson advises the president on issues related to bioterrorism, in particular such agents as anthrax and Henderson's area of specialty, smallpox. "I feel no pleasure or vindication," he told Yochi J. Dreazen for the *Wall Street Journal* (October 24, 2001), speaking of his appointment to his new post. "I wish I was still out there warning people that there might be a problem rather than figuring out how to deal with it." In 2002 Henderson received the Presidential Medal of Freedom, the nation's highest civilian award.

Donald Ainslie Henderson, known as D.A., was born on September 7, 1928 in Lakewood, Ohio, the son of David and Grace (McMillan) Henderson. He attended Oberlin College, in Oberlin, Ohio, and graduated in 1950 with an A.B. degree in chemistry. After earning his M.D., in 1954, from the University of Rochester School of Medicine, in New York State, he remained in New York State to serve his internship (1954–55) at the Mary Imogene Bassett Hospital in Cooperstown. While a medical student he first confronted an epidemic—on that occasion an outbreak of polio, a disease that often paralyzed its victims. Treating people, many of them children, who were in iron lungs to facilitate breathing with partially paralyzed lungs was "a very vivid, depressing experience," he told Melissa Hendricks for the *Johns Hopkins Magazine* (February 1991). In 1955, a time when polio and influenza prevention were of major concern to public-health professionals, Henderson went to Atlanta, Georgia, as the assistant chief of the U.S. government's Epidemic Intelligence Service of the Communicable Disease Center (CDC)—now called the Centers for Disease Control and Prevention. A military deferment allowed him to work in that post rather than serve in the armed forces. He intended to stay in Atlanta only briefly but found that epidemiology suited him well; he remained at the CDC for two years, frequently traveling to the scene of disease outbreaks with the goals of assessing, controlling, and stopping epidemics. "We were a group of 'disease detectives,'" Henderson recalled to Hendricks. In 1957 he returned to Bassett Hospital as a resident in medicine and pathology.

Although he had completed his medical training, Henderson could not envision himself in a traditional hospital or clinical setting, as he admitted to Richard Rhodes: "I decided I was never going to be a practicing doc. It was just too dull, really." He continued his education, by earning a master's degree in public health from Johns Hopkins University in 1960. Intending to work as an epidemiologist, he returned the same year to the CDC, where he supervised investigations such as that of a 1961 hepatitis outbreak, which was traced to infected shellfish that had been harvested from polluted waters and eaten in Atlantic Coast states. "Eating raw shellfish may be said to be a little like playing Russian roulette on the half shell," he quipped to Robert C. Toth for the New York *Herald Tribune* (June 21, 1961). In 1961 the number of cases of hepatitis, a liver disease that is contagious but usually not fatal, grew to more than 60,000 in the U.S., a record level.

Although smallpox had not appeared in the U.S. since 1949, in 1962 the CDC began to keep tabs on outbreaks of the disease around the world, developing vaccines and delivery methods to immunize great numbers of people. In 1965 he became the chief of the CDC's Smallpox Eradication Program. Worldwide smallpox eradication had been quietly suggested as early as 1958 by a Soviet health official, Viktor Zhdanov; in the mid-1960s European scientists suggested that eliminating the disease could save millions in vaccination and treatment costs, and the World Health Organization (WHO) thus took up the task. The president of the United States at that time, Lyndon B. Johnson, "was looking for a health initiative that had some pizzazz," Henderson told Richard Rhodes. "All of a sudden—this was November 1965—the order came from the White House pledging American support for an international program to eradicate smallpox." Henderson, on loan to WHO with the approval of President Johnson, was appointed to lead the group charged with eliminating smallpox worldwide. The choice of an American to lead the project—which upset the Soviets, who had been its first advocates—was a political move on the part of Marcolino Candau, WHO's director-general, as Henderson explained to Rhodes: "[Candau] was very unhappy about the program. He'd been brought up in Brazil, and he knew that there were a lot of tribes in the Amazon that you could never reach, and he never got it through his head that you can stop smallpox without vaccinating everybody. . . . He wanted an American to head the program because he was sure it was going to fail and he wanted an American holding the bag."

While he was reluctant to be at the epicenter of a political/public-health showdown, Henderson moved with his family to Geneva, Switzerland, to kick off what was to be a 10-year project. "The World Health Assembly [the annual meeting of the WHO] proposed a ten-year program, because [President John F.] Kennedy had said we could land a man on the moon in ten years," he explained to Richard Preston for the *New Yorker* (July 12, 1999).

Smallpox was targeted for eradication for several reasons. The virus was found in two forms, the relatively mild *variola minor* and the devastating *variola major*. The virulence of *variola major* was legendary; that strain killed approximately 40 percent of its victims in an ordinary epidemic and up to 80 percent in particularly vicious outbreaks. With its distinctive symptoms, most notably a rash of red, malodorous, pus-filled pox, smallpox had been recorded as far back as the time of ancient Egypt. From the Middle East, historians have speculated, smallpox was carried by conquering armies throughout the world: east to China by the Huns, west to Europe by the Moors, and to the Americas by Spanish conquistadors. Regarded as a common childhood disease, smallpox is thought to have regularly killed 10 percent of the population until the 20th century. For victims who survived, the disease often caused permanent and disfiguring scars, including blindness as a result of scarred eye tissue. A second major reason that smallpox was chosen to be eliminated was the relative ease of tracking it. The disease had a short incubation period, so new cases would appear within three weeks after the virus was transmitted, through close person-to-person contact. Also of great importance was the fact that smallpox could survive only in human hosts; once people all over the world were vaccinated or otherwise made immune, the disease would die out. Effective vaccines were easily manufactured because the *variola* virus, a large and brick-shaped pox virus, had a single, stable form. (Viruses such as influenza and HIV, which have multiple strains or self-modifying DNA, cannot be treated with a single, narrow-spectrum vaccine.) The first smallpox vaccine was developed in the 1790s by a British physician, Edward Jenner, using cowpox, a virus related to smallpox but not fatal to humans. Immunity conferred by vaccination was not lifelong but generally lasted for years, providing the WHO immunization campaign with enough time to chase smallpox from humanity and into small, secure storage facilities in the United States and Russia, where it would be used only for research and vaccine development.

Henderson acknowledged to Richard Preston that the push to eliminate smallpox from the entire world was an enormous undertaking. "I'm one of many in the eradication. . . . I could come up with fifty names. Let alone the tens of thousands who worked in the infected countries." The smallpox-eradication team set out to vaccinate 80 percent of the population in countries where smallpox was known to still exist—in Africa, Asia, Latin America, and Eastern Europe—and pursued an efficacious route of on-the-spot vaccinations; at the same time, smallpox vaccinations ceased in locations such as the United States, which had been smallpox-free for decades. More than 100,000 WHO representatives and local health-care workers tracked down smallpox outbreaks, treated those infected, and vaccinated everyone within a wide radius of each victim. Henderson himself visited scores of smallpox sites, particularly in Africa and Asia, where vaccination efforts were hampered by suspicious governments or a lack of any health-care infrastructure. "By definition, the areas where it still exists are the most difficult ones," he told Bowen Northrup for the *Wall Street Journal* (February 15, 1972). He witnessed the results of outbreaks in hospitals in such countries as Bangladesh, Iran, India, and Yugoslavia; traveling to remote villages, he helped to coordinate vaccination campaigns, some of which used new devices that did not require medical training, such as the jet injector, with which health-care workers or volunteers could administer 1,000 vaccinations per hour.

Henderson had promised to stay in Geneva for 18 months; he stepped down from his position at WHO in 1977 (after more than a decade in Geneva), just before the last naturally occurring cases of *variola major* and *variola minor* were assessed and treated. In the public-health community, he was now a hero of international stature. His signature graces the document, released on December 9, 1979, certifying the eradication of smallpox. The defeat of smallpox was officially announced to the world on May 8, 1980.

From Switzerland, Henderson went to Baltimore, Maryland, where he had accepted the positions of dean and professor of epidemiology and international health at the Johns Hopkins School of Hygiene and Public Health. Influenced by his experiences at WHO, he determinedly expanded the school's program in international health and used his position as a platform from which to advocate vaccination. After the elimination of smallpox, he plotted with other scientists to tackle such diseases as polio and guinea worm, although initially he was "very skeptical," as he admitted to Melissa Hendricks, citing failed attempts to get rid of malaria in the 1960s. Waging war on viruses had become more difficult than it was in the 1970s; polio is a more subtle disease than smallpox, as not every infected person displays symptoms, and for that reason some countries are reluctant to pay for campaigns to combat it. But Henderson knew that preventing disease was ultimately more cost-effective than curing it. In countries where children were not vaccinated against polio, measles, and other childhood diseases, "the countries were spending a lot of money in foreign exchange to procure drugs to *cure* disease," he explained to Hendricks. "If they had bought the vaccines, they wouldn't need to buy so many drugs. Curative care is essential, but to totally ignore the preventive side is foolishness. *The* single most cost-effective tool we have in medicine is vaccination. It's a very powerful tool, preferable to trying to patch up a problem with antibiotics." Henderson threw his support behind a campaign to eradicate polio in the Americas through the Pan American Health Organization (PAHO), with Henderson as chairman of its Technical Advisory Group in Immunization. The PAHO also undertook to eliminate other common childhood diseases, such as measles, from Latin America. Henderson then advised the WHO on a similar project, which is seeking to wipe out polio worldwide by 2005.

Henderson stepped down from the Johns Hopkins deanship in 1990. A few months later he became a presidential adviser in the Office of Science and Technology Policy under President George Herbert Walker Bush. In 1993, under President Bill Clinton, Henderson was appointed as a deputy assistant secretary in the Department of Health and Human Services, where he served for one year before becoming the senior science adviser to the department, also for about one year. Henderson's work on smallpox reentered the news in the mid-1990s, when WHO announced its recommendation that the remaining stocks of the virus, held at the CDC in Atlanta and a remote laboratory in Siberia, be destroyed; vaccines could be developed without them, the organization argued, and the risk of new contamination would be reduced if the virus were eliminated. (The last cases of smallpox occurred in 1978, when two people in England were infected, one fatally, in a contaminated laboratory environment.) Henderson was in full agreement with WHO but increasingly opposed by the many people in the U.S. scientific community who thought that to destroy live smallpox stocks would be to place too much trust in Russia. Russian defectors to the U.S. had indicated that there was a 20-ton stockpile of the smallpox virus distributed among three separate Russian laboratories, and fears arose surrounding the idea that smallpox could be used as a biological weapon. "The issue is, if you do destroy it in the known laboratories and you ask all countries to put the pressure on, are you in some way going to minimize the risk of smallpox virus being used as a bio-terrorist weapon? And there are some of us, and I am one of them, who feel that this would be beneficial. That way we could minimize the risk of having smallpox used again or let[ing] it be loose again," Henderson explained on the ABC News program *20/20*, as reported by Howard L. Rosenberg for *ABCNEWS.com* (March 17, 1999). Henderson also said: "One does not wish to think in terms of having that virus return. I think it would be an absolute catastrophe." (If smallpox were released as a biological weapon, it could have a devastating effect on the targeted population, as many people currently have no immunity to the disease and the immunity of many who were vaccinated decades ago is in doubt.)

Henderson left the government in 1995 and remained on the sidelines of the bioterrorism debate until 1998, when he became the founding director of the Johns Hopkins Center for Civilian Biodefense Strategies, a biological-terrorism think tank. He spent much of the late 1990s presenting his ideas about bioterror threats to state and federal agencies, but, as he told Yochi J. Dreazen, "I was a voice in the wilderness." Still, in June 2001 the Center for Civilian Biodefense Strategies participated in "Dark Winter,"a simulated smallpox attack meant to analyze government and health-care readiness in the event of a real attack. The think tank raised concerns, based in part on the results of "Dark Winter," that the U.S. was unprepared for a large-scale bioweapons attack, particularly on the front lines—hospital emergency rooms.

Because of his expertise, Henderson's semiretirement ended in November 2001. After the September 11 terrorist attacks and a subsequent spate of viral anthrax attacks through the U.S. mail, fears about large-scale biological terrorism increased. Tommy Thompson, the secretary of health and human services under President George W. Bush, asked Henderson to lead a new branch of that department: the Office of Public Health Preparedness. Henderson was willing to put his own political views aside, he explained to Sheryl Gay Stolberg for the *New York Times* (November 18, 2001), and accept that the U.S. smallpox virus would stay alive and well in Atlanta, as stipulated by the policies of both the Clinton and George W. Bush administrations. "I'm a member of the administration at this point in time, and so I necessarily have to be in accord with the administration's position." (Responding to the statement by Peter Jarhling of the U.S. Army's biological facility in Fort Detrick, Maryland, that Henderson sought the destruction of smallpox as "the crown jewel in his career," Henderson told Stolberg that the accusation was "mythology.") Even with public fear at a high level, Henderson proceeded cautiously. While recommending that more doses of the smallpox vaccine be added to the 15.4 million then on hand, he stopped far short of requiring health-care workers to be vaccinated, for fear that they could pass the disease on to unvaccinated patients; he likewise declined to recommend mandatory vaccination in the event that the smallpox virus is released on a large scale. "I think that you're . . . trying to corral people in an appropriate way," he told the Associated Press, as printed in the *St. Louis Post-Dispatch* (November 2, 2001), referring to potential efforts to persuade or force people to get vaccinated. "Without trying to do this by force, you get ahead a lot further."

In addition to the Presidential Medal of Freedom and more than a dozen honorary degrees, Henderson has won such prestigious awards as the Public Welfare Medal from the National Academy of Sciences, in 1978; the International Merit Award from the Gairdner Foundation, in 1983; the Albert Schweitzer International Prize for Medicine, in

1985; the 1986 National Medal of Science; and the 1988 Japan Prize. He and his wife, the former Nana Bragg, live in Baltimore. They have three grown children: Leigh, David, and Douglas. — K.S.

Suggested Reading: *Johns Hopkins Magazine* p15+ Feb. 1991, with photos; *New York Times* B p1 Nov. 18, 2001, with photos; *New Yorker* p44+ July 12, 1999; *Rolling Stone* p43+ Oct. 31, 1991, with photo; *Wall Street Journal* p40 Feb. 15, 1972, B p1 Oct. 24, 2001

---

## Herzog, Jacques, and de Meuron, Pierre

*Architects*

Herzog, Jacques
(HERT-zahg, zhahk)
*Apr. 19, 1950–*

de Meuron, Pierre
(de myoor-AHN, pih-YEHR)
*May 8, 1950–*

*Address: HdM, Rheinschanze 6, CH-4056, Basel, Switzerland*

In April 2001 the Swiss architects Jacques Herzog and Pierre de Meuron, childhood friends and long-time business partners, were awarded the Pritzker Prize, which is known unofficially as the Nobel Prize for architecture. The two architects head the highly acclaimed and much-in-demand architecture firm Herzog de Meuron (HdM), which is based in Basel, Switzerland. Their winning of the Pritzker marked only the second time in the more than 20-year history of the prestigious award that two architects had been chosen to share it, and the first time that a team had won it together. In its 24-year existence, HdM, one of the most celebrated contemporary practitioners of architectural minimalism, has taken on a broad range of projects, including industrial facilities, private houses, apartment buildings, commercial buildings, sports arenas, and museums. Herzog and de Meuron's best-known work is the design of the new Tate Gallery of Modern Art, in London, England, which was completed in 2000. Other highly regarded designs of the Swiss team include the library of the Eberswalde Technical School, in Eberswalde, Germany, the gallery for the private Goetz Collection of modern art, in Munich, Germany, and the Ricola Factory and Storage Building in Mulhouse-Brunstatt, France. In the United States, Herzog and de Meuron have completed the Dominus Winery in Napa Valley, California, which won *Time* magazine's Best Design honor for 1998. As quoted in an article that appears on the Web site *architectureweek.com*, the Pritzker jury, in awarding HdM the prize, praised the team for their "significant contributions to humanity and the built environment through the art of architecture" and their ability, demonstrated in a broad range of projects, to fuse "the artistry of an age-old profession with the fresh approach of a new century's technical capabilities."

Herzog and de Meuron were born in the same neighborhood in Basel, Switzerland, 19 days apart—Herzog on April 19, 1950 and de Meuron on May 8, 1950. They met in kindergarten, grew up as friends, built toys together, and attended the same schools. In 1975 they graduated from the Federal Polytechnical University in Basel (ETH), where they studied architecture under Aldo Rossi and Dolf Schnebli. Herzog and de Meuron formed their own firm in 1978. That was also the year of their first collaboration, a performance piece in Zurich for which Herzog recruited the renowned German sculptor, performance artist, and video artist Joseph Beuys; it involved—among other elements—a brass marching band. Beuys's concept of art as a means of evoking a collective, intuitive knowledge in all people had a strong influence on Herzog; this connection between architecture and contemporary art was one that Herzog and de Meuron would return to in later projects.

One of the first works by Herzog and de Meuron to gain wide attention was a gallery in Munich, Germany, commissioned by Ingvild Goetz to house her private collection of modern art. Completed in 1992, the Goetz Collection building is an elegant rectangle with two translucent glass bands—one separating the structure from the ground and the other crowning it. Between the strips of glass are two horizontal bands of birch wood panels. The writer Martin Filler commented in the *New Republic* (June 19, 2000) that the design made "the concrete-framed structure appear to hover above the park-like landscaped setting." Benjamin Forgey wrote for the *Washington Post* (April 2, 2001), "The succinctness of the shape and the simplicity of the wrapping make the building appear both beautiful and strange." The Goetz Collection building brought Herzog and de Meuron attention in the United States in 1995, when Terence Riley, chief curator of architecture and design at the Museum of Modern Art (MoMA) in New York City, included pictures and drawings of it in an exhibition, which greatly interested the viewing public. In addition to lesser-known residences in Germany and Switzerland, HdM designed the Ricola Factory and Storage Building in Mulhouse-Brunstatt, France, the construction of which was completed in 1993. (Ricola is the manufacturer of popular herbal throat lozenges.) The exterior walls of the building are made of translucent polycarbonate panels, which are commonly used for industrial buildings; over them, Herzog and de Meuron—using a silk-screening process—printed a repeating plant pattern taken from a photograph by the botanical artist Karl Blossfeldt. As the light changes during the course of a day, emerging and receding, so does the appearance of the plant design on the building's exterior. Herzog told Holly Brubach for the *New York Times Magazine* (September 20, 1998), "We

Both photos courtesy of Pritzker Architecture Prize c/o Jensen and Walker Inc.

*Pierre de Meuron (left) and Jacques Herzog*

are interested in the surface not as pure decoration but for its capacity to have an impact on the space." Ricola commissioned Herzog and de Meuron again in 1997, this time to design a new building in Laufen, Switzerland. Martin Filler called the finished project, which features large expanses of glass surrounded by an abundance of plants, a "reiteration of the early modernist ideal of the machine in the garden." Fiberglass poles project outward from the roof of the building, in order to support a mesh canopy for vines; tall trees around the building add to what Filler called "the illusion of a secluded glade," out of which the structure seems to emerge.

Over the course of the 1990s, Herzog and de Meuron designed a series of buildings in and around the railyard in Basel, Switzerland. The most prominent edifice in that group is the Signal Box Auf dem Wolf, which was completed in 1994. The Signal Box, a six-story concrete shell with an insulated exterior, contains electrical equipment for the railway engine depot. Per Herzog and de Meuron's practical design, it is wrapped with copper strips that are twisted, or louvered, to allow daylight to filter in at certain places. Of the exterior, an article on the MoMA Web site stated, "While the copper creates a dynamic architectural skin, its functional role is to provide an electrostatic shield." Benjamin Forgey wrote that the Signal Box was a fine example of the way Herzog and de Meuron "combine elegant materials with succinct, simple shapes. In photographs, the buildings appear at once clear-headed and disturbing." Other critics, however, such as Martin Filler, were of the opinion that the Signal Box, among other Herzog and de Meuron buildings, have not aged well. Filler wrote, "The rapid decay of some of [Herzog and de Meuron's] best-known schemes exposes the unpleasant reality that comes with investing so much importance in the pure physicality of the artifact. Buildings, after all, get left out in the rain. They should be designed so that they are not the worse for wear because of it."

The team's best-known work in the United States is the Dominus Winery in California's Napa Valley, at Yountville, which was commissioned by Christian Moueix, the owner of the vineyard, and completed in 1998. Forgey described the structure as a "long, low box sheathed in mortarless walls of local basalt stones held together by gravity and almost-invisible wire containers." Those "wire containers" are called gabions; the stones range in size from small rocks to large boulders. Inside the building are stark concrete floors, bare glass walls, and wire mesh ceilings. The building has won widespread praise. Holly Brubach called the basalt stone façade of the 330-foot-long winery "at once ancient and innovative." Martin Filler opined that it was a "tantalizingly photogenic structure" that looks like an "alien monolith"; he found the interior less impressive, calling it "cold, clinical, and joyless." The attractive façade has a practical function, in that the stones help to modulate the temperature of the cellar spaces where the wine is stored, making air conditioning unnecessary.

Other Herzog and de Meuron works of note completed in the late 1990s are the Rudin House, in Leymen, France, and the library of the Eberswalde Technical School. For the latter building, Herzog and de Meuron silk-screened news photos by the art photographer Thomas Ruff in repeating patterns over a façade of concrete and glass panels. Observers and critics have commented that Ruff and HdM were clearly inspired by the likes of the artists Andy Warhol and Robert Rauschenberg. In an article posted on *architectureweek.com*, Herzog is quoted as saying, "[Andy Warhol] used common Pop images to say something new. That is exactly what we are interested in: to use well known forms and materials in a new way so that they become alive again. . . . We love to destroy the clichés of architecture."

In 1997 HdM was one of 10 firms selected to participate in a competition held by MoMA to decide which of them would design an expansion of the museum. HdM advanced to the final round of the competition with two other firms, the New York–based Bernard Tschumi and the Tokyo-based Yoshio Taniguchi, whose design was eventually selected as the winner. Herzog and de Meuron's design called for glass structures to be built over and around the existing museum structures. According to Martin Filler, who called the plan "minimal to a fault," the MoMA committee's final response to HdM's design proposal was that it was too simple.

The new branch of the Tate Gallery of Modern Art, on the south bank of the Thames River in London, England, is HdM's largest and costliest work to date. (It cost more than $200 million to design and create.) Completed and opened to the public in 2000, the Tate Modern, as it is known, is in the building that originally housed the Bankside Power Station, a hulking structure designed by Sir Giles Gilbert Scott in the 1940s and completed in 1963. Herzog and de Meuron, instead of scrapping or drastically altering the original "fortress-like" structure built around a 325-foot-high central chimney, decided to use its features to their advantage in the process of turning it into the largest contemporary art museum in the world. On the Web site *architectureweek.com*, Herzog stated, "In the future this will be an increasingly important issue in European cities. You cannot always start from scratch. We think this is the challenge of the Tate Modern as a hybrid of tradition, Art Deco, and super modernism. . . . Our strategy was to accept the physical power of the massive mountain-like brick building and to even enhance it rather than breaking it or trying to diminish it. This is a kind of Aikido strategy where you use your enemy's energy for your own purposes. Instead of fighting it, you take all the energy and shape it in unexpected and new ways." Martin Filler wrote, "Herzog and de Meuron's Tate Modern is the most spectacular transformation of a disused urban landmark into an art museum since Gae Aulenti's conversion of the old Gare d'Orsay in Paris opened as the Musée d'Orsay in 1987."

The Tate Modern has more than 300,000 square feet of space and boasts an enormous entrance hall—formerly the equipment-filled Turbine Hall—which is 500 feet long and 115 feet high. HdM added a long skylight and mounted glass fixtures on the walls. Benjamin Forgey called the Tate Modern "one of the world's most unusual public spaces," while Martin Filler argued that "the revamped Turbine Hall in the end is noteworthy only for its extraordinary size—and for this amazing space Scott, not Herzog and de Meuron, must be given the credit." The Tate Modern contains the largest museum bookstore in the world. Another prominent feature, and the most visible change wrought by HdM to the outside of the edifice, is a narrow, two-story glass penthouse on the roof; referred to by Herzog and de Meuron as the "light beam," the penthouse houses one of the museum's two restaurants and private accommodations for the museum's benefactors. It offers outstanding panoramic views of London. In an editorial for the Web site *eurozine.com*, Marco Meier called HdM's Tate Modern a "staggering feat of moderation." A fair number of critics found the galleries inside disappointing, due to what they saw as their poor lighting and boxy shapes, and several critics felt that the Tate Modern showed that not every interesting structure makes for a good place for the exhibition of art.

Still, since its opening the Tate Modern has attracted huge crowds from around the world and brought HdM international attention and praise, in addition to the Pritzker Prize in 2001. Pritzker juror Carlos Jimenez, a professor at Rice University's School of Architecture, stated in an article posted on *architectureweek.com*, "One of the most compelling aspects of work by Herzog and de Meuron is its capacity to astonish. They are able to transform what might otherwise be an ordinary shape, condition or material, into something truly extraordinary." Other winners of the prestigious Pritzker Prize include Richard Meier, architect of the Getty Museum in Los Angeles, among other well-known projects; Frank Gehry, who designed the Guggenheim Museum in Bilbao, Spain; and Rem Koolhaas, the Dutch architect who created the innovative new home of Prada in New York City and who, as quoted by Martin Filler, said of Herzog and de Meuron, "They ooze smoothness, a kind of otherworldly perfection."

HdM, which now has more than 120 staff members in offices in Europe and the United States, has been commissioned to design, among other projects, a new building for the de Young Museum in San Francisco's Golden Gate Park, due to be completed in 2004, and a $50 million expansion of the Walker Art Center in Minneapolis, Minnesota, due in 2005. Herzog, as quoted on the Web site *greatbuildings.com*, described HdM's philosophy, stating, "A building is a building. It cannot be read like a book; it doesn't have any credits, subtitles or labels like [a] picture in a gallery. In that sense, we are absolutely anti-representational. The strength of our buildings is the immediate, visceral impact they have on a visitor." — C.F.T.

Suggested Reading: *architectureweek.com; eurozine.com*; *greatbuildings.com*; *MoMA.org; New Republic* (on-line) June 19, 2000, with photos; *Washington Post* C p1 Apr. 2, 2001; Wang, Wilfried, ed. *Herzog & de Meuron: Projects and Buildings, 1982-1990*

Mike Fiala/NewsMakers/Getty Images

## Hewitt, Lleyton

(HYOO-it, LAY-ton)

*Feb. 24, 1981– Tennis player*

*Address: c/o ATP Tennis International Group, 20 Alfred St., Milsons Point, 2061 New South Wales, Australia*

Although his aggressive style of play and contentious on-court antics have led him to be compared to the past tennis greats Jimmy Connors and John McEnroe, Lleyton Hewitt, an Australian, represents a new breed of tennis professional. Shorter and lighter than many of his competitors on the Association of Tennis Professionals (ATP) tour, he is known for his agility, athleticism, and stamina, which have carried him swiftly to the pinnacle of the world rankings. He first participated in a Grand Slam tournament in 1997, when, not quite 16 years old, he lost in the initial round of the Australian Open; less than five years later, he won the 2001 U.S. Open and ended the 2001 season as the world's number-one men's player. "I'm not a guy who needs to read motivation books," he told Tim Adams for the London *Observer* (July 1, 2001, online). Having earned his second Grand Slam title by winning Wimbledon in 2002, he stands a good chance of becoming the top-ranked player for a second straight year. His playing has earned praise from Pete Sampras, whom he defeated in the U.S. Open final, former president Bill Clinton, and Australian prime minister John Howard, among others; meanwhile, his fiery nature has led him to run-ins with linesmen, umpires, and the press. Opinions about him aside, no fair assessment of Hewitt would fail to acknowledge his strong work ethic, which drives him to stay in shape by lifting weights, riding his bicycle, running on sand, and taking on opponents in two-on-one tennis drills. "That's what I have to do to get better," he explained to Andrea Leand for *Tennis* (September 2000), "so I go at it with everything I have."

The son of Glynn Hewitt, a financier, and Cherilyn (Rumball) Hewitt, a physical-education teacher, Lleyton Hewitt was born on February 24, 1981 in Adelaide, Australia, where he grew up with a younger sister, Jaslyn. His entire family was athletic: Glynn Hewitt, along with his brother and father, had played Australian Rules Football at the professional level, and Cherilyn Hewitt had played pro netball (similar to team handball). One day when he was four, Lleyton, tagging along with his parents to their tennis club, picked up a racquet and asked to play. After he showed that he could drive the ball over the net consistently, his parents enrolled him in group lessons. Less than two years later, he had a private coach, Peter Smith, who was known for his work with top junior players. "He was just a fantastic pupil—quiet, shy, and respectful—and he tried extremely hard to absorb absolutely everything that I said," Smith told Daniel Williams for *Time South Pacific* (January 14, 2002). The Hewitt family's activities began to revolve around tennis: lessons for Lleyton and Jaslyn, early-morning runs, and summer vacations spent watching match after match at the Australian Open in Melbourne.

At around age eight Hewitt began to compete in junior-level tournaments. "People ask me where I get my fighting spirit," he told Peter Bodo for *Tennis* (February 2002). "Well, I copped a lot of wallopings in the juniors. I was playing kids two, three, four years older and a lot bigger. I had to learn to fight to survive." More than just surviving, he triumphed in competitions. At only 10 years of age, he was placed on the development squad for South Australian junior tennis—among players who were generally three to four years older—and he quickly progressed to the talent squad; still a junior, he found himself groomed for international play at the South Australia Sport Institute and the Australian Institute of Sport. At 13 he gave up Australian Rules Football, which he had played for fun, to devote himself fully to tennis, and two years later he was Australia's top junior-level player. To size up the competition at the international level, he traveled the world as a junior, representing Australia at the International Team Competition for World Junior Tennis in Japan, competing in boys' doubles at Wimbledon, and taking on opponents in Holland and Germany—in the process winning three tournaments on clay, a surface on which he had no prior experience.

In about 1996 Hewitt persuaded Darren Cahill, who had been a Top 25 player on the ATP tour, to be his coach. In January 1997, at the age of 15 years, 11 months, Hewitt became the youngest person ever to play in the Australian Open. (He lost to Sergi Bruguera of Spain in the first round.) Afterward he received his first ATP ranking—797th in the world—and left his 11th-grade studies at Immanuel College to pursue his tennis career full-time. Within a year he had skipped through the rankings to 550th, and at age 16 years, 10 months, he won his first ATP event, in his hometown of Adelaide, at the 1998 Australian Men's Hardcourt Championships. In the process of winning the tournament, he defeated Andre Agassi, his tennis hero, in the semifinals. His victory over fellow Australian Jason Stoltenberg made him both the lowest-ranked ATP titlist in history and the youngest ATP tournament winner since Michael Chang in 1988. In the Adelaide tournament, his first-round victory over countryman Scott Draper occurred while he was wearing a baseball cap backwards; as he told Bill Scott for *Tennis* (June 2000), "I've worn it ever since," as a good-luck token.

Hewitt played in several other tournaments in 1998, on hard courts, clay, and grass, but never progressed past the second round in singles play or the third round in doubles. Despite winning only one tournament in 1998, his year-end ranking catapulted to 113th. In 1999, defending his title in the Australian Men's Hardcourt Championships, he was defeated in the finals by Thomas Enqvist, seeded second in the event. Hewitt reached three other finals during the 1999 season: the Franklin Templeton Tennis Classic, at which he lost to Jan-Michael Gambill; the Grand Prix of Tennis, at which he lost to Nicolas Lapentti; and the Citrix Tennis Championships, a clay-court tournament at which he defeated Xavier Malisse. Hewitt began to perform better in Grand Slam tournaments, reaching the third round in both Wimbledon, where he lost to Boris Becker, and the U.S. Open, where Andrei Medvedev defeated him in a five-set match. He played for Australia in the Davis Cup, a team tournament; although Hewitt lost both of his singles matches, the Australian team won the Davis Cup. Playing for his country, he told Peter Bodo, is "everything to me. I'll play whenever and wherever I'm asked to." (Hewitt had participated in the Davis Cup before, as an "orange boy," a practice partner and aide to the pros.) Having turned professional prior to the 1999 season, he was named the Male Rolex Rookie of the Year for 1999 by *Tennis* magazine. Hewitt ended the 1999 season with an ATP ranking of 22.

During the 2000 tennis season, news of Hewitt's most prominent attributes—his talent and his temper—began to creep past the confines of Australia. He defeated Enqvist to win the 2000 Australian Men's Hardcourt Championships, but not before becoming incensed when his hometown fans rooted for his opponents, particularly Dejan Petrovic, an Australian with Czech roots. "I'm playing in my home crowd and at least three-quarters if not more are going for the Czech guy," he said in a press conference after the match, as reported by Peter Bodo. "It's weird, but I think that's just the stupidity of the Australian public. You always knock the better players." Hewitt was attacked in the Australian press for his remarks, and as a result he has since refused to grant one-on-one interviews to the Australian media. The off-court scuffles did not affect his game; less than one month later he won the Adidas International Tournament in Sydney, Australia. He was victorious at the Franklin Templeton Tennis Classic, in Scottsdale, Arizona, in March 2000, and came out on top in his first grass-court tournament, the Stella Artois Championships, also known as Queen's, defeating Pete Sampras in the final in June 2000. But Hewitt lost to Sampras at their next meeting, in the semifinals of the U.S. Open, Hewitt's highest finish in a Grand Slam tournament in 2000. After finishing up the season at the Davis Cup, which Australia lost to Spain, he was ranked seventh in the world.

Hewitt's career came into full bloom in 2001. He successfully defended his titles at the Adidas International Tournament and the Stella Artois Championships and began to win frequently against the world's best players: Agassi, Magnus Norman, Sampras, Marat Safin, and Sebastian Grosjean, among others. He reached the final of a Grand Slam event for the first time at the U.S. Open, where he defeated Sampras in straight sets, 7–6 (4), 6–1, 6–1. His other titles in 2001 included the Japan Open, the Heineken Trophy, and the Tennis Masters Cup in Sydney; his victory over Grosjean in the Masters Cup elevated him to the top of the world rankings, in turn making him the youngest year-end number-one player in tennis history and the only Australian ever to reach that rank. "It's an unbelievable feeling," he told Parker Holmes for *Tennis* (February 2002). "To become No. 1 at 20 years of age and to do it in Australia, you couldn't have written a better dream." But his achievements were marred by controversy. At the French Open he was fined for calling an umpire a "spastic," and in his five-set, second-round match at the U.S. Open, he made a comment to the umpire strongly implying that an African-American linesman was favoring Hewitt's opponent, James Blake, because of race (Blake's father is black). While neither Blake nor the International Tennis Federation chose to pursue the issue, Hewitt was trailed by the U.S. press for several days, during which he repeatedly insisted that his comment had had nothing to do with race. "I copped a lot of flak for it," he said in a press conference after the U.S. Open finals, as reported by Allen St. John in the *Village Voice* (September 18, 2001). "I knew I was really innocent. That's why I tried to block it out as much as possible and concentrate on my tennis." His brashness, formerly dismissed as healthy competitiveness, had soured the enthusiasm of some fans and journalists, who felt he was a racist and should have been penalized for his comments.

Hewitt had a slow start in 2002, due to illness; stricken with chicken pox during a warm-up event prior to the Australian Open, he refused to pull out of the Open itself, where he was the first Australian since 1976 to be seeded number one. Clearly still under the weather, Hewitt was defeated in four sets in the first round. "If I was covered in spots and still couldn't go near anyone, then I wouldn't have played," he said in a press conference following the match, as reported by the *Washington Post* (January 16, 2002). "But I was pretty much going to walk out on court no matter how bad I was feeling." He bounced back soon afterward, defeating Agassi for the Siebel Open crown and winning his final against Tim Henman to win the Pacific Life Open. Hewitt defeated Henman twice more at the midpoint of the season, once to win the Stella Artois Championships and again in their semifinal match at Wimbledon. Hewitt went on to beat David Nalbandian, 6–1, 6–3, 6–2, in the final of Wimbledon, achieving his childhood dream at only 21 years of age. "As soon as the match was over, I just sort of went numb," he recalled to L. Jon Wertheim for *Sports Illustrated* (July 15–22, 2002). "I'm thinking Wimbledon is over, and you won it." Hewitt led the 2002 ATP Championship Race, which determines the world rankings at the end of the season, and he was a heavy pre-tournament favorite in the 2002 U.S. Open.

At the 2002 U.S. Open, Hewitt, the number-one seed in the tournament, achieved two straight-set victories in the early rounds. In the third round he faced James Blake, who was seeded 25th, in a rematch of their 2001 second-round battle. With the crowd noisily against him, Hewitt was the victor in a hard-fought, five-set match, 6–7, 6–3, 6–4, 3–6, 6–3. After defeating Jiri Novak, seeded 14th, in the fourth round and Younes El Aynaoui, the 20th seed, in the quarterfinals, Hewitt faced his childhood hero, Andre Agassi, in the semifinals. Hewitt had prevailed in four of six previous meetings, but at the 2002 U.S. Open Agassi was victorious in four sets, winning 6–4, 7–6, 6–7, 6–2. He lost to Paradorn Srichaphan of Thailand in the quarterfinals of the Japan Open in Tokyo in late September. He avenged that loss by defeating Srichaphan in the semifinals at the Paris Masters tournament, but succumbed in the finals to Russia's Marat Safin.

When Hewitt is not playing tournaments, he lives with his parents in Adelaide. Besides tennis, his favorite sports are golf, which he plays regularly with a handicap of eight, and Australian Rules Football—he roots for his hometown team, the Adelaide Crows. Hewitt is five feet, ten inches tall and weighs 150 pounds. He is a Global Ambassador for Special Olympics. Hewitt is currently dating Kim Clijsters, a top-ranked Belgian tennis player on the women's professional tour. "Kim has helped me to stay a bit calmer in the easier matches, which I need," he told Tim Adams. "She relaxes me around the big tournaments." — K.S.

Suggested Reading: *Sports Illustrated* p60 July 15–22, 2002, with photo; *Tennis* p18 June 2000, p30+ Feb. 2002, with photos; *Time South Pacific* p54+ Jan. 14, 2002, with photo; *Washington Post* D p1 Sep. 1, 2001

---

## Hewlett, Sylvia Ann

*1946– Economist; social activist; writer*

*Address: National Parenting Association, P.O. Box 77, New York, NY 10113*

Christian Steiner/Courtesy of Royce Carlton Inc.

"The most urgent problem facing modern American women is reconciling the demands of childbirth and child rearing with those of earning a living," Sylvia Ann Hewlett wrote in an opinion piece for the *New York Times* (June 17, 1986). "For them, the conditions are onerous and getting worse." An economist by training, Hewlett has taught economics at Barnard College; served as the executive director of a think tank, the Economic Policy Council; and become a public champion of working parents. In 1993 she founded the National Parenting Association, a nonprofit research and advocacy organization calling upon parents to unite in demanding that the government extend a helping hand to them, through measures and services including tax breaks, quality child care, and better educational opportunities for children. Hewlett's commitment to advocacy grew out of her own experiences in trying to juggle motherhood and a career: beginning in the late 1970s, she became frustrated with the lack of support—in the form of maternity leave, available child care, and flexible hours—from her place of work, and she felt equally frustrated with the federal government, which had no laws requiring her employer to take her family situation into consideration. Her experiences drove her to research the lives of working mothers, and the government policies supporting them, in European nations. She asserted in her 1986 book, *A Lesser Life: The Myth of Women's Liberation in America*, that U.S. policies equating men and women in the workplace were detrimental to working mothers and their families. Some feminists reacted negatively to her ideas, claiming that such thinking would undo the progress that had been made toward parity between the sexes. Hewlett continued to explore the needs of the American family, her research culminating in her 1991 book, *When the Bough Breaks: The Cost of Neglecting Our Children*, and a 1998 book, written with Cornel West, *The War Against Parents: What We Can Do to Help America's Beleaguered Moms and Dads*.

Hewlett's most recent book is *Creating a Life: Professional Women and the Quest for Children* (2002). While working women in general are the focus of *Creating a Life*, Hewlett concentrated in particular on high-achieving career women who delay having children until the point at which doing so becomes risky or biologically impossible. The findings in *Creating a Life* are based on a survey of more than 1,000 successful professional women; in that controversial book and in several magazine articles and television appearances by Hewlett that quickly followed, she urged women who want to be mothers to be as proactive in their personal lives as in their professional lives. Since the mid-1980s, according to Hewlett, the main challenge facing working women has shifted from the necessity of supporting children to the attempt to make time in a busy life to have children at all. "The greatest choice facing modern women is to freely choose to have both, a job and a family, and be supported and admired for it, not be seen as some overweaning yuppie," Hewlett explained to Nancy Gibbs for a cover story, "Making Time for a Baby," in *Time* magazine (April 15, 2002).

The second of the six daughters of Vernon Anthony Hewlett, a teacher, and Jean Hewlett, an artist and homemaker, Sylvia Ann Hewlett was born in 1946 in Pyle, Wales. She was raised in various blue-collar Welsh mining districts, which suffered from high unemployment. The family was poor—they relied on thrift-shop clothes and made do without such conveniences as a car, a telephone, or a refrigerator—but tight-knit. Hewlett's parents instilled in their daughters the value of education, and her father consistently encouraged his daughters to dream about better lives for themselves. "He had feminist instincts before they were fashionable and told us with enormous force and clarity that we had to get ourselves an education and find our own way in life," Hewlett wrote in the preface to *Creating a Life: Professional Women and the Quest for Children*. Although money was scarce, all six girls had music lessons, and Hewlett eventually became a member of the Welsh Youth Orchestra. "My father conventionally wanted sons," she explained to Nessa Rapoport for *Publishers Weekly* (July 12, 1991), "but when he finally looked at his six daughters and realized this was it, he made it clear that early marriage to an out-of-work miner was no solution. When I was 13, although I'd never traveled anywhere, he took me to [the University of] Cambridge and said, 'You can go someplace like this if you work hard.'" Hewlett enrolled at Cambridge University, in England, at age 17; she was the first student from her secondary school to be admitted there. "I was from the wrong side of the tracks," she told Rapoport. "I spoke English the wrong way—and it was very hard crossing all those class barriers."

Hewlett earned a B.A. degree in economics from Cambridge in 1967. Then, having won a Kennedy Scholarship to Harvard University, in Cambridge, Massachusetts, she entered a graduate program in economics there. "I . . . sailed across the Atlantic to the country that, to me, as to so many other immigrants, had always been the Promised Land," she wrote in her book *A Lesser Life*. "The Great Society was then in full swing; America was eradicating poverty and urban decay. . . . Blacks and women were beginning to claim their birthright as free and equal human beings. I still recall the exhilaration I felt being in the right place at the right time—America in the latter part of the twentieth century." Hewlett earned an M.A. degree from Harvard in 1971 and a Ph.D. in economics from the London School of Economics, in England, in 1973. She returned to the United States in 1974, to join the faculty of Barnard College, in New York City, as an assistant professor of economics. She published her first book, *Cruel Dilemmas of Development: Twentieth-Century Brazil*, about social problems accompanying Brazil's economic growth, in 1980. She co-edited her next book, *Brazil and Mexico: Patterns in Late Development* (1982), with Richard S. Weinert, whose specialties include international finance and Third World debt.

Hewlett, who had married Weinert in 1976, gave birth to her first child in 1977. Despite her tenure-track position at Barnard College, she told Nessa Rapoport, "I discovered that I was lucky to get 10 days' maternity leave." Moreover, she continued, "When I came back to work I was doing everything badly. I blamed myself. I thought that if only I could learn to get along on three hours' sleep, everything would slide into place. . . . I was frantic with a sense of failure." Two years later, after miscarrying twins in her sixth month of pregnancy, she was advised by the chairman of her department to postpone having more children until her future at the college was assured. "At that point I realized there was something horrendously indecent about the way academia dealt with an employee's having children," she told Rapoport. "At last I understood that it wasn't me. My head was in the right place. But I was put in the position of choosing between either job security after years of vulnerability or raising a family—but not both." After her third pregnancy, which ended with the premature birth of a healthy son, Barnard denied her tenure, despite the unanimous recommendations of the school's Appointments and Tenure Committee. Eager to sue Barnard but unwilling to do so without co-plaintiffs, she sought in vain for organizations that would join her in litigation. Rather than spend years battling for herself alone, she decided to research and write about the larger problem of women's workplace dilemmas. "Modern [American] superwomen are meant to have children on the side, on their own time, and the less said about the matter the better," she told Marilyn Gardner for the *Christian Science Monitor* (March 7, 1986). She added, "I'm a feminist, and I believe in people being equal. But I also think [men and women are] different in some regards, and you can't ignore that. Equal access to jobs and education is very important. But unless you do something about a woman's double burden in the workplace and in the home, she's never going to achieve equal opportunity with men."

In 1981 Hewlett became the executive director and vice president for economic studies of the Economic Policy Council, a think tank connected with the United Nations Association of the United States (UNA-USA). She spearheaded the formation of a family-policy panel, which included the *Washington Post*'s publisher, Katharine Graham, and other corporate leaders, to explore how businesses might ease the burden placed on parents by work and family responsibilities. "I spent hundreds of hours pursuing reluctant business leaders, telling them over innumerable power breakfasts that they needed to get up to speed on work/family issues and put some support policies in place," she wrote in the preface to her book *When the Bough Breaks: The Cost of Neglecting Our Children.* "Mostly it was an exercise in rejection. Powerful executives just didn't get the connection. How could these 'soft' women's issues be worthy of serious time or attention?" The year 1986 saw the appearance of the Economic Policy Council study "Work and Family in the United States," as well as a book, *Family and Work: Bridging the Gap*, which Hewlett edited with Alice S. Ilchman and John J. Sweeney and which was published by UNA-USA/Economic Policy Council. Hewlett expanded on the themes of the study in her book *A Lesser Life: The Myth of Women's Liberation in America* (1986), in which she contrasted the governmental and societal supports for working mothers in several European nations (France, Italy, Great Britain, and Sweden) with those in the United States. She found the policies of the U.S. lacking compared with the European ones, particularly in the areas of flexible or reduced working hours and child-related leave. "[Europeans] do what they do not because they're gung-ho for women's rights but because they care enormously about the fabric of their society—about making it possible for kids to have a decent start in life, about making it possible for women to be mothers as well as workers," she stated, as quoted by Marilyn Gardner. The book generated a negative reaction from those who thought that Hewlett had failed to acknowledge the substantial gains in women's lives brought about by the feminist movement; that she was actually fueling anti-feminism; that in separating the needs of women from those of men, and urging measures aimed specifically at women, she was in effect advocating inequality in the workplace and "giv[ing] employers reason not to hire women," as Betty Friedan complained to Nina Darnton for the *New York Tmes* (April 21, 1986); and that in light of fundamental differences between European societies and that of the U.S., Hewlett's comparisons were necessarily fallacious. "By and large feminists have been hostile," Hewlett told Marilyn Gardner. "Because I failed a litmus test of feminist orthodoxy—support for the Equal Rights Amendment—they find it very hard to see the book as a legitimate exercise." (She found the Equal Rights Amendment insufficiently supportive of working mothers.) She added, "But the central message of the book is a passionate plea for greater economic justice for women, so feminists should connect with it." Other critics called Hewlett on the carpet for what they viewed as a personal agenda. "It's disappointing that as a scholar and academic, Hewlett doesn't offer more than self-interested opinions on the real needs of young children," Joan Beck wrote for the *Chicago Tribune* (May 11, 1986). "It's also unfortunate that Hewlett did not write more as an economist as well as a tired mother. . . . Hewlett could have steeled her arguments by dealing, as an economist, with the hard-headed objections to what she proposes." Among those who were impressed by *A Lesser Life* was Bronwyn Drainie, who wrote in the Toronto *Globe and Mail*, as quoted in *Contemporary Authors* (1988), that the book is "an exhilarating read. It's honest, well researched and passionate."

Hewlett hoped that the government would take notice of the Economic Policy Council's report and suggestions. "The federal government has to provide a little leadership," she told Marilyn Gardner. "Then the private sector will put its mind to being imaginative and more effective. We expect so little from our public policies in this sphere. It's seen as kind of illegitimate to expect safety nets. We're all supposed to solve our problems ourselves." In Hewlett's opinion, 1988 was a watershed year, during which corporate leaders began to acknowledge the large percentage of women in the workforce. "The number of companies interested in family supports quintupled overnight, and I got upgraded from breakfast to lunch," she wrote in *When the Bough Breaks*. Meanwhile, the demands of her job, which often required her to be in Washington, D.C., while Congress was in session, had grown intolerably burdensome for her. Feeling that her children (two sons, a daughter, and a stepdaughter) needed her more than the Economic Policy Council did, she resigned her position. Remaking her career a second time, she concentrated on freelance writing and also served as a volunteer for children living in shelters in New York City and its suburbs.

She was moved by stories of the children she met, who, she felt, were victims of both the greater reliance on women in the workforce and the government's insufficient support for child care or child-welfare programs. Hewlett wrote her 1991 book, *When the Bough Breaks: The Cost of Neglecting Our Children*, "to chronicle the plight of America's children; to show how and why our attitudes and policies have tilted against young people; and to demonstrate why we must create conditions under which all children can flourish," as she wrote in the book's preface. "Ms. Hewlett blames both public and private neglect for this tragedy: using anecdote, blistering statistics and crusading rhetoric, she hopes to galvanize everyone—liberals and conservatives, public officials, corporate executives and ordinary Americans—to do *something*," Betsy Dworkin wrote in a review for the *New York Times* (June 30, 1991). "Her purpose is admirable, but the results are mixed. Parts of her book are compelling and instructive. But others seem impressionistic, not thought through, and dependent on material recycled from her last book . . . or familiar from the work of others." In the *New York Times* (July 11, 1991), Christopher Lehmann-Haupt praised as "imaginative" Hewlett's solutions, which included more funding for child-centered welfare programs and a more family-friendly corporate America. Still, he noted, "They depend on reversing certain trends in contemporary American culture, and here her book gets into difficulty." He added, "Despite her evangelical tone and an occasional shallowness in her reasoning, what is compelling about Ms. Hewlett's case is her argument that America's greatest weakness of the moment could be turned into its greatest advantage. Any investment now would eventually pay for itself and then some, she reasons."

In 1993 Hewlett founded the National Parenting Association, a nonprofit organization and think tank dedicated to "giving parents a greater voice in the public arena," according to its Web site. Five years later she teamed with Cornel West, who was then a professor of philosophy and Afro-American studies at Harvard University, to write *The War Against Parents: What We Can Do for America's Beleaguered Moms and Dads*. Like Hewlett's previous books, *The War Against Parents* describes the disadvantages of families overwhelmed by work responsibilities and lacking proper government support in the form of parental leave and tax support for family-friendly companies. Unlike her other books, it presents mothers and fathers as being equally burdened in a society that, in the view of Hewlett and West, "does not value or support parents," as Susan McCaffrey wrote for *Library Journal* (February 1, 2001). "We've written a Parents' Bill of Rights," Hewlett told Stefanie Weiss for *NEA Today* (September 1998), "that calls for paid parental leave, income supports for parents of children under six, tax incentives for companies that offer flexible hours, a living wage of at least $7 an hour, mortgage subsidies for families making less than $100,000 a year, incentives for parents to vote, tougher divorce laws, affordable child care, trigger locks on guns, and much more." The book received mixed reviews. "Hewlett and West hit a lot of appropriate targets," Marguerite Kelly wrote for the *Washington Post* (May 10, 1998), "but their proposed solutions have more misses than hits. Although they shuffle taxes and rework regulations to help families, and occasionally suggest smart ways to pay for their ideas . . . their Parents' Bill of Rights is a mix of the good, the bad and the silly: the kind of ideas you might hear in a graduate school coffee shop." Kelly added, "The authors' basic premise, however, is correct. As the richest nation in the world, we clearly must do something to help our beleaguered parents deal with the terrible time and money crunch they face today."

In the late 1990s Hewlett turned her attention to high-achieving women (whom she defined as those earning more than $55,000 a year). After she interviewed 15 women in order to determine the factors that had contributed to their success, she told Neal Conan on National Public Radio's *Talk of the Nation* (April 8, 2002), "I . . . realized the amazing fact that none of the women I was talking to had children." "I was stunned by this fact," Hewlett admitted to Ann Treneman for the London *Times* (April 22, 2002). "I hadn't chosen them because I was seeking childless women. I was seeking prominent women." In a second series of interviews, she learned that the women had not intended to be childless; rather, they told her, the demands of their careers had left them without time to seek a mate, commit to creating a family, or explore fertility treatments. Through the National Parenting Association, Hewlett conducted a survey of 1,168 high-achieving women ages 28 to 55 and found that 33 percent of those who were 40 or older had no children. For women who earned more than $100,000, 49 percent of those who were 40 or older were childless. (An estimated 15 percent of women in the U.S. actively decide not to have children.) Hewlett highlighted the disparity between high-achieving women and men, who were more likely to have children as they became more successful. She published her findings in *Creating a Life: Professional Women and the Quest for Children*, which relates case studies and also contains warnings for younger women. "It's tremendously comforting for a 34- or 36-year-old professional woman to imagine that she has time on her side," Hewlett told Nancy Gibbs. In reality, she noted, a woman's fertility begins to decrease starting when she is about 27; by her early 40s, the attempt to produce a healthy child has come to involve a race against time and an increased risk of chromosomal abnormalities. "Young women have had an extraordinary sense of entitlement," Hewlett said to Vanessa Grigoriadis for *New York* magazine (May 20, 2002). "Somehow they think that they have the *right* to have kids whenever they want." She expressed her hope that women would be "intentional," adding, "You all figure out what you want in your professional lives and then go after it, and you must find a way to do that in your personal lives, too." *Creating a Life* quickly created a buzz in the media: in the spring of 2002 Hewlett appeared on *The Oprah Winfrey Show, Today*, and *The View*, and "baby hunger" was the focus of a cover story in *Time* magazine. As Vanessa Grigoriadis noted, the book led to a great deal of introspection among young professional women who had previously thought that "there was a time for families: later." Some were critical of *Creating a Life*. "The decision of whether to have a child will always be one of the most important anyone makes; the challenge is not allowing time and biology to make it for them," Nancy Gibbs asserted. She also observed, "Biology may be unforgiving, but so is corporate culture: those who voluntarily leave their career to raise children often find that the way back in is extremely difficult." Hewlett took a different view. "You will make some compromises in your career [by having children earlier]. But you will catch up, reinvent yourself, when the time is right," she explained to Gibbs. "Look, there are two approaches you can take," she told Grigoriadis. "You can either stand on the sidelines and be critical. Or you can say: This is the game, and it is a game I want to play, because I want to end up with a husband and a child."

Although Hewlett's controversial thesis and public statements provoked a media frenzy, *Creating a Life* sold surprisingly few copies; as Warren St. John reported for the *New York Times* (May 20, 2002), two months after the book reached stores, only 8,000 to 10,000 copies of the 300,000 hardcovers printed had sold. "The publicity may have backfired," St. John wrote. "The book was portrayed in articles as not merely controversial, but as scary. The headline on the cover of *New York* magazine summed up the anxiety the book was generating: Baby Panic." Many booksellers speculated that women didn't want to read about the difficulties they faced in trying to have both a career and children.

At the age of 51, after four years of treatment with infertility therapies that rely on assisted reproductive technology, Hewlett gave birth to a daughter, Emma. "I'm one of the lucky ones," she admitted to Vanessa Grigoriadis. Her husband, Richared Weinert, is the senior managing director of Multinational Strategies, a private investment bank specializing in emerging markets in Central and Eastern Europe and the former Soviet Union. Hewlett lives with her family in New York City. —K.S.

Suggested Reading: *Christian Science Monitor* p25 Mar. 7, 1986, with photo; *People* p101+ Oct. 26, 1986, with photos; *Publishers Weekly* p49+ July 12, 1991, with photo; *Time* p10+ Aug. 26, 1991, with photo, p48+ Apr. 15, 2002, with photo

Selected Books: *A Lesser Life: The Myth of Women's Liberation in America*, 1986; *When the Bough Breaks: The Cost of Neglecting Our Children*, 1991; *The War Against Parents: What We Can Do for America's Beleaguered Moms and Dads* (with Cornel West), 1998; *Creating a Life: Professional Women and the Quest for Children*, 2002

---

## Higgins, Chester Jr.

*Nov. 1946– Photographer; writer*

*Address:* New York Times, *229 W. 43d St., New York, NY 10036-3959*

"I'm a cultural anthropologist with a camera . . . ," Chester Higgins Jr. told a writer in an interview that appeared on the Web site *abesha.com*. "You know when you write something it's limited to the language that you write in, whereas photographs, it's not limited to English speakers, French speakers, Luciphone speakers, Amharic speakers . . . everyone knows what a photograph is." Higgins has been a staff photographer for the *New York Times* since 1975. He has five books of photography to his credit: *The Black Woman* (1970), *Drums of Life* (1974), *Some Time Ago: A Historical Portrait of Black Americans 1850-1950* (1980), *Feeling the Spirit: Searching the World for the People of Africa* (1994), and *Elder Grace: The Nobility of Aging* (2000)—all of which explore and celebrate, in different ways, African-American or African heritage, culture, and identity. Higgins's photographs have appeared in *Art News, Look*, the *New York Times Magazine, Life, Newsweek, Fortune, Ebony, Essence*, and *Archaeology* in addition to the *New York Times*.

Chester Archer Higgins Jr. was born in November 1946 in Lexington, Kentucky, and grew up in New Brockton, Alabama. He was raised by his mother, Varidee Loretta Young Higgins Smith, and his stepfather, Johnny Frank Smith. In 1970 he graduated from Tuskegee Institute (now Tuskegee University), in Tuskegee, Alabama, with a bachelor's degree in business management. While an undergraduate at Tuskegee, Higgins was mentored by P. H. Polk, the school's official photographer; Polk gave Higgins lessons in photography and interested him in his African-American heritage. Higgins told Clarence Peterson for the *Chicago Tribune* (December 4, 1980), "I became a photographer in 1967 because there were things I thought should be appreciated that were not being seen, and I figured they would only be seen if I went out and shot them." Some of his first pictures were of his great-aunts and great-uncles. In 1968, around the time that Higgins bought his first camera, there were civil rights protests by black students at Tuskegee, and Higgins documented the event, compiling his photographs under the title "Student Unrest at Tuskegee Institute." After graduation

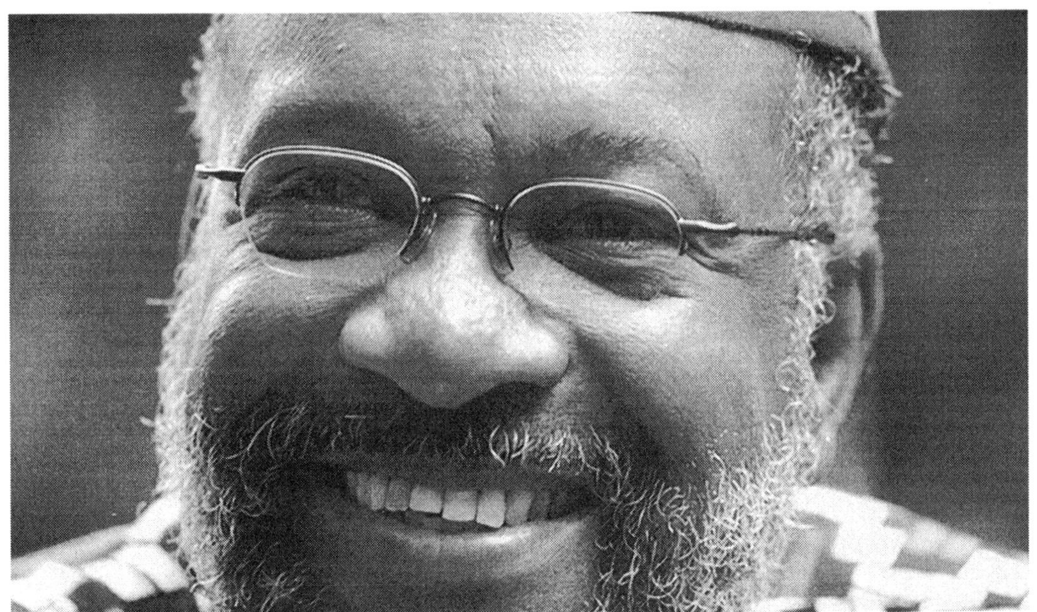

Courtesy of Chester Higgins

*Chester Higgins Jr.*

Higgins was in New York showing some of his pictures to various magazine editors when he met Arthur Rothstein, then director of photography at *Look* magazine. Rothstein became another mentor to Higgins, who discovered, at this time, the work of such master photographers as Alfred Stieglitz, Henri Cartier-Bresson, and Gordon Parks. In 1970 *Look* magazine sent Higgins on his first assignment; his job was to follow and photograph a young civil rights leader named Jesse Jackson as he toured various cities and gave speeches. Higgins was quoted in the *New York Times* (June 9, 1996) as saying, "It got so I could predict how the audience was going to react at a particular moment in the speech, so I could pick a face and be ready with my camera."

In 1970 Higgins published his first book of photographs, *The Black Woman*, as a response to the prevalence of stereotyped and negative images of black women. He told Angela Terrell for the *Washington Post* (August 8, 1974), "I saw the danger of the media was that it could condition people's minds to what other people are supposed to be." *Drums of Life* (1974), a follow-up to *The Black Woman*, features the photographer's positive images of black men, with an accompanying text by the writer Orde Coombs. Much of Higgins's motivation was to help counterbalance what he saw as the "dishonest fantasies" in the common depictions of black men. Higgins commented to Terrell that he was interested in "the need and desire to project black life," and in having viewers see that "my life (the black man) is a full and natural life." In the book, Higgins showed black males as children, young adults, fathers, and husbands. He worked as a part-time photography instructor at the New York University School of Fine Arts from 1975 to 1978 and took a job as a staff photographer at the *New York Times* in 1975. In the meantime he continued his artistic quest to present more realistic images of blacks.

Higgins recalled to Jacqueline Trescott for the *Washington Post* (December 16, 1980), "A teacher of mine told me the story of a man who used to read a bedtime story to his son about a fight between a man and a lion. The man always won and his son asked how that was so, since the lion was king of the jungle. And the father said the lion will win when he writes his own book." In 1980 Higgins again wrote his own book: *Some Time Ago: A Historical Portrait of Black Americans 1850-1950.* For this project Higgins searched over the course of four years through more than 40,000 images—pictures that he found in places ranging from cigar boxes and old trunks to the Library of Congress, in Washington, D.C., and the New York Public Library's Schomburg collection. From these he culled 200 of his favorite photographs for his book, which contains no pictures taken by Higgins himself. *Some Time Ago* features the work of such famous photographers as Dorothea Lange, Gordon Parks, and Walker Evans and includes pictures of famous African-Americans, including the abolitionist and women's rights activist Sojourner Truth, the singer Marian Anderson, and the educator Mary McLeod Bethune. There are also photographs of a barber and his customer, a chain gang, children at prayer, and the whip-scarred back of a man who lived during the era of slavery. Higgins told Clarence Peterson about the book, "Because the records are there, you can go back and see for yourself what people were doing, how they lived, and even how they withstood the conditions that were sometimes intolerable. It makes you feel good to see that, against all those odds, those people survived. And it gives you a sense of continuance, of belonging, that you're part of a long tradition."

*Feeling the Spirit: Searching the World for the People of Africa* was the result of more than 25 years of Higgins's traveling the world to take pictures that represent the African diaspora. This 303-page book captures in more than 200 photographs the traditions, spirituality, and daily lives of people of African heritage—everyone from tribal dancers in Mali, to voodoo practitioners in Haiti, to black Jews in the Harlem section of New York City, to Yoruba people worshipping in Brazil, to black men and women in rural Alabama. Two major exhibits of Higgins's photographs from *Feeling the Spirit* followed the book's publication. One exhibit, which shared the book's title, was held at the International Center of Photography, in New York; the other, organized by the Schomburg Center for Research in Black Culture, was titled *Invoking the Spirit: Worship Traditions in the African World.* The photographs include those of a Brooklyn man holding a Bible, a Ghanaian man blessing his son on a beach, a Mexican statue of a person with African features, the face of a Trinidadian schoolgirl, and a man resting in his boat on the Niger River in Mali, as well as the "Door of No Return" in Senegal, through which enslaved Africans were sent on ships to the Americas. Higgins told Diane M. Bolz for *Smithsonian* (Fall 1997), "We are Africans not because we are born in Africa, but because Africa is born in us." He added, "It's the people's characters themselves speaking through the film, through the lens, that tells the story." Eddy L. Harris reviewed Higgins's book for the *New York Times* (November 20, 1994), writing, "*Feeling the Spirit* is a beautiful book. It is a big book of photographs, all of them in black and white, all of them caught by Mr. Higgins's careful and patient eye. They are images that capture the sometimes difficult, sometimes joyous, sometimes painful, sometimes routine daily lives of black people everywhere."

Higgins's latest book of photography is *Elder Grace: The Nobility of Aging*, which includes photographs from Higgins's traveling exhibit of the same name. The book, with a foreword by Maya Angelou, contains 80 individual portraits of elderly African-Americans. Higgins's wife, Betsy Kissam, who interviewed the subjects, supplied a quotation from each below his or her photograph. Higgins told Lyle Rexer for the *New York Times* (February 25, 2001), "I want people to see my pictures and ask, 'How can I look like that when I get to be that age?' You can't deny the next day, so accept it, embrace it." Rexer wrote, "Mr. Higgins has assembled a gallery of the beautiful, the pensive and the noble. . . . By lavishing attention on his subjects and by seeking to apprehend what he calls their shine, or inner light, he captures qualities that continue to make them physically attractive into late age: humor, elegance and dignity."

During the course of his career, Higgins has had one-man exhibitions at the International Center of Photography, the Smithsonian Institution, the Museum of African Art, the Museum of Photographic Arts, the Schomburg Center, the Newark Museum, the National Civil Rights Museum, and the Field Museum of Natural History. His photographs have also been shown at the Metropolitan Museum of Art, in New York City, and in American embassy galleries around the world. They are included in the permanent collections of the New York Museum of Modern Art, the International Center of Photography, and the Schomburg Center. For his photography Higgins has won a United Nations Award, an American Graphic Design Award, a *Graphics* Magazine Award, and an Art Directors Club of New York Award. Higgins was the subject of the PBS film *An American Photographer: Chester Higgins Jr.*, and his work has aired on the *Sunday Morning News* on CBS, *The News Hour* on PBS, and the ABC programs *Like It Is* and *Freedom Forum*. He has received grants from the National Endowment for the Arts, the Andy Warhol Foundation, the Ford Foundation, the Rockefeller Foundation, and the American Revolution Bicentennial Commission. Higgins has lectured on photography at Harvard University and Dartmouth, and he did special photography for Gordon Park's film *Shaft's Big Score* (1972).

Higgins married and divorced Renalda Walker, with whom he has a son, Chester III (also called Damani), and a daughter, Nataki. Higgins's second wife is Betsy Kissam, a magazine journalist. He lives in the Fort Greene section of Brooklyn, New York. — C.F.T.

Suggested Reading: *Chicago Tribune* I p13 Dec. 4, 1980, with photo; *New York Times* VII p13 Nov. 20, 1994, with photos, C p6 Nov. 24, 1995, II p48 Feb. 25, 2001; *Washington Post* B p4 Dec. 16, 1980, with photos, C p1 Feb. 19, 1997; *Who's Who Among African Americans 1998-99*

Selected Books: *Some Time Ago* (1980), *Feeling the Spirit* (1994), *Elder Grace* (2000)

---

## Hill, Grant

*Oct. 5, 1972– Basketball player*

*Address: Orlando Magic, TD Waterhouse Centre, 600 W. Amelia St., Orlando, FL 32801*

When Orlando Magic forward Grant Hill started his career in the National Basketball Association (NBA), in 1994, ordinary fans and experts alike predicted that he would become one of the greatest players ever. Hill had played on two college championship teams and participated in the Final Four an unprecedented three times during his years at Duke University, prompting the Detroit Pistons to select Hill as its first-round draft choice. (He was the third pick overall.) Basketball pundits immedi-

Courtesy of the Orlando Magic

*Grant Hill*

ately began to tout Hill as the next Michael Jordan, referring to the Chicago Bulls/Washington Wizards player whom many consider to be the best in the game's history. Hill's on-court performance in his first year with the Pistons lived up to expectations, as he led his team in scoring (19.9 points per game) and steals (124). He also proved capable of instilling excitement in those who watched him play, as evidenced by his overwhelming popularity in that year's All-Star balloting: he received more votes than anyone else in the league, becoming the first rookie in NBA history to achieve that feat. Although comparisons to Jordan have all but subsided seven years into Hill's pro career, that is not because of his lack of stellar play. Experts simply have noted the differences in the two players' games. Hill's former coach in Detroit, Doug Collins, in an interview with Jackie MacMullan for *Sports Illustrated* (January 22, 1996), explained, "Grant doesn't have the killer instinct in scoring that Michael has. He can dominate a game more subtly, by getting the ball to open people, by rebounding and, with two dribbles, getting his team into the open floor the way Magic [Johnson] did as a rookie." Following the 1999–2000 NBA season, the Pistons traded Hill to the Orlando Magic. In his first season with the Magic, Hill sat out all but four games due to an ankle injury suffered in the previous year's play-offs; at the commencement of the 2001–02 season, however, Hill's physicians gave him a clean bill of health.

Grant Henry Hill was born on October 5, 1972 in Dallas, Texas, the only child of Calvin and Janet Hill. Calvin Hill had been an All–Ivy League running back at Yale University, in New Haven, Connecticut, and gone on to play for several professional football teams—notably the Dallas Cowboys, the squad on which he won the National Football League (NFL) Rookie of the Year honor in 1969. In addition, he played in four NFL Pro Bowls and two Super Bowls and was named to the Dallas Cowboys' All-Time Team. When Grant Hill was very young, his father was traded to the Washington Redskins; the family then moved to a suburb of Washington, D.C., where Grant spent most of his childhood. After his retirement from professional football, Calvin Hill went on to become a successful businessman, holding managerial positions in various organizations, including the Baltimore Orioles baseball team. Grant Hill's mother attended Wellesley College, in Wellesley, Massachusetts, where she shared a dormitory with future First Lady Hillary Clinton (then Hillary Rodham). After studying mathematics, Janet Hill worked as a special assistant to the secretary of the army, later becoming a partner in the Capitol Hill consulting firm Alexander & Associates.

Fearing that their child would suffer from comparisons with his father, Calvin and Janet Hill forbade Grant from playing football until he entered the ninth grade, at South Lakes High School, near the family home in Reston, Virginia. After watching the team practice on a stifling August afternoon, the teenager decided that football was not his game. He told William Plummer for *People* (January 23, 1995), "I looked [at the football team] and said [to my father], 'I am not going to be out in this hot weather. I'm going to be in that air-conditioned gym.'" He thus focused his efforts on the game of basketball, for which he soon showed extraordinary talent. In his junior and senior years at South Lakes, Hill led his team to two state championships while maintaining a scoring average of 25 and 29 points per game, respectively. He was also named a high-school All-American in both years. While his success on the basketball court made his father proud, Calvin and Janet Hill were determined that their son not let his accomplishments go to his head. To that end, Calvin often gave his son good-natured ribbing, some of which Grant Hill recalled to Alexander Wolff for *Sports Illustrated* (February 1, 1993): "Grant, you're good," he remembers his father saying, "but you've only got half my genes. Imagine if you had the other half." Calvin Hill told Wolff about his son's success, "It's like General Douglas MacArthur. His father was a general too, and the son totally eclipsed him." Grant Hill has acknowledged his parents, and the manner in which they raised him, as the biggest influences on his life. "I know this sounds funny," Hill told Christopher John Farley for *Time* (February 13, 1995), "but it was almost like being born into a royal family and being raised like a prince, being taught one day to become king. Not just how to be an athlete, but how to do things right."

From high school Hill was recruited to play for the basketball team at Duke University, in Durham, North Carolina, where he majored in history. There was considerable hype surrounding the 18-year-old freshman. In an interview with Anthony Cotton for the *Washington Post* (April 27, 1991), Hill explained, "In high school I knew everyone from growing up with them. I was just one of the fellas, it wasn't like 'Ooh you're Grant Hill.' The first day [at Duke] there were people asking me for my autograph and they were expecting so much—it was like if you didn't do what they thought you should be doing you were letting them down." By the end of the regular season, Hill had for the most part lived up to those expectations; on a team that boasted such stars as Bobby Hurley, Christian Laettner, and Bill McCaffrey, Hill averaged 11.2 points per game, shot 52 percent from the field, and had 79 assists, 51 steals, and 30 blocked shots. Hill and his teammates beat Kansas (72–65) in the final game of the 1991 National Collegiate Athletic Association (NCAA) Championships to win the national title at the Hoosier Dome, in Indianapolis, Indiana. Hill was voted to the All-American Freshman team, selected for the All-ACC (Atlantic Coast Conference) Freshman team, and invited to represent the U.S. at the 1991 Pan American Games held in Havana, Cuba—where the U.S. team took the bronze medal after losing to Puerto Rico in the semifinals. Mike Krzyzewski, Hill's coach at Duke, told Cotton for the *Washington Post* (April 1, 1991), "[Hill] just plays so many different positions that he's difficult for people to try and match up with. . . . I can't imagine an 18-year-old playing as well as he has at this level."

Hill's momentum only increased during his sophomore season at Duke. In addition to his valuable play at small forward, he showed remarkable versatility when Hurley was injured during the regular season; stepping into the point-guard role, he averaged 16.4 points and 5.6 assists in five games. In that season's championship game, Duke bested the University of Michigan, 71–51. During an interview with Michael Bradley for the *Sporting News* (April 4, 1994), Hill explained the attitude of his team that year: "On November 1, we knew we were going to win the national championship. There was an air of confidence. Our whole approach was that the [opposing] team had the audacity to be on the court with us. . . . That was that whole feeling and vibe." At the close of the 1991–92 season, Hill was named to the NCAA All-Final Four Team, the Second Team All-American, and the Second Team All-ACC. That summer he also received the opportunity to play on the USA Olympic Development Team, which trained with the U.S. Olympic squad—the "Dream Team" that included Jordan, Charles Barkley, and Magic Johnson.

With the graduation of several key players, Hill was forced into a leadership position in his junior year. Although for the first time in his collegiate career, the team did not win the national championship—being ousted by California in the tournament's second round—Hill led the Blue Devils in scoring for the 1992–93 season, with an average of 18 points per game, despite having suffered a broken toe. He also topped the team in steals (64), which led to his winning the Henry Iba Corinthian Award as the nation's best defensive player. Hill was named to the Second Team All-American and First Team All-ACC.

With the NBA draft approaching, all eyes were on Grant Hill during his senior year. While Duke lost a 76–72 nail-biter to the University of Arkansas in the NCAA final, Hill led his team in four major categories that year: scoring (an average of 17.4 points per game), minutes played (an average of 35.7 per game), assists (176), and steals (64). His efforts earned him a unanimous First Team All-American spot, and he was voted ACC Player of the Year. Hill was also the NCAA Southeastern Regional Most Valuable Player and a finalist for the Naismith, Wooden, and RCA/USBWA National Player of the Year awards. In his four-year tenure at Duke, Hill had compiled 1,924 points (ninth highest in Duke's history), 461 assists (sixth highest), 218 steals (fourth), and 133 blocks (fourth). In honor of his performances on the court, Duke University retired Grant's number, 33; he became only the eighth player at the university to receive that honor. In his interview with Bradley, Hill also described his personal growth. "When I got [to Duke]," he explained, "I was shy. I changed a lot—not for the worse. I've changed. I've grown. I've matured. I've had a great experience at Duke, and I'm a lot different than I was when I first got here."

Shortly after earning his bachelor's degree, Hill was selected by the Detroit Pistons as that team's first pick in the 1994 NBA draft and signed to an eight-year, $45 million deal. Hill's transition from college play to the fast-paced world of the NBA, as many sports reporters noted, appeared to be almost effortless. Averaging 38.3 minutes per game, Hill started all but one of the Pistons' 70 games in his rookie year and led the team in steals (124), points per game (19.9), and total points (1,394). Long noted for his modesty, Hill shrugged off comparisons between himself and Michael Jordan, telling Johnette Howard for the *Washington Post* (December 2, 1994), "I think it's absurd. The only thing Michael Jordan and I have in common is we both played college basketball in North Carolina and won championships our first years. Here [in the NBA], I haven't done anything yet." Basketball fans, however, disagreed, as evidenced by the results of the 1994 All-Star Game balloting, in which Hill emerged as the first rookie in NBA history to lead the league in votes. Joe Dumars, a Pistons veteran and mentor to Hill, told Christopher John Farley, "[The NBA is] a league of guys who are out of control. Fringe behavior is being recognized and accepted, sometimes even rewarded. It's probably not a healthy comment that Grant is being recognized for just being a good person, but it's time we get back to that." Hill was named Co-Rookie of the Year for the 1994–95 season, along with Dallas Mavericks point guard Jason Kidd.

Hill's play was equally good in his second season as a pro. He finished the season as only the 15th player in modern NBA history to lead his team in points (1,618), rebounds (783), and assists (548). He also led the NBA with 10 triple-doubles, or games in which he reached or surpassed the number 10 in each of three categories: points, assists, and rebounds. Fans again expressed their appreciation for Hill through their All-Star voting; for the second consecutive season, Hill led the league in ballots, with 1,358,004 votes. He scored 14 points in the All-Star Game. Following the end of the NBA season, Hill was selected as a member of the 1996 USA Olympic Basketball squad, or Dream Team III. In the Olympic Games, held in Atlanta, Georgia, Hill led the team to a gold medal.

Over the next four seasons, although Hill continued to improve as a player, his team failed to make it past the play-offs. With the emergence of the Los Angeles Lakers star Kobe Bryant, even the comparisons of Hill and Jordan seemed to disappear. Hill told Jackie MacMullan and Marty Burns for *Sports Illustrated* (February 9, 1998), "In some ways, I'm kind of jealous. Kobe is in such a great environment. I'd love to see what it's like to be around three other All-Stars [Shaquille O'Neal, Eddie Jones, and Nick Van Exel]." "I know I'll be criticized until I win a championship," he further explained to MacMullan and Burns. "That's how it was with Michael [Jordan] and Hakeem [Olajuwon]. But it's hard to watch us get further away, instead of closer to that goal. . . . This is the most frustrated I've ever been in my career." During those four seasons Hill started every All-Star Game.

In the Pistons' first-round loss to the Miami Heat in the 2000 NBA play-offs, Hill suffered a broken bone in his left ankle. Three days later he underwent surgery, which entailed the insertion of a pin and left Hill in a cast for four weeks. A full recovery was expected in time for the 2000–01 season. The question remained, however, as to whether Hill would remain in Detroit. The answer came on August 3, when the Orlando Magic signed him to a seven-year, $92.96 million contract. When the season began, in late October, Hill's ankle was still bothering him, and his court time was limited. At the end of 2000, the team announced that Hill would require a second round of surgery, which he underwent on January 3, 2001. Hill had played in only four regular-season games, averaging 13.8 points per game.

While the six-foot, eight-inch forward started the 2001–02 season believing that he was fit, his ankle continued to bother him; he played only 14 games before his condition forced him to bow out for a while. "[My ankle had been] in the healing process, but then I came back and it . . . stopped healing," Hill explained to Marc Stein for the ESPN Web site (October 4, 2002). "It went backwards. The 50 percent that it healed went to 40 percent. When I came back . . . the bone hadn't healed completely." In December 2001 he underwent his fourth ankle surgery. (Continuing without him, the Magic finished third in the Atlantic Division, with a 44–38 record.) During the summer off-season, Hill limited his workouts to an hour a day; he returned to form in training camp in September. The Magic got off to a 5–2 start in the 2002–03 season, with Hill performing outstandingly. Although he played an average of only 28.6 minutes per game, his field goal percentage (.635) was the second-best in the league, and he achieved a free-throw percentage of .842, an average of 5.6 assists per game, and an average of 20.3 points per game. He also ranked first in the NBA in efficiency per 48 minutes. Hill is now surrounded by such established players as Shawn Kemp and Horace Grant as well as highly talented up-and-comers, including Tracey Grady. Having proved himself to be one of the premier players in the NBA, Hill is now focused on helping to win an NBA title. The year before, he told Jonathan Feigan for the *Houston Chronicle* (October 20, 2001), "I want to win, and this injury has put that into perspective. . . . I can get into all the All-Star Games in the world, all the commercials and all the money, but it doesn't mean anything if you don't win."

In 1999 Hill married the Grammy-nominated recording artist Tamia Washington (known professionally as simply Tamia). The couple live in Orlando, Florida. — J.H.

Suggested Reading: *Essence* p80+ Nov. 1995, with photos; *Houston Chronicle* p5 Oct. 20, 2001; *New York Times Magazine* p30+ Oct. 26, 1997, with photos; *Sport* p17+ Apr. 1996, with photos, p96+ Nov. 1999, with photos; *Sporting News* p9 Apr. 4, 1994, with photo; *Sports Illustrated* p59+ Feb. 1, 1993, with photos, p40+ Apr. 24, 1995, with photos, p58+ Jan. 22, 1996, with photo, p40+ Nov. 25, 1996, with photos, p50+ Feb. 9, 1998, with photo; *Washingtonian* p33+ Apr. 1997, with photos

---

## Holm, Ian

*Sep. 12, 1931– Actor*

*Address: c/o Julian Belfrage Associates, 46 Albermarle St., London W1X 4PP, England*

"I know that I have a gift," the British actor Ian Holm told Bruce Kirkland for the *Toronto Sun* (October 15, 1997, on-line). "I know that I am good at what I do. But it took me about 25 or 30 years to accept that. Once I did, I found I could relax more and ply my trade." Nicknamed "Mr. Ubiquitous," Holm is one of the most versatile actors of stage, screen, and television. In his nearly 50-year career, he has portrayed a huge range of character types. "Holm is the purist of conduits for the behaviors and motivations of the characters he plays," Bob Wake wrote for *culturevulture.net* in 2001. "Whether portraying button-down negligence at-

Sion Touhig/Getty Images

*Ian Holm*

torney Mitchell Stephens in *The Sweet Hereafter*, or Greenwich Village gadfly Joe Gould in *Joe Gould's Secret*, Holm disappears into his roles with thorough self-effacement." The actor launched his career in 1954 as a member of the Royal Shakespeare Company. In theater, he has received rave reviews for his depictions of King Lear, Richard II, and other characters created by Shakespeare and also for his work in dramas by such playwrights as Anton Chekhov, Jean Giraudoux, Jean Anouilh, and, most notably, Harold Pinter. But Holm "unequivocally" prefers film to theater, as he declared in an interview with Claire Armitstead for the London *Guardian* (January 20, 1994). "I find it quite difficult to be transported by the theatre in the way that you can be sitting in the cinema," he told her. Holm made his first appearance on the silver screen in 1968, in *The Bofors Gun*, and won a BAFTA (British Academy of Film and Television Arts) award for his efforts. He has since appeared in several dozen feature films, among them *Oh! What a Lovely War, Nicholas and Alexandra, Alien, Chariots of Fire, Brazil, The Sweet Hereafter*, and, most recently, the first installment of Peter Jackson's *Lord of the Rings* trilogy, in which he was cast as Bilbo Baggins. He has also been in many made-for-television movies, such as *The Borrowers*, and TV series, such as *Game, Set and Match*, and lent his voice to numerous documentaries, among them several for the BBC series *The Natural World*. In 1989 he was named a Commander of the Order of the British Empire, and in 1998 Queen Elizabeth II knighted him, citing his "services to drama."

A son of James Harvey Cuthbert and Jean Wilson Cuthbert, Sir Ian Holm was born Ian Holm Cuthbert on September 12, 1931 in Goodmayes, in Greater London, England, at the mental asylum where his father worked as a psychiatrist and superintendent. His mother and father were much older than the average parents of newborns, and by his own account, he never got to know them well. Holm has told several interviewers that for most of his childhood, he felt unhappy both at home and at school (the Chigwell Grammar School, in Essex, near London). He enjoyed going to the theater with his father, though. As a seven-year-old he saw Charles Laughton perform in a stage version of Victor Hugo's novel *Les Misérables* and decided that he, too, would become an actor. When Holm was about 13, his older brother, Eric, died of cancer while serving overseas in the Scots Guard, a British military regiment; according to several sources, Eric's death profoundly affected the rest of the family.

In 1950 Holm enrolled at the Royal Academy of Dramatic Arts, in London. Before he graduated from the academy, in 1953, he spent a year in the British military, to fulfill his National Service requirement. In 1954 he became a member of the famed Royal Shakespeare Company (RSC) in Stratford-upon-Avon, where, that same year, he made his stage debut as a sword carrier in William Shakespeare's *Othello*. He temporarily left the RSC in 1955. His first appearance on the London stage came in 1956, in a West End production of Dulcie Gray's play *Love Affair*. That year he also toured Europe in Laurence Olivier's production of Shakespeare's *Titus Andronicus*; he was cast as Mutius, one of the title character's sons. In 1957 Holm rejoined the RSC, and during the next 10 years, as an RSC contract artist, he gained a reputation as one of the leading young lights in British theater. In 1965 and 1967 he received *Evening Standard* Actor of the Year Awards for his work in Shakespeare's *Henry V* and Pinter's *The Homecoming*, respectively. The 1967 Broadway production of the latter play brought him a Tony Award. After seeing him perform the role of Prince Hal in *Henry IV*, Penelope Gilliatt, in the London *Observer* (April 10, 1966), described him as "brilliant . . . a cool, trim, watcher, mak[ing] the betrayal of his past with Falstaff seem a deeply rooted act of temperamental necessity instead of an expedient piece of ditching by a new monarch." In the London *Guardian* (September 12, 1967), assessing him as a Shakespearean actor, Gareth Lloyd Evans labeled Holm "a self-confessed, intuitive player, more at home with psychologically bunched-up characters than with romantic free-ranging heroes." Evans also wrote that the actor displayed a "combination of tenacious professionalism, warm feeling, loneliness, and something else. He has an extra quality which, at best, is a kind of thoughtful wit, at worst a playful roguishness. This gives him the audacity and the technique always to be trying something new. It often works brilliantly, but occasionally it lets him down." Also with the Royal Shakespeare Company, Holm appeared as Richard III in *The War of the Roses*, in which the troupe performed three of Shakespeare's historical plays in succession. In a review of the televised broadcast of the series, John Horn wrote for the New York *Herald Tribune* (March 28, 1968), "Nothing lacked in Ian Holm's brilliant depiction of the crippled king," and described his performance as "lighted by intelligence and a fine sense of malevolence."

Holm made his film debut in 1968, in *The Bofors Gun*, a military drama set in Germany after World War I. Holm played a British soldier named Flynn, whose life is threatened by a drunken Irish gunner. For his work in *The Bofors Gun*, Holm won a BAFTA award for best supporting actor. Also in 1968 he appeared as Grubeshov in the movie *The Fixer*, directed by John Frankenheimer from a screenplay based on the Pulitzer Prize–winning novel by Bernard Malamud. In his next major role, in the made-for-television film *Moonlight on the Highway* (1969), Holm portrayed a disturbed man whose obsession with the 1930s singer Al Bowlly helps him to forget unpleasant elements from his past.

During the next 10 years, Holm's silver-screen performances included supporting roles in *Oh! What a Lovely War* (1969), *Nicholas and Alexandra* (1971), *Young Winston* (1972), *The Homecoming* (1973), *Robin and Marian* (1976), and *The Man in the Iron Mask* (1976). Among his more prominent appearances, he was cast as the witless wine-taster Martin Lynch-Gibbon in *A Severed Head* (1971); David Riccio in *Mary, Queen of Scots*; and the mute servant Mohammed in the World War I adventure film *Shout at the Devil* (1976). In 1974 he starred as Napoleon in the television miniseries *Napoleon and Love*.

In 1976, during a theatrical production of Eugene O' Neill's *The Iceman Cometh* in which he played the main character, Hickey, Holm developed a severe case of stage fright during one of his monologues and left the stage. "I wasn't domestically going through a particularly happy period at the time," he told an interviewer for *ExxonMobil Masterpiece Theatre Online*, referring to the break-up of his relationship with a photographer named Bee, who had borne two of his children. "I'd just done a long stint of work in a television epic called *Jesus of Nazareth* . . . where I was 16 weeks in the desert in Tunisia, and that's enough to drive anybody mad. . . . Something just snapped. Once the concentration goes, the brain literally closes down. It's like a series of doors slamming shut in a jail. . . . But it was righted by medication. It didn't take that long. I guess I could have gone back probably a lot sooner than I did, but fortuitously I was gainfully employed in the other two media; I started movies seriously and television, where as we all know, if you make a mistake, you can do it again."

Having turned away from theater, Holm played the fierce Arab leader El Krim in the movie *March or Die* (1977). The following year, in two television miniseries, he was cast as Heinrich Himmler in *Holocaust* and then as J. M. Barrie, the author of *Peter Pan*, in *The Lost Boys*. His appearance as Thenardier in the made-for-television movie *Les Misérables* (1978) came 40 years after the stage production of *Les Misérables* that had influenced him so powerfully when he was a child. In 1979, in one of his best-known roles, Holm portrayed Ash, the treacherous spaceship science officer, who turns out to be an android, in the Ridley Scott science-fiction thriller *Alien*. That year, in his first appearance in a play since his experience with stage-fright, he took on the role of Astrov, a doctor, in a production of Chekhov's *Uncle Vanya* mounted at the Hampstead Theatre, in London. (After that, another 14 years passed before he acted in a play.) His performance in the film *Chariots of Fire* (1981) as the Jewish athletic trainer/coach Sam Mussabini, who hopes to prove to the world that Jews are not inferior beings, brought Holm an Oscar nomination and BAFTA and Cannes Film Festival awards for best supporting actor. Holm portrayed Napoleon for the second time in his career in Terry Gilliam's *Time Bandits* (1981). Among his other noteworthy roles in the early 1980s was that of Capitaine Phillippe D'Arnot in *Greystoke: The Legend of Tarzan, Lord of the Apes* (1984). In that film Tarzan rescues D'Arnot from certain death in the jungle, and in return, D'Arnot teaches Tarzan to speak English. He later discovers that the wild man is actually the Earl of Greystoke. Also in 1984 Holm starred in the movie *Laughterhouse* as Ben Singleton, a farmer who, during a strike by his workers, rounds up his hundreds of geese, which he cannot slaughter without help, and leads them on a 100-mile trek to London. The film focuses on the harmfulness of commercial farms.

Holm appeared in four feature films in 1985. In the comedy/horror fantasy *Brazil*—his second Terry Gilliam picture—he played Mr. M. Kurtzmann, the boss of the main character. He took on the role of Stanley Pilborough in the playwright David Hare's first film, *Wetherby*, about an unmarried schoolteacher whose life is disrupted when a student inexplicably commits suicide in her kitchen. Holm portrayed Lewis Carroll (the pen name of Charles L. Dodgson) in *Dreamchild*; written by Dennis Potter and directed by Gavin Millar, *Dreamchild* focuses on the 80-year-old Alice Liddell Hargreaves (depicted by Coral Browne), who, as a child, was the inspiration for Carroll's classic fantasy *Alice in Wonderland*. In Mike Newell's *Dance with a Stranger*, written by Shelagh Delaney, about the real-life Ruth Ellis—the last woman to be executed in England—Holm played Desmond Cussen, who tries in vain to rescue Ellis (Miranda Richardson) from the destructive influence of the lover (Rupert Everett) whom she ultimately kills. Holm's depiction of Cussen is widely considered to be among his finest performances.

In the latter half of the 1980s, Holm was cast in the 13-part British television series *Game, Set and Match* (which earned him a Royal Television Society award as best actor) and two big-screen films: Woody Allen's *Another Woman* (1988) and Kenneth Branagh's rendering of Shakespeare's *Henry V* (1989). In *Another Woman* Holm played an emotionally remote, unfaithful cardiologist, whose wife (Gena Rowlands), a middle-aged philosophy professor, is painfully examining her life. His depiction of Fluellen, a Welsh officer in the king's army, in *Henry V* was highly acclaimed, as was his later portrayal of Polonius, King Claudius's adviser, in Franco Zeffirelli's interpretation of Shakespeare's *Hamlet* (1990), which features Mel Gibson as the title character. "Holm is especially effective in the 'to thine own self be true' speech, evoking memories of his great work as the track coach in *Chariots of Fire*," Roger Ebert noted in his review of *Hamlet* for the *Chicago Sun-Times* (January 18, 1991). In 1991 Holm reprised his performance as Astrov in the made-for-television movie *Uncle Vanya*. That year he also played the evil Dr. Murnau in Steven Soderbergh's feature film *Kafka* and the eccentric writer Tom Frost in David Cronenberg's cinematic adaptation of William S. Burroughs's expressionistic, surreal novel *Naked Lunch*.

In 1993 Holm portrayed the intellectual, lecherous priest Albertus in the film *The Hour of the Pig* (also known as *The Advocate*), a murder mystery/comedy set in medieval France. Also in 1993, in a radically different role, he starred as Pod Clock (opposite his third wife, Penelope Wilton, who was cast as Pod's spouse, Homily) in the children's television movies *The Borrowers* and *Return of the Borrowers*; both were based on Mary Norton's much-loved novels, the first published in 1952, about a family of humans only a few inches tall who live in a normal-size family's house and survive by borrowing all their necessities from their unwitting hosts. Holm earned a BAFTA award as best actor for his work in *The Borrowers*. In 1993, in what he has described as his "real" return to the theater after the stagefright incident, he played the bed-ridden civil servant, Andy, in Harold Pinter's *Moonlight*, creating in the character what Claire Armitstead described as "a towering inferno of impotent rage." For his work in *Moonlight*, Holm was named actor of the year by the *Evening Standard* and earned a Critics Circle Theatre Award, also in England.

In 1994 Holm appeared as Baron Frankenstein, the father of the monster-creator Victor Frankenstein, in Kenneth Branagh's adaptation of Mary Shelley's classic 1818 novel *Frankenstein*. The part was not big, as Holm told Armitstead: "I mean, whoever heard of Frankenstein's father? But I'm finding it fascinating. I've never known a director who worked so intensely." In a meatier movie role, Holm portrayed Dr. Willis, the royal physician, in the much-lauded *Madness of King George* (1994), adapted by Alan Bennett from Bennett's same-titled play, about the mental illness that struck George III of England in 1788–89. "Holm is perfect for the role—stern, unyielding, and dotty," Roger Ebert wrote for the *Chicago Sun-Times* (January 27, 1995). After supporting parts in such films as *Loch Ness* (1995) and *Big Night* (1996), Holm appeared as the tough cop Liam Casey in Sidney Lumet's police melodrama *Night Falls on Manhattan* (1997), based on a Robert Daley novel. He also took on the comic role of Vito Cornelius, a priest, in Luc Besson's science-fiction film *The Fifth Element* (1997).

After some 30 years in film, the 65-year-old Holm got top billing for the first time, in the role of Mitchell Stephens in *The Sweet Hereafter* (1997). An adaptation of a Russell Banks novel written and directed by the Canadian independent filmmaker Atom Egoyan, *The Sweet Hereafter* shows how residents of a small rural community in British Columbia are affected by a school-bus accident that results in the deaths of 14 of the town's children. Stephens is a big-city lawyer who arrives at the scene with the aim of persuading the victims' parents to join in a class-action suit against those who might have been responsible for the disaster; in the process, he reopens wounds festering since even before the children's deaths. Meanwhile, he is repeatedly reminded of his failed relationship with his troubled, adult daughter. "Ian Holm's performance here is bottomless with its subtlety," Roger Ebert wrote for the *Chicago Sun-Times* (December 12, 1997); "he proceeds doggedly through the town, following the routine of his profession, as if this is his penance." In *New York* (November 24, 1997), David Denby declared, "This is Holm's best film role, and his performance is economical but amazingly expressive. He has often played hard, bitter men, but in his role as an intelligent man who does not know himself, he achieves the stature of a tragic villain."

In another dramatic tour de force, Holm appeared in the title role of Shakespeare's *King Lear* at London's National Theater in 1998. In that production, he became the first actor in recent memory to strip completely naked during the storm scene in Act III, an action that many interpreters have suggested is required by the text. Holm's performance brought him an Evening Standard Award, an Olivier Award, and the Critics Circle Theatre Award. The televised version of the play, which aired on the PBS series *Masterpiece Theatre* in 1998, earned Holm an Emmy Award nomination for best actor. Asked by the interviewer for *ExxonMobil Masterpiece Theatre Online* about his approach to acting, he stated, "I grew up with the great Sir Laurence Olivier, and I think it's fair to say that a lot of actors my age were influenced by his very individual vocal delivery. He was a showman who would always play to the gallery. I would tend much more toward that aspect of acting as opposed to the style of some of the great actors like Charles Laughton and Sir John Gielgud, who concentrate almost entirely on the words. Having said that, the words are of paramount importance. The verse tells the story. I try to achieve both. I try to be emotional and big, and at the same time very true to the verse."

In 1999 Holm was cast as Kiri Vinokur in David Cronenberg's virtual-reality adventure *eXistenZ*; as Sirius/Boris in *Simon Magus;* as Big Tam in *The Match*; and as Joseph Maguire in *Shergar*, based on the true story of a champion racehorse that was abducted, some have theorized, by the IRA. His next starring role was that of Joe Gould in *Joe Gould's Secret* (2000), directed by Stanley Tucci. The film was based on the real-life Gould, an eccentric who hung out in New York City's Greenwich Village from 1916 to 1964. Claiming to be a graduate of Harvard, Gould would roam from bar to bar, telling stories, reciting poems, and loudly expressing his opinions. He often talked about his life's work, which was to be a book containing hundreds of overheard conversations. The film also depicts his on-and-off friendship with the journalist Joseph Mitchell, who profiled him in the *New Yorker* in 1942. "Holm is a revelation as Gould, a vivid portrait of a man composed layer by layer of psychosis, genius, nervous tics, need, and self-deception, his staccato, rapid-fire monologues cast a spell of dazed incredulity on the listener," Karl Williams noted for *All Movie Guide* (on-line). In a dissenting view, Charles Taylor wrote for *Salon* (April 7, 2000, on-line), "Ian Holm is one of the actors I most look forward to seeing in the movies. His Fluellen in Kenneth Branagh's film of *Henry V* is unlikely ever to be matched. And his performance as Lewis Carroll in the too-little-seen *Dreamchild* is one of the least-known great performances in the movies. . . . What's missing from Holm's performance [in *Joe Gould's Secret*] is joy in Gould's nonconformity, some zip in his high-hatted rot-gut palaver, a touch of the freeing grossness you see in Michel Simon's performance as the bum in Renoir's *Boudu Saved from Drowning*. For Gould to wind up tragic, he can't start that way."

In 2001 Holm, who had provided the voice of the Hobbit Frodo Baggins in a popular British radio adaptation of *Lord of the Rings* in the 1970s, was seen as Frodo's uncle Bilbo Baggins in *Lord of the Rings: The Fellowship of the Ring*, the first installment of the newest cinematic rendering of J. R.R. Tolkien's epic fantasy. Holm played Bilbo at different ages, and for some scenes he spent up to seven hours in the makeup chair. In an interview with Holm for *E! Online* (May 1, 2001), John Forde mentioned that one day during filming, he had noticed that the actor had "varied the mood and intonation" of his lines for every shot. Holm responded by saying, "I think the filming process, as far as an actor is concerned, is to show the director a kaleidoscope. Which way a director wants to go is up to them, but I can show you umpteen different ways of doing it. And each is marginally different from the other. That's the work. It also keeps it fresh. If you do take after take that's identical, it becomes boring." Holm will reprise his role as Bilbo Baggins in *Lord of the Rings: The Return of the King* (2003).

The five-foot six-inch Holm has been married three times. From his first marriage, to Lynn Mary Shaw, he has two daughters; from his second, to Sophie Baker, he has a son; from his third, to Penelope Wilton, he has one stepdaughter. From his liaison with the photographer Bee, he has a daughter and a son. Holm does not like to give interviews. "I haven't said very much, ever," he told Bruce Kirkland. "I think too much is known about people. There used to be an air of mystery about thespians. Nowadays everybody knows everything there is to know about everybody." He also said, in a reference to his acting or his life, or perhaps both, "I genuinely don't know what I am doing half the time. I just do it." — G.O.

Suggested Reading: *E! Online* (on-line) May 1, 2001, with photo; (London) *Guardian* p5 Sep. 12, 1967, with photo, p20 Jan. 20, 1994, with photo; *Toronto Sun* (on-line) Oct. 15, 1997; *Who's Who 2001*

Selected Films: *Bofors Gun*, 1968; *Moonlight on the Highway*, 1969; *Oh! What a Lovely War*, 1969; *Nicholas and Alexandra*, 1971; *A Severed Head*, 1971; *Mary, Queen of Scots*, 1971; *Young Winston*, 1972; *The Homecoming*, 1973; *Napoleon and Love*, 1974; *Shout at the Devil*, 1976; *Robin and Marian*, 1976; *The Man in the Iron Mask*, 1976; *March or Die*, 1977; *Holocaust*, 1978; *Les Misérables*, 1978; *The Lost Boys*, 1978; *Alien*, 1979; *Chariots of Fire*, 1981; *Time Bandits*, 1981; *Greystoke: The Legend of Tarzan, Lord of the Apes*, 1984; *Laughterhouse*, 1985; *Brazil*, 1985; *Wetherby*, 1985; *Dreamchild*, 1985; *Dance with a Stranger*, 1985; *Another Woman*, 1988; *Henry V*, 1989; *Hamlet*, 1990; *Kafka*, 1990; *Naked Lunch*, 1991; *The Hour of the Pig*, 1993; *The Borrowers*, 1993; *Frankenstein*, 1994; *The Madness of King George*, 1994; *Night Falls on Manhattan*, 1997; *The Fifth Element*, 1997; *The Sweet Hereafter*, 1997; *King Lear*, 1997; *eXistenZ*, 1999; *Simon Magus*, 1999; *The Match*, 1999; *Shergar*, 1999; *Joe Gould's Secret*, 2000; *Esther Kahn*, 2000; *Beautiful Joe*, 2000; *The Last of the Blonde Bombshells*, 2000; *From Hell*, 2001; *Lord of the Rings: The Fellowship of the Ring*, 2001

---

## Hopkins, Bernard

*Jan. 15, 1966– Boxer*

*Address: B. Hopkins Jr. Inc., 2121 N. Venango St., 2d Fl., Philadelphia, PA 19140*

On September 29, 2001 the boxer Bernard Hopkins upset the previously undefeated Puerto Rican champion Felix Trinidad. With his victory, Hopkins became the first man to hold the undisputed middleweight boxing championship since 1987, when Marvelous Marvin Hagler held the middleweight titles in all three of boxing's major organizations: the International Boxing Federation (IBF),

Justin Lane/*New York Times*

*Bernard Hopkins*

the World Boxing Council (WBC), and the World Boxing Association (WBA).

Bernard Hopkins was born in Philadelphia, Pennsylvania, on January 15, 1966. He began boxing at age 10 and embarked on an amateur boxing career in his adolescence; that career was cut short, however, after he was convicted of robbery and sentenced to prison at age 18. "I was a tough kid," Hopkins told *insideboxing.com*, "working the street, wanting a little gold chain and some money in my pocket. You know, a hard case. I thought it was bad, thought it was hip." Hopkins spent almost five years at Graterford, a Pennsylvania state correctional facility. "Graterford is like a city with a wall around," Hopkins told *insideboxing.com*. "There's guys shooting dope, smoking crack, making wine, gambling, all sorts of weird stuff. I'm 18, 19 and I figured now I really got to be tough. It took me just over a year to say: 'Whoa, I gotta get out of here.'" For Hopkins, the way out was through boxing; he joined the prison boxing team and held the Pennsylvania prison-system middleweight championship for three straight years. "The guards gave me respect and I liked it," he continued. "And I gave them respect. Inmates bet cigarettes on me when I fought. I had always known how to fight, but I had used it as a bully. Now I was a real fighter. Rehabilitation has got to be in yourself. You have to want it. No one wanted it more than I did."

While Hopkins has since amended his ways—he is now married and the father of a two-year-old daughter, Latrice—he appears to have transformed his troubled past into something of a professional cachet: often during the verbal sparring that leads up to most big matches, Hopkins speaks of his "bachelor's degree" from state prison. "I think that degree is more suitable for this business," he told those gathered at one press conference, as quoted by Edward Wong in the *New York Times* (April 12, 2001). "I've had a hard life. I smell and sense fear. I didn't get that from Catholic school; I know what fear is."

After he was released from prison, in 1987, Hopkins resumed his boxing career. He made his professional debut in 1988, fighting against Clinton Mitchell in a light-heavyweight bout. Hopkins lost that debut match, then waited 16 months before stepping back into the ring, against Greg Paige, in 1990. Hopkins defeated Paige, then went on to win his next 21 consecutive matches.

At RFK Stadium in Washington, D.C., in May 1993, Hopkins faced Roy Jones, a 1988 Olympic silver medalist. Jones was declared the victor by unanimous decision after 12 rounds, handing Hopkins his second defeat and capturing the previously vacant IBF middleweight title. While Hopkins managed to stay on his feet, Jones dominated the entire match. The result was certainly a disappointment for Hopkins, but it also appears to have strengthened his resolve. "When I lost to Roy in 1993," he later declared at a press conference, as quoted by Clifton Brown in the *New York Times* (April 16, 2001), "I told myself that I don't like losing. From that day on, I haven't." (As of early 2002, that remained the case.)

In late 1994 Hopkins once again made a bid for the IBF middleweight title, this time against Segundo Mercado at a match staged in Quito, Ecuador. Mercado and Hopkins fought each other to a standstill; the match was declared a draw, and a rematch was scheduled for April 1995 in Landover, Maryland. From the beginning of the second fight, Hopkins came on strong. He landed several powerful rights in the early rounds, and by Round 7 Mercado was leaning on the ropes. At that point the referee stopped the match and declared Hopkins the winner by technical knockout. With this victory, Hopkins also captured the IBF middleweight crown.

Between April 1995 and the end of 2000, Hopkins successfully defended the IBF middleweight title 12 times. Despite holding the title, however, he languished in relative obscurity during this period. Such neglect was due chiefly to the drabness of Hopkins's opponents: Richard Hoffer, writing for *Sports Illustrated* (October 8, 2001), described the boxer as having been "stuck in a succession of low-luster bouts against guys like Andrew Council and Syd Vanderpool." Hopkins sought to remedy the situation through theatrics worthy of the World Wrestling Federation: adopting the moniker "The Executioner," he began appearing in the ring alongside halberd-wielding attendants in black hoods. (More recently, Hopkins has shown up at press conferences with bags of rice and beans, symbolically offering his opponents a "last meal.")

Hopkins was given another shot at stardom in 2001, when the promoter Don King recruited the boxer for his Middleweight Championship Series.

The series comprised three matches: two semifinals, pitting Hopkins, the IBF middleweight champion, against Keith Holmes, the WBC middleweight champion, for the unification of those two titles, and Felix Trinidad against William Joppy for the WBA middleweight belt; and a final between the winners of the previous two matches. The winner of that fight would be recognized as champion by all three organizations.

In the April 14 match against Holmes, held in New York's Madison Square Garden, Hopkins was declared the victor by unanimous decision after 12 rounds. Hopkins dominated the fight from the third round on. Neither boxer scored a knockdown, despite Hopkins's prefight predictions of a knockout. "I lied," Hopkins told reporters when asked after the fight about those predictions, as quoted by Clifton Brown. "What can I say? I went for the knockout, but I didn't get it. But I won the fight."

In the September 29 final, Hopkins defeated Felix Trinidad (who had beaten Joppy in May) with a 12th-round technical knockout and captured the WBA championship belt. The loss was the first of Trinidad's 41-fight career. For most, Hopkins's victory over the formidable Puerto Rican boxer came as a surprise. "It wasn't clear what was happening until the fourth round," Hoffer wrote, "when Hopkins realized how baffled Trinidad was. Hopkins would dance in, sometimes throwing stiff jabs, sometimes lone right hands, and drive back Trinidad every time. . . . By the 10th round the punches Trinidad was taking had him close to being out on his feet." By the start of the 12th round, the judges' scorecards had Hopkins far ahead of his opponent. Trinidad knew he needed a knockout to win, but he still thought he stood a fair chance, he later told reporters. All little over one minute into the round, however, Hopkins landed a hard right to the chin that sent Trinidad to the canvas. He struggled unsuccessfully to regain his feet, and Hopkins was declared the victor. "I'm not great yet, but I will be," Hopkins declared shortly after the fight, as quoted by Micah Pollack in the *Washington Post* (September 30, 2001). "I am the American dream. I am the American story." — P.K.

Suggested Reading: *Jet* p51 Oct. 15, 2001, with photos; *New York Times* D p2 Apr. 12, 2001, with photo, D p7 Apr. 16, 2001, with photo; *Sports Illustrated* p54+ Oct. 8, 2001, with photos; *Washington Post* D p1 Sep. 30, 2001

---

## Hopkins, Nancy

*1943– Molecular biologist; social activist*

*Address: Massachusetts Institute of Technology, Dept. of Biology, 77 Massachusetts Ave., Cambridge, MA 02139-4307*

Donna Coveney/Courtesy of MIT

"I went to college thinking I would be a math major," Nancy Hopkins stated in her 1998 convocation address at the Massachusetts Institute of Technology (MIT), as quoted on the PBS Web site. "Then one day I happened to hear a lecture by a professor named James D. Watson. . . . It was apparent to all of us lucky enough to stumble into that classroom that if you understood how genes and their proteins worked you would understand life at the molecular level, and one day—some day—you could even answer every interesting question you had ever wanted to ask about being human. For example: How do you make a hand? What is a memory? How does a cell become cancer? Why do I look like my mother? It was the possibility of finding the answers to these questions that was totally intoxicating, totally passion provoking." Hopkins, the Amgen Inc. Professor of Molecular Biology at MIT, one of the most prestigious science and engineering universities in the country, has been a student, teacher, and researcher in the fields of virology, molecular and developmental biology, and genetics for more than 40 years. She is a fellow of the American Academy of Arts and Sciences, an international society composed of the world's leading scientists, scholars, artists, and businesspeople, and a member of the National Academy of Sciences' Institute of Medicine, whose members are selected in recognition of their distinguished and continuing achievement in original research. Hopkins is best known to the general public, however, for bringing into the national spotlight the issue of gender bias and inequality in academia. Her study during the mid-to-late-1990s of the different treatment afforded male and female professors at MIT led to sweeping changes at the institution and provoked a national debate.

The second of the two daughters of Richard and Marjorie Doe, Nancy Hopkins was born in 1943 in New York City. She attended the exclusive Spence School on Manhattan's Upper East Side from first grade through high school. She skipped the 10th grade and earned early admission to the prestigious Radcliffe College, in Cambridge, Massachusetts. (Radcliffe officially became part of Harvard University in 1999 and is now known as the Radcliffe Institute for Advanced Study.) Hopkins initially chose mathematics as her major, then switched briefly to architecture. It was in her junior year that she took a biology class taught in part by James D. Watson, who, along with Francis Harry Compton Crick, had discovered the structure of deoxyribonucleic acid (DNA), the molecule that makes up genes, in 1953. (In layperson's terms, DNA is a map to the makeup of a human being.) Watson, Crick, and Maurice Hugh Frederick Williams shared the Nobel Prize in physiology or medicine in 1962 for their work with nucleic acids. Speaking of the class that inspired her, Hopkins said in her convocation address at MIT, "At the end of the hour, I was not a math major. I was in love with DNA—for life. The field I had discovered was molecular biology."

After she graduated from Radcliffe, with a degree in biology, in 1964, Hopkins spent a year and a half in a Ph.D. program at Yale University, in New Haven, Connecticut, then returned to Cambridge, where she earned a Ph.D. from Harvard University's Department of Molecular Biology and Biochemistry in 1971. Hopkins's doctoral thesis dealt with the bacterial virus lambda and how it affects genes. She stayed at Harvard to do postdoctoral work with Watson, who had become something of a mentor to the young scientist. Hopkins also joined Robert Pollack, a renowned professor of biological sciences at Columbia University, in New York City, to study tumor viruses at the Cold Spring Harbor Laboratory, a top research and educational institution on Long Island, New York. In 1973 MIT offered Hopkins a position as an assistant professor of biology at its Center for Cancer Research. She undertook research in virology—specifically, the viruses that cause tumors, a new field in which scientists attempted to understand cancer by examining its genetic causes. MIT made Hopkins an associate professor in 1976, granted her tenure in 1979, and promoted her to full professor in 1982.

In the early 1990s Hopkins switched the focus of her research to genetics. She embarked on an ambitious experiment involving zebra fish from the Ganges River, in India. "The possibility of applying genetics in the zebra-fish system—actually finding the genes that were responsible for developmental processes and for behaviors in a vertebrate animal—was something people hadn't imagined you might really be able to do. I thought it would be fun to see whether one could make that possible, I was drawn to that," Hopkins told Rebecca Zacks in an interview for *Technology Review* (July/August 1998). Hopkins developed a research technique called insertional mutagenesis, whereby viruses are inserted into the genes of animals and leave traces, so that when mutations in the animals' development occur, the researchers can isolate the mutated genes, seeing what their specific roles are. Hopkins told Zacks, "We have a very sharp focus, and it's very big but very simple, very clear: We just want to understand how you start with a single cell and make an animal, that's all. And we know that it is done by genes." Since the genetic makeup of zebra fish is 90 percent identical to that of humans, Hopkins's research may reveal some of the secrets of how organs are formed and biological systems constructed, how birth defects and diseases occur, and how our different organ systems function, questions whose answers could have a significant impact on medicine and human health. The industry-leading biotechnology company Amgen Inc. is the major supporter of Hopkins's research. (Her work is not associated with that of the Genome Project.)

In 1994, when Hopkins was fighting for more time, space, and resources from MIT for her research, she became frustrated with what she saw as a lack of support from the university. She observed that there were comparatively very few female professors in the hard sciences at MIT and that those few were paid less than their male counterparts, given less space in which to work, and usually passed over for tenure and promotions to higher positions within their respective departments. Hopkins said to the writer Amy Oringel, in an article that appeared on the Web site *www.ka-Ching.com*, "MIT was a harsher world, but it never occurred to me that it was because I was a woman. Eventually I began to understand by watching what was going on with others . . . my eyes slowly opened. There was something wrong." The dean of the School of Science, Robert J. Birgeneau, and MIT president Charles M. Vest gave the approval for Hopkins and a group of other female faculty members from the School of Science to investigate the matter of gender inequality in their department. The 15 women, with Hopkins as chairwoman, formed the Committee on Women Faculty in the School of Science. For five years they conducted interviews and gathered data concerning the differences between the university's treatment of men and that of women—relating to everything from the square footage of lab space allocated, to the disbursement of salaries, to the filling of positions of authority. Their findings revealed substantial discrepancies, with the women on the losing end in most cases. In 1999 the committee submitted to the administration a document called "A Study on the Status of Women Faculty in Science at MIT," which pointed to many instances of the marginalization of and subtle discrimination against female faculty. The administration took swift action to address the problem, raising women's salaries an average of 20 percent to equal the men's; increasing research money for female faculty; giving women positions in key committees; granting tenure to a larger number of women; and even augmenting the pensions of some women who had already retired. When MIT's faculty newsletter reported the committee's findings and the university's actions, the national media quickly covered the story of the women's victory. In a front-page article in the *New York Times* (March 23, 1999), Carey Goldberg quoted Charles Vest as stating in the school newsletter, "I have always believed that contemporary gender discrimination within universities is part reality and part perception. True, but I now understand that reality is by far the greater part of the balance." Hopkins was hailed as a "Joan of Arc for this century" and a heroine in the battle against sex discrimination. Committees similar to the one begun by Hopkins at MIT were formed at other top universities around the country. Hopkins was interviewed for a CNN story called "Ivy Bias" and was invited to the White House, where she was praised and thanked for her courage by President Bill Clinton and his wife, Hillary Rodham Clinton, on behalf of the nation. Goldberg quoted Hopkins as saying, "I think what was accomplished here was extraordinary. . . . The challenge now is what can you do so that this wonderful thing that has happened can become automatic and institutionalized?"

The initial positive reaction, however, was followed by a number of published critical examinations of the MIT committee's report and the administration's claim that they accepted it because the findings were "data-driven." In the magazine *Heterodoxy* (February/March 2000), Kathryn Jean Lopez quoted Professor Judith S. Kleinfeld of the University of Alaska at Fairbanks as calling the women's report "a political manifesto masquerading as science." Kleinfeld added that MIT had allowed the women to be "judge and jury of their own complaints." The MIT case also gave new fuel to the debate over whether affirmative-action programs—whose purpose is to counteract the effects of past and continuing discrimination—are beneficial.

Hopkins is the author of many papers on topics within the fields of virology and molecular and developmental biology. She was named a Class of 1960 Fellow by MIT for co-developing and teaching the first biology course required of all undergraduate students at MIT. With James D. Watson and three other scientists, Hopkins co-authored the fourth edition of the textbook *The Molecular Biology of the Gene*. She has also served as the co-chair of MIT's first Council on Faculty Diversity, which directs the Gender Equity Project and also the Minority Faculty Project. Hopkins has been awarded the WTS–Boston Chapter's first Diversity Leadership Award and has been named the Women's History Month Honoree of the New York Academy of Sciences. Hopkins also received the MIT Women's League Laya Wiesner Community Award in 2001.

Hopkins married her college sweetheart, Roger Brooke Hopkins III; the couple divorced in 1973. She told Carey Goldberg for the *New York Times* (March 27, 2000, on-line), "I do believe that if these fifteen tenured women at MIT make the lives of a generation of women scientists easier, that would be a wonderful thing. But my passion is really science." — C.F.T.

Suggested Reading: *Chronicle of Higher Education* Web site; *New York Times* I p1+ Mar. 23, 1999, with photos, F p1+ Mar. 27, 2000, with photo; PBS Web site

---

Courtesy of the governor's office

## Hull, Jane Dee

*Aug. 8, 1935– Governor of Arizona (Republican)*

*Address: State Capitol, 1700 W. Washington, Phoenix, AZ 85007*

"I think there's an old independent spirit in Arizona dating from the pioneer women who came out here," Jane Dee Hull told Robert Pittman for the *Business Xpansion Journal* (July 2000, on-line). "We actually had women in the [Arizona] legislature before women got the vote." As the first woman to be elected governor of Arizona in the state's history, Hull is a pioneer herself. After switching careers from education to politics, she won a seat in the Arizona House of Representatives in 1978; she soon gained a reputation for speaking her mind and entrenched herself within the conservative wing of the Republican Party. But as her stature in state government grew, through the 1980s and early 1990s, she moderated her views, realizing the importance of compromise in governing. In 1997, after serving almost three years as Arizona's secretary of state, Hull became its 20th governor, upon the resignation of Governor J. Fife Symington. Having been elected to the governorship in her own right in 1998, Hull relishes her prominent role in U.S. politics, underscoring her policies of cutting taxes, revamping education, and promoting Arizona as a leader in business and technology. "I just happen to be one of those lucky people who are always in the right place at the right time," she explained to Pittman. Her success cannot be contributed solely to serendipity, however; Hull won the 1998 gubernatorial election by an overwhelming margin.

Hull was born Jane Dee Bowersock on August 8, 1935 in Kansas City, Missouri. Her mother, Mildred (Swenson) Bowersock, and father, Justin Bowersock, who was an editor of the *Kansas City Star* newspaper, shared a keen interest in politics. "I grew up with politics at the table," Hull recalled to Shaun McKinnon for the *Arizona Daily Star* (September 4, 1997). She spent most of her childhood in the Kansas City suburb of Mission, Kansas, and was a successful—and very active—student at Shawnee Mission High School. Hull appeared poised to follow in her father's footsteps: she edited the school newspaper and joined the yearbook staff. When she enrolled at the University of Kansas, in 1953, she intended to major in journalism, but her plans were to change; early in 1954 she married her high-school sweetheart, Terry Hull. By the time she graduated, in 1957, she had changed her major to education—since, as she told Chad Bettes for the *Kansan* (November 11, 1999, online), "I was married with two kids and probably more coming and it was a better life to be a teacher."

While her husband attended medical school, Hull taught in the Kansas City, Kansas, public schools. In 1962 the family pulled up stakes and moved to Chinle, Arizona, where Terry Hull worked in a clinic on a Navajo reservation. "It was obviously hard leaving both of our families, but I think we were both intent that we would probably not come back to Kansas," Hull told Chad Bettes. In Chinle she taught junior high school for one year. In 1964 the family moved again, to Phoenix, and Hull left teaching to return to school herself, taking graduate courses in politics, business, and economics at Arizona State University.

Hull began her journey to Arizona's highest office in 1965, when she became a volunteer precinct committeewoman and deputy registrar for the Republican Party. In that capacity she familiarized herself with the local government and its constituency. She had been inspired by Barry Goldwater, the Arizona congressman and 1964 Republican presidential nominee who was known for being fiscally conservative and an opponent of "big government," ever since she heard him speak in Kansas in the early 1960s. "I feel government is necessary," she told Shaun McKinnon. "I just don't think too much government is necessary." In the 1970s Hull worked on several Republican campaigns, including the 1974 governor's race, before becoming a candidate herself. In November 1978 she was elected to the Arizona House of Representatives from District 18, which covered north-central Phoenix. She was reelected several times to that office, at one point heading the Government Operations Committee, and she took on the additional responsibilities of majority whip during 1987 and 1988. (Some sources say 1988 and 1989.) In 1989 she became the Speaker of the Arizona House of Representatives, the first woman to hold that post; in addition, Hull was honored as the National Legislator of the Year by the National Republican Legislators Association. Already sporting the nickname "Iron Lady," during the early 1990s she served as the chair of the Economic Development and International Trade Committee and the chair of the Ethics Committee. As the Speaker of the House, she handled the fallout from the AzScam corruption scandal, after a 1991 police-led sting operation implicated seven of her colleagues in the legislature on charges of trading money for votes.

Hull resigned from the House of Representatives in 1993 to campaign for the office of Arizona's secretary of state. In the following year she became the first Republican elected to that post, the state's second-highest, since 1931. (Arizona has no lieutenant governor; the secretary of state, who runs on a separate ticket from the governor and may have a different political affiliation, is first in line to succeed the governor.) Hull had no designs on the governor's office when she ran for secretary of state: "I honestly ran for secretary of state because I liked the job," which involved a lot of record keeping, as she explained to Shaun McKinnon. She was supportive of Governor J. Fife Symington, also a conservative Republican, particularly in his quest to cut taxes and relax regulations on businesses operating in the state. But Symington's governorship was beset by scandal, which culminated in his conviction on charges of federal bank and wire fraud, mostly in connection with his prior career as a real-estate developer. In September 1997 Symington resigned from office.

Hull ascended to the governorship on September 5, 1997 and was sworn in at the U.S. Capitol several days later by U.S. Supreme Court justice Sandra Day O'Connor, an Arizona native. She immediately set to work, retaining many of Symington's staff members to ease the transition. "I think the main thing [to do upon taking office] would be to let people know I'm competent," she had confided to Shaun McKinnon the day before Symington tendered his resignation. "I would want as few disruptions as possible. I would want to do the best thing for Arizona." Once officially in charge, Hull continued to support tax cuts for residents and tax breaks for Arizona businesses. "There's always room for tax cuts," she told McKinnon. "Government should never take more money from people than it has to. I think the economy booms when you lower taxes." She also focused on health care, particularly for uninsured children; her program KidsCare provided health care for low-income children, using federal funds and money from the state tobacco tax. Additionally, Hull worked to make funding of school districts more equitable, while maintaining Arizona's charter schools and local bond fund-raising programs. Beyond those measures, Hull was willing to step aside and let school decisions take place on a local level. "Everyone wants education improved, but nobody quite knows what to do," she admitted to Robert Pittman. "I get kind of irritated because I think the Legislature tends to act like a school board. I tend to say put decisions down on the local level and let school boards decide, and let the principals and teachers decide how best to use the money. They are, frankly, more informed on educational issues."

Less than a year after she took office, Hull began to campaign for the next gubernatorial election. Several potential opponents, including Republican Arizona congressman Matt Salmon, chose not to run against her in the primary. Ahead in the polls going into the general election, Hull faced Democrat Paul Johnson, a former mayor of Phoenix. Johnson criticized Hull as being too conservative, citing as an example her legislative record on abortion, which she had vigorously opposed while in the Arizona House of Representatives. Hull had since softened her abortion stance, however, explaining to Shaun McKinnon, "There are some places government shouldn't go." Focusing on education issues, Hull won the election with 61 percent of the vote to Johnson's 36 percent and made Arizona history by becoming the state's first elected woman governor. Also in the 1998 balloting, women were elected to the state's top five positions; nicknamed the Fabulous Five by the press and constituents, the four Republicans and one Democrat took their respective places as governor, secretary of state, attorney general, treasurer, and superintendent of public instruction in January 1999, sworn in by Sandra Day O'Connor. "We are five women, but we have a range of political philosophies, we come from different parties, we have a range of experience and a range of interests," Hull told Julie Cart for the *Los Angeles Times* (December 17, 1998). Downplaying the role of gender in the election results, Hull explained to Cart: "The idea that all of a sudden we are all going to go out and put forth a so-called women's agenda makes no sense at all. What they call women's issues—education, child support—are on the forefront of the issues now."

In her second term Hull has tried to focus on longstanding priorities such as promoting business and development, while keeping a close eye on urban sprawl and allocation of water resources. Arizona's diverse economy, embracing such high-tech fields as superconductors and aeronautics and low-tech pursuits including citrus and cotton growing and copper mining, has kept her busy—as have her efforts to boost school funding, build more schools, and keep better track of student progress, thus making good on her campaign promise to improve education. A program encouraging Arizonans to buy alternative-fuel cars proved so popular that Hull was forced to put a moratorium on the measure to prevent the state from overrunning its budget. She also ruffled a few feathers when she announced her support of George W. Bush in the 2000 presidential campaign over Arizona's longtime senator John S. McCain. In July 2001 Hull was appointed to the Advisory Council on Historic Preservation by President Bush, in recognition of her attempts in 2000 to control urban growth through such anti-sprawl measures as her Growing Smarter Program and through land preservation. "I think open space is a part of Arizona's charm," she explained to Robert Pittman, "and a key component to our quality of life."

Hull, who is ineligible to run for a third gubernatorial term, has thus far given no hints about her political ambitions for the future. As the mother of two sons and two daughters and grandmother of eight, who call her "Grammie governor," Hull regards her political career as a surprise gift. "I don't think I ever even thought of a life in politics," she told Chad Bettes. "I was teaching school, raising children, [planning on] going back, after the kids were raised, to a career of sorts. The politics just kind of came along when I wasn't looking, which is the best way for most things to happen." — K.S.

Suggested Reading: *Arizona Daily Star* (on-line) Sep. 4, 1997, with photo; *Business Xpansion Journal* (on-line) July 2000; *Kansan* (on-line) Nov. 11, 1999, with photo; *Los Angeles Times* p1 Dec. 17, 1998

---

## India.Arie

*Oct. 3, 1975– Singer; songwriter*

*Address: c/o Motown Records, 1755 Broadway, 7th Fl., New York, NY 10019*

"All my songs are about me and my own experiences," the singer/songwriter India.Arie told Kathy Cano-Murillo for the *Arizona Republic* (September 13, 2001, on-line). "If there is a message in them, it would have to be about learning about the matters of the heart, the healing of the heart, self-love, confidence, creativity . . ." India.Arie offered that message of hope, healing, and self-acceptance in her debut album, *Acoustic Soul* (2001), which entered the *Billboard* 200 album chart at number 10 and, within six weeks of its release, had gone gold, selling more than half a million copies. (As of early December 2001, that number had surpassed one million.) Striking a chord—particularly with her songs "Video" and "Strength, Courage & Wisdom"—with the many women who are unhappy about being judged by standards of

John Ricard/Retna Ltd.

*India.Arie*

beauty unattainable by all but a few, as well as those who appreciate being loved for what they are, India.Arie has fused soul, folk, and rhythm and blues to create her own sound, supported by her lead on acoustic guitar. "I'm trying to convey a sense of pride, optimism and unconditional love," she told Steve Jones for *USA Today* (April 20, 2001). "It's also about healing—allowing yourself to let go of things and even admit things that you won't admit to yourself." "My goal has never been, and I hope never will be, to see how high I can get on the chart or to try to compete with anybody else," she told Percy Ednalino for the *Denver Post* (September 12, 2001). "I just want to make the songs that I hear in my head. That's what I do, I'm a musician. I'm a singer and songwriter. I'm not in a race." In January 2002 India.Arie was nominated for seven Grammy Awards, in the categories of best new artist; record of the year; song of the year; album of the year; best female R&B vocal performance; R&B album of the year; and best R&B song.

The musician was born India Arie Simpson on October 3, 1975 in Denver, Colorado. She was named in honor of the Indian political and spiritual leader Mohandas K. Gandhi (1869–1948), whose birthday—October 2—was the date on which she was due to be born; her middle name means "lion" in Hebrew. Her father is Ralph Simpson, a basketball standout who played for the Denver Nuggets in the 1970s and is now a minister. Her mother is a fashion designer; known as Simpson, she designs India.Arie's outfits and thus contributes to the singer's funky, eclectic look. Musical from her early years, India.Arie had begun studying the recorder by the time she was in second grade; she later took up the saxophone and French horn as well. From age two she also sang; influenced by her mother, who had been a semiprofessional singer as a teenager in Detroit, she joined her school choirs. Her musical heroes ranged from classic soul artists, among them Marvin Gaye and Donnie Hathaway, to such icons as James Taylor, Karen Carpenter, and Stevie Wonder. "I always loved James Taylor," she told Mark Binelli for *Rolling Stone* (June 21, 2001). "Whenever I'd hear 'You've Got a Friend' on the radio, my whole body got chills. From like ten on, I would always have daydreams of myself being him. Not being him, but being a person with a guitar, someone who could just play, me and my guitar, just play and sing." When she was 12 her parents divorced, and she moved to Atlanta, Georgia, with her mother. Adjusting to her new environment was difficult, she recalled to Binelli: "I looked different—I was different—and people kept reminding me I was different." (By her own account, those "differences" stemmed from her "weird" clothing, permed hair, and acne.) She later told Kenya N. Byrd for *Essence* (September 2001), "I'm a lot better about how I perceive myself now. I still have issues, but who doesn't? I just take it one day at a time."

Dividing her high-school years between Atlanta and Denver, Colorado, where she lived with her father, India.Arie became interested in making jewelry. After she graduated from high school, she enrolled at the Savannah College of Art and Design, in Georgia, where she specialized in metals and jewelry and minored in art history. As she explained to Richard Harrington for the *Washington Post* (August 24, 2001), she had lost interest in "band teachers, sheet music and all that stuff . . . and jewelry was something that I'd always loved. I would stare at it the same way I would stare at instruments. My mom would have fashion shows and I would be out there trying to polish the bracelets."

While in college India.Arie began playing the guitar and trying her hand at songwriting. Feeling that she had a wealth of thoughts and emotions to share, she left school and moved back to Atlanta, where she co-founded the Groovement artists' collective. "We were like, 'Let's play music and see what happens,'" she recalled to Martha Southgate for *O, the Oprah Magazine* (September 2001, online). "Everything I did, I thought, I can't believe I did that. Like when I wrote my first song—I can't believe I did that. I never had a goal of becoming famous." Using a stage name, which she created by joining her first and middle names, she began playing in Atlanta coffeehouses. According to *Rolling Stone*, she also worked in a candy store. In 1997, after setting up a microphone and an eight-track recorder in her bathroom, she produced an acoustic tape. She also contributed to an album that came out on Groovement's Earthseed label (EarthShare, according to some sources). Her singing impressed talent scouts working for the all-female Lilith Fair music festival (which toured during the summers of 1997, 1998, and 1999), and, at their invitation, she performed at a few stops in the summer of 1998.

India.Arie's Lilith Fair act attracted the attention of representatives from several major studio labels, who reportedly thought she might make a fresh-faced complement to well-known neo-soul artists, such as Erykah Badu. In 1999 she signed with Motown Records, securing creative control of her debut album—an unusual achievement for a relative novice. At the same time, she realized that she would have to modify some of her music to make it acceptable for radio play. "That was my challenge," she told Mark Binelli, "how to be current enough and loud enough to be on the radio and still keep the songs alive. It look me a long time to find that balance." Determined to maintain her distinctive sound, she worked on the album for two years. "I thought it was going to be a lot quicker than it was," she admitted to Richard Harrington, "that I would get session players, have them play and then my album would be done. But after I did that and was listening back to it, it wasn't what I wanted." "Translating [the songs] from guitar and vocals to being fully produced and having it keep the same energy was not easy," she told Kathy Cano-Murillo. Learning to work with demanding music professionals helped her greatly, as she explained to Rashaun Hall for *Billboard* (February 24, 2001). "I went from being a student at Savannah State and doing what I wanted to do, to being on Motown and having people wake me up and question my work habits. When that happened, I had to grow up. I had to learn how to organize my stuff and be able to speak my mind in a proper way. I went from all me to having a real career."

*Acoustic Soul* debuted in late March 2001. "Video," the first single released from the album, received wide radio play and soon became an anthem for women tired of being judged by Hollywood and MTV standards of beauty. "I'm not the average girl from your video," she sings in the chorus, "And I ain't built like a supermodel / But I learned to love myself unconditionally / Because I am a queen." After India.Arie sang "Video" on *The Oprah Show*, on June 21, 2001, Oprah Winfrey exclaimed, as quoted by Randy Lewis for the *Los Angeles Times* (July 28, 2001), "We love that song! Not only do we love that song, we love you for writing that song. We needed that song!" "A lady came up to me in New Orleans and said that she and her granddaughter sing 'Video' every day," India.Arie told Randy Lewis. "She just started crying and saying, 'You don't know what you've done for her.' She was like at church almost."

*Acoustic Soul* earned critical success as well. In a review for *People* (April 9, 2001), Chuck Arnold described the album as "a breath of fresh air." Maurice Bottomley, a music critic for *PopMatters.com*, wrote, "The bulk of the material is musically and lyrically impressive. On top of this Arie has a great voice—purer and richer than any of the established new classic women. The acoustic guitar as dominant instrument is, in this context, refreshing and there is enough melodic variety to hold the interest. As a wordsmith Arie is patchy and overreaches herself from time to time but when she hits home, it is a big hit." Within a few months of the release of *Acoustic Soul*, India.Arie had been nominated for an MTV Video Music Award and three *Billboard* magazine Music Video Awards for "Video"; she also captured nominations for two Soul Train Lady of Soul Awards. During this period she toured as the opening act for the British soul singer Sade.

In January 2002 India.Arie was nominated for seven Grammy Awards, among them record of the year and album of the year, for *Acoustic Soul*; she did not win any of them.

On September 24, 2002 Arie's second album, *Voyage to India*, arrived in stores. While recording it, she revealed, she felt that her love of music making had revived. "The heart center, the energy that's right here," she told Anthony DeCurtis for the *New York Times*, "that's where I sing and write from. I can cry so easily just talking about it. My heart is engaged." *Voyage to India* received respectable notices from critics; it debuted at number one on the R&B charts and number six on the *Billboard* Top 200.

At the request of the director Spike Lee, India.Arie contributed to the soundtrack of Lee's 2000 movie *Bamboozled*. (Stevie Wonder, Erykah Badu, and Prince are among the other performers whose songs are on the soundtrack.) Recently, she recorded a duet with the rock musician John Mellencamp; called "Peaceful World," it is the first single on his album *Cuttin' Heads* (2001). She has also modeled clothing for televised Gap ads. India.arie, who is single, has continued to write songs and make appearances on television and at small venues. "I'm happy that the people who inspired me like my music," she told Martha Southgate. "When Elton John said I was one of his favorite artists—now, that was success." — K.S.

Suggested Reading: *Arizona Republic* (on-line) Sep. 13, 2001, with photo; *Los Angeles Times* F p1 July 28, 2001, with photos; *Rolling Stone* p30 June 21, 2001, with photo; *Washington Post* WW p7 Aug. 24, 2001, with photo

Selected Recordings: *Acoustic Soul*, 2001; *Voyage to India*, 2002

## Inkster, Juli

*June 24, 1960– Golfer*

*Address: c/o LPGA, 100 International Golf Dr., Daytona Beach, FL 32124*

"Golf is a stupid game," Juli Inkster told Douglas S. Looney for *Sports Illustrated* (April 10, 1989). "You tee up this little ball, really this tiny ball. Then you hit it, try to find it, hit it. And the goal is to get it into a little hole placed in a hard spot." After dominating women's golf at the collegiate and amateur levels for three straight years in her early 20s, in 1984 Inkster became the first player in the history of the Ladies Professional Golf Association (LPGA) to win two major tournaments in a rookie season. Since then, weathering poor showings, equipment problems, and the difficulties of returning to the green after maternity leaves, Inkster has quietly left her mark on her sport, becoming one of the LPGA's premier players. She completed a career grand slam in 1999, 15 years after she began it, and was inducted into golf's Hall of Fame in the following year. Now past the age of 40, a point at which other golfers' careers have begun to decline, Inkster has continued to shine. In the summer of 2002, in what Clifton Brown in the *New York Times* (July 8, 2002) called "a performance for the ages," she won the U.S. Women's Open for the second time in her career. "No one has ever conquered this game. One week out there and you are God, next time you are the devil," she explained to Looney. "But it does keep you coming back."

Juli Inkster was born Juli Simpson on June 24, 1960 in Santa Cruz, California, the daughter of Jack Simpson, a former professional baseball player, and Carole Simpson. She has two older brothers, Danny and Mike. Her interest in sports began when she was a young girl. In high school, as she told Bob Verdi for *Golf Digest* (February 1999), she played softball and basketball and ran track. During the same period—when she was 15—she turned to golf. (The Simpsons' house was near the 14th hole of the Pasatiempo Golf Club.) The only girl on her high-school golf team, she was encouraged by her teammates and coach. Inkster had the second-best amateur score at the 1978 U.S. Women's Open, only 10 strokes behind the professional winner of the event, Hollis Stacy. Her excellent showing at the Open was a harbinger of her four years as an All-American at San Jose State University, from which she graduated in 1982; she won that year's Broderick Award for Golf, as the top female collegiate golfer in the U.S. In 1980, prior to her junior year in college, she married Brian Inkster, a club professional who had given Juli her first golf lessons. "I was . . . working as the cart girl at the [Pasatiempo] club," she recalled to Bob Ottum for *Sports Illustrated* (August 30, 1982). "That is, Brian would bark 'Get a cart up here!' and I'd have to jump. The secret reason I married him . . . was so I could get a raise and a better job in the office," she joked.

Inkster's amateur career flourished. In 1981 she was the California Women's Amateur champion and California's Amateur of the Year. Ranked the top amateur by *Golf Digest* in both 1981 and 1982, she won the U.S. Women's Amateur title for three straight years—1980 through 1982—becoming the only player to do so between 1934, when Virginia Van Wie achieved the feat, and 1996, when the golf sensation Tiger Woods accomplished it. Inkster turned professional prior to the LPGA's January 1983 qualifying tournament, but she had a disappointing experience there. "I missed my first Q school," she told Bob Verdi, referring to the qualifying tournament to secure professional-level spots on the LPGA tour. "A little humbling. I made a mistake by not playing mini-tour events." Despite her successes as an amateur, she was nearly discouraged from making a second attempt at qualifying. In the end, though, she tried again, this time tying for the low score at the August 1983 LPGA qualifying event and picking up her tour card in the process. She immediately set out on the pro tour and won the fifth tournament she entered, the 1983 Safeco Classic. She made the cut in all eight LPGA events she entered and came away with two top-10 finishes and an LPGA rank of 30. Although she was not technically a rookie (because she played in only a few events and missed some of the majors), *Golf Digest* named her Rookie of the Year for 1983.

In 1984—which the LPGA considers her rookie year—Inkster became the first rookie ever to win two majors. (The four most competitive and lucrative tournaments on the tour—the Nabisco Dinah Shore, the du Maurier Classic, the U.S. Women's Open, and the LPGA Championship—are called majors. The winning of all four majors in a single season is known as a grand slam; victory in all four majors over the course of one's career is called a career grand slam. The Nabisco Dinah Shore is now known as the Kraft Nabisco Championship, and in 2001 the Women's British Open replaced the du Maurier Classic.) In her first major, the 1984 Dinah Shore, she was trailing an LPGA tour veteran, Pat Bradley, when play was delayed in the final round; Bradley lost her rhythm and finished the round tied with Inkster. In a sudden-death play-off, Inkster won the tournament on the first hole. "It was during the delay that I said to myself, I have nothing to lose," Inkster told Gordon S. White Jr. for the *New York Times* (July 7, 1986). "I thought that if I fouled up it was me who was the rookie. That's expected of rookies." The win, she added, "turned my career around right there." She tied for seventh place at the LPGA Championship and for 27th at the U.S. Women's Open, then won the 1984 du Maurier Classic, the last major of the season, and was named the LPGA Rookie of the Year.

Her outstanding rookie year completed, Inkster had only one victory in 1985, at the Lady Keystone Open; she missed the cut after two rounds of the U.S. Women's Open, and her highest finish in a major was at the Nabisco Dinah Shore, in which

*Juli Inkster* Larry Smith/AP

she tied for 19th. But her play improved in 1986, after she had taken private instruction from Leslie King, a London-based golf teacher. "There are a few in the world I'd call master instructors. Leslie King is one," Inkster told Gordon S. White Jr. (King "teaches in London," Brian Inkster told Bob Ottum in 1982, when King was 73 years old. "He's holed up in what used to be squash courts in a beat-up apartment building. . . . There's no golf course, nothing. Just nets. He makes you hit into nets so you can concentrate on your swing and not worry about where the ball's going.") Inkster successfully defended her Lady Keystone title in 1986 and made the cut in all four major events; her best finish in a major was a tie for third at the LPGA Championships. Inkster also won the 1986 Women's Kemper Open, the 1986 McDonald's Championship, and the 1986 Atlantic City Classic, and twice during the season she finished rounds with a score of 64, a career low.

In 1987 Inkster made the cut in all 24 events she set out to enter; she struggled in them, however, failing to finish higher than fourth in a tournament, although she tied for ninth in the LPGA Championship. Returning to her winning form in 1988, she was crowned as the champion in three tournaments, two of them—the Crestar Classic and the Atlantic City Classic—after sudden-death play-off competition. Her 1989 season began terribly, with low finishes and a missed cut. Although, as she told Douglas Looney, "I never blame my equipment," she realized that she "kept missing three- and four-foot putts." She tried a new putter and collected her second career win at the Nabisco Dinah Shore. She ended her season early due to her first pregnancy, but not before a successful defense of her Crestar Classic title. Less than two months after her daughter Hayley was born, in February 1990, she was back on the links to defend her title in the Nabisco Dinah Shore. She finished that tournament tied for 11th and failed to make the cut in any of the other majors during the 1990 season. Adjusting to motherhood was difficult for Inkster, and her game suffered, as she admitted to John Goldstein for *Golf* (June 1993): "My attitude on the golf course was horrible . . . my confidence was down. I was trying to do too many things and do them all perfectly. When I was brought up, my mom was always home. I was having guilty feelings, wondering if it was right to leave Hayley to play golf." Her distraction was evident throughout her abbreviated season; in 18 tournaments she missed the cut five times and had only three top-10 finishes.

Despite the demands of parenthood, Inkster decided not to give up her golf career. Redoubling her efforts to return to contention, she accrued six top-10 finishes in 1991, including her victory at the Bay State Classic, her first win since the 1989 Crestar Classic. She made the cut in three out of four majors and placed ninth in the LPGA Championship. Inkster regained top form—and an LPGA rank of seventh—in 1992, with a win at the JAL Big Apple Classic and 10 top-10 finishes, including all four majors. She finished second in the Nabisco Dinah Shore and in the U.S. Women's Open, leading her competitors in each contest until the playoff round; she admitted to Clifton Brown for the *New York Times* (June 7, 1999) that her defeat in the Open, which had come after she led by two strokes with two holes to play, "was a heartbreak."

Inkster almost disappeared from golf's map in 1993. She missed six cuts, had a top finish of second, and saw her LPGA rank plunge to 47th. Juggling the responsibilities of professional golf and motherhood became further complicated in March 1994, with the birth of her second daughter, Cori. During a shortened playing schedule that year, her best finish was a tie for second; she did not compete in the Kraft Nabisco Championship, and she missed the cut in the du Maurier Classic. "It was more of a struggle mentally, wondering if I was doing the right thing having [the children] out there with me," she explained to James Deacon for *Maclean's* (August 2, 1999). "I was trying to be a good mom and good golfer and not feeling that I was doing well at either of them." With her husband, Brian, who was still her coach, she would "go down [to the golf course] and talk about the kids, talk about everything but golf," she told Steve Popper for the *New York Times* (July 15, 1999). "I just needed a direction, a focus."

Because of her struggles on the course, Inkster considered retirement. "I just didn't like to come out here and be a mediocre player . . . ," she told Kirsten Seaborg for *GolfWeb* (September 28, 1999, on-line). "I felt like I was just out here going through the motions and hauling my kids around and really wasn't accomplishing much. That is when I really decided I needed to start working on my game." She hired a new coach, Mike McGetrick, and began a slow climb up the LPGA rankings. She had five top-10 finishes in 1995 and seven in 1996, and in 1997 she had her best showing in five seasons, making the cut in all 24 events she entered. She won the 1997 Samsung World Championship of Women's Golf in a sudden-death play-off round with two opponents and had nine other top-10 finishes. Her 1997 LPGA ranking rebounded to sixth, from 21st the previous year, and she lowered her stroke average to 70 per 18 holes, a career-best mark. "Being the impatient person that I am, I didn't want [improvement] to take time," she explained to Seaborg. "I wanted it to happen along the way. But basically it did. It took two years to really get back where I was; starting to play consistent golf again." In 1998 Inkster maintained her number-six ranking, successfully defending her Samsung title and notching 11 other top-10 finishes.

In 1999 Inkster put together her best season of the decade. That June, following her victory at the Longs Drugs Challenge, she came out on top at the LPGA Championship, one of the two majors she had not previously won; in July she triumphed at the U.S. Women's Open, picking up her fourth major title (her fifth overall) and completing a career grand slam. The period between the first step of her career grand slam and the last was the longest in women's golf; the other three career grand slams were completed in five, six, and 11 years, by Mickey Wright (in the 1950s and '60s), Pat Bradley (in the 1980s), and Louise Suggs (in the 1940s and '50s), respectively. "As far as accomplishments and records, I don't play for that. I play just to play," she told Steve Popper. "I play for the respect of my peers. I play for my family. I always thought to win the grand slam would be awesome. I won two majors my rookie year and then, I don't know, your goals kind of change. I never thought I'd accomplish it, and then to go ahead and do it is just icing on the cake for me. Everything I'm doing now is just a bonus." In September 1999 she had her 22d career victory—one of five that season—at the Safeway LPGA Golf Championship. She also reached a sufficient number of career points to be elected to the Hall of Fame; she was inducted in November 2000.

Inkster's successes continued into the 21st century. She had three victories in 2000: a successful defense of her title at the 2000 Longs Drugs Challenge, a third Samsung title, and a second win at the LPGA Championship. "It means a lot to me to prove to myself that I'm still one of the top players," she explained to Alan Shipnuck for *Sports Illustrated* (July 3, 2000). "It's in my blood. I love to compete." Even amidst the rise of younger stars, such as Se Ri Pak and Annika Sorenstam, Inkster has maintained her prominence in the sport. She had only one victory in 2001, at the Electrolux USA Championship. Halfway through the 2002 season, she won the Chick-Fil-A Charity Championship and took the U.S. Women's Open, her seventh major title, with a come-from-behind victory over Sorenstam, the LPGA's top-ranked player, at the Prairie Dunes Country Club in Hutchinson, Kansas—where she had won her first amateur title, in 1980. At 42, Inkster was the second-oldest winner in the history of the U.S. Women's Open. "I don't know how many more Opens I'm going to be able to compete in," she told Clifton Brown for the *New York Times* (July 8, 2002). "To beat the best player in the world, you don't get a chance to do that often. This is pretty sweet." She has intimated that she will retire in the next few years, in order to spend more time with her daughters.

Inkster lives in Los Altos, California. She likes to ski and is an avid fan of sports teams in the San Francisco area. In her free time, she coaches her daughters' sports teams. — K.S.

Suggested Reading: *Golf* p110+ June 1993, with photo; *New York Times* D p1 June 7, 1999, with photo; *New York Times* D p4 July 15, 1999, with photo; *Sports Illustrated* p56+Aug. 30, 1982, with photos; *Sports Illustrated* p34+ Apr. 10, 1989, with photo; *USA Today* C p13 June 24, 1999, with photo

John Spellman/Retna Ltd.

## Ja Rule

*Feb. 29, 1976– Rapper; actor*

*Address: c/o Def Jam Records, 825 Eighth Ave., New York, NY 10019*

Combining some of the style and attitude of gangsta rap with, increasingly, spiritual and romantic elements, Ja Rule has established himself in the top ranks of contemporary rappers. He has also achieved considerable crossover success. While his tougher raps attract him to a young, predominately male audience, his more sensitive singles, delivered in a gruff, deep voice that some have likened to that of the soul and R&B icon Barry White, have made him popular with women—even those of middle age. "Everybody can enjoy my music," Ja Rule told Rashaun Hall for *Billboard* (September 29, 2001). "I have 40-year-old and 50-year-old women come up to me and tell me, 'I like that song. It's a nice record.' They're not looking at it as a rap record, because they'll say to me in the same breath, 'I don't listen to rap music.' That's telling me that they're hearing my music and labeling it as just good music." Ja Rule's broad popularity is attributable in part to his integrity. "When he walks into a room, his aura is a star—he's got that," Kevin Liles, the president of Def Jam/Def Soul, Ja Rule's current label, told Alona Wartofsky for the *Washington Post* (April 29, 2001). "He makes you not only hear what he's saying, but feel what he's saying." Three of Ja Rule's albums have gone platinum (that is, sold at least a million copies); several of his singles have ranked in the Top 10 of *Billboard*'s hot-100 singles charts, and he has earned a host of award nominations. "A lot of artists make records to make money," Ja Rule told Rashaun Hall. "Not to make people smile, or make hearts light up, or to warm souls. That's why I make records, and it's starting to show."

Ja Rule was born Jeffrey Atkins in the New York City borough of Queens on February 29, 1976. He grew up in Hollis, a Queens neighborhood that became famous as the home of members of the 1980s rap group Run-D.M.C. Ja Rule's mother was a hospital nurse; his father, a drug addict, was rarely around. When Ja Rule was young he would entertain his mother at night by dancing like the pop star Michael Jackson. Although his family was poor, Ja Rule recalled to Zondra Hughes for *Ebony* (April 2002), "When I was little, my mom and grandmom did little things for me that always made me feel like we were doing well financially. Black people have a knack for that, making bad times feel good. They gave me a lot of strength." Ja Rule's family were Jehovah's Witnesses, and as a child Ja Rule would accompany his mother when, as required by the religion, she went door to door to proselytize. "That background is real strict," Ja Rule told Kris Ex for *Rolling Stone* (March 29, 2001). Speaking of the Jehovah's Witness injunction against celebrating birthdays or Christmas, he said, "It's tough on children. If you're an adult, you can make your own choices—you choose not to celebrate Christmas or you choose not to celebrate your birthday; that's your business. But when you're a kid, it's kind of hard to grasp those ideas when all the other kids in school are getting gifts. And it hurts and it's painful." Ja Rule's mother was once "disfellowshipped" (shunned) by Jehovah's Witnesses for drinking alcohol, which the religion forbids. As part of her punishment, no one, including her parents, was allowed to speak to her. "As I grew older," Ja Rule told Ex, "I started to see, 'I don't think that I want that. Not if it's separating families.'" Ja Rule later practiced Islam for a time; more recently, he has reportedly returned to a more liberal branch of Christianity.

Ja Rule was "mischievous" as a child, as he told Alona Wartofsky. By the time he reached the age of 14, he recalled to Wartofsky, "life got a little different. Got introduced to drugs, started smoking weed, alcohol. Stuff like that changes a young person's mind, so I kind of went on the wrong road for a little while." At around that time, Ja Rule started to date Aisha Murray. Then, during 11th grade, he dropped out of school and started dealing drugs to make a living. A turning point came when Aisha gave birth to his daughter. Becoming a father, he told Wartofsky, "made me feel I had to get serious in life. I had to do something to make a difference in her life, you know?" Ja Rule had been creating rhymes since he was 16 and had occasionally rapped on street corners and in his high-school cafeteria. So he decided to pursue a career as a rapper and adopted as his professional name Ja Rule, forming "Ja" by combining his initials.

Ja Rule's first contribution to a recording came on Mic Geronimo's rap "Time to Build," the B-side of Geronimo's single "Masta I.C." During this period Ja Rule and two friends formed a group called the Cash Money Click and signed an album deal with Blunt/TVT Records. In 1995 they released their first and only single, "Get the Fortune," with "For My Chick" on the B side. "Get the Fortune" aired on New York's influential radio station Hot 97. The producer of the single, Irv Gotti, soon joined Def Jam Records as an A&R (artist and repertoire) representative. Gotti was unable to offer Ja Rule a contract, though, because the rapper was still under contract with TVT—a deal that also cost him his publishing rights to his first album, which was never released. "When you're young and you get into this industry," Ja Rule told Zondra Hughes, "you just see bright lights and big stars. They hit you with this little check and you think, 'I'm going to make hit records; I'm going to be in the videos; I'm going to be the [man].' And when it doesn't all fall into place, that's when you get a real slap of reality, that this is the real world and some people make it, and some don't." Eventually TVT released Ja Rule from his contract, and he signed with Def Jam.

While Ja Rule was recording tracks for his next album, the rapper Jay-Z asked if he could use the hook Ja Rule was developing for a song of his own. Ja Rule agreed, and the hook became the staple for Jay Z's hit single "Can I Get A . . ." (1998), which features Ja Rule in a party-themed rap. Ja Rule's debut album, *Venni, Vetti, Vecci*, was released in 1999 and hit number three on the *Billboard* album charts. The title is a play on the words "Veni, vidi, vici" (ascribed to Julius Caesar), which is Latin for "I came, I saw, I conquered." "It's really not a conquering of the world, but more of a conquering of myself," Ja Rule was quoted as saying on *MTV.com.* The record's first single, the hit "Holla, Holla," became a party anthem; it also aroused controversy over the line "It's murder!" "Let's be realistic about it," Ja Rule told Wartofsky. "I'm a recording artist. The name of the company I record for is Murder Incorporated Records [a subsidiary of Def Jam], which I also happen to have a piece of, a vested interest. So of course I'm gonna scream 'It's murder' for the company, see? And if people don't like it, hey, it's America. Close your eyes, close your ears. I think it's very, very clear that I'm not talking about actual murder." Stephen Thomas Erlewine, in *All Music Guide* (on-line), wrote of *Venni, Vetti, Vecci*, "Ja Rule doesn't bend the rules of East Coast hardcore hip-hop enough to truly distinguish himself, but he does deliver a solid record, filled with tough party jams and good straight-ahead gangsta." The record sold 1.5 million copies in the United States and topped *Billboard*'s R&B/hip-hop albums chart for three weeks. In addition to offering plenty of gangsta-styled rap, such as "It's Murda" and "World's Most Dangerous," the record tackled more spiritual topics, on such songs as "Daddy's Little Baby," which features a performance by the soul legend Ronald Isley, and "Only Begotten Son," a message from Ja Rule to his father. "He may not be versatile enough to carry a whole album—there's loads of filler here," Rob Sheffield wrote for *Rolling Stone* (on-line). "But . . . Ja Rule never comes off as a phony, and at this crossroads moment for hip-hop, it's a pleasure to hear a rapper who just wants to make you *feel* something."

Ja Rule next sang on *Irv Gotti Presents Murderers*, a gangsta-rap compilation that also features performances by Jay-Z, DMX, Busta Rhymes, and Memphis Bleek. In 2000 Ja Rule released his sophomore album, *Rule 3:36*, which was recorded in Hollywood Hills, California. The title refers to John 3:36, from the New Testament: "He that believeth in the Son hath everlasting life: and he that believeth not the Son shall not see life; but the wrath of God abideth in Him." In his liner notes, Ja Rule wrote, "He who believes in Ja shall have everlasting love. He who does not shall not see life, but the wrath of my vengeance." "Some people [are] just naturally leaders," Ja Rule explained to Wartofsky, "and they really believe in these visions that they see. I see visions, and I believe in my heart that I can carry out these visions. And as long as I believe it, I feel the people around me should believe it—if they [are] with me." Slicker and more diverse than its predecessor, *Rule 3:36* debuted at the top of the *Billboard* R&B/hip-hop albums chart and in time became a triple-platinum seller. Critics were less impressed than record-buyers apparently were. "Ja Rule plays it painfully safe on his second album," Kathryn Farr wrote for *Rolling Stone* (on-line), "doling out pop hooks over gimmicky production. His gruff voice hasn't changed, but aside from the nimble singsong flow he flexes on the fluffy radio hit 'Between Me and You,' Rule doesn't push himself much; he simply musters the requisite rawness . . . or throaty sentimentality . . . and moves on." In contrast to the many tougher raps on the album, "Between Me and You" focuses on discreet relationships between married men and single women. The single, featuring the vocalist Christina Milian, became a Top Five hip-hop hit on the *Billboard* charts. Next on the album is "Put It on Me (What Would I Be without You)," a duet with Li'l Mo. A song about faithful lovers, the rap includes the lyrics "When you need a shoulder to lean on / Never hesitate knowing you can call on / Your soul-mate / And vice versa." "Put It on Me" won a *Source* Hip-Hop Music Award for single of the year.

In 2001 Ja Rule appeared in the film *The Fast and the Furious*, starring Vin Diesel and Paul Walker. The movie is about Los Angeles street gangs who race cars to display power. Ja Rule played the character Edwin, a drag racer; he also contributed several songs to the soundtrack. Also in 2001 Ja Rule released his third album, *Pain Is Love*; offering a mixture of spiritual reflections and love songs along with edgier material, it is his most topically diverse album to date. "My lyrical direction has become more uplifting, more spiritual, more passionate; I'm looking to live, but I'm not afraid of death," Ja Rule told Matt Diehl for *Rolling Stone* (December 6, 2001). "It's inspired by the things going on in the world, period." The title of the record echoes a sentiment tattooed on Ja Rule's chest. "It's about the sacrifices you go through for the ones that come next," Ja Rule told Diehl, "all the pain and suffering you experience so that they receive a little love. 'Pain is love' is like what Malcolm X and Martin Luther King did for black people, what Jesus Christ did for mankind. *That's* sacrifice." Although the record earned mostly lukewarm reviews, *Pain Is Love* debuted at the number-one position on the *Billboard* albums chart, hit the top of the R&B/hip-hop charts, and went platinum within five weeks of its appearance. The record includes "So Much Pain," a remake of the late Tupac Shakur's "Pain" done as a duet with Ja Rule, made possible through digital technology. It also contains Ja Rule's remix of the Jennifer Lopez song "I'm Real"; the remix, on which Ja Rule guest rapped, hit the number-one spot on *Billboard*'s singles chart. "[The remix] opened a lot of doors for me to become something that's maybe never been before," Ja Rule told Rashaun Hall. "That's the goal I've been shooting for—to be a different artist." "Livin' It Up," another single from *Pain Is Love*, also reached *Billboard*'s Top 10 in 2001. At the end of that year, Ja Rule was named the number-one Hot 100 male artist in *Billboard*'s year-end charts.

In 2002 Ja Rule was nominated for three Grammy Awards, for best album; best rap performance by a duo or group, for "Put It on Me"; and best rap/sung collaboration, for "Livin' It Up." He also earned a nomination for an American Music Award, for favorite rap/hip-hop artist. "Always On Time"—a duet with the R&B singer Ashanti on *Pain Is Love*—topped the *Billboard* singles chart in 2002, as did his remix of Jennifer Lopez's single "Ain't It Funny." In March 2002 Ja Rule was named the world's best-selling rap artist at the World Music Awards ceremony. His fourth album, *The Last Temptation*, was scheduled for release in November 2002.

Despite his success, Ja Rule has stated on several occasions that he does not plan to focus permanently on solo recording. "Making a solo album is a real grind because it's you against the world," he told Zondra Hughes. "But if I stop making solo albums and concentrate on making films, I'll become a much better actor and I can do soundtracks. I really want to start concentrating on making music and writing songs for other artists." Ja Rule has completed shooting for *Half Past Dead*, starring Steven Seagal, which is scheduled to open late in 2002. He is also slated to appear with Vin Diesel in a sequel to the sci-fi picture *Pitch Black* (2000).

Ja Rule has been featured in ads for Coca-Cola and Calvin Klein. Although many women regard him as a sex symbol, Ja Rule told Hughes, "I didn't know I was a major sex symbol. I know I'm a husband. I don't see [the fans' reaction] as that. I see it as love from the people, just an appreciation of the music and what I'm doing." Ja Rule lives in New Jersey with Aisha Murray Atkins (whom he married in April 2001) and their two children. —G.O.

Suggested Reading: *Billboard* p12 Sep. 29, 2001, with photo; Def Jam Web site; *Ebony* p138+ Apr. 2002; *MTV.com*; *Rolling Stone* p28 Mar. 29, 2001, with photo; *Rolling Stone* (on-line) Dec. 6, 2001, with photo; *TV Guide* p38+ Dec. 29, 2001–Jan. 4, 2002; *Vibe* p84+ Jan. 2002, with photo; *Washington Post* G p1 Apr. 29, 2001; *YM* p152+ Apr. 2002, with photo

Selected Albums: *Venni, Vetti, Vecci*, 1999; *Rule 3:36*, 2000; *Pain Is Love*, 2001

---

Jimi Celeste/Getty Images

## Jackson, Hal

*Nov. 3, 1915– Radio personality; entrepreneur*

*Address: c/o WBLS, Inner City Broadcasting Corp., Empire State Bldg., 350 Fifth Ave., New York, NY 10118*

The broadcasting pioneer Hal Jackson has amassed a long string of achievements in his 63 years in the field. The first African-American announcer on network radio, Jackson was a catalyst of racial integration in music, television, and professional sports. From his base in then-segregated Washington, D.C., where he reached the airwaves through careful planning and craftiness, he opened up new frontiers for African-American musicians and broadcasters through one of his first shows, *The House that Jack Built*, which was heard on different stations in Washington, Baltimore, Annapolis, and New York. Jackson's influence has reached all levels of the radio world; in the early 1970s he and several other investors became the first African-American radio-station owners. In 1984, at an age by which many have retired, he renewed his commitment to broadcasting by becoming a deejay once again. His new show, *Sunday Morning Classics*, has since become an institution on New York's WBLS-FM, mixing pop, salsa, reggae, jazz, gospel, and blues in a friendly format. "I get up some Sunday mornings, and I think, 'What am I still doing on the air?'" he admitted to Paul Colford for *Newsday* (May 25, 1988). "But I come here, and I do the show, and it seems to work. I guess I love the communication with people." A memoir describing his unique career in broadcasting, *The House that Jack Built*, which he wrote with James Haskins, was published in 2001.

Harold Baron Jackson, known as Hal, was born on November 3, 1915 in Charleston, South Carolina, the youngest of the five children of Eugene Jackson, a tailor, and Laura Rivers Jackson, a homemaker. He attended the Avery Normal Institute, a private school for black children, for a few years, until his life was disrupted by the deaths of his parents (from unrelated illnesses) within a few months of each other, when he was about nine. He spent the next several years shuttling between his sisters' families in New York and Washington, D.C.; for one year during that period, he attended the Troy Academy, a boarding school in Vermont. At 13 Jackson moved into a boarding house in Washington and began to support himself by shining shoes, cleaning bathrooms, and busing tables, all while attending public school. As a teenager he developed a passion for sports; after befriending football and basketball players at Howard University, in Washington, he became the mascot of the teams. He got a job picking up trash at Griffith Stadium, chiefly because it gave him a way to attend the home games of the Washington Senators baseball team for free. (The team moved to Texas in 1972 and was renamed the Rangers.) At Dunbar High School he lettered in five sports: football, basketball, track, tennis, and baseball. Jackson attended Howard University, where he began broadcasting sporting events. Through his mentor Sam Lacey, the national sports editor for the *Afro-American* newspaper chain, Jackson got jobs writing on local sports for the Washington *Afro-American* and broadcasting Negro League baseball games from Griffith Stadium. (He did not graduate from Howard.)

Although Jackson had many broadcasting gigs, his audience remained small. In the late 1930s no black-hosted or -themed radio programs were allowed on the air, except for religious programming, so his sports broadcasts were restricted to the stadiums where the games were played. In 1939 he engineered a plan to begin a daily 15-minute program, which he christened *The Bronze Review*, on the *Washington Post*–owned station WINX. The station manager had told him, in no uncertain terms, that no African-American would ever broadcast from WINX. "I remember it well," Jackson told Valerie Gladstone for the New York *Daily News* (July 27, 1986). He added, perhaps referring to segregation on the airwaves, "From then on I was determined to break this thing down." Jackson lined up a restaurant owner to sponsor the program, booked time at the station through Cal Erlich and Merrick, a white-owned advertising agency, and promoted the program himself, using newspapers, handbills, and word-of-mouth—all without revealing the nature of the program to anyone at the radio station. "Even with all that promotion, the people at WINX, the city's third-largest radio station, owned by the biggest newspaper, the *Washington Post*, never caught on," he wrote in *The House that Jack Built*. Only 15 minutes before the show's 11:00 p.m. premiere, in November 1939, Jackson appeared at WINX with his first guest: Mary McLeod Bethune, an African-American member of President Franklin D. Roosevelt's administration. "Everybody was stunned, and I was scheduled to go on. They couldn't locate the manager, wherever he was. Anyway, we went on the air and the phones just lit up," he told Nancy Marshall for National Public Radio's *Weekend Edition Sunday* (July 15, 2001). *The Bronze Review* was an overnight success and stayed on the air for more than two years, as Jackson played host to some of the biggest names in the black community: Congressman Adam Clayton Powell Jr.; the heavyweight boxing champion Joe Louis; the physician Charles Drew, a pioneer in the preservation of blood plasma; the magazine publisher John Johnson; and many others. By the mid-1940s, while working at the station seven days a week, he was handling talk-radio programming or sports broadcasts. In addition to regular broadcasting on WINX, part-time radio work for other stations, and sports reporting for the *Afro-American*, he used his charm and business savvy to bring professional basketball to Washington, D.C., assembling a team—called the Bears—of early 1940s African-American basketball standouts. Before proving to be financially unsustainable, the Bears went undefeated in 1942 and 1943, against both white teams and black teams, and won the 1943 Chicago World Professional Basketball Tournament.

Jackson expanded from part-time shows on various radio stations to a full-time position at WOOK, a station in the Maryland suburbs, in the mid-1940s. The station's owner, Richard Eaton, allowed him to select his own music, with the expectation that he would appeal to African-American listeners. Jackson was on the air from six in the morning until sundown, with a three-hour lunch break, and was also expected to solicit advertising, at which he became very adept. He named his show *The House that Jack Built* because, as he explained in his memoir, "it was the era of 'personality' radio, and the most important thing that a successful host did was to create a personality and the setting to go with it." As Nancy Marshall described the show, "Jackson invented an imaginary house and took listeners on a tour. He started by introducing guests from the living room, and then spun the hottest hits from the kitchen, songs by B.B. King, Frank Sinatra." The program was extremely successful. Jackson eventually divided his time among WOOK (mornings), WANN in Annapolis, Maryland (early afternoons), WSID in Baltimore, Maryland (late afternoons), and WINX (late nights). Because he reached so many listeners, he assumed the mantle of a local celebrity and community leader. He raised funds for charity, started the Good Deed Club, which encouraged people to donate time and gifts to hospitals, and hosted hundreds of benefits. Jackson also lent his name and star power to political causes, joining forces with the National Association for the Advancement of Colored People (NAACP) to picket stores and unionize staffers at WOOK.

In 1949 Jackson became the first African-American to host a television variety show, which was taped in Washington at the Howard Theater and sponsored by Emerson, a manufacturer of radios and televisions. The show, which lasted less than a year, featured many entertainment luminaries, including Duke Ellington, Dinah Washington, and Sarah Vaughn. Also in 1949 Jackson was persuaded to move his show to New York City, where he debuted on WLIB. Gearing his show toward Harlem's large African-American population, Jackson duplicated the formula that had been successful for him in Washington. He was on the air twice a day, hosting a parade of celebrity guests and weighing in on events of the era, which ranged from the funerals of famous entertainers such as the tap dancer Bill "Mr. Bojangles" Robinson to visits of foreign dignitaries including Emperor Haile Selassie of Ethiopia, whom Jackson interviewed.

After his one-year contract with WLIB was up, in 1950, Jackson returned to Washington. He took over an ailing station in suburban Maryland, changed the call letters to WUST—for U Street, in the heart of Washington's black community—and reinvigorated the operation, in part with a music show and a sports show that included racing reports. In the early 1950s Jackson was lured back to New York by the promise of access to a station, WAMC, with an open signal—much more powerful than WLIB's. WAMC's owner, Nathan Strauss, encouraged him to appeal to all New Yorkers, not just those living in Harlem, with the music he played on the show, called *The All-American Revue*. "Strauss had never had a black on the air at the time, and he was intrigued," Jackson explained in an interview with *Broadcasting* magazine (October 22, 1990). "He told me: 'I don't want you to identify with the black person on the air, I want you to do pop things.'" By the mid-1950s Jackson was again broadcasting on three local stations at all hours of the day and night, hosting shows that included a live, daily midnight jazz broadcast from the Birdland club for WABC, a network station whose programs were heard across the country. He had another brief foray into television when he hosted a Sunday-morning talent show for children, called *Uncle Hal's Kiddie Show*. By the late 1950s Jackson had returned to WLIB, which boasted a new, more powerful signal, because he wanted to redouble his efforts on behalf of the black community. To that end he played a great deal of jazz and rhythm and blues on the radio, raised funds for Martin Luther King Jr.'s Southern Christian Leadership Conference, and participated in civil rights protests around the eastern United States.

In the late 1950s Jackson's career stalled. In what came to be called the payola scandal, he and several other deejays were accused of accepting gifts from record companies in return for playing their artists' songs on the radio. Charges against Jackson were never proven, but he was fired and forced to battle the accusations in court. "I had no job, no way to take care of my family after that," he told Nancy Marshall. "So here I was, Mr. Big Shot, cleaning buildings at night so I could take care of my family." According to his autobiography, he also drove a New York City taxicab during this period. But he soon found radio work again, in Philadelphia, where he alternated between classical music and a rhythm-and-blues show at two different stations. Within months, he was back on the air in New York, beginning at a small station in the borough of Queens, WWRL, and building a new fan base for the station around his popularity. He continued to put in scores of personal appearances a year and regularly broadcast variety shows from the Palisades Amusement Park, in New Jersey. In the late 1960s he produced an annual Miss Black Teenage America contest, as a response to the Miss America Pageant, which was then all-white. The Miss Black Teenage America contest later evolved into Hal Jackson's Talented Teens International competition.

As part of a group of investors, the Inner City Broadcasting Corp. (ICBC), Jackson became a part owner of WLIB-AM in 1971; the consortium later purchased a sister station, WBLS-FM in New York, as well as radio stations in Detroit, Philadelphia, San Francisco, and Los Angeles. Jackson, who was the vice president of the ICBC, relocated to Los Angeles in the late 1970s to look after the two ICBC stations there. Within a few years, he was back on the air. "For a long time, I had worried that the classics were missing from the airwaves," he wrote in *The House that Jack Built*. "There was no radio show where you could hear Bobby Blue Bland along with Barbra Streisand, B.B. King along with Peggy Lee, Count Basie along with Sade. There were a number of White artists who were really getting into the blues and gospel and jazz, but you couldn't find them on radio stations aimed at the Black market. I had been thinking about this a lot when a slot on Sunday mornings opened up at WBLS." Jackson moved back to New York and returned to the air with *Sunday Morning Classics*, a two-hour show, in 1984. It steadily grew in popularity and increased its hours; by 1993 he was on the air every Sunday from 8:00 a.m. to 4:00 p.m with two co-hosts. Jackson himself selects all the music, which ranges from gospel to jazz to salsa to pop. "I can't follow that trend that says that you can't play certain things together," he told Alison France for the *New York Times* (October 23, 1993). "Why can't you?" He does not, however, care for rap music. "I relate to very little of it," he explained to France. "I try, because I don't want to be on the outside looking in. But some of this rap is pretty rough."

Jackson was inducted into the National Association of Broadcasters Hall of Fame in 1990 and the Radio Hall of Fame in 1995; he was the first African-American to be honored by either institution. He was inducted into the *Broadcasting and Cable* Hall of Fame in 2001. He has been honored by four presidents: Franklin D. Roosevelt, Harry S. Truman, Dwight D. Eisenhower, and John F. Kennedy. Jackson is currently married to his fourth wife, Debi, who is one of his co-hosts on *Sunday Morning Classics.* (His three previous marriages ended in divorce.) From his first marriage he has a daughter, Jane, a teacher and school administrator; from his second marriage, he has a son, Hal Jr., a judge, and a daughter, Jewell Jackson McCabe, a publicist and the founder of the National Coalition of 100 Black Women. — K.S.

Suggested Reading: *Broadcasting* p103 Oct. 22, 1990, with photo; New York *Daily News* p22 July 27, 1986, with photo; *New York Times* I p49 Oct. 23, 1993, with photo; *Newsday* II p15 May 25, 1988, with photo; Jackson, Hal, and James Haskins. *The House that Jack Built*, 2001

Selected Radio Shows: *The House that Jack Built*; *Sunday Morning Classics*

---

Rob Hann/Retna

## Jackson, Peter

*Oct. 31, 1961– Film director; screenwriter; producer*

*Address: WingNut Films Ltd., P.O. Box 15-208, Miramar, Wellington, New Zealand*

Peter Jackson, who has directed and co-written the screenplays for the *Lord of the Rings* film trilogy, is a longtime fan of the J.R.R. Tolkien novels on which the movies are based. (The first of the films, which were shot simultaneously, was released at the end of 2001.) "As a director, [the series] has given me an enormous canvas on which to try all sorts of things," Jackson said, as quoted on the films' official Web site. "The story has so much variety to it. In each installment there is intimate, heart-wrenching drama, huge battle scenes, intense special effects, sudden changes for the characters, every emotion in the realm. It was a continual challenge for me." When he started the project, he recalled for that Web site, he had "one goal: to take moviegoers into the fantastical world of Middle-earth in a way that is believable and powerful. I wanted to take all the great moments from the books and use modern technology to give audiences nights at the movies unlike anything they've experienced before." In her review of the first installment for *Salon* (December 18, 2001, on-line), Stephanie Zacharek described *Lord of the Rings: The Fellowship of the Ring* as "one of the best fantasy pictures ever made" and added, "It's a lovely example of how, with care and thought and not all that much money . . . a director can successfully capture the mood and feel of a book on the big screen."

Earlier in his career, Jackson gained experience in the use of special effects to enhance cinematic fantasies. Working with some of his friends, he produced the low-budget cult classic *Bad Taste* (1987) and two additional low-budget films, *Meet the Feebles* (1989) and *Braindead* (1992), that have also become underground favorites; all three pictures feature gory special effects and dark humor. Jackson surprised many critics with *Heavenly Creatures* (1992), which tells the true-life story of two New Zealand girls who became close friends and eventually murdered the mother of one of them. Jackson's direction of *Forgotten Silver* (1995) and *The Frighteners* (1996) have solidified his reputation as a wide-ranging and imaginative filmmaker.

The only child of Bill Jackson, a civil engineer, and Joan Jackson, Peter Jackson was born on October 31, 1961 in Pukerua Bay, a small town on the west coast of New Zealand. When he was eight he and his friends began shooting short films with an 8mm movie camera that his parents had bought.

Lacking deep pockets, he thought up ingenious, cost-free methods for creating special effects. In a movie he made in 1973 about World War II, for example, he punched holes in the film to simulate the effects of gunfire. Among his other cinematic projects, Jackson reproduced several Monty Python skits word for word. He also experimented with animation, opening and closing the camera's shutter very quickly in order to create the sort of stop-motion effects associated with Ray Harryhausen, whose work enhanced such fantasy or science-fiction films as *The Beast from 20,000 Fathoms* (1953) and *Jason and the Argonauts* (1963).

When he was 17 Jackson left school and found a job as a photoengraver with the *Evening Post*, a Wellington, New Zealand, newspaper. He saved enough money from his wages to buy a used Bolex 16mm camera, which was both easy to handle and versatile. Jackson and his friends soon began making another film, which had the working title "Roast of the Day"; they intended to keep it short, but Jackson kept adding to it, and before long it had reached nearly feature length. "We had no script," Jackson told Hal Hinson for the *Washington Post* (July 28, 1996). "Not a word was ever committed to paper. It was, like, all in my head. Each week, I'd think of more stuff, so the thing just kept on growing and growing and growing." Up to that point Jackson had financed "Roast of the Day" entirely with his own money; none of the actors or crew, all of whom were friends of Jackson's, were paid. When the film was three-quarters completed, Jackson applied to the New Zealand Film Commission (NZFC) for money to help with postproduction. Unlike the other board members, the NZFC's chairman, Jim Booth, expressed enthusiasm for the project; he used a discretionary fund to help finance the last quarter of shooting.

"Roast of the Day," renamed *Bad Taste*, was completed in 1987. Although he had not originally planned to act in it, Jackson portrayed the film's hero, Derek, one of four witless men from the New Zealand Air and Space Defense League who journey to a small fishing town to investigate reports of UFO landings. Before long the men are battling a large army of aliens, who have butchered the townspeople for use as an ingredient in items served in their intergalactic chain of fast-food eateries. A friend of Jackson's in the movie industry persuaded the director to enter *Bad Taste* at the Cannes Film Festival, in France; it won a great deal of acclaim there and recouped its costs within a few days through distribution deals. *Bad Taste* has since become a cult classic on the strength of its outrageous humor and notable, albeit amateurish, special effects. "Despite being little more than a rambling selection of lame characters and imaginative—if hammy—executions, the film's farcical energy and glorious B-movie schlock keeps you hooked until the apocalyptic finale," Matt Ford wrote in a review for *BBC Online*. "This is a film without heroes, and it's sometimes hard to decide whether the aliens or the hillbilly locals are the more repulsive—never mind actually care about any of them. All you can do is sit back, hold on, and watch the roller coaster carnage unfold."

On the heels of *Bad Taste*'s success, Jim Booth left the NZFC to join Jackson as a partner in WingNut Films, which Jackson had founded. Earlier, while making *Bad Taste*, Jackson had met Frances Walsh (with whom he became romantically involved) and Stephen Sinclair, and he now began collaborating with them on a script about zombies. Although Jackson succeeded in supplementing funds from the NZFC with money from Japanese and Spanish investors, he soon realized that he did not have enough cash to shoot this new project. Proceeding on the assumption that greater commercial success would attract more investors, he took the remainder of the profits from *Bad Taste* and wrote another script, this one with his friend Danny Mulheron as well as Walsh and Sinclair. The result was *Meet the Feebles* (1989), made on a budget of $750,000. Directed, produced, and animated by Jackson, the film is about Heidi the Hippo, the star of a show called *Meet the Feebles Variety Hour*, who discovers that her husband, Bletch the Walrus, is cheating on her. The troubles of other Feebles—portrayed by puppets and actors in animal suits—involve drug abuse, extortion, robbery, the AIDS virus, and murder. "I'd like to view it as a satire of human behaviour," Jackson told Jorgen Broms, as reprinted on *Peter Jackson Online*. "Imagine a scenario where the Muppets just finished a TV show. What would happen if they went backstage and behaved like normal people, smoking, drinking and having sex? That's what we were aiming at." Thanks to sufficient backing, what was originally planned as a short picture grew into a full-length film. In a review for *BBC Online*, Nick Cramp wrote, "With its wilful grotesquery and soap opera storyline this is novelty trash, but nevertheless succeeds in rising above itself." *Meet the Feebles* was shown at several festivals; the interest it generated enabled Jackson to secure the necessary funding for the zombie film.

Released in 1992 as *Braindead* in the United Kingdom and *Dead Alive* in the United States, the zombie picture was billed as the goriest movie ever made. The plot features a poisonous "rat monkey" that arrives in a New Zealand zoo. After the hero's mother is bitten by the monkey, she slowly turns into a zombie and starts hunting people. Each person she bites also becomes a zombie. In a gruesome showdown the hero and his girlfriend face hundreds of zombies. A number of critics enjoyed the film's dark, tongue-in-cheek humor; among them was Mark Savlov, who described *Dead Alive* in the *Austin Chronicle* (April 16, 1993) as "a film so gleefully over-the-top that it's decidedly hard not to gag while you're laughing yourself incontinent." Soon after the picture opened in the U.S., New Line Cinema asked Jackson to write a script for the sixth film in the *Nightmare on Elm Street* series. After he handed it in, the studio turned it down in favor of another writer's script.

In a change of pace from their previous two films, Jackson and Walsh began writing the screenplay for *Heavenly Creatures*, a movie based on the true story of two teenage girls—Juliet Hulme, a young British newcomer to New Zealand, and Pauline Parker, a New Zealand native—who enter into an obsessive friendship at a repressive school for girls. Hulme, whose personality dominates their relationship, creates an intricate fantasy world that the girls come to believe is more important than reality. In 1954 the girls killed Pauline's mother, because she had refused to give Pauline permission to accompany Juliet to South Africa, where the Hulme family planned to move. (Juliet, who later adopted the name Anne Perry, is now a successful mystery novelist.) "What attracted me to this story was that it was complicated, about two people who are not evil, not psychopaths but totally out of their depth," Jackson told Bernard Weinraub for the *New York Times* (November 24, 1994). "Their emotions got out of control."

With the goal of re-creating the girls' story accurately, Jackson and Walsh painstakingly researched the murder case, which is among New Zealand's most notorious, and interviewed people who had known Juliet and Pauline and their families. Many people refused to cooperate with them, however, as did administrators at the school the teenagers had attended, complaining that they did not want a film to be made about the case. "A lot of the people who were involved at the time are still alive, and I have had all sorts of anguish over whether we should have done it," Jackson told an interviewer for the New Zealand supplement to *Cinema Papers*, as reprinted on *Peter Jackson Online*. "Ultimately there is no justification. I do feel bad about having done it, and in a sense I shouldn't have. The only justification, and it is not real justification, is that if I hadn't made the film, other people would have. There were two or three other features lined up to go, based on the same case. Two or three other New Zealand filmmakers also had scripts. One was a tele-movie based on a play that came out about a year or so ago in New Zealand. It was unsympathetic towards the girls and basically just dramatized the sensational headlines of the 1950s without having any regard to their being a couple of human beings. The girls must have had a reason for doing what they did—they weren't just mad—but the play portrayed them as psychos. So, it was a story that was going to be made. And we felt that if it had to be done by somebody, we should do it properly ourselves. We knew we could do a good job of it, and that we had uncovered facts about the case which no one else had."

Casting the part of Pauline proved to be enormously time-consuming. Jackson wanted an unknown actress who looked similar to the real Pauline. Walsh drove across southern New Zealand and stopped in many towns, where she showed school superintendents a photo of the teenage Pauline. A few days before the deadline for starting the shoot, she found what she was seeking in Melanie Lynskey, a student at the New Plymouth Girls High School, who was then about 14. The British-born actress Kate Winslet was chosen to play Juliet.

Financed by the NZFC and German backers, *Heavenly Creatures* was released in 1994. In his review of the movie for *Leonard Maltin's Movie & Video Guide*, as reprinted on the Internet Movie Database (on-line), Maltin wrote that the film was "very well acted, particularly by Lynskey and Winslet, and stunningly directed by Jackson, who plunges us into the bizarre fantasy world that the girls create for themselves." Hal Hinson, writing for the *Washington Post* (November 23, 1994), was equally impressed. "Hundreds, perhaps thousands of movies have been made about girlfriends and their unique bond, but I can't think of another one where the topic is addressed more frankly or openly. Though the film's subject is sensationalistic in the extreme, Jackson's style is poetic. He presents Pauline and Juliet . . . as singularly blessed. And he raises the question of whether there is any love purer or more gratifying than this same-sex soulmating. Because their love ends in murder, it's at least implied that the romance is tainted somehow. Does the fault lie with the girls, or with the cramped morality of the time? Thankfully, this powerful, evocative movie leaves the question wide open."

Although several critics regarded *Heavenly Creatures* as a turning point in Jackson's career, the filmmaker had a different view. "I have no set plan for my career," he told the interviewer for *Cinema Papers*. "To me it was simply that I was interested in making this film. It's something new and that is good. But I have always seen my other films as being different from each other in certain ways. This is obviously a greater leap, however. It is much more of a mainstream film; there is no doubt about that. It's interesting that people whom I have never met have all these assumptions about my career. People immediately assume that filmmakers do things because of a grand plan. People are no doubt saying, 'Oh, Jackson wants to be taken as a serious filmmaker now. He's sick of being branded as a splatter filmmaker and he wants to do arty mainstream films.' That's not true. I do intend to do other splatter films. I have intentions of doing all sorts of films." *Heavenly Creatures* earned Jackson and Walsh an Academy Award nomination for best original screenplay.

Jackson's next project was *Forgotten Silver* (1995), which he co-wrote and directed, with Costa Botes, and executive produced. The film, which premiered on New Zealand television, was a mock documentary about a fictional New Zealand filmmaker named Colin McKenzie and the amazing advances he made in cinema, such as creating a picture with a soundtrack in 1908 and using color film in 1911. (In actuality, the world's first successful commercial "talkie," as movies with sound were once called, was shown in 1926, and the first commercial film in color came out in 1935.) *Forgotten Silver* combined interviews with real people (among them Leonard Maltin, the actor Sam Neill, and Harvey Weinstein, the co-chairman of Miramax Films) with intricate silent footage and still pictures supposedly dating from about 1900 through the 1920s. The mockumentary was so realistic that many New Zealand moviegoers believed McKenzie had actually existed. In his review of the film for the *New York Times* (October 3, 1997), Lawrence Van Gelder described *Forgotten Silver* as "a delightful spoof" that "at once positions its hero in the path of great events while sending up its subject—film history—with informed skill, much affection and mischievous glee."

At around this time, the American film director Bob Zemeckis asked Jackson to draft a screenplay for another installment of *Tales from the Crypt*, a low-budget series of horror movies. Jackson turned in his screenplay a few weeks later, and Zemeckis liked it so much that he decided it should stand apart from the series. Co-written with Fran Walsh, *The Frighteners* (1996) stars Michael J. Fox as a psychic private detective with a couple of ghostly partners. His investigation of the mysterious deaths of people in a small town leads alarmingly to what may be the spirit of death itself. The film, made on a budget of $30 million, used digital effects in more than 570 shots, ranging from about one second to minutes in duration. (By the time that movie came out, Jackson had set up his own digital-effects company, WETA Ltd.) Although it was a success at the box office, grossing more than $16 million in the United States, critical reaction was mixed. "Shrill, overproduced and crammed with clever visual effects and sound cues, *The Frighteners* starts off with a simple idea—a small-time ghostbuster meets his match in a sinister poltergeist—but smothers whatever merits it may have had in a rush of bells, whistles, bombast and smoke," Edward Guthmann wrote in his review for the *San Francisco Chronicle* (July 19, 1996). Kenneth Turan was more enthusiastic, noting in an assessment for the *Los Angeles Times* (July 19, 1996), "Jackson, at home with all kinds of excess, keeps everything spinning nicely, not even losing a step when the mood turns increasingly disturbing."

Jackson was next commissioned to write a script for a remake of *King Kong*, one of his favorite films. After he finished the script, he accepted an invitation to direct the film. Although all seemed to be going well, *King Kong* was never made. With *Godzilla* already in the works and remakes of *Mighty Joe Young* and *Attack of the 50 Ft. Woman* soon to be released, executives at Universal Studios feared that the market would be flooded with too-similar films, and they suspended production. At about the same time, Jackson had been offered the chance to write and direct "Freddy vs. Jason," a horror film in which the supernatural villains of the *Nightmare on Elm Street* and *Friday the 13th* series face off. Jackson turned down the job, because he was busy working on *King Kong*.

Not long afterward Jackson agreed to direct a film adaptation of the *Lord of the Rings* trilogy, based on the hugely popular 1950s fantasy novels by J. R. R. Tolkien. (An earlier, completely animated version, directed by Ralph Bakshi, came out in 1978.) Along with Walsh, Stephen Sinclair, and Philippa Boyens, a newcomer to cinema, Jackson co-wrote the screenplay. "I'm a real believer in trying to push yourself," he told Mark Burman for the London *Guardian* (July 30, 1999). "And if you're a film-maker, I don't think there's anything more amazing to be involved with than *The Lord of the Rings*. It's the holy grail of film-making. It's a once in a lifetime experience, and if [my wife and I] do it and we can be proud, then we want to retire when it's all over." All three films were shot in 2001 in New Zealand. "Shooting three separate movies back to back has never been done before," Jackson told Burman. "But I think it's unfair to say to an audience, 'Come to *The Fellowship of the Ring* and, if it's successful, we make part two'. That's not what we're doing. We are making the entire trilogy, one long film shoot and then we'll cut them all together. I guess it's a certain form of madness." The focal point of the saga are the hobbits, small humanoids with large, furry feet. Jackson used various special effects to give moviegoers the impression that normal-size actors are hobbit size, and a year before shooting began, he had 5,000 cubic meters of suitable vegetation planted in the area chosen to be the hobbits' home.

*Lord of the Rings: The Fellowship of the Ring* opened in December 2001. The film was made at a cost of about $109 million, a relatively low figure in light of its exceedingly intricate visual effects and Jackson's use of as many as nine film crews to shoot footage in remote parts of New Zealand. A huge success at the box office, the movie grossed over $313 million in the United States alone and received mostly favorable reviews. "Made with intelligence, imagination, passion and skill, propulsively paced and shot through with an aged-in-oak sense of wonder, the trilogy's first film so thrillingly catches us up in its sweeping story that nothing matters but the vivid and compelling events unfolding on the screen," Kenneth Turan wrote in a review for the *Los Angeles Times* (December 19, 2001, on-line). Turan also noted, "Having someone who has an interest in, and insight into, the intricacies of human nature in charge here brings substance and authenticity to the table. It's the rarest thing to have a director with that kind of perception eager to take on an action-adventure epic with a massive budget, and it makes all the difference." For Stephanie Zacharek, who reviewed it for *Salon*, the film was a reminder of "why we go to the movies in the first place." "Jackson unfurls the action so that it drifts into graceful peaks and valleys," Zacharek wrote; "the picture is a marvel of pacing, built on the premise that the proper flow of tension and suspense is the most powerful special effect of all." Roger Ebert, in his review for the *Chicago Sun-Times* (December 19, 2001, on-line), acknowledged that the picture "is remarkably well made." But then he complained, "It does go on, and on, and on—more vistas, more forests, more sounds in the night, more fearsome creatures, more prophecies, more visions, more dire warnings, more close calls, until we realize this sort of thing can continue indefinitely." *The Fellowship of the Ring* was nominated for 13 Academy Awards, for best picture, best director, and best writing of a screenplay based on previously written material, among others; it won Oscars in the categories of makeup, score, cinematography, and visual effects. In addition, the British Academy of Film and Television Arts (BAFTA) named it best picture.

The other two films in the *Ring* trilogy, subtitled *The Two Towers* and *The Return of the King*, are slated to premiere in December 2002 and December 2003, respectively.

Although Jackson has made some high-budget mainstream films, he has little interest in moving to Hollywood or being the sort of director-for-hire who signs on to projects half-heartedly. "Too often you see film makers from other countries who have made interesting, original films, and then they come here and get homogenized into being hack Hollywood directors. I don't want to fall into that," he told Bernard Weinraub. "I have a freedom that's incredibly valuable. Obviously my freedom is far smaller in scale than people like Zemeckis and [the filmmaker Steven] Spielberg have here. But it's comparable. I can dream up a project, develop it, make it, control it, release it." Jackson lives in New Zealand with Fran Walsh and their two children. — G.O.

Suggested Reading: *BBC News* (on-line) Feb. 24, 2002, with photos; (London) *Guardian* (on-line), July 30, 1999; *New York Times* C p11 Nov. 24, 1994, with photo; *Washington Post* G p2 July 28, 1996, with photo

Selected Films: *Bad Taste*, 1987; *Meet the Feebles*, 1989; *Braindead*, 1992; *Heavenly Creatures*, 1994; *Forgotten Silver*, 1995; *The Frighteners*, 1996; *Lord of the Rings: The Fellowship of the Ring*, 2001

---

## James, Edgerrin

*Aug. 1, 1978– Football player*

*Address: Indianapolis Colts, P.O. Box 535000, Indianapolis, IN 46253*

Reuters/Colin Braley/Hultin Archive by Getty Images

While his dreadlocks and five gold teeth made the Indianapolis Colts' running back Edgerrin James easily recognizable in 1999, his rookie year, he stood out even more because of his exceptional play. A power runner, the 214-pound, six-foot James is capable of bruising running inside, and with his quickness and athleticism, he is adept at eluding tacklers in the open field. In his first season in the National Football League (NFL), James, who wears the number 32, helped the Indianapolis Colts rise from last to first place in their division as he led the league in rushing yardage and easily captured the Rookie of the Year award with his tenacious play. He immediately impressed his teammates and coaches with his hard work in practice and soon won over skeptical Colts fans with his dominant running. James's remarkable stamina allows him to wear down defenders over the course of a game, and his sure hands make him a threat as a receiver as well.

Born on August 1, 1978, Edgerrin James grew up in a migrant farming town called Immokalee, near the Florida Everglades. His mother, Julie James, worked in a school cafeteria. She created her son's name by joining parts of the given name and surname of his father, Edward German, whose job as a harvesting contractor often kept him away from Immokalee. Except at harvesttime, Immokalee's economy was depressed, and, like many families who lived there, the Jameses had little money; food stamps helped them to survive. When he became old enough, Edgerrin worked in the fields to supplement the family's income. Often, in the summers, he joined relatives in Georgia to pick watermelons. From morning to night, often in 110-degree heat, he would load a truck with 30-pound watermelons that had been passed along by lines of other workers. As his half-brother, Edward, explained to John Ed Bradley for *Sports Illustrated* (September 20, 1999), James's position was more difficult than those of the other migrants. "The person farthest from the truck throws [the watermelon] to the next person, who throws it to the next one," Edward said. "If you're the person right next to the truck, you touch every last watermelon. They call that bumpin'. Well, Edgerrin did mostly bumpin'. He was so strong, he could touch the watermelon with one hand and just throw it up in the truck without any effort. He had stamina like nobody else. He could go all day."

As a boy James played in the Pop Warner youth football league (named for the celebrated Glenn Scobey "Pop" Warner, Stanford University's head football coach from 1923 until 1932). As he literally ran over the other players, he liked to pretend that he was the football star Walter Payton. "People in Immokalee called it the Edgerrin James show," James's uncle John James told Bradley. In high school James continued to excel as a running back and was named a *Parade* All-American. He let his studies slide, though, and often cut classes. Nearly all of the many universities initially interested in recruiting James lost interest after he did poorly on his college entrance exams. Only the University of Miami offered him a scholarship.

While sharing the stage with other talented running backs on Miami's football team, the Hurricanes, James played well and, after his junior year, became the first Hurricane ever to rush for 1,000 yards in two consecutive seasons. The team's running-back coach, Don Soldinger, raved about James to Bradley: "The kid can do so many things. To start, he has receiver-like hands. . . . He's afraid of nothing. On his blitz pickups Edgerrin hurts people. He gets in great position; then he just nails you—and, yes, I'm talking about linebackers. His running ability is phenomenal. Plus, the guy is smart."

James's standout game in college came in December 1998, in his junior year, against the UCLA (University of California at Los Angeles) Bruins, who were vying for a chance to play in the national college football championship game. The Hurricanes upset the Bruins behind the incredible running of James, who rushed for 299 yards (a Big East division record) and three touchdowns. After the 1998 season James made the decision to leave school early to play for the NFL. Though he had been impressive in college, the fact that he had shared playing time with other running backs (he had started only 17 games for Miami) led some people to doubt his prowess. Thus, it was a surprise to many when, in 1999, James was drafted as the fourth overall pick by the Indianapolis Colts, who passed over the 1998 Heisman Trophy winner, the running back Ricky Williams.

Colts fans were skeptical about James. The team had just traded their star running back Marshall Faulk, and fans thought Ricky Williams would have been a better pick to fill Faulk's shoes. Then, as the Colts' training camp began, James and his agent held out for more money, fueling fans' ill-feelings. James signed a seven-year deal that, provided certain conditions came to pass, was worth $49 million. The Colts had had a 3–13 season the year before, and the front office placed its hopes on James to turn the team around. Furthermore, early indications of the Colts' running game in the 1999 preseason did not look good. In the second preseason game, against the Cincinnati Bengals, the Colts rushed for only 34 yards, and their starting running back, Darick Holmes, broke his leg in the process. As quoted by Sean Deveney in the *Sporting News* (January 20, 2000), the Colts' head coach, Jim Mora, said after that game, "It's going to take Superman to make yardage the way we're blocking."

If James wasn't a Superman in 1999, he came close. He was a diligent worker in training camp, and he quickly mastered the Colts' offensive scheme. Almost every day during the season, he arrived at the team's practice facility by 6:30 a.m."Nobody puts more pressure on me than I put on myself," James said to Steve Herman for the *Detroit News* (November 23, 1999, on-line). "I'm in the NFL, this is my dream, and I've always said that once I get to the NFL, I'm going to try to make the best out of it." In his first professional game, James rushed for 112 yards and a touchdown as the Colts beat their arch rivals, the Buffalo Bills, 31–14. He ran for 118 yards and another touchdown in his second game. In November, against the Philadelphia Eagles, James racked up 152 yards and two touchdowns and caught five passes for 47 more yards and a third touchdown. James proved durable and never missed a game, while Ricky Williams—whom many had thought a better running back than James—missed most of the season due to injury. In his 16 regular-season games, James never had fewer than 80 yards in total offense. He led the league in total rushing yards with 1,553 and gained an additional 586 yards receiving. Adding to his list of achievements, James broke an NFL rookie record by running for 100 or more yards in 10 games, while also scoring an impressive 17 touchdowns in the season.

"All my life has been about proving myself," James told Bradley. "I've been through so much that what I'm going through now is nothing. You get so accustomed to hearing bad things said about you. People used to say I'd never make it in college because of where I came from, and I've proved them wrong. Nothing I love more than turning a negative into a positive." By a vote of 49 out of 50, he was named the 1999 Rookie of the Year. He was also elected to the Pro Bowl.

Unlike some NFL stars, James remained levelheaded about his success. During the 1999 season he bought a relatively modest $350,000 home in Indianapolis. He also made sure that his mother no longer had to work (she volunteered at the school cafeteria nevertheless). Though many had encouraged James to adopt a more conservative look in the interest of cultivating sponsorship contracts, James refused to change his appearance. "People are always telling me, 'You're losing all these opportunities,'" James said, as quoted by Bob Kravitz in the *Indianapolis Star* (September 8, 2000, on-line). "But what sense does it make if I'm not happy with what I'm doing? Why should I change who I am? My mom's got gold teeth. My brother's got gold teeth. Growing up in South Florida, you go down there, you see a lot of people with gold teeth." Kravitz wrote of James, "It's not often you get to use these words in sports anymore, but here it is: refreshing. Edgerrin James is refreshing. There is no artifice here, no pretense. He is proud of who he is and how he looks and from whence he came."

Because the Colts led their division with a 13–3 record, they did not have to play in the wild-card round of the 1999 NFL play-offs. In the second round they met the formidable Tennessee Titans and engaged them in a tough defensive battle. The Titans' swarming defense effectively shut down the Colts' offense, including James, who rushed for only 56 yards on 20 carries. Thus, a great season was cut short, as the Colts lost to the Titans, 19–16.

During the off-season James had special charts made showing his statistics for the 1999 season, so that he might compare his performances from that and upcoming seasons. In the 2000 season the Colts exhibited both the adeptness of their 1999 regular-season play and the deficiency of their post-season play. In their first game of the season, on September 3, 2000, the Colts went to Kansas City to play the Chiefs, a team notorious for being tough at home. After committing some early errors in the oppressive heat, the Colts appeared to wear the Chiefs down. James gained about half of his 124 rushing yards in the fourth quarter of the game as the Colts won, 27–14. After the game James said to Bob Kravitz for the *Indianapolis Star* (September 4, 2000, on-line), "Shoot, this heat ain't nothing compared to where I'm from. Try playing Pop Warner ball in the deep, deep South, 11 o'clock, 1 o'clock, and nobody's watching. This ain't nothing." In their second game of the season, the Colts came up short against the Oakland Raiders, losing 38–31 after squandering a chance to tie the game in the final minutes. James rushed for 91 yards and a touchdown. The Colts' 10–6 record was enough to give them a wildcard berth in the play-offs, where they lost in the first round to the Miami Dolphins, 23–17, in overtime.

During the sixth game of the 2001 season, James sustained a knee injury that ended his playing for the year. After his departure the Colts achieved only mediocre performances. Through the first seven games of the 2002 season, James rushed for 523 yards on 154 attempts, and the Colts posted a 4–3 record to lead the American Football Conference South Division.

James lives in Indianapolis during the season; at other times he lives in Immokalee, where he keeps to a rigorous training regimen. As he said to Herman, "Every day, I'm working and trying to get better, because you never know how long it's going to last. And you want to be remembered for being one of the great players of the NFL." — P.G.H.

Suggested Reading: *Detroit News* (on-line) Nov. 23, 1999; *Indianapolis Star* (on-line) Sep. 4, 2000, Sep. 8, 2000; *Sport* p41+ Jul. 2000, with photos; *Sporting News* (on-line) Jan. 20, 2000; *Sports Illustrated* p40+ Dec. 14, 1998, p44+ Sep. 20, 1999, with photos

---

# Jay-Z

*Dec. 4, 1970– Rapper; entrepreneur*

*Address: Roca Wear, 463 Seventh Ave., #1600, New York, NY 10018*

In the dog-eat-dog music business, few entertainers who rise to the top remain there for long. This is especially true in the world of hip-hop, where this week's hot young rapper quickly becomes a has-been. Jay-Z has defied that truism, achieving critical acclaim and commercial success since the release of his debut album, *Reasonable Doubt*, in 1996. Many of his studio albums, in fact, have debuted at number one on the *Billboard* charts, confirming his reputation as one of the preeminent rappers in the U.S. Although critics have occasionally criticized his posturing and braggadocio, and some fans have accused him of becoming too commercial, his influence as a reconciling force between hardcore gangsta rap and pop-rap has been widely acknowledged. In addition to his skills behind the microphone, Jay-Z is one of the few rap musicians to own a record label. In 1995, with his longtime friends Damon Dash and Kareem "Biggs" Burke, he formed Roc-A-Fella Records, which has signed such up-and-coming artists as Memphis Bleek, Beanie Sigel, and Amil. Rock-A-Fella is now involved in film and concert promotion and has expanded to include a clothing line, Roc Wear.

Jay-Z was born Shawn Carter on December 4, 1970 in the New York City borough of Brooklyn. His father deserted the family when Shawn was 12; his mother, Gloria Carter, worked as a supervising clerk in an investment firm and struggled to raise her two sons and two daughters alone. Shawn grew up in the Marcy Houses, a city-run dwelling in Brooklyn's Bedford-Stuyvesant section, a tough neighborhood where drugs and violence were a part of the backdrop of his everyday experience. Although he did well in school and displayed an agreeable personality, in his teens he took to selling drugs, and he was shot at on several occasions. While he now hesitates to speak to interviewers about his drug dealing, his music is infused with references to the subject.

Phil Knott/Camera Press/Retna Ltd.

*Jay-Z*

In Bedford-Stuyvesant Shawn was nicknamed Jazzy; he later shortened the moniker to Jay-Z. Having become known locally for his ability to remember complex lyrics and rhymes without writing them down, the teenaged Jay-Z began trying to make a name for himself as a rapper. Partly with the aim of devoting himself to his fledgling music career, he abandoned his lucrative drug business. "It wasn't specifically one thing," Jay-Z explained in an interview with Richard Harrington for the *Washington Post* (January 2, 2000). "It was more so out of fear. You can't run on the streets forever. What are you going to be doing when you're 30 years old, or 35 or 40? I had a fear of being nothing—that pretty much drove me."

Around that time Jay-Z became good friends with a local rapper named Jaz-O (also known as Big Jaz or the Jaz), who had a record deal and had made a single called "Hawaiian Sophie." In 1988 Jay-Z contributed to an album by Jaz-O. Dismayed by Jaz's treatment at the hands of his record label, which kept the lion's share of the profits from the single, Jay-Z returned to the drug world for a while. "I was young and foolish," he told Harrington. Still, he never lost sight of his dream of becoming a rap star.

In 1995 Jay-Z made a 12-inch single called "In My Lifetime" and sold it from the trunk of his car. Soon afterward he was signed by Priority Records, which released *Reasonable Doubt*, his first LP, in the following year. The recording became tremendously popular, especially in New York City, and landed in the Top 25 on *Billboard*'s album charts—an impressive feat for an unknown rapper. Rap lovers were impressed with Jay-Z's fresh, conversational tone, quick timing, and smooth rhymes, as well as with his choice of collaborators, among them the Notorious B.I.G. and DJ Premier. The album yielded a single, "Ain't No Nigga," a duet with the female newcomer Foxy Brown that went gold, and three additional hit singles—"Can't Knock the Hustle," "Dead Presidents," and "Feelin' It."

Although *Reasonable Doubt* quickly went platinum (selling more than a million copies), Jay-Z felt unhappy about Priority Records' promotion and distribution of his work. Along with Biggs Burke and Damon Dash, he formed a new record label—Roc-A-Fella Records, named after Nelson A. Rockefeller, who was responsible for the extremely tough antidrug laws that went into effect while he was governor of New York State (1959–73).

Jay-Z's next album, *In My Lifetime, Vol. 1* (1997), was an even bigger success than his debut, moving to the number-three position on the *Billboard* charts. Adding to the album's marketability were contributions by the popular guest artists Puff Daddy and Teddy Riley, who brought Jay-Z's sound closer to pop-rap. Such singles as "Sunshine" and "The City Is Mine" (the latter a tribute to Notorious B.I.G., who was killed in a drive-by shooting on March 9, 1997) displayed Jay-Z's willingness to become a more commercial rapper. That flexibility distressed many of his original fans, who preferred his gangsta-style rap. As a reviewer for *Vibe* (November 1997) wrote, "Due to the current pop climate, *In My Lifetime, Vol. 1* will surely enjoy a healthy dose of mainstream consumption. But both playas [i.e. fans] and haters can be assured that Jay-Z's new, easy-to-swallow coating dulls the ruff 'n'ready active ingredient that made his first release the classic cure."

Jay-Z next released *Vol. 2: Hard Knock Life* (1998), an infectious pop-rap album that topped the *Billboard* charts for five weeks and went multiplatinum. The recording produced three hit singles: "Can I Get a . . . ," "Cash, Money, Hoes," and "Hard Knock Life (Ghetto Anthem)." The last-named piece contains a segment featuring the chorus of singing orphans from the Broadway musical *Annie*, which Jay-Z remembered from his childhood. As he recalled to Richard Harrington, "When I heard [the original song], I thought, whoa, that's amazing—those kids are too strong to let the ghetto life bring them down! That's the emotion of the ghetto, that's how people feel right now: 'Instead of treats, we get tricked; instead of kisses, we get kicked.'" Although three other singles, "Jigga What?," "It's Alright," and "Money Ain't a Thang," soon became hits, too, some critics felt the recording lacked coherence; as Richard Harrington observed for the *Washington Post* (October 28, 1999), "Jay-Z's fluid flow and assured presence are . . . responsible for the album's success, though *Vol. 2* is nowhere near as consistent as his 1996 debut, *Reasonable Doubt*. For one thing, Jay-Z spends too much time dissing the competition ('Ride or Die'), self-mythologizing ('If I Should Die') and belaboring the obvious ('Money, Cash, Hoes')." Despite such criticism, the songs had a great deal of airplay on radio and on MTV, and the album won a Grammy Award for best rap album of the year. (Jay-Z boycotted the ceremony to protest what he considered the Grammy committee's dismissal of most rappers.) *Backstage*, a documentary about the *Hard Knock Life* concert tour, was released by Dimension Films, a division of Miramax, in 2000.

In late 1999 Jay-Z released his album *Vol 3: The Life and Times of S. Carter*. Like its predecessors, it sold well, debuting at number one on the album charts. Its hit singles included "Big Pimpin'" and "Do It Again (Put Ya Hands Up)." In a January 2, 2000 review (separate from the feature article of the same date) for the *Washington Post*, Richard Harrington proclaimed the album to be "solid platinum, chock-full of hot tracks and sharp lyric attacks on pretenders, player-haters and critics of hip-hop's current No. 1 hit man."

The success of the album was overshadowed in the press by news of Jay-Z's arrest for the stabbing of the record executive Lance "Un" Rivera at a party at the Kit Kat Club, in New York City. Jay-Z turned himself in to law-enforcement officers shortly after the stabbing and was released on $50,000 bail. According to Allison Samuels in *Newsweek* (December 13, 1999), Jay-Z and Rivera had argued over Jay-Z's accusation that Rivera had been leaking pirated copies of the rapper's unfinished album to bootleggers. In October 2001 Jay-Z was sentenced to three years' probation; he also paid Rivera an undisclosed amount to settle the civil suit Rivera had brought against him. (An unrelated gun-possession charge from the year before, related to a weapon found in Jay-Z's vehicle, was dropped at around the same time; Jay-Z's chauffeur admitted to owning it and was sentenced to one year in prison.)

*The Dynasty: Roc La Familia* (2000), Jay-Z's fifth album, is a group effort that displays the talents of Roc-A-Fella's growing roster, which included Beanie Sigel, Amil, and Memphis Bleek; it also features the popular rap artists Scarface, Snoop Dogg, and R. Kelly. Although the LP produced a hit single—"I Just Wanna Love U (Give It 2 Me)"—many critics felt that it was not up to Jay-Z's usual standards. In the *Village Voice* (January 23, 2001), Robert Christgau gave the album a grade of "B" but wrote, "This is a major falloff, a lazy cash-in no matter who won't admit it." Still, the album had multiplatinum sales and was nominated for a Soul Train Music Award.

Jay-Z released *The Blueprint* in 2001. Referring to the single "Renegade," which features the controversial rapper Eminem, Will Hermes wrote for *Entertainment Weekly* (September 28, 2001), "Jay just replays his hard-knock life, while Em carps yet again about being a cultural scapegoat. Alas: two of the world's greatest rappers, afraid to talk about anything but the same ol' shtick." Some other critics felt that Jay-Z's references to Jehovah, on such tracks as "Izzo (H.O.V.A.)" and "Hola Hovito," were self-aggrandizing. But most reviewers praised *The Blueprint* as a return to form for the rapper, and the LP sold almost 500,000 copies within its first week in stores. Jay-Z released two more albums in 2001: *Unplugged*, recorded live from MTV's performance series, and *The Best of Both Worlds*, a collaboration with R. Kelly. Jay-Z's album *Blueprint 2: The Gift and the Curse* was expected to be released in mid-November 2002.

In addition to its record business, Roc-A-Fella has successfully segued into movie production (the company currently has a distribution deal with Miramax films) and has helped to promote some of the biggest national tours in rap history. Jay-Z and some of his associates have also started a clothing line, Roc Wear. "We know how we like our stuff," he told Richard Harrington. "If I see something that I like, I'll maybe take it and alter it to my specifications. Fashion pirates—that's what they call us!"

Jay-Z's songs have been featured on several movie soundtracks, among them *Space Jam* (1996), *Soul Food* (1997), *The Players Club* (1998), *The Nutty Professor II: The Klumps* (2000), and *Rush Hour 2* (2001). In addition to the Grammy Award, his honors include being named lyricist of the year at the 1999 Source Hip-Hop Music Awards ceremony, and earning the 1999 MTV Video Music Award for best rap video (for "Can I Get a . . ."), the 1999 *Billboard* Music Award as rap artist of the year, and the 2001 Black Entertainment Television Award for best male hip-hop artist.

Jay-Z has a home in Fort Lee, New Jersey. "The bigger you are, that doesn't change you as a person," he told Nick Charles for *People* (April 5, 1999), "unless you let it." — C.M.

Suggested Reading: *Entertainment Weekly* p18 Dec. 17, 1999, p16 Feb. 11, 2000, p72 Sep. 28, 2001, with photo, p68 Jan. 11, 2002, with photo, p72 Apr. 12, 2002, with photos; *Jet* p62+ Sep. 27, 1999; *New York Times* B p9 Mar. 6, 1999, B p7 Feb. 1, 2000, B p4 Apr. 14, 2001, D p2 Oct. 18, 2001, with photo, 9 p1+ Jan. 6, 2002, with photo; *Newsweek* p84+ Dec. 13, 1999; *People* p161+ Apr. 5, 1999; *Vibe* p 144 Nov. 1997, with photo, p 119+ Dec. 1998/Jan. 1999, with photos, p98+ Apr. 1999; *Washington Post* Dp7 Oct. 28, 1998, with photos, G p1 Jan. 2, 2000, G p12 Jan. 2, 2000

Selected Works: *Reasonable Doubt*, 1996; *In My Lifetime, Vol. 1*, 1997; *Vol. 2: Hard Knock Life*, 1998; *Vol. 3: The Life and Times of S. Carter*, 1999; *The Dynasty: Roc La Familia*, 2000; *The Blueprint*, 2001; *Unplugged*, 2001

Courtesy of Crossroad Publishing Co.

## Johnson, Elizabeth A.

*Dec. 6, 1941– Theologian; writer; educator*

*Address: Fordham University, Theology Dept., 441 E. Fordham Rd., Bronx, NY 10458-9993*

"The goal of feminist theology is not to make women equal partners in an oppressive system," Elizabeth A. Johnson wrote in her seminal work, *She Who Is: The Mystery of God in Feminist Theological Discourse*. "It is to transform the system." To that end, Johnson, a Distinguished Professor of Theology at Fordham University and a nun in the order of the Sisters of St. Joseph, uses biblical and classical Christian sources to argue for the equal use of both feminine and masculine language and imagery to characterize God. To constantly refer to God as "He," she argues, is not only to limit the full divinity of God, but also to suggest that men are closer to the divine than are women. "Language doesn't just reflect what we think," she told Karen Houppert for the *Village Voice* (October 10, 1995); "it shapes what we think and defines our world." Johnson's theology, as she explained it in *She Who Is* and other books, lectures, and numerous articles, calls into question the traditional, patriarchal ways of understanding God, community, world, and self, and seeks to establish a new understanding based on the individual and collective experiences of women.

Elizabeth A. Johnson was born on December 6, 1941 in the New York City borough of Brooklyn. In 1959 she became a nun in the order of the Sisters of St. Joseph, whose members live and work in ordinary communities with the aim of facilitating the union of all people with one another and with God. She received a bachelor's degree in classics from Brentwood College (now defunct), on Long Island, New York, in 1964, a master's degree in theology from Manhattan College, in the New York City borough of the Bronx, in 1970, and a doctorate in theology from Catholic University of America, in Washington, D.C., in 1981. For the next 10 years, Johnson served as an associate professor of theology at Catholic University. In 1990 she published her first book, *Consider Jesus: Waves of Renewal in Christology*, a survey of Catholic thought regarding Christ since the mid-20th century. In 1991 Johnson left Catholic University to become an associate professor at the Bronx campus of Fordham University.

Johnson published *She Who Is* in 1992. That work, which many consider to be the finest book to date in feminist theology, advocates a christology of "trinitarian feminism," as it has come to be known. In order to amend the hitherto solely masculine image of God, Johnson turned to the Hebrew scriptures to retrieve the symbol of Sophia (which means "wisdom" in Greek). In the biblical text, Sophia is presented as another name for God; when Sophia acts, the reader is to understand that action as the work of God. Johnson applied that feminine symbol of the divine to the Christian tradition, asserting that Jesus can justifiably be identified as the son of Sophia. Within this context, the author reinterpreted the Trinity, seeing Sophia in each of its three Persons (which she identified as Spirit-Sophia, Jesus-Sophia, and Mother-Sophia) as well as in the unity of the three—the essence of God. It is significant that in her interpretation of the Trinity, Johnson began with the Spirit rather than the Father or the unity of God; she contended that the traditional approach—in which the Trinity is referred to as the Father, the Son, and the Holy Spirit, in that order—reinforces a patriarchal hierarchy and implies the subordination of the Second and Third Persons of the Trinity to the First Person. Beginning instead with Spirit-Sophia—the active presence of God in each of us—not only restores the quality of the Three Persons in the Trinity but also, as Johnson wrote in her book, "allows a starting point more closely allied to the human experience of salvation, without which there would be no speech about the triune God at all." Johnson further argued that Christian, and in particular Catholic, churches must use more-inclusive language and equivalent imagery when talking about the Divine. To refer to images with one gender rather than the other, and to use pronouns that refer to one sex rather than the other, is to render God finite, she asserted. Language is a critical issue for Johnson because, as she told Karen Houppert, "the way in which a faith community shapes language about God implicitly represents what it takes to be the highest good, the profoundest truth, the most appealing beauty." Thus, to refer to God exclusively as He implies that the masculine is inherently better than the feminine. In her call for doctrinal change, Johnson has insisted, she is trying not to destroy the Catholic Church but to preserve it. As she told Houppert, "If the idea of God does not keep pace with developing reality, the power of experience pulls people on and the god dies, fading from memory." *She Who Is* received the University of Louisville Grawemeyer Award in Religion and the Crossroad Women's Studies Award. It has been translated into several languages, among them German, Portuguese, French, and Korean.

In 1993, at Saint Mary's College, in Notre Dame, Indiana, Johnson gave the Madeleva Lecture in Spirituality, which addresses the concerns of women in the Catholic Church. Her talk, "Women, Earth, and Creator Spirit," drew a connection between the exploitation of Earth's resources and the exploitation of women. The lecture was subsequently published as a 79-page book with the same title by the Paulist Press. Johnson's article "Does God Play Dice? Divine Providence and Chance," published in the journal *Theological Studies* in March 1996, explores the relationship between science and religion. In it, Johnson discussed whether God's providential role in the universe—that is, God's role in guiding human and natural destiny—can still be affirmed when science continuously shows the significant role of chance in various phenomena. Based on the assertion by Thomas Aquinas, the 13th-century Catholic philosopher and theologian, that a created being exists only insofar as it participates in creating Being, or God, it can be said that a created being, by way of that participation, is empowered to act as an autonomous agent. Johnson thereby concluded that God's providence works *through* chance. "Divine governance," she wrote, "involves God in waiting upon the world, so to speak, patiently acting through its natural processes including unpredictable, uncontrollable random events to bring about the emergence of the new while consistently urging the whole toward fullness of life."

In *Friends of God and Prophets: A Feminist Theological Reading of the Communion of Saints* (1998), Johnson reevaluated the doctrinal symbol referred to as the communion of the saints—the spiritual union in the Church of the faithful on Earth, the saints in heaven, and the souls in Purgatory. The doctrine is presented in liturgy, Johnson noted, in terms of a hierarchy: those on Earth need intercession to God, and the saints (most of whom are men) provide that intercession. Johnson described this rendering of the doctrine as "profoundly patriarchal, shaped according to a graded pyramid of power with an elite corps near the top and a male ruling figure at the point." This conceptualization, according to Johnson, also implies that only an elite few are in direct communion with God. In her reinterpretation of the doctrine, Johnson turned to women's experiences of being united in a community through struggle, and thus came to see the communion of the saints as a community of living and dead who equally and collectively participate in the holiness of God. "The whole point," she wrote in the introduction to *Friends of God and Prophets*, "is to retrieve this symbol in such a way that it itself functions in a befriending and prophetic way, nourishing women in the struggle for life and equal human dignity and nurturing the church through memory and hope into being a true community of the friends of God and prophets." The book received the American Academy of Religion Award of Excellence in the Study of Religion and was the Catholic Book Club's featured book for May 1998.

In addition to her duties at Fordham University, Johnson contributes regularly to many scholarly and religious publications and serves on the editorial boards of *Theological Studies*, *Horizons: Journal of the College Theology Society*, and *Theoforum*. She is a member of the American Academy of Religion, the College Theology Society, and the Catholic Theological Society of America, the last of which she served as president between 1996 and 1997. Johnson has received honorary degrees from St. Mary's College (1992), Maryknoll School of Theology (1994), Chicago Theological Union (1997), and Siena College (1998). Most recently, she edited the book *The Church Women Want: Catholic Women in Dialogue*, which was scheduled for publication in December 2002. — H.T.

Suggested Reading: (Lakeland, Florida) *Ledger* D p1+ Mar. 14, 1999; *New York Times* A p12 June 20, 1995, with photo; *Theology Today* p330+ Oct. 1995; *U.S. Catholic* p6+ Apr. 1992; *Village Voice* p37+ Oct. 10, 1995, with photo; Tilley, Terence, and Phyllis Zagano, eds. *Things New and Old: Essays on the Theology of Elizabeth Johnson*, 1999

Selected Books: as author—*Consider Jesus: Waves of Renewal in Christology*, 1990; *She Who Is: The Mystery of God in Feminist Theological Discourse*, 1992; *Women, Earth, and Creator Spirit*, 1993; *Friends of God and Prophets: A Feminist Theological Reading of the Communion of Saints*, 1998; as editor—*The Church Women Want: Catholic Women in Dialogue*, 2002

---

## Jones, Bobby

*1939– Vocalist; television broadcaster; educator*

*Address: Millennium Entertainment, 1314 Fifth Ave. N., Nashville, TN 37208*

"What Dick Clark is to rock 'n' roll and Don Cornelius is to soul, Bobby Jones is to gospel music," Mike Joyce declared in the *Washington Post* (July 7, 1995). Thanks to Bobby Jones and his television show *The Bobby Jones Gospel Hour*, gospel artists have had the opportunity to perform for millions of people around the world. One of the first programs to air on Black Entertainment Television (BET), *The Bobby Jones Gospel Hour* debuted on that network in 1980. The longest-running weekly show in cable-television history, it is still the only nationally syndicated black gospel television

Courtesy of BET

*Bobby Jones*

show; as such, it provides rare access to national exposure for top gospel acts. "It's catapulted gospel into a whole new era," Jones told James D. Davis for the Fort Lauderdale, Florida, *Sun-Sentinel* (May 10, 1997). "Before, you had only radio and concerts. TV has opened gospel up to a lot of people." Nicknamed "The Goodwill Ambassador of Gospel Music," Jones has also had a successful gospel career of his own. He has recorded 10 albums, most of them with his group, New Life. "Gospel music brings people together," he told Christopher Heron for *GospelCity.com* (March 2001). "It makes you feel good about your fellow men, and more importantly, makes you believe in yourself. The messages in the music may be old as time itself, but those messages are as appropriate today as the day they were delivered."

Bobby Louis Jones was born in 1939 in the small town of Hindreas, Tennessee, which had a population of roughly 500 people. During his childhood his family moved to Paris, Tennessee (population about 12,000). "It was a very simple and closed community," Jones told Christopher Heron. "We were very poor, as most Black Americans were during that period." As a youngster he did farm work, including picking cotton. Early on, he told Christopher Heron, "I recognized the God force . . . and it was awe-inspiring. The spirit led me to my course in life and the opportunity to spread the word of God through Gospel music." Jones always dreamed of a musical career but was also devoted to academics. He excelled in his classes and graduated from high school in 1955, at the age of 15. Four years later he received a bachelor's degree in elementary education from Tennessee State University, in Nashville. While working at the same school toward a master's degree, also in education, he taught in elementary schools in both Tennessee and Missouri, according to an on-line press release issued by Tennessee representative Bob Clement, who honored Jones on the floor of Congress on June 27, 2001. After he earned his master's degree, he continued to teach before being hired as a textbook consultant for an educational publishing house. "I had an opportunity to be a linguist, travel around the world and work with reading and science material for elementary children. It was a wonderful platform," he told Christopher Heron for *Gospel City.com.* Later, in 1980, Jones earned a Ph.D. in reading and special education from Vanderbilt University, in Nashville.

In 1972 Jones began working at Tennessee State University as an instructor in reading and study skills, a position he held until mid-1985. "I tried to get students to realize that learning can be simplified through diligence, discipline, honest, hard work and having respect for one's self and others," he told Christopher Heron. Also in the early 1970s, Jones began a second career, as a gospel singer, performing at local venues. His introduction to television began during this period, when he was hired as the host and producer of the children's program *Fun City 5*, which aired on WTBF in Nashville. In 1975 he formed the gospel group New Life, whose members have included, at various times, Francine Belcher, Nuana Dunlap, Stefania Stone Frierson, Emily Harris, and Beverly Crawford, among other singers. New Life released its first album, *Sooner or Later*, in 1976. That same year Jones helped to create the first Black Expo, in Nashville, Tennessee. The Black Expo is held in cities across the nation and was inspired in part by Operation PUSH (People United to Save Humanity), an organization founded in 1971 by the Reverend Jesse Jackson. The expo, which resembles a large fair, "is designed to promote African American economic development and to offer companies, large and small, the opportunity to access" the African-American market, as one of its Web sites states; it also showcases the contributions of African-Americans to their communities and features musical performances. The success of the 1976 Nashville expo—50,000 people attended Natalie Cole's concert there, and it attracted much local media attention—led to Jones's getting a contract for his first television gospel show. "At that time affirmative action was in place and Channel 4 in Nashville didn't have its complete number of black programmers in place," he told Mike Joyce, as quoted on *African American Publications* (on-line). "So we asked if we could do a pilot for a gospel show—and it's been running ever since."

In 1980 Jones's gospel show was picked up by the newly created BET. At the time BET was broadcasting only a few hours each week, due to a lack of funds. *The Bobby Jones Gospel Hour* helped the fledgling network gain a sizable viewership and brought gospel to a larger audience. "We basically built the show around unknown talents who were just interested in being presented on television," Jones told Christopher Heron for *GospelCity.com.* "Every now and then, we would get a colorful character, but personalities like [gospel singer] James Cleveland were never presented on my show." As the series evolved, talented gospel artists who had received little previous publicity were given the chance to perform before a national audience. Because the program was taped in Washington, D.C., Jones had to fly in from Nashville each week. Jones, who estimates that a substantial portion of the show's audience is white, told Joe Edwards for the *Chicago Tribune* (October 24, 1985), "I want to be one of the people to bring gospel music to the real marketplace by educating people about its marvelous and unique features. It should be placed where any good music is." In addition to the *Gospel Hour*, from 1978 to 1984 Jones hosted *Bobby Jones World*, a magazine-style show that combined gospel music with features on politicians, authors, and entertainers, among other topics. In 1982 he made his acting debut, in the TV movie *Sister Sister*, starring Diahann Carroll, Paul Winfield, and Irene Cara. "That movie was just a fabulous experience for me," he told Christopher Heron.

In 1980 Jones's gospel opera, *Make a Joyful Noise*, aired on PBS. Jones, who also starred in the opera, won a Gabriel Award and an International Film Festival Award for his writing and performance. Meanwhile, he continued to record with New Life. Among their releases were *There Is Hope in This World* (1978), *Caught Up* (1979), and *Tin Gladje* (1981). Their 1982 album, *Soul Set Free*, was nominated for a Grammy Award for best performance by a black contemporary gospel group. *Come Together* (1984) received the Dove Award for black contemporary album of the year from the Gospel Music Association (GMA), and Jones's duet with the country music singer Barbara Mandrell, "I'm So Glad I'm Standing Here Today," won a Grammy Award in 1984. Mandrell later appeared on Jones's show and toured with him until she was severely injured in an automobile accident, in 1984. Marty Robbins, Ricky Skaggs, and other country-music stars also appeared on the program, all of them singing gospel. "We're trying to bridge ideologies to the focal point—the works of Jesus," Jones told Joe Edwards. He added, "Our goal is to bring one's attention to the wonderful design of the Bible." In 1989 a new Jones show, *Video Gospel*, premiered on BET; currently, it is the only nationally syndicated televison program to broadcast gospel videos. Also in 1989 he launched the Bobby Jones Gospel Explosion, a live tour of gospel acts, which is still active. His "mini-Explosions" have brought gospel performances to the smaller cities of Europe and the Caribbean.

In the 1990s, in collaboration with New Life, Jones released the albums *I'll Never Forget* (1990), *Bring It to Jesus* (1993), *Another Time* (1996), and *Just Churchin'* (1998), the last of which features a then-new group, the Nashville Superchoir. "I've worked with the New Life Singers who've generated a lot of attention, but with the departure of Beverly Crawford into her own ministry, we didn't have the same kind of impact," Jones told Christopher Heron. "I thought that now would be an excellent time to bring in talent within our local community. Many of the members of the Nashville Superchoir are songwriters, producers, choir directors who've recorded their own albums. They're just great people. . . . [Making the record] was [meant] to provide an opportunity for those people to experience and express their work with Gospel music and Jesus Christ." *Just Churchin'* features performances by such gospel luminaries as Vicki Winans, Vanessa Bell Armstrong, Donald Lawrence, and James Moore as well as by the noted poet and writer Maya Angelou. "This is my best work," Jones said of the album, as quoted on *iMusic Urban Showcase* (on-line). "It has all the right elements to bring gospel music to a broad audience." Although it includes hip-hop and other contemporary styles, the record does not stray from its religious message. "I wanted to make traditional hymns and update them," Jones said, as quoted on *iMusic Urban Showcase*. Jones's autobiography, *Make a Joyful Noise: My 25 Years in Gospel Music* (2000), which he wrote with Lesley Sussman, caused something of a commotion in the gospel world because of Jones's recollections of some negative experiences with prominent people.

Jones, who loves to attend gospel performances in Las Vegas, Nevada, lives in Nashville with his wife, Ethel Williams Jones. *The Bobby Jones Gospel Hour* is currently seen on Sundays on BET and is also broadcast on the American Christian Network and the Armed Forces radio and television stations. It is also seen in 17 other countries worldwide. His radio program, *The Bobby Jones Gospel Countdown*, has been syndicated on the Sheridan Network. His shows *Bobby Jones Presents . . . Gospel on Stage* and *Bobby Jones Presents . . . Gospel Classics*, the latter of which consists of vintage performances from the *Bobby Jones Gospel Hour*, began airing in 2001 on the Word Network. Recently, he has made the problem of AIDS a focus of his program and has had as guests people who help educate the public about the disease. "The biggest thing is awareness," he told Randy Boyd for *BlackAIDS.org*. "We want to eradicate this epidemic, to share with our television audience the effect of AIDS on the black community, and to sensitize the church to the plight of AIDS and become more friendly to those who have it." Jones also told Boyd, "All of us need to become involved in each other's lives. This whole foolishness about gay people, straight people is nonsense. Nobody's going away. We're all here. Get over it. Get over this Puritanical church notion that some are better than others. Hope you can effect others in a positive way. We ought to be on the front lines defending everybody." Jones plans to begin the Humanity Relief Tour to raise money for those struck by natural catastrophes. He coordinates the Executive International Record Label Gospel Artists Retreat, organized to provide a forum for discussing the gospel-music business. In 1990 he received the GMA's Commonwealth Award for outstanding contribution to gospel music, and in 1994 he was nominated for a CableACE Award. Payne Theological Seminary, in Wilberforce Ohio, awarded him an honorary doctorate in theology in 1991. Jones told James D. Davis, "I would like to be known for completing what the Lord gave me to do, bringing people together, spreading love. . . . Without that, I am nothing." — G.O.

Suggested Reading: *African American Publications* (on-line); *BlackAIDS.org*; *Chicago Tribune* C p101 Oct. 24, 1985, with photo, D p13 Nov. 7, 1985; *GospelCity.com*; *iMusic Urban Showcase* (on-line); *Washington Post* N p13 July 7, 1995, D p1 July 17, 1995

Selected Recordings: with New Life—*Sooner or Later*, 1976; *There Is Hope in This World*, 1978; *Caught Up*, 1979; *Tin Gladje*, 1981; *Soul Set Free*, 1982; *Come Together*, 1984; *I'll Never Forget*, 1990; *Bring It to Jesus*, 1993; *Another Time*, 1996; with the Nashville Superchoir—*Just Churchin'*, 1998

---

Courtesy of ABC Radio Networks

## Joyner, Tom

*1942(?)– Radio personality*

*Address: ABC Radio Networks, 13725 Montfort Dr., Dallas, TX 75240*

"First we get people laughing, then we get 'em to listen. If you can get people to listen, then they begin to think, and that's when they start making a difference," Tom Joyner, the host of the country's number-one nationally syndicated urban radio program, the *Tom Joyner Morning Show*, was quoted as saying on *99jamz.com*. Begun in 1994, the *Tom Joyner Morning Show*, which is heard daily over ABC Radio Networks by millions of listeners in more than 100 cities, is the first syndicated radio program hosted and produced by an African-American; it has won *Billboard*'s R&B Network Syndicated Program of the Year Award 10 times. The show has won a loyal following not only because of Joyner's comedic on-air personality but because of his activism and philanthropy, which have brought him a number of awards. Joyner, who has worked in radio since the 1960s, is the first African-American to be elected to the Radio Hall of Fame.

Thomas Joyner was born in around 1942 in Tuskegee, Alabama. (According to his publicist, he prefers not to reveal the month and day of his birth.) He is the second son of Frances Joyner, a secretary for the military and for Tuskegee Institute, and Hercules Joyner, an accountant. When Joyner was young, he joined many other blacks in the South in fighting for their civil rights, taking to the streets every week in what was known as the "Tuskegee Boycott." On one occasion, between his high-school graduation and his undergraduate years, Joyner was part of a protest against a local radio station in Tuskegee that seemed to have a policy against playing music by African-Americans. When the station owner relented and asked if someone from the crowd of protesters would agree to serve as a disc jockey, Joyner raised his hand. As a result he began hosting a weekend show, called the *Soul Matinee*, at the station. While broadcasting, Joyner tried rhyming. "I wasn't good at it, because I couldn't think of rhymes on the spot," he told Kristal Brent Zook for *Savoy* (February 2002). "I had a briefcase full of slips of paper with rhymes on them. I used to say things like ''Right on' and 'Be free.'" Joyner's early inspirations were Father Rock, a fast-talking, rhyming deejay in Montgomery, Alabama; John R., a blues and soul deejay broadcasting out of Nashville, Tennessee; and the legendary Doug "Jocko" Henderson, who commuted between top-rated radio shows in New York City and Philadelphia.

Joyner attended Tuskegee Institute, in his hometown, earning a bachelor's degree in sociology in 1970. (The school is now known as Tuskegee University.) Joyner and his friends, who included the future recording star Lionel Richie, entered the Tuskegee freshman talent show as a singing group called the DuPonts; they performed at local clubs throughout Joyner's college years. Just out of school, Joyner accepted a job as a radio news announcer at WRMA, an AM radio station in Montgomery, Alabama. "I fell into radio. It was just dumb luck. But once I was there, I discovered it was something that I could do pretty well, and I enjoyed it," he told Muriel L. Sims for *imdiversity.com*. "I learned how to cut commercials and do a little production work. I became the 'fill-in jock,' filling in whenever someone got sick, or was on vacation, or got drunk the night before and couldn't come in. I had finally found my niche and the money—$90 a week—wasn't bad either." Joyner was mentored in part by Tracy Larkin, who was known as "The Voice" of WRMA. "One of the things I got from [Larkin] was that radio needed to be involved in the community," Joyner told Sandra Gregg for *Emerge* (November 1998). "We were the eyes and ears. We had a responsibility to the people."

A succession of on-air radio jobs followed. Joyner's first full-time music show was on WLOK-AM, a station in Memphis, Tennessee. A stint at KWK-AM in St. Louis, Missouri, led to another at KKDA, in Dallas, Texas, in 1972. Along with his winning personality, Joyner made his mark at KKDA by getting major celebrities, including the boxing legend Muhammad Ali, to sit in on his program. "I would get Ali on the air and he would make noise and do a few rhymes before his Joe Frazier fight . . . ," Joyner recalled for Sims. "He'd be out training and I'd call him and I just kept calling and calling. Most of the time I wouldn't get him, but sometimes I would." Joyner moved next to Chicago, where he continued to win over radio listeners with his energy and sense of humor as a disc jockey on WVON-AM. He then went to station WBMX-FM—"black music experience"—where he caught the attention of the African-American media mogul John H. Johnson, who hired Joyner in the hope of boosting ratings at his station WJPC-FM in Chicago. Johnson, publisher of *Ebony* and *Jet* magazines, became a mentor to Joyner and helped increase the deejay's national profile by running a number of stories about him, with pictures, in his magazines.

In 1983 Joyner returned to Dallas, where he took over the morning shift at KKDA, heard by many listeners as they drove to work. Within six months he had surpassed all of his competitors in the ratings. His popularity inspired the local media to give him the nickname "Mr. Dallas." No African-American deejay had ever enjoyed such popularity in that city. According to *Emerge* (November 1998), Joyner had a brief stint in 1983 on the television program *Ebony/Jet Showcase*. In 1985, just as Joyner was renegotiating his contract with KKDA, the Chicago station WGCI-FM offered him its afternoon time slot. "Dallas and Chicago are in the same time zone," the deejay told Carlton Stowers for *People* (January 20, 1986). "There was plenty of time between the morning and afternoon shows, so . . ." Looking into the possibility of working in both Chicago and Dallas—approximately 800 miles apart—Joyner checked daily airline schedules and consulted a doctor, who told Joyner that if he took care of himself, exercised regularly, and quit drinking, the frequent flying would not have any adverse effects on him. Joyner decided to take both jobs, requiring him to fly to Chicago every day after doing the morning show on KKDA in Dallas, then fly back home to Dallas for the night. Although some observers and industry insiders initially dismissed Joyner's outlandish commute as a publicity stunt, Joyner worked both jobs for eight years, traveling an average of 8,000 miles each week and compiling seven million frequent-flier miles in the process. Executives at the two stations, who did not know that Joyner was working two jobs until months after he had begun doing so, were angry with the deejay at first. They acquiesced, however, because KKDA and WCGI were not competing for the same listeners. In addition to a handsome income (according to some sources, more than $1 million per year from each of his two employers), the feat earned Joyner national attention and the nicknames "radio iron man" and the "Fly Jock." Both his morning show, on KKDA, and his afternoon program, on WGCI, reached number one in the ratings. During this time Joyner also hosted *On the Move*, a syndicated weekend show on CBS radio.

In 1993 Joyner gave up both jobs and considered retiring from radio. Then ABC Radio Networks offered the popular deejay a five-year, $15 million contract to host a weekly morning show. The Dallas-based *Tom Joyner Morning Show* debuted in January 1994. The program, whose target audience is 25-to-54-year-old urban African-Americans, broadcasts from five to nine every weekday morning; it is carried on more than 100 stations around the country and, according to Frank Ahrens in the *Washington Post* (July 10, 2001), has a weekly audience of 10 million listeners nationwide. (Several sources put the daily listenership of the *Tom Joyner Morning Show* at five million people and its annual revenues at more than $30 million. With these numbers Joyner joins Rush Limbaugh and Howard Stern as the most powerful radio personalities in the country.) The show offers a combination of music, gossip, news, sports, serious discussion, comedy routines, and celebrity guest interviews held with the likes of Oprah Winfrey, Bill Cosby, Spike Lee, Evander Holyfield, and former president Bill Clinton.

Joyner, who introduces himself every morning on the air by saying, "This is the haaardest-working man in radio," has assembled a popular cast of performers and other personalities for the *Tom Joyner Morning Show*, including the comedian J. Anthony Brown, Joyner's sidekick; news anchor Sybil Wilkes; Jedda Jones, a writer and comedian whose on-air persona is Ms. Dupree, a self-styled voodoo priestess and psychic; the writer and comedian Myra J., who performs the segment "Momma's Tips"; and the comedian George Wallace, who is responsible for the humorous segment "That's the Way I See It, That's the Way It Ought to Be." Other features of the show include the daily soap opera

"It's Your World"; "Thursday Morning Mom," a weekly segment spotlighting letters from listeners, each explaining why the listener's mother is the world's best and deserves to be honored; and the popular musical portion, called the "Tom Joyner Old School Breakfast Mix." (A recording based on that segment and titled "Tom Joyner's Old School Mix" was released by Rhino Records in 1999.) The show's various performers broadcast from different locations—several of them from Los Angeles—while Joyner leads the proceedings from a studio in Dallas. About 30 times a year, Joyner takes his show on the road and broadcasts from different cities; these so-called Sky Shows, which were started in 1996 and feature contests, live music, and fund-raising and voter-registration drives, have become enormously popular with listeners. Also popular are the shows broadcast during the Fantastic Voyage Cruise, an event produced annually since 1999 by the Tom Joyner Foundation and various corporations; listeners are invited to join Joyner, his team of regular performers, and various guest stars on a seven-day cruise. In 2000 Joyner signed a distribution deal with the black-owned Radio One to broadcast from stations owned by the company. In 2001 the *Tom Joyner Morning Show* was picked up for the first time by a station (WRKS, known as "Kiss FM") in New York City, the country's largest media market.

Joyner has long used his radio show to speak out against racial discrimination and to raise social awareness. "You're always going to be challenged because you're Black. You're always going to have to double-step," Joyner told Muriel L. Sims. "You're going to have to overcompensate for what people think. That's going to happen in any field and radio is no different." On the subject of using radio as a vehicle for social activism, Joyner told a writer for the *Black Collegian*'s Web site, "When we were growing up, the disc jockey was entertaining you, but he was also telling you what was going on in the community. I think a lot of activism left black radio. I'm just trying to bring it back. I have to, because that's the way I was raised." On the same theme, he told Vern Smith and Allison Samuels for *Newsweek* (February 23, 1998), "If I can get you laughing, I can get some information to you, too, and that's what we try to do." Among the many examples of Joyner's activism is the occasion in 1997 when Joyner and his morning radio-show team spoke out against the planned sale at Christie's International Auction House, in New York City, of three antique posters advertising rewards for runaway slaves. With the help of Tavis Smiley, a TV talk-show host and correspondent, radio commentator, and member of the *Tom Joyner Morning Show*, Joyner inspired listeners to call Christie's Auction House to express their opposition to the planned sale. After Christie's was deluged for days with thousands of phone calls from *Tom Joyner Morning Show* listeners, the auction house canceled the sale of the posters. In 1999 Joyner and Smiley took issue on the air with CompUSA, the largest computer retailer in the U.S., among other companies, for making large profits from the black community but not buying advertising in black media. Again, the response from listeners was overwhelming, and after weeks of discussion, the chief executive officer of CompUSA promised on the *Tom Joyner Morning Show* to enlist the services of a black-owned advertising agency and to offer each listener who had protested a 10 percent discount on his or her next purchase. Through their on-air lobbying, Joyner and Smiley helped bring about the 1999 awarding of a Congressional Gold Medal to Rosa Parks, the black woman who sparked a new era in the civil rights movement by refusing to give her seat to a white passenger on a segregated bus in Montgomery, Alabama, in 1955.

The Tom Joyner Foundation, a charitable, non-profit organization set up by the popular deejay in 1998, awards scholarships to deserving students at historically black colleges and universities in the United States. Kristal Brent Zook reported in *Savoy* (February 2002) that in its first three years, the Tom Joyner Foundation had raised more than $9 million for black students. As of mid-summer 2002, the foundation had raised more than $12 million. Part of the inspiration for this program, called Dollars for Scholars, came from Joyner's mother, Frances, who was active in helping struggling students in the Tuskegee community. Along with other charity work, the foundation grants wishes throughout the year to individuals and organizations dedicated to helping young people in urban areas. The foundation is a family-run affair: Joyner is president; his son Thomas Jr. is CEO; Joyner's father, Hercules, is treasurer; and Joyner's son Oscar is a board member. In 1998 the United Negro College Fund (UNCF) entered into a partnership with the Tom Joyner Foundation to form the Tom Joyner/UNCF Black College Fund, which donates money to a different black college or university each month.

In 2001 Joyner launched the news, information, and commercial Web site *BlackAmericaWeb.com*, which he has publicized as a "mall for all things black." "What we're trying to do is reach African Americans through media—whatever media source that might be," he told Frank Ahrens. "The mother ship, of course, is the radio show. Now, we've extended that through BlackAmericaWeb. We want to be the one-stop shop. When you want to reach blacks to advertise, to vote, to shop, that one stop will be here." According to the February 2002 issue of *Savoy* magazine, *BlackAmericaWeb.com* receives 3.5 million hits per month. Joyner's son Oscar has served as the Web site's CEO and president. Joyner was inducted into the National Association of Broadcasters Hall of Fame and has received *Impact* magazine's Joe Loris Award for Excellence in Broadcasting. *Impact*, in recognition of the many times it has honored Joyner, renamed its Best DJ of the Year Award the Tom Joyner Award, and *Savoy* named Joyner the magazine's 2002 Person of the Year. The deejay has also been named by *Billboard* magazine the Best Urban Contemporary Air Personality a number of times. The January 18, 1999 issue of *Newsweek* named Joyner as one of the 20 people responsible for changing the way Americans get their news. Among the other honors he has received for using his radio power for social causes, Joyner was given the Mickey Leland Humanitarian Award, sponsored by the Congressional Black Caucus; the President's Award from the National Association for the Advancement of Colored People (NAACP); and the Harold Washington Award for his work in getting citizens to participate in Census 2000.

Joyner has written two books: *Clearing the Air: The Making of a Radio Personality* (1995) and *Amen, Brother: Somebody Had to Say It* (1997). He lives in Dallas with his second wife, Donna Richardson, a fitness expert, writer, and maker of exercise videos, who contributes to NBC's *Weekend Today Edition.* The two met when Richardson was a guest on Joyner's show; she occasionally serves as a fitness adviser on the *Morning Show.* Thomas Joyner Jr., nicknamed Killer, and Oscar Joyner, nicknamed Thriller, are the deejay's sons from his marriage to Dora Chatmon. Joyner and Chatmon divorced in 1996, after 27 years of marriage. With the help of his second wife's fitness and nutrition advice, Joyner, a fairly large man, has been losing weight. — C.F.T.

Suggested Reading: *abc.go.com*; *abcradio.com*; *black-collegian.com*; *Emerge* p46+ Nov. 1998, with photos; *imdiversity.com*; *Savoy* p80+ Feb. 2002, with photos; *tomjoyner.com*

---

Virginia Sherwood/Courtesy of ABC

## Judd, Jackie

*Nov. 29, 1952– Broadcast journalist*

*Address: ABC News Washington Bureau, 1717 Desales St. N.W., Washington, DC 20036-4407*

Jacqueline Dee Judd, known as Jackie, is an Emmy Award–winning correspondent for ABC News and one of the most respected journalists in the nation. Judd began her career in broadcast journalism in the early 1970s as a college student, taking a job as a desk assistant at ABC News in Washington, D.C. She has reported on some of the major stories of the past 15 years, including the Tiananmen Square massacre, in Beijing, China, in 1989; Operation Desert Storm, the U.S.-led military response to the Iraqi leader Saddam Hussein's 1990 invasion of Kuwait; and Bill Clinton's first presidential campaign, in 1992. Judd was the first television network reporter to broadcast allegations of the sexual relationship between then–President Bill Clinton and the former White House intern Monica Lewinsky, which surfaced in 1998, and served as ABC's lead reporter on the scandal, which became a national obsession and the focus of a debate within the media concerning journalistic ethics. She has covered the nation's politics for a number of broadcast-news organizations since 1974. In 1994 Judd was named special assignment correspondent for ABC News's *World News Tonight with Peter Jennings.*

Jackie Judd was born in Johnstown, Pennsylvania, on November 29, 1952. She attended American University, in Washington, D.C., and graduated in 1974 with a bachelor's degree in journalism and political science. After college she entered the world of radio broadcasting, serving as a reporter for WKXL Radio in Concord, New Hampshire, and then for WBAL Radio, in Baltimore, Maryland. From 1979 to 1982, she worked at National Public Radio (NPR) in Washington, D.C., as a news anchor for the program *Morning Edition* and as the weekend news anchor for the award-winning program *All Things Considered. (Morning Edition,* hosted by Bob Edwards since its inception, recently celebrated 20 years as one of the premier news programs on the air. Begun in 1971, *All Things Considered* is NPR's acclaimed daily afternoon news program.) Judd is still an occasional guest host for *Morning Edition*, bringing listeners newsworthy items and conducting on-air interviews. Her recent stories include interviews in February 2002 with the *Washington Post* reporter Douglas Farah on the finances of the terrorist network Al Qaeda and with NPR's Peter Kenyon on developments in the Middle East; a preview of the 2001 Tony Awards ceremony, in New York City; and a remembrance of James Edward Brown, a veteran of World War I who died in 2001 at the age of 107.

In 1982 Judd joined CBS News Radio Network, in New York City. Two years later she covered the presidential primaries and broadcast reports from the Democratic and Republican National Conventions. During the elections of 1986, she anchored CBS News Radio's Senate/Governor desk, covering the results of U.S. Senate and gubernatorial contests. She also anchored hourly news broadcasts for CBS. Judd joined ABC-TV News as a general assignment correspondent in 1987. In the following year, for ABC's *World News Tonight*, she covered the 1988 presidential primaries, the Republican National Convention, and the campaigns of the Republican vice-presidential nominee, Dan Quayle, as well as the Democratic presidential nominee, Michael Dukakis. In 1992 Judd covered Bill Clinton's presidential campaign and Al Gore's vice-presidential campaign, in addition to the Democratic National Convention.

While contributing to ABC News's coverage of presidential elections, Judd also filed dramatic reports from abroad. The year 1989 found her in Beijing, China, covering the student protests and subsequent violence in Tiananmen Square, and she reported from Japan on the funeral of Emperor Hirohito. Judd also went to Eastern Europe that year to provide coverage of democratic movements there. During that time she filed an exclusive story for ABC's *PrimeTime Live* on the Czechoslovakian secret police, for which she was awarded an Overseas Press Club Citation of Excellence.

From 1990 to 1992 Judd was a correspondent for the ABC News program *Nightline*. In that capacity, in 1990, she reported from Saudi Arabia on the preparations for Desert Storm and from Israel on that year's Palestinian uprising. In 1991 Judd won an Emmy Award from the American Academy of Arts and Sciences in New York City for *Nightline's* coverage of Iraq's invasion of Kuwait. Judd's next post at ABC News was congressional correspondent. During 1996 Judd covered the Republican Jack Kemp's vice-presidential campaign as well as the Republican National Convention.

Judd was named special assignment correspondent for ABC News's *World News Tonight with Peter Jennings* in 1994. Two years later she won her second Emmy Award, for her contributions to a series on juvenile crime that aired on the program. In 1998 Judd was at the scene of perhaps the biggest political scandal of the 1990s—that surrounding President Clinton's extramarital sexual relationship with Monica Lewinsky. In late January Judd—using two of her own sources, in accordance with ABC's policy—became the first network journalist to report the story to a shocked and fascinated nation. As quoted by Lawrence K. Grossman in the *Columbia Journalism Review* (November/December 1998, on-line), Peter Jennings introduced Judd's segment by saying, "Today, someone with specific knowledge of what it is that Monica Lewinsky says really took place between her and the president has been talking to ABC's Jackie Judd." In the aftermath of the broadcast, ABC and Judd were criticized for going forward with a story taken from what some called dubious and biased sources. For her part, Judd insisted that she had gotten the story from two legitimate and reliable sources, and she was supported in that claim by then–ABC News senior vice president Richard C. Wald, who was charged with enforcing the network's news standards. Months later Steve Brill, the media critic and founder of the magazine *Brill's Content*, wrote, as quoted by Grossman, "Judd's every utterance is infected with the clear assumption that the president is guilty at a time when no reporter can know that." Judd told Grossman, "Of all the stories we reported involving the president and Monica Lewinsky, ABC was most vilified for our reports about [Lewinsky's] semen-stained dress"—the item reportedly proving Clinton's involvement with Lewinsky. "Critics kept asking, 'where's the proof?'" Vindication for Judd came more than six months after her initial on-air report, when legal sources revealed that Lewinsky had turned over to special prosecutor Kenneth Starr a dress she said she had saved because it was stained with Clinton's semen. While Judd and ABC had proven their professionalism in that instance, the Committee of Concerned Journalists found that in the initial flurry of reporting on the scandal, many news outlets had put forth speculation and opinion in place of fact-based, well-sourced reporting.

As special assignment correspondent for *World News Tonight*, Judd also contributes to the network's evening newscast, *Nightline*; *Good Morning America*; and other ABC News broadcasts. Recently, she has reported on such high-profile stories as the American military involvement in Afghanistan; the trials of the alleged terrorists John Walker Lindh and Zacarias Moussaoui; and the effects of the Enron collapse. In 1994 Judd received both a duPont Award and a commendation from Women in Radio and Television for a series on women's health issues that ran on *World News Tonight with Peter Jennings*. In a 1999 report by the Center for Media and Public Affairs, Judd was found to be the most visible female reporter on network evening news, with 99 on-air reports in 1998, which placed her 13th overall among journalists that year. Reflecting that achievement, in 1999 Judd received several honors, including a Murrow Award (named for the legendary newsman Edward R. Murrow and awarded by the Radio-Television News Directors Association for outstanding achievements in electronic journalism); Clarion and Headliner Awards, both given by the Association for Women in Communications for excellence in communications; and a Joan S. Barone Award, which recognizes excellence in reporting on national affairs and public policy. In 2001 *Washingtonian* magazine named Judd one of Washington's top 50 journalists. Judd is a member of the Radio and Television Correspondents' Association of Capital Hill, and from 1993 to 1996 she served on the association's executive committee. She is also a member of the American Federation of Radio and Television Artists. — C.F.T.

Suggested Reading: ABC News Web site; *Columbia Journalism Review* Nov./Dec. 1998 (online); NPR Web site; *Who'sWho in America 2001*

---

Bill Pugliano/Getty Images

## Kamen, Dean

*Apr. 5, 1951– CEO and president, Deka Research and Development Corp.; founder, U.S. FIRST; inventor*

*Address: Deka Research & Development Corp., 340 Commercial St., Manchester, NH 03101*

"You have teenagers thinking they're going to make millions as [basketball] stars when that's not realistic for even 1 percent of them. Becoming a scientist or engineer is." Dean Kamen, who made that observation, became a millionaire by the time he was 25 years old, thanks to his invention, as an undergraduate, of an automatic syringe (also known as an infusion pump) that injects precise quantities of insulin or other medications at set times. That and other Kamen inventions—notably, a portable dialysis machine and a wheelchair that can raise and lower the user to useful heights and can also climb stairs—have significantly improved the lives of thousands. Most recently, he developed a scooter-like, self-balancing, one-person vehicle, the Segway Human Transporter, or Segway HT, whose speed and direction are controlled by changes in the rider's center of gravity. The prospect of Segway HTs' being in use everywhere "is about more than money for Dean," Michael Schmertzler, a managing director at Credit Suisse First Boston, a major Segway investor, told John Heilemann for *Time* (December 2, 2001, on-line). "Pardon the cliche, but he really does want to change the world." Largely self-educated in mechanical engineering, Kamen and/or his businesses hold more than 200 U.S. and foreign patents, many emanating from Deka Research and Development Corp., of which he is the founder, president, and CEO. He also owns and heads Segway LLC and Teletrol Energy Systems Inc., the latter of which manufactures electronic climate-control systems for large commercial buildings. In 2000 President Bill Clinton presented him with the National Medal of Technology, the highest honor in the United States in that field.

In addition to helping people by means of technology, Kamen's expressed mission in life is to increase junior-high and high-school students' interest in science and engineering. Toward that end, he established U.S. FIRST (Foundation for the Inspiration and Recognition of Science and Technology), which sponsors an annual student robotics competition. "Math and science isn't a cold, dry, dismal subject where the answers are all in the back of the book," he remarked to Ann Kellan for CNN (April 6, 2001, on-line). "In fact, more than any other human endeavor, engineering is about creating things that have never been created before." Thousands of students from all over the U.S. have participated in the competition, and some of them have gone on to pursue careers in science.

Kamen is regarded as a genius by those who know his work. "Dean is one of the premier electromechanical engineers in the world," Jerry Fisher, head of the renal division of Baxter Healthcare Corp., told Glenn Rifkin for the *New York Times* (February 14, 1993). "There just isn't a problem he can't attack. He invariably comes up with a half-dozen ideas that can make inroads into a problem. And he's relentless." Roland Schmitt, a former president of Rensselaer Polytechnic Institute and former chair of the National Science Board, told Steve Kemper for *Smithsonian* (November 1994), "Dean is the best technologist I've ever encountered, and I've known some great ones. He has the ability to synthesize knowledge about so many areas—sensors, materials, mechanics, electronics." The Internet pioneer Stewart Brand told Joel Garreau for the *Washington Post* (January 12, 2001), "He's in the tradition of Carl Djerassi and the birth control pill, Thomas Edison and the light bulb, Benjamin Franklin and the Franklin stove. And they really did change everything."

The second of three sons, Dean Kamen was born on April 5, 1951 in Rockville Centre, a village on Long Island, New York. His father, Jack Kamen, was a comic-book artist whose drawings appeared in *Weird Science* and *MAD* magazines. His mother, Evelyn, was an accounting teacher; currently, she does bookkeeping for his businesses. Despite his unusual intelligence, Dean Kamen nearly flunked out of high school, because he felt bored in class. "I used to like to sit and think about things and I would always question what the teachers said," he told Glenn Rifkin. "They used to get furious with me. But I was very frustrated and became pretty belligerent." At home he enjoyed tinkering in the basement, building such apparatuses as control systems for sound-and-light shows. While still in high school, he did various kinds of technical jobs in New York City, for the Hayden Planetarium (now part of the Rose Center for Earth and Space, at the American Museum of Natural History), the Four Seasons Hotel, and the Museum of the City of New York; he also worked on the mechanism that lowers the huge crystal ball atop One Times Square to usher in the new year at midnight every December 31. By the time he graduated from high school, in 1974, he was earning $60,000 a year.

Kamen attended Worcester Polytechnic Institute (WPI), in Worcester, Massachusetts. As an undergraduate he spent most of his time reading on his own and working on his inventions. "Dean was one of those rare kids who really wants to understand and get to the bottom of things," Harold Hilsinger, a WPI physics professor, told Rifkin. "He was in my office every day for as many hours as I could stand. He has a great excitement about life and his passion is his work. He understands natural philosophy as few people do." In 1979 he acceded to WPI's request that he leave, because in his five years there he still had not earned enough credits to graduate. He stayed briefly on Long Island before moving to New Hampshire, which attracted him because the state imposes neither an income tax on individuals nor a general sales tax and because its population is small. "I saw the license plates that read LIVE FREE OR DIE, and that sounded pretty good to me," he told Scott Kirsner for *Wired* (September 2000, on-line).

Earlier, when Dean had started college, his older brother, Bart (then a medical student), asked him to invent a syringe that could administer precise amounts of drugs to patients without human monitoring. In a matter of weeks, Kamen devised the auto-syringe, a pocket-size infusion pump that, wherever the patient may be, can inject exact amounts of medication intravenously at set times, eliminating the need for frequent trips to the hospital and significantly reducing childbirth-related risks for diabetic women. That same year he founded AutoSyringe Inc., which produced wearable infusion pumps. Working in the Kamen family home with parts manufactured elsewhere, he, his younger brother, Mitch, and friends of his assembled the pumps, while his mother tested the circuit boards used in the device.

In around 1979, after leaving WPI, Kamen founded Deka (using the first two letters of his first and last names to form its name), to work on his inventions and do research and development for other businesses. Kamen is CEO and president of the company, which is located on the banks of the Merrimack River in Manchester, New Hampshire, and currently employs 300 people. "Deka is one of the highest-morale operations I've ever seen," Ray Price, president of the Economic Club of New York and a close friend of Kamen's, told Kirsner. "There's no bureaucracy, and very little structure. Dean expects performance, but how [his employees] get to solutions is up to them." But some people have found the atmosphere less than congenial. "Dean is so intense and so aggressive that you always have to worry whether he'll get frustrated at not moving fast enough," Robert Z. Gussin, Johnson & Johnson's recently retired chief scientific officer, told Kirsner. "Sometimes his intensity is almost frightening." (Gussin met Kamen in connection with the iBOT, Kamen's radically new kind of wheelchair; he persuaded Johnson & Johnson to buy the rights to iBOT's technology and manufacture the device.)

Kamen's next major invention after the auto-syringe was a portable kidney-dialysis machine, which Deka developed at the request of Baxter International, a major medical-products and -services company. Roughly the size of a telephone directory, Kamen's machine enables people with kidney failure to dialyze—that is, undergo the process of hemodialysis, whereby impurities are removed from the blood—at home while they sleep; previously, nearly all patients had to visit a clinic three times weekly for a four- to six-hour procedure involving a machine the size of a dishwasher. The average annual cost of the new system—$10,000—is covered by Medicare or another insurance plan, in most cases. "We didn't believe it could be done," Vernon R. Loucks Jr., the former chair of Baxter International, told Kirsner. "Now it's all over the world. Dean is the brightest guy I've ever met in this business, bar none."

In 2001 Kamen unveiled the iBOT, a wheelchair that can go over curbs and up stairs; negotiate bumpy surfaces; balance on two wheels; and raise the sitter to various heights—for example, high enough to position its user within reach of high shelves or at eye level with a person standing. Kamen refers to the iBOT not as a wheelchair but as "the world's most sophisticated robot," according to John Heilemann. What inspired Kamen to invent the iBOT was the sight of a young man struggling to get his wheelchair over a curb. "I just fixated on how unreasonable that condition really is," he told John Hockenberry for MSNBC (June 30, 2001, on-line). "And it just seemed to me that the fundamental issue was the world has not been architected for people that are sitting down at 39 inches." "The solution came later," Joseph P. Shapiro reported for *U.S. News & World Report* (December 25, 2000–January 1, 2001), "when Kamen slipped in the shower, then caught himself by swinging his arms"; he then realized, Shapiro wrote, that "walking is really a controlled fall." The iBOT—nicknamed Fred Upstairs, or Freddie, by its developers, after the phenomenally agile dancer Fred Astaire—balances by means of six gyroscopes and three computer systems. With its added equipment and six wheels, it is heavy (200 pounds), but it is more compact and narrower than a traditional wheelchair. Johnson & Johnson hopes to start marketing the iBOT by 2003; the retail cost will be about $30,000 for each device—three to six times that of the average motorized wheelchair. Offsetting the high purchase price will be financial benefits: users will not have the expense of customizing their homes with ramps and wider doorways to accommodate traditional wheelchairs; moreover, by increasing their mobility, iBOT may enable them to get better-paying jobs. "At first blush, you'd stay away from developing something like the [iBOT], just because of the legal implications," Woodie Flowers, a professor of mechanical engineering at MIT and a friend of Kamen's, told Kirsner. "You're going to put a human in it and it'll go up stairs? That's nuts. But he did it. He's not one to get caught up in conventional wisdom."

News leaks in January 2001 about another Kamen project, now known as the Segway Human Transporter, triggered a media frenzy, with wild speculations that the invention would profoundly change the way humans live, work, and even think. Before its public debut, in December 2001, the device, which was more than a decade in the making, was referred to as both Ginger—after Fred Astaire's frequent dance partner, Ginger Rogers—and IT. Looking like "a cross between a hand mower and a Razor scooter," according to *USA Today* (December 3, 2001, on-line), it is a two-wheeled, gyroscope-stabilized, battery-powered scooter that can carry a person weighing up to 250 pounds along with up to 75 pounds of cargo. Developed at a cost of $100 million, it has been called an engineering marvel that mimics the human body's ability to maintain balance. There is no brake, engine, throttle, gearshift, or steering wheel. Instead, tilt sensors monitor the rider's center of gravity more than 100 times a second; by leaning to the left or right, the rider signals to the wheels which way to turn; leaning forward or backward indicates a desire to speed up or slow down, respectively. The Segway HT can roll smoothly over pavement, gravel, grass, sand, and small obstacles (but cannot climb stairs). Its average speed is eight miles per hour, about three times faster than the average walker; its maximum speed is 12 miles per hour. It can travel a distance of up to 17 miles on a six-hour charge that uses just 10 cents of electricity—and thus is far cheaper, cleaner, and more efficient than cars. Kamen would like to see cars banned from city streets to make way for pedestrians and Segway HT riders. "Cars are great for going long distances, but it makes no sense at all for people in cities to use a 4,000-lb. piece of metal to haul their 150-lb. [bodies] around town . . . ," he said to Amy Harmon for the *New York Times* (December 3, 2001, online). "A bike is too slow and light to mix with trucks in the street but too large and fast to mix with pedestrians on the sidewalk. Our machine is compatible with the sidewalk. If a Segway hits you, it's like being hit by another pedestrian."

Instead of having another company manufacture and sell the human transporter, as he has done with most of Deka's products, Kamen formed his own firm, Segway, to produce and market it. With some of the $90 million he has collected from investors, he has built a 77,000-square-foot factory on the outskirts of Manchester. Models are currently available to commercial users and government agencies; they have not yet received approval for sale to individuals. Early Segway HT purchasers include the U.S. Postal Service, the National Parks Service, General Electric, and the police departments of Manchester, New Hampshire, and Boston. The consumer model of the Segway HT is expected to sell for about $3,000. Kamen believes that the device will initially be more marketable overseas, particularly in developing countries that lack or have insufficient public-transportation systems and do not have to deal with a huge car-owning public, automobile-industry lobbyists, or other likely opponents. Kamen predicted to Heilemann that "10 years from now, this will be the way many people in many places get around. If all we end up with are a few billion-dollar niche markets, that would be a disappointment."

Kamen and his team are currently trying to come up with a practical and affordable version of the Stirling engine, a remarkably efficient hot-air machine invented in 1816 by Robert Stirling, a Scottish minister. In the past, extremely high costs had thwarted people who had tried to mass produce the engine. Kamen hopes that Deka's Stirlings, in development for seven years, will bring portable electricity to Third World nations. "It can burn any fuel, and you can do all kinds of things with it," he told Kirsner.

In a very different type of endeavor, in 1985 Kamen established Science Enrichment Encounters (SEE), a science museum for children in Manchester, New Hampshire. Some 70 hands-on exhibits are designed to show young students that science and technology can be exciting and rewarding. Four years later he launched U.S. FIRST, a non-profit organization dedicated to improving the attitudes of American teenagers toward science and technology, specifically with the goal of inspiring them to consider entering those fields as careers. U.S. FIRST holds an annual contest in which students work at their high schools with an engineer from a corporation or university (AT&T, Boeing, Delco Electronics, General Electric, Raytheon, Nynex, MIT, Harvard, and Dartmouth have all participated) to build a robot that must accomplish a specific task. (Kamen formulates a different task each year.) They then compete against teams from other schools. Seventeen regional contests are followed by a national championship event, held at Walt Disney World's EPCOT Center, in Orlando, Florida, in April. Prizes include college scholarships and, sometimes, a meeting with the U.S. president or vice president. In 2002 more than 600 teams from the U.S. and abroad were eligible for the national FIRST competition. Commenting on the lively atmosphere at the event, Bill Slocum wrote for the *New York Times* (March 28, 1999), "Calling it a science fair is like calling the Super Bowl a shoulder-pad scrimmage." Kamen hopes that someday, every student in the country will participate, and the final contest will be televised. "In a democracy, we get what we celebrate," Kamen told Slocum. "Every kid 7 to 17 dreams about the Super Bowl, but no one can tell you what a superconductor is. Every kid knows who won the Heisman Trophy, but no one can tell you who won the Nobel Prize for Physics." Kamen believes that to increase appreciation for science and technology among students, American culture must shift to those subjects and their practitioners some of the attention paid to professional athletes and performers—in effect, create science and technology superstars. "We've created demand for sports and entertainment figures because our culture makes them seem very accessible," he told Emily M. Smith for *ASME News* (September 2001, on-line), a publication of the American Society of Mechanical Engineers. "In reality, only a few dozen people are going to start playing basketball every year at the professional level. But, last year, there were two million technical jobs that went unfilled in the U.S. because nobody was there to do them. Young people aren't being told often enough, and when they're young enough, that if they started putting as much energy into learning some algebra, some trigonometry and develop even just a little bit of analytical capability, they would be able to have an exciting career, make a lot of money and fill any of these unfilled jobs. Nobody is explaining to them that being an engineer and a scientist is fun. It's accessible. It's exciting to create things." Thanks to his efforts, New Hampshire state office-holders have become visible supporters of FIRST. In addition, during presidential-election years, Kamen makes FIRST headquarters and his huge home available for political rallies, parties, and speeches. FIRST has also collaborated with the Lego company to hold little-league robotics competitions, known as the FIRST Lego League Challenge, for nine-to-14-year-olds.

"Of all the things I've worked on . . . the one that has had the potential for the greatest positive impact on the world is FIRST . . . ," Kamen said to Smith. "When you're sitting at the nationals and looking out at 20,000 kids in the arena at EPCOT . . . you realize that they are the ones who are going to pretty much take over the leadership role in inventing and creating the products and services of the future, dealing with global warming, energy issues and health issues. And you look out there and think, because FIRST got them thinking about engineering and science, one of these kids is going to cure cancer. One of these kids is going to come up with some extraordinary technical achievement that'll create an entirely new field. . . . The possibilities are just awesome."

In addition to the National Medal of Technology, Kamen's many honors include the 1994 Kilby Award, the 1995 Hoover Medal, the 1997 Edwin F. Church Medal, from ASME, the 1998 Heinz Award in Technology, the Economy and Employment, and the 2002 Lemelson-MIT Prize. He was named Engineer of the Year by *Design News* in 1994 and elected to the National Academy of Engineering in 1997. He is a fellow of the American Institute of Medical and Biological Engineering.

Never married, Kamen lives in a 32,000-square-foot, hexagonal, multilevel house, called Westwind, on a hill overlooking Manchester. Of his own design, it is built around a 150-year-old steam engine once owned by Henry Ford and contains secret passageways, a pulley system for moving wine bottles from the kitchen to the bedroom, and a foundry, machine shop, and computer room in the basement. Its power is generated by a wind turbine; also on the grounds is a fully lit baseball diamond. A licensed pilot, Kamen owns two Enstrom helicopters (he has invented devices for helicopters) and a Citation jet. In the late 1980s he purchased an island off the coast of Connecticut. Kamen treats the island, named North Dumpling, as his own tiny country; it has a flag, an anthem, a navy (one boat), currency (with each bill's value that of pi), and a mutual nonaggression pact with the U.S. signed by Kamen and President George Herbert Walker Bush. A photograph of the island hangs in his office at Deka, with the tag "The Only 100 Percent Science-Literate Society."

No matter what the occasion—even the National Medal of Technology awards ceremony at the White House—Kamen dresses in the same outfit: blue jeans, a denim work shirt, and Timberland boots. On a typical day, he arrives at work at 9:30 a.m. and works until 9:00 or 10:00 p.m., when he has supper with one or two employees to talk business. "If I'm awake, I'm working," he told Kirsner. "Deka and First are my work, my family, my hobby. They're everything." He is planning to set up a science-and-technology hall of fame in one of his buildings; to make it especially attractive to tourists, he will devote one wing to science fiction. He dreams of having the film director Steven Spielberg and the science-fiction writer Ray Bradbury attend its opening. — K.E.D.

Suggested Reading: *ASME News* (on-line) Sep. 2001, with photo; CBS News (on-line) Feb. 6, 2001, with photo; *ID* [*International Design*] p46+ June 2002; *New York Times* III p10 Feb. 14, 1993, with photos; *Newsweek* p56+ May 27, 2002; *Scientific American* p36+ Sep. 1999; *Smithsonian* p98+ Nov. 1994; *Time* (on-line) Dec. 2, 2001, with photo; *Vanity Fair* p184+, p222+ May 2002; *Wired* (on-line) Sep. 2000

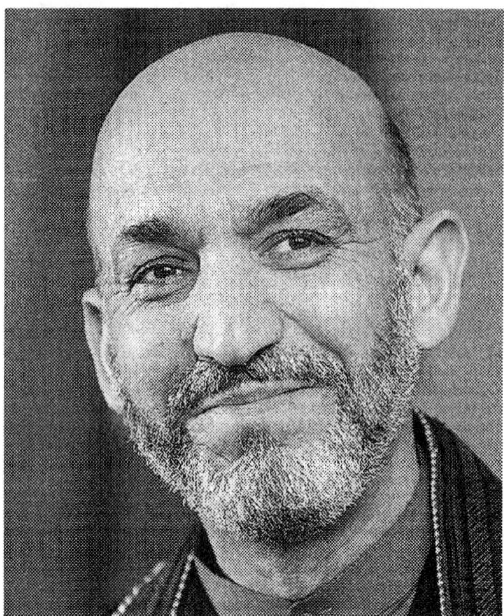
Sean Gallup/Getty Images

## Karzai, Hamid

(KAR-zeye, ha-MEED)

*Dec. 24, 1957– President of Afghanistan*

*Address: c/o Afghanistan Consulate General, 360 Lexington Ave., 11th Fl., New York, NY 10017*

Afghanistan has long been a country without real leadership. Although it has been ruled by tribal kings for centuries, infighting and cultural clashes have crippled the nation time and again. In 1979 Afghanistan was invaded by the Soviet army, and its people spent a decade fighting the interlopers. After the Soviet retreat at the end of the 1980s, the Afghan people again sought to rebuild their struggling nation. However, corruption and amoral leadership led to the rise of the Taliban, a fundamentalist Islamic group that ruled more than 90 percent of the country, killing those who did not follow them and engaging in brutal treatment of women. Following the terrorist attacks on the U.S. on September 11, 2001, the Taliban was driven from power by American and British forces, working in tandem with anti-Taliban Afghan units. Once again, Afghanistan found itself seeking someone to lead its people. In December 2001 Hamid Karzai was chosen as interim leader; six months later he was elected president of Afghanistan.

Karzai is a part of the Popalzai clan, a respected and influential Pashtun tribe, numbering around 500,000. (The Pashtun are the people of the eastern and southern parts of the country, as well as adjacent regions of Pakistan. They make up more than half of Afghanistan's population. Nearly every Afghan king since 1747 has come from the Popalzai.) Those who know Karzai describe him as quiet and unassuming, qualities they believe will allow him to lead a country that has long been torn apart by conflict. "He is not an obstreperous warlord with blood on his hands, plunder on his mind and a ragtag army," Babak Dehghanpisheh and Ron Moreau wrote for *Newsweek* (December 31, 2001). "He is not tainted by association with the mujahedin who flattened Kabul after driving out the Soviets, or with the fanatical Taliban who took their place. He is not a bully, or a crook, or a chauvinist or a zealot—he is none of the things that has defined Afghan leaders over the past 23 years." Karzai's administration is slated to serve until 2004.

Hamid Karzai was born on December 24, 1957 in Kandahar, the capital city of Afghanistan's Kandahar Province, into a family of seven other sons and one daughter. (Some sources say there were six other sons.) Five of his siblings currently live in the United States, where they run a chain of Afghan restaurants. Karzai's grandfather was, during Afghanistan's monarchical era, speaker of the Parliament. His father, Abdul Ahad Karzai, was the head of the influential Popalzai clan and assumed several high-level posts under the rule of King Mohammed Zahir Shah, who reigned from 1933 to 1973, providing a few decades of relative stability to the region. Throughout the Pashtun world, the Karzai name was a respected one.

Part of Karzai's education took place in India, where he studied political science and learned to speak six languages fluently—English, French, Pushtu, Dari, Urdu, and Hindi. Rajendra Chauhan, one of Karzai's professors, was impressed with him even then. "If I go back to 1981 and remember his thought and vision," he told Christiane Amanpour and Andrea Koppel for *CNN.com* (December 22, 2001), "I am confident he will bring peace to Afghanistan."

In 1979, when the Soviet Union invaded Afghanistan in a bid to bolster its crumbling empire, Karzai and his father fled to Pakistan. From there they helped the efforts of the anti-Soviet fighters by providing supply lines for them and acting in an advisory capacity. During this period Karzai fostered a relationship with the Central Intelligence Agency (CIA), which was involved in the Afghan struggle at the time. He also ran a small hotel in Peshawar. While Karzai was in Pakistan, his father taught him about Pashtun culture and the intricate practices of tribal etiquette. "One of his strengths is that he knows intimately the very complex, southern Pashtun tribal society," Edmund McWilliams, a former U.S. envoy to Afghanistan, told Ron Moreau for *Newsweek* (December 24, 2001).

After the Soviets withdrew from Afghanistan, in the late 1980s, Karzai returned to his homeland, briefly serving as deputy foreign minister under President Burhanuddin Rabbani. Distrust and infighting during Rabbani's administration led Karzai to leave within two years. He briefly aligned himself with the Taliban, although he declined an offer to be their U.N. ambassador. "Like so many [mujahedin] I believed in the Taliban when they first appeared on the scene in 1994 and they promised to end the warlordism, establish law and order and then call a Loya Jirga [national grand council] to decide upon who should rule Afghanistan," he told Ahmed Rashid in an interview for *Eurasia Insight* (December 10, 2001). Karzai gave the Taliban $50,000 (U.S.) and supplied them with a large cache of weapons he had hidden away. During this time Karzai also worked as a consultant for the U.S. oil company Unocal, which briefly supported the Taliban; the company planned to build a pipeline to transport oil and gas from Central Asia to Pakistan via Afghanistan.

Karzai soon grew disgusted with the Taliban's fundamentalist approach to the Islamic religion. In particular, he abhorred their treatment of women, which included forcing them to keep their faces and bodies hidden and preventing them from leaving their houses, getting education, or holding jobs. (Karzai believes strongly in equal opportunity for women; his interim cabinet includes two female ministers.) He also became concerned when the Taliban harbored Osama bin Laden, the fundamentalist Islamic militant who had strong links to terrorist activity. "By 1997 it was clear to most Afghans that the Taliban were unacceptable because Osama bin Laden was playing a leadership role in the movement," he told Rashid. "I warned the Americans many times, but who was listening—nobody." Karzai suspected that the root of the Taliban's corruption had been its infiltration by anti-Afghan influences, specifically Pakistan's Interservices Intelligence (ISI). ISI had reportedly allowed Arabs and other foreigners into Afghanistan, where they began setting up terrorist training camps. "These Arabs, together with their foreign supporters and the [Taliban], destroyed miles and miles of homes and orchards and vineyards," he said, as quoted on the Web site *afghan-info.com*. "They have killed Afghans. They have trained their guns on Afghan lives. These Arabs are in Afghanistan to learn to shoot. They learn to shoot on live targets and those live targets are the Afghan people, our children our women. We want them out." He returned to Pakistan, where he and his father began an active crusade against the Taliban. "[Karzai] has been the strongest foe of the Taliban," his brother Mahmood told Tim McGirk for *Time Atlantic* (December 17, 2001). "I always told him to leave Pakistan because I thought he was in danger, but he stayed long because he is hardheaded." Karzai began to organize opposition against the Taliban; he formed ties with Pashtun chiefs with similar grudges against the group and asked for support from the U.S. in creating an armed anti-Taliban movement that would take the country back by force.

In 1999 Karzai's father was shot to death while walking home from a mosque in Quetta, Pakistan. The murder was believed to have been perpetrated by Taliban agents. Karzai was quickly appointed the new Popalzai chief. His father's death spurred him in his crusade against the Taliban. He again approached members of the U.S. government in Washington, D.C., proposing a resistance movement that could unseat the organization, but met with little success.

On September 11, 2001 the word "Taliban" entered the American public's consciousness. That morning two airplanes smashed into the towers of New York City's World Trade Center, collapsing them both. A third plane hit the Pentagon, in Washington, D.C., causing a portion of that structure to crumble. A final plane, thanks to the intervention of a group of passengers, crashed in a field in Pennsylvania, rather than the government building that had undoubtedly been its target. Almost instantly the U.S. government named bin Laden as being the most likely instigator of the attack. Karzai had long been aware of bin Laden's ties to Al Qaeda, a terrorist group, but he had never suspected that the organization could execute an attack of that magnitude. "The Afghans I used to meet outside of the country used to tell me that I was underestimating these people," he told Lally Weymouth for *Newsweek* (February 4, 2002). "I would tell them, 'You are cowards, you have lost heart.' But I found out that those people were right and I was wrong." The events of September 11 galvanized Karzai into action. Only a few days after the attack, he began to stockpile weapons, communications gear, and money in order to create a tribal *lashkar* (militia) to overtake the Taliban. In October he slipped into Afghanistan in an effort to rally his fellow Pashtuns to fight. He traveled first to Karz, his ancestral village, then to the mountains of Orguzan, recruiting tribal elders to his cause as he went. He also helped to assemble a Loya Jirga, the multifaction council that would establish a new Afghan government once the Taliban were overthrown. Karzai had little money, few supplies, and almost no outside support. Nonetheless, he found himself among allies. "I was surprised, truly, to find out that the people were absolutely in support of an honorable life for Afghans and the return of peace, in support of Loya Jirga," he told an interviewer for *CNN.com* (December 22, 2001). The Taliban soon discovered Karzai's presence and set up an ambush, but Karzai escaped with the help of U.S. forces, who ferried him away by helicopter. Around this time President George W. Bush issued an ultimatum to the Taliban: turn over bin Laden, or face military action. When the Taliban refused, Allied forces launched a vigorous campaign against them. By December, the Taliban's reign over Afghanistan had crumbled and they had fled from the capital city, Kabul.

The fall of the Taliban regime left Afghanistan at a crossroads. The country was now faced with choosing someone who could lead its people, as well as help rebuild its infrastructure. At a conference held in Bonn, Germany, in early December 2001, Karzai was selected as the country's interim leader by the council, which was composed of members of four Afghan factions. The selection was made in part because Karzai had fewer enemies than the other candidates. The plan outlined at Bonn called for Karzai to remain in power for six months as head of a 30-member multi-faction administration. In June 2002 a tribal assembly of 1,500 Afghans would meet to choose a transitional government. (Mohammed Zahir Shah, the former king, plans to return from exile to preside over the gathering.)

While Karzai had numerous supporters, there were some who balked at the Bonn committee's suggestion. "He is alone, doesn't represent a party, has no political base outside his tribe and is not widely known in Afghanistan," a Western diplomat from Islamabad told Ron Moreau for *Newsweek* (December 24, 2001). Karzai's detractors felt he was too quiet and introspective to lead such a harsh and violent country. Others felt that those qualities would serve him well. "He's a very peaceful person," his brother Qayum told the reporter for *CNN.com*. "He has enormous capabilities of dialogue and enormous diplomatic skill to negotiate, and is a person who really believes that Afghan national unity is the fundamental resource that we have to establish peace in Afghanistan."

Karzai was sworn in on December 22, 2001, making him the first person in nearly 30 years to take control of Afghanistan peacefully. "The significance of this day in Afghan history really depends on what happens in the future," he said at the ceremony, as quoted by Patricia Smith for the teen magazine *New York Times Upfront* (February 11, 2002). "If we deliver, this will be a great day. If we don't deliver, this will go into oblivion." In setting up his administration, Karzai took on the difficult task of assembling a competent cabinet while still appeasing the powerful warlords who maintain control of many Afghan provinces. The Uzbek leader Abdul Rashid, who controls a large part of northern Afghanistan, had already formally stated that the Uzbeks would not support Karzai's government. Additionally, reports have surfaced saying that Rabbani, one of the country's former presidents, is paying off Pashtun elders in the eastern regions to oppose Karzai.

Not long after he was named interim prime minister, Karzai was nearly killed. At work in his temporary headquarters in the desert near Shahwalikot, Karzai was in the midst of preparing to meet with high-ranking Taliban officials to discuss the surrender of Kandahar. Overhead, U.S. bombers continued their assault on the Taliban. Without warning, a 2,000-pound stray bomb slammed into the ground a few hundred yards away. The resulting explosion blew out the windows of Karzai's office, pelting his face with glass. Three American servicemen and seven Afghans—two of them among Karzai's top lieutenants—died in the blast.

Karzai's administration faces numerous other difficulties, as well. He currently has no police force or army, leaving much illegal activity unchecked. Pat Lancaster, in an article for *Middle East* (February 2002), quoted a *New York Times* correspondent as writing, "Now the Taliban are gone, and the city and the surrounding [area] are run again by warlords and guerillas, whose rackets have almost instantly turned the place into Afghanistan's version of Shakedown Street, the land where almost everything is corrupt."

The country's opium trade also poses a serious problem for the Karzai administration. During the reign of the Taliban, the growing of opium poppies was forbidden. However, since the group's hold on the country was broken, farmers have begun planting the poppies during the winter months. The crop is expected to reach 2,700 tons, reestablishing Afghanistan as the largest producer of illegal opium in the world. (At one time the country was the source of 75 percent of the world's supply of the drug.) Karzai placed a new ban on the growing of opium poppies, but most of the areas in which they are cultivated fall outside of the new government's jurisdiction. "If we don't deal with the drugs properly," Kemal Kurspahic, spokesman for the United Nations Drug Control Programme, told Andrew Purvis for *Time* (March 25, 2002), "then everything else we do in Afghanistan may be in vain." In early April a bomb exploded near a convoy carrying Karzai's defense minister, who was traveling in Jalalabad to promote a government program to pay farmers for destroying their poppy crops. He was unharmed, but the blast killed four others and wounded six.

In February 2002 Karzai was returning from Jalalabad, where he was continuing his efforts to appease the warlords. Arriving at the airport, he was greeted by a mob of Muslims who were waiting for planes to take them to the holy city of Mecca, in Saudi Arabia. (According to Islamic law, every Muslim must make the pilgrimage, or *hajj*, to Mecca at least once in his or her life.) Because of the war on terrorism, planes were in limited supply, and the mob soon turned angry. According to Michael Hirsh and Scott Johnson in *Newsweek* (February 25, 2002), Karzai told the crowd, "If you want to kill me, I'm ready." Karzai escaped harm, but Abdul Rahman, the head of air transport, was stabbed to death and his body thrown down the steps of the plane he was boarding. Karzai has stated that he believes the killing was part of a plot by his own government ministers. Senior officials denied the charges, saying the blame for the incident fell strictly on the shoulders of the mob. Nonetheless, eight men, including a general and the deputy chief of intelligence, were either arrested or had warrants issued for them. On the day of Rahman's funeral, President Bush sent a 90-man squad from Special Forces to Kabul. Since then, at least 160 people have been arrested on suspicion of plotting against Karzai in an effort to destabilize the interim government. (Mohammed Zahir Shah has also been threatened, making his return to Afghanistan uncertain.)

On June 13, 2002 Karzai was elected president of Afghanistan by a Loya Girga, with 1,295 of 1,575 ballots distributed. That month Karzai swore in five vice presidents. Among them were Karim Khalili and Hajji Abdul Qadir, both leaders of anti-

Taliban forces. On July 6, 2002 Qadir was assassinated in an ambush outside a government ministry building in Kabul. To date, his killers have not been identified.

Two months later Karzai himself was the victim of an assassination attempt. On September 5, 2002 a gunman in uniform fired on the president's car in Kandahar. One of Karzai's bodyguards returned fire; both he and the gunman were killed in the exchange. Gul Agha Sherzai, Kandahar's governor, was wounded during the shooting. An investigation into the shootings revealed that the assassin was Abdul Rahman, a Taliban fighter who had been released from prison the previous June. Also on September 5 a car bomb exploded in Kabul, killing 26 people. Most observers believe that the Taliban and Al Qaeda were responsible for both those deaths and those of the president's companions.

Continuing his attempts to assert control beyond Kabul, in November 2002 Karzai fired several high-ranking officials, after accusing them of corruption, drug trafficking, and abuse of power. He is working to remove several warlords and militiamen from outlying regions and has called for the expansion of a 4,800-person international security force to help him do so.

Hamid Karzai currently makes his home in Kabul. Although traditionally men in Afghanistan marry in their 20s, he remained a bachelor until his early 40s. He was married in January 1999; his wife, Zinat, is a doctor, active in assisting refugees in Pakistan. In the days since he took office, he has traveled to 15 world capitals, striving to maintain international interest in Afghanistan. He is developing a plan to spend $4.5 billion in foreign aid on hospitals, schools, and highways. Much of the country does not have contact with Karzai or the other members of the central government, as there are few telephones or highways. "Indeed, Mr. Karzai often appears to be less a head of state than a mayor," Dexter Filkins wrote for the *New York Times* (March 26, 2002). "In his three months in power, Mr. Karzai has ventured only occasionally into the provinces, which, with their mud-brick huts and oxcarts, sometimes seem separated from Kabul by centuries." Nonetheless, when he does visit the people, he is often warmly received.

"We will keep working against [terrorism], together with the U.S. and other allied forces," Karzai told Weymouth. "We will try to make sure that we seek them out from their caves and put them on trial. I would like the TV cameras to show their faces to the American and the Afghan people, so that our people and yours will get a sense that justice is being done." — J.K.B.

Suggested Reading: *Afghan-info* Web site; *Beijing Review* p10+ July 4, 2002, with photo; *Eurasia Insight* (on-line) Dec. 10, 2001; *New York Times* A p1 Mar. 26, 2002, with photos; *New York Times Upfront* p22+ Feb. 11, 2002, with photos; *Newsweek* p32+ Dec. 24, 2001, with photos, p22+ Dec. 31, 2001, with photos, p36 Feb. 4, 2002, with photo; *Time* p41+ Dec. 17, 2001, with photos, p36+ Mar. 4, 2002, with photo

## Kass, Leon R.

*Feb. 12, 1939– Bioethicist*

*Address: Olin Center, University of Chicago, 1116 E. 59th St., Chicago, IL 60637*

Leon R. Kass is widely considered a pioneer in the field of bioethics, which explores the ethics of such medical and biotechnological issues as in-vitro fertilization, abortion, surrogate motherhood, doctor-assisted suicide, fetal and stem-cell research, and cloning. Kass, who began his career as a researcher in molecular biology, turned his back on scientific research in the late 1960s to devote himself to warning the public, through the medium of print, of the dangers of medical discoveries and new medical technologies. Rather than improve the human condition, he cautioned, such findings and innovations might lead to dehumanization and even enslavement. Kass is a co-founder of the Hastings Center, a think tank that focuses on ethical questions on biotechnology, medicine and health care, and the environment. On August 9, 2001 President George W. Bush appointed Kass chairman of the President's Council on Bioethics, an advisory body of lawyers, physicians, academics, and theologians charged with the task of exploring ethical questions related to advances in biomedical science and technology and recommending guidelines for the use of such new technologies. Kass dismissed predictions that he would use his post to block scientific and medical progress. "I esteem scientific discovery, and I treasure medical advance," he declared to Jeremy Manier and Ron Grossman for the *Chicago Tribune* (August 12, 2001). "But it's very clear that the powers we are now acquiring to alter the human body and mind also pose a certain threat to the long-term future of the things that make us human."

The son of Samuel and Anna (Shoichet) Kass, Jewish immigrants from Eastern Europe, Leon Richard Kass was born on February 12, 1939 in Chicago, Illinois. His parents, who spoke Yiddish at home, ran a clothing store. Kass told Manier and Grossman that his father and mother imbued in him "a certain sense that there is something called human dignity, and doing the right thing which goes beyond what is easy or comfortable." An excellent student, he gained admission to the University of Chicago at age 15. He majored in biology, earning a B.S. degree with honors in 1958. He then enrolled at the University of Chicago's medical school, from which he earned an M.D. degree with honors four years later. After completing an internship in medicine at the Beth Israel Hospital in Boston, Massachusetts, in 1963, he entered Harvard University, in Cambridge, Massachusetts, as a doctoral student in biochemistry. He received a Ph.D. degree in that specialty in 1967.

That same year Kass joined the National Institutes of Health (NIH) in Bethesda, Maryland, where, as a staff fellow, he conducted research in molecular biology. (At about the same time, he be-

Leon R. Kass

Courtesy of the University of Chicago

came affiliated with the United States Public Health Service in Washington, D.C., as a surgeon.) Over the next several years, he wrote or co-wrote several highly technical papers for such publications as the *Journal of Biological Chemistry* and *Methods in Enzymology*.

In 1967 Kass read an article in the *Washington Post* by the geneticist Joshua Lederberg, a winner of the 1958 Nobel Prize for Medicine, about the prospect that human beings would someday be cloned. "[Lederberg] suggested that cloning could help us overcome the unpredictable variety that still rules human reproduction, and allow us to benefit from perpetuating superior genetic endowments," Kass wrote for the *New Republic* (June 2, 1997). "These writings sparked a small public debate in which I became a participant. At the time a young researcher in molecular biology at the National Institutes of Health (NIH), I wrote a reply to the *Post*, arguing against Lederberg's amoral treatment of this morally weighty subject and insisting on the urgency of confronting a series of questions and objections, culminating in the suggestion that 'the programmed reproduction of man will, in fact, dehumanize him.'"

In another piece, published in the *Washington Post* on January 14, 1968, Kass argued that the transplantation of organs from one person to another, though beneficial, raised several ethical questions that he believed had to be addressed by the medical community and the larger society. In particular, he pointed to the possible eroding of trust between a dying patient and his or her physician, the possibility that organ transplantation would encourage euthanasia, and the dilemmas associated with selecting the recipients of the ever-scarce organs, all of whose survival depended on transplants, including those who had damaged their health by smoking or drinking. Although he offered no specific answers or guidelines, Kass maintained that society would have to resolve these problems as transplants became more common. "All of medical manipulation must be viewed not as an end in itself; not even as a means for the preservation of life," he concluded. "It must be viewed as a means for enabling the individual to live a life that is more than merely biological, a life of dignity and freedom, a life appropriate to a human being. Whenever medicine threatens the end it rightly serves, we must refuse to pay the price."

In part, Kass has traced his growing skepticism of the unalloyed benefits of medical advancement to two books: Aldous Huxley's novel *Brave New World* (1932) and C. S. Lewis's nonfictional *The Abolition of Man* (1944), both of which warned that the abuse of science could lead to loss of freedom and of the emotional, spiritual, and psychological characteristics we associate with humanity. Kass explained to Manier and Grossman that both books "show how the perfectly reasonable and laudatory humanitarian project to conquer disease, master nature, relieve suffering, could, if we are not careful, lead to our degradation." During this period—the late 1960s—he also began reading widely in classical Greek literature.

A growing number of professionals, including scientists, physicians, philosophers, scholars, and theologians, publicly expressed similar concerns about the possible negative consequences for society of advances in medical technology and about the near absence of public discussion of difficult new ethical dilemmas. In 1969 Kass and several colleagues, including the philosopher and author Daniel Callahan, the Protestant theologian Paul Ramsey, and the psychoanalyst Willard Gaylin, co-founded the Hastings Center, a think tank devoted to the emerging field of bioethics. In the *Hastings Center Report* (January 1990), Kass recalled that some of the center's co-founders were "inclined toward hope, eager to have the benefits of new technologies, but with protections against error and folly," while others were "inclined toward fear, repelled by certain prospects of biomedical intervention and concerned that even the well-intentioned uses of the new powers over the human body and mind might inadvertently diminish our humanity." The Hastings Center (currently located in Garrison, New York) has become one of the nation's leading think tanks, successfully keeping the issue of ethics in medicine and science in the public eye. Scholars affiliated with the center, prominent among them Kass and Callahan, have published many articles and books on bioethical controversies in the last three decades. They have also been interviewed frequently by the media for their opinions on such issues as abortion; in-vitro fertilization; surrogate motherhood; sterilization; prenatal genetic testing; end-of-life matters, including the care of the dying and doctor-assisted suicide; the selling of organ transplants; ethical implications of agricultural biotechnology; ethical and legal questions connected with HIV/AIDS, among them balancing the good of society with individual liberties; the ethics of animal research; racial, ethnic, and gender disparities in health care; and ethical concerns in managed care.

In 1970 Kass left the NIH and the United States Public Health Service to serve as the executive secretary of the Committee on the Life Sciences and Social Policy, a branch of the National Research Council (NRC), which in turn is part of the National Academy of Sciences (a private, nonprofit society). During his two years with the NRC, Kass helped produce the committee's report *Assessing Biomedical Technologies*, which, according to a press release (August 20, 2001) on the University of Chicago's Web site, "provided one of the first overviews of the emerging moral and social questions posed by biomedical science." In 1972 Kass began teaching at St. John's College in Annapolis, Maryland. Concurrently, two years later he was named the Joseph P. Kennedy Sr. Research Professor in Bioethics at the Kennedy Institute of Ethics at Georgetown University, in Washington, D.C. In 1976 Kass left both St. John's and Georgetown to join the faculty of the College and Committee on Social Thought at the University of Chicago, as a teacher of courses on ethics, classical Greek literature, and philosophy. From 1976 to 1984 he held the title Henry R. Luce Professor of the Liberal Arts of Human Biology at the college; in 1990 he was named the Addie Clark Harding Professor.

In addition to teaching, Kass has written many articles on bioethical controversies and other issues for such periodicals as the *Public Interest*, *Science*, *Theology Today*, *Commentary*, the *New Republic*, *First Things*, *Hastings Center Report*, the *American Scholar*, and *Commonweal*. In an article for the *Public Interest* (Winter 1972), Kass expressed opposition to in-vitro fertilization, arguing that it dehumanized individuals and could be abused for eugenic purposes. "There are more and less human ways of bringing a child into the world," he observed. "I am arguing that the laboratory production of human beings is no longer *human* procreation, that making babies in laboratories—even 'perfect' babies—means a degradation of parenthood." Although he gradually changed his mind about in-vitro fertilization, which has enabled about one million couples to conceive children, Kass is still concerned that the procedure might unleash evils that far outweigh its benefits.

In an article published in the *American Scholar* (Spring 1983), Kass criticized scientific research that sought ways to prolong human life, and possibly achieve immortality, by slowing down or even stopping the aging process. Natural death, he argued, is necessary for human society as a whole. The prolonging of life by a decade or longer, Kass wrote, would have such negative consequences as increasing unemployment and burdening the medical and social-service systems. About a year after that article's publication, Richard Lamm, who was then the Democratic governor of Colorado, cited it in a reference to terminally ill elderly people, declaring, "We've got a duty to die and get out of the way with all of our machines and artificial hearts, so that our kids can build a reasonable life," as quoted in *Time* (April 8, 1984). Lamm's comments were widely viewed as callous and interpreted as an endorsement of euthanasia, and they sparked an uproar, especially among senior-citizens' organizations. (Lamm denied to *Time* that he favored involuntary euthanasia, but he insisted that "people have the right to die without medical science intervening.") Kass, who was inundated with telephone calls from the press, was outraged that Lamm had cited his article and charged that the governor had taken what he wrote out of context. According to Dana Wilkie in the Catholic magazine *Crisis* (June 2002), the incident made Kass wary of the press, and he often refused to speak to reporters "unless they agree[d] to tell him which of his quotes they plan[ned] to use."

In 1985 Kass published his first book, *Toward a More Natural Science: Biology and Human Affairs*, a collection of his articles. In a review for *Choice* (October 1985), R. F. White described the book as the "best popular work to date exploring the tension among biology, medicine, and ethics. Writing in a straightforward style sparsely footnoted, Kass emerges as an outspoken critic of the growing manipulative mentality in biology and medicine." Kass has also written about social customs and relationships. In his book *The Hungry Soul: Eating and the Perfecting of Our Nature* (1994), he discussed the moral and sociological significance of the everyday act of eating. Kass asserted that besides nourishing the body, eating and the rituals that lead up to it, such as cooking and setting the table, provide human beings with the opportunity to socialize. In a lengthy article for the *Public Interest* (January 1997), he analyzed the decline of courtship, as traditionally understood, between men and women—a ritual that, in his opinion, helped to foster strong marriages and happy family lives.

During the 1990s Kass became visible as an opponent of doctor-assisted suicide and human cloning. "A physician-euthanizer is a contradiction in terms," Kass told Rogers Worthington for the *Chicago Tribune* (May 8, 1994). "People ought to be very wary of breaking down this absolute prohibition against physicians directly assisting in the taking of life." In the *New Republic* (June 2, 1997), Kass condemned the cloning of human beings (which is still a possibility only, not a reality) as both unethical and dangerous, writing that it "threatens confusion of identity and individuality," "represents a giant step . . . toward transforming procreation into manufacture," and "represents a form of despotism of the cloners over the cloned." In appearances before congressional committees and elsewhere, Kass has strongly supported efforts to outlaw human cloning. Many scientists and medical experts have argued against a complete ban on human cloning, on the grounds that the technology could be used to produce replacement organs and tissue for those who need them. Kass's *New Republic* essay appears in the book *The Ethics of Human Cloning* (1998), which he co-wrote with the political scientist James Q. Wilson.

During the spring of 2001, President George W. Bush grappled with the politically explosive question of whether the federal government should fund stem-cell research. Scientist advocates of such funding contended that research on stem cells (a type of cell that can give rise to many other types) might lead to the invention of effective treatments or cures for such debilitating illnesses as Alzheimer's disease and Parkinson's disease, techniques for rebuilding blood vessels, and ways to repair injured spinal cords. Stem cells are usually harvested from embryos, which are destroyed in the process. Many American pro-life organizations, virtually all of which supported Bush in the 2000 election, as well as Roman Catholic and evangelical Christian leaders strongly objected to stem-cell research, because they consider embryos to be human from the moment of conception and therefore entitled to protection. Those who shared that view urged that researchers be permitted to use only stem cells harvested from adults and discarded umbilical cords.

To assist him in formulating a policy regarding stem-cell research, President Bush turned to Kass and Daniel Callahan, who met with him at the White House on July 9, 2001. "I was invited not so much to tell [Bush] what to do, but to help him think through the various moral issues," Kass told Manier and Grossman. Earlier, on June 7, 2001, in testimony before the House Judiciary Committee Subcommittee on Crime, Kass had expressed approval of adult stem-cell research; by "pouring our resources into adult stem cell research—or, more accurately, nonembryonic stem cell research—we can also avoid the morally and legally vexing issues into embryo research," he said, as quoted by Mary Leonard in the *Boston Globe* (August 12, 2001).

After hearing from both Kass and Callahan, President Bush opted for a compromise. "As a result of private research, more than 60 genetically diverse stem cell lines already exist," Bush announced in a nationally televised address on August 9, 2001, as quoted on the White House Web site. "They were created from embryos that have already been destroyed, and they have the ability to regenerate themselves indefinitely, creating ongoing opportunities for research. I have concluded that we should allow federal funds to be used for research on these existing stem cell lines, where the life and death decision has already been made." The president added that his administration would allocate $250 million for stem-cell research using newborns' umbilical cords, thus avoiding the moral dilemmas associated with the use of embryonic stem cells. At the same time Bush named Kass chairman of a proposed council of doctors, lawyers, ethicists, philosophers, and theologians that would monitor stem-cell research and make recommendations on that and other biomedical issues. (Bush officially established the President's Council on Bioethics through an executive order on November 28, 2001; unlike many other presidential appointees, its members did not require Senate approval.) In a talk with Linda Wertheimer for *All Things Considered* (August 10, 2001), on National Public Radio, Kass explained that his role as the chairman of the President's Council on Bioethics was "to convene a group of people representing multiple points of view and various kinds of expertise to try to make clear what the moral issues are and to help people understand the deeper meaning of what is at stake in these issues and, of course, to be a group of advisers to whom the president can turn for assistance."

The reception to his appointment was mixed. In the *American Prospect* (September 24, 2001), Chris Mooney depicted him as a scaremonger who would block scientific progress. Several others, including some who did not share Kass's opinions, thought Kass was an excellent choice to lead the new panel. Among those was Alexander Capron, a bioethicist and professor of law and medicine at the University of Southern California, who told Manier and Grossman, "[Kass] makes arguments that are engaging, insightful and attention-grabbing. But they're not the kinds of arguments that some of us slide into—they're not just rhetorical, or done for shock value." Responding to various critics, Kass denied that he opposed scientific progress; as he told Nell Boyce for *U.S. News & World Report* (February 11, 2002), "I would have been dead three or four times over if it weren't for modern medicine. The claim that I'm some kind of Luddite is just ridiculous."

The terrorist attacks on the World Trade Center and the Pentagon on September 11, 2001 and the launching of the war in Afghanistan delayed the appointment of members of the council for several months. Then, on January 16, 2002 the White House announced the names of 17 people who would serve on the council under Kass. The appointments included James Q. Wilson; the well-known author and social scientist Francis Fukuyama; Mary Ann Glendon, a professor of law at Harvard University; the syndicated columnist and psychiatrist Charles Krauthammer; and Robert P. George, the McCormick Professor of Jurisprudence and director of the James Madison Program in American Ideals and Institutions at Princeton University, in New Jersey. The announcement sparked some complaints that the council was stacked with conservatives and opponents of cloning and would not be open to alternative viewpoints.

The President's Council on Bioethics met for the first time in Washington, D.C., for two days in mid-January 2002. (Complete transcripts of each meeting, along with the texts of academic papers discussed, are available on the council's Web site.) On the first day Kass requested that council members read and discuss Nathaniel Hawthorne's short story "The Birthmark" (1846), in which Aylmer, an alchemist, devises a treatment to eradicate a minor blemish from the beautiful face of his wife. The blemish disappears, but the treatment kills her. According to the transcript of the meeting, Kass explained that the story deals "with certain important driving forces behind the growth and appreciation of modern biology and medicine, our human aspiration to eliminate defects and to pursue some kind of perfection. Goals to which science and technology more and more have been put into service." "The Birthmark" sparked a lively discussion among members of the council. Daniel Foster, a physician with the Texas Southwestern Medical School, said that most scientists that he knew were not like Aylmer and "are just talking about advances that might be helpful to the community at large." Robert P. George noted that it was "profoundly important that we not . . . move as a culture towards identifying the worth and dignity of the human being with the absence of such defects," noting that Aylmer had lost sight of human beings "as worthy intrinsically—as having an intrinsic dignity."

The council's second meeting, held February 13–14, 2002, was devoted to the issue of cloning. According to Laura Meckler in the *Chicago Tribune* (February 15, 2002), members failed to reach a consensus on the ethics of human cloning, because they disagreed on the moral status of the human embryo—that is, whether the embryo has the same rights as a person (or any rights at all). At the third meeting, held April 25–26, 2002, experts explained the medical promise of both embryonic and adult stem-cell research. The council also discussed the paper "The Ethics of Stem Cell Research," presented by Gene Outka, the Dwight Professor of Philosophy & Christian Ethics at Yale University. The group discussed cloning and the patentability of human organisms at its fourth meeting, held June 20–21, and the same subjects—along with stem-cell research and the potential for genetic enhancement in sports—at its fifth session, held July 11–12. At the sixth gathering, September 12–13, the members discussed pharmacological aspects of depression, the genetic enhancement of muscle, and Hans Jonas's paper "Philosophical Reflections on Experimenting with Human Subjects." Unless President Bush extends its term, the council will disband on November 28, 2003.

Kass served as a National Institutes of Health postdoctoral fellow (1963–67), a Guggenheim Memorial Foundation fellow (1972–73), a National Humanities Center fellow (1984–85), and as the William H. Brady Jr. Distinguished Fellow at the American Enterprise Institute, in Washington, D.C. (1991–92 and 1998–99). His honors also include the University of Chicago's Llewellyn John and Harriet Manchester Quantrell Award for Excellence in Undergraduate Teaching (1983) and the Amoco Foundation Award for Distinguished Contributions to Undergraduate Teaching (1993). He received an honorary doctorate from the University of Dallas, in Texas, in 1997.

In 2002 Kass published his book *Life, Liberty, and the Defense of Dignity: The Challenge for Bioethics.* He and his wife, the former Amy Apfel, married in 1961. The couple co-edited the book *Wing to Wing, Oar to Oar: Readings on Courting and Marrying* (2000). They have two daughters, Sarah and Miriam, and live in Hyde Park, Illinois. —D.C.

Suggested Reading: *American Prospect* (on-line) Sep. 24, 2001; *American Scholar* p173+ Spring 1983; *Boston Globe* A p1+ Aug. 12, 2001, with photo; *Chicago Tribune* p13 May 8, 1994, p1 Aug. 12, 2001, with photo, p24 Feb. 15, 2002; *Crisis* p11+ June 2002, with photos; *Hastings Center Report* p5+ Jan. 1990; *New Republic* p17+ Jun. 2, 1997; President's Council on Bioethics Web site; *Public Interest* p18+ Winter 1972, p39+ Jan. 1997; *U.S. News & World Report* p58+ Feb. 11, 2002, with photo; University of Chicago Web site; *Weekly Standard* p13+ Feb. 4, 2002

Selected Books: *Toward a More Natural Science: Biology and Human Affairs*, 1985; *The Hungry Soul: Eating and the Perfecting of our Nature*, 1994; *The Ethics of Human* Cloning (with James Q. Wilson), 1998; *Life, Liberty, and the Defense of Dignity: The Challenge for Bioethics*, 2002; as editor—*Wing to Wing, Oar to Oar: Readings on Courting and Marrying* (with Amy Kass), 2000

Robert Mora/Getty Images

## Keener, Catherine

*1961– Actress*

*Address: c/o Publicity, Signature Theatre Company, 1650 Broadway, New York, NY 10019*

The characters portrayed by the actress Catherine Keener have come "to represent a contemporary type," Stephen Holden wrote for the *New York Times* (June 28, 2002): "Headstrong, brutally candid, radiating a free-floating hostility that seems to stem from some deep, gnawing disappointment (especially in men), she is the embodiment of what might be called a postfeminist malcontent." Keener began her acting career in the mid-1980s, with a bit part in the movie *About Last Night . . .*, and in the early 1990s she landed roles in several independent films. While her penchant for playing offbeat, tradition-defying roles made her a favorite among independent-film fans and filmmakers alike, it also meant that she was virtually ignored by Hollywood. That changed in 1999, with Keener's Academy Award–nominated performance in Spike Jonze's *Being John Malkovich.* Since then, she has appeared in an increasing number of mainstream movies, such as Joel Schumacher's *8mm* (1999) and Danny DeVito's *Death to Smoochy* (2002). She has also continued to choose roles she finds personally meaningful, in "small" films including Nicole Holofcener's *Lovely and Amazing* (2002). "I don't think about fame," she told Stephen Schaefer in an interview for the *Boston Herald* (July 15, 2002). "You need to work for many reasons, not just that you need money but that you love what you're doing. If you don't have other objectives than money and fame, it's going to be a frustrating experience."

The third of Evelyn and Jim Keener's five children, Catherine Keener was born in 1961 in the Little Havana section of Miami, Florida. Later the family moved to Hialeah, Florida, where Keener spent the rest of her childhood. After graduating from high school, Keener attended Wheaton College, a private women's school in Norton, Massachusetts, where she studied English and history. She was first exposed to the pleasures of acting during her sophomore year, when, closed out of a photography course, she signed up for a theater-ensemble class. Much to her surprise, her teacher cast her in a production of Wendy Wasserstein's *Uncommon Women and Others.* Although Keener had never acted before, she accepted the part. As she told Rene Rodriguez in an interview for the *London Free Press* (November 27, 1999), the experience made a deep impression on her: "[I] was encouraged by both the experience and other people to continue [acting]. I never knew what it was like to be on stage and hear an audience laugh at something that came out of your mouth. It was so much fun."

For a time Keener saw acting as just that: fun, but not a potential career. After graduating from Wheaton, she worked as an assistant to the New York–based casting director Gail Eisenstadt. When Eisenstadt relocated to Los Angeles, Keener went with her. After being diagnosed with lung cancer, Eisenstadt had a heart-to-heart talk with Keener. "She asked me what I wanted to do, and I told her I was embarrassed to admit it, but I'd done some acting in college . . . ," Keener told Jennifer Aniston for *Interview* (May 1, 2002). "She gave me some script pages and said, 'Come back and read for me.' I was terrible, but she really encouraged me and even called an agent for me. I think she wanted to set me up before she [died]." Eisenstadt pulled strings to land Keener a bit part as a cocktail waitress in the 1986 film *About Last Night . . . .* The part consisted of only one line, which was enough to earn Keener membership in the Screen Actors Guild.

Keener then decided to pursue acting as a full-time career, but found that jobs were not easy to come by. She has recalled being told time and time again that she was not sexy enough or that she was too "hard." As she told Terry Gross in a July 11, 2002 interview for the National Public Radio program *Fresh Air,* "I remember I had an audition once, and the director thought that I'd done a fairly good job in the reading, but my problem was that I wasn't sexy. And he didn't say 'sexy enough for this part,' or anything. He just said, you know, it's basically labeled me that way. And it was good, because, you know, it gave me some perspective on how arbitrary it all is, you know? Because at the time I just thought, 'Well, God, I really can't do anything about that. You know, I can't work that out, you know.'" Instead of trying to become what directors and others in the business thought she should be, or giving up on acting entirely, Keener chose to simply be herself. "I realized that I just have to kind of be who I am because I can't fight those forces who are just going to decide what they think about me. . . . I can't do anything about that," she explained to Gross.

Fortunately for Keener, in the early 1990s the independent-film industry began to flourish. Independent films (or those not connected with major Hollywood studios) provided an outlet for unconventional voices—a blessing for the supposedly "too-hard" Keener. Since her 1986 debut she had found work in only one film, *Survival Quest* (1989), and had appeared in a few television shows, among them *The Alan King Show* pilot episode and the short-lived *O'Hara*. Now she found filmmakers willing to work with her. One of them was Tom DiCillo, a cinematographer turned writer and director who in 1991 was casting his first film, the low-budget *Johnny Suede*. The film tells the story of a cocky young rockabilly musician, played by Brad Pitt, who belatedly grows up. DiCillo cast Keener in the part of Yvonne, the teacher with whom Suede falls in love and who spurs him on to maturity. Although *Johnny Suede* received mixed reviews, Keener's role earned her her first Independent Spirit Award nomination for best actress. Over the next seven years, Keener and DiCillo made three more movies together: *Living in Oblivion* (1995), *Box of Moonlight* (1996), and *The Real Blonde* (1998).

In 1996 Keener co-starred with Anne Heche in *Walking and Talking*, written and directed by Nicole Holofcener. The actress played Amelia, the neurotic, single friend of the newly engaged Laura (Heche). Like DiCillo, Holofcener recognized Keener's theatrical gifts. As the filmmaker told Margy Rochlin in an interview for the *New York Times* (January 23, 2000), "She uses her whole body to play a scene. She does these things that are so lovely and unique. Things you can't write. Things you can't say to an actress, like 'When you run into the lake, make your arms go up and down like a chicken.' If a director said that to an actress, she'd look at them like they were crazy." The movie was well-received by critics. In a July 26, 1996 review for the *Boston Globe*, Jay Carr described *Walking and Talking* as a "note-perfect" romantic comedy that has a "lively survivor's humor, which, despite some imperfections, carries it miles beyond most entries in this genre." And Michael Rechtshaffen noted in *BPI Entertainment News Wire* (July 22, 1996), "Particularly satisfying are leads Keener and Heche, both of whom should see their stars rise considerably after this outing." For the second time Keener was nominated for an Independent Spirit Award in the category of best actress. Over the next two years, Keener appeared in Neil LaBute's *Your Friends and Neighbors* (1998) and Steven Soderbergh's *Out of Sight* (1998), as well as DiCillo's *Real Blonde*.

In 1999 Keener landed the part that would change her career. She was cast in Spike Jonze's *Being John Malkovich*, the bizarre tale of a lonely puppeteer named Craig (played by John Cusack), who discovers a portal that allows whoever enters it to "become" the titular actor—that is, to experience life from Malkovich's perspective—for 15 minutes. Keener played Maxine, Craig's sexy, aloof co-worker, with whom he falls hopelessly in love; her character is so venomous and self-assured that at one point she tells Craig, "If you ever got me, you wouldn't have a clue what to do with me." To further complicate matters, Craig's frumpy wife, Lotte (played by Cameron Diaz), also falls in love with Maxine. When Jonze first approached Keener about playing Maxine, she was startled. As she told Gross, "I just kept trying to convince Spike that he was casting the wrong person, because I thought, you've got me confused with somebody else. . . . I really honestly thought that I should have auditioned for Lotte. . . . But he kept saying, 'No, I think that, you know, you would be righter for this part, Maxine.' So we read practically the whole script in like a two-hour marathon audition, and I was nervous and scared, and I kept thinking, this isn't me, this isn't me, this isn't me. And he, you know, kept giving me an encouraging pat and saying, 'Yeah, I think you can do it. I do.'" Jonze said that Keener's particularly acerbic reading of an exchange with Cusack's character convinced him that she was perfect for the role. "She did it so casually and so unforced," he told Lorenza Munoz in an interview for the Bergen County, New Jersey, *Record* (January 26, 2002). "It was sort of the quintessential Maxine with a zippy line. She had the ability to play Maxine in a way that she would say the harshest things to somebody, but you almost didn't know you got stung until afterward. She didn't do it venomously, which is more interesting than playing those lines as a villain." Keener won the New York Critics Circle Award for best supporting actress and was also nominated for an Academy Award, a Screen Actors Guild Award, and a Golden Globe Award. (The film also garnered Oscar nominations for best screenplay and best director.)

By all reports, Keener is nothing like Maxine. Married to fellow actor Dermot Mulroney and mother to their three-year-old son, Clyde, she is described by interviewers as warm and unassuming. Munoz noted, "At a recent interview, it was hard to believe that the nervous, ponytailed young woman wearing an oversized, moth-eaten green sweater could be the same razor-edged woman she plays on screen." Unlike many actors, Keener seems shy about discussing her success. Margy Rochlin wrote that during their interview, whenever she asked Keener about her future, the actress would whisper her replies. When pressed, Keener said, "Maybe I'm embarrassed to say I already get really good parts. And that I'm lucky. And that I don't know what the next step will be."

Keener followed *Malkovich* with *8mm* (1999), which was directed by Joel Schumacher and starred Nicolas Cage. The film centers on a private investigator's search for the source of an eight-millimeter reel of pornographic film. Keener had a small role as Cage's anxious wife. Her next film was *Simpatico* (2000), an adaptation of a 1994 Sam Shepard play, featuring Nick Nolte, Jeff Bridges, Albert Finney, and Sharon Stone. Keener played a lonely supermarket clerk who unwittingly becomes involved in a horse-racing scam. Neither of those films did well at the box office.

Keener had no fewer than five movie credits for 2002. In February she appeared with Robin Williams and Edward Norton in the critically and commercially disappointing *Death to Smoochy*, playing a television-studio executive who falls for the rhinoceros-clad host of a children's show. Next the actress starred in *Lovely and Amazing*, a film that reunited her with the filmmaker Nicole Holofcener. She played the eldest of three sisters, a frustrated artist unhappy in her marriage and insecure about her looks. Holofcener wrote the part especially for Keener. The film also features Keener's husband, although the two had no scenes together. Both the picture and Keener's performance in it received favorable reviews. Matt Wolf wrote for the Associated Press (June 25, 2002) that the film's title "perfectly characterizes its leading performance." While he noted that the cast as a whole is excellent, he found that Keener "has something special that sets her apart . . . she possesses the face of a Modigliani canvas and a faultless insight into human truths." Steven Soderbergh's *Full Frontal*, starring Keener, Julia Roberts, and David Duchovny, was released in August. Keener admitted to Meyer that she was "never quite sure what [Soderbergh] was up to" during filming but was nevertheless "blown away" by the finished product. Said to be an unofficial sequal to Soderbergh's 1989 film, *sex, lies, and videotape*, *Full Frontal* follows eight characters for 24 hours in Los Angeles. Most critics panned the movie, complaining that the characters were underdeveloped and the plot too confusing to follow. Andrew Niccol's *Simone* finds Keener playing a film-studio executive married to the character portrayed by Al Pacino. Scheduled for release in December 2002 was Spike Jonze's *Adaptation*, in which Keener, Jonze, and John Cusack reportedly play themselves re-creating the set of *Being John Malkovich*.

From September 19 through November 9, 2002, Keener appeared onstage with her *Smoochy* co-star Ed Norton in the Signature Theatre Company's revival of Lanford Wilson's *Burn This*, at the Union Square Theater in New York. Keener portrayed the roommate of a gay dancer whose accidental death disrupts her life and those of three other New Yorkers. In a review for the *New York Times* (September 29, 2002), Ben Brantley described the production as a "soulful, eye-opening new revival," and wrote that Keener gave "a beautifully natural, unshowy performance that grows on you by stealth."

Talking with Margy Rochlin for the *New York Times*, Spike Jonze described Keener's acting style as "very real, but complicated. Naturalistic. More like you're watching a person as opposed to a character." Perhaps that explains why audiences find the people she portrays likable in spite of their unappealing traits. An example is the character Michelle in *Lovely and Amazing*, whom Keener "plays . . . so sympathetically that your heart goes out to her even as you want to strangle her," in the words of Stephanie Zacharek in *Salon.com* (June 28, 2002). Keener feels compelled to play such characters because, as she explained to Carla Meyer for the *San Francisco Chronicle* (July 14, 2002), "there really are people like this—and we're friends with them, or we have them in our families. It doesn't take courage [to take these roles]. There aren't many parts like that around—I get the ones actors dream of." — H.T.

Suggested Reading: (Bergen County, New Jersey) *Record* Y p2+ Jan. 26, 2000, with photo; *Boston Herald* Arts & Life p31 July 15, 2002; *Interview* p108+ May 1, 2002; *London Free Press* C p12+ Nov. 27, 1999, with photo; National Public Radio July 11, 2002; *New York Times* II p11+ Jan. 23, 2000, with photos; *St. Paul Pioneer Press* E p1+ July 18, 2002; *San Francisco Chronicle* Sunday Datebook p38 July 14, 2002, with photo

Selected Films: *Living in Oblivion*, 1995; *Walking and Talking*, 1996; *Your Friends and Neighbors*, 1998; *Being John Malkovich*, 1999; *Lovely and Amazing*, 2002

Selected Plays: *Burn This*, 2002–

---

## Kennedy, Randall

*Sep. 10, 1954– Writer; educator*

*Address: Law School, Harvard University, Cambridge, MA 02138*

Randall Kennedy is a professor of law at Harvard University and one of the most authoritative voices in the nation when it comes to issues of race relations and criminal justice. His first book, the highly praised *Race, Crime, and the Law* (1997), which examines the racial aspects of both the formulation and the enforcement of criminal laws in the United States, won the prestigious Robert F. Kennedy Book Award in 1998. His next book, *Nigger: The Strange Career of a Troublesome Word* (2002), which has caused a stir in the media and among the public due to the provocative nature of its title and subject, is Kennedy's attempt, as he wrote in the book, to "put a tracer on *nigger*, report on its use, and assess the controversies to which it gives rise." The professor explained his purpose in writing the book to Linton Weeks for the *Washington Post* (December 11, 2001, on-line), saying, "I want to defang the word by making people knowledgeable about the word." Kennedy's articles can often be found in scholarly and general-interest magazines, including the *Nation*, *American Prospect*, *Journal of Criminal Justice*, *Time*, and the *New Republic*. As a scholar, teacher, and writer, Kennedy is

Courtesy of Randall Kennedy

*Randall Kennedy*

known, in the words of a *Publishers Weekly* writer quoted in *Contemporary Authors* (1998), "for his nuanced views on racial issues."

The second of Henry and Rachel Kennedy's three children, Randall Kennedy was born on September 10, 1954 in Columbia, South Carolina, and grew up in the Takoma section of Washington, D.C. His father was a postman, and his mother a teacher; both are now retired. Kennedy's older brother, Henry Jr., is a district court judge in Washington, D.C., and his younger sister, Angela Acree, is an attorney with the District of Columbia Public Defender Service. Kennedy attended St. Albans School, a private institution in Washington, before enrolling at Princeton University, in Princeton, New Jersey, where he received a B.A. degree in history in 1977. He won a prestigious Rhodes Scholarship to attend the University of Oxford, in England, where he lived and studied from 1977 to 1979. (First awarded in 1902, Rhodes Scholarships are the oldest international fellowships; they bring outstanding students from all over the world to study at Oxford, one of the oldest and most distinguished universities in the world.) After returning to the United States, Kennedy won an Earl Warren Legal Training Scholarship and earned a doctorate in jurisprudence in 1982 from Yale University Law School, in New Haven, Connecticut, considered by many to be the finest law program in the country. From 1982 to 1984 Kennedy served as a law clerk for Judge Skelly Wright of the U.S. Court of Appeals in the District of Columbia and for Thurgood Marshall, the first black justice of the U.S. Supreme Court. Kennedy began teaching law at Harvard University, in Cambridge, Massachusetts, in 1984. For a year he was an assistant professor of law; he became an associate professor in 1985 and then, in 1989, a full professor. His teaching has included courses on contracts, freedom of expression, and the law as it applies to race relations.

Like his early mentor Thurgood Marshall, Kennedy has an abiding faith in the U.S. legal system, despite what he acknowledges as its inevitable limitations. In his 1997 book, *Race, Crime, and the Law,* Kennedy examined a number of issues regarding the extent to which justice is served under the law and the ways in which the law affects African-Americans. Among other topics, he addressed the use by police of race as a grounds for suspicion, the disparity between the number of whites and blacks sentenced to death, race as a factor in the selection of juries, and the prevalence of unequal prison sentences for blacks and whites convicted of similar offenses. Kennedy's overall purpose, he wrote in *Race, Crime, and the Law,* as quoted in *Contemporary Authors,* is "to facilitate the emergence of a polity that is overwhelmingly indifferent to racial differences, a polity that looks beyond looks." Richard Bernstein wrote for the *New York Times* (May 21, 1997), "Rarely if ever has anyone systematically and cogently addressed as many of the vexing issues persisting in American society as Randall Kennedy does in *Race, Crime, and the Law* . . . a book that is deeply informed, all encompassing in its transracial humanity, and firmly anchored in a kind of impassioned common sense."

In the book Kennedy also discussed what he views as the contradictory judgments of Supreme Court justice William Rehnquist on matters involving race; the 1991 beating of a black man, Rodney King, at the hands of white Los Angeles police officers who were acquitted of wrongdoing by an all-white jury, a decision that ignited the Los Angeles riots of 1992; and the infamous case of the black performer and former athlete O. J. Simpson, a high-profile, racially charged murder trial that ended with Simpson's acquittal in 1995—a result that polarized public opinion largely along racial lines. "[Kennedy's] basic strategy is to insist that for all the serious, race-linked shortcomings of American criminal justice, it is the only game in town, and that African Americans above almost all others have a stake in a tough and effective system of law enforcement. Most of the racially objectionable impacts of the legal order can be ameliorated, Kennedy argues, if racial categories are rigorously and actively exorcized from the criminal justice system," Daniel D. Polsby wrote for *Reason* (December 1997). "*Race, Crime, and the Law* is a thoroughly, and characteristically, decent performance, by a scholar and teacher who has achieved great distinction by patiently expounding on the vices of racial sorting and promoting the ideal of treating people as individuals rather than as vectors of some abstract, mandatory racial identity. But there remain serious questions—not so much about Kennedy's aspirations for our country as about the means he offers for getting there." In another review of *Race, Crime, and the Law*, Judith A. M. Scully wrote for *Criminal Justice Ethics* (Winter/Spring 2000), "From reading this historical account of race and the criminal legal system, it is obvious that Kennedy is keenly aware of the detrimental impact that racial discrimination has had on the criminal legal system. It is also obvious that Kennedy believes that racism has shaped criminal policies as recently as the late 1980s and early 1990s. What is surprising, however, is that Kennedy often dismisses the influence of racial discrimination in his analysis of current public policies. . . . My criticism of Professor Kennedy's approach is that his commitment to 'historical optimism' and 'the politics of respectability'"—Kennedy's argument that it is up to blacks to behave in a respectable way that will incline more white Americans to support causes of racial justice—"provides interesting narrative but does not offer an adequate solution to the current racial justice crises in the criminal legal system." *Race, Crime, and the Law* won the 1998 Robert F. Kennedy Book Award, named for the slain U.S. senator and presidential candidate. As stated on the Robert F. Kennedy Memorial Web site, the award is given each year to the book that "most faithfully and forcefully reflects Robert Kennedy's purposes—his concern for the poor and the powerless, his struggle for honest and even-handed justice . . ."

Kennedy's second book, *Nigger: The Strange Career of a Troublesome Word*, was published in early 2002. "One of the courses I have taught at Harvard Law School is a course on race relations, and in teaching that course I have often done lectures which had as their starting point a word, a key word . . . ," Kennedy told Daniel Smith in an interview for the *Atlantic Unbound* (January 17, 2002, on-line). "'Nigger' is sort of a familiar word, and one day I was thinking about it a little bit and I looked at my computer and I typed n-i-g-g-e-r into the Lexis-Nexis computer bank and asked for the citation list of any state or federal court that had reported a decision. I got thousands of entries. Then I started reading these cases, and I saw that I was onto something, because the cases were just really interesting." What he found as he traced the word's course through American history led, first, to a series of lectures he gave at Stanford University in 1999, and then to the book. "If you're going to write a book with a title like this, you're going to, as Samuel Johnson said, 'disturb the peace,'" Kennedy told Linton Weeks, acknowledging the word's ability to shock people. "I'm glad the word nigger is a stigmatized word," Kennedy said to Smith. "I'm glad that it is a word that causes people to have anxieties. I'm glad that for the most part it's a word that is presumptively wrongful to use. I think that's fine. But that's not the end of the conversation. It's presumptively wrong to use nigger, but a presumption can be overcome. So if a white guy uses the word nigger—if anybody uses the word nigger—I'd say presumptively there's a problem. But then dig a little deeper and say, Well, what's going on? What is this person saying? Why did he say it? What is he attempting to accomplish? There may be answers to all those questions that are perfectly fine." The author told Weeks, "I've been on the receiving end of the N-word, across the spectrum. Affectionately and hurtfully."

In the book Kennedy traced the history of the title word, from its beginnings as the Latin *niger*, for black, to its use during the colonial era in the U.S., the long period of slavery (which continued after the nation won its independence), the Civil War and Reconstruction, and the 20th century, to all its present-day uses. In doing so he examined the word's role in American legal history, in works of literature, such as Mark Twain's *The Adventures of Huckleberry Finn*, in the comedy of black performers such as Richard Pryor and Chris Rock, and in current rap and hip-hop music, in which the word often has positive connotations. "There is much to be gained by allowing people of all backgrounds to yank *nigger* away from white supremacists, to subvert its ugliest denotation, and to convert the N-word from a negative into a positive appellation," Kennedy told Weeks. The columnist and author Earl Ofari Hutchinson, president of the National Alliance for Positive Action, expressed the common dissenting opinion, arguing in an article posted on the *Hutchinson Report*, his Web site, "If color-phobia is a deep-rooted standard in American life, then a word, as emotionally charged as nigger, will always reinforce and perpetuate stereotypes. It can't be sanitized, cleansed, inverted, or redeemed as a culturally liberating word. Nigger can't and shouldn't be made acceptable, no matter whose mouth it comes out of or what excuse they give for using it." As to why attention should be given to just one racial slur when there are epithets for every race, Kennedy told Daniel Smith, "From a broad sociological view, [the word 'nigger'] is associated with more havoc in American society than other racial slurs, in terms of the bloodshed, misery, injury that have been inflicted in episodes in which the N-word has figured prominently. Now, obviously there are all sorts of ethnic, racial conflicts in American society, but there's one that is deeper than all the others and that's the white/black racial conflict."

In the *New York Times Book Review* (March 3, 2002, on-line), Gerald Early wrote, "Randall Kennedy's *Nigger: The Strange Career of a Troublesome Word* has everything to make it popular: it is short, easy to read and provocative. But a book must be more than that to be good or to have been worth writing. . . . Kennedy's book feels a bit like an inflated essay and a bit hastily composed. It is often engaging and informative, but the arguments don't seem quite telling or convincing." Some reviewers and cultural observers have criticized Kennedy for using the word in his title as simply a ploy to sell more books. (His book is not the first to have the "N-word" in its title; its predecessors include the comedian and activist Dick Gregory's 1964 autobiography, *Nigger*.) "Give Randall Kennedy credit, though, for guts, thoroughness and a remarkable media achievement. Thanks to him, the issue is right here in your family newspaper, in black and white," Carlin Romano wrote for the *Philadelphia Inquirer* (January 20, 2002).

Kennedy has written prolifically on a wide number of topics involving race and the law. His published articles include "Orphans of Separatism: The Painful Politics of Transracial Adoption," in the *American Prospect* (Spring 1994); "Is All Discrimination Created Equal?," in *Time* (October 16, 1995); "On Racial Integration," in *Dissent* (Summer 1996); "You Can't Judge a Crook by His Color," in the *Utne Reader* (January/February 2000); "The Marital Color Line," in the *Nation* (December 25, 2000); and "Contempt of Court," in the *American Prospect* (January 1, 2001), in which Kennedy attacked the U.S. Supreme Court's intervention in the 2000 presidential election. He wrote the introduction to the book *Blacks at Harvard: A Documentary History of African-American Experience at Harvard and Radcliffe* (1993), edited by Werner Sollors.

Kennedy has been a guest on the *Today Show*, *Nightly News with Tom Brokaw*, and the National Public Radio shows *Fresh Air* and *The Connection*. He has also been interviewed widely, and has given many talks, since the publication of *Nigger: The Strange Career of a Troublesome Word*. Kennedy's next book, *Interracial Intimacies: Sex, Marriage, Identity, and Adoption*, is due to be published in early 2003. He has sat on the editorial boards of the *Nation*, *Dissent*, and the *American Prospect*. In 1990 Kennedy began publishing his own short-lived magazine, *Reconstruction*, which was intended to provide a forum for discussion and debate on key issues affecting black Americans. He is a member of the American Law Institute, the American Academy of Arts and Sciences, and the American Philosophical Society. Kennedy was awarded an honorary degree from Haverford College, near Philadelphia, and was once a trustee of Princeton University.

Kennedy met his wife, Yvedt Matory, a surgical oncologist, at a dance when they were both in eighth grade. The couple have three children. —C.F.T.

Suggested Reading: *Atlantic Unbound* (on-line) Jan. 17, 2002; *Criminal Justice Ethics* (on-line) Winter/Spring 2000; *Mother Jones* (on-line); *New York Times* B p6 Jan. 5, 1990; *Philadelphia Inquirer* (on-line) Jan. 20, 2002; *Reason* (on-line) Dec. 1997; *Washington Post* C p1 Dec. 11, 2001; *Contemporary Authors* vol. 162, 1998

Selected Books: *Race, Crime, and the Law*, 1997; *Nigger: The Strange Career of a Troublesome Word*, 2002

---

## Kidd, Jason

*Mar. 23, 1973– Basketball player*

*Address: New Jersey Nets, Nets Champion Center, 390 Murray Hill Pkwy., East Rutherford, NJ 07073*

The basketball player Jason Kidd, currently a member of the New Jersey Nets, is regarded as one of the best passers in the game. Aspiring since childhood to duplicate the smooth moves of Earvin "Magic" Johnson, Kidd has also set his sights on John Stockton's National Basketball Association (NBA) record of more than 15,000 assists. (Kidd recorded his 5,000th career assist on January 21, 2002.) Commenting for *Sports Illustrated for Kids* (February 2000) on his skill at passing, he said, "I think it's a combination of work, studying my teammates, and understanding where they are on the court. It's also about being unselfish. Being part of a play is just as much fun as scoring a basket." Kidd has the ability to be "part of a play" in a variety of ways: an all-around star, he excels at defending in addition to rebounding, assisting, and scoring. Frequently mentioned as one of the best among active point guards, he has improved the records of each of the three teams for which he has played. Kidd, who blows a kiss to his wife before every free throw, hopes that his third team, the Nets, will be the "charm"—the team he helps to win an NBA championship.

Mark Mann/Retna Ltd.

Jason Frederick Kidd was born on March 23, 1973 in San Francisco, California. He and his younger sisters, Denise and Kimberly, were raised on a small ranch outside Oakland, California, by

Steve Kidd, a TWA employee, and Anne Kidd, a computer analyst at Bank of America. "I was different from the day I was born," he told Michael J. Goodman for the *Sporting News* (October 3, 1994). "Dad is black. Mom is white. I had two different cultures and two different backgrounds to learn from." His parents were his role models when he was young, as he explained in the interview with *Sports Illustrated for Kids*: "They always reminded me to treat others the way I wanted to be treated." Kidd was involved in sports from his elementary-school years onward, playing on select soccer teams and in a Catholic Youth Organization (CYO) basketball league. He studied the moves of Los Angeles Lakers superstar Magic Johnson—"I enjoyed watching him on TV, and I tried to play like him on the playground," he recalled to *Sports Illustrated for Kids*—and became an excellent passer. In fourth grade, he set his first basketball record by scoring 21 of his team's 30 points in a CYO game. As his skills developed, he garnered a following and dreamed of playing for the NBA. His parents, however, attempted to keep him grounded, as he explained to *Sports Illustrated for Kids*: "I wasn't doing well in school when I was in the eighth grade. My parents threatened to take basketball away if I didn't pick up my studies. At that point, I realized school had to be first."

Kidd attended St. Joseph of Notre Dame, a small Catholic high school in Alameda, California, and turned it into a basketball power. During his four years at St. Joseph of Notre Dame, the basketball team had a 122–14 win–loss record, and Kidd's playing drew crowds so large that some games were moved to the Oakland Coliseum. The team won Division I state titles in Kidd's junior and senior years, and he was twice named the California Player of the Year. During his senior season, in which he averaged 25 points, 10 assists, seven blocks, and seven rebounds per game, he was showered with accolades: he won the Naismith Award, honoring the best high-school player; he was named the high school Player of the Year by *Parade* magazine and *USA Today*; and he played in the McDonald's High School All-American Game. But not all of the scrutiny was welcome; news of Kidd's struggles to earn good marks on college entrance exams made the pages of the *Oakland Tribune*. "It was an unreal childhood," he recalled to Jill Lieber for *USA Today* (December 13, 2001). "It was like I was Michael Jackson or some other young superstar entertainer."

Highly sought-after for college basketball, Kidd decided to remain close to home. He attended the University of California at Berkeley, a member of the Pacific-10 Conference of the National Collegiate Athletic Association (NCAA), and made a mark even as a freshman. His average of 3.8 steals per game set an NCAA freshman record, and after posting game averages of 13 points, 7.7 assists, and 4.9 rebounds, he became only the fifth first-year player in league history to earn a spot on the All-Pac-10. He was named Freshman of the Year by the *Sporting News*, and his underdog team, the Golden Bears, which had posted a 23–33 record during the two seasons before Kidd arrived, upset the two-time defending champions, Duke, in the NCAA tournament. (There was controversy off the court, as a mutiny by the players forced out veteran Golden Bears coach Lou Campanelli, who had a reputation for encouraging players to attend classes regularly and take full course loads in addition to meeting his strict standards on the court. The general feeling in the NCAA community was that Campanelli's firing was "suspicious"; whether Kidd was a bystander or an instigator was never determined.) Kidd's sophomore season, in which he averaged 16.7 points, 9.3 rebounds, and 9.1 assists per game, was even more storied than his first year with the team; he was the first player from the University of California–Berkeley and the first sophomore ever to be named the Pac-10 Player of the Year. He was also a First-Team All-American player and a finalist for both the college-level Naismith Award and the John Wooden Award. Placing on the back burner his hopes to one day teach history, Kidd left school, and the California Golden Bears, after his second year and entered the 1994 NBA draft. He was drafted in the first round, second overall, by the Dallas Mavericks, who signed him to a nine-year, $54.2 million contract, starting in the 1994–95 season.

Before the draft, Kidd had found himself in various scrapes. He was named in a paternity suit and eventually agreed to pay child support for his son, Jason, who was born in November 1993. He also gained a reputation for heavy drinking, and an acquaintance, Tameka Tate, filed a criminal complaint and sued him for $250,000, reportedly because he refused to apologize after allegedly hitting and verbally abusing her. (Because of conflicting accounts from witnesses, the local district attorney decided not to take legal action against Kidd.) A month before his NBA career officially began, he was charged with speeding and misdemeanor hit-and-run after he left the scene of a freeway accident he may have caused. (Pleading no contest, Kidd was fined $1,000 and sentenced to two years of probation as well as 100 hours of community service, which he served at a Boys and Girls Club.) "I've got to develop a strategy to deal with this, to protect myself," he told Michael Goodman, acknowledging that events had spiraled out of control. "I've got to find out how to be the real Jason Kidd."

Perhaps making a start in that direction, Kidd immediately won over Dallas fans by contributing money to local charities. The Mavericks had performed dismally during the 1993–94 season, finishing with a 13–69 record, but Kidd's contribution helped bring the team out of its slump. Dallas's record improved to 36–46 while Kidd averaged 11.7 points, 7.7 assists, and 5.4 rebounds per game. He participated in the 1995 NBA All-Star Rookie Challenge and shared the Rookie of the Year title with Grant Hill of the Detroit Pistons.

Kidd achieved his first NBA triple-double against the Los Angeles Lakers on April 5, 1995; he led the league that season with four. (A triple-double occurs when a player records double figures in three statistical categories in a single game.) In Kidd's second pro season, 1995–96, his statistics improved further, to 16.6 points, 9.7 assists, and 6.8 rebounds per game. Finishing the year with 1,348 points, 783 assists, and 553 rebounds, he became only the third player in NBA history to amass at least 700 assists and 500 rebounds in a single season. (Magic Johnson and Oscar Robertson each achieved the feat six times in their respective careers.) He was elected to start in the 1996 NBA All-Star Game. Overall, however, the Mavericks worsened, finishing with a record of 26 wins and 56 losses.

Meanwhile, Kidd frequently clashed with Jimmy Jackson, another young star of the Mavericks. In a controversy that seemed made for the media, Kidd publicly announced before the 1996–97 season his feeling that either he or Jackson would have to be traded—and then, in a reversal, claimed that they would work out their differences. He attributed the two men's squabbling to the stress of playing on a losing team, as he explained to Johnette Howard for *Sports Illustrated* (November 11, 1996): "I didn't know how to get the team to respond to me. I didn't know how to come at somebody without them thinking I'm trying to degrade them." In December 1996, with more than six years remaining on his contract, Kidd was traded to the Phoenix Suns. Confident that he would be able to make a mark in Phoenix, he chose 32 as his uniform number (with the numerals 3 and 2 representing triple and double, respectively), signifying his hope that he would one day have a triple-double season average, as only Oscar Robertson has done, in 1961–62. "I'd love to do it," he told David Sabino for *Sports Illustrated* (December 4, 2000). "A lot of people say it can't be done. I'm more interested in winning a championship, but I'd like to take a run at it." Although the Suns were performing abysmally before Kidd arrived—the team had a 0–13 start—they ended the regular season in play-off position, seeded seventh in the Western Conference with a 40–42 record. Kidd played in only 55 games over the course of the season—22 of them in Dallas—and posted average numbers, 10.9 points per game and fewer than 500 assists for the season. The Suns could not outplay the Seattle SuperSonics, their opponents in the first round of the play-offs, who beat them after the fifth game of the seven-game series.

The Suns attempted to build their team around Kidd, who had an extremely successful 1997–98 season. He played a career-high 3,118 minutes and averaged 11.6 points per game. For the second time as a pro, he finished with more than 700 assists and 500 rebounds (745 and 510, respectively). Kidd's average of 9.1 assists per game was second-highest in the NBA, and he posted four triple-doubles over the course of the season (thus tying Grant Hill for the most triple-doubles). He went to the 1998 All-Star Game as a reserve player and led the Suns, who were seeded fourth with a 56–26 record, to the NBA play-offs. (In the first round they lost to the San Antonio Spurs after the fourth game of a five-game series.) A championship season eluded the Suns again the following season, 1998–99, when they lost to the Portland Trailblazers after the third game of first-round play-off action. Due to a lockout, that season was truncated by about 30 games. Kidd had a superb offensive season, averaging 16.9 points per game and 10.8 assists per game, the best assisting average in the NBA. He also logged seven triple-doubles; the rest of the NBA combined posted only 11. For a week in April 1999 Kidd was simultaneously the NBA's player of the week and player of the month.

Kidd's first major injury occurred during the 1999–2000 season; he sat out several games in March and April 2000 due to a fractured bone in his left ankle. Prior to his injury, he had won a spot as a Western Conference starter for the 2000 All-Star Game, managed five triple-doubles (the most in the NBA that season), led the NBA in assists with 10.1 per game, and averaged 14.3 points per game. Kidd missed the Suns' first three games in the 2000 play-offs but returned in time to help Phoenix complete their first-round victory over the San Antonio Spurs. "When you're in a good situation, a winning situation, you want to enjoy it as much as possible," he told Sabino. "You want to be on the floor as much as possible." The Suns, however, lost the next round to the dominant Los Angeles Lakers, despite a good showing from Kidd, who in Game Four posted his first-ever play-off triple-double. After the season ended he traveled to Sydney, Australia, as a member of the U.S. Olympic team. Kidd was one of three captains and the starting point guard for the team, which won the gold medal.

Kidd continued to be a driving offensive force for the Suns in 2000–2001. For the second time in his career, he averaged 16.9 points per game, and for the third season in a row, he led the NBA in assists (9.8) and triple-doubles (seven). He was voted the starting point guard for the Western Conference in the 2001 NBA All-Star Game. In 77 games for the Suns over the regular season, he logged 3,065 minutes of playing time. His style, he told David Sabino, had remained consistent through his years as a professional. "I don't think I'm less flashy than I used to be. I look for the best way to deliver the ball, whether it's a bounce pass or a behind-the-back pass."

Although Kidd's basketball game had never been better, his personal life soured in January 2001. He was arrested on charges of spousal abuse for hitting his wife of four years, the former Joumana Samaha—who, fearing for her safety and that of the couple's two-year-old son, Trey, had called 911 after an argument with her husband turned violent. Kidd, who spent a night in jail, paid a fine and underwent counseling with a sports psychologist. He realized that he had been experiencing career-related stress and as a result was not giving his family the attention it needed; he had also been struggling to accept his father's death from a heart attack in May 1999. The arrest led him to readjust his priorities, as he told S. L. Price for *Sports Illustrated* (January 28, 2002): "I've learned a lot at home and been able to take what I've learned at home to the court. My body feels better. My mind's a lot clearer." While Kidd was still forced to deal with media disapproval of his actions as well as fans' displeasure, he saw himself as a changed man. "I felt as good as I ever had," he told Price. "I felt like a ton of bricks had been lifted off me, and I was doing the right thing, proving to my wife that I loved her." Still under contract, in July 2001 Kidd was traded by the Suns to the New Jersey Nets despite his reputation as one of the game's best point guards. In the deal, the Suns got Stephon Marbury, a number-one draft pick who is four years younger than Kidd. Rumors swirled that Kidd was traded due to his arrest or for his disagreements with the management and coaching staff.

When Kidd arrived in New Jersey, he was named a co-captain of the Nets. Soon, the team, which had not had a winning season since 1997–98, began rolling over their opponents. Kidd brought to New Jersey the style of play for which he had been lauded in Phoenix and Dallas; he moved the ball and passed it to open players, and he encouraged his teammates to play the same way. "Passing, and the desire to pass, can be catching, like a cold," he told Ira Berkow for the *New York Times* (December 26, 2001). "I've told all of our guys that when one of you is hot, you'll get the ball. The others have to be patient. They'll get their turn." Keith Van Horn, a top scorer for the Nets, told Berkow, "Jason always gives you the ball in your rhythm, in your stride. His timing and court vision are unparalleled in this league. It makes you more alert, and that naturally improves the play of everyone." The team improved so much, in fact, that in 2001–02 they became the first Nets squad to win 50 games in a season. (The team had notched only 26 wins the year before.) One week before the regular season ended, the Nets emerged as the Atlantic Division champions of the Eastern Conference, bound for the play-offs as a top-seeded team. With Kidd leading them, the Nets defeated the Indiana Pacers and Charlotte Hornets in the first two rounds of the 2002 play-offs, then won the Eastern Conference Championship by defeating the Boston Celtics, in the process earning the team's first trip to the NBA Finals. In the finals the Nets succumbed to the powerful defending champions, the Los Angeles Lakers. Kidd played in the 2002 NBA All-Star Game and was again a league leader in assists and triple-doubles. He ended the 2001–02 season with 46 career triple-doubles, a number topped only four times in the history of the NBA. The lowest moment of the season for Kidd occurred in a March 2002 game in Phoenix, in which he was fined $5,000 by the NBA for making an obscene gesture to heckling fans.

Kidd and his family, which has included twin daughters, Miah and Jazelle, since November 2001, live in Saddle River, New Jersey. Kidd supports several children's charities, including the Jason Kidd Foundation, which he founded in March 1999. He enjoys playing and watching golf; he organizes an annual celebrity golf tournament for the Jason Kidd Foundation. — K.S.

Suggested Reading: *New York Times* S p1 Dec. 26, 2001, with photo; *Sporting News* p47+ Oct. 3, 1994, with photos; *Sports Illustrated* p94+ Nov. 11, 1996, with photos, p62+ Dec. 4, 2000, with photos

---

Koichi Kamoshida/Getty Images

## Koizumi, Junichiro

(koy-ee-zoo-mee, jew-nee-cheer-oh)

*Jan. 8, 1942– Prime minister of Japan*

*Address: 3-1, Nagatacho 2-chome, Chiyoda-ku, Tokyo 100-0014, Japan*

"Koizumi is the best thing to happen to Japan in years . . . ," Bill Powell declared in *Fortune* (September 3, 2001). "The veteran of the Liberal Democratic Party is the sole reason people in Tokyo can say the words 'Japanese politics' and 'hopeful' in the same sentence and not get laughed at." Junichiro Koizumi, a member of the Diet, Japan's Parliament, for three decades and, since the spring of 2001, the country's prime minister, is "definitely in the dry, elderly upper echelons" of his party, the LDP, as Stephanie Strom reported for the *New York Times* (April 12, 2001), but he is far from being just another middle-aged face among the many in his nation's political crowd. His wit, ability to converse in English, status as a divorced father, professed love of rock and roll, fashionable attire, and even his permanent-waved hair all set him apart, and have contributed to popular support unprecedented for a Japanese politician: less than three months after his election, according to *mainichi.co.jp* (July 8, 2001, on-line), the public had purchased more than 600,000 Koizumi posters, tens of thousands of T-shirts bearing his image, and thousands of mobile-phone straps adorned with "Koizumi dolls," among other such items. But among his political colleagues, Koizumi has distinguished himself even more through his determination to reform the political, economic, and social systems of Japan and through the passionate rhetoric with which he has pushed for such changes. Often described as a maverick, and sometimes as an eccentric, he is "the closest thing to a rebel that Japan has," Stephanie Strom wrote for the *New York Times* (April 25, 2001).

Koizumi is the 10th person to become prime minister of Japan in the last 12 years. When he took office, Japan's economic situation was growing increasingly grim. As Bill Powell wrote, "After nearly a decade of teetering on the edge of a deflationary abyss, Japan, it's now clear, tipped into it earlier this year. Wholesale and consumer prices are plunging. Industrial production is down, as is consumer spending for every month this year compared with last. Unemployment is rising quickly, so consumers are likely to cut back even more, and that will lead to additional cuts in production, more unemployment, further declines in prices . . . : a classic, vicious deflationary cycle the likes of which the world hasn't seen in a developed country since, well, the Great Depression."

"No pain, no gain" was part of Koizumi's message during his most recent electoral campaign. On April 26, 2001, the day of his appointment as prime minister, according to the Japanese government Web site *kantei.go.jp*, he declared that what he dubbed his "Ceaseless Reform Cabinet" would be guided by the conviction that "without structural reform there can be no economic recovery." "I will advance political structural reform while at the same time leaving no sacred areas exempt from reforms in Japan's social and economic structures . . . ," he said. "In implementing reform, I intend to put into practice 'politics of trust,' that consider both the benefits of policies and their shortfalls from the viewpoint of the people of our nation, without prejudice or reserve, and without regard for vested interests of institutional theories. This process will be fully open to public review as I seek the broad understanding of the people." "People in the private sector are prepared to cope with and accept change . . . ," he declared, as quoted by Strom. "What is lacking is political and administrative will."

Junichiro Koizumi was born to Junya Koizumi and his wife, Yoshie, on January 8, 1942 in Yokosuka, in the Kanagawa Prefecture (one of 47 such provincial divisions in Japan), south of Tokyo. He has five siblings. His father (who took his wife's surname) and his maternal grandfather, Matajiro Koizumi, were both LDP members, and both served in the Japanese government—Matajiro as minister of posts and telecommunications as well as vice speaker of the lower house of Parliament, and Junya as minister of state for defense and director general of the Defense Agency. Junichiro Koizumi attended the prestigious Keio University, in Tokyo, from which he earned a degree in economics in 1967.

Koizumi's graduate studies, at the London School of Economics, in England, ended abruptly in 1968, when his father died. He immediately returned to Japan, where he ran for his father's seat in Parliament; Junya Koizumi had represented the Kanagawa Prefecture's 11th district, which encompasses the cities of Yokosuka and Miura. Junichiro Koizumi lost the election, though by only 4,000 votes. He then took a post as a secretary to Takeo Fukuda, a member of the House of Representatives who later served as Japan's prime minister (1976–78). In 1972 Koizumi resigned from that job to make another bid for the parliamentary seat his father had held. This time, thanks both to his association with Fukuda and to his many public appearances while in Fukuda's service, Koizumi triumphed. Shortly thereafter Koizumi married Kayoko Miyamoto, whose grandfather had founded a major Japanese pharmaceutical company. The couple had two sons, Kotaro and Shinjiro, before they divorced, in 1982.

Earlier, in 1979, Koizumi was named the parliamentary vice minister of finance (according to some sources, his title was state secretary for finance). The next year he was appointed chairman of the LDP's finance division, an arm of the party's Policy Research Council. In 1986 he became chairman of the House of Representatives' Committee on Finance, and the following year, chief deputy chairman of the LDP's Diet Affairs Committee. In 1988 he received his first cabinet position, as minister of health and welfare, during the administration of Prime Minister Noboru Takeshita (November 1987 to June 1989). He retained that post under the next prime minister, Sosuke Uno, who served from June to August 1989. In addition, Uno named Koizumi chairman of the LDP's National Organization Committee and chairman of the LDP's Research Commission on Fundamental Policies for Medical Care. In 1991 Koizumi became the chief deputy secretary-general of the LDP. The next year, which marked his 20th anniversary as a member of the House of Representatives, he was recognized as a senior politician—a formal designation in Japan.

Following in his grandfather's footsteps, in 1992 Koizumi became Japan's minister of posts and telecommunications, in the cabinet of Prime Minister Kiichi Miyazawa (who served from November 1991 to August 1993). On the very day of his appointment, Koizumi broke a Japanese political taboo by speaking out against what Michiyo Nakamoto in the London *Financial Times* (November 15, 1994) described as "a key policy" of the postal ministry; he thus became, in Nakamoto's words, "the man whom bureaucrats love[d] to hate." In 1994 Koizumi caused another stir by calling for the privatization of the postal service. He explained to Nakamoto why he believed the nation should take that step: "What private business can do should be left to the private sector and the government's role should be restricted to a small number of essential functions. . . . If the government continues to do what private businesses can do just as well, the size of the administration will continue to swell. People need to realise that in order to avoid having to continuously raise taxes, it is crucial to reduce the functions of the government's bloated administration."

Koizumi's proposal met with widespread opposition, not least because of the huge role the postal service plays in the lives of Japan's citizenry: unlike those of most other industrialized nations, Japan's postal ministry not only handles mail delivery but also maintains a savings bank (in monetary terms, by far the largest such enterprise in the world) and an insurance company (also the world's largest), and, because of its government status, can offer people better rates than can private banks and insurance providers. Moreover, as Stephanie Strom reported in the *New York Times* (November 18, 1997), "Postmasters [in Japan] think nothing of picking up an old man's passbook on their way to work and dropping off his withdrawal on their way home at night. They run errands for elderly widows, find jobs for customers' children and organize local festivals and events." In addition, although the law forbids such activity, postmasters routinely recruit new members for the LDP. Not surprisingly, the postal unions exert great influence in Japanese elections. Although Koizumi recognized that his proposal had little chance of success—"Most people still think it is not necessary to take such a drastic step," he conceded to Nakamoto—in the following years he continued to press for privatization of the postal ministry.

In 1995 Koizumi campaigned for the presidency of the LDP. He was easily defeated by Ryutaro Hashimoto, who was sworn in as prime minister in January 1996. Koizumi served as minister of health and welfare in two of Hashimoto's cabinets, in 1996 and 1997. In that post he again aroused the ire of many politicians, by advocating that the government launch an anti-smoking campaign. As in the United States, purchases of cigarettes are taxed and thus provide funds for government services. The Japanese Ministry of Finance depends heavily on the money that cigarette taxes generate.

In 1997, having served 25 years in Parliament, Koizumi became eligible for a $2,400 monthly stipend (in addition to his regular salary), but he declined the payment, saying that he would not accept it while the national deficit was so high. The move embarrassed his colleagues in the Diet but won him the admiration of many Japanese. He also refused the honor of having his official portrait painted, thus saving the Ministry of Finance an additional $8,000.

In July 1998 the LDP suffered a humiliating defeat in the upper house of the Diet, and Hashimoto resigned. Koizumi then made another bid for the LDP presidency. This time, in a four-way race, he lost to Keizo Obuchi, the nation's foreign minister, who, according to Stephanie Strom in the *New York Times* (July 16, 1998), gained the support of his colleagues "largely because his turn [had come] on the seniority ladder." The election spurred younger members of Parliament and the LDP to question openly the party's rigid rules of seniority and the practice of holding secret party meetings from which junior members were excluded. "Those who support that system argue that it projects unanimity and strength—something voters and international investors are looking for—and produces the best candidate," Strom wrote. "But others, especially newer members, argue that it is time for party decisions to come out of the shadows. They want deliberations about the next premier to be public and a requirement that each candidate stand up and declare his positions on key issues. . . . This will help guarantee that a candidate will be selected on merit and policy positions, they say, not on friends, connections and seniority."

In April 2000 Keizo Obuchi fell into a stroke-induced coma; he died the following month. He was succeeded by the number-two figure in the LDP, its secretary-general, Yoshiro Mori, who was widely described as an old-school, "backroom" politician. Less than a year later, Mori was "clearly on the way out," as Brian Bremner, Chester Dawson, and Irene M. Kunii wrote for *Business Week* (March 26, 2001). According to those *Business Week* writers and other observers, with Japan mired in a recession, the public had grown increasingly impatient with political corruption and the seeming dearth among Mori and other politicians of ideas for rallying the economy. Meanwhile, after controlling the government almost continuously since 1955, when the party was founded, the LDP appeared to be in danger of losing its leadership position. Koizumi seized the opportunity to try to win the hearts of voters and, by so doing, to show his fellow LDP members that the party's continued primacy required his election as its president. In July 2001, three months after the LDP was to pick its president, the public was to vote in parliamentary elections, the outcome of which would decide the party's fate. The installation of yet another hidebound member of the old guard in the LDP's top post, Koizumi warned, would push voters into the camps of other parties.

Upon declaring his candidacy, on April 11, 2001, Koizumi announced as his campaign slogan "Change the Liberal Democratic Party, change Japan." He was determined, he said, to end the factionalism within the LDP and thus the power wielded by those factions. As evidence of his resolve, in an extraordinarily unusual step for a Japanese politician, he announced at a press conference that he was ending his longtime affiliation with the faction headed by Yoshiro Mori, and he promised not to resume that association after the party elections. As for his plans for Japan, foremost among them was the privatization of the postal savings system, which, by then, held $2.5 trillion in citizens' accounts. He also proposed drastic cuts in government borrowing and spending, including among the latter a halt to costly government bailouts of failing companies. "There will be companies going bankrupt and increased unemployment, but if we are fearful of unemployment, we will never see the recovery of the Japanese economy," he said, as quoted by Stephanie Strom in the *New York Times* (April 12, 2001). "The economy has not recovered because we have not adopted reforms."

Koizumi's chief rival for leadership of the LDP was again Ryutaro Hashimoto, the choice of the LDP's main faction. Although, as prime minister, Hashimoto had been blamed for seriously weakening the Japanese economy, largely by raising consumption and social taxes, and had resigned in disgrace, many observers believed that he had a strong chance of making a comeback. Fully aware that he faced a serious competitor, Koizumi launched a full-scale media campaign to solidify his standing with the Japanese public. In this effort, he made far better use of television than Hashimoto (and just about all of his other political predecessors or contemporaries). As William Schneider pointed out in his *Los Angeles Times* piece, other world leaders—among them the American presidents Ronald Reagan and Bill Clinton, Prime Minister Tony Blair of Great Britain, and Russian president Vladimir Putin—had demonstrated how to use television to great advantage. "The power of these leaders is essentially personal," Schneider explained. "Voters support them, not their party or ideology. They don't need a party or ideology. They have television. Of course, Japan has had the tube for as long as the U.S., but it has also had a powerful political machine that resisted the personalization of politics for decades. In the end, even in Japan, television, which allows direct, personal communication between politicians and voters, won out." She then noted, "Koizumi's greatest skill is his ability to communicate with voters." Indeed, Koizumi succeeded in getting voters excited not only about him but also about parliamentary activities. As Stephanie Strom reported in the *New York Times* (June 5, 2001), "Japanese politicians in general seem uncomfortable and stiff in public settings but Mr. Koizumi thrives in the spotlight. His performances in Parliament are spiked with pithy jokes, wordplay and barbed repartee. . . . During a particularly heated moment in a budget committee debate . . . a record 13.1 percent of households with a television were watching."

On April 24, 2001 the LDP elected Koizumi president by an almost two-to-one ratio. What apparently ensured his victory was a newly instituted system giving greater weight to the presidential choices of the rank-and-file of the LDP chapter in each prefecture. "The new voting system, in which each . . . party chapter received three votes [in the balloting for LDP president] and each Diet member received one, was widely credited with making possible the unprecedented defeat of a candidate of the majority faction," *Facts on File* (April 26, 2001) explained. On April 26, 2001 the LDP members of the House of Representatives elected Koizumi prime minister by a vote of 298 to 155.

Koizumi immediately shattered precedent by appointing among the 17 members of his cabinet 11 politicians who were unaffiliated with any of the LDP's factions. He also named five women to that body—more women than had ever been in a Japanese cabinet—among them, as foreign minister, the popular, outspoken Makiko Tanaka (the daughter of Kakuei Tanaka, Japan's prime minister from July 1972 to December 1974), who thus became the first woman to hold that post in Japan. (Koizumi dismissed Tanaka in January 2002, in response to feuding between her and other foreign-ministry officials.)

In a policy speech to the Diet on May 7, 2001 that was transcribed on *kantei.go.jp*, Koizumi said, "The top priority that I must address is to rebuild our economy and reconstruct our society into one full of pride and confidence. Moreover, Japan must fulfill a constructive role as a member of the global community. In the belief that 'without structural reform there can be no rebirth for Japan,' I am resolved to ceaselessly advance structural reforms, including economic reforms, fiscal reforms, administrative reforms, social reforms and political reforms." He repeated his campaign promise to let insolvent companies fold rather than prop them up with government funds, even though their collapse would increase unemployment and thus create hardships for many citizens. To emphasize the wisdom of that approach, he made use of a parable: "At the beginning of the Meiji era [1868–1912], the Nagaoka Region was in a state of severe poverty. As a gesture of assistance, an offering of 100 sacks of rice was sent [there]. If consumed immediately, this would have been enough to fill the hungry stomachs of the people . . . for a few days. However, the wise leader of the region chose to forgo the immediate satisfaction of feeding his people in favor of selling the food and investing the proceeds in the establishment of a school to educate the people, thereby ensuring a future harvest of thousands and even tens of thousands of sacks of rice." "My promise is not to fear pain, not to flinch from the barriers erected by vested interests and not to be shackled by past experiences," he declared, as quoted in *Facts on File* (May 17, 2001). He also promised greater transparency in policy-making processes and public accounting systems, to bring back "politics of trust." As chairman of the Council for Science and Technology Policy, he said, he intended to work to make Japan "the most advanced IT [information technology] state in the world within five years." To revitalize the nation's cities, he announced the creation of the so-called Urban Rejuvenation Headquarters, which he himself would direct. As part of his commitment to make Japanese society "one that is truly gender equal," he pledged to "take measures aimed at ensuring that there are sufficient day care facilities for all children so that no one has to wait for a day care place, and creating facilities to provide care for children after the end of a school day in all areas where they are needed." Koizumi has also expressed his belief that the Japanese constitution should be changed to allow female children of the emperor as well as male children to ascend to the nation's throne.

In June 2001 the Koizumi administration proposed a cap of 30 trillion yen ($242 billion) on government bonds issued in the next fiscal year and recommended that government spending be redirected from road-building and other such activities to educational programs and IT projects. It also pushed for the privatization of various state-owned enterprises (for example, the Japan National Housing Corp.) in addition to the postal system. With the unemployment rate continuing to rise—it reached a postwar record of 4.9 percent in August—the administration announced that the budget for fiscal year 2002 would be drawn up with the goal of rigorously limiting federal expenditures to items "that truly contribute to the progress of Japan."

In October 2001, acting upon his declaration, in his May 7 speech, that "we must maintain and enhance Japan's friendly relations with its neighbors, including the People's Republic of China [and] the Republic of Korea," among others, Koizumi visited China and then South Korea. Because of Japan's half-century occupation of Korea, beginning in the early 1900s, and its invasion of China in 1937, which left many thousands of Chinese dead, its relations with both of those neighbors had long been strained. Koizumi had fueled Korean and Chinese resentment of Japan when, a few months earlier, he had visited the Yasukuni Shrine, which honors—along with the 2.6 million other Japanese victims of war since the 19th century—several convicted World War II criminals. Koreans and Chinese had been further angered when Koizumi refused to order Japanese schools to discard a recently adopted history textbook that, according to Japan's neighbors, whitewashed Japanese wartime atrocities. During his visit to South Korea, the *BBC News* (October 15, 2001, on-line) reported, Koizumi said, "I sincerely apologise for the pain and sorrow Japan inflicted on the Korean people under Japanese colonial rule."

On October 18, five weeks after the terrorist attacks on the World Trade Center, in New York City, and the Pentagon, in Washington, D.C., the Diet approved legislation that would enable Japan to contribute military assistance to the U.S. effort to combat terrorism. Previously, the nation's constitution (drawn up under the guidance of the American general Douglas MacArthur after the Japanese surrender to the U.S., in 1945, ended World War II) had expressly forbidden the use of Japanese troops for any reason except self-defense. In November 2001 three Japanese warships with several hundred sailors aboard set out for the Indian Ocean, to provide whatever noncombat military support the U.S. military might need. Since September 11 Koizumi has also met twice with President George W. Bush, in Washington, D.C.

By the end of his first year as prime minister, Koizumi's popularity had plummeted. The economy showed no signs of improvement, and conservatives in the LDP had forced Koizumi to compromise on aspects of his reform agenda. His plans to privatize the post office, for example, met with strenuous objections; the final plan allowed for limited competition for mail delivery only. The public grew so disillusioned with Koizumi's seemingly empty promises that some critics began to call him the "NATO" prime minister—"No Action, Talk Only." In July 2002 politicians from the opposition Democratic Party, called for a vote of confidence for Koizumi and his administration. The prime minister easily passed this test, by a vote of 280 to 150, but the fact that it occurred at all was an embarrassment. In September Koizumi reshuffled his cabinet, replacing opponents of a bank rescue plan with ministers more inclined to reform. Many saw the cabinet shake-up as a reassertion of Koizumi's resolve to turn the Japanese economy around as well as an attempt to reclaim the popularity he had enjoyed early in his term.

By that time, however, his approval rating had soared to 70 percent, thanks to an historic summit meeting held a few weeks earlier with North Korea's leader, Kim Jong Il. Although Japan had established diplomatic relations with South Korea in 1965, it had never done so with North Korea. On September 17, 2002 Koizumi and Kim agreed to begin normalizing diplomatic relations. At their meeting Kim admitted that during the late 1970s North Korean agents had kidnapped 11 Japanese nationals, six of whom had died in the intervening years. In response, Koizumi apologized for the suffering Japan had caused the Korean people while occupying Korea during World War II. Though some in the international community criticized Koizumi for softening Japan's stance with regard to North Korea, the prime minister maintained that repairing the relationship between Japan and North Korea "[does] not just benefit the two countries," as Howard K. French quoted him as saying in the *New York Times* (September 18, 2002, online). "It affects peace on the Korean peninsula and all of Northeastern Asia. It also contributes greatly to the peace and stability of South Korea, the United States, Russia, China, other neighboring nations and the international community as a whole."

Koizumi lives in the Kantei, the official residence of his country's prime minister. Although he has reportedly dated many women, he has never remarried and has publicly stated his intention to remain single. —M.H.

Suggested Reading: *Boston Globe* A p1 July 30, 2001, with photo; *Economist* (on-line) Aug. 4, 2001, with photo, p13+ July 13, 2002, p39 July 27, 2002; *Far Eastern Economic Review* p17+ May 2, 2002; *Financial Times* p5 Nov. 15, 1994, with photo; *Fortune* p175+ Sep. 3, 2001; (London) *Guardian* p12 July 31, 2001, with photo; *Los Angeles Times* M p2 Aug. 5, 2001, with photo; *New York Times* D p1 Nov. 18, 1997, A p3 July 24, 1998, with photo, A p4 July 22, 1998, with photo, A p16 Apr. 12, 2001, A p10 Apr. 25, 2001, A p15 May 29, 2001, A p4 June 5, 2001, with photo, A p3 June 26, 2001, with photo, p6 Aug. 1, 2001, p3 Aug. 3, 2001, with photo; *Washington Post* A p24 July 16, 1998, A p16 July 31, 2001

---

Stewart Mark/Retna

## Kournikova, Anna

*June 7, 1981– Tennis player*

*Address: c/o Octagon Worldwide, 1114 Ave. of the Americas, 18th Fl., New York, NY 10036*

Although she has yet to win a singles Grand Slam title, Anna Kournikova is probably the tennis world's most celebrated female athlete. With approximately $10 million in annual earnings from advertising endorsements, the Russian-born Kournikova ranks 58th on the 2001 Forbes worldwide celebrity power list—just behind U.S. secretary of state Colin L. Powell and comfortably ahead of such fellow women's tennis stars as Venus and Serena Williams and Martina Hingis. While some have suggested that Kournikova's celebrity is due largely to her physical beauty and is disproportionate to her athletic ability (at least as manifested thus far), she is without question a talented player, especially in doubles matches. Whether or not she goes on to become one of the game's greats, Kournikova has already succeeded in boosting the popularity of women's tennis.

Anna Kournikova was born in Moscow, in what was then the Soviet Union, on June 7, 1981. Both of her parents have athletic backgrounds: her father, Sergei, was a Greco-Roman wrestling champion and later became a professor at the University for Physical Culture and Sport in Moscow. Her mother, Alla, is a former 400-meter runner. "We were young and we liked the clean, physical life," Kournikova's father told Peter Bodo for *Tennis* (May 2001), "so Anna was in a good environment for sport from the beginning."

Encouraged by her grandparents as well as her parents, Kournikova began playing tennis at age five. Two years later she entered her first tournament and became a member of the Spartak Athletic Club, an organization associated with the Russian tennis player Olga Morozova. "I had dolls, but I was never really into girly stuff," Kournikova recalled to Bodo. "My favorite toys were my stuffed animals, although I didn't give them enough of my time. I would just visit with them for maybe five minutes every morning, and then I was running off to find something more active to do. I had too much energy. I was always hanging around with the boys, but just for the reason that they were the ones like me, running around, playing games. Mostly, I just wanted to play tennis for eight hours a day, watch tennis videos, eat, and fall into bed, dead."

In 1991 Kournikova was "discovered" by Eugene L. Scott, the publisher and editor in chief of *Tennis Week* magazine, while she was participating in a tournament he had organized in Moscow. Scott subsequently discussed her strong points with Paul Theofanous, a talent scout for the International Management Group (IMG), the world's largest sports-management and -marketing firm. "I kind of laughed it off at first," Theofanous told Robin Finn for the *New York Times* (April 23, 1992), "but then I saw her hit at the 1991 Kremlin Cup, and I started hearing from too many other people that this one was one extraordinary talent." Theofanous talked briefly with Kournikova's mother over the phone, and soon afterward the gifted preteen signed a contract with IMG.

A few months later Kournikova, accompanied by her mother, traveled to Bradenton, Florida, where she enrolled in the Bollettieri Tennis Academy, an IMG-owned facility that counts among its alumni such tennis legends as Jim Courier, Andre Agassi, and Monica Seles. Almost immediately, Kournikova was hailed as a rising star. "I've seen them all, but this one actually frightens me," Nick Bollettieri, the academy's head coach, told Finn. "She knows everything—what she wants to do and how she's going to get there. She's not only the youngest real prospect I've ever had, but the best. We've had Andre [Agassi]. We've had Courier. We've had Seles, but I can say without hesitation that when I see how this girl can play, at age 10, I'm shocked." Eight years later, speaking with Frank Deford for *Sports Illustrated* (June 5, 2000), Bollettieri mentioned other characteristics he had observed in Kournikova: "Everything about her said, Here I am! She knows who she is and how to take over. No matter who I was working with—Seles, Agassi, whoever—she would call out, 'Nick, my turn.' She was very impatient. She had to be the center of attention. We had a little weekend campout, and Anna wanted to know why she had to get her own meal, why she couldn't be served her dinner."

From the moment she arrived in Florida, Kournikova was clear about her intention to turn pro. When asked when she planned to do so, she told Finn, "Soon, really soon, the sooner the better." Yet, despite strong showings at a number of youth tournaments and talk of her turning professional at age 12, Kournikova did not make her professional debut until October 1995, after her 14th birthday. (In a 1995 interview Bollettieri suggested that the delay could be attributed to Kournikova's frequent absences from the sports academy—and the resulting lapses in instruction—when she played junior tournaments in Europe or visited relatives in Russia.)

Over the course of the next two years, Kournikova made steady, if unspectacular, headway. By the end of 1996, she had climbed 224 places in the world tennis rankings to occupy the number 57 spot. She reached the fourth round of the 1996 U.S. Open, and in 1997, in her fourth Grand Slam tournament, she advanced to the semifinals at Wimbledon. (Kournikova lost there to Martina Hingis, who went on to win the tournament in straight sets.) Then, in March 1998, at the Lipton Championships in Key Biscayne, Florida, Kournikova turned heads by defeating four top-10 players in a single week: the number two–ranked Lindsay Davenport, Monica Seles (number four), Arantxa Sanchez-Vicario (eight), and Conchita Martinez (nine). Not only tennis fans and commentators but Kournikova herself seemed surprised by that accomplishment: "Even after I lost the first set against [Sanchez-Vicario], I thought, Wow!," she told Carter Coleman for *Women's Sports & Fitness* (June 1998). "This is great, I'm playing! I didn't try to go for winners right away. I kept the ball in play, three, four, five times, and then I went for it when I had a good shot. I proved to everybody that I can play good tennis, a lot of matches in a row." (She was defeated in the finals by Venus Williams.) Later that year, although she failed to capture a singles title, Kournikova defeated both Martina Hingis—then the top-ranking player—and Steffi Graf.

At the 1999 Australian Open, Kournikova teamed up with Hingis as a doubles partner to win her first Grand Slam title. Her other principal athletic accomplishment that year was advancing to the semifinals of the IGA Superthrift Tennis Classic in Oklahoma City. (Kournikova lost to Amanda Coetzer in two sets.) Kournikova reached the semifinals in a number of important tournaments in 2000 and 2001 but was hampered by a string of injuries, including two stress fractures and a torn ankle ligament.

Kournikova had a disappointing year in 2002, losing in the first round of each of the four Grand Slam events—the Australian Open, the French Open (also known as Roland Garros), Wimbledon, and the U.S. Open. In January, at the Australian Open, she suffered a first-round loss to number eight–ranked Justine Henin, but teamed with Hingis to upset top-seeds Lisa Raymond and Rennae Stubbs for the doubles title, her second career Grand Slam title. Playing at the French Open for the first time in two years in May, she was defeated in the first round. At Wimbledon in June, she was a doubles semifinalist with Chanda Rubin and a quarterfinalist in mixed doubles with Jonas Bjorkman; in women's singles she was eliminated after the first round. In August she succumbed in the first round of the U.S. Open; spectators booed her off the court after her poor performance against Angelique Widjaja of Indonesia, which included 40 unforced errors.

Kournikova reached her fourth singles final—and the first in nearly two years—in September 2002 in Shanghai, China, where she fell to top-seeded Anna Smashnova of Israel. Paired with Janet lee, she won the doubles title at that event. As a wild card in the Moscow Open in October, she sprained and partially tore a ligament in her left ankle, forcing her to withdraw from the tournament as well as subsequent competitions. Ranked number eight in the world in women's tennis at the end of 2000, she has since slipped to 36th place.

In May 2002 Kournikova hired as her coach Harold Solomon, who had worked with Jennifer Capriati and helped her make a comeback. "Not one to put up with attitude, Solomon has been trying to strip away the hype, and funnel [Kournikova's] attention into tennis and get her mind right on the big points," Selena Roberts wrote for the *New York Times* (June 25, 2002), pointing out that many tennis insiders believe Kournikova must rearrange her priorities and change her behavior, which has been described as "divalike."

Meanwhile, Kournikova's popularity among youthful male tennis fans surged to levels unprecedented in the sport. At matches, she has regularly been greeted by young men chanting her name or clamoring for an autograph, and her more zealous admirers have even been known to prowl tournament grounds in the hope of finding a keepsake, such as one of her towels. Kournikova's romantic life has been the subject of intense, ongoing scrutiny in the tabloid press, and she is said to be the athlete whose name is most often fed into Internet search engines—a fact cunningly exploited in early 2001 by the so-called Kournikova Virus, which purported to contain pictures of the tennis star and thereby tricked computer operaters into downloading a malicious programming code.

While some of Kournikova's competitors have taken swipes at her because of the publicity she receives, others—particularly older or retired players no longer vying for media attention—have offered a more pragmatic viewpoint. "We have a chance to do what no other women's sport has done, to gain equity with comparable men's sports," the tennis legend Billie Jean King told Frank Deford for *Sports Illustrated* (June 5, 2000). "That's done at the box office. It doesn't bother me at all if some of the guys come out to watch women's tennis because they want to see a beautiful woman. Who could hold that against Anna? Still, it is unfortunate when others with a high skill factor don't win the endorsements. Sure, the good-looking guys get more endorsements, but the difference in men's sports is that the ugly ones get their share, too." That sentiment was echoed by Martina Navratilova, the Czech-born tennis player who won Wimbledon nine times between 1978 and 1990. "You know, she's good for the game," Navratilova told Rachel Alexander for the *Washington Post* (June 28, 2000). "She brings attention. I just wish she'd play better. She's a better player than she's shown."

Kournikova has established a one-woman virtual embassy on the World Wide Web. Her official Web site, *www.kournikova.com*, features a photo archive, her tennis statistics, a schedule of upcoming matches, news items relating to the athlete, a personal journal, and links to Kournikova's advertising sponsors (among them Adidas shoes, Omega watches, Yonex tennis racquets, Berlei sports bras, and the Lycos search engine). It also houses an online store that sells a variety of Kournikova-themed merchandise, including a swimsuit calendar replete with what her Web site describes as "sensational pictures of the Russian taken in Acapulco."

Kournikova's name appeared on *People*'s 50 Most Beautiful People list in 1998; only one other athletes was included. In 2000 she was one of five female tennis players selected for *Forbes*'s Power 100 in Fame and Fortune (she was ranked number 58). The five-foot, eight-inch athlete weighs 123 pounds and is known for her long blond hair. In recent years she has earned $10 million in endorsements annually. In 2001 she released an exercise video, *Basic Elements: My Complete Fitness Guide*, in which she demonstrates a challenging 52-minute workout for experienced athletes. Kournikova lives in Miami, Florida. — P.K.

Suggested Reading: *New York Times* B p13 Apr 23, 1992, with photo; *Sports Illustrated* p94+ June 5, 2001, with photos, p56+ Mar. 30, 1998, with photos; *Sports Illustrated Women* p86+ Oct. 2002, with photos; *Tennis* p30+ May 2001, with photos, p22+ June 1997; *Washington Post* A p1 June 28, 2000; *Women's Sports and Fitness* p98+ June 1998, with photos

---

## Krause, David W.

*Feb. 15, 1950– Paleontologist; anatomist*

*Address: Department of Anatomical Sciences, 100 Nicholls Rd., Stony Brook University, Stony Brook, NY 11794*

In six expeditions to Madagascar, the world's fourth-largest island, David W. Krause has found what he described to Laura Banish for *Newsday* (July 30, 2001) as "an unbelievable abundance of dinosaur, crocodile and bird fossils." Almost as big as Texas, Madagascar lies in the Indian Ocean off the southeastern coast of Africa. Separated from that continent for tens of millions of years, the island is home to lemurs and many other species of animals and plants found nowhere else on Earth, and its sedimentary rocks contain the fossilized remains of many extinct species that are also unique to Madagascar. Supported by the National Geographic Society, the National Science Foundation, and other sources, Krause has sought answers to questions regarding paleontology, evolution, and the geological history of Earth that have fascinated him since his late teens. A member of the faculty of Stony Brook University since 1982, Krause conducted research in the U.S. and Canadian West for nearly two decades before switching his focus to Madagascar, in the early 1990s. He and his multinational teams of scientists have filled in many of the gaps in the island's fossil record from as far back as the Late Cretaceous period, which began about 100 million years ago. Krause has served as an officer of the Society of Vertebrate Paleontology and has participated in the struggle to stop commercial fossil hunting on public lands. He is the founder and director of the Madagascar Ankizy Fund, a nonprofit organization whose goal is to build schools and health clinics in remote parts of Madagascar. He also serves as vice president on the board of trustees of Aiza Biby, a nonprofit organization dedicated to conservation education for young people ages three through 18.

The youngest of six children, David W. Krause was born on February 15, 1950 in Medicine Hat, in southeastern Alberta, Canada, not far from the border with Montana. He grew up 60 miles from Medicine Hat, on a cattle ranch and farm owned and operated by his parents; during his early years their home lacked electricity, indoor plumbing, and a

M. Stewart, courtesy of David W. Krause

*David W. Krause*

telephone. The nearest neighbors (also ranchers) in this sparsely populated area were relatives—his mother's sister and brother were married to his father's brother and sister, respectively. When not in school, Krause was often outdoors, helping with ranch and farm chores; in his few free moments, he enjoyed reading and hunting. He attended first grade at a one-room schoolhouse with only 15 other students (nine of whom were his siblings or cousins), usually getting there by horse and buggy. He completed grades two through nine in a slightly larger school in the nearby town of Hilda. His high school was in Medicine Hat, too far for a commute, so he boarded with another family during the week and returned to the ranch to work on weekends.

Krause's first experience with paleontology occurred when he was 11. Allowed to tag along on an amateur fossil-hunting expedition, he explored badlands on the fringes of his family's ranch. "It was rare for me to be allowed time for such leisure activities . . . ," he told *Current Biography,* "but it was Sunday and it was between calving, roundup, seeding, and harvesting seasons. . . . It was my first exposure to fossils and I was lucky enough to find a tail vertebra of a duck-billed dinosaur." When he enrolled at the University of Alberta at Edmonton, in 1968, Krause anticipated returning to the family business and becoming a cattle rancher when he graduated. An unexpected job as a field research assistant during the summer after his freshman year led him to change his career goal. Under the direction of Richard C. Fox, one of his professors, he worked in and around Dinosaur Provincial Park (now a World Heritage Site), in Alberta. "The thrill of scientific discovery could not be matched by anything I had experienced on the ranch," he told *Current Biography.* With the idea of seeking a career involving paleontology and evolution—despite his parents' skepticism regarding the practicality of his choices—he earned a B.S. degree, in 1971, and an M.S., in 1976, both in zoology, from the University of Alberta. He then did graduate work in geology at the University of Michigan, under the direction of the noted paleontologist Philip D. Gingerich. In 1981 he won the Anna M. Jackson Award from the American Society of Mammalogists, for best student paper. He received his Ph.D. in 1982.

That same year Krause accepted an assistant professorship in the Department of Anatomical Sciences at Stony Brook University (a division of the State University of New York also known as SUNY-Stony Brook), where he has taught courses in such subjects as paleontology, human anatomy, and mammalian evolution. He was promoted to associate professor in 1987 and to full professor in 1993. In 1996 he earned the Stony Brook University School of Medicine's prestigious Aesculapius Award, which recognizes outstanding teaching. Concurrently, from 1987 to 1990, he served as editor of the *Journal of Vertebrate Paleontology.* He was vice president of the Society of Vertebrate Paleontology from 1992 to 1994 and president from 1994 to 1996. The issue of fossil collection by individuals on federal lands was high on Krause's agenda during his presidency. At the behest of commercial fossil hunters, in early 1996 Democratic representative (now U.S. senator) Tim Johnson of South Dakota introduced in Congress the Fossil Preservation Act, which would have permitted any taxpayer or group of taxpayers to excavate for fossils on public lands without a permit and to sell for personal profit whatever they found. Strongly opposed to such amateur excavations, the Society of Vertebrate Paleontology, in collaboration with the East Islip, New York–based Dinosaur Society, mobilized to prevent passage of the bill; toward that end, Krause helped to found the nonprofit organization Save America's Fossils for Everyone (SAFE). "If fossils are simply regarded as curios and items for interior decoration, that's all they'll ever be," he said to Vivien Kellerman for the *New York Times* (November 2, 1997). "But there's much more to fossils. They were once part of real animals. Fossils yield a great deal of information about past life on this planet, information about how extinct animals lived and died, and how they interacted with each other and their environment. That information is fascinating to many people, but can only be revealed if fossils are excavated with extreme care, if data on their geological context are collected, if they are carefully removed from the rock by skilled technicians and if they are studied by trained paleontologists. Each fossil has a story to tell, and if fossils are torn from the earth in haste, sold into private collections and left unstudied, many of the pages of each of those stories will be lost forever." The Fossil Preservation Act did not pass. (New legislation, called the Paleontological Resources Preservation Act, which the Society of Vertebrate Paleontology and SAFE supports, was introduced in the House of Representatives in October 2001.)

From the mid-1970s through the early 1990s, Krause's primary research focused on the evolution of mammals during the Mesozoic era (which extended from approximately 245 million to 65 million years ago and is subdivided into the Triassic, Jurassic, and Cretaceous periods) and the Paleocene epoch of the Cenozoic era (approximately 65 million to 55 million years ago). He led and participated in many field research expeditions, some as far away as Pakistan but most in western areas of the United States and Canada.

In 1993 Krause turned his attention to Madagascar, an island in the Indian Ocean 250 miles from the eastern coast of Africa. (The whole island is one nation, called the Malagasy Republic.) Madagascar "has this incredible and unusual and bizarre flora and fauna," Krause explained to Steve Wick for *Newsday* (April 25, 1999). "Anything that was able to get there, or was left there, evolved in isolation for 85 million years." Like many others, he hoped to find clues to the question of whether Madagascar is geologically and paleontologically most closely related to Africa, India, or South America, the last of which is believed to have been attached to Antarctica 70 million years ago. Another goal was to fill in the huge gaps in the island's fossil record. "[Eighty] to 90 percent of the species of plants and animals that live on Madagascar today are unique to the island," Krause told Keith Griffith for the Stony Brook edition of *Academic Science News & Review* (October 1996); "there are entire groups, like lemurs and tenrecs, that are known from nowhere else in the world. The basal stocks of these groups must have come to Madagascar long ago and evolved and diversified in isolation. The problem is, the fossil record is so poor that no one really has a clue when or how those basal stocks got to the island, or from where."

"My team had more hope than clues in 1993 when I led an expedition to northwestern Madagascar with scientists from five U.S. institutions and Madagascar's University of Antananaviro," Krause wrote for *National Geographic* (August 2000). "We went in search of late Cretaceous dinosaurs and other animals, but all we had were sketchy accounts of fragmentary bones and teeth, first noted by a French infantryman participating in an 1895 invasion." On their first day of searching, in a remote area called the Mahajanga (pronounced "Majoonga") Basin, close to the Mozambique Channel, a graduate student named Christine Wall discovered a tooth that proved to have come from a mammal that lived 70 million years ago. "Our primary goal was to find the first remains of early mammals from that part of the world," Krause told Keith Griffith, "which we did in the first 20 minutes of the expedition! We were tremendously excited—little did we know that we wouldn't find any more evidence of mammals for the rest of that trip." The crew discovered the remains of hundreds of bones and teeth belonging to other classes of animals, however (among them fishes, frogs, turtles, snakes, crocodiles, dinosaurs, and birds), thus, in a single expedition, more than doubling the number of extinct species associated with Madagascar and helping to fill in the spotty fossil record for the island.

The success of the 1993 trip—and the determination to find more mammalian fossils—spurred Krause and his colleagues to return to Madagascar in 1995 and again in 1996, 1998, 1999, and 2001. Several fossil finds from those expeditions have proven to be crucial in testing plate-tectonic theories about the timing and sequence of fragmentation during the Mesozoic era of what was once a single entity—a supercontinent called Gondwana (now divided into the separate landmasses of India, Australia, Antarctica, South America, Africa, and Madagascar). Early in the Cretaceous period (135 million to 120 million years ago), some paleogeographers theorized, while Madagascar and India remained fused and, like the tip of South America, attached to Antarctica, the African continent broke free. (It is generally agreed that Madagascar became a discrete entity 90 million to 80 million years ago. The findings of Krause's expeditions indicate that many modern-era species arrived on Madagascar, via the Mozambique Channel, after it became an island.) The fossilized mammal teeth uncovered in Madagascar matched fossilized teeth found in South America and India, supporting the idea that those land masses were once connected, presumably through Antarctica. Krause told Kelly Campbell for *Newsday* (January 20, 1998) that the teeth belonged to unique mammals called gondwanatheres. "There's no other mammal during the huge interval of time during the age of dinosaurs that have tooth crowns that are so high," he explained to Campbell. "These animals, whatever they are, obviously ate a very abrasive diet." He added: "Until we made that discovery [of the teeth in Madagascar] we had no reason to believe that that group of animals would be found anywhere outside of South America." In India, he said, evidence of their existence was "just one fragmentary tooth. It was really just a small scrap. It was hard to recognize as a mammal tooth. Only when our discovery came to light did they [the Indian scientists] realize it was the same type."

A superb find from the 1995 expedition was that of a 50-foot skeleton of a new species of titanosaurid dinosaur (an herbivore of the sauropod suborder) that was 85 percent complete—by far the most complete skeleton ever unearthed of a member of that family. In the summer of 2001, Krause's Stony Brook colleague Catherine Forster and his graduate student Kristina Curry Rogers, both of whom had accompanied Krause on several digs, announced that they would christen the new species *Rapetosaurus krausei* in his honor. ("Rapeto" is a mythical Malagasy giant.) This sauropod became the seventh extinct species—and first dinosaur—to bear Krause's name.

The 1996 expedition to Madagascar yielded dinosaur fossils never before seen, among them a lower jawbone (found by Catherine Forster) containing long, splayed, cone-shaped front teeth. "To be honest, none of us had a clue what this animal was," Krause told Martha Pickerill for *Time for Kids* (February 9, 2001). "We thought it could be a crocodile or even a flying reptile—a pterosaur." Other unearthed fossilized bones formed 40 percent of the skeleton of a previously unknown species of dinosaur: it was a five-to-six-foot-long, 80-pound carnivore that might have used its spiky teeth to spear fish or insects. The creature was named *Masiakasaurus knopfleri*, using "masiaka," the Malagasy world for "vicious," and honoring Mark Knopfler, the singer/songwriter of the rock band Dire Straits and Krause's favorite rock musician. ("We would frequently find bones of this previously unknown beast in one particular excavation site while playing tapes of Knopfler's music to while away the time," Krause explained to *Current Biography*.)

Another extraordinary discovery of Krause's 1996 expedition was that of the almost-complete and exquisitely preserved skull of a 30-foot-long predatory dinosaur known as *Majungatholus*. "After discovering mostly isolated teeth and a few bone fragments in 1993 and 1995, our search for more complete remains of *Majungatholus* had become an obsession," Krause recalled to *Current Biography*. Over the course of the six expeditions, he and his co-workers have also found fossil remains of an extraordinary diversity of crocodiles—at least seven kinds—including a new species that was named *Simosuchus clarki*. "It lacked the typical crocodilian long snout and conical teeth," Krause wrote for *National Geographic*. "Instead, this pug-nosed croc bore teeth clearly made for vegetation, not flesh, and a snout that looked as if it had run headlong into a tree." The excavations also uncovered many avian fossils, helping to support the theory that birds evolved from dinosaurs. The most significant bird fossil discovered was a partial skeleton of *Rahonavis ostromi*, a creature that lived during the Late Cretaceous period (70 million years ago). Evidence of a hyper-extendable claw, used for killing, on the rear of the foot links the animal to the similarly clawed theropods, bipedal carnivorous dinosaurs that lived at the same time.

In 2001 Krause reported the discovery of a 70-million-year-old marsupial tooth—the oldest marsupial fossil ever found on Gondwana. (Present-day marsupials, or pouched mammals, include opossums and kangaroos.) "Until now, the earliest known remains of a marsupial in the [Southern Hemisphere] dated back to the Paleocene Epoch . . . ," Karen W. Arenson wrote for the *New York Times* (August 1, 2001). "This find suggests that marsupials were in the Southern Hemisphere during the late Cretaceous period." All told, Krause and his teams have identified five times the number of extinct species previously known from the Late Cretaceous period of Madagascar.

The village closest to Krause's excavation sites is Berivotra, which, when he first arrived there, had no running water, no electricity, and no school. Krause and his team were eager to repay the villagers for what he described to Phyllis Lader for the *Smithtown* [New York] *News* (June 15, 2000) as "their many kindnesses—letting us work on the land and helping us with the dinosaur bones." The 1996 team contributed $500 of their own money to hire a teacher, who set up shop in the village church, the only public building in the area, and taught there for two years. Upon their return in 1998, Krause and his colleagues discovered that many of the community's children had not gone to the school, because their parents' traditional religion forbid them to be in a Christian church. Krause immediately made plans to erect a separate school building so that all of the children in the community could attend. He established the non-profit Madagascar Ankizy Fund—"Ankizy" means "children" in Malagasy— and, with the help of his colleagues, began to raise funds from individuals, groups, and children in American elementary and middle schools. For about $10,000, the fund built and staffed Sekoly Riambato—in Malagasy, "The Stony Brook School"—which opened in July 2001. Other funds were used to dig wells and build toilets in Berivotra. In addition, the Ankizy Fund has acquired and donated medical supplies to several other remote communities and sponsored a small group of medical and dental professionals from SUNY-Stony Brook who treated 300 patients during each of the 1999 and 2001 paleontological expeditions. The Madagascar Ankizy Fund (whose Web address is *www.ankizy.org*) continues to raise funds to help impoverished children in remote areas of the island by building schools and clinics.

Krause and his wife, the former Susan Knispel, who is the outreach educator at the Sweetbriar Nature Center, in Smithtown, New York, have been married since 1978. The couple live in St. James, New York, with their teenage sons, Wyatt and Tyler. In his free time Krause coaches the Smithtown Kickers, a youth-league soccer team. — K.S.

Suggested Reading: *Chicago Tribune* II p1+ Jan. 18, 1996; Madagascar Ankizy Fund Web site; *National Geographic* p44+ Aug. 2000, with photos; *New York Times* XIV p3 Nov. 2, 1997, with photo, B p8 Aug. 1, 2001; *San Francisco Chronicle* A p12+ Jan. 19, 2000, with photo; *Time for Kids* p4+ Feb. 9, 2001, with photo

## Kushner, Tony

*July 16, 1956– Playwright; director*

*Address: c/o Steven Barclay Agency, 12 Western Ave., Petaluma, CA 94952*

Speaking of his epic two-part drama, *Angels in America*, the playwright Tony Kushner told Bob Ickes for *New York* (April 12, 1993), "I never thought *Angels* would come to Broadway. Never in my wildest dreams did I think that every producer here would want it. . . . I'm just not a mainstream writer." Broadway producers did indeed clamor to present Kushner's seven-hour work, which concerns homosexuality, AIDS, Mormonism, and Judaism and includes among its dramatis personae an angel and the McCarthy-era right-wing lawyer Roy Cohn (one of its four major homosexual characters). Parts I and II of *Angels in America—Millennium Approaches* and *Perestroika*, respectively—are far from what many people would consider standard Broadway fare. One of the major theater events of the 20th century, *Angels in America*, the first part of which premiered in 1991, was among the few decidedly left-leaning dramas to achieve widespread acclaim and attract mainstream audiences. Kushner, who is Jewish, has impassioned political views and has at times struggled with his homosexuality. He began his career in theater as a director, and *Angels in America* was only the second full-length play he had ever written. In 1993 *Millennium Approaches* won the Pulitzer Prize for drama and Tony Awards for best play, best actor (Ron Liebman), best actor in a featured role (Stephen Spinella), and best director (George C. Wolfe); it also won five Drama Desk Awards and awards from the New York Drama Critics' Circle, the London *Evening Standard*, and the San Francisco Drama Critics, among other honors. *Perestroika* earned three Tony Awards, three Drama Desk Awards, three Outer Critics Circle Awards, and the Los Angeles Drama Critics' Circle Award, among other prizes. Kushner's most recent play, *Homebody/Kabul*, examines Western perceptions of Afghanistan as articulated by a British woman who is killed by the Taliban while she is visiting that country in 1998. Three years in gestation, *Homebody/Kabul* premiered in New York in December 2001, three months after the September 11 attacks on the World Trade Center and the Pentagon. Despite those events, and the subsequent U.S.-led war on the Taliban, all of which profoundly affected the relationship between Afghanistan and the West, Kushner did not revise his play.

The second of the three children of William Kushner and Sylvia Deutscher Kushner, Tony Kushner was born in New York City on July 16, 1956. When he was two his parents moved to Lake Charles, Louisiana, a short distance from the Texas border, where his father had inherited the family lumber business. Members of a well-established Jewish community in Lake Charles, the Kushners attended a synagogue affiliated with Reform Judaism, a branch of the Jewish religion that emphasizes the absolute equality of women in all aspects of Jewish life and the importance of working toward social justice everywhere. "My parents were always adamant that I never take [expletive] from anyone about being Jewish," Kushner told Robert Leiter for the Jewish weekly the *Forward* (February 24, 1995). "If there was ever any sense in the schools that I was being forced to participate in Christian, unconstitutional activities, they would be on the phone in a minute. This was New Deal-liberal, WPA Judaism," he continued, referring to the Work Projects Administration, a Depression-era federal program that supported many theater, art, and literature projects in which Jews were prominent. "And I consider myself very much a descendant of it."

Kushner's parents were both classical musicians, his father a clarinetist and his mother a bassoonist. Before the move to Lake Charles, where his father has conducted the city's symphony orchestra, his mother had played in the New York City Opera orchestra. In Louisiana she diverted her energies into teaching, acting, and homemaking. She and her husband made sure that their two sons and one daughter got a good cultural education. As a youngster Tony was given synopses of Richard Wagner's *Ring Cycle* operas to read, and his parents would reward him and his siblings with a dollar when any of them memorized a poem. As a child Tony saw his mother perform in local productions, among them a mounting of Arthur Miller's drama *Death of a Salesman*, in which she portrayed Linda Loman, the wife of the title character. "I think that's the major reason I went into theater," he told Susan Cheever for the *New York Times* (September 13, 1992). "I saw some of her performances when I was four or five years old and they were so powerful. I had vivid dreams afterwards."

Politics was another of the Kushners' passions; having heated discussions about political issues was a favorite family pastime. As a teenager Kushner read Fred J. Cook's *Nightmare Decade: The Life and Times of Senator Joe McCarthy* (1971), about the senator's campaign in the early 1950s to root out communism in the U.S. " Kushner has traced to that book his fascination with Roy M. Cohn, the chief counsel to the Senate committee that McCarthy headed. In high school, thanks to his wide-ranging knowledge, verbal skills, and dramatic flair, Kushner became the star of the student debate team.

Speaking with Robert Leiter about his political development, Kushner said, "I think I inherited a certain style of thinking and fascination with history and a certain kind of moralism from my father. And I think I inherited a certain passion and anger and outspokenness from my mother. She had, from her childhood in the '30s and '40s in New York, a Communist Party-USA sense of martyrology and sacrificing for the cause."

Courtesy of Steven Barclay Agency

*Tony Kushner*

In 1974 Kushner entered Columbia University, in New York City, where he was exposed to the philosophies of Marxism and feminism and to psychoanalytic theory, all of which have influenced his work and political views. During his college years he saw many theatrical productions, ranging from Broadway musicals to avant-garde Off-Off-Broadway works. In his senior year he met Kimberly T. Flynn, a student at Barnard College (called Columbia's "sister college"), with whom he had many inspiring discussions; he has long considered Flynn, a dramaturge, his closest friend. In writing *Angels in America*, he drew on his experience of ministering to her after she sustained brain damage in a car accident. In an article for the *New York Times* (November 21, 1993) adapted from the print version of *Angels in America: Perestroika*, Kushner described Flynn as his teacher as well as his friend. He also noted, "As both writer and talker, Kimberly employs a rich variety of rhetorical strategies and effects, even while expressing deep emotion. . . . This relationship to language, blended with Jewish and gay versions of the same strategies, is evident in my plays, in the ways my characters speak."

As an undergraduate, in what he described to Cheever as "an error of closeted youth," Kushner began seeing a psychoanalyst in the hope of curing himself of his homosexuality. "I have fairly clear memories of being gay since I was six," Kushner told Richard Stayton for the *Los Angeles Times* (May 13, 1990). "I knew that I felt slightly different than most of the boys I was growing up with. By the time I was 11 there was no doubt. But I was completely in the closet." He did not speak openly to others about his sexual orientation; he kept it from his parents, too, because, despite their progressiveness and liberalism, he knew that they would not accept his homosexuality. Then one day, three years after his college graduation and after treatment by another, gay therapist, he called his mother from a pay phone in New York City's East Village and revealed to her that he was gay. She burst into tears at that news. Soon afterward he sent his parents "that angry letter that you write," as he put it. For months following his disclosure, his mother cried every time he spoke with her. Many years passed before she and Kushner's father came to terms with their son's homosexuality.

After earning a B.A. degree in medieval studies from Columbia, in 1978, Kushner enrolled at New York University, also in New York City. He studied stage direction rather than playwriting, because, as he admitted to Richard Christiansen for the *Chicago Tribune* (December 26, 1993), "I was afraid I couldn't write the kind of plays I admire." Among his favorites were works by William Shakespeare, Bertolt Brecht, Samuel Beckett, and Johann Wolfgang Goethe as well as the contemporary British writers Caryl Churchill and David Hare. Concurrently, for six years beginning in 1979, Kushner worked as a switchboard operator at a New York City hotel. He still had that job when, after he completed his master of fine arts degree, in 1984, he started writing what became his first play, *A Bright Room Called Day*. A preliminary version of *Angels in America: Millennium Approaches*, *A Bright Room Called Day* is a political drama that points up similarities between the United States in 1990—two years into the presidency of George Herbert Walker Bush, who succeeded the two-term president Ronald Reagan—to Germany in 1932–

33, when the Weimar Republic was coming to an end and Nazism was taking hold. The plot involves a present-day graduate student who visits Berlin, where—magically—she watches a group of artists and liberals in the days before the collapse of the Weimar Republic. *A Bright Room Called Day* was produced at the Joseph Papp Public Theater, in New York City, in 1991. Directed by Michael Greif, it received mostly negative reviews, with critics complaining that its political point was unoriginal and overstated.

Earlier, however, a 1985 workshop production of the play had attracted the attention of Oskar Eustis, at that time the artistic director of the Eureka Theater Company, in San Francisco, California. Eustis directed and produced a successful mounting of *A Bright Room Called Day* at the Eureka in the fall of 1987. He then commissioned Kushner to write a new play for the theater, in part so that they could jointly apply for a National Endowment for the Arts (NEA) grant. Acting upon Eustis's request that he write a short play with songs in it, that year Kushner began working from a poem about the paradoxes of Mormonism that he had written earlier, while on a directing fellowship at the St. Louis Repertory Theater, in Missouri, in 1985–86. Commenting on the play's unlikely genesis, Kushner told Bruce Weber for the *New York Times Magazine* (April 28, 1993), "All I knew was that I wanted to write a play about gay men, Mormons, and Roy Cohn." Kushner finished his draft, behind schedule, in 1988. It was 240 pages long and did not come to a conventional resolution; rather, it ended with an angel bursting through the ceiling of a hospital room where a man lay dying of AIDS. Despite Eustis and Kushner's fears that they would never win NEA support for the play because of its politically left-wing viewpoint and its themes of homosexuality and religion, they were awarded a $57,000 grant ($10,000 of which went to Kushner). With this money, along with a $30,000 Whiting Writers' Award, which he won in 1990, Kushner earned his living as a playwright for the first time. Later, joking about the unwieldy length of *Angels*, he told Christiansen, "I wanted to give the taxpayers their money's worth."

In its long process of development, *Angels* went through numerous readings and revisions and a workshop production with an $80,000 budget at the Mark Taper Forum, in Los Angeles, in 1990. The following summer the Eureka put a lot of pressure on Kushner to put the finishing touches on the script, a task that became far more difficult for him after his mother died of cancer, in August 1991. As a break from his work on *Angels*, Kushner wrote a loose adaptation of *The Illusion*, by the 17th-century French playwright Pierre Corneille, completing the script in only 10 days. In reviews for the *Boston Globe* of productions of *The Illusion* mounted five years apart, Richard Dyer (February 17, 1995) described Kushner's adaptation as "brilliant" and Ryan McKittrick (May 19, 2000) characterized it as "spellbinding"; Dolores Whiskeyman, in the *Washington Post* (June 29, 2001), wrote that Kushner's "witty, poetic script achieves the heightened reality of fable."

The official premiere of *Angels in America: Millennium Approaches*, at the Eureka in 1991, was a great success, despite the collapse of the scenery during several performances. "Angry, funny, disturbing and deeply moving," Steven Winn wrote for the *San Francisco Chronicle* (December 29, 1991), "*Angels in America* was the single most exhilarating theatrical experience of the year. Audiences who filled the Eureka for the regrettably short run knew they were in the presence of something rare—a new American masterpiece in the making." In 1992 Declan Donnellan, from England's Royal National Theatre, who had seen the workshop presentation of *Millennium Approaches* at the Mark Taper Forum, staged the play in London. Echoing the words of Steven Winn, Nicholas De Jongh wrote in a review for the London *Evening Standard* (January 24, 1992), "Something rare, dangerous and harrowing has erupted upon the London stage. . . . *Angels in America* is like a roman candle hurled into a drawing room. For three hours and 40 minutes the air is full of its particular incandescence, a mingling of horrors and the blackest shade of humour."

Eager to have it seen by the largest audience possible, Kushner sought a producer for a Broadway mounting of the play. One or more of the 11 people who agreed to produce it tried to persuade him to drop the play's subtitle ("A Gay Fantasia on National Themes"), but Kushner refused. He also stipulated that cheaper tickets be made available for those of lesser means, the lowest being $7.50 for the Wednesday matinee.

*Angels in America* revolves around Louis and his lover, Prior, who has AIDS. The other central characters are Joe and Harper, a devout Mormon couple who live in Salt Lake City, Utah. Joe works for Roy Cohn, who, when the play's action takes place, is a Reagan-era power broker in Washington, D.C. Joe eventually confesses to Harper that he is gay and begins an affair with Louis, who has left Prior because he is unable to deal with Prior's illness. Harper becomes addicted to Valium and is plagued by delusions of being in Antarctica. Roy Cohn, meanwhile, contracts AIDS but vehemently denies his homosexuality. *Millennium Approaches* ends with an angel announcing to Prior that Prior is a prophet. *Perestroika* continues the surprising interweaving of the characters' lives. Joe's mother befriends Prior; Prior's ex-lover turns out to be Cohn's nurse. Other characters include the ghost of Ethel Rosenberg; an old Bolshevik; and an elderly rabbi (portrayed by a young actress). The setting jumps back and forth, from Joe and Harper's average, middle-class home, to the men's room in a federal courthouse, to the Antarctica of Harper's visions, among other places. Sometimes, scenes in different settings take place on stage simultaneously. In the *New York Times* (March 5, 1992), the critic Frank Rich wrote, "Mr. Kushner has created an original theatrical world of his own, poetic and churning, that once entered by an open-minded viewer of any political or sexual persuasion, simply cannot be escaped."

The great success of *Angels* turned Kushner into an overnight celebrity—he even posed for a Gap clothing ad—but he soon became eager to get back to business as usual. "I don't want to be a poo-bah," he told Christiansen. "I don't want to make a life out of being a celebrity in what is, after all, the very private and isolated field of writing." Kushner's next play was the 80-minute *Slavs! (Thinking About the Longstanding Problems of Virtue and Happiness)*, which was created out of four scenes that had been cut from *Perestroika* in its very early stages. Its characters include the last Bolshevik (a character from *Angels*) as well as a bevy of Soviet bureaucrats who assess the future and the past as Mikhail Gorbachev, the last president to lead the Soviet Union before its collapse, comes to power. Other main characters include a lesbian who guards the preserved brains of Russia's great past leaders (played by Marisa Tomei in a 1994 production at the New York Theater Workshop) and a little Siberian girl who dies of cancer, a result of having lived too close to a nuclear-waste dump. The play was commissioned by the annual Humana Festival for New American Plays at the Actors Theater of Louisville, in Kentucky, where it premiered early in 1994. A critic for the *New York Times* (April 4, 1994) called it an "extremely funny intellectual vaudeville."

In about 1993 the Hartford Stage Company, knowing of Kushner's interest in classic Yiddish plays, invited him to create an adaptation of *The Dybbuk: Between Two Worlds*, written by S. Ansky in 1914. Ansky was an ethnographer who gathered traditional folktales in *shtetyls*—villages populated by Jews—in the Ukraine from 1911 to 1914; *The Dybbuk* was the first play to depict this way of life. It tells the story of Khonen, a young rabbinical student who dies of a broken heart when the woman he loves marries another man. His dybbuk—spirit—returns from the dead and takes possession of her body, and the head rabbi is summoned to exorcise it. When the Hartford Stage Company approached him, Kushner had never seen the play, which is perhaps the best-known and most popular work of Yiddish theater. At first he found some of the play's language and its references to obscure Hasidic Jewish doctrine cumbersome, but after doing further research, he "began to fall more in love with the play," as he told *New York* (November 10, 1997), "and paradoxically, the more I fell in love with it, the freer I felt to change it." Kushner's version, reworked from the original Yiddish with the help of a translator, Joachim Neugroschel, retains the central story while updating the language and emphasizing the theme of religious doubt. Kushner also added elements that foreshadow the Holocaust, which led to the extinction of the way of life portrayed in *The Dybbuk*. Kushner's adaptation was produced in Hartford in 1995 and in New York, at the Joseph Papp Public Theater, in 1997. In a lukewarm review of the production for the *New York Times* (November 17, 1997), Ben Brantley conceded that "Kushner and Neugroschel have imbued much of their adaptation's language with an exquisite sense of poetry."

After *The Dybbuk*, Kushner wrote essays for various publications, including the *Nation*, made lecture circuits of college campuses and elsewhere, and worked on other adaptations, including ones of Goethe's *Stella* and Brecht's *The Good Person of Setzuan*. In 2000 he published a collection of his plays, *Death and Taxes: Hydriotaphia and Other Plays*. Kushner had been writing a play about Afghanistan, entitled *Homebody/Kabul*, for several years and had recently completed it when terrorists attacked New York City and Washington, D.C., on September 11, 2001. An avid Socialist, Kushner had been interested in Afghanistan ever since the Soviet Union invaded that country in 1980. "I'd always been moved and disturbed," he told Peter Marks for the *New York Times* (November 25, 2001), "both because of what the Soviet Union did there, and then there was the American complicity in arming the mujahedeen [Muslim soldiers] and leading to a decade of slaughter." *Homebody/Kabul* was scheduled to premiere in December 2001, and Kushner faced a tough choice in deciding whether or not to proceed with his plans. He knew that in the wake of the September 11 tragedy, the play might scour some raw wounds. For example, with uncanny prescience, Kushner had one character in it predict that the Taliban would be coming to New York.

Kushner decided to present the play as planned, and it opened at the New York Theater Workshop, in New York City, on December 19, 2001. The four-hour, three-act play begins with a monologue presented by an Englishwoman, known as the Homebody, who discusses her encounter with a disfigured Afghani shopkeeper as well as her troubled relationships with her husband, Milton Ceiling, and her daughter, Priscilla. The second act finds Milton and Priscilla in Kabul, Afghanistan, investigating the Homebody's disappearance. Priscilla, noting inconsistencies in the official reports of her mother's death, decides to search for her. She is aided by a Tajik poet and a young Afghan obsessed with Frank Sinatra, who tells her that her mother is still alive. During her search Priscilla witnesses the desperately poor conditions in which many Afghans live, and her father falls into a drug-induced decline. Kushner told Michael Phillips for the *Los Angeles Times* (September 22, 2001, on-line), "A certain misinterpretation of Islam may give some of these [terrorists] the courage to do what they do, but they're not doing it because they're Muslim. They're doing it because they come from a part of the world where life is so desperate, they quite literally feel they have nothing to lose, or at least they know people who have nothing to lose."

In a critique of *Homebody/Kabul* for the *New Republic* (March 18, 2002), Robert Brustein wrote, "The destruction of the World Trade Center and America's subsequent pursuit of the Taliban and Al Qaeda has radically altered our consciousness about that country in a way that no prophet could have possibly foreseen. As a result, *Homebody/Kabul* . . . is a schizophrenic entity, at the same time relevant to the point of prescience and woefully out-of-date." In the *Christian Science Monitor* (December 28, 2001), Iris Fanger wrote, "If the aim of theater is to incite emotions and stir discussion, Kushner has succeeded. However, it's less certain that he's made up his mind as to his intentions. Kushner has created a dream play in which characters appear never to return, daily objects take on ominous significance, and dialogue conjures up illusions as often as the truth." Charles Isherwood wrote for *Variety* (December 24, 2001), "Merely by putting on a single stage, however messily or, occasionally, polemically, the friction between the cultures of Afghanistan and the industrialized West, Kushner's play is vividly illustrating the point at the heart of his play: For better or, all too often, for worse, these seemingly disparate worlds have long been and always will be connected by infinitely complicated networks of cultural, political and human interaction. The suffering of one cannot be—must not be—separated from the suffering of the other. To pretend otherwise is only to sow more pain, and reap more pain."

Kushner's children's book, *Brundibar,* illustrated by Maurice Sendak, was published in 2002. Since 1997 Kushner has been planning to stage *Henry Box Brown*, his dramatization of the real-life story of a black American slave who mailed himself to freedom and ended up in England, where he urged British textile workers against using cotton picked by slaves. *Angels in America* is scheduled to be made into a six-part miniseries for HBO, starring Al Pacino, Meryl Streep, and Emma Thompson. The playwright's other current projects include writing the text for a musical, "Caroline or Change," set in Louisiana in 1963; the composer Jeanine Tesori is writing the score. He is also rewriting *Homebody/Kabul* for future performances.

Kushner has established an acting scholarship at New York University that bears the name of his mother. According to Patrick Pacheco, writing for the *Los Angeles Times* (July 31, 1994), his mother's death was "the most emotionally wrenching experience of his life." Speaking of her death and those of some of his friends—among them the actress Ellen McLaughlin, whom Kushner had envisioned as the angel in *Angels in America* but who died before its debut—Kushner told Pacheco, "If you know that life is basically going to be horrendously difficult, at best, and all but unlivable at worst, or possibly even unlivable, do you go on? And the choice to go on is the only thing that I think can be called hope. Because if hope isn't forced to encounter the worst possibility, then it's a lie." — P.G.H.

Suggested Reading: *Forward* p1+ Feb. 24, 1995, with photo; *Los Angeles Times* p45 May 13, 1990, with photo, p3 July 31, 1994, with photos; *Mother Jones* p59+ July/Aug. 1995, with photo; *New York* p42+ Apr. 12, 1993, with photo; *New York Times* II p7 Sep. 13, 1992, with photo, II p19+ Nov. 21, 1993, with photos, II p1+ Nov. 25, 2001, with photo; *New Yorker* p59+ Nov. 30, 1992; *Vanity Fair* p72+ Mar. 1993, with photo; *Vogue* p158+ Nov. 1992, with photo; Vorlicky, Robert, ed. *Tony Kushner in Conversation*, 1998

Selected Plays: *Angels in America: Millennium Approaches*, 1993; *Illusion*, 1994; *A Bright Room Called Day*, 1995; *Angels in America: A Gay Fantasia on National Themes*, 1995; *The Dybbuk and Other Tales of the Supernatural* (with Joachim Neugroschel), 1997; *Death & Taxes: Hydriotaphia, and Other Plays*, 2000; *Homebody/Kabul*, 2002

Selected Books: fiction—*Brundibar*, 2002; nonfiction—*Thinking about the Longstanding Problems of Virtue and Happiness: Essays, a Play, Two Poems, and a Prayer*, 1995

---

## La India

*Mar. 9, 1969– Salsa singer*

*Address: c/o RMM Records, 568 Broadway, Suite 806, New York, NY 10012*

Known in the Latin music world as the "Princess of Salsa" (in deference to the "Queen of Salsa," Celia Cruz), the singer La India has helped to transform salsa from a genre that, in the United States, attracted primarily Hispanic-Americans past their youth to one that is also popular among young people of many different backgrounds. A major reason for her success is her extraordinarily powerful soprano voice—"the world's most magnificent pop voice since Fafá De Belém of Brazil," as Tom Smucker described it in the *Village Voice* (February 2, 2000, on-line); La India's voice, he wrote, combines "the earnestness of Carole King, the skill and depth of Aretha Franklin, the breadth of Linda Ronstadt, the power of Janis Joplin, the energy of Celia Cruz, and the strength of La Lupe." In collaboration with some of the most influential figures in Latin music, among them Eddie Palmieri, Tito Puente, and Marc Anthony, La India has released four albums of salsa music and has earned two Grammy Award nominations. Her songs offer support and hope for women who have been emotionally abused or are having difficulties in relationships. "Beyond her raw vocal talent, India's appeal is her style," Alisa Valdes wrote for the *Boston Globe* (August 22, 1995, on-line). "With her no-nonsense lyrics about not needing men, being disappointed by men, finding men stupid and insolent, India represents a new generation of Latina women. She sings anthems many Latinas have been longing to sing for centuries."

Yael/Retna Ltd.

*La India*

Often referred to simply as India, La India was born Linda Viera Caballero on March 9, 1969 in Rio Piedras, Puerto Rico. She was nicknamed India by one of her grandmothers, who thought she looked Indian. When La India was an infant, her family moved to the borough of the Bronx, in New York City, where she grew up. As a native of Puerto Rico who is also a New Yorker, she is part of a group known informally as Nuyoricans. From a very young age, La India enjoyed singing. "I always sang at home and whenever I did it in front of people, despite being a bit shy, I never felt embarrassed," she was quoted as saying on *Music of Puerto Rico* (on-line). When La India was 10, her parents enrolled her in opera lessons, but she soon lost interest, after realizing that no one she knew listened to opera on the radio. As she explained to Marla Friedler for *Salsaweb* (on-line), "I used to say in my mind, 'I don't want to sound like this. The radio doesn't sound like that. I don't hear anybody singing opera style on the radio. So, you know, I don't think this is gonna be my ticket to fame.' So I stopped the school immediately." At the age of 14, La India began singing backup for the Latin hip-hop group TKA. "I loved singing rock-and-roll, jazz, anything on radio, anything commercial," she told Peter Watrous for the *New York Times* (June 6, 1994). "I was able to do anything, but I didn't know what direction to go in." Although she modeled a little as a teenager, her heart remained set on music. At 18 she recorded for Jellybean Records, in English, her debut single, the pop-style "Dancing in the Fire." "I always loved Latin music, but half of the time I was fighting with my parents about it," she told Marla Fiedler. "I wanted them to give English pop hits a chance, too. They would always play salsa, and I'd be like 'But, Mom, we want to hear disco. Let us listen to Gloria Gaynor's 'I Will Survive.'"

In 1990 La India married the disc jockey and producer Little Louie Vega, who encouraged her to build her career. Vega co-wrote and co-produced many of the songs on her debut album, *Breaking Night,* which was released in the same year on the Warner Bros. label. Offering hip-hop-influenced dance-pop that included elements of world music and jazz fusion, the record "sound[ed] confused at times," according to Ron Wynn in *All Music Guide* (on-line). "It confused audiences and the record company as well," Wynn added. At around this time Ralph Mercado of RMM Records took La India out to dinner and gave her some pointed advice. "He told me that he felt that females in salsa were going nowhere," she recalled to Marla Friedler. "It was dead. There was nobody after Celia Cruz. Everybody wanted to sound like her. There was no new activity. He was upset about it. He spoke with a lot of seriousness. 'You can spend your life making English music or come to Latin music and get noticed.'" His words struck a chord, because La India had begun to feel uneasy in the English-language pop world. "Everybody kept confronting me about my Latin roots," she told Peter Watrous, "and I'd say, 'Right now I'm having a great time singing and I'm comfortable.' But I felt pressure to follow in Madonna's footsteps, and I didn't want to base my career on sex. So I began to change how I saw myself."

La India spent a year writing material for an English-language album for Marc Anthony. Then she signed with RMM records and, in 1992, released the salsa record *Llego La India,* made with the noted producer and pianist Eddie Palmieri. *Llego La India* (La India Has Arrived) was widely hailed as one of the best salsa albums of the year. After touring with Palmieri to promote *Llego La India,* she made her second album, *Dicen Que Soy* (1994; They Say That I Am). Her most commercially successful disk, it went triple platinum (selling three million copies), became a Top 10 hit in the U.S. and Puerto Rico, and spent several months on the *Billboard* Latin Top 50 albums chart. Produced by Sergio George, it features the song "Vivir Lo Nuestro" (To Live with Ours), a duet sung with Marc Anthony. Also in 1994 La India and Little Louie Vega released the EP *Love and Happiness,* a collection of dance music based partly on the Santeriá chants that are part of the foundation of Afro-Cuban music.

In her 1996 album, *Jazzin',* La India expanded her musical horizons by recording such classic pop standards as "Love for Sale" and "Going Out of My Head" in addition to salsa music. The record was produced by Tito Puente and features Puente's Latin Jazz Ensemble as well as the Count Basie Orchestra. That same year La India released *Mega Mix,* which includes several of her songs as remixed by Little Louie Vega and Kenny "Dope" Gonzalez. Describing a concert that La India gave the next year, Alisa Valdes—referring to the mixture of English and Spanish spoken by many Puerto Rican immigrants to the U.S. mainland—wrote that the singer was reaching "a hip, young generation of Spanglish-speaking, bicultural Latinos. This duality is reflected in her music, which manages to capture the essence and energy of East Coast hip-hop while retaining and paying homage to traditional salsa."

La India's next album, *Sobre El Fuego* (1997; Through the Fire), includes "La Voz De La Experiencia" (The Voice of Experience), a duet with Celia Cruz. "Sobre El Fuego," a hit single, was nominated for a Grammy Award for best Latin tropical performance. "For so many years I felt like I was putting out the best music I could and I never got nominated before and then all of a sudden this is just a big surprise to me," La India told Marla Friedler. "I never make music for nominations because if you do that, most of the time you're going to be let down. I've known that from the start."

After attending a La India concert in 1997, the *New York Times* (December 31, 1997) music critic Jon Pareles wrote, "She was singing for women who had been deceived and betrayed, with tough, unforgiving songs that insisted she wasn't going to give any man the satisfaction of seeing her suffer. . . . And whether she was singing about love or faith, she worked her way toward improvisatory ecstasy." Pareles also observed, "Her singing has not left her dance-pop experience completely behind. Along with the clarion phrases of traditional salsa, she unleashes the gospelly swoops and growls of dance-music divas." India's next record, *Sola* (1999), was nominated for a Grammy Award for best salsa performance. "The fact that India doesn't shake things up much at all is actually a benefit," Terry Jenkins wrote of *Sola* for *All Music Guide* (on-line); "her rich voice and percolating, infectious music prove that 'traditional' doesn't mean 'conventional.'" Tom Smucker, writing for the *Village Voice* (February 2, 2000, on-line), agreed, calling *Sola* "the most satisfying pop CD of [the year]." La India's "greatest hits" album, *The Best . . .*, was released in 2001.

The full-figured La India has long, curly black hair; she often appears on stage wearing tight-fitting outfits and holding her trademark cigar. In a *New York Times* (July 13, 1999) review of a La India concert, Ben Ratliff wrote, "Everything about her is hard work and optimism." La India is the national spokesperson for the Grammy's Concert Series for Young People; she also serves as a panelist for the Grammy in the Schools Careers in Music program, in which capacity she visits high schools nationwide and talks to students about career opportunities in the music industry. She is also an advocate for various causes related to health and social issues and is known for propounding the importance of a positive attitude and self-respect. "My dream is about love," she told Marla Friedler, "everybody loving each other. But, before you can love somebody else, you have to love yourself. You have to deal with yourself. Each day is a new day and a new chance to take a step forward. When you take those steps, it is good to know that God is by your side." — G.O.

Suggested Reading: *Boston Globe* (on-line) Aug. 22, 1995, with photo; *New York Times* C p11+ June 6, 1994, with photo, II p6 Aug. 11, 1996, p10 Dec. 31, 1997; *SalsaWeb* (on-line), with photo; *Village Voice* (on-line) Feb. 2, 2000, with photo

Selected Albums: *Breaking Night*, 1990; *Llego La India*, 1992; *Dicen Que Soy*, 1994; *Jazzin'*, 1996; *Sobre El Fuego*, 1997; *Sola*, 1999; *Best Of . . .*, 2001

---

Michael Dwyer/AP

## Law, Ty

*Feb. 10, 1974– Football player*

*Address: New England Patriots, 60 Washington St., Foxboro, MA 02035-1388*

"Ty Law is a gambler. You can tell he studies people. If he gets a chance, if he reads a pattern, especially an out route, he'll just sit out there and make some plays." The former Pittsburgh Steelers' wide-receiver coach Dave Culley made that observation about the ace New England Patriots cornerback in a conversation with Gerry Dulac for the Pittsburgh *Post-Gazette* (December 5, 1998, on-line). A star in both football and basketball in high school, Law was in his eighth season with the Patriots in 2002, having played with them since he began his professional career. As of October 2002 he was the all-time Patriots leader in interception returns for touchdowns, having made five. One example of Law in top form was his performance during Super Bowl XXXVI, held on February 3, 2002, when the Patriots beat the St. Louis Rams, 20–17. In the second quarter Law intercepted a pass from the Rams quarterback Marshall Faulk intended for Isaac Bruce and ran with it for 47 yards, scoring the first Patriots touchdown of the night. Although he faced one of the most potent offenses in the National Football League (NFL), Law made seven tackles over the course of the game. "They say [the Rams are] the best track team in the National Football League," Law said later, as quoted by the Associated Press (February 3, 2002, on-line), "but I never saw anybody win a 100-yard dash with someone standing in front of them."

The son of Raymond and Diane Law, the cornerback was born Tajuan Law on February 10, 1974 in the town of Aliquippa, in western Pennsylvania, a few miles from the West Virginia border. He attended Aliquippa High School, where he was twice named most valuable player (MVP) on the school's football team and earned that honor once as a member of its basketball team. In addition, both *Parade* magazine and Tom Lemming's *Prep Football Report* named him a First-Team All-American football player. As a high-school senior, Law played five positions—tailback, cornerback, safety, wide receiver, and return specialist—while helping to lead his team to the Class AA state title. That year he averaged 22.1 yards on 23 receptions, 10.1 yards on 45 rushes, and 21.1 yards per punt return. He also notched 71 tackles and picked off eight passes. "I don't know where I'd be today, what kind of football player I'd be, if I didn't play for the Aliquippa Quips," Law told Gerry Dulac. "That made me the type of guy that I am, the competitiveness, the expectations from everyone in the city. They expected me to come out there and play well. That's just how it is."

Law attended the University of Michigan at Ann Arbor, where he studied sports management and communications. As a freshman member of the campus football team, the Wolverines, he played in every game and started the final six games of the season as weakside cornerback. That year he had 49 tackles, 37 of them solos. During his sophomore year Law was named First-Team Sophomore All-American; he led the Wolverines with six interceptions and finished fourth on the team in number of tackles, with 57, 47 of them solo. In one game that season, he made two interceptions against Ohio State, one in the end zone and the other at the five-yard line, both of which stopped touchdown drives. His achievements earned him recognition as national player of the week by the *Sporting News* and *Sports Illustrated*, as well as Big Ten Conference defensive player of the week. In his third year he earned First-Team All-American honors from the Walter Camp Football Foundation and *Football News*. That year he made 58 tackles, including 45 solos, as well as two interceptions.

Law left college before earning a degree. He was drafted by the New England Patriots in the first round (23d overall) of the 1995 draft and signed by the team on July 20, 1995. In his rookie season he started seven games and played in 14. He missed two games due to a hip-flexor injury (such injuries involve a major hip muscle) but nevertheless finished the year ranked 10th on the team in total tackles, with 47 (40 solo), and made his first sack of a quarterback. In addition, he defended nine passes and made an interception in each of three consecutive games. His debut as a starter came on October 1, 1995, as a nickel back in a game against the Atlanta Falcons. Despite Law's contributions, the Patriots floundered that year and finished with a record of six wins and 10 losses. The following season Law started the first nine games at left cornerback. In the season opener he made five solo tackles against the Miami Dolphins. He missed three games and four starts due to a knee injury; after his return he succeeded in compiling a total of 62 tackles, good enough to be ranked seventh best on the team; with his 56 solo tackles, he ranked third in that category among Patriots. In a game against the New York Jets on December 8, 1996, Law ran an interception for a touchdown for the first time in his professional career. The Patriots finished the regular season with 11 wins and five losses and then faced off against the Pittsburgh Steelers in the divisional play-offs. Law made two tackles in that game, which the Patriots won, 28–3. In the American Football Conference (AFC) play-offs, the Patriots defeated the Jacksonville Jaguars 20–6. Law made three tackles in the play-offs and another three in Super Bowl XXXI against the Green Bay Packers, which the Patriots lost, 25–21.

In 1997 the Patriots continued their winning ways, compiling a record of 10–6. On September 21, 1997 Law made the first fumble recovery of his professional career, in a contest with the Chicago Bears. He set career highs that season with 77 tackles (70 of them solo) and 11 passes defensed. In addition, he made three interceptions. The Patriots once again made it to the play-offs, where they defeated the Miami Dolphins 17–3 in the AFC Wild Card game; in the divisional play-offs they were defeated by the Pittsburgh Steelers 7–6. In the 1998 season Law played 16 games and made 70 tackles (60 of them solo) with a career-high 27 passes defensed, including nine interceptions returned, for a total of 133 yards. Although the Patriots were among the NFL teams that allowed the most passing yards and most touchdowns that season, they also intercepted more passes than almost any other team in the NFL. "It's deceiving because we feel like we've played better than what our stats indicate," Law told Dulac. "A lot of teams are throwing more on us because they can't run on us, so that's why our pass defense is not rated where it should be, talent-wise. Nobody can run on us, so everybody has to throw the ball." The Patriots finished with a record of 9–7, good enough for a third straight play-off appearance. However, they were unable to make it past the first round, suffering defeat by the Jacksonville Jaguars, 25–10.

During the off-season that year, Law signed a seven-year contract extension that could potentially total $50 million. That deal and his $14.2 million signing bonus were the largest in Patriots history. Before the start of the 1999 season, Law's teammates voted him defensive co-captain. At the end of the season, Patriots defense finished eighth overall and seventh in defense against passing plays, thus becoming the highest-rated defensive squad on a Patriots team since 1988. Law started the first 13 games of 1999 at left cornerback before breaking a bone in his right hand in a game against Dallas. He managed to play the following week against the Indianapolis Colts but missed the final two games of the season. He finished with 59 tackles (50 solo) and 10 passes defensed, including two interceptions. Over the course of the season, Law had his third career interception returned for a touchdown, setting a new Patriots record. "When I retire, five years later I want to be inducted into the Hall of Fame," Law declared, according to a writer for the *Washington Post* (August 21, 1999). The Patriots finished the 1999 season with a record of eight wins and eight losses and did not make the play-offs.

In the 2000 season Law started 15 games at cornerback; he ranked second among defensive backs and sixth on the Patriots defensive squad with 74 tackles, 63 of them solo. He had 11 passes defended and two interceptions. He ended the season on a sour note: on December 20 he was suspended from the team (and thus prevented from participating in the season's final game) after being caught on the Canadian border with the illegal drug Ecstasy. In 2000 the Patriots won only five games and lost 11. A writer for the *Sporting News* (June 25, 2001) offered an explanation for their poor showing: "Two years ago [Law] was a top cover man and an interception machine. He signed a big contract extension and hasn't been the same. Law was hurt, in part by a scheme that stresses zones and disguised coverages. He's best playing press coverage at the line and going one-on-one all over the field." In order to improve, according to the *Sporting News* writer, the Patriots had to restore Law's level of production. Although Law's statistics in 2001 resembled those of his 2000 season, the Patriots did much better overall. Law totaled 70 tackles (61 solo) and nine passes defensed, including three interceptions for 91 yards and two touchdowns. The Patriots lost three of their first four games that season and then won the last six games, ending in a tie for first place in the AFC East division. Considered the underdogs in the first round of the play-offs, the Patriots secured a dramatic 16–13 overtime victory against the Oakland Raiders. In that game Law racked up 10 tackles. Prior to the next play-off game, against the heavily favored Pittsburgh Steelers, Law said, as quoted by a reporter for the *Pittsburgh Tribune-Review* (January 23, 2002), that the Steelers were acting too confident and needed to be "smacked in the face." The remark caused a furor among Steelers fans, but Law stood by his comments. "By this time of the year . . . if you can't get hyped and get ready to play you shouldn't be here on either team," an Associated Press reporter quoted him as saying. "I never said anything disrespectful or intentionally to point out any individual player." The Patriots ended up defeating the Steelers 24–7, with Law making seven tackles. In Super Bowl XXXVI, which some have called the best Super Bowl ever played, the Patriots defeated the St. Louis Rams by 20 to 17 in the closing seconds of the fourth quarter. Law's interception and touchdown, along with seven tackles, helped the team. The Patriots opened the 2002 season with three consecutive wins, then proceeded to lose four straight, showing little resemblance to the confident team that had captured the Super Bowl the year before. Law, however, seemed to be putting together what promised to be his strongest NFL season yet. In those seven games he made a total of 36 tackles, 30 of them solo. He also made two interceptions and three passes defended.

Ty Law stands five feet, 11 inches tall and weighs 199 pounds. He has one daughter, Tya. During the 2001 season he participated with other Patriots players in a multimedia public-awareness campaign to encourage donations of blood platelets, an essential component in the treatment of certain cancers. — G.O.

Suggested Reading: *ESPN.com* (on-line); (Pittsburgh) *Post-Gazette* (on-line) Dec. 5, 1998

---

## Leakey, Meave

(mayv)

*1942– Paleontologist*

*Address: Leakey Foundation, P.O. Box 29346, 1002A O'Reilly Avenue, San Francisco, CA 94129-0346*

The Leakey name has been practically synonymous with paleontology for many years, beginning with Louis Leakey, an African-born son of British missionaries, who began digging for fossils in Kenya in the early 1930s. Louis Leakey's wife, Mary, and his son Richard also earned reputations as accomplished paleontologists. His daughter-in-law Meave Leakey, who headed the division of paleontology for the National Museums of Kenya from 1982 to 2001, is perhaps the most accomplished of the lot. "[Meave Leakey's] years of hard-earned experience in the field and laboratory," John Noble Wilford wrote for the *New York Times* (November 7, 1995), "along with [her] respected academic credentials, make her better prepared than any previous family member to carry on the Leakey tradition." Focusing on early hominids, humankind's most primitive bipedal ancestors, Meave Leakey has already done as much as anyone to clarify our

Courtesy of Royce Carlton Inc.

*Meave Leakey*

picture of early human evolution. Fossil remains she unearthed in 1995 showed that primates began walking upright at least four million years ago, 500,000 years earlier than any previous research had shown. (Hominid fossils as old as six million years have since been found.) The 3.2-million-year-old skull that she discovered in 1999 helped prove that the human evolutionary tree has been branching ever since the emergence of hominids—discrediting previous theories that it did not begin to do so until some 2.5 million years ago. Unlike Louis Leakey, who developed a reputation for sometimes inflating the significance of his contributions to the field, Meave Leakey prefers to view paleontology as a multidisciplinary team effort rather than an individual pursuit. Her colleagues, however, have a different view. "Meave is overly modest," the renowned paleontologist Donald Johanson told Karen E. Lange for *National Geographic* (October 2001), adding that she is "the embodiment of paleontology."

The eldest of the three children of Phil Epps, a surgeon, and Jo Epps, Leakey was born Meave Epps in London, England, in 1942. As a child growing up in Sussex, Meave was fond of collecting beetles, caterpillars, and other creatures and storing them in glass jars. She was so good at puzzles that, in order to make them more difficult, she often turned the pieces upside down and worked by shape alone. One of her friends, impressed by her ability, repeatedly tried to confound her by carving complex puzzles out of blocks of wood, but Meave was always able to put them together with ease. These skills later served her well in the field of paleontology, which, as she told Jennifer Frey for the *Washington Post* (April 9, 2001), is "multidisciplinary teamwork. It's like a big jigsaw puzzle, all of us putting together the pieces."

Leakey grew up in a time when girls were not generally encouraged to seriously pursue academics, particularly the sciences. She was initially educated in various all-girls schools, first in a convent and then a boarding school. "My early education," she wrote for *Archaeology* (August 1999, on-line), "was designed to instill a sense of security, stability, and lack of change. We were taught literature, history, the Christian religion, art, and music, with a little math thrown in. Science was not considered relevant for a girl's future. As an adult, and having overcome the limitations of my schooling by attending a technical college and then a university, I have found that the essence of life is its instability, insecurity, and constant change."

Leakey attended a technical college and university before going on to earn her B.S. degree, in marine zoology, from the University of North Wales. By 1965 Leakey was starting to be discouraged by the lack of positions available to women in marine zoology. She therefore decided to answer an ad for a position at the Tigoni Primate Research Centre, operated by Richard Leakey outside Nairobi, Kenya, in Africa. Leakey was hired and began performing her doctoral research on the forelimb skeleton of modern monkeys, completing the degree in zoology, from the University of North Wales, in 1968. That year Richard Leakey invited her to join his expedition at Koobi Fora, Kenya, along the shore of Lake Turkana. Leakey, as she recalled to John Noble Wilford for the *New York Times* (November 7, 1995), was interested in delving as deeply into the hominid past as possible. "I had a choice of concentrating on gaps in the time period already being worked or going to earlier sediments," she said. "We found fossils in the earlier sediments clearly worth a look. It was so much more exciting. We now have a chance of finding the earliest hominids or ancestors of both apes and hominids." The Lake Turkana site was located in the East African Rift Valley, a 1,800-mile-long gash in the earth that gives paleontologists access to deep, stratified layers of dirt and rock that are rich in fossils. Long ago, volcanic activity in the valley produced ash and lava, which have radioactive elements that make it easy to date specimens. Because research on early hominids was still relatively sparse at that time, Leakey's early days in the valley were full of discovery. "It was incredible," she told Keith K. Howell for *California Wild* (Summer 1999, on-line). "The area was unexplored, with no roads and no people. It was sort of [a] no man's land as far as the local tribes were concerned. When they came into the area they would fight each other, so they tended to keep out. We were pretty much on our own. And in terms of the paleontology, it was completely unexplored, too, and everywhere we went we found completely new things. It was amazingly exciting, and I love to be in remote places and be in the bush. It was an experience I felt very privileged to be part of."

In 1970 Meave married Richard Leakey and became part of the Leakey paleontological dynasty. Richard Leakey had already proven to be as great a paleontologist as his parents, and Meave soon proved to be a fine paleontologist in her own right. In 1972 Meave and Richard Leakey, again searching near Lake Turkana, made an important discovery, finding numerous, tiny pieces of a 1.9-million-year-old cranium that belonged to a member of a previously undiscovered species later named *H. rudolfensis.* "I had the privilege of reconstructing the most exciting three-dimensional jigsaw puzzle I have ever attempted," she recalled for *Archaeology.* "As each small fragment found its place, the braincase gradually came together: The brain was surprisingly large, although a lot smaller than ours." In 1975 the Leakeys discovered another important fossil, a 1.8-million-year-old cranium belonging to the *H. erectus* species, which possessed a brain case slightly larger than the *H. rudolfensis* sample. In 1983 Meave and Richard Leakey excavated Kenya's only known evidence of an archaic *H. sapiens,* or human. The fossil, a skull, was several hundred thousand years old and had a braincase comparable in size to those of modern humans.

In 1989 Richard Leakey, who had become increasingly involved in conservation work as head of the Kenya Wildlife Service, turned over most of the family's paleontological fieldwork to his wife. Then, in 1993, after Richard lost both of his legs below the knee in an airplane crash, Meave assumed sole responsibility for the fieldwork. She caused a stir in September 1995 when she discovered evidence that human ancestors had been walking upright for at least four million years, well before they developed the enlarged brains typical of *H. sapiens.* The four-million-year-old skeletal remains that Leakey found—which included complete upper and lower jaws, teeth, a skull fragment, arm bones, and a leg bone—were half a million years older than any other known hominid fossil. The skull and jaws of the new species, which Leakey dubbed *Australopithecus anamensis,* were more apelike than human, but the morphology of the leg bones clearly indicated bipedalism. "[The discovery] demonstrates . . . that brain enlargement was the latest in a series of significant adaptions," Leakey explained for *Archaeology,* "and one that is largely associated with the emergence of *H. erectus* and evolution of the earliest *H. sapiens.*"

In March 2001 Leakey attracted worldwide notice with her announcement of the discovery of a new species, *Kenyanthropis platyops.* In 1999 she had unearthed a 3.2-million-year-old skull, and by 2001 she had become convinced that its existence proved the need for a reassessment of early human evolution. A front page *New York Times* (March 22, 2001) headline declared, "Skull May Alter Experts' View of Human Descent's Branches." Previous evidence had suggested that between 2.5 million and one million years ago, there were multiple hominid species living in Africa, most of which eventually died out. However, most paleontologists agreed that from the emergence of hominids (six million to eight million years ago) until approximately 2.5 million years ago, there was a single line of evolution from which all later hominids, including humans, had evolved. The most well-documented species of that line was *Australopithecus afarensis,* which lived three million to four million years ago and had become famous with Donald Johanson's uncovering of the "Lucy" skeleton in 1974. But Leakey's finding suggested that there were other hominids during Lucy's time and that *Kenyanthropis platyops* was as likely a progenitor of the human race as was *Australopithecus afarensis.* The *Kenyanthropis platyops* skull was flatter on top than that of *Australopithecus afarensis* and had smaller teeth. It was so different from other *Australopithecus* remains that Leakey postulated that it belonged not only to a different species (the smallest category of classification) but a different genus, *Kenyanthropis* (the next-smallest category). "For more than 20 years we thought that *Australopithecus afarensis* was our common ancestor," Leakey told Sharon Begley for *Newsweek* (April 2, 2001). "With this find, we now have at least two possibilities for who our ancestor was."

Leakey has published extensively in scientific journals and is the editor or co-editor of several books, including *Koobi Fora Research Project* (1978) and *Lothagam: The Dawn of Humanity in Eastern Africa* (2001). She and Richard Leakey have two daughters, Samira and Louise. (She also has a stepdaughter, Anna, from her husband's first marriage.) Louise Leakey works with Meave at their favored site in Koobi Fora. "We now run joint expeditions and so she works with me in the field . . . ," Leakey told Howell. "We go off in our separate directions through the week and then come together at weekends to compare notes and to catch up on the curating and packing and cataloging problems. It works incredibly well. It's really lovely to have her with me." — P.G.H.

Suggested Reading: *Archaeology* (on-line) Aug. 1999; *California Wild* (on-line) Summer 1999; *National Geographic* (on-line) Apr. 18, 2001, p84+ Oct. 2001, with photos; *New York Times* C p1 Nov. 7, 1995, F p3 May 12, 1998; *Newsweek* p46+ Apr. 2, 2001; *Time* p58+ Aug. 28, 1995, (on-line) Mar. 26, 2001; *Scientific American* p32+ Oct. 2001, with photos; *Washington Post* C p1 Apr. 9, 2001

Selected Books: as editor—*Koobi Fora Research Project,* 1978; *Lothagam: The Dawn of Humanity in Eastern Africa* (with John Harris), 2001

John Spellman/Retna Ltd.

## Lee, Jeanette

*July 9, 1971– Professional pool player*

*Address: Jeanette Lee Foundation, 1427 W. 86th St., Suite 183, Indianapolis, IN 46260*

Leveling dark stares across the pool table, dressed all in black, and wearing her black hair hanging down her back, Jeanette Lee leaves no question as to how she earned the nickname "the Black Widow." Lee's aggressive play and striking looks have made her one of the most recognized pool players in the world; partly due to her appeal, the Women's Professional Billiard Association (WPBA), and women's pool in general, have recently surged in popularity, overshadowing men's professional pool. As Kristin Pires, the editor of *Billiards Digest*, told Patricia Babcock McGraw for the Arlington Heights, Illinois, *Daily Herald* (January 12, 2002), "I don't think there's ever been a pool player as popular and as widely recognized as Jeanette. She's made this incredible image for herself." Lee has appeared on *Good Morning America*, *Extra*, *Vibe TV*, *Hard Copy*, and HBO's *Arliss*, among other TV shows, and has been featured in such publications as *People*, *Glamour*, *USA Today*, and *Sports Illustrated*. A professional since 1993, she has stayed in the top ranks of the WPBA despite being legally blind (without corrective lenses) and undergoing at least eight operations to correct a severe scoliosis.

The youngest of the three children of Korean immigrants, Jeanette Lee was born in the New York City borough of Brooklyn on July 9, 1971. Her father, Bo Chun Lee, owned a smoke shop; her mother, Sonja, worked as a nurse. From a fairly early age, Lee made a point of defying both parents. After discovering how much it irked her mother, she took to wearing all-black outfits. When Lee was 12 she was diagnosed with a serious case of scoliosis, a curvature of the spine. She underwent surgery, which involved breaking her back and planting two 18-inch steel rods from the top of her spine to her pelvic bone. "I didn't know what the heck was going on," Lee recalled to Abe Aamidor for the *Indianapolis Star* (February 21, 1999). "All they told me was they were going to make my back straight. I can tell you I was in the most pain you can imagine." She was in a cast for two months, after which she was forced to wear a bulky brace that kept her from participating in sports with her schoolmates. At present Lee can bend over at no farther than an 80-degree angle, barely enough to lean over a pool table.

Lee's superior performance on a competitive exam gained her entrance to the prestigious Bronx High School of Science. While still attending the school, she left home to live with friends in their own apartment. She became enamored of pool at 18, when she walked into Chelsea Billiards, in Manhattan, and saw an older man shooting pool. "I was just mesmerized by his playing," Lee told Brian Meehan for the *Oregonian* (January 17, 2002). "He was brilliant and graceful and kind of gentle. He hardly ever missed a ball. He had the cue on a string and he could make it dance. I just fell in love with the game." After that, Lee played at every opportunity and even took to sleeping with her fingers taped in the shape of a cue bridge. Once, after playing for 37 hours straight, she suffered such pain in her back that friends had to carry her home. Within two months she was playing for money—she once won $900 in less than 20 minutes—capitalizing on the misconceptions of men who assumed they could beat the quiet young woman.

Playing pool significantly improved Lee's self-image. "When I was growing up, I never felt good about myself," she told McGraw. "I had a sister who was a lot smarter than me. I was pretty misunderstood by my parents, and I had this back that made me wimpy and different from all the other girls. But playing pool made me feel good about myself because I was actually good at it. My back didn't have to be as much of a factor as it is with every other sport. It was all hand-eye coordination and strategy. And once I got that down, I was beating guys."

In the first professional pool event for which she qualified, in 1992, Lee placed third. In 1993, less than three years after her introduction to the game, she turned pro—and within a year she ranked in the WPBA's Top 10. Lee became an immediate standout in the WPBA not only because of her exceptional skills but also because of her mystique. The nickname Black Widow, given to her by the owner of the Howard Beach Billiard Club, remained a private joke between him and Lee until Lee mentioned it off the record to a *New York Times* reporter, who nevertheless included it in an article. From then on the name stuck—despite the best efforts of Lee's mother, a devout Christian, who found its wicked connotations disconcerting. At one tournament Sonja Lee told journalists that her daughter had a new nickname, "the Lily of the Valley," but none of them ever adopted it.

From the start of her career, Lee has used intimidation and bravado to her advantage. The first time she played against Helena Thornfeldt, who, as of October 28, 2002, ranked fourth in the WPBA, Lee told her that she considered herself the best female straight pool player in the world. (Straight pool is a game in which 15 balls worth one point apiece may be pocketed in any order.) To drive the point home, she sank 94 balls in succession. "Jeanette was awesome," Thornfeldt told Kimberly Wong for *Sports Illustrated* (July 8, 1996). "She was the best woman pool player I ever saw. Jeanette says a lot of things, but she backs them up." In 1993 Lee was the runner-up in the World Pool-Billiard Association (WPA) World Championship events, in Konigswinter, Germany. Continuing to climb the ranks in 1994, she placed first in five of the WPBA's 12 official tournaments—the Baltimore Billiard Classic, the Kasson Twin Cities Classic, the BCA (Billiard Congress of America) San Francisco Classic, the U.S. Open 9-Ball Championships, and the Connelly WPBA National Championships—and second in the WPA World Championship events. Those victories were enough to earn her player-of-the-year honors from the WPBA. By 1995, less than two years after turning pro, Lee had become the world's number-one-ranked female pool player. That year she won the Olhausen Los Angeles Classic and the Brunswick New York Classic. In 1996, still ranked number one, she won the Billiard Congress of America Charlotte Classic.

In 1997 Lee married the professional pool player George "the Flamethrower" Breedlove and settled with him in Indianapolis, Indiana. That year she won two WPBA tournaments, the Hubler Cues Nashville Classic and the Olhausen San Diego Classic. In 1998 she won the ESPN Ultimate 9-Ball Challenge, the Penn Ray Recreational Arizona Classic, and the Cuetec Cues Hawaii Classic, and the WPBA voted her the sports person of the year. While suffering severe back pain in 1999, Lee nevertheless chalked up victories at the Gentleman Jack Great Dallas Shoot-out, the Viejas Southern California Classic, and the Tournament of Champions. During the first six months of 2000, she underwent three back operations and did not play pool at all. During that time she dropped in the rankings to number five. (Rankings, updated monthly, are based on the total of points earned in the most recent 12-month period, with a first-place finish worth 200 points, second-place, 160, etc.) Then, in midyear, she returned to the circuit with the announcement "I fully intend on reclaiming the No. 1 ranking," as quoted by Ellen Horrow in *USA Today* (June 26, 2000). She did not win any of the remaining WPBA tournaments that year, however.

Lee, who plays in nearly constant pain, is active in several scoliosis foundations. She is a member of the board of directors and handles the job of vice president of funding for the Scoliosis Association; in addition, she currently serves as its national spokesperson. She also has ties with the Arc of Northern Essex County, a Massachusetts chapter of a national nonprofit organization serving people with mental and developmental disabilities. In 1998 she established the Jeanette Lee Foundation, which raises money to fight scoliosis. "Now I can understand why God put me through this," Lee told Elijah Gosier for the *St. Petersburg Times* (February 18, 2002). "If you can just survive the bad times, you'll be an inspiration for somebody else."

With Allan Scott Gershenson, Lee co-wrote *The Black Widow's Guide to Killer Pool* (2000), which is part memoir and part manual, offering Lee's ideas on psychological aspects of the game as well as techniques for playing. In August 2001, after undergoing yet another operation, Lee competed in the first-ever billiards event at the 6th World Games, held in Akita, Japan. (A multi-sports competition held every four years, the World Games are sponsored by the Netherlands-based International World Games Association.) Competing in the finals against the WPBA's number-one-ranked player, Karen Corr, who represented Great Britain, Lee beat her 9–3 to capture the gold medal. She defeated Corr again to win the 2001 BCA Open 9-Ball Championships, one of the five top-10 finishes she achieved in the six tournaments in which she played in 2001. Toward the end of 2001, the cable-TV station ESPN voted Lee the third-sexiest female athlete in the world (behind the tennis player Anna Kournikova and the track-and-field athlete Marion Jones). Lee, whose sleek pool attire has sometimes drawn criticism, told Joseph Sanchez for the *Denver Post* (March 12, 2002), "I think women should be very proud to be women and celebrate their femininity, and that's something that I do. I'm very proud to be a woman. I want to be feminine and still be able to be great and hold myself with class and dignity, and that's what I try to do." As a member of the Diverse Races Committee of the Women's Sports Foundation, Lee promotes the cause of women athletes; at the White House, according to Elijah Gosier, she urged President George W. Bush to promote equitable funding between men's and women's college sports programs.

Ranked number three in the WPBA as of October 28, 2002 (behind Karen Corr and Allison Fisher), Lee lives in Indianapolis with her husband. She has two stepdaughters, Morgan and Olivia. Lee told McGraw, "I love playing pool and I don't see myself stopping anytime soon—at least not until I get back to being No. 1 in the world again. If I have to, I'll use my cue as a cane to get around the table. Just as long as I can keep playing." — P.G.H.

Suggested Reading: (Arlington Heights, Illinois) *Daily Herald* p1 Jan. 12, 2002; *Denver Post* D p10 Mar. 12, 2002, with photo; *Indianapolis Star* J p1 Feb. 21, 1999; Jeanette Lee Web site; *New York*

*Times* B p3 Aug. 8, 1998; *People* p86 Mar. 13, 1995, with photo ; *St. Petersburg Times* D p1 Feb. 18, 2002, with photo; *Sports Illustrated* p10+ July 8, 1996; *USA Today* C p3 June 26, 2000, with photo; WPBA Web site

---

Courtesy of the New York Mets

## Leiter, Al

*Oct. 23, 1965– Pitcher for the New York Mets*

*Address: New York Mets, 123-10 Roosevelt Rd., Flushing, NY 11368*

"I'm a grown man—by rights, I should have a real job, with a briefcase and a suit and tie and flipping some papers around and staring at a computer. Instead, I get to take my civvies off, put on this funny outfit, and act like a 10-year-old," the New York Mets pitcher Al Leiter told Harry Stein in an interview for the *American Spectator* (June 2001). A standout baseball player during his high-school days in New Jersey, Leiter has since weathered debilitating injuries, unwanted trades, and pressure-packed innings in pro seasons that have ranged from uneven to outstanding, in both the American and National Leagues. In 1998 he was traded to the Mets and became the ace of the team he followed as a child, when he studied the technique of the star pitcher Tom Seaver. "I'm living out my boyhood dream," he told Bill Shannon for *Mets Magazine* (September 14, 2001).

Alois Terry Leiter, known as Al, was born on October 23, 1965 in Toms River, New Jersey. He and his twin sister were among the seven children of Alex Leiter, a merchant seaman, and Maria Leiter, a homemaker. The Leiter family, living on the New Jersey seashore, cheered for the Mets, as Al Leiter recalled to Howard Z. Unger for the *Village Voice* (May 19, 1998): "I grew up a total Mets fan. My father was from the Flushing area and he got my brothers and me to really root for them. I remember my oldest brother used to emulate Tom Seaver's pitching motion as a kid. I guess that's why we all became pitchers." (Two of Leiter's brothers, Kurt and Mark, have also had careers in Major League Baseball.) Leiter's father was often away from home on business for several months at a time, and his parents divorced when Al was a freshman in high school; Leiter has credited his mother with maintaining a solid family life in spite of such turmoil. "There were some breakups and stuff like that, probably very typical of a lot of families, but she stuck in there for the kids," he told Jack Curry for the *New York Times* (May 10, 1998). "Her thing was she was always going to be there when we came home [from school]." An all-around athlete, Leiter ran track and played football and basketball at Central Regional High School in Bayville, New Jersey, earning All-County honors for football in his senior season. But he was most outstanding in baseball, the sport in which he was named an All-American in 1984, his senior year. In his final high-school season, he pitched four no-hitters, had a record of 10 wins and zero losses, and helped his team win the state championship. During high school he had also become a serious student, electing to take Advanced Placement science courses and contemplating a career in mechanical engineering. "I saw I had to do more with myself, and ended up getting really into schoolwork," he explained to Harry Stein. Although he had been accepted at Northwestern University, Stanford University, and the University of Florida, his college plans were put on hold when the New York Yankees picked him in the second round of the June 1984 amateur draft. "I ended up taking the bonus. A hundred thousand dollars is a lot of money," Leiter admitted to Stein.

After his high-school graduation, Leiter immediately began his career in minor-league baseball. He played first with the single-A Oneonta, New York, Yankees, then moved to Fort Lauderdale, Florida, to play for another Yankees-affiliated single-A team before graduating to the double-A Albany-Colonie Yankees. He also spent a short season playing for the Arecibo Lobos in the Puerto Rico Winter League. By the 1987 season he was with the triple-A Columbus Clippers, aided by his left-handed throwing and his good, if inconsistent, pitches—a formidable fastball primary among them. In his four minor-league seasons, he amassed a record of 15 wins and 25 losses, with an earned run average (ERA) of 4.32. He made his major-league debut, with the New York Yankees, on September 15, 1987. In four major-league starts that season, his record was 2–2, with an unimpressive ERA of 6.35. In 1988, after adjusting to major-league hitting, Leiter cut his ERA to 3.92 in 14 starts, but he ended the year with a 4–4 record, having frequently been optioned to the Clippers for more minor-league experience and often nursing blisters on his left hand.

In 1989, after earning a 1–2 record and an ERA of over six in four starts, Leiter was traded to the Toronto Blue Jays for the outfielder and power hitter Jesse Barfield, in a move that the Yankees hoped would improve their offense. In retrospect, Leiter admitted to Jason Diamos for the *New York Times* (June 26, 1998), "I don't feel like [the Yankees] dissed me or like it was any kind of raw deal. If anything, I don't feel like I did as well as you are supposed to do as a Yankee." He started in only one game for the Blue Jays—a no-decision—before suffering a string of injuries to his shoulder and elbow that required numerous surgical procedures and difficult stints in rehabilitation. In 1990 he saw only six innings of bullpen work in four games. His pitching elbow remained irritated in the following season, and after struggling through less than two innings over three games, during which his ERA shot past 27, he was assigned to the Class A team in Dunedin, Florida. Originally slated to remain in Florida for 20 days, he spent the remainder of the 1991 season there, and he languished in the minors for most of 1992 as well, starting in 27 games for the triple-A Syracuse SkyChiefs while the Blue Jays ended the season as winners of the 1992 American League pennant. On October 4 of that year, Leiter threw for just one inning in Toronto, as a relief pitcher. "There were a lot of depressing moments wondering if I would ever get back," he told Jack Curry for the *New York Times* (October 18, 1993).

As the 1993 season approached, Leiter returned to health. He was a spot starter and bullpen regular for the Blue Jays, appearing in 34 games and finishing with a 9–6 record, two saves, and a 4.11 ERA. The first of his 12 starts that season—and his first since May 6, 1989—took place on April 10, 1993; that day, after pitching seven shutout innings, he recorded his first major-league win since April 14, 1989. "I never doubted I could get back to where I could compete on the major league level," he told Murray Chass for the *New York Times* (April 11, 1993). "People want to hear negative, doomsday things, but it never has happened. I guess I'm a positive person. Not only have I learned to pitch, but the adversity I've gone through has made me a better person. This spring I went in the underdog. Nobody thought of me and I came through. I worked hard to earn it. It's a wonderful feeling." Toronto won the American League pennant again in 1993 and faced the Philadelphia Phillies in the World Series. Leiter had a key role in Game One of the series, earning a win by pitching two-plus scoreless innings. "If it was the bottom of the ninth and the seventh game, that's what you dream about when you're playing in the backyard as a kid," he told Jack Curry, describing the experience of pitching with the bases loaded in a tied game. "It was tense. At that moment, I wasn't thinking about it. I was just trying to stay aggressive and get [the ball] over the plate." Leiter also pitched in the fourth and sixth games of the World Series, which the Blue Jays won in six games.

By 1994 Leiter had earned a regular spot in the Toronto pitching rotation. He suffered injuries again, however, and started only 20 games that year, finishing the season with a 6–7 record and a 5.08 ERA. In 1995, his first full injury-free season in the majors, he started 28 games and had a record of 11–11; his ERA was the best of his career up to that point, ending at 3.64. That December Leiter, a free agent, signed an $8.6 million contract to go to the two-year-old Florida Marlins for three years, in part because he lived in southern Florida during the off-season. Dave Dombrowski, the Marlins' general manager, "took some heat for supposedly spending too much on me," Leiter told Tim Kurkjian for *Sports Illustrated* (May 20, 1996). "That was drummed up by the media. But the people who know baseball—the players, scouts, etcetera—they kind of know what I'm about."

In 1996 Leiter had the best season of his career up to that time, achieving a 16–12 record in 33 starts, striking out 200 batters, lowering his ERA to 2.93—the third lowest in the National League—and receiving his first invitation to the All-Star Game, in which he pitched for part of the ninth inning. He also pitched the first no-hitter in the Marlins' history, on May 11, 1996, against Colorado; after the first inning, in which he walked two batters and hit another, he did not give up a hit, and he struck out six men. Leiter did not fare as well in 1997, finishing with an 11–9 record and a 4.34 ERA. But both he and the Marlins were able to improve their game in the postseason, easily defeating the San Francisco Giants in the National League Division Series (NLDS) and winning four of six games against the Atlanta Braves to win the National League Championship Series (NLCS). Florida faced the Cleveland Indians in that year's World Series. Leiter was on the mound for the decisive Game Seven; after shaky postseason starts, which included a loss and two no-decisions, Leiter pitched well, leaving the game after six innings, with the Marlins down 2–0. After scoring runs in the seventh and ninth innings, the Marlins won the World Series in the bottom of the 11th.

The Marlins were not able to keep up with the salary demands of their players, and many members of the World Championship team were traded during the off-season. Leiter, who had one year left on his contract, was dealt to the New York Mets. He played the best season of his career to date in 1998, ending with a 17–6 record, 174 strikeouts, and a 2.47 ERA, despite missing several starts and the 1998 All-Star Game because of a knee injury. After his outstanding pitching performances, the Mets offered Leiter a four-year, $32-million contract through 2002. Going into the 1999 season, he was considered the staff ace—a nickname that put pressure on Leiter, particularly after his troubling start: in his first eight games, he was 1–4 with an ERA of 6.12. "Right now, I'm letting other people affect me," he admitted to Jason Diamos for the *New York Times* (May 20, 1999). "Who am I? What am I doing? How did I get here? What am I all about? I'm dismissing all that just based on a number and a start of a baseball season. I'm allowing it to penetrate me as a person, to affect my job. I'm allowing some of it to enter into my mix of what I have to do to be who I know I am, and can be, and will be. And that's a good pitcher." Leiter quickly recovered from his rocky beginning to be named June's National League Pitcher of the Month for his 5–0 record. He ended the year with a 13–12 record and a 4.23 ERA. His clutch performance in the last game of the season, a two-hit shutout against the Cincinnati Reds, allowed the Mets to advance to the play-offs for the first time since 1988. The Mets defeated the Arizona Diamondbacks in the NLDS, taking three of four games, but fell to the Atlanta Braves in six games in the NLCS.

In 2000 Leiter played in the World Series as a member of his childhood-favorite team. His regular-season record was 16–8, with an ERA of 3.20 over 31 starts, and he matched his career high of 200 strikeouts. He notched his 100th career victory on July 1, 2000 and pitched that summer in his second All-Star Game, in which he had the misfortune to take the loss—that is, throw the ball that won the game for the American League—in the third inning of the contest. The Mets finished the season in the wild-card slot, as they had in 1999, and faced the San Francisco Giants in the NLDS and the St. Louis Cardinals in the NLCS. This time they emerged victorious in their contest with the Cardinals and took on their crosstown rivals, the New York Yankees, in the 2000 World Series. In the fifth game of the best-of-seven series, with the Yankees up three games to one, Leiter gave an excellent performance, giving up only two runs over the first eight innings. But he faltered after two strikeouts in the ninth, allowing a walk, two singles, and two more runs, and the Yankees won the series. Leiter took the loss to heart, particularly since he had asked to be allowed to pitch as much of the game as possible. "I told Bobby [Valentine, the Mets' manager] yesterday that I didn't care if I had to throw 150 pitches, because I wanted to be out there," he told Bob Klapisch for *ESPN.com* (October 27, 2000) after the series. "I said, 'I've got four months to rest. I've had a good career, but I'm 35 years old. I'd really like the chance to win this game.' . . . It really hurts that I couldn't get the last out. It's just amazing that three hours of great pitching, a terrific game, all of it could be wiped away in just 3–4 minutes."

Leiter was on the disabled list for almost a month at the beginning of the 2001 season, due to a strained elbow ligament. After recovering, he finished the year with an 11–11 record and a 3.31 ERA, the eighth best in the National League. The Mets' pitching rotation was not as deep as in seasons past, however, and the team failed to make the play-offs. In 2002 Leiter accumulated a 13–13 win-loss record and an ERA of 3.48, as well as two shutout games and 172 strikeouts. (The Mets had a dismal season, ending up in last place in the National League East division.) On April 30, 2002, in a contest with the Diamondbacks, Leiter became the only active pitcher to notch a win against all 30 teams in Major League Baseball.

With his contract expiring at the end of the season, there was speculation about Leiter's future with the team. Although he had made it clear before the season began that he wished to stay with the Mets until his retirement as a pitcher, the team's general manager, Steve Phillips, was slow to offer him a new deal. "I hope not [to go to another team] because I like it here and this has been a great five years," Leiter said, as Jack Curry reported for the *New York Times* (July 17, 2002). "Even as upsetting and frustrating as this year has been off and on, I'd still rather be wearing a Mets uniform than any other uniform. Period." A new contract appeared, and he signed it on July 24; under its terms, he will be paid a total of $18 million for two years, with a mutual option for a third year. (He earned $9.25 million for the 2002 season, and it is believed he could have received as much as $12 million a year had he signed with another team.) He has hinted that he may retire when his current contract expires and has discussed the possibility of coaching baseball, becoming a broadcaster, or even running for public office. "Being around the game gets in your blood; it's not easy to give up," he told Harry Stein.

In 1998, with his wife, Lori, the pitcher founded Leiter's Landing, a charitable foundation focusing on children. Leiter's Landing has funded a wide range of projects, from a new Little League field in Berkeley, New Jersey, to computers for schools in the New York City neighborhood of Harlem, to a playroom at the New York University Medical Center. "I'm making a tremendous living because of a baseball game," he told Doug Mittler for *Mets Magazine* (April 12, 1999). "I'm just grateful and I want to give something back." He chose to donate primarily to small organizations, he explained to Mittler, because "I always felt like the underdog. I don't feel like a star or enjoy being called an ace. I like the little guy. I'd like to make a difference with the smaller groups who will appreciate it more." Leiter's contributions, including a pledge of $1 million from his most recent contract, attracted the notice of baseball officials. He was honored with the 1999 Branch Rickey Award, sponsored by the Rotary Club of Denver, and the 2000 Roberto Clemente Award, given annually by Major League Baseball to a player who demonstrates excellence both in baseball and in community involvement.

Al and Lori Leiter live in Manhattan. They have two daughters and a son. — K.S.

Suggested Reading: *American Spectator* p59+ June 2001, with photo; *New York Times* C p5 Oct. 18, 1993, with photo, C p3 June 26, 1998, with photo; *Sports Illustrated* p69 May 20, 1996, with photo

Christopher Little/CBS/Getty Images

## Letterman, David

*Apr. 12, 1947– Host of* Late Show with David Letterman

*Address: Ed Sullivan Theater, 1697 Broadway, New York, NY 10019*

With his loony, sophomoric stunts and sight gags, irreverence toward celebrities, and remarkably quick, often biting wit, David Letterman has been credited with reinventing the late-night television talk show and creating in his long-running programs what some have called a parody of the genre. "Letterman and his writers have opened up comedy, revealing humor in the simplest and silliest of notions," the television journalist Barbara Walters said when she interviewed him on January 29, 1992 for *The Barbara Walters Special*. "His interview approach is sometimes considered mean-spirited, but many guests say that sitting down with Letterman is better described as a sort of survival test." To date, only one talk-show host has appeared on late-night television longer than Letterman: Johnny Carson, who presided over *The Tonight Show* for three decades. The first of Letterman's own programs was *The David Letterman Show*, which debuted on NBC in 1980 and aired during a daytime slot for three months before its cancellation. Next, beginning in 1982, also on NBC, he appeared on *Late Night with David Letterman*, televised immediately after *The Tonight Show*. "Letterman was doing the most innovative, ironic comedy on the air," Ken Tucker wrote for *Salon* (July 20, 1999, on-line) about Letterman's work during that period. Widespread speculation as to whether Letterman would succeed Carson as host of *The Tonight Show* upon Carson's retirement ended when NBC tapped Jay Leno for the job. Long dissatisfied by NBC's treatment of him and disappointed about the network's choice of Leno to replace Carson, Letterman promptly accepted a generous contract from CBS to create a new show. Broadcast during the coveted 11:30 p.m. time slot, *Late Show with David Letterman* was launched on August 30, 1993. The five-night-a-week show, which currently earns CBS about $120 million a year in advertising revenues and, according to Ronald Grover in *Business Week* (March 8, 2002, on-line), $25 million a year in profits, is syndicated worldwide and has spawned many imitators in the U.S. and overseas. Letterman, his shows, and other people associated with them have earned a total of 15 Emmy Awards, in such categories as as outstanding host in a variety series; outstanding individual achievement; and outstanding variety, music, or comedy series, among others. In a February 20, 1996 interview with Mark McEwen on *CBS This Morning*, Letterman said about his work, "When it goes great, it can be the best fun. . . . It can be more fun than you ever imagined."

The second of the three children of Harry Joseph Letterman and his wife, Dorothy, David Letterman was born in Indianapolis, Indiana, on April 12, 1947. His older sister, Janice, is a homemaker; his younger sister, Gretchen, is an editor with the *St. Petersburg Times*. His father owned a florist shop, where his mother helped out; she later became a church secretary. (Widowed in the 1970s, she remarried in 1983.) "It was a solid *Father Knows Best* or *Leave It to Beaver* type of lower middle-class family," Letterman told Kay Gardella for the New York *Daily News* (January 29, 1980). Letterman has described himself as a "wiseass" and comedian since childhood. "I grew up watching Steve Allen, Johnny Carson, and Jonathan Winters," he told Fran Carpenter for *Parade* (April 21, 1980). "They're the three I really paid attention to. With those three, I see myself—and I catch myself doing things that I feel are an amalgam of their influences."

After earning a bachelor's degree in radio and television broadcasting at Ball State University, in Muncie, Indiana, in 1969, Letterman worked for four years as a television announcer for the ABC affiliate in Indianapolis. He irritated his superiors when he signed off the late-night television movie by blowing up a cardboard replica of the building that housed the station, and, on other occasions, when he interjected into the news such items as the announcement that Guam had purchased the tall Soldiers and Sailors' Monument in the center of Indianapolis and planned to paint it green to honor asparagus, which he called Guam's national vegetable. Speaking of his experiences as a replacement weatherman, he told David Gritten for the *Los Angeles Times* (December 19, 1979), "You can only announce the weather, the highs and the lows, so many times before you go insane. In my case, it took two weeks. I started clowning. I'd draw peculiar objects on the cloud maps, and invent disasters in fictitious cities. I made up my own measurements for hail, and said hailstones the size of canned hams were falling." In his fifth, and final, year with the ABC affiliate, Letterman served as a radio talk jockey, which better suited his fondness for whimsicality, clownishness, and the absurd.

Seeing no future for himself in Indianapolis, in 1975 Letterman moved to Los Angeles, where he tried without success to sell six situation-comedy scripts he had written. He began performing at the Comedy Store, a club still considered a showcase for aspiring comedians. One night Jimmie Walker, then starring in the CBS sitcom *Good Times*, saw his act and hired him as a writer. Before long Letterman was earning television writing assignments for the singer John Denver and the comedians Bob Hope and Paul Lynde; he also did gigs on the *Gong Show*, *Rock Concert*, and *The Peeping Times*. In 1977 he wrote for and performed on *The Starland Vocal Band Show*, a summer-replacement variety show, and the next year he appeared in Mary Tyler Moore's short-lived comedy-variety hour *Mary*.

Letterman's big break came when talent scouts for *The Tonight Show*, hosted by Johnny Carson, saw him on *Mary*; he made his first appearance on *The Tonight Show* on November 26, 1978. During Letterman's third booking Fred De Cordova, the series' producer, invited him to become a guest host. Within a year he had filled in for Carson 20 times, more than any other substitute. In April 1979 Carson announced his intention to leave *Tonight*, prompting speculation that Letterman would succeed him. When Carson changed his mind, NBC signed Letterman to an exclusive two-year contract to create his own program. *The David Letterman Show* premiered at 10:00 a.m. on June 23, 1980, with its host backed by a house band. Segments spotlighted guest singers; Edwin Newman, providing news updates; Mark Goldstein, reporting during a cross-country bus trip; and comedic bits with such regulars as Edie McClurg, Valri Bromfield, and Paul Raley. Unlike other talk shows, Letterman's interviewees were not celebrities but people of dubious distinction: a woman who raised a chimpanzee in her apartment, for example, and a couple searching for the world's largest ball of string. On one occasion, Letterman sent a burly member of the audience for a cup of coffee and then—to much laughter and applause from others in the studio—tipped the reluctant go-fer when he returned. On another installment, he used a portable TV to see what was being broadcast on other channels. He once told his audience after a commercial break that the mayor of New York had just appeared nude on the set. Some sources of his humor, Letterman told Larry Kart for the *Chicago Tribune* (January 6, 1980), were what he called "setups"—ridiculous or ludicrous statements that triggered ideas for funny punch lines. For example, while in a supermarket, he noticed a headline in the *National Inquirer* that read, "How to Lose Weight Without Diet or Exercise." "So I think to myself, 'That leaves disease,'" he explained to Kart. "I've been doing that word for word for four years, and it never fails to get a laugh. Or there was the time I was driving my pickup truck and I heard a guy on the radio screaming, 'Now you can buy breakfast at McDonalds!' And I thought, 'Boy, there's a dream come true.' They're not so much jokes as they are sarcastic comments, expressions of an attitude."

In the Toronto *Globe and Mail* (June 25, 1980), Rick Groen characterized *The David Letterman Show* as "television at its most ironic" and its host as "a cross between Carson and [the talk-show host Dick] Cavett, with an incisive but amiable wit." In *Newsweek* (July 7, 1980), Harry F. Waters called the program "a laudable if somewhat erratic TV departure" that "in its best moments exudes the inspired mischief of Martin Mull's *America 2Night* along with a refreshing whiff of the late [comedian] Ernie Kovacs." Waters also wrote that Letterman "keeps things percolating with his easy blend of boyish charm and trigger-quick ad libs" and that "both Carson and Letterman possess the same effortless wit, but David seems closer to his audience." The show failed to attract viewers in sufficiently large numbers, however; poor ratings led to its cancellation. The last installment aired on October 24, 1980.

NBC's decision to give Letterman another try in a different time slot resulted in *Late Night with David Letterman*, which premiered in February 1982 at 12:30 a.m. Eastern Time. Popular features included the top-10 list (the "top 10 things about living longer," for example, included "shoulder-length ear hair" and "Every time you sneeze, you break your hip"); stupid pet tricks; stupid human tricks; and viewer mail. Since *Late Night* aired immediately after *The Tonight Show*, "from the very beginning, . . . we all knew and understood and wanted to do something that was different so that we could not be accused of, 'Oh, they're just trying to be Johnny. They're trying to do the same kind of show that Carson is doing,'" Letterman told Walters. "And we were lucky enough that it succeeded in some measure." The show was actually a huge hit, especially among college students and others in their 20s; during its 11-year run, it grossed about $50 million annually and earned five Emmy Awards.

Carson's announcement that he would retire in May 1992, after 30 years on the air, triggered a frenzy of speculation in the media as to whether his successor would be Letterman or Jay Leno, the permanent (that is, sole) guest host of *The Tonight Show* since 1987. Letterman did not campaign for Carson's job. "It wasn't a matter of hubris, but rather the fact that it is simply not in Letterman's character to seek the favor of anyone, be it audience or network brass," Ken Tucker wrote for *Salon*. NBC's choice of Leno for the job led Letterman, in January 1993, to announce that he would be leaving NBC for CBS, which reportedly offered him $14 million a year, double his NBC salary, along with more creative control over his show and the preferred,

11:30 p.m time slot. Letterman has also revealed that for some years he had felt angry about what he regarded as NBC's ill treatment of him after General Electric acquired the network, in 1986. In particular, he has cited what he viewed as unwarranted "nickel-and-dime" attempts to cut his budget and NBC's decision to sell *Late Night* reruns to the Arts & Entertainment Network without consulting or compensating him or allowing him to edit out inordinately dated or embarrassing material. A book about these events, *The Late Shift: Letterman, Leno, and the Network Battle for the Night* (1994), by Bill Carter, was adapted for a movie that aired on cable TV in 1996.

Broadcasting from the Ed Sullivan Theater in New York City, *Late Show with David Letterman* premiered in August 1993. In his first two years at CBS, Letterman led the ratings among 11:30 p.m. shows, but Leno has surpassed him since 1995, and at times the ABC news program *Nightline*, with Ted Koppel, has taken second place. Letterman has traced his ratings problems to CBS's poor ratings in prime time; indeed, *Late Show*'s popularity rose when CBS's prime-time lineup began attracting more viewers. In March 2002 some 4.4 million viewers tuned in to *Late Show*, an increase of 12 percent over the previous year. (In the same month Leno's audience totaled about 5.7 million.)

The *Late Show* has been described as slightly flashier and less acerbic than Letterman's previous late-night program—a change generally regarded as an improvement. "Some of Dave's most inventive and delightful new bursts of creative humor come from his unexpected display of affection and newfound social ease . . . ," Lisa Schwarzbaum wrote for *Entertainment Weekly* (December 31, 1993). "He runs out into traffic, he kisses pro bowlers, he talks to cabbies. . . . The surprise discovery about David Letterman in 1993 is not only that he has a brain and courage, but that he also has a heart." Some of Letterman's humor involves unlikely interviewers, among them people in the neighborhood surrounding his studio. In 1994, for example, he sent Mujibur Rahman and Sirajul Islam, souvenir-shop owners, on a cross-country tour as his "good-will ambassadors." Also in 1994 Letterman's mother, Dorothy Mengering, covered the Winter Olympics for *Late Show*, winning fans with her wry observations; she has appeared on the show from time to time ever since.

Letterman is known as his own toughest critic; he told Ken Tucker for *Entertainment Weekly* (December 1, 1995) that when a show was unsatisfactory, the blame rested with him. "I'm the catalyst, I'm the reactor through which the audience interprets the show, so it's up to me to be in control and give out the right vibe," he explained. He told Fred Schruers for *Rolling Stone* (May 30, 1996) that spontaneity is what keeps the show fresh: "You always would rather have something haywire. . . . But it's hard to orchestrate anarchy every night." He also said that after producing dozens of "perfect" shows, "you realize, 'Yeah, it's perfect, but something unpleasant and ugly and sloppy is more memorable.'"

Letterman, who has expressed his anxiety about maintaining the quality of his show and has set extremely high standards for himself, is said to work longer hours than most other talk-show hosts. Eager not to repeat his mistakes, he often spends hours reviewing tapes of his broadcasts. "Dave is an absolute perfectionist," Leslie Moonves, the president of CBS Entertainment, told Schruers, "I've never seen anybody who cared about detail as much as he does. He has one of the best work ethics of anybody I've ever been in business with."

Despite his self-criticism and the fact that his show's ratings are lower than those of *The Tonight Show*, many television writers and reporters have called Letterman the "king" of late-night comedy and have credited him with popularizing comedic irony. Tucker, writing for *Salon*, called him "the most important talk-show host of his era and arguably second only to Johnny Carson as the best of all time." According to *Entertainment Weekly* (Winter 1999), "Letterman raised smarmy-pants irony to high art, and, in the process, recast the late-show persona. . . . Before Letterman, there was no shameless slagging [mocking] of network bosses, no tossing of melons off rooftops, no celebration of tomfoolery . . . and fratboy stupidity." Conan O'Brien, who hosts *Late Night with Conan O'Brien* in the spot Letterman's show once occupied on NBC, told the *Entertainment Weekly* interviewer, "What attracted me to Dave was that he was going by his own compass. This wasn't a slick operation. He wasn't trying to win you over. He was doing things he thought were funny." Writing for *GQ* (August 1993), Gerri Hirshey said, "He's puerile and he's proud. Brave, too. Dave's never quailed at physical comedy, descending into deafening fizz in his Alka-Seltzer suit, driving hard at the terrifying Wall of Condiments in his notorious Golf Cart of Death." In *Saturday Night* (September 1996), Mark Kingwell expressed a dissenting view, complaining that Letterman's act had gone downhill since he moved to the earlier time slot on CBS. "The genius of Letterman used to be that he showed clear signs of discomfort with the culture of celebrity," Kingwell wrote. "His show acted almost as a late-night tonic, an antidote to the straight-ahead endorsements of *The Tonight Show*. . . . What a difference an hour makes. Now that he's running at 11:30 instead of 12:30, Letterman no longer eases his own boredom by indulging in the manic gags and sarcasm that made his show so worth watching in the late 1980s."

Letterman has sometimes been called a mean-spirited interviewer, and several guests have walked off the set because of his antics. He is also known for his frostiness toward guests during commercial breaks. (The title character on the 1992–98 HBO sitcom *The Larry Sanders Show*, who behaves rudely to his guests, was said to be modeled on Letterman; Letterman has said that he recognized aspects of himself in the Sanders character, who was portrayed by Garry Shandling.) But he insisted to Jennet Conant for *GQ* (June 1990), "It's never been my intention to cause ill will among the fraternity and sorority of celebrities. I think some people may feel that they're not being treated with enough respect or that their work is diminished through some flip attitude on my part. But I'm a wiseass and a smart ass. . . . I think I know in my heart I'm not trying to be mean. And I try to get as many laughs at my own expense so others will kind of get the idea." Indeed, he has often directed his critical barbs at himself. Joel Goodman, the director of the Humor Project—which, according to its Web site, seeks "to help people get more smileage out of their lives and jobs by applying the practical, positive power of humor and creativity"—told Barron, "Letterman's self-depreciating style is what saves him. Otherwise, he'd be too hard or harsh for people if he's always putting down somebody without taking himself with a grain of salt. He appears to be genuinely bemused by where he finds himself each night."

On January 14, 2000, after the discovery of five blockages in his coronary arteries, Letterman underwent an emergency quintuple-bypass operation. In public he made light of the surgery, telling George Watson for the Associated Press, according to the ABC News Web site (January 15, 2000), "I feel fantastic. In addition to rerouting the arteries, they . . . installed an E-Z pass" (a device for paying highway tolls electronically). During his recovery he taped only two or three shows a week, with guest hosts filling in on the other days. (In his previous 18 years in late-night TV, he had not missed a single workday due to illness and had never employed guest hosts.) Upon his return to the *Late Show*, on February 21, 2000, he introduced on the air the team of doctors and nurses from his surgery and gave to members of the audience Official Dave Letterman Bypass T-Shirts; subsequently, the shirts were sold via the Internet, with the proceeds being donated to the American Heart Association.

Letterman was the first late-night talk-show host to return to the airwaves after the September 11, 2001 terrorist attacks on New York City and Washington, D.C. Instead of starting the show as he usually does, with a humorous monologue, he spoke in somber tones, praising New York City's mayor, Rudolph Giuliani, and the city's firefighters and police officers, mourning those lost in the disaster, and telling the audience, "There is only one requirement for any of us, and that is to be courageous, because courage, as you might know, defines all other human behavior." The usually unflappable Letterman and his guest, the veteran CBS anchorman Dan Rather, broke down in tears during the broadcast. Rather later told a *People* (December 31, 2001) interviewer, "It was Dave's finest hour."

In early March 2002, while Letterman was involved in what were said to be contentious negotiations with CBS over the renewal of his contract, news leaked that ABC was courting him, with the aim of airing his show on ABC in place of Ted Koppel's *Nightline*. ABC's action sparked worried discussions about the future of network news and the networks' emphasis on younger viewers at the expense of older ones. Later that month CBS agreed to pay Letterman more than $30 million annually for five years ($10 million more per year that he had been earning) and to market *Late Show* more aggressively; Letterman announced that he would stay at CBS and hoped to end his career there. "This has not been an easy decision," he said on his show on March 25, 2002, as reported on the CNN Web site (March 27, 2002). He went on to praise Koppel as representing "the absolute highest echelon of broadcast achievement."

Through the years Letterman has experienced problems with overzealous fans. Notable among them was Margaret M. Ray, a mentally ill woman who trespassed on his property and broke into his $1.2 million home in New Canaan, Connecticut, at least eight times; once, she was caught driving his Porsche. Ray was arrested and tried; although he testified against her, Letterman also voiced compassion for her. In March 1990 Ray was sentenced to a year in prison. After her suicide, eight years later, Letterman issued a statement calling her death the "sad end to a confused life," as reported by Tom Gliatto in *People* (October 26, 1998).

Letterman is the founder and co-owner of the production company Worldwide Pants, which produces the *Late Show*, the sitcom *Everybody Loves Raymond*, and the *Late Late Show with Craig Kilborn*, all on CBS, and *Ed*, on NBC. His talk shows have won 15 Emmys: two for *The David Letterman Show*, five for *Late Night with David Letterman*, and eight for the *Late Show with David Letterman*, including six for outstanding variety, music, or comedy series. His debut on the silver screen was in a cameo role in the dismally received comedy *Cabin Boy* (1994), a vehicle for Chris Elliott, who appeared in many *Late Night* skits. Letterman has since played himself in three feature films: the Whoopi Goldberg comedy *Eddie* (1996), Howard Stern's autobiographical *Private Parts* (1997), and Milos Forman's *Man on the Moon* (1999), in which Jim Carrey portrayed the late comic Andy Kaufman.

An avid runner and dog lover, the six-foot, two-inch Letterman is known for his gap-toothed grin, his thin frame, his wire-rimmed glasses, his reluctance to be interviewed, and his fondness for good cigars. (He recently told the talk-show host Larry King that he has quit smoking.) He has shunned all endorsement offers, including one worth $25 million from the dog-food division of Ralston Purina; in the early 1990s he bought out of a multifilm deal with the Disney Co. In 1996 Letterman, who enjoyed watching Indianapolis 500 auto races while growing up, bought a minority interest in Team Rahal, owned by the race-car champion Bobby Rahal.

Letterman's eight-year marriage to his college sweetheart, Michelle Cook, ended in divorce in 1977. His decade-long relationship with Merrill Markoe, the first head writer for his show, was followed by a similarly lengthy romantic involvement with Regina Lasko, who worked behind the scenes on *Late Night* and *Saturday Night Live*. In 1991 Letterman received the prestigious George Foster Peabody Award, for managing to "take one of TV's most conventional and least inventive forms—the talk show—and infuse it with freshness and imagination," according to the Peabody's Web site. In 1994 he received an American Comedy Award for *The Late Show Video Special with David Letterman*, and in December 1996 *TV Guide* named him one of the "50 Greatest TV Stars of All Time." — K.E.D.

Suggested Reading: ABC News (on-line) Jan. 15, 2000, with photo; *Entertainment Weekly* p24 + Dec. 1, 1995, with photos; *GQ* p166+ June 1990, with photos; *People* p56+ Feb. 11, 2002, with photos; *Rolling Stone* (on-line) May 30, 1996; *Salon* (on-line) July 20, 1999

---

Joseph Marzullo/Retna

## Levy, Eugene

*Dec. 17, 1946– Actor; director; screenwriter; producer*

*Address: c/o William Morris Agency, 1 William Morris Pl., Beverly Hills, CA 90212*

Since he got his start, in the Canadian sketch-comedy program *Second City Television* (*SCTV*), the actor Eugene Levy has built a career that now spans a quarter-century and includes more than 50 films and dozens of television shows, some of which he wrote or directed. Levy entered American households in the late 1970s, when *SCTV* was licensed by a variety of stateside local, network, and cable outlets, including Cinemax and NBC. The show was an instant success in the U.S., gaining a loyal cult following, and by the end of its seven-year run in its adopted country, Levy had earned two Emmy Awards for his work on the Toronto-based show. (*SCTV* was an offshoot of the Second City performance troupe in Toronto; there is also a Second City company in Chicago. Alumni of either *SCTV* or one of the troupes include John Candy, Rick Moranis, Martin Short, Dan Aykroyd, John Belushi, and Bill Murray.) Levy has recently solidified his reputation among American audiences by appearing in the film comedy *American Pie* (1999) as well as its sequel, *American Pie 2* (2001). In those movies Levy played the awkward but understanding father to Jim (Jason Biggs), whose mature awakenings are central to the stories' comic lewdness. Among Levy's other celebrated roles are the car salesman in *National Lampoon's Vacation* (1983), Walter Kornbluth in *Splash* (1984), Barry Steinberg in *Club Paradise* (1986), Dr. Allan Pearl in *Waiting for Guffman* (1996), Gerry Fleck in *Best in Show* (2000), and Macall Polay in *Serendipity* (2001). Beginning with his tenure on *SCTV*, Levy has been noted for his extraordinary talent for improvisational acting. In an on-line interview with *urbancinefile.com*, Levy said, "The thing that works best for me is riding a very fine reality line, and having people wonder: is it supposed to be funny or not? I like that line kind of blurred, and when it rides dangerously close to that line, that's when I get the most excited."

Of Jewish descent, Eugene Levy was born on December 17, 1946 in Hamilton, Ontario, a suburb of Toronto, in Canada. In an interview with Jeremy Taggart for *ChartAttack* (2000, on-line), Levy explained that his brother contributed to his interest in performing. "He was the one who got me onto a stage," Levy told Taggart. "You see, he had a really hot singing quartet and they were so good that it inspired me to start a singing group. So that's how I got all my insecurities out onstage." Eugene Levy's own group later turned to writing and performing skits. Levy himself had long had an interest in comedy. "I grew up watching all of the great comics of the [1950s]," he told *urbancinefile.com*, "but where my skewed sensibilities come from, I have no idea."

After graduating from Westdale High School in Hamilton, Levy enrolled at nearby McMaster University, where he earned his bachelor's degree in sociology and became friends with several of his schoolmates, including the director and producer Ivan Reitman and the actor Martin Short. Through Reitman's McMaster Film Board—of which Levy was vice president during the 1967–68 academic year—the actor landed his first feature-film role, in

Reitman's 1973 horror/comedy *Cannibal Girls*. At around the same time, he appeared in a Toronto production of the musical *Godspell* along with Short and other future celebrities, including Gilda Radner and Paul Shaffer. Shortly afterward, Levy moved to Pasadena, California, with future *SCTV* cohorts John Candy and Joe Flaherty. The three had dreams of a business venture, but those plans fell apart on Levy's arrival, and Levy soon went back to the Toronto area, where he joined the Second City troupe.

In 1976 Levy teamed up with members of the troupe for the first season of *SCTV*, which kept up Second City's tradition of sophisticated satire. Among Levy's numerous characters were Sid Dithers, a mumbling Jewish grandfather; game-show host Alex Trebel; anchorman Earl Camembert; sleazy salesman Mel Slurp; the financial adviser Brian Johns; and the two whom American audiences found most memorable—polka king Stan Shmenge and Las Vegas comic Bobby Bittman. The show enjoyed success on both sides of the border, leading Larry Kart to write for the *Chicago Tribune* (August 10, 1986), "*SCTV* was the best ensemble-comedy effort to grace the tube since the days of Sid Caesar and *Your Show of Shows*." Levy told Kart, "I know without a question that *SCTV* was a good show. And I don't think there's anything that any of us has done since, on film or anywhere else, that has given us the same kind of creative highs." By the end of the show's run, in 1983, Levy realized that much of that magic had disappeared. "It had gotten to the point where we just couldn't think of another thing to parody," he recalled to Kart. "It seemed like we'd done everything; and if we hadn't, somebody else had. We couldn't come up with any more original ideas, so we knew it was time to end the show."

Levy's exposure on *SCTV*, as well as the two Emmys he had won for his work on the show, brought him many assignments. The first was the role of a seedy car salesman, opposite Chevy Chase, in *SCTV* alum Harold Ramis's 1983 film, *National Lampoon's Vacation*. The part, a relatively small one, taught Levy about the differences between television and film acting. "The big transition for me—or at least the hardest thing I've had to deal with in making films—has been how to do it without a whole lot of makeup on . . . ," Levy explained to Kart. "I mean for seven years on *SCTV* we really hid behind a lot of makeup. We kind of became the characters we played because we looked like those people. . . . On film, though, you're really out there on your own, looking pretty much like yourself."

In 1984 Levy scored a larger part, in Ron Howard's *Splash*, which stars Tom Hanks and Daryl Hannah. His character, a scientist trying to capture a mermaid (Hannah) for research purposes, earned him kudos from critics. Levy, however, told Kart, "*Splash* was a wonderful film, and I've gotten some nice acclaim from it, but when I first saw it I wasn't impressed with myself at all." Later that year Levy teamed up with John Candy for *The Last Polka*, a one-hour HBO special on which the two men reprised their *SCTV* roles as the Shmenges, polka-playing "rock stars" giving their final concert appearance. Levy and Candy wrote and produced the special as well. Howard Rosenberg wrote for the *Los Angeles Times* (March 11, 1985), "[*The Last Polka*] is a wonderfully imaginative spoof of rock group farewells . . . [leaving] you pining for more *SCTV*." Among other of his projects during that period, Levy appeared in Ramis's *Club Paradise* (1986), which stars Robin Williams and features a host of former *SCTV* players, including Flaherty, Moranis, and Andrea Martin. Levy also starred, again with John Candy, in *Armed and Dangerous* (1986). Over the next six years, Levy would play small parts in a number of television productions and films, most notably in Charles Shyer's *Father of the Bride* (1991), starring Steve Martin and Diane Keaton. Also during this period, as a member of the Northern Lights music group, Levy contributed to the track "Tears Are Not Enough" for the album *We Are the World*, whose proceeds went toward famine relief.

Levy's directorial debut was *Once Upon a Crime* (1992), a comedy with Candy, James Belushi, and Cybill Shepherd. A remake of the 1960 Italian movie *Crimen*, *Once Upon a Crime* failed to impress either critics or audiences. Later that year Levy acted in and directed the made-for-TV *Partners 'n Love*, an homage to the 1940s romantic comedies starring such legends as Katharine Hepburn, Spencer Tracy, and Cary Grant; that project, too, was a critical disappointment.

After minor roles in *I Love Trouble* (1994), *Father of the Bride, Part II* (1995), and other movies, Levy teamed up with Christopher Guest—of *This Is Spinal Tap* (1984) fame—to write *Waiting for Guffman* (1996). Directed by Guest, with a cast that included both men, the movie was performed largely in the improvisational style of *SCTV*. The fictional town of Blaine, Missouri, is the setting for this mock documentary, which offers a satirical look at small-town theater companies. The story follows a small troupe of untalented amateurs who put on a musical to commemorate Blaine's 150th anniversary. The film received rave reviews from critics. In the *Los Angeles Times* (January 31, 1997), Kenneth Turan wrote, "[*Waiting for Guffman* is] a sly and gleeful comedy showcase that pokes clever fun at the American musical, amateur theatricals and anything else that's not nailed down." Joe Morgenstern, in the *Wall Street Journal* (February 4, 1997), called the movie "very funny and subversively original," and added, "The best . . . of the bunch includes Eugene Levy's lazy-eyed dentist, Allan Pearl."

In 1999 Levy appeared in the coming-of-age comedy *American Pie*, which went on to gross more than $100 million at box offices. Although his was a supporting role, it was well received by both audiences and critics and introduced Levy to a new generation of movie viewers, many of whom were born after the heyday of *SCTV*. Steven Rosen, writing for the *Denver Post* (July 9, 1999), referred to Levy's character as "perfectly played." In an online interview with *romanticmovies.about.com* (August 3, 2001), Levy admitted, "I'm very pleased with the way the character has kind of hit. . . . I'm kind of proud to carry the moniker of 'Jim's Dad' now." Cast with a group of teenage and 20-something stars, Levy was given free rein with his character; the result was a great deal of improvisation, which is seen as his strength. Levy's character was brought back for the movie's 2001 sequel, *American Pie 2*.

A year earlier Levy had teamed up with Christopher Guest to co-write another mock documentary, this time lampooning the dog-show circuit. *Best in Show*, like Guest and Levy's *Guffman*, was a success with critics. Calling the film "hilarious," David Willoughby wrote for the London *Times* (March 10, 2001), "In selecting the ultra kitsch world of dog shows, Guest and Levy could be accused of having chosen an easy target for derision. But behind this mercilessly incisive satire lurks a genuine affection for the subject matter and real empathy with the protagonists." Although it was only a modest success at the box office, *Best in Show* earned Guest and Levy nominations for the best original screenplay award from the Writers Guild of America in 2001. Most recently Levy turned up in Peter Chelsom's *Serendipity* (2001), a romantic comedy starring John Cusack and Kate Beckinsale.

In 2002 Levy had a co-starring role in the television comedy series *Greg the Bunny*, in which people and puppets co-exist in a fictional world. Levy played the director of a children's show onto which the title character, a crude, boorish rabbit, bluffs his way. *Greg the Bunny* was canceled within two months of its March 27, 2002 debut. In 2003 Levy will appear in the film *A Mighty Wind*, along with Guest and several other cast members of *Waiting for Guffman* and *Best in Show*. A parody of the folk-music movement of the 1960s, *A Mighty Wind* follows the Folksmen, an aging trio of singers who reunite to embark on what they hope will be a comeback tour. Levy co-wrote the screenplay with Guest, who will direct the film.

Eugene Levy resides in Toronto, during the brief spells when he is not filming in Hollywood or on location in other parts of the world. Levy, who is a father, said in his interview for *urbancinefile.com*, "I made a choice to stay in Toronto to raise my family. I felt very strongly about NOT raising a family in Los Angeles. Also, I did not have this huge penchant for building a career; my thing was to try and make a good living." — J.H.

Suggested Reading: *Chicago Tribune* III p10 Aug. 10, 1986, with photo; *Denver Post* E p3 July 9, 1999; *Houston Chronicle* p6 Mar. 9, 1992; *Los Angeles Times* p10 Mar. 11, 1985, with photo, p26 Nov. 27, 1992, F p1 Jan. 31, 1997

Selected Films: as actor—*Cannibal Girls*, 1973; *National Lampoon's Vacation*, 1983; *Splash*, 1984; *Armed and Dangerous*, 1986; *Club Paradise*, 1986; *Father of the Bride*, 1991; *I Love Trouble*, 1994; *Father of the Bride, Part II*, 1995; *American Pie*, 1999; *American Pie 2*, 2001; *Serendipity*, 2001; as actor and director—*Once Upon a Crime*, 1992; *Partners 'N Love*, 1992; as actor and writer—*Waiting for Guffman*, 1996; *Best in Show*, 2000; as actor, writer, and producer—*The Last Polka*, 1984

John Sann/Courtesy of Universal Music Group

## Lincoln, Abbey

*Aug. 6, 1930– Jazz singer; songwriter; actress*

*Address: c/o Publicity, Verve Music Group, 1755 Broadway, Third Fl., New York, NY 10019*

"When I came to the stage," the jazz singer Abbey Lincoln recalled to Lara Pellegrinelli for the *New York Times* (March 3, 2002), "the women, the divas, were singing about a man who wasn't much." Lincoln was referring to the 1950s, when songs such as "Happiness Is Just a Thing Called Joe," "My Man," and "Glad to Be Unhappy" were typical fare, representing a seeming masochism most commonly associated with the legendary jazz singer Billie Holiday. "I did that for a minute," she explained, "and thought: 'Well, this is a drag. If he's nothin', I'm nothin' neither.'" Lincoln, who would eventually emerge as a prolific songwriter in her own right—as well as one of the most prominent and respected of jazz vocalists—followed a long and winding path to success. After starting off as a sultry West Coast nightclub singer performing under the name Gaby Lee, Lincoln joined up with the bebop percussionist Max Roach (her future husband) on the East Coast, contributing vocals to his landmark protest album about race relations and African-American history, *We Insist! Freedom Now Suite* (1960). The record's hard-edged politics, combined with Lincoln's performance on it—one track features her screeching as if in pain—proved to be too controversial for the music establishment of the time, and following the release of her 1961 album, *Straight Ahead*, Lincoln's singing career was curtailed. After a brief stint as an up-and-coming actress during the 1960s, Lincoln disappeared from public view for much of the next two decades. It was not until the 1990s, with the release of such critically acclaimed albums as *The World Is Falling Down* (1990), *You Gotta Pay the Band* (1991), *Devil's Got Your Tongue* (1992), and *A Turtle's Dream* (1994), that Lincoln came into her own as a jazz vocalist and songwriter.

Lincoln is frequently compared to Holiday, whom she has cited as one of the most important influences on her career. Her singing is technically imperfect, and unlike most jazz singers, she does not scat or improvise. Where she excels is in her empathy: her ability to plumb the emotional depths of a lyric, employing subtle alterations of rhythm and tempo in a voice that is described as forceful, raw, and worldly-wise. "There is an undeniably searing quality to her interpretations, a direct and unadorned way of communicating that consistently recalls Holiday," Howard Reich noted for the *Chicago Tribune* (June 14, 1993). "More intellectual than sensual, more dramatic than lyric, Lincoln's best work far transcends her vocal limitations." As one of the few jazz vocalists to write her own songs, Lincoln seizes the opportunity to express what is on her mind. She moves between advocating the empowerment of black women through defiance and independence and celebrating, as she has in her most recent albums, love, family, and the changes that come with aging. "The best thing you can do," she told Lara Pellegrinelli, "is to be a woman and stand before the world and speak your heart."

Abbey Lincoln was born Anna Marie Wooldridge on August 6, 1930 in Chicago, Illinois. She was raised on a farm in rural Calvin Center, Michigan. Her mother "was the griot [or culture-bearer] of the family," Lincoln told Gene Seymour for *Newsday* (November 17, 1991). "She told us who was in our family history, where we came from. I learned from her the art of being well." Her father worked as a handyman; he frequently borrowed records from his customers to bring home and play on the family's Victrola phonograph, which was housed in a cabinet. "I was looking for the people who were making the music inside the cabinet," Lincoln recalled to Michael Bourne in an interview for the Newark, New Jersey, jazz radio station WBGO. "I would look in there and see if I could find somebody who was making all this wonderful music." The family, while poor, had an upright piano in the living room, and at the age of five Lincoln began to play songs. As the 10th of 12 children, she found solace in music. "Nobody bothered me in the music room," she told Michael Bourne. "They didn't tell me when to play and when not to play, and I started to figure out the spaces between the notes because I didn't know anything about notes and changes or anything. . . . If I could sing the song, I would learn to play it." She joined a singing group at school and sang with the church choir. When she was 14 she heard a Billie Holiday recording for the first time, on the Victrola, and was "knocked out by the sound of her voice—it was so real," she told Howard Reich for the *Chicago Tribune* (September 3, 1995).

Lincoln began listening to other great singers, including Ella Fitzgerald, Sarah Vaughan, and Lena Horne. At 19 she won an amateur singing contest, and shortly afterward she moved to Los Angeles, California, to perform in nightclubs. In 1952 she left for Honolulu, Hawaii, where she spent two years as a resident singer at a club. She then returned to Los Angeles and started singing at a French-themed club in Hollywood called the Moulin Rouge. The club's owners had her perform as Gaby Lee (a name they thought sounded French) and wear feathered hats and provocative dresses onstage. "I was innocent and inexperienced, and in Hollywood there were people who were interested in selling me," she explained to Jill Nelson for *Essence* (April 1992). She told Les Payne for *Newsday* (July 2, 2000), "I was told not to 'sound like a Negro' when I spoke and I sang the more titillating standards and phony folk tunes." In Hollywood she met the lyricist Bob Russell (the writer of such standards as "Don't Get Around Much Anymore"), who became her manager and changed her name to Abbey Lincoln—a name inspired by Westminster Abbey, in London, England, and President Abraham Lincoln. Through Russell she landed a deal with Liberty Records, and in 1956 she recorded her first album, *Affair: A Story of a Girl in Love*, whose cover showed her in a provocative pose. Later that year she appeared in the film *The Girl Can't Help It*, starring Jayne Mansfield. Although she had only a small singing role, she attracted a lot of attention by wearing a dress that Marilyn Monroe had worn in *Gentlemen Prefer Blondes*, prompting *Ebony* magazine to feature her on the cover of its June 1957 issue as "The Girl in Marilyn Monroe's Dress." As her profile as a sex symbol grew, however, Lincoln began to worry that it might undermine her singing career. "[It] was making a mess of my life," she recalled to Howard Reich during their 1995 conversation, "because they weren't taking me seriously, though how would you expect them to, in that Marilyn Monroe dress?"

Lincoln's relationship with Max Roach, whom she met in the mid-1950s and married in 1962, helped convince her that her music should take precedence over her glamorous image. In the late 1950s she acted on the advice of Roach, a renowned jazz percussionist, and moved to New York City, where she met and worked with such jazz legends as John Coltrane, Sonny Rollins, Thelonious Monk, and Oscar Brown Jr. "After being involved in the insincere approach to the stage [in Hollywood]," she explained to Howard Reich, "coming to New York and discovering all these artists was like finding a haven. . . . It changed my life." In 1957 Lincoln recorded for Riverside Records what is considered to be her first real jazz album, *That's Him*, with Roach, Rollins, Kenny Dorham, Paul Chambers, and Wynton Kelly. She followed it up with *It's Magic* (1958) and *Abbey Is Blue* (1959). "With those discs began the long-running and apt comparisons to Holiday that describe Lincoln's behind-the-beat attack and stark tonal qualities," Gene Santoro observed in the *Nation* (July 3, 1995).

Lincoln meanwhile found herself drawn to the emerging civil rights movement, which brought her into contact with such prominent black intellectuals and writers as Amiri Baraka (then known as LeRoi Jones) and Maya Angelou. As she traveled around the country, she was dismayed to discover the extent to which African-American communities were mired in poverty. In an expression of pride in her cultural heritage, she began wearing her hair in an Afro, becoming one of the first stage singers to do so. In 1960 she sang on Roach's controversial civil rights anthem, *We Insist! Freedom Now Suite*, for Candid Records. One of the tracks on the avant-garde album features Lincoln screaming along with Roach's drumming—a performance that shocked many listeners. Although Lincoln embraced the album's message of racial equality, she felt the music was not right for her. "I was really looking for myself and for my material at that time, but I also was a partner with Roach," she explained to Howard Reich. "So it was an enriching experience to work on that music, but it was traumatic, too, to stand on the stage and holler and scream in people's ears."

It was also during this period that Lincoln began to write lyrics, mostly for other jazz composers' previously wordless tunes. She supplied lyrics for John Coltrane's "Africa" and Thelonious Monk's "Blue Monk," the latter of which she recorded on her 1961 album *Straight Ahead* (also for Candid). The effort won praise from Monk, who said she would make a great composer. The album piqued some critics, however, because of its outspoken racial politics. Ira Gitler, a reviewer for *Down Beat* magazine, faulted Lincoln for becoming "a professional Negro," as quoted by Nat Hentoff in the *New York Times* (March 3, 2002). "We don't need the Elijah Muhammad type of thinking in jazz," Gitler wrote, referring to the founder of the black-nationalist religious movement known as the Nation of Islam. Although her performances on *We Insist!* and *Straight Ahead* led some to celebrate Lincoln as a bold and forward-thinking vocalist, others branded her as a radical, and she found that fewer record offers came her way afterward.

In the mid-1960s the door to a promising film career opened for Lincoln, beginning with a starring role in Michael Roemer's 1964 film, *Nothing But a Man*, about racial relations in Alabama. In *Newsday* (November 17, 1991), Gene Seymour called the film, in which Lincoln and Ivan Dixon portray a couple, "one of the most realistic depictions of an African-American marriage." In 1968 she starred opposite the award-winning actor Sidney Poitier in Daniel Mann's romantic comedy *For the Love of Ivy*. Both films were notable "for their low-key, sensitive portrayals of black men and women," as John Leland noted for *Newsweek* (January 6, 1992). A future as a major actress failed to materialize, however, as Lincoln refused to appear in the "blaxploitation" films that began to proliferate around that time—movies that almost invariably stereotyped blacks as criminals seeking power and revenge on a corrupt white establishment. The film historian David Bogle remarked to John Leland, "[Lincoln] was able to project intelligence and poise and sensitivity. She had color. She wasn't a nurturing mammy figure or over-sexed. . . . It's an image that the media is not interested in or not comfortable with from an African-American woman."

Following an emotionally scarring divorce from Roach in 1970, Lincoln checked herself into a psychiatric hospital in upstate New York. After a five-week stay, she moved back to Los Angeles, where she took care of her ailing mother. Lincoln spent the next decade out of the limelight, working on personal projects and trying to find peace in her life. She took minor parts in television shows, read a great deal, learned to paint, and wrote poetry. In 1972 she spent two months in Africa, accompanying the South African singer Miriam Makeba, who was on tour there at the time. She met the president of Guinea, Sekou Touré, who honored her with the African name "Aminata," in recognition of her inner strength and determination. She also received the name "Moseka"—that of the goddess of love—from Zaire's minister of information. Those experiences inspired her, and upon her return to the United States she composed the songs for *People in Me* (1973). The album, though little-noticed, held much personal importance for Lincoln. "It really relieved me of whatever anxieties I had been carrying around, and it helped me to make peace with myself," she told Don Heckman for the *Los Angeles Times* (October 27, 2000). She continued to write lyrics and train as a vocalist, all to the apparent indifference of the music industry.

Lincoln moved back to New York City in 1981. She started performing in nightclubs again, and in 1983 she recorded *Talking to the Sun*. Two other albums followed—volumes one and two of *Abbey Sings Billie*—but it was not until 1989, when Jean-Phillippe Allard of Polygram France signed Lincoln to the label, that her luck began to change. The following year's release of *The World Is Falling Down*, on Verve Records (a subsidiary of Polygram), marked the beginning of Lincoln's highly celebrated career comeback. In *Time* (May 17, 1993), Jack E. White described the writing on some of the tracks as "prickly proclamations of self-esteem," offering as an example the lyrics from "I Got Thunder (And It Rings)": "I'm a woman hard to handle, if you need to handle things. / Better run when I start coming. I've got thunder and it rings." Eric Levin, reviewing the album for *People* (December 17, 1990), described Lincoln's singing as "relaxed, certain and emotionally rounded. . . . Her voice here has a crackling vivacity that brings lyrics to life and a tactile sauciness that dances the syllables over the beat." Also in 1990 Lincoln found herself in the movie business once again, when the director Spike Lee cast her in a small role in his film *Mo' Better Blues*.

Lincoln's next release, *You Gotta Pay the Band* (1991), which paired her with the eminent jazz saxophonist Stan Getz, fared even better than her previous album, reaching number two on *Billboard*'s jazz album chart. Mike Joyce, in the *Washington Post* (January 8, 1992), called it a "marvelous recording, full of intimate yet soul-stirring performances." *Devil's Got Your Tongue* (1992), for which Lincoln wrote nine of the 11 songs, also reached the top of the jazz charts. On the title track from that album, Lincoln offers a harsh critique of rap singers who denigrate black culture: "Tell a dirty story, / of a lowly jerk," she sings, as quoted by Jack E. White. "Even though the joke's on us, it's supposed to work." Another song on the album, "Story of My Father," evokes "a sense of roots that go back through segregation and slavery all the way to Africa," White observed.

The highly acclaimed *A Turtle's Dream* (1994), nine of whose 11 songs are originals, earned Lincoln a Grammy Award nomination and appeared on numerous critics' album-of-the-year lists. "Laying back seductively on the beat, she wraps her warm contralto around a melody and entices listeners to hang on every word of a song," David Grogan wrote for *People* (September 11, 1995). "On the title track of this album, arguably her best effort since she made her recording debut nearly four decades ago, Lincoln adopts the persona of a turtle who dreams of soaring like an eagle but ultimately finds comfort in the realization that 'I can swim the ocean / And it's deep and wide / And in the house above me abide.'" Stephen Holden of the *New York Times* (November 10, 1995) called *A Turtle's Dream* "profoundly beautiful. . . . A piercing pain is balanced by an exhilarating sense of self-determination and a childlike wonder."

Lincoln wrote seven of the 10 songs on *Wholly Earth* (1998). "Her writing proves every bit as impressive as her singing," Geoffrey Himes noted in a review of the album for the *Washington Post* (January 8, 1999). "More often than not, her words prove fresh and clever without ever losing their conversational flow or their comfortable fit with the insinuating melodies. The lead-off track, 'And It's Supposed to Be Love,' may well become a standard." Lincoln's most recent album, *Over the Years* (2000), includes five original tunes as well as renditions of such songs as Leonard Bernstein's "Lucky to Be Me," the World War II song "When the Lights Go on Again," and a Mexican love song, "Somos Novios," which Lincoln sang in Spanish. "An album full of traditional and original ballads, all of which are treated to Lincoln's inimitable style, *Over the Years* soothes like an old friend calling you on a lonely night," Natalie Bullock opined for *NPR On-line*. "With her round, full sound, edges coarse from experience and wisdom, Lincoln sings a perfect set exactly for the listener, as if she knows just what your soul needs to hear."

Lincoln, who turned 70 in 2000, continues to perform at venues across the United States and in Europe. She was recently honored with a retrospective, "Abbey Lincoln: Over the Years," presented by New York City's Jazz at Lincoln Center. "I don't know what's before us," Lincoln remarked in an interview posted on the Verve Music Group Web site. "No one knows. It's sobering, but we're still all-powerful human beings. If you can keep hope, you can live on. And there's the music—it always leaves footprints in the sand." — A.I.C.

Suggested Reading: *Chicago Tribune* I p16 June 14, 1993, XIII p9 Sep. 3, 1995; *Essence* p72 Apr. 1992; *Los Angeles Times* F p24 Oct. 27, 2000; *Nation* p30 July 3, 1995; *New York Times* C p1 Nov. 10, 1995, II p31 Mar. 3, 2002; *Newsday* p15 Nov. 17, 1991, B p6 July 2, 2000; *Newsweek* p50 Jan. 6, 1992; *People* p25 Dec. 17, 1990, p23 Sep. 11, 1995; *Time* p59 May 17, 1993; *Washington Post* C p7 Jan. 8, 1992, N p17 Jan. 8, 1999

Selected Albums: *Affair: A Story of a Girl in Love*, 1956; *That's Him*, 1957; *It's Magic*, 1958; *Abbey Is Blue*, 1959; *We Insist! Freedom Now Suite*, 1960; *Straight Ahead*, 1961; *People in Me*, 1973; *The World Is Falling Down*, 1990; *You Gotta Pay the Band*, 1991; *Devil's Got Your Tongue*, 1992; *A Turtle's Dream*, 1994; *Wholly Earth*, 1998; *Over the Years*, 2000

---

## Lincoln, Blanche Lambert

*Sep. 30, 1960– U.S. senator from Arkansas (Democrat)*

*Address: 355 Dirksen Senate Office Bldg., Washington, DC 20510*

When she was elected to the United States Senate in November 1998, Arkansas Democrat Blanche Lambert Lincoln became the youngest woman ever elected to the upper chamber of the United States Congress, and only the second woman in her state's history (the first was Hattie Carraway in 1932) to win a Senate seat.

The daughter of Jordan Lambert Jr. and Martha Kelly Lambert, Blanche Lambert Lincoln was born on September 30, 1960 in Helena, Arkansas, a small town situated in the flat agricultural country

Courtesy of Senator Lincoln's office

*Blanche Lambert Lincoln*

along the Mississippi River. A sixth-generation farm family, the Lamberts grew rice, wheat, soybeans, and cotton on their property. They kept their daughter in the public schools after those schools were integrated during the civil rights movement of the 1960s. "My parents raised independent-minded kids," Lincoln has said, as quoted by the *Almanac of American Politics 2000.*

Lincoln studied briefly at the University of Arkansas, in Fayetteville, before going on to earn a bachelor's degree from Randolph-Macon Women's College, in Lynchburg, Virginia, in 1982. After completing her education, Lincoln found employment as a staffer for the Democratic congressman Bill Alexander, then representing the First Congressional District of Arkansas. She worked with Alexander for two years, then went to Washington, D.C., to work for the businessman and lobbyist Billy Broadhurst.

In 1992 Lincoln returned to Arkansas in order to run against her former boss, Bill Alexander, for a seat in Congress representing the First District. (Lincoln later told Melinda Henneberger for the *New York Times* [June 13, 1998] that when she informed Alexander of her plans to run against him, "he laughed and said, 'Why not run for the Senate?'") Aided by the wave of anti-incumbent sentiment then sweeping the nation, Lincoln defeated Alexander in the primary, taking 61 percent of the ballots cast and carrying 23 of the district's 25 counties. In the general election Lincoln did even better, soundly defeating Terry Hayes, the Republican challenger, with 70 percent of the vote. That occasion was the first on which a woman had been elected to the House of Representatives from Arkansas's First District. Two years later, in 1994, Lincoln was reelected, this time by a much narrower margin—53 percent to 47 percent.

Lincoln, who has been variously characterized as both a moderate and a conservative Democrat, won seats on the Commerce Committee and the Democratic Steering and Policy Committee during her first term. She came out in favor of limited abortion rights, believing in a woman's right to choose but opposing late-term abortions, except in cases in which "the treating physician deems it necessary to protect the life or serious health of the mother," as she told Roy Maynard for *World* (September 12, 1998). She supported a ban on the manufacture of assault rifles, but also endorsed many of the items in the so-called Contract with America, the legislation proposed by the Republican Party, which gained control of both the Senate and the House in 1994. She strongly advocated a balanced-budget amendment (one of the key provisos of the contract), supported the North American Free Trade Agreement (NAFTA), and was a founding member of the "Blue Dog" Coalition, an association of socially moderate, fiscally conservative Democrats. According to the National Taxpayers Union Foundation, Lincoln ranked as the eighth-lowest-spending Democrat in the House during her tenure. Over the course of her two terms, Lincoln voted with President Bill Clinton, a Democrat, about two-thirds of the time (on average, House Democrat support for the president was 75 percent).

In January 1996, having just learned that she was pregnant with twins, Lincoln announced that she would not run for reelection in the House that coming November. The decision not to run, Lincoln has said, was prompted by concerns about keeping an arduous campaign schedule during a high-risk pregnancy. Two years later Lincoln declared her candidacy for the U.S. Senate after the Democrat Dale Bumpers, a former governor and the state's senior senator, announced that he would not run for reelection in 1998.

In the primary Lincoln beat her chief Democratic rival, the state attorney general, Winston Bryant, by a margin of 45 percent to 27 percent. (Bryant nonetheless drew the support of organized labor, in large part because Lincoln had voted for NAFTA in Congress.) In the general election Lincoln defeated by a margin of 55 percent to 42 percent the Republican Fay Boozman, an ophthalmologist and state senator known primarily for his staunch opposition to the so-called "partial-birth abortion" procedure. (Boozman was hurt by his statement that women rarely get pregnant when raped because fear triggers a hormonal change that blocks conception. He denied reports that he had referred to that phenomenon as "God's little shield.") Lincoln, by contrast, made much of her maternal status during the campaign ("Daughter, wife, mother, Congresswoman," intoned the voice-over in one of her television advertisements, as quoted by Henneberger, "living our rock-solid Arkansas values"), and promised to dedicate herself to women's and children's health issues—without, however, offering many specific proposals. She further declared herself in favor of cutting taxes, proposed diverting a portion of the federal budget surplus to Social Security and Medicare, and said that she supported charter schools but not vouchers, which in her view would drain resources from the public-school system.

Lincoln currently serves on the Senate Finance Committee, with subcommittee assignments on Health Care, International Trade, Taxation, and IRS Oversight. In addition, she serves on the Agriculture, Nutrition and Forestry Committee and the Special Committee on Aging. Along with the Republican Louisiana congressman W. J. 'Billy' Tauzin, she received an award from the Alliance for Aging Research in 2002, for supporting medical research on health and aging. Lincoln is a founding member of the Senate New Democrat Coalition, an association of moderate Democrats, and a member of the Senate Centrist Coalition, a bipartisan group. Her current term is set to expire in January 2005.

In collaboration with her female colleagues in the Senate, Lincoln co-authored *Nine and Counting* (there were nine female senators after the 1998 elections), an account of the women's experiences in the Senate.

Lincoln's husband, Steve, whom she married in July 1993, is an obstetrician with a private practice in Fairfax County, Virginia. The couple have twin boys, Reece and Bennett Lincoln. In her spare time Lincoln enjoys duck hunting, fishing, and attending yard sales. She is an active member of her local Episcopal church. — P.K.

Suggested Reading: *New York Times* A p1 July 13, 1998, with photos, p4 Nov. 5, 1998, with photo; *Washington Post* A p6 Apr. 24, 1995, with photo; *Almanac of American Politics 2000*

---

## Linkin Park

*Rock band*

Bennington, Chester
*Mar. 20, 1976– Singer*

Bourdon, Rob
*Jan. 20, 1979– Drummer*

Delson, Brad
*Dec. 1, 1977– Guitarist*

Shinoda, Mike
*Feb. 11, 1977– Singer*

Hahn, Joseph
*Mar. 15, 1977– DJ*

Phoenix
*Feb. 8, 1977– Bassist*

*Address: c/o Warner Bros. Records, P.O. Box 6868, Burbank, CA 91510*

Achieving new heights in transgenre musical success, the rock band Linkin Park released their debut album, *Hybrid Theory*, in October 2000. After premiering at number 16 on the *Billboard* Top 200 chart, the record quickly climbed into the Top 10, where it has remained for over a year. The album delivers a high-intensity performance in a style combining punk and so-called rap-metal, meshing electric guitar and bass lines with hip-hop–inspired lyrics and rhythms. (Two of the six members of Linkin Park are, respectively, a rapping MC and a deejay who mans turntables and handles electronic sampling.) The band resists being categorized with others. "I see how we can be classified with [bands such as Papa Roach and Disturbed], because that's the closest thing to what we sound like," Linkin Park's guitarist, Brad Delson, explained to Ernest A. Jasmin for the Tacoma, Washington, *News Tribune* (January 26, 2001), "but when we started writing songs five years ago none of those bands had come out." Linkin Park's lyrics are intended especially for angry or angst-ridden young men who are unable to express themselves. The band's MC, Mike Shinoda, told Jenny Eliscu for *Rolling Stone* (January 18, 2001) that *Hybrid Theory* discusses "the everyday struggle that you get stressed out by." He added: "The topics of the songs may not be positive, but I think people can relate to them in a positive way." Fans have shown their appreciation by purchasing millions of copies of *Hybrid Theory*; the album has been certified quintuple platinum (five million units) in the United States. It was the best-selling rock record in 2001.

Linkin Park evolved in Los Angeles, the hometown of five of its six members. Shinoda, born on February 11, 1977, and Delson, born on December 1, 1977, met in the seventh grade, when both were becoming interested in music. Delson had started guitar lessons around that time and got his own guitar in 1989. Shinoda, who had had piano and music-theory instruction, was inspired to write songs when he first attended a rock concert. As he recalled to Lina Lecaro for the *Los Angeles Times* (February 1, 2001), going to hear the metal band Anthrax and the rap group Public Enemy, who toured together in 1991, "was a really important thing in my life. . . . It was this mixing of all these different types of music." Shinoda and Delson graduated from colleges in the Los Angeles area, Delson having studied at the University of California at Los Angeles (UCLA) and Shinoda having majored in illustration at the Pasadena Art Center College of Design. Each found outlets for his musical talents with new friends. A classmate of Shinoda's, Joseph Hahn (born on March 15, 1977), was recruited as a deejay to spin the turntable and create

Reuters/Steve Marcus/Las Vegas Sun/Hulton/Archive by Getty Images

*The members of Linkin Park (left to right): Mike Shinoda, Joseph Hahn, Chester Bennington, Phoenix, Bob Bourdon, Brad Delson*

samples, and Delson's roommate, Dave Farrell (born on February 8, 1977), who goes by the name Phoenix, proved to be a talented bass player. In around 1996 Shinoda, Hahn, Delson, and Phoenix persuaded a fellow southern Californian, Rob Bourdon (born on January 20, 1979), to join the group as a drummer; Bourdon had been playing drums since the age of 10. With a lead vocalist who has since departed, the band, then called Xero (pronounced "zero"), began to write music and play small gigs.

The band dropped the name Xero in favor of Hybrid Theory, a testament to their blending of musical styles. But as they discovered when threatened with a lawsuit, another group already had that name. The musicians then called themselves Linkin Park, after the Santa Monica, California, landmark Lincoln Park. The misspelling was purposeful, as Shinoda explained to Lina Lecaro: "We wanted our own Web site, and the official spelling would have been too expensive. Plus we wanted our fans to be able to find us easily on the Internet." The lineup of the band changed around 1998 to include a new vocalist, Chester Bennington, born on March 20, 1976. A native of Phoenix, Arizona, Bennington had adopted music as his calling at a young age. Captured on tape singing Foreigner songs at age two, he developed a liking for hip-hop in junior high school and later became a fan of heavy metal. The front man for the Phoenix band Grey Daze in the mid-1990s, Bennington devoted himself to songwriting, drawing on rough childhood experiences that included sexual abuse, his parents' divorce, and a teenage addiction to cocaine and methamphetamine. "I think that's where a lot of the anger in my songs comes from," he told Rob Sheffield for *Rolling Stone* (March 29, 2001). "I've never written a song about it, because I don't think it should matter to people. But I don't hide it, because I don't think you should ever be ashamed or afraid of who you are, or anything that's happened to you. . . . If it helps kids to hear me talk about it, if they can relate, that's cool."

Bennington was an excellent fit for the group, a skilled singer and songwriter who always had his mind on the needs of the listeners. He and Shinoda began to collaborate on lyrics for an album. (Early fans were treated to a 1998 EP released with the name *Hybrid Theory*, as the band was still calling itself then.) To the surprise of both, none of the 12 tracks they wrote together contained a single curse word, allowing the CD to avoid the industry's parental-advisory sticker—a highly unusual feat for a rap-metal band. "When Mike and I sat down and wrote the lyrics [for *Hybrid Theory*] we wanted to be as honest and open as we could," Bennington told Rob Sheffield. "We wanted something people could connect with, not just vulgarity and violence. We didn't want to make a big point of not cussing, but we don't have to hide behind anything to show how tough we can be." While the lyrics are not profane, they are often emotionally raw or brooding. "A lot of it is really frustrated emotion," Shinoda told Bill Jensen for *New York Newsday* (August 8, 2001). "We put that out there—'This is how we feel about it'—and people can listen and know they're not alone."

The band began to put samples of their music on the Internet, occasionally playing small venues in Los Angeles but refusing to go on cross-country tours of tiny clubs. "We're songwriters at heart and we didn't play that many shows," Shinoda told

Lina Lecaro, "so the Internet was a good way to meet a lot of kids and get feedback." During a gig at the Los Angeles club Whiskey, however, Linkin Park was noticed by Warner Bros. Records, which signed the group to a contract in early 2000. In August of that year, after making the record, they went on tour. *Hybrid Theory*, which was released on October 24, 2000 to considerable Internet fan-site buzz, debuted at number 16 on *Billboard*'s Top 200 album chart. Reuniting with bassist Phoenix, who had left the group for a year, Linkin Park continued to tour in support of their rapidly selling album, which had been certified platinum (one million sold) by March 2001. The group performed at Ozzfest in the summer of 2001, joining bands such as Slipknot and Disturbed, and at the Family Values Tour in the fall of 2001, side by side with Stone Temple Pilots and Staind, among others. In addition, the band toured on its own, with five separate trips to Europe, Asia, and Australia, each for about two weeks. In Europe they had the opportunity to open for the Deftones, a band they greatly admire. "In the past, a lot of bands have been discouraged from coming to other countries, because they're not used to starting all over," Joseph Hahn told Paul Sexton for *Billboard* (October 6, 2001). "We consider ourselves a worldwide band, and we really want to reach as many people as possible." He continued: "It's real hard for us to make time to come overseas, but it pays off." Indeed, *Hybrid Theory* went double platinum (two million units sold) in Australia and platinum in each of four markets—Canada, the United Kingdom, Germany, and the Asian Pacific (Japan, Singapore, and Malaysia).

Loneliness and frustration are two of the major themes of the album. On one of the singles from *Hybrid Theory*, "One Step Closer," Bennington bellows, "Everything you say takes me one step closer to the edge / I'm about to break!" "As far as the lyrics, it's very self-explanatory. I think that's one reason that it's being as well-received as it is," Shinoda told Jill Pesselnick for *Billboard* (October 21, 2000). "One Step Closer" debuted at number 34 on *Billboard*'s modern rock tracks chart a few weeks in advance of the album's release. Further explaining the song, Shinoda added: "It was written at a time when we were in the studio and things with our social lives and our music were getting a little bit stressful. We were at the end of our ropes, so to speak." Other well-received tracks from the album include "Papercut" and "In the End." "Crawling," which was released as a single in early summer 2001 and vaulted into the Top 10 of *Billboard*'s modern rock tracks chart, is a lyrical tour through feelings of isolation. "It was an expression of those feelings of insecurity and self-doubt that everyone goes through," Delson told Jill Pesselnick for *Billboard* (June 30, 2001). "The emotional unburdening [of the album] is accompanied by jolting fuzz-guitar riffs and knob-twirling sound effects that make this a consistently interesting set of dysfunctional, get-out-of-my-way rock," Steve Morse noted in his review of *Hybrid Theory* for the *Boston Globe* (January 25, 2001). In December 2001 the band was named the Modern Rock Artist of the Year at the *Billboard* Music Awards.

Linkin Park was nominated for an American Music Award for favorite artist—alternative music in January 2002. In March of that year, the song "Crawling" won the group a Grammy for best hard-rock performance. In mid-summer the band released *Reanimation*, a remix of *Hybrid Theory*, featuring radically reworked versions of the latter record's songs. While some critics regarded its appearance as merely a chance for Linkin Park to buy some time before having to record an entirely new album, others applauded its daring. "Commercially expedient though it may be," Rob Sheffield wrote for *Rolling Stone* (August 8, 2002), "it's also a labor of love." In August 2002 the band's "In the End" won an MTV Music Video Award for best rock video.

As dark as the themes of their songs may be, the members of Linkin Park are generally chipper in public—a surprise to many in the media, though not to the group's fans. "Most of the time, we're pretty upbeat guys, pretty mellow," Shinoda revealed to Bill Jensen. "The fans know that. It's the press that expect us to be these depressed, torn souls, always gloomy and—off." While they perform songs about isolation, several of the band members are in serious romantic relationships; Hahn and his girlfriend are expecting the birth of twins, and Bennington and his wife, Samantha, who married five years ago, are due to become parents in May. As unusual as the group's profanity-free album is its alcohol- and cigarette-free tour bus. "We're not a bunch of straight-edge goody-two-shoes, but we have responsibilities to ourselves and our families and the people in this group, and we respect that," Bennington told Rob Sheffield. "If you're getting wasted, you should be spending that energy out there meeting your fans. I love to get compliments from the janitors in the clubs—'Dude, thanks for not destroying the place, I can go home early tonight.'"

The response to *Hybrid Theory* was overwhelming, as Bennington explained to Rob Sheffield for *Rolling Stone* (December 6–13, 2001): "It's insane. We have the same intensity we had a year ago, but now it's to five times the audience." Connecting with the audience remains crucial to Linkin Park, who spend hours after each show signing autographs and talking to their fans, who are eagerly anticipating the late 2002 sophomore CD release from the incessantly touring band. "A lot of times, we'll sign [autographs] for twice as long as we play," Shinoda told Bill Jensen. "It's just important to us. We've always been about that. We love our kids. We have a lot of kids that say, 'This helped me through this situation'—they related to that song and it helps them out." "In this country, people do not think about the sensitivity of young men," Bennington observed to Jenny Eliscu. "It's a real tragedy. For kids to be able to listen to bands like us who are able to express ourselves—not through violence and vulgarity—I think it helps them learn to express themselves." — K.S.

Suggested Reading: *Los Angeles Times* F p37 Feb.1, 2001, with photo; *New York Newsday* C p1 Aug. 8, 2001; *Rolling Stone* p29 Jan. 18, 2001, with photo, p39+ Mar. 29, 2001, with photos

Selected Recordings: *Hybrid Theory*, 2000; *Reanimation*, 2002

---

D. Darr/Courtesy of ECM Records

## Lloyd, Charles

*Mar. 15, 1938– Jazz saxophonist*

*Address: c/o ECM Records, Postfach 600 331, D-81203, Munich, Germany*

During the mid-to-late-1960s, there were few jazz groups more popular than the quartet led by the tenor saxophonist Charles Lloyd. Heavily indebted to pop, Lloyd's album *Forest Flower: Live at Monterey*, recorded at the 1966 Monterey Jazz Festival on California's northern coast, was one of the first jazz albums ever to sell more than a million copies. The Charles Lloyd Quartet, which also included pianist Keith Jarrett, bassist Cecil McBee, and drummer Jack DeJohnette, became the first jazz group ever to play at the world-famous Fillmore West concert hall in San Francisco, California, which had normally been reserved for such behemoths of rock and roll as Jimi Hendrix, the Grateful Dead, and Janis Joplin. The Lloyd troupe then embarked upon a tour of what was then the Soviet Union, becoming the first jazz ensemble to make that journey. Despite derision from critics who regarded him as a kind of diet alternative to the legendary jazz saxophonist John Coltrane, Lloyd enjoyed a huge following among ordinary listeners and was referred to on many occasions as the "jazzman of the hippies."

His spot at the pinnacle of popular music, however, did not bring Lloyd personal fulfillment. In 1969 he "got off the bus," in his words, seeking a spiritual haven on the beaches of Malibu, California, before settling down for the better part of two decades in Big Sur, located south of San Francisco. In 1981 Lloyd was persuaded by the French pianist Michel Petrucciani to join him on a handful of European tours, which produced two live albums. The collaboration was short-lived, though, and Lloyd returned to his hillside retreat at Big Sur. It was not until later in the decade, after he had experienced a near-fatal illness, that Lloyd made a full-fledged comeback. In 1988 he played at the Montreux Jazz Festival, in Switzerland, where he had dazzled crowds throughout the 1960s, leading the Swiss critic Yvan Ischer to write, as quoted on *jazzvalley.com*, "To see and hear Charles Lloyd in concert is always an event, as this saxophonist has been at quite a few crossroads, but also because he seems to hold an impalpable truth which makes him a thoroughly original musician permitting us to capture the essence of a quartet that was practically being born under our eyes. This is what we call Grace!" Lloyd's late-1980s quartet included pianist Bobo Stenson, bassist Palle Danielsson, and drummer Jon Christensen. A year after their appearance at Montreux, the group recorded and released *Fish Out of Water*, marking Lloyd's return to the forefront of jazz. Since then, with various bandmates, Lloyd has released eight albums with the Munich, Germany–based ECM Records. His latest, *Hyperion with Higgins* (2001), was dedicated to Lloyd's friend and longtime collaborator Billy Higgins, who died earlier that year.

Charles Lloyd was born in Memphis, Tennessee, on March 15, 1938 into a family of African, Cherokee, Mongolian, and Irish lineages. Long noted for its musical tradition, Memphis was an especially rich environment for blues and jazz during Lloyd's formative years. During the 1940s the work of the jazz giants Billie Holiday, Lester Young, and, most important, Charlie Parker inspired Lloyd to take up music as a career. (He has also claimed to remember seeing Elvis Presley working as a local iceman.) Lloyd received his first saxophone at age nine and his first music lessons, from the jazz pianist Phineas Newborn, three years later. When he entered high school, Lloyd was immediately surrounded by talent. His classmates included such budding musicians as Booker Little, Harold Mabern, Frank Storzier, and Hank Crawford. At about this time Lloyd began appearing in Memphis clubs, playing with the blues legends B.B. King and Howlin' Wolf.

Following their high-school graduations, in the mid-1950s, most of Lloyd's peers went to Chicago, which had a long history as a scene of jazz innovation. Lloyd, however, took an unorthodox route west to Los Angeles, California, where he enrolled at the University of Southern California to major in composition. While in Los Angeles Lloyd found a community of talented jazz musicians that included the drummer Billy Higgins, the saxophonist Ornette Coleman, the trumpeter Don Cherry, and the reedman and flutist Buddy Collette. Collette recommended Lloyd to the drummer Chico Hamilton, in whose band Lloyd promptly found a place. Before long, Booker Little, who had now made his home in New York City, asked Lloyd to join him there; eager for Lloyd to stay in Los Angeles, Hamilton offered him a job as the band's musical director, which he accepted. Lloyd's musical direction represented an attempt, as Ben Waltzer noted for the *New York Times* (October 7, 2001), "to synthesize two streams of the early 60's jazz avant-garde: John Coltrane's ecstatic spirit and Eastern overtones and Ornette Coleman's rocketlike melodic declarations." The group's most popular recordings, made with the help of then-unknown Hungarian guitarist Gábor Szabó, were *Man from Two Worlds* and *Passin' Thru*. But New York and Booker Little continued to beckon, and in 1961 Lloyd joined his childhood friend in the Big Apple. Only six months after Lloyd's arrival in New York, however, Little was dead, at 23, of kidney failure. As quoted by Michael Burgess in the California weekly *La Jolla Village News* (May 24, 2000, online), Lloyd recalled, "When I first came to this work I wanted to jump in the fast lane. And Booker said, 'No, you've got to have quality of character.' It still haunts me how beautiful Booker was."

Lloyd briefly joined alto saxophonist Julian "Cannonball" Adderley's group on tenor sax. In 1965 Lloyd teamed up with Szabó, the bassist Ron Carter, and the drummer Tony Williams to record the album *Of Course, Of Course*, which inspired *Down Beat* magazine to name Lloyd best new jazz artist of 1965. Soon thereafter Lloyd formed a band with the young musicians Keith Jarrett, Jack DeJohnette, and Cecil McBee and made the landmark 1966 recording *Forest Flower: Live in Monterey*. As noted by Waltzer, the album's music "appealed to the same audiences that followed psychedelic rock groups," helping to lend a popularity to jazz that it had not enjoyed since the advent of rock and roll; *Forest Flower* sold a million copies. Lloyd's quartet traveled across the U.S. and to Europe, playing to packed houses wherever they stopped. The European tour included an historic, "unauthorized" stop at the 1967 Tallinn Festival in Estonia, which was then a constituent republic of the Soviet Union. Making their appearance there during the decades-long Cold War between the Soviet Union and the U.S., Lloyd's quartet faced immense pressure from local officials. "For three days, they wouldn't let us play the festival," Lloyd recalled to Thomas Conrad for *Down Beat* (July 1997). "They wanted us to do a clinic. They even offered to put us on television. I said, 'I'm here to play for human beings.' Finally, I asked them an interesting question. I asked them if they were practicing racism. The Soviet guys couldn't deal with that question. They said, 'You'll play tomorrow.'" He was also told, however, that his musical set would be limited to 20 minutes. But, as Lloyd told Conrad, "we came in the spirit of music, which transcends politics." The band performed for 50 minutes, marking the first time modern jazz was played by Americans in the Soviet Union. (Lloyd returned 30 years later to the Tallinn Festival in a now-independent Estonia. As quoted by Conrad, Lloyd announced to a sold-out crowd, "I feel to be a part of your past. Thirty years ago the people had a very difficult time, and I could feel it so much. Tonight, I feel your freedom.")

Back in the U.S. Lloyd continued to play to capacity crowds throughout the country, including several gigs at the famed Fillmore West, in San Francisco. He was also named *Down Beat*'s jazzman of the year for 1967. A couple of years later, however, Lloyd—who had earned a quarter of a million dollars a year since 1966—began to realize his disillusionment with the business of making music. "Something was nagging me," he explained to Peter Watrous for the *New York Times* (June 24, 1992). "I was still a young man, but I wasn't satisfied. I saw something quite magical in music, but I was frustrated with the world and life and travel: I didn't have enough inner life." Compounding his difficulties were his drug habit and the recent death of his mother, at age 54. The resulting turmoil led him to abandon music for a time. "I walked away from a gold mine," Lloyd later told Zan Stewart for the *Los Angeles Times* (December 2, 1994), "but that wasn't the most important thing in my life to me. The inner call was so strong that I realized that if I didn't deal with it, no amount of bread would make up for it."

Lloyd retreated first to the beaches of Malibu. "I was looking for a quiet place to nest," Lloyd told Watrous. "I stayed [in Malibu] for a few years on the beach; [the actors] Larry Hagman and Peter Fonda were there and showed me brotherhood. Larry had a kind of childlike nature so we hit it off well. I became a vegetarian, and lived simply." He later went to the mountainous terrain of Big Sur, where he began to focus on the study and practice of Eastern religious thought.

In the 1970s Lloyd released only a handful of records—"low-key albums," as Josef Woodard put it in *Down Beat* (June 1990), "the persistent airiness of which presaged new age music." These include *Geeta* (1974), *Weavings* (1978), and *Autumn in New York* (1979). Then, in 1982, Lloyd was visited at his Big Sur retreat by a 17-year-old piano virtuoso from France, Michel Petrucciani. The diminutive pianist, who suffered from a rare degenerative bone disorder (he died in 1999, at age 36), managed to coax Lloyd from his hermitage. In 1982 Lloyd and Petrucciani won the Prix d'excellence when they performed together at the Montreux International Jazz Festival. They recorded two live albums together on the Blue Note record label during 1982 and 1983 tours of Europe. (One of the albums, *A Night in Copenhagen*, has recently been reissued by Blue Note.) Lloyd then returned to his solitude in Big Sur. In the mid-1980s, though, he was led back to music after an intestinal ailment threatened his life. One of Lloyd's closest friends, Steven Cloud, later told Tom Conrad for *Down Beat* (April 1994), "Charles was a few hours from death. When he survived, he came out of the hospital with a decision: To rededicate himself to the great tradition, the jazz art form." Lloyd then formed a new quartet with the pianist Bobo Stenson, the bassist Palle Danielsson, and the drummer Jon Christensen. He made his triumphant return at the Montreux Festival in 1988, a year before signing a long-term contract with ECM Records. Through that alliance Lloyd, as Josef Woodard wrote for *Down Beat* (November 2000), "produced his strongest body of work in his career."

Lloyd's first ECM recording was *Fish Out of Water* (1989). In *Down Beat* (June 1990), Woodard hailed the album as Lloyd's "best in years—maybe decades." "He's again making a bid for life in the external world," Woodard continued. "With the help of an icily eloquent European rhythm section . . . an ethereal sense of poise governs the proceedings. Lloyd's own tone and ideas on the tenor teem with freshness, dark beauty, and repose."

As Danielsson and Christensen went on to solo success, Lloyd and Stenson recruited bassist Anders Jormin and drummer Billy Hart to fill the gaps. The new quartet's release *All My Relations* (1994)—made up, like Lloyd's other ECM recordings, of original material—earned critical kudos. John Corbett, for example, wrote for *Down Beat* (July 1995) that *All My Relations* "contains at once a certain softness and clear sense of definition." By the end of the 1990s, Lloyd's band had re-formed once again, this time to include drummer Billy Higgins, guitarist John Abercrombie, and bassist Dave Holland. That group's 1999 release, *Voice in the Night*, was "Lloyd's most lyrically beautiful album ever. Even blissful," in the opinion of Jeff Bradley, writing for the *Denver Post* (May 20, 1999).

In late December of that year, the band, with the addition of Brad Mehldau at piano and Larry Grenadier replacing Holland on bass, returned to the studio to record what Lloyd envisioned as a double CD. ECM executives decided instead to make two separate CDs from the sessions. The first, *The Water Is Wide* (2000), prompted Steve Futterman, writing for the *Washington Post* (November 22, 2000), to call Lloyd "a marvel." "On many tracks," Futterman continued, "he creates that most magical of moments: He makes you forget how the resplendent sounds he is making came to be. . . . Lloyd is ready to take his place with the masters." Especially noted by some critics was the interplay between Lloyd and his drummer, Higgins. Mike Joyce wrote for the *Washington Post* (September 29, 2000), "As always, the pairing of Lloyd and Higgins is its own reward for listeners. . . . Their understated but obvious rapport is among the album's great virtues."

The second recording from the December 1999 sessions was meant to be dedicated to Higgins's mother, who, herself a drummer, had died in early 2001 at the age of 97. On May 3 of that year, however, Higgins himself died of liver and kidney failure. The album, released later that year and titled *Hyperion with Higgins*, was therefore dedicated to both mother and son. Jeff Gordinier wrote for *Fortune* (October 1, 2001), "Lloyd has always been a spiritual man, but the soulful undercurrent on his latest disk runs deeper than usual: The album serves as a farewell from drummer Billy Higgins. . . . It's hard to imagine a more radiant elegy." Lloyd talked to Steve Graybow for *Billboard* (August 25, 2001, on-line) about the decision to release the two records separately: "[ECM was] worried that these children of mine would not find as many homes if they were introduced on a double CD. However, if you spend any time with them, you will find that they need their siblings. The music belongs together."

Charles Lloyd lives near Santa Barbara, California, with his wife and manager, Deborah Darr. "Tomorrow's not a given," he told Jeff Bradley. "But I do know that I love what I'm doing now. . . . A world without music is a miserable place." — J.H.

Suggested Reading: *Denver Post* E p5 May 20, 1999, with photo; *Down Beat* p48 June 1990, with photo, p34 Apr. 1994, p30+ July 1997, with photo, p44+ Nov. 2000, with photos; *New York Times* p2.31 Oct. 7, 2001, with photo

Selected Recordings: *Of Course, Of Course*, 1965; *Forest Flower: Live in Monterey*, 1966; *Charles Lloyd in the Soviet Union*, 1967; *A Night in Copenhagen*, 1983; *Fish Out of Water*, 1989; *Notes from Big Sur*, 1991; *The Call*, 1993; *All My Relations*, 1994; *Canto*, 1996; *Voice in the Night*, 1999; *The Water Is Wide*, 2000; *Hyperion with Higgins*, 2001

---

## Lucas, George

*May 14, 1944– Film director; producer; screenwriter*

*Address: Lucasfilm, 5858 Lucas Valley Rd., Nicasio, CA, 94946*

The acclaimed filmmaker, producer, and screenwriter George Lucas has had a hand in the creation of nearly every movie made in the past 25 years. While that may sound like an overstatement, a look at the scope of Lucas's filmmaking empire shows it to be true. From his production company, Lucasfilm, to his pioneering special-effects house, Industrial Light & Magic (ILM), down to THX Sound, which handles the mixing of movie soundtracks and even audio quality in movie theaters, Lucas's contribution to the world of movies is seemingly

In-Focus/Adrian Groom/Getty Images

*George Lucas*

endless. Additionally, Lucas helped to revitalize the world of moviemaking by reworking time-tested ideas into entirely new concepts. He is perhaps most famous for two series that radically changed the cinematic landscape. For the first, the *Star Wars* series, Lucas borrowed from sources as disparate as the films of Akira Kurosawa, the writings of Joseph Campbell, and *Flash Gordon* movie serials and comic books to create an entire science-fiction universe—so successfully that, a quarter-century later, many directors are still trying to emulate his achievement. His other series, the *Indiana Jones* films, paid homage to 1930s movie serials, telling of a swashbuckling archaeologist and his globetrotting hunts for lost treasure.

In his more than 30 years in the movie business, George Lucas has revolutionized special effects, sound design, and even the way movies are distributed. His film *Star Wars* (1977) was dumped into theaters on May 25, a time of year that movie distributors then viewed as a "dead zone," when patrons tended not to go to theaters and films often disappeared quickly. *Star Wars* changed all that, becoming a blockbuster, spawning a fan base that is almost religious in its zeal, and generating four sequels to date. "George Lucas effectively moved the summer forward two weeks, from the middle of June to the end of May," Tom Sherak, president of distribution for 20th Century Fox, told Aljean Harmetz for the *New York Times* (May 21, 1987). "The Wednesday before Memorial Day is called George Lucas Day."

In addition to being a huge moneymaker, *Star Wars* ushered in a new era in cinematic special effects. Whereas, prior to 1977, sci-fi films had used such low-tech items as fishing wire, Roman candles, and papier-mâché models to provide the illusion of spaceships in flight, Lucas employed a computer-controlled camera system that produced images of ships flying at incredible speeds, performing deft aeriel maneuvers, and hurtling directly at the camera. He also made quantum leaps forward in makeup, creating a cast of creatures, including robots and aliens, still unparalleled in their design. In the ensuing years he has continued to push boundaries with each successive film. For the first *Star Wars* sequel, *The Empire Strikes Back* (1980), he created the character Yoda, a wizened, three-foot-tall creature who mentors the film's hero. Yoda was brought to life entirely through elaborate puppetry, marking one of the few times that a lead actor has convincingly shared the screen with a puppet. In the late 1980s Lucas experimented further with computer-generated special effects, helping to bring to life the dinosaurs in *Jurassic Park* (1993) and creating fully realized digital sets for the television series *The Young Indiana Jones Chronicles.* In 1999 he wrote, directed, and produced *Star Wars: Episode I—The Phantom Menace*, the first in a series of prequels to the original trilogy. For that film, Lucas constructed physical sets that were no higher than six feet, adding the remainder of what appeared onscreen by using computers. In addition, that film was the first to employ a leading character, the comic foil Jar-Jar Binks, created entirely by digital technology. For the second film in the series of prequels, *Star Wars: Episode II—Attack of the Clones* (2002), Lucas used digital cameras exclusively, removing film entirely from the filmmaking process. "There's no physical print to get dirty," he told Steve Daly for *Entertainment Weekly* (March 26, 1999). "And it's much easier to [adjust] colors in portions of a shot in a digital print than it is with a chemical print. Chemical prints are so inexact, it's like working in the dark ages. It's depressing." Lucas objects to the widely held view that he is a technological wizard who would rather work with machines than actors and who employs a strictly mechanical approach to moviemaking. "I know I have this reputation for being this technical guy," he told Ty Burr for *Entertainment Weekly* (May 4, 2001, on-line), "but I'm not. All I know is I need to tell a story, and I'm most interested in quality."

For a man who has inspired generations of moviegoers to look toward the stars, George Walton Lucas Jr. had very down-to-earth beginnings. He was born on May 14, 1944 in Modesto, California, a small town south of San Francisco. "Even though it's California," Lucas told Charles Champlin, author of *George Lucas: The Creative Impulse* (1992), "it was a quiet, Midwestern kind of upbringing. There wasn't much going on." His father, George Lucas Sr., ran a successful office-supply store in town, with the help of Lucas's mother, the former Dorothy Bomberger. Lucas's mother was often ill, for reasons that doctors could never fully determine. She was in and out of the hospital, and Lucas, along with his two older sisters and one younger sister, was cared for by a housekeeper named Mildred Shelley, called "Till" around the house.

Lucas was a creative and imaginative child. He and his friends would often devise elaborate games; at one point, they built a carnival in Lucas's backyard, complete with a funhouse, a petting zoo, and a fully functional roller coaster. He was also fascinated with comic books, eventually owning so many that his father devoted an entire section of their shed to Lucas's collection. Lucas would spend hours drawing his own comics, as well as creating greeting cards and elaborate panoramas. He became a devotee of television, too, in the early 1950s. His favorite program was *Adventure Theater*, a nightly series that featured 1930s and 1940s movies. During this time Lucas enjoyed a steady diet of such characters as Flash Gordon, Tailspin Tommy, and the Masked Marvel. These serials made an indelible impression on him, particularly because of their cliff-hanger endings, each of which found the lead character in a seemingly hopeless situation that would not be resolved until the next installment. Many of his films, including the *Star Wars* and *Indiana Jones* series, stemmed from his love of movie serials.

When Lucas was 15 the family moved from their house in Modesto's residential section to a ranch set on 13 acres of walnut trees. Isolated from his friends, as the town was too far away to reach by bicycle, Lucas became somewhat withdrawn, spending a lot of time in his room listening to rock-and-roll music, for which he quickly developed a passion. He also became very interested in photography at this age, after his father bought him a 35mm camera. During this period Lucas began experimenting with film, taking low-angle and trick shots and oil-tinting the photos with the use of Q-Tips.

At Thomas Downey High School, Lucas was a relatively poor student, earning low grades and even attending summer school one year. He has since admitted to being bored by school, seeing the existing educational system as being pointless. "I would have learned to read eventually—the same with writing," he told Dana White for her book *George Lucas* (2000), published in association with A&E's *Biography* series. "You pick that stuff up because you have to. I think it's a waste of time to spend a lot of energy trying to beat education into somebody's head. They're never going to get it unless they want to get it."

Perhaps another reason Lucas couldn't always concentrate on his studies was his love of cars, which blossomed when his father bought the 15-year-old a Fiat Bianchina. "I had my own life once I had my car," he told White. "Along with the sense of power and freedom came competitiveness." He soon began spending his afternoons working on the car, modifying it until it was fit for racing. Although he was too young to compete officially, he began racing in small meets held at fairgrounds and in parking lots. Soon he was winning trophies not only in Modesto, but also in nearby towns. In addition, he spent his nights in Modesto immersed in the ritual known as "cruising." In his treatment for *American Graffitti* (1973), a film inspired by his teenage years, Lucas described cruising as "an endless parade of kids bombing around in dagoed, moondisked, flamed, chopped, tuck-and-rolled machines rumbling through a seemingly adultless, heat-drugged little town." Lucas was so enamored of cruising and racing that he wanted to devote his life to those pursuits. His father was displeased to hear of this, as he had hoped that Lucas would eventually take over the family business. "At eighteen, we had this big break, when he wanted me to go into the business," Lucas told John Seabrook for the *New Yorker* (January 6, 1997), "and I refused, and I told him, 'There are two things I know for sure. One is that I will end up doing something with cars, whether I'm a racer, a mechanic, or whatever, and, two, that I will never be president of a company.' I guess I got outwitted."

Lucas's dreams of becoming a racer came to a halt on June 12, 1962, when, while he was driving home, his car was broadsided by an oncoming vehicle. Lucas's seatbelt snapped, and he was thrown from the car, which struck a tree moments later. Lucas suffered major injuries, including several broken bones, a fractured scapula, and crushed lungs. While recovering in the hospital, he reevaluated his life. Concluding that he had been wasting his time, he decided to go to college. He attended Modesto Junior College, where he began studying in earnest. Two years later he transferred to the film school at the University of Southern California (USC). It was there that he discovered that his true passion was film. "Within one semester, I was completely hooked," he told Mike Duffy for Knight-Ridder Newspapers (January 25, 2002). "Film was my life. Cars weren't important to me. Nothing was important to me except film. . . . The best feeling in the world is to discover yourself. To discover what it is you're good at."

At USC Lucas began experimenting with various filmmaking styles, creating movies that thematically, visually, and musically broke the rules of directing. His first film was *Look at Life*. Using still photographs from *Life* magazine, Lucas alternated between violent and peaceful images, set to a thunderous soundtrack. The movie made an impression on the cinema department at USC, as well as on Lucas's classmates. *Look at Life* won Lucas several prizes at amateur film competitions. Over the next two years, he made several noteworthy student films, including *1:42:08*, about an auto race, and *Freiheit* (the German word for "freedom"), about a young student attempting to escape from East Germany to West Germany.

After graduating from film school, Lucas began looking for jobs in the movie business. He worked on a documentary for the United States Information Agency and served in the evenings as a teaching assistant at USC, where he also began taking graduate courses. As a grad student Lucas shot

*THX 1138: 4EB* (also known as *Electronic Labyrinth*), an imaginative science-fiction film set in a dystopian future in which people are given numbers instead of names. The film won first prize at the Third National Student Film Festival, among other awards. It also caught the attention of many people in Hollywood, including Francis Ford Coppola, then an up-and-coming director. With Coppola's permission, Lucas sat in on the shooting of his film *Finian's Rainbow* (1968). Lucas then shot a documentary, *Filmmaker*, which chronicled the making of Coppola's next picture, *The Rain People* (1969). During this period Lucas also made a short documentary entitled *6-18-67*. Originally intended to be about the making of the film *Mackenna's Gold* (1969), *6-18-67* became more of a visual tone poem about the film's desert locales.

With Coppola's help, Lucas secured financing from Warner Bros. to make *THX 1138: 4EB* into a feature-length film. Retitled *THX 1138*, and starring Robert Duvall and Donald Pleasance, the film expanded on Lucas's vision, showing a more detailed vision of the authoritarian world of the 25th century. When the film was shown to Warner Bros., the studio demanded that it be recut to make it more palatable to a mass audience. Though enraged at having his vision of the film compromised, Lucas accepted the studio's terms. The finished film, which attracted a small audience, still lost money for the studio. In the ensuing years it has earned a loyal following and remains one of Lucas's favorites among his films.

After the frustrating experience of making *THX 1138*, Lucas felt eager to direct a film that would be successful financially while remaining true to his artistic vision. To that end, he began drafting a treatment for a movie based on his teenage years in Modesto. The movie, *American Graffiti*, centers on four friends who face life-affecting decisions on the night before their high-school graduation. The film features the music of the 1950s and 1960s, the era in which it is set. "It was the first script I'd ever read where the soundtrack *was* the script," Ned Tanen, a former executive at Universal Pictures, told Chris Nashawaty for *Entertainment Weekly* (March 1, 1999). "What amazed me was that I was the last person in town to ever see this screenplay. Every company in town passed on it." *American Graffiti* opened on August 1, 1973 and proceeded to set box-office records; its tag line—"Where were you in '62?"—became a catchphrase. Its soundtrack also became a big seller, ushering in an era of nostalgia for the 1950s and early 1960s. The movie was nominated for five Academy Awards, including best director and best picture.

The astounding success of *American Graffiti* put Lucas in the position of being able to choose his projects. He had long dreamed of creating a space adventure story in the vein of the *Flash Gordon* films he had seen as a child, but with more modern special effects. Additionally, he wanted to make a positive film, one unlike the increasingly bleak and occasionally brutal films then being released. In an interview with Bruce Handy for *Time* (February 10, 1997), Lucas said that his primary reason for making *Star Wars* was "to give young people an honest, wholesome fantasy life, the kind my generation had."

He began work on an epic saga entitled "The Star Wars," a sprawling tale that featured a princess in need of rescue, an evil empire bent on dominating the universe, and a band of "Jedi" knights sent to quell the brewing conflict. The story borrowed elements from the films of Akira Kurosawa, such novels as Frank Herbert's *Dune*, and various ancient myths and legends. One of the script's concepts was that of the Force (called the "Force of Others" in early treatments), an energy field generated by all living things; the Jedi knights believed strongly in the Force and could often use it to their advantage. This concept added a touch of religious mysticism to what was otherwise a star-hopping swashbuckler. Although Lucas was a hot property in Hollywood, most studios did not understand his script for "The Star Wars" (originally titled "The Adventures of the Starkiller, Episode One of the Star Wars") and turned it down. However, Alan Ladd Jr., an executive at 20th Century Fox, saw something in the script and agreed to produce it. Once financing was secured, Lucas began reworking the script. Realizing that his story was too long for one film, he turned its three acts into separate movies. If the first was a hit, he reasoned, he could always complete the story later. He also shelved the elaborate backstories he had devised for the characters, saving them for a possible future series. Eventually, he whittled his script down to a compact story involving Luke Skywalker, a naive boy from a desert planet who, along with his mentor, Obi-Wan Kenobi, travels across the galaxy to rescue Princess Leia from the clutches of the Empire's chief enforcer, the evil Jedi knight Darth Vader. Along the way he meets a rogue space pirate named Han Solo and his co-pilot, the apelike Chewbacca, a "Wookie." Lucas also included a pair of robots, C-3PO and R2D2, who served as comic relief.

From the start, the shooting of the movie—now called simply *Star Wars*—was plagued with technical, financial, and personnel-related problems. Additionally, after having spent $1 million of their $2 million budget, Lucas's special-effects company had only three usable shots. The situation reached its breaking point when, during a flight to San Francisco, Lucas felt sharp pains in his chest. His wife, Marcia, rushed him to the hospital, where he was told that he was suffering from hypertension and exhaustion. (Some reports say that his condition may have been exacerbated by diabetes, with which he had been diagnosed in 1966.)

Lucas returned from his brief stay in the hospital determined to finish *Star Wars* and never direct again. By the spring of 1977, he had completed the film. He arranged an advance public screening in San Francisco, which he attended. Seeing the movie's first shot, in which a seemingly endless spaceship rumbles overhead with laser guns blazing, the audience erupted in cheers. The screening was a rousing success, validating all of Lucas's hard work. Still, he remained skeptical that the film would turn a profit.

His fears were eased on May 25, 1977, the day *Star Wars* officially hit theaters. That day Lucas and his wife were on their way to lunch at a Hollywood restaurant when they found themselves amid throngs of people—most of whom, it turned out, were going to see Lucas's movie. "One lane of traffic was blocked off," Lucas told White. "There were police there. There were limousines in front of the theater. There were lines, eight or nine people *wide*, going both ways and around the block. [I thought] 'My God, what's going on here? It must be a premiere or something.' I looked at the marquee, and it was *Star Wars*." The film became the highest-grossing movie of its day and still ranks in the top 10 movies of all time in terms of box-office receipts. Moreover, it spawned a legion of fans, some of whom saw the film hundreds of times. Those viewers were impressed by the concept of a futuristic world that had a lived-in look; the set designers for *Star Wars* had been asked to dirty the sets and nick the robots with saws, and the result was a fictional world that seemed much more real than the brightly polished universes of previous science-fiction films. As a testament to Lucas's vision, nearly every sci-fi film released since *Star Wars* presents the future largely as he imagined it.

*Star Wars* is also noteworthy as the first film to demonstrate the power of merchandising. Before long, stores were inundated with *Star Wars* T-shirts, beach towels, bed linen, and, perhaps most famously, action figures. The merchandising boom created by *Star Wars* made Lucas, who owned the lion's share of the merchandising rights, a millionaire many times over. *Star Wars* was also nominated for 10 Academy Awards; it collected six, including one for Lucas's wife for best editing and awards for best original costume design and best special effects.

The success of *Star Wars* caused a reverberation in the movie community. Soon, studios were dusting off sci-fi scripts neglected for years. (One of these was a feature-film version of the television series *Star Trek*, which arrived in theaters in 1979 and has since spawned nine sequels.) By 1978 *Star Wars* fans and studio executives were clamoring for a sequel to *Star Wars*. While Lucas had two waiting in the wings, he did not want to direct them, preferring to serve as executive producer. He turned the reins over to Irvin Kershner, who had directed such films as *Return of a Man Called Horse* (1976) and *Eyes of Laura Mars* (1978). Lucas penned a story treatment for the film and asked the screenwriter Leigh Brackett to write the script. After Brackett turned in a first draft, she succumbed to cancer. Lucas then turned to the up-and-coming writer Lawrence Kasdan to pick up where Brackett had left off. A much darker film than its predecessor, *The Empire Strikes Back* finds the main characters scattered across the galaxy. Luke begins his Jedi knight training under the watchful eye of Yoda, while Leia, Han, Chewbacca, and the robots find themselves relentlessly pursued by Darth Vader, who wants to use them as bait to trap Luke. The film ends with a nod to the cliffhangers of Lucas's youth, with the heroes beaten by the Empire and Han in the clutches of a galactic crime lord. Making the film, Lucas encountered some budgetary concerns, and at times did not entirely approve of Kershner's directorial decisions. Still, the overall experience was much more positive for Lucas than making *Star Wars* had been.

*The Empire Strikes Back* was released on May 21, 1980. Critics' reactions to it were divided. David Sterritt wrote for the *Christian Science Monitor* (May 21, 1980), "Rarely have high filmic art and Saturday-matinee excitement been so successfully combined." Vincent Canby, however, wrote for the *New York Times* (June 15, 1980), "I found myself glancing at my watch almost as often as I did when I was sitting through a truly terrible movie called *The Island*." Still, audiences embraced the film. By the end of the summer, it had bested *Star Wars* in box-office receipts to become the biggest moneymaker in movie history. It is still regarded by many fans as the best film in the *Star Wars* series. After it was re-released, in 1997, Lisa Schwarzbaum wrote for *Entertainment Weekly* (February 7, 1997), "The storytelling is the series' best, with a zingy balance of drama, humor and Deep Thoughts. . . . The boffo action sequences are more gracefully integrated into the whole than they are in *Star Wars*. And the psychological underpinnings . . . are smoothly, even wittily present, without distracting from the corking saga."

In the wake of the success of *The Empire Strikes Back*, Lucas began building Skywalker Ranch, a 3,000-acre haven for filmmakers, located in Nicasio, California, where creativity was stressed above all else. There, Lucas designed a Victorian-style headquarters for his company, Lucasfilm. Lucas told Champlin that the ranch would be "like a big *home*, a big fraternity where filmmakers could work together and create together." Describing the complex for the *New York Times* (July 13, 1981), Aljean Harmetz wrote, "Through a redwood forest, over a newly built wood bridge, is a Victorian village—octagonal buildings with casement windows and stained glass, tongue-and-groove oak paneling that can rarely be found in homes less than 80 years old, gables, cupolas, immense flagstone fireplaces—all of the quaint, eccentric buildings painted ice-cream white and blueberry gray. There are meadows of wild flowers everywhere, and the 10th deer of the morning grazes on a hillside clotted with the frail orange petals of California poppies."

During this time Lucas also began work on *Raiders of the Lost Ark* (1981). Based on an idea that he and the highly successful filmmaker Steven Spielberg hammered out on the beach in Hawaii, the film—with Spielberg as director and Lucas as a producer—was a direct homage to the movie serials Lucas had seen while watching *Adventure Theater.* For the movie's hero, Lucas created Indiana Jones, an unshaven, gun- and whip-toting archaeologist with a fear of snakes and a penchant for getting into danger. The U.S. government sends Jones on a globe-spanning race to find the Ark of the Covenant (a chest that, according to biblical lore, once held the tablets containing the Ten Commandments) before the Nazis do. To play Jones, Lucas and Spielberg hired Harrison Ford, who had become famous as Han Solo in the first two *Star Wars* films. When it opened, on June 12, 1981, *Raiders of the Lost Ark* became a smash hit, earning over $200 million and cementing Lucas's and Spielberg's reputations as the new kings of Hollywood.

While Lucas had reinvented the way people looked at movies, the way they heard them was another story. He was frustrated with the state of sound in most movie theaters and felt that there must be a way to improve it. He tapped Tom Holman, then a technical director at Skywalker Sound, to create a revolutionary sound system that would bring audiences the purest sound possible. Holman devised a method of using the walls of the theaters themselves to generate better sound. "Two things mainly distinguished this system," the sound designer Randy Thom told John Baxter for *Mythmaker: The Life and Work of George Lucas* (1999). "One was Holman's idea to mount the speakers behind the screen into a solid wall rather than having them just hanging or sitting freely by themselves. They were imbedded, with the surface of the speaker flush with the wall. In theory, that gives you better low-frequency response; the wall becomes part of the speaker. The second is what they call a crossover network. All these elaborate sound systems have one. It's an electronic circuit which determines which frequencies of sound will go to which parts of the speaker system, so that you don't waste the energy of the speakers sending high frequencies to the part of the speaker [that's] only supposed to produce low frequencies." Holman christened the design THX. (There is some dispute as to the origin of this name. Some say that it stands for Tom Holman's eXperiment or Tom Holman's Crossover. However, the official Lucasfilm site points to Lucas's film *THX 1138* to explain the name's origin.) Today, more than 2,000 theaters around the world employ THX technology, which is also the standard for dubbing and mixing feature films.

In 1983 Lucas released the third *Star Wars* film, *Return of the Jedi*, directed by Richard Marquand. Originally titled *Revenge of the Jedi* (the title was changed when Lucas determined that "revenge" was too ignoble a concept for a Jedi knight), the film tied up all the loose ends from *The Empire Strikes Back.* Han is freed from the clutches of the gangster Jabba the Hutt, Leia learns the truth about her family, and Luke engages in a final showdown with Vader. Many critics felt that this film traded in some of the previous movies' wit and intelligence for slapstick humor and an emphasis on such cute, merchandisable creatures as the teddy-bear-like characters called Ewoks. "*Return of the Jedi* is not a movie, it's a shopping mall," David Denby wrote for *New York* (May 30, 1983). "At the beginning, as John Williams's music started blaring away, my heart sank a bit, because the big brass theme has become the anthem of a merchandising concept that has completely triumphed." Nonetheless, the film broke box-office records on its first day in wide release and continued to dominate the movie world in the summer of 1983.

After *Return of the Jedi*, Lucas decided to put the *Star Wars* series on hold indefinitely. Not only did he feel that technology had not yet reached a level at which he could make the kind of effects he wanted, but his companies were having trouble staying on their feet. "I had gotten all of these things, but they couldn't sustain themselves," he told Anne Thompson for *Premiere* (May 1999). Licensing the merchandising rights for the *Star Wars* films solved the companies' financial troubles but created potential dangers—such as falling into a pattern of making *Star Wars* movies simply to pay the bills. Lucas recalled to Anne Thompson, "After every movie ILM would come back and say, 'Make another *Star Wars* movie because we need the money.' And I finally said, 'This isn't the way it was supposed to be. The company was supposed to work for me. I wasn't supposed to end up working for the company.' I said I wasn't going to go back and do any more *Star Wars* films until the company could stand on its own two feet. Once that happened, once I had the technology I needed, once my family was grown up to a point where they were more manageable, *then* I would go back and make the films."

Throughout the 1980s Lucas devoted much of his time to maintaining his various film companies and raising his family. Before divorcing, in 1983, he and his wife adopted a child together, Amanda. Since then, Lucas has adopted two more children, Katie and Jett. Lucas didn't entirely retire from filmmaking; he was very active in the production of the two sequels to *Raiders of the Lost Ark*, *Indiana Jones and the Temple of Doom* (1984) and *Indiana Jones and the Last Crusade* (1989), as well as one of the most notorious failures in motion-picture history, *Howard the Duck* (1986). In 1988 he produced the fantasy film *Willow*, directed by Ron Howard. Based on a story by Lucas, the movie told the tale of the diminutive Willow Ufgood, who is charged with rescuing an infant princess. Though the film was not a box-office smash, it earned a loyal following in the ensuing years, so much so that Lucas continued Willow's story in three novels: *Shadow Moon*, *Shadow Dawn*, and *Shadow Star.* The novels were written by Lucas, along with Chris Claremont, who has penned some of the more popular stories in the *X-Men* comic-book series.

In March 1990 18 middle schools in San Francisco began using a multimedia learning system developed by Lucas's educational company, Lucas Learning. Titled "GTV: A Geographic Perspective on American History," the program consisted of 40 video segments, each running about two hours and covering a pivotal event in history. GTV was the first step in Lucas's attempt to use technology to make education more engaging and fun for children. "It's kind of what I brought to the movie business," Lucas told Bernard Weinraub for the *New York Times* (January 27, 1992). "I said when I began, 'Why can't I make the most exciting two-hour movie?' And I did it. And then I realized that I can take the same technique and move it into the classroom just by respecting the material." Today, Lucas Learning provides classrooms with interactive computer games and programs that teach such subjects as math, science, and critical thinking. Additionally, Lucas has founded the George Lucas Educational Fund, a nonprofit organization that promotes new methods to improve education for students from kindergarten through 12th grade.

In 1992 Lucas introduced the television series *The Young Indiana Jones Chronicles*, which he produced. The show aimed to blend the thrills of the three *Indiana Jones* films with educational elements. The episodes shuttled between Jones's boyhood and young manhood, and found him interacting with such historical figures as Lawrence of Arabia, Sigmund Freud, and Pablo Picasso. Although the series was canceled after 32 episodes, it lived on in a number of made-for-TV and direct-to-video movies, including *Young Indiana Jones and the Hollywood Follies* (1994), *Young Indiana Jones and the Attack of the Hawkmen* (1995), and *Young Indiana Jones and the Mystery of the Blues* (1999). The last-named episode was notable, as it featured Harrison Ford playing the older incarnation of the title character.

*The Young Indiana Jones Chronicles* helped to reinvigorate Lucas. Despite its comparative failure in the ratings, the series showed the director what could be done with computer-generated images (CGI). In 1993 his company ILM had amazed audiences by creating realistic-looking dinosaurs for Spielberg's *Jurassic Park*. Now Lucas was able to create crowds, cityscapes, and whole sets using computers. Additionally, he felt thrilled by the challenge of creating a bold new series. "That was the most fun thing I've done," he told Thompson. "It wasn't really television; it was a chance for me to *not* do television and have television pay for it. But it was a little too esoteric, I think, for that medium." Still, Lucas now felt that technology had caught up with his imagination. He realized that it would be possible to create environments digitally that would be indistinguishable from the real thing. To test this theory, he dusted off an idea he had for a murder mystery set in a radio station in 1939. For the film, *Radioland Murders* (1994), Lucas's team created a number of innovative digital shots, including an elaborate tracking shot that begins atop a radio tower and spirals down into the station itself. Although the film did not do well critically or commercially, it convinced Lucas that computers were the tools that would allow him to return to the *Star Wars* universe.

In the years following *Return of the Jedi, Star Wars* had lain dormant on the pop-culture landscape. Save for two made-for-TV movies, *The Ewok Adventure* (1984) and *Ewoks: The Battle for Endor* (1985), there had been no new material from the Lucas camp. The toys were no longer selling, and, while the *Star Wars* series had greatly influenced the way subsequent movies were made, there was little mention anywhere of the series itself, aside from a few scattered references in movies or TV shows. That changed in 1991, when the science-fiction author Timothy Zahn published the novel *Heir to the Empire*. The first of a three-book cycle, authorized by Lucasfilm, the book picked up the *Star Wars* saga five years after the period covered in the last film. In the book, Han Solo and Leia are married and expecting twins; Luke is the first in a new line of Jedi knights; and the galaxy is still struggling through a period of reconstruction after so many years of war. The book shot to number one on the *New York Times* best-seller list, an unheard-of achievement for a science-fiction novel. Its two sequels, *Dark Force Rising* (1992) and *The Last Command* (1993), did equally well. Soon, the market was flooded with *Star Wars* novels, comic books, toys, and role-playing games. Watching this renaissance unfold, Lucas decided to re-release the movies, first on home video and then on the big screen. The video launch of *Star Wars* broke records, selling more than 30 million copies. The re-release of *Star Wars* in theaters on January 31, 1997, proved to be an even bigger event. People waited for hours for tickets, and lines stretched around corners. Lucas had made a bet with some of his colleagues that the film would make $10 million in its opening weekend. When that figure turned out to be $36.2 million, he was as stunned as he had been 20 years before. "I am flabbergasted, just flabbergasted," he told the *New York Times* (February 2, 1997). "It's a 20-year-old movie. I just did not expect this to happen."

Part of the attraction of the *Star Wars* re-release was that Lucas had touched up the movie, adding new scenes and cleaning up old ones. "It's like that old screen door in back that never fits right," he told David A. Kaplan and Adam Rogers for *Newsweek* (January 20, 1997). "I wanted to fix little things that have bugged me for 20 years. I was furious at the time *Star Wars* came out because it was a half-finished movie that just got thrown into the marketplace. And one day you have the energy and the stuff you need to fix it, and you do and it feels so good."

*The Empire Strikes Back* and *Return of the Jedi* were released in February and March, respectively, and also did brisk business. That summer Lucas began shooting the first *Star Wars* prequel in a planned series of three. The film, entitled *Star*

*Wars: Episode I—The Phantom Menace*, focuses on Anakin Skywalker, Luke's father, and how he became a Jedi knight. It also contains a labyrinthine plot involving a scheming senator who plans the downfall of the Republic and creates the Empire; a greedy Trade Federation's attempts to take over a peaceful backwater planet; and the return of the Sith, a race of evil Jedi bent on destroying the Jedi Council. The cast includes notable actors, among them Liam Neeson, who played a venerable Jedi master, Ewan McGregor, playing Obi-Wan Kenobi as a young man, and Natalie Portman, as the benevolent queen who will one day marry Anakin. Breaking new ground, the film introduced the first major character ever created through digital effects: Jar-Jar Binks, an amphibious, bipedal creature, served as *The Phantom Menace*'s comic relief, often getting in the way of the protagonists with his clumsiness but ultimately emerging as the film's unlikely hero. Jar-Jar was brought to life by the actor Ahmed Best, formerly of the Off-Broadway show *Stomp*. After Best filmed his scenes, ILM experts animated the character in accordance with his movements. The result is a seamless integration of digital technology with live action.

The hype leading up to the release of *Star Wars: Episode I—The Phantom Menace* dwarfed that for any other film of the period. Legions of fans slept outside theaters for months in advance. The Internet was abuzz with fake scripts, fan-made artwork, and rumors about casting. In November 1998 Lucasfilm released a teaser trailer attached to such films as *Meet Joe Black* and *The Siege*. In an unusual move, Fox placed the trailer both before and after the movies. "We tried to pick the markets with the biggest fan bases and do something special for the die-hard fans," Tom Sherak of 20th Century Fox told Daniel Fierman and Jeff Jensen for *Entertainment Weekly* (November 27, 1998). "This was a way they could see it twice without having to pay again." Fans flocked to theaters in droves, often lining up strictly to watch the trailer.

*Star Wars: Episode I—The Phantom Menace* opened on May 19, 1999. Screenings were held around the clock, and *Star Wars* enthusiasts, whipped into a frenzy, turned the premiere into a communal gathering reminiscent of Woodstock, the famous three-day music festival held in 1969. In addition to camping out in front of movie houses, some fans engaged in playful light-saber duels in theater lobbies or arrived at screenings dressed as their favorite characters. Once again, critical response to the movie was split. "While the new film is certainly serviceable," Kenneth Turan wrote for the *Los Angeles Times* (May 18, 1999), "it's noticeably lacking in warmth and humor, and though its visual strengths are real and considerable, from a dramatic point of view it's ponderous and plodding." Janet Maslin's review for the *New York Times* (May 19, 1999) was more complimentary. "Whether dreaming up blow-dryer-headed soldiers who move in lifelike formation or a planet made entirely of skyscrapers," she wrote, "Lucas still champions wondrous visions over bleak ones and sustains his love of escapist fun. There's no better tour guide for a trip back to the future." Audience response to *The Phantom Menace* was overwhelmingly positive. By May 23 receipts had already passed the $100 million mark, making the movie the first in history to earn that much money in so few days. By the time it had ended its theatrical run, the movie had amassed nearly $1 billion in profits, making it one of the biggest cinematic moneymakers ever.

Almost immediately after the release of *The Phantom Menace*, Lucas threw himself into the writing and directing of *Star Wars: Episode II—Attack of the Clones*. The film chronicles the exploits of Anakin, now a young man and full-fledged Jedi knight, and outlines the rise of the Empire against the backdrop of a galactic civil war between an army of cloned soldiers and a band of separatists. Additionally, the film follows Anakin's romance with Queen Amidala, Portman's character from the first episode. Their relationship is hindered by the Jedi order's prohibition against knights' falling in love. In an interview with David Kamp for *Variety* (March 2002), Lucas called the film "a love story in the *Star Wars* tradition." "I'd call it a love haiku more than a love sonnet," he went on. "It's shorter than a traditional love story, and thinner than a traditional love story, but still, hopefully, has the same impact as a traditional love story."

Continuing to break new ground, Lucas opted to shoot the film exclusively with digital cameras. Removing film from the moviemaking process freed Lucas considerably, as many of the technical constraints ordinarily placed on him disappeared. Thanks to digital technology, Lucas was able to shorten the shooting schedule of *Attack of the Clones* from 65 days to 61 and set up 37 shots a day, as opposed to the 26 he completed per day for *The Phantom Menace*. In addition, almost immediately after calling "Cut," he could watch the footage that had been shot. Using digital film also enabled Lucas to get better performances from his actors. "You don't want a lot of time between takes," he told Burr. "If you have to stop to reload the camera, it has a tendency to dissipate a lot of the energy that an actor's developing to get the performance right."

*Attack of the Clones*, which opened on May 16, 2002, drew decidedly mixed reactions among critics. In his review for the *New York Times* (May 10, 2002), A.O. Scott wrote, "While *Attack of the Clones* is many things—a two-hour-and-12-minute action-figure commercial, a demo reel heralding the latest advances in digital filmmaking, a chance for gifted actors to be handsomely paid for delivering the worst line readings of their careers—it is really not much of a movie at all, if by movie you mean a work of visual storytelling about the dramatic actions of a group of interesting characters." Joe Leydon, writing for the *San Francisco Examiner* (May 16, 2002, on-line), wrote that the film "abounds in A-budget variations of Saturday-matinee B-movie excitement." Fan reaction to *Attack of the Clones* was more positive; the film went on to reap more than $600 million in box-office receipts around the world. On November 1, 2002 Lucas released an IMAX version of *Attack of the Clones*, which, through the art of digital remastering, fills eight-story-high screens.

Lucas's next project will be the third, and final, film in the *Star Wars* saga, provisionally titled "Star Wars: Episode III." At one point it was thought that Lucas would make a total of nine films; the next trilogy would reveal what becomes of Luke Skywalker and his companions from the first series. Lucas has insisted, however, that the series will end after "Episode III." "I never had a story for the sequels, for the later ones," he told David Kamp for *Vanity Fair* (February 1999), "and also, I'll be to a point in my age where to do another trilogy would take 10 years." In the same interview, he quelled many fans' fears by explaining that the six-film cycle will represent his complete vision of the *Star Wars* saga. "When you see it in six parts, you'll understand," he said. "It really ends at part six."

Lucas has occasionally come under fire from critics who blame him for the recent onslaught of big-budget "event movies" that emphasize special effects, trading plot and character development for eye-popping visuals. Lucas dismisses such criticism. "I am an independent filmmaker," he asserted to Anne Thompson. "I've always had a rather strained relationship with Hollywood. I've lived in San Francisco all my life. I went to college in Los Angeles for a few years and came right back here. And I've managed to stay up here and avoid making movies in Hollywood. People say, 'Yeah, but they're just like Hollywood movies.' And I say, 'They're *my* movies. I can't help it if Hollywood copies.'"

George Lucas lives a very quiet existence in Marin County, California. "For being sort of a state-of-the-art guy, my personal life is very *un*state-of-the-art," he told Kevin Kelly and Paula Parisi for *Wired* (February 1997). "It's very Victorian, actually. I like to sit on a porch and listen to the flies buzz if I have five minutes, because most of my life is interacting with people all the time. I interact with a couple of hundred people every single day, and it's very intense. I've got three kids, so I interact with them whatever's left of the day. The few brief seconds I have before I fall asleep are usually more meditative in nature."

A devoted single father, Lucas begins every day by having breakfast with his children and then dropping them off at school before heading to work. When he is not shooting on location, he is always home in time for dinner. "Children are the whole point of life," he told Orville Schell for the *New York Times* (March 22, 1999). "Even as I was getting divorced, I decided that taking care of the kids was the most important thing I could do. You have to open yourself up to it, but I don't think there is any greater spiritual joy." There is, he told Schell, "a lonely part to having kids alone. Even though society has shifted its view on single parents, two parents are still a good idea. Without two, the emotional need is always there. You don't have that level of sharing. But also, you don't have to compromise. But, face it, I'd rather be married. But I'm not. As you grow up, you understand that there is no such thing as a perfect life." — J.K.B.

Suggested Reading: *Entertainment Weekly* p 95+ Mar. 1, 1999, with photos; *New York Times* C p25 May 25, 1987, with photos, C p17+ Jan. 27, 1992, with photos, (on-line) Mar. 22, 1999; *New Yorker* p40+ Jan. 6, 1997; *Newsweek* p52+ Jan. 20, 1997, with photos; *Premiere* p68+ May, 1999, with photos; *Time* p68+ Feb. 10, 1997, with photos; *Vanity Fair*, p118+ Feb. 1999, with photos, p198+ Mar. 2002, with photos; *Wired* p160+ Feb. 1997, with photos; Champlin, Charles. *George Lucas: The Creative Impulse*, 1992

Selected Films: as director—*THX 1138*, 1970; *American Graffiti*, 1973; *Star Wars*, 1977; *Star Wars: Episode I—The Phantom Menace*, 1999; *Star Wars: Episode II—Attack of the Clones*, 2002; as producer—*The Rain People*, 1969; *Star Wars*, 1977; *The Empire Strikes Back*, 1980; *Raiders of the Lost Ark*, 1981; *Return of the Jedi*, 1983; *Indiana Jones and the Temple of Doom*, 1984; *Labyrinth*, 1986; *Captain Eo*, 1986; *Willow*, 1988; *Tucker: The Man and His Dream*, 1988; *The Land Before Time*, 1988; *Indiana Jones and the Last Crusade*, 1989; *Star Wars: Episode I—The Phantom Menace*, 1999; *Star Wars: Episode II—Attack of the Clones*, 2002; as writer—*THX 1138* (with Walter Murch), 1970; *American Graffiti* (with Gloria Katz and Williard Huyck), 1973; *Star Wars*, 1977; *The Empire Strikes Back* (story treatment), 1980; *Raiders of the Lost Ark* (story treatment), 1981; *Return of the Jedi* (story treatment), 1983; *Indiana Jones and the Temple of Doom*, (story treatment) 1984; *Willow* (story treatment), 1988; *Indiana Jones and the Last Crusade*, 1989; *Radioland Murders* (story treatment), 1994; *Star Wars: Episode I— The Phantom Menace*, 1999; *Star Wars: Episode II—Attack of the Clones*, 2002

Selected Television Shows: as producer—*The Ewok Adventure*, 1984; *Ewoks: The Battle for Endor*, 1985; *Ewoks*, 1985; *Droids*, 1985; *The Young Indiana Jones Chronicles*, 1992; *Young Indiana Jones and the Hollywood Follies*, 1994; *Young Indiana Jones and the Treasure of the Peacock's Eye*, 1995; *Young Indiana Jones and the Attack of the Hawkmen*, 1995

Walter McBride/Retna Ltd.

## Mac, Bernie

*1957– Comedian; actor*

*Address: P.O. Box 900, Attn: Bernie Mac, Beverly Hills, CA 90213-0900*

Although the comedian Bernie Mac has appeared in movies, television shows, and stage tours pitched primarily to African-Americans, he has refused to be categorized as a certain type of performer. "I don't consider myself a Black comic," he explained to a writer for *Jet* magazine (September 20, 1999). "I don't consider myself a White comic. I consider myself a comedian. You have to know your audience and know what they want to see. I can make them all laugh. . . . You've got to be able to do everything." After toiling in small clubs and shows for more than a decade, Mac joined the ranks of an elite group of comedians in the early 1990s. Performances with the *Def Comedy Jam* led to film roles, cable television specials, and a spot with the 1998 *Original Kings of Comedy* tour, a wildly successful production that showcased some of the most popular contemporary African-American comedians. At the height of this recognition of his talents, Mac signed on as the star of a unique sitcom, *The Bernie Mac Show*, which premiered on the Fox network in November 2001 to thunderous applause from critics and viewers. On that show, the comedian plays a surrogate father; unlike the sweet, gentle approach to parenting usually depicted in mainstream television comedy, the Mac character's style of fatherhood involves shouts and threats. Viewers have been disarmed, however, by the character's underlying affection for the children.

Bernie Mac was born Bernard Jeffrey McCullough in Chicago, Illinois, in the autumn of 1957. He was raised in the Englewood section of Chicago's South Side, a poor, rough neighborhood, in a home he shared with his mother, several siblings, and a large extended family that included his grandparents. "I came from a place where there wasn't a lot of joy," Mac admitted to Frazier Moore of the Associated Press, as printed in the *Detroit News* (November 21, 2001), but he has repeatedly acknowledged the solid emotional foundation that his grandparents provided for the household through their "tough love." Mac was determined from childhood to make people laugh when he grew up. "I was about four or five," he recalled for *Entertainment Tonight* (November 28, 2001, online). "I saw my mamma crying one night. . . . But Ed Sullivan was on, and he was introducing Bill Cosby. Bill did a routine about snakes in the bathroom. When I saw her laughing, I told her that I was going to be a comedian so she'd never cry again." His career as a comedian began at a church social when he was eight. He has recalled that he was a bright boy but a poor student and a jokester; after his mother's death from breast cancer, when he was 16, however, he began to apply himself to his studies at the Chicago Vocational High School. By the time he graduated, he had gained a serious outlook on life, hoping to find success and respect through being funny. As he related to *Entertainment Tonight*: "I won 'Class Clown' my senior year and I turned it down because I said, 'I'm funny. I'm a comedian, I'm not a clown.' My humor had changed from foolishness to making sense!"

After graduating from high school, Mac took several jobs, working as a janitor, a mover, a bread salesman, and a school-bus driver. He married his high-school sweetheart in 1976; in the following year he settled into a job at a General Motors plant and became the father of a daughter. He performed comedy on the weekends, perfecting an act that has been characterized as sly and witty. He also entertained for tips in the Chicago subway system. "Chicago was brutal in the winter time, and I was up at 6 o'clock," he told Phil Rosenthal for the *Chicago Sun Times* (January 29, 2002). "I worked the [elevated trains] all the way to downtown Chicago and I made $400, sometimes $500 a day. But I stopped doing that . . . I felt like I was begging." In the era when he started performing as a comedian, he explained to Phyllis Croom for the *Washington Post* (February 13, 1994), "you couldn't use certain language or certain gestures, you had to paint a picture. You had to be a little more cunning, a little bit more witty." He played tiny venues and squeezed in a few minutes of his own material while acting as an emcee for other entertainers at bigger clubs. "When I started in the clubs, I had to work places where didn't nobody else want to work," he told Croom. "I had to do clubs where street gangs were, had to do motorcycle gangs, gay balls and things of that nature."

In 1983 Mac's stable life was rocked when he was laid off by General Motors. He then took several jobs in quick succession. His family seemed unable to land on its feet; they moved in with relatives for a time and were forced to apply for welfare in 1985, which was "one of the hardest parts of my life," Mac recalled to Allan Johnson for the *Chicago Tribune* (October 5, 1995). Mac's wife suggested that he give up comedy to concentrate on more lucrative pursuits, but he had realized that performing was his lifeblood. "If you take that away from me, I'm gonna die," he remembered explaining, as reported by Johnson. Mac told Roy S. Johnson for *Savoy* (October 2001), "When GM laid me off, it taught me a valuable lesson: Don't be complacent, be dedicated. I made an oath that I'd never be broke again. For five years I did amateur hour. I was an opening act for two and a half years. I emceed at every club. I wanted them to call *my* name! I wanted that more than the money."

With his family's blessing, Mac plunged into more and more comedy, found steady gigs at bigger clubs, and unexpectedly drew support from the legendary comic performers Redd Foxx and Slappy White, who invited him to perform off-the-cuff in Las Vegas, Nevada, in 1989. "That was good for me, man," Mac explained to Mike Weatherford for the Las Vegas *Review-Journal* (November 3, 2000). "That was my legitimacy for the big leagues, coming from [Foxx]." His true breakthrough came in 1990, when he won a national comedy contest sponsored by a brewing company. He was invited to perform in two shows with the *Def Comedy Jam*, a touring act featuring African-American comics that was also broadcast on the cable channel HBO. His performances captured the attention of Hollywood, and he landed small comedic roles in such movies as *Mo' Money* (1992) and *Who's The Man* (1993). Mac was selected to host the *Def Comedy Jam* on another tour, during which he further developed his stage persona and made an impression on audiences with his sharp observations and blue language. There were few subjects that he would not tackle in his act, as he explained to Phyllis Croom: "I try to touch on a lot of things from politics to more serious issues such as child abuse, drug relations etc. Nothing is sacred in comedy. Comedy comes from adversity. I know mine does." Still, as he told Rebecca J. Coudret for the Evansville (Illinois) *Courier & Press* (April 27, 2000), "I don't joke about rape—and in a movie I will not do any kind of rape scene. . . . And I won't complain about God. He's been too good to me. He knows my heart. God has a great sense of humor—but I don't do God jokes."

In 1994 Mac headlined his own show in the *Who Ya Wit* tour, mixing in elements that included a nine-piece rhythm-and-blues band and a troupe of seven dancers, the Macaronis. "I've been working in clubs for 21 years," he told Chuck Crisafulli for the *Los Angeles Times* (November 18, 1994), "but I got the feeling that the comedy world was at a standstill. I wanted to get back to the basics of entertainment, when audiences were so excited about what they were going to see. The lights go down, the curtain goes up, and it's 'Wow.'" Also in 1994 Mac was seen in his first dramatic movie role, portraying a former professional basketball player in *Above the Rim*. While the ensemble cast, including Mac, was praised, the film got mixed reviews, with critics complaining about the script and direction. Executives at the television cable channel HBO, familiar with his work from the *Def Comedy Jam*, invited Mac to develop his own variety show. *Midnight Mac*, which was filmed on Chicago's North Side and featured many of the same elements from his *Who Ya Wit* tour, lasted only one season but prompted Mac's nomination for a CableACE Award.

Mac began to take on more film and television roles in the mid-1990s. Some were comic roles, such as his parts in the movies *Friday* (1995) and the parody *Don't Be a Menace to South Central While Drinking Your Juice in the Hood* (1996), or his recurring role as "Uncle Bernie" on the United Paramount Network's touchstone sitcom *Moesha*. Mac had a dramatic role in the 1995 film *The Walking Dead*, set in the Vietnam War era, and was part of an ensemble cast in Spike Lee's film *Get On the Bus* (1996), about the 1995 Million Man March in Washington, D.C.

Despite the frequent work in Hollywood, Mac's heart remained with comedy. He was eager to participate in the *Original Kings of Comedy* production, a 1998 national tour that featured Mac, Steve Harvey, D. L. Hughley, and Cedric "The Entertainer," all considered to be among the top African-American comedians. *The Original Kings of Comedy* garnered good reviews and drew sold-out audiences; the tour's gross of $59 million was the highest ever achieved by a comedy tour. HBO broadcast several shows based on the tour, and a performance in North Carolina was taped and adapted for the 2000 film *The Original Kings of Comedy*, directed by Spike Lee. A second tour kicked off in 1999, and a third—called *The Crown Royal Kings of Comedy* and including the "Queens of Comedy," among them Adele Givens and Mo'Nique—drew large audiences in 2001. Mac attributed the success of the tours to laughter's healing powers. "We're doctors," he told the writer for *Jet*. "We're medicine. . . . People come and can forget about their hardships. The world is hurting. Most of the people who come may be crying and arguing, but they come to get away and to laugh for a couple of hours." Mac also conducted the *All About You* solo tour in 1999.

The idea of starring in a network television show did not initially appeal to Mac. "To be honest with you, television is not something I've wanted to do, because of the politics," he explained to Lillian A. Jackson for *Electronic Media* (February 3, 2002). "I'm a student of the game, and I've seen what television has done to so many great . . . comedians. I've seen them take all their hard work, plus their style, and flushed it down the toilet. . . . The people come to see you, the person they fell in love with, but when they see you on TV you become a whole other character, another person, and they become disappointed, and I wasn't going to allow that to happen to me." But Mac was coaxed to come to television by Larry Wilmore, who created and developed a sitcom based on story lines from Mac's real life. *The Bernie Mac Show* premiered in November 2001. In the show, Mac plays a successful comedian, happily married and happily childless, who agrees to care for his nephew and nieces while his sister undergoes drug rehabilitation. (In his off-stage life, Mac had helped to raise a niece and a grand-niece, and a friend of his had taken in nieces and a nephew; the two stories were intertwined to create the premise of *The Bernie Mac Show.*) The show has elements that are unusual for a sitcom, including a few minutes of each episode during which Mac speaks directly to the camera, a segment similar to the confessional portion of the MTV "reality" show *The Real World.* Mac and Wilmore took risks by leaving Mac's edgy stage persona intact; his character's child-rearing methods are authoritarian and traditional, contrasting with the warm and fuzzy parent-child interaction portrayed on many other television shows. "Nowadays parents don't want to be parents, they want to be friends with the kids," Mac told Bernard Weinraub of the *New York Times* (December 5, 2001). "We always say we want to give our kids more than we ever had, but more is not better." A few critics were uncomfortable with the Mac character's vociferous approach to parenting, but the majority were impressed with his shake-up of the sitcom standard. Ken Tucker of *Entertainment Weekly* (November 16, 2001) called *The Bernie Mac Show* "a mighty sitcom bursting with juicy ideas and energy. . . . [It] may remind you how puny and derivative most comedies have become."

*The Bernie Mac Show* had good ratings throughout its freshman season, coming in second only to NBC's hit drama *The West Wing* in its time period and becoming one of the Fox network's biggest hits. Mac was nominated for an Emmy for best lead actor in a comedy series (he lost to Ray Romano of *Everybody Loves Raymond*); the series' executive producer, Larry Wilmore, won an Emmy for outstanding writing for a comedy series for the pilot episode. The show also won a Peabody Award and two honors from the Television Critics Association, one for the program itself, for being the best comedy, and the other for Mac, for individual achievement.

After airing at 9:00 p.m. Eastern Time during the 2001–02 season, the show was scheduled to move to the 8:00 p.m. time slot in 2002–03. The announcement of the proposed change set off a minor controversy, as it pitted *The Bernie Mac Show* against *My Wife and Kids*, one of the few other popular series starring African-Americans. Damon Wayans, the star of the latter show, publicly aired his displeasure, predicting that, with one show siphoning black viewers from the other, a drop in ratings for both series would result. Wayans tried without success to persuade Mac, a friend of his, to protest the scheduling decision. "I have no problem with Fox . . . ," Mac explained to Glenn Garvin for the *Miami Herald* (July 23, 2002). "That was a business decision." Wilmore, meanwhile, insisted that the assumption that only African-Americans watched both shows was incorrect. "Because you have two shows that have the same racial makeup, doesn't necessarily mean they have the same creative makeup," he told Rob Owen for the *Pittsburgh Post-Gazette* (July 23, 2002, on-line). "To just think of our show in the light of being an African-American show kind of marginalizes what *The Bernie Mac Show* is." Sandy Grushow, the chair of the Fox Television Entertainment Group, pointed out that according to Fox research, 86 percent of *Bernie Mac* viewers did not watch *My Wife and Kids* and that neither show would necessarily lose viewers if they competed head-to-head. Wayans disagreed. "It's the same audience, and they're lying if they say it's not," he told Owen. "Me and Bernie go out on tour together and the same audience go to see both of us." (According to the BET Web site, the Neilsen ratings ranked *The Bernie Mac Show* first among black households and *My Wife and Kids* fifth; neither show made the top 20 among white viewers.) As it turned out, because of the broadcasting of the baseball play-offs on Fox, the shows did not compete against each other for most of the fall season.

Earlier, while *The Bernie Mac Show* was in development, its star tackled other projects. He had supporting roles in *What's the Worst That Could Happen?* (2001) and *Ocean's Eleven* (2001); he also wrote a book that was published late in 2001: *I Ain't Scared of You: Bernie Mac on How Life Is.* "The book is about getting over fears, not being afraid to fail . . . ," he told *Ebony* (February 2002). "But there's a lot of funny stuff in there, too." Mac will appear in three movies slated for release in 2003: *Charlie's Angels: Full Throttle*, *Head of State*, and *Bad Santa.* He will also lend his voice to *Lil' Pimp.*

Mac lives in the Chicago suburb of Crete with his wife of 25 years, Rhonda, a former nurse who is now president of her husband's production company, Mac Man Enterprises Inc. Their daughter, Je'Niece, is a Ph.D. candidate in child psychology. — K.S.

Suggested Reading: *Chicago Tribune* V p1 Oct. 5, 1995, with photos; *Los Angeles Times* p24 Nov. 18, 1994, with photo; *New York Times* E p1 Dec. 5, 2001, with photo; *Savoy* p54 Oct. 2001, with photo; *Washington Post* G p3 Feb. 13, 1994, with photo

Selected Television Shows: *The Bernie Mac Show*

Selected Films: *Mo' Money*, 1992; *Above the Rim*, 1994; *Booty Call*, 1997; *The Original Kings of Comedy*, 2000; *Ocean's Eleven*, 2001

Selected Books: *I Ain't Scared of You: Bernie Mac on How Life Is*, 2001

Armando Gallo/Retna Ltd.

## Maguire, Tobey

*June 27, 1975– Actor*

*Address: c/o Gersh Agency, 232 N. Canon Dr., Beverley Hills, CA 90210*

During the late 1990s Tobey Maguire emerged as one of the most promising young actors in Hollywood. Maguire earned critical acclaim for his portrayals of shy, sensitive, introverted, offbeat antiheroes in such films as *The Ice Storm* (1997), *Pleasantville* (1998), *The Cider House Rules* (1999), and *Wonder Boys* (2000). In *Spider-Man* (2002) he was cast in the title role, one that is both similar to and very different from his previous parts: that of Peter Parker, a timid high-school student who is also a crime fighter with superhuman powers. Although some Hollywood insiders, and many fans of Marvel Comics' popular *Spider-Man* series, expressed misgivings about the casting of the soft-spoken, five-foot eight-inch, 140-pound Maguire as a superhero, critics raved about his performance, and moviegoers flocked to see the film: within 11 weeks of its early May 2002 release, its box-office receipts had topped $400 million. The success of *Spider-Man* has established Maguire's appeal to mainstream audiences. The actor, who earned $4 million for his work in *Spider-Man*, will reportedly collect $26 million for appearing in the two *Spider-Man* sequels currently planned. Maguire told Jess Cagle for *Time* (May 20, 2002), however, that he is "not really concerned about money." "I just want to make good movies," he explained to Cagle. "If there's a script I like with a character I like and a filmmaker I like, I would do the movie."

Tobias Vincent Maguire was born on June 27, 1975 in Los Angeles, California. "My mother was eighteen and my father was twenty when they had me," Maguire told Ingrid Sischy for *Interview* (October 1998). "They got married when I was two, and I think they got divorced when I was two as well, so they would move around separately." His father, Vincent, worked as a cook; his mother, Wendy, held various jobs, most of them secretarial. Maguire has four half-brothers, whom he rarely saw during his childhood because of his frequent moves from parent to parent and to the homes of various other relatives, in California, Oregon, Washington State, and Canada. Maguire's family had little money to spare. "I needed braces when I was a kid but they were too expensive," he told Sischy. "My [mom] would still get me these crazy gifts, though. On Christmas or my birthday she would get me something completely beyond our means. She got me a keyboard piano one year, a nice one, even though she couldn't afford it." She also encouraged him to develop his creative side, with piano and ballet lessons, and often accompanied him to the movies. When Maguire was 11—he was then living with his father and paternal grandmother—his mother gave him $100 to enroll in a drama workshop. "At the time it was a gigantic sum of money," Maguire told Sischy.

Up to that point Maguire had done well academically, though he had often felt so nervous that he would vomit before leaving for school in the morning. Then, when he was in the sixth grade, perhaps because of the cumulated stress of repeatedly relocating, he lost interest in school; on many days he would play hooky, and his marks began to suffer. Before he entered the eighth grade, he returned to Los Angeles to live with his mother. Displeased about his frequent truancy, she offered him the choice of attending a regular school or a professional school where he could concentrate on acting. He opted for the latter. According to Maguire, the school "had shortened hours, the lunches were long, and if you were late or took a little longer at lunch they didn't really say anything to you," as he described it to Luaine Lee for the Knight-Ridder/Tribune New Service (April 22, 2002, online). "And I did the work I wanted to do, turned it in when I felt like it." In an apparent understatement, he added, "There were only like six students in the entire school, and you could go off and work and it was fine."

After one year at the professional school, Maguire enrolled at a private high school. "In the tenth grade I took home study but cheated the entire year—didn't answer one question myself," he told Lee. "They sent you all the answers and your parents are supposed to check them but they sent you answers for the tests and everything, so I did my entire year in two days, copying all the answers." Maguire dropped out of school after completing the 10th grade. He later obtained the equivalent of a high-school diploma by passing the California High School Proficiency Exam.

During his high-school years, Maguire had acted in several plays in Los Angeles. After quitting school he turned his complete attention to acting. He appeared in several television commercials and such TV shows as *Blossom, Roseanne, Eerie, Indiana,* and *Walker, Texas Ranger.* In a big break for him, in 1992 he was cast in the title role in the Fox network sitcom *Great Scott!* His character, Scott Melrod, was a shy teenager who spent a lot of his time daydreaming. Although the series was canceled after nine weeks, Maguire earned a nomination from the Young Artist Awards for best young actor in a new television series.

Maguire made his feature-film debut in 1993, in a small part in the British director Michael Caton-Jones's *This Boy's Life*, an adaptation of a coming-of-age memoir by Tobias Wolff. The picture starred Ellen Barkin as Tobias's mother, Robert De Niro as his brutal stepfather, and Leonardo DiCaprio as Tobias—a role for which Maguire had auditioned unsuccessfully. (Earlier, he and DiCaprio had met at many other auditions and had become good friends.)

Maguire next appeared in such made-for-television movies as *Spoils of War* (1994), *A Child's Cry for Help* (1994), and *Seduced by Madness: The Diane Borchardt Story* (1996). Maguire tried out for a role in Allan Moyle's silver-screen film *Empire Records* (1995), about a group of music-store employees who fight to keep the business from shutting down, but he arrived at the audition unprepared and thus "sabotaged my chance of getting a big part," as he admitted to Sischy. "I disappointed Allan and I disappointed myself, but my agent got me a small part in the film." During the shooting of *Empire Records*, in North Carolina, Maguire felt isolated from the rest of the cast, who had been working together for over a month. With Moyle's approval, he left the project and returned to Los Angeles. About 20 years old at that time, he took six months off to relax and think about his future. "I had a kind of semi-breakdown . . . ," he told Sischy. "For the next year, none of the external things in life mattered to me anymore. . . . Then all the inner work started paying off externally. Things started to turn around and I began to participate in life, and, no matter how much fear I had about being judged, I would get out there and dance a bit and start talking to people, even though I was almost trembling at times. It became like a personal triumph to walk through fear like that. And what happened was that I started getting good work and girls began paying attention to me."

Maguire bounced back with a part in Griffin Dunne's *The Duke of Groove* (1996), which co-starred Kate Capshaw and Uma Thurman and earned an Academy Award nomination for best live-action short film. His first lead role in cinema came in Quinton Peeples's thriller *Joyride* (1996), in which he was cast as a boy who steals the car of a professional killer; that picture went directly to video. Also in 1996 Maguire appeared in Woody Allen's *Deconstructing Harry*. In 1997 he portrayed a principal character in Ang Lee's critically acclaimed film *The Ice Storm*. Set in 1973 in a posh Connecticut suburb, *The Ice Storm* focuses on two dysfunctional families, each of which suffers from a near-absence of communication between husband and wife (Kevin Kline and Joan Allen as the Hoods, Jamey Sheridan and Sigourney Weaver as the Carvers) and parents and children (Elijah Wood and Adam Hann-Byrd as the Carver brothers, Maguire and Christina Ricci as the Hood siblings). "The acting is flawless, including Tobey Maguire's performance as Kline's 16-year-old son and the film's narrator, who experiences a less than fulfilling night when he takes the train into Manhattan to try his luck," Jay Carr wrote in his review for the *Boston Globe* (October 17, 1997). "A younger version of his father, more earnest, less obtuse, [Maguire] gives the film its voice of unwarranted hope."

Maguire was cast in the supporting role of a hitchhiker in *Fear and Loathing in Las Vegas* (1998), with Johnny Depp and Benicio Del Toro co-starring. Based on the "gonzo" journalist Hunter S. Thompson's fictionalized account of his drug-drenched, "savage journey to the heart of the American dream," as his 1971 book is subtitled, *Fear and Loathing in Las Vegas* was directed by Terry Gilliam. In the movie *Pleasantville* (1998), written and directed by Gary Ross, Maguire co-starred as David Parker, a 1990s teenager who loves a popular 1950s TV sitcom (called *Pleasantville*) and much prefers the seemingly perfect lives of the sitcom's characters to the harshness of the real world. One day he and his twin sister, Jennifer (Reese Witherspoon), get magically transported into the show's black-and-white landscape and become characters themselves—the children of ideal parents (William H. Macy and Joan Allen). While David enjoys this new world, Jennifer becomes bored with life in Pleasantville, where all the pages in the library books are blank and the high-school basketball players never miss a shot. Eager for change, she introduces new ideas to the townspeople—teaching teenagers about sex, for example—and David later follows suit. To depict the residents' emotional and intellectual awakenings, which enable them for the first time to experience joy, lust, and other genuine feelings, the filmmaker (with the help of state-of-the-art colorization techniques) turned their monochromatic world into one filled with colors. *Pleasantville* impressed most critics and many moviegoers, who enjoyed its sendup of such 1950s-era sitcoms as *Father Knows Best* and *Leave It to Beaver*. Maguire's performance earned him a Saturn Award from the Academy of Science Fiction, Fantasy & Horror Films for best performance by a young actor.

In 1999, working again with the Taiwanese-born Ang Lee, Maguire appeared in the director's *Ride with the Devil*, an adventure set during the Civil

War. Maguire's character, Jake Roedel, joins a group of Confederate guerrillas, called bushwhackers, whose numbers include a freed slave (Jeffrey Wright). The film received mixed reviews and did poorly at the box office. His next film, *The Cider House Rules* (1999), directed by Lasse Hallstrom, met with great success. An adaptation by John Irving of one of his own novels, *The Cider House Rules* explores the quest for identity and such issues as abortion and incest. Maguire was cast as Homer Wells, an orphan raised by the kindly doctor Wilbur Larch (Michael Caine) at his orphanage in rural, 1940s Maine. Larch grooms Homer to succeed him, teaching him everything he knows, including abortion techniques. After setting out on his own, Homer finds work as an apple picker and love with a woman whose fiancé is fighting in World War II. A crisis of conscience arises for him when Homer, an opponent of abortion, must decide whether to use his skills to end the pregnancy of an incest victim. "Anchoring the movie is Mr. Maguire's sober, wide-eyed Homer, a wounded, moon-faced innocent who, in leaving the institution that nurtured him, blindly follows his heart and finds fulfillment working outdoors," Stephen Holden wrote for the *New York Times* (December 10, 1999). In a dissenting view, Roger Ebert, in the *Chicago Sun-Times* (December 12, 1999, on-line), faulted Maguire's performance, describing it as "almost maddeningly monotone." The Screen Actors Guild nominated Maguire and his co-stars for an award for outstanding performance by a cast in a theatrical motion picture.

For his next film, *Wonder Boys* (2000), based on a novel by Michael Chabon and directed by Curtis Hanson, Maguire was teamed with the screen veteran Michael Douglas. Douglas played Grady Tripp, a middle-aged professor of creative writing whose personal life is a shambles; in the seven years since his first, successful book was published, he has written 2,000 pages of his second novel but has failed to complete it. Meanwhile, he has become both mentor and father figure to one of his most talented students, James (portrayed by Maguire), who, by the story's conclusion, has embarked on what promises to be an outstanding literary career. A box-office failure, *Wonder Boys* received qualified praise from most critics. Carrie Rickley, who gave the film three-and-a-half stars in her review for the *Philadelphia Inquirer* (February 25, 2000), extolled Maguire's performance: "The supremely understated Maguire, who moves fewer facial muscles than Buster Keaton, is sensational as the aspiring author poised to replace Grady as the next Wonder Boy," Rickley wrote. "His James is a compulsive liar, and thus an ideal storyteller, who snares Grady in his tangled web. The young actor brings out the warmth and paternal wisdom long latent in Douglas, whose character's evolution from eternal boy stuck in the eternal [1970s] to mature man of the millennium is unexpectedly moving to witness."

In 2002 Tobey Maguire scored a big hit as the title character in *Spider-Man*, a big-screen adaptation of the Marvel Comics series created in 1962 by the illustrator Steve Ditko and the writer Stan Lee. Sam Raimi, the director of *Spider-Man*, rejected many other prominent young actors who lobbied to play the arachnoid hero, instead casting Maguire after seeing a tape of *The Cider House Rules*. "I thought 'this guy is just great' and looked like he could play 17 years old," Raimi told Rory Ford for the *Edinburgh Evening News* (June 6, 2002, online). "So I then met with Tobey and he seemed very personable, intelligent, had a charisma and we could communicate very well." In a conversation with David Hochman for the *New York Times* (April 28, 2002), Raimi said, "I sensed that Tobey had this powerful, sexier side that his previous roles simply didn't capture. His work, particularly in *Cider House Rules*, possessed a great power in its stillness. Even when Tobey was quiet, he commanded the screen." Executives at Sony Pictures balked at Raimi's choice of Maguire, complaining that a smallish actor who had become identified with sensitive and offbeat characters would be wrong for a big-budget action film. They relented after Maguire—at their insistence—screentested for the role twice, once as Peter Parker and then while wearing the Spider-Man costume. The demand for the second test made Maguire "a little agitated . . . ," as he told David Hochman. "Then I realized the only reason I wouldn't do it was ego, and that wasn't a good enough reason."

As a child Maguire had never read *Spider-Man* or any other comic books. To familiarize himself with the character, he read all the *Spider-Man* installments published during the series' first four years. He also undertook an extensive exercise regimen to get himself into shape for the role. "I trained for five months, six days a week, anywhere from an hour-and-a-half to four hours a day," he told Sean Daly for the *Toronto Star* (April 23, 2002). "I was doing a combination of gymnastics, yoga, martial arts, weight training and high-end cardio"—the last item referring to cardiovascular, or aerobic, exercise.

In Raimi's film, whose screenplay is by David Koepp, Peter Parker is a lonely orphan who lives with his aunt and uncle in the New York City borough of Queens. One day, during a trip with his high-school class to a scientific laboratory, Peter is bitten by a genetically altered spider. (In the comic book, the spider had been irradiated.) When he wakes up the next day, Peter discovers that he no longer needs his glasses to see properly and has a well-sculpted physique. Peter can climb and stick to walls and sense impending danger. He can also produce spider silk—the sticky, phenomenally strong material with which spiders build their webs—and shoot it from his wrists. At first, Peter uses his new powers for personal gain—for example, impressing Mary Jane Watson (Kirsten Dunst), the girl he has a crush on. After his beloved uncle (Cliff Roberston) is killed by a carjacker, Peter decides to use his abilities to fight crime and evil. He adopts the persona of Spider-Man, a costumed superhero, who soon finds himself batting a villain called the Green Goblin (Willem Dafoe)—who is also the father of his best friend.

In a mixed assessment of both the film and Maguire's acting for *Entertainment Weekly* (May 10, 2002), Owen Gleiberman wrote, "At first, the offbeat casting of Tobey Maguire, with his gurgly-voiced passivity, works well. He brings his own cuddly conviction to the 'divided' role of a clandestine teen superhero, weighing each and every word as though he were stoned. He's that rarity, an entirely sincere actor, so earnest in his cuteness that at times he's like an oversize baby. . . . Maguire, winning as he is, never quite gets the chance to bring the two sides of Spidey—the boy and the man, the romantic and the avenger—together. That hesitant voice starts to sound a little odd issuing from behind Spider-Man's mask, and after a while you may start to ask: Is our hero's big-eyed daze of wonder hiding something, or is there not much there to hide?" A. O. Scott, writing for the *New York Times* (May 3, 2002), found more to like in the film. After reporting that *Spider-Man*'s makers had "succeeded in rejuvenating the [comic-book character] while staying faithful to his roots," he wrote, "They have been helped by the inspired casting of Tobey Maguire as Peter Parker. . . . With his wide eyes and soft, mobile mouth, Mr. Maguire seems at once knowing and vulnerable; more than any other actor in his 20s, he embodies the generational trait of expressing irony and earnestness as if there were no difference between them. He sometimes appears too smart for his own good, observing his own performance with skeptical cool; but here this detachment is consistent with his character's predicament. Peter himself, after all, is something of an actor, forced to improvise a performance that is both dangerous and ridiculous."

Maguire's next film, *Seabiscuit*, co-starring Jeff Bridges and William H. Macy, has a tentative release date of July 2003. The movie, written and directed by Gary Ross, is based on Laura Hillenbrand's best-selling nonfiction book *Seabiscuit: An American Legend*, about an improbably but phenomenally successful Thoroughbred racehorse who, in the U.S. during the Great Depression of the 1930s, became as famous as Franklin Delano Roosevelt, the nation's president during that time. Maguire will play Red Pollard, who—despite being blind in one eye—rode Seabiscuit in more races than any other jockey.

Maguire lives in a mansion that he recently bought in Beverly Hills, California. The actor, a vegetarian, enjoys cooking, practices yoga, and is an avid fan of the Los Angeles Lakers basketball team. Maguire told David Hochman that he "didn't really want to" commit himself to appearing in *Spider-Man 2* (in which the hero will square off against Doctor Octopus) and *Spider-Man 3*, and did so only because "they weren't going to hire me [to act in *Spider-Man*] otherwise." He also told Hochman, "Although I do contain the young, wise, open, naive guy I always play, I do have other aspects of my personality I'd like to exploit. Look at Jack Nicholson's career. He's sustained it by doing a little of everything. . . . I want to do movies in different genres." — D.C.

Suggested Reading: *Boston Globe* C p1 Oct. 17, 1997; *Chicago Sun-Times* (on-line) Dec. 12, 1999; *Edinburgh Evening News* (on-line) Jun. 6, 2002; *Interview* p142+ Oct. 1998, with photos; Knight-Ridder/ Tribune News Service (on-line) Apr. 22, 2002; *New York Times* E p1 Dec. 10, 1999, II p1+ Apr. 28, 2002, with photo; *Philadelphia Inquirer* Features Weekend p3 Feb. 25, 2000; *Time* p74 May 20, 2002, with photo; *Toronto Star* D p1 Apr. 23, 2002, with photo

Selected Films: *This Boy's Life*, 1993; *The Duke of Groove*, 1996; *Joyride*, 1996; *Deconstructing Harry*, 1997; *The Ice Storm*, 1997; *Fear And Loathing in Las Vegas*, 1998; *Pleasantville*, 1998; *Ride With the Devil*, 1999; *The Cider House Rules*, 1999; *Wonder Boys*, 2000; *Cats and Dogs*, 2001; *Spider-Man*, 2002

---

## Mann, Emily

*Apr. 12, 1952– Theater director; playwright*

*Address: McCarter Theatre, 91 University Pl., Princeton, NJ 08540*

Emily Mann has been the artistic director of the renowned McCarter Theatre Center for the Performing Arts, in Princeton, New Jersey, since 1990. At the McCarter, which was honored with a Tony Award for outstanding regional theater four years after her arrival, she has directed productions of some of her own dramas as well as works by many others, among them Anton Chekhov, Henrik Ibsen, and Tennessee Williams. In her own plays Mann has focused on actual instances of social injustice, creating much of her dialogue from words spoken by the real people involved; for that reason her work has often been referred to as "theater of testimony." "I feel the need to tell people's stories . . . ," she told Maria LoBiondo for *Princeton Online* in the mid-1990s. "I think it is important, for me, to be, in a way, invisible. I give voice to the voiceless." Mann's best-known plays are *Still Life*, in which a man and two women talk about the Vietnam War from their personal perspectives; *Execution of Justice*, about the trial of the man who murdered the San Francisco mayor and city supervisor in 1978; and the smash hit *Having Our Say*, based on the 1991 nonfiction best-seller in which Bessie and Sadie Delany, centenarian African-American sisters, talked about their lives and shared their thoughts. "Community building—that's what theater's all about," Mann told Maria LoBiondo. "It's where a community comes togeth-

Courtesy of McCarter Theatre

*Emily Mann*

er to share an event, a forum where significant ideas can be batted around. It's also a place to laugh together. There has to be a balance."

One of the two daughters of Arthur Mann and the former Sylvia Blut, Emily Betsy Mann was born on April 12, 1952 in Boston, Massachusetts. Her father, an historian who specialized in American reform politics, taught at the Massachusetts Institute of Technology and Smith College, both in Massachusetts, and then, starting in 1966, at the University of Chicago; he wrote seven books, among them two volumes about Fiorello La Guardia, the mayor of New York City from 1934 to 1945. At the dinner table, Arthur Mann liked to engage Emily and her sister, Carol, in discussions about such subjects as ethnicity and history; during such conversations Mann first learned about her Jewish heritage and philosophies of social justice. When she was seven Mann attended a production of S. Ansky's play *The Dybbuk* (1920) at a Yiddish theater in New York City. A classic tale of ghostly possession, *The Dybbuk* is about a young man who dies when the father of the woman he loves refuses to let her marry him; the young man promptly becomes an evil spirit that enters the woman's body and causes mischief, which leads to a dramatic scene of exorcism. Shortly after that Mann saw the Pulitzer Prize and Tony Award–winning musical *Fiorello!*, which deals with the life of former mayor LaGuardia. Both plays made a powerful impression on Mann and had a lasting influence on her. Another of Mann's vivid memories concerns the 1965 "Freedom March," led by the Reverend Martin Luther King Jr., in which several thousand blacks and whites walked from Selma to Montgomery, Alabama, in support of voting rights for African-Americans. Mann's father participated in the march along with the black historian John Hope Franklin, whom Dudley Clendinen, in the *New York Times* (February 4, 1996), described as Arthur Mann's "mentor and best friend." The possibility that her father would be killed along the march, Clendinen reported, "terrified" the 12-year-old Emily, who had seen televised scenes of people being beaten by law-enforcement officers during previous civil rights demonstrations in the South.

As a young girl Mann enjoyed writing short stories, painting, sculpting, dancing, and listening to music. In her teens she discovered that theater encompassed all of those interests. While still in high school, she got her first job in theater, at the University of Chicago, where she helped to make props. She worked with Louise Grafton, with whom she has remained friends and who currently makes costumes, builds sets, and produces other items necessary for theatrical productions.

Mann attended Harvard University, in Cambridge, Massachusetts, where she studied playwriting with the school's beloved professor William Alfred, an accomplished poet and writer for the stage. She graduated with a bachelor's degree in 1974. She earned her master's degree in fine arts from the University of Minnesota in 1976. That same year she was hired as the resident director of the Guthrie Theater, in Minneapolis, Minnesota, which is among the most respected regional theaters in the country. Mann directed at the Guthrie for three years, during which time she guided an acclaimed revival of Tennessee Williams's *The Glass Menagerie*. In 1980 she moved to New York City to become resident director of the theater company of the Brooklyn Academy of Music. She held that job until 1981.

*Annulla: An Autobiography*, the first play Mann wrote, was inspired in part by her discovery among her father's papers of transcribed oral recollections by World War II concentration-camp survivors. The papers included an interview between a Czech mother and daughter in which the mother described how she had endured the inhuman conditions of the camps. Her words deeply affected Mann, whose own mother had lost many relatives during the Holocaust. The Czech mother "had been a ballerina, and she used her memory of a perfect moment on stage—of a perfect pose, a perfect turn, a perfect ray of lighting—to get through her camp experiences," Mann told Sid Smith for the *Chicago Tribune* (March 3, 1996). "She kept reliving this moment of perfect beauty." At the suggestion of her father, who advised her to find a story of her own, Mann traveled to Poland, where she met with her best friend's aunt, whom she described to *Current Biography* as "a Jew and a survivor." The result of that meeting was *Annulla*, in which the main character relates her concentration-camp memories to the audience while cooking chicken soup in her kitchen. In *Annulla* Mann blended techniques of both the documentary and live theater and brought moral issues to the stage. Mann told Kathleen

Betsko and Rachel Koenig for their book *Interviews with Contemporary Women Playwrights* (1987), "Most of what I know about human experience comes from listening. That's why it's very natural for me to believe in direct address in the theater. It's an extension of listening: I hear the stories, then I let *you* the audience have the same experience I had as a listener." *Annulla*, which Mann wrote in 1977, made its New York premiere at the New Theater of Brooklyn in 1988, with Linda Hunt in the title role.

Mann's play *Still Life* premiered at the Goodman Theatre, in Chicago, and then opened in New York City Off-Broadway under her own direction in 1981. The play's central characters are a man, his wife, and his mistress, each of whom relates from a personal perspective the effects of the Vietnam War. In a review for the *New York Times* (February 20, 1981), the theater critic Frank Rich wrote, "The setting is a conference table, complete with water pitchers and ashtrays, at which three characters sit to address the audience for 90 minutes. Though Miss Mann, who also directed, occasionally allows her capable actors to stretch their legs, her play's title all too literally describes its method." Despite such criticism, *Still Life* garnered six Obie Awards, including ones for distinguished playwriting and distinguished direction. (Introduced by the *Village Voice* in 1956, the Obies are considered the highest honors for Off-Broadway theater.) Mann made her Broadway debut as both playwright and director in 1986, with her courtroom drama *Execution of Justice*, about the tragic and highly politicized case of Dan White's assassination in 1978 of George Moscone, who was then the mayor of San Francisco, and the openly gay Harvey Milk, the city supervisor. Mann used transcripts from White's trial and included in the cast of characters actual witnesses to the crimes. In the *New York Times* (March 14, 1986), Mel Gussow described *Execution of Justice* as a "bold attempt to explore not just one crime but contemporary moral values and the criminal justice system." The play, which ran on Broadway for only a short time, won a playwriting award from the Women's Committee of the Dramatists Guild for dramatizing issues of conscience, a Helen Hayes Award, a Bay Area Theater Critics Circle Award, a Burns Mantle Yearbook best-play citation, and a Drama Desk nomination. It also shared first place in that year's Great American Play Contest, held by the Actors Theater of Louisville, Kentucky.

In 1990 Mann took over as the artistic director of the McCarter Theatre Center for the Performing Arts, in Princeton, New Jersey, one of the most esteemed and successful regional theaters in the U.S. The theater, which opened in 1930, was originally built as the home of Princeton University's Triangle Club; because of its large seating capacity, its big stage, and its location—a short distance from New York City—it quickly became a popular pre-Broadway showcase for many productions. By the time of Mann's arrival, the McCarter had lost some of the luster of its star-studded past and was in financial trouble. Mann turned the situation around, bringing in recognizable names—for example, the award-winning South African playwright Athol Fugard, who has made the McCarter the site for debuts of his work in the U.S., and the actresses Mary Stuart Masterson, Linda Hunt, and Frances McDormand for Mann's 1992 production of Chekhov's *Three Sisters*. Moreover, by the end of her first four years as artistic director—at which time McCarter won the Tony Award—the number of season subscribers had increased by 80 percent. Mann has also brought to the stage new and unique work, such as Anna Deavere Smith's look at the Los Angeles riots of 1992, *Twilight: Los Angeles, 1992*, for which Mann won an award for best director from the Los Angeles chapter of the National Association for the Advancement of Colored People (NAACP), and *Betsey Brown: A Rhythm and Blues Musical*, which Mann created in collaboration with the poet Ntozake Shange and the composer Baikida Carroll.

Mann's most successful play to date is *Having Our Say*, based on the best-selling 1993 memoir *Having Our Say: The Delany Sisters' First 100 Years*, by two African-American women, Sadie and Bessie Delany, in collaboration with Amy Hill Hearth. The work opened on Broadway at the Booth Theatre in 1995 after a trial run that broke the audience-attendance record at the McCarter. Like the book, the play is about the lives and times of Sadie and Bessie Delany, who, when the book was published, were each more than 100 years old. The sisters reminisce about their experiences with family and work and discuss their views of historic events that took place during the century they witnessed. Mann discussed her idea of bringing the book to the stage with her friends Judith Rutherford James and Camille O. Cosby (the wife of the comedian Bill Cosby), both of whom helped to produce *Having Our Say* on Broadway. Concerning the appeal of the Delany sisters, Mann told Tom Sime for the *Dallas Morning News* (April 7, 1998, on-line), "They're loving and funny, and old and harmless. . . . The Delany sisters make us glad that we are part of the human race. . . . I think we all need to bask in that glow now and then. . . . You can live well, you can be a good person. It's possible." Some critics noted that Mann did not so much write the play as simply transpose the book to the stage. In a different view of her accomplishment, Kevin K. Gaines, a history professor at the University of Texas and the author of the best-selling book *Uplifting the Race: Black Leadership, Politics and Culture Since the Turn of the Century*, said to Tom Sime, "Her staging of the play is brilliant in making the historical material work as theater." Gaines felt that other historians would also applaud Mann for her "commitment to accuracy." After the Delany sisters came to see the show on Broadway, Mann told Sid Smith, "Watching them watch the show was amazing. They got a standing ovation from the audience at the end, and to see them honored was one of the most beautiful moments of my life." For her work on *Having Our Say,* Mann received the Hull-Warriner Award, presented by the Dramatists Guild (it is the only award given by playwrights to one of their peers); two Joseph Jefferson Awards; Drama Desk and Outer Critics Circle Award nominations; and Tony Award nominations for best play and best director. *Having Our Say* also toured nationally and debuted internationally in South Africa in 1998. The TV movie, adapted from the play by Mann, won a Peabody Award for Broadcast and Cable Excellence in 1999.

In 1996 Mann's *Greensboro: A Requiem* premiered at the McCarter under the direction of Mark Wing-Davey. The play documents an incident in which a dozen Ku Klux Klansmen and members of the American Nazi Party killed five anti–Ku Klux Klan demonstrators and wounded eight others in Greensboro, North Carolina, in November 1979. Involved in the episode were, among others, members of the Communist Workers Party (both black and white) who were trying to unionize three local mills; several Jewish students from the Duke University Medical School (some of whom were among those murdered); and local police officers who, despite prior warnings, took no steps to try to prevent the tragedy. The three trials held afterward did not result in any convictions. For the dialogue in her script—which is another example of her style of documentary theater, or theater of testimony (a phrase credited to the South African director Barney Simon)—Mann used only statements from police and court transcripts, newspaper accounts, television footage, and interviews she had taped with some of the actual protagonists. She relied solely on those sources, Dudley Clendinen wrote, "because she loves the idiomatic character of real speech, and because she believes that a 'heightened reality' comes from the re-enactment of real words and real people in real events." Speaking of *Greensboro: A Requiem*, Mann told Clendinen, "No one's getting off easy here"; according to Clendinen, Mann wanted the play to awaken audiences to the possibility that "there may be more issues, and more levels of responsibility in this story than first appear."

Mann directed her adaptation of Isaac Bashevis Singer's 1994 novel *Meshugah* at the McCarter Theatre in 1998. (The title is the Yiddish word for "crazy.") In the *New York Times* (December 27, 1998), Alvin Klein wrote, "The piece gave stage life to Singer's complex, resonant story about an impossible quest for happiness after the Holocaust." After describing the play as "understated" and "underappreciated," Klein wrote that "Mann's loving fidelity" to Singer's tale "was unfairly misconstrued as undramatic." *Meshugah*, he concluded, is a "life-enhancing play about an inexorable death wish."

Over the years Mann has directed revivals of such well-known plays as Henrik Ibsen's *A Doll's House*, Tennessee Williams's *Cat on a Hot Tin Roof*, and Anton Chekhov's *The Cherry Orchard*, among many others. Venues at which she has directed include the Mark Taper Forum, in Los Angeles; the La Jolla Playhouse, in California; and the Hartford Stage, in Connecticut. Her plays have been published in such collections as *Coming to Terms: American Plays and the Vietnam War* (1985), *The Ten Best Plays of 1986*, *Out Front* (1988), and *Testimonies: Four Plays by Emily Mann* (1996). With David Roessel, she co-edited the anthology *Political Stages: Plays That Shaped a Century* (2002). Mann has received fellowships from the Guggenheim Foundation and the National Endowment for the Arts. Her honors also include the 1995 Brandeis University Women of Achievement Award, the 1996 Douglass College of New Jersey Woman of Achievement Award, the Rosamond Gilder Award for Outstanding Achievement in the Theater, in 1999, and, from Radcliffe College, a division of Harvard University, an Alumnae Recognition Award, also in 1999.

Paraphrasing Mann, LoBiondo wrote that "wherever she goes—sitting on a plane, for example—people open up to her." "Her gaze may be a large part of the reason; it is compassionate and nonjudgmental," LoBiondo wrote. "Her dark eyes seem able to take all of a story in and hold it there." Louise Grafton described the playwright to LoBiondo as a "terrifically fair person. In theater there typically are a lot of temperaments, a lot of high emotions. Emily always seems to make the right decision." From her marriage to the actor Gerry Bamman, which ended in divorce, Mann has one son, Nicholas. In 1994, shortly after the McCarter won the Tony Award, she was diagnosed with multiple sclerosis. "There's a blessing in the curse," she told LoBiondo. "In some ways it has been a rebirth. I've had to re-examine my priorities. It's very clear what matters to me now, and who matters to me now. With fewer hours in the day, my work has improved. I find that I value the goodness in people more, and I don't put up with less than the best." — C.F.T.

Suggested Reading: McCarter Theater Web site; *New York Times* C p13 Apr. 18, 1995, II p5 Feb. 4, 1996, with photos; *Newsday* II p3 Mar. 9, 1986; *Princeton Online*; Betsko, Kathleen, and Rachel Koenig. *Interviews with Contemporary Women Playwrights*, 1987; Frick, John W., and Vallillo, Stephen M., eds. *Theatrical Directors*, 1994; Robinson, Alice M., et al., eds. *Notable Women in the American Theatre*, 1989; Shapiro, Ann R., ed. *Jewish American Women Writers*, 1994; *Who's Who in America 2001*

Selected Plays: *Annulla: An Autobiography*; *Execution of Justice*; *Greensboro: A Requiem*; *Having our Say*; *Still Life*

Selected Television Shows: *Having Our Say*

## Marcy, Geoffrey W., and Butler, R. Paul

Marcy, Geoffrey W.
*Sep. 29, 1954– Astrophysicist*

*Address: 417 Campbell Hall, University of California, Berkeley, CA 95064*

Butler, R. Paul
*1960– Astrophysicist*

*Address: Dept. of Terrestrial Magnetism, Carnegie Institution of Washington, 5241 Broad Branch Rd., N.W., Washington, DC 20015-1305*

Since 1995 the astrophysicists Geoffrey W. Marcy and R. Paul Butler have discovered or co-discovered 70 planets beyond the borders of our solar system—a number that represents over two-thirds of all extrasolar planets known to date. "The discovery of other planets was something I had pondered when I was a kid," Marcy told Francine Tyler for the University of California (UC)–Santa Cruz campus magazine *Review* (Winter 1997, on-line). "As a researcher, I wanted to tackle a question that many children ask: 'Are there planets around the stars I see at night?'" Before they reaped any results, the researchers spent eight years pioneering a new technique for discovering objects orbiting distant stars; all the while they endured the criticism and ridicule of many of their peers, who felt the mission to find planets beyond the reaches of our own solar system was a fool's errand. Marcy and Butler are now recognized as the greatest team of planet hunters in the world; indeed, the radical degree to which their work has challenged astronomical paradigms has led them to be compared to Copernicus and Columbus.

Geoffrey W. Marcy was born in Detroit, Michigan, on September 29, 1954. His father, Robert, was a mechanical and aerospace engineer; his mother, Gloria, an elementary-school teacher. He has two sisters, Renee and Susan. When he was 14 his parents bought him a poster of the solar system—the sun and its planets: Mercury, Venus, Earth, Mars, Jupiter, Saturn, Uranus, Neptune, and Pluto. His parents also gave him a four-inch telescope (that is, a telescope whose mirror measures four inches in diameter). "I was kind of a sports-oriented kid, but when I got that telescope I was completely taken," he told David Perlman for the *San Francisco Chronicle* (May 22, 2000). "I remember seeing the rings around Saturn and I was stunned. And when I saw the four moons around Jupiter—that Galileo saw, too—it was unbelievable, and I could even chart their orbits. Pretty soon all the kids were looking at my telescope and it became a kind of a neighborhood circus."

In 1976 Marcy earned a B.A. degree in physics and astronomy from UC–Los Angeles (UCLA), where he was elected to Phi Beta Kappa. He earned a Ph.D. in astronomy and astrophysics from UC–Santa Cruz in 1982. Then, as a Carnegie Fellow working at the Carnegie Institution's observatories in Pasadena, California, he began studying the magnetic properties of stars. But the work did not interest him "on a gut human level," as he told William Speed Weed for a *Salon* article reprinted in *Reader's Digest* (March 2000). "I asked myself, What would appeal to me even if I wasn't an astronomer?" The answer was a question that had been in his mind for many years: Is there life on other planets in the universe? In 1983, while at the Carnegie Institution, he began his search for planets outside our solar system. In the following year he joined the faculty of San Francisco State University (SFSU) as an associate professor of physics and astronomy. It was at SFSU that he met Butler, then a graduate student, and found an eager collaborator for his work.

Robert Paul Butler was born in San Diego in 1960 to Donald A. Butler, who has retired from the Los Angeles Police Department, and Karen I. Butler. He has one brother, Ronald "Carl" Butler, now a doctor. Known informally as Paul, Butler earned a B.A. degree in physics in 1985 and a B.S. in chemistry in the following year from SFSU. He was working on his M.A. degree in physics (which he received in 1989) at SFSU when he made Marcy's acquaintance. In 1993 he was awarded a Ph.D. in astronomy from the University of Maryland. Concurrently for the next four years, he held the posts of visiting research fellow at UC–Berkeley and research scientist at SFSU.

In 1987 Marcy and Butler, using the giant telescope at the Lick Observatory (a University of California facility near San Jose), began to record measurements of the white light emanating from 120 stars similar in size to the star that we call the sun. (White light contains all the colors of the spectrum; measurements of a star's spectra provide much information about the star.) Because distant planets are far too dim to be seen against the glare of the stars they orbit (much the way a 30-watt bulb would be invisible in front of a billion-watt source of light), their presence is detectable only by monitoring their stars for telltale motions. The gravity exerted by an orbiting planet causes a star to wobble slightly as it travels across the sky—"much like a dog owner gets yanked around by a little poodle," as Marcy told Greg Lefevre for CNN, according to the *Literacy Net* (April 14, 1999, on-line). Detecting such motion with traditional optical astronomical devices was not possible. A major refurbishment of the Lick spectrograph in the late 1980s, along with the introduction of methods pioneered by Marcy and Butler, made possible the measurement of tiny changes in the light spectra of stars. The changes, called Doppler shifts, indicate subtle increases toward blue or red light in a star's spectra. A larger planet will cause its star to wobble more than a smaller planet will, with the extent of the wobble reflected in distinctive changes in the star's spectrum.

As they labored to come up with a way to analyze the changes in spectra, Marcy and Butler endured criticism and derision from the scientific

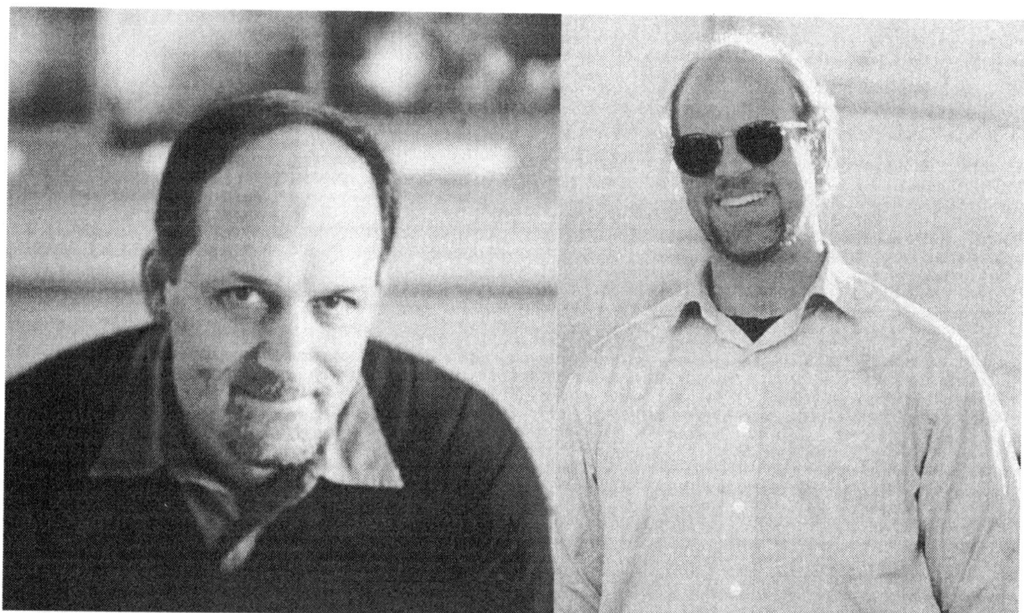

*Geoffrey W. Marcy (left) and R. Paul Butler*

Courtesy of UC Berkeley (left) and R. Paul Butler

community. "Paul and I were very worried for many years," Marcy admitted to Kathy Sawyer for the *Washington Post* (December 25, 1996). "I mean, we were getting bad results . . . not only were we clearly unsuccessful, but there was a certain amount of embarrassment." Butler concurred, telling Sawyer, "It was an extraordinarily depressing six or seven years." The signal they sought was in the data, but they had trouble finding it. "We just didn't know how to pull it out, sort of like Dorothy didn't know how to get back home. We had to learn how to click our heels together three times." In December 1995, after eight years of observations, Marcy and Butler discovered two planets between 40 light-years and 70 light-years from Earth. The planets—70 Virginis b in the constellation Virgo and 47 Ursae Majoris b in Ursa Major (the Big Dipper)—were only the second and third to be discovered outside the solar system. (Discovery of the first extrasolar planet, which circles the star 51 Pegasi, had been announced two months earlier by the Swiss researchers Michel Mayor and Didier Queloz.) "After the discovery of 51 Peg everyone wondered if it was a freak, a one in a million observation," Marcy said in a January 17, 1996 UC–Berkeley news release. "The answer is no. Planets aren't rare at all." The planet 70 Virginis b appears to be 7.5 times more massive than Jupiter (the largest planet in the solar system by far, Jupiter is 318 times bigger than Earth) and orbits its star every 116.7 days; 47 Ursae Majoris b is about 2.3 times the mass of Jupiter and orbits its star in 1,100 days. The surface temperature of 70 Virginis b is estimated to be about 90 degrees Celsius (194 degrees Fahrenheit)—less than the boiling point of water, which means that water might exist there but the likelihood is small that any living organisms could survive. The presence of the planets, however, indicated that there might be other planets, possibly ones that support life, in the Milky Way, a galaxy that contains more than 100 billion stars (including the sun). "We are at a watershed," Marcy said when announcing the discovery of the two planets, as reported by Paul Recer for the Associated Press (January 18, 1996) and printed in the Toronto *Globe and Mail*. "There is a dawning of a new field in science. These new planets offer a challenge to us to compare them with those in our solar system." He went on to say that the finding of 47 Ursae Majoris b was particularly significant. "It is the first find with characteristics of mass and orbit that are similar to the solar system," he told Recer. "We know of only one way to get such a thing, and that is to have an event around that star that is the same event that happened around the sun. And that event produced an Earth, the one planet [in our solar system] that does support life. This is the first evidence that what occurred around the sun [formation of a family of planets] has occurred around at least one other star."

Since then, Marcy and Butler, along with collaborators including Steven Vogt of UC–Santa Cruz, Debra Fischer of UC–Berkeley, and Chris McCarthy of the Carnegie Institution, have discovered or co-discovered 70 of the 102 currently known extrasolar (or exosolar, as they are also called) planets. Marcy and Butler quickly became known as the most successful planet-hunting team in the world. Meanwhile, the pace and scope of their discoveries increased, when they began making observations from the Keck Telescope, on the summit of Hawaii's dormant Mauna Kea volcano. In September 1998 they discovered the first planets to be detected with the Keck Telescope. One of the two planets, orbiting the star HD187123, in the constellation Cygnus, was discovered with the help of Kevin Apps, a sophomore astrophysics student at the University of Sussex, England. The other planet, which orbits the star HD210277, near the constellation Aquarius, is the first extrasolar planet that appears to have an Earth-like orbit in terms of duration (its year lasts 437 days) and average distance from its star. (However, while orbiting its star, it passes much closer to and much farther from that star than Earth does from the sun.) Referring to the average distance of HD210277's planet from its sun, Marcy told a Reuters reporter, according to the ABC News Web site (September 24, 1998), "We wondered if nature rarely puts planets at one Earth-Sun distance. Now we know that such planets are not rare."

In April 1999 Butler, Marcy, and Fischer announced the discovery of the first solar system, or planetary system (a system in which two or more planets orbit the same star) other than our own. While studying the spectrograph of the star Upsilon Andromedae, around which a planet had been discovered in 1996, the researchers saw a pattern different from anything they had encountered before. They later realized that the pattern was a result of the gravitational pulls of three planets. The star, approximately 44 light-years away, is slightly larger than our sun, while the planets are roughly the size of Jupiter. "With the discovery of the first planetary system beyond our own, we are witnessing, I think, the emergence of a new era in human exploration," Marcy told Earl Lane for *Newsday* (April 16, 1999). The finding implied that solar systems may form readily, which would mean that our own solar system is not unusual, a theory Marcy embraced at the time. "When I watch *Star Wars* and *Star Trek* movies, I see people like Jean-Luc Picard darting from planet to planet in the Milky Way Galaxy, and it seems utterly obvious, at least to the writers, that there would be a multitude of planets out there," Marcy said in a press release issued by SFSU (April 24, 1999). "But scientifically, we had no evidence of this until today with this Upsilon planetary system. Now we have the first clear evidence that there are indeed planetary systems out there and probably most of the stars in the Galaxy harbor some sorts of planets." The discovery was puzzling as well as thrilling, because no current theory could account for how several giant planets could form and co-exist around one star.

As of fall 1999 the planet-hunting team led by Marcy and Butler had gathered mathematical evidence of 18 planets but could infer their existence only by measuring the wobble of nearby stars caused by the gravitational pull exerted by the planets as they orbited. On November 5, 1999, working at the Keck Telescope, the dozen-member team detected a wobble in the star HD 209458, in the Pegasus constellation. They notified the astronomer Greg Henry of Tennessee State University, who operates a cluster of remote-controlled telescopes in the Patagonia Mountains of Arizona. After focusing one of the telescopes on the star, Henry observed that it dimmed visibly as the planet crossed in front of it, as Marcy and Butler had predicted. That finding provided the first visual proof of an extrasolar planet. "This is the first independent confirmation of a planet discovered through changes in a star's radial velocity and demonstrates that our indirect evidence for planets really is due to planets," Marcy said in a press release from UC–Berkeley (November 12, 1999). "With this one, everything hangs together. This is what we've been waiting for." Based on their observations, team members calculated that the planet orbits HD 209458 every three-and-a-half days. A gaseous giant similar to Jupiter, the planet has only 63 percent of Jupiter's mass but is roughly 60 percent larger in diameter. Its star is 153 light-years from Earth and is relatively close to the star 51 Pegasi, around which the first extrasolar planet was discovered, in 1995.

In January 2001 Marcy and Butler made an announcement that shocked the scientific world: their discovery of two immense planets—one at least 7.7 times and the other between 17 and 42 times the mass of Jupiter—orbiting the star HD168443, 123 light-years away in the constellation Serpens. The size of the second planet was far greater than that of any other planet discovered up to that time, and in fact placed it, in terms of size, in a category previously reserved for stars and various other large extraterrestrial objects. "We never expected nature would make such gargantuan planets, and indeed maybe they aren't planets at all," Butler told David L. Chandler for the *Boston Globe* (January 10, 2001). However, he warned against identifying the large object as a brown dwarf, a "failed star" that never got large enough to produce the nuclear fire that is a hallmark of a star. "To say it's a brown dwarf is just sweeping all the mystery under a rug," Butler said. (The brown-dwarf theory, too, is puzzling, because it is believed to be impossible for a brown dwarf to form so close to another star.) Existing astronomical theory could not account for the formation of such a large planet. "To find a planet 17 times the mass of Jupiter says there's got to be another way to make planets," Alan Boss of the Carnegie Institution told Sharon Begley and Jamie Rend for *Newsweek* (January 22, 2001). "Nature has thrown a monkey wrench into what we thought we understood about planetary formation." Marcy and Butler also announced the discovery of a pair of planets, one roughly half the mass of Jupiter and the other nearly double Jupiter's mass, that whirl around their home star, Gliese 876, with synchronized orbits; one circles the star in 30 days while the other takes twice that long to make a complete orbit. Four of Jupiter's moons (there are at least 39)—Io, Europa, Ganymede, and Callisto—also have synchronized (or resonant) orbits, but the phenomenon had not been seen before among planets. Even more startling is that the system appears to be on the brink of instability, meaning that a slight change in masses or orbits would cause the planets to crash into their star or fly out into space. "After finding so many exoplanets, we thought we understood their masses and orbits," Marcy said at the 2001 annual meeting of the American Astronomical Society, as quoted by Govert Schilling in *Science* (January 19, 2001). "Maybe we became a little cocky. But the new systems, with two planets each, are unique and a little frightening. These systems stump us."

On June 13, 2002 Marcy and Butler announced the discovery of 15 more extrasolar planets, including a planet orbiting the star 55 Cancri that is remarkably like Jupiter. It is only 3.5 to 5 times Jupiter's mass, orbits its star at a distance of 510 million miles (Jupiter's orbit averages about 480 million miles from the sun), and circles the star in 13 years (compared with Jupiter's 12-year orbit). The presence of a planet of this size at such a distance from a star is thought to be essential to the development of smaller inner planets like Earth, as the gravitational pull exerted by such a large planet would attract many comets and asteroids that, without the large planet to act as a sort of buffer, would travel closer to the star and thereby prevent the formation of planets like the inner ones in our own solar system. Also distinguishing the new planet was its almost circular orbit; the orbits of other extrasolar planets often take them closer to their stars than Mercury is to the sun. "An Earth-like planet can't get established when a Jupiter-size wrecking ball is sailing through," Butler told Jeffrey Kluger for *Time* (June 24, 2002). The discovery raises hopes that smaller planets that could support life may exist around 55 Cancri or other stars. "We have the first sign of a planetary system that has an architecture qualitatively similar to [that of] our own solar system," Marcy said when announcing the discovery, as reported by William Harwood in the *Washington Post* (June 14, 2002). "Clearly, finding another solar system like our own begs the question, are there other Earths, Earth-like planets in this system?"

It is not surprising that all extrasolar planets discovered thus far are comparable in size to the huge, gaseous, outer planets of our solar system, since objects much smaller cannot be detected with currently available equipment. But astronomers *were* surprised to find the majority of the planets so close to their parent stars; they often approach their stars to a distance smaller than the nearest distance at which Mercury, the innermost planet in our solar system, orbits the sun. (Mercury's path is an ellipse, ranging in distance from the sun from 29 million to 43 million miles.) Marcy believes that these glimpses of other solar systems could be a preview of the fate of our own. Almost undoubtedly, according to Marcy, within 10 billion to 20 billion years, Mercury and Pluto, the smallest planets in the solar system, will be "tossed out into the galaxy," as he told Perlman, while the bigger ones will remain. Thus, he continued, "the gas giants we've already detected" orbiting other stars may be "the debris of some great big bumper-car era where there's only one car left." One explanation proposed to explain the existence of such massive planets so close to stars is that they formed at a much greater distance from the star and have moved inward over time. Giant planets cannot form too close to a star, because there is too little gas and dust in the inner regions of the gaseous, dusty rings (known as protoplanetary disks) surrounding young stars. Another startling finding is the extreme elliptical orbits of most of the extrasolar planets; since the planets in our own solar system (except for Mercury) have nearly circular orbits, that was what astronomers expected to find among extrasolar orbiting planets. "We should consider ourselves lucky that Jupiter ended up in a nearly circular orbit," Marcy and Butler wrote in a paper that appears on Marcy's Web page on the UC–Berkeley Web site. "If it had careened into an oval orbit, Jupiter might have scattered Earth, thwacking it out of the solar system. Without stable orbits for Earth and Jupiter, life might never have emerged."

Present technology is not sufficient to determine the compositions of the newly discovered planets. They are assumed to be gaseous, because they most closely resemble Jupiter in mass. Marcy theorizes that the existence of life on any given planet depends on the planet's distance from its star and the shape of its orbit. In order for a planet to support life, circumstances must be just right—producing the "Goldilocks effect," in Marcy's words: the planet's temperature cannot be too hot or too cold, and its orbit must be fairly circular and not too close or too far from the star. The extrasolar planets discovered so far do not exhibit the Goldilocks effect. "By the time we're up to 100 planets, I strongly suspect most will be in elliptical orbits," Marcy told a reporter for the Scripps Howard News Service, according to ABC News (January 20, 1999, online). "The question then arises: Why are we so lucky to live on a planet that's circular in orbit? Clearly, circular orbits are critical to the survival and evolution of life. We are here, in other words, because this is the only kind of planetary system amenable to the onset of biochemistry."

Marcy and Butler believe that with current technology, it is possible to detect Neptune-size planets (roughly 15 to 17 times Earth's mass) but not Earth-size ones. "We'll be out of business, we think, in 10 years when we've found the Saturns and the Neptunes and the Jupiters," Marcy told Alan Boyle for the MSNBC Web site (March 29, 2000). Referring to the National Aeronautics and Space Administration, he added, "We will need indeed to turn to the new technology that NASA is developing—spaceborne telescopes without which we will never detect Earthlike planets." NASA expects two such telescopes to be operational within the next decade. The Space Interferometry Mission (SIM) telescope, scheduled for launch in 2009, will orbit the sun 60 million miles from Earth for five years. With 30-foot telescopic arms (comparable in total dimensions to the Keck

Telescope), it will be capable of measuring characteristics of approximately 40 million stars, along with their distances from Earth. The second NASA telescope, the Terrestrial Planet Finder, may be launched in 2011. The progress of the two projects depends on continued funding for NASA, which the U.S. Congress has targeted for budget cuts in 2003, because of the current economic slump. While some critics claim that the search for extrasolar worlds has no direct benefit for humankind, Marcy believes we need to take the long view. "Discovering planets, even life in the universe, isn't going to affect corporate profits," he told Don Sheron for the *San Antonio Express-News* (October 30, 2001). "But understanding the uniqueness of Earth is a value that comes within"—apparently meaning that it is valuable in and of itself.

Every month Marcy and Butler, whose research is supported by the NASA Origins Program and the National Science Foundation, travel to the Keck Telescope in Hawaii; they use the telescope for three nights to scan about 800 of the approximately 200 billion stars in the Milky Way Galaxy. (They scan the same 800 stars each time.) The data are sent by Internet to computers at UC–Berkeley and the Carnegie Institution, where Marcy and Butler painstakingly analyze them over the next months. "We're not geniuses," Marcy told Sawyer. "We just work hard, and that's what has paid off."

In 1996 Marcy received the Alumni Achievement Award from the UC–Santa Cruz Alumni Association. Among his many other honors are the Manne Siegbahn Award, from the physics committee of the Swedish Academy (1996); the UCLA Alumni Professional Achievement Award (1999); the inaugural Bioastronomy Medal of Honor from Commission 51 of the International Astronomical Union (IAU); and the first-ever Certificate of Recognition from the Extrasolar Planetary Foundation (1999). He was named a California Academy of Sciences Fellow in 1996. He has served on the board of councilors of the American Astronomical Society, the board of directors of the Astronomical Society of the Pacific, and an American Astronomical Society committee on the status of women in astronomy. He is a member of NASA working groups on the origins of solar systems and on the Terrestrial Planet Finder. In 1991 he became a visiting scholar at UC–Berkleley; he was given the title professor of astronomy there in 1999, the year in which his position at SFSU changed to adjunct professor. He is an avid tennis player, fitting a game into his schedule nearly every day, and is dedicated to preserving open spaces, especially natural and wildlife habitats. He lives in the San Francisco area with his wife, Susan E. Kegley, a chemist who serves as the staff scientist/program coordinator for the Pesticide Action Network.

Butler received a NASA Graduate Student Researchers Fellowship for 1991–92, as well as the California State University Alumni Award (1996), the SFSU Alumnus of the Year Award (1996), and the International Astronomical Union Bioastronomy Medal (1997). He received a Certificate of Recognition from the California State Senate in May 1996. In 1997 he was named one of 100 Americans for the Next Century by *Newsweek* and was inducted into the SFSU Hall of Fame. Among Butler's other honors are the Bernard Oliver Memorial Award from the Extrasolar Planetary Foundation (1998), the Achievement in Science Award from *Popular Science* magazine (1999), the Henry Draper Medal from the National Academy of Sciences (2001), and the University of Maryland College of Physical Sciences Distinguished Alumnus Award (2001). From 1997 to 1999 he worked as a staff astronomer at the Anglo-Australian Observatory, in Australia, which has headquarters near Sydney and a telescope on Siding Spring Mountain, near Coonabarbarbran; he often commuted between Australia and Hawaii to monitor sun-like stars within 50 parsecs (150 light-years) from Earth. Currently he spends a total of about two months a year at telescopes in Hawaii, Australia, and Chile, with the goal of observing all 2,000 such stars for the presence of planets; about 65 percent of them are currently under survey. Since 1999 he has been a staff scientist in the Department of Terrestrial Magnetism at the Carnegie Institution of Washington, D.C. — K.E.D.

Suggested Reading: ABC News (on-line) Jan. 20, 1999; MSNBC (on-line) Mar. 29, 2000; *Newsweek* p52+ Jan. 22, 2001, with photos; *Reader's Digest* p26+ Mar. 2000, with photo; *San Francisco Chronicle* A p6 May 22, 2000, with photo; University of California–Berkeley Web site; *Time* p53 June 24, 2002; *Washington Post* A p1 Dec. 25, 1996, with photos

---

## Marlette, Doug

*Dec. 6, 1949– Cartoonist; writer*

*Address: c/o* Newsday, *2 Park Ave., Rm. 601, New York, NY 10016-5679*

"A great political cartoon is a monster jam, a scud missile, a drive-by shooting," the cartoonist Doug Marlette told an assembly of journalism students at the University of North Carolina at Chapel Hill, as quoted by Cyndi Soter for the *Carolina Communicator* (January 2001). "It's also a poem, a prayer, a religious experience. It can strike at the heart like a lightning bolt from above and change the way you see and think and feel." The recipient of the 1988 Pulitzer Prize for editorial cartooning, Marlette has been poking fun at public figures for almost 30 years. "He produces strong, uncomplicated, hit-the-mark kind of work that reflects an innocent refusal to be tricked," Jerry Shin, the editorial-page editor for the *Charlotte Observer*, wrote for *Esquire*, as quoted by *Contemporary Authors*. One recent cartoon by Marlette, for example, satirized President George W. Bush's attempts to appeal to

Courtesy of the University of North Carolina School of Journalism and Mass Communications

*Doug Marlette*

African-American voters in the 2000 presidential campaign; the cartoon featured the candidate dressed, like a rapper, in baggy pants, unlaced sneakers, and an outsized "W" medallion while carrying a boom box and shouting "Whaaasssuuuuup?" to three representatives of the NAACP. Another cartoon took aim at former president Bill Clinton's philandering, showing a giant zipper with a caption reading "Clinton Memorial."

Marlette's work has appeared in more than 200 newspapers and magazines worldwide, including the *New York Times*, the *Washington Post*, *Newsday*, *Time*, *Newsweek*, *Christian Century*, *Rolling Stone*, *Der Spiegel*, and *Esquire*. In addition to the Pulitzer Prize, Marlette has won three National Headliners Awards for consistently outstanding editorial cartoons; two Robert F. Kennedy Awards for editorial cartooning; two first prizes in the John Fischetti Memorial Cartoon Competition; and a citation from the Overseas Press Club for cartoons about foreign affairs. Beyond his work as an editorial cartoonist, Marlette is known for his comic strip *Kudzu*; a musical based on *Kudzu*; and *The Bridge*, a novel.

Douglas Nigel Marlette was born on December 6, 1949 in Greensboro, North Carolina. His father served as a medic in the Marine Corps during World War II, an occupation he continued to practice after the war ended. The cartoonist's mother was a homemaker. Speaking with Bob Minzesheimer for *USA Today* (November 1, 2001), Marlette described his family as "conservative Southern Baptists who I thought of as benighted political reactionaries." The family moved around the South as Marlette's father was transferred from one military installation to another; in addition to Greensboro, Marlette spent his childhood in Durham, North Carolina, Laurel, Mississippi, and Sanford, Florida. "I grew up in towns so backwards even the Episcopalians handle snakes," he quipped, as quoted by Cyndi Soter.

Marlette took up cartooning at an early age: he has recalled bartering his sketches of Donald Duck and Mickey Mouse for sweets or toys with his kindergarten classmates. Later on he drew for the school paper and created election posters for friends running for class office. At first, Marlette has said, his approach to drawing was intuitive and unsystematic, but as he grew older he took a more methodical tack, studying the drawings of other artists and reading everything about drawing he could get his hands on. However, an irreverent streak prevented him from fully embracing the traditional fine arts. "I took straight art courses all the way from 8th grade, where I did still life and figure drawings, but I was never serious," he told Catherine Edgerton for *Dream/Girl Magazine* (Spring 1998, on-line). "That was my problem. I would do a still life, but I would have the apple saying something to the banana."

If the fine arts were too staid for his temperament, Marlette soon learned that political cartooning put a premium on playful iconoclasm. He first discovered political cartoons in the 1960s, in the midst of the civil rights movement and the growing public opposition to the Vietnam War; he was immediately impressed. "For a Southern Baptist Marine Corps military brat, such images come to you like fire, like a flaming pillar leading you out of the darkness and into the Promised Land," he recalled, as quoted by Soter. "They spoke to me in unknown tongues of peace and racial equality and social justice and the brotherhood of man. They taught me a reverence for irreverence." In 1966, at the age of 16, Marlette made his first sale, publishing a cartoon in the *Sanford Herald*, the local newspaper.

By the time he graduated from high school, in about 1967, Marlette had decided to pursue a career in cartooning. As he told Edgerton, however, "I didn't get encouraged much, because nobody would encourage you to be a cartoonist. It's like encouraging someone to be an actor or a songwriter. I mean, no responsible high school guidance counselor would tell someone, 'Live in an attic and starve.'" As a result, when he enrolled in Seminole Community College, in Sanford, he studied advertising and commercial art. On the side, though, he continued to pursue cartooning, regularly publishing his work in the *Orlando Sentinel-Star*.

Marlette transferred to Florida State University in Tallahassee in 1969. For the next two years, while pursuing a degree in philosophy, he published editorial cartoons in the *Florida Flambeau*, the campus newspaper. In 1972 Marlette left Florida to take a job as editorial cartoonist for the *Charlotte Observer*, in Charlotte, North Carolina. Because he was one foreign-language course shy of the graduation requirement, Marlette did not receive a bachelor's degree from Florida State at that time. (In 1998 the university waived the requirement and awarded him a degree in philosophy.)

For the next 15 years, Marlette remained with the *Charlotte Observer*, steadily winning a reputation as an astute and sometimes controversial editorial cartoonist. During this period he published three collections of his cartoons, which had begun to appear in national syndication: *The Emperor Has No Clothes* (1975), *If You Can't Say Something Nice* (1978), and *Drawing Blood* (1980). In 1980 Marlette won a Nieman Fellowship from Harvard University, awarded "to working journalists of particular accomplishment and promise for an academic year of study," according to the *Harvard University Gazette* (May 27, 1999). He was the first cartoonist to receive the prestigious fellowship.

While producing editorial cartoons for the *Charlotte Observer*, Marlette began publishing *Kudzu*, a loosely autobiographical comic strip that chronicles the life of Kudzu Dubose, an aspiring writer growing up in the American South. Set in the fictional town of Bypass, *Kudzu* also features the preacher Will B. Dunn, Kudzu's mother (whom Marlette, as quoted by Soter, characterized as the "Southern equivalent of a Jewish mother"), and Uncle Dub, "the classic good ol' boy." In creating the strip, Marlette has said, he was particularly influenced by Johnny Hart, the cartoonist who created *The Wizard of Id* and *B.C.*, and Al Capp, the writer and illustrator of the comic strip *Lil' Abner*.

In an article adapted from *In Your Face: A Cartoonist at Work* (1991), as quoted by *Contemporary Authors*, Marlette stressed that the editorial cartoon and the comic strip are entirely different media. "It didn't take me long to discover that drawing a comic strip has about as much in common with doing a one-panel editorial cartoon as shooting a jump shot has to do with playing the violin. . . . My political cartoons deal with the outside world. . . . But *Kudzu* is more personal, dealing with more basic themes, like those eternal strivings for love, power, and chocolate." *Kudzu* has been collected in a number of bound volumes, including *Kudzu* (1982), *Preacher: The Wit and Wisdom of Reverend Will B. Dunn* (1984), *I Am Not a Televangelist: The Continuing Saga of Will B. Dunn* (1988), *Even White Boys Get the Blues: Kudzu's First Ten Years* (1992), and *Gone with the Kudzu* (1995). As of late 2002 the comic strip remained in national syndication.

Marlette left the *Charlotte Observer* in 1987 to become an editorial cartoonist for the *Atlanta Constitution*, in Georgia. When Bill Kovacs, the editor of the *Constitution*, was fired one year later, Marlette left the paper and joined *Newsday*, a New York newspaper, once again as editorial cartoonist. Throughout the 1980s and 1990s, he continued to publish collections of his political cartoons, including *It's a Dirty Job—But Somebody Has to Do It!* (1984), *Shred This Book! The Scandalous Cartoons of Doug Marlette* (1988), *Faux Bubba: Bill and Hillary Go to Washington* (1993), and *I Feel Your Pain* (1996).

In March 1998 Marlette made his first foray into musical theater, with *Kudzu: A Southern Musical*. Based on his comic strip, *Kudzu* was written in collaboration with Jack Herrick and Bland Simpson of the Red Clay Ramblers, a string band. "There's a lot of talent involved in *Kudzu* . . . ," Lloyd Rose wrote for the *Washington Post* (March 12, 1998), "and the show is so good-hearted that you automatically root for it. Musical comedy is a tough form, though—and in spite of Marlette's wit and the lively musical contributions from Bland Simpson and Jack Herrick of the Red Clay Ramblers, the evening, which starts with some spark, ends up diffuse and energyless."

Meanwhile, the rediscovery of a forgotten episode from his family history spurred Marlette to begin work on his first novel. After moving to Hillsborough, North Carolina, near Raleigh, in 1991, Marlette learned that his grandmother had worked at a local cotton mill. In fact, Mama Gracie, as Marlette's grandmother was known, whom the cartoonist described in *Esquire* (April 1996) as a tiny woman "who had a black belt in passive aggression and was into child abuse long before it hit *Oprah*," had been bayoneted by a national guardsman in the General Textile strike of 1934. (She survived the incident.)

*The Bridge*, Marlette's fictionalized account of his family history, was published in October 2001 to mixed reviews. "In the tradition of Pat Conroy, Reynolds Price, and Clyde Edgerton, Marlette adds a new voice to southern family fiction," Carol Haggas wrote for *Booklist* (September 15, 2001). "The Pulitzer Prize-winning political cartoonist turns his kinetic powers of observation on familiar turf—the dysfunctional southern family—to bring us a portrait of reflection, resolution, and redemption that explosively transcends time and place to bridge generations and build legends." Jon Garelick, writing for the *New York Times Book Review* (November 4, 2001), was less enthusiastic. "There's been plenty of complaint about the memoir glut," he noted, "but Marlette's first novel might make you wish [he] had taken his family history, and a chapter of American labor unionism, head-on instead of giving us this awkwardly fictionalized account. . . . Marlette has identified his real-life grandmother as the source of some of this material, but these sections of the book read like bad memoir—labor union history served up in ungainly chunks of dialogue or woodenly staged scenes. There are also specious subplots. . . . At its best, Marlette's prose has a straightforward immediacy, but his storytelling could benefit from a cartoonist's economy of expression."

Since 1980 Marlette has been married to Melinda Hartley. The couple have one son, Jackson Douglas, who was born in 1986. — P.K.

Suggested Reading: *Carolina Communicator* (on-line) Jan. 2001, with photo; *Dream/Girl Magazine* (on-line) Spring 1998; *Publishers Weekly* p46+ Aug. 6, 2001, with photo; *USA Today* (on-line) Nov. 1, 2001

Selected Books: *The Emperor Has No Clothes*, 1975; *If You Can't Say Something Nice*, 1978; *Drawing Blood*, 1980; *Kudzu*, 1982; *Preacher: The Wit and Wisdom of Reverend Will B. Dunn*, 1984; *It's a Dirty Job—But Somebody Has to Do It!* 1984; *Just a Simple Country Preacher: More Wit and Wisdom of Reverend Will B. Dunn*, 1985; *There's No Business Like Soul Business*, 1987; *I Am Not a Televangelist: The Continuing Saga of Will B. Dunn*, 1988; *Shred This Book! The Scandalous Cartoons of Doug Marlette*, 1988; *A Doublewide with a View: The Kudzu Chronicles*, 1989; *In Your Face: A Cartoonist at Work*, 1991; *Faux Bubba: Bill and Hillary Go to Washington*, 1993; *I Feel Your Pain*, 1996; *The Bridge*, 2001

---

Courtesy of Girl Scouts of the USA

## Matsui, Connie L.

(mat-soo-ee)

*Jan. 11, 1954– National president of Girl Scouts of the USA; pharmaceutical company executive*

*Address: Girl Scouts of the USA, 420 Fifth Ave., 14th Fl., New York, NY 10018; IDEC Pharmaceuti-cals Corp., 3030 Callan Rd., San Diego, CA 92121*

On October 17, 1999 Connie L. Matsui was elected to a three-year term as the national president of Girl Scouts of the USA (GSUSA), the highest volunteer position in the organization. GSUSA's first Asian-American president, Matsui brought to the job not only more than 20 years of experience with Girl Scouts but also the skills she has developed in a successful career in business. Currently, Matsui is a senior vice president of planning and resource development at IDEC Pharmaceuticals Corp., a San Diego–based biotechnology company that creates therapies for people with cancer and autoimmune diseases. Her corporate expertise includes strategic planning, organizational development, finance, and general management. Matsui has been honored with the Girl Scouts' highest award for adults, the Thanks Badge, and *a Magazine* (December 2001/January 2002), which celebrates Asian America, listed her among the 25 most-notable people of Asian descent in the U.S. Matsui's strong belief in the importance of expanding the reach of the Girl Scouts and fostering tolerance and inclusion in the organization informs her approach to the GSUSA presidency. "We really want to dispel that image that we're just a white, middle-class 'craft, cookies and camping' organization," she told Robert Ito for *a Magazine* (December 2001/January 2002). "We're so much more than that now."

Connie L. Matsui was born on January 11, 1954. She earned a B.A. degree in English from Stanford University, in Stanford, California, in 1975 and a master's degree in business administration from the Stanford Graduate School of Business in 1977. At the suggestion of a colleague, shortly after she completed her MBA, Matsui volunteered to serve as a board member and officer of the San Francisco Bay Girl Scout Council, in Oakland, California. "Girl Scouts matched my desire to contribute to social welfare with my expectations of a well-run organization," Matsui recalled to Ross Atkin for the *Christian Science Monitor* (February 2, 2002). She told Cherian George for an article that appears on the official Web site of the Stanford Graduate School of Business, "Once I joined the local board, I soon learned how well managed and capable the organization was and how much Girl Scouts contributes to the lives of girls throughout the country." Although Matsui had never been a Girl Scout, she quickly embraced what she described to Atkin as "the vision" of the organization—a commitment to people from all cultures and walks of life and a mission to help all girls to reach their full potentials. "Despite my earlier experiences in high school and college, I was readily accepted for who I am and what I could contribute, not just what I looked like, whom I associated with, or how long I had been in the business or Girl Scout world," Matsui told Cherian George.

Girl Scouts of the USA, the world's largest organization for girls, was founded by Juliette Gordon Low in Savannah, Georgia, in 1912. It was originally called Girl Guides, like the Girl Guides of England, on which the American version was based. The first Girl Scout handbook, *How Girls Can Help Their Country*, was published in 1913, and the popular magazine the *American Girl* was published by Girl Scouts from 1917 to 1979. Four years after it came into being, the organization moved its national headquarters from Washington, D.C., to New York City, where it remains today. In 1950

Girl Scouts of the USA was reincorporated under a congressional charter. Its members currently total 2.8 million girls, ages five to 17, with nearly a million adult volunteers. As stated on the official Web site of Girl Scouts of the USA, its goal from the beginning has been to help girls to "build character and skills for success in the real world." Famous as door-to-door cookie sellers, Girl Scouts have sold cookies since the organization's early days; the organization's first official sale of commercially baked cookies took place in the Philadelphia area in 1936. (The most popular Girl Scout Cookies—a trademarked name—have been the Thin Mints.) Other Girl Scout activities include "career exploration," field trips, participation in sports skill-building clinics, community-service projects, and cultural exchanges. According to the organization's Web site, more than 50 million women in the U.S. have been Girl Scouts.

Matsui was elected to the Girl Scouts' national board of directors in 1984, then served three terms as a member-at-large. She was elected national secretary in 1993 and first vice president in 1996. As president of GSUSA, Matsui has made a concerted effort to expand the organization's scope. In 2001 she and the national board of directors launched "Girl Scouts for Every Girl, Everywhere," a campaign to increase membership among Hispanic and Asian-American girls. In addition, because many people still regard the Girl Scouts as merely a camping and cookie-selling organization, Matsui hopes to gain greater recognition of other Girl Scout programs, among them competitive sports, computer literacy, education, and community service.

A controversy concerning Matsui and GSUSA came to a head toward the end of 2000, when members of the conservative press and right-wing Christian groups attacked the organization's values. (This public criticism came on the heels of the Boy Scouts' well-publicized, successful legal fight to bar homosexuals from serving as scoutmasters.) After a screening at the White House in December 2000, Matsui commended the video *That's a Family!* for its focus on the needs of all children. The official Web site of the American Family Association objected to *That's a Family!*, however, calling it "an instructional video for children which equates same-sex relationships with marriage and claims that same-sex couples with children are families." The American Family Association's attack on the Girl Scouts' spirit and values was not the first to which conservative critics had subjected GSUSA. In another instance, Kathryn Jean Lopez, an associate editor of the *National Review* (October 23, 2000, on-line), wrote for that publication, "The Girl Scouts' leaders hope to make their youthful charges the shock troops of an ongoing feminist revolution. It's been a long slide for the Girl Scouts. . . . They dropped 'loyalty' from their oath in 1972, in favor of 'I will do my best to be honest and fair.' In 1975, a Catholic archdiocese cut off all support of the Girl Scouts because of their sex-ed program. In 1993, the Girl Scouts made 'God' optional in the Girl Scout promise." In an article posted to the Web site *gaytoday.com*, Bill Berkowitz quoted Lopez as writing of "a tendency from the Girl Scouts to be liberal feminists and to bring issues of sex and sexual orientation into the Girl Scouts rather prominently." Lopez also decried the presence of lesbians in the Girl Scouts and what she called the group's supposed overall "homosexual agenda." Matsui won praise for standing firm and reaffirming the organization's long-standing policy of nondiscrimination. "Being open to all people has always been part of the heritage of the organization," she told Robert Ito. "That's not about to change."

Before she joined IDEC Pharmaceuticals, Matsui held management positions at Wells Fargo Bank. She was a 2001 International Year of Volunteers honoree for her work with GSUSA. She has been a board member of the California School of Professional Psychology Alumnae Resources and a trustee of the San Francisco Bay Area United Way.

Matsui lives in San Diego with her husband, a real-estate developer, their teenage son, and their younger daughter, who is a member of the Girl Scouts. — C.F.T.

Suggested Reading: *a Magazine* p59 Dec. 2001/Jan. 2002, with photo; *Christian Science Monitor* Feb. 2, 2002, with photo; Girl Scouts of the USA Web site; Stanford Business School Web site

---

## McGraw, Phillip

*Sep. 1, 1950– Psychologist; writer; television personality*

*Address: P.O. Box 140143, Irving, TX 75014-0143*

From his Tuesday appearances on *The Oprah Winfrey Show*, Phillip McGraw became known to many as "Dr. Phil"—and, because of his forthright style, as "Tell It Like It Is Phil" (a nickname bestowed by Winfrey). A psychologist with a Ph.D. from the University of North Texas in Denton, McGraw launched his own program, the *Dr. Phil Show*, in September 2002; on it, he questions and advises guests on a variety of topics, eschewing clinical terms in favor of plain language and snappy one-liners that reflect his Texas background. His three self-help books have all made the *New York Times* best-seller list, and his nationally syndicated talk show debuted in the fall of 2002. "I've been very blessed in my life," he told an interviewer for *Entertainment Tonight* (August 31, 2001, online). "Things that I've done and things that I do now have been very successful, because we've always worked hard, been committed to excellence, and done a good job. I'm not a stranger to success, and I'm committed to sharing what has worked for me with other people." He is a frequent lecturer

Danny Turner/Courtesy of Simon & Schuster

*Phillip McGraw*

and also president of Courtroom Science Inc., a Dallas-area trial-strategy service.

Phillip McGraw was born on September 1, 1950 in Vinita, Oklahoma, and raised in Oklahoma, Kansas, and Colorado. His father, Joe, held a number of jobs—including high-school football coach and pilot carrying equipment to oil-field workers—before returning to school at age 40 to become a psychologist. His mother, Jerry, stayed at home to raise Phillip and his three sisters. In a conversation with Jane Pauley for *Dateline NBC* (January 27, 2002, on-line), he recalled realizing in junior high school that his family was poor. "We had so little money we lived in a little apartment near the school I went to. And we couldn't turn on the utilities for two months. We just didn't have money for groceries either. And one night we had some bread and some ketchup and some mustard. And that was dinner." During that time the family survived on the money Phillip and his father earned from a newspaper route. "That was rent money, that was grocery money," he told Pauley. "That wasn't . . . extra money, that's how we lived at the time. [The route] was 52 miles long if you can believe it and so every morning at 3:30 we would get up and fold papers. . . . They had two newspapers so we threw the papers in the morning and threw them again in the afternoon. Over a hundred miles a day throwing newspapers."

As a six-foot four-inch, 175-pound high-school linebacker in Kansas City, Kansas, McGraw won a football scholarship to the University of Tulsa. When his athletic career was cut short by an injury in his sophomore year, he left college and moved in with his parents and sisters in Wichita Falls, Texas. He went to work selling health-club memberships and was such a persuasive salesman that after six months he owned half the club. After three years in that business, he decided that a change was in order. He briefly considered a career in law or medicine before deciding to follow in his father's footsteps and study psychology. McGraw earned his bachelor's degree from Midwestern State University, in Wichita Falls, in 1975, and went on to receive his master's and Ph.D. degrees from the University of North Texas. After establishing a practice in Wichita Falls, he soon realized that interpersonal therapy was not his strong suit. "I was the worst relationship therapist in the world," he told Wes Smith for *Biography* (July 2000). "People would come in and start bitching and whining at each other and I'd think, 'My God, I'd slap him if he said that to me!' . . . I was teaching methods that I'd learned in school, but they didn't work—they never had. So I started looking for nontraditional ways to use my training." While maintaining his practice for several more years, he used his training in the industrial psychology, management, and training fields to establish, with his father and another partner, a company that conducted self-motivation and life-skills seminars across the United States. In 1988, a year before McGraw quit his practice, the Texas Board of Examiners and Psychologists reprimanded him for hiring a patient who was under his care; according to the *New York Times* (September 24, 2002), the board described McGraw as both caregiver and employer to the individual and referred to their association as an "inappropriate dual relationship."

McGraw's expertise in neuropsychology, the study of the brain and central nervous system, led to involvement as an expert witness in civil and personal-injury lawsuits involving brain damage. Because of his ability to explain complex science in easily grasped terms, he spent a lot of time on the witness stand, and he discovered that he enjoyed the orderliness of court proceedings. By contrast, "as a psychologist, I'd treat somebody and they'd be better one day but worse the next," he told Smith. "You don't cure people, you give them tools to manage their disorders, and that frustrated me." He soon began to assist in trial strategy as well. In 1989 he and his next-door neighbor, attorney Gary Dobbs, founded Courtroom Science Inc. (CSI) to help lawyers and their clients prepare for and go through the trial process. CSI's headquarters in the Dallas suburb of Irving boasts a million-dollar replica of a federal courtroom and a state-of-the-art television studio. Among the services offered by CSI are mock trials, assembling of mirror juries (in which CSI employees interview private citizens whose responses to trial testimony give attorneys an idea of the feelings of actual jurors), and assistance in selection of jurors. The company brings in an estimated $20 million a year. As reported by Smith, the price for CSI's services is steep: $29,500 a day for mock trials, $17,500 a day for mirror juries, and $400 an hour for McGraw to personally help select the real jurors. As president of CSI, McGraw traveled extensively throughout the United States, Europe, and the Far East to consult with clients that included Fortune 500 companies, major television networks, and airlines.

Though he was known in legal circles as a top predictor of jury behavior, McGraw kept a low public profile until Oprah Winfrey's legal battle with Texas cattle ranchers put him on the map. He met the queen of daytime talk shows in 1998, during the trial stemming from Winfrey's remark—made during a 1996 installment of her show—that because of mad cow disease she might never eat hamburger again. After cattle prices dropped, a group of Texas cattlemen filed suit against Winfrey, charging her with causing them to lose some $10 million in profits. With her reputation and millions of dollars at stake, Winfrey's lawyer, Chip Babcock, called in McGraw, with whom he had worked before. McGraw has recalled that the talk-show host felt depressed and unfairly attacked, and that he feared her state of mind would influence the way the jury perceived her. He told her to get over her hurt feelings and commit herself to fighting back. "There was a point in the trial where she was really asking why, why, why," he told Pauley. "And I just had to give her a wake up call. It doesn't matter why. It is and you'd better get in the game, or it's going to go bad. And I tell you, the day she plugged in, that case was over." Jurors ruled in the television star's favor after five weeks of testimony. An ebullient Winfrey called McGraw "one of the smartest men in the world" and credited him in part with her court victory. She then showed her thanks by inviting him to appear on her show; his appearances, which began in 1998, quickly became a regular feature. Known for his straightforward, often blunt style, he became so popular that the program enjoyed a distinct ratings surge every Tuesday, the day he dispensed advice. Winfrey also encouraged him to write a book, and to date he has written three: *Life Strategies: Doing What Works, Doing What Matters* (1999), *Relationship Rescue: A Seven-Step Strategy for Reconnecting with Your Partner* (2000), and *Self Matters: Creating Your Life from the Inside-Out* (2001), each of which topped the *New York Times* best-seller list in the advice category. He also writes a column on relationships for Winfrey's monthly publication, *O, the Oprah Magazine.* With more than five million copies of his books in print in 27 languages, he has become a sought-after public speaker, earning up to $75,000 per appearance. The 230-pound, balding psychologist was named sexiest self-help guru in *People* magazine's November 26, 2001 issue.

"From a very early age I just really got interested in success," McGraw told Pauley. "I wondered why some people who had every advantage in the world seemed to be just sorry, just worthless. And others who seemed to have every disadvantage in the world just seemed to be absolute stars." One of the keys to a fulfilling, successful life, he has said, is knowing what one wants, a concept that—in McGraw's view—Americans ignore too often. "Everybody thinks we're a selfish society. I think we're a selfless society. I mean we're pretty good sheep in America. We're so programmed we don't stop and say, 'Wait a minute, what do I want?' . . . And if . . . you don't know what you want, how do you ever expect to get it?"

McGraw's own national television show debuted on September 16, 2002, in partnership with Paramount Television, King World Inc., and Winfrey's Harpo Productions. Unlike many talk shows, McGraw's program does not center on celebrity guests. "People in America are really interested and committed to having a good life and we don't prepare people well in our society," he told *Entertainment Tonight.* "You go to school, you learn how to read, write, add and subtract, but nobody teaches you how to be a husband or wife, mother or father . . . or friend to yourself. They don't teach you how to deal with the challenges that you face in this world. So I intend to bring quality television with meaningful content to people in an entertaining way. We are going to talk about things that others might not want to talk about. There are silent epidemics in America that are raging throughout society, and we are going to get to the bottom line and talk about things that matter. I want to create appointment television for people who have a mission, a purpose in their lives." McGraw developed the show with Winfrey's assistance. "In 15 years, I've never come across anyone who understood human functioning better than Phil," Winfrey said, as reported by Joe Schlosser for *Broadcasting & Cable* (July 2, 2001). "He knows how to . . . get to the bottom line of what really matters. He has become America's therapist."

The *Dr. Phil Show* is syndicated to all but a tiny part of the U.S. and airs every weekday for one hour. In its first four days, the *Dr. Phil Show* received the highest ratings of any daytime talk show since Winfrey's debut, in 1986; for the week of October 7–13, 2002, *Dr. Phil* averaged a national household rating of 4.3. That share of the viewing audience was larger than that for any talk show in syndication, except for the *Oprah Winfrey Show.* Not surprisingly, the program generated much excitement in the television industry. King World Productions, which distributes it domestically, began selling the program in July 2001 and had sold it to more than 80 percent of U.S. markets within five weeks and 90 percent by mid-December. "I think Dr. Phil probably has one of the best chances of succeeding, because he has really proven himself to the audience," Jay Cascio, vice president of programming and creative services for the NBC affiliate KING-TV in Seattle, told Daisy Whitney for *Electronic Media* (December 31, 2001). "What Oprah has done with him is absolutely brilliant," Greg Meidel, the president of Paramount Domestic TV Programming, said, according to Schlosser. "She has single-handedly taken advantage of his skills, groomed him and nurtured him into stardom. We have someone who will have developed his instincts and style for four years."

Others were more reserved in their predictions. "It remains to be seen whether Mr. McGraw's personal style—which fans call folksy, plain-spoken and tell-it-like-it-is, and detractors call dismissive victim-blaming—will make the transition from weekly to daily exposure," Brian McCormick wrote for *Crain's Chicago Business* (February 11, 2002). "And some question whether the Dr. Phil phenomenon can stand on its own without Ms. Winfrey by his side. . . . Mr. McGraw's tough, sometimes insulting, talk with fragile guests also may pose potential dangers. He alternately chides and scolds guests who bare their deepest personal secrets before a national audience." Indeed, McGraw's critics claim that the format of his appearances on Winfrey's show has set up unrealistic expectations that complex problems can be remedied quickly. Some have also found fault with his tendency to chastise victims for allowing themselves to be used and to conclude discussions with witty one-liners. In an article in the *Washington Post* (June 26, 2000), Libby Copeland criticized the dismissive attitude she thinks he evinces to those who come to him with problems. "Dr. Phil promises to Tell It Like It Is, and he does so with equal measures of confrontation and compassion. It's a tough love that Dr. Phil doles out—advice for smart women who aren't acting smart. Wake up, woman! Treat yourself right! . . . Tough, tough love. Difficult questions. Little time, alas, to dwell on the answers. One guest has hardly chastised the inner demons that have turned her off sex when we're off! Next dilemma! A woman who can't get her husband to clean up! Even in a quick-fix culture, the glibness of these solutions is startling." For his part McGraw acknowledged to *Entertainment Tonight* that he is well aware that some people reject his approach. "I'm very direct, and I may not be fair, but maybe people will feel a little bit safer with a couple of thousand miles and a television screen between them and me where they can get the information in a safe environment . . . ," he said. "I certainly don't think I'm going to cure America on Wednesday afternoon on the 'Dr. Phil' show. I tell you what I can do, I give people information they can use, I can give them a tool belt that they can strap on and use in their life, and I think we're going to have some fun doing it." Earlier in the same interview, he noted, "The message we are trying to convey is to take control of your life, take control of your family, take control of your goals and objectives, treat yourself with dignity and respect and get the tools you need to get busy in your own life. As a society I see things that scare me, we are circling the drain and I don't want that to happen. . . . We are going to give a wake-up call to America in some areas that maybe are a little touchy to talk about sometimes."

McGraw has become a frequent target of the late-night talk-show host David Letterman. (The mockery may have something to do with Letterman's frosty relationship with McGraw's television mentor, Oprah Winfrey; Winfrey has banned Letterman from her show and refused to appear on his.) In addition, there have been reports that *Dr. Phil* staff members are extremely unhappy due to poor working conditions that allegedly include grueling hours and a lack of empathy from McGraw. "He doesn't suffer fools gladly, and he thinks that a lot of people are fools," one insider told Jeannette Walls for "The Scoop," her column on the MSNBC Web site (October 23, 2002). "There's a lot of yelling and unhappiness. He's a shrink, but making people feel good about themselves is not his specialty."

McGraw does not hide his contempt for many self-help gurus. "Most of these guys who write these gimmicky books have everything but verbs in their sentences," he told Skip Hollandsworth for *Texas Monthly* (September 1999). He is impatient with those who he feels ignore the sometimes harsh realities of life. "There are therapists out there telling people they need to discover their 'inner child' and to rock themselves like a baby with a blanket wrapped around them in order to find happiness. Good God, we've got people trying to get their rent paid, trying to keep their kids off drugs, trying to make their marriages work, trying to get their careers in gear, trying to manage their own impulses—and they are supposed to go rock themselves? Come on. Life is a full contact sport, and if you don't have a really good strategy to get through it, if you don't come up with a very specific plan to make your life better, then you're never going to change." Hollandsworth, referring to the legendary football coach, called McGraw "the Vince Lombardi of therapy—a tough taskmaster with an unblinking stare who tells his audiences to get over such obsessions as why they had 'negative feelings' or who treated them unfairly in the past."

Surprisingly, perhaps, McGraw has said that he has a hard time talking to people outside of his professional activities. "I am shy," he told Jane Pauley. "Painfully shy. People would think, no way . . . because I come on very directly and maybe strong sometimes. That's because I have a task in front of me. You give me something to do, put me in front of 10,000 people to give a talk, or millions of people on television, it doesn't bother me a bit. My pulse doesn't go up a beat. Put me in a cocktail party to make small talk, I'd rather get a root canal. I mean, it's just painful. I don't know what to say. And I think why would anybody be interested in what I have to say anyway?"

McGraw told Pauley that while his mission is to help others, he does not claim to be perfect himself. "I'll tell you, for sure, I've made every mistake you can make. I learned by running it off in the ditch," he said. "I've been a workaholic to the point that it was just almost physically crippling. I was just missing marriage, kids, family, even if I was there in body, I wasn't there in spirit. And I still have to work and struggle against that today. . . . I would hate for people to ever think that I hold myself up as the paragon of what to do in life or marriage. But I tell you what I am, though, is committed to learning." He also seems a little bemused at his transformation from a little-known if respected local psychologist to a national icon. "You know, all I wanted to do was pass on some common-sense advice," he told Hollandsworth, reflecting on the success of his first book. "I'm still amazed that it could create so much attention."

McGraw has published numerous scholarly articles and has testified before Congress as an expert on human functioning. He received an honorary doctorate of humanities from Parker College of Chiropractic in Dallas in December 2001. He is an avid golfer, tennis player, scuba diver, and Little League baseball coach. He married Robin Jameson in 1976; the couple live in Texas with their two sons, Jay and Jordan. Jay McGraw is the author of the best-selling self-help books *Life Strategies for Teens* and *Closing the Gap: A Strategy For Reconnecting Parents And Teens.* — K.E.D.

Suggested Reading: *Biography* p82+ July 2000, with photos; *Broadcasting & Cable* p7 July 2001; *Crain's Chicago Business* p34 Feb. 11, 2002, with photos; *Dateline NBC* (on-line) Jan. 27, 2002; *Electronic Media* p19 Dec. 31, 2001, with photos; *Entertainment Tonight* (on-line) Aug. 31, 2001; *People* p96 Nov. 26, 2001, with photo; *Television Quarterly* p70+ Winter 2002; *Texas Monthly* p142+ Sep. 1999, with photos; *Washington Post* C p1 June 26, 2000

Selected Television Shows: *The Dr. Phil Show,* 2001–

Selected Books: *Life Strategies: Doing What Works, Doing What Matters,* 1999; *Relationship Rescue: A Seven-Step Strategy for Reconnecting with Your Partner,* 2000; *Self Matters: Creating Your Life from the Inside-Out,* 2001

---

Morrison/Wulffraat/Retna Ltd.

## McGraw, Tim

*May 1, 1967– Country singer; guitarist*

*Address: 49 Music Square East, Nashville, TN 37203*

Although some might think of him as simply "Mr. Faith Hill," Tim McGraw is as much a country-music icon as his wife. The son of the famous baseball pitcher Tug McGraw, he first made waves in 1994, with the somewhat controversial novelty song "Indian Outlaw." Since then he has sold more than 19 million albums, notched 13 number-one hits, and earned a slew of prizes, including nine Academy of Country Music (ACM) Awards and six Country Music Association (CMA) Awards. More than a million copies of his 2001 record, *Set This Circus Down,* were purchased before its official release, and it debuted at number one and number two on the *Billboard* country charts and the *Billboard* 200, respectively. McGraw's music, a mixture of country, folk, and boisterous rock, appeals to a wide range of listeners, and he himself has readily acknowledged the influences of artists ranging from Merle Haggard to Rush. A sense of individualism, according to McGraw, best defines his image. "I don't think that you can be successful as an artist if you're not being true to yourself," he told Ray Waddell in an interview accompanying a *Billboard* (October 6, 2001) article by Jim Bessman. "If you start doing things according to what the critics say or start changing what you do because of what people say, then you're a puppet. What do they want you to be if you're not doing it the way you want to do it?" A devoted family man who was voted Father of the Year by the National Fatherhood Initiative, McGraw has been married to Hill since 1996; the couple have three daughters. Reflecting sentiments expressed in a single from his most recent album, he told Michael McCall for *Country Music* (June 2001), "Once the kids start school, we're definitely going to be winding off the road and at least be home during the school year. Someday I want to coach football or something. You know, I was somebody before I started making music, and I'll be somebody afterward."

When he was born, on May 1, 1967 in Delhi, Louisiana, after his mother's brief fling with Tug McGraw (who was then in the minor leagues), the singer was given the first and middle names Samuel Timothy. When he was seven months old, his mother, Betty, married Horace Smith, a truck driver, and the family moved to Start, in northeastern Louisiana. "It's just a farming community—cotton, beans, rice," McGraw told Jim Bessman. "No red light, just a flashing yellow light, couple convenience stores and a cotton gin. But there's a lot of good, salt-of-the-earth people there who value family. It's one of those places where, if you were over at somebody's house and you messed up, their parent would take you out and switch you. It was a great place to grow up."

As a child, McGraw would often accompany his stepfather on trucking runs, hauling cottonseed through Louisiana and Texas. Along the way he would listen endlessly to Horace Smith's eight-track country-music tapes. "By the time I was six," he told Christopher John Farley for *Time* (June 28, 1999), "I felt as if I knew the words to every album Merle Haggard ever recorded." He was also raised on a steady diet of rock music, thanks to his mother, who "loved music, too," as he told Ray Waddell. "She's from Jacksonville, and she was more into the Beach Boys, the Beatles. And, of course, I loved rock 'n' roll, Rush, Styx, like every kid in junior high in the '70s. I liked what was on the radio."

As he grew older McGraw enjoyed hunting, fishing, and playing baseball with his friends. "I had a driver's license at 15," he told Bessman. "Some people got 'em at 13 or 14 if they worked on farms. All the police knew you. We used to go to what we called bar pits, out in the country, where you'd dig all the topsoil out, and we'd steal tires from the co-op, build a big fire to keep the mosquitoes away, back the trucks up and drink Miller ponies. Hank Williams, Jr. was our hero, and we'd crank him up. Nobody ever got in any trouble."

One day when he was 11, while rifling through his mother's closet looking for an old photo, McGraw stumbled upon his birth certificate, which named Frank Edwin "Tug" McGraw as his biological father. "That was the first I knew of it," he told Bessman, "so there was a mild freakout, I guess. But it was probably less traumatic for me than for the people who were around me, like my mother, who had been living with this for 11 years." His mother told Jeremy Helligar for *People* (April 27, 1998), "The funny thing was that he did have his father's baseball cards hanging on the wall before he knew it was his father." McGraw finally met with his father during his senior year in high school. "When our relationship began," Tug McGraw told Helligar, "we decided it was a look-forward kind of relationship and we'd move on, not look back." While Tim McGraw remains close to Tug, he has said that he considers Smith to be his father.

After graduating from Monroe Christian High School, where he excelled at baseball and basketball, McGraw turned down several offers of sports scholarships and enrolled instead at Northeast Louisiana University (now named the University of Louisiana at Monroe), with the intention of becoming a lawyer. "Then I got my grades back the first semester," he told a writer for *Artist Direct* (1999, on-line), "and I knew that wasn't going to work." He then began preparing for a career in sports medicine. During the summer following his freshman year, he lived alone in the fraternity house that he had shared with several other men during the fall and spring terms. He whiled away his time watching the country-music channel on TV and idly strumming a guitar acquired in a pawnshop. Then he began thinking, "I could play this thing, there's only six strings," as he recalled to Bessman. The self-taught McGraw soon became proficient enough to play a dozen songs, and he began performing for tips here and there in Monroe.

After his junior year of college, McGraw dropped out of school and headed to Nashville, Tennessee, the capital of the country-music world. On May 9, 1989, the day he arrived there, the country singer Keith Whitley, one of McGraw's musical heroes, died of an alcohol overdose. "It was really a shock," McGraw told Mike Joyce for the *Washington Post* (November 24, 1994). "Part of my plan was to see if I could hook up with him and hang out a little. I still think he was one of the greatest soul singers country music has had."

Not long after settling down in Nashville, McGraw formed a band with some fellow musicians and began playing in clubs around town. After two years, during which he had made a demo tape, McGraw came to the attention of the record producer Mike Curb, of Curb Records, who had "found out Tug McGraw had a son in town who wanted to be a singer . . . ," as McGraw told Bessman. McGraw added, "Tug made a whole helluva lot of payback with that one meeting." With Curb, he cut his first album, titled *Tim McGraw* (1993). The disk, which included the singles "Welcome to the Club" and "Two Steppin' Mind," did not fare well commercially. "I thought we had a good record," McGraw recalled to Bessman, "but I also knew it wouldn't blow anybody's skirt up. It was my first time in the studio, and I had to work to find the songs at that stage. It took a while to get my feet wet and develop some sort of idea about what I was doing."

The singer's next album, *Not a Moment Too Soon* (1994), catapulted him to fame. "When I recorded *Not A Moment Too Soon*," he told *Artist Direct*, "we thought we were onto something, that we had a good album with a good variety of songs. But I don't think we had any idea of what we actually had." The first single from the record, "Indian Outlaw," written by Tommy Barnes, blends honky-tonk and Native American rhythms; it became a smash hit, rocketing into the Top 15 on the pop charts and pushing *Not a Moment Too Soon* to number one on the country charts. It also brought on a storm of protest, spearheaded by Wilma P. Mankiller, the first female chief of the Cherokee Nation, who objected to what she and others considered clichés and stereotypes in the songs. (For example, the lyrics included the lines "You can find me in my wigwam / I'll be beating on my tom-tom / Pull out the pipe and smoke you some / Hey and pass it around".) In a letter that she sent to several radio stations, Mankiller described "Indian Outlaw" as "crass, exploitative commercialism at the expense of Indians," according to Peter Cronin in *Billboard* (March 19, 1994), and she wrote that the song "promotes bigotry." Some radio stations acceded to Mankiller's request that "Indian Outlaw" not be aired. Meanwhile, protesters demonstrated their disapproval of the lyrics outside venues where McGraw was performing. Not all Native Americans were offended, however. "The kids here like to dance to it," Gerald Parker, a Cherokee vice chief from North Carolina, told Steve Dougherty and Meg Grant for *People* (April 25, 1994). "If I wasn't old and crippled, I'd dance to it too." McGraw told Joyce that he had performed "Indian Outlaw" in clubs for years, apparently with no complaints from audiences. "When we went to record that song . . . I wasn't going in to set a political agenda," he said to Joyce. "I wasn't going to try to make a social statement or try to influence anybody. I was just trying to make a good country record. And that was all there was to it. In this day and age you can't please everyone. I go by my judgment, my instincts and the values I was raised with. I trust that." The negative publicity notwithstanding, the Academy of Country Music named *Not a Moment Too Soon* album of the year; *Billboard* voted *Not a Moment Too Soon* the year's top country album; and McGraw received a "best new artist" award from Country Music Television.

McGraw's next record, *All I Want* (1995), debuted at number four on the *Billboard* 200 (which ranks the top 200 albums each week). Its first single, "I Like It, I Love It," spent five weeks at number one on the country charts. "I can breathe now. There was a collective, exhaustive breath," McGraw told Deborah Price Evans for *Billboard* (August 19, 1995), indicating his nervousness—and that of others involved in the making of *All I Want*—about the fate of the album. Referring to "I Like It, I Love It," he said, "It was a cool, fun, back-to-school song. It doesn't really say a lot. . . . We put it out because it's a fun sing-along song, and it will call attention to some of the meat songs on the album that I really want people to hear." *All I Want* sold 2.5 million copies and earned McGraw the American Music Awards title "favorite new country artist."

To promote *All I Want*, McGraw embarked on the Spontaneous Combustion tour, which made stops in 100 cities. McGraw's co-headliner was Faith Hill, whose album *It Matters to Me* was also soaring on the charts. By the end of the tour, the pair were engaged to be married. By McGraw's own account, the relationship led him to reassess his priorities: after years of "wanting to be on the road, singing and playing and that's about it," he found himself "wanting to have a family and wanting to take care of business," as he told a reporter for the Associated Press (September 23, 1996). "And still be singing on the road and having a good time." McGraw and Hill married on October 6, 1996. The couple's first child, Gracie, was born the following May.

A month later McGraw released his next studio album, *Everywhere*. Bolstered by the first single, "It's Your Love," a duet with Hill, the album broke records upon its release. Ultimately, *Everywhere* went quadruple platinum, selling four million copies. "It's Your Love" was named single of the year by the Country Music Association, Country Music Television, and *Billboard*. *Everywhere* was the Country Music Association 1998 album of the year, and McGraw won a Country Radio Music Award as best artist. That same year marked the birth of McGraw and Hill's second child, Maggie.

McGraw's next record, *A Place in the Sun* (1999), earned respectable notices. "At times, Tim McGraw seems to thrive in a rut, spewing out whiny, line-dance-ready songs with sing-songy arrangements," Ralph Novak wrote for *People* (May 4, 1999). "So it's a pleasure to hear him branch out a little on this album." *A Place in the Sun* produced several hit singles, including "Please Remember Me," "Something Like That," and "My Next Thirty Years." The album sold 3.1 million copies and received the CMA award for album of the year.

Released in 2000, *Greatest Hits* contains 15 of McGraw's most popular and best-selling songs. "This is one of the rare modern day incidences of a Greatest Hits that really offers all the hits, and nothing but," Steven Thomas Erlewine wrote for the *All Music Guide* (on-line), "which not only makes it a boon to fans, but also makes it the most consistent record in McGraw's catalog." The album went double platinum and was *Billboard*'s 2001 country album of the year. McGraw also captured the 2001 American Music Awards title of favorite male country artist.

On June 3, 2000 McGraw ran afoul of police in Buffalo, New York. The incident began when, after a concert at Ralph Wilson Stadium, the country star Kenny Chesney asked a mounted police officer if he could ride his horse. The officer gave Chesney permission to sit on the horse but not to ride it. But Chesney disregarded the policeman's words and rode off, ignoring requests to stop. As deputies approached Chesney, McGraw allegedly grabbed one of them, who later claimed that the singer had held him in a choke hold. In a press release quoted by the *Calgary Sun* (June 17, 2000), McGraw, who was arrested, denied the charges. "At no time did I ever throw any punches or put anyone in anything remotely resembling a choke hold," he stated in the release. "One of the officers pulled his nightstick and hit me at least three times on my leg." McGraw was released on bail the following morning. In May 2001, after a trial lasting more than a week, McGraw and Chesney were acquitted.

Earlier, in April 2001, McGraw released *Set This Circus Down*, his sixth studio album. "Out of all the records I've made," he told a reporter for *guitarcenter.com*, "I feel I'm closest to the mark of the sound and the feel that I had in my head when I wanted to make a record. I feel like I've improved every album and gotten better and gotten closer to that mark. But this is the closest to what I've actually heard and tried to get down on the tape as any record I've done." In *Set This Circus Down*, McGraw's sound is calmer and less raucous. The change in tone is evident in the title track, written by Bill Luther and Josh Kear, about a man who hopes to stop going on the road, as his job requires and as he has long enjoyed doing, and retreat to a quieter life as a husband and father. "I wish that I could have written the song because it really does sound autobiographical," he said in a question-and-answer section of his Web site. Unlike his previous albums, *Set This Circus Down* has no images of McGraw's face on the cover or in the accompanying booklet. Instead, the cover art is a commissioned painting, which shows, as McGraw requested, a circus tent in a stark landscape under a lowering sky. "You get tired of seeing your mug plastered on the top of everything," McGraw told the questioner on his Web site. "I wanted something that people could hold in their hand and look at like a book." Another success, *Set This Circus Down* reached platinum status before it appeared in stores, thanks to pre-release orders, and it debuted at the top spot on the *Billboard* country chart. In 2002 the record and McGraw received American Music Awards, for best country album and favorite male country artist, respectively. Additionally, *Set This Circus Down* was nominated for album of the year by the Academy of Country Music (it lost to the soundtrack album of *O Brother, Where Art Thou?*). McGraw was also nominated for entertainer of the year and favorite male vocalist, but lost to Brooks & Dunn and Alan Jackson, respectively. His next album is scheduled for release in November 2002.

In his *Country Music* (June 2001) article, published shortly after *Set This Circus Down* reached stores, Michael McCall, the author of the on-line music commentary *The NashvilleScene*, offered an explanation for McGraw's success: "When you first hear him, McGraw isn't an obvious candidate for superstardom. His talents aren't immediate, they're cumulative. McGraw is far from Music Row's most powerful vocalist. But he makes great use of the intimate quality of his husky, mid-range voice. Instead of dazzling listeners with roof-shaking force, he concentrates on communicating the themes of his songs in a clear, friendly, believable style. He also excels at presenting songs that celebrate the settings, relationships, and simple, positive pleasures of life in Middle America. As a performer, he comes across as a genuine, principled guy with a bit of a mysterious wild streak, whose passion translates into a charismatic presence. At the same time, . . . McGraw also has an everyman appeal, and he can make the basics of life seem exciting and important."

McGraw planned to release *Tim McGraw and the Dancehall Doctors*, a new album of original material, on November 26, 2002. The album bears the name of his touring band; for a change of pace, he recorded the album with the band rather than with the usual roster of Nashville studio musicians. "Making this record was the most fun I've ever had in the studio and the most rewarding musical experience I've ever had," he said in a press release posted on his official Web site. "I think I sang more honestly on this record, and that came from the honesty that the music was played with." At the same time that the album arrives in stores, McGraw's book, *Tim McGraw and the Dancehall Doctors: This Is Ours*, will go on sale. The book chronicles the recording of the album, along with accounts of what McGraw and the band have experienced during 10 years of tours.

McGraw lives on a farm near Nashville with Faith Hill and their children. (Their third daughter, Audrey, was born in 2001.) "Every day when I wake up with this goddess, I'm amazed she chose me," he told Johanna Schneller for *InStyle* (April 2001). "Not as amazed as the guys I went to college with. But I don't mind running into them now." Citing the importance of his home, he has cut down on the number of stops on his tours. "Family is absolutely [number one]," he told Ray Waddell. "People are always asking how we balance career and family. Well, you don't. If you try to balance career and family, you're screwing up to begin with and you're doing your family a disservice. Career or anything else isn't on the same level as family. Family is first, and everything else is way down the line." — J.K.B.

Suggested Reading: *Billboard* p26+ Oct. 6, 2001; *Country Music* p30+ June 2001, with photos; *InStyle* p373+ Apr. 2001, with photos; *People* p85+ Apr. 27, 1998, with photos, p95+ July 12, 1999, with photos, p86+ Aug. 21, 2000, with photo; *Time* p69 June 28, 1999, with photos; *TV Guide* p12+ Sep. 23–29, 2000, with photo

Selected Recordings: *Tim McGraw*, 1993; *Not a Moment Too Soon*, 1994; *All I Want*, 1995; *Everywhere*, 1997; *A Place in the Sun*, 1999; *Greatest Hits*, 2000; *Set This Circus Down*, 2001

---

## McQueen, Alexander

*1969(?)– Fashion designer*

*Address: c/o Amie Witton, Alexander McQueen, 10 Amwell St., London EC1R 1UQ, England*

According to Melanie Rickey, the editor of the London Sunday *Times* styles section, Alexander McQueen "represents all that is great about British fashion: energy, talent, creativity, tradition and a huge flair for adrenaline-pumping theatrics," as she wrote for the London *Times* (August 13, 2001, on-line). Often referred to as the "bad boy" of British fashion, McQueen is "one of the industry's most electrifying stars and controversial characters" and has become well known for both his "devilish personality" and the "magic and madness" in his shows, as Robin Givhan wrote for the *Washington Post* (December 5, 2001). Also re-

Dumoulin/Java/Retna

*Alexander McQueen*

nowned for his extraordinary skills as a tailor and cutter, McQueen has been named the British Designer of the Year at the London Fashion Awards three times, and he won a Special Achievement Award at that awards ceremony in 1998.

The product of a lower-class environment, McQueen got first-hand training in the shops of elite London tailors before attending a prestigious London school of art and design. In 1996 he became the chief designer for Givenchy, one of the top houses of couture in Paris; simultaneously, he produced collections for his private label, Alexander McQueen. Months before his five-year contract with Givenchy was due to expire, he joined another major player in the world of high fashion—the Italian corporation Gucci Group N.V., which purchased a controlling stake in McQueen's personal label but granted him total artistic freedom, with the title of creative director. "My label and the future of 'Alexander McQueen' are incredibly important to me," he said on December 4, 2000, when his move to Gucci was announced, as quoted on *Fashionclick* (on-line). McQueen operates boutiques in London and Tokyo and plans to open a store in New York City in the near future.

The youngest of the six children of a cab driver and his wife, Lee Alexander McQueen was born in London, England, in about 1969. (His family and close friends still address him as Lee.) With his two brothers and three sisters, he grew up in London's East End, in the down-at-the-heels Stratford section. Dominated almost entirely by council estates (government housing projects), his Stratford neighborhood afforded McQueen few opportunities to express his early interest in fashion. He attended the all-boys Rokeby comprehensive school, where, he told Alix Sharkey for the London *Guardian* (July 6, 1996), he "didn't learn a thing. I just drew clothes in class." He also participated in such traditional activities as rugby and swimming. At age nine he suffered a serious accident: misjudging a dive, he landed face-first on the edge of a pool and shattered many of his front teeth. Seven years went by before he had his teeth capped.

McQueen left Rokeby at age 16 and worked briefly as a dishwasher in a local pub. A turning point in his life came when he and his mother saw a televised documentary that described the dearth of new apprentices on London's Savile Row, a street renowned for shops that produce bespoke (custom-made) men's suits. The documentary warned that the art of fine tailoring was in danger of extinction in Great Britain. "So me mum said, 'Why don't you go down there, give it a go?'" McQueen recalled to Sharkey. "So I just walked into Anderson & Sheppard, got a job on the spot." For the next two and a half years, McQueen worked at Anderson & Sheppard, one of the most prominent establishments on Savile Row, and learned the art of tailoring men's suit jackets. He then found a job at another renowned Savile Row emporium, Gieves & Hawkes, where he learned how to make trousers. Displaying his soon-to-be-famous rebellious tendencies, McQueen (according to what may be an apocryphal story) used his tailor's chalk to scribble something on the lining of a suit fashioned for Prince Charles, a Savile Row devotee. (Sources do not agree about the exact words or even the nature of the message.) McQueen next moved to Bermans & Nathans, a firm specializing in costumes for theater and film. "I was interested in the technical side, learning all these old techniques, 16th-century pattern cutting and stuff like that," he told Sharkey. From Bermans & Nathans he went to Koji Tatsuno, also in London, who, McQueen told Sharkey, made "fantastic clothes using antique fabrics [and] tailored jackets with beautiful linings." His tenure at Tatsuno was short-lived; soon after his arrival, the business failed. McQueen then traveled to Milan, Italy, where he secured a job as a pattern cutter with the designer Romeo Gigli.

After nine months in Italy, McQueen returned to London, where he went to the Central St. Martins College of Art and Design in the hope of getting a teaching job. He interviewed with Bobbie Hillson, the founder/director of the Central St. Martins master-of-arts course in fashion design and a one-time *Vogue* editor. Although McQueen had not completed high school, Hillson admitted him without hesitation to the postgraduate course. As she explained to Sharkey, "To have left school at 16, studied at Savile Row, gone to Italy alone and found a job with Gigli—that was incredible. He was also technically brilliant." McQueen earned an M.A. degree in 1992. The early-1993 show of his Central St. Martins work, held in association with his graduation, was well received. Among the attendees was Isabella Blow, a wealthy patron of the arts whom Godfrey Deeny, in the London *Sunday Times* (October 1, 2001, on-line), described as "one of fashion's most influential stylists, muses and talent finders." Blow immediately became McQueen's unofficial public-relations representative. She also provided the young designer with a home in Gloucestershire, England, which contained space for him to work. Blow reportedly persuaded McQueen to drop the "Lee" from his name and be known professionally as Alexander McQueen.

In the first collection of his post-school career, McQueen adorned his models in styles that both shocked and excited onlookers. Describing those garments, which were seen on London runways in October 1993, in a show called "Taxi Driver," Amy M. Spindler wrote for the *New York Times* (October 20, 1993), "The last show of the [London fashion] season gave editors the aggressive British attitude they had been expecting. A little of it, of course, goes a long way, and Alexander McQueen provided a lot: models extending middle fingers to the audience, punked hair and raccoon eyes and some dresses washed or hand-printed with paint the color of dried blood." McQueen also introduced audiences to "bumsters," a term he coined for the very-low-slung jeans and trousers of his own design, which revealed the cleavage in the wearer's posterior. He gained additional attention when the pop singer Madonna sported a pair of bumsters in a television commercial for the cable television station MTV.

In "Nihilism," his spring/summer 1994 show, McQueen presented Edwardian-style jackets worn over shell tops that had been spattered with dirt and blood. Acknowledging the influence of the Arts and Crafts Movement (1870–1910) in England and the United States, he incorporated prints designed by William Morris, the movement's most prominent practitioner. For "Banshee," his fall/winter 1994–95 show, he hired both "a pregnant skinhead and vogue fashion editor," as he described them on his Web site, to model various designs, as a way of "reflecting conflicting appearances," in his words. The inspiration for "The Birds," his spring/summer 1995 show, according to McQueen's Web site, was Alfred Hitchcock's classic horror movie of the same name; the styles included jackets printed with avian silhouettes.

McQueen's fall/winter 1995–96 collection, shown in London in March of that year, was among his most controversial to date. Entitled "Highland Rape" (in a reference to the forced uprooting, in the late 17th and early 18th centuries, of tens of thousands of Scots and the clearing of their land by English noblemen who used it to raise sheep), it featured dresses with violently torn bodices and spatters of a substance that resembled blood. The models walked on a runway covered with heather and bracken, plants commonly associated with the Scottish Highlands. Tony Scott's 1983 vampire picture, *The Hunger*, which stars Catherine Deneuve, Susan Sarandon, and David Bowie, was the impetus for McQueen's spring/summer 1996 show, also called "The Hunger." That collection included, for the first time in McQueen's career, designs for men, including suits made of taffeta.

McQueen staged his fall/winter 1996 show, called "Dante," in the famous Christ Church in London's Spitalfields section, near Stratford. (The Christ Church cemetery is the final resting place for many of the designer's forebears, among them French Huguenots who came to England to escape religious persecution in France.) In an article for the *Houston Chronicle* (March 14, 1996), McQueen was quoted as saying that the show was "about war and peace through the years." "I think religion has caused every war in the world, which is why I showed in a church," he added. The collection featured apparel made of luxurious fabrics on which were printed images of war (such as that of a Vietnam-era American soldier) or the effects of war (for example, a picture of a crippled Vietnamese civilian). In the *New York Times* (October 1, 1996), Amy M. Spindler wrote of the show, "There is nothing that gets fashion people on their feet faster than a good shock. But the standing ovation [McQueen received] was for the work." In 1996 McQueen was named the Designer of the Year at the British Fashion Awards ceremony.

Weeks later, Bernard Arnault, the chairman and chief executive officer of Moet Hennessy Louis Vuitton (LVMH), the world's largest and most successful luxury-goods conglomerate, announced that the company had signed McQueen to a five-year contract to head the much-celebrated House of Givenchy in Paris, France. (McQueen succeeded his fellow British designer John Galliano, who had been made head of the Christian Dior label, another LVMH property.) The move dismayed many fashion aficionados, who feared that McQueen would upend Givenchy's time-honored traditions. But he surprised them by presenting in his debut show for Givenchy, in March 1997, a collection that Sally Brampton, in the London *Guardian* (March 13, 1997), described as "dangerously polite," one that "looked as if it came not from McQueen's heart, but from his head." "Neither fake leopard-skin nor skin-tight black patent leather, not the wickedly high stilettos in which the models teetered across the cobbles, could disguise that at heart, this was a collection that lacked soul, radical or otherwise," Brampton wrote. The universally negative response it generated contrasted markedly with the enthusiastic critical reception that had greeted McQueen's private-label collection a month earlier, in Paris. Titled "It's a Jungle Out There," that show was an effort to compare "animal instincts in the natural world" to the "'animal' aggression of the urban jungle," according to McQueen's Web site. In October 1997 the British Fashion Awards again named McQueen Designer of the Year; this time, though, he shared that honor with Galliano.

In his October 1998 private-label show, called "#13," which unveiled apparel for spring/summer 1999, the designer included among his models women with physical disabilities. One was the American athlete, model, and double amputee Aimee Mullins, who wore a leather bodice and ruffled skirt over a pair of finely crafted wooden prosthetic legs. "I selected Aimee not to attract media but to break a fixed idea on beauty," McQueen explained, as quoted on the Deco Orthopedic Web site. To end the show, one theme of which was "the way in which man relates to machine" at the turn of the 21st century, as his Web site put it, McQueen had two robotic arms spray black and yellow paint at the multilayered white dress worn by the supermodel Shalom Harlow as she revolved on a wooden turntable.

While McQueen's private-label shows were getting admiring reviews, those he was doing for Givenchy—while not the total flops that his debut collection had been—were generating little excitement. McQueen blamed his lack of innovation on his heavy Givenchy workload; he was required to produce six shows a year for the fashion house. As he explained to Cathy Horyn for the *New York Times* (February 27, 2001), "Give me the time and I'll give you revolutionary." By all accounts, he grew increasingly unhappy at Givenchy, not least because, unlike Galliano, who received subsidies from Dior to maintain his private label, McQueen got no financial help from LVMH for his. Rumors that he would leave Givenchy became reality when, in early December 2000, LVMH announced that McQueen was joining the Milan-based Gucci Group, which owns the Gucci, Yves Saint Laurent, Sergio Rossi, Bedat & C, Stella McCartney, and Boucheron labels and whose corporate headquarters are currently in Amsterdam, the Netherlands. In a statement quoted by *CNN.com* (December 4, 2000), McQueen said, "I believe that this partnership will prove a great success." He later told Robin Givhan for the *Washington Post* (May 25, 2001), "As far as Givenchy, I think that was the biggest mistake of my life." Then, referring to the movie actress Audrey Hepburn, whose association with Hubert de Givenchy spanned four decades (Givenchy designed the costumes for such Hepburn vehicles as *Sabrina*, *Funny Face*, *Love in the Afternoon*, *Breakfast at Tiffany's*, and *Charade*, among others), McQueen added, "I could never grasp the Audrey Hepburn of it. I don't find it modern."Although McQueen's contract with LVMH extended until October 2001, the collection he created for Givenchy for the fall of 2001, shown in March of that year, was his last as a Givenchy employee. A month earlier McQueen had been named British Designer of the Year for the third time. The award was presented to him by Prince Charles at a ceremony at the British Natural History Museum held during London Fashion Week, an event, organized by the British Fashion Council, that was attended by several thousand buyers, fashion writers, and other visitors.

The Gucci Group currently owns 51 percent of the Alexander McQueen label; McQueen retains ownership of the balance. "The business will be established and managed as a separate entity within our Group, and Mr. McQueen will have full creative independence for his brand," Domenico De Sole, the president and chief executive officer of the Gucci Group N.V., said in December 2000, as quoted on *Fashionclick* (on-line). With the Gucci Group's financial backing, McQueen opened a 1,500-square-foot boutique in Tokyo, Japan. According to Jenny Bailly in *fashionwindows.com* (November 13, 2001, on-line), the shop's "curved walls, suspended columns and engraved quotations from Dante's *Inferno* create an other-worldly setting for McQueen's often visionary pieces." The first McQueen retail outlet, a 2,000-square-foot establishment, opened in London in 1999. His third store, which is under construction, will occupy 4,000 square feet in what is known as New York City's meatpacking district, a now-trendy area where many upscale restaurants are located. YSL (Yves Saint Laurent) Beauté is currently collaborating with McQueen to develop the first McQueen women's fragrance, due to be launched in the spring of 2003.

In his December 2000 interview with Robin Givhan, Domenico De Sole said that McQueen "works like a maniac." In 2000 McQueen married George Forsyth, who works in the film industry. According to the fashion-world gossip columnists Horacio Silva and Ben Widdicombe in *hintmag.com* (August 22, 2001), the two men separated one year later. — J.H.

Suggested Reading: *fashionclick.com*; *Harper's Bazaar* p130+ June 1996; *hellomagazine.com* (Dec. 28, 2001); (London) *Guardian* T p38 July 6, 1996, with photos; (London) *Sunday Times* (on-line) Oct. 1, 2001; (London) *Times* p12 Aug. 13, 2001, with photo; *New York* p86+ Dec. 21–28, with photo; *New York Times* B p9 Feb. 27, 2001, with photos; *New Yorker* p62+ Apr. 1, 1996; *Vogue* p323+ Oct. 1997, with photos; *Washington Post* C p1 Dec. 5, 2000, C p2 May 25, 2001

---

## Mendes, Sam

*Aug. 1, 1965– Stage director; filmmaker*

*Address: c/o Creative Artists Agency, 9830 Wilshire Blvd., Beverly Hills, CA 90212-1825*

"He has the eye of a camera even when he's staging theater," the filmmaker Steven Spielberg told Lynn Hirschberg for the *New York Times Magazine* (July 7, 2002), referring to Sam Mendes. "His theater is cinematic, and his cinema is theatrical." A wunderkind of British theater, Mendes rose quickly in the 1980s and early 1990s to become one of the most lauded young talents in England, producing successful plays at the National Theatre and elsewhere before taking on the directorship of the Donmar Warehouse Theatre, in London, in 1992 at the

Armando Gallo/Retna Ltd.

*Sam Mendes*

age of 27. He has overseen numerous hit productions at the Donmar, some of which, such as *Cabaret*, *Othello*, and *The Blue Room*, have gone on to runs in New York City. Simon Russell Beale, who played the title role in Mendes's production of Shakespeare's *Richard III*, praised the director, telling Claire Armitstead for the London *Guardian* (September 21, 1992): "He can quote gags that were used in Tyrone Guthrie's *Troilus and Cressida* or Brook's *A Midsummer Night's Dream*. His man management is superb. He is very acute in requirements of all actors. He certainly doesn't let the older ones off the hook but he treats them slightly differently. And as a teacher, he is marvelous, especially with verse-speaking." In the late 1990s Mendes turned his attention to directing movies. His first film, *American Beauty* (1999), which won an Academy Award for best picture, brought Mendes an Oscar for best director, and his second, *Road to Perdition* (2002), opened to several glowing reviews. Mendes has accomplished all of this with confidence, charisma, and an air of ease that have made him a favorite among actors. "[Mendes] was constantly focused on the story, and that comes from the theater," Annette Bening, one of the stars of *American Beauty*, told Bernard Weinraub for the *New York Times* (September 12, 1999) about the making of that film. "The camera never calls attention to itself. This is someone who didn't go to film school. You can tell. There's nothing fancy about the way the story is told. It's simple in the best sense of the word."

Samuel Alexander Mendes—named for the playwright and novelist Samuel Beckett and the poet Alexander Pope—was born in Redding, England, on August 1, 1965, the only child of Peter Mendes, a university lecturer in English literature, and his wife, Valerie, who worked in publishing and wrote children's books. In an interview with Andrew L. Urban for *Urban Cinefile* (on-line), Mendes said that Redding is "one of the more boring towns . . . not a great place to be born. I wish I'd been born in a more glamorous place . . . " Mendes's parents divorced when he was a small boy, and he went to live with his mother, who was later diagnosed as a schizophrenic. Mendes would recall his childhood as a lonely one. "I was a troubled fantasist," he told Bernard Weinraub. "Well, most fantasists are troubled. I was escaping from my parents' divorce. It was just me and my mother, and so I lived in my head a great deal of the time." Mendes revealed to Lynn Hirschberg, "I was a television kid. *Fawlty Towers*, Monty Python, all comedians. The first play I remember seeing was *Godspell*, around 1978. I thought it was brilliant. I remember the woman who played the voluptuous madam stopping at the end of my row and saying, 'How are you doing, big boy?' That scarred me for life. I'm sure that moment has affected every performance I've staged since." When Mendes was 12 he and his mother moved to Oxford. He attended the Magdalen College School, where he focused less on academics than on cricket, becoming captain of his school's team. In an interview with Stephen Hunter for the *Washington Post* (September 26, 1999), Mendes noted, "I learned the principles of leadership from sports teams. When you're the captain of a team, your first responsibility is to exercise authority without arrogance, to get people to work together for a common goal. And that of course is what you're doing as a director."

Mendes attended Cambridge University, where he was awarded a first (the equivalent of graduating cum laude) in English. During his university years he played cricket and was very active in theater, directing numerous plays and founding the Works Theater Co-operative, now a prestigious company. "At a certain point in my life I was desperate for structure," Mendes told Hunter. "Then I stumbled on it. I went as a schoolboy to Stratford and I saw three plays—*Antony and Cleopatra, The Merchant of Venice* and *The Tempest*—and I can still remember every detail and can recite from them exactly. I knew: That's it. When I got to Cambridge, I got into a rehearsal room, and I just wanted to have a go at it. I got hooked. That was it. That was life." He explained to Hirschberg, "I began to realize that there's a big difference between loving a play and having something to say about it, having a secret. When I staged *Cyrano de Bergerac* at school, that was the first time I found a secret that was mine alone. . . . After *Cyrano*, I thought, I can do this, because I did *that*."

After graduating Mendes briefly considered a career in journalism before deciding to continue in theater. Seeking a director's apprenticeship, he sent 70 letters to theater groups in London. "I offered to do anything they wanted for nothing yet got few responses," he recalled to Graham Hassell for *Plays and Players* (May 1989). "But one of those few was John Gale, the artistic director at Chichester. He gave me a start as assistant director for two months on £40 per week, although for the first week I was little more than ASM [assistant stage manager]." By "being a little pushy," however, he was able to direct plays on his own, mounting successful productions of Anton Chekhov's works *The Bear* and *The Proposal.* (According to Lynn Hirschberg, Gale hired Mendes at least in part because of his skill at cricket; Chichester played every year against the Royal Shakespeare Company.) After working at the Chichester for only a short while, Mendes was called in to take over the play *London Assurance*—which he had never read—when the original director left. Under Mendes's direction, the production was a hit. Paul Eddington, a veteran English actor who performed in the play, told Claire Armitstead, "It is quite daunting for a director to work with senior members of the acting profession for the first time, but Sam showed no sign of that. He has a natural authority." During this time Mendes also worked with Kenneth Branagh's Renaissance Theatre Company and Michael Bogdanov's English Shakespeare Company.

After *London Assurance*, Mendes, then 24, directed the celebrated actress Judi Dench in *The Cherry Orchard*. In the same year he became the artistic director of the new Minerva Studio, a 250-seat theater run by the Chichester. Mendes told Weinraub, "I found that I loved directing. I loved the company of other people, because I had so little of it when I was a kid. When I walked in and did it, I thought, 'Oh, this is so great.' And it combined the company of people and the visual arts, which I had studied. I was able to paint, to a degree, on a stage. And I'm not a very gifted painter." In the late 1980s Mendes won a bursary award, under the Hamburg Shakespeare Prize, allowing him to participate in German theater for a six-month term. Soon Mendes was being associated with a group of young English directors known as Britain's "next generation," which also included Katie Mitchell and Matthew Warchus. Some in the press, noting that Mendes was less interested in experimentation than were his contemporaries, complained that his productions were too commercial. Mendes told Armitstead, "I feel quite comfortable working on plays that are for a commercial setting but not plays that don't have anything to say." Over the next several years, Mendes staged successful productions with the National Theatre and the Royal Shakespeare Company (RSC). One such production was the *Fall of Little Voice*, which starred Jane Horrocks, with whom Mendes would have a long-term romantic relationship.

In 1992 Mendes took a gamble, renovating and reestablishing the Donmar Warehouse Theatre in London—a rehearsal space for the RSC that had been closed since the 1960s—and installing himself as artistic director. "I had this idea to revive it as a theater . . . that was light on its feet and could respond to the zeitgeist," Mendes explained to Hirschberg. "I asked the R.S.C., and I thought they'd surely say no, but they didn't. Suddenly, I had a theater to run. It was terrifying." The theater had a medium-sized seating capacity, meaning that it could not recoup production expenses through ticket sales alone. Increasing the financial risk, Mendes's vision for the new theater was that it would put on primarily house productions (that is, productions mounted by the theater's staff). The Donmar opened in late 1992, with Mendes's production of Stephen Sondheim's musical *Assassins.* The theater soon became critically acclaimed for such productions as *Company, The Glass Menagerie*, and *Othello*, which won two Olivier Awards. Mendes's new production of *Cabaret*, starring Alan Cumming, was especially noted for the director's dark interpretation and for the cleverness of the set design. For the production, which opened in December 1993, Mendes converted the Donmar to resemble a 1930s Berlin nightclub; since the tables at which the actors sat were close to the stage, audience members became, in effect, part of the show. Mendes noted that his mother's being Jewish contributed to his decision to direct the play, which is set in Nazi Germany.

Despite enthusiastic reviews of its productions and good attendance, by 1995 the Donmar Warehouse was in financial jeopardy. As a result, the theater began mounting fewer in-house productions and a greater number put on by outsiders; still, in order to remain open, the Donmar would need a subsidy. "We've fought a valiant battle," Mendes told Matt Wolf for *Variety* (September 25, 1995), "and I think we've proved that the work here is worthy of financing. I am willing to sit at any table with anyone and argue that this theater does some of the best work in London. If London wants this theater, somebody's got to help me fight for it." Although the Donmnar continued to have financial difficulties, it managed to stay afloat, and Mendes began to branch out once more, directing the Royal Shakespeare Company's production of Shakespeare's *Othello*, starring Simon Russell Beale. In 1996 Mendes signed on to direct his new version of *Cabaret* at the Roundabout Theater in New York City, which marked his U.S. directorial debut. The play opened in March of that year and received enthusiastic reviews. Richard Zoglin noted in *Time* (March 30, 1998), "Mendes has deglamorized *Cabaret*, broadened its human scope and brilliantly re-energized it for the '90s." *Cabaret* was one of the major Broadway plays of the year. Also in New York, Mendes's production of Shakespeare's *Othello* premiered at the Brooklyn Academy of Music in 1998, and *The Blue Room*, starring Nicole Kidman, turned many heads, first at the Donmar, in 1998, and on Broadway the next year, in part because of Kidman's semi-nude scene.

Steven Spielberg, who had been impressed with Mendes's *Othello*, was so taken with the direction of *Cabaret* that he invited Mendes to direct a feature film for his studio, DreamWorks. Mendes had been looking for a directorial project in movies for three years but had not found one that interested him. Spielberg gave Mendes copies of several scripts, including one called "American Beauty," Alan Ball's darkly comic study of American suburban life. "I read ['American Beauty'] on the flight back to London," Mendes told Hunter, "and the first thing I did when I was done was read it again. I saw it in my mind right away, filmically, if you will. I called my agent and said, 'I really want to get this.'" In an interview for *Virgin Net Cinema* (online), Mendes told Chris Roberts, "I always thought I'd make a British film, but when I saw this script I thought if anyone else does this movie, I'll have to kill myself. . . . I like to think of this [film] as 'featuring' America, rather than being 'about' America. It's not a state-of-the-nation address. It's just a great story: a fable about one man's search for redemption." He added, "I wanted the movie to hover a foot above reality all the time. I wanted a slightly surreal, peaceful poetry in this very emotional story . . . something dislocated. Often, that's down to holding a shot longer than you'd think, having tension in the frame . . . it was only when I started making this that I realised I had opinions on camera shots!" Mendes also found that he could identify with the script on a personal level. "I'm an only child," he told Weinraub. "This was about dysfunctional families. And without wanting to sound rude about it, my family was not entirely functional."

Despite his enthusiasm, Mendes's first few days on the set were disastrous. "I just got everything wrong," he told Jeff Gordinier for *Entertainment Weekly* (March 2000). "The costumes were too cartoony. The cinematography had no peace in it. The performances were too theatrical. It was too comic, too broad. I looked at the dailies and I just said, 'Look, guys, this isn't what I wanted to shoot.' And luckily the studio agreed with me." One of the movie's stars, Annette Bening, told Gordinier, "There was something very smart about the way [Mendes] handled that. There's a lot of different ways to confront that kind of moment. You can be in denial. You can be unsure. But Sam was remarkably sane. He knew it wasn't right, so he said, 'We've got to do this again.'" Mendes told Weinraub, "The biggest surprise was how mundane filmmaking is in many ways, how it's a mosaic and you polish every little piece and it was very slow, very practical. Even bigger than that was the sheer joy of editing. I mean, it was the most creative thing I've ever done. The interesting thing about the theater is [that] the creative thing is at the very beginning of the process. The rehearsals are great. With movies, the creative thing was at the end. I didn't realize the incredible pleasure of, once you've got your footage, manipulating it and beginning to tell a story and cutting to a close-up or adding a music track. That astonished me."

*American Beauty* is about a dysfunctional suburban household. The husband, Lester Burnham, played by Kevin Spacey, undergoes a midlife crisis; in the process he quits his dead-end job and starts smoking marijuana again, working out, and lusting after his teenage daughter's friend, a high-school cheerleader (portrayed by Mena Suvari). His wife, Carolyn (Annette Bening), an ambitious, desperately self-motivated real-estate agent, becomes involved in an extramarital affair with another realtor. Neither parent pays much attention to their angry, morose daughter (Thora Birch), who becomes involved with a young drug-pushing neighbor (Wes Bentley). Reviews of *American Beauty* were overwhelmingly positive. Glenn Kenny noted in *Premiere* (October 1999), "Shooting in hard-to-master widescreen, Mendes achieves a wonderfully skewed visual style, often framing his characters against vast and textured but peculiarly blank backdrops that highlight their isolation." David Ansen wrote in *Newsweek* (September 27, 1999), "Mendes . . . uses the screen like a born filmmaker. He and cinematographer Conrad Hall create bold, spare images suspended somewhere between Caravaggio and comic strip. His film examines a malaise that's been plaguing the affluent, deracinated middle class since the suburbs were invented." *American Beauty* was nominated for five Academy Awards and won four, including best picture and best director. In addition, it captured four British Film Critics awards and brought Mendes a Director's Guild award.

Mendes's second film, *Road to Perdition*, is based on a graphic novel by Max Allen Collins and Richard Pier Rayner. Its plot, set in 1931, revolves around a hit man, Michael Sullivan (played by Tom Hanks), who works for a Chicago crime lord—his foster father (Paul Newman). After his older son sees Sullivan and an associate commit murder, the boy is targeted by the mob; Sullivan's wife and younger boy are then murdered by mistake, and Sullivan is forced to live life on the run with his surviving son. "With 'Perdition,'" Mendes told Lynn Hirschberg for the *New York Times Magazine* (July 7, 2002), "there are two layers. First, there's a subtle, complex layer about violence and redemption and the secret life our parents lead that we never really know about. That's the secret movie. Then there's the other movie, which is a more conventional narrative about fathers and sons. *That* movie appeals across the board." Released in July 2002, the film received mixed reviews. The enthusiastic notices included one by Kenneth Turan, who, in the *Los Angeles Times* (July 12, 2002, on-line), wrote that Mendes had "told this surprisingly resonant story with the potent, unrelenting fatalism of a previously unknown Greek myth." In another positive assessment, this one for the *New York Times* (July 12, 2002, on-line), Stephen Holden wrote that Mendes and his cinematographer, Conrad L. Hall, had "created a truly majestic visual tone poem, one that is so much more stylized than [*American Beauty*'s] that it inspires a continuing and deeply satisfying awareness of the best movies as monumental 'picture shows.'" David Edelstein disagreed, writing for *Slate* (July 11, 2002, on-line) that Mendes's stylization of "most of the action" gave the film "bogus moral/religious weight, and it has little impact. This is a by-the-numbers vigilante flick that comes with a handy anti-violence message—delivered with perfect timing, after the bad guys have been blown away."

Mendes returned to the Donmar Warehouse in September 2002 to direct productions of William Shakespeare's *Twelfth Night* and Anton Chekhov's *Uncle Vanya*, both starring Emily Watson and Simon Russell Beale. The two plays were also performed in repertory, marking a first for Mendes. They received highly laudatory reviews.

In the *International Herald Tribune* (October 30, 2002, on-line), Sheridan Morley wrote, "I have never seen a more complex or fascinating *Twelfth Night*. This is no longer a mindless frolic of mistaken identity, but a strange, soulful tragi-comedy about bisexuality, depression and misplaced power, closer to the later Shakespeare of *Winter's Tale* or *Cymbeline* in its many moods and internal conflicts." Steve Schifferes, a critic for *BBC News* (September 19, 2002, on-line), was similarly impressed with the Donmar's *Uncle Vanya*, calling the production "spectacular." In January 2003 Mendes is scheduled to begin rehearsals of the musical *Gypsy*, starring Bernadette Peters, in what will be his first production to premiere on Broadway.

Mendes has been described as being "shortish" and "chubbyish" and as having long, prominent eyelashes, which in Claire Armitstead's estimation "create an illusion of coyness, of modest withdrawal from eye contact or of closed-eyed contemplation." Mendes plans to step down as head of the Donmar at the end of 2002; according to Lynn Hirschberg, he would like to produce movies. Of late, he has been romantically linked with the actress Kate Winslet. He lives in London. — G.O.

Suggested Reading: *Guardian* p19 Sep. 21, 1992; *New York Times* II p9 Feb. 1, 1998, II p71 Sep. 12, 1999; *New York Times Magazine* p16+ July 7, 2002, with photos; *Plays and Players* p20+ May 1989; *Washington Post* Arts p1 Sep. 26, 1999

Selected Films: *American Beauty*, 1999; *Road to Perdition*, 2002

Selected Plays: *London Assurance*, 1989; *The Cherry Orchard*, 1989; *Troilus and Cressida*, 1990; *The Sea*, 1992; *Richard III*, 1992; *Assassins*, 1992; *Cabaret*, 1993, 1998; *The Tempest*, 1993; *The Birthday Party*, 1994; *Oliver!*, 1994; *Glengarry Glen Ross*, 1995; *The Glass Menagerie*, 1995; *Company*, 1995; *Habeas Corpus*, 1996; *The Front Page*, 1997; *Othello*, 1997; *The Fix*, 1998; *The Blue Room*, 1998; *To the Green Fields Beyond*, 2000; *Twelfth Night*, 2002; *Uncle Vanya*, 2002

---

Courtesy of Vivendi Universal

## Messier, Jean-Marie

(mess-ee-AY, zhon-ma-REE)

*Dec. 13, 1956– Businessman*

*Address: Vivendi Universal, 800 Third Ave., 38th Fl., New York, NY 10022-7604*

"I am not realising a dream to become a media mogul. I am realising my dream of creating a truly global media company that is neither European or American-centric." According to the London *Sun-*

*day Times* (June 25, 2000), as quoted on *Justpeople.com*, those words were uttered by Jean-Marie Messier, then the chairman and CEO of the highly diversified French company Vivendi. Messier was speaking at a news conference at which he and Edgar Bronfman Jr., the head of the Canadian beverage and entertainment company Seagram's, announced the merger of their firms with the French concern Canal Plus to form what is now called Vivendi Universal. The deal brought under one umbrella Vivendi's operations, which ranged from waste management, to the provision of utilities, to publishing, to television and phone service; Seagram's holdings, which included Universal Pictures and Polygram Records as well as distilleries; and Canal Plus, one of the biggest pay-TV businesses in Europe. A year later, according to Seth Schiesel in the *New York Times* (August 27, 2001), Vivendi Universal ranked as the fourth-largest media conglomerate on Earth, behind AOL Time Warner, Disney, and Viacom. (In terms of total revenues, it was second to AOL Time Warner.)

Messier spent a dozen years in government service before entering the private sector, in 1989. He worked for the investment bank Lazard Frères before joining, in 1994, Compagnie Générale des Eaux (General Water Co.), one of France's oldest and most respected utility firms. Within two years he had become its head, and in 1998 he changed its name to Vivendi. As the chairman of Vivendi Universal, Messier directed an empire valued at about $55 billion, one that encompassed one of Europe's main cable companies as well as Universal Pictures and Universal Music Group. In contrast to the stereotypical corporate European modus operandi, which is characterized by caution and insularity, Messier conducted business at a fast pace and espoused a global vision.

Yet even more rapidly than Vivendi had been transformed into a leading player in the world media market, it collapsed, due to massive debt and a series of missteps by Messier that alienated both Vivendi investors and a large segment of the French citizenry. People who had once regarded him as a hero came to view him as a traitor because of his all-but-stated objective of ending the French government's heavy subsidization of the nation's film industry, on one hand, and spreading American-style pop culture on the other. Throughout the first half of 2002, Messier tried to turn his company around, but on July 1, 2002, yielding to growing pressure from others within the firm, he announced his resignation. "In some respects, Mr. Messier set out to be an exception to the French exception," Mark Landler wrote for the *New York Times* (July 7, 2002). "In other respects, however, he was simply walking the treacherous path trod by other moguls who tried to straddle national and cultural divides."

The son of Pierre Messier and the former Janine Delapierre, Jean-Marie Raymond Pierre Messier was born into a middle-class family on December 13, 1956 in Grenoble, France. He attended the École Polytechnique, an elite business college in Paris, from 1976 to 1979. From 1980 to 1982, also in Paris, he studied at the École Nationale d'Administration, which trains French civil servants. Upon graduating he was hired by the French Ministry of Economy and Finance as inspector of finances, a position he held from 1982 to 1986. In 1986 he was selected to lead the Finance Ministry team that was preparing the first privatization of state companies in France. In this position he served as adviser to Finance Minister Edouard Balladur, who later served as France's prime minister. With the resignation in 1988 of the right-wing prime minister Jacques Chirac and his replacement by a Socialist, Michel Rocard, a new Finance Ministry staff was appointed, and Messier lost his job. In 1989 Messier joined the investment bank Lazard Frères & Co. as a general partner, thus becoming the youngest partner in the history of the century-old bank. During the five years he worked for Lazard Frères, he spent five months in New York City, where he learned American business practices.

In 1994 Messier was named chief executive of the executive committee at Compagnie Générale des Eaux, a Paris-based water, waste-management, public-transport, and construction company. (Essentially, he was the company's second in command.) Générale supplied potable water to business, industry, municipalities, and residences; reaching about 70 million people, including 25 million in France, it was Europe's largest supplier of water. Messier assumed control of Générale in 1996, after his predecessor as chief executive officer, Guy Dejouany, stepped down. At the time of Messier's ascendancy, Dejouany and other Générale managers were being investigated for making illegal donations to political parties. In addition, in 1995, for the first time in its almost 150-year history, Générale had reported a loss—one amounting to $624 million. The company had also accumulated $9.6 billion in debt due to unsound real-estate investments and the acquisition of a vast array of holdings, ranging from casinos to laundry services.

Recognizing that Générale had to divest itself of many of its holdings in order to stay afloat, Messier instituted radical changes. In his first few months at the helm, he trimmed the workforce by 10 percent (although, with 220,000 employees remaining, Générale was still the largest private employer in France). He also raised money by selling $1.6 billion worth of property in Europe, the company's health-care assets, and Générale's majority stake in a private cable-television company. He then refocused the company by dividing it into two entities, one handling water service and waste management and the other dealing with communications. "We had to reform strongly and abruptly," Messier told John Tagliabue for the *New York Times* (October 14, 1997). "Now we are in a position to be more aggressive."

Armed with the money earned from divesting Générale of many of its assets and from financing through eurobonds (bonds issued by an international syndicate and offered to investors in a number of countries simultaneously), Messier reinvested in water and waste-management facilities. In 1997 he bought out Leigh Interest, a British waste-management company, for $187.4 million; in 1998, for $6.2 billion, he bought the US Filter Corp., the largest private American water company as well as the largest global supplier of industrial water-treatment equipment and services. By 1998 Générale had become active in more than 80 countries. It ranked as the top energy supplier and the leading waste-management company in Europe, operating 187 municipal heating works (which provide heat to homes and businesses) and collecting more than 15 tons of household and nonhazardous industrial waste annually. In addition, Générale had become Europe's leading private transport operator, with a fleet of 8,000 local and intercity buses and 2,400 train cars transporting more than 600 million passengers a year.

With regard to communications and the media, Générale's goal, Seth Schiesel quoted Messier as saying, was "to be the world market leader in the five fields of content that we consider as key for this digital age: music, movies, games, education and sport." Through a stock swap, in early 1997 Messier increased Générale's share in the French multimedia group Havas to 30 percent. Among other products, Havas publishes the Larousse encyclopedias and the weekly French magazine *L'Express*. Of greater importance to Messier was Havas's controlling interest in Canal Plus, Europe's largest cable- and pay-TV company. In 1998 Messier became the leading shareholder in Havas, thus giving Générale control of Havas's stock in Canal Plus. Earlier, in 1997, Générale had completed a deal in which British Telecom, Mannesmann, and SBC Communications acquired minority stakes in Générale's telecommunications subsidiary, Cégétel, currently the second-largest telecommunications operator in France and the owner of SFR, a French wireless operator. In Messier's first year and a half as Générale's head, the company reported net profits of $320 million on revenues of $28.5 billion. "The changes at Générale have been significant during the last eighteen months," Messier told an interviewer for *Director* magazine, as quoted on the Web site of Jeremy Josephs, a journalist whose specialty is France. "Not just by French, but also by international standards. If you look at our divestitures during this period, they are close to 10 billion dollars—and I don't think that there are many groups in the world that have gone through such a revamping in such a short period of time. I have made some new choices and tried to recover some of the flexibility of the group. I feel that we are well-placed too, because in so far as utilities and communications are concerned, there is much to be done in the years ahead."

In mid-1998 Messier changed the company's name to Vivendi, which is a form of the French word for "living." The following year he acquired Pathe S.A. for Vivendi for $2 billion in stock. The largest film production and distribution company in France, Pathe S.A. also held stock in Canal Plus, which helped Vivendi tighten its grip on the satellite television network. In addition, the deal gave Messier Pathe's 17 percent stake in British Sky Broadcasting, a Canal Plus rival that was controlled by Rupert Murdoch's News Corp. With the aim of trying to merge Canal Plus and British Sky Broadcasting, Vivendi increased its stake in Canal Plus to 24.5 percent. Negotiations toward a merger failed, however, because the question of who would run the blended company could not be resolved. Messier later sold his stake in British Sky Broadcasting to satisfy the European Competition Commission.

Vivendi made additional strides toward becoming a major global multimedia power when, in June 2000, it acquired the Canadian-owned firm Seagram's for $34 billion. (At the same time, Vivendi and Canal Plus merged.) The merger was approved by the European Commission in October 2000 after the companies promised concessions to dilute the power of their combined business. Seagram's holdings included Universal Pictures, a major Hollywood studio that owned a library of more than 24,000 television episodes and 3,000 feature films, and the Polygram music group, which, with its many labels (among them Motown, Mojo, Island, and Def Jam Records), was the largest record company in the United States in terms of sales. Vivendi also acquired Seagram's beverage business, which it later sold for $8.15 billion. (Edgar Bronfman Jr., the head of Seagram's before its merger with Vivendi, served as executive vice chairman of the new company until his resignation, on December 6, 2001.)

When the Vivendi-Seagram's deal was announced, Vivendi stocks dropped, reflecting stockholders' doubts about the wisdom of such a massive expansion. (By September 2001 stocks of Vivendi-Universal, as its name had become in December 2000, were still 31 percent lower in value than Vivendi's had been before the purchase.) Other large corporations had passed up the opportunity to buy Seagram's, and many in the business world thought that Vivendi had paid too much for the company. (According to Carol Matlack in *Business Week* [July 3, 2000], Vivendi paid "a 46% premium on Seagram's pre-bid price.") Moreover, many observers warned that Vivendi had greatly overestimated its ability to manage Universal. Expressing a widely held view, one analyst told Reuters, as quoted by David Ignatius, "The chance of the French succeeding in running a U.S. music and film business properly is about zero." "Most of the reactions were skeptical," Messier acknowledged to Peter S. Goodman for the *Washington Post* (June 23, 2000). "Basically, the classic French, European reaction: 'OK, that's the concept, but if it could exist, a U.S. company would have done it already.'"

Despite the merger, more than half of Vivendi's roughly $40 billion in revenue continued to come from water distribution, waste management, and construction. Determined to increase the size and scope of Vivendi Universal, in 2001 Messier made a series of additional purchases: he spent $2 billion for 35 percent of a Moroccan telephone company, $2.2 billion for the Boston-based educational publisher Houghton Mifflin, and $372 million for the Internet site *MP3.com.* In partnership with the United Kingdom–based Vodafone AirTouch, the world's largest wireless telephone provider, Messier also prepared to launch a new European Internet portal to be known as Vizzavi. As Messier envisioned it, Vizzavi would be accessible by mobile telephones, desktop computers, and hand-held devices and would generate a whole new market for a subscription service to Universal's music catalog. "Can you tell me how to reach 100 million people across Europe?" Messier said to Peter S. Goodman. "That's what Vizzavi is." The launch of Vizzavi was delayed, because Web-enhanced, rapid-action cell phones were not yet available to consumers.

In 2001, after several failed attempts due to insufficient demand from institutional investors, Messier siphoned off Vivendi's water and construction business into Vivendi Environment, a separate stock offering. Also in 2001 Vivendi and the Sony Corp., headquartered in Tokyo, Japan, announced their joint formation of a new company to rival Napster's on-line music-sharing service. Pressplay, as it was called, covered Vivendi's and Sony's music catalogs through an exclusive licensing agreement and is offered as a paid subscription service. "No one can imagine launching online music without the world's number one and number two companies," Messier declared, as quoted on *BBC News* (February 23, 2001, on-line). He added, "We hope to licence 50% of the world's music." The subscription service was one of Messier's favorite tools for furthering business. "It's through a subscription relationship that you can identify what the customer is really doing and not doing, loving and not loving," he told Seth Schiesel. In late summer 2001 Cégétel announced the creation of Universal Music Mobile, a new service available through its SFR mobile-phone operation in France. The service included such benefits as personal voice-mail greetings recorded by pop stars. With the goal of expanding Vivendi's horizons in another direction, Messier (in collaboration with four other major Hollywood studios) announced plans for a system that would allow consumers to download movies over the Internet.

In early 2002 Vivendi's Universal Music Group was the world's largest music operation, with annual sales totaling around $6 billion. As of August 2001 Universal Pictures had the largest share of the box-office market for that year. By that time Vivendi had also become the second-largest publisher of computer games; its Blizzard games, which included the "Diablo" series, among others, were highly lauded. Canal Plus, which aimed to expand throughout Europe, began to take losses. Meanwhile, Cégétel had enrolled more than 12 million customers in France. Eager to keep his company's image up to date, Messier moved the Paris headquarters of Vivendi to modern offices near the Arc de Triomphe; the new site featured a cyber café (also called an Internet café) on the ground floor. Messier also shifted his personal base of operations to New York City, proclaiming a love for the city and becoming heavily involved in its social and philanthropic scene.

In December 2001 Vivendi Universal purchased, for $1.5 billion, 10 percent of EchoStar, a satellite television company that had made inroads into the suburban American cable-television markets and had more than five million subscribers in the United States. At the time Messier and his colleagues believed that Vivendi could fortify EchoStar with new technology and Universal movies and television programs. Shortly afterward Messier announced a $10.3 billion deal to set up a new company called Vivendi Universal Entertainment, which would run the conglomerate's American movie, television, and theme-park business. To head this company Messier hired the former ABC, Paramount, and Fox mogul Barry Diller, who also retained control of the USA Networks. With hopes high for the success of this venture, American depository receipts for Vivendi Universal rose 6.43 percent on the New York Stock Exchange after the deal. In the spring of 2002, Vivendi gained control of the entertainment assets of USA Networks; with the acquisition of USA Interactive, as it was renamed, Vivendi secured majority control of the Home Shopping Network, Ticketmaster, Hotel Reservations Network, and the Web site Expedia, among other businesses.

All was not well with Vivendi Universal, however. In 2001 Canal Plus, which aimed to expand throughout Europe, had suffered large losses for the fifth straight year, as a result of rising programming costs. In March 2002 Vivendi reported an astounding $12 billion loss, attributed to Canal Plus's troubles, Vizzavi's faltering business, and reduced values of other Vivendi acquisitions. With investor pressure mounting, on April 16, 2002 Messier fired the head of Canal Plus, Pierre Lescure. The reason, Messier told the *New York Times* (April 17, 2002), was the need to "change the team, to give it a fresh start. Canal Plus used to have a soul and profit. The impression is that it has lost a little bit of both." But an angry Lescure charged, according to Tagliabue, that his removal showed that Messier's intention was really "to reduce the channel to a simple editor, with distribution passing into the hands of foreigners responsible for audiovisual material." Although Vivendi's share price revived somewhat following the shakeup at Canal Plus (which included the resignation of Lescure's right-hand assistant), it remained at about 50 percent below what it had been when the Seagram trade had been completed. Many French people resented Messier's actions, not least because Canal Plus acted as a funnel through which the French government financed 80 percent of all French films. Moreover, many still felt angry about a a December 2001 interview in which Messier said, as quoted by Alan Riding in the *New York Times* (December 24, 2001), "The Franco-French cultural exception is dead"—a reference to the French system of promoting films made in France through subsidies and mandatory investment, and by requiring 40 percent of movies broadcast on French television to be French productions. Messier insisted in vain that he had been misquoted; even the president of France, Jacques Chirac, and members of the nation's cabinet criticized him.

In mid-April 2002 Vivendi announced that it would sell one of its publishing units, so as to reduce the company's overall $33 billion debt by about $1 billion (in euros). At a Vivendi Universal shareholders' meeting later that month, the attendees—angered about a fall of 35 percent in the value of Vivendi stock since the beginning of the year—heckled Messier and urged him to resign. Messier, however, announced that Vivendi Universal had had a better-than-ffexpected first quarter, thanks to a rise of 16.5 percent in revenues over the previous year's first quarter from its telecommunications and media units. Displaying an unusual level of humility, Messier confessed to the shareholders, as quoted by Alan Cowell in the *New York Times* (April 25, 2002), "I was clumsy and involuntarily contributed to a certain measure of misunderstanding by communicating too much. I got the message, and I'm fixing it." Messier also announced that he would invest his previous year's bonus in Vivendi stock.

Whatever Messier gained in good will at that meeting evaporated a week later, when Vivendi announced that it intended to ask a Paris court to annul the results of two shareholder votes. (The shareholders had rejected two of Messier's proposals: to set aside 5 percent of the company's shares for stock options for senior managers, and to raise some $2.7 billion by issuing new shares of stock.) Messier claimed that the balloting system had been tampered with. While his board of directors continued to support him, members of the Bronfman family, who held seats on Vivendi Universal's board of directors, led a growing chorus calling for his resignation.

Nevertheless, Messier pressed on. He announced that, to lower Vivendi Universal's debt, he had reduced his company's stake in Vivendi Environmental by 15.5 percent, through sales of stock. With Vivendi Universal's share in Vivendi Environmental reduced to less than 50 percent, Vivendi Universal would no longer be required to consolidate Vivendi Environmental's debt on its books. However, Messier's indecision over how to rid Vivendi of the shares gave investors the impression that the company was desperate to raise cash; panicky investors sold large amounts of stock, thus lowering the value of Vivendi Universal's shares by 25 percent. With prices down 67 percent since the start of the year, Vivendi's stock offering was now lower than it had been in 13 years. The value of Vivendi Environmental stock also dropped. As a result, Messier's prediction that he would raise about 1.7 billion euros fell short by about 200 million euros. Further weakening Messier's position was the decision of one of his closest allies, Bernard Arnault, the head of the luxury-goods conglomerate LVMH, to step down from the board, on June 25. On July 1, 2002, faced with an increasing lack of confidence in him and bad news from Moody's Investors Service (Moody's downgraded Vivendi's debt to junk-bond status and lowered the rating on the firm's long-term debt to below investment grade), Messier resigned as chief executive and chairman of Vivendi Universal. "I am leaving so that Vivendi Universal stays," Messier declared in an announcement, according to Suzanne Kapner and Laura M. Holson in the *New York Times* (July 2, 2002). "You cannot lead a company if the board is divided." Messier was soon replaced by Jean-René Fourtou, the vice chairman of the French-German pharmaceuticals company Aventis. The day after Messier's resignation, disclosures about Vivendi Universal's shady accounting practices regarding British Sky Broadcasting sent its stock price plummeting, as investors feared that new revelations might send the company into bankruptcy, as happened to such American companies as Enron and Worldcom.

Messier has been called J6M, an abbreviation of his long nickname—*Jean-Marie Messier, moi-même, maître du monde*, which means "Jean-Marie, myself, master of the world." His autobiography, *j6m.com* (2001), was a best-seller in France. A practicing Roman Catholic, he has been married since 1983 to the former Antoinette Fleisch; the couple have three sons and two daughters. In his spare time Messier enjoys skiing, playing tennis, watching James Bond films and movies directed by Steven Spielberg, and listening to New Orleans–style jazz. He dresses casually and is known for his easy-going manner, strong grasp of figures, and—before his departure from Vivendi, at least— brilliant salesmanship. He remains a member of Vivendi Universal's board of directors and has also served on the boards of directors of Alcatel; BNP-Paribas; Cégétel; Compagnie de Saint-Gobain; LVMH-Moet Hennessy Louis Vuitton; UGC (a European chain of movie theaters); USA Networks; the Whitney Museum of American Art, in New York City; and the New York Stock Exchange (he was only the second non-American to sit on that board). In recognition of his achievements, the French government named him a chevalier of the French Legion of Honor. Fluent in English, Messier maintains homes in both Paris and New York City.
— G.O.

Suggested Reading: *BBC News* (on-line) Feb. 23, 2000; *Business Week* p57+ May 20, 2002, p64+ July 1, 2002, with photo, p48+ July 8, 2002; *Fortune* p136+ Sep. 3, 2001, with photo, p51

May 13, 2002, p32+ June 10, 2002, with photo; *JeremyJosephs.com*; *Justpeople.com*; *New York* p24+ May 13, 2002; *New York Times* D p1 Oct. 14, 1997, C p1+ Aug. 27, 2001, with photos, A p1+ July 2, 2002; *New Yorker* p31 July 15, 2002; *Time* (on-line) Sep. 13, 1999; *Vanity Fair* p194+ Oct. 2002, with photo; *Washington Post* A p23 June 21, 2000, E p1 June 23, 2000; *International Who's Who 2001*

---

Armando Gallo/Retna

## Messing, Debra

*Aug. 15, 1968– Actress*

*Address: c/o Allen Agency, 23852 Pacific Coast Hwy., Suite #401, Malibu, CA 90265*

"I think Debra Messing is almost our modern day Audrey Hepburn. There's always something magical about the way she looks," Merle Ginsberg, the entertainment editor of *Women's Wear Daily*, told an interviewer for *Entertainment Tonight* (December 21, 2001, on-line). A classically trained stage, television, and film actress, Messing is best known for her portrayal of the interior designer Grace Adler on NBC's award-winning sitcom *Will & Grace*, which debuted in 1998 and has completed four successful seasons. In her most prominent movie role to date, Messing played opposite Woody Allen in Allen's film *Hollywood Ending* (2002). "Smart, well-spoken, down-to-earth. She comes to work without makeup. She orders McDonald's more than she should. She listens. She is the least flaky actress I know," Eric McCormack, Messing's co-star on *Will & Grace*, has said, as quoted on the Web site *askmen.com*. Woody Allen described Messing to Jeannie Williams for *USA Today* (April 3, 2002, on-line) as a "natural comic talent . . . beautiful, very, very gifted. She lights up everything she does."

Debra Messing was born into a Jewish family in the New York City borough of Brooklyn on August 15, 1968. When she was three she moved with her parents and her older brother, Brett, to a quiet town outside Providence, Rhode Island. Her father, Brian Messing, is a sales executive for a jewelry manufacturer; her mother, Sandy Messing, has worked as a professional singer, banker, travel agent, and real-estate agent. As a youngster Messing took lessons in dance, singing, and acting. "I remember watching the television show *Fame* and wanting to dance on top of a taxi," Messing told Jennifer Kasle Furmaniak for *Cosmopolitan* (February 2001). She recalled to Roz Brooks for *Complete Woman* (September 1999), "I was always singing and dancing for my mother when I wasn't glued to the television watching *I Love Lucy* or the *Carol Burnett Show*." While Messing's parents encouraged her dream of becoming an actress, they also urged her to get a standard liberal-arts education before deciding on acting as a career. Heeding their advice, she attended Brandeis University, in Walsham, Massachusetts. During her junior year she studied theater at the prestigious British European Studio Group of London program, in England, an experience that fueled her desire to act. After graduating summa cum laude from Brandeis, in 1990, with a bachelor's degree in theater arts, Messing gained admission to the elite Graduate Acting Program at New York University (NYU), which accepts only about 15 new students annually. Three years later she earned a master's degree in fine arts from NYU.

Later in 1993 Messing won praise for her acting in the pre-Broadway workshop production of Tony Kushner's much-lauded play *Angels in America: Perestroika*. Before long she broke into television, playing the part of Dana Abandando—the conniving sister of one of the main characters—in three episodes of the award-winning television series *NYPD Blue;* those installments aired in late 1994 and early 1995. In 1995 Messing made her film debut, in the director Alfonso Arau's love story *A Walk in the Clouds*, in which she had a small role as the wife of a World War II veteran (Keanu Reeves). This exposure led the Fox network to make her the co-star of the television sitcom *Ned and Stacey*; the series, about a young man and young woman who marry for reasons other than love after knowing each other for only a week, lasted for two seasons (1995–97). "I had no idea what I was doing," Messing told David Martindale for *Biography* (May 2001). "I was thrown into the fire and learning on my feet in front of millions of viewers. I hardly even remember the first six months, because I was just terrified. I feel so much more at home [acting in a prime-time show] now." Messing appeared as Jerry Seinfeld's date in two episodes of the hit television show *Seinfeld*: "The Wait Out," in 1996, and "The Yada Yada," in 1997.

The actress turned down a starring role in another television sitcom to appear in Donald Margulies's two-character play *Collected Stories*, which opened at the Manhattan Theater Club, an Off-Broadway venue, in 1997. Messing portrayed the protégé—and, ultimately, literary betrayer—of a famous short-story writer (Maria Tucci). Speaking of her rejection of the TV role in favor of acting on the stage, she told Furmaniak, "One was going to afford me money and fame. The other would take me back to the reason I'm an actor—the theater. . . . It was the most important decision I've ever made in my professional life. It was about risk taking and not looking back." But Messing also acknowledged to Brooks, "I love the theater, but if I wanted to pay my bills, I had to be open to film and television."

In 1998 Messing had a lead role as the bioanthropologist Sloan Parker on ABC's dramatic science-fiction television series *Prey*, about a vicious new species of humans, spawned by global warming, who are determined to kill off all other humans. Although the show developed something of a cult following, *Prey* was canceled after one season. Meanwhile, Messing's agent had approached the actress with the pilot script for the television show *Will & Grace*, in which a heterosexual woman lives with a gay man who is also her best friend. Feeling tired after her stint on *Prey*, Messing was inclined to take some time off, but the pilot for *Will & Grace* intrigued her. In a conversation with Ian Williams for *P.O.V.* (November 1999), Messing described the visit to her apartment by the producers of *Will & Grace* one night; armed with a bottle of vodka and some limes, they tried to persuade her to join the show, which would pose a professional risk for everyone involved, because Will was to be depicted as openly gay. "I had to be assured by the producers that the very first priority, always, would be to make people laugh," Messing said to Williams. "Not to be critical. Not to proselytize. To make people laugh. People come home from work and they're tired and they want distraction; they want to laugh. And now, much to my shock, there hasn't been a right-wing revolt or picketing or exposes about how we're ruining America. Because the show is funny first."

Will, played by Eric McCormack (who is not himself homosexual), is a gay lawyer living in New York City with Grace (Messing), an endearingly clumsy and spirited interior designer who has been Will's friend since college. The story line revolves around the roommates' search for love and romance. Other characters are Will's hilarious gay friend Jack (Sean Hayes), and Karen, Grace's pampered secretary (Megan Mullally). In portraying Grace, Messing has often been described as a beautiful woman who is not afraid to act like a clown; Grace is known for her pratfalls and facial contortions. According to Ian Williams, "[*Will & Grace*] . . . owes much to Messing's ricochet-like comic timing and rat-a-tat-tat delivery." Tom Carson wrote for *Esquire* (October 2000), "What makes Grace the perfect sitcom heroine for these excessively briefed, motivationally addled times is that she keeps deciding to be impetuous—usually as a last resort and one that never works any better than her other instant stratagems for coping. It just turns her disasters into a form of self-expression. . . . [Messing] is unique and something splendidly unprecedented on TV."

Directed by James Burrows, who also directed *Cheers*, *Frasier*, *Seinfeld*, and *Friends*, and created by Max Mutchnik and David Kohan, *Will & Grace* was an instant success. Messing has attributed its popularity in part to the earlier airing of *Ellen*, a sitcom about a bookstore owner who, in the course of the series (1994–98), realizes that she is a lesbian. That show was written by and starred the well-known comedian Ellen DeGeneres, who announced publicly during the show's third season that she herself is homosexual. After that revelation, *Ellen* lost viewers, and a year later ABC canceled the series, after its fourth season. "There's never been a leading man on TV who is gay," Messing said to Furmaniak. "*Ellen* broke the door down, and we were able to walk through." "Men relationships are very different," John Catania, a producer for PBS's *In the Life*, a television news magazine series that focuses on gays and lesbians, said to Patricia Brennan for the *Washington Post* (February 14, 1999) in an attempt to explain how *Will & Grace* has escaped the backlash that *Ellen* suffered. "[*Will & Grace*] is as out there as *Ellen* was, exploring the issues, so either the public has matured, which I don't think it has, or there's something else."

"I come from the New York theatre world, and I have a lot of gay male friends, so this friendship of Will and Grace's isn't such a stretch," Messing told Brooks. She said to David Martindale, "It's a show about friendship. That's what drew me to it, just the fact that these two characters know each other so well that they can practically read each other's minds." Since its premiere, in September 1998, *Will & Grace* has been one of the most-watched shows on television. In 1999 *Will & Grace* won the People's Choice Award (whose recipient is determined through a Gallup poll of the public) for favorite new comedy series, and in 2000 it won an Emmy Award for outstanding comedy series. For her work on *Will & Grace*, Messing won the 2001 *TV Guide* Award for actress of the year in a comedy series; a 2001 Screen Actors Guild Award as a member of the show's ensemble cast; and a 2002 Golden Satellite Award, from the International Press Academy, among other honors. She was nominated for an Emmy Award as outstanding lead actress in a comedy series in 2000, 2001, and 2002, received Golden Globe Award nominations in each of those years, and has been nominated several times for an American Comedy Award. After the show's successful first year, the producers gave a Porsche Boxer sports car to each of the sitcom's four principal actors.

Messing was hand-picked by Woody Allen for a small role in his movie *Celebrity* (1998). When she learned that she had won the prominent role of Allen's girlfriend in his film *Hollywood Ending* (2002), a huge scream "erupted" from her, as she put it to Jeannie Williams. "It was as if I went blind for a minute with joy and shock," she told Williams. She recalled to Williams that she then told her agent, "Yes, yes, yes—say no to everything else, this is it, this is a dream come true. I grew up watching [Allen's] films. They defined for me what comedy in American cinema is." *Hollywood Ending* is about a washed-up director named Val (Allen), who tries to make a comeback. Messing's character, Lori, is an aspiring actress who is "convinced she's destined to be the next Julia Roberts," as Messing said to Stephen Schaefer for the *Boston Herald* (May 6, 2002, on-line). "There is no doubt in her mind that is her destiny and she will either do it being 'discovered' on the street walking, like Michelle Pfeiffer was going to the grocery store, or she will do it with the help of Val. . . . She's someone who wants to take the easy road." In an interview with the on-line entertainment magazine *UniverCity* (May 23, 2002), Messing described the method Allen used to enable her to discover the essence of her character—one that resulted in nerve-racking uncertainty for the actress, who during her first four days on the set got no feedback from Allen. After he offered his first words of guidance, on the fifth day, Messing felt herself undergoing a transformation. As she recalled to the *UniverCity* interviewer: "My voice starts to change and my body starts to do something different. And [Allen] was like: 'You just found the character.' . . . And I thought, 'Okay, this is going to be the greatest lesson of my life; I'm going to sit back [and] trust this genius because, you know, he's earned trust.' . . . And from that point on, it was heaven. Because I knew exactly what he needed." Reviews of the movie and of Messing's performance in it were mixed.

Messing's big-screen roles also include turns as a happily married but ill-fated wife in the supernatural thriller *The Mothman Prophecies* (2002), which stars Richard Gere; Lieutenant Penelope Carpenter in the inconsequential remake of the military comedy *McHale's Navy* (1997); and Mary Magdalene in CBS's biblical television movie *Jesus* (1999). Her stage work includes a stint as an understudy to Mary-Louise Parker and Polly Draper in the Off-Broadway production of *Four Dogs and a Bone* (1993) and a co-starring role in Paul Rudnick's play *The Naked Truth* (1994). In the early 1990s she also had a role in a Seattle production of Oscar Wilde's play *The Importance of Being Earnest.*

With her recognized talent for physical comedy and her luxurious head of curly auburn hair (which is sometimes described as red and has brought her jobs as a spokesperson for hair-care products), Messing has drawn comparisons to the legendary redheaded comedic television actress Lucille Ball. *Cosmopolitan* (February 2001) named Messing the magazine's Fun Fearless Female of the Year. "I love to do glamorous things, like wear Valentino," the photogenic Messing told Furmaniak, referring to the celebrated Italian fashion designer. "That's a part of me that will never go away, playing dress up in my mom's closet and looking at pictures of old Hollywood stars." Messing is a supporter of the charities AmFAR, an organization that combats AIDS; the Gay Men's Health Crisis; and Best Friend's Animal Sanctuary.

Messing met her future husband, Daniel Zelman, an actor and screenwriter, on their first day as graduate students at NYU. "He was different from anyone I'd been interested in before. I'm so right out on the table. But he was quiet and introspective. I couldn't stop wondering about him," Messing recalled in an article that appeared on *Entertainment Tonight* (February 12, 2002, on-line). She and Zelman, who were married on September 3, 2000, live in Los Angeles. "Debra and her husband still basically live like they did when they were acting students," Eric McCormack told Josh Rottenberg for *InStyle* (March 2002). "You go to their house, and they're watching TV on a nine-year-old couch, and the place is still barely furnished. She still loves going to McDonald's at midnight." One of Messing's long-term goals is to move back to New York with her husband and start a family. — C.F.T.

Suggested Reading: *askmen.com*; *Biography* (on-line) May 2001, with photos; *Cosmopolitan* Feb. 2001, with photos; *Entertainment Tonight* (on-line); *Esquire* p170+ Oct. 2000, with photos; *InStyle* p394+ Mar. 2002, with photo; *Glamour* p276+ Nov. 2000, with photo, p134+ Jan. 2002, with photo; *TV Guide* p34+ Oct. 17–23, 1998, with photos; *UniverCity* (on-line) May 23, 2002, with photo; *Washington Post* (on-line) Feb. 14, 1999

Selected Television Shows: *McHale's Navy*, 1997; *Prey*, 1998; *Will & Grace*, 1998–

Selected Films: *A Walk in the Clouds*, 1995; *Celebrity*, 1998; *Hollywood Ending*, 2002; *The Mothman Prophecies*, 2002

---

## Meta, Ilir

(MAY-tah, IL-yir)

*1969– Albanian politician*

*Address: c/o Embassy of Albania, 2100 S St., N.W., Washington, DC 20008*

On October 27, 1999 President Rexhep Meidani of Albania approved the Socialist Party's nomination of Ilir Meta, a political economist and member of that party, to replace Pandeli Majko as prime minister. The Socialist Party holds a majority in the Albanian Parliament and thus is entitled to nominate the prime minister (who must also be a member of Parliament); Meta defeated the only other candidate, Mekbule Cecosi, by a 67–46 vote among So-

Hulton/Archive by Getty Images

*Ilir Meta*

cialist Party leaders. When Meta accepted the appointment, Bernhard Kueppers reported for the *Sueddeutsche Zeitung* (October 28, 1999, on-line), he spoke of a "government of continuity" and pledged to continue the policies of his predecessor. In particular, he sought to reassure the European Union and other international institutions that are active and influential in the region that he was not planning any surprises. "I guarantee to our partners in the European Union, the Council of Europe, the World Bank, the International Monetary Fund and NATO that we are ready to fulfill all our obligations in the international community," he said. Sympathetic to the West, Meta has advocated eventual Albanian membership in NATO and the European Union. In late January 2002 Meta resigned because of a dispute with Fatos Nano, head of the Socialist Party. In September 2001 Nano had charged that Meta and his cabinet were corrupt and incompetent. After several members of Meta's cabinet resigned, Nano and his supporters in Parliament refused to accept Meta's replacements for the posts. Meta remains a member of Parliament, and in August 2002 he was named deputy prime minister and foreign minister.

Albania, Europe's poorest country, has had to confront more urgent problems: banditry is common, especially in the rural north, and a wave of civil unrest that swept through the south in 1997 has only recently subsided; in 1999 more than 400,000 ethnic Albanian refugees fleeing the Serbian military campaign in neighboring Kosovo took refuge in Albania (nearly all of them have since returned); corruption is widespread; and the country continues to be a transit point for drug smugglers and illegal immigration. In spite of such formidable difficulties, Meta has made progress in restoring civil order and resuscitating the economy; in the words of a correspondent for the *Economist* (April 29, 2000), Albania has, "in a small way, begun to forge ahead."

For most of its recent history, Albania has been one of the most isolated countries in Europe. To some extent, the country's historical seclusion can be attributed to geography: situated on the eastern shore of the Adriatic Sea, Albania is encircled by rugged mountains to the north, south, and east. (To the east, its neighbors, from north to south, are Yugoslavia, Macedonia, and Greece.) The official language, Albanian, is not closely related to any other European tongue (it is the sole member of its linguistic family in the Indo-European group), and the country's traditionally Muslim faith—a product of the more than 400 years that it spent as a suzerainty of the Ottoman Empire, before it gained independence, in 1912—further distinguishes it from other European countries. Albania's cultural and geographic isolation was reinforced by government policy throughout much of the post–World War II era: although, under Enver Hoxha's hard-line Communist regime, the nation had been a staunch ally of the Soviet Union in the late 1940s and early 1950s, that relationship deteriorated after the death of the Soviet leader Joseph Stalin, in 1953. In 1957 Hoxha denounced Nikita S. Khrushchev's reformist policy of "de-Stalinization," and four years later his government severed diplomatic ties with the Soviet Union altogether. Throughout the 1960s and 1970s, Hoxha aligned his country with the People's Republic of China; that alliance soured in the late 1970s, when, after the death of Mao Zedong, the Chinese government moved toward détente with the West—a policy that Hoxha condemned as an "imperialist-revisionist" betrayal of Socialist principles. After China suspended all economic and military ties, in 1978, the Albanian government embarked on an increasingly isolationist course, becoming one of the most rigidly governed countries in the Communist bloc.

In 1985 Hoxha died. Ramiz Alia, his designated successor as head of the ruling Albanian Party of Labor, or PPS, proclaimed in April 1990 an end to the policy of diplomatic isolation, as the social and political changes then sweeping Eastern Europe began to take hold in Albania as well. Late that year and early in 1991, strikes and student protests around the country led to a nullification of the bans on opposition parties and, in the spring of 1991, on multiparty balloting. By securing a majority of 168 out of 250 seats in the People's Assembly, Albania's unicameral Parliament, the PPS retained its hold on power; however, continued unrest soon forced the party to participate in a multiparty governing coalition, at which time the PPS was reformed and renamed the Socialist Party of Albania, or PSS. More protests in December 1991 led to open general elections in March 1992. This time the opposition Democratic Party of Albania, or PDS, won a two-thirds majority in the Assembly (now reduced to 140 seats); Sali Berisha, head of the right-wing Democratic Party, became president.

Ilir Meta, who was born in 1969 in Skrapar (a region southeast of Albania's capital, Tirana), began his political career in the midst of this turbulent period. Meta, who had studied political economy at the University of Tirana, emerged as a student leader in 1990 and took an active role in the protests that helped bring an end to the one-party state. In 1991, shortly after it was re-formed, Meta joined the Socialist Party. One year later he was elected to a four-year term in the People's Assembly. In 1993 Meta was appointed vice chairman of the Socialist Party, a post that he held until 1996; he also served as his party's secretary for foreign affairs. In 1996 he was reelected to the People's Assembly. Throughout this period Meta's Socialist Party was in the opposition.

According to Meta, the Berisha government of the mid-1990s resumed many of the repressive practices of the former, Communist regime. As he explained in a 1997 speech at the Olof Palme Center, an organization founded by the Swedish Social Democratic Party, "In the name of combating communism, Berisha built up an authoritarian government. He violated human rights and persecuted political opponents. The president controlled the media and made all forms of public meetings difficult." Meta further stated, "The international community and the EU [European Union] made the mistake of believing that democracy had been secured because Berisha came to power in a free election. They lived in the illusion that stability in the area was safeguarded by a strong leader, as Berisha was considered to be. So they pretended not to notice his human rights violations." For the most part, human rights organizations corroborated such allegations: Amnesty International, for example, in a March 13, 1997 account that appeared on its Web site, reported, "Arrests, ill-treatment and violent attacks on opposition politicians and journalists—which have increased considerably over the past year—have contributed to the extreme polarization of the population and the lack of respect for law and order which now make the achievement of a peaceful consensus so difficult."

The situation in Albania deteriorated dramatically in 1997 after the collapse of widespread "pyramid" financial schemes precipitated a rebellion in the south of the country. Angry investors—who by some estimates lost as much as $1 billion in total—took to the streets to demand repayment. (The schemes, which promised returns as high as several hundred percent and attracted many Albanians, had been endorsed by the government.) Meanwhile, the exiled son of King Zog, the pre–World War II ruler of Albania, had returned to the country to promote the restoration of the monarchy. Eight neighboring countries responded to the Albanian government's call for military assistance by dispatching troops to Albania to help police the south, and under pressure from the European Union abroad and the opposition at home, Berisha invited members of the Socialist Party into an interim coalition government pending new elections in late June. In those elections the Socialists made a resounding comeback; Berisha subsequently resigned, to be replaced by Rexhep Meidani of the Socialist Party. "It is easy to wonder why people did not realize the risks of these pyramid schemes . . . ," Meta told the Olof Palme Center. "For 50 years, they had been trained to obey authority. When the government and the president openly supported the schemes, people trusted them."

With the Socialists' return to power, Meta, as the Socialist Party secretary for foreign affairs, became the Albanian secretary of state. In 1998 he made an unsuccessful bid for the office of prime minister after Fatos Nano, the previous prime minister, stepped down. According to a correspondent for the *Sueddeutsche Zeitung* (September 30, 1998), Pandeli Majko, who eventually prevailed, was unable to secure an absolute majority in a vote taken by the Socialist Party leadership; rather than force a runoff, Meta ceded the contest and accepted a position as deputy prime minister. In the fall of 1999, in the wake of the Kosovo crisis, Majko angered his Socialist colleagues by meeting with opposition leaders; on October 26 he was forced out of office. This time, Meta's bid for the post of prime minister was successful.

"We are working to create a strong and functioning democracy," Meta declared on May 9, 2000, shortly after becoming prime minister, in a speech at Harvard University's John F. Kennedy School of Government that was quoted on the Web. "Political dialogue and increased participation with the opposition in joint projects is our goal. We are encouraging cooperation with civil society; we consider them an asset that spurs better governance. We are working heavily on our economy, increasing private participation in infrastructure and services. We are trying to strengthen our institutions and enforce our laws better. We are fighting corruption and increasing citizen participation in decision-making. We are trying to build up a stronger safety net and provide employment opportunities."

Thus Meta views economic development and democratic reform as inextricably linked. More specifically, he feels that institutions such as the International Monetary Fund (IMF) and the World Bank, which recent critics have charged with aggravating world poverty and inequality, play a crucial role in facilitating democratic reform in countries like Albania. As he further explained in his Harvard speech, "I also want to say a few words about the role of the IMF and World Bank in the development of Albania. A few weeks ago there was a demonstration in Washington, D.C. against them. The intellectual debate centers on the fact that [as] Bretton Woods institutions [the IMF and the World Bank were founded in 1944 at the so-called Bretton Woods Conference], they were set up to do different things than what they are doing today. For example, the world does not have the fixed exchange rate system based on gold any more. But the world has countries like Albania and others that are still in a stage of development where they need these institutions to help with fiscal and monetary advice, as well as with soft loans. We do not have a significant amount of experience on our shoulders to foresee every crisis and provide a solution to it. We also do not have access to capital or an affluent capital market where we can go freely to borrow funds for development. For some countries like mine, this is not an option. But I know that we need these institutions, in this form or in another form. We need what they provide to us and we can not get it elsewhere."

In June 2001 Meta's Socialist Party retained control of the government in Albania's first general elections since the crisis of 1997. While balloting was marred by violence—a man in Tirana shot two election officials after a dispute—international observers judged the voting to have been generally fair. The Socialist Party had campaigned on its successes in reestablishing order after the collapse of the pyramid schemes in 1997; it also pointed to Meta's handling of the refugee crisis during the 1999 Kosovo fighting.

On January 29, 2002 Meta resigned, and Berisha's opposition coalition announced that they would end their six-month boycott of Parliament. Meta's decision to step down was prompted by a dispute between the Socialist Party leader, Fatos Nano, and Meta that had begun in September 2001, when Nano accused Meta of corruption and incompetence. The Socialists split into two groups, with one supporting Nano and the other Meta. Four members of Meta's cabinet resigned in December 2001 after Nano accused them of corruption, power abuse, and nepotism; Meta was unable to replace them, because Nano's faction of the party refused to attend cabinet meetings or support Meta's candidates. "During my mandate as the head of government, I have been the butt of accusations and irresponsible defamations on the part of Mr. Nano," Meta said upon his resignation, as quoted in the *New York Times* (January 30, 2002). "It is unprecedented for the head of a party to attack a government and a prime minister from his own party in such an aggressive manner." Meta said the intra-party quarrels had crippled his cabinet and its ability to deal with the economic consequences of a winter so severe that officials had to declare a state of emergency in parts of Albania. He accused Nano of instigating the crisis because of Meta's refusal to support him as a candidate for the presidency—a charge that Nano denied. (Nano himself had been the target of corruption allegations some time before.) Defense Minister Pandeli Majko (who has served as prime minister from 1998 to 2000 and whom Meta picked as his replacement) succeeded Meta and began forming a new cabinet in early February.

Even after Meta's resignation, Parliament remained deadlocked. Majko needed the votes of Nano's deputies in Parliament to win approval for his new cabinet, but Nano and his supporters refused to endorse them. That situation changed after the International Monetary Fund froze a $30 million loan to Albania, and the World Bank warned that further funding was at stake. Despite the approval of Majko's cabinet, the ruling Socialist Party remained deeply divided by internal quarrels. Meanwhile, the Democratic Party demanded a government comprising all parties represented in the legislative chamber. Unable to govern without the support of his own party, Majko resigned in late July, after just six months as prime minister, and Nano assumed the position on August 1, 2002. (Earlier, on June 24, Alfred Moisiu had been elected president; he was sworn in on July 24.)

As of late October 2002, Meta continued to serve in the cabinet, as deputy prime minister and foreign minister. In the latter capacity he has traveled to Macedonia, Serbia, Russia, and Greece. One of his primary goals is the negotiation of a Stabilization and Association Agreement between Albania and the European Union. He has campaigned for more U.S. assistance to develop Albania's agriculture and economy. Since 1991 the United States has given over $265 million in assistance to the small Balkan nation, including $35 million in 2002. The U.S. has budgeted $28 million in aid for Albania in 2003, with an additional $1.5 million allocated for disarmament efforts.

In addition to his native Albanian, Meta speaks English and Italian. In his free time he enjoys weightlifting. — P.K.

Suggested Reading: *Economist* (on-line) Oct. 30, 1999, with photo, Apr. 29, 2000, May 19, 2001; *New York Times* A p16 Oct. 28, 1999

---

## Meyer, Edgar

*Nov. 24, 1960– Bass player; composer*

*Address: c/o Sony Classical, 550 Madison Ave, New York, NY 10022-3211*

From as far back as he can remember, Edgar Meyer has thought of himself as a bass player. Indeed, his self-image is inextricably bound with the instrument itself—to the extent that, as he declared to Mark Levine for the *New Yorker* (July 24, 2000), "I *am* the bass." Echoing that observation, Susan Ranney, the principal bass player of the Los Angeles Chamber Orchestra, told Levine, "I don't consider that Edgar and I play the same instrument. He is a soul that has decided to locate itself in a bass." Widely considered among the greatest double bassists of all time—one who is "unquestionably up there with the great players on any instrument," as David Finckel, the cellist with the Emerson String Quartet, told Levine—Meyer is known for his abili-

Christian Steiner/Courtesy of IMG Artists
*Edgar Meyer*

ty to make the bass "sing" in tones as rich as the human voice, even in the lowest and highest registers of the instrument, and his virtuosity in musical genres ranges from classical to bluegrass. With an "open-to-everything" attitude, as Michael McCall put it in *NashvilleScene* (December 15, 1997, on-line), he has traveled an extraordinarily eclectic musical path, collaborating with such stellar figures or groups in the world of classical music as the cellist Yo-Yo Ma, the violinist Joshua Bell, and the Guarneri Quartet; renowned bluegrass innovators, such as the banjoist Bela Fleck and the mandolinist Sam Bush; the jazz pianist Chick Corea; the country singers Bruce Cockburn, Mary Chapin Carpenter, Emmylou Harris, and Reba McIntyre; and the folk-rock singers the Indigo Girls and James Taylor. His many albums range from his interpretations, on double bass, of Bach's Unaccompanied Suites for Cello to his Grammy Award–winning *Appalachian Journey*, which he recorded with Yo-Yo Ma and the fiddler Mark O'Connor. "Most of the music I've become interested in is hybrid in its origins," Meyer, who plays double bass equally well with or without a bow, told Levine. "It's real hard to find a pure strain of anything. Classical music, of course, is unbelievably hybrid. Jazz is an obvious amalgam. Bluegrass comes from eighteenth-century Scottish and Irish folk music that made contact with the Blues. By exploring music, you're exploring everything." The winner of many competitions and awards, Meyer has performed in solo recitals as well as with chamber groups and orchestras. He is a composer, too; among other works, he has written a violin concerto, a concerto for double bass, and a double concerto for bass and cello as well as "bluegrass-classical fusion" pieces for such albums as *Uncommon Ritual*. "Music," he declared to Mark Levine, "is just the best place to be."

Edgar Meyer was born in Tulsa, Oklahoma, on November 24, 1960 to Edgar A. Meyer and the former Anna Mary Metzel. A few years after his birth, his family moved to Oak Ridge, Tennessee, where his father taught music; a double-bass player who at one time had performed with jazz bands throughout the southern United States, the senior Meyer later studied the classical repertoire. According to the *Oak Ridger Online* (February 28, 2002), Meyer's father (who died in 1988) "rejuvenated the strings program" in the city's schools.

As a toddler Meyer would imitate his father by "playing" a broomstick as if it were a double bass. "I grew up in a house where there was a lot of classical music played and a lot of jazz music played," he told Brittany A. Frompovich for *Bass Frontiers* (1996, on-line). "My father's enthusiasm for it was unbridled. He really loved this music. Although we went to church I would say that those records had more of a religious overtone in our house than church did. They were at the center of what [my father] thought was important. That was just transferred to me. . . . That's what I cared about and that's what made everything worthwhile or interesting. In that sense my father is the biggest influence there will ever be on me since he just implanted a love of music at an early age." (Later, in an interview with Katinka Welz for *Double Bassist* [Autumn 2001, on-line], he said, "If I were to list the people who have influenced me strongly, I always feel I ought to make a list of at least 500 people. There are so many players, singers and composers that I would be afraid to leave out.")

Under his father's tutelage, Meyer began playing the bass when he was five years of age. He learned rapidly, even though he practiced only about 45 minutes a day. When he was 10 his father presented him with his own instrument—a 1933 Czechoslovakian double bass that someone had apparently hung from a ceiling and used (minus its top) as a container for a plant. "I grew up really laid back on the instrument, thinking it was just a blast," Meyer recalled to Mark Levine. He also became proficient on piano, violin, and cello. Meanwhile, starting at an early age, Meyer had also been composing music. His first pieces were "little pop songs," as he told Levine. Later, he wrote classical pieces to play along with friends; if the friends could improvise, he would write only the melody. "I spent a lot of time jamming with a couple of buddies—a trombonist and a bassoonist—just doing free-improv stuff," he recalled to Levine. In his high school, in Oak Ridge, he played in jazz bands. During his teens he also served as the bass accompanist for a church choir and, with his father, performed at weddings and bar mitzvahs.

Meyer graduated from high school in 1978. Although his primary interest was music, he enrolled at the Georgia Institute of Technology, in Atlanta, with the goal of becoming a mathematician. At the end of his freshman year, after acknowledging to himself that he felt far more attracted to music as a career, he transferred to the Indiana University (IU) School of Music, in Bloomington. There, he studied with the double bassist and composer Stuart Sankey and, because he was "eager to absorb everything that was offered," as Katinka Welz wrote, he "made sure he had got to play for every member of the string faculty, including [the violinist] Josef Gingold and [the cellist] János Starker, by the time he graduated." Despite Sankey's opposition, Meyer explored an array of approaches to playing the bass as well as various avenues for performance. In addition to his classical studies, he played improvisational jazz piano at bars and, on bass, performed with a black gospel choir, a Latin band, and a country singer. While at the university he met the prodigiously talented violinist Joshua Bell, a fellow student seven years his junior, with whom he played in chamber-music classes. In 1981 he won the Zimmerman-Mingus Competition, an international event hosted by the International Society of Bassists. In the following year, while playing for tips outside an Aspen, Colorado, ice-cream parlor, he met Bela Fleck, who promptly joined him in an impromptu sidewalk concert. Meyer earned a bachelor of music degree from Indiana University in 1984.

Finding unattractive the prospect of being relegated to the fringes of a symphony orchestra, as are the vast majority of classical bass players, Meyer moved to Nashville, Tennessee, where he became fascinated by a complex, progressive style of bluegrass music often referred to as "newgrass." The pioneer of this approach to bluegrass is Bela Fleck, on whose record *Double Time* (1982) Meyer made his first billed appearance. (Earlier, he had played in some recorded string sessions but had not been credited on the resulting albums.) Meyer soon put together a demo tape of his own music, on which he was assisted by four other musicians—Fleck, Mark O'Connor, Sam Bush, and the Dobroist Jerry Douglas. After being signed to MCA on the strength of the tape, Meyer was backed by those four musicians on his first solo record, *Unfolding* (1986). Dubbing themselves Strength in Numbers, the quintet performed onstage together for the first time at the 1987 Summer Lights Festival, in Nashville; later, they performed at bluegrass festivals in Telluride, Colorado, and elsewhere. "All of those guys are my teachers," Meyer told Brittany A. Frompovich. "Being with those guys is like going to college again. All of them have had a very profound impact on me. Each of them in a different way." In his talk with Michael McCall, he said that while with Strength in Numbers, he came in particular "to see what a defining thing rhythm is in all music." Strength in Numbers released one album, *The Telluride Sessions* (1989), which contains 10 compositions, each written by a different pair from the group. Thom Owens, writing for *All Music Guide* (on-line), called the record "adventurous and unpredictable, revealing more levels upon each listen." In a review for *Amazon.com*, Marc Greilsamer described it as "a true landmark in 'new acoustic' music" and added, "What makes the album special is the uncanny blend of precision and freedom, of improvisation and structure." Strength in Numbers disbanded in 1992.

Earlier, in 1985, Meyer became the first regular bass player for the Santa Fe Chamber Music Festival. Later in the 1980s, on the MCA label, he released the recordings *Dreams of Flight* (1987) and *Love of a Lifetime* (1988), which offer mixtures of jazz, blues, and contemporary classical and so-called ambient music. In the opinion of Mark Levine, the albums "pushed the vogue for eclecticism to the point of incoherence"; Wendell Norman, by contrast, in his article about Meyer for *nashville.com*, called them "masterpieces." In 1990 Meyer collaborated with the country musician Kathy Mattea on "Where Have You Been," which won a Grammy, a Country Music Award, and an Academy of Country Music Association Award for country song of the year.

The year 1993 marked the premiere of Meyer's concerto for bass, with Meyer as soloist and Edo de Waart conducting the Minnesota Orchestra. Also in 1993 Meyer ended his association with the Santa Fe Chamber Music Festival, for which, during the previous eight years, he had written six new works. "In my own vision of my life, composition was something that I was gonna do when I was 50 or 60," he told Katinka Welz. "But when you get these opportunities to play with wonderful artists of all different stripes, it's a real issue what one plays, and not being crazy about the choices, you have to address it. . . . My biggest interest was in 18th- and 19th-century classical music, and also in music just being played today, whether it's jazz or old-time fiddle music. Those were the reasons why I was in music, and so writing for me was going to be about those things." He also told Welz, "Writing is a very fulfilling activity. There is a strong need to express, but also just a curiosity. I have a lot of curiosity about how music works, and writing is the best way for me to explore that." "A large percentage of the material I write today is involved with very specific ways of playing the instrument and sounds that I can hear in my head but I can't totally notate," Meyer told Brittany A. Frompovich. "But there are a lot of things in between the notes and not just nuances or pitch related things or slides. It is a whole sense of phrasing and timing that is important to these pieces. That phrasing and timing is very hard to get right."

In 1994 Meyer joined the Chamber Music Society of Lincoln Center, in New York City, where he has continued to perform regularly. In 1995, in collaboration with the Emerson String Quartet, he served as soloist in the debut performance of his Quintet for Bass and String Quartet. Also that year the premiere of Meyer's Double Concerto for Bass and Cello took place, with the cellist Carter Brey and the San Luis Obispo Mozart Festival Orchestra. The following year he recorded the album *Appalachia Waltz* with Yo-Yo Ma and Mark

O'Connor. The pieces on the record, which combined bluegrass with classical music, were written primarily by Meyer. *Appalachia Waltz* appeared on the *Billboard* classical albums chart for over a year and at number one for 16 weeks in a row.

In 1997 Meyer released the album *Uncommon Ritual* (1997), which he recorded with Bela Fleck and the mandolin player Mike Marshall; that disk reached the Top 10 on *Billboard*'s classical albums chart. The pieces on *Uncommon Ritual* range from a transcription of a Bach fugue to bluegrass and swing-style numbers. An exploration of the fusion of classical music and bluegrass by a quartet that Meyer formed with Joshua Bell, Mark Marshall, and Sam Bush led to their Grammy-nominated record *Short Trip Home* (1999). Featuring pieces written mostly by Meyer, it is the bassist's "most exhilarating album" up to that date, according to Mark Levine, who also described it as "a brilliantly fresh argument for bluegrass as a smart, unpredictable—and completely unpretentious—form of American classical music." That same year saw the release of Meyer's album *Bach Unaccompanied Cello Suites Performed on a Double Bass*, which made it to *Billboard*'s classical albums chart. In 2000 Meyer's Violin Concerto premiered, in a performance by the violinist Hilary Hahn (for whom he wrote it) and the St. Paul Chamber Orchestra. In 2000 Meyer, Ma, and O'Connor reunited to record *Appalachian Journey* (2000), for which James Taylor and the fiddler and singer Alison Krauss performed as guest soloists. The record won a Grammy Award in 2001 for best classical crossover album. That year Meyer also collaborated with Bela Fleck on *Perpetual Motion*, which includes their new arrangements of short works or portions of works by such classical composers as Johann Sebastian Bach (who, Meyer has said, is one of his biggest influences), Ludwig van Beethoven, Claude Debussy, and Peter Ilich Tchaikovsky. Fleck and Meyer received Grammy Awards for their bluegrass treatment of Debussy's "Doctor Gradus ad Parnassum," from his *Children's Corner Suite*, and for best classical crossover album. Meyer's most recent record release, on the Sony label, contains his three-movement Double Concerto for cello and double bass (with YoYo Ma as cellist) and his Concerto for Double Bass, along with two pieces by the 19th-century Italian composer, conductor, and virtuoso double bassist Giovanni Bottesini: Concerto for Double Bass no. 2 in B minor and Gran Duo Concertante for violin and orchestra (with Joshua Bell as violinist). Hugh Wolff conducted the St. Paul Chamber Orchestra on that 2002 album.

As a visiting professor, Meyer has taught double bass at the Royal Academy of Music in London, England. He has also performed at the Aspen, Caramoor, and Marlboro festivals. In 2000 he debuted with the Boston Symphony Orchestra at Tanglewood, Massachusetts, performing his Double Concerto with Yo-Yo Ma. That same year he received the Avery Fisher Prize, becoming one of only 16 people to have won it in the last 26 years. In 2002 he was named a MacArthur Fellow by the John D. and Catherine T. MacArthur Foundation. The so-called genius grant from the foundation amounted to $500,000, to be awarded to him in $100,000 increments each year for the next five years. Meyer has played a 1769 Gabrielli double bass since his father purchased it for him in 1983 and uses the same $10 bow he has had since he was a child.

When Michael McCall met Meyer in 1997, he found that the musician never "quite relaxes: Meyer, one imagines, would be a tightly wound bundle of anxious energy even on a meditative day at the beach." Speaking of Meyer to McCall, Fred Sherry, a cellist with the Chamber Music Society of Lincoln Center, described him as "a genius, and that's not a word I toss around lightly. He's also the sweetest, nicest, most interesting guy to hang around with. He has incredible patience. But he also expects everybody to be great, and he really won't accept anything less. He expects you to be in tune and in time, and he expects you to have perfect intonation and to phrase things beautifully. He expects that because that's the way he does it."

Meyer has been married since 1988 to the violinist Cornelia Heard (called Connie), who teaches at Vanderbilt University and is a member of the Blair String Quartet. The couple live with their son, George, who was born in 1992, in the Green Hills section of Nashville. — G.O.

Suggested Reading: *Bass Frontiers* (on-line); *Double Bassist* (on-line) Autumn 2001; Edgar Meyer Web site; *Oak Ridger Online* Feb. 28, 2002; *nashville.com*; *NashvilleScene* (on-line) Dec. 15, 1997; *New Yorker* p82+ July 24, 2000, with photo

Selected Albums: *Unfolding*, 1986; *Dreams of Flight*, 1987; *Love of a Lifetime*, 1988; *Work in Progress*, 1990; *Bach Unaccompanied Cello Suites Performed on a Double Bass*, 1999; with Bela Fleck—*Perpetual Motion*, 2001; with Bela Fleck and Mike Marshall—*Uncommon Ritual*, 1997; with the Emerson String Quartet: *Quintet*; with Joshua Bell, Sam Bush, and Mike Marshall—*Short Trip Home*, 1999; with Strength in Numbers—*The Telluride Sessions*, 1989; with Yo-Yo Ma and Mark O'Connor—*Appalachia Waltz*, 1996; *Appalachian Journey*, 2000; *Bottesini/Meyer: Concertos for Double Bass*, 2002

Armando Gallo/Retna Ltd.

## Meyers, Nancy

*Dec. 8, 1949– Filmmaker; screenwriter*

*Address: Paramount Pictures, 5555 Melrose Ave., Los Angeles, CA 90038*

For many years the writer, producer, and director Nancy Meyers was known in Hollywood for the films on which she collaborated with her longtime partner and eventual husband, Charles Shyer. "Their togetherness extended to the giving of joint interviews in which they had a habit of completing each other's sentences," as Margy Rochlin wrote for the *New York Times* (December 10, 2000). The pair's "glossy, mainstream productions," to use Rochlin's words, include the popular comedies *Private Benjamin*, *Baby Boom*, *Father of the Bride* and its sequel, and *The Parent Trap*. In the late 1990s, for the first time in decades, Meyers embarked on a movie project that did not involve Shyer. The result, *What Women Want* (2000), which stars Mel Gibson and Helen Hunt, broke box-office records for a female-directed Hollywood film and served to demonstrate Meyers's prowess as a director and writer working on her own.

The youngest daughter of Irving Meyers, a voting-machine manufacturer, and Patricia Meyers, Nancy Jane Meyers was born on December 8, 1949 and grew up in the Philadelphia area. As she revealed in a conversation with Margy Rochlin, the idea of making films entered her consciousness at least as early as her teens. While under anesthesia at the dentist's office, she had a dream that she made a romantic comedy starring Rock Hudson and Doris Day. "When I came to, I was telling the dentist the entire plot," she recalled to Rochlin. "That's the only time I've been unconscious. And it's always stuck with me that that happened." In 1972, after earning a degree in journalism at American University, in Washington, D.C., she moved to Los Angeles in search of work. "All I knew was that I wanted a job with a desk and a swivel chair," she told Laurie Halpern Benenson for the *New York Times* (December 15, 1991). She quickly found a job as a production assistant on the CBS game show *The Price Is Right*. "I planned the prizes and took hysterical women away from [the show's host,] Bob Barker," Meyers explained to Benenson. Tiring of those duties before long, she went to work as a story editor for Ray Stark, the producer of several Hollywood hits, including *Funny Girl* (1968), *Seems Like Old Times* (1980), and *Annie* (1982).

It was while working for Stark that she met Charles Shyer, then a writer for the television series *The Odd Couple*. In 1976 Shyer and Meyers became romantically involved. The two shared a passion for golden-age Hollywood films, particularly those directed by Frank Capra. Interviewed along with Shyer by Paul Rosenfield for the *Los Angeles Times* (July 12, 1987, on-line), Meyers recalled the moment that the couple knew they were in love and one that epitomized their twin sensibilities: "In bed, we were watching Preston Sturges's *Miracle of Morgan's Creek*, and there was this moment when Eddie Bracken collapsed . . . and Chuck and I both fell out of bed laughing. That was the moment."

Following her tenure at Ray Stark's company, Meyers concentrated on writing screenplays. "Charles would help me a lot with my writing," she told Benenson, "and Harvey Miller, who was a friend of ours, kind of like one of those TV next-door neighbors, would come by a lot. And every night we'd talk about this idea I'd had, this girl in the Army. It just kind of snowballed, and we said, 'Why don't we try it. We'll do it for six weeks, and if anything comes out, fine.'" Even though the actress Goldie Hawn expressed interest in the project, the script was rejected by a number of film companies before being purchased by Warner Brothers. The film, *Private Benjamin*, was directed by Howard Zieff, with Meyers and Shyer as producers. Critics warmed to the comedy about a spoiled woman (Hawn) who joins the army; Meyers, Shyer, and Miller shared an Academy Award nomination for best original screenplay, while Hawn was nominated for best actress. The three writers also won an award from the Writers Guild of America for best comedy written directly for the screen.

Capitalizing on the success of *Private Benjamin*, Meyers and Shyer co-wrote *Irreconcilable Differences* (1984), about a girl who seeks a divorce from her squabbling parents. Considered by reviewers to be likable fluff, the movie, directed by Shyer, performed well at the box office. Next up was *Protocol* (1984); written by Meyers, Shyer, and Miller and directed by Herbert Ross, that film stars Goldie Hawn as an accidental heroine who is rewarded with a cushy government job and then gets drawn into an international crisis. While critics were lukewarm in their reviews of the picture, *Protocol* did solid box-office business. In 1987 Shyer was back in the director's chair with *Baby Boom* (1987), another Meyers–Shyer screenplay collaboration. The film stars Diane Keaton as J.C. Wiatt, a career-minded woman who finds herself caring for the infant of a deceased relative. *Baby Boom* spawned a television series, starring Kate Jackson, which was also written by Shyer and Meyers and aired for one year.

Following a hiatus, the pair served as co-writers, with others, on *Father of the Bride* (1991), a comedy that found Steve Martin and Diane Keaton cast as the parents of a soon-to-be-wed daughter. (The picture was a remake of the same-named 1950 film starring Spencer Tracy.) Directed by Shyer, the film was a huge success. "There are no great revelations [or] stunning insights in their films. Just everyday life, warmly observed," Roger Ebert wrote for the *Chicago Sun Times* (December 20, 1991, online). Meyers and Shyer were brought in to write a screenplay for *Once Upon a Crime* (1992), a remake of the Italian film *Crimen* (1960). Directed by Eugene Levy, the ensemble piece was packed with well-known performers, among them John Candy, James Belushi, Richard Lewis, Sean Young, Cybill Shepherd, and George Hamilton, but failed to impress moviegoers or critics. Meyers and Shyer wrote the similarly unsuccessful *I Love Trouble* (1994), an action/comedy—starring Nick Nolte and Julia Roberts and directed by Shyer—about two rival reporters who try to solve the mystery behind a train derailment. The couple bounced back with Shyer's *Father of the Bride, Part II* (1995), which was both a sequel to the 1991 film and a remake of *Father's Little Dividend* (1951). Steve Martin and Diane Keaton reprised their roles for the movie, which proved popular with audiences. On the strength of that success, the couple inked a movie-development deal with the Walt Disney Co.

As part of that agreement, Meyers made her directorial debut, with *The Parent Trap* (1998). That movie, which she scripted with Shyer, is an update of the 1961 film about separated twins who meet and try to get their parents back together. In directing the film Meyers made several adjustments to the story. First, she lowered the age of the twins from 14 to 11. "We tried to figure out what today equals 14 in 1961 and came up with 11. Fourteen-year-olds today are wearing makeup, starting to dress like women, and boys are on their minds," she told James Ryan for the *New York Times* (July 26, 1998). Another difference was Meyers's use of digital editing, which made it easier for one actress (Lindsay Lohan) to appears as twins. Aside from those adjustments, Meyers tried to remain true to the spirit of the original film, which she loved as a child. "It's a movie I've seen over and over with my daughters. It's a classic girls' story, of which there are very few. Plus, the fantasy that you have a twin somewhere makes it a really terrific story," Meyers told Janet Weeks for the *Los Angeles Daily News* (December 9, 1995). The remake did brisk business at the box office and was generally well-liked by critics. "In a summer marked by the nuclear-powered vulgarity of *There's Something About Mary* and the harrowing brutality of *Saving Private Ryan*, Disney's almost pathologically innocuous remake of *The Parent Trap* seems a relief," a reviewer for the *Los Angeles Daily News* (July 31, 1998) wrote. Ironically, given the theme of *The Parent Trap*, Meyers and Shyer, who had had two daughters together and gotten married in 1995, separated at about the time that the movie was made. "Something ran its course," Meyers told Margy Rochlin. "But I don't know what that something is. But it was obvious to both of us. I don't think anybody can articulate the thing, can they? It's not just *a* thing. If it were *a* thing, it would probably be easier for everybody."

Meyers's next film project was the romantic comedy *What Women Want* (2000). Starring Mel Gibson and Helen Hunt, the film concerns an advertising executive (Gibson) who finds, after an electrical mishap, that he can hear the thoughts of the women around him. The film was based on two scripts, one by Josh Goldsmith and Cathy Yuspa and the other by Diane Drake; Walt Disney had brought in Meyers in 1998 to synthesize the two versions of the story. She completed that assignment, only to find that Disney was no longer interested in the project. In the end, the movie was released by Paramount Pictures, with Meyers as director. *What Women Want* is the first film on which Meyers worked without Shyer; demonstrating Meyers's prowess as a writer and director in her own right, the film pulled in $33 million in the first weekend of its release, in late 2000, and went on to earn $182 million, making it the highest-grossing movie directed by a woman in Hollywood history.

In 2001 Meyers produced *The Affair of the Necklace*, a film directed by Shyer and featuring Hillary Swank's first performance in a leading role since her Academy Award–winning work in *Boys Don't Cry* (1999).

The five-foot-one-inch Nancy Meyers currently lives in Los Angeles. Annie and Hallie, her daughters from her relationship with Shyer, have had cameo roles in a number of the films on which their parents collaborated. — A.T.

Suggested Reading: *Atlanta Journal-Constitution* p6+ Dec. 11, 1995, with photos; *Flak Mag* (online) Dec. 21, 2000; *Los Angeles Times* p4+ Jul. 12, 1987, with photos, p24+ July 3, 1994, with photos; *Times Union* p6 Dec. 9, 1995, with photos

Selected Films: as co-writer—*Private Benjamin*, 1980; *Protocol*, 1984; *Irreconcilable Differences*, 1984; *Baby Boom*, 1987; *Father of the Bride*, 1991; *Once Upon a Crime*, 1992; *I Love Trouble*, 1994; *Father of the Bride, Part II*, 1995; as director—*The Parent Trap*, 1998; *What Women Want*, 2000

Irwin Daugherty/Liaison Agency

## Mickelson, Phil

(MICK-el-son)

*June 16, 1970– Golfer*

*Address: c/o PGA Tour, 13000 Sawgrass Village Circle, Ponte Vedra Beach, FL 32082*

The world's number-two golfer, Phil Mickelson, Michael Bamberger wrote for *Sports Illustrated* (August 27, 2001), is "the best player never to have won a major." (A major is one of the four most important professional tournaments in golf; on the men's tour, these events are the Masters, the U.S. Open, the British Open, and the PGA [Professional Golfers' Association] Championship.) As of October 2002, Michelson had accumulated 21 PGA Tour victories, and many aficionados of the sport have speculated that he would very likely be the greatest golfer of his day, if not for the remarkable Tiger Woods. Since Woods's entrance on the PGA Tour, in 1996, Mickelson has been overshadowed by Woods's brilliance. Still, his accomplishments are impressive. In 2000, for example, he won four PGA Tour events and earned almost $4.5 million for his efforts. But both of these statistics were surpassed by those of Woods, who fell just short of $10 million in earnings and captured nine wins, including three major championships (the U.S. Open, the British Open, and the PGA Championship). "No one can argue that Mickelson is among the most gifted players of his generation," Leonard Shapiro wrote for the *Washington Post* (July 5, 2001). "But until he wins his first major championship, his place in history will be well back in the pack." "I think I've gotten closer and closer [to winning a major] each year since I've been out on tour . . . ," Mickelson told John Hawkins for *Golf Digest* (January 2001). "I feel like it's just a matter of time as opposed to 'Will it happen?'"

Philip Alfred Mickelson was born on June 16, 1970 in San Diego, California. His father, Philip Sr., was a flight instructor at the Miramar Naval Air Base and also worked as a commercial pilot; his mother, Mary, was the marketing director of a retirement home. When Mickelson was 18 months old, his father placed a golf club in his hands—after shortening the shaft—and although the toddler was decidedly right-handed, he learned to swing a golf club from the left side by standing in front of his father and mirroring his motions. Mickelson played a round of golf for the first time at age four; as he approached the 18th green, he began crying, because he didn't want the game to end. In 1980 he won his first junior tournament; afterward, while driving home with his father, he announced that he "wanted to play golf for a living," as he recalled to John Hawkins. By the age of 18, Mickelson had participated in 162 junior tournaments throughout the United States; he had won 34 of those events, had come in second 22 times, and had placed in the top five 104 times.

In 1988, when Mickelson enrolled at Arizona State University (ASU) at Tempe, he was already being touted as a future star of the game. His collegiate performance lived up to expectations. In 50 National Collegiate Athletic Association (NCAA) events during the next four years, Mickelson won 16 times, including three NCAA Championships, and finished out of the top 10 only seven times. He also competed on the amateur circuit, representing the United States in the Walker Cup, and in 1990 he became only the second player (after the golf legend Jack Nicklaus) to win both the NCAA Championship and the U.S. Amateur in the same year. (In 1996 Tiger Woods became the third player to accomplish that feat.) The next year Mickelson gained berths in several PGA Tour events by virtue of his U.S. Amateur title. In January 1991 he won the Northern Telecom Open, held in Tucson, Arizona, thus becoming only the fourth player in history to win a PGA Tour event while still an amateur—something Woods did not accomplish. Having won an official tournament, Mickelson had the option of withdrawing from the university and joining the PGA Tour full time; he chose to remain at ASU. In 1992 he won his third NCAA Championship, setting several scoring records in the process, and was named to the First Team All-America for the fourth consecutive year. Immediately after he graduated from ASU, in 1992, with a bachelor's degree in psychology, he turned professional. He did so, John Hopkins wrote metaphorically for the London *Financial Times Weekend* (June 20, 1992), "to a roll of drums and a fanfare of trumpets." "Not since Jack Nicklaus . . . has a young amateur excited the world of golf like Mickelson," Hopkins added.

The first event in which Mickelson competed as a professional was the June 1992 U.S. Open, held at the Pebble Beach Golf Links, in California. Although he did not make the cut—that is, shoot a low enough score in the first two rounds to qualify for weekend play—he shot a four-under-par 68 in the first round. In the *New York Times* (June 19, 1992), after noting that Mickelson had "joined the PGA Tour with the stature as the most dominant amateur golfer in more than three decades," Dave Anderson reported, "On the 373-yard first hole of his first tournament as a touring pro, he justified that stature with a birdie 3 after spinning a 9-iron to within 18 inches of the cup."

During the remainder of the 1992 season, Mickelson placed second at the New England Classic but failed to win any tournaments. He ended his losing streak in 1993, at the fourth tournament of his first full year on the PGA Tour: the Buick Invitational, at the Torrey Pines Golf Course in La Jolla, California, near San Diego. Mickelson was very familiar with the course, having played there many times as a junior golfer. Closely pursued by Tour veterans Payne Stewart and Dave Rummells going into the final round, Mickelson quickly pulled away from the field with a seven-under-par 65 en route to a four-stroke win over Rummells, who posted a final round 70. Stewart, who also shot 70, finished five strokes behind Mickelson. "I personally think [Mickelson] is going to be one of the greatest players of all time," Rummels told Bob Green for the Associated Press, as printed in the *Washington Post* (February 22, 1993). "He hits it long and is good with his irons and is a great putter. . . . I was really impressed." Mickelson's mature conduct in the face of pressure led Jaime Diaz to write for the *New York Times* (March 25, 1993), "Despite the impressive depth of his dimples and the improbable length of his backswing, Phil Mickelson is no longer a golf Wunderkind. His air is too serene, his shots too controlled, and his putter too steady." Mickelson followed his win in La Jolla with a strong showing two weeks later at the Players Championship, finishing in a tie for sixth. Six weeks into the season, he was only 12 places behind the top money winner. Later in the year, in his second victory as a professional, he captured the Sprint International. When he completed his 24th event of the 1993 season, he had finished in the top 10 four times and ranked 22d on the list of biggest earners. In addition to his two wins on American soil, Mickelson captured the 1993 Perrier Open, held in Lyon, France.

In the 1994 season's opener, the Mercedes Championship, Mickelson overcame Fred Couples in a play-off to win his fourth PGA Tour event. During the next five tournaments, he finished in the top 10 three times. His best outing came at the Buick Invitational, where he finished third. After that contest Mickelson took a week off from golf and went skiing. While skiing downhill he slipped on a sheet of ice and crashed into a tree, breaking his left femur and right ankle. The injuries sidelined Mickelson for the next three months. In late May, though still walking with a bad limp, Mickelson returned to the tour, competing in the Southwestern Bell Colonial in Texas. Hitting a seven-under-par 65 on the last day, Mickelson claimed eighth place, his fifth top-10 finish of his injury-shortened year. Although he did not win again in 1994, a host of strong showings enabled him to finish 15th on the money list. He also recorded his first PGA Tour hole-in-one, at the Kemper Open (now called the Kemper Insurance Open), in Montgomery County, Maryland, where he finished in a tie for fourth. In 1995, as the victor at the Northern Telecom Open in Tucson, Mickelson accomplished perhaps the most impressive feat of his career: he became the first player in PGA Tour history to win the same tournament both as a professional and as an amateur. He also made his strongest appearances in two of that year's four majors, finishing in a tie for seventh at the Masters tournament in Augusta, Georgia, in April and in a tie for fourth at the U.S. Open in June at the Shinnecock Hills Golf Course, in Southampton, New York. These outings earned Mickelson a place on the U.S. Ryder Cup team, which competes in a biennial event pitting the best American golfers against the best Europeans. The U.S. team lost to the Europeans that year; Mickelson himself did well, going undefeated in three matches. He ended the year in the 28th spot on the PGA Tour money list.

The year 1996 witnessed the much-anticipated arrival of Tiger Woods on the PGA Tour. The media hype that surrounded Woods's professional debut put some pressure on Mickelson, whose successes, although significant, fell short of the expectations others had had for him at the beginning of his career. Confronted by Woods's entrance on the scene, he played better than ever—perhaps because, as Larry Dorman noted in the *New York Times* (January 17, 1996), "he is the type of player who needs a challenge." After winning his third Northern Telecom Open, Mickelson took the top prizes at three other events: the Phoenix Open, the GTE Byron Nelson Classic, and the NEC World Series of Golf. His performances led the California Golf Writers Association to name Mickelson Player of the Year. (Woods came in a close second in the voting.) Mickelson also earned $1,697,799 by virtue of his eight top-10 finishes. His winnings were second only to the total earned by Tom Lehman, who eclipsed Mickelson by $80,000.

The next season, while Woods was stealing the spotlight, Mickelson won the Bay Hill Invitational in Orlando, Florida, and the Sprint International, held in Castle Rock, Colorado. He earned a total of $1,225,390 in 1997, and with his two victories, which brought his career total to 11, he became the youngest player since Jack Nicklaus to win more than 10 tournaments on the PGA Tour. But Mickelson, now a four-year veteran, began to be faulted for his poor performances in major championships, especially in light of Woods's triumph at the Masters in his second season as a professional. Mickelson responded to the criticism by concentrating on his game. He won another two tournaments in 1998 and earned an additional

$1,837,246, a career high. His $6.96 million total winnings raised him to 17th on the PGA Tour career-earnings list. He also became the only player to have at least one win in six consecutive years.

Winless since February 1998, Mickelson entered the final day of the 1999 U.S. Open in a tie for the lead with Payne Stewart. Competing at the historic Number Two Course in Pinehurst, North Carolina, the two golfers battled each other throughout the day. Leading Mickelson by a single stroke, Stewart needed to sink a winding 15-foot putt at the final hole to avoid a tie with his opponent, which would have led to a play-off the next day. Stewart succeeded in draining his putt, yet again denying Mickelson his claim to a major title. The media, meanwhile, had been focusing on something else: Mickelson's wife, Amy, was pregnant and due to go into labor at any moment. Before the tournament began, Mickelson had vowed to leave the course to be with his wife if labor started. He had even hired a Hawker 700 airplane to rush him home, and his caddy, Jim "Bones" Mackay, carried a beeper to enable Amy to call Mickelson. In an unsigned article in *People* (July 12, 1999), Mickelson was quoted as saying, "There's going to be a U.S. Open every year. The birth of my child was an experience that I will cherish for the rest of my life." After his loss to Stewart, Mickelson flew home on his rented plane, and about nine hours later, at about the time the play-off would have begun had Stewart missed his putt, the Mickelsons' daughter was born. In October 1999 Payne Stewart died in a plane crash; a few days later Mickelson told Clifton Brown for the *New York Times* (October 31, 1999), "It's hard for me to believe I'm saying this, but I'm glad Payne won that tournament now. I never expected that I would feel that way, because at the time, it was a tough tournament for me to lose. But I anticipate having many chances to win major championships, and as it turned out, it was Payne's last chance. I believe things happen for a reason." Mickelson earned over $1.7 million in prize money in 1999, but he did not win a tournament that season, marking his first full year on the PGA Tour without at least one victory.

As the 1999 season drew to a close and the next one began, Tiger Woods seemed to be unstoppable. He had accumulated victories in six tournaments in a row before he entered the Buick Invitational in February 2000. The contest was held on the Torrey Pines Golf Course. Going into the final round, Mickelson led Woods by six strokes. Woods then fired a four-under-par 68 to cut Mickelson's lead to two strokes. But Mickelson held his course, shooting a final round 70 and eclipsing Woods by four strokes. Later in 2000, at the Tour Championship, in Atlanta, Georgia, Mickelson ended another of Woods's winning streaks (this one extending for 19 games): Woods entered the last round with a one-stroke lead over Mickelson, whereupon Mickelson fired a barrage of birdies en route to a final-round four-under-par 66. Woods's score stood at 69, and Mickelson took the title by two strokes. The win was Mickelson's fourth of the year, equaling his career best. (Earlier, he had won the MasterCard Colonial and the BellSouth Classic.) Mickelson finished the year 2000 with $4,746,457 in winnings, the second-biggest annual total in golf; the record was set that year by Woods, whose total came to $9.1 million. (Woods's nine wins included three majors.)

In 2001 Mickelson captured a record third Buick Invitational as well as the Greater Hartford Open. But he failed for the ninth straight season to capture a major championship. As Vartan Kupelian pointed out in the *Detroit News* (July 17, 2001, online), Mickelson had "won 19 times on the PGA Tour. He's won the Greater Hartfords and the Bay Hills and the Buick Invitationals. But no Masters or U.S. Opens, or PGA Championships. In that sense, his career has been defined: He's a terrific player, maybe the second-best of his era." "What I need to do really is to come through in a major championship, and I realize that," Mickelson acknowledged to Kupelian. "I have been working hard towards that. I know I did not win the Masters and U.S. Open where I had good opportunities. But instead of seeing that as failure and not winning, I see it as success. Last year I didn't even have those chances, and for me to improve enough to get to a level where I have a great opportunity to win, I see that as a significant accomplishment."

In his first appearance of the 2002 season, at the Bob Hope Chrysler Classic, Mickelson shot an impressive 66 in the final round to win the event. The victory was the 20th of his PGA career, a milestone that assured him lifetime membership on the PGA tour. Mickelson also triumphed at the Canon Greater Hartford Open; with that, his 21st career PGA win, he moved into a tie for 25th on the all-time PGA Tour victories list. Again coming tantalizingly close to winning a major tournament, Mickelson finished third at the 2002 Masters Tournament and second to Woods at the 2002 U.S. Open, thus gaining seven top-three finishes in 40 major-championship appearances.

Mickelson told Fran Blineberry for the *Houston Chronicle* (April 6, 2001), "I think the next 10 years, what I do, how I play, the things that I accomplish will ultimately decide how I'm looked at as a player generations from now. So these 10 years are important, because I want to be viewed in a certain light. I want to be a guy who has won majors, not the one who never could. . . . I don't feel it's that far away." Mickelson has acknowledged the crucial role of his caddy, Jim "Bones" Mackay, in his career. According to Mickelson, Mackay, who has worked with him since he turned professional, is "one of those guys that, under the gun, when it's a critical time, he thinks his clearest," as he put it to David Noonan for *Newsweek* (July 16, 2001).

The six-foot two-inch, 190-pound Mickelson, whose career earnings total almost $22 million, has secured tens of millions of dollars' worth of endorsement contracts. Currently, he has corporate affiliations with Titleist, which manufactures golf equipment and accessories; Hugo Boss golf apparel; KPMG Consulting, which advises businesses; Grayhawk, a real-estate developer; and *Golf Digest*. His own company, the Mickelson Group, manufactures the Sportscope, a periscope that enables a spectator surrounded by crowds at a golf tournament to see the action on the putting green. Mickelson, who owns a jet plane, lives in a mansion in Scottsdale, Arizona, with his wife, Amy, and their daughter, Amanda. — J.H.

Suggested Reading: *Detroit News* (on-line) July 17, 2001, with photo; *Golf Magazine* p82+ Apr. 1991, with photos, p76+ May 1997, with photos; *Golf Digest* p114 Jan. 2001, with photo; Houston Chronicle B p1 Apr. 6, 2001; (London) *Financial Times Weekend* II p8 June 20, 1992, with photo; *New York Times* B p13 June 19, 1992, with photo, B p17 Mar. 25, 1993, B p11 Jan. 17, 1996, with photo, VIII p14 Oct. 31, 1999, with photo; *Newsweek* p34+ July 16, 2001, with photo; *People* p52 July 12, 1999, with photos; *Sport* p82+ Oct. 1996, with photo; *Sports Illustrated* p12 Jan. 21, 1991, with photo, p40+ May 6, 1991, with photos, p58+ June 15, 1992, with photos, p48 Mar. 1, 1993, with photo, p40+ Aug. 27, 2001, with photo; *Washington Post* G p3 May 23, 2001, D p07 July 5, 2001

---

Courtesy of Dan Millman

## Millman, Dan

*Feb. 22, 1946– Writer; former champion gymnast*

*Address: c/o New World Library, 14 Pamaron Way, Novato, CA 94949*

Dan Millman, a former world-champion gymnast, has written a dozen books on spiritual living, which, all together, have been translated into more than 20 languages and have sold millions of copies. While not adhering to any particular religion, Millman has drawn lessons from the world's great faiths, written about them in language accessible to laypeople, and applied them to such practical matters as the management of finances and to other areas that include human sexuality. "I've found that the basic spiritual truths are simple and easy to know," Millman told Tony Cecala for *Holistic Networker* (on-line). "However, the trick is turning what we know into what we DO. When we apply our knowledge, we turn it into wisdom. Reading about spiritual concepts is not enough to change a person, taking the concepts and applying them brings about true change in our lives." Over two decades after it first came out, *Way of the Peaceful Warrior* (1980), perhaps his best-known book, is still widely read among high-school and college students as an introduction to spiritual thought and enlightenment. Millman has spawned a thriving cottage industry: in addition to his books, he offers more than 30 audiotapes, a videotape, a popular seminar, literary coaching, personal consultations, and spiritually based vacation retreats.

One of the two children of Herman and Vivian Millman, Dan Millman was born on February 22, 1946 in Los Angeles, California. The grandchild of Russian Jews, Millman grew up in a nonreligious household. As a child he enjoyed the outdoors and various athletic activities. One day at the age of six, he recalled to Cathleen Hodgson and Steve Sanchez for the Arcana Celestia Spiritual Rights Foundation Web site, he jumped off a roof onto a pile of sand, after one of his friends, having grown impatient as Millman stood undecided at the roof's edge, yelled to him, "Stop thinking and jump." "That's what I have done my whole life since then," Millman said to Hodgson and Sanchez.

Millman attended accelerated classes in a Los Angeles elementary school. When he was about 10 years old, he discovered an old trampoline at summer day camp and began practicing on it. After he entered the Thomas Starr King Junior High School, he joined a tumbling and trampoline club started by his homeroom teacher; he later continued his trampoline training at a facility in Burbank, California. "When I discovered the trampoline," Millman wrote in an essay submitted to *Current Biography*, "it was like I had found my tool, my special path—like I was really born in a new way." Millman, who has described himself at that time as an introverted loner, attended John Marshall High School, also in Los Angeles, where his coaches soon noticed his great gymnastic potential. He won the Los Angeles City tumbling championship, and his high school came in fourth in the competition—with Millman as the only competitor from his school. The summer after his junior year in high school, Millman won the United States Gymnastics Federation (USGF) Championship. He was named senior athlete of the year during his final year in high school.

Millman attended the University of California at Berkeley on a gymnastics scholarship. As a freshman, in 1964, he won the first World Trampoline Championship, in London, England. He went on to become a three-time All American, a National Collegiate Athletic Association (NCAA) vaulting champion, and USGF National Floor Exercise champion. In 1966 he participated in the Maccabiah Games, in Israel. That same year, as a potential Olympian, he was invited to observe the World Games, in Lubiana, Yugoslavia. At the beginning of his senior year—shortly before his scheduled departure for Lubiana—Millman shattered his right femur in a motorcycle accident. His doctor told him it was unlikely that he would ever be able to return to gymnastics.

Around this time Millman met an elderly man at a Texaco station in Berkeley at 3:00 a.m. The man became the basis for the character named Socrates in *Way of the Peaceful Warrior*, published over a decade later. As quoted in an excerpt of the book published on the Amazon Booksellers Web site, the man told Millman, "You must cleanse your body of tension, free your mind of stagnant knowledge, and open your heart to the energy of true emotion." The man told Millman that his belief in academics, athletics, and achievement was misplaced and urged him to develop better spiritual awareness. With this new outlook Millman successfully underwent arduous physical rehabilitation and returned to his college gymnastics team as co-captain, leading his teammates to their first NCAA Gymnastics Championships. In 1968 he won the Gimbel Award for top student athlete and was also selected by Berkeley as senior athlete of the year. That same year he graduated with a B.A. degree in psychology.

Millman had married during his senior year at Berkeley. He and his wife, Linda, soon became expectant parents and needed more income, so he decided not to try out for the 1968 Olympic team. Later that year he was appointed director of gymnastics at Stanford University, in California. Over the next four years, he transformed the school's losing gymnastics team into winners at the highly competitive Pacific-8 Conference. At the peak of his success, he retired. "I stopped coaching when I realized I was admiring the other team as much as my own athletes," he told Simon Hunt for *Spiritual Endeavors* (on-line). "I didn't care who won. I cared if everybody played a good game and did their best. . . . I treated opposing athletes not as the enemy, but as potential teachers. So I decided it wasn't really appropriate for me anymore."

In 1972 the Millman family moved to Oberlin, Ohio, where Millman became an assistant professor of physical education at Oberlin College. "No matter what I learned, no matter what I gained [through gymnastics], it only benefitted one person, and I was aware I was going to take that one person to the worms one day," Millman told Steve McCardell for the *New Times* (September 2000). "But I wanted to make a difference, and I felt if I could teach *other* people, they might share with other people, and I could have a bigger positive impact." At Oberlin he taught several cutting-edge courses, including East/West Concepts of Physical Education, Mirthful Movement (a circus course), and Way of the Peaceful Warrior—a type of martial art expanded to encompass a way of life. During his tenure at Oberlin, having won a grant, Millman studied yoga, martial arts, and meditative techniques in other parts of the world. He also completed a 40-day period of training at the Arica Institute, founded by the controversial Bolivian scientist and mystic Oscar Ichazo.

In 1975 Millman and his family returned to California. His marriage had suffered stress since Millman had begun focusing on the spiritual side of his life, and he and Linda divorced later that year. Before long a woman named Joy, whom he had met at Oberlin, moved to California to be with him. The two married in 1976. Millman held a series of jobs over the next few years. By the time he was appointed women's gymnastics coach at the University of California at Berkeley, in 1978, he had begun to write. "I started my writing career with articles about natural principles of training for a gymnastics magazine," he told Simon Hunt. "Later, these principles expanded to the broader arena of skill training, including other sports, such as dance, martial arts, and music." After the Millmans returned to Oberlin College, to serve as residence-hall directors, Millman published his first book, *The Inner Athlete* (1979); two decades later his updated edition came out under the title *Body Mind Mastery: Creating Success in Sports and Life.*

In 1980 Millman published his second, and arguably best-known, book, *Way of the Peaceful Warrior: A Basically True Story.* A fictionalized account of his life after he shattered his femur, it focuses on the life-changing experiences Millman underwent because of Socrates, a teacher based on the man he had met at a Berkeley gas station years before. The subtitle of the book caused some confusion as to whether the volume was fiction or nonfiction, so it was later reworded as *A Book That Changes Lives.* On his Web site Millman wrote, "Socrates became a means to convey what I had learned from a number of different mentors and experiences in my life, both external and internal." He added that he sometimes told people, "Socrates is real; Dan Millman is a fictional character." Many readers were impressed by Millman's descriptions of Socrates' superhuman feats, such as jumping from the ground to a high rooftop, but Millman has denied that such exploits ever took place. "Some people are very disappointed to learn that it's not all factual," he told Simon Hunt, "because they are so strongly hoping for 'magic' in the world that contrasts with what appears to be a mundane existence."

In his third book, *Sacred Journey of the Peaceful Warrior* (1991), which is entirely fictional, Millman meets Mama Chia, a Hawaiian shamanistic healer who takes him to the island of Molokia, where she introduces him to the so-called path of service. "I constructed *Sacred Journey* almost entirely out of my creative imagination," Millman wrote for his Web site. "Mama Chia is a composite of various women I've known. I wrote this book to provide . . . higher models of our human and spiritual evolution that explain much about the inner workings of the human being." A writer for the *New Age Journal*, as quoted on *Amazon.com*, called the book "entrancing," "decidedly down-to-earth," and "a fun, enjoyable read sure to inspire you in your own endeavors." In 1991 Millman also published a children's book, *Secret of the Peaceful Warrior: A Story about Courage and Love*. The story is about a boy named Danny who, with the help of an old man whom he first dreams about and then actually meets, finds the courage and love that enable him to deal with a neighborhood bully.

Millman followed in 1992 with another children's book, *Quest for the Crystal Castle: A Peaceful Warrior Children's Book*, about a boy who travels with a magical teacher into another world. There, he learns through his quest for a crystal castle that it is the quest itself, not the object being sought, that is important. That same year Millman published *No Ordinary Moments: A Peaceful Warrior's Guide to Daily Life*. Next came *The Life You Were Born to Live: A Guide to Finding Your Life Purpose* (1993), in which Millman unveiled his "Life Purpose System," a numerological guide to living well. In *Laws of Spirit: Simple, Powerful Truths for Making Life Work* (1995), Millman described a fictionalized meeting with a mystical mountain sage as a way of introducing 12 principles that, in his view, can help people live happier and more fulfilling lives. Among the principles are what he called the laws of balance, choices, process, and compassion.

Millman's *Everyday Enlightenment: The Twelve Gateways to Personal Growth* (1998) was favorably reviewed in several New Age periodicals. A critic for *Publishers Weekly* (March 2, 1998), by contrast, described it as "exuberantly optimistic, if simplistic" and wrote, "Claiming that 'you don't have to think or feel enlightened. You only have to behave that way,' [Millman] all but ignores important psychological, philosophical and political issues, encouraging addicts to 'just stop,' for example, without recommending that they enter a treatment program."

*Divine Interventions: True Stories of Mystery and Miracles that Change Lives* (1999), which Millman wrote with Doug Childers, consists of tales of ordinary people's reported encounters with the divine. The volume also includes brief sections on the 15th-century French heroine Joan of Arc, the pioneering Swiss psychologist Carl Jung, and a founder of Alcoholics Anonymous. Millman next published *Living on Purpose: Straight Answers to Life's Tough Questions* (2000), in which he sought to answer common questions about the meaning of life, death, and the "right" spiritual path. "To me," Millman told Steve McCardell, "life is questions and answers; the whole history of humanity has involved problems and solutions. Rather than just in some idealistic philosophical way, I get down to 'What can we actually do?' 'How does life work?'"

Millman lives in Marin County, in northern California, with his second wife and the two children from their marriage. He has one child from his first marriage. He is currently working on a novel, tentatively titled "The Journal of Socrates." In his leisure time Millman enjoys bike riding, trampoline training, practicing various martial arts, and hiking. On his Web site Millman noted, "Anyone who observed my day-to-day life would likely find qualities that reflect an expanded perspective of life. I sincerely practice what I teach, and believe I serve as a good example of a life well lived. I can claim no more, and do no less than this." — G.O.

Suggested Reading: Dan Millman's Web site; *New Times* (on-line) Sep. 2000; *Philadelphia Inquirer* (on-line) Nov. 10, 1999; *San Francisco Chronicle* p2 Aug. 30, 1992; *Spiritual Endeavors* (on-line); Millman, Dan. *Way of the Peaceful Warrior: A Book That Changes Lives*, 1984

Selected Books: *The Inner Athlete*, 1979; *Way of the Peaceful Warrior*, 1980; *Sacred Journey of the Peaceful Warrior*, 1991; *Secret of the Peaceful Warrior: A Story about Courage and Love*, 1991; *Quest for the Crystal Castle: A Peaceful Warrior Children's Book*, 1992; *No Ordinary Moments: A Peaceful Warrior's Guide to Daily Life*, 1992; *The Life You Were Born to Live: A Guide to Finding Your Life Purpose*, 1993; *Laws of Spirit: Simple, Powerful Truths for Making Life Work*, 1995; *Everyday Enlightenment: The Twelve Gateways to Personal Growth*, 1998; *Divine Interventions: True Stories of Mystery and Miracles that Change Lives* (with Doug Childers), 1999; *Living on Purpose: Straight Answers to Life's Tough Questions*, 2000

Carlos Llano/Courtesy of Silver Wave Records

## Mirabal, Robert

*Oct. 6, 1966– Flutist; percussionist; singer; songwriter*

*Address: c/o Silver Wave Records, P.O. Box 7943, Boulder, CO 80306*

In a style that he has dubbed "Alter-Native," the multitalented instrumentalist, singer, and songwriter Robert Mirabal has fused the sounds and rhythms of traditional Native American music—particularly those of his own tribe, the Pueblo—with elements of jazz, rock, hip-hop, techno, and other relatively recent musical genres. "I'm very much a part of two different worlds," Mirabal has said, as quoted on *Imusic* (on-line). "There is the Native culture that's my heritage, and the rock & roll culture I grew up with. I can separate the two, of course, but they're both part of who I am, so one goal of my music is to express that combination." Mirabal has mastered both the playing and the making of the Native American flute and is accomplished on percussion and the Australian didgeridoo, among other instruments. He has incorporated stories in many of his songs, because, as he explained in an interview quoted on *Imusic* (on-line), "if you can do that, people will listen from beginning to end. They'll be interested in who you are and where you come from. It could be a hunter's dream, or a man running up the hill or whatever." "Then," he continued, "you've got this basic rhythm that comes from the heartbeat, your stomp, and you speed it up or slow it down, add to it, make it fit the story. With all of that put together, I bring you in and give you a peek at my world—like if you came in and had a bowl of chili with me. You don't have to understand my politics or my religion. You're just listening to my stories, and it so happens that with the color of my skin and the part of America I come from, this is what my stories are like." Describing his development as a musician for the Janson Television Web site, Mirabal said, "My evolution has come from the Pueblo to Japanese Butoh dancers, to cowboy poets, Hawaiian chants, Australian Aborigines, and more—so much more. The world I live in has been full of dancers, geniuses, storytellers, sorcerers, and kisses—and I have had an appetite for them all."

Robert Mirabal was born on October 6, 1966 in Taos Pueblo, in northeastern New Mexico, a Native American community that the Pueblo Indians believe has existed for about a thousand years. (The habitations and ceremonial centers have collectively been designated a UNESCO World Heritage Site.) The residents, who number about 4,500, rely on tourism for most of their income. Mirabal "didn't have much connection" with his father, as he revealed on his Web site; rather, his primary caretakers during his early years were his maternal grandparents and his mother. He remembers other women, too, as being prominent in his life. "When you grow up in a very traditional society you are raised by people that are involved in that society for generations and generations and so when a child is born you teach it the language and teach it the songs and you teach it rhythm and you teach it stomp,. . . you know, to the Earth," Mirabal told Peggy Randall for the *Alternative Press* (on-line). "So I was raised in a community of dancers and singers, painters, drum makers, all these different people." Mirabal was also influenced by the Western music his mother often listened to and by musicians who performed in Taos Pueblo, among them the blues guitarist and singer B.B. King, a bagpiper from Scotland, and a Flamenco dancer from Spain. Mirabal told Randall, "My mom was a Country music fan and she turned me onto Don Williams and just the way he approached music in such a simple way that it hit me and I really got involved with [the rock musician John] Mellencamp, they both [told] stories about the common man." He attended a government school in Taos Pueblo. According to Mirabal, his music teacher at the school could play some 40 instruments, and "every year, I'd learn a different instrument," as he told Mark Holan, as quoted on Mirabal's Web site. "Clarinet and saxophone first, but I eventually ended up on drums." During his student years he also helped care for his grandparents.

When Mirabal was 18 a man who belonged to the same Native American association as his grandfather donated a traditional Native American flute for use at a ceremony. "For some reason I really wanted that flute," Mirabal has recalled, according to his official Web site. He proceeded to learn how to play the instrument. "The New Age thing was getting big back then, and as soon as I began playing, people would ask me to perform," he wrote for his Web site. "They say the flute chooses you, and it certainly has changed my life—since then, I've spent most of my time traveling and playing music." Within a year Mirabal had started to make his own flutes. (Handmade of wood and often embellished with carved designs, the traditional Native American flute is used in ceremonies as well as for entertainment. The instrument is of a type known as the block flute, which is played like a recorder rather than like a transverse flute. Some of Mirabal's flutes have been displayed at the Smithsonian Institution, in Washington, D.C.) With money borrowed from his grandmother, he recorded his self-titled debut album at a local studio. Available only on cassette, it was released in 1988. While *Robert Mirabal* is more traditional than much of his later work, it includes experimental blends of elements of jazz (in the manner of such masters as Miles Davis, Charlie Parker, and Thelonious Monk) and Native American flute music. "I've mostly been influenced by jazz mostly because it's so obscure," Mirabal said to Peggy Randall. "My native language and culture has always been considered obscure, so it's obvious that I would choose a genre that would be considered very obscure." The material from Mirabal's debut and from others among his cassette-only releases was later remixed for his albums *Song Carrier* (1995) and *Warrior Magician* (1996). In the *New York Times* (November 7, 1991), Anna Kisselgoff referred to Mirabal's "exquisitely nuanced flute playing . . . [and] captivating birdlike melodies."

For a few years after the release of his debut album, Mirabal toured frequently and sold thousands of his cassettes. "I had no clue what was going to happen with all of it," he said, as quoted on *Imusic* (on-line), "but after a while I realized how valuable the flute was for me. That piece of wood gave me a life, a way to survive. And it gave me a way to communicate." In 1990 the Japanese modern dancers Eiko and Koma performed at Taos Pueblo and commissioned Mirabal to write and perform a score for a dance piece they created, having gained inspiration from what they experienced in the Pueblo community. In 1992 Mirabal won a Dance Theater Workshop Dance and Performance Award, known as a Bessie Award, for the music he contributed to the dance piece, which was titled *Land.* Mirabal thus became the first—and so far only—Native American to earn that accolade. At the Bessie Awards ceremony, held in the Delacorte Theater in New York City's Central Park, the singers Sekou Sundiata and Pura Fe performed to Mirabal's flute accompaniment in what Jack Anderson, writing for the *New York Times* (September 11, 1992), described as "a ritual of chanting and . . . music in memory of members of the dance world who had died in the last year."

During this period Mirabal expanded his knowledge of world and rock music by playing with the band Kraze Kunoe Tribesmen, which was popular in New York City. In addition to Mirabal, the group featured an Australian digeridoo player, a Jamaican keyboardist, and an instrumentalist from Barbados. "It was all these tribal rhythms," Mirabal told Peggy Randall. "It was kind of like dance music. We were really ahead of our times. So that's where I picked up how to use my language in the four-four pattern—how to accommodate how I feel in dance rhythms and basic Western rhythmic tracks.

A collection of poetry, prose, and short stories that Mirabal recalled from his childhood was published under the title *A Skeleton of a Bridge* in 1994. At about the same time, he signed a contract with Warner Bros., which released his album *Land* in 1995. *Land*, Stephen E. McDonald wrote for *All Music Guide* (on-line), is "worth finding just for the sheer sonic force Mirabal creates here." The disk, which focuses on vocals and percussion rather than flute, was recorded with the drummer Reynaldo Lujan, a cousin and frequent collaborator of Mirabal's. The following year Mirabal played flute and contributed vocals to the Native American singer-songwriter Bill Miller's album *Native Suite—Chants, Dances, and the Remembered Earth.* Next came *Mirabal* (1997), an album that combined Native American rhythms with rock. The songs include "Witch Hunt," in which Mirabal meditated on social evolution, and "Hope," which considers spiritual quests as difficult but rewarding journeys. The song "Tony & Allison" earned praise from various critics, including one who wrote for *Imusic* (on-line), "The stark, brooding piece is almost novelistic in depth. Like good fiction puts the reader in the scene, the song immediately makes the listener eyewitness to head-on collisions between good and evil . . . , the ritualistic past and a relentlessly violent present." "I wanted to make an album that explored all of the things people experience," Mirabal said, according to his official Web site, "love, hate, fear, confusion, and especially the loneliness that seems to be so pervasive in modern society. And I wanted it to have a rock'n'roll edge."

In 1999 Mirabal released *Taos Tales*, which struck Paige La Grone, writing for *Amazon.com*, as a work that "aurally gives form, function, and sacred breath to the commanding vision and essence of the magnificent Taos Valley. Flute, strings, and keyboard reflect the wide blue sky stretching over the high road into the town below. Percussion and samples capture the essence of the wind's spirit as it sculpts and buffets the rain-splashed earth." *Taos Tales* joins Native American chants and rhythms with music for cello and guitar, among other innovative touches. In an interview for *Amazon.com*, Mirabal called the album "reservation chamber music." On several tracks, Mirabal tells stories; others contain songs, among them "Onate," about Juan de Onate, a Spanish conqueror whose actions caused the deaths of many people from the Pueblo and other tribes four centuries ago, and "Quiet Season," about the time during the winter when the Pueblo forgo the use of cars and avoid making loud noises. *Taos Tales* did well on New Age voice charts; *Amazon.com* named Mirabal the 2000 New Age Artist of the Year. Earlier, in 1999,

Mirabal performed on a nationwide tour as a flutist and percussionist in the theater piece *Spirit: A Journey in Dance, Drum, and Song*, conceived by Peter Buffett, who also wrote the music. The work, which earned critical praise, concerns a modern-day everyman who rejects what he views as the excessive automation of contemporary life and embarks on a journey into the spirit world. "The way I approach collaborations is that I really consume them as my own also," Mirabal told *Borders.com*, according to Mirabal's Web site. "And so, when I do take them on, they become my children too."

Mirabal made his next album, *Music from a Painted Cave* (2001), with his band and dance group, Rare Tribal Mob. The title refers to multimedia concerts in which, through special lighting, Mirabal created the impression that the performance was taking place in a cave. The music on the album was culled from those concerts and ranged from traditional Native American and world music to pieces featuring synthesizers and modern electronic beats. On the Web site of Janson Television, Mirabal was quoted as saying that *Music from a Painted Cave* "is based on all the endeavors that I have chosen to do on stage. An evolution is the best word I can use to describe it. . . . *Music from a Painted Cave* is an evolutionary vision of one man, from birth, breath, through the metamorphosis of time."

Mirabal has won four Native American Music Awards (known informally as the Nammies), which are sponsored by the Native American Music Association: songwriter of the year (2000 and 2001), artist of the year (2001), and record of the year (2001) for *Music from a Painted Cave*. He has appeared on TV in two PBS specials—*Music from a Painted Cave* and *Spirit* (the Peter Buffett work). Mirabal has received a National Endowment for the Arts award and Meet the Composer grants (awarded by the New York State Council on the Arts). A New York Japanese Foundation fellowship enabled him to study with the Japanese High Court musicians for two years.

Mirabal, who rarely discusses political issues in public, told Peggy Randall, "One thing I get sad about is how come [Native American musicians] don't have a section in the Grammys? It's like we are still pushed into the ancient times. I speak my language. I sing the ancient songs so that means they're not ancient, they are not of the past. I sing them today and they are contemporary. . . . I believe everybody keeps putting Native people into the past."

Mirabal lives in Taos Pueblo with his wife, Dawn, and their daughter, Aspen. Speaking of his wife, Mirabal told an interviewer for *Ladyfire* (on-line), "As I got older I realized how unique the culture that we have here at the pueblo was. It became apparent for me when I went out in the world. I needed somebody to take on the road to live with and to also come home with to experience and explore the traditional side of who I am. Both worlds were lonely at one time but now it's becoming pretty fun, I've realized I've found somebody that I can live in both of those worlds with. I can understand her conflicts without saying anything and she can understand my conflicts." As an artist-in-residence at Dartmouth College, in Hanover, New Hampshire, and as a lecturer at Colorado College, in Colorado Springs, Mirabal has taught courses in ecology, multiculturalism, and Native American traditions. — G.O.

Suggested Reading: *Alternate Music Press* (on-line), with photo; *Amazon.com*; *Borders.com*; *Imusic* (on-line), with photo; *Ladyfire* (on-line), with photos; Mirabal Web site

Selected Recordings: *Land*, 1995; *Song Carrier*, 1995; *Warrior Magician*, 1996; *Mirabal*, 1997; *Taos Tales*, 1999; *Music from a Painted Cave*, 2001

Selected Books: *A Skeleton of a Bridge*, 1994

Courtesy of Bryant Galleries

## Mitchell, Dean

*1957– Artist*

*Address: 11918 England, Overland Park, KS 66213*

"Dean Mitchell's paintings are all about dignity," Marilynne S. Mason observed in the *Christian Science Monitor* (April 12, 1993), referring to the noted African-American artist. "His portraits shimmer with it. Even his landscapes capture nature in its quiet composure—no grandeur, just simple dignity and grace in its light and air, trees and water. In his street scenes, just as in his portraits, Mitchell honors the common men and women (most of them African-American) who have achieved or maintained dignity, despite whatever difficulties they have encountered in poverty or social censure." Working primarily in watercolor, oil, and acrylic paints, Mitchell has been compared to some of the greatest portrait artists in history, among them the 17th-century Dutch painter Vermeer, especially for his depictions of African-Americans in moments of quiet strength. In sensitive, frank images of people of different ages and races and from different walks of life, he has explored subjects as diverse as death, familial connections, and inner-city life, and, in doing so, has brought out the spiritual meaning in ordinary moments of existence. "I have inherited a passion for the simple things of life," he was quoted as saying on the Web site of Hearne Fine Art. "In this we retain the essence of time and the true meaning of life." "I think art should reflect the inner energy that created it," Mitchell wrote for *International Artist* (December/January 2000). "So as an artist, I have to paint from the heart, to paint what I love. When I do, it's as if a God-like light illuminates the work, which only increases my passion for making art."

Dean Mitchell was born in Pittsburgh, Pennsylvania, in 1957. When he was 11 months old, his family moved to the town of Quincy, Florida, which at that time had a population of 6,000. There, while his mother attended college, Mitchell was raised primarily by his maternal grandmother, Marie Mitchell, in an all-black neighborhood; along with his mother, they shared a small, concrete-block house with Mitchell's uncle and his cousin Carolyn, who became something of an older sister to him. Mitchell's father often visited the boy's paternal grandparents, one street away from where Mitchell lived in Quincy, but until recently Mitchell and his father had never met. "When I would hear he was in town, I would go over there and just watch him through the bushes, but I never approached him," he told John Ferri for the *Tampa Tribune* (May 29, 1997). Mitchell also told Ferri that he recalls growing up with a sense of abandonment. His grandmother told him that when he first came to live with her, he would often rock back and forth; he now believes that this movement was his way of comforting himself in the absence of sufficient physical contact with others. "I don't think that will ever go away," he told Ferri. "I like telling the story, and if someone can find inspiration in that, then great. Maybe part of my being an artist is not so much about the art as being an inspiration." Mitchell has often referred to his grandmother, who supported her family with a small welfare paycheck and the $15 a week she earned as a cook, as one of the primary inspirations for his work. "My grandmother had great dignity," Mitchell told Mason, adding that she "gave me a sense of self-worth and a strong foundation." Through his grandmother Mitchell learned a great deal about the importance of accepting, and having confidence in, oneself. "I always considered my grandmother a wise woman," he told Mason. "I watched her work for rich people in Florida. She never complained. . . . I thought even though my mom had a college education, my grandmother had a lot more foresight in terms of having you dream and believing in what you could do."

Mitchell—who by his own account was an introverted child—was fascinated by cartoons when he was very young. At the age of five, he was given a paint-by-number set; after completing the first picture according to the directions in the kit, he painted the next one the way he wanted. When Mitchell was 12, his family moved to Philadelphia, Pennsylvania. Over the next three years, he became seriously interested in art. He responded to an ad in a magazine for a correspondence course available through the Famous Artists School, but after learning of the prohibitive cost of the course, he decided to work on his own. He bought his first set of oil paints at the age of 12, and for inspiration he began studying Norman Rockwell's famous cover art for the *Saturday Evening Post* magazine. Most members of his family discouraged his artistic pursuits. As Mitchell recalled to Tim Janicke for the *Kansas City Star* (March 3, 2002), his aunt once said of him, "That boy is going to wind up on the street. Black people don't buy pictures." For his first commission, for which he was paid $10, Mitchell painted murals in a child's bedroom. Before Mitchell started ninth grade, his family moved back to Quincy. There, to pay for art supplies, he found work shaking pecans from trees and picking beans, among other jobs. At one point when he was in junior high school, he was ready to quit painting, but a talk with his art teacher, Tom Harris, changed his mind. As Mitchell recalled to Dottie Indyke for *Southwest Art* (May 2002), "We were sitting outside on a bench and [Harris] said, 'You have a keen eye for composition and an abstract way of seeing things. Technique can be taught but not a way of seeing.'" Harris encouraged his gifted students to enter art shows and took them to art fairs where they would compete for prizes. In the first competition that he entered, Mitchell won two awards.

In 1975 Mitchell enrolled at the Columbus College of Art and Design, in Columbus, Ohio, where he began to paint in watercolor. He paid for his schooling through grants, scholarships, and, eventually, sales of his paintings. Finding himself far behind students who had been able to afford earlier training in art and to travel to the museums and galleries of Europe, Mitchell, by his own estimation, worked three to four times the number of hours that his professors required. In the summer after his freshman year, Mitchell worked in Quincy, both in a cannery and in nearby tobacco fields. During his sophomore year his artwork began to win awards, much to his relief. "I studied hard," Mitchell told Janicke. "But I was in tears. I thought I was not going to make it in that school." On the strength of the publicity surrounding the prize he won at an art show in Panama City, Mitchell was hired to teach art at a Boys and Girls Club in that city. Through the show he also met JoAnn Dickerson, who introduced him to many Florida gallery owners. Mitchell sold his work—for about $20 per painting—to a couple of them. After he graduated from Columbus College, in 1980, with a bachelor's degree in fine art, Mitchell moved to Kansas City, Kansas, where he supported himself for several years by painting pictures for Hallmark greeting cards while continuing to work on his own art.

A difficult few years followed for Mitchell. By November 1983 his relationship with Hallmark had grown strained; Mitchell was entering and winning many art contests, which, he has said, made his supervisor and several co-workers jealous. After other co-workers began to submit their work to art competitions, Mitchell was fired, because, he was told, he was not focusing on his Hallmark assignments. After applying for positions at several other companies, Mitchell was told by one interviewer that he would have to decide if he wanted to be a fine artist or an illustrator. Mitchell then decided not to interview anymore but to concentrate on his own art. At around the same time Mitchell was fired, his grandmother died and his marriage broke up under the financial strain that had resulted from his unemployment. Although he was distraught to the point of contemplating suicide during that period, Mitchell was ultimately able to channel his energy into his work. "I felt like my grandmother provided an opportunity for me," he told Ferri, "and how dare I let that go wasting energy on self-pity." To make ends meet, Mitchell worked as a freelance artist for other greeting-card companies as well as for Anheuser-Busch, the Olympics, and McDonald's. His art appeared in galleries, but he became frustrated at how little money he was earning from those shows. He thus began entering more contests, in which he won several cash prizes. He desperately needed money in those days, for, as he recalled to a writer for *Ingram's* (February 2002), "All I had was a box springs, a mattress, and my drawing table."

During this period of intensive work and soul-searching, Mitchell began to explore the theme that would inform much of his art for the next few decades: positive portrayals of African-Americans. "It's always been inside my soul to lift black people," he told Janicke. "My grandmother had a really strong moral fiber. The people I grew up around were hard-working, God-fearing people and they wanted the best for their kids. I wanted to portray that sort of dignity. Even though black people didn't have a lot of money or wealth they had this dignity." In 1990 Mitchell moved from Kansas City to Overland Park, Kansas. Over the next decade he slowly gained recognition for his depictions of ordinary people. Commenting on Mitchell's 1991 painting of a church usher, *Usher of Hope*, Robert W. Duffy wrote for the *St. Louis Post-Dispatch* (August 24, 1994), "[It] is more than a likeness, it is an exploration of a soul. It is not only the fact that the usher's eyes are windows through which a viewer can begin to understand the character of the man portrayed. But his character, his nobility is also communicated through his white gloved hands, which hold an alms basin that flashes like lightning in a painting that is overall an arrangement of tones of black and white, and brown. His grasp is strong but also sensitive. It is also, altogether, the definition of dignity." In another work, *Bright Gesture*, painted in 1992, an African-American woman wearing a yellow dress stands at a street corner, pondering which way to turn. "A simple decision about crossing the street can change the course of a life," Mitchell wrote for *International Artist*. "But this woman radiates that she's bright enough to make the right choices to survive." Another of Mitchell's paintings that has received acclaim is *Common Dignity* (1993), an inner-city street scene in which three people wait for a bus. Through the painting, Mitchell has said, he tried to tell Americans that there is nothing wrong with being ordinary. "My grandmother was a common woman," he told Mason. "We had very little money, but money does not define dignity. Some of the most wonderful people have been common and have changed the world. And you don't want to be complacent. I have worked and tried to make a better life for myself, and so can you, but there is nothing to feel ashamed about. A lot of times poor people think ill of themselves."

Best known for his portraits, Mitchell has also painted still-lifes, landscapes, and depictions of buildings. The sense of isolation and timelessness in his landscapes has reminded various critics of that found in many works by Edward Hopper. Some buildings Mitchell has painted, such as *Mr. Earnest's Pecan Shop* (1992), have personal meanings for him. He has also focused on buildings that exhibit the richness that comes with age. "I've liked those old buildings," Mitchell told Steve Penn for the *Kansas City Star* (May 8, 1997). "It has an appeal to me. I'm just attracted to older things." Mitchell treasures age in human subjects as well. "I like faces and objects that are worn," he wrote for *International Artist*, "that show the strength and endurance of their lives and that have a connection with humanity."

*The Art of Dean Mitchell: The Early Years*, a 100-page collection of the painter's watercolors, drawings, and oil paintings, was published in book form in 1999 by Mitchell himself. The artist paid $25,000 of the $60,000 cost of publishing from his own funds; he raised the balance through presales of the book (with each copy accompanied by a reproduction of one of his drawings). Although he had received offers from a couple of publishing companies to print the collection, Mitchell turned them down because of the creative restrictions involved. "A lot of black artists don't get offers from mainstream publishing companies because we're still a risk," Mitchell told Steve Penn. Referring to such African-American artists as Romare Bearden, who died before any book of his work was published, Mitchell told Penn, "I looked at prior history and I told myself, 'I'm not waiting until I'm 80 years old before I get a book out.'" In addition to dozens of Mitchell's often-praised portraits of African-Americans, the book includes a wide range of other subject matter, such as a still life of a propped-up wheelbarrow, several picturesque landscapes, and a portrait of a Scottish bagpiper. Remarking on Mitchell's ability to paint diverse subjects and moods, Robert W. Duffy wrote, "He celebrates the irrepressible joy of living that is manifest in the face of a clear-eyed man in a ball camp. He knows the rough, romantic beauty of the dock where the shrimping boat is tied up in a shining sea. He reveals the stark ochre beauty of Ozark winter in beautiful landscapes." Mitchell wrote for *International Artist*, "As a young artist, I found a style that was successful and I stuck with it so that my work would be recognized and accepted. But then I visited the Picasso museum in Spain, and I was blown away by the variety of work that he did. It was such an inspiration to me! Now, I'm exploring new ways of painting and new subjects, and people are responding in a very positive way. They appreciate that I'm growing and changing, and I'm having fun with it."

Mitchell has won more than 400 awards, including the grand prize from the prestigious Arts for the Parks 1999 Juried Exhibition for his painting *French Quarter Coachman*, which brought a cash award of $50,000, and the gold medal from the American Watercolor Society. He has been honored by the Florida legislature, which declared April 6 Dean Mitchell Day in Gadsden County. In 1995 the U.S. Postal Service commissioned him to paint portraits for stamps depicting the jazz legends Louis Armstrong, John Coltrane, Erroll Garner, Charles Mingus, Charlie Parker, and Coleman Hawkins.

Mitchell currently lives in Overland Park and paints in the basement of his condominium; he has expressed interest in moving to Florida, where he feels his work is better appreciated. Among Mitchell's favorite painters are Rembrandt, Leonardo da Vinci, Richard Diebenkorn, Franz Kline, and Robert Motherwell. Mitchell's work can be found in the permanent collections of several museums, among them the Nelson-Atkins Museum of Art, the St. Louis Museum, the Kemper Museum of Contemporary Art, the Margaret Harwell Art Museum, the Hubbard Museum, the Mississippi Museum of Art, and the Arkansas Art Center. Mitchell believes that his work displays the types of images of contemporary African-Americans that are not shown in most mainstream museums. "Most museums cater to the stereotypical view of minorities," he told Penn. "But I don't deal with slavery. My subjects are actual living people." Mitchell, who was awarded an honorary master's degree from Columbus College in 1994, is a member of the Miniature Artists of America (some of his paintings measure just a few inches on each side), Allied Artists of America, the National Society of Painters in Casein and Acrylic, Knickerbocker Artists, and the Santa Fe Watercolor Society, for which he served as president for one year. He collaborated with the noted poet Maya Angelou on a limited-edition printing of her poem on jazz, which includes etchings both designed by Mitchell and produced individually by him on a press. "My work is an avenue to bring a feeling of peace to people," Mitchell was quoted as saying on the Bay Art & Frame Web site. "Not just the people I paint, but also the people who identify with them. Never think of an individual as just a collection of features, or a landscape as just trees and grass. Look deeper for the essence, the inherent spirituality. My painting expresses who I am, as well as who my subject is, and explores the bond between us." — G.O.

Suggested Reading: *American Spectator* p72+ Apr. 2001, with photos; *Christian Science Monitor* p16+ Apr. 12, 1993, with photos; *International Artist* Dec./Jan 2000, with photos; *Kansas City Star* p8 May 8, 1997, Mar. 3, 2002, with photos; *SouthwestArt* May 2002, with photos; *St. Louis Post-Dispatch* p28 Aug. 24, 1995; *Tampa Tribune* Baylife p1 May 29, 1997

---

## Monk, T. S.

(munk)

*Dec. 27, 1949– Jazz drummer*

*Address: Thelonious Monk Institute of Jazz, 5225 Wisconsin Ave., N.W., Suite 605, Washington, DC 20015*

In the 1990s T. S. Monk, the son of the legendary jazz pianist Thelonious Monk, embarked on his own widely celebrated career as a jazz drummer and the leader of his own sextet. Playing new interpretations of tunes by hard-bop artists of the 1960s, Monk and his outfit have won praise for both their professionalism and their refusal to merely recreate other musicians' recordings. The sextet's 1997 album, *Monk on Monk*, drew accolades from much of the jazz press for its sensitive updating of Thelonious Monk's music. T. S. Monk, who started out as a funk artist, incorporated that style in his group's 1999 album, *Cross Talk*. Monk also heads the Thelonious Monk Institute of Jazz, which supports a variety of musical and educational endeavors.

Thelonious Sphere Monk III was born on December 27, 1949 in New York City. His father helped to revolutionize jazz in the mid-20th century; he was famed for his innovative, often dissonant playing style and for dozens of compositions that would become jazz standards. The home T. S. Monk shared with his father and mother, Nellie Monk, was the gathering place of a virtual roster of jazz legends, such as Art Blakey, John Coltrane, Miles Davis, Dizzy Gillespie, and Max Roach. While music was always present in T. S. Monk's life, his father never steered him toward a career as

Warren Mantooth

*T. S. Monk*

a jazz musician. "I had a very strong relationship with my father," Monk told Charles J. Gans for the Associated Press, as quoted in the western Connecticut–based *News-Times* (October 2, 1997, on-line). "He gave me his name but then he said, 'You're not required to do anything but be my son.' Thelonious in his genius allowed me to grow into what I am. I wasn't forced into it." As a small child Monk played the trumpet and the piano, but at the age of seven—when his father brought him to a recording session for the now-legendary *Brilliant Corners* album—he became enamored of a different instrument. "I remember looking out into the studio at Max Roach's drums and beautiful timpanis, kettle drums with beautiful copper bottoms," Monk told Martin Renzhofer for the *Salt Lake Tribune*, as quoted on *Jazz Voice On-line*. "Max looked like an executive at a big desk taking care of business." When he was 13 Monk secretly began practicing the drums, and at 15 he told his father that he wanted to be a drummer. Thelonious Monk immediately had the drummer Art Blakey get his son a set of drums, and soon the young man was taking lessons from Max Roach himself. Monk practiced diligently. "From day one I loved gadgets . . . and the drums was the instrument that looked like a huge gadget and I understood it from day one," Monk told an interviewer for *Jerry Jazz Musician* (on-line). "It seemed like a no brainer for me."

In 1970 Monk performed with his father on a television program, marking his first public appearance as a musician. "Thelonious came in the door of his home and said to his son, 'Are you ready to play?' 2 days later, I was on national TV with Thelonious," Monk stated in a chat on *Jazz Central Station* (on- line). "No rehearsal, no conference." Monk toured with his father's quartet for the next year before joining the nine-piece fusion band Natural Essence, in which he met his future girlfriend Yvonne Fletcher. Monk also played with the Paul Jeffrey Big Band during this time. In 1976 he formed the group Cycles with Yvonne and his sister, Barbara; the band, which played R&B and funk, later changed its name to T. S. Monk. In 1980 the group released its first album, *House of Music*, which made the Top 100 on the U.S. album chart while the debut single "Bon Bon Vie" hit the U.S. R&B Top 20. "Bon Bon Vie" also made an impression on the U.K. charts, as did the follow-up single, "Candidate for Love." The T. S. Monk band followed with the less successful *More of the Good Life* (1981); Monk himself recorded the album *Merc 'N Monk* with the composer Eric Mercury. Shortly afterward, a series of deaths caused Monk to put his music aside for a time. In 1982 Thelonious Monk died, at the age of 64. Not long afterward, T. S. Monk's sister and his girlfriend both died of breast cancer, only four months apart.

In 1986 Monk formed the Thelonious Monk Institute of Jazz, with the aim of celebrating and promoting his father's music. The institute hosts an annual competition that has brought fame to some of its winners, among them Joshua Redman and Jacky Terrason. Perhaps more importantly, the institute acts as an umbrella organization for several groups that sponsor the Jazz in the Classroom program, as well as after-school athletic programs and full scholarships for music students. Through his work with the organization and with the trumpeter and arranger Don Sickler, Monk slowly returned to music and jazz. "I realized I was in a unique position," he told Martin Renzhofer. "Between 1986 and 1990, I had honed my spokesperson skills. Then someone found out that I had played with dad. When I sat down at the instrument, I realized I had never stopped playing in my head." Monk played drums in Clifford Jordan's big band and with Walter Davis before putting together his own sextet, which consisted of Sickler, the tenor saxophonist Willie Williams, the bassist James Genus, the pianist Ronnie Mathews, and the alto saxophonist Bobby Porcelli—all experienced professionals. In 1991 T. S. Monk released *Take One*, his first album as leader. Playing hard bop, the group performed little-known numbers by such artists as Kenny Dorham, Hank Mobley, Idrees Sulieman, Elmo Hope, Walter Davis Jr., Clifford Jordan, Donald Brown, and Tommy Turrentine. The album received strong reviews, as did Monk's next two records, *Changing of the Guard* (1993) and *The Charm* (1995). Meanwhile, the band was also impressing critics with its live performances. "The accuracy with which each musician entered and exited the ensemble texture, the precision with which the band built to climaxes, then eased away from them, underscored just how polished this ensemble is," Howard Reich wrote for the *Chicago Tribune* (October 27, 1994) in his review of one of the group's shows. While Monk's group did not perform vocals at that time, the drummer often told stories to the audience in between songs. "I can do it in between the instrumental music and it has the same effect as if I was singing with the music," Monk told the interviewer for *Jerry Jazz Musician* (on-line), "or rapping with the music, because people want to be talked to . . . they want to know that you know they appreciate you."

In 1997 T. S. Monk came into the spotlight with the release of *Monk on Monk*. For that recording, a celebration of what would have been his father's 80th birthday, Monk assembled an all-star group of jazz musicians—in addition to his core sextet—to perform tunes Thelonious Monk had composed in honor of family and friends. Among the jazz luminaries who joined T. S. Monk for the record and the subsequent national tour were the trumpeter Roy Hargrove, the saxmen Wayne Shorter and Grover Washington Jr., and the pianist Herbie Hancock. *Monk on Monk* received many favorable reviews and won the New York Jazz Awards' first annual Recording of the Year prize and *Downbeat*'s 63d Reader's Poll Award. "I just felt that probably the best justice I could do Thelonious is to expose more of his music," Monk told Charles J. Gans. "Thelonious supplied the harmonic foundation that was the launching pad to move the music into the era of modern jazz. . . . I think Thelonious would have dug this record because he liked you to play your own thing. We certainly don't try to play the music like he did. It's got his flavor but everybody is playing their own stuff." The group followed *Monk on Monk* with *Cross Talk*, which found the sextet delving into light funk, world music, and classical styles while featuring the first vocalist (Patricia Barber) on a Monk record in 15 years. "I am truly a child of the 60's," Monk told the interviewer for *Jerry Jazz Musician*. "I grew up with the Beatles and the Byrds and Motown and Jimi Hendrix. I went to Prep School, so I was exposed to the Beach Boys and the Four Seasons, and at the same time in the other ear I was listening to Monk and Parker and Coltrane and Dizzy and Miles and Art and Max and all those cats, and I truly am . . . in the middle." Monk's group planned to release their sixth album, *Higher Ground*, in late 2002.

In addition to his work as a jazz drummer and bandleader, Monk continues to head the Thelonious Monk Institute and, with his brother-in-law, Peter Gain, has formed the label Thelonious Records. The label plans to put out nine previously unreleased recordings of concerts given by Thelonious Monk in Paris. T. S. Monk served as artistic director of *A Tribute to America's Music*, which was produced by the Thelonious Monk Institute and aired on ABC. In addition, he hosted the nationally televised *Jazz at the White House*. Monk has been a leading advocate for improved marketing of jazz. "We can sell jazz just like bubblegum if we only apply a hip marketing strategy to the problem at hand," he said, as quoted by the interviewer for *Jerry Jazz Musician*. "My approach is about marketing. My approach is . . . be valid be solid but be loud, be visible, be entertaining, be charming. . . . Be all those things and do things in a fashion that [makes] people take notice."

T. S. Monk has one son, Thelonious IV. "Like my father, I would love it if my son gets involved in music, but I ain't going to push him," he told Charles J. Gans. "If he wants music, the bug is going to bite him like it bit me." — G.O.

Suggested Reading: *Jazz Central Station* (online); *Jazz Voice On-line*; *Jerry Jazz Musician* (online); (Western Connecticut) *News-Times* (online) Oct. 2, 1997

Selected Recordings: *Take One*, 1991; *Changing of the Guard*, 1993; *The Charm*, 1995; *Monk on Monk*, 1997; *Cross Talk*, 1999

---

Courtesy of *www.intel.com*

## Moore, Gordon E.

*Jan. 3, 1929– Computer pioneer; chairman emeritus of Intel; philanthropist*

*Address: Intel Corp., 2200 Mission College Blvd., P.O. Box 58119, Santa Clara, CA. 95052*

Few pioneers of the computer age have had as reverberating an effect on information technology as Gordon E. Moore. In 1965 Moore published a paper in *Electronics* magazine in which he predicted that the power of microchip technology would double every year for the next decade. Moore's Law, as it was dubbed, came to be seen as an informal target for the designers and builders of computers, and progress in the field has proved it to be remarkably accurate. Three years after issuing his famous prediction, Moore co-founded the Intel Corp., one of the giants of the computer industry and the world's premier maker of silicon-based microchips. Moore served as executive vice president (1979–87), president and chief executive officer (1975–79), chairman and CEO (1979–87), and chairman (1987–95) of Intel; since his retirement, he has held the title of chairman emeritus. Moore "didn't invent things," Arthur Rock, a venture capitalist who invested in Intel in its infancy, told Brian O'Reilly for *Fortune* (April 26, 1997), "but he clearly saw the way to get somewhere. He more than anyone else set his eyes on a goal and got everybody to go there."

Quiet, unassuming, and amiable, Moore has a reputation for extraordinary patience and attentiveness to whoever is speaking to him. He rarely uses the word "I" in conversation, preferring to call attention to the roles of others in his success. His approach to life and business has earned him tremendous respect among his peers. Currently, he devotes much of his time to the Gordon E. & Betty Moore Foundation, which supports unconventional university research (such as programs that search for extraterrestrial intelligence) and projects to preserve the environment. The Moores plan to donate to their foundation a total of $5 billion (which amounted to about half their estimated wealth in early 2002). In 1990 President George Herbert Walker Bush presented Gordon Moore with the National Medal of Technology, which honors the country's greatest technical innovators.

Gordon E. Moore was born on January 3, 1929 in San Francisco, California, to Walter Harold Moore and Florence (Williamson) Moore. He spent his first 10 years in the small farming community of Pescadero, north of the city. "Pescadero was really my hometown," he told an interviewer for the Stanford University Web site. "Its only distinction is that it's the only town I know of in California that's smaller now than it was sixty years ago. The main street used to go through it and then they moved the highway onto the coast and Pescadero became a bit of a backwater." In about 1939 Moore's father, a deputy sheriff, landed a promotion, which necessitated the family's move to Redwood City, California.

During his childhood Moore became interested in science, and early on he decided to pursue a career in chemistry. "My next door neighbor got a chemistry set for Christmas," he recalled to Jill Wolfson and Teo Cervantes for the *San Jose Mercury News*, as reprinted on the Web site *thetech.org*. "I started playing with him and that set. In those days you got really neat chemicals in the chemistry set. You could make explosives and a variety of things." In high school Moore's aptitude for mathematics and skill at sports were evident. "Math came fairly easy for me," he told Wolfson and Cervantes. "I took all the math courses around, but I was interested in athletics, too. In high school, I had four letters in four different sports. I was never the best, but I was always good enough to play in the games. I spent a lot more time playing sports than I did doing homework, I have to admit. It wasn't really until my senior year in high school that I settled down and really started to study a bit."

The first person in his family to attend college, Moore studied for two years at San Jose State University before transferring to the University of California at Berkeley. He earned a B.S. degree in chemistry in 1950 and then enrolled at the California Institute of Technology (Caltech), in Pasadena, where he received a Ph.D. in physics and chemistry in 1954. After searching in vain for a job in his specialty in California, he looked farther afield, and found work at the Applied Physics Laboratory of Johns Hopkins University, in Maryland, just outside Washington, D.C. But he soon became dissatisfied there. "First of all, the team I was with was breaking up, and my two bosses were moving out," he told W. Wayt Gibbs, who interviewed him for *Scientific American* (September 1997, on-line). "I started calculating the cost per word in the published articles [that emanated from the lab] and decided that at $5 a word, I wasn't sure that the government was getting its money's worth. . . . I decided I really wanted to get closer to something with practical application. I was looking for some technical stuff that would lead to a real product."

Meanwhile, the physicist William Shockley, who had recently set up Shockley Semiconductor Laboratories as a division of Beckman Instruments, was trying to recruit a chemist to work on semiconductors and thermonuclear devices in his lab. Moore's name came to his attention, and in 1956 the young chemist joined Shockley's staff. (Shockley shared the Nobel Prize in physics that year, for his co-invention of the transistor in 1947. He later became notorious for propounding the theory that, on average, whites were more intelligent than blacks, and that because blacks, on average, were having more children than whites, the human race was regressing.) For Moore, working for Shockley was both challenging and frustrating. As he told W. Wayt Gibbs, "When I first went to work for him, he was thinking of making a transistor. But then he decided he wanted to make a rather obscure device called a four-layer diode. Mainly [the problem] was just that while Shockley was a technical genius, he really didn't understand how people worked very well. He stirred things up internally." After about a year and a half, Moore and seven of his co-workers complained about Shockley to Arnold O. Beckman, the founder of Beckman Instruments. "Beckman finally told us that Shockley was the boss, and we'd just have to learn to live with him," Moore recalled to Gibbs. The situation at Shockley Semiconductor for Moore and the other seven grew uncomfortable—they were dubbed "the Traitorous Eight and a variety of other things," as Moore explained to Gibbs—so, in 1957, they decided to strike out on their own. (Besides Moore, the partners were C. Sheldon Roberts, Eugene Kleiner, Robert N. Noyce, Victor H. Grinich, Julius Blank, Jay T. Last, and Jean A. Hoerni.)

Using $3,500 of their own funds, the men invented a way to mass-produce silicon transistors; it became known as the "mesa process." They then began scouring the *Wall Street Journal* for companies on the New York Stock Exchange that they thought might be interested in investing in their invention. After being rejected by more than 30 companies, the group found an ally in Sherman M. Fairchild, a pioneer in the fields of photography and aviation and the founder of the Fairchild Camera and Instrument Corp. and the Fairchild Engine and Airplane Corp. With a $1.5 million investment from the endlessly curious and inventive Fairchild, Moore and his partners founded Fairchild Semiconductor. (Officially, Moore's title was manager of engineering from 1957 to 1959 and then, until 1968, director of research and development at Fairchild Camera and Instrument Corp.)

Fairchild Semiconductor then began producing transistors, which, in essence, are the on/off switches that form the foundation for all digital logic. The firm sold its first 100 to IBM at $150 apiece. "Fairchild really was in the right place at the right time," Moore told the interviewer for the Stanford Web site. "Not only did we have a lot of technical contributions, that was a time period where it seems like every new idea that came along spawned one to five new companies. It really was the period of time when the 'silicon valley effect' of all the spin-offs really blossomed." Many companies, he added, "can trace their origins back to Fairchild."

In 1959 Moore's colleague Robert Noyce realized that an entire circuit could be created on a single chip. In the spring of that year, Fairchild began work on what it dubbed "unitary circuits." In April 1961 the U.S. patent office awarded the first patent for an integrated circuit to Fairchild (which thus beat out Texas Instruments, which was working on a similar project). Thus was launched the age of the microchip, the cornerstone of nearly all contemporary information technology. Moore understood the enormous implications of the microchip; as he wrote in his seminal article for *Electronics* (April 19, 1965), "The future of integrated electronics is the future of electronics itself. . . . Integrated circuits will lead to such wonders as home computers—or at least terminals connected to a central computer—automatic controls for automobiles, and personal portable communications equipment." In the same article Moore predicted that each year engineers would figure out a way to double the number of transistors implanted on computer chips. "We had just gotten some of the first [integrated circuits] out, making some a bit more complex, and I looked at what was happening on those and saw that the number of components—that is the number of transistors or resistors—in an integrated circuit was about doubling every year. So I just took that and said, 'What's gonna happen in components is going to continue to happen for the next ten years, so things will be a thousand times as complex in 1975 as they were in 1965,'" Moore recalled to the Stanford University interviewer. During the next three decades, Moore's Law, as it became known, correctly described progress in the computer industry. Meanwhile, as Moore explained to *PC Magazine* (March 25, 1997, on-line), the operations of Fairchild Semiconductor had eclipsed those of its parent company; as he put it, "The Semiconductor Division at that time was a West Coast operation, it was kind of, this tail that was wagging the dog, where the dog was Fairchild Camera and Instrument, which was an East-coast-based company."

In 1968 Moore and Noyce resigned from their jobs at Fairchild. Noyce left, Moore told *PC Magazine*, because when the post of CEO became vacant at Fairchild, the board of directors sought a replacement from outside the company rather than tapping him for the position. Moore quit in part because as head of the laboratory, he had become "frustrated with the increasing difficulty of moving things from the laboratory into production," as he explained to *PC Magazine*. Moreover, he said, "I could see that if they were going outside to hire somebody [as CEO] the company was going to change rather significantly. So I thought I'd better leave before it happened rather than after." Moore and Noyce teamed up with the idea of forming a new business. They typed a one-page proposal outlining their plan for a company called Intel that would make complex integrated circuits. Although they had developed fairly concrete plans, they deliberately made their proposal "completely and utterly vague," as Moore told *Scientific American*. Its lack of specifics notwithstanding, the plan intrigued Arthur Rock, a venture capitalist who already knew Noyce. Rock limited his investments to companies that were a short drive from his San Francisco offices; with its Santa Clara, California, address, Intel filled the bill. Within two days Rock had lined up 25 investors, and Intel had its funding. In 1969 the company manufactured its first product, a bipolar microchip, the uses of which soon proved to be highly diverse: it was incorporated in electronic marijuana sniffers (which replaced dogs) at airports; machines that analyzed blood; and equipment that automated operations in chicken houses. Moore and Noyce and their workers apparently had much to celebrate in those early years; on the spur of the moment, they would gather in their little coffee room to drink champagne. In an article for *Daedalus* (Spring 1996), Moore wrote, "By the time we outgrew this facility, the tiles in the ceiling were peppered with the imprints of all these champagne corks."

Not long afterward, Busicom, a Japanese start-up company that wanted to produce scientific calculators, enlisted Intel to build and supply its chips. Busicom had already mapped out a design for 13 complex circuits that would perform the calculations. Intel accepted the job even though Moore felt that it was more than the small engineering staff of the fledgling company could handle. Then one of Intel's engineers, Ted Hoff, ascertained that, thanks to improvements in Intel's technology, all the functions of the calculator could be controlled with a single chip. Moore thereupon persuaded Busicom, as he recalled to Wolfson and Cervantes, "To abandon all the design work they had done, and adopt this method of using a central computer chip, with programs and memory to do all of the calculations." Busicom agreed, and that is what led Intel, in 1969, to create microprocessors, a basic component of computers.

Since Busicom had fronted the lion's share of the money needed to develop microprocessors, they held the rights to them. Then, financial pressures and the desire to lower the cost of microprocessors spurred Busicom to negotiate a deal with Intel. By returning the $65,000 that Busicom had advanced for research, Intel acquired all the rights to sell the chip for other applications; Busicom could still use the chip for their calculators. "So the Japanese initially owned all the rights to microprocessors, but sold them for 65 grand," Moore told *Scientific American*. "In retrospect, it was kind of like the purchase of Manhattan." (According to a story for which no proof exists, Peter Minuit, a director of the Dutch West India Trading Co., acquired the island of Manhattan by giving representatives of the local Indians beads valued at $24.)

Early on, Intel developed by using what Moore has called the "Goldilocks strategy." In essence, the company considered the possibility of manufacturing one of three chips: one that would be easy to produce and therefore could be easily copied by competitors; a very complicated one, which might bankrupt the company in the process of being created; or a chip with a moderately complicated design. Intel chose the last alternative. "The key was the right degree of difficulty," Moore told Robert Lezner for *Forbes* (September 11, 1995). Nevertheless, Intel found itself struggling. At one point, to generate revenue, the company sold much of its core technology to a Canadian concern. "Throughout most of the '70s, we sold more development systems to companies designing products that were going to use microprocessors than we actually sold microprocessors," Moore explained to Anthony B. Perkins for *Red Herring* (September 1995). In the latter part of the decade, an oil crisis caused a downturn in the economy, and Intel was forced to cut a third of its workforce in order to stay afloat.

Intel's fortunes took a turn for the better in 1981, when IBM selected the Intel 8086 microprocessor for the personal computer (PC) that it was planning to launch. At that time most people—including Moore—believed that such a product would find few if any buyers. "If you asked me in 1980, I would have missed the PC," Moore admitted to Michael Kanellos for *CNET News.com*. "I didn't see much future for it. I thought automobiles would be a bigger market [for microprocessors]. But the IBM PC kind of hit it off with the public." Before long the IBM PC was much in demand; by the end of the 1980s, the fraction of U.S. households owning at least one personal computer was approaching one-third.

Intel suffered a setback in 1985, when Japanese semiconductor companies flooded the U.S. market with cheap microprocessor chips. After securing a loan from IBM, Intel developed the Intel386; with 275,000 transistors on one chip, the machine was among the most advanced microprocessors of its day. In 1997 Intel developed the Pentium microprocessor, which contains 3.1 million transistors. True to Moore's Law, the capabilities of the Pentium chip have increased exponentially since then. Its most recent descendant, the Pentium IV, has 42 million transistors.

Earlier, in 1979, Moore had succeeded Noyce as Intel's CEO. During that time he earned a reputation for being a patient leader and a good listener. According to Brian O'Reilly, "Engineers could plop down uninvited beside him in the cafeteria and in 15 minutes get insight into a problem that had bedeviled them for years." In 1987 Moore retired as CEO and became chairman. "I was getting lazy," he told O'Reilly. "I got tired of jumping on a plane at the drop of a hat and flying around the world to meet with a customer." Moore gradually reduced his workload and workweek before he retired, in 1997.

Since then, Moore has devoted much of his time to philanthropic and environmental causes. He is a member of the board of directors of Conservation International, an organization that seeks to preserve biological diversity through ecologically, economically, and socially sound solutions. In 1998 Moore and his wife donated $35 million to Conservation International. In December 2001 he announced that he and his wife planned to donate $261 million to the organization over the next 10 years. In 2000 the Moores established the multibillion-dollar Gordon E. and Betty Moore Foundation, which focuses on education, scientific research, and the environment. "It's something I've wanted to do for a long time," he told John Boudreau for the *San Jose Mercury News* (November 15, 2000). "It's hard work to give money away intelligently. A major problem was finding someone I felt comfortable with who could take it on." (He solved that problem by relying on himself.) Earlier, in 1997, Moore, along with William R. Hewlett and David Packard, the co-founders of the electronics giant Hewlett-Packard, donated $18 million to the privately funded SETI [Search for Extraterrestrial Intelligence] Institute, in Mountain View, California. "My view is statistically it's likely that there is intelligent life someplace else in the universe," Moore told Robert Buderi for *Technology Review* (May 2001). Moore and his wife have also donated substantial sums to United Way Silicon Valley and Cambridge University. Speaking of his wealth, he told Boudreau, "You've got to do something with it. If you don't give it away, the government will take most of it. There is only so much that makes sense to give to your kids."

Moore's honors include the 1984 Computer Society Pioneer Medal, from the Institute of Electrical and Electronic Engineers (IEEE); an award for advancing research, from the American Society of Metals, in 1985; and a Founder's Award from the National Academy of Engineering, in 1988. Moore has served on the boards of directors of Varian Associates, Gilead Sciences Inc., and Transamerica Corp. and was on the technology committee that advised George W. Bush during his campaign for the presidency. He is a member of the U.S. National Academy of Engineering, a fellow of the IEEE, and chairman of the board of trustees of the California Institute of Technology.

Moore has been married since 1950 to the former Betty I. Whittaker. He and his wife, who both love to fish, have two grown sons, Kenneth and Steven. — P.G.H., J.K.B.

Suggested Reading: *Electronic News* p1+ July 27, 1992; *Forbes* p167+ Sep. 11, 1995, with photos; *Fortune* p166+ Apr. 26, 1999, with photos; *Red Herring* (on-line), Sep. 1995; *Technology Review*, p64+ May 2001; *U.S. News & World Report* p38 July 10, 2000; *Who's Who in America, 2001*

---

Courtesy of the City of New Orleans

## Moriál, Marc

*Jan. 3, 1958– Former mayor of New Orleans; lawyer*

*Address: Adams and Reese LLP, 4500 One Shell Sq., New Orleans, LA 70139*

Marc Morial was elected to the first of his two terms as mayor of New Orleans in 1994, during one of the most difficult periods in the city's history. That year 424 murders were committed in New Orleans, giving the city the nation's highest per capita homicide rate. That development, together with the skyrocketing rate of crime in several other categories as well, affected the financial well-being of New Orleans. Businesses began pulling up stakes, and the much-depended-upon tourist trade dwindled considerably following a great deal of negative media attention. Compounding the problems, the New Orleans Police Department (NOPD) was not only rendered impotent in the face of such widespread crime—it was accused of corruption.

Morial, in short, inherited a city in trouble. In response, he immediately implemented a series of drastic reforms that put New Orleans on the path to recovery. Unprecedented teenage curfews, the enlisting of Federal Bureau of Investigation (FBI) assistance in cleaning up the NOPD, and substantial government investment brought about such dramatic results that the U.S. Conference of Mayors presented New Orleans with the 2000 City Livability Award. By 2001 New Orleans's murder rate had dropped more than 60 percent, prompting the National Civic League to recognize it as an All-American City, which marked the first time New Orleans had received that honor in more than 50 years. In 2001 Morial was elected president of the U.S. Conference of Mayors. That year he attempted without success to amend the City Charter so that he would be exempted from New Orleans's two-term limit for mayors. Since he left office, in May 2002, he has worked in New Orleans and Washington, D.C., as a special counsel with the law firm Adams and Reese. He is also on the roster of Leading Authorities, a speakers' bureau, and gives talks on such topics as leadership, education, and diversity issues.

The second of the five children of Sybil Haydel and Ernest N. "Dutch" Morial, Marc H. Morial was born on January 3, 1958 in New Orleans. Growing up in the upper-middle-class, predominantly black Ponchartrain Park neighborhood of New Orleans, Morial was exposed to politics and civil rights activism throughout his childhood. His mother, a schoolteacher, was active in the civil rights movement, and his father rose through the ranks of New Orleans politics, first as a prominent attorney, then as a local legislator and judge, and finally, beginning in 1978, as the city's first African-American mayor. Like his son, Dutch Morial would serve two consecutive four-year terms and earn a place as one of New Orleans's most popular mayors before his death, in 1989. After graduating from Jesuit High School, in 1976, Marc Morial went on to study economics at the University of Pennsylvania, in Philadelphia. In 1977, during his undergraduate years, Morial served as his father's campaign coordinator. Upon receiving his B.A. degree, in 1980, he enrolled in law school at Georgetown University, in Washington, D.C., earning his J.D. degree three years later. Returning to New Orleans, he accepted an associate partner position at the Barham & Churchill law firm. Morial spent two years with the firm before founding the Marc H. Morial Professional Law

Corp. in 1985. In 1991, in the historic *Chisom v. Roemer* case, he argued in front of the U.S. Supreme Court against a redistricting plan that, in effect, would have negated the votes of residents of certain largely minority-inhabited communities in contests for state Supreme Court judges. The nation's highest court ruled in Morial's favor, stating that judicial elections were covered by the 1964 Voting Rights Act. Later, as a result of that decision, Louisiana's first black Supreme Court justice was elected. During that period, in a case that was brought before the Louisiana Supreme Court, Morial argued successfully that police reports should be regarded as public records.

Despite the demands of his law practice, Morial found time for politics. During the Reverend Jesse Jackson's ultimately unsuccessful campaign for the 1988 Democratic presidential nomination, Morial was a key player in the New Orleans organization that supported the candidate. Morial also served as a Louisiana delegate to the 1988 Democratic National Convention, held in Atlanta, Georgia.

Shortly after scoring his victory in *Chisom v. Roemer*, Morial himself ran for office, winning the 1991 race for Louisiana state senator, representing District Four. In his short tenure as state senator, he authored more than 50 bills and co-authorized 90 others that became law. The *Baton Rouge Business Report* named Morial its political Rookie of the Year for 1992. A year later the Louisiana political columnist John Maginnis named Morial to his All-Rookie Team for 1993. Morial took liberal positions, supporting reproductive rights for women and opposing the death penalty.

In December 1993 Morial announced his plans to seek the mayorship of New Orleans. The city had recently fallen on hard times under Mayor Sidney Barthelemy; among other problems, New Orleans had seen much corruption on the part of its high-ranking officials. As quoted in an undated article on *Africanpubs.com*, Morial proclaimed at the press conference at which he declared his candidacy, "We need to clean up City Hall with a shovel and not a broom!" The road to City Hall was rife with obstacles for the son of the former mayor. One was his relative inexperience. Nonetheless, when the primaries were held, in February 1994, Morial secured 32 percent of the vote, coming in second to—and forcing a run-off with—New Orleans lawyer Donald Mintz, who had lost the mayoral race to Barthelemy four years earlier.

In the weeks leading up to the run-off, reports emerged concerning a pair of anonymous anti-black and anti-Semitic fliers that had begun to circulate. Morial then made the stunning charge that Mintz, who was Jewish, had had the fliers sent himself, in an attempt to generate sympathy for his candidacy. Morial's accusation took on credibility when Mintz's aide Napoleon Moses was indicted for distributing anonymous campaign literature, in violation of state law. It was further discovered that the Mintz campaign had raised hundreds of thousands of dollars by appealing to Jewish organizations after what were thought to be anti-Semitic threats. The mayoral race, in which Mintz had led his opponent by more than 10 percentage points, took a sharp turn in Morial's favor. The state senator defeated Mintz, earning 54 percent of the vote to his opponent's 46 percent. Race proved a crucial factor in a city whose population was 61 percent black; Morial won 85 percent of the black vote, while Mintz secured 91 percent of the white vote. As reported in an Associated Press article that ran in the *Washington Post* (March 7, 1994), Morial announced at his victory party, "I hope that tomorrow we can begin the process of building an administration and a new government, but more importantly, we can begin rebuilding our city."

One of Morial's first acts after taking office on May 2 was to recruit Richard Pennington, formerly with the Washington, D.C., police department, to head New Orleans's crumbling law-enforcement agency. Morial and his new police chief then spent the next year weeding out corrupt officers. By March 1995, 74 New Orleans police officers had been either fired, suspended, or reprimanded. More than 30 of those officers faced felony charges for rape, drug trafficking, and, in three cases, murder. The mayor then awarded the remaining officers with a 5 percent pay increase, their first raise in more than eight years. (The NOPD had previously ranked among the lowest-paid police departments of any major American city.) Several more crime-reduction measures were put into place, including the establishment of a controversial community-policing program, whereby New Orleans citizens took an active role in reclaiming the streets, and the moving of the citizen-complaint department out of a police precinct building, which reduced fear of reprisals by police. (Earlier, a police officer had been convicted of hiring a drug dealer to murder a woman who had filed an assault complaint against the officer.) Morial also imposed a curfew on the city's juvenile residents. The curfew required youths under 17 to be indoors from 8 p.m. until 6 a.m. during weekdays from September to May and from 9 p.m. until 6 a.m. from June through August. On weekends, juveniles were required to return home before 11 p.m. Curfew offenders, as well as their parents, were forced to attend counseling with social-service professionals. Repeat offenders were subject to substantial fines. By the end of 1995, New Orleans's murder rate had dropped 18 percent. The curfew program proved so successful that it was nationally recognized and praised by both major candidates in the 1996 presidential race, President Bill Clinton and U.S. senator Bob Dole.

As the crime rate continued to plummet, Morial ran away with the 1998 mayoral race, earning 93 percent of the black vote and even taking 43 percent of the white vote. Morial told Rick Bragg for the *New York Times* (February 17, 1998), "This city [before 1994] was in the prone position. It was like a patient and the family was sitting around, trying to decide whether to pull the plug. It was plagued by this coffee table rhetoric of, 'I'm frightened, I'm getting out.' Well, you don't hear that anymore."

In October 1998 Morial became the first mayor to file a legal suit against the gun industry, arguing that gun manufacturers had failed to incorporate available safety devices in handgun designs and had thus directly contributed to many of the city's shooting deaths. In an editorial published in the *New York Times* (November 14, 1998), Morial was cited as arguing that by failing to include safety devices with handguns, the companies had manufactured "unreasonably dangerous" products. Several other cities followed suit, including Atlanta, Georgia; Chicago, Illinois; Miami, Florida; Detroit, Michigan; and Cincinnati, Ohio. While the cities approached the issue from different angles, all sought the same outcome, namely the culpability of gun makers who failed to guard against accidental injuries or deaths. With Morial at its center, the issue received national attention, as had lawsuits brought against the tobacco industry by several state attorneys general. Unlike the plaintiffs in the tobacco cases, however, Morial hit a legal brick wall, when the Louisiana state legislature voted in 1999 to stymie New Orleans's lawsuit. The vote was endorsed by the state's Republican governor, Mike Foster, an opponent of gun controls; soon afterward, a law was passed that prevented Louisiana cities from suing the gun industry. The new law, which was approved without a dissenting vote, included a retroactivity clause that nullified the suit already filed by Morial.

Shaking off that loss, Morial vowed to continue his fight in the appellate courts. In February 2000 Louisiana Civil District Court judge Lloyd Medley ruled that the legislature's earlier attempt to block New Orleans's suit was unconstitutional. Less than a month later Morial joined President Clinton and others to announce a settlement with the gun manufacturer Smith & Wesson. Under the settlement, the company agreed to provide safety locks on all its handguns within 60 days and, within a year, to make all handguns unusable by young children. (By 2002 the company's products are to include internal safety locks.) Financially, Smith & Wesson promised to devote 2 percent of its annual revenues to developing smart-gun technology, which would make gunfire possible only by authorized persons. In a statement published on the mayor's official Web site, Morial announced, "The war to keep guns out of the hands of criminals and to keep our children safe is not over; but this major breakthrough shows that the whole nation agrees with what we are doing."

Morial continued the revitalization program for New Orleans, which he had implemented some years earlier. Dubbed "Rebuild New Orleans Now!," the five-year, $172 million initiative sought to rebuild the city's landscape with repairs to streets, public buildings, and recreational facilities. Included in the plan was the restoration of more than 30 parks and playgrounds, which, paired with "The Mayor's Team Summer Jobs," put more than 1,000 underprivileged youths to work each summer. In 2000 a second phase of "Rebuild New Orleans Now!" was approved by voters, and an additional $177 million was allotted to the continued rebuilding of the city.

In 2001 the U.S. Conference of Mayors (USCM) elected Morial as its president. Morial thus became the fourth New Orleans mayor—including his father—to hold that post. (Marc Morial had previously served as the organization's vice president.) The conference is a nonpartisan organization comprising the mayors of cities with populations of at least 30,000. As reported in the New Orleans *Times-Picayune* (June 26, 2001), "[The USCM] is probably the most powerful lobby there is on issues that relate directly to the well-being of the nation's urban areas."

Morial was barred by the City Charter from serving a third term as mayor. Eager to circumvent that restriction legally, he asked for a special referendum in which voters would decide whether to make a one-time exception to the City Charter specifically for him. (Dutch Morial had attempted to do the same thing, in 1986.) "To justify the need for a third term, Mr. Morial says that much of his work is not yet finished, especially regarding New Orleans Public Schools . . . ," Christopher Johnson wrote for the *Tulane Hullabaloo* (October 19, 2001), a publication of Tulane University, in New Orleans. "While it is undoubtedly true that there's still much work to do for the public schools, it is not unreasonable to ask why Mr. Morial didn't think of that some time during the last seven years. . . . Perhaps the best reason [the amendment to the law] should not pass is the fact that it is merely a one-time change. In other words, the term limit law would still be in place, just not for Morial. That's not 'concern for the schools,' that's egotism." Like his father's proposed change to the City Charter, Marc Morial's fell short of the needed votes; on Election Day, held in mid-October 2001, 61 percent of those who cast their ballots chose to uphold the two-term limit for mayors. On March 2, 2002 C. Ray Nagin was elected mayor of New Orleans; his inauguration took place the first week of the following May.

"In many ways, Marc Morial will rank among New Orleans' most successful modern mayors," Clancy DuBois wrote for the *Best of New Orleans* Web site (May 7, 2002). "He leaves office with the highest voter approval ratings in memory, and no one can say that the city isn't substantially better off than when he arrived at City Hall eight years ago. A recent University of New Orleans survey shows voters are incredibly optimistic about the city's future—a tribute . . . to Morial's accomplishments. . . . Among Morial's obvious legacies are a vastly improved police department, an ambitious capital construction program and a revised City Charter. Other elements of his legacy include improved race relations, a stable political climate, and a feeling that New Orleans can turn itself around." DuBois criticized Morial, too, citing the slowness of infrastructure maintenance, including street repairs; his failure to make more of an effort to improve public education; and his failure to set up an office of inspector general and an ethics commission, both of which were authorized by changes to the City Charter during his first year in office.

Marc Morial married the TV newswoman Michelle Miller in 1999. He has a daughter, Kemah, from a previous relationship. From 1987 to 1990 he taught political science as an adjunct professor at Xavier University of Louisiana, in New Orleans. That university awarded him an honorary doctor of laws degree in 2002. Also that year he was recognized by the National Organization on Disability for encouraging mayors throughout the United States to increase opportunities for people with disabilities to take part in civic and community activities. Among his other honors are the Richard J. Daley Award; the United States Conference of Mayors City Livability Award; the Americans for Arts Award; the Torch of Liberty Award; and the Pro Bono Publico Award from the Louisiana State Bar Association. — J.H.

Suggested Reading: *Ebony* p80 Nov. 1994; *Jet* p48+ July 16, 2001, with photo; *New York Times* A p10 Mar. 7, 1994, with photo, A p10 Feb 17, 1998, with photo, A p12 Nov. 14, 1998; *USA Today* A p3 Apr. 12, 1995; *Wall Street Journal* A p38 Nov. 16, 1998

---

## Moses, Robert P.

*Jan. 23, 1935– Educator; civil rights activist; founder and president of the Algebra Project*

*Address: Algebra Project Inc., 99 Bishop Allen Dr., Cambridge, MA 02139; Lanier High School, 933 Maple St., Jackson, MS 39203-3814*

A hero of the American civil rights movement of the 1960s, Robert P. Moses is the creator of the Algebra Project, an unusual and highly effective program of school reform that aims to increase middle-school students' chances for academic success and, consequently, lifelong economic prosperity. In his book *Radical Equations: Math Literacy and Civil Rights* (2001), which he co-wrote with Charles E. Cobb Jr., Moses explained that the lessons he learned as a civil rights activist about empowerment, problem solving, and organizing underlie the philosophy and pedagogical tactics of the Algebra Project. In the early 1960s Moses, then commonly known as Bob, led the Mississippi voter-registration project organized by the Student Nonviolent Coordinating Committee (SNCC, pronounced "snick"). Despite considerable—and sometimes violent—opposition from whites, he and his fellow activists refused to end SNCC's efforts to increase the number of blacks on Mississippi voting rolls, and he gained a reputation for fearlessness, strong leadership, and quiet strength. "Moses pioneered an alternative style of leadership from the princely church leader that King epitomized," the civil rights historian Taylor Branch told Julia Cass for *Mother Jones* (May/June 2002, on-line). "He was the thoughtful, self-effacing loner. He is really the father of grassroots organizing—not the Moses summoning his people on the mountaintop as King did, but, ironically, the anti-Moses, going door-to-door, listening to people, letting them lead." He later turned his attention to protesting the Vietnam War. After he was drafted into the military, he fled the U.S. He worked as a schoolteacher in Tanzania for half a dozen years before he returned to the States.

Moses, who had taught math in the U.S. in the late 1950s, founded the Algebra Project in 1982, with the goal of teaching algebra to poor, predominantly minority children by the time they reached eighth grade. In Moses's system, math problems are expressed in vernacular English and made applicable to the students' lives. Skeptics predicted that the program would not work, because, they implied, the youngsters he was targeting had little interest in learning, but Moses has proven them wrong. Since its inception the Algebra Project has helped thousands of students improve their academic performance. The program currently serves roughly 10,000 students annually in 28 cities across the country and involves more than 300 teachers. "Like sharecroppers demanding the right to vote 40 years ago, students will have to demand education from those in power," Moses told an interviewer for *4word* (June 2001, on-line). "Math literacy is a civil right. Just as black people in Mississippi saw the vote as a tool to elevate them into the first class politically, math is the tool to elevate the young into the first class economically." He also said, "Change can't just come from the top, it must come from communities of people who organize to make demands, and in the process transform themselves." In a conversation with Alexis Jetter for the *New York Times Magazine* (February 21, 1993), Moses's longtime friend the Reverend James P. Breeden, who is also a civil rights activist and educator, said, "Bob combines Calvinist, absolute certainty with a deep commitment to democracy and poor folks. He can be the most charming, open guy you'll ever want to meet or a totally inside-himself, enigmatic mystic. But one rarely runs into such an implacable being." Moses won a MacArthur Foundation "genius" grant in 1982.

Robert Parris Moses was born on January 23, 1935 in Harlem, a section of New York City, and grew up in a public housing project there. His father had a low-paying job as a security guard at the historic 369th Regiment Armory, in Harlem. "He and my mother scrimped and saved to ensure that

*Robert P. Moses* AP/Rogelio Solis

my brothers and I would get ahead," Moses is quoted as saying in William Heath's novelistic biography *The Children Bob Moses Led* (1995), which includes Moses's reminiscences and many factual references to his life and work. "The stress and strain took their toll: my mother once suffered a minor breakdown, and my father would sometimes slip into fantasies that his name was not Gregory Moses but Gary Cooper—a man brave enough, in spite of his cowardly town, to stand up for what was right." Thanks to his high score on a special entrance exam, Moses was admitted to Stuyvesant High School, a New York City public school known for its excellent mathematics and science programs. In his senior year he was elected president of his class.

After graduating from Stuyvesant, in 1952, Moses attended Hamilton College, in Clinton, New York, on a scholarship; he majored in philosophy and French. Thanks to one of his French professors, he began reading works by the humanist philosopher and writer Albert Camus; by his own account, Camus's ideas influenced him profoundly. In *The Children Bob Moses Led*, he was quoted as saying that during this period he "began asking hard political questions: 'Can revolution be humane?' 'Can the "victim" overthrow the "executioner" without assuming his office?'" For a time Moses belonged to a group of Pentecostal Christians at Hamilton; on weekends he would travel with them to New York City's Times Square to preach. When Moses told his father that he was thinking of becoming a preacher, as his grandfather had been, his father successfully dissuaded him, telling him, as Moses recalled for *The Children Bob Moses Led*, "That's not just any job. You've got to be called." As an undergraduate Moses traveled elsewhere as well; one summer, impressed by the Quakers' pacifist philosophy, he attended an American Friends Service Committee international work camp in France. The following year he went to Japan to help build wooden steps for juvenile residents of a mental hospital. By the time he earned a bachelor's degree at Hamilton, in 1956, Moses had become committed to the ideas of nonviolence and leadership through example.

After completing college Moses began graduate study in philosophy at Harvard University, in Cambridge, Massachusetts. He earned an M.A. degree in 1957 and then started working toward his Ph.D. But the abstract aspects of that discipline increasingly troubled him. "I tired of thinking about thinking and the meaning of meaning," he explained, as quoted in *The Children Bob Moses Led*. "In that remote realm of tautologies, indexes, and surds, I was in danger of forgetting that the meaning of life was no abstract speculation but my immediate and concrete concern." In the spring of 1958, Moses's mother died of cancer, and his distraught father had to be hospitalized for months. Moses cut his studies short and returned to New York City, where he found work teaching junior-high-level math at the Horace Mann School, an elite private school in the Riverdale section of the Bronx. At around this time he became increasingly aware of the civil rights movement, reading in the *New York Times* about the first sit-ins and student protests taking place in the South. Moses was especially affected by the photos of determined young protesters. "They weren't cowed," he recalled in *The Children Bob Moses Led*, "and they weren't apathetic—they meant to finish what they had begun. Here was something that could be done. I simply had to get involved."

Over spring break in 1960, Moses visited an uncle of his in Hampton, Virginia. During his stay he witnessed students picketing segregated stores in nearby Newport News, and he decided to join them. The experience left him feeling exhilarated, and he resolved to work in the movement. After he returned to New York, he volunteered with the Committee to Defend Martin Luther King, helping the group organize a rally to raise funds to defend the civil rights leader from legal prosecution. He soon realized that he did not feel comfortable working in an office while others were putting themselves in harm's way. At the suggestion of a friend, in the summer of 1960 he traveled to Atlanta, Georgia, to work for the Southern Christian Leadership Conference (SCLC). To his dismay, Moses again found himself assigned to office tasks. Moreover, as he was quoted as saying in *The Children Bob Moses Led*, SCLC struck him as "too hero-worshiping, media-centered, preacher-dominated, and authoritarian." He felt far more attracted to SNCC, which was attempting to build a grassroots civil rights movement. Although viewed with suspicion by some SNCC members because of his college degree and soft-spoken manner, Moses left SCLC and joined protests and picket lines organized by SNCC.

Later in the summer of 1960, Moses went to Mississippi, then the most racially segregated state in the nation, to view for himself the conditions of blacks and try to organize people to come to Atlanta in October for a SNCC conference. Upon arriving in Mississippi, he met Amzie Moore, a local official of the National Association for the Advancement of Colored People (NAACP), who made Moses aware of the plight of several poor black Mississippi families. In *The Children Bob Moses Led*, Moses recalled, "[Moore] showed me scenes that I'll never forget: children with swollen ankles, bloated bellies, and suppurating sores; children whose one meal a day was grits and gravy; children who didn't know the taste of milk, meat, fruits, or vegetables; children who drank contaminated water from a distant well, slept five in a bed, and didn't have the energy to brush the flies from their faces." Moore and Moses then planned a campaign to register African-Americans to vote—a huge and dangerous undertaking, the goal of which was to rid Mississippi of the racist politicians who controlled the state. At the time of the project's inception, less than 5 percent of black Mississippians had been registered to vote, although 40 percent of the state's population was black.

The next summer, after teaching one more year at Horace Mann, Moses returned to Mississippi, choosing the railroad town of McComb as his base. As he recalled in *The Children Bob Moses Led*, his purpose was "to break the Solid South by applying pressure at its strongest point. I sought out the worst part of the most intransigent stage, placed myself on the charity of the black community, located a few brave souls who would support civil rights workers, and set up a voter registration school. If enough people could find the courage to go down to the courthouse, confronting the system designed to oppress them, then blacks all over the South would take heart, the country would take notice, and maybe, one hundred years too late, the federal government would take action." The registration process was designed to make it almost impossible for the mostly poor and illiterate black population to gain the franchise; even blacks who could read were turned away, after failing tests that were nearly impossible to pass—tests on which whites were given passing grades, no matter how poorly they had performed. Moreover, armed white bigots harassed and even injured blacks who attempted to register. As a result, African-American Mississippians were fearful of taking any empowering action.

Moses and his SNCC colleagues began organizing classes in what they dubbed "freedom schools," to help local residents understand the voter-registration process. As their activity continued, racist whites targeted Moses and his fellow SNCC members for attacks and beatings. Pickup trucks filled with shotgun-toting whites would follow SNCC members. "You were always looking in your rearview mirror for headlights," Moses told Bruce Watson for *Smithsonian* (February 1996). One day in February 1963, a car filled with angry whites followed Moses and a colleague of his as they were traveling by car. The two men managed to shake that car, only to be attacked by people in a second car, who opened fire after pulling up alongside them. A bullet just missed Moses but hit the driver in the neck. Moses grabbed the wheel, pulled the car over to the side of the road, and drove his colleague to the hospital. In this instance and many others, law-enforcement officers did not help the civil rights workers; rather, they ignored and even encouraged the violence against them. In addition, they repeatedly placed many SNCC members, including Moses, under arrest. Despite such actions, the federal government refused to become involved on SNCC's behalf.

The violence and formidable odds did not faze Moses, and before long he had become known for his bravery. Once, he was found napping in a SNCC office that had been attacked by an angry white mob only hours before. Another time, he was beaten while accompanying two blacks to a registrar. Bleeding heavily from his wounds, Moses continued to lead the two to the registration site. Afterward, he pressed charges against his attacker, an action virtually unheard-of for a black man in Mississippi at that time.

In 1963 Moses co-founded and became the director of the Council of Federated Organizations (COFO), an association that aimed to coordinate the activities of all civil rights groups in Mississippi. As a way of publicizing blacks' unhappiness about their disenfranchisement, he organized the so-called Freedom Vote, a mock election in which 80,000 blacks participated. Encouraged by the turnout, in 1964 SNCC initiated Freedom Summer, a massive registration drive for blacks. After a lengthy debate SNCC members decided to recruit white students from the North to help in the effort. After a weeklong orientation, more than 1,000 students traveled to Mississippi to canvass cities and small towns to encourage blacks to register. Although the number of people who did so was small, the drive made more African-Americans aware of the civil rights movement, and it brought national attention to both SNCC and the civil rights struggle in Mississippi. Concurrently, attacks on SNCC members and volunteers increased. That summer at least 80 people were beaten, some 70 churches, homes, and businesses were destroyed by racists, and, most notoriously, three civil rights workers—James Chaney, who was black, and Andrew Goodman and Michael Schwerner, who were white—were murdered by members of the Ku Klux Klan. The publicity provoked by their deaths aroused resentment among African-American volunteers, who recognized that the murders were generating far more attention than had earlier killings in which all the victims were black. Many African-American volunteers also bristled at the behavior of white civil rights workers who acted as if they thought they were better equipped than their black counterparts to assume leadership roles in Freedom Summer activities. For those and other reasons, relations between white and black SNCC workers began to deteriorate. "That summer, people who were talking to each other stopped," Moses told Alexis Jetter. "People who had been working together left. The whole spectrum of race relations compressed, broke down and washed us away."

Another disappointment for Moses and SNCC was connected with their efforts at the 1964 Democratic National Convention, held in Atlantic City, New Jersey. Joining with other civil rights organizations, SNCC formed the Mississippi Freedom Democratic Party (MFDP), to protest the all-white composition of the official Mississippi delegation to the convention. Although the MFDP received nationwide publicity and a member of the protest delegation was given the opportunity to address the convention, the delegates were not allowed to participate in convention activities. As the summer wore on, Moses became increasingly disturbed by the slow progress of voter registration and the deaths of SNCC workers, for which he felt partially responsible. He was also angered by the federal government's lack of involvement in the registration effort. As United States military activities in Vietnam increased, Moses began to focus more on the antiwar movement. (A fictionalized version of Moses's experiences with SNCC was presented in the 2000 TNT made-for-television film *Freedom Song*, starring Danny Glover.)

In 1966 Moses was drafted into the army. To avoid having to serve in the Vietnam War, he fled to Canada with his second wife, Janet Jemmott, a former SNCC activist. He lived there under the name Bob Parris for two years. The couple then moved to the African nation of Tanzania, where Moses taught math. In Tanzania, as Moses told Julia Cass, he "lived a life as just another person. That helped me get grounded again and helped our family be just a family." He and his wife returned to the United States with their four children in 1976. (President Jimmy Carter issued a blanket pardon of draft dodgers in January 1977.) With his family, Moses settled in Cambridge, Massachusetts, where he resumed working toward his Ph.D. in the philosophy of mathematics at Harvard University. In 1982 he became sidetracked from his studies once again, after finding out, to his surprise and dismay, that the school attended by his eldest child—his daughter Maisha—did not offer instruction in algebra. (According to the Harvard Archives, Moses has not yet earned a doctorate.) He asked the girl's teacher if Maisha could sit by herself in her math class and work on more advanced material. The teacher responded by inviting Moses to teach Maisha and other students at her level of math proficiency. That invitation led Moses to design the Algebra Project, with the aim of teaching poor children algebra by eighth grade and the ultimate goal of stemming the number of school dropouts and the resulting high unemployment rate among minority teenagers. Since math is crucial in today's industrial and technological world, Moses hopes that impoverished communities can be uplifted with the help of the Algebra Project. Those who can learn algebra by eighth grade, Moses has theorized, will have a greater chance of getting into academically superior high schools, enrolling at college, and building successful careers. In his book *Radical Equations: Math Literacy and Civil Rights* (2001), he described how his experiences during the civil rights movement led to his creation of the Algebra Project. A nonprofit corporation, the project currently operates with an annual budget of $2.5 million and employs 22 people full-time.

The Algebra Project is built around the idea that youngsters will be more excited about math if it is applied to everyday life and taught in everyday language. In one exercise, the notion of negative and positive integers is conveyed by means of a field trip; from a designated starting point, the students walk in one direction, retrace their steps, and then walk in the opposite direction. Upon returning to the classroom, the youngsters are asked to assign negative and positive numbers to the places where they stopped on their outing. Another technique teaches ratios through African drumming. The results of such pedagogic methods have been striking. According to Amelia Newcomb in the *Christian Science Monitor* (April 12, 2001, online), researchers at Lesley College, in Cambridge, Massachusetts, found that 92 percent of Algebra Project graduates in Cambridge had enrolled in upper-level math courses in ninth grade—a percentage twice as great as that in a control group of their local peers. Test scores among students in the project have shot up, while the number of students being sent to detention and dropping out has fallen substantially. Educators across the country have praised Moses and his program. Speaking with Newcomb, Freeman A. Hrabowski III, an African-American mathematician who is the president of the University of Maryland, Baltimore County, said, "The most important thing the Algebra Project shows is that kids from all backgrounds can succeed in math. It bridges the culture of the child and the world of math." "Each one, teach one," an Algebra Project motto, conveys Moses's conviction that, as *4word* quoted him as saying, "there is a way that young people reach young people, are able to touch each other, that in my view is central to the future shape of the Algebra Project. It is not about simply transferring a body of knowledge to children, it is about using that knowledge as a tool to a much larger end. Young people in Mississippi changed the country. Now we are asking young people to step out into a different way of seeing themselves."

Moses, whose home is in Cambridge, Massachusetts, where the Algebra Project is based, spends most weeks teaching at Lanier High School, in Jackson, Mississippi. He is a devotee of the yogi Paramhasana Yogananda and is a vegetarian. Each morning he wakes before dawn to swim 1,000 yards at a gym, an activity he repeats at the end of the day. His wife, Janet (Jemmott) Moses, earned an M.D. degree in 1987; currently, she teaches at the Harvard-MIT Division of Health Sciences and Technology and is on the pediatric staffs at two Boston hospitals. The couple's four children—Maisha, Omowale, Tabasuri, and Malaika—have all worked to increase math literacy among schoolchildren. Maisha teaches her father's classes on Mondays and trains teachers in Algebra Project methods. Omowale and Tabasuri co-founded, and Omowale directs, an arm of the Algebra Project known as the Young People's Project, which, according to the Algebra Project Web site, "recruits, trains and deploys high school and college-age youth to work with their younger peers in a variety of math learning opportunities." In 2002 Moses and the Algebra Project were awarded the prestigious James Bryant Conant Award by the Education Commission of the States. Earlier that year he received the 2001 Margaret Chase Smith American Democracy Award, given by the National Association of Secretaries of States. — G.O.

Suggested Reading: *4word* (on-line) p1+ June 2001, with photos; Algebra Project Web site; *Christian Science Monitor* (on-line) Apr. 12, 2001; *Educational Leadership* p6+ Oct. 2001, with photo; *New York Times* p30+ Jan. 7, 2001, with photos; *New York Times Magazine* p28+ Feb. 21, 1993, with photos; *Smithsonian* p114+ Feb. 1996, with photos; Burner, Eric R. *And Gently He Shall Lead Them: Robert Parris Moses and Civil Rights in Mississippi*, 1994; Heath, William. *The Children Bob Moses Led*, 1995; Moses, Robert P., and Charles E. Cobb Jr. *Radical Equations: Math Literacy and Civil Rights*, 2001

Courtesy of Xerox Corp.

## Mulcahy, Anne M.

*Oct. 21, 1952– Chair and CEO of Xerox*

*Address: Xerox, 800 Long Ridge Rd., Stamford, CT 06904*

When Anne M. Mulcahy became the CEO of Xerox, in August 2001, she raised to five the number of women concurrently heading Fortune 500 companies—and thus made history, because never before had so many women held the top posts in that elite group of firms. Mulcahy, who held the title of president as well, faced a herculean task when she took charge. Xerox had once been so dominant in the copier market that its name became a generic verb for copying, and it has been credited with developing the graphic user interface (used in computer software), the laser printer, and aspects of Internet technology, but since late 1999 the company had been struggling under the weight of massive debt. Moreover, Canon, Ricoh, Heidelberger, and other competitors were making inroads into Xerox's sales. Mulcahy also had to grapple with severe dissatisfaction among Xerox employees. "This was clearly a case of the responsibility being thrust upon me," Mulcahy said in a presentation to the Executives' Club of Chicago on March 14, 2002. "And I accepted it with equal parts of pride and dread, confidence and doubt, conviction and uncertainty." In January 2002 Mulcahy became Xerox's chair as well as its CEO. (The position of president was eliminated.) Under her leadership, Xerox has improved its financial fortunes considerably. In the second quarter of 2002, the company had its strongest showing in two years. Nevertheless, Xerox still has a long way to go before it completely recovers.

The only girl among five siblings, Anne M. Mulcahy was born Anne Dolan on October 21, 1952 in Rockville Centre, a suburb of New York City. Her father was an English professor before becoming an editor in a publishing firm; her mother was a homemaker and handled the family finances. "My upbringing was my greatest advantage. I was comfortable around men, and I learned to love contention," Mulcahy told Claudia H. Deutsch for the *New York Times* (May 13, 2000). Her oldest brother, Thomas J. Dolan, head of Xerox's Global Solutions Group, told Deutsch that his sister "wouldn't let us exclude her from anything, even shooting basketball hoops. Dinnertime in our home was a time for debating ideas, and Anne was as outspoken as the rest of us."

Mulcahy chose to attend Marymount College, in Tarrytown, New York, partly because the school admitted only women. But she grew to dislike the campus environment intensely, and after her junior year, she joined VISTA (Volunteers in Service to America, now known as Americorps VISTA), a federal program that is the domestic equivalent of the Peace Corps. For 15 months Mulcahy worked with preschool children, prisoners, and juvenile delinquents in poor areas of Kentucky. She then returned to Marymount, where she earned a bachelor's degree in journalism and math in 1974, having considered a career as a reporter. "I took a tryout at *Cosmo* and got weeded out real quick," she told Deutsch. Seeking an alternative, she took a position in the training department at Chase Manhattan Bank. Then, in 1976, she joined her husband in Boston, Massachusetts, and found a sales job at Xerox. "She was the first woman on our sales team," Thomas A. Horne, a Xerox vice president who was a sales manager when he hired Mulcahy, told Deutsch. He added that while she had few qualifications for the job, "she seemed professional [and] organized," and he "just sensed she was committed to being successful."

Mulcahy began her employment at Xerox as a field sales representative. She next managed sales territories in New York City and Boston. In 1985, with her promotion to head of human resources, she became the company's first female officer. She served as vice president for human resources from 1992 to 1995, when she was promoted to vice president and staff officer for customer operations, taking charge of markets in South America, Central America, Europe, Asia, and Africa. Her next title, earned in 1998, was that of senior vice president and chief staff officer, with responsibility for human resources, quality, communications, advertising, Internet marketing, and government relations. She next became president of the 6,000-worker General Markets Operation, a worldwide, $6 billion business, launched in January 1999, that soon accounted for about 30 percent of Xerox's total revenue. "Every time I was tempted to leave [Xerox], they'd find something interesting [for me]," Mulcahy told Deutsch.

While Mulcahy's career was advancing, Xerox as a whole had been suffering from a host of severe problems, among them increasing competition and correspondingly poor sales; a huge drop in the value of its stock; massive dissatisfaction among its workers and the departure of some of its account executives, following what by all reports was a poorly planned reorganization; and, as Anthony Bianco and Pamela L. Moore described it for *Business Week* (March 5, 2001), "executive-suite discord so intractable as to amount to corporate civil war." (Later, Mulcahy offered the Executives Club of Chicago a partial explanation for the company's troubles: "We attempted too much change too fast," she said. "Competition stiffened while economies here at home and around the world weakened. . . . And we took some actions that in the broad daylight of hindsight were dumb.") Talk of bankruptcy had been in the air for months when, on May 11, 2000, Mulcahy was named Xerox's president and chief operating officer. At the same time, the company ousted its CEO, G. Richard Thoman; in what Xerox announced was a temporary measure, Thoman was replaced by his predecessor—Paul A. Allaire, Xerox's chair, a title that he continued to hold as well. The shakeup clearly indicated that Mulcahy was being groomed to succeed Allaire as CEO.

Xerox suffered another blow in October 2000, when the Securities and Exchange Commission (SEC) began investigating the company's accounting practices, after Xerox disclosed accounting irregularities in its Mexican operation dating from the previous June. In April 2002—without admitting any wrongdoing—Xerox paid a $10 million fine, the largest ever, as part of its settlement with the SEC, and two months later the company filed restatements of financial reports dating back to 1997. The SEC also ordered the company to reevaluate its internal financial controls and criticized Xerox for its lack of cooperation during the SEC's probe.

Meanwhile, to reverse the company's downhill slide, Mulcahy had formulated a three-pronged agenda that emphasized generating cash, reducing costs, and planning for long-term growth. In October 2000 Xerox announced that it intended to cut expenses by $1 billion and would divest itself of $2 billion to $4 billion in assets to help pay part of its staggering debt. Toward that end, the company sold half its 50 percent interest in Fuji Xerox (for $1.3 billion) and its entire China operation (for $550 million). In addition, in the last quarter of 2000 and first quarter of 2001, Xerox eliminated a total of 6,000 jobs, bringing to more than 16,000 the number of positions wiped out since 1998. Then, on June 14, 2001, the company decided to scrap Mulcahy's pet project—its line of desktop inkjet printers—because the year-old enterprise, which employed 1,500 people across the globe, was not expected to produce a profit for several years. "In a year of tough decisions, this one was toughest," Mulcahy told Pamela Moore for *Business Week*

(August 6, 2001). She also vowed to reduce Xerox's manufacturing costs, which were believed to be far higher than those of the company's competitors. But she promised not to shrink the research-and-development (R&D) department. "We're leaving R&D virtually untouched and we will preserve investments in technology," she told Michael R. Zimmerman for *eWeek* (November 16, 2000, on-line). Indeed, Xerox's spending on research and development increased 11 percent in the first quarter of 2001, with much of that money going toward color technologies; in May 2001 the company invested another $100 million in R&D. In response to the advent of digital document processing, which blurs the line between copying and printing, Mulcahy has been trying to shift Xerox's focus from copiers to products that combine scanning, storage, and printing capacities for digital documents.

On July 26, 2001 Xerox's board of directors announced Mulcahy's appointment as president and CEO, effective August 1. Explaining the board's choice, Paul Allaire told Claudia H. Deutsch for the *New York Times* (July 26, 2001, on-line) that Mulcahy was "a driver of our turnaround plan, and she's shown a great willingness to embrace change. She is definitely the right person for the job." Sheila Wellington, who has worked with Mulcahy on the board of Catalyst, a nonprofit research and advisory group specializing in women's issues, agreed. "Anne's had an exceptional breadth of experience within Xerox, she has a superb analytic mind, and she's a crisp, decisive leader," Wellington told Deutsch. Others wondered whether Mulcahy could institute the radical changes the company needed. "The good news or the bad news is she has the soul of Xerox. The risk is, maybe she's too close to it," an adviser to Xerox told Pamela Moore. For her part, Mulcahy told Moore that she was ready to make necessary changes. "There needs to be far more innovation and receptivity to new ideas," she said. "I have very little time for endless debate and consensus."

According to many observers, Xerox's difficulties had resulted as much from its corporate culture as from the company's slowness in incorporating new technology into its products, and therefore Mulcahy would have to work as hard to change the former as she would the company's product line. "Xerox has more red tape than most government bureaucracies," Gary Peterson wrote for *Spotlight* (February 15, 2001, on-line), the newsletter of ARS, a market-research firm. "Every type of decision must gain a stamp of approval by dozens of managers, supervisors, and consultants. . . . This culture worked in the past when Xerox dominated the high-end, high-dollar copier and print production markets. Xerox was generating the revenue to support this culture because the technology was roughly 30 years old and slow to change, and the company had little to no competition. Now the world has gone digital; IT [information technology] prices are plummeting, and aggressive competitors from Japan and Germany have entered the spectrum. Today, Xerox's bogged down culture is simply too slow to keep up and react to the increasingly complex world in which it exists."

Mulcahy has shown that she is not afraid to take bold action on various fronts. For example, she was a major player in Xerox's $950 million acquisition of Tektronix Inc.'s color-printer business in early 2000—the firm's first major acquisition since the 1970s—and she has led Xerox's first forays into providing services via the Internet. She is also much more accessible than the company's top brass has traditionally been; during her first three months as president and COO, she traveled across the country, holding dozens of meetings with employees. She has promised to fly anywhere, anytime to help salespeople close tough deals, and she has tried to announce layoffs in person. Mulcahy has said that she wants Xerox to offer services to help businesses manage documents, not just reproduce them. "It's the ability to walk and chew gum," she told Moore. "We can't be [just] the giant copier company."

Xerox hopes to break into the printer market, by means of both its addition of direct-imaging lithographic presses to its product line and the launch of its Premier Partner program. The latter offers what Mulcahy described to Bob Hall for *Quick Printing* (November 2000, on-line) as "the virtual printing company of the future": making use of the Internet, Xerox channels printing jobs to selected graphic-arts service providers; it also offers graphic-arts training courses, workflow tools, and a way of sharing jobs through arrangements by on-line global directors. As Mulcahy explained to Hall, the Premier Partner program "creates a global electronic hub to connect supply and demand in the printing industry. We are offering our partners access to an expensive infrastructure without having to invest in their own. They will now have the ability to say 'yes' to virtually any new business opportunity."

Xerox lost $167 million in the third quarter of 2000; as of March 2001 the company had a $17 billion debt, of which $2.7 billion came due later that year. Later in 2001 its financial health began to improve. At the end of the first quarter, its operating losses totaled $86 million, or 12 cents a share—less than the 28 cents a share that analysts had predicted or the 31 cents a share that Xerox had expected. The company had a net income gain of $158 million for the period, including the proceeds from asset sales and restructuring. Xerox returned to operational profitability in the fourth quarter of 2001; in the second quarter of 2002, the company had its strongest showing in two years, with earnings of 12 cents a share and an operating cash flow of $541 million. Xerox drew ahead of schedule in cutting costs, largely by removing overseas management positions and reducing the need for technicians (since digital machines don't break down as often as older, nondigital copiers). The sales of newer divisions, Mulcahy has pointed out, has enabled Xerox to concentrate on such core businesses as document management services and superfast and color copiers. "Though we are reducing costs in many areas, we are actually ramping up the color investments that are critical to our future," Mulcahy said in a March 20, 2001 Xerox press release. "Our goal is to make the vast majority of Xerox products color enabled over the next three to five years." In 2000 revenues from such products amounted to $3 billion, double the total for 1997.

On December 3, 2001 Xerox's board of directors elected Mulcahy to the post of chair, effective January 1, 2002. She continued to hold the position of CEO, while the post of president was eradicated.

Mulcahy is well liked among Xerox employees. She has attributed her popularity to her honesty and willingness to tackle thorny questions. "I get out in front of our people every day and am willing to answer the really ugly questions," she told *Darwin* magazine (August 2001, on-line). "If you do that in front of thousands of people, they know you're not hiding from the tough issues. They understand that this company may be changing, but if you're a part of it going forward, you won't have to keep looking in the rearview mirror and wonder if it's something you want to be a part of."

Mulcahy is known for her low-key demeanor. She has sometimes been mistaken for Carly Fiorina, the CEO of Hewlett-Packard, as the two have similar builds and short blond hair. Mulcahy's first marriage, to Charles Roy, ended in divorce. In 1981 she married Joe Mulcahy, a now-retired Xerox regional sales manager, whom she met on a company ski trip. The couple have two sons—Michael, born in 1983, and Kevin, born in 1987. Mulcahy is a member of Xerox's four-member office of the chairman as well as the company's board of directors. She also sits on the boards of directors of Fuji Xerox Co., Xerox (Europe) Ltd., the Target Corp., Axel Johnson Inc., Catalyst, and Fannie Mae. — K.E.D.

Suggested Reading: *ARS Spotlight* (on-line) Feb. 15, 2001; *Business Week* p47+ Aug. 6, 2001, with photos; Executives' Club of Chicago Web site; *New York Times* C p1 May 13, 2000, with photo; *New York Times* (on-line) July 26, 2001

---

## Murray, Ty

*October 11, 1969– Rodeo performer*

*Address: c/o Tony Garritano, 8076 W. Sahara, Las Vegas, NV 89117*

The rodeo champion Ty Murray has been called "King of the Cowboys," "Superman in Boots," and, perhaps inevitably, "the Michael Jordan of professional rodeo." During his career as a professional cowboy, which began in the late 1980s, Murray won the World Championship in bull riding twice, and in 1998 he became the first cowboy to win seven All-Around Championship titles at the Professional Rodeo Cowboy Association (PRCA) National Finals. (The previous record of six such titles was set by Larry Mahan, in the 1970s.) Moreover, in a sport in which few athletes earn enough to quit their day jobs (and in which those who do often have trouble covering travel expenses and tournament entry fees), Murray set records for the most money earned at a single rodeo event. His prize money totaled more than $3 million when, on May 14, 2002, he announced his retirement. "I've been thinking about it all year, because I don't have the focus, drive and intensity I've had in the past," he explained on his Web site. "You have to have a fire in you for this sport, because it's way too dangerous to do it as an afterthought, and I've never been interested in competing at any capacity less than that of a serious contender. I've always promised myself that I'd retire before I started to backslide, and I'm keeping that promise."

As a cultural phenomenon, professional rodeo exists in a limbo between past and present. In some respects the sport is a relic of a vanished way of life: contemporary ranchers don't have much need to break wild horses (they can buy tame animals at auction), and the frontier passed out of living memory long ago. Few professional cowboys grew up on ranches, and most have at least a partial college education. At the same time, rodeo has become a modern professional sport: some 23 million fans attend the more than 700 rodeos staged by the PRCA annually around the nation, and each week more than 1.5 million television viewers tune in to the PBR [Professional Bull Riders] Bud Light Cup, broadcast on the Nashville Network.

A typical rodeo features three so-called roughstock events—bareback riding, saddle bronc riding, and bull riding—and often includes timed events, such as team roping, calf roping, steer wrestling, and barrel racing. Because the roughstock events are more demanding and more dangerous than the timed events, they confer more status on those who compete in them. (That status also carries a price: few roughstock cowboys remain sufficiently physically fit to compete beyond their early 30s.) Unlike most rodeo cowboys, who specialize in only one of the roughstock events, Murray excelled at all three.

In bareback riding, a contestant seeks to remain astride a bucking bronco for a full eight seconds by hanging on, with only one hand, to a thin rawhide rigging. For the duration of the ride, the cowboy must continually spur the horse; if he achieves a scoring ride, by staying mounted until the eight-second buzzer sounds, he is then judged on his

Andy Watson/Courtesy of PBR

*Ty Murray*

control and spurring technique. Physically, bareback riding is probably the most punishing of the roughstock events, since the horse's hindquarters slam into the rider's head and back when it kicks with its hind legs. As J. Pat Evans, a rodeo physician and former team physician for the Dallas Cowboys, explained to Skip Hollandsworth for *Texas Monthly* (May 1999), a bareback rider "can take as many hard hits in eight seconds as a professional football player does in an entire game." (Unlike pro football players, bareback riders do not wear protective gear.)

Saddle bronc riding differs from bareback riding in that the horse is outfitted with a modified western-style saddle. Again, a cowboy must remain mounted for a full eight seconds in order to score, after which he is judged on his form and spurring technique. (The spurring in saddle bronc riding differs from that of the bareback competition in that it is executed in a front-to-back, rather than an up-and-down, motion. Ideally, the spurring is synchronized with the horse's bucking.)

Bull riding is without question the most glamorous rodeo event, and the most dangerous as well. Walt Garrison, a rodeo cowboy and former Dallas Cowboys running back, told Jeff Coplon for the *New York Times* (April 12, 1992) that riding a bull is "like reachin' out with a hay hook and grabbin' a freight train goin' 60." A rodeo bull can weigh up to a ton—over 10 times the weight of the typical cowboy—and is as quick as or quicker than a bronco. In bull riding, as in bareback and saddle bronc riding, a cowboy must hang on for a full eight seconds in order to score. The bull, meanwhile, in an effort to throw the rider, executes an array of maneuvers that includes leaping up to four feet in the air, crashing down to the ground, charging forward, pivoting, and tilting its back from side to side. The challenge for the cowboy is to anticipate what the bull will do next. "Bull riding is counteracting whatever the bull does," Murray explained to Hank Whittemore for *Parade* (November 22, 1992), "and no matter what you might plan, it's different each time. So I try not to plan too much. The hardest thing, with the animal being so strong and things happening at 90 miles an hour, is just to stay loose and focused at the same time." "If you make one small shift the wrong way on a good bull," he told Hollandsworth, "you do not stay on. And it's when you're down that you become the most vulnerable, because that's when a bull will try to trample you or hook you with his horns."

Murray has survived the flailings and pummelings of broncos and bulls for some 23 years. The only son of Harold "Butch" Murray and his wife, Joy, he was born on October 11, 1969 in Phoenix, Arizona. He has two sisters, Kerri and Kim. Both of his parents participated in rodeos as teenagers, and they encouraged in their son a love of the sport. "If there was someone born to ride, I imagine it was me," Murray told Skip Hollandsworth. "As a family, we didn't ski or bowl or play golf. We went to participate in rodeos on weekends." Ty's first words, his mother told Hollandsworth, were "boo wider" ("bull rider"), and soon after he learned to walk, he would sit astride her sewing-machine cover and pretend to ride.

By age two Murray was riding calves with his father's assistance, and one year later he was able to stay mounted by himself. By the time he entered grade school, Murray was already set on becoming a rodeo champion. To improve his balance, he would practice walking along fence posts or riding a unicycle; with the money he saved from doing odd jobs and chores, he bought himself a mechanical bull. Later, in high school, he joined the student gymnastic team, to further build his strength and coordination.

Murray mounted his first bull at age nine. As he later admitted, it was a frightening experience: "When you first start riding bulls, it's so scary that everything kind of goes black," he told Whittemore. On his second attempt, he suffered a broken jaw after the bull threw him and stepped on him. Undaunted, he began riding again as soon as he recovered. "He knew that hard knocks were part of the sport," Murray's father told Hollandsworth. Nowadays, Murray explained to Whittemore, "I tell kids in rodeo school that [seeing everything go black] happens out of fear, but each time they ride things will get a little clearer. When you do something over and over, your body gets to where it reacts. You get to where things seem to slow down and you can think."

At age 12 Murray entered his first rodeo, riding in the bareback competition. One year later he competed in the Little Britches National Finals, a junior rodeo, in Colorado. Larry Mahan, who at the time held the PRCA record for the most All-Around Championship titles, was deeply impressed by the ability Murray displayed at that event. "I thought, 'My God, he's riding bulls better than I did when I was a world champion,'" he recalled to Hollandsworth. "He was already a master of his mind and body, almost Zen-like in his control."

In 1987 Murray won the National High School Rodeo all-around title. That same year he matriculated at Odessa College, a two-year school in Odessa, Texas, with a strong extracurricular rodeo program. While at Odessa he turned professional, and in 1988 the PRCA named him Rookie of the Year. In 1989 he qualified for the PRCA's National Finals in Las Vegas, where he ended up winning the first of several All-Around Championship titles. He was the youngest all-around champion in the history of the PRCA.

For six consecutive years beginning in 1989, Murray competed in the PRCA's annual National Finals, and each time he captured the All-Around Championship title. During those years he regularly qualified for the finals in the bareback, saddle bronc, and bull riding competitions, and in 1993 he took first place in bull riding. From 1995 to 1997 Murray was sidelined by injuries; he underwent reconstructive surgery on both knees and both shoulders. Upon returning to competition, in 1998, he once again won the PRCA All-Around Championship title, as well as the Bull Riding Championship title. He later began concentrating on his PBR career. (He is a founding member and original shareholder of the PBR.) In 1999 Murray won the PBR Bud Light Cup World Championships in Las Vegas. (He also qualified for the PRCA finals that year, but did not take the title.) In 2000 he was inducted into the ProRodeo Hall of Fame.

In announcing his retirement, on May 14, 2002, Murray declared, as quoted on his Web site, "I've had a great career, and I don't feel like I have anything to gain by staying out there if my heart's not in it. I always said I'd ride as long as I could be competitive at the world-class level and as long as it continued to be fun. I feel like I've accomplished everything I wanted to, so there's no other brass ring for me to grab."

In collaboration with Kendra Santos (the editor of *Pro Bull Rider* magazine), Murray wrote a memoir, *Roughstock: The Mud, the Blood and the Beer* (2001). He has served as an occasional television commentator for rodeo events broadcast on ESPN. He lives outside Stephenville, Texas, on a ranch he purchased with his rodeo prize money. (Stephenville, home to a dozen or so top rodeo cowboys, is known as the "Cowboy Capital of the World.") In his free time he enjoys fishing and other outdoor pursuits. Murray has been linked romantically with the singer/songwriter, poet, and memoirist Jewel. — P.K.

Suggested Reading: *New York Times* VI p34+ Apr. 12, 1992, with photos; *Parade* p4+ Nov. 22, 1992, with photos; *Texas Monthly* p118+ May 1999, with photos; Ty Murray Web site

Selected Books: *Roughstock: The Mud, the Blood and the Beer* (with Kendra Santos), 2001

---

## Myers, Richard B.

*Mar. 1, 1942– Chairman of the Joint Chiefs of Staff; U.S. Air Force general*

*Address: Chairman of the Joint Chiefs of Staff, The Pentagon, Washington, DC 20318-9999*

On August 24, 2001 President George W. Bush announced his selection of air force general Richard B. Myers to serve as the next chairman of the Joint Chiefs of Staff, the nation's highest-ranking military leader after the president. The chairman of the Joint Chiefs advises the president, the secretary of defense, and the National Security Council on military matters; helps plan all military operations; and makes decisions about the acquisition of new weapons and other matters that affect the armed services. Myers's diverse military experience, which began four decades ago, includes service as a fighter pilot during the Vietnam War and as commander of the U.S. Air Force Fighter Weapons School, U.S. forces in Japan, Pacific air forces in Hawaii, the North American Aerospace Defense Command, and the U.S. Space Command. Myers assumed the position of chairman of the Joint Chiefs on October 1, 2001, after serving as vice chairman for 19 months.

By his own account, before he was sworn in as chairman, General Myers anticipated as his top priorities modernizing the military, streamlining the bloated Pentagon bureaucracy, and fighting for

Alex Wong/Getty Images

*Richard B. Myers*

the development and deployment of technologically advanced weapons systems, such as the missile defense shield. Then, on September 11, 2001, three days before his appointment was confirmed by the U.S. Senate, terrorist hijackers flew planes into the twin towers of the World Trade Center, in New York City, and the Pentagon, in Washington, D.C., killing nearly 3,000 people. In response, President Bush vowed to bring to justice those who sponsored terrorists and punish any nation that sheltered or supported them, singling out as enemies of the U.S. the terrorist leader Osama bin Laden and the Taliban regime in Afghanistan. Myers helped plan the American military response to the terrorist attacks, and he has continued to play a key role in the ongoing U.S. campaign against worldwide terrorism. By the end of 2002, Myers was preparing for a possible U.S. attack on Iraq, to remove Saddam Hussein, the Iraqi president, from power and prevent him from using the weapons of mass destruction that some observers believe he has developed, in violation of United Nations resolutions.

General Myers's appointment as chairman of the Joint Chiefs was widely praised. In an interview with Vernon Loeb for the *Washington Post* (August 24, 2001), retired general Merrill "Tony" McPeak, a former air force chief of staff and colleague of Myers's, described the incoming chairman as "a levelheaded guy, he doesn't panic, he eats pressure for breakfast, and doesn't have a personal agenda." Referring to two popular movie actors, the first known for his air of quiet strength on screen and the second for his rugged, two-fisted brand of heroism, McPeak added, "He's more of a Gary Cooper than a John Wayne."

The son of a hardware-store owner, Richard B. Myers was born on March 1, 1942 in Kansas City, Missouri, and grew up in Merriam, Kansas. As a child he witnessed the crash of a small military plane. The sight traumatized him and left him terrified of aircraft. To cure him of his phobia and convince him that airplanes would not harm him, Richard's pediatrician advised his parents to take him to the local airport. After many trips over several months, the boy overcame his fear.

In high school Myers was an outstanding athlete, earning letters in football and track. After his graduation he enrolled at Kansas State University, in Manhattan, Kansas. There, he joined the Reserve Officer Training Corps (ROTC) of the U.S. Air Force. In 1965 he earned a bachelor's degree in mechanical engineering (BSME) and was commissioned a second lieutenant in the air force.

That June Myers trained as a fighter pilot at Vance Air Force Base (AFB), in Oklahoma. When he completed his training, he was promoted to first lieutenant and assigned to the 417th Tactical Fighter Squadron at Ramstein AFB, in what was then West Germany. He flew the F-4D Phantom II, a long-range fighter-bomber. After spending time at bases in Idaho and Florida, Myers was promoted to captain and transferred to the 13th Tactical Fighter Squadron at the Udorn Royal Thai AFB, in Thailand, in December 1969. During the Vietnam War he flew missions over Southeast Asia, ultimately logging more than 600 combat hours.

In December 1970 Myers began an assignment in Japan, first as a pilot with the 80th Tactical Fighter Squadron at Yokota AFB and then with the 67th Tactical Fighter Squadron at Kadena AFB as an F-4 weapons-and-tactics officer and flight commander. Myers left Japan in September 1973 to become a flight instructor and "air-to-surface" flight commander at Nellis AFB, in Nevada. In addition to the F-4, Myers flew such combat aircraft as the T-33, the F-15, and the F-16, logging a total of more than 4,000 flight hours.

In 1976 Myers, who by then held the rank of major, broadened his education, receiving a diploma from the Air Command and Staff College at Maxwell AFB, in Alabama. The next year he received a master's degree in business (MBA) from Auburn University, in Alabama. From August 1980 to June 1981, he studied at the prestigious Army War College, in Pennsylvania. Later in 1981 he participated in the Program for Senior Executives in National and International Security at the John F. Kennedy School of Government at Harvard University, in Cambridge, Massachusetts.

In 1977 Myers was given his first post in Washington, D.C., at the headquarters of the U.S. Air Force, where he served as an operational test and evaluation staff officer in the directorate of operations and later as the deputy chief of staff of plans and operations. During the 1980s he assumed additional command and administrative duties. Promoted to full colonel in 1984, he was assigned to the headquarters of the Tactical Air Command at

Langley AFB, in Virginia. The next year he was appointed commandant of the U.S. Air Force Fighter Weapons School, in Nevada. In 1987 he returned to Langley AFB, first to serve as the commander of the 1st Tactical Fighter Wing and then to work in various administrative capacities. During this period he rose to the rank of colonel. On April 1, 1990 Myers was promoted to brigadier general. In December 1991 he became the director of fighter, command and control, and weapons programs in the office of the assistant secretary of the air force for acquisition, in Washington, D.C. In that post he was responsible for procuring new aircraft.

In November 1993 Myers, who had by then risen to lieutenant general, earned his first command, as the head of U.S. forces in Japan and the Fifth Air Force at Yokota AFB. In September 1995 a political crisis erupted, when three U.S. servicemen (one marine and two navy men) were charged with abducting and raping a 12-year-old girl from the Japanese island of Okinawa. The incident sparked widespread outrage against the American military in Japan. Some Japanese officials and members of the press even called for the scrapping of an agreement between the U.S. and Japan that gave special legal status to American military personnel. In an effort to cool the anger of the Japanese, Myers and former U.S. vice president Walter Mondale, who was then the U.S. ambassador to Japan, expressed publicly their "sincere apologies for the suffering this crime has brought to the child, her family, and the people of Okinawa," as quoted in the *Los Angeles Times* (September 20, 1995). In another conciliatory gesture, Myers and Mondale met with Masahide Ota, the governor of Okinawa. (In March 1996 a Japanese court found the servicemen guilty and sentenced them to prison.)

As commander of U.S. forces in Japan, one of Myers's top priorities was keeping American personnel at a high state of preparedness in the event that North Korea, one of the world's last hard-line Communist regimes, invaded South Korea. The general himself often flew F-15s from Okinawa in training exercises. In an interview with Kevin Sullivan for the *Washington Post* (June 7, 1996), Myers explained, "Our business is to be ready, and so to be ready, quite often the scenarios used by our F-15s will be threats that replicate what the North Koreans have and the tactics we've seen them execute."

In July 1996 General John Shalikashvili, who was then the chairman of the Joint Chiefs of Staff, tapped Myers to be his assistant at the Pentagon. "Quite often you find people who rise to that level who have a bravado about them, and it gets in the way of getting the job done," Shalikashvili observed to Vernon Loeb. "Dick doesn't have any of that. He's very confident—free of the sort of thing you would normally associate with people who have risen to senior ranks in the military." Among other duties, Myers served as Shalikashvili's liaison to the State Department and often accompanied Secretary of State Madeleine K. Albright on foreign trips, as a military adviser.

Myers left the Pentagon in 1997 to assume command of the Pacific Air Forces in Hawaii. In July 1998 he was appointed commander-in-chief of three important Colorado-based installations: the North American Aerospace Defense Command (NORAD), a binational U.S.-Canadian organization, which is responsible for monitoring the airspace over the U.S. and Canada for possible security threats; the U.S. Space Command; and the Air Force Space Command. Heading these posts, Myers became visible as an advocate for developing technologically advanced and space-based systems for national defense, such as satellites that enhance surveillance and also provide military personnel in cockpits, jeeps, tanks, and ships with maps, intelligence information, and orders in "real time." In *Aviation Week & Space Technology* (January 1, 2000), Myers pointed out that existing space-based technology had contributed to NATO's successful 1999 bombing campaign against Serbian forces in Kosovo, launched to end the Serb military's brutal aggression against civilians and the Kosovo Liberation Army. Myers cited as an example the Global Positioning System (GPS), which made possible highly accurate targeting of bombing sites and thereby helped to keep to a minimum the number of casualties among NATO forces and civilians. "Today the United States is the world's space superpower, the leader in the once-exclusive club," Myers wrote. "But unless we act now to protect and modernize our space systems, this advantage will quickly dissolve and eventually turn against us." The general also supported the development of a missile defense system for the United States, despite opposition from members of Congress who believed that such an approach to defense, while enormously expensive, would accomplish little. In 1999 the Pentagon unveiled a "cyberwarfare center" in Colorado Springs, Colorado, designed to protect American military computer systems from hackers and impair an enemy's computer networks. The center was placed under Myers's command.

In 1999 President Bill Clinton appointed Myers vice chairman of the Joint Chiefs Staff under General Henry Shelton, who was then chairman. (Members of the Joint Chiefs of Staff include, in addition to the chairman and vice chairman, the chief of staff of the army, the chief of naval operations, the chief of staff of the air force, and the commandant of the Marine Corps.) In a statement published in the *Weekly Compilation of Presidential Documents* (October 18, 1999), Clinton declared that he had "the utmost trust and confidence" in General Myers's ability to meet challenges "ranging from preserving and enhancing military readiness to modernizing and transforming our forces to maintain our military superiority in the 21st century." On November 1, 1999 the U.S. Senate confirmed Myers's appointment. As vice chairman Myers worked with Deputy Defense Secretary Paul D. Wolfowitz in drawing up the *Quadrennial Defense Review*, a lengthy report—issued by the Bush administration and published on September 2, 2001—that called for a major reassessment of the capabilities of the nation's armed forces.

In 2000 General Shelton announced that he would retire as chairman when his second two-year term expired, on September 30, 2001. Among the candidates whom President George W. Bush and his advisers considered to succeed Shelton were Myers; General Ralph E. Eberhart of the air force, the commander-in-chief of NORAD, the U.S. Space Command, and the Air Force Space Command; Admiral Vern Clark, the chief of naval operations; and another naval officer, Admiral Dennis C. Blair, the commander of the Pacific Command. Among the factors that led to the president's decision to select Myers was the general's broad experience. Additionally, Myers, like Bush, supported the development of a missile defense system and thus would serve as a powerful and influential voice in the effort to gain congressional and defense-community support for the project. Myers was also seen as someone whose interpersonal skills would complement those of Donald H. Rumsfeld, the secretary of defense. One of Rumsfeld's top priorities was modernizing the military and scaling back the Pentagon bureaucracy. But Rumsfeld was unpopular with many Pentagon officials, according to various accounts in the press, because of his heavy-handed management style. Myers, by contrast, who had the reputation of being diplomatic and politically savvy, was highly regarded at the Pentagon and would thus be able to help Rumsfeld push through his reforms. "General Myers is a man of steady resolve and determined leadership," Bush explained to the press, as quoted by the *Washington Post* (August 25, 2001). "His is a skilled and steady hand. He is someone who understands that the strengths of America's armed forces are our people and our technological superiority, and we must invest in both." Myers's nomination was regarded favorably by many members of Congress, other military leaders, and Pentagon observers. The Senate was expected to confirm Myers's appointment without any opposition or controversy.

On the morning of September 11, 2001, a few days before the Senate's scheduled hearings on Myers's nomination, terrorists hijacked four commercial airliners, crashing two (American Airlines Flight 11 and United Airlines Flight 175) into the twin towers of the World Trade Center, in New York City, and one into the Pentagon. The fourth plane, United Airlines Flight 93, crashed 80 miles southeast of Pittsburgh, Pennsylvania, after passengers foiled the hijackers' suspected plan to crash the plane into the White House or another federal building. Testifying before the Senate Armed Services Committee a few days later, Myers revealed that NORAD had received a report of the first hijacking at 8:38 a.m. Several minutes later two F-15 fighters were scrambled from Otis AFB, in Massachusetts. At 8:45 a.m. the hijackers flew American Airlines Flight 11 into the north tower of the trade center. When United Airlines Flight 175 crashed into the south tower, at 9:03 a.m., the two fighters were still 70 miles away. At 9:35 a.m., after the military received reports that another airliner has been hijacked and was bound for Washington, D.C., two F-16 fighters were launched from Langley AFB. A few minutes later, the terrorists crashed American Airlines Flight 77 into the Pentagon; an explosion shook the entire building, and one of its sides partially collapsed. At that moment most of the Pentagon's 20,000 civilian and military personnel were following the unfolding events in New York City on television and radio. Immediately after the crash, the Pentagon was evacuated, and rescue efforts were begun to help those trapped in the rubble. Myers and other top officials remained in the building, meeting in the National Military Command Center, a fortified and secure area below Secretary Rumsfeld's office, to monitor the crisis and discuss military options. By 10:30 a.m. both towers of the World Trade Center had collapsed. Including those aboard the planes, nearly 3,000 people were killed in the World Trade Center attacks and the crash of the hijacked plane in Pennsylvania; the death toll at the Pentagon totaled 189, including those aboard the plane. (The number at the Pentagon was far less than had initially been feared, because the plane crashed into an area of the building that was closed for renovations.) In response to the attacks, every airport in the United States was shut down, grounding all air traffic, and fighter jets were dispatched throughout the country to patrol the skies. That day, and again in an address to Congress on September 21, President Bush declared war on terrorism, vowing reprisals against those who had sponsored the September 11 attacks and any nation that aided or sheltered terrorists.

During Myers's Senate confirmation hearing, members of the Senate Armed Services Committee questioned him about why the fighter jets had failed to intercept the hijacked planes before they crashed into the World Trade Center and the Pentagon. Myers told the panel that the nation's intelligence agencies did not have any information or evidence that a terrorist attack of such scope was going to take place. He added that the military was trained to respond to airborne threats coming from outside the country, not from commercial aircraft departing from domestic airports. "We're pretty good if the threat is coming from outside," Myers said, as quoted by Bradley Graham in the *Washington Post* (September 14, 2001); "we're not so good if it's coming from inside." The general agreed with the senators that the nation's intelligence-gathering capabilities had to be greatly improved. He also warned that the role of the military in providing domestic security had to be clearly defined in order to alleviate fears that civil liberties would be ignored. "What will keep me awake in this job will be the things we haven't thought about," Myers said, as quoted by Graham. "There are probably more surprises out there." On September 14 the

Senate approved Myers's appointment unanimously. He was sworn in as the nation's 15th chairman of the Joint Chiefs of Staff on October 1.

The terrorist attacks of September 11 were blamed on Osama bin Laden, an Islamic extremist and wealthy Saudi Arabian exile who had masterminded the creation of the terrorist Al Qaeda network. In November 1998 a federal grand jury had indicted bin Laden on charges related to the bombings the previous August of the American embassies in Kenya and Tanzania, which killed hundreds of people. He was later implicated in the bombing in October 2000 of the *U.S.S. Cole* as it was docked in the Yemeni port of Aden; 17 sailors died in that attack. It was widely reported that bin Laden was hiding somewhere in Afghanistan. Most of Afghanistan was under the control of the Taliban, a fanatical group of Islamic clerics who seized power in 1995, in the aftermath of the nation's five-year civil war, which followed a decade of military occupation by what was then the Soviet Union. In 1998 the U.N. Security Council, to no avail, ordered the Taliban regime to stop providing shelter and training to terrorist groups; similarly, the Taliban ignored international expressions of deep concern about the brutal repression of Afghanistan's civilian population. In his September 21 speech to Congress, President Bush condemned the Taliban and demanded that it turn bin Laden over to the United States. Taliban representatives refused, denying that they knew where bin Laden was and claiming that there was no evidence that he had had any role in the attacks on the U.S.

Having failed to elicit any signs of cooperation from the Taliban, on October 7, 2001 the United States began military operations against suspected terrorist hideouts in Afghanistan. Both Myers and Rumsfeld helped plan the campaign, which was dubbed "Operation Enduring Freedom." General Tommy R. Franks, who headed the United States Central Command (Centcom), in Tampa, Florida, was placed in charge of the day-to-day effort. Throughout the rest of October, American bombers, fighters, and Tomahawk missiles launched from submarines struck the Taliban's air defenses and airfields and Al Qaeda terrorist camps. About two weeks after the air strikes began, the U.S. Special Forces, U.S. Army Rangers, and other elite military units arrived in Afghanistan to gather intelligence and attack special targets, such as the compound of the Taliban leader Mohammad Omar, near the city of Kandahar. Every day Franks conferred with Myers and Rumsfeld to update them on the progress of the campaign and discuss targeting strategies to minimize civilian casualties. Myers and Rumsfeld also held daily media briefings at the Pentagon.

Myers has warned Americans not to expect a quick and easy victory in Afghanistan or in the larger war against terrorism. During an appearance on the ABC television program *This Week* on October 21, 2001, the general said that American troops would try to capture Osama bin Laden alive but were prepared to kill him. "It depends on the circumstances," Myers said, as quoted by Peter Pae in the *Los Angeles Times* (October 22, 2001). "If it's a defensive situation, then you know bullets will fly. But if we can capture somebody, then we'll do that."

After three months of nonstop U.S. attacks, the Taliban regime collapsed, and many Taliban and Al Qaeda fighters fled or were captured. By December 2001 an interim government headed by the pro-Western Hamid Karzai took power in Afghanistan. Both Myers and Rumsfeld have declined to speculate as to whether bin Laden and Omar are still alive and hiding in Afghanistan or another country.

In 2002 U.S. troops in Afghanistan intensified their efforts to capture or destroy the remaining Taliban and Al Qaeda forces, believed to be hiding in the mountains and preparing to regroup. In May of that year, Myers visited U.S. forces in Afghanistan. Two months later he called for the continued improvement of the military. "While we have a war on terrorism, the last thing we can afford to do is halt any efforts towards making our forces more responsible in the 21st century," he said, as quoted by Amanda Riddle for the Associated Press State & Local Wire (July 30, 2002, on-line). "We do not have the luxury of waiting to transform to make ourselves better. We need every good idea."

Also in 2002 President Bush began to devote more attention to Iraq, demanding that President Saddam Hussein comply with a series of U.N. resolutions and dismantle the weapons of mass destruction that he had reportedly developed in the last few years or face a U.S.-led invasion. Bush feared that Hussein might use such weapons in a war or provide them to terrorists, who might use them to kill civilians, and he expressed support for a "regime change" in Iraq. Commenting on Bush's stance, Myers told William C. Mann for the Associated Press (September 8, 2002, on-line), "We think [Iraq's] capabilities today are much less than [they] were during Desert Storm. On the other hand, the U.S. armed forces and the armed forces of our friends and allies are much stronger. . . . The only thing I would say is that if the president decides that military action is needed against Iraq, the U.S. armed forces and our allies will prevail."

In October 2002 both houses of Congress approved President Bush's resolution authorizing the use of force against Iraq. U.S. forces in the Middle East began preparing for a possible attack. "No one wants a war," Myers told Adnan Malik for the Associated Press (October 29, 2002, on-line), "but the bottom line is the disarmament of Iraq."

Myers's honors include the Defense Distinguished Service Medal with one oak-leaf cluster, the Distinguished Service Medal, the Legion of Merit, the Distinguished Flying Cross with one oak-leaf cluster, the Meritorious Service Medal with three oak-leaf clusters, the Air Force Medal with 18 oak-leaf clusters, the Air Force Commendation Medal, the Joint Meritorious Unit Award with one oak-leaf cluster, and the Air Force Outstanding Unit Award with the "V" device and three oak-leaf clusters.

For recreation, Myers enjoys playing golf and riding his Harley-Davidson motorcycle. He and his wife have two daughters and a son. — D.C.

Suggested Reading: *Aviation Week & Space Technology* p54+ Jan. 1, 2000; Joint Chiefs of Staff Web site; *Los Angeles Times* p4 Sep. 20, 1995, A p1 Aug. 24, 2001, with photo, A p1 Oct. 22, 2001, with photos; *New York Times* A p5+ Sep. 12, 2001, with photos, B p4 Oct. 8, 2001, B p1 Oct. 24, 2001, A p18 May 6, 2002, with photo; U.S. Department of Defense Web site; *Washington Post* A p30 June 7, 1996, A p1 Aug 24, 2001, with photo, A p6 Aug. 25, 2001, A p8 Sep. 14, 2001, A p18 Sep. 15, 2001; *Weekly Compilation of Presidential Documents* p2051+ Oct. 18, 1999

---

Arnaldo Magnani/Liaison/Getty Images

## Najimy, Kathy

(nah-JEE-mee)

*Feb. 6, 1957– Actress; director; producer; playwright*

*Address: c/o International Creative Management, 8942 Wilshire Blvd., Beverly Hills, CA 90211*

The award-winning actress, director, playwright, activist, and self-described feminist Kathy Najimy first made a name for herself in the late 1980s, when she and Mo Gaffney wrote and performed the celebrated Off-Broadway comedy and HBO special *The Kathy and Mo Show.* Najimy's prominent stage work also includes her 2000 Broadway performance as Mae West in the play *Dirty Blonde* and her appearances in Eve Ensler's wildly successful *Vagina Monologues.* Her television credits include her role as a witty executive on the prime-time sitcom *Veronica's Closet,* which starred Kirstie Alley, and as the voice of Peggy Hill on the animated, Emmy Award–winning series *King of the Hill.* Often cast in humorous supporting roles, Najimy has appeared in more than 30 films since 1991, among them the hit movie *Sister Act* (1992), for which she won an American Comedy Award with her turn as the pathologically cheerful nun Sister Mary Patrick. A longtime AIDS and gay-rights activist, Najimy has been honored for her passionate and steadfast support of many causes and charities. "I'm really proud of myself," she told Marianne Schnall in an interview posted on the Web site *feminist.com* (August 16, 1994). "I worked really, really hard—but I also know that even with all the hard work . . . I wouldn't have [succeeded] if it wasn't for the women's movement and the performers before me and the people who take chances and the people who fought for their rights and fought to be heard and fought not to just be silly little women in the background. . . . It's . . . because of Gloria Steinem and Whoopi Goldberg's one woman show and Lily Tomlin's one woman show . . . people who came before us, that said, 'You need to listen to us. And feminists are funny.'"

Kathy Najimy was born to Fred and Samia Najimy, Lebanese immigrants, in San Diego, California, on February 6, 1957. Her father, who died in 1971, was a postal worker. "Being Lebanese is something I have grown up being very proud of," Najimy was quoted as saying on the *Lebanese Women's Association* Web site. "As a kid I wore it like a badge. I was a different breed as far as I was concerned." Her first television appearance was as a contestant with other members of her family on the game show *Family Feud* in 1981. (The Najimy family won the $10,000 grand prize.) She studied drama at San Diego State University. During a speech at the American-Arab Anti-Discrimination Committee Convention in 1997, which appears on *Caféarabica.com,* Najimy spoke of the early influences on her career, saying, "I was particularly influenced in my life by Marlo Thomas," an actress and the daughter of the famous Lebanese-American actor Danny Thomas. "She was Arabic and beautiful and smart and feminist, an author, actress and activist and the first woman character on T.V. who was single, a career woman, not living at home and not supported by a man." (In 2000 Marlo Thomas narrated an episode of *Intimate Portrait,* a series on Lifetime Television, about Najimy.)

In the mid-1980s Najimy, who had been working as a telephone operator, left San Diego for New York City with her friend Maureen "Mo" Gaffney, a comedic actress with whom she had begun writing and performing in San Diego's theater world. In New York the two wrote *The Kathy and Mo Show: Parallel Lives,* frequently referred to as a feminist comedy, which they began performing publicly at comedy clubs and other venues in 1986. Najimy and Gaffney toured the country with *Parallel Lives*, then performed the show Off-Broadway in New York for two years in the late 1980s. *Parallel Lives* consisted of a number of skits, with Najimy and Gaffney playing a variety of roles, including angels discussing sex and unsophisticated urban girls arguing over *West Side Story*. Stephen Holden of the *New York Times* (May 12, 1989) described *Parallel Lives* as "an evening of brilliantly observant two-character comedy sketches with a feminist slant." *Parallel Lives* gained popularity through word of mouth, and Najimy and Gaffney won an Obie Award in 1989. (The Obie Awards were created by the *Village Voice* in 1956 and recognize distinguished achievement in Off-Broadway and Off-Off-Broadway productions.) The cable channel HBO taped a 1991 performance of *Parallel Lives* in San Francisco and aired it as an hour-long special, for which Najimy and Gaffney were honored with CableACE Awards for best comedy special and best performance in a comedy special. (As of the summer of 2002, *Parallel Lives* was being performed by various acting companies around the country.) In 1995, in Los Angeles, HBO filmed *Kathy and Mo: The Dark Side*, which includes material from the stage version of *Parallel Lives* that was not used in the original HBO special. *The Dark Side* found Najimy and Gaffney playing, among other roles, an elderly Jewish woman dealing with her nephew's homosexuality and the specter of AIDS; an anti-abortion protester; and children fond of misquoting the Bible to each other during arguments. Like *Parallel Lives*, *The Dark Side* aired on HBO's *Comedy Hour*, and again the comedy team won CableACE Awards for best comedy special and best performance in a comedy special.

Meanwhile, with *Parallel Lives* having launched her career, Najimy began appearing in movies, including *The Hard Way* (1991), which starred James Woods and Michael J. Fox; *Soapdish* (1991), in which Sally Field and Kevin Kline headed a cast of high-profile actors; and *The Fisher King* (1991), with Robin Williams and Jeff Bridges. In 1992 Najimy played Sister Mary Patrick in the film *Sister Act*, which starred Whoopi Goldberg as a singer who, to escape the Mafia, disguises herself as a nun and lives in a convent. While the critical response to *Sister Act* was largely negative, the film garnered nearly $140 million at the box office. Roger Ebert wrote for the *Chicago Sun-Times* (May 29, 1992, on-line), "At least Goldberg and her fellow nuns (especially Kathy Najimy as the jolly Sister Mary Patrick) are able to create life and humor when the camera is upon them." "Najimy . . . may have to do penance for scene stealing; she's a comic wonder," a reviewer wrote for *Rolling Stone* (June 25, 1992, on-line). For her turn as Sister Mary Patrick, Najimy won an American Comedy Award in 1993 for funniest supporting actress and was also honored by the Hollywood Women's Press Club with a nomination for female discovery of the year. Najimy reprised the role in *Sister Act 2: Back in the Habit* (1993), which was not as big a hit with audiences as the original. In the comedy *Hocus Pocus* (1993), about three witches seeking immortality, Najimy starred alongside Bette Midler and Sarah Jessica Parker. The actress also starred in the Emmy Award–winning Turner Network Television (TNT) special *In Search of Dr. Seuss* (1994), as a reporter, Kathy Lane, who interviews various Dr. Seuss characters, portrayed by such actors as Christopher Lloyd and Patrick Stewart. Other movies in which Najimy appeared include *It's Pat* (1994), *Alien Encounter* (1995), *Nevada* (1997), *Zack and Reba* (1998), *Hope Floats* (1998), *Leaving Peoria* (2000), *The Wedding Planner* (2001), and *Rat Race* (2001). Najimy was the voice of Tillie Hippo in the animated movie *Cats Don't Dance* (1997), lent her voice to Harvey Fierstein's animated movie *The Sissy Duckling* (1999), which aired on HBO, sang and danced in the Fox special *Cinderelmo* (1999), and played the gynecologist of Sharon Stone's character in the 2000 HBO movie *If These Walls Could Talk 2*, which consisted of three stories about lesbian couples in different decades. She will star as one of three benevolent spirits who help two teenagers fight a ghost in the Disney Channel's original movie *The Soul Patrol*, which is scheduled to air in October 2002.

In three episodes of the CBS television series *Chicago Hope* that aired in February 1996, Najimy played Dr. Barbara "Bix" Konstadt, a psychiatrist struggling with manic depression. Between 1994 and 1998 she appeared on three episodes of *Ellen*, the hit television series that starred the actress and comedian Ellen DeGeneres. For three years beginning in 1997, Najimy had a role on the NBC sitcom *Veronica's Closet*, which starred Kirstie Alley as a self-help/romance writer and founder of a successful lingerie business; Najimy played Olive Massery, a savvy Lebanese-American executive in Alley's company. She received an American Comedy Award nomination for her performance in the series. In early 2000, in order to concentrate on her family and her film career, she left the show, which was canceled later that year. Since 1997 Najimy has provided the voice of the character Peggy Hill, the energetic substitute teacher and wife of Hank Hill, on the Emmy Award–winning animated Fox series *King of the Hill*, which revolves around the life of a quirky Texas family. As the voice of Peggy, Najimy has received two Annie Award nominations. (The Annie Awards, which include honors for voice talent, are the highest recognition of excellence in animation.) Najimy has also lent her voice to animated characters on the television programs *Hey Arnold!*, *Pepper Ann*, *Duckman*, *Hercules*, and *Little Bill*. Her other television credits include appearances on *She TV*, *The College of Comedy with Alan King*, and the drama *Early Edition*.

On the stage, in addition to *Parallel Lives* and *The Dark Side*, Najimy has performed in more than a dozen musicals, including productions of *Grease* and *Godspell.* She has appeared in a number of plays at the Old Globe Theater in San Diego. For five years Najimy was a member of the feminist theater company Sisters on Stage, for which she created and performed *It's My Party*, a one-woman show. Najimy also served as the resident director of the award-winning New Image Teen Theater in San Diego for four years. (The New Image Teen Theater is now known as Images; sponsored by Planned Parenthood of San Diego and Riverside Counties, it is a peer-education theater group for teenagers, who create and perform scenes based on real-life experiences involving sexuality and abuse issues.) In 1992 and 1993 Najimy directed the critically acclaimed Off-Broadway production of *Back to Bacharach and David*, a light-hearted musical revue celebrating the music of Burt Bacharach and the lyrics of Hal David. She also directed the Off-Off-Broadway plays *Don't Get Me Started* and *I Can Put My Fist in My Mouth.*

Along with Susan Sarandon, Glenn Close, Gloria Steinem, Jane Fonda, Oprah Winfrey, Whoopi Goldberg, Winona Ryder, and Alanis Morissette, among many other women, Najimy has performed in Eve Ensler's smash hit *The Vagina Monologues* in New York and California. Several of her appearances in the show were part of V-Day, a global movement to stop violence against women; V-day has been celebrated since 1998 through benefit performances held each year on and around Valentine's Day. With humor and candor, *The Vagina Monologues* explores many issues concerning women's sexuality and their bodies. "Eve Ensler is sent from the universe to heal the planet and has . . . ," Najimy told Tony Phillips in an interview that appeared on the *Next* magazine Web site. "Just the title is political in nature and moves people. Every word in the monologues is something that frees people, especially women."

In the well-received 2000 Broadway play *Dirty Blonde*, which tells the story of two eccentric New Yorkers whose shared obsession with the stage and screen idol Mae West leads to romance, Najimy reprised the roles of Jo and Mae West (played in the original Broadway run of the show, in early 2000, by Claudia Shear, who also wrote the play). Comparing Najimy with Shear in a review that appeared on the Web site *curtainup.com*, Elyse Sommer wrote, "The come-hither look is a tad less come-hithery, the strut and shimmying not quite aggressive. On the other hand, Kathy Najimy brings terrific comic timing to her interpretation of Jo, the actress-temp[,] and her idol, the legendary Mae West. While Najimy is a more actory Jo-Mae than her predecessor, Claudia Shear can go to London, where she's scheduled to reprise the tough girl, with the assurance that Najimy will do honor to her play on Broadway." Najimy told David Bahr for the *Advocate* (March 13, 2001), "I never played somebody who was a real person before. The characters I've played were closer to myself. The great thing was, director James Lapine said, 'Look, I don't want an impersonation. If I wanted an impersonation, I could get a drag queen who could do it better than anybody. We just want the spirit of the woman and her story.' . . . It's beautifully written and it deals with sexuality, tolerance, and Mae West. What more could you want?"

Najimy has served as a guest speaker or performer at many functions, benefits, and other events. She was, for example, the grand marshall of the 1997 Gay and Lesbian West Hollywood Pride March in Hollywood, California, and she sang and danced with Tim Curry in the opening act of the 1995 Academy Awards. For more than 20 years, Najimy has been involved in the fight for gay and lesbian rights and has been an AIDS activist. She has received the Daniel P. Warner Founders Award from L.A. Shanti, a Los Angeles–based organization dedicated to AIDS prevention and education and support for people infected with HIV/AIDS, as well as the L.A. Gay and Lesbian Center's Rand Schrader Distinguished Achievement Award. A vegetarian and an outspoken advocate of animal rights as well, Najimy is a longtime supporter of People for the Ethical Treatment of Animals (PETA), which has honored Najimy for her efforts. She has worked in support of Project Angel Food, AIDS Project Los Angeles (APLA), the Gay and Lesbian Alliance Against Defamation (GLAAD), Human Rights Campaign Fund, Broadway Cares, Equity Fights AIDS, the American Foundation for AIDS Research (amfAR), Planned Parenthood, Voters for Choice, the Arab Anti-Defamation League, and the National Abortion and Reproductive Rights Action League (NARAL). "I have been a feminist since I was about nine without knowing that there was a name for it," Najimy told Tony Phillips. "I have a really low tolerance for injustice and things that are unfair. . . . When I was 18, I hung out at a gay disco in San Diego. I used to stand outside and scream at the religious right zealots all night. I just never understood hate. Of course, now as an adult, I understand it is fear and shame, but when it starts to affect the world . . . then it becomes my business. " "Being a political person, the good has far outweighed the bad," Najimy told Jeanann Pannasch for *Ms.* (August/September 2001). "I get frustrated and I get angry, I get desperate. I get tired. But overall, it's so fulfilling to me that I will never stop. It's the most fulfilling thing that I do."

Najimy has published pieces in the *New York Times* and several national magazines. In addition, she contributed a chapter to the book *The Choices We Made* (1991), in which 25 men and women address the subject of abortion, and lent her voice to the audiotape version of Wally Lamb's best-selling novel *She's Come Undone*. Najimy will be featured in the book *Starpower*, which is scheduled for publication in late 2002 and focuses on politically active celebrities. Some sources list skydiving and playing in a band, Hail Mary, as Najimy's pastimes.

Najimy married Dan Finnerty in 1995. Thirteen years her junior, Finnerty is the front man for the Dan Band as well as an actor. The couple's daughter, Samia, whose godmother is Ellen DeGeneres, was born in 1996. "I'm most in my skin when I'm being a mother or an activist," Najimy told Betty DeGeneres in an interview for the Human Rights Campaign Web site. — C.F.T.

Suggested Reading: *Caféarabica: The Arab-American Online Community Center*; Kathy Najimy Web site; *Ms.* p73+ Aug./Sep. 2001, with photos; *New York Times* C p1 May 12, 1989, with photo, II p25 July 2, 1995, with photo; *Nextmagazine.net*

Selected Films: *Soapdish*, 1991; *Sister Act*, 1992; *Sister Act 2: Back in the Habit*, 1993; *Hocus Pocus*, 1993; *In Search of Dr. Seuss*, 1994; *It's Pat*, 1994; *Nevada*, 1997; *Cats Don't Dance*, 1997; *Hope Floats*, 1998; *The Wedding Planner*, 2001; *Rat Race*, 2001

Selected Television Shows: *Veronica's Closet*, 1997–2000; *King of the Hill*, 1997–

---

HY/NewsMakers/Getty Images

## Nelly

*Nov. 2, 1978– Rapper*

*Address: c/o Tony Davis, 4246 Forrest Park Ave., St. Louis, MO 63108*

"This is undeniable: Nelly is a gifted, witty MC in possession of one of the catchiest rhyme flows to ever hit the pop charts," Rob Marriott wrote for *Rolling Stone* (July 2, 2002, on-line). Nelly's first album, *Country Grammar* (2000), which features the Midwest flavor of his native St. Louis and the hit singles "Country Grammar," "Ride Wit Me," and "E.I.," rose to number one on the *Billboard* album charts and sold more than eight million copies, in the process making Nelly a rap icon and putting St. Louis on the hip-hop map. He followed up that success with the album *Nellyville*, which also went to number one, as did its singles "Hot in Herre" and "Dilemma." "I don't sound like anyone," Nelly told a writer for *Jet* (July 30, 2001). "I've got a style that's all my own. I'm rappin' the blues. I like to think of my music as a jazz form of hip hop." Nelly was nominated for two Grammy Awards each in 2001 and 2002 and has won a number of honors, including an American Music Award for favorite rap/hip-hop artist in 2002.

Nelly was born Cornell Haynes Jr. in Austin, Texas, on November 2, 1978. His father was in the United States Air Force, and the family moved often—at one point living in Spain—as Nelly was growing up. After they moved to St. Louis, Missouri, Nelly's parents divorced. Nelly then found himself "moving around amongst friends and family, and . . . just always on the go," as he told a reporter for MTV, as quoted on the Web site *NellyHQ.com.* A talented baseball player as a teenager, Nelly attended the training camps of the Atlanta Braves and the Pittsburgh Pirates before deciding to pursue a career in music. During this time, Nelly, who did not graduate from high school, worked jobs at McDonald's and the United Parcel Service. In 1993 he formed the St. Lunatics, a rap group that included his high-school friends Robert "Kyjuan" Cleveland, Tohri "Murphy Lee" Harper, Ali "Big Lee" Jones, Corey "Slow Down" Edwards, and Lavell "City Spud" Webb, Nelly's younger half-brother. The group achieved a measure of success in 1996 with the single "Gimme What Ya Got," which sold nearly 10,000 copies and was a hit in the St. Louis area. Nelly told MTV, "Well my man Big Lee's the oldest. He went away to college. And me, Kyjuan, and City Spud, my little brother, Murphy Lee, Kyjuan's little brother, we were back at home and, so to speak, rapping for the 'hood. My man Big Lee came home with a new outlook. He helped motivate us a little bit, like, 'Yo, we should try to do it this way. We should try to listen to what St. Louis is doing. Just listen to the other groups and just differentiate ourselves from all that.' That's what we did. We just took time and kept planting it, kept planting it, kept working in the studio for years in a row. I'm talking 'bout every day was a studio day. Even if we was just dropping by, grabbing a beat, or whatever, I [was in] the studio every day for three years. We just really pressed hard, man. It took hard work to get here." When asked by the MTV reporter about the group's relationship with their hometown, Nelly responded, "St. Louis is our foundation. No matter what we do right now, we always can fall back on the Lou', 'cause they've been loving us. They've been holding us up for so long. Any time we go down, they can give us that boost to come back up, and I think everybody needs that. Lock down home first, 'cause that's very important, we think." Nelly explained that because of its central location in the U.S., St. Louis absorbs the rap and hip-hop styles of both the East and West Coasts, in addition to southern and midwestern musical influences. "I listen to everybody from 2Pac [Shakur], Biggie [Smalls] . . . ," Nelly told MTV. "When you say L.L. [Cool J], man, you know that's a big influence right there. Snoop [Dogg], Goodie M.O.B, Outkast. We just pump it all right there. If it's hot, it's definitely in St. Louis."

In 1999 Nelly signed a solo deal with Universal Records. "Well, it wasn't my idea, it was a group idea," the rapper told MTV. "We sat down, and I want to tell everybody that it's not Nelly and The St. Lunatics, it's Nelly from The St. Lunatics, 'cause I'm still in the group, always will be in the group, started in the group, and I ain't never leaving the group. But it was something we all decided on." The St. Lunatics were having trouble acquiring a record deal and thought that Nelly, with his charisma and rhyming skills, might be able to achieve success more easily by himself and then be in a position to assist the others. In an article on the *Teen People* Web site, Nelly is quoted as saying, "I don't necessarily feel like a solo artist . . . I'm just the key in the door for the rest of the St. Lunatics. I'm the first to release an album. But we're all family. We came up together from nothing. So it's St. Lunatics for life."

In May 2000 Nelly released the single "Country Grammar," which reached number one on the *Billboard* rap singles chart—a spot it occupied for four weeks. The song featured the catchy refrain "down, down, baby," which was taken from a children's song, and the words "shimmy, shimmy ko-ko bop," borrowed from an old song by Little Anthony and the Imperials. "Country Grammar" was played often on the radio and could be heard blasting from cars and clubs in cities nationwide. In June Nelly's debut album, also titled *Country Grammar*, appeared. When asked by the MTV reporter about the meaning of the title, Nelly said, "I'm basically representing for everybody [in the] Midwest, South . . . everybody with that slur on their English, or everybody with that pronunciation that sounds a little off." For the album, in a smooth, sing-song style, Nelly took on such typical rap themes as crime, on the song "Greed, Hate, Envy," and sex, on the track "Thicky Thick Girl." The song "Batter Up" exemplifies bravado and male posturing, and in "Ride Wit Me" Nelly rapped breezily about an intoxicated spin in a Mercedes Benz. In a review of the album for VH1, which appears on the Web site *cdnow.com*, a critic commented, "Not only does [Nelly] deserve to take his place as the leading exponent of Midwest rap thanks to his spicy rhymes, innovative country slanguage, and diverse street dreams, but Nelly proves the true strength of 'outer borough' hip-hop with every track. . . . Nelly raps with a knowledge that he has nothing to lose. And that degree of street and craft passion soars high," as Nelly injects "strong doses of dirty Mississippi blues and earthy jazz rhythms into his jangly, bounce-driven rhymology."

By September 2000 *Country Grammar* had sold more than three million copies and reached number one on the *Billboard* album charts, where it stayed for several weeks, supplanting the rapper Eminem's album *The Marshall Mathers LP*. Nelly performed "Country Grammar" at the MTV Video Music Awards, and the video for the song topped MTV's listing of Top 20 videos. In December Nelly's "E.I.," a party anthem with the infectious arms-in-the-air refrain "Ohhh! Ohhh!," became the second cut from *Country Grammar* to reach the Top 10. In 2000 Nelly was named the world's best-selling new artist at the World Music Awards ceremony in Monaco. He was nominated the following year for Grammy Awards for best rap solo performance, for the song "Country Grammar," and for best rap album. That same year he won a Blockbuster Entertainment Award for favorite new male artist; a Black Entertainment Television (BET) Award for best new artist; an MTV Video Music Award for best rap video for "Ride Wit Me," which was also nominated for best male video and a viewer's choice award; two *Source* Awards, for album of the year and new artist of the year; and a Soul Train Music Award for best rhythm & blues/soul or rap new artist. Nelly's popularity earned him a spot alongside Aerosmith, Britney Spears, and 'N Sync as a performer at the 2001 Super Bowl halftime show, and Nelly could be heard singing with other famous performers on the All-Star Tribute benefit single "What's Going On," an updated version of a classic Marvin Gaye song, the proceeds from which were donated to the fight against AIDS and to the United Way's September 11th Fund, which was set up in the wake of the September 11, 2001 terrorist attacks. By the end of 2001, *Country Grammar* had sold more than eight million copies.

After achieving success as a solo artist, Nelly helped the St. Lunatics acquire their own record deal, then joined them to record the album *Free City* (2001). The title expressed the group's desire to see Nelly's younger brother and bandmate City Spud, who raps on and produced the Nelly hit "Ride Wit Me," freed from prison, where he is serving time on charges of armed robbery. *Free City*, which features the hit single "Midwest Swing," debuted at number three on the *Billboard* 200 albums chart and quickly sold more than a million copies. (Jason Epperson, who produced most of *Country Grammar*, produced most of *Free City* as well.) In a review of *Free City* posted on the Web site *dotmusic.com*, John Mulvey pronounced the record to be almost as good as Nelly's *Country Grammar* and praised the atmosphere of fun that resulted from its celebration of cars, girls, and partying. "There's something improbably good-natured about these low-slung grooves," Mulvey wrote.

In January 2002 Nelly was in the Top 10 again, with the song "#1," which he contributed to the soundtrack for the movie *Training Day* (2001) and later included on his second album. In June 2002 Nelly's single "Hot in Herre" went to number one on the *Billboard* Hot 100 chart. (Nelly added the extra "r" to the title "Hot in Herre" to emphasize the way in which fellow natives of St. Louis and the Midwest pronounce certain words—another example of the "country grammar" he celebrated on his first album.) The August 5, 2002 issue of *Jet* estimated the song's radio audience during one record-setting week at 163.1 million people. That same month his second album, *Nellyville,* was released. "Nelly's music moves forward in funk-rooted blips and starts, embellished with high vocal whoops, asides, and exclamations that function as hooks," Tom Sinclair wrote in a review of *Nellyville* for *Entertainment Weekly* (June 28–July 5, 2002, on-line). "He works with a variety of producers (including young St. Louis native Jason 'Jay E' Epperson and, on 'Hot in Herre,' the Neptunes), rapping with an easy confidence and a steady, steamrolling flow. . . . Nelly offers some words of advice to his rivals: 'If what you got ain't hot, then check your flame/If what you're spittin' ain't hittin', then check your aim.' On the evidence of *Nellyville,* our man seems to be in control of his flame and on top of his game as he takes aim at the pop charts once again. If you like your rap loose and funny, Nelly's the man for you." Sinclair also praised the album's nods to older works, including the music of the go-go pioneer Chuck Brown. While most other reviews of the album were positive, some critics qualified their praise. "It's a solid dance record, peppered with clever punch lines and very likable, yet it fails to capture the imagination," Rob Marriott wrote. "Outside of 'Pimp Juice,' the album sounds weighed down by the commercial pressures of going multiplatinum the last time out. After five tracks, one cannot help but wonder what might have been had Nelly not gotten so pop so quickly." Other songs on the album include "Splurge," in which Nelly sang about the benefits of success; the title track, for which he imagined a fictional city where marijuana is legal, everyone is rich, and children are given cars and diamonds; and "Work It," for which Justin Timberlake of the group 'N Sync joined Nelly. Cedric "The Entertainer," a St. Louis comedian and actor who was one of the stars of the Spike Lee movie *The Original Kings of Comedy* (2000), is featured in several humorous segments on *Nellyville.*

July 2002 found "Hot in Herre" at the top of three *Billboard* charts: those for Hot R&B/Hip-Hop Singles and Tracks, Hot Rap Tracks, and the Hot 100. In addition, Nelly's song "Dilemma," which is also on *Nellyville* and features Kelly Rowland from the music group Destiny's Child, was the fastest-climbing song on the *Billboard* Hot 100 chart and reached number one in August 2002, bumping "Hot in Herre" to number two. *Nellyville* topped the *Billboard* 200 albums chart and the Hot R&B/Hip-Hop Albums chart, selling more than 700,000 copies in its first week alone and eclipsing Eminem's 2002 CD, *The Eminem Show.* A month after its release, *Nellyville* had sold nearly two million copies. In 2002 Nelly was again nominated for two Grammy Awards, for best rap solo performance for "Ride Wit Me" and best rap/sung collaboration for "Where the Party At," a song by the Atlanta-based soul-music quartet Jagged Edge, which features a performance by Nelly and entered *Billboard* Top 10 lists in the second half of 2001.

Nelly sang with 'N Sync on their hit song "Girlfriend." He made his big-screen debut in the independent movie *Snipes* (2001), a drama in which he played a hip-hop star who is kidnapped. As of July 2002 Nelly was in talks with Paramount Network Television concerning a possible starring role in a new television sitcom. Nelly has appeared on the late-night Fox comedy show *Mad TV.* He helps the St. Louis community in a variety of ways, which include running a nonprofit foundation called 4Sho4Kids; that organization sponsors programs and events, such as basketball games and literacy drives, donates goods to schools, and assists children affected by drug addiction and Down syndrome. The rapper also runs his own clothing line, Vokal. — C.F.T.

Suggested Reading: *Billboard.com*; *Entertainment Weekly* (on-line) June 28–July 5, 2002; *Jet* p32+ July 30, 2001, with photos; *mtv.com*; *NellyHQ.com*; *rockonthenet.com*; *Rolling Stone* (on-line) July 2, 2002

Selected Recordings: *Country Grammar,* 2000; *Free City* (with the St. Lunatics), 2001; *Nellyville,* 2002

---

## Novacek, Michael J.

(NOH-vuh-chek)

*June 3, 1948– Paleontologist; museum curator*

*Address: Dept. of Paleontology, American Museum of Natural History, Central Park West at 79th St., New York, NY 10024*

Part intrepid explorer and part exacting scientist, the paleontologist Michael J. Novacek has made some of the most important discoveries of dinosaur bones ever recorded. Through his work in the desolate but beautiful Gobi Desert of Mongolia over the past dozen years, he has taken steps toward answering many questions about the Cretaceous period (146 million–65 million years ago), also known as the age of dinosaurs. Novacek has been fascinated by the desert since his childhood—when his favorite family-vacation spot was the Grand Canyon, in Arizona—and as an elementary-school student he was enraptured by paleontology. Explaining his success in a highly competitive field to Claudia Dreifus for the *New York Times* (January 8, 2002), he said, "I didn't get diverted. A lot of kids have their first intellectual experience learning about dinosaurs. But a lot of them, quite naturally, get diverted as they go along and develop interests in other things. I didn't get diverted." Novacek, who had a brief stint as a college teacher, has been asso-

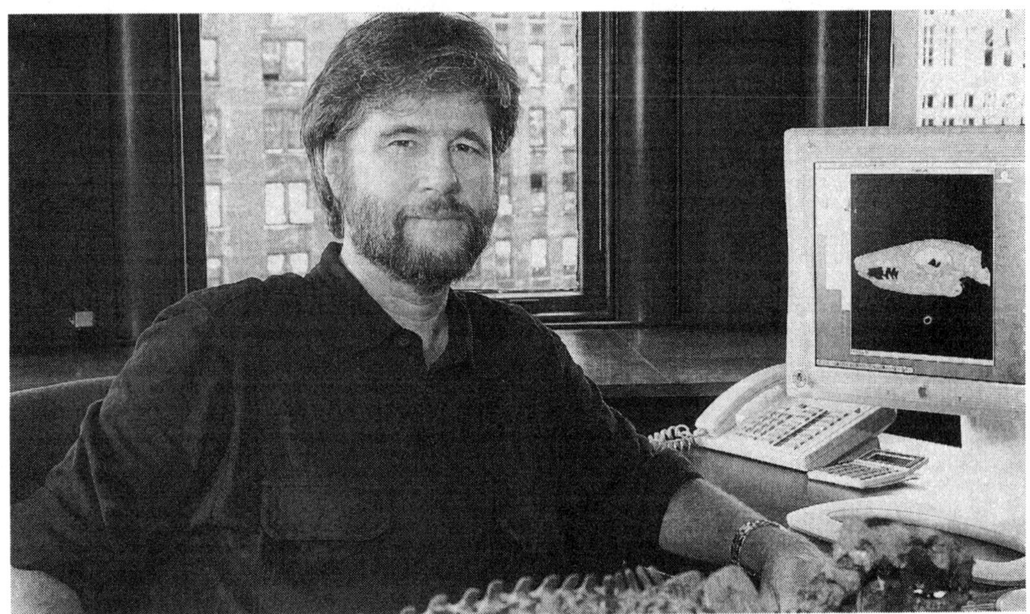

Courtesy of American Museum of Natural History

*Michael J. Novacek*

ciated with the American Museum of Natural History for 20 years as a curator and administrator, jobs that have allowed him at least one field trip a year since 1983. "I often feel this typical wanderlust thing," he admitted to Dreifus. "When I get back from the field, I say, 'I'm not going anywhere for the next 10 years.' But then the months go on and you find yourself jumping, ready to go. Again."

One of the four sons of Albin Novacek, a professional musician, and June (White) Novacek, a homemaker, Michael John Novacek was born on June 3, 1948 in Evanston, Illinois, and grew up primarily in Los Angeles, California. He first read *All About Dinosaurs*, by the early-20th-century adventurer and scientist Roy Chapman Andrews, at age seven. "I know that when I was a kid, my attraction to dinosaurs had a lot to do with the fact that they were big and scary," he told Claudia Dreifus. "Also, they existed in a time and place totally alien to my experience. At the same time, they were real." Although his Catholic-school teachers chided him for his interest in dinosaurs and Ice Age Mammals, referring to them as "monsters," and he lived in an urban area, where dinosaur remains were unlikely to be discovered, his fascination with the subject never wavered. "I wished I had grown up in Bozeman, Mont., or someplace where I could be surrounded by a lot of old and weird fossils," he told Dreifus. "But now that I think about it, I spent a lot of time fantasizing about what L.A. might have looked like millions of years ago. And it was fantastic to have the La Brea Tar Pits and to see the 10,000-year-old bones from there at the Los Angeles County Natural History Museum, which was my second home." When he was 10 his family moved to northern Wisconsin, where Novacek eagerly participated in amateur fossil hunts with a cousin; on one such outing he found a well-preserved trilobite, which his cousin sent to the Field Museum in Chicago. (He never found out what the museum did with it.) At age 13 Novacek returned to Los Angeles; as a teenager there he pursued other interests, including surfing and playing in rock bands.

After enrolling at Santa Monica City College, in California, through a student deferment that prevented him from being drafted into the military during the Vietnam War, Novacek transferred to the University of California at Los Angeles (UCLA), where he majored in zoology. With other students, he accompanied his mentor, Peter Vaughn, a UCLA professor, on a trip to New Mexico, Colorado, and Utah during the summer of 1969. "The dig that I went on in New Mexico . . . gave me my first real experience," he wrote for McGraw Hill—Invitation to Science, found on the *National Geographic* Web site. While he had a rough-and-tumble experience in the fiercely hot desert, he explained to Claudia Dreifus, "One of the lucky things was that when I was in college . . . there was a lot of reverence for basics. Backpacking was popular. It was fun not to take a bath all the time." The trip to the Southwest was a revealing one for Novacek, who discovered that "field paleontology could be boring, especially when you weren't finding anything," as he wrote in his book *Time Traveler* (2002). "But even boring field paleontology could take you to nice places." The ragtag group had greater success in Colorado than in New Mexico. Novacek explained in *Time Traveler* that the work, unearthing fossils and wrapping them in plaster for shipment, "was hard. But I liked the routine, I felt useful; we were a chain gang in the service of science." Although he knew it would be difficult to find a full-time position in paleontology, his summer experience solidified his commitment to the field. He worked with Vaughn again in the summer of 1970 and, with Vaughn's help, found a position connected to the Los Angeles County Natural History Museum. "As though in compensation for suffering persecution from nuns eleven years before in elementary school, I was offered employment in the La Brea Tar Pits," Novacek wrote in *Time Traveler.* He oversaw the extraction of bones from the pits on weekends and also identified and catalogued the finds.

While still harboring some hopes for a career as a rock guitarist, Novacek continued his studies after graduating from UCLA, in 1971. As his grades in chemistry could not gain him entry into UCLA's prestigious paleontology program, he enrolled instead at San Diego State University, to study for a master's degree in biology. Working with his professor Jay Lillegraven in San Diego, Novacek had the opportunity to practice the painstaking tasks required to find and identify tiny bits of bones and teeth; the Mission Valley area of San Diego was known to hold myriad specimens of small insectivores that lived during the Eocene period (55 million–34 million years ago), and he wrote his master's thesis on this topic. He earned his master's degree in 1973 and then entered a Ph.D. program at the University of California at Berkeley. In the summer of 1974, he accompanied two professors, Bill Clemens and Don Savage, to excavations in Wyoming and Montana. Aside from a brief bout of illness caused by intestinal bacteria from creek water, Novacek spent the summer uncovering bones from dinosaurs, ancient mammals, and reptiles. Afterward, he became so busy with academic and laboratory research that he did not return to Wyoming for several years. He earned his Ph.D. in 1978; even before graduating, he had taken a position as a teacher at San Diego State University. In 1982 he led a small expedition to Wyoming, his first field trip in years.

Also in 1982 Novacek was presented with a career-making opportunity. He moved across the country to become an assistant curator in the Paleontology Department at the American Museum of Natural History (AMNH), in New York City. In 1983, 1984, and 1985, with the help of funding from the National Geographic Society, he organized small trips to Baja California, where he had excavated remains of Eocene mammals as a graduate student; his team regularly found fossils from rodents, mammals, including antecedents of modern horses, and the extinct mesonychids, believed to be the closest land relatives of whales. Some of the fossil findings in Baja matched those made much farther north, in Colorado, Montana, Wyoming, and New Mexico. Based on these findings and other evidence, Novacek and a paleogeologist, John Flynn, offered the theory that the climate over much of the North American continent had been uniform 55 million years ago. "The combined results yielded a picture of the early Eocene earth as a hothouse that nurtured a Garden of Eden—with dense forest, lakes and rivers, and diverse mammals, birds, amphibians, and reptiles—that has not reappeared over such a wide swath of the earth's surface anytime since," Novacek explained in *Time Traveler.*

In the mid- and late 1980s, Novacek undertook several trips to South America under the auspices of the AMNH. Near the Chilean-Argentinian border, he and the members of his team found evidence of rodents, early species of horses, and glyptodonts, armadillo-like mammals, all of it estimated to be 15 million to 20 million years old. Invited by Paul Raty, a veterinarian in a small Chilean town high in the Andes Mountains, near a site where whale vertebrae had been unearthed, an AMNH team found fossilized remains of marine life, including oysters, shark teeth, and whale bones. The evidence of aquatic creatures added weight to the theory that the Andes are "among the fastest-growing mountains in the world," as Novacek wrote for *Smithsonian* (December 2001); 15 million to 20 million years ago, they were close to sea level, and the fossil remains trapped inside them were later carried to elevations of over 10,000 feet.

As Novacek advanced in the administration of the AMNH—in 1989 he was appointed a curator and took the titles of vice president and dean of science—he continued his globetrotting ways. A trip to Yemen in the summer of 1989 was not as successful as he had hoped. Then, in 1990, Novacek embarked on what he regarded as his most important scientific project: a series of expeditions to the Gobi Desert of Mongolia. (Mongolia had long been a Soviet republic and closed to scientific researchers from the West. When it became an independent nation, in 1990, the government allowed expeditions into the desert for the first time in more than 60 years.) Novacek was excited to be following in the footsteps of Roy Chapman Andrews, who spent his entire career at the AMNH and who, as leader of the famed Central Asiatic Expeditions, had named a swath of the desert the Flaming Cliffs, because of the hills of red, rocky sand there. Still, as Novacek told Jerry Adler and Adam Rogers for *Newsweek* (June 5, 1995), it was "just as hard to get into the desert from Beijing . . . as it was 70 years ago." The first joint American-Mongolian delegation reached the windswept badlands after a week-long journey via train, truck, and jeep from Ulaan Baatar, Mongolia's capital. The expedition yielded the skeleton of an ankylosaur (a low-slung herbivore covered in bony plates), dinosaur eggs, mammalian bones, and a skull of a previously undiscovered species of venomous lizard. Novacek and others from the AMNH returned to Mongolia in the summer of 1991 and again in 1992, joining the Mongolian paleontologist Demberylin Dashzeveg and a team from the Mongolian Academy of Sciences. The expedition found specimens of the dinosaurs *Velociraptor* and *Protoceratops*; *Mononykus*, a flightless bird; and *Zalambdalestes*, a mammal that hopped. All of those bones were found in locales previously known to researchers, either through the writings of Andrews or Mongolian expeditions that had taken place in the 1960s and 1970s. "We had not yet found the right new spot at the right time—the first time," Novacek wrote in *Time Traveler*. "There was after all nothing like the first time, when you walk into a gully strewn with skeletons and know it hasn't been walked before. Where were those localities? Had we entirely missed a mountain range and another valley behind it?"

Novacek's team stumbled onto a significant find in the summer of 1993. Forced to camp near a truck that had gotten stuck in the sand, the team noticed bones at the surface of the desert, just beneath their feet. After finding about three dozen skulls of lizards and mammals in only three hours, they decided to stay put and keep digging. "It's sort of out-of-body," Novacek recalled for Claudia Dreifus, describing the excitement of the experience. "I remember at one point, I felt like I was vibrating. The next day, there is a little bit of withdrawal because you wonder if this will ever happen to you again in your life." On the second day Novacek found six ankylosaurs and a skull identified as that of a Troodon, a small dinosaur—a rare fossil find. Over 10 days, the locale—named Ukhaa Tolgod by the Mongolian scientists—yielded fossil evidence of 13 theropod dinosaurs (meat eaters, among them *Tyrannosaurus rex*, that walked on their hind legs), 147 mammals, and 175 lizards. The researchers also found several dinosaur eggs, some with embryos preserved inside, and a dinosaur that had died while sitting on a nest of eggs. "What we found—and there is no doubt we were here first—is perhaps the richest little pocket of bones in the Cretaceous Gobi, or the Cretaceous anywhere for that matter," Novacek told John Noble Wilford for the *New York Times* (April 5, 1994). There were so many fossils at the site that, because of space limitations, it was impossible to transport them all right away; many were put away for safekeeping and taken away on later trips. "It's such an enriched vision of a Cretaceous world that almost transcends our capacities to understand it," he explained to Dreifus. "It's like finding Pompeii or something like that. The site will be mined for centuries." In 1996 Novacek published the well-reviewed *Dinosaurs of the Flaming Cliffs*, a detailed account of his first five expeditions to the Gobi Desert, with vivid descriptions of the fossil finds.

The rich fossil deposits at Ukhaa Tolgod, particularly in a section nicknamed Xanadu, after the beautiful, savage land in Samuel Taylor Coleridge's poem "Kubla Khan," brought Novacek back to Mongolia for several weeks every summer, despite the harsh working conditions. Because the Gobi is so vast, so dry, and so empty, the researchers were forced to transport all of their necessities there, some on water trucks that went into the desert from the closest spring, 80 miles away. "We only get to shower once or twice a summer," Novacek told *Science World* (December 11, 2000). In an on-line chat hosted by *Omni* magazine (December 8, 1996), he admitted, "Actually, there are times in the Gobi when I'd much rather be somewhere else. It's a great adventure, it's fun, I like deserts, there's a lot of beauty there, I feel comfortable sleeping on the ground, I've done it a lot of my life. Yet those hot fly-ridden days, the sun, the flash-floods are things I could really do without. On those days, the only things that keep us going are the knowledge of our previous triumphs and the anticipation of others to come." Beginning several years after the finding of Ukhaa Tolgod, Novacek would devote part of each summer to geological mapping and descriptions of the site, which were important for theorizing about the environment during the Cretaceous period and also helpful to the caravan of researchers trying to find the site again following months of sandstorms. "There's no orientation in the desert," Novacek explained to *Science World*. "We get lost a lot."

Novacek and his fellow scientists, including Mark Novell and Malcolm McKenna of the AMNH, began to put forth theories based on what they had found in the Gobi Desert. They echoed the already existing view that modern birds had evolved from Cretaceous dinosaurs and pointed to what they believed were links between placental mammals and marsupials, based on evidence found in the skeleton of *Zalambdalestes*. Additionally, they tried to solve the mystery of what had killed the dinosaurs, lizards, and mammals whose remains were secreted beneath the sand for 65 million years; among the plausible explanations were disease, starvation, or a series of cataclysmic sandstorms or flash floods, the latter of which might have combined with the sand to create enormous avalanches or mudslides. "The good sites, like Ukhaa Tolgod and the Flaming Cliffs, concentrated the remains of animals that may have come to feed and to breed in comparatively sheltered areas," Novacek wrote in *Time Traveler*. "These animals thrived in oases in the middle of a desert—oases that were not always oases, not always secure from elements like rain, floods, and mudflows. The harsh oscillations of drought and flood, starvation and bounty, pestilence and health on the Serengeti or the Okavango Delta in Africa are a reenactment of the timeless tension between survival and catastrophe that is integral to the evolutionary history of life on earth." What Novacek and his associates had uncovered in Mongolia, and witnessed while doing so, served as a warning about Earth's resources and capriciousness, Novacek believed. "I have a lot of colleagues in the field that basically say, 'Well, I'm not really trying to save the Earth. I'm just trying to get a census on what's left, and, so, people will know.' I would like to sort of diverge from that viewpoint," he told Bill Moyers on the PBS program *Earth on Edge* (June 19, 2001). "I really do think that there are a lot of scientists, a lot of professionals who understand this biodiversity loss better than anyone else . . . who really believe that that kind of information, that kind of work with conservation action and with government and policy, can lead to sustainable conditions that are better than we have now."

Novacek has been a provost of science and senior vice president at the AMNH since 1994. His second book, *Time Traveler: In Search of Dinosaurs and Ancient Mammals from Montana to Mongolia*, was published in 2002. He has also written many articles for professional journals and written, edited, or co-edited several technical books, among them *Mammal Phylogeny* (1993) and *Biodiversity Crisis: Losing What Counts* (2001). He and his wife, Vera, have a daughter, Julie, and live in New York City. — K.S.

Suggested Reading: *Natural History* p40+ Apr. 1994; *New York Times* C p1 Apr. 5, 1994, with photos, F p3 Jan. 8, 2002, with photo; *Science World* p14 Dec. 11, 2000; *Smithsonian* p98+ Dec. 2001; Novacek, Michael J. *Dinosaurs of the Flaming Cliffs*, 1996, *Time Traveler: In Search of Dinosaurs and Ancient Mammals from Montana to Mongolia*, 2002

Selected Books: *Dinosaurs of the Flaming Cliffs*, 1996; *Time Traveler: In Search of Dinosaurs and Ancient Mammals from Montana to Mongolia*, 2002

---

Courtesy of the Dallas Mavericks

## Nowitzki, Dirk

*June 19, 1978– Basketball player with the Dallas Mavericks*

*Address: Dallas Mavericks, 777 Sports St., Dallas, TX 75207*

In 1997, not long before Dirk Nowitzki joined the National Basketball Association (NBA), Charles Barkley and a group of other NBA superstars met him in Berlin, Germany, on a Nike-sponsored European tour. A skinny 19-year-old playing in a minor German basketball league at that time, Nowitzki impressed the American players; after the game Barkley told the German press, as quoted by Sönke Iwersen for *Sport* (March 1999), "He can call me if he wants to get to the U.S." By the next year Nowitzki had made the move to the States, primarily because of the persistent interest of the Dallas Mavericks' general manager and coach, Don Nelson. Now in his fifth season with the Mavericks, Nowitzki is an NBA star in his own right. Averaging an outstanding 23.4 points and 9.9 rebounds per game for the 2001–02 regular season (each figure eighth-best in the league), Nowitzki helped get the Mavericks to the play-offs. Because he is an extremely mobile seven-footer who, unlike most of the NBA's plodding big men, can shoot well from long-range and score close to the basket, too, Nowitzki, along with Kevin Garnett, the star forward for the Minnesota Timberwolves, represents a new kind of talent in the NBA. Named an All-Star for the first time in 2001–02, Nowitzki is among the best and the most exciting of the NBA's new crop of foreign-born players, a still relatively small group whose numbers are increasing partly due to his success.

Dirk Nowitzki was born in Würzburg, Germany, a scenic and tranquil town in the north of Bavaria, on June 19, 1978. His family was exceptionally athletic. His father, Joerg, played team handball with a West German crew; his mother, Helga, starred on the West German women's national basketball team; and his sister, Silke, has played professional basketball. Nowitzki didn't play basketball until he was 13 years old. "I was always playing soccer, tennis and team handball," he recalled to L. Jon Wertheim for *Sports Illustrated* (January 10, 2000), "but not at such a high level as the rest of my family. When I finally discovered basketball, I didn't know how to play, but it became my favorite right away." Holger Geschwindner, captain of West Germany's 1972 Olympic basketball team and the record holder for the most games played on the German national team, discovered Nowitzki at 15, when he was practicing basketball in a gym in Würzburg. Nowitzki, though skinny and still somewhat awkward, was dominating the other players in the gym that day, and Geschwindner saw in him unlimited potential. Geschwindner, who had become the owner of a project-management company after ending his career as a player, became Nowitzki's basketball mentor, coach, and unofficial agent. He put Nowitzki on a training regimen and devoted many of his lunch breaks to 90-minute basketball sessions with his student. Nowitzki's sister, Silke, told Iwersen, "Holger sees a bit of himself in Dirk. He's living his dream through Dirk. Let's face it, when Holger was playing, nobody here really cared for basketball."

In 1993 Nowitzki was a member of the German Bavarian Select team. By the middle of the next year, when he turned 16, he already stood six feet, seven inches. While attending Roentgen High School and helping his family run a house-painting business, he began playing basketball for the DJK Oliver Würzburg X-Rays, a second-division professional team. "I was having a simple, happy life" in Würzburg, he told Wertheim. In 1996 Nowitzki played on the German National Junior Team, the European Junior Select Team, the World Junior Select Team, and the German Under-22 National Team. Meanwhile, he continued to play outstanding basketball for DJK Oliver Würzburg. The American basketball player Paul Howard, who was a member of a German team from 1996 to 1997, told Iwersen, "He just does everything. He's tall, he's fast, and he scores from all over the court. Just like Toni Kukoc, only better." (Kukoc, a three-time European Player of the Year from Croatia, went on to develop a fine NBA career, winning three consecutive championships with Michael Jordan and the Chicago Bulls from 1995 to 1998; he now plays for the Atlanta Hawks.) There were questions, however, as to whether Nowitzki could play well against stiff competition; DJK Oliver Würzburg was, after all, only a second-division team. For his part, Nowitzki seemed content where he was and decided to play another year for his hometown team. Holger Geschwindner would tell anyone who asked that Nowitzki still had things to learn about basketball. Nowitzki told Iwersen, "In Würzburg, I was totally unrestricted. I could play any position I liked, so I really completed my game there. Besides, I wanted to move up to the first division with my team, and I just have absolute trust in Holger." Averaging 17.5 points and 9.9 rebounds per game over the course of 20 games, Nowitzki achieved his goal by leading DJK Oliver Würzburg to a division title in the 1997–98 season, which allowed the team to move up to the first division. He managed this while also serving a mandatory stint in the German army, from September 1997 to June 1998.

A pivotal moment for Nowitzki came in March 1998, when he was invited to play on the International Select Team in a game against top American high-school players in the Nike Hoop Summit, held that year in San Antonio, Texas. Nowitzki dazzled the crowd with 33 points and 14 rebounds in leading the international team to a 104–99 upset of the young American standouts, several of whom were on their way to the NBA. "Perhaps never before," Iwersen wrote, "has a non-American player come out of nowhere and shocked the community of coaches and agents the way Nowitzki did that day." The basketball great Larry Bird, as quoted by Iwersen, said of Nowitzki's performance, "If you went by that tape alone, you'd think he was the best ever."

The attention the German unknown received after his display in San Antonio was enormous. Suddenly, dozens of American colleges and a number of NBA teams were interested in him, and top Spanish and Italian teams offered him millions of dollars to play for them. Nowitzki was a bit bewildered by the options and consulted with Geschwindner and his parents to decide what to do. Though he elected to declare his eligibility for the 1998 NBA draft, he felt in his heart that it was too soon to make such a large jump. "I'm not ready for the NBA. I'm going to stay in Europe for another two or three years," he said, according to Iwersen. Despite that declaration Nowitzki was drafted ninth overall by the Milwaukee Bucks and then traded immediately to the Dallas Mavericks. Nowitzki and Geschwindner heard the news in Germany at around 4:00 a.m., when they called the house of a friend who was watching the NBA draft on TV via satellite. The Mavericks' Don Nelson had gambled on the chance that he could persuade Nowitzki to play for his team. He had traded his number-six pick in the draft, Robert Traylor, to Milwaukee for Nowitzki and the 19th pick. In an effort to persuade Nowitzki to join their team, Nelson and his son, the assistant coach, Donnie Nelson, flew to Germany, where they met Nowitzki and the Mavericks' owner, Ross Perot Jr. (who was not yet convinced that Nowitzki was worth all the trouble). Nowitzki hesitated, saying that he didn't feel ready for the NBA. Iwersen quoted Don Nelson as saying at the time, "He's a star. The kid doesn't know how good he is. I keep telling him he's got to let us worry about that." The Nelsons succeeded in their mission; Nowitzki and Geschwindner flew back with them to Dallas, where Nowitzki met the Mavericks players and decided, on the advice of Geschwindner, to join the team. By the time he left for the U.S. and the NBA, Nowitzki was leading the German first division in scoring with an average of 21.4 points-per-game, and was third in rebounding, with an average of 8.4 per game. Nowitzki also played in eight games for the German National Team in 1998, in the European Championships 22-and-Under tournament. (Germany finished seventh in the tournament, with a 5–3 record.) Germany's *Basket* magazine named Nowitzki the player of the year for 1998.

The 1998 NBA season was delayed by a dispute between the team owners and the players; in the meantime, Nowitzki had returned to Germany and rejoined DJK Oliver Würzburg. During the lockout-shortened 1998–99 season, Nowitzki played in 47 games as a small forward for the Mavericks. He started slowly, averaging only 8.2 points and 3.4 rebounds per game, but showed flashes of his enormous potential. Nelson held to his belief that Nowitzki was going to be a star player. In the 1999–2000 season, Nowitzki finished second in the balloting for the league's most improved player. He and Michael Finley were the only Maverick players to participate in all 82 games. Nowitzki led the Mavericks with 116 three-pointers (15th-best in the NBA), and was second on the team in both scoring (averaging 17.5 points per game) and rebounds (averaging 6.5 per game). Among the European players in the league, he was the third-leading scorer. During the 2000 NBA All-Star Game Weekend, he participated in the annual AT&T Shootout, in which players try to make as many three-point shots as possible in a limited time; Nowitzki placed second. He also played on the team of second-year players in the Schick Rookie Challenge, an annual All-Star Game Weekend event that pits rookies against second-year players.

During the 2000–01 season, Nowitzki established himself as one of the NBA's elite players, becoming the first Maverick in team history to be named to the All-NBA Team. (The members of that team are selected by a panel of writers, broadcasters, and media representatives.) He led the Mavericks to an impressive 53 wins, once again playing in all 82 games, while averaging 21.8 points and 9.2 rebounds per game. (Both averages were team highs.) The now seven-foot, 245-pound Nowitzki, known for his ability to score from anywhere on the court, was successful on 47 percent of his shots. He became only the second player in the history of the league to compile more than 100 three-pointers (151) and more than 100 blocks (101) in one season. (The other was Robert Horry, who achieved triple figures in those two categories for the Houston Rockets in the 1995–96 season.) Nowitzki also finished eighth in the NBA with 38 double-doubles, meaning that he recorded double figures in two different statistical categories in a single game. He led the Mavericks to the play-offs—it was the team's first appearance in the play-offs in 11 years—where they beat the Utah Jazz three games to two in the first round before falling to the San Antonio Spurs in the second round, four games to one. Before the start of the 2001–02 season, Nowitzki signed a six-year deal with the team worth an estimated $90 million. In January 2002 Nowitzki and his teammate Steve Nash were selected by coaches as reserves on the Western Conference All-Star team. Nowitzki told Jodie Valade for the *Dallas Morning News* (January 30, 2002), "I really wanted to make it once in my career. To get it now when I'm only twenty-three years old, after just four years in the league, is a dream come true." The occasion marked the first time that two Maverick players have gone to the All-Star Game since 1988, when Mark Aguirre and James Donaldson were chosen. Nowitzki led the Mavericks again in scoring and rebounding, helping the team to an impressive 57-win season in 2001–02. In the first round of the play-offs, Nowitzki and the Mavericks swept the Minnesota Timberwolves, but for the second year in a row, the team lost in the second round, this time to the Sacramento Kings. With his performance during the 2002 play-offs, Nowitzki joined Kareem Abdul-Jabbar as the only players since 1970 to tally at least 30 points and 15 rebounds in four consecutive play-off games. Nowitzki was named to the All-NBA Second Team for his outstanding season. Some NBA watchers say that the Mavericks' awesome trio of Finley, Nash, and Nowitzki is as good as the legendary Boston Celtics' trio of Robert Parrish, Kevin McHale, and Larry Bird.

Each NBA off-season Nowitzki returns to Germany to play for the national basketball team. In the 2002 Basketball World Championships, he led Germany to a bronze medal, the country's first in the annual competition. He was named most valuable player of the tournament. Nowitzki enjoys reading and playing the saxophone. When his mother was asked by L. Jon Wertheim how she felt about her son's NBA career, she replied, "Would I like it if he weren't so far away? Ja, of course. But the way Dirk has been playing this season, we're all *ganz stolz*. Very proud." — C.F.T.

Suggested Reading: *cnnsi.com*; *nba.com*; *Sport* p38+ Mar. 1999, with photos; *Sports Illustrated* p44+ Jan. 10, 2000, with photos

---

## Ollila, Jorma

(OH-lee-la, YORE-ma)

*Aug. 15, 1950– Chairman and CEO of Nokia*

*Address: Nokia Head Office, Keilalahdentie 2-4, FIN-02150 Espoo; P.O. Box 226, FIN-00045 Nokia Group, Finland*

"I never thought of going into industry," Jorma Ollila, the chairman and chief executive officer of Nokia, said at a 1996 conference held at Switzerland's University of St. Gallen, according to the school's Web site. "I thought I would be an academician giving lectures on different things." Based in Finland, Nokia is currently the world's largest manufacturer of cell phones. When Ollila joined the firm, in 1985, Nokia was a medium-sized conglomerate whose many products included televisions and consumer electronics; mobile phones and wireless telecommunication accounted for only a small portion of its income. Named president and CEO in early 1992, Ollila led the company out of debt by shedding its traditional product lines and focusing on cellular phones and mobile communication. Nokia has even altered the fortunes of Finland, accounting for a large portion of the country's stock-market transactions. "We badly needed a third leg, after forest products and metals, to support our economy," the Finnish prime minister, Paavo Lipponen, told T. R. Reid for the *Washington Post* (September 5, 1999). "And now we have it in communications." Since 1999 Ollila has

Courtesy of the Ms. Foundation Picture Gallery
*Jorma Ollila*

served Nokia as chairman and CEO. In September 2001 Nokia's executive committee approved his retention of those positions for another five years.

Jorma Ollila was born on August 15, 1950 in the small coastal town of Seinajoki, Finland. His father was an engineer and owned an electronics business. When he was 17 years old, Ollila won a scholarship to Atlantic College, a newly established boarding school in Wales, whose founder, the German educator Kurt Hahn, sought to bring together future leaders from around the world. (Ollila's English bears traces of a Welsh accent.) In 1976 Ollila earned a master's degree in political science from the University of Helsinki; two years later he earned a second master's degree, this one in economics from the London School of Economics. In 1981 he earned a third master's, in engineering, from the Helsinki University of Technology.

Ollila began his professional life in 1978 as an account manager for London's Citibank N.A. Corporate Bank; from 1980 to 1982 he worked as an account officer at Citibank in Helsinki. In 1982 he became a member of Citibank's board of management, a position he held until 1985, when he left the company to become vice president for international operations at Nokia. Nokia was established in 1865 as a lumber mill, situated on the banks of the Nokia River, in Tampere, Finland. In time Nokia also manufactured a line of paper products. In 1967 it merged with the Finnish Cable Works and the Finnish Rubber Works. The cable company made power transmission cables, phone lines, and, more recently, televisions and computers, while the rubber company manufactured tires and fishing boots. Among the cable division's most popular products were radio telephones—useful devices in a country as sparsely populated as Finland. The nordic region's cellular system began operating in 1981; it had excellent coverage, fairly low prices, and international roaming capabilities, and it soon became the world's most heavily used cellular network. Nokia made one of the first phones for use within the system. (Inventors in both the United States and Japan have taken credit for inventing the cellular phone, in the early 1970s.)

In 1986, about a year after he joined Nokia, Ollila became the company's senior vice president of finance. In December 1988 Nokia's CEO, Kari Kairamo, committed suicide. His death was the first of a series of problems that beset the company. Its mobile-phone division was then struggling against such international rivals as the American firm Motorola and Sweden's Ericsson, and its TV and computer businesses were floundering. The recession in Russia that followed the breakup of the Soviet Union soon spread to Finland and affected Nokia (along with other Finnish companies). In February 1990 Ollila was put in charge of the mobile-phone division, with instructions to decide within six months whether the department could be made competitive or should be sold. His knack for organization soon set the troubled division on the right course, and within four months he recommended that Nokia retain its mobile-phone interests. Still, there was no sense among the firm's executives that this small product line, which accounted for less than 20 percent of Nokia's sales, held the key to the company's financial recovery. "In 1991, people were telling me, 'Now that you've been able to get [your mobile-phone business] into the black, you should sell it quick, because the Japanese will eat you all up,'" Ollila told Maryanne Murray Buechner for *Time* (May 29, 2000).

The announcement of Ollila's appointment as CEO and president of the company, in early 1992, shocked many observers, and the company's stock tumbled. Ollila immediately began selling off most of Nokia's businesses to concentrate on cell phones. "Retired Nokia people tell me that I'm unholy, I'm a traitor, for selling off the fishing boots and the pulp and paper and the PCs," he told Reid in 1999. "But we are now in one of the fastest-growing and fastest-changing markets in the world. To play that game, you have to be completely focused on what the market wants." The strategy paid off handsomely. In 1993, when the company was still producing tires, tissue paper, televisions, and boots, its sales totaled just over $2 billion. In 1999, by which time it was manufacturing only cellular phones and related products, it recorded sales of $10 billion. "We realized that the key to recovery was to find something that took advantage of our know-how and gave us global, not just local, growth opportunities," Ollila told Reid. "And the more we moved into mobile phones and the infrastructure for mobile networks, we understood that we had to concentrate almost completely on that business. It was very, very hard to sell the pulp and paper business, and the rubber products, because that was what Nokia had been about since the 19th century. But we had to focus or die."

In the early 1990s mobile phones were seen almost exclusively as expensive business tools. Ollila foresaw that they could become a popular consumer item as they became cheaper, lighter, and more stylish. In addition to jettisoning Nokia's other product lines, he set out to distinguish the firm's products from the competition's by promoting cell phones as fashion accessories as well as communication tools; to this end he hired designers from Europe and California to give Nokia phones their distinctive look.

In 1994 Nokia gained a listing on the New York Stock Exchange. Ollila believed that besides providing an infusion of capital, trading on the exchange would increase visibility and sales. His prediction came true; Nokia began to attract more investors and make inroads against Motorola and Ericsson. By 1998 Nokia had grabbed first place in the global cell-phone market and was registering record earnings, while other competitors were announcing layoffs. Profits jumped more than 70 percent that year. Nokia also moved faster than its rivals into digital networks and wireless Internet access. The company was the first to launch digital phones, create data products (combining personal organizers and telephones), sell mobile phones specially designed for Asian customers, market mobile phones with user-changeable face plates, and produce cell phones with unique short-message chat functions, which, much like an Internet chat room, enables users to send text messages to other users. In 1999 Ollila was appointed chairman of the company, and Pekka Ala-Pietila assumed the presidency.

In 2001 Nokia sold 140 million cell phones and increased its share of the mobile-phone market to 37 percent, more than double that of Motorola, its nearest competitor, and almost twice Nokia's market share in 1999. "It would take a moon shot to make a dent in Nokia's position," Bryan Prohm, an industry analyst, told Buechner.

Ollila encourages a corporate culture that Buechner called "remarkably free of politics and oversize egos," and his management style has been described as generous and forgiving. He wears a photo ID and waits in line in the cafeteria along with others among the 1,000 workers at Nokia headquarters, in Espoo, a suburb of Helsinki on the Gulf of Finland. Ollila believes that giving employees permission to fail at some job-related endeavors is one reason for the company's success. "It's the way the organization creates a meeting of minds among people," he told Justin Fox for *Fortune* (May 1, 2000). "How do you send a very strong signal that this is a meritocracy, and this is a place where you are allowed to have a bit of fun, to think unlike the norm, where you are allowed to make a mistake?"

While the idea of teaming up with competitors would be anathema to many CEOs, Ollila has been involved in several such partnerships. One was with AT&T in 1997, to develop a phone for the launch of the carrier's Digital One Rate; that joint venture proved to be crucial to establishing the Nokia brand in the U.S. In another venture, announced on July 9, 2002, Nokia and IBM will jointly create a way to deliver music through cell phones. "When you come from a little country this far north, you learn to be a bit humble; you can't do everything yourself," Ollila told Maryanne Murray Buechner. Nokia's excellent relationship with consumers is also considered to be one of its unique strengths. Neil Barton, a Merrill Lynch analyst, told Rahul Jacob for *Fortune* (February 1996), "Motorola and Ericsson are pioneers in technology. Nokia is much closer to customers." He continued, "[Nokia] doesn't pioneer technology. It just gives customers what they want."

Nokia posted $4.8 billion in operating profits in 2001, when other telecom giants were losing money, and its unit sales of cell phones grew 9 percent even as industry sales overall dropped. Ollila has predicted that by 2003 about a third of the one billion cell phones expected to be in use will have Internet capabilities and that more people will be logging on to the Internet via mobile phones than via computers. Ollila plans to capitalize on that change. The company is now backing new standards for third-generation (3G) wireless phones that will handle Internet connections as fast as cable modems. (Those in the industry refer to analog phones as first generation, digital phones as second, and high-speed digital-data phones as third.) The advent of mobile phones with links to the World Wide Web may lead to some conflict with the computer-software giant Microsoft, but many observers believe that Nokia will withstand any such friction. "If any cell phone maker can thrive in this new world, Nokia can," Janet Guyon and Paola Hjelt wrote for *Fortune* (March 4, 2002). "The company is a little bit Wintel, a little bit Apple, a little bit Dell, and a whole lot Coca-Cola."

The prognosis isn't completely positive, however. Cell phone prices, and thus profits, have been declining in recent years, and sales of the wireless access protocol (WAP) phones in which Nokia has invested heavily have been disappointing. Still, Ollila is undeterred in his mission to bring the Internet to people via mobile phones, and Nokia—along with its competitors—is racing to introduce 3G cell phones to consumers. Nokia unveiled its first 3G model in September 2002 and expected to begin selling it commercially in 2003.

Often described as modest yet outgoing, Ollila addressed industry and political leaders at a June 2000 United Nations Economic and Social Council meeting on the role of information technology in the global economy. He is a member of the European Roundtable of Industrialists, the Science and Technology Policy Council of Finland, and the boards of the Ford Motor Co., Otava Books, and

UPM-Kymmene Corp. He serves as deputy chair of the board of the Confederation of Finnish Industries and Employers, as the overseas advisory trustee for the American-Scandinavian Foundation, and as chair of both the Council of the Finnish Foreign Trade Association and the advisory committee of the Helsinki University of Technology. He is on the executive board of the Association for the Finnish Cultural Foundation and is a member of the dean's council of Harvard University's John F. Kennedy School of Government. Among other honors, he has received the Order of the White Star, Estonia (1995); the Order of Merit of the Hungarian Republic, the Officer's Cross (1996); and the Commander's Cross of the Order of Merit of the Federal Republic of Germany (1997). In 2000 *Industry Week* magazine named him CEO of the year.

Ollila is fluent in Swedish as well as Finnish and English. His many interests include tennis, which he plays three mornings a week. He and his wife, Liisa Annikki, and their three children, Jaakko, Anna, and Matti, often retreat to a cottage 150 miles north of Helsinki. "You can't be a good people manager unless you have a balanced life yourself," he told John S. McClenahen for *Industry Week* (November 20, 2000). — K.E.D.

Suggested Reading: *AnchorDesk* (on-line) Nov. 14, 2001; *Cahners Business Information* p4 Apr. 22, 2002; *Fortune* p86+ Feb. 19, 1996, with photos, p160+ May 1, 2000, with photos, p115+ Mar. 4, 2002 with photos; *Industry Week* p38+ Nov. 20, 2000; *New York Times* (on-line) Jan. 25, 2002; *Time* p64+ May 29, 2000, with photos; *Washington Post* H p1 Sep. 5, 1999

---

## Ortner, Sherry B.

*Sep. 19, 1941– Anthropologist*

*Address: Dept. of Anthropology, 452 Schermerhorn Extension, Columbia University, 1200 Amsterdam Ave., New York, NY 10027*

Sherry B. Ortner has been called a founder of feminist anthropology, a designation based on the influence of her 1972 paper "Is Female to Male as Nature Is to Culture?" In it, she argued that male dominance was universal and was based partly on the fact that women's bodies were associated with nature while those of men were connected in people's minds with culture, or a subduing of nature. The article sparked controversy among feminists and scholars and has since become required reading in many universities around the world. While that paper remains the work for which she is best known outside the field of anthropology, Ortner's research on the Sherpa people of Nepal has yielded three books as well as a film, and she has recently completed a yet-to-be-published book about the relationships among class, race, ethnicity, and gender in American culture. She teaches at Columbia University, in New York City.

Of Jewish descent, Sherry Beth Ortner was born in the New York City borough of Brooklyn on September 19, 1941 to Samuel and Gertrude (Panitch) Ortner. She grew up in Newark, New Jersey, where she had what she has called a conventional, middle-class upbringing in a Jewish section of the city. Her father ran a packaging-supply business (which was relocated to Colorado by her younger brother in the early 1990s). Ortner graduated from Weequahic High School in 1958. Four years later she earned a bachelor's degree in anthropology from Bryn Mawr College, in Bryn Mawr, Pennsylvania; there, she had become involved in the civil rights movement, participating in lunch-counter sit-ins and in activities (including tenants' strikes) to help residents of Newark housing projects. Ortner has said that she chose to study anthropology partly because it offered the chance to explore a world other than the one in which she was raised. "I loved the idea of this privileged, Jewish, urban—I wouldn't say 'princess,' but someone who had never really done anything very hard or uncomfortable—going out in the field to live in these difficult conditions," she told Joe Levine for the *University of Chicago Magazine* (February 1996). "That was very important to me, this kind of Margaret Mead image of the intrepid young woman in the field with a tape recorder."

Ortner continued to study anthropology at the University of Chicago, receiving her master's degree in 1966 and her Ph.D. in 1970. While there, she studied under and became a follower of Clifford Geertz, who was developing an interpretive, humanities-oriented theory of culture, in contrast to the scientific approach dominant at the time; she was also influenced by the work of the social anthropologist Claude Lévi-Strauss and the political philosopher Karl Marx. More recently she has added practice theory, associated especially with Pierre Bourdieu, to her theoretical approach. Practice theory is concerned with the ways in which everyday practices can maintain or change power relations in the social order. "Sherry doesn't satisfy herself with theoretical ruminations," Geertz, now a professor of social science and founder of the School of Social Science at the Institute for Advanced Study at Princeton University, told Levine. "She doesn't take the easy way out; she wants to understand what's out there, and she explicates what's really going on."

Ortner began her first fieldwork in Nepal in 1966 among the Sherpas, a small ethnic group living in the high valleys of the Himalayas; she was interested in them because they practiced Mahayana Buddhism, the religion of the Dalai Lama. She traveled there with her first husband, fellow anthropologist Robert A. Paul, hoping to study the relationship between shamans—local folk healers among the Sherpas—and Buddhist lamas, only to discover that the Buddhist religious establishment had all but ended the influence of the shamans; nevertheless, she decided to stay. Ortner has called the 14 months she lived in a remote Sherpa village (10 days' walk from the nearest city, Kathmandu) her most difficult period of fieldwork. "I think about how young I was," she told Levine. "I felt, in retrospect, that I wasn't old enough, I wasn't wise enough or deep enough. I thought, God, it's amazing that they put up with this shallow young person who had almost no life experience."

Ortner has continued her explorations of the Sherpa culture, publishing *Sherpas Through Their Rituals* (1978), *High Religion: A Cultural and Political History of Sherpa Buddhism* (1989), and *Life and Death on Mt. Everest: Sherpas and Himalayan Mountaineering* (1999). In a review of the last-named book, Michael Parfit wrote for the *New York Times* (October 24, 1999): "It's written so clearly and with such evident fascination with the subject that it's more than just accessible to lay readers—it's captivating. I've had anthropology texts put me to sleep right after morning coffee, but this one kept me awake at night." Ortner's books and papers have described the enormous impact of the advent of mountaineering on the Sherpa people; before that pursuit became popular among European and American adventurers in the second half of the 19th century, the Sherpas generally avoided mountain peaks, believing mountains to be the homes of irritable gods—whereas now the Sherpas are known as excellent guides and load carriers on expeditions in the Himalayas. Ortner also served as a consultant on the 1976 film *Sherpas*, part of the Disappearing Worlds series that aired on British television.

In early 1968, after she completed her first fieldwork, Ortner returned to the U.S. This was a time of tumult in the nation, one that saw the murders of the civil rights leader Martin Luther King Jr. and Senator Robert F. Kennedy, nationwide political protests that included riots at the Democratic National Convention, in Chicago, and the emergence of the modern feminist movement. The latter would greatly influence Ortner's work. In 1972 she published a paper, "Is Female to Male as Nature Is to Culture?," in the journal *Feminist Studies*. The paper has become required reading in many anthropology courses; it has been translated into several foreign languages and reprinted in at least a dozen professional journals and collections of essays. In the paper, Ortner argued that male domination exists in all cultures because men are equated with culture, or the attempts of humans to subdue nature, while women are equated with nature itself. The paper upset many feminists, who had hoped that anthropological research would find societies in which power was shared between the sexes. "The belief at the time was that there was egalitarianism. It was argued that cultures existed where women had an equal role as men. I said that in a larger context, male dominance persisted," Ortner told Fernando Quintero for the *Berkeleyan* (February 1, 1995, on-line), the campus newspaper of the University of California at Berkeley. Tanya Luhrmann wrote in the *New York Times* (November 24, 1996), "Many feminists fiercely attacked [Ortner's paper], partly out of the fear that talk about universal domination (symbolic or otherwise) made that domination seem inevitable." Ortner had no idea that her paper would have such an impact on feminist and anthropological discourse. "I didn't set out to write a classic—I was just a young, white, middle-class academic trying to figure out how to live as an embodied woman while embarking on a career as a disembodied mind," she said at a meeting of the American Anthropological Association, as quoted by Levine. "I guess it just touched a chord." With Harriet Whitehead, she co-edited the 1981 book *Sexual Meanings: The Cultural Construction of Gender and Sexuality*, which reaffirmed the thesis she had laid out in her controversial paper, but in *Gender Hegemonies* (1993), she made a partial retraction. "I said the critics were more right than I admitted early on," she told Quintero. "If you look at the issue a certain way, you come up with male dominance. . . . [You need] a more complex picture of dominance. You can see societies where women have strong roles. Overall, I believe there is a trap in putting societies into boxes."

When Ortner returned to Newark for a high-school reunion in 1988, she was pursuing another research project: studying the lives of 100 members of her high-school class by interviewing them and their children. The anthropologist, who sees social class as one of the overlooked factors in the public discourse and in scholarly work (maintaining that it is often subsumed by discussions of ethnicity, race, and gender), found ample evidence, in her investigation into the marriages, divorces, careers, and children of her former classmates, that the American class system is alive and well. "Overall, what I see is a very strong mechanism of class reproduction," she told Quintero. "When the middle class is successful, it really watches out for itself. For many of my classmates, that means a shift rightward."

Ortner is known as a centrist in the otherwise sharply divided world of anthropology, because she typically rejects extreme positions and is often able to clarify differences between opposing sets of ideas. "One reason Sherry's so well-known is that she frames issues very clearly, in a way that has made a lot of productive debate possible," Paul Rabinow, who taught with Ortner at Berkeley, told Levine. "People may not agree with her, but the debate always seems to come back to how she poses it." She is also known for her commitment to ethnography, a method that combines participation and observation as a way of understanding particular social and cultural worlds. Ortner was co-editor of *Culture/Power/History: A Reader in Contemporary Social Theory*, which appeared in 1994; a collection of her feminist essays, *Making Gender: The Politics and Erotics of Culture*, was published in 1996. In 1999 she served as editor of *The Fate of "Culture": Geertz and Beyond*. Her most recently completed book, to be titled "New Jersey Dreaming: Capital, Culture, and the Class of '58," is based on her interviews of her high-school classmates. Anthropology is "in the process of remaking itself," Ortner told Quintero. "It's trying to hang on to a concern with other people's experience as well as the here and now. On one hand, we don't want to be known as just someone who studies exotic natives somewhere in a distant land. On the other, there is a real commitment to cross cultural and international perspective. If we aren't thinking about indigenous peoples of the fourth world, who will?"

Ortner taught at Sarah Lawrence College, in Bronxville, New York, from 1971 to 1977. She then relocated to the University of Michigan, where she remained for 17 years, working in the women's studies department as well as in anthropology. (She was Sylvia L. Thrupp Professor of Anthropology and Women's Studies at the school from 1992 to 1994.) From 1994 to 1996 she taught at the University of California at Berkeley, leaving for a position at Columbia University, where she is currently professor of anthropology.

In 1990 Ortner received a five-year, $295,000 MacArthur Award (commonly referred to as the "genius grant") for her work in anthropology. Her other honors include a Solomon R. Guggenheim Memorial fellowship (1982–83), two faculty-recognition awards from the University of Michigan (1989 and 1990), and the Retzius Medal from the Swedish Society of Anthropology and Geography (2001). She has given lectures to the Israeli Anthropological Association and the Finnish Anthropological Society and has also lectured at many universities in the U.S. and abroad. She was a visiting member of the Institute for Advanced Study at Princeton University (1989–90) and an Invited Senior Fellow at the National Humanities Center (1999–2000). She is a fellow of the American Anthropological Association and the American Academy of Arts and Sciences. Her other memberships include the Nepal Studies Association, the Tibet Society, the American Ethnological Society, and the Society for Cultural Anthropology. She was elected to the American Academy of Arts and Sciences in 1992. In addition, she has served on the editorial boards of *Feminist Studies, Cultural Anthropology, Social Analysis, Comparative Studies in Society and History, Representations, Ethnography*, and the *Journal of Social Archaeology*, and she has sat on the executive boards of the Society for Cultural Anthropology and the American Council of Learned Societies. She has received many grants and fellowships to fund her research, from sources including the National Institutes of Mental Health, the National Science Foundation, the Wenner-Gren Foundation for Anthropological Research, the American Institute of Indian Studies, the University of Michigan, the National Endowment for the Humanities, and the Henry Luce Foundation.

Ortner's first marriage, to Robert A. Paul, ended in divorce in 1976, after 12 years. She married Raymond C. Kelly in 1979 and has a daughter, Gwendolyn, from that union. She and Kelly, a University of Michigan professor of anthropology, divorced in 1989. In 1994 she married Timothy D. Taylor, who teaches music at Columbia University; his specialties, according to his Columbia Web site, include "music as it relates to globalization, postmodernism, colonialism and postcolonialism, gender, race and ethnicity, and technology." — K.E.D.

Suggested Reading: *Berkeleyan* (on-line) Feb. 1, 1995; *University of Chicago Magazine* (on-line) Feb. 1996, with photo

Selected Books: as writer—*Sherpas Through Their Rituals*, 1978; *Sexual Meanings: The Cultural Construction of Gender and Sexuality*, 1981; *High Religion: A Cultural and Political History of Sherpa Buddhism*, 1989; *Gender Hegemonies*, 1993; *Making Gender: The Politics and Erotics of Culture*, 1996; *Life and Death on Mt. Everest: Sherpas and Himalayan Mountaineering*, 1999; as editor or co-editor—*Culture/Power/History: A Reader in Contemporary Social Theory*, 1994; *The Fate of "Culture": Geertz and Beyond*, 1999

Klaus Pollmeier/Courtesy of Clarion Books

## Park, Linda Sue

*Mar. 25, 1960– Children's writer*

*Address: Author Mail, c/o Houghton Mifflin Children's Books, 8th Fl., 222 Berkeley St., Boston, MA 02116-3764*

The children's writer Linda Sue Park, who won the prestigious 2002 Newbery Medal for her third book, *A Single Shard*, has used writing to express the connections between her Korean heritage and her American sensibilities. When Park was growing up, in 1960s Chicago, there was virtually no Asian-American literature for children. "I gradually came to realize that for most of my American neighbors . . . Asian comprised a confusion of monochromatic images: kimonos and Confucius, karate and chop suey, Charlie Chan and Mr. Moto," she wrote for *Booklist* (January 1/January 15, 2000). "Asian meant Chinese and Japanese icons in an indistinguishable jumble." Park's four novels, aimed at children ages seven and older, are each set in Korea in different historical periods—the 17th century, the 15th century, the 12th century, and the 20th century—but broach universal themes: wondering about the unknown, fitting in, and overcoming adversity. "I came to writing for children via a lengthy, circuitous route that included public relations, advertising, teaching, and food journalism," Park wrote in the article for *Booklist*. A cooking contest sponsored by the British newspaper the *Independent*, she added, provided her with the initial motivation to blend Korean and American elements in her work. "I ended up making marinated quails on a nest of rice," she wrote. "I used wild rice, which grows only in North America, and a Korean marinade. Although I didn't realize it at the time, I was doing in the kitchen what I wanted to do in life: putting Korean and American together in a seamless way."

The oldest of three children, Linda Sue Park was born on March 25, 1960 in Urbana, Illinois. She was raised in the Chicago suburb of Park Forest by Ed Park, a civil engineer, and Susie Park, a piano teacher, who had both emigrated from South Korea in the 1950s. (Ed Park later became a computer systems analyst, and Susie Park went on to teach English as a second language.) Park had a "very American" upbringing, as she explained to *Time for Kids* (February 8, 2002, on-line): "We celebrated certain holidays and upheld a few [Korean] traditions, but I don't actually speak Korean." The family did, however, visit South Korea when Park was about 12. Her mother taught her to read when she was four, using a series of cartoons that involved phonics, which she clipped from a Chicago newspaper. "Now that I think about it, it's pretty amazing, because English was her second language," Park told *Current Biography*. "When I got to kindergarten, I was the only child in the class who could read, because she had already taught me." As she told *Time for Kids*, she credits her father with encouraging the voracious reading she did as a youngster, because "he took me to the library every two weeks without fail. Because he didn't know much about American children's books himself, he just took me there to learn. I read everything growing up." Among her favorite books were those in the *Little House* series, by Laura Ingalls Wilder, and *Roosevelt Grady*, by Louisa Shotwell. Park began writing at an early age as well, as she told *Current Biography*: "I was a huge reader, and I think that the gap, the jump from reading to writing never felt like a huge one. Because I loved reading so much, it seemed logical to try writing as well." When, at age nine, Park sold her first piece—a haiku—to *Trailblazer*, a church publication, her father framed and proudly displayed the $1 check she received for her work. She continued to write poetry, and her work was published in magazines for children and young adults.

Park attended Stanford University, in California, where she majored in English and, as she had in high school, competed on the gymnastics team. Upon graduating she took an entry-level writing job in the public-relations department of the Amoco Oil Co., where she composed a newsletter for Amoco–Standard Oil retirees. "I actually really enjoyed [the work]," she told *Current Biography*. "It was like a small town newspaper, almost. . . . I learned that if a writer is interested, any topic can be interesting." In 1983, after two years at Amoco, she moved to Dublin, Ireland, where she spent a year studying Anglo-Irish Literature at Trinity College. "It was an unbelievable year," she told an interviewer for *Moveo Angelus Literary Arts* (Spring 2000, on-line). "Ireland's really special . . . Dublin was like a small town then—the mid-eighties—you'd study modern poets and go to the pub and they'd be there drinking." Once she completed her program at Trinity, she followed her Irish boyfriend, whom she had met in the United States, to England on a "fiancee visa," which required them to be married within three months of her arrival. "On day eighty-nine we did the deed," she told *Moveo Angelus Literary Arts*. The couple lived in London, where Park taught English as a second language (ESL) and attended graduate school part-time, earning a master's degree in modern British literature from the University of London in two years. "I wanted to be a travel writer," Park explained on her Web site in May 2001. "At 23, I thought I was off to a pretty good start: I left the U.S. and went to Ireland to study. Alas, it was not to be: The very next year I was a stay-home mom with a beautiful infant son and I had to reknit my dream considerably. I became, instead, a food writer. That way, I could at least attempt reasonable facsimiles of what they might be eating in all the places I couldn't travel to." After winning the *Independent*'s cooking contest, she wrote food articles for the paper—beginning with an article on Korean food that coincided with the 1988 Olympic Games, in Seoul, South Korea—and other British publications.

In 1990 Park and her family, which included a daughter by then, moved to New York City. She taught ESL at Brooklyn College and, later, at the Rochester Institute of Technology's English Language Center, after the family moved to upstate New York, in 1993. She wrote poems and essays, which were published in such magazines as *Cricket*, a literary magazine for children, *Contemporary Poetry*, an on-line magazine, and the *Alsop Review*, a literary journal.

In 1997, inspired by her husband's advice that she follow her dream of writing children's books, Park began to compose stories. Her first efforts, which were based on Korean folktales, were met with "encouraging rejections," as she told *Current Biography*. Her book *Seesaw Girl* was accepted by Clarion Books, a Houghton Mifflin imprint, in October 1997 and published in 1999. The book explores the life of Jade Blossom, an inquisitive 12-year-old girl in 17th-century Korea. Because of her family's high station, Jade Blossom is not permitted to leave her family compound, but she longs to see the world outside its walls. She engineers a brief escape but ultimately returns home and accepts the rules by which her society operates. Her compromise is to fashion a seesaw, which allows her glimpses of the outside world. Park—who had not been to South Korea since childhood but used the traditional architecture of an aunt's house as inspiration for the setting of the book—did most of her research for *Seesaw Girl* through books, magazines, and the Internet. "I do almost all of my reading and research before I begin writing; I like to know the subject so well that I don't have to refer to my notes very often," she explained to Julia Durango for the "By the Book" column in the Ottawa, Illinois, *Daily News* (July 18, 2000). *Seesaw Girl* received warm critical reviews, which lauded both the book's plot and its detailed depiction of 17th-century Korean life. "In descriptive, engaging prose, the story portrays the culture, traditions, and daily lives of the Korean aristocracy in a time of political and cultural change," Shelle Rosenfeld wrote for *Booklist*, as quoted on *Amazon.com*. "Park sympathetically conveys the challenges and joys of becoming an adult, and offers perspective on the many meanings of 'privileged.'" *Seesaw Girl* was included on the "best books of the year" lists of several organizations, including the New York Public Library and the Virginia Center for Children's Books. It was also placed on the Texas Bluebonnet Award list and the lists for the West Virginia and the South Carolina State Children's Book Awards, all of which are voted on by young readers.

Stories of her father's childhood pastime in Korea, kite fighting, sparked Park's second book, *The Kite Fighters* (2000). The book, set in 15th-century Korea, captures the sometimes fractious relationship between two brothers, Kee-sup and Young-sup, who design, build, and fly kites competitively. "Though the story is set in medieval times, the brothers have many of the same issues facing siblings today," Barbara Scotto wrote in a starred review of the book for *School Library Journal* (June 2000). "They play and argue, they compete for their father's attention, and eventually develop a greater understanding of one another. The author has drawn her characters with a sure touch, creating two very different boys struggling to figure out who they are. With ease and grace, Park brings these long-ago children to life." *The Kite Fighters*, for which Park's father drew the chapter-heading illustrations, was a spring 2000 Junior Library Guild selection.

Park set her third children's novel, *A Single Shard*, in the 12th century. "In doing my research on Korea for my first two books, I kept coming upon the fact that in the 11th and 12th centuries Korea was considered the best in the world at pottery," she told *Time for Kids*. "I thought it was amazing." *A Single Shard*, about Tree-ear, a poor orphan who becomes an apprentice to Min, a master potter, was published in 2001. The book was critically lauded, earning starred reviews from the *School Library Journal*, *Kirkus Reviews*, *Booklist*, and *Publishers Weekly*. In January 2002 the Association for Library Service to Children, a division of the American Library Association (ALA), named *A Single Shard* the winner of the 2002 John Newbery Medal, one of the most prestigious honors in American children's literature. "Tree-ear's determination and bravery in pursuing his dream of becoming a potter takes readers on a literary journey that demonstrates how courage, honor and perseverance can overcome great odds and bring happiness," the Newbery Medal Committee chair, Kathleen Odean, explained in an ALA press release (January 21, 2002). "The story shines with dignity and strong values. Park's writing is powerful and precise as she explores universal themes about loyalty and art." In South Korea, where Park's books were published in Korean in the fall of 2002, the award brought an enthusiastic reaction—something that "was really surprising and very moving, just completely unexpected," as Park told *Current Biography*. She planned to visit Korea in November 2002, on a trip that will coincide with the publication there of *A Single Shard*.

Park stopped teaching ESL, for the first time in 15 years, in the fall of 2001 due to her full slate of writing projects, which are currently under contract with Clarion Books and are slated to be published in the next couple of years. Her fourth book, *When My Name Was Keoko*, was published in March 2002 and earned starred reviews from *Kirkus* and *Publishers Weekly*. The events depicted in *When My Name Was Keoko* take place in 1940, when Korea was occupied by Japan. Expressions of Korean culture were banned by the ruling Japanese, and citizens were required to take Japanese names. (Park's parents lived in Korea during this period; her mother's Japanese name was Keoko.)

As Park told *Current Biography*, she hopes that children's interest in the unfamiliar survives the computer age. "For kids nowadays, their worlds have gotten paradoxically larger and smaller. Smaller because of the Internet. . . . At the same time, because of that, they need to know about places a great deal more than they used to." She added, "Curiosity and interest in something that's 'not you': I hope that's something that a post-electronic age doesn't wipe out. If, as I think, it is universal, then books that satisfy that need will always be important."

Park lives in upstate New York with her husband, Ben, a journalist; their son, Sean; their daughter, Anna; and the family dog, Cosmo. She enjoys traveling, cooking, reading, and doing crossword puzzles. — K.S.

Suggested Reading: *Booklist* p832 Jan.1/Jan.15, 2002; Linda Sue Park Web site; (Rochester, New York) *Democrat and Chronicle* (on-line) Jan. 22, 2002, with photo; *Time for Kids* (on-line) Feb. 8, 2002, with photo

Selected Books: *Seesaw Girl*, 1999; *The Kite Fighters*, 2000; *A Single Shard*, 2001; *When My Name Was Keoko*, 2002

---

## Pascal, Amy

*1958– Chairwoman of Columbia Pictures*

*Address: Columbia Pictures, 10202 Washington Blvd., Culver City, CA 90232*

Reuters/Fred Prouser/Hulton/Archive by Getty Images

"I always knew I wanted to be in the movie business," Amy Pascal, the chairwoman of Columbia Pictures, told John H. Richardson for *Premiere* (May 1990). After rising from production assistant to studio executive in only five years, Pascal carried her passion for movies to Columbia; before the age of 40, following a brief stint at Turner Pictures Worldwide, she returned as president. She was named the chairwoman in December 1999. Acknowledging that deciding which movies to champion and shepherd through production can be risky, she told Chris Nashawaty for *Entertainment Weekly* (June 18, 1999): "Well, it's an *educated* gamble. But sometimes you can think you know everything and be wrong." She has often been right, however, as proven by the long list of hit movies she has helped to grow from script to finished product.

The daughter of a bookstore owner and an economist, Amy Pascal was born in 1958 and raised in Los Angeles. She graduated in 1981 from the University of California at Los Angeles (UCLA), where, despite her desire to work in the film industry, she majored in international relations (some sources say political science). (She told John H. Richardson that she would have been "locked out of the house" if she had pursued a more creative course of study.) Pascal signed on as a secretary to the producer Tony Garnett at Kestral, an independent production company, quickly becoming his assistant and later business partner. Together they developed *Follow That Bird* (1995), a full-length film featuring Big Bird and other characters from the PBS children's series *Sesame Street*. (The development of a movie, which begins before directors, actors, or producers sign on, involves either writing or purchasing and revising a story and then working out a budget.)

In 1985 Pascal took her first studio job, as the vice president of production at 20th Century–Fox. There she had successes and failures, developing the teenage sleeper hit *Say Anything . . .* (1989) as well as having a hand in the poorly received *Revenge of the Nerds II* (1987). She joined Columbia Pictures in 1988—some sources say 1987—as a vice president of production and garnered a reputation as a fierce negotiator (in the areas of budgets and casting, for example) for the films she backed. Despite a less than ideal working environment at Columbia, which was then struggling to overcome a reputation for financial failure, Pascal pushed the movie *Awakenings* (1990) through to production. That picture, starring Robert DeNiro as a formerly catatonic patient and Robin Williams as his doctor, turned out to be an enormous critical and popular success, receiving three Academy Award nominations. Promoted to executive vice president of production at Columbia Pictures, she approved and oversaw production of films including *Single White Female* (1992), *Groundhog Day* (1993), and the two most celebrated movies with which she was associated during the period: *A League of Their Own* (1992), based on the true story of American 1940s professional women's baseball teams, and *Little Women* (1994), a sparkling remake of the classic Louisa May Alcott novel that earned three Oscar nominations.

In 1994 Pascal left Columbia to become the president of production at a new studio, Turner Pictures Worldwide. She held the post for two years before the studio's owner, Ted Turner, merged his film outfit with Time Warner, the parent company of Warner Bros. studios. During her tenure at Turner Pictures Worldwide, Pascal sent five films into production, including the Nora Ephron–directed *Michael* (1996), starring John Travolta, and *City of Angels*, a 1998 drama with Nicolas Cage and Meg Ryan. Pascal reunited with Columbia Pictures in 1996, accepting an appointment as president of the studio, which had suffered under management shake-ups during the 1990s. By 1999, as Chris Nashawaty noted, Columbia had "risen from the dead. . . . By hitting moneymaking singles and doubles [*I Know What You Did Last Summer*, *Stepmom*, *Big Daddy*] instead of swinging for the fences, Pascal and [CEO John] Calley have turned Columbia into one of Hollywood's smoothest-operating studios." Columbia hoped to build on the success of the horror flick *I Know What You Did Last Summer* (1997) with a run of other movies aimed at the teen market, but neither the 1998 sequel to that movie, nor the comedy-romance *Can't Hardly Wait* (1998), performed as well as expected. "You don't have to put $20 million movie stars in [those films] . . . so far those stars don't cost that much. They will," Pascal told Nashawaty, explaining Columbia's decision to gamble on teen-market films. Referring to the runaway success of *I Know What You Did* and the lackluster performance of its sequel, she added: "I think [the teenage audience] is very fickle." Under her guidance, the studio released *Stepmom* (1998), starring Susan Sarandon as a terminally ill mother and Julia Roberts as her former husband's girlfriend, and *Big Daddy* (1999), a popular comedy starring Adam Sandler—movies that buoyed Columbia through the summer of 1999. To her chagrin, audiences shunned *Go* (1999), a critically well-received drama aimed at teenagers but saddled with an R rating, and *8MM* (1999), a story set in the sexual underworld. "It was an intense psychological thriller," she told Nashawaty about *8MM*. "We had hoped that audiences would respond more enthusiastically." Columbia and its parent company, Sony, shared criticism for the failures of movies such as *8MM* and *Jakob the Liar* (1999); Pascal, along with others, was tagged for the low grosses of films such as *Girl, Interrupted* (1999), a critical success but something of a box-office disappointment. Despite the ebbs and flows of the movie business and the resulting threats to her job security, she has always loved her position; as she explained to Claudia Eller for the *Los Angeles Times* (October 27, 2000), "I wake up every day, even on the worst days, and I love this job."

Pascal was promoted to chairwoman of Columbia Pictures in December 1999. She was at the helm during the successful Christmas 1999 release of *Stuart Little*, based on the classic children's book by E. B. White and heavily reliant on computer graphics. In the summer of 2000, *Charlie's Angels*, a movie adaptation of the popular 1970s television series, proved to be a hit with the moviegoing public; Pascal had approved the project and guided it through several bouts of expensive production problems. "I really want this one to work because it hasn't been the world's greatest year, and it would be great for this to be the beginning of the turnaround," she had told Claudia Eller at the time of the movie's premiere.

In 2002 Columbia released *Spider-Man*, a film version of the popular comic book, with Tobey Maguire as the title character. Made for just over $100 million, the movie grossed four times that amount at the box office, making it the most profitable movie of the year. *Men in Black II*, the studio's other major summer film, collected nearly $200 million in box-office receipts. Other films produced by Pascal's studio in 2002 were *Punch-Drunk Love*, *I-Spy*, and *Adaptation*. Upcoming projects include *Charlie's Angels: Full Throttle* and the screen adaptation of Arthur Golden's acclaimed novel *Memoirs of a Geisha*.

Pascal's professional awards include the 2001 Crystal Award for Women in Film and the inaugural Motion Picture Business Leader Award, given in 1999 by the Carl DeSantis Business and Economics Center for the Study and Development of the Motion Picture and Entertainment Industry, at Florida Atlantic University. A resident of southern California, Pascal is married to the *New York Times* entertainment reporter Bernard Weinraub. The couple have one child. — K.S.

Suggested Reading: *Entertainment Weekly* p31+ June 18, 1999, with photo; *New York Times* C p8 Dec. 16, 1999; *Premiere* p70 May 1990

---

Hulton/Archive by Getty Images

## Pau, Peter

(pow)

*1951(?)– Cinematographer*

*Address: c/o Gersh Agency, 232 N. Canyon Dr., Beverly Hills, CA 90210*

One of the most successful and well-respected cinematographers in the Hong Kong film industry, Peter Pau has recently made his mark in Hollywood as well. The recipient of three Hong Kong Film Awards for best cinematography (and nine additional nominations), Pau won the 2001 Academy Award for best cinematography for his work on Ang Lee's epic martial-arts fantasy *Crouching Tiger, Hidden Dragon* (2000).

Peter Pau was born in Hong Kong in about 1951. His father, Pau Fong, was an actor and director. When he was 15, Peter Pau moved from Hong Kong to Canton, China. "My father sent me there for the discipline," he told David E. Williams for *American Cinematographer* (October 1998). "The schools there were better than those in Hong Kong. But the following year, the Cultural Revolution began and I could not leave." Pau was forced to remain on the Chinese mainland for 12 years. By the time he returned to Hong Kong, at age 27, he had decided to pursue a career in filmmaking; with his family's support, he enrolled in a film program at the San Francisco Art Institute, where he earned a bachelor's degree in 1983.

Upon returning to Hong Kong, Pau directed and photographed *Temptation of Dance* (1984), thereby making himself known in the local film industry. "[*Temptation of Dance*] gained me a lot of attention from other directors, who wanted me to work with them as a director of photography," Pau told Williams. In the following years Pau served as cinematographer on a number of low-budget Chinese-language features, including John Woo's *The Killer* (1989), a hyperkinetic action film about a hired assassin (Chow Yun-Fat) who wants to leave that business but must take one last contract; *A Fishy Story* (1989); *To Be Number One* (1991), about a Chinese peasant who becomes a crime boss in Hong Kong; *Saviour of the Soul* (1992), a medieval postapocalyptic samurai action comedy; Ronnie Yu's *The Bride with White Hair* (1993), an epic fantasy about a swordsman and heir to the Wu-Tang clan throne, whose existential crisis is relieved by romance; and *The Phantom Lover* (1995), a romance set in 1930s China. Pau won three Hong Kong Film Awards for best cinematography for his work on *A Fishy Story*, *Saviour of the Soul*, and *The Bride with White Hair*, respectively.

While establishing a reputation as one of Hong Kong's most capable cinematographers, Pau continued to refine his professional skills. "I've been lucky to practice my craft often," he told Williams. "The Hong Kong film industry grew up with limited budgets and limited amounts of production time. We had to learn how to work with great precision. I would have to account for every light, and even determine rental time in terms of hours! But that allowed us to maximize the visual presentation, and nothing was wasted. It was good training."

Pau made his American debut with Tsui Hark's *Double Team* (1997), an action thriller featuring the high-octane triumvirate of Jean-Claude Van Damme, Dennis Rodman, and Mickey Rourke. According to Janet Maslin in the *New York Times* (April 4, 1997), the three principals "meet violently in Rome for a showdown in the Colosseum involving land mines, a baby and a Bengal tiger, eventually leaving the great landmark engulfed in special-effects flames. If you have to ask why, then the flashy, cheesy, overheated *Double Team* is not for you." Maslin also made note of Pau's "dynamic cinematography."

After *Double Team*, Pau collaborated again with the director Ronnie Yu, this time on *Warriors of Virtue* (1997) and then *Bride of Chucky* (1998). *Warriors of Virtue*, an adolescent action fantasy combining elements of *The Karate Kid* and *Star Wars*, features a race of kangaroo warriors; it was widely panned. *Bride of Chucky*, the fourth installment in the *Child's Play* horror series, about a homicidal children's doll, fared no better. Still, *Bride of Chucky* gave Pau a chance to expand his range: "*Chucky* is very different from the other fantasy films I have shot," he told Williams, "because 'horror' is its main concept. This affected how the camera should see Chucky and Tiffany [Chucky's 'bride'] as characters. After reading the script, I saw in my mind that we had to make them larger than life, not only in their size, but also in their expressions. In a way, they are the heroes of the film, and their personalities are bigger than those of the adult characters. But they are both less than three feet tall, very small in comparison to an adult, so we had to work hard to make them seem impressive. For example, whenever we saw Chucky's face, I wanted to make the audience jump back a bit. To do that, I tried to always shoot his close-ups with the camera extremely close to his face, usually using a 40mm lens, and often at a slightly low angle. On the screen, this gave Chucky the exact same presence that a grown man might have, and ensured that all of his facial expressions would be clear to the audience."

Despite his reputation as one of Hong Kong's top cinematographers, Pau came to work on *Crouching Tiger, Hidden Dragon* (2000), the Mandarin-language martial-arts epic for which he won an Academy Award, almost by default. The producers of the film, Bill Kong and Chui Po Chu, approached Pau only after having considered two other cinematographers, both of whom had scant experience with action movies. "The producers were so worried about finishing the film—not even saying finishing on time—but just finishing the film," Pau told An Tran for *Cinematographer.com* (December 20, 2000). "So they introduced me to [the director Ang Lee]. I went to Beijing to meet him and an hour later, I got the job."

At their meeting, Pau asked Lee—who had previously specialized in such character-driven dramas as *The Wedding Banquet* (1993), *Sense and Sensibility* (1995), and *The Ice Storm* (1997)—to name the action films he found most visually appealing. "Ang told me, 'None of them,'" Pau recalled to Williams. "He was serious!" While most Hong Kong action films employ a full palette of colors, stark contrasts, and bright lighting (as well as liberal smoke-and-fog effects), Lee felt that such a visual style would overdramatize *Crouching Tiger*, which already had a dramatic storyline and strong characters. Consequently, Lee and Pau decided to start from scratch in developing a visual approach to the film. "Ang and I discussed particularly that the film should look like a Chinese watercolor painting," Pau told Tran. "I wanted to make everything have a mild contrast. It's not like the hip movies of today, which have deep, deep blacks or bright, bright whites. We wanted everything in the middle range of the contrast to show the most detail of the costumes, the sets and the background."

Not only did Pau and Lee depart from the traditional look of most Hong Kong action films, they also sought to handle the film's fight scenes in a novel fashion. "For the action we asked, 'Why don't we move together with the action? Move as they move?,'" Pau told Tran. "The drama would be very still and we wanted the action running like a rabbit as well as the camera. . . . We wanted the fights to be convincing, even though it is a fantasy-like setting with great leaping and flying. . . . We wanted to show all of the actions by shooting at human eye level, basically trying to find what is inside their fights, what is between them." In order to accomplish that, Pau used lens distances of 25mm, 35mm, 40mm, and 50mm. "These are what the human eyes see," he explained to Tran. "To show the dynamic of the action, you had to get close. I think when you look at the scenes very closely, the action sequences have a very good human touch instead of a purely 'video game' framing. Ang said, 'Everything is a personal fight. I want to get into the personal feelings of each person.'"

In addition to Pau's Oscar for best cinematography, *Crouching Tiger, Hidden Dragon* garnered Academy Awards for best foreign film, best art direction, and best music, and was nominated for six more honors. The movie also pleased critics. "*Crouching Tiger, Hidden Dragon* is the most exhilarating martial arts movie I have ever seen . . . ," Roger Ebert wrote for the *Chicago Sun-Times* (December 22, 2000). "But like all ambitious movies, *Crouching Tiger, Hidden Dragon* transcends its origins and becomes one of a kind. It's glorious, unashamed escapism and surprisingly touching at the same time." Desson Howe wrote for the *Washington Post* (December 22, 2000), "Lee has created the year's most visually wondrous movie; and all this without the expensive benefit of computerized, digital effects."

Pau was also responsible for the cinematography in *Dracula 2000* (2000), a remake of the Dracula legend that Stephen Holden, in the *New York Times* (December 23, 2000), characterized as "Dracula Meets Stigmata and They Fly to New Orleans via Hong Kong. That's because on top of all the Christian imagery (electrically illuminated crosses exploding into showers of sparks and such), the action sequences sometimes find the characters doing combat in the air."

Pau made his debut as a director with *The Touch* (2002); starring Michelle Yeoh, Ben Chaplin, and Brandon Chang, the film is about a family of circus acrobats who are trying to track down a stolen artifact. According to *Asiaweek* (April 13, 2001), Pau earned "about seven times his normal fee" to direct and handle the cinematography for *The Touch*. Reviews of the picture ranged from scathing—"a movie so bad, it has to be seen to be believed," in the words of Helmi Yusof, writing for the *Straits Times* (on-line)—to decidedly mixed. Among the latter was Bryan Walsh's, who wrote for the Asian edition of *Time* (August 19–26, 2002), "The most fun part of watching *The Touch* . . . is figuring out the movie's most unrealistic element. . . . [The director] can frame a gorgeous scene, but has trouble keeping his story moving." "You can't help but wonder what *The Touch* would have been like if possessed of a good story and consistent execution," Lee Alon commented in *City Weekend* (August 15, 2002), a biweekly publication that focuses on contemporary China.

Earlier, in an interview with Yuan Jo Mei for CNN.com (July 9, 2001), Pau indicated that, praise and criticism notwithstanding, he is guided by what he labeled an "old saying": "You are only as good as your last picture." Then he added, "So you've got to do something new, you've got to move forward." — P.K.

Suggested Reading: *American Cinematographer* p24+ Oct. 1998, with photos, p54+ Jan. 2001, with photos; *Cinematographer.com* Dec. 2000, with photos; *CNN.com*; *Kodak.com*

Selected Films: as cinematographer—*Temptation of Dance*, 1984; *The Killer*, 1989; *A Fishy Story*, 1989; *To Be Number One*, 1991; *Saviour of the Soul*, 1992; *The Bride With White Hair*, 1993; *The Phantom Lover*, 1995; *Double Team*, 1997; *Warriors of Virtue*, 1997; *Bride of Chucky*, 1998; *Crouching Tiger, Hidden Dragon*, 2000; *Dracula 2000*, 2000; as director and cinematographer—*The Touch*, 2002

---

Associated Press

## Paulson, Henry M. Jr.

*Mar. 28, 1946– Chairman and chief executive officer of the Goldman Sachs Group*

*Address: Goldman Sachs Group Inc., 85 Broad St., New York, NY 10004*

In 1999, a quarter-century after joining the firm in an entry-level position, Henry M. Paulson Jr. was named chairman of the Goldman Sachs Group Inc., one of the premier investment banks and asset-management firms in the world. Paulson began his professional life as an employee of the U.S. government, first with the Department of Defense and then as a White House aide during the presidency of Richard Nixon. In 1977, within four years of his arrival at Goldman Sachs, he had become a vice president, and five years after that, a partner. Rising further, he became the co-head of the firm's investment-banking division and then was named to Goldman Sachs's five-person management committee. In 1994 he was named the vice chairman of the committee as well as Goldman Sachs's chief operating officer, thus attaining the company's second-highest position, below Jon S. Corzine. For about six months in 1998, he and Corzine worked together as co-heads of Goldman Sachs. Then, in early 1999, in a coup engineered by Paulson, Corzine lost his titles, and on the day the firm went public, a few months later, he resigned, leaving Paulson in the top spot.

In June 2002 Paulson made headlines when, in response to what he called "mounting evidence of gross mismanagement and malfeasance" by executives at some of the nation's most prominent companies, he gave a speech at the National Press Club in which he urged corporations to adopt an "agenda for change" to restore investor confidence. "The stakes, after all, are enormous," he declared, according to the Goldman Sachs Web site. "And they transcend those of individual firms or investors. The US economy and its financial markets are, rightly, the envy of the world. . . . But our markets are not just beneficiaries of our remarkable economic performance. They also drive it by mobilizing capital, unlocking value, encouraging entrepreneurship, and rewarding good management. Our financial markets are the deepest, most efficient, and fairest to be found anywhere; they are models that others, in developed and developing economies alike, strive to emulate. But they are not perfect. And it's time that we fix them."

The son of Henry Merritt Paulson Sr., a wholesale jeweler, and Marianna (Gallaeur) Paulson, Henry Merritt Paulson Jr. was born on March 28, 1946 in Palm Beach, Florida. Goldman Sachs press releases refer to him by his nickname, Hank. Paulson grew up on a farm in Barrington, Illinois, a suburb of Chicago, where he developed a love of the outdoors while spending time with his father. "When we went horseback riding, he'd point out sparrows and meadowlarks," Paulson told Emily Thornton for *Business Week* (March 4, 2002). During his four years at Barrington Consolidated High School, he shone academically and was a member of the wrestling and football squads. In his late teens he worked as a counselor and instructor at a Colorado summer camp, teaching mountaineering and other wilderness skills. During his second year at the camp, when he was 19, he led rafting excursions and horseback-riding trips and was placed in charge of a dozen counselors. "That was the first time I had an opportunity to have a certain amount of management responsibility and learn about working with people, and it was the first time I really needed to stand up and speak in front of a group," he told Evan McGlinn for *Polo.com* (2001). Paulson attended Dartmouth College, in Hanover, New Hampshire, where he displayed his athletic talents as a lineman for the Dartmouth football team, whose members nicknamed him "The Hammer" because of the intensity with which he played. He was named to the First Team All-Ivy, All-New England, and All-East and earned the 1967 National Collegiate Athletic Association (NCAA) Scholar-Athlete Award. He was elected to Phi Beta Kappa and graduated in 1968 with a B.A. degree in English.

In 1970, after receiving a master's degree in business from Harvard University, in Cambridge, Massachusetts, Paulson took a job with the U.S. Defense Department at the Pentagon, in Washington, D.C. He worked there as part of a group that investigated huge cost overruns associated with a project of the Lockheed Corp., a major military contractor. Lockheed had developed a transport plane for the U.S. Air Force (the C-5A Galaxy) and then billed the government for a total amount equal to nearly twice the company's estimated worth; nevertheless, the project had continued, with congressional approval. Within two years Paulson had transferred to the White House to serve as an aide to John Ehrlichman, a close adviser to President Richard Nixon. But in 1973, as the Watergate scandal (which involved a break-in by Republican-hired operatives at the Democratic National Committee headquarters and its subsequent cover-up) enveloped the presidency and Ehrlichman resigned, Paulson became disheartened. He left the White House when he concluded that "the President was lying," as Emily Thornton wrote.

Then, his interest in finance having been piqued during his work on the Lockheed problem, Paulson sought to join a Wall Street firm. In early 1974, impressed by the people with whom he interviewed at Goldman Sachs, he accepted a position there as an entry-level associate. An investment bank, trading house, and asset-management institution founded in 1869, Goldman Sachs was regarded as a bastion of conservative management and keen business sense; it had been known to recruit candidates from top business schools as early as the 1920s. "When I picked Goldman Sachs, they weren't close to being the premier firm in the industry," he explained, according to the Web site *justpeople.com*, "but the thing I learned in Washington is that just as important, or more so, as what you do is who you do it with." He eagerly accepted an offer of work in the firm's Chicago office, and with his wife he resettled in Barrington, after buying several acres from his father and building a house on the property.

In Paulson's early years with Goldman Sachs, he learned the investment-banking trade with the help of James P. Gorter, the head of the Chicago office, who became his mentor. By Paulson's own account, Gorter also helped him learn how to balance his professional responsibilities with his home life, after he realized that he was neglecting his wife and two children, who were then about one and three years of age. "I came home late from the office [one night], and I walked through the door, and I hardly acknowledged my family," he recalled to Evan McGlinn. Guided by Gorter, Paulson "developed a pattern in which I would take the early train home," as he told McGlinn. "I would give the kids a bath, and I would read them a good night story, and then I'd put them to bed. Then I would get on the phone and do work. If you take that same energy and creativity and figure out how to make things work with regard to your family, it will make all the difference."

Often characterized as hardworking and driven and as having uncommonly good business sense, Paulson was promoted to one of the vice-presidential positions at Goldman Sachs in 1977. Five years later, in recognition of his potential as a future leader of the firm, he was named a partner in the investment-banking division of the Chicago office. (Worldwide, Goldman Sachs had several dozen partners.)

The investment-banking segment of Goldman Sachs analyzes potential and actual corporate mergers and acquisitions, assists in corporate restructurings, and underwrites debt and equity, among other services. Paulson cultivated clients from his Chicago office, including Archer-Daniels-Midland, a huge food and food-products company; the Sara Lee Corp., which sells foods, clothing, and household goods; and Allstate Insurance. Paulson's solicitous service and frequent site visits made him popular among his clients. "[Site visits let] you see what's happening on the battlefield," he told Emily Thornton. He was also known for his discretion. "Clients don't want to read about their investment bankers [in the newspaper]," he told Patrick McGeehan for the *New York Times* (June 16, 2002). In 1984 the domain of his partnership was expanded to include the entire U.S. Midwest.

In 1990 Paulson was again promoted, to the position of co-head of Goldman Sachs's investment-banking division. He spent the workweek in New York City, where he lived in a hotel, and commuted to Illinois on weekends. He was also awarded a seat on Goldman Sachs's management committee, which developed corporate policies and strategies. In 1994 he settled with his family on the Upper West Side of Manhattan, eschewing the tony Upper East Side neighborhoods popular among his peers in the top echelons of banking. Late in 1994 he was named vice chairman of the management committee and chief operating officer of Goldman Sachs, second in command only to Jon S. Corzine, who, at the same time, was named the senior partner, chief executive officer, and chairman of the management committee. The two men operated the firm together, although, as Paulson told Leah Nathans Spiro for *Business Week* (September 26, 1994), "stylistically we're very different. He's a big, cuddly teddy bear. I can't get people to look at me like that." In 1997 Paulson was made president of the firm, a position in which he was still subordinate to Corzine.

One of the biggest issues facing Paulson and Corzine was the firm's status as a private institution. (In 1996 the partners rejected a plan to sell a percentage of the company to outside shareholders.) Although they had succeeded in trimming costs in the mid-1990s, Corzine, who had come to the firm as a trader, was eager to make an initial public offering (IPO) to raise an estimated $3 billion in capital, by making approximately 10 to 15 percent of shares available to the public. Paulson and other executives, however, hesitated to go against Goldman Sachs's tradition, and pointed out that mergers had followed the IPOs of some of their competitors, leading to the formation of Credit Suisse First Boston and Shearson Lehman Brothers/American Express, for example. According to Joseph Kahn in the *New York Times* (January 13, 1999), Paulson agreed to a public offering only "when Mr. Corzine agreed to make him his full equal." Once Paulson was installed as co-CEO, in June 1998, Goldman Sachs executives approved a plan for an IPO. But after the economy faltered a bit toward the end of the same year, and Goldman Sachs suffered trading losses of between $500 million and $1 billion, the firm put the plan on hold. As Goldman Sachs's most high-profile trader, Corzine found himself in an awkward spot; in January 1999 Paulson, with the support of two other executive-committee members, John Thain and John Thornton, forced Corzine to step down as co-CEO, thus leaving Paulson as the sole company head. Paulson described the tripartite decision to Leah Nathans Spiro for *Business Week* (January 25, 1999) as being "in the best interests in terms of how we manage the firm." Explaining the importance of making the change in management before the firm's IPO, he said to Spiro, "We saw a window of opportunity and decided it was the best time to make that change." Corzine resigned from Goldman Sachs on May 4, 1999, when the firm made its highly successful IPO.

On the day of the IPO, 69 million shares of the Goldman Sachs Group (the firm's new name), totaling $3.7 billion, were made available to the public, and the price rose from $53 to $70.375 per share by the time the closing bell rang at the New York Stock Exchange (NYSE). Among the beneficiaries of the IPO were Goldman Sachs employees who had stock options; these included Paulson, whose stock in the firm rose in value from $95 million on May 3 to $315 million the next day. On the negative side, after becoming a publicly held company, Goldman Sachs—for the first time in its long history—saw some of its missteps become public knowledge. (In one instance of carelessness, a security breach enabled a temporary employee to steal and sell information about mergers.)

Between 1995 and 2000 Goldman Sachs reportedly spent $5 billion on state-of-the-art software, high-tech equipment, and their installation. "Trading is part of what makes Goldman Sachs special and what differentiates this firm from our competitors," Paulson told Michael Carroll for *Institutional Investor* (January 2000). "For Goldman Sachs to be Goldman Sachs, we need to be in the middle of capital flows. That's why you see us embracing electronic trading and the latest technologies—to ensure we remain at the heart of capital flows and global markets." In September 2000 Goldman Sachs paid $6.5 billion to acquire Spear, Leeds & Kellogg, a powerful stock-exchange specialist and industry leader in securities processing and electronic-trade execution. At that time Spear, Leeds & Kellogg specialized in more than 400 NYSE stocks and, according to the *Economist* (September 16, 2000), served as a "deal maker in a fifth of all transactions" on that exchange. Thus, as Justin Schack wrote for *Institutional Investor* (October 2000), the acquisition provided Goldman Sachs "with a unique window on the retail market." For some time before Goldman Sachs gained possession of Spear, Leeds & Kellogg, Paulson had repeatedly called for a major overhaul of the NYSE with an eye toward shifting to electronic transactions exclusively. For that reason the acquisition surprised many financiers and other businesspeople, since it represented an investment in the traditional way of conducting NYSE trades. Still, as Paulson revealed about eight months later in an interview with *Future Banker* (May 2001), Goldman Sachs had been "driving technology very, very hard" in its own operations. "Even in this very tough year, when we're cutting expenses every way we know how," he said, "we're maintaining our technology spending, because it's just essential to continue to change our existing businesses to be more efficient."

On June 5, 2002, in a highly unusual action that followed a deluge of financial scandals involving such heavyweights in the corporate world as Enron, Worldcom, Tyco, and the prominent accounting and auditing firm Arthur Andersen, Paulson made a speech at the National Press Club, in Washington, D.C., in which he urged American corporations to "clean house." "In my lifetime," he said, according to the Goldman Sachs Web site, "American business has never been under such scrutiny. To be blunt, much of it is deserved." He also said, referring to the Financial Accounting Standards Board (FASB), a private organization that the federal Securities and Exchange Commission has relied on to establish standards of financial accounting and reporting, "If the outcome of all that we have been through in the past six months, all the soul-searching and debate, is business as usual at the FASB, then we will have missed an enormous opportunity." He later told Patrick McGeehan, "I wasn't putting myself or Goldman Sachs up as paragons of virtue. But if you don't speak out on these things, it could be construed as tacit approval." Among the business and political leaders who praised Paulson for publicly condemning corporate misconduct were the billionaire investor Warren Buffett and Jon S. Corzine, who had won a seat to represent New Jersey in the U.S. Senate in 2000.

An avid outdoorsman, Paulson has a passion for fly-fishing. "I find it very relaxing. It is difficult, and it takes my mind off everything else," he told Patrick McGeehan. A Republican, Paulson has been compared to the early-20th-century Republican president Theodore Roosevelt for his commitment to wildlife conservation. He sits on the board of directors of the Peregrine Fund, a nonprofit organization devoted to preserving birds of prey in the wild, and is the co-chairman of the Asia/Pacific Council of the Nature Conservancy. According to a thumbnail sketch of him for *Business Week* (March 4, 2002, on-line), he has worked with the Nature Conservancy and China's president, Jiang Zemin, to preserve the 10,000-foot-deep Tiger Leaping Gorge, in Yunnan Province, China, a natural site whose widely acknowledged beauty is being destroyed by the construction of new roads and other projects designed to attract tourists. Paulson's wife, the former Wendy Judge, a naturalist and Nature Conservancy trustee, leads birdwatching expeditions in New York City. The couple, who maintain homes in New York City and Barrington, Illinois, have a son, Henry Merritt III, and a daughter, Amanda. — K.S.

Suggested Reading: *Business Week* p84+ Jan. 25, 1999, with photo, p178 Mar. 29, 1999, with photo, p82+ Mar. 4, 2002, with photo; *Institutional Investor* p20 July 1998, with photo; *New York Times* III p1 June 16, 2002, with photo; *Polo.com* 2001 (on-line)

---

Courtesy of D-Esprit

## Pelzer, Dave

*Dec. 1960– Writer; self-help promoter*

*Address: P.O. Box 1385, Guerneville, CA 95446*

The victim of horrendous brutality at the hands of his mother, who nearly caused him to die on several occasions during his childhood, Dave Pelzer has come to terms with his past and forged a highly successful career as a writer and inspirational speaker. Pelzer, whose books have all been best-sellers, is one of only a handful of authors ever to have had four books simultaneously on the *New York Times* best-seller list. In his first three books—*A Child Called "It"*, *The Lost Boy*, and *A Man Named Dave*—Pelzer described experiences he had under his mother's roof and then as a foster child; his service in the U.S. Air Force; and his decision to share his history with others. In his most recent book, *Help Yourself*, Pelzer attempted to apply the lessons he has learned in life to situations other people often face in theirs.

One of the five children of Stephen Pelzer and Catherine Roerva Pelzer, David J. Pelzer was born in December 1960 in Daly City, California. His father was a fireman, and his mother a homemaker. During his early years his mother, who was an alcoholic, increasingly singled him out among her children for extremely harsh treatment. At various times she almost killed him, by starving him for days on end and forcing him to endure exposure to bitter temperatures. Once his mother actually stabbed him; the wound became infected, and he had to clean it himself with a rag. Another time his mother locked him in the bathroom, where he was exposed to potentially fatal fumes from a mixture of ammonia and Clorox that his mother had poured into a bucket. By his own account, he survived by placing his mouth over a heating duct and breathing through it. The more his mother drank, the greater the frequency and intensity of her violent reactions toward him became. By the time he was eight, his mother had stopped calling him by his name; instead, she referred to him as "The Boy" and, later, as "It."

In January 1973 Pelzer's parents separated. Although his father had ignored his mother's behavior toward him, Pelzer had always felt safer in his presence. With his father gone from the house, Pelzer lived in constant fear that his mother would murder him. By this time his mother had turned him into a virtual slave with regard to housework and forced him to sleep in the garage. As Pelzer recalled in his book *A Man Named Dave: A Story of Triumph and Forgiveness*, his mother told him, "If *It* wants to be fed, then it's simple: *It* does exactly as It's told. If It doesn't want to be punished, then It stays out of trouble. It knows the rules. I don't treat you any different than anybody else. It simply refuses to obey." Although, as his mother ordered him to, Pelzer gave various excuses to his teachers when they asked him about his bruises, eventually the school nurse and several teachers reported Pelzer's condition to authorities. In doing so, according to various sources, they put their careers on the line, because in those years—the early 1970s—few laws existed to protect abused children.

Reportedly identified as one of the most severely abused children in the state of California, Pelzer seemed destined for a grim future; various professionals predicted that before his 18th birthday, he would either be imprisoned for criminal behavior or be killed in a fight. He spent his teenage years in a series of five foster homes, trying to build a decent life for himself. Worried that he would never amount to anything and knowing that after he turned 18 he would no longer be a ward of the court, while in high school he took various part-time jobs, among them shining shoes and serving as a busboy. By his own account, he worked almost to the point of collapse before cutting back on his hours.

At the age of 18, Pelzer dropped out of high school and joined the U.S. Air Force, with the goal of getting training in firefighting. But all the fireman positions had been filled, so he was given the job of cook. After some years in that position, he was reassigned to begin training as an air-crew member; he also began to take college courses. During his approximately 13 years in the air force, he also worked as a counselor in juvenile-detention facilities and as a member of Youth Service America. As an air-force air crewman, he helped to refuel jet planes in midair. During Operations Just Cause, Desert Shield, and Desert Storm, the military actions taken by the United States and its allies against Iraq during the 1991 Persian Gulf War, Pelzer was chosen to refuel the secret SR-71 Blackbird and F-117 Stealth Fighter war planes.

After his honorable discharge from the air force, in 1991, Pelzer wrote *A Child Called "It": One Child's Courage to Survive* (1993). The book details his early years from his own child's-eye point of view. It was followed by another best-seller, *The Lost Boy: A Foster Child's Search for the Love of a Family* (1994). In *A Man Named Dave* (1999), Pelzer chronicled his life from the time he left his last foster family through his career in the air force and his experiences as a writer, husband, and father. The book also describes his encounters with his father shortly before the older man's death and with his mother when he was 32. While looking at a wedding picture of his parents before his mother's funeral, Pelzer was struck by the hope and joy evident in her expression. "With the frame shaking in my hand, I emptied my chest," he wrote in *A Man Named Dave*. "I forgave her. I forgave 'The Mother.'" In *Help Yourself: Celebrating the Rewards of Resilience and Gratitude* (2000), Pelzer offered advice based on the lessons he has learned in his life, emphasizing the importance of the qualities named in the subtitle. "If I learned anything from my unfortunate childhood it is that there is nothing that can dominate or conquer the human spirit," he wrote in *Help Yourself*. "This is the essence of the message I wish to present to you."

Pelzer has worked in California as a counselor for children at risk. He currently travels in the U.S. for two-thirds of each year, speaking to groups of business, human-services, and education professionals. He also gives talks to audiences of students in junior high and high schools.

Pelzer has received personal commendations from former presidents Ronald Reagan, George Herbert Walker Bush, and Bill Clinton. He was awarded the J. C. Penney Golden Rule Award in 1990, thus becoming the California Volunteer of the Year. The United States Junior Chamber of Commerce named him one of the Ten Outstanding Young Americans in 1993 and honored him the following year as the only American among the Outstanding Young Persons of the World. In 1996 he was one of the carriers of the centennial flame for the Summer Olympics. He has appeared on television on *The Oprah Winfrey Show*, *The Montel Williams Show*, the *Sally Jesse Raphael Show*, *Leeza*, and *The View*, co-hosted by Barbara Walters. He currently lives with his second wife, Marsha, in Guerneville, California. He has one son, Stephen, from his previous marriage. His activities include serving as the national adviser for the Missing Youth Foundation and sitting on the board of directors of Foster Care Independent Living Program; he also counsels members of the armed forces who have discipline problems or other troubles. In his leisure time he reads and watches television and films. — G.O.

Suggested Reading: *New York Times Magazine* p22+ July 28, 2002, with photo; Pelzer, Dave. *A Child Called "It"*, 1993, *The Lost Boy*, 1994, *A Man Named Dave*, 1999, *Help Yourself*, 2000

Selected Books: *A Child Called "It"*, 1993; *The Lost Boy*, 1994; *A Man Named Dave*, 1999; *Help Yourself*, 2000

---

## Pierce, Paul

*Oct. 13, 1977– Basketball player*

*Address: c/o National Basketball Association, 645 Fifth Ave., 10th Fl., New York, NY 10022*

After four seasons with the National Basketball Association (NBA), the Boston Celtics' Paul Pierce has proven himself to be one of the most formidable scorers in the game. Alternating between shooting guard and small forward (a position also called swingman), Pierce shoots well from the outside, excelling at three-pointers, and is proficient at driving to the basket. "Paul is a classic swingman," Sachin Shenolikar wrote for *Sports Illustrated for Kids* (May 2002): "6' 6", 230 pounds, with smooth footwork and a sugar-sweet jumper. When he posts

Robert Mora/Getty Images

*Paul Pierce*

up, he sheds defenders with a shake and a shimmy, often laying it up and drawing a foul. The high release of his jumper allows him to shoot over opponents' arms." During the 2001–02 season Pierce helped the Celtics get to the play-offs (it was their first trip since 1995) and racked up 2,144 points, the most in the NBA. In the *New York Times* (January 5, 2002), Mike Wise declared Pierce—who has been nicknamed "The Truth" by the basketball great Shaquille O'Neal—to be part of "the group of pro basketball's best swingmen, alongside Kobe Bryant, Tracy McGrady and Vince Carter."

The youngest of the three sons of Lorraine Hosey, Paul Pierce was born on October 13, 1977 and grew up outside Los Angeles, California. An avid Los Angeles Lakers fan, he and his friends used to sneak into their arena to see Earvin "Magic" Johnson and Kareem Abdul-Jabbar play. "There was a side door that maintenance used to go through," Pierce recalled to Shenolikar. "When they came in and out, we'd sneak in." Pierce attended Inglewood High School, where he became a star basketball player. In one play-off game he scored 20 points in two minutes. During the time he played high-school ball, Pierce, a tough leader, got into fistfights with six of his 11 teammates because he thought they were not playing hard enough. In his senior year, during which he averaged 24.5 points and 11.5 rebounds per game, he was named California's high-school player of the year and a McDonald's All-American.

Widely recruited by colleges, Pierce decided on Kansas University, in Lawrence, known for its disciplined basketball program and its group of established stars, including Raef LaFrentz. "I wanted to go somewhere where someone would push me," Pierce told Bob Dutton for the *Sporting News* (February 2, 1998). "If I went to a team where everything was built around me, I'd probably get lazy and spoiled. I wanted to go to a team that also had a chance to win a national championship, where I'd get good exposure and have a good head coach—somewhere where I could learn." In his freshman season with the Jayhawks, 1995–96, Pierce averaged 11.9 points per game, helping his team finish first in the Big 12 conference and make it to the regional finals of the National Collegiate Athletic Association (NCAA) basketball tournament. In the 1996–97 season, he brought his scoring average to 16.3 per game, and the Jayhawks again finished first in the Big 12 and made it to the NCAA regional finals. The Jayhawks advanced just as far the next season, and Pierce, who averaged 20.4 points per game and played spectacularly during the postseason, was named a first-team All-American.

Pierce left college after his junior year and made himself eligible for the NBA draft. The Boston Celtics chose him 10th overall, which made him a later pick than he and many commentators had predicted. Feeling slighted by the teams that had passed him up, Pierce used his frustration to drive him through the rigorous preseason practices led by the Celtics' coach, Rick Pitino. "Whatever little thing I can find, I use to motivate myself," Pierce told Jackie MacMullan for *Sports Illustrated* (March 15, 1999). The 1998–99 NBA season was shortened by a strike, so Pierce did not make his professional debut until February 5, 1999, against the Toronto Raptors; in that game he exceeded all expectations by scoring 19 points and racking up nine rebounds, five assists, and four blocked shots. Pierce also wasted no time proving his boldness: in another early-season game against the Raptors, he tussled with the six-foot nine-inch, 250-pound Charles Oakley, who is known for being tough. "I just felt like if I backed down, I would be dead for the rest of my career," he told Mike Wise. "Everybody would think of me as soft." Pierce finished the season with an average of 16.5 points and 6.4 rebounds per game (both second-best among rookies that year) and was selected to the All-Rookie First Team. Perhaps more importantly, he meshed well with the Celtics' star forward, Antoine Walker, although their team did not make it to the play-offs. Pierce worked hard during the off-season and in the 1999–2000 season averaged 19.5 points per game.

During the following off-season, on September 25, 2000, Pierce nearly died in a stabbing incident at a Boston club. He was talking to a woman when three men approached him, one of them claiming to be the woman's brother. Pierce was then hit over the head with a bottle and stabbed more than a dozen times, in the back, torso, and neck. He also sustained surface wounds to his face. Doctors performed emergency surgery to repair a collapsed lung and said that Pierce's leather jacket may have saved his life. "It was a real crowded place," Pierce recalled to Wise. "I don't know what people thought, but there was no way I was hitting on a girl. It was no more than a minute conversation and the next thing you know, my life is changed. Things just happened so fast, I didn't even know it was three people. I thought it was 10 or 15 people. You don't realize what's going on until it's over." Afterward, Pierce was plagued by nightmares. His family supported him during that difficult time. "[The incident has] changed my life," Pierce told Ian Thomsen for *Sports Illustrated* (April 16, 2001). "It helped me grow up a lot faster and become closer with my family. You never know when your time will come. I realize you can't take the people around you for granted, including the fans—they helped me through this."

Pierce was healed and ready to play basketball in less than four weeks, just in time for the beginning of the 2000–01 season. Remarkably, he did not miss any games that season (he was the only Celtic who didn't), and he elevated his play to a distinctly higher level. In his first game after the stabbing, he scored 28 points. In March 2001 he was named player of the month, becoming the first Celtic to win that honor in 15 years. His 25.3-point-per-game average was the eighth-best in the NBA, and he became the first Celtic to score more than 2,000 points in a season since Larry Bird in 1988.

Pierce continued to improve during the 2001–02 season. In December 2001, after missing 15 of 16 shots against the New Jersey Nets, he scored 46 points in the second half, totaling a career-high 48 points. He scored a total of 2,144 points that season, the most in the league, and averaged 26.1 points per game, the third-highest in the NBA. His performance earned him a spot on the All-Star team and helped carry his team to the play-offs for the first time since 1995. In the first round of the play-offs, Boston defeated the Philadelphia 76ers. Pierce played impressively in the series, particularly in the fifth and final game, in which he scored 46 points in a 120–87 rout. Next, Pierce helped his team past the Detroit Pistons, a matchup the Celtics won fairly easily in five out of a possible seven games. In the Eastern Conference finals, the Celtics faced the New Jersey Nets, a team against which Pierce had played well all season. In Game Three, with the series tied 1–1 and the Nets ahead by 21 points in the beginning of the fourth quarter, it looked as though the Celtics would fall to 1–2 in the series. But Pierce, who had hit only two of 14 shots in the first three quarters, led the charge—scoring 19 points to clinch a 94–90 victory and the most dramatic comeback in NBA play-off history. In Game Four Pierce scored 31 points but let his team down with 1.1 seconds left in the game by missing two free throws in a 94–92 loss to the Nets. The Nets went on to win the series in six games. After the series Pierce told Dan Ventura for the *Boston Herald* (June 1, 2002), "We have nothing to hang our heads down for, we had a great year. I think this is just the beginning of a young team taking our steps toward something that can be pretty special down the line. . . . In time we can be a championship team."

Pierce, who is single, often works out during the off-season at the University of California at Los Angeles, where he occasionally gets pointers from Magic Johnson. "He's a throwback," Johnson told Steve Bulpett for the *Boston Herald* (June 14, 2002) about Pierce. "He's like one of the old guys because he wants to improve and he'll work at it." — P.G.H.

Suggested Reading: *New York Times* D p1 Jan. 5, 2002, with photos; *Orlando Sentinel* June 23, 1998; *Providence Journal-Bulletin* Oct. 27, 1999; *Sporting News* Feb. 2, 1998, with photos; *Sports Illustrated* July 6, 1998, with photo, p77+ Apr. 16, 2001, p48+ Nov. 26, 2001, with photos; *Sports Illustrated for Kids* p25+ May 2002, with photos

---

Alex Wong/Getty Images

## Pitt, Harvey

*Feb. 28, 1945– Former chairman of the U.S. Securities and Exchange Commission*

*Address: c/o Fried Frank Harris Shriver & Jacobson, Suite 800, 1001 Pennsylvania Ave. N.W., Washington, DC 20004-2505*

Since the latter half of 2001, as financial scandals at Enron, WorldCom, and other corporations have plagued the U.S. economy, causing a crisis in investor confidence, few have drawn more of the blame than Harvey Pitt, who served as the chairman of the the U.S. Securities and Exchange Commission (SEC) for 15 months, beginning on August 3, 2001. Pitt began his career as an attorney in 1968, when he joined the SEC, the government agency responsible for protecting investors and maintaining the integrity of the securities markets. He rose through the ranks of the commission for 10 years, before essentially switching sides and going into private practice to defend corporations and business organizations against charges brought by the SEC. Representing virtually all of the largest accounting firms—such as Arthur Andersen, which has been implicated in the Enron scandal—Pitt became one of the most sought-after counsels by those facing charges of financial misconduct. Kathleen Day wrote for the *Washington Post* (July 25, 2002, on-line), "Past and current colleagues describe Pitt as an intense, sometimes volatile workaholic whose hands-on micro-management style has tended throughout his career as a securities attorney to divide those he works with, but that also produces sparks of brilliance."

When he was instated as SEC chairman, Pitt appeared ready to chart a course quite different from that of his predecessor, Arthur Levitt, who was known for aggressively policing corporate business practices. Pitt proposed a more cooperative approach, maintaining that illegal accounting and financial-reporting practices could be effectively prevented if corporations were less afraid to communicate with the SEC. This stance soon became unpopular; as illegal business practices were uncovered in more and more corporations, many blamed Pitt for being too lenient, ignoring his insistence that the problems had been caused by the restrictive and secretive atmosphere imposed by Levitt. In July 2002 several members of Congress publicly called for Pitt's resignation. President George W. Bush, however, repeatedly expressed his support for Pitt, and Representative Dick Armey, Republican of Texas, said, as quoted by the Cox News Service (July 12, 2002), "I think [Pitt] is being scapegoated. It would be unreasonable for us to say to anybody, 'Get this straightened out in 12 months.'" On November 5, 2002, in the midst of the uproar sparked by the revelation that he had withheld damaging information connected with William Webster, whom the SEC had chosen to head a newly established accounting-industry oversight board, Pitt tendered his resignation to President Bush.

Harvey Lloyd Pitt was born to Morris and Sara (Sapir) Pitt on February 28, 1945. He grew up in the New York City borough of Brooklyn and attended Stuyvesant High School and Brooklyn College before earning his law degree from St. John's University, in New York City, in 1968. Upon graduating, Pitt joined the SEC as a staff attorney in the office of the general counsel. In 1969 he became a legal assistant for then–SEC commissioner Francis M. Wheat, after which he served as special counsel in the office of the general counsel (1970–72), editor of the SEC's *Institutional Investor Study Report* (1972), chief counsel in the division of market regulation (1972–73), and executive assistant to then–SEC chairman Ray Garrett Jr. (1973–75).

In 1975 Pitt was appointed general counsel of the SEC, becoming the youngest person ever to hold that position. As general counsel, he helped curb accounting abuses at United Brands, Lockheed, and other large corporations and accounting firms. "We brought 20 cases against the Big Eight accounting firms," Stanley Sporkin, a former SEC enforcement director, told Mike McNamee, Amy Borrus, and David Henry for *Business Week* (March 25, 2002). "Harvey was in on every one of them." From 1974 to 1982 Pitt was an adjunct professor of law at George Washington University Law School, in Washington, D.C.; he also held that position from 1975 to 1984 at Georgetown University, in Washington, D.C., and from 1983 to 1984 at the University of Pennsylvania, in Philadelphia.

In 1978 Pitt left the SEC to join the law firm of Fried, Frank, Harris, Shriver, & Jacobson, where he became the top-billing partner for many years and represented some of the most powerful companies and organizations in the financial industry, including the Securities Industry Association, the American Institute of Certified Public Accountants (AICPA), the Investment Company Institute, the New York Stock Exchange, America Online, Merrill Lynch, and Arthur Andersen. According to Stephen Labaton in the *New York Times* (May 8, 2001), Pitt, as a private counsel, was "a top lobbyist for an industry-led initiative that made significant changes in the securities laws in 1995 that have helped to insulate companies from class actions filed by investors."

In a highly publicized case in 1987, Pitt represented the financier Ivan F. Boesky, who was accused of illegally using inside information to profit from stock transactions. Boesky was fined $50 million out of a possible $150 million and charged with one felony; many attributed the relative moderateness of his punishment to Pitt's skill. Arthur Fleischer, a partner at Fried, Frank, Harris, Shriver, & Jacobson, told Kirk Victor for the *National Law Journal* (December 1, 1986), "I was very instrumental in attracting Harvey to Fried Frank. I knew him perhaps better than any other partner. I was more aware of his capacity and capabilities. Whenever I had the opportunity, I tried to get him involved. He's the kind of lawyer you always want involved." In 2000 Pitt helped the AICPA to make a deal on behalf of the accounting industry that countered efforts by the then–SEC chairman, Arthur Levitt, to steer accounting firms away from potential conflicts of interest, such as might arise from consulting for the corporations they audit.

Pitt was installed as chairman of the SEC on August 3, 2001, at a time when the U.S. economy was suffering a downturn and the SEC had recently initiated several major investigations into investment banks. Pitt's appointment by President Bush caused immediate controversy. Some, such as Senator Charles E. Schumer, Democrat of New York—who called Pitt "the Zeus of the [securities] field," according to Stephen Labaton in the *New York Times* (July 20, 2001)—argued that Pitt's extensive experience defending big businesses would prove invaluable in helping him regulate some of those same businesses. Others argued that because of Pitt's former ties to corporate executives and accounting firms, his appointment was a major coup for corporate lobbyists. "The various professional groups associated with Wall Street have organized to win themselves the most lenient possible treatment," Jonathan Chait wrote for the *New Republic* (December 17, 2001). "Thus the appointment of Harvey Pitt." At a meeting with the Senate Banking Committee on July 19, 2001, Pitt was asked by the head of the committee, Senator Paul Sarbanes, Democrat of Maryland, whether his corporate ties would make him overly sympathetic to corporate interests. Pitt, as quoted by Labaton, responded, "I was known as a vigorous enforcer of the law and the public interest. My success in private practice has been attributed to the fact that I tell my clients what they need to hear, not what they want to hear. Sometimes it's been unpleasant and I have been fired for expressing my views. I haven't worked this hard in 33 years to come before this committee to risk my reputation by doing anything other than what the public interest requires."

In one of his first public speeches as SEC chairman, on October 22, 2001 before the AICPA governing council, Pitt inflamed his detractors by showing what some read as sympathy toward the accounting industry. In the speech, as posted on the SEC's Web site, Pitt said, "Somewhere along the way, accountants became afraid to talk to the SEC, and the SEC appeared to be unwilling to listen to the profession. Those days are ended. I speak for the entire Commission when I say that we want to have a continuing dialogue, and partnership, with the accounting profession, and we will do everything in our power to evidence a new era of respect and cooperation." Fuel was added to the fire the next day, when David S. Hilzenrath reported for the *Washington Post* that Pitt had declared in an interview his intention to make the SEC "a kinder, gentler place for everyone," not only accountants. Less publicized were Pitt's warnings to the AICPA, such as his declaration in his speech that "practices that reflect venality and disservice to public investors . . . will not be tolerated." Reactions to Pitt's speech to the AICPA continued to plague him well into the next year, often overshadowing his efforts to regulate corporations. "People took out of context what I said," Pitt told Jackie Spinner for the *Washington Post* (February 13, 2002), "and the result of that was those words have been used to suggest things that are wholly at odds with what I stand for."

In the fall of 2001, shortly after Pitt took office, the revelation of serious problems in Arthur Andersen's accounting for the energy giant Enron Corp. shook the financial world at its foundations. Enron filed for bankruptcy on December 2, 2001, and in the wake of that development a string of financial scandals hit U.S. corporations such as Kmart, Adelphia, WorldCom, Qwest, Global Crossing, Dynegy, Merrill Lynch, and Tyco. Furthermore, the SEC was short-staffed in its upper-level positions because the Bush administration had failed to nominate replacements for departed officials. In a speech delivered on March 7, 2002, addressing the subject of the economy, President Bush, as quoted in *Business Week* (March 25, 2002), said, "Today, I call upon the Securities & Exchange Commission to take action. Reform should improve investor confidence and help our economy to flourish and grow." In response to the uneasiness caused by the scandals, Pitt had increasingly begun to emphasize the importance of directly regulating companies, rather than allowing them to oversee many of their own activities. "I have moved off a notion of self-regulation," he told Jackie Spinner in February 2002, "and I've moved into a notion of what I call private regulation. I am not willing to try to solve this by having the accounting profession regulate itself. Even if I thought it could be done, and I don't, it wouldn't sell."

During the first six months of Pitt's tenure, the SEC issued more suspensions and subpoenas than in the year before he arrived; in the first three months of 2002, the commission launched 64 financial-reporting investigations. In late June, after WorldCom admitted accounting irregularities in its operation, the SEC filed civil-fraud charges within 24 hours. The SEC's efforts to step up regulation notwithstanding, Pitt generally discouraged any major new regulatory legislation, instead pointing to the prosecution of Arthur Andersen by the U.S. Department of Justice and emphasizing the formation of new SEC rules, to be issued under its existing legal authority. Those rules included stronger penalties for illegal behavior, clearer and more efficient financial reporting, and structural changes in auditing. As a deterrent to dishonest business practices, the SEC announced that guilty executives would be banned from leading other businesses and would lose their compensation packages. In order to improve financial reporting, Pitt ordered companies to inform their investors of bookkeeping issues that would likely have significant effects on reported profits. CEOs, under Pitt's direction, had to state plainly, in the "management discussion and analysis" section of reports, any upcoming financial risks being taken by their companies. Also, executives were required to disclose all stock sales within 48 hours, as opposed to the 13-month period they enjoyed before.

Taking further strides to correct abuses, Pitt, on March 21, 2002, offered a proposal before the Senate Banking Committee to set up the Public Accountability Board, which would monitor accounting firms. His plan, however, was fraught with difficulties, and the way he went about pushing for its adoption proved problematic as well. Before explaining it to Congress or the Public Oversight Board (which had been established by Levitt to perform duties similar to those that would be handled by Pitt's proposed board), Pitt had first met with the AICPA and representatives of the "Big

Five" accounting firms. Pitt also proposed the inclusion of accountants on his new board, though his plan did not call for giving them subpoena power to gather evidence. Some members of Congress felt slighted because Pitt had approached the AICPA first, and the Public Oversight Board, which in effect would have been replaced, disbanded in protest. Pitt also elected not to meet with the Council of Institutional Investors, an organization for pension holders. "That's just bad management," Sarah Teslik, the executive director of the council, told Jackie Spinner. "Even if you want to sell us down the river, you still meet with us because it looks good." The result of Pitt's actions was that his proposal for a new oversight board was widely viewed as weak and compromised by his ties to the accounting industry.

Pitt attracted more criticism in April 2002, when he reportedly met with executives at Xerox and KPMG (a company that was auditing Xerox), around the time that the SEC planned to fine Xerox $10 million for bad accounting. Critics charged that Pitt was tipping off these companies to impending investigations. When asked about the meetings by Ron Insana for *Money* (August 2002), Pitt responded, "The meetings that I have had have all been for the purpose of serving the public interest. If we regulate a major firm and they are subject to our regulation and they have a new CEO who wants to meet us and make it clear that we can call on them to do what they're supposed to do in the public interest, that's a meeting that helps investors. It doesn't hurt investors. Much of the criticism that I've seen, in my view, is both ill-informed and misdirected."

Just as critics were questioning Pitt's ability to clean up corporate America, Congress came up with its own solutions to the economic slump. On June 18, three days after Arthur Andersen was declared guilty of obstructing justice in the investigation of Enron, the Senate Banking Committee approved an accounting-reform bill. Senator Paul Sarbanes had introduced the bill, which proposed a new oversight board (Pitt's had not yet materialized) to review audits of publicly traded companies and to restrict accounting firms from providing consulting services to the companies they audit. The latter provision was one that Pitt had consistently resisted, despite the fact that many believed that the Enron scandal—in which it was revealed that Arthur Andersen had earned $25 million from Enron for consulting fees, the same amount it had collected for auditing—proved the importance of removing such potential conflicts of interest. Pitt told Mike McNamee and Amy Borrus for *Business Week* (March 25, 2002) that if the restriction on consulting went through, "in the next five years we will have far worse audits than we have now. With all the bashing of accountants, it's hard to see the best and brightest minds going into this field." He also said to McNamee and Borrus, "If accounting firms are more dependent on audit clients, then by definition they're less independent. Independence is important. But the real issue is the quality of audits."

Disapproval over Pitt's performance reached a fever pitch in July, when both Republicans and Democrats began to call for his resignation. Senate Majority Leader Tom Daschle, Democrat of South Dakota, said, as quoted by the Cox News Service (July 12, 2002), "I have to say that at this point, we could do a lot better than Harvey Pitt in that position today," while Representative Spencer Bachus, Republican of Alabama, said, "There is now some question over whether [Pitt] is the right person, and this is the right time for him to be chairman of the Securities and Exchange Commission." Later in July Pitt suggested to Congress that, as an addition to its accounting bill, his SEC chairmanship should be elevated to a Cabinet position, with a concomitant 21 percent pay raise (from $138,200 to $166,700). Senator Daschle, as quoted by *CNN Money* (July 24, 2002, on-line), responded, "This is further proof and a clear illustration of why it is many of us feel the time has come for a change in that position. I am surprised and saddened by the insensitivity of Mr. Pitt." Pitt himself emphatically dismissed the notion that he ought to resign. "I have absolutely no intention of stepping down," he said on the NBC program *Meet the Press*, as quoted by the New York *Daily News* (July 15, 2002). "Anybody who looks at what we've really done," Pitt added, "what our record is, instead of these politically crass sound bites, will understand this is the most aggressive, most effective SEC that there has ever been in the 68 years of this agency."

While the White House's and Pitt's initial plan to stem the economic crisis had not involved significant new legislation, Senator Sarbanes's accounting-reform bill and a similar, less radical, bill initiated by Representative Michael Oxley, Republican of Ohio, gathered momentum in Congress. In a speech delivered on June 20, 2002, Pitt said, as posted on the SEC Web site, "Some speculate we are competing with Congress to see who gets to solve our crisis of confidence. No such rivalry exists—the only important thing is that this crisis is resolved. We've said all along, and proven, that we will work with both Houses of Congress in the development of legislative solutions to problems we've identified." However, aides to Senator Sarbanes claimed, as reported by Kathleen Day for the *Washington Post* (July 25, 2002), that Pitt met with Republicans in the Senate Banking Committee in an unsuccessful effort to derail the bill before a crucial vote; he then further agitated Sarbanes and his team by declaring on a talk show in early July that he was working with Sarbanes to facilitate passage of the bill. On July 30, 2002 President Bush signed into law the Sarbanes-Oxley Act of 2002, which, in addition to setting up an accounting oversight board and promoting the independence of accounting firms from the companies they audit, increases penalties for corporate wrongdoing, expands corporate financial disclosure, and increases the SEC budget.

In October 2002 Pitt made what some believe to be his most grievous mistake as SEC chairman. Charged with naming a head for the new accounting oversight panel created by Congress, Pitt at first supported the appointment of John H. Biggs, the chairman and CEO of TIAA-CREF (the nation's largest teachers' pension fund) and a well-known advocate of stricter rules for accountants; both Alan Greenspan, the chairman of the Federal Reserve Board, and Paul H. O'Neill, the secretary of the treasury, approved the choice of Biggs. But many accounting-industry executives expressed fierce opposition to Biggs, as did Republican congressman Michael G. Oxley of Ohio, the chairman of the House Financial Services Committee. Yielding to their protests, Pitt backed away from Biggs and instead offered the job to William H. Webster, a former head of the FBI and the CIA who had no accounting experience; by a vote of three to two (with the three Republicans on the SEC in favor and the two Democrats opposed), Webster won the appointment. Pitt, however, had failed to inform his fellow SEC commissioners or the White House that Webster had led an audit panel for a company called U.S. Technologies Inc., which has been accused of defrauding shareholders of millions of dollars while Webster served on that panel. After that bombshell and the revelation of other events that indicated Webster's unsuitability for his new position, the SEC's inspector general, the General Accounting Office (the investigative arm of Congress), and Congress itself launched investigations into the circumstances surrounding Webster's appointment. "What we have here is the worst self-inflicted wound in the history of the commission," Joel Seligman, the dean of Washington University Law School and an expert on the history of the SEC, told Diana B. Henriques for the *New York Times* (November 3, 2002). "This is really an issue of an S.E.C. chairman not choosing to share material information with his colleagues. That is absolutely unprecedented."

On Election Night, November 5, 2002, the White House announced that Pitt had given up his position. In the letter of resignation that he sent to President Bush earlier that day, Pitt wrote, as quoted by T. K. Maloy on the Web site of United Press International (November 12, 2002), "Unfortunately, the turmoil surrounding my chairmanship and the agency makes it very difficult for the commissioners and the dedicated SEC staffers to perform their critical assignments. Rather than be a burden to you or the agency, I feel it is in everyone's best interest if I step aside now, to allow the agency to continue the important efforts we have started."

Pitt's honors include the Outstanding Young Lawyer Award from the Federal Bar Association, in 1975, and the Learned Hand Award from the Institute for Human Relations, in 1988. Pitt has two children with his wife, Saree Ruffin, and two from a former marriage. Remarking on the state of the U.S. economy, he told Insana, "We have seen this at other periods of our history, such as in the 1920s. This time, however, when you see some of the dramatic consequences of [unlawful] behavior, there's a real opportunity to make far-reaching changes, and that's why I think this is a historic time to be at the SEC." Pitt added that people should continue to invest in business because "owning shares of stock in American companies gives people the chance to realize the American dream. It doesn't work if the game is rigged, so we are here to make certain that the game can't be rigged. . . . Americans should be proud to invest in American companies as long as the markets are fair to everyone and nobody has a special break." — P.G.H.

Suggested Reading: *Business Week* p72 Mar. 25, 2002; *Money* p57+ Aug. 2002; *National Law Journal* p6+ Dec. 1, 1986; *New Republic* p14+ Dec. 17, 2001; *New York Times* C p1 Jan. 17, 2002, A p1 May 8, 2001, C p1 July 20, 2001; *Salon* (on-line) July 10, 2002; *Traders* Aug. 1, 2001; *U.S. News & World Report* p132 May 20, 2002; *Washington Post* E p1 Oct. 23, 2001, E p1 Feb. 13, 2002, with photos

Selected Books: as author—*Evolving Financial Services Industry*, 1985; *The Law of Financial Services*, 1988; *Pitt on Corporate Control*, 1988; *28th Annual Institute on Securities Regulation*, 1996; as editor—*Securities in ihe Electronic Age: A Practical Guide to the Law and Regulation* (with John F. Olson), 1997

---

## Plimpton, Martha

*Nov. 16, 1970– Actress*

*Address: Steppenwolf Theatre Company, 1650 N. Halstead St., Chicago, IL 60614-5530*

Unlike many performers who become famous at a young age, Martha Plimpton has avoided many of the pitfalls of childhood celebrity to thrive in her profession as an adult. Plimpton made her cinematic debut at age 11, in *Rollover* (1981). Three years later she gained recognition as the co-star, alongside Tommy Lee Jones, in *The River Rat*. She went on to appear in a number of teen and family films, including *The Goonies* (1985), *Parenthood* (1989), and *Josh and S.A.M.* (1993), and also took on major roles in more troubling motion pictures, among them *The Mosquito Coast* (1986), *Running on Empty* (1988), and *Another Woman* (1988). "While most actors her age are ghettoized in teen-problem movies . . . , she has made real films for real people," Susan Linfield observed in *Premiere* (February 1990). In recent years Plimpton has appeared in a string of independent films, among them *Pecker* and *The Sleepy Time Gal* (2001), while also concentrating on a stage career. In 1998 she joined the prestigious Steppenwolf Theatre Company; as a member of that Chicago-based troupe, she has been seen in productions of *Hedda Gabler*, *The Glass Menagerie*, *The Playboy of the*

Joseph Marzullo/Retna Ltd.

*Martha Plimpton*

*Western World*, and *The Libertine*. She has also acted in theaters in New York City; New Haven, Connecticut; and Seattle, Washington. In the Atlantic Theater Company's production of the 1915 comedy *Hobson's Choice*, Plimpton, who played Maggie, the strong-minded eldest daughter of the title character, "breathed life into a tricky role, managing to convey a sense of authority without sacrificing her openness and humor"; such was the opinion of the play's director, David Warren, as paraphrased by the Associated Press reporter Mark Kennedy in January 2002. (Kennedy was quoted in the on-line edition of the *Columbia [Missouri] Daily Tribune*.) Warren added, "What she has naturally is power and strength. She's also very vulnerable and very warm and very kind. She seems to have both of them at the same time. Maybe that's why she's so special."

Martha Plimpton was born on November 16, 1970 in New York City. Her parents, Shelley Plimpton and Keith Carradine, are both actors. Her mother is perhaps best known for being among the first performers to appear nude on Broadway, in the 1969 musical *Hair*. Her father, another *Hair* cast member, has many big-screen and television movies to his credit and has also acted on stage. Shelley Plimpton and Keith Carradine separated before the birth of their daughter. Martha Plimpton was raised in New York City by her mother.

When she was eight Plimpton was introduced to the composer, dramatist, and writer Elizabeth Swados, a friend of her mother's, who included the young girl in an acting workshop that she was leading. By age 11 Plimpton was appearing in television commercials for Calvin Klein jeans. The ads, which featured preadolescent girls talking suggestively to the camera, generated some controversy. "Oh, God, I don't even want to talk about them," Plimpton told Linfield.

That same year Plimpton landed her first film role, in the Alan J. Pakula thriller *Rollover*. The film, which features Jane Fonda, Kris Kristofferson, and Hume Cronyn, was a commercial and critical failure, but it helped open doors in Hollywood for her. She next played the daughter of an ex-con (Tommy Lee Jones) in Thomas Rickman's movie *The River Rat* (1984), in which father and daughter regain their former closeness while traveling down the Mississippi River in search of hidden money. Speaking of his decision to cast Plimpton, Rickman told Linfield, "I was looking for a little southern girl, a 1980s Huckleberry Finn, and I'd been testing *lots* of actresses from all over. I had seen Martha in the [Calvin Klein] ads, and I thought, 'I can't have Calvin Klein going down the Mississippi!' But the minute she tested, it was love at first sight. I knew she was it, no question about it. The folks at Paramount agreed; Michael Eisner said, 'Book her.'"

After *The River Rat* Plimpton won a role in Richard Donner's *The Goonies* (1985), an adventure film whose story came from Steven Spielberg. The title characters are misfits who set out in search of a pirate's treasure in the hope of saving their town from land developers. The cast included some of the hottest young actors of the 1980s, among them Sean Astin, Corey Feldman, and Kerri Green. Plimpton played Stefanie, a popular teenager who inadvertently gets roped into accompanying the Goonies on their adventures. *The Goonies* was a smash hit, earning more than $60 million at the box office, and it propelled Plimpton and other members of its cast to stardom.

Plimpton was next seen playing a minister's daughter in Peter Weir's *The Mosquito Coast* (1986). Based on a novel by Paul Theroux, the picture focuses on Allie Fox (portrayed by Harrison Ford), whose disgust with the materialism and erosion of morals in contemporary society spurs him to relocate his family to a Central American rainforest. His attempts to create a little utopia end disastrously. *The Mosquito Coast*, which earned few positive reviews, marked the first time Plimpton appeared on screen with River Phoenix, who played Charlie, Allie's older son.

Over the next few years, Plimpton was cast in a number of modest films, including Woody Allen's Bergmanesque *Another Woman* (1988), before reuniting with Phoenix in Sidney Lumet's *Running on Empty* (1988). Plimpton played Lorna Phillips, a small-town teenager who falls for Danny Pope (Phoenix), whose parents have been on the run from the FBI since the 1960s, when they helped to blow up a weapons lab as a way of protesting the Vietnam War. "There was an element of trust" between her and Phoenix that strengthened her work in the movie, Plimpton told Alan Mirabella for the New York *Daily News* (September 11, 1988). "I think my performance would not have been the same had it not been for River. For the first time, I'm pleased with my performance. But I'm still growing and changing as an actress and there's a lot I have to learn." Responding to widespread media speculation that she and Phoenix were romantically involved, she told Linfield. "We're not an *item*. . . . It's nothing like that. We're related. We're connected. We're bonded. We're great friends. And even if we *were* romantically involved, I wouldn't sit here and tell you about it." The romantic nature of their relationship became public knowledge after Plimpton had split up with Phoenix, as a result of his continued drug use. (The young actor died of a drug overdose on October 31, 1993.)

Plimpton was next seen in Ron Howard's *Parenthood* (1989), an ensemble comedy starring Steve Martin, Mary Steenburgen, Jason Robards Jr., Dianne Wiest, and a host of other noted actors. The film shows how three families cope with raising children of varying ages. Plimpton, playing a rebellious teenage daughter, earned positive notices from critics. In 1990 she appeared in *Stanley & Iris*, with Robert De Niro and Jane Fonda in the title roles. She took the part of Kelly, Iris's daughter, who gets pregnant by an unnamed man. "My character in this film is different from anything I've played," Plimpton told Linfield. "She's precocious, and she's a smartass, and I guess she's tough. But she's also full of fear. That's something I haven't had a chance yet to play, and I like having something else there to do." After remarking that the actress "to some extent" was "reprising some of her old characters" in *Stanley & Iris*, Linfield wrote, "But Plimpton is also doing new things, things we've never seen her do before on-screen: in addition to the bravado, there is uncertainty, vulnerability, and a deep hurt."

Plimpton subsequently appeared in several lower-profile movies, among them the independent films *Inside Monkey Zetherland* (1992), *Mrs. Parker & the Vicious Circle* (1994), *Last Summer in the Hamptons* (1995), and *I Shot Andy Warhol* (1996). She also had roles in such successful mainstream films as Ted Demme's *Beautiful Girls* (1996) and Herb Gardner's *I'm Not Rappaport* (1996), as well as such failures as *Josh and S.A.M.* (1993) and *200 Cigarettes* (1999). In 1997 and 1998 she co-starred with E. G. Marshall and Beau Bridges in a trilogy of television movies inspired by the 1950s TV series *The Defenders*. Plimpton played a lawyer who, along with her father, takes on a series of cases involving murder, racism, and corruption. The actress was seen in a recurring guest role on the television series *ER* in the latter half of 1999.

In the mid-1990s Plimpton began doing a great deal of stage work. She made her theatrical debut with the Steppenwolf Theatre Company in 1996, in Stephen Jeffreys's contemporary play *The Libertine*. Two years later she officially joined the ensemble, whose current members include Joan Allen, John Malkovich, Austin Pendleton, and Gary Sinise; she has since appeared in Steppenwolf productions of Tennessee Williams's *The Glass Menagerie* and J. M. Synge's *The Playboy of the Western World* and has directed the group's mounting of Robert William Sherwood's psychological thriller *Absolution*. In 2001 she played the title role in Steppenwolf's production of Henrik Ibsen's *Hedda Gabler*. Preparing her characterization was a challenge for Plimpton, albeit a welcome one. "The more I read, the less possible it was to see any kind of arc [in Hedda's character]," she told Martha Hostetter for *American Theatre* (December 2001). "She struck me as a series of actions that were disconnected on the surface and very much living in a sort of Brechtian vacuum. She does not have a master plan—she's smart, but she's not a wicked weaver of spells. You know, we have in our culture this need to sort of stamp everything, put it in a box, give it a name." Alluding to the popular talk-show host Oprah Winfrey, she continued, "It's what I refer to as the 'Oprah-fication' of the nation—and I think *Hedda Gabler* is not a play that you can do that with, really. This is not a story that has clear answers." In a review of the production for *Center Stage*, Samantha McKinnon wrote that Plimpton "ignites the role with the perfect balance of longing[,] boredom, evil charm and playful desire. Plimpton's Hedda is all-consuming. We see Hedda in every cell of Plimpton's body, as she curls her fingers at her sides like claws, paces through the space and interacts with the forces that shape her life."

Plimpton has also been seen in productions of *Uncle Vanya* and *Robbers* at the Seattle Repertory Theatre, in Washington State; *Hedda Gabler* at the Long Wharf Theatre, in New Haven, Connecticut; and, in New York City, in *Suburbia* at the Lincoln Center Theater, *Runaways* at the Public Theater, and *Hobson's Choice* at the Atlantic Theatre. In the last-named play, by Harold Brighouse, which was first performed in 1915, Plimpton created a "quietly commanding Maggie," according to John Simon in *New York* (February 4, 2002).

In 1998 Plimpton was present at the White House, along with 31 other Steppenwolf actors, when President Bill Clinton presented the company with the National Medal of Arts. Plimpton lives in New York City with her dog, Alice. — J.K.B.

Suggested Reading: *American Theatre* p24+ Dec. 2001, with photos; (New York) *Daily News* C p25 Sep. 11, 1998, with photos; *Premiere* p69+ Feb. 1990, with photos; *Seventeen* p85+ Nov. 1984, with photos; Hardy, Karen, and Kevin J. Koffler. *The New Breed: Actors Coming of Age*, 1988

Selected Films: *Rollover*, 1981; *The River Rat*, 1984; *The Goonies*, 1985; *The Mosquito Coast*, 1986; *Another Woman*, 1988; *Parenthood*, 1989; *Stanley & Iris*, 1990; *Josh and S.A.M.*, 1993; *Mrs. Parker and the Vicious Circle*, 1994; *Last Summer in the Hamptons*, 1995; *I Shot Andy Warhol*, 1996; *Beautiful Girls*, 1996; *Pecker*, 1998; *200 Cigarettes*, 1999; *The Sleepy Time Gal*, 2001

Selected Television Shows: *The Defenders: Payback*, 1997; *The Defenders: Choice of Evils*, 1998; *The Defenders: Taking the First*, 1998

---

Paul Mattick/Courtesy of Random House, Inc.

## Pollitt, Katha

*Oct. 14, 1949– Essayist; poet; social activist*

*Address:* Nation, *33 Irving Place, New York, NY 10003*

"For me, to be a feminist is to answer the question 'Are women human?' with a yes," Katha Pollitt wrote in her book *Reasonable Creatures: Essays on Women and Feminism* (1994). "It is not about whether women are better than, worse than or identical with men. . . . It's about justice, fairness and access to the broad range of human experience." A poet as well as an essayist, Pollitt won the 1983 National Book Critics Circle poetry prize for her collection *Antarctic Traveller*. She has also become known for her column "Subject to Debate," which has appeared in the *Nation* every other week since 1994. (More than 80 of her pieces for the column were collected in a single volume in 2001.) The *Washington Post* called the column in that progressive weekly "the best place to go for original thinking on the left," according to the *Nation*'s Web site, which named among her devotees the novelist and essayist Susan Sontag, the feminist activist and writer Gloria Steinem, and the feminist author Naomi Wolf. Pollitt has also written essays for the *New Yorker*, the *Atlantic Monthly*, the *New Republic*, *Harper's*, *Mirabella*, *Ms.*, *Glamour*, *Mother Jones*, and the *New York Times*, among other publications. Her poems, too, have appeared in many periodicals. "I think the most fun writing is the writing that is an extension of what you are really thinking about," Pollitt told Joan Smith for the *San Francisco Examiner* (January 23, 1995). "Which is one reason I seem to write so often about women. The other is that I would like, during my little time on Earth, to make things better for women. I want the world to be better for my daughter than it was for me."

The only child of Basil Riddiford Pollitt, a lawyer, and Leanora (Levine) Pollitt, a real estate agent, Katha Pollitt was born on October 14, 1949 in the New York City borough of Brooklyn. She became interested in poetry as a sixth-grader, and she came to admire the poets Lord Byron, John Keats, Emma Goldman, and Emily Brontë. "I always loved to write," she recalled to Ruth Conniff for the *Progressive* (December 1994). "And I used to come home from school and go up to my room and sit on my bed and write my poems. And I was writing angry letters to the newspaper." She also told Conniff, "My mother had always wanted to be a writer, and I think because of that she was particularly encouraging. She was always finding poems and sending me poems when I was in summer camp, encouraging me to read, and sharing books with me and reading what I wrote with great interest. Both my parents were very encouraging. I was very lucky that way." Political liberals, her mother and father welcomed Katha's participation in political discussions at mealtimes. "They never gave me the message that you grow up, you get married, that you have to get a man by pretending to be less intelligent than you are—which was a very common idea in young girls then and, I'm sure, still is in many cases now," she told Alice Steinbach for the *Baltimore Sun* (January 8, 1995). "So I think I had some freedom to think about what I would want in life that wasn't so determined by fitting into some role."

Pollitt attended the Packer Collegiate Institute, a private girls' prep school (now co-ed) in Brooklyn. According to the Web site of Washington University, where she gave a reading in 1995, during her years at Packer the school's administration was socially conservative; the principal, a man, once told her, for example, "I've always felt that a woman only needs to know as much math as she needs to do her grocery list." In 1967 Pollitt enrolled at Radcliffe College, in Cambridge, Massachusetts, a women's school associated with Harvard University. (It has since been renamed the Radcliffe Institute for Advanced Study.) When her parents learned that she had participated in the student takeover of Harvard University's ROTC facilities to protest the Vietnam War, they sent her flowers. Also as an undergraduate, in what she has remembered as her first encounter with feminist thought, she read *Sexual Politics*, by Kate Millet, which "put into a framework of ideas all the feelings I had," as she told Steinbach. After she earned a B.A. degree, in philosophy, in 1972, she took a job as an assistant to the *New Yorker* staff writer Ved Mehta, aiding the blind journalist, novelist, and essayist with reading and research. She next worked as a proofreader at *Esquire*, while continuing to write poetry in her free time. In the early 1970s *Mademoiselle* magazine printed three poems by Pollitt. The *New Yorker*, the *Nation*, and the *Atlantic* published poems by her in 1975, the year in which she earned a master of fine arts degree in creative writing from Columbia University, in New York City. Many of her poems have since appeared in the *New Republic*, *Grand Street*, the *Yale Review*, *Poetry*, and *Antaeus*, among other publications.

Pollitt's first book, *Antarctic Traveller* (1982), won critical praise and inspired comparisons of her poems to those of Wallace Stevens. "Her lines are almost always exactly right, and there is a sense of finish and finality to her work one rarely sees in poets young or old—the diction clean and precise, the rhythms clear and effective," the poet Dana Gioia wrote for the *Hudson Review* (Winter 1982–83). In the *Georgia Review* (Summer 1982), the essayist and editor Peter Stitt wrote that Pollitt's "best poems have a spare delicacy reflective of a rigorous sense of decorum."

At around this time Pollitt began writing book reviews for various publications; in 1982 she was hired as literary editor of the *Nation*, and also in the early 1980s, became a regular book critic for *Mother Jones*. Writing about books led her in a new direction, as she explained to Conniff: "At a certain point I was more interested in what I had to say than in the book I was reviewing. I started more and more using book reviews as a kind of jumping off place for my own reflections. And then at a certain point the book dropped out. And I started writing on my own." Pollitt began writing the "Subject to Debate" column for the *Nation* in January 1994. In her columns, many of which have been reprinted in other publications nationwide, she has addressed such topics as "family values"; surrogate motherhood; teenage mothers; abortion as related to health-care reform; the Million Mom March against gun violence, held in 2000; and Shakespeare's place in the literary canon. She has also sharply criticized welfare reform, as carried out during President Bill Clinton's administration and at present; school vouchers; the removal of evolution theories from public-school curriculums in Kansas; the New York City shelter system for the homeless; the death penalty; and police brutality. She has written in support of reproductive rights; affirmative action; the firm separation of church and state; and freedom of speech, and has reported on her recent conversations with women from the Revolutionary Association of the Women of Afghanistan (RAWA), a group working to improve conditions for women in that country. "I believe that if I keep writing my column, eventually I will have written about every single facet of feminism since time began," she joked to Conniff. Later in the interview she added that she felt an obligation to continue writing "Subject to Debate" because it was the only space in the *Nation* reserved for specifically feminist views. "So I feel, well, this is my brief in life. If I don't do this, then that's that much less representation of feminism."

Speaking of the effects of the feminist movement on society, Pollitt told Alice Steinbach, "I would say there are areas in which feminism has been extremely successful. I think that it's been quite a socially revolutionary force at the individual level—even for women who don't think of themselves as feminists. It's raised women's expectations of the amount of respect they're due in life, both from other women and from men. And it's raised their sights in terms of what they can accomplish in the world of work." In her interview with Mina Kumar for *Sojourner* (May 1995), she said, "I think [feminism] offers both gains and losses to men. Having to do more housework—most people would consider that as a loss. But there are gains also—more real intimacy in marriage, more flexibility to your own work life if there are two incomes, and a different relationship to children. Men get a lot more of what they want from life because society is structured to take it away from women and give it to men. At the same time, [men] don't seem very happy. . . . You could say that men would be better off if they were less 'manly.' Feminism offers them the choice to lay down some of that masculine armor."

In a moderated chat on the Web site of the American Civil Liberties Union (ACLU) on January 18, 1995, Pollitt talked about the stigma attached to the word "feminist." "I think there are some people of either sex who find the very word 'feminist' so upsetting that they can hardly take in what you're saying on any given subject . . . ," she said. "Any woman who calls herself a feminist is going to get . . . criticism, and it doesn't matter how many boyfriends they have, or how many husbands they have, or how polite and receptive their social manner is." Discussing the way she believes the media often stereotype feminists, she told Steinbach, "Feminists are portrayed as man-hating—in two contrary ways. One is the woman who is sexual the way a man is sexual—too aggressive and demanding. And then there's the contrary stereotype which is feminism as man-hating lesbian."

"I think Katha Pollitt represents what she might call 'equality' feminism," the social critic and feminist writer Barbara Ehrenreich told Steinbach. "She represents a point of view . . . that mentally, intellectually, emotionally there's not that much difference between the sexes. This distinguishes her from the difference feminists who say women are intellectually different, think a different way and have a superior emotional or moral sensibility." Pollitt coined the phrase "difference feminism" to describe the viewpoint propounded by the Harvard psychologist Carol Gilligan, who believes that men and women use different criteria to make moral choices. In a conversation with Michael Kinsley on CNN, she called difference feminism "the view that women, either by nature or nurture or socialization or whatever, are different than men in that they're more sharing and caring and loving and cooperative and they're not mean and hierarchical and they're not interested in power, whereas, of course, men are interested in nothing but power." She went on to tell Kinsley, "I think that . . . it basically is . . . a restatement of the 19th century idea of separate spheres. It's basically saying men get power because women don't want power." "I completely disagree with the idea that there are these innate feminine qualities," Pollitt told Smith. "I don't think you can prove it. And I think it's dangerous because the difference feminists talk about it as if this were a good thing. . . . They completely miss the point, which is that the culture is set up to produce men and women who don't get along very well." Later in the same interview, she noted, "A lot of people will say, 'We tried to raise our son or daughter so they won't have any gender ideas and, lo and behold, she plays with a doll and he plays with trucks.' But you don't raise your child in a bubble. You have a relationship with the opposite sex, you watch television, the child has friends, and so on. There's this idea that you can get out of the culture and take your child with you, and you can't." Pollitt also discussed difference feminism in "Are Women Morally Superior to Men?," a *Nation* cover story (December 28, 1992).

Pollitt has expressed her frustration with the success that so-called anti-pornography feminists—prominent among them Catharine A. MacKinnon and Andrea Dworkin—have had in gaining national attention. Unlike MacKinnon and Dworkin, Pollitt does not think that pornography should be an issue in feminist politics unless it surfaces in the workplace. "I guess I am a First Amendment absolutist, partly because one person's hate speech is another person's honest attempt at expression of an unpopular idea . . . ," she said during the ACLU chat. "I think in the workplace, where people are forced to be together for economic survival, it's ok to ask people to be on their best behavior, or at least on pretty good behavior. . . . Outside the workplace, I do not support restrictions on speech." She has also voiced her concern that the topic of pornography has drawn attention away from issues that bear more directly on the daily lives of women in the U.S. "I think that it's very interesting that the women's movement in thirty years has not been able to get paid parental leave, something that many other countries have, something that's very modest, but actually would help people a lot," she told Conniff. "It has not been able to get a national system of day care—something else that exists in many countries. But it has been able to inject into the public discourse the views of Andrea Dworkin and Catharine MacKinnon on pornography."

Pollitt is a pragmatist rather than an idealist, and while her politics are left-wing, she has faulted the Democratic Party and progressive organizations when she believed criticism was warranted. "I don't think there is a Left in this country," she told Conniff in 1994. "There are liberals in this country. But I don't know of any movement, really, that mounts any kind of fundamental challenge to capitalism, and to the basic way this country is organized." Pollitt added that people cling to what she described as "the whole lesser-of-two-evils, this-is-our-last-best-hope, we-have-to-go-along-to-get-along-mentality. Instead of trying to create some sort of independent basis for social change you piggy-back on the conservative wing of the Democratic Party."

A collection of Pollitt's writings, *Reasonable Creatures: Essays on Women and Feminism*, was published in 1994. (The title comes from a line written by the 18th-century feminist Mary Wollstonecraft: "I wish to see women neither heroines nor brutes, but reasonable creatures.") Pollitt's book was nominated for a National Book Critics Circle award. "Both for those already familiar with Pollitt's work and for those coming to it for the first time, *Reasonable Creatures* . . . will confirm her standing as one of the most incisive, principled, and articulate cultural critics writing today," Boyd Zanner wrote in a review for *Belles Lettres* (Spring 1995). He concluded, "Pollitt's graceful style and frequent flashes of real wit are reason enough for rejoicing, but even more impressive is the fact that they never obscure the power and urgency of what she has to say." In the *New York Times* (October 9, 1994), the literary critic Susan Shapiro praised Pollitt's "razor-sharp wit and her impatience with sound-bite solutions," but also questioned the accuracy of her statistics. "Although she criticizes others for shoddy data, Ms. Pollitt's own statistics are not carefully annotated and at times seem questionable," she complained.

Pollitt's third book, *Subject to Debate: Sense and Dissents on Women, Politics, and Culture* (2001) is a collection of 88 of her *Nation* columns. "*Subject to Debate* is a stunningly good read," the Cornell University law professor Kathryn Abrams wrote for the *Women's Review of Books* (April 2001). "It seems almost indecent that so much insight, ferocity, wit and old-fashioned common sense should be combined in a single person. The individual essays are completely absorbing: virtually every one uses familiar controversies to make eye-opening points about the persistence of inequality or the foibles of public actors, in a distinctively witty and pungent prose." Dissenters to Abrams's view included Lynn Crosbie, who, in the *Toronto Star* (March 18, 2001), wrote that Pollitt had presented "theories that Germaine Greer has already ably covered at great length in *The Whole Woman*" and took issue with her "scornful dismissal" of several conservative female writers. She also wrote, "*Subject to Debate* serves as a nice refresher course in well-integrated politics, and perhaps a revelation to her students and the like: While Pollitt makes a lot of noise about race and class, she is ultimately concerned with the demographic that NOW [National Organization for

Women] originally targeted: the celery-nibbling, degree-driven babes whose problem has no name."

Pollitt became the subject of strenuous criticism from some quarters for the "Subject to Debate" column published in the on-line edition of the *Nation* on September 20, 2001, nine days after the terrorist attacks on New York City and Washington, D.C., and in the print edition on October 8. In that essay Pollitt revealed her opposition to her teenage daughter's request that an American flag be placed in the window of their apartment. "Definitely not, I say. The flag stands for jingoism and vengeance and war," she wrote. She also expressed her hope that the U.S. would not take military action against Afghanistan, whose government was harboring the terrorist group believed to be responsible for the attacks. "Bombing Afghanistan to 'fight terrorism' is to punish not the Taliban but the victims of the Taliban, the people we should be supporting," she wrote. In a harsh response to Pollitt's column, Ross Douthat, an intern at the *National Review*, wrote for the on-line edition of that magazine (September 24, 2001), "In Pollitt's worldview, it is always 1969, Richard Nixon is always president, and the bombs are always falling on innocent Cambodia."

Pollitt served as a contributing editor of the *Nation* from 1986 to 1992, when she became associate editor; she held that position until the late 1990s. On radio, Pollitt has been a guest on the National Public Radio series *Fresh Air* and *All Things Considered*; on television, she has appeared on CNN, the BBC, *Charlie Rose*, *The McLaughlin Group*, and *Dateline NBC*. Her honors include the 1984 Peter I. B. Lavan Younger Poets Award from the Academy of American Poets; a 1984 National Endowment for the Arts grant; a 1985 Fulbright Writers Grant for travel in Yugoslavia; a 1986 Arvon Foundation Prize; a 1987 Guggenheim Fellowship; a 1987 New York Foundation for the Arts Grant; a 1983 Whiting Writers Fellowship; the 1995 Freethought Heroine Award from the Freedom from Religion Foundation; and a 1996 Alumnae Recognition Award from Radcliffe College. Her 1992 essay "Why We Read: Canon to the Right of Me . . ." won the National Magazine Award for essays and criticism. Also in 1992 she won the Whiting Foundation Writing Award, and the following year her essay "Why Do We Romanticize the Fetus?" received the Maggie Award from the Planned Parenthood Federation of America. She has taught at Princeton, Barnard College (where she was also poet-in-residence), the State University of New York at Purchase, and the New School for Social Research (now the New School University), as well as at the 92d Street YM-YWHA in New York City. She is a fellow of the New York Institute for the Humanities.

Pollitt's marriage to the television-humor writer Randy Cohen ended in divorce. She lives on New York City's Upper West Side with her daughter, Sophie, from that marriage; her partner, the philosophy teacher and art critic Paul Mattick; and four cats. — K.E.D.

Suggested Reading: ACLU Web site Jan. 18, 1995; *Baltimore Sun* K p1 Jan. 8, 1995, with photos; CNN June 25, 1994; *LiP Magazine* (on-line) Apr. 2, 2001; *Nation* p9 Oct. 8, 2001; *Progressive* p34+ Dec. 1994, with photo; *San Francisco Examiner* C p1 Jan. 23, 1995, with photo; *Sojourner* p1+ May 1995

Selected Books: Poetry—*Antarctic Traveller*, 1982; Essays—*Reasonable Creatures: Essays on Women and Feminism*, 1994; *Subject to Debate: Sense and Dissents on Women, Politics, and Culture*, 2001

---

www.jpl.nasa.gov

## Queloz, Didier

(KAY-lohz, DEE-dee-yay)

*Feb. 23, 1966– Astrophysicist*

*Address: Geneva Observatory, 51 chemin des Maillettes, 1290 Sauverny, Switzerland*

In December 1994 Didier Queloz and Michel Mayor of the Geneva Observatory, in Switzerland, discovered a planet orbiting the star 51 Pegasi, located about 40 light-years from Earth in the constellation Pegasus. The object—called an extrasolar planet, or "exoplanet"—was the first heavenly body to be detected in orbit around a Sun-like star. A gaseous giant like the planets Jupiter, Saturn, Uranus, and Neptune, it appears to be orbiting 51 Pegasi approximately five million miles from the star. (By contrast, Earth orbits the Sun at a distance of about 93 million miles.) Moreover, although the exoplanet is as big as Jupiter (the diameter of which is 11 times that of Earth and the mass of which is 318 times that of Earth), it completes its revolution around 51 Pegasi in less than five days. (Earth travels once around the Sun every 365 days; Jupiter makes the same journey only once in almost 12 years.) The exoplanet's size, combined with its nearness to the star, struck Queloz and Mayor as "something completely crazy," as Queloz told a reporter for the *BBC* (June 17, 1999, on-line). "Nobody was expecting this," he added. "Even us."

Queloz and Mayor resolved to keep their discovery a secret until they could double-check their data. "We had to be sure that this was real," Queloz told the *BBC*. "We had to work a lot to be convinced that the only explanation for this phenomena was a planet." On October 6, 1995, after another 10 months of investigation, the two astronomers went public with their findings. The discovery, which made headlines worldwide, was subsequently confirmed by other astronomers, working independently. Since then, planet-hunting has experienced a boom, and astronomers (among them the Geneva team to which Queloz belongs) have reported a flurry of discoveries: at the latest count, they have detected 76 exoplanets orbiting stars relatively near Earth.

Didier Queloz was born in Geneva, Switzerland, on February 23, 1966. Queloz told *Current Biography* that he has always been interested in general science. As a youth he read books by the American astronomer Carl Sagan. He studied physics at Geneva University, where he earned a diploma in 1990, and still considers himself primarily a physicist. Because the faculty at Geneva University was particularly strong in astrophysics, Queloz found himself specializing in that field "by chance"; he was philosophically attracted to astrophysics, he told *Current Biography*, because of its affinity to nuclear physics, another of his interests. He also liked the idea of working in an observatory and hoped to travel someday to the Atacama Desert, in northern Chile (where several observatories are situated). After completing his diploma Queloz began graduate work at Geneva University, with Mayor serving as his thesis adviser.

Part of Queloz's doctoral work involved designing and operating the software for ELODIE, a spectroscopic device for measuring the radial velocity of stars (how fast they are moving directly toward or away from Earth). "The idea," he told *Current Biography*, "was to search for a planet, but a planet [that took four days to revolve around its star] was really unexpected. . . . I thought, well, that's a great subject, and I went into [it] and I made the breakthrough with Michel. . . . It was very exciting already but it became real!" Queloz completed his doctoral work in 1995; his thesis was titled "Research by Cross-Correlation Techniques." Afterward, while continuing to do research, he taught at Geneva University and Caltech.

The idea that there might be other planets or Earth-like worlds in the universe is far from new. While Aristotle (384–322 B.C.) ruled out the existence of any other worlds, another Greek philosopher, Epicurus (341–270 B.C.), declared, "There are an infinite number of worlds both like and unlike this world of ours." Similarly, the Roman poet and philosopher Lucretius (98–55 B.C.), in his long, didactic philosophic poem *De Rerum Natura* (*On the Nature of Things*), argued, "There are such congregations of matter elsewhere as this our world, which the vast abyss holds in its embrace," and the philosopher Metrodorus of Chios (who lived during fourth century B.C.), who, like Lucretius, was a student of Epicurus, wrote, "To consider the Earth as the only populated world in infinite space is as absurd as to assert that in an entire field sown with millet only one grain will grow." The ancients had no way of testing their theories by means of empirical evidence, though. While they could identify the five planets of the Sun that are visible with the naked eye (Mercury, Venus, Mars, Jupiter, and Saturn), they were unable to demonstrate that these "wandering stars" ("planet" comes from the Greek word for "wanderer") were in fact celestial bodies like Earth.

That changed during the Renaissance, with the rise of Copernican astronomy. After years of painstaking observation, the Polish astronomer Copernicus (1473–1543) concluded that Earth circled the Sun, rather than the other way around, as most people then believed. (While the Greek astronomer Aristarchus had advanced the same theory 1,800 years before, his ideas were never widely accepted.) One of Copernicus's followers, Giordano Bruno, went a step further; in his *De l'Infinito Universo e Mondi* (*On the Infinite Universe and Worlds*), Bruno argued, "Innumerable suns exist; innumerable earths revolve around these suns in a manner similar to the way the seven planets [among which Bruno counted the moon] revolve around our sun. Living beings inhabit these worlds." (Church authorities later consigned Bruno to the Secular Arm for chastisement, which, in effect, meant capital punishment by the civil authorities; in 1600 he was burned at the stake as a heretic.) Another disciple of Copernicus, Galileo Galilei (1564–1632), was the first to produce scientific evidence that the planets were more or less Earth-like worlds: by training a telescope on the night sky, Galileo was able to observe the mountains of the moon, the phases of Venus, and the satellites of Jupiter.

The invention of the telescope led to the discovery of other planets in our solar system: Uranus, the seventh planet, was first observed in 1781, and Neptune, the eighth, in 1846. Pluto, the ninth and outermost planet, was first sighted in 1930. (In the opinion of some astronomers, Pluto, a hunk of ice and rock that is smaller than a number of moons in the solar system, ought to be stripped of its planetary status; those scientists feel it is more appropriate to label Pluto a "planetoid" or a "minor planet." On the other hand, partisans of Plutonian planethood argue that while it may be rather petite, it is roughly spherical in shape, and it orbits the sun—two important criteria in most astronomers' definition of a planet. The "Pluto question" is currently unresolved.)

Although planetary science has made considerable advances since the discovery of Pluto (the *Mariner*, *Viking*, *Pioneer*, and *Voyager* space probes have relayed to Earth information gained at close range about all the planets except Pluto), until 1994 almost nothing was known about extrasolar planets. But scientists long suspected their existence. If there is any lesson to be drawn from the history of modern astronomy, it is that our particular corner of the cosmos is in no way remarkable; consequently, scientists have long suspected that the Sun is not the only star orbited by planets. But extrasolar planets are extremely difficult to detect, because they produce no light of their own; rather, they are aggregates of nonluminous matter, what John Milton, in *Paradise Lost*, described as "the black, tartareous, cold, infernal dregs" of stellar creation, which never attained sufficient mass to trigger nuclear fusion. Like the moon, they only reflect light. Seen from a great distance, a planet can appear thousands or even millions of times less luminous than its star—roughly comparable to how a firefly might appear in the glare of a nuclear explosion. While several of the planets in our own solar system reflect enough light to be visible to the naked eye at night, even the most sophisticated astronomical instruments are currently incapable of directly observing planets across the vastness of interstellar space.

Thus, astronomers have had to employ other, indirect methods to detect extrasolar planets. The first breakthrough occurred in 1994, when Alexander Wolszczan, a radio astronomer at Pennsylvania State University, used a radio telescope to detect two and perhaps three planets orbiting a pulsar in the Virgo constellation. (Composed of densely packed neutrons, a pulsar is the remnant of a collapsed star; essentially, it is a dead star. The name "pulsar" derives from the fact that the remnant emits regular bursts, or pulses, of electromagnetic radiation. Wolszczan deduced the planets' existence from irregularities in the Virgo pulsar's signal; like most other exoplanets, they cannot be seen by any telescopes currently available to scientists.) Wolszczan's was an important first step toward detecting extrasolar Earth-like worlds. However, planets in the vicinity of a pulsar would lack sunlight; they would also be flooded with intense radiation. Such environments could not possibly support life as we know it.

Queloz and Mayor's discovery of a planet orbiting 51 Pegasi was crucial because that star is similar to the Sun. That very similarity rendered the radio techniques used by Wolszczan impractical: unlike the pulsar in Virgo, 51 Pegasi does not emit powerful bursts of radiation that could be examined for signs of a planet. Rather, Queloz and Mayor used another indirect method, known as spectroscopy, to make their discovery.

Spectroscopy relies on the fact that a planet (or any mass orbiting another) is not orbiting its star's center of gravity; rather, both the planet and the star orbit the common center of gravity, or barycenter, of the sun-planet system. (Because stars are usually so much more massive than planets, the barycenter is often quite close to the star's own center of gravity.) The gravitational tug of an orbiting planet produces a telltale wobble in the orbit of the star. By carefully measuring the period and amplitude of this wobble, astronomers can deduce the mass and orbit of the planet—provided they know the mass of the star (which, in the case of most nearby stars, they do).

Astronomers using the spectroscopic method look for wobbles in a star's radial velocity by studying the frequency of its light. (Another technique, astrometry, measures wobbles in a star's angular, or lateral, velocity by carefully charting the star's course against the sky. Like the sound of an ambulance siren, which, to a bystander, suddenly drops in pitch the moment it passes by, the apparent frequency of light emitted by an object is affected by that object's velocity relative to the observer—a phenomenon known as the Doppler effect. Light from an object moving toward an observer will be "compressed"—that is to say, it will have shorter wavelengths (a higher frequency) and will thus acquire a bluish tint—and light from an object moving away from an observer will be "stretched out," or reddish. By precisely measuring the respective redshift or blueshift of a star's light—that is, the deviation of its spectral lines from those of an object of identical chemical composition at rest—astronomers are able to determine oscillations in its radial velocity as caused by orbiting planets.

In the search for exoplanets, recent efforts to separate starlight reflected by an orbiting planet from the light of the star itself have borne some fruit; astronomers have also detected the slight dimming of a star as an orbiting planet crosses between the star and Earth. But the vast majority of exoplanets known to astronomers have been detected by spectroscopy. Spectroscopy is not currently capable of distinguishing between planets whose environments resemble that of Earth and those whose environments do not. (Most scientists suspect that planets similar to Earth do indeed exist.) Such small planets will probably elude detection until the next generation of satellite-based observational instruments is operational, perhaps in a decade or so.

On April 4, 2001 the international team of astronomers of which Queloz is a member announced the discovery of 11 new exoplanets, thus bringing the total of known exoplanets with a minimum mass of under 10 Jupiter masses (one Jupiter mass equals 318 Earth masses) to 63. (An idiosyncracy of the radial-velocity method is that it allows scientists to determine only a lower mass limit for a given planet.) Among the planets discovered was one with an orbit almost identical to that of Earth. "This new planet," according to a press release from the European Southern Observatory (April 4, 2000, on-line), "is therefore located in the 'habitable zone' where temperatures like those on the Earth are possible." While the newly discovered planet is a gaseous giant with a mass at least 3.5 times that of Jupiter, and thus an unlikely candidate for life as we know it, the press release reported that it "may be orbited by one or more moons on which a more bio-friendly environment has evolved. The presence of natural satellites ('moons') around giant extra-solar planets is not a far-fetched idea; just look at our own Solar System."

Queloz has taught at Caltech and at Geneva University and has remained active on the planet-hunting team associated with the Geneva Observatory. From 1997 to 1999 he served as a distinguished visiting scientist at NASA's Jet Propulsion Laboratory; managed by Caltech, the laboratory is located in the San Gabriel Mountains near Pasadena. When not working, he enjoys being outdoors. He is an avid swimmer, hiker, and skier. — P.K.

Suggested Reading: *BBC* (on-line) Jun. 17, 1999; *New York Times* 1p1 Feb. 9, 1997, with photo; *Scientific American* (on-line) May 1996; *Christian Science Monitor* p3 Jan. 19, 1996, with photo

---

## Raimi, Sam

(RAY-mee)

*Oct. 23, 1959– Filmmaker*

*Address: c/o Creative Artists Agency, 9830 Wilshire Blvd., Beverly Hills, CA 90212*

"He's like the kid in school who wouldn't get into trouble himself but would get *you* into trouble," the writer Scott Smith told Rebecca Mead for the *New Yorker* (November 23, 1998) about the filmmaker Sam Raimi. For many years Raimi, who has directed and acted in more than 30 films, was best known for his cult-classic horror trilogy, comprising *The Evil Dead* (1982), *Evil Dead II: Dead by Dawn* (1987), and *Army of Darkness* (1993). After his initial attempts at mainstream filmmaking resulted in two big-budget flops—*Darkman* in 1990 and *The Quick and the Dead* in 1995—Raimi turned to television, where he developed and produced movies and series, most notably *Xena: Warrior Princess*, one of the most successful syndicated shows in history. In 1998 Raimi renewed his efforts at making mainstream pictures, this time scoring a success with *A Simple Plan*, starring Bill Paxton and Billy Bob Thornton. With the release of *Spider-Man*, in May 2002, Raimi struck box-office gold and, perhaps, joined the "A" list of Hollywood directors. While he has now found a following beyond the world of horror movies, Raimi does not look down on his past work, instead dubbing it a testament to his unconventional development as a film director. "I wasn't attracted to 'the movies,'" he told Mead. "I've often read about these filmmakers who were attracted to great movies, and that had nothing to do with it for me." Rather, he first developed an interest in film because of his father's home movies. "I remember seeing footage of my seventh-birthday party," he said. "It was a Halloween party, and he showed all the kids playing party games outside, and then he showed them leaving the party, and then, on the same reel, he showed them arriving at the party. I was so taken with the fact that he had shuffled the order of reality. I thought, This is unbelievable. Something about it made me giddy. It seemed like we were tampering with God's world, altering something that was far beyond our ken."

The fourth of five children, Samuel M. Raimi was born on October 23, 1959 in Franklin, Michigan. His mother, Celia, owned an intimate-apparel store called Lulu's Lingerie, and his father, Leonard, ran an appliance shop begun by Sam's grandfather. "Our house was littered with comic books, Three Stooges paraphernalia, and Fig Newton bars—that was our reality," Sam's older brother Ivan, now a doctor and Sam's writing partner, told Mead. Another older brother, Sander, drowned in a swimming pool while studying in Israel on a high-school scholarship. By all accounts a smart young man and natural leader, Sander played a large part in Sam's development. "[Sander] used to perform magic at my parties when I was younger," Sam Raimi told Mead. "Incredible magic, with electricity and chemicals and fire." After Sander's death, Sam—inspired by his brother—learned how to perform magic tricks himself. He told Mead, "My parents pulled their strength together to make sure we survived [Sander's death]. But it colors everything you do the rest of your life."

Raimi made his directorial debut at the age of 13, when he and a group of friends began using the Super-8 video camera his father had given him. "We were making skits . . . every day after school . . . ," he told Mead. "At that stage, it wasn't even about making *bad* movies—we were making movies that no one could understand. The movies had to improve, just so that people could understand what were trying to tell them. They had to improve for people even to realize that it was a bad movie. We didn't even have that." Raimi's earliest film crew consisted of John Cameron, who would later produce films for the Coen brothers; Scott Spiegel, now a screenwriter and director; and Bruce Campbell, who "remember[s] seeing Sam dressed as Sherlock Holmes and sitting on the floor at the school playing with little dolls, and [knowing] immediately the guy was different," as he told Mead. "Me and those boys made *The Jimmy Hoffa Story*, Part 1, Part 2, and Part 3," Raimi added. "We read in the paper about him being kidnapped, and the next Sunday we went to the place where it happened and shot it. We made *James Bombed* starring Bruce Campbell. . . . Up until the eighth grade, we would play the women's roles in drag. Our backward social skills prevented us from knowing women, but finally we overcame that."

Retna Ltd.

*Sam Raimi*

Raimi and his friends continued to make films throughout high school. Then, in the fall of 1977, college separated them. Raimi attended Michigan State University, where he met his future collaborator, his roommate Rob Tapert, who shared his love of filmmaking. Together, the two produced their first movie, *The Happy Valley Kid*, which was filmed with a Super-8 camera and cost $700 to make. About a college student who becomes violently insane a week before finals, the film grossed $3,500. "It was a big hit on campus, because the kids really liked watching the professors get blown away," Raimi told Mead. "I learned, 'Oh, it is the exploitation aspect that sells.'"

After a year and half at Michigan State, Raimi and Tapert left the university, enlisted the acting help of Bruce Campbell, and began raising money for their next project, while supporting themselves through various jobs in food service. Concluding that making a horror film was the best way to recoup the money they planned to invest, Raimi and his brother Ivan sat down to write a script. "[Initially] I didn't really like horror films—they frightened me," Raimi told Mead. "But, as I studied them, I began to see that there is an art to them, and there is a craft to making suspense, and I realized how interesting the process was. I would watch the suspense build in a picture, and it would be released and the audience would jump and scream, and I thought, This is kind of fantastic: they are being brought to a level here, and how long can we sustain that level? . . . I began to understand that making a horror film was like writing a piece of music: it's like watching the work of a composer." Having shot a half-hour version of what would become *The Evil Dead*, Raimi, Tapert, and Campbell approached potential investors in the Detroit area. After months of peddling the project, the trio, who had begun calling their partnership Renaissance Pictures, had the money they needed. Shooting the film in a cold, dingy cabin in Tennessee over a period of 12 weeks, Raimi improvised with the camera to make up for the group's limited funds and lack of state-of-the-art equipment. For example, in an attempt to simulate the perspective of the monster as it chased its victims, he nailed a camera to a two-by-four-foot board and had the cameraman run while keeping the camera just above ground level. The technique, highly innovative for its time, has since become Raimi's hallmark. "Back then, it was a much more infantile goal," he told Mead. "Get a response, a visceral, audible response. Will they jump, and how high? And can we measure their movement in inches?" In 1983 *The Evil Dead* was picked up for screening at the prestigious Cannes Film Festival, in France. Extremely graphic—Raimi had heeded the advice of a theater owner who had told him to "make the blood run down the screen"—and with a grainy, low-budget look, the film was released without a rating in the United States, pulled from theaters in England, and slapped with an eight-year ban in Germany.

For the next few years, Raimi played bit parts in such films as *Spies Like Us* (1985), starring Dan Aykroyd and Chevy Chase; *Stryker's War* (1985); and *Maniac Cop* (1988). He returned to directing in 1985 with *Crimewave*, a film co-written by the brothers Joel and Ethan Coen. Raimi does not think of the film fondly; referring to it as "Slimewave," he told Henry Sheehan for *Premiere* (August 1990), "I wouldn't use it for filler in a porno movie." After that project was finished, Raimi and his brother Ivan began fashioning a script for the sequel to *The Evil Dead*.

Raimi approached the making of *Evil Dead II: Dead by Dawn* differently from the way he had gone about directing its predecessor; while still focusing on gore, he also added elements of slapstick to the script. Embraced by Raimi's now-substantial cult following, *Evil Dead II* made a tidy profit. It too went unrated in the U.S., but the picture's success caused the major studios to take notice. Universal Studios agreed to pick up the tab for Sam and Ivan Raimi's next film, *Darkman*, about a scientist who has the ability to take on the appearance of others and who seeks revenge on the gangsters who tried to kill him. The movie, Raimi's first attempt at a big-studio picture, bombed at the box office, leading Raimi to conclude that the world of big-budget filmmaking was simply not for him. Discouraged, he returned to his home in Los Angeles and began developing the third installment of the *Evil Dead* story line.

In the new film, entitled *Army of Darkness*, the protagonist (Campbell) finds himself in 14th-century Europe. With its sarcastic bite and array of one-liners, the movie was a hit worldwide. As Richard Harrington wrote for the *Washington Post* (February 19, 1993), "Raimi shows he's quite capable of bringing his quirky vision to life on a larger, action-oriented scale." With a third hit film to his credit and his reputation restored, Raimi once again took on the world of big-budget movies, and soon found himself directing Sharon Stone and Leonardo DiCaprio in the Western *The Quick and the Dead* (1995). In general, while critics lauded the filmmaker's intentions, particularly his having Sharon Stone attempt to break away from the femme-fatale persona she had developed in the film *Basic Instinct*, they did not shower the movie with praise. After *The Quick and the Dead* proved to be a commercial failure, Raimi took time out from directing feature films to work in television, which allowed him to "drive to work every day and be back for dinner," as he told Mead.

On the heels of the success of the Coen brothers' 1994 film, *The Hudsucker Proxy*, which he co-wrote, Raimi developed two series for national television syndication. *Hercules: The Legendary Journeys*, starring Kevin Sorbo, began as a series of television movies in 1994, before hitting the airwaves as a regular series in 1995. Later that year its spin-off, *Xena: Warrior Princess*, debuted. With Lucy Lawless in the title role, *Xena* developed a substantial following; the show featured less-than-subtle dialogue that insinuated a lesbian relationship between Xena and her sidekick, Gabrielle, played by Renee O'Connor. Also starring Raimi's younger brother, Ted, as the character Joxer, a warrior with low self-esteem, the series became one of the most successful shows of the 1990s. Both *Hercules* and *Xena* enjoyed long runs, airing until 1999 and 2001, respectively. The hour-long *Hercules* was replaced by two fairly short-lived shows produced by Renaissance Pictures: *Jack of All Trades*, about an American spy in the Napoleonic era, and *Cleopatra 2525*, which focused on "three tightly dressed women battling aliens," as J. D. Biersdorfer described it in the *New York Times* (February 6, 2000). Meanwhile, Raimi attempted to cash in on the success of *Hercules* and *Xena* with the television series *American Gothic*, a collaborative effort between Raimi, as executive producer, and the 1970s teen heartthrob Shaun Cassidy. That show, which debuted on CBS in October 1995, and *M.A.N.T.I.S.*, which Raimi co-wrote and produced for Fox, were both canceled within their first seasons. *Spy Game*, another series that Raimi helped to create, began its brief run in 1997. Also during the 1990s Raimi took small roles in such films as *The Flintstones* (1994) and *Galaxis* (1995) and in made-for-TV movies including *Journey to the Center of the Earth* (1993), *Body Bags* (1993), and *The Stand* (1994).

In the late 1990s Raimi began to hint that he wanted to return to directing. He had expressed interest in making the film version of *A Simple Plan*, a mainstream 1993 novel by Scott Smith, but many industry insiders had trouble seeing him as anything other than a director of horror films. As Raimi recounted to Mead, "[The producer] Scott Rudin told me, 'You know, I want to work with you, but truthfully, there are a lot of other directors that I think are more right for this project, and you are, like, number fifteen down on the list.'" After a number of big-name directors pulled out of the project, Raimi got the nod. *A Simple Plan* (1998) is about two brothers who, finding $4 million in a duffel bag inside a crashed airplane, slowly descend into greed, debauchery, and madness. The film was a critical and commercial success, but Raimi worried that he had alienated his fan base by directing a movie outside the horror genre. In his defense, he told Chris Nashawaty for *Entertainment Weekly*, "I'd be surprised if people thought this was a mainstream movie. God, it's about brothers who are thieves and murderers. That won't exactly sell more tickets." Janet Maslin disagreed, writing for the *New York Times* (December 11, 1998) that Raimi had made "a flawless segue into mainstream storytelling." Raimi's longtime partner Rob Tapert told Mead, "I think *A Simple Plan* is the first time Sam has shown his potential. I have always felt that he is a better director and filmmaker than the reception that the movies have received would suggest." The film garnered Oscar nominations for the actor Billy Bob Thornton and for Smith, who adapted his novel for the screen.

Raimi directed Kevin Costner in the mainstream baseball film *For Love of the Game*, released in 1999. He followed that up in 2001 with *The Gift*, whose screenplay, by Billy Bob Thornton, is about a woman (played by Cate Blanchett) who uses her psychic abilities in attempting to help residents of the small town where she lives. In the *New York Times* (January 19, 2001), A. O. Scott complained that *The Gift* had "gaps in logic big enough for [a] pickup truck," but he also noted, "The picture is saved from mediocrity by Mr. Raimi's smooth competence, and by the unusually high quality of the acting."

May 2002 saw the release of *Spider-Man*, Raimi's film based on the comic-book character created in the 1960s by the writer Stan Lee and the artist Steve Ditko. In the story, the awkward teenager Peter Parker (Tobey Maguire) develops arachnoid abilities after he is bitten by a genetically altered spider; he then dons a costume and uses his new powers to defend New York City from the villainous Green Goblin (Willem Dafoe). Meanwhile, he pursues a romance with his fellow high-school student Mary Jane (Kirsten Dunst). In the *New York Times* (May 3, 2002), A. O. Scott wrote, "Mr. Raimi is a master of pop realism, unafraid of easy jokes and corny sentiment and willing to give the actors room to find moments of offhand wit and genuine tenderness." Scott found *Spider-Man* to be "disarmingly likable, and touching in unexpected ways." Anthony Lane, on the other hand, asked in the *New Yorker* (May 13, 2002), "How come *Spider-Man* begins in such good humor and ends, like Eensy-Weensy, completely up the spout?" Specifically, he found fault with the "ill-fitting sequences" of the movie's second half, which "could have been made by a committee." That criticism notwithstanding, *Spider-Man* proved to be a box-office hit; a sequel is scheduled for 2004.

"Sam, you know, he's misunderstood. Even by himself," Ethan Coen told Mead. Joel Coen added, "[Raimi is] very polite. He has always helped little old ladies across the street. That has always been a part of Sam, along with evisceration and dismemberment." Sam Raimi lives with his wife, Gillian, a daughter of the late actor Lorne Greene, in Brentwood, California. They have three children. — C.T.

Suggested Reading: *Entertainment Weekly* p44+ Sep. 19, 1999, with photos; *Films and Filming* p18+ July 1987, with photos; *New York* p108+ Feb. 27, 1995, with photos; *New York Times* C p10 Feb. 19, 1993, with photo, B p27 Feb. 26, 1995, with photo, B p37 Oct. 22, 1995, with photos, E p16 Dec. 11, 1998, with photo; *New Yorker* p40+ Nov. 23, 1998, with photos; *Premiere* p74+ Mar. 1995, with photos; *International Motion Picture Almanac 2002*

Selected Films: *The Evil Dead*, 1982; *Crimewave*, 1985; *Evil Dead II: Dead by Dawn*, 1987; *Darkman*, 1990; *Army of Darkness*, 1993; *The Quick and the Dead*, 1995; *A Simple Plan*, 1998; *For Love of the Game*, 1999; *Spider-Man*, 2002

Selected Television Shows: *Hercules: The Legendary Journeys*, 1995–1999; *Xena: Warrior Princess*, 1995–2001; *American Gothic*, 1995

---

## Rall, Ted

*Aug. 26, 1963– Editorial cartoonist; newspaper columnist*

*Address: P.O. Box 2092, Times Square Station, New York, NY 10108; c/o Sue Roush, Universal Press Syndicate, 4520 Main St., Kansas City, MO 64111*

Courtesy of Universal Press Syndicate

The editorial cartoonist Ted Rall has taken aim at myriad targets, ranging from the media, to politicians, to big business, to consumer culture, to the attitudes of the U.S. populace. In much of his work, he has lamented the problems that beset 30-somethings like himself, such as unemployment or uninspiring employment; the high divorce rate; the ever-increasing cost of a college education; and the deterioration of the environment. "His attitude is so rotten, he's on the way to becoming the spokesperson for his generation," Rall's fellow cartoonist Stan Mack has said of him, as quoted in *Columbia* (Winter 1993). Rall's blocky, asymmetrical cartoon characters are inked in bold, dark lines—the style he deems best for documenting "the decline of America," as he told David Astor for *Editor & Publisher* (December 18, 1993), and for grabbing a reader's attention.

Rall's sense of humor leans toward sarcasm. While his detractors accuse him of unrelenting cynicism, his fans consider him an accurate and insightful observer of contemporary society. Typical of Rall's penchant for combining worst-case scenarios with a touch of the absurd is a cartoon, posted on *Ucomics.com*, in which a reporter sits at a desk in front of a TV camera and declares, "The story you're about to hear is so shocking that it could very well shake American society down to its foundations. On the other hand, I may be making the whole thing up." In another cartoon, reprinted in *Columbia* (Winter 1993), a man holding several bags of luggage, presumably at an airport, has paused before a sign that reads, "Welcome to McUSA: 18 million unemployed, 45 million underemployed." Yet Rall doesn't limit himself to the targets often chosen by other liberal-leaning cartoonists. As Bettijane Levine noted for the *Los Angeles Times* (July 2, 1998), "He has been called a liberal for the way he jabs boomers who loot successful corporations while putting thousands out of work. He has been called a conservative for his almost retro stand on morals and family values." Rall often picks on the public for failing to keep informed, as in one cartoon, posted on *Ucomics.com*, that pictures a man and a woman conversing on a city street. The woman, dressed conservatively in a business suit, says, "I have no idea what [President] Bush is doing, but whatever that is, is fine with me." The man, who is wearing a T-shirt that reads, "U.S. Out of *Wherever*," replies, "Whatever that is, I'm against it." The cartoon's caption reads, "America, United."

Ted Rall was born on August 26, 1963 in Cambridge, Massachusetts, and grew up in Dayton, Ohio. His parents separated when he was two; afterward he was raised by his mother, a schoolteacher. As Rall has acknowledged, his oft-expressed distrust of the older generation stems partly from his experience of his parents' separation (they divorced when he was five). "I wish that all musicians, authors, bankers, mayors, professors, and cartoonists were under thirty," he told *Columbia* (Winter 1993) when he was about 30 himself. "If the current state of America is a good indication, its aged ruling class could use a rest." Rall's mother is French, and he learned to speak French before he learned English.

Rall's first published cartoons appeared in a small Ohio newspaper—the *Kettering-Oakwood Times*, located near Dayton—in 1980. Soon, seven other local papers were carrying his cartoons. a high-school junior, he won a contest sponsored by an Ohio cartoonists' association. Mike Peters, a Pulitzer Prize–winning Dayton editorial cartoonist, came to Rall's school to present the award to him. "I really think you have some talent, why don't you come down to my office and watch me draw?" Peters suggested to him, as reported by Kent Worcester in the *Comics Journal* (August 1998), transcribed on the Ted Rall Web site. Every week or two thereafter, the teenager would visit Peters at the *Dayton Daily News* offices and chat with him about cartooning. "I thought if . . . I can ever make a living drawing political cartoons then this is definitely what I want to do," Rall told Worcester.

In 1981 Rall graduated from high school, and—ignoring Peters's advice that he attend Ohio State University, which had an excellent campus newspaper, or attend a school of graphic arts—he enrolled at the engineering school of Columbia University, in New York City, to study physics. At Columbia Rall showed more interest in making mischief than studying. Once, he caused an uproar by rewiring his dorm's phone system. In 1984 the college expelled him for academic and disciplinary reasons. By claiming to prospective employers that he had earned his bachelor's degree, he secured a trader-trainee position at Bear, Stearns & Co. Inc., a New York City brokerage firm. To supplement his $10,000-per-year salary—which even then was considered very low—he drove a taxi at night and worked as a telemarketer. In 1986 he was hired by the New York City branch of the Industrial Bank of Japan. That year one of the bank's clients, Mitsui Real Estate Ltd., decided to purchase the Exxon Building, in Manhattan; to oversee the deal, Mitsui hired Rall's company, which assigned the task to Rall's division. Though Exxon's asking price was $375 million, Mitsui insisted on offering $610 million, because the company's president wanted to break the record—$600 million—for the highest price ever paid for a single building. As Rall recalled in an article for *Harper's* (August 1995), he and his boss told Mitsui's president, "We called the New York City Board of Education: [the additional $235 million] would bring the facilities at every public school in all five boroughs up to current standards. The press would be huge! Isn't that better than some listing in the Guinness Book?" Rall continued, "[The president] listened politely as we pleaded for his quarter-billion. Then he left to sign the papers. We went back to our offices. I've never felt so dirty."

That experience and others like it eventually led Rall to quit the field of business and, in 1990, to return to Columbia; this time he enrolled at the School of General Studies (GS) and focused on history instead of physics. He earned a bachelor's degree, with honors in history, in 1991 and later that year began selling his cartoons to various papers through the *San Francisco Chronicle* syndicate. "I'm super, super grateful to GS," Rall told Abigail Beshkin for the *Columbia University News* (April 18, 2000, on-line). "GS really offers something that is very rare in our society, which is a second chance, an opportunity for people who messed up once to go back once they're a little older and a little wiser, and get a second chance to redeem themselves and finish their education."

In 1992 Rall published a collection of his cartoons entitled *Waking Up in America*. "With bemused cynicism," Gordon Flagg wrote of the collection for *Booklist* (September 15, 1992), "Rall's cartoons reflect the concerns of the post–Baby Boomer generation—mind-numbing jobs; the alternative to mind-numbing jobs: unemployment; and neurotic sexual relationships—as well as occasional forays into electoral politics and other mainstays of conventional editorial cartooning. . . . [Rall's] refreshing radicalism shows up mainstream editorial cartoonists for the wienies they are." Rall's no-holds-barred style appeared to have dire consequences in 1992: shortly after a newspaper published a cartoon of his entitled "12 Ways to Kill Your Parents," a copy of that cartoon was found in the pocket of a boy who had killed his parents. "Did the cartoon plant the idea? I don't know and that disturbs me," Rall told Tim Yohannan for *Manhattan Spirit*, as reprinted on Rall's Web site. "I hate to resort to the [underground comic icon] R. Crumb defense, but to a certain extent as a creative person, you're not responsible for what comes out of you. What comes out of me is lots of gunfire and killing your parents. We all have these demons." Later, in a conversation with Alex Beam for the *Boston Globe* (June 12, 2001), he labeled the controversy sparked by the killings "good." "You can see what happens when people get stirred up over cartoons," he told Beam. "These things do have incredible power."

Rall's second collection of cartoons, *All the Rules Have Changed*, appeared in 1995. That year he also won first place in the Robert F. Kennedy Journalism Awards for cartoons. (He earned that honor again in 2000.) Despite such recognition, Rall was still not earning enough money through cartooning to make a comfortable living. The money he earned from syndication came irregularly, and he was unable to get a full-time job with a daily newspaper, both because such jobs were scarce and because the contents of his cartoons were often considered too controversial. He was forced to work a day job and do freelance illustrations in addition to his editorial cartoons, making for a schedule that was, as he joked to David Astor for *Editor & Publisher* (August 12, 1995), "good" for his work because it kept him "angry, tired and irritable."

In 1996 Rall was one of three finalists for the Pulitzer Prize for editorial cartoons; that recognition seemed to boost his career. In 1997 the *New York Times* reprinted more of Rall's cartoons in its Sunday section "News of the Week in Review" than those of any other cartoonist, and the next year he began producing color cartoon strips regularly for *Time* and *Fortune*. Also in 1998 he published *Revenge of the Latchkey Kids: An Illustrated Guide to Surviving the 90s and Beyond*, in which he once again bashed the Baby Boomer generation for neglecting younger generations. In 1998 Rall published *My War with Brian*, a fictionalized, cartoon account of his experiences in high school, where he had been regularly harassed by the resident bully. (The bully's real name was not Brian.) In *My War with Brian*, Rall gets no help from his teachers and takes matters into his own hands, using his smarts to get even with Brian. "Will this book speak to high school readers?" Francisca Goldsmith wrote for *School Library Journal* (January 1999). "Absolutely. But adults who have forgotten how gruesome those years can be also need to read it." In 1999 Rall's cartoons again outnumbered those of any other cartoonist represented in the Sunday *New York Times*. He also began writing "Search and Destroy," a column for the New York City alternative weekly the *Village Voice*, in which he weighed in on an array of topics. Two books by Rall were published in 2001: a collection of cartoons entitled *Search and Destroy* and a graphic novel, *2024*, based on George Orwell's cautionary, dystopian novel *1984*. Rather than the totalitarian government that looms over the characters in *1984*, the main enemies in *2024* are mega-corporations and consumer culture, whose influence is such that Rall's characters are helpless to do anything but try to stave off boredom with WebTV, shopping, and other forms of entertainment. In an assessment of *2024* for *Publishers Weekly* (September 3, 2001), Jeff Zaleski wrote, "Rall's view of the future's social contract is a razor-sharp, irony-saturated parody of today's pop culture/consumerist consciousness. But his bleak lampoon of the mindless consumer state requires a lot of exposition, and, at times, his bold-faced text boxes threaten to visually overwhelm the exploits of his characters."

Rall's most recent book, *To Afghanistan and Back* (2002), is a compilation of cartoons, essays, and photographs that he took in 2001 while he was reporting on the U.S. military's antiterrorist actions in Afghanistan. Rall entered Afghanistan with a convoy of 45 reporters, three of whom were killed within two weeks. "Producing [*To Afghanistan and Back*] was a unique experience," Rall wrote for *Amazon.com*. "I wrote and drew it beginning just days after my return from Afghanistan, so my impressions and memories of the trip were still amazingly fresh. I've tried to incorporate that sense of immediacy with a view to the long term, so that someone who wants to know (a) what Afghanistan is like and (b) what the American bombing campaign was really like might come away with a fairly accurate impression. Much of the reporting from the war was spun and edited beyond recognition. This is my attempt to set the record—the part I saw, anyway—straight." An anthology that Rall edited, entitled *Attitude: The New Subversive Political Cartoonists*, was published in mid-2002. That fall a compilation of five essays by Rall appeared, with the title *My Government Went to Afghanistan and All I Got Was This Stupid Pipeline: The Complete Truth About the U.S. Attack on Afghanistan*. In that book he suggested, among other convictions, that one motive behind the military assault on Afghanistan that followed the September 11th terrorist attacks on the U.S. was the administration's determination to make Afghanistan safe for the construction of oil and gas pipelines.

Though Rall has increasingly enjoyed success and widespread publication in such newspapers as the *New York Times*, the *Village Voice*, and the *Los Angeles Times*, he has not abandoned his provocative approach to cartooning, perhaps disproving his 1993 prediction in *Columbia* (Winter 1993) that "one of two things will happen. . . . You won't hit success and [therefore] end up a cult figure, dark and bleak, like [the radical journalist] I. F. Stone, or you hit it and get co-opted." His Web site, *www.Rall.com*, includes half a dozen illuminating interviews reprinted from various publications. Rall is married and lives in New York City. —P.G.H.

Suggested Reading: *Boston Globe* D p1 June 12, 2001; *Columbia* p34+ Winter 1993, with photo; *Columbia University News* (on-line) Apr. 18, 2000; *Editor & Publisher* p42+ Dec. 18, 1993, with photo; *Los Angeles Times* p1 July 2, 1998; *New York Observer* (on-line) Jan. 25, 2002; *New York Times* A p27 Nov. 1, 1994, A p23 Apr. 25, 1995, p41 July 3, 1995; *San Francisco Chronicle* p60 July 29, 2001; Ted Rall Web site

Selected Books: *Waking Up in America*, 1992; *All the Rules Have Changed*, 1995; *My War with Brian*, 1998; *Revenge of the Latchkey Kids: An Illustrated Guide to Surviving the 90s and Beyond*, 1998; *Search and Destroy*, 2001; *2024*, 2001; *To Afghanistan and Back*, 2002; *Attitude: The New Subversive Political Cartoonists*, 2002

---

## Ramirez, Manny

*May 30, 1972– Baseball player with the Boston Red Sox*

*Address: Boston Red Sox, Fenway Park, 4 Yawkey Way, Boston, MA 02215*

"I don't really care where I play," Manny Ramirez told the *New York Times* (May 15, 1993) shortly before starting his Major League Baseball career. "I just want to play every day." He got his wish in September 1993, when the Cleveland Indians, who had drafted him in 1991 as the first pick for their minor-league system, called him up to the big leagues. By the end of seven spectacular seasons with the Indians, however, Ramirez had decided he did care about what team he played for. He spent the off-season of 2000 deep in contract negotiations and ultimately decided to join the Boston Red Sox, who added him to an already strong offensive lineup that included shortstop Nomar Garciaparra and designated hitter Carl Everett. The eight-year, $160 million contract that drew him to Boston was the second-richest in the major leagues at the time. Ramirez helped assure himself a warm welcome in his new home by pledging $1 million to Boston-area charities focused on Latino youth. The Red Sox are counting on the 30-year-old to help overcome their nemesis: the New York Yankees, the team that Ramirez and his friends rooted for as kids in Washington Heights, a poor New York City neighborhood.

Manuel Aristides Ramirez was born in Santo Domingo, Dominican Republic, on May 30, 1972. After Manny and his family—which included his three older sisters—relocated to the New York City

Ezra Shaw/Getty Images

borough of Manhattan, in 1985, Manny's father, Aristides, took a job as a livery-cab driver, and his mother, Onelcidad, found work as a seamstress in a garment factory. The Washington Heights neighborhood where Manny spent his teenage years was rough, with a high homicide rate and much drug-related crime.

Ramirez's fascination with baseball started in the Dominican Republic, when one of his grandmothers returned from a trip to the U.S. bearing a baseball glove and a child-sized Dodgers uniform for him. Lacking the proper equipment, Ramirez and his friends played stickball rather than baseball. After the move to New York, baseball helped insulate him from the neighborhood's seamier elements. "All my friends and I were so into baseball, it probably kept us out of trouble," he recalled to Gordon Edes for the *Boston Globe* (December 17, 2000). Ramirez played baseball all over New York City—with a sandlot team in Brooklyn; in the Pablo Morales and the Alexis Ferreiras Little Leagues; and with a Washington Heights team sponsored by Las Tres Marias, a restaurant that now displays a huge collection of Manny Ramirez memorabilia. The owner of Las Tres Marias, Miguelina Barbuena—who often served Ramirez orange juice, steak, and fried plaintains, beginning when the boy was in Little League—expressed the feelings of many Washington Heights residents who had begun rooting for Ramirez when he became a local teen star: "He's from our country. He's from our neighborhood. He's our guy," she told Sara Rimer for the *New York Times* (June 3, 1991).

Ramirez attended George Washington High School, in Manhattan, whose graduates include former U.S. secretary of state Henry Kissinger and the baseball Hall of Famer Rod Carew. Ramirez played third base with his school baseball team and quickly gained attention with his powerful hitting and his devotion to training; he regularly rose at 4:30 a.m. for workout sessions that included running up the half-mile incline of Fort George Hill, the longest hill in Washington Heights, while dragging an automobile tire tied to his waist. In the afternoons he practiced with the school team, and on weekends he went to Brooklyn to play with his sandlot team, coached by Mel Zitter, who also ran the Youth Service League in Brooklyn. Ramirez's high-school coach, Steve Mandl, told Ira Berkow for the *New York Times* (June 18, 1995), "Manny's a legend around here. I can talk to my kids all about goals and they can make it by hard work, but unless they see it firsthand, it doesn't have the same impact. But Manny's something tangible. They all know him. Know what he had to do to get where he is. He's something for them to grasp. He's one of them."

Hitting has always been Ramirez's outstanding talent. In 1991, when he was a senior, he was named the New York City public-high-school player of the year; that season he hit 14 home runs and posted a .650 batting average (some sources say .643 or .633). On June 3 he entered the amateur draft and was selected as the first choice of the Cleveland Indians and the 13th pick overall. "It's like a dream," Ramirez told Sara Rimer for the *New York Times* (June 4, 1991). Joe DeLucca, who scouted Ramirez for the Indians, felt the same way. "I have never seen a high school kid who can swing a bat like that," the veteran scout told Rimer. "We think he's probably the best hitter in the draft."

Ramirez left school a semester short of earning a high-school diploma (he later earned his GED) and headed for North Carolina, where he spent the summer playing with the Burlington Indians, the Cleveland Indians affiliate in the rookie Appalachian League. After some initial nervousness and homesickness, he settled in, racking up a .326 batting average and leading the Appalachian League with 19 home runs and 63 runs batted in (RBIs). He was voted the Appalachian League's most valuable player of 1991.

It was obvious that the Indians were grooming Ramirez to progress rapidly through the ranks. In 1992 he moved up to Class-A ball, playing with the Kinston Indians in the Carolina League. There he changed positions from third base to the outfield, playing both center and right field. His batting average and RBI totals were steadily climbing when a severe bruise of the hamate bone in his left hand ended his season prematurely, in July. Ramirez began the 1993 season playing Class AA ball in Canton-Akron; in mid-July he was promoted to Class AAA in Charlotte. Before joining the Charlotte team, he had been the leading batter in the Class AA league, hitting .340 with 17 home runs and 79 RBIs. Though he spent less than a month and a half in Charlotte, he posted a .317 average with 14 home runs and 36 RBIs. Then, on September 1, 1993, the Cleveland Indians—taking advantage of a Major League Baseball rule entitling them to expand their roster from 25 to 40 in the month of September—called Ramirez to join the team.

Ramirez's major-league debut, on the night of September 2, 1993 against the Minnesota Twins, was almost ruined when lost luggage delayed his arrival at the Indians' Metrodome. It was a less than memorable debut; he went 0-for-4 that night. On the following night Ramirez came home to play against the New York Yankees. "I'm excited to go back to New York, where all my friends will see me," he had told Ira Berkow for the *New York Times* (September 2, 1993). "I heard they're going to be bringing signs about me." In front of his high-school and neighborhood friends and his family, Ramirez hit a double in his first at-bat and followed that with two home runs later in the game. It was the first time his family had seen him play because, as his sister Rosa Rosario told Rimer, "he was always shy. He always told us not to come. He said he gets nervous." Although Ramirez finished the 1993 season with a batting average of only .176, in late September *Baseball America* named him the minor-league player of the year.

In 1994 Ramirez became the Cleveland Indians' starting right fielder. He was hitting .269 with 17 home runs and 60 RBIs when the season came to an abrupt end due to a players' strike. In 1995 he returned in sparkling form, posting a season batting average of .308, with 31 home runs and 107 RBIs. Midway through the 1995 season, Mike Hargrove, the Indians' manager, told Ira Berkow for the *New York Times* (June 18, 1995), "A year ago, in spring training, I thought we'd have to farm [Ramirez] out [to the minor leagues] again, mostly because of his defense. But Manny came to me and said, 'I know I can make the club.' And he worked very, very hard. And he turned things around for himself, where we just had to keep him. He still has a lot to learn, but he's coming to the park early and working in the weight room and talking with the older players—doing everything to learn, to adapt to the major leagues." The year 1995 was punctuated with career firsts for Ramirez: he won his first Silver Slugger Award; hit his first career grand slam (on August 4); and made his first appearance in the postseason. Cleveland won the American League (AL) Championship Series before succumbing to the Atlanta Braves in the World Series.

Ramirez's numbers improved in 1996: he hit 33 home runs and had 112 RBIs. During the season he hit three grand slams and helped the Indians reach the postseason for the second year in a row. His defensive skills improved markedly, and he led American League outfielders with 19 assists. In 1997 Ramirez's home-run and RBI totals dropped, but his batting average jumped to .328. The Indians again found their way to the postseason before losing the World Series to the Florida Marlins. Ramirez's fine season was marred somewhat by some trouble on the base paths. In 1997, in a game against the Detroit Tigers, Ramirez safely stole second base but returned to first and was tagged out.

He explained to Hargrove that he thought that Jim Thome, who was in the batter's box, had hit a foul ball. Hargrove, however, was incensed. "I've never seen anything like that in all my years in baseball," he told Steve Herrick for the *Sporting News* (March 9, 1998). By 1997 Ramirez had established an unfortunate reputation for being forgetful not only during base-running but also during at-bats. On occasion, he lost count of balls and strikes, necessitating reminders to go to first base after ball four, or having to be recalled from first base after ball three. During Game 2 of the 1995 World Series, he was tagged out at first base by Braves pitcher Javy Lopez immediately after the Indians' first-base coach had reminded him that Lopez often tries to pick off base runners.

After the 1997 season Al Bumbry was hired as the Indians' new outfield and first-base coach, partly to help Ramirez with his base running and concentration on the field. The Indians also acquired a team psychologist, Charles Maher, in an effort to help Ramirez with his focus. Maher, who stated publicly that Ramirez's concentration problems were not caused by attention deficit disorder, soon saw results: in 1998 Ramirez slammed 45 home runs and 145 RBIs, the best offensive showing by a Cleveland Indians right fielder in franchise history. The Indians made it to the postseason again but were defeated in the AL Championship Series by the New York Yankees. (In the *New York Times* [October 14, 1998], Selena Roberts blamed the Indians' loss of the series-ending Game 6 on Ramirez's less-than-stellar offensive performance and a fielding mistake that allowed the Yankees' Derek Jeter to make a run-scoring triple.) Ramirez won the club's 1998 most valuable player award, which he promptly gave to Maher in a show of appreciation. "Charlie helps me a lot," Ramirez told Bob Nightengale for the *USA Today Baseball Weekly* (May 12, 1999). "He helps me to concentrate. I wanted to do something for him, and thank him for that."

Behind great hitting from Ramirez, the Indians made it to the postseason for the fifth straight season in 1999. Ramirez hit 44 home runs, managed a .333 batting average, and totaled 165 RBIs. It was the first time in 60 years that a player had more than 160 RBIs in a season. (Jimmie Foxx had last done it, in 1938.) Ramirez, who received his second Silver Slugger Award, also earned accolades from the press and his peers. In *Sports Illustrated* (April 5, 1999) Gerry Callahan crowned him as the successor to the great Cubs outfielder Sammy Sosa: "At 6 feet and 205 pounds, he is almost the same size as Sosa [who is 6 feet, 210 pounds], plays the same position, comes from the same country, has similar power to all fields and had a similar rap against him (lacks focus) as a young player."

Although he was on the disabled list for six weeks in 2000 because of a strained left hamstring, Ramirez had an excellent season in the batter's box. He boosted his average to .351, hit 38 home runs, and had 122 RBIs while playing only 118 out of 162 regular-season games. He captured the media spotlight, however, not for his hitting but for his contract negotiations. In December 2000 he signed a contract with the Boston Red Sox worth $160 million over eight years, with the option to earn $20 million in both 2009 and 2010. This seemed an unusual about-face for Ramirez, who had been characterized as not caring much about his salary. Once, he had dropped his paycheck into a boot and accidentally left it in the visiting-team locker room at the Texas Rangers' ball park. In 1999 Ray Negron, the Indians' media liaison for Latin players, had told Callahan, "Manny is the single most unpretentious, unassuming guy I've ever met in baseball. If he didn't have an agent, he probably wouldn't know how much money he made—and wouldn't care." Further evidence of a changed Manny Ramirez emerged during a press conference in Boston: while he had often refused interviews in the past, claiming his English was insufficient, he chatted freely at the conference and gave interviews to whoever asked. Edes speculated that "his agents have impressed upon him the added demands that come with becoming the second-highest-paid player in baseball [after Alex Rodriguez]." Ramirez told Edes, "I think it is important to show everybody what kind of player I am. To me, coming to Boston is like starting all over again. Nobody knows me here. I have to start all over again."

In 2001 Ramirez opened the season with an explosion of offense. Initially posted at the designated-hitter spot, in April alone he was named the American League player of the month and hit .408, with nine home runs and 31 RBIs. After several weeks he settled into left field, a position in which he played only 55 games. (He was the designated hitter in 87 games.) Despite a slump toward the end of the season, he finished with a .306 batting average, with 41 home runs and 125 RBIs, winning another Silver Slugger Award. Ramirez remained steady despite the managerial uproar that plagued the Red Sox in 2001; coach Jimy Williams was fired, and there were open hostilities between general manager Dan Duquette and the team. "When I played [in Cleveland] it was relaxed," Ramirez told Tom Withers for *sportserver.com* (July 3, 2001). "But in Boston, it's all about winning. You go into the clubhouse and you don't see nobody jumping or playing around. It's all about going out there and beating somebody." After a tight race between the Red Sox and the Yankees for much of the season, the Red Sox faded in the last weeks, during which time Ramirez sat out several games because of hamstring and wrist injuries. Boston finished just three games over .500, with a record of 82 wins and 79 losses.

In 2002, during which he missed 42 regular-season games because of a broken finger, Ramirez won the American League batting title, with a batting average of .349. He also accumulated 33 home runs and 107 RBIs.

In November 2001 Ramirez married Juliana Monterio. — K.S.

Suggested Reading: *Boston Globe* A p1 Dec. 17, 2000; Boston Red Sox Web page; *New York Times* B p1 June 3, 1991, with photos, *New York Times* (on-line) Dec. 13, 2000; *Sport* p40+ Aug. 2000, with photo; *Sporting News* p40+ Mar. 9, 1998, with photos; *Sports Illustrated* p100 Sep. 28, 1998, with photo, p62+ Apr. 5, 1999, with photos, p112+ oct. 2, 2000, with photos, p54+ June 4, 2001, with photos; *USA Today Baseball Weekly* p6+ May 12, 1999, with photos

Andrew Crowley/Camera Press/Retna Ltd.

## Rampling, Charlotte

*Feb 5, 1946– Actress*

*Address: c/o Artmédia, 20 ave. Rapp, 75007 Paris, France*

The British actress Charlotte Rampling is famous for choosing many controversial film roles over the past three decades. After beginning her career with such comedies as *Rotten to the Core* (1965), *The Knack* (1965), and *Georgy Girl* (1966), Rampling opted for darker roles; in 1969 she was cast as a member of a decadent family of industrialists in early Nazi Germany in Luchino Visconti's *The Damned*, and she received international notoriety for her role in *The Night Porter* (1974), in which she played a Holocaust survivor who has a sado-masochistic affair with a former concentration-camp guard. While Rampling has also acted in a number of mainstream films, including *Farewell, My Lovely* (1975), *Stardust Memories* (1980), and *The Verdict* (1982), she has for the most part shunned Hollywood, preferring to spend her time in her adopted country of France and make films that interest her. A bout with depression during the 1990s led to fewer and less notable parts. By the end of the decade, however, Rampling was enjoying a comeback with impressive performances in *The Wings of the Dove* (1997), the television film *Great Expectations* (1999), *Aberdeen* (2000), *Signs and Wonders* (2001), and the highly regarded *Under the Sand* (2001). "I may have made some odd films, but I've never made crap," she told Brian Libby for *Salon* (January 24, 2002, on-line), "and I've never done it for the money. It's about honor. Honor is a warm thing, a caressing thing. I'd rather go to bed with honor than a bank balance. I'll feel much better in the morning."

Charlotte Rampling was born on February 5, 1946 in Sturmer, England. Her father, Godfrey Rampling, was a gold medalist at the 1936 Berlin Olympic Games and a British army officer assigned to the North Atlantic Treaty Organization (NATO). "I was an army brat, and we'd be constantly on the move," the actress recalled to Iain Blair for the *Chicago Tribune* (April 12, 1987). "The disadvantages were that you'd never stay in one place long enough to make great friends, but then you'd be thrown back on your own resources, and perhaps that's how I first got the taste for performing." For several years Rampling's family lived in France, and she attended a Catholic school in Fontainebleau. "It wasn't a particularly happy memory but at least it ingrained French language and culture into me," Rampling told Charles Bremner for the London *Times* (October 1, 1994). Around 1958 the family returned to England, where Rampling continued her education.

Rampling expressed an interest in acting at an early age, often performing plays with her sister. During the early 1960s Rampling began acting in theater productions outside London and found work as a model. At her father's urging she also attended secretarial school. While working as a typist, Rampling was cast in the 1965 film *Rotten to the Core*, a comedy about several inept bank robbers. A review in *Time* (August 20, 1965) described her character as "a pert socialite making her criminal debut as the temptress assigned to dazzle a lieutenant of the armed guards, though much of her wickedness is spent in murdering the Queen's English with such nauseous effusions as 'how rave-making' or 'supremo!'" The same year Rampling had a small part in the comedy *The Knack*.

In 1966 Rampling co-starred with Lynn Redgrave in *Georgy Girl* as Meredith, a beautiful and icy cellist who neglects her baby while enjoying the sexual revolution in London. By contrast, her roommate, Georgy, played by Redgrave, is a good-hearted but awkward young woman who envies Meredith's lifestyle. *Georgy Girl* was a hit with both critics and audiences worldwide.

When she was 20 Rampling took a leave of absence from acting, after her 23-year-old sister died of a brain hemorrhage and her mother suffered a stroke at about the same time. "My whole life fell apart," Rampling recalled to Alan Riding for the

*New York Times* (April 29, 2001). "I couldn't be in films for entertainment. I had to be in films for another reason if I was to carry on making films." She began traveling, living with gypsies in Afghanistan and spending two months in a Tibetan monastery in Scotland. She also took up yoga and studied Eastern religions.

In 1969 Rampling appeared in two noteworthy films, *Three* and *The Damned*. In *Three*, she starred as a young British woman who, while vacationing in Italy, becomes the object of desire for two American college students. A review of the film in *Time* (January 19, 1970) asserted, "Charlotte Rampling, all angles and sensuality, is that rare thing, a beautiful woman who can also be fairly called an actress." Rampling went to Italy to make *The Damned*, an erotic film directed by Luchino Visconti and set in early Nazi Germany. "There I was . . . still quite green, and to be literally swept away by Visconti and taken under his wing, it was an incredible experience," Rampling told Blair. "I became his sort of protégé and stayed at his villa for a long time, which was all a great training for me. Everything he did was on such a grandiose scale and very operatic."

Rampling told Blair that after making *The Damned*, she fell in love with Italy, remaining there for the next few years. The actress kept busy with roles in *'Tis Pity She's a Whore* (1971), *The Ski Bum* (1971), *Corky* (1972), *Asylum* (1972), *Henry VIII and His Six Wives* (1972), and the science-fiction film *Zardoz* (1974), with Sean Connery.

During Rampling's stay in Italy, the British actor Dirk Bogarde, who had worked with her on *The Damned*, asked her to co-star with him in *The Night Porter*, which was written and directed by Liliana Cavani. Rampling told Blair that, at first, Cavani was reluctant to cast her because she thought the actress was still relatively unknown. Bogarde then told Cavani that he would make *The Night Porter* only if Rampling was in it, insisting that she was the only actress who could play the female lead. Cavani finally agreed after meeting with both Bogarde and Rampling. Released in Europe and the United States in 1974, *The Night Porter* is one of Rampling's (and Bogarde's) most controversial films. Rampling played Lucia, a Holocaust survivor who comes to stay at a Vienna hotel with her husband in 1957. Lucia recognizes Max, the hotel's night porter (Bogarde), as the SS guard who raped and tortured her when she was a 14-year-old inmate of a Nazi concentration camp. Lucia and Max begin a bizarre relationship built around sadomasochistic sex. "[My character] was not a passive victim," Rampling told Michael Zwerin for the *Washington Post* (February 23, 1981). "She was a victim [who] won. She was taken over mentally and physically by something totally corrupt. And the corruption turned her on. Even though it was a bizarre love, it was the only love she had known, and she decided to live her destiny to the very end. She chose, in fact, not to be a victim by deciding to accept whatever happens." Although *The Night Porter* was a hit in Europe and generated much publicity, it failed to impress most critics in the United States. In her review for the *New York Times* (October 2, 1974), Nora Sayre wrote that *The Night Porter* was "handsomely filmed in dark, rich tones," but objected to its exploitation of the Nazi victims "for the sake of sensationalism," adding that "their suffering is almost made to seem chic." Sayre observed, "Rampling's elegant sternness and low, bitter voice are suitable for her role, but she's a one-dimensional actress who can't convey much beyond tension. Toward the end, she produces one sulky scowl that makes you grateful for a new facial expression." Despite the negative reviews and the controversy, *The Night Porter* made Rampling into an international star, although one with a less-than-flattering image. For example, a reporter for *Newsweek* (September 9, 1974) observed that Rampling was known as "the kinky queen of the Continent." The actress was then offered similar "kinky" roles, including that of a corpse in a necrophiliac's fantasy, but she declined them all.

In 1975 Rampling appeared with Peter O'Toole in *Foxtrot*, which received little attention, and with Robert Mitchum in *Farewell, My Lovely*, a crime thriller based on Raymond Chandler's novel of the same name. Mitchum was cast as Philip Marlowe, the private detective Chandler created, and Rampling as the femme fatale. Reviewing the film for *Newsweek* (August 18, 1975), Charles Michener wrote, "Cast, seemingly, for her superficial vocal and physical resemblance to Lauren Bacall [a film-noir veteran], Rampling comes across as merely a scrubbed-up mannequin of her smoky predecessor." Rampling was also seen in Yves Boisett's *The Purple Taxi* (1977) and *Orca* (1977), a box-office disappointment, in which Richard Harris, as the captain of a whaling ship, and his crew are menaced by a killer whale. She then took a hiatus from acting and, to escape England's high taxes, moved to France with her husband, the composer and musician Jean-Michel Jarre, whom she had married in 1977.

In 1980 the director Woody Allen offered Rampling a part in his film *Stardust Memories*. At first Rampling declined, preferring not to leave her family. However, Allen persisted, even traveling to France to persuade her. Rampling finally agreed and, during the filming in New York City, frequently returned to France to see her family. Released in 1980, *Stardust Memories*, which Allen also wrote and co-starred in, was autobiographical and borrowed from Federico Fellini's *8½* (1963). Allen played Sandy Bates, a popular director who attends a film festival devoted to his work during a weekend at the Stardust Hotel. Disillusioned with the films he has made, Bates looks back on his life and career, which included a brief relationship he had with a neurotic actress, played by Rampling. "Woody Allen was the perfect person to start me off again," Rampling told Joan Juliet Buck for *Vanity Fair* (April 1988). "He gave me the possibility of playing a really screwed-up character in a very loving environment." *Stardust Memories* sharply divided reviewers. Some critics, among them Vincent Canby of the *New York Times* (September 28, 1980), thought it was a brilliant satire of moviemaking, while other reviewers—such as Pauline Kael of the *New Yorker* (October 27, 1980)—accused Allen of treating with contempt audiences who had enjoyed his previous comedies. Such views notwithstanding, *Stardust Memories* is now widely considered one of Woody Allen's best films.

Rampling's next role was as Paul Newman's love interest—a woman with something to hide—in Sidney Lumet's courtroom drama *The Verdict* (1982), which was a hit with both critics and audiences. She also made several films in France, including *Max, Mon Amour* (1986), in which her character has an affair with a chimpanzee. Discussing with Brian Libby her unusual role choices, Rampling said, "Provocative subjects provoke me, and I need that. Otherwise, I'll get bored. I've always searched out that type of work, and it's not just a coincidence that I chose these particular films. They are related to me, because I see myself in them."

Rampling then turned to comedy with *Mascara* (1987), which earned her best-actress awards from the Flanders International Film Festival and Portugal's Fantasporto festival; also that year she had a supporting role in the thriller *Angel Heart.* In 1988 she played a right-wing British politician in *Paris by Night* and was also cast in the remake of the 1950 noir thriller *D.O.A.*, alongside Meg Ryan and Dennis Quaid.

During the 1990s Rampling battled depression and greatly scaled back her acting, taking only a handful of roles that interested her. "I couldn't work," she told Michael Atkinson for the *Village Voice* (May 15, 2001). "I had to go underground. Film is about light, and I couldn't go into the light." After nearly fading from public view, Rampling began her comeback, in the critically acclaimed period piece *The Wings of the Dove* (1997), which is based on the Henry James novel of the same name. Set in 1910, the film co-starred Helena Bonham Carter as Kate Croy, a woman who hatches a scheme to have the man she loves marry a dying heiress. Rampling played Kate's snobbish aunt, who constantly pressures Kate to marry for money. In 1999 Rampling was cast as Miss Havisham in *Great Expectations*, an adaptation of the Charles Dickens novel broadcast on the PBS network.

In 2000 Rampling made two films with the Swedish actor Stellan Skarsgård. In *Aberdeen*, which received mixed reviews, Rampling played a woman who reunites with her alcoholic ex-husband (Skarsgård), who had abandoned her 15 years earlier. Most critics were impressed with *Signs and Wonders*, which found Skarsgård and Rampling portraying a married couple living in Athens, Greece, who are unfaithful to each other. "With a passionate, intelligent performance, Rampling is the sane, seductive center of the film," Loren King wrote in a review for the *Boston Globe* (July 27, 2001).

Rampling earned international acclaim for her performance in *Under the Sand* (2001), a French film directed by François Ozon. She starred as Marie, a woman whose happy life is shattered when, while she is napping at a beach, her husband—who had gone swimming—mysteriously disappears. Unable to handle the pain and the shock of his loss, Marie goes into denial and acts as if he is still alive. Rampling closely identified with Marie. "I lived through this," she told Susan King for the *Los Angeles Times* (May 17, 2001). "I was in complete denial when my sister [died]." In his review of *Under the Sand* for the *San Francisco Chronicle* (May 25, 2001), Edward Guthmann praised Ozon's decision to cast Rampling in the role, writing that the actress was "surprisingly sympathetic in this intimate tale of love and grief." Guthmann added that with "her high cheekbones and lithe body, her funny, ambiguous smile and her aura of strength and intelligence, she's endlessly fascinating in a film that places her in every scene." For her performance, Rampling received nominations for best actress from the European Film Awards and the César Awards, France's equivalent of the Academy Awards.

In 2001 Rampling also narrated the documentary *Clouds: Letters to My Son* and had a cameo in the action film *Spy Game*, with Robert Redford and Brad Pitt in the lead roles. That same year Rampling co-starred in *The Fourth Angel* and played a nun and psychiatrist who investigates a murder in *Superstition.* Rampling's next role was in the French comedy *Embrassez qui vous voulez*, which was released in October 2002 in several European countries and screened at the Montreal Film Festival, in Canada. In 2003 she will co-star in François Ozon's *The Swimming Pool* (known in France as *Huit Femmes*, meaning "Eight Women"), and Mike Hodges's thriller *I'll Sleep When I'm Dead.*

In 2000 Charlotte Rampling was named an Officer of the British Empire (OBE), an honorary title, by Queen Elizabeth II. The next year she earned an honorary César Award. Rampling's first marriage, to Bryan Southcombe, a public relations agent, ended in divorce in 1976. Her marriage to Jean-Michel Jarre also ended recently. Rampling has a son from her first marriage and a son from her marriage to Jarre; she also has one stepdaughter. —D.C.

Suggested Reading: *Boston Globe* D p6 Jul. 27, 2001; *Cahiers du Cinéma* p54+ Feb. 2001, with photos; *Chicago Tribune* Arts p20+ Apr. 12, 1987 with photos; *Los Angeles Times* p11 May 11, 2001; *New York Times* p58 Oct. 2, 1974 with photos, II p17 Apr. 29, 2001 with photo; *Newsweek* p73 Aug. 18, 1975 with photo; *Salon* (on-line) Jan. 24, 2002; *San Francisco Chronicle* C p3 May 25, 2001; *Time* p67 Jan. 19, 1970 with photo; *Vanity Fair* p104+ Apr. 1988 with photos; *Washington Post* B p3 Feb. 23, 1981

Selected Films: *Rotten to the Core*, 1965; *The Knack*, 1965; *Georgy Girl*, 1966; *The Long Duel*, 1967; *Three*, 1969; *The Damned*, 1969; *Zardoz*, 1974; *The Night Porter*, 1974; *Foxtrot*, 1975; *Farewell, My Lovely*, 1975; *Orca*, 1977; *Stardust Memories*, 1980; *The Verdict*, 1982; *Max Mon Amour*, 1986; *Angel Heart*; 1987, *Paris By Night*, 1988; *D.O.A.*, 1988; *The Wings of the Dove*, 1997; *Great Expectations*, 1999; *Aberdeen*, 2000; *Signs and Wonders*, 2000; *Under the Sand*, 2001; *Spy Game*, 2001; *Superstition*, 2001; *The Fourth Angel*, 2001; *Embrassez qui vous voulez*, 2002

---

Louis Myrie/LMI

## Ressler, Robert K.

*1937– Criminologist; writer*

*Address: c/o Lavin Agency, 872 Massachusetts Ave., Suite 2-2, Cambridge, MA 02139*

Robert K. Ressler is one of the world's foremost experts on violent criminals, particularly those guilty of serial and sexual homicides. It was Ressler, in fact, who coined the phrase "serial killer," in the mid-1970s. At that time he was a supervisory special agent and criminologist with the Behavioral Science Unit (BSU) of the Federal Bureau of Investigation (FBI), a division set up some years earlier to strengthen the bureau's ability to solve heinous crimes. Ressler helped develop criminal profiling, a now widely used process of creating a probable physical and behavioral portrait of an unknown perpetrator based on evidence gathered from one or more crime scenes. Over the course of his more than 30-year career, Ressler has interviewed many of the nation's most notorious serial killers to gain information and insights that might assist him and other law-enforcement officials in apprehending other violent criminals. Murderers interviewed by Ressler include John Wayne Gacy (the killer of 33 young men and boys), Ted Bundy (who slaughtered at least 36 young women in the 1970s), Charles Manson (who is serving a life sentence for the murders of the actress Sharon Tate and four others in 1969), and Jeffrey Dahmer (convicted in 1991 of killing 17 men and boys). In 1990 Ressler retired from the FBI and, that year, set up Forensic Behavioral Services International, whose activities include training others in psychological profiling. Ressler directs the group, which is based in Virginia. During the 1990s Ressler also served as a consultant in many high-profile cases, including the as-yet unsolved murder of six-year-old JonBenet Ramsey in Colorado in 1996. Ressler's expertise extends to hostage negotiation, threat assessment, and criminal-investigation analysis, all of which he has taught and researched. He served as the FBI's hostage-negotiation instructor in 1977 and 1978. Ressler's many awards for his achievements in criminology include the prestigious Jefferson Award from the University of Virginia, in Charlottesville (which he earned twice), an Amicus Award from the American Academy of Psychiatry and the Law, and a Psychiatry and Behavioral Science Section Award from the American Academy of Forensic Sciences. He has also co-written five books, among them the textbook *Sexual Homicide: Patterns and Motives* and the memoir *Whoever Fights Monsters*.

Robert K. Ressler was born in 1937 in Chicago, Illinois. He was introduced to the world of violent crime through reading the *Chicago Tribune*, his father's employer. When he was nine years old, he became consumed with details in the newspaper's accounts of the abduction and brutal murder of a six-year-old girl from his northwest Chicago neighborhood. As he recalled to John M. McGuire for the *St. Louis Post-Dispatch* (June 3, 1999), he was especially struck when he read that the killer—who was later caught and identified as a 17-year-old University of Chicago student named William Heirens—had scribbled with lipstick at the crime scene the words "For heaven's sake, catch me before I kill more, I cannot control myself."

In 1955 Ressler enrolled at Michigan State University (MSU), in East Lansing. He interrupted his studies two years later to enlist in the U.S. Army. He served active duty in Okinawa, Japan, from 1957 to 1959. After his military discharge he returned to MSU, where he earned a B.S. degree in 1962. Through that university's Reserve Officers Training Corps (ROTC) program, he was commissioned as a second lieutenant in the Military Police Corps. In that capacity he served in Europe, the U.S., and Southeast Asia from 1962 to 1970, in turn holding the titles of provost marshal, criminal-investigation supervisor, and military-police operations and intelligence officer. In recognition of his outstanding performance, he was awarded the

Meritorious Service Medal, the Vietnam Service Medal, the National Defense Medal, and the Army Commendation Medal with oak leaf clusters. He was honorably discharged in 1970, with the rank of major. For the next 22 years, he continued his military service, as a reservist with the U.S. Army Criminal Investigation Command in Washington, D.C. and as commander of a Theater Army Support Group in Richmond, Virginia. When he retired from the military, in 1992, he held the rank of colonel. Earlier, in 1968, while stationed in the U.S., he earned an M.S. degree from MSU.

On February 2, 1970 Ressler became a special agent for the FBI. During stints in Chicago, New Orleans, and Cleveland, he investigated interstate thefts, forgeries, and securities frauds as well as prostitution, pornography, and organized crime. In January 1974 Special Agent Ressler was selected to be a counselor at the 96th session of the FBI National Academy, held in Quantico, Virginia. Soon afterward he was promoted to special agent supervisor and assigned to the BSU as a criminology instructor. At around this time Ressler was also appointed program manager of the FBI's Criminal Personality Research Project, in which information on serial murderers, rapists, child abductors, and other violent criminals was gathered. That work led him to interview three dozen serial killers, among them Richard Speck (who murdered eight student nurses in Chicago in 1966), David Berkowitz (known as "Son of Sam," who murdered six people in New York City in 1976 and 1977), and Edmund Kemper (who was arraigned in 1973 on eight counts of first-degree murder, including that of his mother, and was sentenced to life in prison). Ressler described his encounters with the killers in his 1992 memoir, *Whoever Fights Monsters*, which Tom Shachtman co-authored.

In compiling information that he elicited from his interviewees, Ressler coined the label "serial killers" to refer to murderers of two or more people. Previously, such criminals had been called "stranger killers," in the belief that they had not known their victims. Ressler discovered that in some cases the victims and their killers were not strangers; sometimes, as in the case of Kemper and his mother, they were related. The phrase "serial killer" was immediately adopted by criminologists as well as the media.

In the course of his research, Ressler helped to develop the process known as criminal profiling, whereby what is discovered at a crime scene is used to generate a hypothesis regarding the perpetrator's personality, mannerisms, living habits, and personal history. Although not always completely accurate, profiling often provides local law-enforcement agents with starting points from which to conduct their investigations. In an excerpt from *Whoever Fights Monsters* posted on Ressler's Web page (*robertkressler.com*), he explained, "Profiles don't catch killers, cops on the beat do, often through dogged persistence and with the help of ordinary citizens, and certainly with a little bit of luck." Referring to his profile of the serial killer Richard Trenton Chase, he noted that it had "markedly narrowed the search for a dangerous killer." "Did my work help catch Chase? You bet, and I'm proud of it," he wrote. "Did I catch him myself? No."

Ressler's professional life has inspired many writers. Among those who have cited him as a driving force behind their work are Chris Carter (creator of the TV show *The X-Files*), the novelist Mary Higgins Clark, and the makers of such films as *Silence of the Lambs* (1991), for which Ressler reviewed scripts; *Copycat* (1995); and *Red Dragon* (2002). Although admittedly flattered by such attention, Ressler is quick to point out that the portrayal of his work in motion pictures is far from accurate. In an interview with *Time.com* (July 20, 1997), Ressler explained, "What you don't see in the media is the lengthy examination of the crime scene, photographs and videotapes, careful examinations of the autopsy and the photos. Oftentimes this takes a considerable amount of time, and there's coordination with the investigating officers to reach a logical conclusion to come up with a profile. The movie portrayal usually shortcuts the lengthy process by mindflashes of the profiler at the scene of the crime which would indicate that some sort of psychic experience is going on. And of course this is nonsense." Other TV shows inspired by aspects of Ressler's life are *Millennium* (1996–99) and *Profiler* (1996–2000).

In 1984 Ressler helped to set up the FBI's National Center for the Analysis of Violent Crime (NCAVC). The following year he developed the Violent Criminal Apprehension Program (VICAP), with the aim of evaluating unsolved crimes and detecting similarities in past and recent crimes. Ressler was the program's first director. In 1986 he received the Jefferson Award from the University of Virginia, given to a faculty member of the FBI Academy for outstanding research and published works. His second Jefferson Award came in 1988, the year of publication of *Sexual Homicide: Patterns and Motives*, co-written with Ann W. Burgess and John E. Douglas.

In August 1990 Ressler retired from his post at the FBI. Later that year he established Forensic Behavioral Services International, a Virginia-based organization that focuses on education, consultation, and the furnishing of expert-witness testimony in the courtroom. In the following years he helped out with several high-profile cases throughout the world, including that of Richard Jewell, who was accused—erroneously, as it turned out—of the bombing of the Centennial Olympic Park in Atlanta, Georgia, during the 1996 Summer Olympics. Ressler has taught hundreds of courses at law-enforcement agencies, universities, and medical schools, among them Georgetown University, the University of Virginia, the U.S. Army Criminal Investigation Command, and Bramshill British Police College. He has also made many television appearances, on such programs as *Good Morning*

*America*, the *Today* show, *Geraldo*, and *Larry King Live*.

Ressler wrote the textbook *Sexual Homicide: Patterns and Motives* (1988) with John E. Douglas and Ann W. Burgess. With Douglas, Burgess, and Allen G. Burgess, he wrote *Crime Classification Manual: A Standard System for Investigating and Classifying Violent Crimes* (1997), which presents the results of a 10-year project conducted by the NCAVC. The International Association of Law Enforcement Intelligence Analysts named that book the most significant contribution of 1994 to the literature of law-enforcement intelligence. Ressler's other books, co-written with Tom Shachtman, are *Whoever Fights Monsters: My Twenty Years Tracking Serial Killers for the FBI* (1992); *Justice Is Served* (1994), about his successful efforts to prove the guilt of a judge who had his wife murdered; and *I Have Lived in the Monster: Inside the Minds of the World's Most Notorious Serial Killers* (1997). Ressler, who lives in Virginia, is reportedly at work on another book. — J.H.

Suggested Reading: *New York Times* I p3 Sep. 30, 1995; *Publishers Weekly* p73+ May 26, 1997; *St. Louis Post-Dispatch* G p1 June 3, 1999; *Time.com* July 20, 1997; Ressler, Robert K., and Tom Schachtman. *Whoever Fights Monsters*, 1992

Selected Books: with Ann W. Burgess and John E. Douglas—*Sexual Homicide: Patterns and Motives*, 1988; with Ann W. Burgess, John E. Douglas, and Allen G. Burgess—*Crime Classification Manual*, 1997; with Tom Shachtman—*Whoever Fights Monsters*, 1992; *Justice Is Served*, 1994; *I Have Lived in the Monster*, 1997

---

Courtesy of UC Davis School of Law

## Reynoso, Cruz

*May 2, 1931– Lawyer; judge*

*Address: Kaye, Scholer, Fierman, Hays & Handler, 1999 Ave. of the Stars, Suite 1600, Los Angeles, CA 90067*

A pillar of the civil rights community, Cruz Reynoso has spent most of his life battling discrimination, as a lawyer, judge, teacher, and, currently, as vice chairperson of the United States Commission on Civil Rights. Focusing his energies on fighting for better education and greater economic resources for poor minorities, he has received several awards for his perseverence and dedication to the cause. Now in his fifth decade of activism, he continues to advocate affirmative action and push for policy changes to protect minorities from civil rights abuses.

One of five siblings, Cruz Reynoso was born on May 2, 1931 in Brea, California. His father worked as a railroad laborer and later became a farmer and irrigator of citrus groves. Reynoso, who grew up speaking both Spanish and English, soon realized that little attention was being paid in the mainstream press to Latinos. "It was [as] if we were invisible," he gold Debra Gersh for *Editor & Publisher* (July 31, 1993). When he was seven, the Reynoso family moved to a small barrio, or village, on the outskirts of northern Orange County, in California. There, Reynoso and his two older brothers attempted to go to a public school but were turned back by the segregated establishment. After sixth grade, he was sent to a desegregated junior high school where Latinos were punished if they spoke any Spanish and were told to inform on friends who did. In Reynoso's high school, because of discrimination, many Latino students were given grades of C or lower in Spanish class, even though they were being taught their own language and performed as well as non-Latinos. "Segregation has not served us well," he explained to Kelly Howard for the *PCC Courier* (October 29, 1998, on-line).

At about the age of 14, Reynoso noticed that adults in his barrio complained of not having rural mail delivery; instead, they had to go to the nearest town to get their mail. "When I heard this, my justice bone started hurting," Reynoso recalled to Howard. The teenager went to see the town's postmaster, who told him to write to the state or federal postmaster. Reynoso not only wrote to him but started a petition in his barrio to get mail delivered to individual homes there. Three to four months later, all the villagers received notes in their mailboxes advising them to prepare for the beginning of rural-delivery service.

After graduating from high school, Reynoso attended Fullerton Junior College, in Fullerton, California, where he received an A.A. degree. He then enrolled at Pomona College, in Claremont, California, where he was involved with student government and decided to become a lawyer. He earned a B.A. degree there in 1953. Drafted into the U.S. Army that same year, he served in the counterintelligence corps during the last stages of the Korean War. After returning to the United States, he attended Boalt Hall, as the law school at the University of California, Berkeley, is familiarly known; he received an LL.B. degree there in 1958. He was admitted to the California Bar in 1959, and after one year as a legislative assistant in the California State Senate, he began to practice law in El Centro, California, as a founding member of the firm Reynoso and Duddy. The firm often represented Latino clients in civil rights cases, such as one involving a woman who was not allowed to vote in an election because of her ethnicity.

In 1966, while continuing to practice law, Reynoso was appointed assistant chief of the state Fair Employment Practices Commission, a position he held for one year. He was appointed the following year as staff secretary of the California governor's office, and in 1967 he gave up his practice to became associate general counsel of the U.S. Equal Employment Opportunities Commission, in Washington, D.C. Reynoso returned to California in 1968 to serve as director of the San Francisco office of the California Rural Legal Assistance program. Regarded as one of the groundbreaking programs of the legal-services movement, it set out to provide low-income people with access to quality legal representation. In 1972 Reynoso left that position to become a professor of law at the University of New Mexico, where he stayed until 1976, when he was appointed associate justice of the state Court of Appeals in the Third District of California. In 1982 he was appointed associate justice of the Supreme Court of California, where he remained until his term expired, in January 1987.

Reynoso then returned to private law practice, working in addition as a private judge. (Such a judge most often serves in the resolution of disputes through arbitration or mediation.) From 1987 to 1988 he was counsel to the law firm of O'Donnell and Gordon in Los Angeles and Sacramento, California, and he is currently special counsel to the law firm of Kay, Scholer, Fierman, Hays & Handler. Reynoso also continues to teach, as a professor at the University of California, Los Angeles (UCLA) School of Law and at the Stanford University Graduate School of Business. In addition, he has taught law at Boalt Hall. His areas of specialty include professional responsibility, remedies, and appellate advocacy.

Most prominently, Reynoso serves as the vice chairperson of the U.S. Commission on Civil Rights, a bipartisan committee that investigates citizen complaints of discrimination and examines federal law for components that violate civil rights. Appointed to the commission in April 1993 by the then–U.S. Senate majority leader, George J. Mitchell, Reynoso has been involved in several high-profile investigations, including one concerning the treatment of blacks and Hispanics by the New York City Police Department. In 2000 the commission made headlines when it opposed Florida governor Jeb Bush's plans to curb his state's affirmative-action program. That same year it made 15 recommendations of ways to help end racial tension between whites and Native Americans in South Dakota and northern Nebraska. "[I've] not been in an area where the divide [between Native Americans and whites] seems to be as great," Reynoso told Dan Anderson for *Indian Country* (April 5, 2001, on-line). "Suspicion has been more intense here than I have seen in Los Angeles, New York, or Miami." He criticized California governor Gray Davis's 4 percent admission plan—according to which the top 4 percent of all California public-school students are admitted to the University of California—as little more than a public-relations move disguised as a way to help low-income and minority students, a purpose Reynoso felt it would not serve. Reynoso has also come out strongly against California proposals that he believes hurt illegal immigrants, such as a 1994 statewide ballot proposal to deny them health care, education, and other public services. Reynoso has stated his belief that standardized tests such as the SAT should not be factors in student admissions to colleges, even though test scores determine the institutions' rankings. "We have become victims of our own circumstances," he said to David King for the UCLA *Daily Bruin* (April 26, 2000, on-line). "We have to take a minute, analyze and do what's right."

Reynoso has been appointed to many government-sponsored committees. He served from 1978 to 1979 as a member of the Presidential Committee to Recommend Potential Appointees as Director of Federal Bureau of Investigation. During the same time he was a member of the California State Commission on Government Reform (the Post Commission) and of the Ethics Advisory Board of the U.S. Department of Health, Education and Welfare (now the Department of Health and Human Services). He was appointed as a U.S. delegate to the 1980 session of the United Nations Commission on Human Rights, in Geneva, Switzerland. He also served as a presidential appointee on the national Select Commission on Immigration and Refugee Policy, 1979–81; a member of the California State Commission on the Teaching Profession, 1984–89; and a member of the California Post Secondary Education Commission, 1987–90. He has written a number of articles published in legal journals and is the co-author of *Built to Last: Successful Habits of Visionary Companies*. Reynoso has been a board member of the Mexican American Legal Defense and Educational Fund and has served on the boards of directors of the Rosenberg Foundation, the Community Board Program, and the Council on Foundations. He is a member of the California Judges' Association, the American Bar Association, the Los Angeles Bar Association, the La Raza Lawyers Association, and the Mexican American and National Hispanic Bar Associations. In addition, he serves on the boards of Latino Issues Forum, the Natural Resources Defense Council, and Children Now. Reynoso has been awarded five honorary doctorates as well as the Loren Miller Legal Services Award, from the California State Bar; the Brillante Award, presented by the National Society of Hispanic MBAs; and the 1993 Society of American Law Teachers Achievement Award for Contributions to Legal Education.

Reynoso currently lives near Sacramento with his wife, Jeannene. The couple have four married children. The California La Raza Lawyers' Association currently gives awards in his honor for "significant contributions to the advancement of Latino lawyers and the Latino community." In 2000 he received the nation's highest civilian award, the Presidential Medal of Freedom, at a White House ceremony. — G.O.

Suggested Reading: *Editor & Publisher* p12+ July 31, 1993; *Indian Country* (on-line) Apr. 5, 2000; *PCC Courier* (on-line) Oct. 29, 1998; UCLA *Daily Bruin* (on-line) Apr. 26, 2000

---

Thomas Struth/Courtesy of Marian Goodman Gallery

## Richter, Gerhard

(RIK-ter)

*Feb. 9, 1932– Artist*

*Address: c/o Distributed Art Publishers, 155 Sixth Ave., 2d Fl., New York, NY 10013*

For more than 40 years, Gerhard Richter has fascinated and baffled the art world by refusing to paint in a single style. Of the styles he has chosen—primarily photorealism, still life, and abstract art—all have been purposely undermined in some way by Richter, who has called into question, for example, the distinctions between naturalistic and abstract art. Through his multiplicity of styles, he has produced a sort of "anti-style," through which he attempts to downplay his personality and point of view and emphasize the paintings themselves as the objects of scrutiny. His subject matter has been equally varied: he has painted a portrait of Jacqueline Kennedy Onassis, a variation on Titian's painting *Annunciation*, portraits of his family, and landscapes as well as representations of Nazis, airstrike sites, warplanes, mass-murder victims, coffins, and skulls. Throughout most of his career, his work—produced most recently in his tidy studio in Cologne, Germany—has earned him the highest praise. Tom McDonough noted for *Art Journal* (Fall 1996), "[Richter] has achieved an almost unheard-of acclaim, earning equal respect from critics, collectors, and curators. Not that his work has been well understood, particularly by its English-speaking audience—critics typically express a rather puzzled approval, unable to place it in any particular cognitive niche but enjoying it nonetheless." Even as Richter has been relentlessly experimental, he has remained loyal to painting's traditional ideals, including the ideal of beauty. He told Michael Kimmelman for the *New York Times Magazine* (January 27, 2002), "The big problem for painting today, the terrible side of modern art, [is that] you can now do anything and simply declare it to be art—with no sense of quality." Richter's commitment to quality, and his insistence that quality is measurable even in today's chaotic artistic environment, has helped to secure his high status among painters. "He may be the contemporary painter who matters most today," Jay Tolson wrote for *U.S. News & World Report* (February 11, 2000): "[his legacy is] a wary but resilient commitment to beauty, truth, and other universals that the assorted ideologies of the past century did their best to corrupt or contaminate."

Gerhard Richter was born in Dresden, Germany, on February 9, 1932. His mother's husband, Horst Richter, was a schoolteacher who joined the Nazi Party because of tacit threats that he would lose his job if he did not. Horst fought for Germany in World War II; he was captured by the U.S. and released and returned to Germany in 1946. By this time young Gerhard was alienated from Horst Richter, partly because his mother, Hildegard

(Schonfelder) Richter, the daughter of a concert pianist, had taken a lover during the war and had intimated to Gerhard that her relationship with his father had been a loveless one. The artist confided to Michael Kimmelman that Horst Richter "was not my father anyway. My mother had let me know this in different ways."

Because of Horst Richter's involvement with the Nazi Party, Gerhard was placed in the German Young Folk, a Nazi organization for young children. After finishing grammar school he enrolled at a trade school, studying accounting, stenography, and Russian. His mother, meanwhile, had always encouraged his interest in the arts, and as a shy young man of 15, he started to draw, partly to fill his solitary hours. In 1949 the eastern portion of Germany became an independent Communist state known as the German Democratic Republic (commonly called East Germany). Richter soon found a job making Communist banners for the government. Wanting to pursue art as a career, he applied to the Art Academy in Dresden but was at first rejected. Finally, in 1952 (1951, according to one source), he was accepted and began to study under Heinz Lothmar, who headed the school's mural-painting department. Artistic expression was restricted under the Communist government, and Richter was obliged to work primarily in the style of social realism, a broad term used to describe naturalistic art that comments overtly on social conditions.

After graduating from the Art Academy, Richter made a good living by painting murals. In 1957 he married Ema Eufinger. Richter's success meant that he was granted traveling privileges by the East German government. In 1959, during a trip to West Germany, he saw modern abstract paintings by Jackson Pollock and Lucio Fontana and realized that by comparison his own work was conservative. (By East German standards he was rather experimental; one of his works, in fact, had been featured in a BBC special to demonstrate that modern art had not been fully suppressed by the government.) Craving artistic freedom, Richter sneaked out of East Germany with his wife in 1961. They settled in Düsseldorf, West Germany, where he enrolled at the Academy of Art and became acquainted with a number of avant-garde artists, such as Sigmar Polke and Blinky Palermo. Absorbing his new, culturally rich surroundings, Richter painted and experimented assiduously. "I started to paint like crazy, from figurative to abstract," he recalled to Kimmelman. "Then after a year, I put it all on a bonfire in the courtyard of the academy. I suppose there was some ritual involved, but I didn't tell anyone before I did it, so it wasn't public, and I felt the work had to be burned because people were already taking things and paintings were starting to circulate. I had to prevent that because I realized it was time to start from scratch. Photographs were the way forward. I'm shocked now that the story seems clear, because it didn't seem clear at the time."

In 1962 Richter began to paint from photographs. His technique consisted of projecting a photograph onto a canvas with a slide projector, tracing in the outlines and colors, and then deliberately blurring or obscuring the image and adding subdued colors. Sometimes he chose ordinary subject matter culled from his own snapshots and from magazines, in the manner of such Pop artists as Andy Warhol and Roy Lichtenstein, who liked to work with images from everyday life (one result was Warhol's famous *Campbell's Soup Can*). Richter also chose more provocative photographs, such as the image of aerial bombardment that he used to paint *Mustang Squadron* in 1964 and the picture of a beaming Nazi soldier that served as the basis for the 1965 painting *Uncle Rudi* (the subject of which was indeed Richter's uncle). "I was surprised by photography," Richter told Kimmelman, "which we all use so massively every day. Suddenly, I saw it in a new way, as a picture that offered me a new view, free of all the conventional criteria I had always associated with art. It had no style, no composition, no judgment. It freed me from personal experience. For the first time, there was nothing to it: it was pure picture. That's why I wanted to have it, to show it—not use it as a means to painting, but use painting as a means to photography." At the same time, Richter's deliberate obscuring of the images reminded viewers not to confuse representations with reality and "accentuated the artificiality rather than the verisimilitude of the images," as stated in the abbreviated catalog for the 2002 show *Gerhard Richter: Forty Years of Painting*, held at the Museum of Modern (MoMA) in New York.

Since the late 20th century, many critics have suggested that painting has become irrelevant; some have said that it is too closely linked to the world of privilege, while others have maintained that it offers escape from reality rather than any significant commentary on it. Still others have said that the possibilities of painting have simply been exhausted by 500 years of experimentation. Some art critics have interpreted Richter's faded, blurred realist paintings—and his insistence on alternating between greatly disparate styles—as deliberate comments on painting's lack of vitality as an artistic medium. Richter, however, has repeatedly defended painting. He told Benjamin Buchloh, as quoted by Kenneth Baker in the *San Francisco Chronicle* (March 26, 1989), that declaring painting to be defunct "seems to me like saying that language is no longer useful because it's a bourgeois inheritance, or that now we should print texts on cups or chair legs instead of in books. I'm still bourgeois enough to eat with a knife and fork, and to paint with oil on canvas." On the Web site for MoMA's 2002 *Gerhard Richter* show, it is noted that painting is "an art form fewer and fewer of [Richter's] closest supporters have believed in and much of the general public has taken for granted, at high cost to painting's ability to convey fresh meaning. In any event, it is a medium that has come to depend for its survival on Richter's severe scrutiny—and it has survived and thrived in large measure because of it."

Richter, who had produced some abstract paintings when he first arrived in West Germany, began experimenting with abstraction again in the mid-1960s, mainly through the painting of color charts. In 1966, for example, he painted *Six Colors*, a large (approximately six feet by five feet) canvas consisting of six equal-sized rectangular blocks of color separated by narrow white borders. *Six Colors* and other, similar works seemed to fall under the heading of minimalism—an abstract form that usually employs large, geometric shapes—but they are also realistic works, in that they are representations of the actual color charts used in paint stores. "It was one of the few pretexts for making an abstract painting that Richter could find," Kenneth Baker surmised, "embarrassed as he was by all the 'spiritual' baggage attached to abstraction by painters such as Piet Mondrian and Josef Albers."

It was not until the late 1970s that Richter returned unapologetically to abstract painting. These works, which usually featured bright colors and thick, bold strokes, are dramatic and attention-grabbing in a way that is quite different from his photo-based portraits and landscapes. At the same time, they have a precision and apparent calculatedness that flies in the face of Abstract Expressionism, a still-dominant movement begun in the 1940s and exemplified by the passionate artistic freedom of Jackson Pollock. Describing to Kimmelman the process of painting his abstractions, Richter said, "At the beginning, I am totally free, and it's fun, like being a child. The paintings can look good for a day or an hour. Over time, they change. In the end, you become like a chess player. . . . Finally, one day I enter the room and say, 'Checkmate.' Then sometimes I need a break, a quiet job, like a landscape. But I always need to paint abstracts again. I need that pleasure." (Between 1993 and 1998 Richter produced more than 250 abstract paintings.)

Throughout the 1970s and much of the 1980s, Richter worked primarily in two modes: photograph-based landscapes and portraits, and abstract paintings. In the early 1980s he also created a series of paintings of skulls and candles, including *Two Candles* (1982), which shows two burning white candles against a subdued, gray background that suggests a dimly lit room. Critics and others were puzzled by the religious undertones of the paintings, and they did not sell well—at least not until Richter began to gain worldwide recognition in the late 1980s.

Much of that recognition came from a series of 15 paintings collectively titled *October 18, 1977*. The black-and-white paintings were derived from photographs of members of the Red Army Faction (also known as the Baader-Meinhof Group), a West German, leftist terrorist group founded by Andreas Baader and Ulrike Meinhof. Protesting against materialism, the Cold War, and the Vietnam War, among other things, the Red Army Faction conducted a series of robberies, shootings, and bombings on U.S. army bases. Six members were caught and imprisoned in 1972. Over the next several years, various protests were made for the release of the six prisoners. On the morning of October 18, 1977, hijackers of a plane negotiated to exchange hostages for the release of the four remaining Red Army prisoners (two had died in jail). By the end of the day, all but one of the hijackers had been killed, the hostages had been released, and three of the four prisoners had died in jail. (The fourth survived a stab wound in the chest.) Officials announced that the cause of death of the three prisoners was suicide. The events of that day caused an uproar in Germany and abroad, polarizing the left and right. Richter's paintings include portraits as well as representations of the dead bodies, of a phonograph in which one Red Army Faction member was said to have hidden the gun he used to kill himself, and of Red Army Faction coffins as they were carried through a crowd of supporters and police. The paintings are seemingly neutral in terms of their viewpoint, their hazy, black-and-white images offering little concrete grounds for interpretation. But when they were made public, more than 10 years after the incident, the paintings caused an uproar. Those sympathetic to the Red Army Faction members found the images too disparaging; those unsympathetic found them too complimentary. "I was standing outside watching how people, on both sides, ignored the truth because of their beliefs, beliefs that made them crazy," Richter told Kimmelman. "That was the point of the pictures." Richter further explained, "I suppose they also had to do with my father, the Nazis, being skeptical of all systems, all manias. In the 70s, political positions were so clearly split in Germany—the country was so divided over the Baader-Meinhof group—and I was annoyed by both sides."

After the Baader-Meinhof paintings put him in the public eye, Richter's work began to appear in more exhibitions, both in Germany and elsewhere. In the winter and spring of 1989, the San Francisco Museum of Modern Art put on a retrospective of Richter's work. Baker, commenting on the show, noted, "There is a strong conceptual streak in Richter's art. That is, it is not for the eye alone, and many people will feel that it is not enough for the eye. You are forced to consider how the image and object you see have been processed and why." In 1994 another retrospective of Richter's work was mounted in various places around the world. Max Kozloff, reviewing the mounting at the Paris Museum of Modern Art for *Art in America* (September 1994), declared that it "reaffirmed [that Richter is] someone to reckon with," but he also stated that Richter is "self-repressed. He doesn't know how to get his feelings out, and disguises this inability with his strange procedures. This continues to be his plight as an artist, one that was driven home by an exhibition that managed to be both stifled and grandiose."

The new millennium saw continued interest in Richter's art. On February 14, 2002 MoMA launched a retrospective of his work, *Gerhard Richter: Forty Years of Painting.* Shortly before the exhibit opened, Richter was featured on the covers of *Artforum, Art in America,* and the *New York Times Magazine.* A gala black-tie preview dinner for the MoMA show lured 500 guests. The exhibition itself, which consisted of 188 of his paintings, was received enthusiastically. Blake Gopnik, writing for the *Washington Post* (March 24, 2002), called it "one of the most important and impressive exhibitions of the last decade." Jerry Saltz, who referred to the show in the *Village Voice* (March 5, 2002) as a "Gerhard-is-God moment," wrote, "I find much of Richter's work strangely unsatisfying, mechanical, and dour. He is praised for being exceptionally 'changeable,' but his veerings between abstraction and representation have a predictable rhythm." Saltz conceded, however, that Richter's work is "done so well—with such intelligence, doggedness, and self-conscious belief in painting's power—and it's been so influential that not granting Richter his due is foolhardy, blind, and more my problem than his."

Richter lives in a suburb of Cologne, Germany, with his third wife, Sabine Moritz, and their two children, Moritz, seven, and Ella, five. — P.G.H.

Suggested Reading: *Art in America* p98+ Sep. 1994; *Art Journal* p89+ Fall 1996; *New York Times Magazine* p6+ Jan. 27, 2002; *San Francisco Chronicle* p14 Mar. 26, 1989, p6 Jan. 21, 1996; *U.S. News & World Report* p54+ Feb. 11, 2002; *Village Voice* p49 May 23, 1995, with photos; Storr, Robert. *Gerhard Richter: Forty Years of Painting,* 2002

Selected Books: *Gerhard Richter: Abstract Paintings,* 1979; *Gerhard Richter,* 1993; *Daily Practice of Painting: Writings and Interviews, 1962-1993,* 1995; *Gerhard Richter: 100 Pictures,* 1996; *Atlas: Of the Photographs Collages and Sketches,* 1997; *Gerhard Richter: Paintings,* 1997; *Gerhard Richter: Landscapes,* 1998; *Gerhard Richter: October 18, 1977,* 2000; Gerhard Richter: Watercolors: 1964-1997 (with Robert Storr), 2000

---

## Riley, Terry

*June 24, 1935– Composer; musician*

*Address: c/o Robert Friedman Presents, 1353 Fourth Ave., San Francisco, CA 94122*

One of the trailblazers of minimalist music, the composer and musician Terry Riley has gone far beyond the achievement of his well-known 1964 composition *In C* to influence musicians ranging from the composer Philip Glass to the rocker Pete Townshend. With more than 35 recordings of his work released since 1966, Riley is a prolific artist who has drawn inspiration from myriad musical styles: ragtime, jazz, classical, Indian raga, and many others. Originally focused on keyboard and violin, he has gone on to compose works for saxophone, voice, guitar, Eastern instruments, and orchestras. "Something in me still wants to do everything," he told Christian Kiefer for the *Sacto News and Review* (May 10, 2001, on-line). Acknowledging to John Allison of the London *Times* (October 20, 1998) that he could be called an American pioneer, he said, "Well, I kind of fit that label, if anybody in America does. I've been interested in very singular sorts of musical pursuits, usually right outside mainstream ideas. I didn't purposely set out to do that, I guess it's just my nature."

Betty Freeman/Courtesy of Robert Friedman Presents

Terry Riley was born on June 24, 1935 in Colfax, California, and grew up in two small northern California towns, Weimar and Redding. His interest in music began when he was a child. The first instrument to engage his attention was the violin; he later took up the piano as well, learning to play by ear, as he told Mark Towns in an interview for *Jazz Houston* (February 13, 2001, on-line): "I had teachers, but essentially I was teaching myself." In high school he was part of a band that played standards at school dances and other events. He also became well versed in classical piano music, as well as other styles. Riley attended San Francisco State College (now San Francisco State University) and earned a master's degree in music at the University of California at Berkeley in 1962 (some sources say 1961). To pay for school, he played ragtime at San Francisco bars.

At Berkeley Riley became a friend and collaborator of LaMonte Young, a budding musician and minimalist composer who had studied jazz; both Riley and Young were influenced by the growing trends of atonal music and psychedelic drugs. While in graduate school Riley found work with Anna Halprin's Dance Company, and in 1960 he composed *Mescalin Mix* for the company. "I was working with tape loops. . . . I had very funky primitive equipment, in fact technology wasn't very good no matter how much money you had," he recalled for Gamall and Ammon Haggerty in an October 1992 interview posted on *qaswa.com*. "Using these machines I would take tapes and run them into my yard and around a wine bottle. . . . I would cut the tape into all different sizes . . . and I would record onto one machine just sound on sound. I would build up this kind of unintelligible layer. . . . It was like primitive sampling." Riley became intrigued by the possibility of creating, in a live performance, sounds similar to those he had produced by machine. The idea, he explained to Gamall and Ammon Haggerty, was "to take repetition, take music fragments and make it live. Musicians would be able to play it and create this kind of abstract fabric of sound." Out of this concept came the 1964 composition *In C*, a seminal piece that earned Riley a reputation as the "father of minimalism." Minimalist music, David Sterritt explained in the *Christian Science Monitor* (January 19, 2001), is meant to be "—well, minimal. Its rhythms are steady, its textures are consistent, its melodies are closer to scales and arpeggios than to the tunes you hum in the shower."

The score of *In C* occupies less than a page of sheet music. The piece can be performed by any number of musicians playing any variety of instruments. Even the length of the piece can vary in performance from 30 minutes to over three hours. *In C* consists of 53 short riffs in the key of C, beginning with a chord made up of C and E. Each musician plays each riff, in order, for as long as he or she desires; the piece ends with all of the musicians playing the 53d pattern in unison. Over the course of the piece, there are two anomalies—an F-sharp toward the middle and a B-flat near the end—but the overriding effect of *In C* has been described variously as "melodic" and "hypnotic." "Usually, once you get the thing started, it just runs on and on," Riley told T. R. Reid for the *Washington Post* (November 15, 1998). "The only danger is that the players like to stop every once in a while to listen to what's happening. And if too many of them do that at once—there's no piece." "*In C* was a more psychedelic thing," Riley explained to Ed Ward for the *Wall Street Journal* (February 12, 1997, on-line). "We were more interested in states of consciousness, out-of-the-body experiences, and so on." The piece also presaged Riley's later compositions in that it grew from a meld of different influences, as the composer recalled to John Allison for the London *Times* (October 20, 1998, on-line): "I'd been working with tape loops and repetition, but all the jazz and world music pushed me in the direction of trance music based on repetition." *In C* was first recorded and marketed by Columbia Records in the late 1960s and has been performed thousands of times since its debut, in November 1964.

In 1965 Riley moved to New York, learned to play the soprano saxophone, and embarked on new compositions for saxophone and electronic keyboards, including *Poppy Nogood and the Phantom Band* (1968) and *A Rainbow in Curved Air* (1968). Also in the late 1960s, he began a series of 10 p.m.-to-sunrise performances (laid-back predecessors of all-night rave dance parties), the first of which was staged at the Philadelphia College of Art on November 17, 1967. The college "wanted to have a concert in an art gallery where people could bring their families and sleep in hammocks and sleeping bags," Riley explained to Theresa Stern for the on-line music magazine *Perfect Sound Forever* (March 1997). "They could relax, listen to music or sleep." Riley took his all-night concerts on tour with a visual artist, Bob Benson, who set up strobe lights and Mylar screens, inviting people to dance or perform acrobatics during the show. "One of my specialties was to be able to play for a really long time without stopping," Riley told Gamall and Ammon Haggerty, "and I would play these repeated patterns for hours and hours and I wouldn't seem to get tired. I guess I have a lot of energy." Riley's work inspired rock-and-roll artists of the era, including The Who, who named the song "Baba O'Riley" in his honor, and the Velvet Underground. "In the '60s, the work that I was doing was more parallel to the work that was going on in rock," he told Stern. "There was the similarities and the kinetic energy that both musics had. I think it was only natural."

Riley took his music in a new direction in 1970. Turning his back on increasing recognition in America, he went to India to study raga, vocal and instrumental techniques fundamental to classical Indian music; his teacher was Pandit Pran Nath, a vocalist popular in India who had also worked with LaMonte Young. "Commercial success would have greatly limited what I wanted to do, I wouldn't have been free," the composer told John Allison. "But it was really my passion for Indian music that made me change direction." After several trips to India through the 1970s, he resettled in California and taught music composition and North Indian raga at Mills College, in Oakland, "setting aside a large amount of time for my studies in North Indian classical music, which I felt needed to have six to eight hours a day of my attention and practice," as he explained to K. Robert Schwarz for the *New York Times* (May 6, 1990).

One of Riley's most crucial decisions came in the mid-1970s, when he moved his family to a 26-acre ranch, which he named the Sri Moonshine Ranch, in the remote Sierra Nevada Mountains, close to where he grew up. He welcomed the geographic isolation, which shielded him from outside distractions and helped him to concentrate on his music. "Working at home is like being on retreat," he explained to John Allison, "and if I don't have to deal too much with the outside world I can focus on whatever I want to do. It's hard to be exact, but the nature of the Sierra Nevada has a lot do to with the way I like to create music." While he emerges from that relative isolation to make recordings or collaborate with others, he has always enjoyed returning to his home and routine. "I live a pretty hermetic existence: I just get up and work, day in and day out," he told Howard Hersh for the *Los Angeles Times* (January 10, 1993). "I don't have a social life to speak of and I don't need—or want—one; work is the biggest enjoyment I have. Certainly, we live in the world, I go out and do concerts and get to see people, but it's in little spurts—then I come back."

In 1978 Riley became acquainted with the members of the Kronos Quartet, who were also teaching at Mills. David Harrington, one of the quartet's violinists, persuaded Riley to compose a piece for the group. Riley did not finish the unusual *Sunrise of the Planetary Dream Collector* until 1981, because, he told K. Robert Schwarz, "it took me a while to change gears from being a solo performer who composed music just for myself, to trying to write everything down. At first I tried to make improvisation charts, but that wasn't the way to work with the Kronos; they preferred to have everything written down—at least all the notes." Discovering that he enjoyed composing for string quartets, Riley wrote music for Kronos over the next decade that included nine pieces for string quartet, among them *Cadenza on the Night Plain* (1984) and *Salome Dances for Peace* (1986), the latter of which was recorded and nominated for a Grammy Award in 1989; he also wrote for Kronos a quintet for strings and piano and a concerto for string quartet and orchestra. *Salome Dances for Peace*, a two-hour piece that demonstrates the influences of Asian music, Arabic melodies, jazzy beats, and other elements, required two years to compose. "All the kinds of music Terry loves are in that piece," David Harrington told Schwarz. Harrington added: "It took Terry two years to write, but it took us three years to learn to play."

Continuing to follow his passion for Eastern music, Riley composed pieces based on Indian classical works. In 1989 he formed the group Khayal—the Urdu word for "imagination"—with which he played until 1993. Khayal consisted of between five and 10 musicians, including keyboardists, percussionists, wind instrumentalists, and vocalists. "I've arranged things for the group, but they're more like a head arrangement in a jazz chart for a big band. We'll come into sections where there's an arrangement to pull us all together, and then from there it goes into improvisation," Riley told Schwarz.

Riley left Khayal to devote more time to an orchestral-operatic project based on the life of Adolf Wolfli, an early-20th-century Swiss artist who, as a schizophrenic, had spent much of his life confined to an asylum. In October 1992 at the Los Angeles County Museum, Riley organized a multimedia theater event called "The St. Adolf Ring," based on Wolfli's life and presented by his newly minted theater company, the Travelling-Avantt-Gaard. Riley's *Four Wolfli Portraits* (1993) is a piece in three movements, one of which—"The Violincellist of Salamanca"—is based on one of Wolfli's paintings of the same title. "I feel a kinship with Wolfli," the composer explained to Howard Hersh. "I keep thinking about him. All artists work out of some inner necessity but his was a compulsion, and it was the only refuge he had. . . . Discovering Wolfli was like finding a colleague, but it's more like a teacher or a kindred spirit—but for sure, someone who's farther advanced. The only thing I could do was create a piece as a way of honoring someone who has been a teacher through his work."

Over his decades of learning and composing, Riley has outgrown his original label as a "minimalist," a development that suits him, as he told John Allison: "Yes, *In C* defined minimalism, but if you're looking for the real father, it has to be LaMonte Young. My piece had a form that was greatly imitated, but it is also only a little part of the way I make music. It's always a mistake for musicians to work under a single banner, to say, OK, I'm going to write a Minimalist piece now—that's not what creativity's about." His most recent works include *Three Requiem Quartets*, for strings; *The Dream*, an evening-length micro-tonal piano solo, commissioned by the Kanagawa Foundation in Yokohama, Japan; and *The Book of Abbeyozzud*, a set of 24 pieces for solo guitar and guitar ensemble. He has recently formed a new musical group, Terry Riley and the All-Stars, which includes his son Gyan as a guitarist.

Riley and his wife, Ann, continue to live in the Sierra Nevada Mountains. They have three grown children: Gyan, Shahn, and Colleen. — K.S.

Suggested Reading: (London) *Times* p36 Oct. 20, 1998, with photo; *Los Angeles Times* p51 Jan. 10, 1993, with photo; *New York Times* II p21+ May 6, 1990; *Wall Street Journal* A p14 Feb. 12, 1997; *Washington Post* G p13 Nov. 15, 1998, with photo

Selected Compositions: *In C*, 1964; *A Rainbow in Curved Air*, 1968; *Cadenza on the Night Plain*, 1984; *Salome Dances for Peace*, 1986; *Cactus Rosary*, 1990; *Four Wolfli Portraits*, 1993

Selected Recordings: *Reed Streams*, 1966; *In C*, 1968; *The Persian Surgery Dervishes*, 1972; *Salome Dances for Peace*, 1989; *The Book of Abbeyozzud*, 1999

Courtesy of Sylvia Rimm

## Rimm, Sylvia B.

*Apr. 16, 1935– Educational psychologist; writer; radio talk-show host*

*Address: Family Achievement Clinic, P.O. Box 24242, Cleveland, OH 44124-0242*

The parenting expert Sylvia B. Rimm has frequently dispensed this tip to mothers and fathers: "If you don't feel in charge, pretend you are." Trained as an educational psychologist, Rimm originally specialized in the psychology of academically gifted and otherwise talented youngsters. She has since worked within other realms of child psychology and parenting. Summarizing her philosophy, she told Christopher Evans for the Cleveland, Ohio, *Plain Dealer* (May 8, 1994), "Kids can't bring themselves up. Parents, adults, teachers really need to take the responsibility for guiding and leading them." Rimm has shared her advice in her books, among them *How to Parent So Children Will Learn, Sylvia Rimm on Raising Kids*, and *See Jane Win: The Rimm Report on How 1,000 Girls Became Successful Women*, the last of which she co-wrote with her two daughters. She has also offered guidance in her weekly syndicated newspaper advice column and articles for magazines and journals; in her weekly public-radio call-in show, *Sylvia Rimm on Raising Kids*; and on NBC's *Today* show, for which she serves as a consultant.

The youngest of three daughters, Rimm was born Sylvia Barkan on April 16, 1935 in Perth Amboy, New Jersey. Her parents, Harry and Reva Barkan, were Jewish immigrants who had fled the growing anti-Semitism in Latvia in 1929. After settling in New Jersey, Harry Barkan got a factory job, and his wife took in laundry. The couple eventually saved enough to open a small grocery store, where they worked seven days a week, aided by their daughters. "The message was that my parents were working that hard so that their life and my life would be better, and that work was the way you did that. It was really the American dream," Rimm told Kristin Choo for the *Chicago Tribune* (September 6, 1998). Rimm was a straight-A student in high school, and her guidance counselor encouraged her to attend college. Money was scarce, but she succeeded in winning several scholarships, and her eldest sister, Vivian, who was working as a secretary, purchased a new wardrobe for her to wear at school.

Rimm chose to enroll at Douglass College, the women's division of Rutgers University, in New Brunswick, New Jersey. She thus became, in 1953, the first member of her family to attend college. The courses were harder than she had anticipated, as she explained to Evans: "I didn't know what to expect. It was a hard adjustment. . . . I was an excellent student in high school but I never really studied. There wasn't any need to. When I got to college I got a shock." She was distraught when she was not invited to join the campus honor society, but she succeeded in overcoming the blow to her confidence, by "making a personal commitment to find a place where I could make a small contribution to society," as she told Evans. "That's a reasonable goal and that's kind of what has guided me."

Rimm graduated from Rutgers with a B.A. in sociology in 1957. That year she married another Rutgers graduate, Alfred "Buck" Rimm. She taught elementary school for a year, and then both Rimms pursued advanced degrees, she in educational psychology and he in epidemiology. Her studies were interrupted by pregnancies as well as by moves required by Buck Rimm's participation in the Reserve Officers Training Corps (ROTC). "First place I went back to graduate school was Rutgers," she told Evans. "Got pregnant. Dropped out. Then I went to the University of New York at Buffalo. Got pregnant. Dropped out." Nevertheless, Rimm was determined to finish her education and fulfill her goals. She told Evans, "I wanted a career. It was very important to me. I wanted to do more than just be a housewife and a homemaker." In between moves and homemaking, Rimm taught elementary school. In the late 1960s, with three children in tow, the Rimms moved to Wisconsin, settling on 500 acres halfway between Madison and Milwaukee. They planted 10,000 apple trees and turned the land into a working fruit farm. The family called the business Apple Bapple Orchards and harvested and sold the fruit themselves. "It was hard work," Rimm recalled to Evans, "but it was wonderful training for the children. The kids really learned how to be workers in partnership with Mom and Dad."

Rimm later returned to graduate school, as a part-time student at the University of Wisconsin at Madison. She again got pregnant, but two weeks after giving birth to her fourth child, she returned to her classes. It took some effort for her to persuade her advisers to permit her to make gifted children the focus of her graduate studies. "I was told there was no need to work with gifted children and there would *never* be a need, and they were quite adamant about it," she explained to Mary Mihaly for *Ohio Week* (November 26–December 2, 1993). "There was not a single course I could have taken. I had to really create my own arena." Rimm earned a master's degree in educational psychology in 1971 and a Ph.D. in the same field in 1976. (Her daughter Ilonna, who was then 18, received her bachelor's degree in molecular biology on the same day that Rimm was awarded her doctorate.)

Earlier, in 1973, Rimm had begun working as the director of the Educational Assessment Service Inc., in Watertown, Wisconsin, a testing service for both gifted children and those labeled underachievers. While there she came to the realization that many intellectually gifted children did not work up to their potential and a portion were at risk of dropping out of school. She discussed her ideas with members of her local school board and, in addition, members of the Wisconsin school superintendent's office, working with them to develop testing procedures to recognize gifted youngsters and to create enrichment programs for them. In the late 1970s and early 1980s, Rimm also taught courses in psychology and education at Mount Mary College, a small women's school in Milwaukee.

In 1981 Rimm founded the Family Achievement Clinic, a counseling service for children and families. Originally intended to help gifted but underachieving students, it has since expanded to serve children with any kind of academic or familial problem that impedes educational progress. According to Rimm, parents and the media have actually encouraged underachievement, albeit unwittingly. As she explained to Cheryl Heckler-Feltz for *Ohio Magazine* (November 1998), "Here we have paraded on television all these characters who don't want to do work and don't value success, and kids take them on as models. We also have a society of loving parents, but they're terribly afraid to watch their kids struggle. When kids say things are hard, their parents assume they have to bail them out. So kids aren't taught to enjoy challenge. They are taught instead to enjoy what is easy." By 1993 the Family Achievement Clinic was operating at four sites in Wisconsin.

In the mid-1980s Rimm began to write and self-publish books. Her book *Underachievement Syndrome: Causes and Cures* (1986), which contains material culled from her work at the Educational Assessment Service and the Family Achievement Clinic, sold 80,000 copies and brought her national attention. She undertook a cross-country speaking tour in support of the book, and the year it was published she was invited to be a regular guest on the psychologist Tom Clark's call-in show, broadcast on Wisconsin Public Radio; that arrangement continued until 1991. Her own small company, Apple Publishing, issued *How to Parent So Children Will Learn* (1990) and *Sylvia Rimm on Raising Kids* (1992). In 1991 Rimm began to write a newspaper advice column on parenting; the following year Creators Syndicate picked it up for distribution to 35 newspapers across the country.

As Rimm was building her reputation, she drew strength and inspiration from her husband and four children—Ilonna, David, Eric, and Sara, all of whom have earned Ph.D. degrees and two of whom have M.D. degrees as well. "My kids are so well-adjusted it's embarrassing," she told Mary Mihaly. "[They] were parented by two people who worked together at parenting them. And they're nice, normal kids. They're not geniuses, but they love challenges, love to think, love to learn." Rimm has said that she developed some of her common-sense parenting ideas by using her children as models. "I tried a lot of things I learned about in the classroom on my kids," she told Kristin Choo. "Especially poor Sara. She was one big experiment." In the Rimm household the parents always presented a united front, even if they disagreed privately. Perhaps even more unusual, they did not own a television. "My husband and I felt that if we had a television, it would probably be on all the time and would take away from our family life," Rimm told Cheryl Heckler-Feltz. "I know it seems strange, but we felt it would be a constant battle."

Although she has not achieved the wide popularity of such child-care experts as the pediatrician T. Berry Brazelton or the psychologist Penelope Leach, Sylvia Rimm has gained greater recognition since the early 1990s, thanks in part to her weekly, hour-long radio call-in program, *Sylvia Rimm on Raising Kids*; produced and distributed by Wisconsin Public Radio, it debuted in 1992. In 1993 Rimm moved to Cleveland, Ohio, after her husband became the chair of the Department of Epidemiology and Biostatistics at Case Western Reserve University. "Being the good husband that he is, he said 'That sounds like a good opportunity, but you'll have to make something for my wife, too,'" she told Mary Mihaly. She accepted the university's offer of a position as clinical professor of psychiatry and pediatrics at its medical school. (Benjamin Spock, the author of *The Common Sense Book of Baby and Child Care* [1946], who was considered one of the foremost child-care experts in the world during his lifetime, was also affiliated with Case Western Reserve.) Rimm also opened a Cleveland branch of her Family Achievement Clinic. But the standing that she had enjoyed in Wisconsin was slow to build in her new environment. "I didn't want to come to Cleveland," she admitted to Christopher Evans in 1994. "Why would I want to leave home where we'd lived for 26 years? Where I worked very hard to become successful?" She added: "I'm still much better known in Wisconsin than I am in Ohio. When I first came here and went to talk at a school, I had six people who came to hear me. I was just crushed. I'm accustomed to hundreds coming."

Within a year of her move to Cleveland, Rimm was invited to be a contributing consultant to the *Today* show, NBC's morning television news and variety program. She believes that one of the show's producer's becoming pregnant contributed to NBC's decision to hire her. "People who have children are much more interested in putting me on television or radio than people who don't," she explained to Carol Lawson for the *New York Times* (October 10, 1996). Once a month beginning in February 1994, Rimm has traveled to New York for a live morning taping with the anchor Katie Couric. She has appeared regularly on local Cleveland morning television programs, too, and production of her weekly radio call-in show was transferred from Wisconsin to Ohio Public Radio. In addition, she signed a three-book deal with Crown, a New York–based publisher. The books appeared in rapid succession: *Why Bright Kids Get Poor Grades and What You Can Do About It*, in 1995; *Dr. Sylvia Rimm's Smart Parenting: How to Raise a Happy Achieving Child*, in 1996; and a revised edition of *How to Parent So Children Will Learn*, in 1997.

One of Rimm's most successful projects to date is a three-year study she undertook with her daughters, Ilonna Rimm, a pediatric oncologist, and Sara Rimm-Kaufman, a clinical psychologist, to determine what factors help to create successful, high-achieving, happy women. She and her daughters conducted more than 1,200 interviews in the course of their study. "We looked at [the women's] pasts to see how they were motivated to achieve," Sylvia Rimm explained to Barbara Sandler for *People* (October 18, 1999). The Rimms discovered that participating in competitive activities, traveling either with family or alone, and having strong, supportive role models were critical elements of their subjects' development. "It's important to be in an environment where people believe in you," Sylvia Rimm told Sandler. The book that emerged from their research, *See Jane Win: The Rimm Report on How 1,000 Girls Became Successful Women* (1999), received mixed critical reviews but became a *New York Times* best-seller. A companion volume, *How Jane Won: 55 Women Share How They Grew from Ordinary Girls to Extraordinary Women*, written by Rimm and Sara Rimm-Kaufman, came out in 2001. *How Jane Won* includes interviews with and biographical information from, among others, the space-shuttle commander Eileen Collins; Christine Todd Whitman, the head of the Environmental Protection Agency and former governor of New Jersey; Supreme Court justice Sandra Day O'Connor; the news anchor Jane Pauley; the singer and actress Florence Henderson; the novelist Jacquelyn Mitchard; and Connie Matsui, the head of Girl Scouts of America.

Rimm has received many honors, including a 1987 Meritorious Service Award from the Wisconsin Association of Educators of the Gifted and Talented, a 1994 Distinguished Woman Scholar Award from the Virginia Commonwealth University School of Education, a 1996 Distinguished Achievement Award from the Douglass Society of Rutgers University, and a 1998 Excellence in Education Honor Award from Pi Lamda Theta. She told Kristin Choo, "That decision I made in freshman or sophomore year of college worked out pretty well. Maybe I didn't set the world on fire, but I made a little contribution, a little difference. And I'm having fun in the process. It's creative, it's interesting, it's helpful. And I'm not done yet." Rimm and her husband have at least six grandchildren. —K.S.

Suggested Reading: *Chicago Tribune* Womanews p3 Sep. 6, 1998, with photos; (Cleveland, Ohio) *Plain Dealer Sunday* p8+ May 8, 1994, with photos; *New York Times* C p8 Oct. 10, 1996, with photo; *People* p137+ Oct. 18, 1999, with photos; *Ohio Week* p16+ Nov. 26–Dec. 2, 1993, with photos

Selected Books: *Underachievement Syndrome: Causes and Cures*, 1986; *How to Parent So Children Will Learn*, 1990; *Sylvia Rimm on Raising Kids*, 1992; *Why Bright Kids Get Poor Grades and What You Can Do About It*, 1995; with Sara Rimm-Kaufman and Ilonna Rimm—*See Jane Win: The Rimm Report on How 1,000 Girls Became Successful Women*, 1999; with Sara Rimm-Kaufman—*How Jane Won: 55 Women Share How They Grew from Ordinary Girls to Extraordinary Women*, 2001

---

## Rimsza, Skip

(RIM-zuh)

*Mar. 31, 1955– Mayor of Phoenix (Republican)*

*Address: Phoenix City Hall, 200 Washington St., 11th Fl., Phoenix, AZ 85003*

Skip Rimsza, the mayor of Phoenix, Arizona, likes to refer to the residents of the city he governs as "customers," and he views his job as clear and simple: to provide those residents with good service. In an essay by Rimsza titled "City Government 101," which appeared on the Web site *Ad 2 Phoenix*, the mayor wrote, "Unlike state government (and most certainly unlike the federal government) city officials don't sit around debating lofty philosophical issues on a mostly partisan basis. While the United States Congress debates special prosecutors, campaign finance reform and who should be our ambassador to Mexico—the city of Phoenix picks up your garbage twice a week, for about 11 bucks a month, and we supply the containers." On October 25, 1994, having won a special mayoral election—which followed the departure of the incumbent mayor, Paul Johnson, in a bid for the Arizona governorship—Rimsza became one of the youngest mayors in the history of Phoenix, the seventh-largest city in the United States. He was reelected to four-year terms in 1995 and 1999. Rim-

Matt York/AP

*Skip Rimsza*

sza, a moderate Republican who had served as a Phoenix city councilman from 1990 to 1994 before becoming the city's 50th mayor, has distinguished himself during his eight years in the mayor's office by running an efficient, nonpartisan local government.

The mayor was born Anton Rimsza in Chicago, Illinois, on March 31, 1955. He moved with his parents to Phoenix at an early age and has never left. He received his bachelor's degree from Phoenix College, and he owned a realty business before entering politics. In 1990 he was elected to a four-year term on the Phoenix City Council as the representative of District 3. He served as vice mayor during 1993, and the next year he became the mayor of Phoenix; with 57 percent of the vote, he beat his closest competitor, the former city councilwoman Linda Nadolski, who captured about 30 percent of the ballots. (According to an Associated Press article dated October 26, 1994, only about 16 percent of eligible voters turned out for the election.) Rimsza took 60 percent of the ballots in the 1995 mayoral election. His three goals from early on have been, in Rimsza's own words, "to renew our neighborhoods, to expand our economy, and to protect our families." His vision of his responsibilities as mayor is centered on a commitment to service. He explained that vision to Evan St. Lifer for *Library Journal* (September 15, 2000): "We all know how we want to be treated as customers, and I want my organization to understand that whether it is checking out a book or applying for a building permit, we always need to keep in mind what the customer wants. We want people to see our long list of amenities and conclude that Phoenix is the best place for them to live." Rimsza does not attend Republican or Democratic national conventions or national political meetings of any other kind, including the U.S. Conference of Mayors. He told St. Lifer, "Those meetings are run by organizations that talk about philosophy. I'm about product. Citizens want the service, the end-product." The mayor also told St. Lifer, "I'm not willing to play the politician's game; I'm just not good at it." Rimsza explained his approach further in his essay on the *Ad 2 Phoenix* Web site: "The best way to describe what city government does," he wrote, "is simple: We provide basic services that, if you weren't buying them from us, you would buy them someplace else. . . . City government is nothing more than customer service. . . . Lastly, the city differs from other levels of government in that it is run on a non-partisan basis. We don't run as Republicans, Democrats, Independents or libertarians. We run as Phoenicians. Why? Because when it comes right down to it, there isn't a Republican way and a Democratic way to fill a pothole. There's just a right way, a professional way. And we've got it down pretty good."

In Phoenix, as in various other western cities, the mayor is not the chief administrative officer. The mayor runs the city council, which appoints a city manager to run the government. Still, as mayor, Rimsza has successfully applied his vision. He has been hard at work, for example, on a housing plan for Phoenix, which is considered to have one of the best real-estate markets in the U.S. in terms of growth and affordability. In 1997 the construction of more than 30,000 new family homes was authorized in the Phoenix area. Rimsza also led a campaign to eradicate graffiti. In his 2001 State of the City address, which appeared on the City of Phoenix Web site, Rimsza noted, "We opened and closed over 36,000 property maintenance issues. . . . We painted out 24,000 pieces of criminal graffiti." Regarding the goal of protecting Phoenix's families, Rimsza stated in the same address that through the Family Advocacy Center, the city had addressed the needs of more than 4,000 victims of domestic violence; and that under his administration violent crimes and property crimes were down by 15 percent, assaults by 21 percent, homicides by 21 percent, burglaries by 27 percent, and auto thefts by 10 percent. Rimsza increased Phoenix's police force by more than 200 officers and established a new unit of the Phoenix Police Department that is dedicated to fighting so-called hate crimes. He introduced a successful truancy program to make sure that children attend school, and he has been a supporter of Phoenix's public-library system. Rimsza, who has been awarded *Library Journal's* Politician of the Year Award four times, was a vital part of a program that has given every first-grader in Phoenix a library card. He also raised over $100,000 for Phoenix's teachers so that they could buy basic teaching materials.

Phoenix, Arizona's capital and largest city, lies on the Salt River in a valley just south of the Grand Canyon. It is known for its natural beauty, boasting an impressive landscape of mountains and desert. One of Rimsza's most ambitious plans as mayor is to purchase and preserve 15,000 acres of the Sonoran Desert directly south of Phoenix to protect it from unchecked development. The people of Phoenix have embraced the plan, and the purchasing of the land began in 2000. Rimsza has added many city parks to Phoenix, including 16 in the year 2000 alone. The mayor also initiated projects to improve the South Phoenix Youth Center, the Cortez Park Lagoon, Mountain Vista Park, and Paradise Valley Park.

Under Rimsza's direction Phoenix passed the first successful bond program since 1988, which has resulted in more than $750 million for city improvements with no tax increases. In the 1990s Phoenix was one of the fastest-growing cities in the U.S., and its population now exceeds 1.3 million. As a result, traffic congestion and jams have become concerns. As a way to combat congestion on the freeways, the construction of a 20.3-mile light electric rail line between Phoenix and Mesa is underway; it is expected to be completed in 2006. Rimsza has pushed for an expansion of the light-rail system. Phoenix's economy has thrived under Rimsza's direction. The city boasts strong technology, electronics manufacturing, trade, and tourism industries. Two major plans that Rimsza put forward in his 2001 State of the City address are to expand downtown Civic Plaza and to create what he has called an "educational cluster" in Copper Square, adding to and expanding the strength of Arizona State University, in downtown Phoenix. In 1993, when Rimsza was vice mayor of the city, Phoenix was named the best-run city in the world by the Bertelsmann Foundation. In his State of the City address on March 20, 2001, which appears on the City of Phoenix Web site, Rimsza noted that *Governing* magazine had named Phoenix the best-run city in the country and that "a whopping 92 percent" of Phoenix residents described the city as "a good place to live."

The mayor is not without detractors. In the *Phoenix New Times* (June 24, 1999), after she complained that Phoenix's elections unfairly favor the incumbent because voter turnout in the city is "historically abysmal," Amy Silverman wrote, "Skip Rimsza's not a bad mayor, per se. I'd say he's been more of a non-mayor. A snoozer, a caretaker . . . with no vision for the future of our city. . . . Skip Rimsza's got a group-hug style of governing: During his last campaign, he handed out pots of flowers, and as mayor he sends out reams of birthday and Christmas cards. . . . But for the most part, he keeps his mouth shut regarding the issues of the day. Rimsza's been lucky. He's been able to keep Phoenix fat and happy—on the surface at least . . ."

Rimsza currently sits on the board of directors of the Stewart Title and Trust Company, and he is a features writer for various trade journals. The mayor is the director of the National Association of Realtors and the Arizona Association of Realtors. He is also a member of the Executive Association of Greater Phoenix. Rimsza lives in Phoenix with his wife, Kim Gill-Rimsza, who runs her own business, the Gill Group. They have a son, Brian, a daughter, Jenny, and triplets, Alexander, Taylor, and Nicole, who were born in 1996. As a young man, Rimsza worked with his brother in Alaska as a hunting guide. He still travels to Alaska, often accompanied by his oldest son, Brian. Rimsza, who drives a 1956 Ford pickup truck, enjoys restoring old cars and trucks. He also likes to make stained glass in his free time. He is fond of riding his bicycle 14 miles to work several times a week.

Concerning the city to which he gives so much of his energy and time, Rimsza told its inhabitants in his May 24, 2000 State of the Neighborhoods address, which appears on the City of Phoenix Web site, "Phoenix, Arizona is as much a part of me as my heart and my soul. I've lived here all my life and I have no plans to leave. I love this place. And it's obvious that you do too." — C.F.T.

Suggested Reading: *azcentral.com*; City of Phoenix Web site; *Library Journal* (on-line) Sep.15, 2000, with photos; U.S. Conference of Mayors Web site; *Who's Who in American Politics 2001-2002*

---

## Romero, Anthony

*1965(?)– Executive director of the American Civil Liberties Union*

*Address: ACLU, 125 Broad St., 18th Fl., New York, NY 10004*

"I learned from my mom and dad the importance of believing in yourself and fighting for what you believe," Anthony Romero, the executive director of the American Civil Liberties Union, told Chris Bull for the *Advocate* (June 19, 2001). "They taught me to treat others with respect but also to demand it in return." The ACLU, founded in 1920, is a nonpartisan organization devoted to defending the civil rights of people in the United States as those rights are delineated in the Constitution and the Bill of Rights. Romero came to the organization in 2001, after a decade of defending human rights in the U.S. and around the world on behalf of the Rockefeller Foundation and then the Ford Foundation. The first Latino and first openly gay man to lead the organization, he arrived with an "overarching goal": "to promote a new generation of committed civil libertarians and civil rights activists," as he stated in an ACLU press release, as quoted in the *Newsletter on Intellectual Freedom* (July 2001). In a prescient statement not long before the September 11, 2001 terrorist attacks on the World Trade Center and the Pentagon, he told Lisa Balmesada for the *Miami Herald* (June 18, 2001), "Our own complacency is our greatest enemy. We give up a lot of our civil liberties because we

Courtesy of the ACLU

*Anthony Romero*

choose not to fight. Americans have been lulled into a false sense of security." After the September 11 attacks, Romero and the ACLU worked assiduously to protect American freedoms, some of which the U.S. government sought to limit (through such procedures as wire tapping, racial profiling, and detention of immigrants) as a means of preventing further attacks or meting out immediate justice for terror victims. "We need to defend security and at the same time protect freedom," Romero explained to Arian Campo-Flores for *Newsweek* (December 31, 2001/January 7, 2002). "The two don't have to be on a collision course."

The son of Demetrio and Coralie Romero, both of whom had immigrated from rural Puerto Rico, Anthony Romero was born in about 1965 in the New York City borough of the Bronx. He has one sister. His father held jobs as a janitor and maintenance worker at a big hotel. Impressed by her son's interest in reading, young Anthony's mother encouraged him to focus on school. He attended a Catholic elementary school in New York City until the family moved to Little Falls, New Jersey, when Demetrio Romero secured a job as a banquet waiter at the hotel. The move followed a long-fought racial discrimination battle that the elder Romero had won with the help of the hotel workers' union. Anthony Romero excelled in school, but because neither of his parents had completed high school, he never thought about attending college. His academic achievement, however—he graduated second in his high-school class—led college recruiters to seek him out. As a result, he enrolled at Princeton University, in Princeton, New Jersey.

At Princeton, Romero studied at the Woodrow Wilson School of Public and International Affairs. "I loved the focus on undergraduate teaching, and my interests were always in international affairs and human rights," he told Katherine Hobson for the *Princeton Alumni Weekly* (March 13, 2002, online). He spent his junior year at a college in Colombia. Fluent in Spanish, he wrote his senior thesis on a topic close to his heart: Latin Americans' immigration to the United States. After he graduated from Princeton, in 1987, he entered Stanford Law School (a division of Stanford University), in Stanford, California, where he again excelled. At both Princeton and Stanford, Romero was a beneficiary of affirmative action, a practice he staunchly supports. "I earned the grades, but affirmative action got me through the door," he told Lynda Richardson for the *New York Times* (January 8, 2002). "Very often, it's misunderstood as being about quotas or being unmeritorious. It's about leveling the playing field."

After earning a law degree, in 1990, Romero felt a pull toward public-interest law. Focusing on charitable foundations, he returned to New York to work for the Rockefeller Foundation, where he oversaw the organization's civil rights endeavors. After two years he moved to the Ford Foundation, a global nonprofit organization that works to distribute grants and funding for various projects. In his first position there, he served as the foundation's program officer for civil rights and racial justice; after five years he was promoted to director of human rights and international cooperation. Through his work at the Ford Foundation, Romero traveled to far-flung locales, including China and Kenya. He also learned to manage funds and grants, a key qualification for working for the ACLU. In May 2001 he was named the ACLU's sixth director, succeeding Ira Glasser, who had headed the organization for 23 years. In a rare display of complete harmony, the 83-member ACLU board voted unanimously for Romero's appointment. "What I have achieved is an enormous testament to this country, so I am incredibly patriotic," he told Arian Campo-Flores. Defending civil liberties and human rights, he added, is "the ultimate act of patriotism."

As the director of the ACLU, Romero became responsible for overseeing a huge spectrum of activities. "Most civil rights and civil liberties organizations focus on a specific issue or a particular constituency," he explained in an ACLU press release (May 1, 2001). "The ACLU, in contrast, is the only organization that defends the civil liberties and civil rights of all Americans." As he explained to Rose Gutfeld for the *Ford Foundation Report* (Winter 2002), he believes there are four issues of particular importance to the ACLU: "The first has to do with free speech and new technologies. . . . The next generation of advocacy will require us to ensure that speech on the Internet is not just uncensored but free—in the sense of being open and available to all, and free from the restrictions on content and opinion that take place in the print and broadcast media, where powerful individuals and a handful of media companies exercise control." The second area of concern to the ACLU, Romero stated, is the U.S. criminal-justice system and the country's huge prison population—nearly two million men and women, the large majority of whom are members of ethnic minorities and are poorly educated or uneducated and were underemployed or unemployed before their incarceration. The ACLU opposes the death penalty and mandatory sentencing and advocates prison reform and a halt to racial profiling. "We may be headed for a situation where prison building is pursued with the same type of civic pride and support enjoyed by the national highway-building program of the 1950s," Romero told Gutfeld. The third priority of the ACLU is affirmative action—particularly with regard to redistricting, to equalize minority representation, and voting reform, to ensure that no registered voters are denied the opportunity to cast their ballots and that all votes are counted. As for the fourth issue, the ACLU has continued to pursue its goal of maintaining privacy for American citizens and visitors to the country. "Solutions to the privacy issues will not be easy because these involve highly technical matters and ethically complex choices," Romero told Gutfeld. Using the mapping of the human genome as an example, he added, "It is an awesome development, but it could be wrongly used. . . . That information can be used to map your propensity for illness and disease, life expectancy and behavioral disposition. Such personal information can now be compiled in private databases, bought by the highest bidder and transacted cross-country with the stroke of a key."

One week after Romero took office, the United States was attacked by terrorists. In the weeks and months that followed, Romero and many other ACLU staffers worked overtime in an attempt to maintain the line between personal safety and violations of civil rights. "Civil libertarians are just like anyone else," he told Rose Gutfeld. "We understand the importance of increasing our safety and increasing our security. . . . At the same time, we believe that we should not lose the basic freedoms and basic liberties that are the hallmarks of our democracy because of this fear and uncertainty. The terrorist attacks were meant not only to destroy; they were also meant to intimidate us as a people and to force us to take actions that are not in our best interests." Romero realized that the terrorist attacks marked a pivotal time for civil liberties. "We've been sounding the note that the U.S. must stay safe and free," he told Katherine Hobson. "Right now, young people will grow up in a new climate of civil liberties and civil rights that are being defined at this moment." Following the attacks, the ACLU protested the harassment of Arab-Americans as well as new federal policies allowing for the detainment of more than 1,200 immigrants whose names the Department of Justice refused to reveal. "By all accounts, the overwhelming majority of [the] detainees are Muslims or Arabs, come from Middle Eastern countries, and are noncitizens," according to testimony presented before the Senate Judiciary Committee on December 4, 2001 by the ACLU's president, Nadine Strossen. "Most of these folks have nothing to do with the terrorist attacks, but we are treating them a certain way because of their national origin," Romero said to Gutfeld. "That's not right, and it cuts against our core principles of fairness and equality under the law." The ACLU filed lawsuits in protest, claiming that these immigrants had been denied due process. "Very little information is coming from our government on this key issue," Romero said during a San Francisco press conference, as reported by Alexis Chiu for the San Jose *Mercury News* (January 30, 2002). "That impedes the public's ability to know whether due process of law is alive and well." Further, the ACLU sent letters to consulates, such as Pakistan's and Egypt's, offering legal advice and assistance for their detained citizens. "Our main concern is that there is a growing momentum focusing on a specific community, regarding them as suspicious merely because of where they are from. The government should focus on what they have done, not where they were born," Romero told Jennifer Barrett for *Newsweek* (January 18, 2002, online). The ACLU has also urged the U.S. government to honor guaranteed rights to privacy when crafting new legislation on issues ranging from airport security to the possibility of standardizing the licensing of drivers throughout the U.S., which would result in de facto national IDs for all drivers. "I worry about another attack and the loss of human life," Romero admitted to Lynda Richardson, "then the repercussions that would follow with a second attack, with a further curtailment of civil liberties and civil rights." Romero's office, close to where the World Trade Center once stood, overlooks New York Harbor and the Statue of Liberty. "My job," he told Richardson, "is to make sure no one extinguishes her flame. So far, so good."

Romero, who enjoys cooking in his spare time, lives in Manhattan with his partner. — K.S.

Suggested Reading: *Miami Herald* (on-line) June 18, 2001; *New York Times* A p20 Jan. 8, 2002, with photo; *Newsweek* p78 Dec. 31, 2001/Jan. 7, 2002, with photo; *Wall Street Journal* B p1 Nov. 19, 2001

Courtesy of Robert Ross

## Ross, Robert

*1918(?)– Entrepreneur; medical-school founder*

*Address: Eastern Europe Inc., 345 Third Ave., 17th Fl., New York, NY 10022*

"Entrepreneurship is something you are born with," Robert Ross wrote in a reminiscence for the "Money and Business" section of the *New York Times* (June 10, 2001). "I had it. What is an entrepreneur? One who takes great risks. In many cases you are not successful, but you have to be tenacious." A worker since the age of eight, Ross earned millions of dollars after launching Eastern Europe Inc., an import-export business, in the 1960s; his focus, as its name indicates, was Eastern Europe and the Soviet Union. When N. R. Kleinfield interviewed Ross for the *New York Times* (January 24, 1992), he reported that Ross was doing "in excess of $100 million of business a year, the preponderance of it through barter. Someone wants tennis shoes, he'll take lumber as payment. Give him wheat for fax machines, steel for jeans." Ross struck Kleinfield as "an old-fashioned diehard New York entrepreneur, an individual filled with rhapsodic fantasies who is always playing hunches and looking for angles." At the age of 73, Kleinfield wrote, Ross "remain[ed] obsessed with the new, the different, well, the outlandish."

In the late 1970s Ross founded the Ross University School of Medicine, which to date has produced more than 3,500 doctors. Located on the Caribbean island nation of Dominica, it is the largest offshore medical school in the world, according to its Web site. "Until now, people unable to enter a U.S. medical school had to go to Mexico, Italy or Spain if they really wanted to be doctors," Ross told Jon Schriber for *Forbes* (March 14, 1983). "With us, they have an English-speaking school where most of the teachers are American and know the U.S. medical system." Ross also established a school of veterinary medicine, on the Caribbean island of St. Kitts, in 1982. He is now chairman emeritus of both schools, which he sold in 2000. "With Dr. Ross, the first word that comes to mind would be entrepreneurial, and to that end, a visionary entrepreneur," Richard Ditizio, the managing director of the Palm Beach office of the Citigroup Private Bank and a friend of Ross's, told Stephanie Murphy for the *Palm Beach Daily News* (January 27, 2002). "Despite his chronological age, he has the energy and drive of a much younger man. He's engaging and always interesting. He sees opportunity where others don't. He has enough life experience to be really opportunistic, to create something out of nothing."

The youngest of the four daughters and two sons of Nathan Rosen, a paint contractor, and Minnie Rosen, Robert Ross was born with the surname Rosen in about 1918 and grew up in Detroit, Michigan. When he was eight years old, his father died. To help support his family, he got a job delivering newspapers. By the time he was 15, his route—which included morning and afternoon deliveries—had become one of the biggest in Detroit, and although the Great Depression was raging, he was netting over $100 a week—four times the average weekly salary in the U.S. in 1933. "I got up at 4 a.m. to deliver 200 copies of *The Detroit Free Press*, the morning paper," he recalled in his *New York Times* essay, which was entitled "My First Job" and was written with Jenny Holland. "But I wasn't satisfied with a small paper route. I wanted a huge paper route. So after school I delivered 200 copies of the afternoon paper, *The Detroit News*, to the same apartment buildings." "I was tired a lot," he admitted to N. R. Kleinfield. After his graduation from high school, in about 1936, Ross continued to deliver papers, until a brother-in-law of his persuaded him to join him in the wholesale-pharmaceuticals business. Dissatisfied with his salary—$15 a week—Ross supplemented his pay by selling over-the-counter drugs and other items to grocery stores, which few salesmen had done before then. After concluding that there was little future for him in wholesale drugs, Ross quit his job and enrolled in a business course at the University of Michigan at Ann Arbor. He later abandoned the course to engage in various entrepreneurial pursuits. By age 25 he had married and become a father. In 1944, toward the end of World War II, he was drafted into the U.S. Army. He was shipped to Europe along with many other servicemen to replenish Allied forces after the disastrous Battle of the Bulge, on the German-Belgium border, which had ended with more than 81,000 U.S. casualties. "I stepped off the train and saw dead Americans, dead Germans, and smoldering vehicles and tanks," Ross recalled to Bill Stokes for *50 Plus Lifestyles* (April 2000). "The stench was awful." Unlike many of his friends in his Division, Ross, as a rifleman, survived without injury two major Allied campaigns. While overseas he earned a handsome sum by buying 20 Mickey Mouse watches from a Frenchman and then selling them to Russian soldiers at a price many times what he had paid. Successfully avoiding an army assignment to a bomb-disposal group after the war in Europe ended, he used his experience in buying and selling to obtain a job managing a post exchange (known as a PX, a retail store on an army base that caters to soldiers). He also worked at the Stuttgart Coca-Cola bottling plant, which made it possible for him to trade soft drinks for food for his supply-short unit.

After his military discharge, in 1945, Ross returned to the U.S. and settled with his family near New York City; at the same time, he told Stokes, "I kept my business eye on Europe." He soon discovered two small companies that were manufacturing seven-inch television sets. Recognizing the potential of television, he became the exclusive Midwest distributor for the TVs and for television-related equipment; he hired others to help him as well. Even in areas without TV signals, he and his workers succeeded in persuading tavern owners of the wisdom of buying the seven-inch sets (which cost a fraction of the price of larger TVs) to attract patrons interested in seeing broadcasts of sports events. In New York and Detroit, he told Stokes, "we made a lot of money." In 1946 Ross moved his growing family and his business to Chicago and expanded his sales territory to include Wisconsin, Minnesota, Florida, and portions of the West Coast. Two years later he returned to New York, where DuMont—a television network and manufacturer of TVs—hired him to supply it with electron tubes, which it had had difficulty locating. Ross found an ample quantity at an army-surplus store, and before long he added RCA, General Electric, and Sylvania to his roster of clients. Later he opened a transistor factory; in time, he told Stokes, his company "became the nation's third largest manufacturer of transistors."

One day in the 1960s, Ross's lawyer, William J. Casey (who later headed the Central Intelligence Agency), suggested to him that he investigate the new markets that were opening up in the Soviet Union and other parts of Eastern European. Ross—who closed his factory around that time, because he could not keep up with advances in technology—took Casey's advice. On an exploratory trip to Moscow, in Russia, Ross made an immediate impression, in part by means of his distinctive appearance: as he recalled to Stokes, he wore a homburg and an eye-catching overcoat and carried a big, expensive, unlit cigar wherever he went. Soon afterward he founded Eastern Europe Inc. and began importing, exporting, and trading in lumber, plastic, grain, crude oil, textiles, electronics, and aluminum and other metals. Ross's business continued to thrive in the 1970s, despite occasional setbacks, such as the failure of his plan to import and market a Romanian car in the U.S. (The car failed tests conducted by the Environmental Protection Agency.) Eastern Europe Inc. was among 150 U.S. companies invited to Communist China in 1973, after U.S. president Richard Nixon and Mao Zedong, the leader of the Communist Chinese government, agreed to normalize relations between the two nations. His business dealings with China included sales of 50,000 tons of fertilizer. According to Lawrence Van Gelder in the *New York Times* (December 5, 1982), Ross also founded the companies International Farmers Grain Inc., American-China Inc., and Crimson Inc. "Once I get into a project," Ross told Van Gelder, "I don't let it go."

In 1976 Ross learned that a staff member's son had been rejected by every U.S. medical school to which he had applied. At the suggestion of his employee, Ross resolved to establish a medical school outside the U.S. for would-be medical students who had not gained acceptance to any of the nation's 125 medical schools. Set up with the help of various consultants, the Ross University School of Medicine opened in 1979 in Dominica, with about a dozen students. Classes were held in a motel in Roseau, Dominica's capital city, until the building's destruction by Hurricane David later that year. Afterward, Ross built a new facility on the 46-acre campus of a defunct college.

For less than the cost of a medical education at most U.S. institutions, the Ross University School of Medicine offers an accelerated program that enables its students to continue their training in teaching hospitals in the U.S., provided that they pass steps one and two of the U.S. Medical Licensing Examination and the Clinical Skills Assessment. The U.S. government has approved the school as a recipient of federal funds, in the form of guaranteed student loans; qualified overseas students who lack the money for tuition will be admitted if they can secure a barter agreement whereby—usually in return for their promise to provide medical services in their countries after earning their M.D. degrees—their governments give Ross some commodity in exchange for free tuition. As N. R. Kleinfield reported, "A few tons of steel could make a person a doctor." About 95 percent of the school's graduates gain acceptance into U.S. mainland residency programs, though usually not those considered the most prestigious. "One thing is clear," Jon Schriber wrote for *Forbes* (March 14, 1983): "Ross U. doctors are very welcome in hospitals in rundown areas like Brooklyn's Sunset Park and Jersey City, snubbed by graduates of the better-established schools. Says an administrator at Lutheran Medical Center in Brooklyn: 'They are a godsend.'" As of mid-2002, according to the Ross University Web site, more than 3,500 physicians had graduated from the school. The chairman of the school's board of directors is Benno C. Schmidt Jr., who is also chairman of the board of the Edison Schools and a former president of Yale University; also on the board, among others, are William F. Weld, a former governor of Massachusetts, and

Thomas F. McLarty III, former president Bill Clinton's first chief of staff. The school's roster of graduates and respected board members notwithstanding, the American Medical Association (AMA) has refused to accredit the Ross medical school (or any other non-mainland school), in part because until 2000, Ross students, unlike mainland medical students, did not have to take the Medical College Admission Test (commonly referred to as the MCAT) as a requirement of admission. Moreover, as Chana R. Schoenberger noted in *Forbes* (May 14, 2001), "The American medical school cartel . . . uses tight accreditation rules to restrict the supply of doctors."

In the late 1990s Ross made plans to open a branch of his medical school in Wyoming, one of the few states without such a school. It would have been the first for-profit medical school to open in the United States in almost a century. Although it was endorsed by Wyoming community, business, and political leaders, the project stalled because the medical establishment feared that if one foreign medical school were allowed to open a branch in the U.S., many other unlicenced and unregulated schools would do the same. The AMA urged Ross to move his school from Dominica to the U.S. and seek domestic accreditation, but he refused, on the grounds that the school had become important to Dominica's economy. In early 1982 he opened another educational institution: the Ross University School of Veterinary Medicine, which since 1983 has been located on the Caribbean island of St. Kitts. To date, according to its Web site, the school is the alma mater of more than 900 veterinarians. In 2000 Ross sold both his schools for $135 million; the chief buyer was Leeds Weld & Co., an investment firm that also started the Edison Project, a venture involving for-profit primary schools.

Earlier, in 1987, Ross had founded International Nurses Recruiting (INR), as a response to the recurring shortages of nurses in the U.S. INR recruits qualified nurses from other countries for temporary assignments, usually extending not more than two years; candidates must pass an examination geared to graduates of overseas nursing schools as well as an English proficiency test. The company helps the nurses to relocate to the U.S., finds provisional housing for them, and assists them with immigration paperwork. Although a nursing association has lobbied against the group, perhaps for fear of increased competition from overseas workers, Ross has kept the business afloat. He has also announced plans to start similar programs for overseas pharmacists and teachers.

In 1995, through Eastern Europe Inc., Ross began importing from China an herbal remedy called Y-snore, which purportedly cures or reduces snoring. The product, which did not require approval from the U.S. Food and Drug Administration, is available over-the-counter as both drops and a spray. Ross's latest venture is in the field of remote learning, in which American universities offer courses through the Internet.

Ross and his wife, Anne, have six children; they are now great-grandparents. The couple maintain homes in both Palm Beach, Florida, and New York City. Ross has established six awards for achievement in government or science in memory of his mother and father, his brother, and three of his sisters, respectively. In 1982 he earned a doctor of humane letters degree from the Southern School of Optometry, in Memphis, Tennessee; on the Ross University Web site, he is identified as Dr. Ross. In addition, he bought the title of Lord of the Manor of Halton Lea, Northumberland, at a London auction; he did so, he has said, on the advice of friends, who told him that the title would enable him to get good tables in restaurants. "My wife keeps telling me to hang up my track shoes," Ross told N. R. Kleinfield. "I just can't. I like the action." — G.O.

Suggested Reading: *50 Plus Lifestyles* p4+ Apr. 2000, with photo; *Forbes* p90 May 14, 2001; *New York Times* B p8 June 30, 1999, with photo, B p1 Jan. 24, 1992, with photos, III p2 June 10, 2001, with photo; *Palm Beach Daily News* Dec. 31, 1987, with photo, D p1+ Jan. 27, 2002, with photo

---

## Rumsfeld, Donald H.

*July 9, 1932– U.S. secretary of defense*

*Address: Office of the Secretary, 1000 Defense Pentagon, Washington, DC 20301-1000*

Donald H. Rumsfeld, the U.S. secretary of defense, is one of the most experienced members of President George W. Bush's Cabinet. The quintessential Washington insider, Rumsfeld brings 40 years of experience in government and the private sector to the post, having served as a U.S. congressman from his home state of Illinois, the director of the Office of Economic Opportunity (OEO) in the administration of President Richard Nixon, counselor in the Nixon White House, U.S. ambassador and permanent representative to NATO, chief of staff under President Gerald R. Ford, secretary of defense in the Ford administration, and President Ronald Reagan's special envoy to the Middle East, among other positions. Rumsfeld has also served as the chief executive officer (CEO) of G. D. Searle, a pharmaceutical company, and General Instrument, an electronics manufacturer, and earned acclaim for guiding both companies to profitability.

In 2001, beginning his second stint as secretary of defense, Rumsfeld vowed to drastically overhaul the military, cut back the bloated Pentagon bureaucracy, and shift more resources to the development of a missile-defense shield. During his first eight months as Bush's defense chief, Rumsfeld inspired a great deal of criticism. Top military officials at the Pentagon, who found many powerful allies in Congress, frustrated his efforts to reform

Courtesy of Defense Link/U.S. Department of Defense
*Donald H. Rumsfeld*

the armed forces. Detractors asserted that his reforms would weaken the military and blamed his heavy-handed management style for failing to win support for his proposals at the Pentagon.

By the end of the year, however, Rumsfeld had come to be considered one of the most effective members of the Cabinet. In the aftermath of the September 11, 2001 terrorist attacks on the U.S., Rumsfeld showed great courage and leadership, attending to the wounded at the Pentagon—which had been struck by a hijacked airliner—and assuring the American public that evening that the Pentagon would be open for business the following day. Rumsfeld helped plan President Bush's military response, which began on October 7 in Afghanistan and targeted the Taliban regime and Osama bin Laden's Al Qaeda terrorist network. Rumsfeld provided the media with daily updates of the campaign; the briefings, which were often televised, turned the defense chief into a popular figure and even, in some circles, a sex symbol. Millions of viewers found themselves charmed by Rumsfeld's old-school manners, honesty, and refusal to engage in "spin." In 2002 Rumsfeld helped to defuse a crisis that threatened to escalate into nuclear war between India and Pakistan; he also helped the Bush administration prepare for a possible war in Iraq. Seeking to explain Rumsfeld's sudden popularity, Jay Nordlinger wrote for the *National Review* (December 31, 2001) that in "feminized society—whose idea of a male sex symbol has been the Brad Pitt–style pretty boy," Rumsfeld is "a relief, or a rediscovery. He has walked out of *Father Knows Best*, or some WWII flick. . . . Whereas [former president Bill] Clinton was a pain-feeler, Rumsfeld is more of a pain-inflicter, at least where the country's enemies are concerned."

Donald Henry Rumsfeld was born on July 9, 1932 in Chicago, Illinois. His father, George, operated a successful real-estate agency. In 1937 the family moved to Winnetka, an affluent suburb of Chicago, where Donald and his sister, Joan, were educated in the town's public schools. Rumsfeld was an excellent student, earning an academic scholarship to Princeton University, in Princeton, New Jersey, in 1950. Rumsfeld, who is short and stocky, became the captain of the school's wrestling team, rarely losing a match. After graduating from Princeton, in 1954, with an A.B. degree in political science, Rumsfeld joined the U.S. Navy. For the next three years, he flew jets and served as a flight instructor.

After leaving the navy, in 1957, Rumsfeld settled in Washington, D.C., joining the staff of David Dennison, a Republican congressman from Ohio. Two years later Congressman Robert Griffin of Michigan, who was later elected to the U.S. Senate, hired Rumsfeld as an administrative assistant. About a year later Rumsfeld returned to Chicago to work for A. G. Becker and Co., an investment-banking firm.

Finding that he missed politics, Rumsfeld decided to run for public office. In 1962 he entered the Republican primary for Illinois's 13th Congressional District, which included a small part of Chicago and several towns just north of the city. Before the primary election Rumsfeld caught a break when the Illinois State Department of Insurance suspended his opponent's insurance company. Rumsfeld, whose campaign attracted thousands of young volunteers, won the primary. In the general election he ran a campaign that stressed conservative values, calling for lower taxes and a reduction of federal regulations on business. He won the election by a two-to-one margin. At age 30, Rumsfeld became one of the youngest members of the U.S. Congress.

In Congress, Rumsfeld compiled a generally conservative voting record, supporting U.S. involvement in Vietnam, taking a hard line against the Cuban dictator Fidel Castro, and opposing President John F. Kennedy's "New Frontier" and President Lyndon B. Johnson's "Great Society" social programs. Rumsfeld did, however, support the landmark 1964 Civil Rights Act as well as greater public access to records of campaign contributions. He was easily reelected in 1964, 1966, and 1968.

In August 1966 Rumsfeld gained national attention by vocally opposing the "Mohole Project," an initiative backed by President Johnson and the National Science Foundation (NSF) that would allocate $20 million to probe the earth's crust. Rumsfeld revealed that one of the project's contractors, Brown and Root Inc. of Houston, Texas, had made substantial contributions to the President's Club, a Democratic Party slush fund. As a direct result the Senate refused to fund the project.

In 1968 Rumsfeld backed former vice president Richard Nixon in the Republican presidential primary. At the Republican National Convention in Miami, Florida, Rumsfeld served as Nixon's assistant floor manager, helping to secure delegates for his nomination. During the general election, in which Nixon squared off against the Democratic nominee, Vice President Hubert Humphrey, Rumsfeld energetically campaigned for the Republican ticket, delivering many speeches on Nixon's behalf. Rumsfeld and Senator Hugh Scott of Pennsylvania also ran the Republican campaign's "truth squad," which dogged the Humphrey campaign throughout the country. Nixon won the election by a narrow margin.

After the election the politically ambitious Rumsfeld pondered his future. While he had frequently considered running for the U.S. Senate, at the time both of Illinois's seats were held by Republicans—Everett Dirksen, the Senate minority leader, and Charles Percy. Impressed with his support during the campaign, President Nixon, in April 1969, asked Rumsfeld to serve as the director of the Office of Economic Opportunity (OEO), a Cabinet-level agency established in 1964 to combat poverty. In the late 1960s the agency faced increasing criticism—from corners including the Nixon campaign—for inefficiency and mismanagement. Rumsfeld, who had voted against the creation of the OEO, was reluctant to accept the appointment, expressing reservations about running an agency that would probably be abolished. After Nixon assured him that the OEO would remain in existence, Rumsfeld agreed to serve as its director. "I wouldn't be accepting the position if I didn't feel it would be a challenging one and an important one," he said in a press conference, as quoted by Robert B. Semple Jr. in the *New York Times* (April 22, 1969). As soon as he was sworn in, Rumsfeld attempted to overhaul the agency, scaling back its operations. His efforts were often frustrated by subordinates, who opposed his reforms and disliked his management style. "There was a group of very dedicated and sincere people here who could not literally believe anyone else could care about the poor as much as they did," Rumsfeld explained to a reporter for *Newsweek* (December 28, 1970).

In 1970 Rumsfeld left the OEO to become Nixon's counselor at the White House. Rumsfeld, who enjoyed daily access to the president, became a dependable member of Nixon's inner circle, which included H. R. Haldeman, the White House chief of staff; John Ehrlichman and Robert Finch, domestic policy advisers; Henry Kissinger, then the president's foreign-affairs adviser and later secretary of state; and George P. Shultz, the director of the Office of Management and Budget (OMB) and future secretary of state in the administration of Ronald Reagan. In 1971 Rumsfeld became director of Nixon's Cost of Living Council, an agency dealing with economic and poverty issues. Late in the following year, Rumsfeld left Washington when the president appointed him U.S. ambassador and permanent representative to NATO in Brussels, Belgium. Rumsfeld enjoyed the post, which allowed him to spend more time with his wife and children.

The Watergate scandal—which involved a break-in at Democratic National Committee headquarters and a subsequent cover-up—led to President Nixon's resignation, on August 8, 1974. Nixon was replaced by Vice President Gerald R. Ford, a former congressman from Michigan and a good friend of Rumsfeld's. Rumsfeld returned to Washington for a brief time to serve as the chairman of Ford's transition team, then resumed his diplomatic post in Brussels. A short time later Ford telephoned Rumsfeld, asking him to serve as his chief of staff. In *A Time to Heal: The Autobiography of Gerald R. Ford* (1979), the president recalled that Rumsfeld was initially unwilling to accept the position. As Ford recalled it, Rumsfeld explained to him that "each member of your senior staff . . . is supposed to have equal access to you. In theory, that sounds fine. It projects the openness you want. In practice, however, it won't work. You don't have the time to run the administrative machinery of the White House yourself. I know you don't want a Haldeman-type chief of staff, but someone has to fill that role, and unless I can have that authority, I won't be able to serve you effectively." Ford concluded that Rumsfeld's assessment was correct and urged him to come on board, arguing that he "would be performing a real service for the country." Rumsfeld agreed, beginning his new duties at the White House at the end of September 1974.

Although Rumsfeld was in effect the president's chief of staff, his job title was assistant to the president. (The name of the position had been changed since it was so closely identified with Rumsfeld's two predecessors, the controversial Alexander Haig and Haldeman, a key figure in the Watergate scandal.) Rumsfeld's first priority as Ford's assistant was to reduce the size of the White House staff, which had grown during the Nixon years. In his autobiography, *It Sure Looks Different from the Inside*, (1978), Ron Nessen, Ford's colorful press secretary, recalled that Rumsfeld often feuded with Robert Hartmann—the president's counselor and longtime aide—over issues such as office space and the circulation of the drafts of presidential speeches to other departments for revision and review. Rumsfeld also clashed with Vice President Nelson Rockefeller, opposing his efforts to make the Domestic Council, an advisory board that made policy recommendations to the president, an autonomous unit that reported directly to Rockefeller. Ford explained in his book that Rumsfeld had no personal animosity toward Rockefeller, but "argued that it would be a serious mistake to allow the council to operate as an autonomous unit outside the organization that Rumsfeld had set up and that he controlled." Ford sided with Rumsfeld; relations between Rumsfeld and Rockefeller remained tense.

In 1975, in a major shake-up of the Cabinet that became known as the "Halloween Massacre," President Ford fired Secretary of Defense James Schlesinger, requested the resignation of CIA director William Colby, and stripped Henry Kissinger (who stayed on as secretary of state) of his duties as national security adviser. Ford replaced Schlesinger with Rumsfeld, who expressed reservations about the changes, thinking that they would not be well received by the public. Rumsfeld was also reluctant to take charge of the Defense Department, but Ford felt—as he recalled in his book—that Rumsfeld, with "his experience and ability, . . . could convince Congress to appropriate necessary funds for the military." Rumsfeld accepted the appointment and, at 43 years of age, became the youngest secretary of defense in the nation's history. (Rumsfeld's fears turned out to be well-founded; the press interpreted the Cabinet changes as a sign of panic and chaos at the White House. For example, in an article for *Newsweek* [November 17, 1975], Peter Goldmann and Thomas M. DeFrank observed that "Ford's great shuffle was hastily planned, badly timed and clumsily executed, and in the end it only inflamed doubts it was intended to settle: whether he really is in control of his unelected Presidency and his uncertain political fortunes.")

In an interview for *U.S. News & World Report* (March 15, 1976), Rumsfeld outlined his views on national defense and military spending. While asserting that the military strength of the United States was roughly equivalent to that of the Soviet Union, he warned that if "the trends of the past 5 or 10 or 15 years—of Soviet military expansion and U.S. contraction—are permitted to continue, we would clearly arrive, at some point, where we could not say that we had sufficiency or rough equivalence" with the Soviets. To address this problem, Rumsfeld called for increasing the defense budget in order to keep pace with the Soviet Union. As for President Ford's policy of détente, which called for easing tensions with the Soviet Union in order to avoid violent conflicts, Rumsfeld agreed that the policy was in the best interests of the United States but cautioned that it should not be interpreted to mean "that the Russians are our friends—that we can trust them . . . , or that they will not continue to develop substantial military strength to serve their interests." Rumsfeld's distrust of the Soviet Union led to disagreements with Kissinger, who was more open to negotiating with the Soviets to reach arms-control agreements. During his term Rumsfeld authorized the acquisition of the B-1 strategic bomber, the F-16 fighter jet, and the M-1 tank, which remain essential parts of the U.S. military's arsenal today. The secretary was also successful in securing increases in defense spending from Congress.

Battered by a recession, high inflation, a bruising primary challenge from former California governor Ronald Reagan, and widespread public disapproval of his unconditional pardon of Richard Nixon, President Ford narrowly lost his 1976 presidential election bid to Jimmy Carter, the Democratic former governor of Georgia. Rumsfeld returned to the private sector for the first time in 15 years, becoming the president and CEO of G. D. Searle & Co., a diversified pharmaceutical manufacturer in Skokie, Illinois. According to an article by Jeffrey H. Birnbaum in *Fortune* (March 19, 2001), Rumsfeld helped turn the struggling company around by selling off its non-drug businesses and using his "Washington savvy" to secure approval from the Food and Drug Administration (FDA) for NutraSweet, the popular sweetener that made billions of dollars for the company. In 1980 *Fortune* magazine named Rumsfeld one of the "10 Toughest Bosses in America."

Rumsfeld took a brief leave of absence from Searle in 1983, when President Ronald Reagan asked him to serve as his special envoy to the Middle East. According to an article in *U.S. News & World Report* (November 14, 1983), Rumsfeld's responsibilities included helping to reconcile the different factions in Lebanon, where a civil war was then raging and where President Reagan had dispatched thousands of troops to act as peacekeeping forces. (On October 23, 1983, 241 marines were killed when a terrorist drove a truck loaded with explosives into the barracks where they were housed.) Rumsfeld was also charged with winning support for Reagan's Mideast peace plan, which had been announced in 1982 and called for talks between Israel and Jordan over the creation of a Palestinian homeland.

In 1984 Rumsfeld left the diplomatic post to return to Searle. A year later he sold the company to the Monsanto Co., an international conglomerate, a move that made him wealthy. He then joined William Blair & Co., an investment-banking firm in Chicago. Republicans in Illinois urged Rumsfeld to run for the U.S. Senate in 1986 against Alan Dixon, the incumbent Democrat. Rumsfeld declined to do so, instead returning to politics by seeking the Republican Party's 1988 presidential nomination. Rumsfeld formed an exploratory committee to raise campaign funds, made frequent campaign appearances in Iowa and New Hampshire, and attended several candidates' forums. Then, on April 2, 1987, he announced that he would not run for president, citing campaign-finance laws that he said made it difficult for him to raise the money he needed. In the primary Rumsfeld endorsed and actively campaigned for Robert Dole, the former Senate majority leader, over Vice President George Herbert Walker Bush, who went on to win the general election. (Though Rumsfeld was mentioned as a possible secretary of defense in the Bush administration, the president ultimately selected Richard B. Cheney, who had served under Rumsfeld at the OEO and later, under the second President Bush, became vice president.)

In 1990 Rumsfeld became the CEO of General Instrument, an electronics manufacturer. Jeffrey H. Birnbaum wrote that "Rumsfeld streamlined, reorganized, and focused the business on promising products like set-top boxes and high-definition TV. After three years he took the company public, made another boatload [of money], and left."

Rumsfeld joined Dole's 1996 presidential campaign as a policy coordinator. Rumsfeld was the chief architect of Dole's pledge to cut taxes by 15 percent, which became the cornerstone of the campaign. In August he became the national chairman of the campaign, which proved to be lackluster; Dole frequently trailed the incumbent, President Bill Clinton, by double-digit margins in polls. In the end Clinton won reelection in a three-way race with Dole and Ross Perot, the Reform Party candidate.

In 1997 Rumsfeld became chairman of the board of directors of Gilead Sciences Inc., a biotechnology company based in Foster City, California. The former defense chief devoted the bulk of his attention, however, to public policy. In 1998 he served as chairman of the Commission to Assess the Ballistic Missile Threat to the United States, whose nine members were nominated by the Republican and Democratic leadership of Congress and approved by the CIA director, George Tenet. (The Republicans nominated six members, while the Democrats picked three.) The commission studied the issue and, on July 15, 1998, presented its findings in a 307-page secret report to the House and Senate intelligence committees and a 27-page summary that was released to the public. In his article for the *Bulletin of the Atomic Scientists* (November/December 1998), Richard L. Garwin, who served on the commission, quoted "the Rumsfeld report," as it was described in the press, as saying, "Concerted efforts by a number of overtly or potentially hostile nations to acquire ballistic missiles with biological or nuclear payloads pose a growing threat to the United States, its deployed forces, and its friends and allies. These newer and developing threats in North Korea, Iran, and Iraq are in addition to those still posed by the existing ballistic missile arsenals of Russia and China, nations with which we are not now in conflict but which remain in uncertain transitions." The developing nuclear powers, the report warned, would acquire the capability to inflict substantial damage to the United States in five to 10 years. The report added that the capabilities of the intelligence community to provide timely and accurate estimates of ballistic missile threats to the United States were eroding and asserted that there were possible scenarios in which the United States would have little or no warning if a missile were launched. Those who supported the deployment of a missile-defense shield, such as the editorial board of the *Wall Street Journal*, cited the report to support their position. (The commission itself did not specifically endorse a missile-defense shield.)

In a press conference on December 28, 2000, President-elect George W. Bush announced that Donald H. Rumsfeld would return for his second tour of duty as secretary of defense. "This is a man who has got great judgment," Bush said, as quoted in the *New York Times* (December 29, 2000). "He has got strong vision. And he's going to be a great secretary of defense, again." Like Bush, Rumsfeld supported the development and deployment of a missile-defense shield, which may have been a factor in his selection; Bush said that he was impressed with Rumsfeld's work with the commission on ballistic-missile threats. "Our nation is positioned well to use technologies to redefine the military," Bush added, as quoted in the *New York Times* article. "And so one of Secretary Rumsfeld's first tasks will be to challenge the status quo inside the Pentagon to develop a strategy necessary to have a force equipped for warfare of the 21st century."

Rumsfeld's nomination got a mixed reception. Some observers thought that the experienced former defense secretary was an excellent choice; others considered him little more than a bureaucrat and leftover cold warrior whose ideology was limited to his support for the development of a missile-defense shield. Rumsfeld's support for missile defense attracted controversy. Critics charged that missile defense was both costly and impractical and violated the 1972 Anti-Ballistic Missile (ABM) Treaty, signed by the United States and the Soviet Union, which prohibited such defenses. During his confirmation hearings before the Senate Armed Services Committee, Rumsfeld, as quoted by Steven Lee Myers in the *New York Times* (January 12, 2001), asserted that the ABM Treaty was "ancient history," saying that it "dates back even farther than when I was last in the Pentagon." Rumsfeld pledged that one of his first acts as secretary would be to conduct a comprehensive review of military policy to see if new threats such as "cyberattacks" and ballistic missiles from emerging nuclear states could be adequately addressed. Rumsfeld testified that he didn't know if he had adhered to the federal "conflict of interest" laws while serving as the CEO of G. D. Searle and General Instrument. He promised, however, that if confirmed as secretary of defense he would divest himself of any financial holdings that posed a potential conflict of interest. Rumsfeld also faced questions about a tape recording of a 1971 meeting he had with Nixon, in which the president made racist comments. According to the transcript of the tape, which was published in the *Chicago Tribune* (January 7, 2001), Rumsfeld agreed with Nixon's statements. Rumsfeld said he did not recall the meeting, but denied that he agreed with Nixon's "offensive and wrong characterizations." The White House defended Rumsfeld by pointing to his having supported civil rights legislation as a congressman and observing that on the tape Rumsfeld's voice could be heard tightening with discomfort as Nixon made his racist statements. On January 20, 2001, with no further controversy, the Senate confirmed Rumsfeld's nomination. Rumsfeld was expected to help realize Bush's goals of shifting more resources to missile defense, cutting the bloated Pentagon bureaucracy, modernizing the military by developing more advanced technologies, and boosting the morale of the military personnel with pay raises and other benefits.

In February 2001 Rumsfeld attended a conference in Munich, Germany, with several European defense ministers. There, Rumsfeld defended the Bush administration's support for a missile-defense shield and discussed other issues, such as the establishment of a military force for the European Union (EU). The United States expressed concern that such a force could undermine NATO. For their part, many European leaders, such as French president Jacques Chirac and German chancellor Gerhard Schroeder, opposed the missile-defense shield, arguing that it would compromise the security of Europe and lead to a renewed arms race. As quoted by Thomas E. Ricks in the *Washington Post* (February 4, 2001), Rumsfeld insisted that the shield "will be a threat to no one" and that it "should be of concern to no one, save those who would threaten others." Bush vowed to extend the shield's protection to Europe, which did not appease his critics or opponents of the system there.

In a meeting with President Bush on March 22, 2001, Rumsfeld submitted his proposal to drastically overhaul the military. According to Ricks's article in the *Washington Post* (March 23, 2001), Rumsfeld's plan included having the navy stop building large aircraft carriers, which were vulnerable to missile attack, and start designing smaller and less costly ones; directing the air force to devote more resources to long-range bombers and unmanned aircraft while cutting back on short-range fighters; reorganizing defense policy to strengthen the United States's military position in the Pacific Ocean to keep up with China, which is gradually displacing Russia as the most powerful nation in the region; and cutting back on older weapons systems that will be obsolete within 10 years. Ricks reported that some high-ranking military officials at the Pentagon were disappointed that Rumsfeld did not seek their input when drawing up his plans. Ricks added that Rumsfeld "was brusque in presenting his findings" to the top brass at the Pentagon.

Rumsfeld made reducing the Pentagon's inefficiency—which was costing billions of dollars that might have gone to purchasing new weapons systems—a top priority. Although mismanagement and inefficiency at the Pentagon had been public knowledge for decades, the secretary told Stan Crock and Richard S. Dunham for *Business Week* (July 2, 2001) that the actual situation was "worse than I had been led to believe." He added that if "you ran a business this way, you'd go broke awful fast." To cut costs and improve efficiency, Rumsfeld tried implementing "business-accounting practices" that are used in major corporations to keep track of money. To that end, he placed in key posts in the Defense Department several corporate executives with excellent track records in reducing costs and mismanagement, including Gordon R. England from General Dynamics as the secretary of the navy, Thomas White from Enron as the secretary of the army, and James G. Roche from Northrop Grumman as the secretary of the air force. These appointments, along with Rumsfeld's hands-on management style, which had served him well in the business world, were seen, in the words of *Business Week* reporters and others, as a "hostile takeover" of the Pentagon. Many top military officials at the Pentagon, displeased by Rumsfeld's approach to leadership and his plans to overhaul the military, resisted his reforms and took their case to Capitol Hill.

By the summer of 2001, Rumsfeld was facing increasing criticism from an unexpected source: conservatives. Several Republican members of Congress thought that his reforms were weakening the military. In their editorial for the conservative *Weekly Standard* (July 23, 2001), Robert Kagan and William Kristol called on Rumsfeld and Paul Wolfowitz, the deputy secretary of defense, to resign. "Right now that may be the best service they could perform for their country," Kagan and Kristol wrote, "for it may be the only way to focus the attention of the American people—and the Bush administration—on the impending evisceration of the American military." The expectations for Rumsfeld's performance were so high that his failure to overcome resistance to his reforms made him appear to be one of the more ineffective members of the Bush Cabinet. In his article for *Newsweek* (September 3, 2001), Fareed Zakaria stated that Rumsfeld had made a tactical mistake in not seeking support for his reforms from the Joint Chiefs of Staff, other top military officials, and Congress. "Power in a corporation is concentrated and vertically structured," Zakaria observed. "Power in Washington is diffuse and horizontally spread out. The secretary might think he's in charge of his agency. But the chairman of the congressional committee funding that agency feels the same."

Questions about Rumsfeld's plans to overhaul the military were placed on the back burner on the morning of September 11, 2001, when terrorists flew hijacked commercial airliners into both towers of the World Trade Center in New York City and the Pentagon, killing nearly 3,000 people. Rumsfeld was in his Pentagon office, following the unfolding events in New York City, when American Airlines Flight 77 crashed into the Pentagon. An explosion shook the entire building, which collapsed on one side. The Pentagon's 20,000 military and civilian personnel were immediately evacuated. Rumsfeld left the building and helped load the wounded into ambulances. He then went to an underground bunker at the Pentagon to monitor the crisis with General Richard B. Myers, the incoming chairman of the Joint Chiefs of Staff, and other senior military officials. Throughout the day, smoke from the fires caused by the crash leaked into the bunker. In the evening

Rumsfeld held a televised press conference, assuring the public, as quoted by Todd S. Purdum and Robin Toner in the *New York Times* (September 12, 2001), that "the United States government is functioning in the face of this terrible act." The defense chief added that the Pentagon would be open for business the next day. At first, the number of people killed at the Pentagon was estimated at more than 800. The death toll was later found to be 189, a figure that included those aboard the plane. (Casualties were minimized because the plane crashed into an area that was closed for renovations.) Rumsfeld earned immediate praise, even from those who had previously criticized him, for his handling of the crisis.

President Bush declared a war on terrorism, vowing to bring to justice those who sponsored the September 11 attacks and punish any nation that sheltered or aided terrorists. Bush blamed the attacks on Osama bin Laden, the Islamic extremist who founded the Al Qaeda terrorist network and was implicated in previous terrorist attacks. Bin Laden was thought to be hiding in Afghanistan, which was under control of the Taliban, a fanatical group of Islamic clerics who had seized power in the aftermath of the nation's bloody civil war. Bush condemned the Taliban, demanding that it turn over bin Laden and shut down his terrorist operations in Afghanistan. The Taliban refused, denying knowledge of bin Laden's whereabouts and accusations that it sponsored terrorism.

After weighing the options, Bush decided to strike back with military force against bin Laden, Al Qaeda, and the Taliban. The president also decided to support the Northern Alliance, a coalition of groups that controlled part of Afghanistan and was fighting the Taliban. On October 7 the United States began military operations against the Taliban and Al Qaeda. Both Rumsfeld and Myers helped plan the campaign, which was dubbed by the president Operation Enduring Freedom. General Tommy Franks was placed in charge of the day-to-day effort, which involved air strikes against terrorist camps and the Taliban's air defenses and airfields. While the Pentagon gave Franks considerable authority in running the campaign, the general communicated daily with Rumsfeld and Myers to update them on the progress of the war and discuss targeting strategies that would minimize civilian casualties. Although bin Laden and the Taliban leader, Mohammed Omar, escaped capture, Operation Enduring Freedom was a success. In three months of nonstop attacks, the Taliban regime gradually crumbled as U.S. troops and the Northern Alliance gained control of the country. The campaign went so quickly that in December Hamid Karzai was installed as Afghanistan's interim leader. That month Rumsfeld visited American troops in Afghanistan and also met with members of the new Afghan government.

During the military campaign, Rumsfeld and Myers held daily media briefings at the Pentagon. Through those briefings, which were frequently broadcast in their entirety on cable television, Rumsfeld became popular with millions of television viewers for his blunt talk, folksy manner, sense of humor, ability to spar with journalists, unapologetic unwillingness to reveal information that he believed would jeopardize the campaign, and refusal to engage in "spin control" or use euphemisms such as "collateral damage" when referring to the deaths of enemy troops or civilians. In the *Wall Street Journal* (December 31, 2001), Claudia Rosett cited several examples: Rumsfeld told reporters that the U.S. military was trying to "capture or kill all the Al Qaeda"; admitted that it did not know where bin Laden was, but had "certain knowledge, that he is either in Afghanistan or in some other country, or dead"; and said, "I could, but I haven't decided if I want to" discuss with the press the captured leaders of Al Qaeda and the Taliban, adding that he didn't yet know how to pronounce their names. When asked by a reporter why the military were using heavy bombs, the secretary replied, as quoted by Nordlinger, that they "are being used on frontline al-Quaeda and Taliban troops to try to kill them," and quipped that the military isn't "running out of targets; Afghanistan is." Rumsfeld repeatedly cautioned against expecting a quick and easy victory in the war against terrorism, saying that the campaign would be a "tough, long, grinding, dirty business." Discussing Rumsfeld's sudden popularity, several writers even described the 69-year-old defense chief, who became a favorite with many female viewers, as a sex symbol. When asked by the CNN talk-show host Larry King what he thought of that label, Rumsfeld replied, according to the Department of Defense Web site, "Oh, come on. . . . I'm pushing 70," but conceded that he might be a sex symbol for the American Association of Retired Persons.

In a speech he delivered on January 31, 2002 at the National Defense University, in Norfolk, Virginia, as quoted by Thom Shanker in the *New York Times* (February 1, 2002), Rumsfeld called for "new ways of thinking and new ways of fighting," observing that the challenge of the 21st century was "to defend our nation against the unknown, the uncertain and what we have to understand will be the unexpected." In February 2002 President Bush requested that Congress approve $379 billion in defense spending, a figure that represented the largest one-year increase since the Reagan administration. Appearing before the Senate Armed Services Committee on February 4, 2002, Rumsfeld testified that the increase was necessary to enhance national security and continue the war against terrorism. "Our adversaries are watching what we do," Rumsfeld said, as quoted on the CNN Web site (February 5, 2002). "They're studying how we have been successfully attacked, how we are responding and how we may be vulnerable in the future." Despite vocal opposition from some members of Congress and Pentagon officials, Rumsfeld canceled the army's $11 billion Crusader artillery system in May. The defense chief argued that the Crusader was obsolete and said that the funds originally earmarked for it would be spent on more technologically advanced systems. In late June both houses of Congress approved by wide margins substantial increases to the defense budget.

Also in June 2002 President Bush dispatched Rumsfeld to Asia to help ease tensions between India and Pakistan; once again, the two nations' longstanding conflict over the disputed Kashmir region threatened to unleash a nuclear war. The defense chief met separately with the leaders of both countries, urging them to resolve their disagreements peacefully and warning them of the dangers of nuclear war. "You can't have two countries living next to each other for very long with a million people staring at each other with weapons and not recognize that there are certain things that would be desirable," Rumsfeld said, as quoted by Thom Shanker and Seth Mydans for the *New York Times* (June 14, 2002). "One would be to have less shelling. Another might be to have more talking." Rumsfeld accomplished his mission, and although tensions remained high between India and Pakistan, the two nations gradually retreated from the brink of nuclear war.

In 2002 President Bush devoted more attention to Iraq, demanding that its president, Saddam Hussein, comply with a series of United Nations resolutions and dismantle the weapons of mass destruction that he had reportedly developed in the last few years; the alternative would be a U.S.-led attack. Bush feared that Hussein could use such weapons in a war or provide them to terrorists, who would use them to kill civilians, and expressed support for a "regime change" in Iraq. Rumsfeld asserted that the United States had evidence that Hussein had chemical weapons and was developing nuclear and biological weapons in violation of the UN resolutions. Rumsfeld scoffed at Hussein's denials, calling him "a world-class liar," as quoted by Shanker in the *New York Times* (June 11, 2002). Rumsfeld urged Congress to approve the authorization of force against Iraq. In testimony before the House Armed Services Committee, Rumsfeld said that Iraq could avoid war with the United States only if Saddam Hussein resigned or was overthrown. In October 2002 both houses of Congress passed resolutions authorizing President Bush to use force against Iraq if he deemed it necessary. U.S. forces stationed in that part of the world thereupon began preparing for a possible attack.

The well-known set of management guidelines that Rumsfeld has gathered over the decades will be published in 2003 in the slender book *Rumsfeld's Rules: Wisdom for a Good Life.* The rules are divided into eight sections, among them "Serving in the White House," "Serving in Government," and "On Business." The first section, which is intended for White House chiefs of staff and senior staff, contains such rules as "Don't divide the world into 'them' and 'us.' Avoid infatuation with or resentment of the press, the Congress, rivals, or opponents. Accept them as facts. They have their jobs and you have yours." The section entitled "On Life (and Other Things)" advises, among other rules, "Persuasion is a two edged sword—reason and emotion—plunge it deep."

Rumsfeld has received many honors, including honorary degrees from 10 colleges, the George Catlett Marshall Award, the Woodrow Wilson Award, the Dwight David Eisenhower Medal, and the Presidential Medal of Freedom, the nation's highest civilian honor. The secretary of defense enjoys skiing and hunting. Rumsfeld has been married to the former Joyce Pierson since 1954. The couple have three children— Valerie, Marcy, and Nicholas — and five grandchildren. ..

Suggested Reading: *Business Week* p45 July 2, 2001; *Chicago Tribune* II p2 Jan. 7, 2001; Department of Defense Web site; *Fortune* p140+ Mar. 19, 2001, with photos; *New York Times* A p18 Dec. 29, 2000, with photos, A p1+ Jan. 12, 2001, A p1+ Oct. 13, 2001, with photo, A p1+ May 18, 2001, with photo; *U.S. News & World Report* p26 Nov. 4, 1974, with photo, p57+ Mar. 17, 1975, with photo, p29+ Mar. 15, 1976, with photo, p13 Nov. 14, 1983, p20+ Dec. 17, 2001, with photo; *Wall Street Journal* A p7 Dec. 31, 2001; *Washington Post* A p24 Feb. 4, 2001, A p23 Sep. 20, 2001, with photos; *Weekly Standard* (on-line) July 23, 2001; *Who's Who in America, 2001*; Krames, Jeffrey A. *The Rumsfeld Way: The Leadership and Wisdom of a Battle-Hardened Maverick*, 2002

---

## Sandford, John

*Feb. 23, 1944– Crime novelist*

*Address: c/o Megan Bradley, G. P. Putnam's Sons, 375 Hudson St., New York, NY 10014*

John Camp is a former journalist and the recipient of a 1986 Pulitzer Prize for feature writing for his work at the *St. Paul Pioneer Press.* He is much better known, however, as John Sandford, the author of 13 detective novels in the best-selling *Prey* series as well as several other works of crime fiction. *Rules of Prey* (1989) was the first novel to feature the Minneapolis police detective Lucas Davenport, a well-to-do ladies' man who routinely risks his life to track down murderers. Speaking to Chris Waddington for the *Minneapolis Star Tribune* (May 20, 2001), Sandford said of his books, "They're morality tales—not the Ten Commandments, exactly, but the bad guy always gets caught."

The writer was born John Roswell Camp on February 23, 1944 in Cedar Rapids, Iowa, the son of Roswell Sandford Camp and Anne (Barron) Camp. After graduating from high school in Cedar Rapids, Sandford enrolled at the University of Iowa, in Iowa City. There, he met his wife-to-be, Susan Lee

John Earle

*John Sandford*

Jones, and graduated in 1966 with a B.A. degree in American history. In the mid-1960s, faced with the prospect of being drafted into the military, Sandford volunteered for duty, in order to expand his options for placement. Choosing to be a journalist, he was assigned as a reporter for a military newspaper in Korea. Upon his discharge, Sandford spent 10 months in Cape Girardeau, Missouri, as a reporter for the town's *Se Missourian* newspaper. He then returned to the University of Iowa, where he earned an M.A. degree in journalism.

After the birth of their first child, Roswell Anthony, in 1969, Sandford and his wife moved to Miami, Florida, where two years later their second child, Emily, was born. Sandford found work at the *Miami Herald* as a general-assignment reporter. Among his colleagues there were Carl Hiaasen and the Pulitzer Prize–winning journalist Edna Buchanan, both of whom also became best-selling crime novelists. For the next seven years Sandford covered a variety of subjects that included murders and drug cases. His experience in Miami helped to shape the thematic content of his fiction.

In 1978 Sandford returned with his family to the north, settling in St. Paul, Minnesota, where he took a job as a features writer for the *St. Paul Pioneer Press.* A year later he became a daily columnist for the paper; an article he wrote that year, about the social inequities plaguing Native American communities in Minnesota and North Dakota, made him a finalist for the Pulitzer Prize. In 1986, while still with the *Pioneer Press*, Sandford produced a series of articles that charted the trials and tribulations of a single farming family in southwest Minnesota, during the height of the farmers' crisis—in which thousands of farmers were forced off their properties by bank foreclosures. The five-part series, "Life on the Land: An American Farm Family," not only won the ASNE (American Society of Newspaper Editors) Award for non-deadline feature writing but earned Sandford (who then wrote as John Camp) a Pulitzer Prize for feature writing.

At that point Sandford began to explore other directions for his career. Between 1986 and 1989 he published two books of nonfiction, one focusing on watercolor painting and the other on plastic surgery. He then turned to popular fiction. In his interview with Chris Waddington, Sandford explained, "I started writing fiction because I saw that I couldn't put two kids through college on a reporter's salary. Winning a Pulitzer didn't change that." In 1989 Sandford sold his first novel, *The Fool's Run*, to the publishing company Henry Holt. Both that book and *The Empress File*, published two years later, were considered "small" novels, or books that would not find a mass audience—and brought the author little financial reward. During a conversation with Louis Burke Frumkes for the *Writer* (September 2000), Sandford recalled, "I asked my agent, 'How do I get out of this small book category into a bestseller category?' She told me in about thirty-five seconds that there has to be some love interest; there has to be a back story. And I said, 'Well, I can do that.' And so, when I wrote the first *Prey* book, she called me back and said, 'We're going to make a lot more money with this. This is what you ought to do.'"

Sandford's first installment of the *Prey* series, *Rules of Prey*, was immediately picked up by the Putnam publishing company. Because Henry Holt had already published two books that Sandford had written under the name John Camp, and because Putnam did not want Henry Holt to take advantage of the success of books printed by Putnam, the writer was urged to find a pseudonym. Using his father's middle name, John Camp began writing as John Sandford.

*Rules of Prey*, published in 1989, introduced readers to the character Lucas Davenport, a Minneapolis police detective charged with solving an assortment of gruesome, puzzling murders. Davenport always finds the culprit, often coming perilously close to his own death in the process. He is very handsome; has a fortune that he earned by creating computer games; drives a Porsche; and attracts a bevy of beautiful women. The character, and the book in which he was introduced, quickly became popular with readers.

Shortly after the publication of *Rules of Prey*, Sandford and his wife divorced; the couple, who remained on good terms, remarried years later. Meanwhile, Putnam published the second and third installments of Sandford's *Prey* series, *Shadow Prey* in 1990 and *Eyes of Prey* in 1991. In the latter year Sandford left his job at *Pioneer Press*; he rented a vacant room in the newspaper's building and used it to write his fiction. A close friend and fellow author, Chuck Logan, explained to Chris

Waddington, "John leaped over the wall, and then he tunneled back in. He's at home in the old newspaper culture. He likes the give and take, but he didn't want to rely on the tender mercies of [*Pioneer Press* owner] Knight-Ridder to carry him to retirement."

Over the next decade Sandford offered readers annual additions to the Davenport saga. Nine of these novels made the *New York Times* best-seller lists in both their hardcover and paperback editions. *Easy Prey*, published in 2000, reached number one on both lists. Jo Ann Vicarel wrote for *Library Journal* (April 1, 2000), "[*Easy Prey*] takes off like a roller coaster ride, and the tension never stops. Sandford . . . has spun a truly engrossing mystery that leaves the reader guessing to the end." Only one year during the 1990s—1997—passed without the publication of a *Prey* book; that year Sandford came out with *The Night Crew*, a novel about a group of ambitious freelance photojournalists in Los Angeles, who risk life and limb to file the "big story." The book introduced readers to the character Anna Batory. Sandford explained to Brian Knapp for *BarnesandNoble.com* (May 22, 1997), "I like the Anna Batory character. . . . I'm not sure I'm done with [her]." Jacqueline Seewald, reviewing *The Night Crew* for *Library Journal* (April 1, 1997), wrote, "Sandford here provides an action-packed novel. . . . The dialogue is clever and hard-edged, black humor abounds, and the romance factor is handled deftly. . . . This is an exciting thriller."

In addition to *Easy Prey*, the year 2000 saw the publication of *The Devil's Code*, which brought back characters from *The Fool's Run* and *The Empress File*: the artist, computer genius, and professional criminal Kidd and his sometime partner/sometime lover, LuEllen. In a review of *The Devil's Code* for *BookBrowser.com* (September 1, 2000), Harriet Klausner wrote, "Perhaps the earlier Kidd tales were ahead of the times, but with the Internet, Intranet, and Extranet explosion, *The Devil's Code* plays like a modern day electronic thriller. The tale is well executed due to Kidd's intellect, witticism, and ethical beliefs. Although it may seem hard to accept [that] an electronic thief has scruples, Kidd does and that propels his compulsion to investigate. Best selling author John Sandford has returned with one of his great characters in a story that will please more than just net conspiracy buffs because of its fast-paced, gigabit loaded hard driving plot."

Sandford's next novel, *Chosen Prey*, was published in hardcover on May 7, 2001. Susan Haas wrote for *USA Today* (May 17, 2001), "*Chosen Prey* is terrific. . . . It's a particular treat for old fans: Sandford tosses in updates on supporting characters and story lines from previous *Prey* books without leaving new readers scratching their heads. As an added wink, the author works in a cameo for Kidd." Shortly before the release of *Chosen Prey*, Sandford had signed a three-book, $12 million contract with Putnam, which calls for a book a year from 2003 through 2005. Sandford explained to Chris Waddington, "I'm a workaholic. At 57, you feel your body losing a little bit, you see the end of heavy-duty work life looming, but I'll probably keep going with the novels until I have a heart attack."

In *Mortal Prey* (2000), the 13th installment of the *Prey* series, Lucas Davenport matches wits with a vengeful assassin named Clara Rinker. According to a writer for the *Kirkus Review* (March 1, 2002), Sandford is distinguished by his ability to create "good villains"; Clara Rinker, for example, "kills for money," but Sandford "puts so human a face on her it requires an act of will to resist her appeal." The *Kirkus* reviewer concluded with the enthusiastic declaration that *Mortal Prey* possesses a "vivid cast, bristling action, neat surprises—and it's funny. Probably the cop novel of the year."

Sandford's interests are not limited to writing. For the last several years, he has been involved in an archaeological excavation in Israel. While the project is sponsored by the Hebrew Museum of Jerusalem, Sandford has poured a great deal of his own money into it. "I've had a life-long reading interest in history and archaeology . . . ," he told Brian Knapp. "I got serious about archaeology a few years back, went around looking at digs and sites. . . . It's *very* hot, dusty, butt-kicking work, and totally fascinating."

John Sandford lives in St. Paul with his wife, Susan. — J.H.

Suggested Reading: *BarnesandNoble.com* May 22, 1997; *BookBrowser.com* Sep. 1, 2000; *Library Journal* p131 Apr. 1, 1997, p132 Apr. 1, 2000; *Minneapolis Star Tribune* F p1+ May 20, 2001, with photos; *Publishers Weekly* p79 Sep. 4, 2000; *USA Today* D p4 May 17, 2001; *Washington Post* X p13 Nov. 5, 1995; *Writer* p26+ Sep. 2000

Selected Books: *The Fool's Run*, 1989; *Rules of Prey*, 1989; *Shadow Prey*, 1990; *The Empress File*, 1991; *Eyes of Prey*, 1991; *Silent Prey*, 1992; *Winter Prey*, 1993; *Night Prey*, 1994; *Mind Prey*, 1995; *Sudden Prey*, 1996; *The Night Crew*, 1997; *Secret Prey*, 1998; *Certain Prey*, 1999; *The Devil's Code*, 2000; *Easy Prey*, 2000; *Chosen Prey*, 2001; *Mortal Prey*, 2002

---

## Saramago, José

(sah-rah-MAH-goh, zhoh-SAY)

*Nov. 16, 1922– Novelist; poet; playwright; journalist*

*Address: c/o Los Topes 3, 35572 Tias, Lanzarote, Canaries, Spain*

In 1998 José Saramago became the first Portuguese-language author ever to win the Nobel Prize for Literature. In awarding the prize, the Swedish Academy praised Saramago as a writer "who with para-

Armando Franca/AP

*José Saramago*

bles sustained by imagination, compassion and irony continually enables us once again to apprehend an illusory reality." Saramago's writing, often characterized as magical realism, has been described as allegorical, outspoken, philosophical, and wildly imaginative and has drawn comparisons to the work of the literary giants Gabriel García Márquez and Franz Kafka. Saramago's best-known works are the novels *Memorial do convento* (published in English as *Baltasar and Blimunda*), which in 1982 brought Saramago, at the age of 60, his first international recognition; *A jangada de pedra* (*The Stone Raft*, 1986); *História do Cerco de Lisboa* (*The History of the Siege of Lisbon*, 1989); *O Evangelho segundo Jesus Cristo* (*The Gospel According to Jesus Christ*, 1991); and *Eusaio sobre a Cegueira* (*Blindness*, 1995). A man of poor, working-class origins and limited formal education, Saramago worked as a mechanic before devoting his life to literature. In his more than 50 years of writing, Saramago has published more than 10 novels, several books of poems, many newspaper articles, and a collection of short stories as well as a number of plays, opera libretti, diaries, and travelogues. His work has been translated into more than 25 languages. He also worked for many years as a translator of French classics and as an editor, manager, and contributor to several Portuguese newspapers. In an article on the Finnish literary Web site *Pegasos*, Saramago is quoted as saying, "The possibility of the impossible, dreams and illusions, are the subjects of my novels."

The son of José de Sousa and Maria de Piedade, poor, landless peasants, José Saramago was born in the small village of Azinhaga, in the central, Ribatejo section of Portugal, on November 16, 1922. "Saramago," the name of a wild plant whose leaves were eaten by the poor in those times, was the villagers' nickname for his father's family; when the writer was born, the village registrar put "Saramago," perhaps by mistake, after the boy's first name—where it remained. Saramago's older brother Francisco died of bronchopneumonia when José was two. (Saramago has called Francisco a "co-author" of his novel *Todos os nomes* [*All the Names*, 1997], as the strange but true story of Francisco's never having been officially registered as dead was an inspiration for the plot and many of the ideas explored in the book.) Saramago's father had served in World War I as an artillery soldier in France. He left farm work and moved his family to Lisbon in 1924, finding work in the capital as a policeman. When Saramago was 14, the family moved into their own house for the first time. Saramago did well in school, but his parents could not afford to send him for very long, and so he had to learn a trade. He studied mechanics at a technical school for five years and subsequently worked for two years as a mechanic in a car-repair shop in Lisbon. The technical school had also offered a literature course, and Saramago has said that to this day he can remember poetry he read in the Portuguese anthology from which the course was taught. The course opened the door for him into the world of literature. He began going to a public library in Lisbon in the evenings after work, and there his taste for reading matured.

Saramago worked in the Social Welfare Service in Lisbon as an administrative civil servant. He published his first book, a novel, in 1947. He had titled it "The Widow," a name that was changed to *The Land of Sin*. He wrote a second novel, "The Skylight," which remains unpublished, then began a third; feeling that he had nothing important to say, however, he abandoned the project and, without regrets, disappeared from the Portuguese literary scene for almost 20 years. Saramago has stated that his long period of silence was not caused by the repressive regime of António de Oliveira Salazar in Portugal, as some have suggested; rather, he has insisted that it was simply a matter of having had nothing of interest to write.

Saramago reappeared with the publication of *Os poemas possiveis* (*Possible Poems*) in 1966. In the late 1950s, meanwhile, he had found work as the production manager of the Lisbon publishing company Estúdios Cor. Through that job, he made friends with some of the more important Portuguese writers of the time. To earn extra money Saramago began translating the work of Jean Cassou, Maupassant, Baudelaire, and, from the French, Tolstoy, among others; he enjoyed translating and continued the work into the 1980s. He also worked as a literary critic during 1967 and 1968. Saramago left Estúdios Cor in 1971 and spent the next two years at the newspaper *Diário de Lisboa*, where he served as an editor and the manager of a cultural supplement. In 1974 he published a collection of essays, editorials, and articles he had written for the *Diário de Lisboa*, under the title *Os opiniões que o D.L. teve* (*The Opinions the DL Had*). The collection captures the political and social state of Portugal at the end of Salazar's dictatorship. The following year Saramago became the deputy director of the morning paper *Diário de Nóticias*. Also in 1975, in the aftermath of an anti-Communist coup, which set back the revolution that had helped topple the Salazar dictatorship the previous year, Saramago—a member of the Portuguese Communist Party since 1969—was fired from his post. Again he collected his newspaper writings, this time from *Diário de Nóticias*, and published them under the title *Os apontamentos* (*Notes*, 1996). *Deste mundo e do outro* (*From This World and the Other*, 1971) and *A bagagem do viajante* (*The Traveller's Baggage*, 1973) are additional collections of Saramago's newspaper articles. Critics consider these books important for understanding the writer's later work. Meanwhile, in 1970 another book of Saramago's poems, *Provavelmente Alegria* (*Probably Joy*), had appeared, and in 1975 he published the long poem *O ano de 1993* (*The Year of 1993*).

For various reasons, Saramago found himself unemployed in the mid-1970s. Regarding his thoughts at that time in his life, Saramago wrote, in a short autobiography for the official Web site of the Nobel Foundation, "I decided to devote myself to literature: it was about time to find out what I was worth as a writer." In 1976 he went to the country village of Lavre for a few weeks to write and study, and he has credited that time of quiet observation with leading to his novel *Levantado do chao* (*Risen from the Ground*, 1980)—which won the City of Lisbon Prize—and with helping him to develop the narrative style he would employ in his future novels. *Risen from the Ground* (sometimes translated as *Raised from the Ground*) is the saga of three generations of a poor Portuguese farming family; it was inspired by memories of Saramago's own parents and grandparents. Also during this period, in addition to *Manual de pintura e caligrafia* (*Manual of Painting and Calligraphy*, 1976), a novel that focuses on the idea of the development of an artist, and *Objecto quase* (*Quasi Object*, 1978), a collection of short stories, Saramago wrote the play *A noite* (*The Night*, 1979). Other plays in Saramago's oeuvre are *Que farei com este livro?* (*What Shall I Do with This Book?*, 1980), *A segunda vida de Francisco de Assisi* (*The Second Life of Francis of Assisi*, 1987), and *In nomine dei* (1993), which was inspired by the history of a 16th-century religious war in Munster, Germany, and from which Saramago would create the opera libretto *Divara* (1993).

For Saramago the 1980s were devoted mainly to the writing of novels. *Baltasar and Blimunda* proved to be Saramago's first big success, bringing the writer, then 60 years old, international acclaim. The story intertwines an account of the building of the convent of Mafra, outside Lisbon, and an anachronistic fantasy involving the two eponymous lovers as they try to flee the Inquisition in a flying machine. In the book, Saramago juxtaposed the privilege and power of the royal court and the hard lives of the laborers and other common people. Irving Howe, as quoted by Alan Riding in the *New York Times* (October 9, 1998), wrote in a review of *Baltasar and Blimunda* for the *New York Times Book Review*, "Mr. Saramago is constantly present as a voice of European skepticism, a connoisseur of ironies. I think I hear in his prose echoes of Enlightenment sensibility, caustic and shrewd." A press release on the official Nobel Foundation Web site (October 8, 1998) stated, "[*Baltasar and Blimunda*] is a rich, multifaceted and polysemous text that at the same time has a historical, a social and an individual perspective. The insight and wealth of imagination to which it gives expression is characteristic of Saramago's works as a whole." Saramago adapted the novel for the libretto of the opera *Blimunda*, with music by the Italian composer Azio Corghi (who collaborated with Saramago on the opera *Divara* as well). *Blimunda* was first performed at Milan's La Scala in 1990.

Saramago followed with *O ano da morte de Ricardo Reis* (*The Year of the Death of Ricardo Reis*, 1984), which takes the form of a dialogue between the great Portuguese poet Fernando Pessoa, who died in 1935, and a fictional version of Pessoa's real alter ego, Ricardo Reis. The impossible meeting between the two leads to the discussion of profound questions. Herbert Mitgang wrote for the *New York Times* (April 30, 1991) that the book is "a rare, old-fashioned novel—at once lyrical, symbolic and meditative." The fantastic event at the heart of *The Stone Raft* (1986)—the Iberian peninsula's breaking off from the rest of the European landmass—allows Saramago to explore notions of Portugal's sometimes tense relationship with the rest of Europe and its place in the world. *The History of the Siege of Lisbon* (1989) tells the story of proofreader Raimundo Silva, who, while proofing the scholarly text of a history of the siege of Lisbon in 1147, mischievously replaces one use of the word "yes" in the text with the word "not." This act of tampering has ramifications that include Raimundo's discovery of love. In a commentary on the book for the Webster University Web site, Bob Corbett wrote, "Perhaps the central puzzle that gets raised in the novel is the question of how much historical truth can we have to begin with?" Saramago told Katherine Vaz for an article that appeared on the *Bomb* magazine Web site, "In fiction, the narrative is obviously about individuals, but to do that effectively, to convey the personal situation of one, two, or three people, the author must understand that everything is set in the context of history. We are 'subjected,' the subjects of history. One can't forget what is behind us and what exists now in a world that is fragmented, chaotic, corrupted, and always moving toward the unknown."

The Portuguese government vetoed the nomination of Saramago's novel *The Gospel According to Jesus Christ* (1991) for the European Union's Ariosto Literary Prize, on the grounds that the book was offensive to Catholics. In the book Saramago retold many of the Gospel stories from an ironic point of view, imagined new prophesies, depicted God as something of a villain, and had Jesus enter into sexual relations with Mary Magdalene. As quoted in *Contemporary Authors*, John Butt described the book in the *Times Literary Supplement* as "an idiosyncratic, satirical, bitter and frequently comical account of Jesus' life." Some were offended by the book, including representatives of the Vatican, who issued statements of protest. Because of the Portuguese government's opposition to the book, which it later retracted, Saramago decided to leave Portugal with his wife, Pilar del Rio, moving to Lanzarote in the Canary Islands. Since 1993 Saramago has kept a dairy, and over the years he has published several volumes of it under the title *Cadernos de Lanzarote* (*Diaries of Lanzarote*).

In the 1995 novel *Blindness*, Saramago used the affliction of the title—which in the book sweeps over the world—as an allegory for the horrors of human society in the 20th century. In an article that appears on the CNN Web site, Saramago is quoted as saying, "This blindness isn't a real blindness, it's a blindness of rationality. We're rational beings but we don't behave rationally."

*All the Names*, published in 1997, tells the story of a civil-service clerk who goes on an obsessive hunt for a mysterious woman after coming across her birth certificate. The story explores themes of identity, loneliness, and human relationships. While some readers and reviewers found *All the Names* to be a compelling fable on a par with Saramago's previous books, others found it to be one of the writer's minor works. He followed that book up with *Conto da ilha descohecida* (*The Tale of the Unknown Island*, 1999), a short, simple tale of a brave man who petitions a corrupt king for a boat in which to search for an undiscovered island. An English translation of Saramago's travelogue *Viagem a Portugal* (1981), which grew out of a cross-country trip through his homeland in 1979, was published in 2001 as *Journey to Portugal*.

*La Caverna* (*The Cave*), first published in 2000, made its English-language debut the following year. (The book was translated by Saramago's wife, the Spanish journalist Pilar del Rio.) In this story, an elderly potter lives with his daughter and her husband in a small country village near a sprawling shopping center. Changing tastes among consumers, and the resulting drop in the potter's income, force the family to move to a site in that same commercial zone. "Profound disorientation and a shocking discovery set their world on edge," Bruce Jensen wrote for *Library Journal* (June 1, 2001). Jensen also wrote that the novel "has the abundant compassion, subtlety, and wit of [Saramago's] earlier works . . . , with rich character development and touches of his familiar magical realism. This uncomplicated story about complex modern issues is as troubling and revelatory as it is deeply humanistic." "*La Caverna* . . . is more than a novel: it is an ax that breaks through the frozen ocean of our consciousness," Pablo Gámez wrote for *Arena*, the cultural supplement of the Mexican publication *Excélsior* (February 25, 2001), as quoted in *World Press Review* (May 2001, on-line). "And this is the only thing that Saramago intends to accomplish in his works: to awaken the consciousness of his readers and force them to react to the world's problems. For the last 10 years, Saramago has managed to create a gigantic x-ray that reveals not just what we are, but also what we are becoming."

Saramago's distinctive prose style is characterized by long, unpunctuated passages, in which the narrative and the characters' dialogue, set down without quotation marks, are intermingled. Regarding his approach to writing a novel, Saramago said to Katherine Vaz, "Sometimes I say that writing a novel is the same as constructing a chair: a person must be able to sit in it, to be balanced on it. If I can produce a great chair, even better. But above all I have to make sure that it has four stable feet."

In addition to the Nobel Prize, Saramago has won three prestigious literary awards from Italy: the Grinzane Cavour Prize, the Mondello Prize, and the Flaiano. In 1995 he also won the Luís de Camoes Prize, named for the great 16th-century Portuguese poet. Saramago was awarded honorary degrees from the University of Turin, Italy, and the University of Sevilla, Spain, in 1991. He married Ilda Reis, his first wife, in 1944. Their only child, Violante, was born in 1947; the couple divorced in 1970. After the divorce Saramago began a relationship with the Portuguese writer Isabel da Nóbrega, which lasted until 1986. He then met the Spanish journalist Pilar del Rio, whom he married in 1988.

The tall, thin, bespectacled Saramago told Katherine Vaz, "Writing is my job. It's the work I do, what I build. I don't believe in inspiration. I don't even know what that is. What I know is that I have to decide to sit down at my desk, and inspiration isn't going to push me there. The first condition for writing is sitting—then writing." — C.F.T.

Suggested Reading: *Bomb* magazine Web site; *Grand Street* p110+ Winter 1999; *Literature Awards* Web site; *New York Times* A p12 Oct. 9, 1998; Nobel Foundation electronic-museum Web site; *Paris Review* p54+ Winter 1998; *World Press Review* p40+ Jan. 1999, with photo; *Contemporary Authors* vol. 153, 1997; *International Who's Who 2002*

Selected Books: *The Land of Sin*, 1947; *Possible Poems*, 1966; *Probably Joy*, 1970; *From This World and the Other*, 1971; *The Traveller's Baggage*, 1973; *The Opinions the DL Had*, 1974; *The Year of 1993*, 1975; *Manual of Painting and Calligraphy*, 1976; *Quasi Object*, 1978; *The Night*, 1979; *Risen from the Ground*, 1980; *What Shall I Do with This Book?*, 1980; *Baltasar and*

*Blimunda*, 1982; *The Year of the Death of Ricardo Reis*, 1984; *The Stone Raft*, 1986; *The Second Life of Francis of Assisi*, 1987; *The History of the Siege of Lisbon*, 1989; *The Gospel According to Jesus Christ*, 1991; *Blindness*, 1995; *Notes*, 1996; *All the Names*, 1997; *The Tale of the Unknown Island*, 1999; *Journey to Portugal*, 2001; *The Cave*, 2001

---

John Spellman/Retna

## Scott, Jill

*1972– Singer; songwriter*

*Address: c/o Hidden Beach Recordings, 3030 Nebraska Ave., Penthouse Suite, Santa Monica, CA 90404; c/o Richard De La Font Agency, 4845 S. Sheridan Rd., #505, Tulsa, OK 74145-5719*

"What I write about isn't complicated," the singer and songwriter Jill Scott told Allison Samuels for *Rolling Stone* (October 12, 2000). "I write about the basics of life, love and friendship. My grandmother used to get up at five in the morning to have some time by herself. She'd take long baths, singing old-school songs from North Carolina, where she's from. Good, deep-down soul songs, full of vigor and meaning—that's how my days would start, and that's stayed with me until this day." Scott began singing professionally when she was in her early 20s, performing her songs and reading her poetry at open-mike nights at small venues. She co-wrote the lyrics to the song "You Got Me," which became a hit for the Philadelphia-based hip-hop group Roots and won a 1999 Grammy Award. Thanks to the attention generated by that honor, Scott signed on to work with the rap musician and producer Jeff Townes. Her first album, *Who Is Jill Scott? Words and Sounds, Vol. 1*, was released in July 2000; within a year it had earned a double platinum rating (selling over two million copies) and three Grammy nominations. That recording was followed, in November 2001, by *Experience: Jill Scott (826 Plus)*, a double CD that captured a live performance at Constitution Hall in Washington, D.C., on August 26, 2001. *Experience* also offers several previously unreleased studio tracks. Noted for her on-stage energy and the apparent honesty of the emotions she conveys in her songs, Scott is counted—along with such musicians as Erykah Badu and Musiq Soulchild—among the neo-soul artists, who blend traditional soul riffs or themes with such newer musical styles as rap or hip-hop.

An only child, Jill Scott was born in 1972 in North Philadelphia, Pennsylvania. "I call it the ghetto because it was kinda poor, but you guys think it's all gang-bangin' and crack-dealing, right?" she said during a conversation with Michael Odell for the London *Guardian* (November 10, 2000). "Well, the truth is more straightforward. . . . Mostly it's people going to work at six, coming home at 10. They sweep their step like everybody else. They say 'Hi' like everyone else. There is a fabric there. There is a community. People just have to work a helluva lot harder to keep it together." Scott was raised by her maternal grandmother, who was called Blue Babe, and her mother, Joyce, whom she described to Kristal Brent Zook for the *Washington Post* (December 24, 2000) as "a Renaissance woman: dental technician, acupuncturist, tiler, drywaller and antique refurbisher." Both her mother and grandmother have "been behind me 100 percent no matter what road I chose. To have unconditional love from your family is a godsend," she told Allison Samuels. Scott's father, a policeman, was present in her life, though not every day. Her stepfather, who lived with her family until she was five, physically abused both Jill and her mother; Scott has since channeled her anguish from that period into her poems and music.

Scott's mother loved rhythm and blues, jazz, and soul music, and mother and daughter often sang along to recordings by artists including Aretha Franklin, Donny Hathaway, and Otis Redding. Unhappy and repeatedly involved in fights at Thomas M. Pierce Elementary School, Scott was allowed to switch to the well-regarded Albert M. Greenfield School, in the Center City section of South Philadelphia. There, her teacher Fran Danish enthralled her. "She was a lady," Scott recalled for Kristal Brent Zook. "We'd have spelling bees and if I did really well, she'd paint my nails during recess and just talk to me." An assignment from Danish led to Scott's discovery of the black poet Nikki Giovanni. "When I saw it was poetry about little black girls, I was so excited," she told Allison Samuels. She recalled to Kristal Brent Zook, "[Giovanni] was my grandmother, my mother. She was me. It was a real revelation, that writing could be this way." That year Scott wrote her first poem and began to put words to music, sometimes as a memory device to help her with spelling. "I had songs for everything," she said to Samuels. "I would sing about catching the bus. My locker combination. I sang to myself all the time, making a melody out of the three syllables of a word. That's how I learned to spell—because I wanted to have lunch with Miss Danish." According to *getmusic.com*, she attended the Philadelphia High School for Girls, a public college-preparatory magnet school, where she sang classical music in German and Latin.

While she dreamed of performing, Scott enrolled at Temple University, in Philadelphia, with the intention of majoring in English and becoming a teacher, one who would use music as part of her lessons. But by her third year at Temple, she had grown frustrated. "The buildings were gray. Gray walls. Gray lockers. Gray floors. That's no way to teach a child," she explained to Kristal Brent Zook. "Children need stimulation. So because I would say things like that, teachers would pat me on the back and call me 'young and idealistic.' I was just tired. I felt disrespected. Every day was a battle. And I just thought, 'I know I have more to offer than this.'" Scott quit school and got a low-paying job as a set builder and toilet cleaner at the Ardent Theater Company, in Philadelphia. "Cleaning toilets is a good way of getting in touch with your creativity," she told Michael Odell. "That's when you find out if you got anything going on in your head." Meanwhile, in her free time she continued to write poetry and songs; she began performing at coffeehouses and other small venues, such as the October Gallery, in Philadelphia, which exhibits work by African-American artists. On some nights there would be as many as 100 people in the audience. "Being a poet in Philadelphia and New York put me standing in front of an audience [with only] words," she told Alan Sculley for *Cincinnati City-Beat* (May 10–16, 2001, on-line). "So it made me realize how very important words are. You want to say something. You don't want it to go in one ear and out the other without making an impression. Being able to stand there on stage with just words and no more, it made me a better artist. It made me a better performer, because I'm not afraid." In 1998 Scott spent three months in the cast of Jonathan Larson's multi-award-winning rock musical *Rent*, as a member of a company touring Canada. She served as a soloist in the signature song "Seasons of Love."

Word about Scott's talents reached Ahmir "?uestlove" Thompson, the drummer and leader of the hip-hop/rap band the Roots. Soon after he attended one of her performances, Thompson gave her a lyric-writing assignment. To fulfill it, in collaboration with one or more members of the Roots, she wrote the lyrics to "You Got Me," which became the band's first single from their fifth album, *Everything Falls Apart* (1999). Scott had hoped to deliver the vocal hook of the song on the studio recording, but she was passed over in favor of the then–better-known singer/songwriter Erykah Badu. "It was a disappointment," she admitted to Alan Sculley. "[I thought] I had gotten my first big break. In reality, I did. . . . I got a lot of attention as a writer." "You Got Me" won the 1999 Grammy Award for best rap performance by a duo or group. At the invitation of the Roots, Scott performed the song with the band on tour; her version is included on their live album, *The Roots Come Alive* (1999), made during that tour.

At around this time Scott began to work with the producer Jeff Townes, who had performed with Will Smith in a duo called DJ Jazzy Jeff and the Fresh Prince. For Will Smith's album *Willennium* (1999), Scott contributed some background vocals and had a guest spot as a singer and lyricist. Meanwhile, she had started to send demo tapes to music companies, in hopes of landing a record deal. In 2000 Scott signed with Hidden Beach Records, a new label to which the basketball player Michael Jordan had contributed start-up funds. The company appealed to her partly because it did not demand a photo of her before it offered the contract. "I didn't want labels to say, 'Oh, she's not what we're looking for,' and not listen to the music," she told Evelyn McDonnell for the *Houston Chronicle* (August 2, 2001). "That's why I'm in it, not for fashion, not for hair. It's about being creative." Scott wrote prolifically for her debut album and recorded 52 songs before Hidden Beach "made me stop," as she confessed to McDonnell. "They told me I wasn't allowed to go in the studio anymore. I write something every day, just because that's what I do. This is what I enjoy." *Who Is Jill Scott? Words and Sounds, Vol. 1*, which contains 18 selections, was released in July 2000. Like most neo-soul albums, it got little airplay on mainstream radio stations at first. Initially, it also got no publicity other than what was generated through word-of-mouth. "I didn't expect anything," Scott told Alan Sculley. "I just wanted to offer it, not sell it, not force it down people's throats, and see what would happen."

Sales of the record were spurred by positive reviews. In one, for the *Washington Post* (December 22, 2000), Curt Fields wrote, "*Who Is Jill Scott?* is like the perfect weekend couple's getaway—comfortable, fun, sexy and occasionally surprising. [Scott] imbues her songs with relaxed, confident charm. . . . [But] she often adds unexpected grit." "With her lush, jazzy vocals and neosoul sensibility, Scott . . . sounds like Billie Holiday crossed with Erykah Badu," Allison Samuels wrote for *Newsweek* (July 24, 2000), adding that the record is a "shimmering collection." Less than four months after its release, *Who Is Jill Scott?* was certified gold, with at least 500,000 copies sold. By February 2001 it had been certified platinum (one million copies sold). In 2000 Scott herself earned three Grammy nominations, in the categories of best new artist, best female R&B vocal performance, and best

R&B album of the year; in early 2001 she won three *Soul Train* Lady of Soul Awards.

Accustomed to traveling undisturbed, Scott was now frequently recognized in public. "I hoped that I would be able to remain myself," she told Kristal Brent Zook. "That I would be able to go to the market and pick out my fish and squeeze my lemons. I don't want to lose that. Fame? . . . I gotta tell you, it's bittersweet. There's nothing like going to buy your tampons and all of a sudden you've got a crowd." She told Clarence Waldron for *Jet* (August 20, 2001), "I hope I don't sound unappreciative. That is not my intention. The biggest cross I have to bear at this moment is dealing with fame. I want everybody to know that I am not that comfortable with it."

Scott's celebrity, which was bolstered by her performances in small halls throughout the U.S., got a big boost when she appeared as the opening act for Sting in the spring of 2001. Her hectic schedule exacted a toll, though: a lung infection caused her to miss the first week of the Sting tour dates, and, even more frightening, in September 2000 she suffered a bout of sudden sensorineural hearing loss—so-called sudden deafness syndrome—and lost 85 percent of her hearing in her right ear. In time she recovered completely from the disorder, which was attributed to stress and frequent air flights. In July 2001 Scott embarked on her first national tour as a headliner; another Hidden Beach Records artist, Mike Phillips, provided her opening act, at such venues as the New Jersey Performing Arts Center, in Newark, and the Chicago Theater. Her performance at Constitution Hall in the nation's capital in August 2001 formed the basis of her recent two-CD live album, *Experience: Jill Scott (826 Plus)*. According to *MTV News Online*, the album also contains 10 new studio tracks (other sources claim fewer) that Scott recorded with her supporting band, Fatback Taffy. "Few live albums actually capture the magic that occurs when a performer and an audience are vibing on all cylinders . . . but here's another candidate," Michael Paoletta wrote for *Billboard* (November 24, 2001). (Two versions of the album were released, one bearing a parental advisory label and the other designated as "clean.")

Scott recently married her longtime friend Lyzel Williams, a graphic artist. Their relationship is well-documented on her first album; "A Long Walk" was inspired by their first date, and "He Loves Me (Lyzel in E Flat)" is dedicated to him. Scott maintains a home in Philadelphia. "I'm just a regular chick from North Philly," she explained to Clarence Waldron. "I do what I do because I love to do what I do. It's natural. It's right. It fits me. It belongs to me, and those are the reasons why I do it. Fame was never even a thought." — K.S.

Suggested Reading: *Ebony* p100+ July 2001, with photos; *Houston Chronicle* F p5 Aug. 2, 2001; *Jet* p58+ Aug. 20, 2001, with photos; *Rolling Stone* p46 Oct. 12, 2000, with photo; *Washington Post* G p1 Dec. 24, 2000

Selected Recordings: *Who is Jill Scott? Words and Sounds, Vol. 1*, 2000; *Experience: Jill Scott (826 Plus)*, 2001

---

## Sedaris, Amy

(seh-DAR-iss)

*1961(?)– Actress; playwright*

*Address: c/o 3 Arts Entertainment, 9460 Wilshire Blvd., 7th Fl., Beverly Hills, CA 90212-2732*

Described by some as a perverse descendant of the comedian Lucille Ball, the playwright and actress Amy Sedaris has developed a cult following for her work on television and the downtown New York stage. Sedaris has co-authored several plays with her brother David Sedaris, a humorist and satirist who has written three best-sellers (two collections of essays and one book of short stories). Amy Sedaris has performed in all their plays, portraying characters ranging from an odorous donkey to a maker of cheese balls who belongs to a bizarre religious sect. Cleverly satirizing government, television, the media, and a bevy of other subjects, Amy and David Sedaris are among the most profane contemporary creators of theatrical comedy. Ben Brantley, writing for the *New York Times* (March 28, 2001), described the Sedarises as "invaluable guides to a synthetic, self-recycling world" who "share an appalled and amused eye for the grotesque in popular culture." In her performances, the physically attractive Amy Sedaris has often transformed herself into weird-looking and oddly dressed women. When Sedaris is "in character," Ty Wenzel wrote for *Privy Magazine* (on-line) in late 1999, "she is the most twisted person you will ever meet. She is not beyond cursing like a truck driver, wearing fat suits, painting her pretty face with bloody open gashes and black, bruised eyes. . . . Nothing is safe from Amy. But her brand of humor will leave you wondering about the state of the world. These piteous characters she becomes take over our collective consciousness, and we recognize ourselves. . . . We can always relate somewhere in our dark and moldy closets to the myriad of dejected qualities her characters wear like a badge of honor. Sedaris' success for comedy is that it spotlights all of our social skills at the point of breakdown, that moment when we are confronted with a situation so amoral, strange, or maybe just plain crude that we have no idea what to do but laugh. And we love her for it." Sedaris co-wrote and starred in *Strangers with Candy*, a television series that poked fun at the moral-laden after-

Joe Marzullo/Retna Ltd.

*Amy Sedaris*

school specials of the 1970s. Although she has received accolades for both her writing and her acting, she remains modest about her accomplishments. "I think I have a sense of humor," she told David Rakoff for *Interview* (May 2001), "but I wouldn't say I'm funny any more than I'd say I'm an actress. I don't know what you'd call what I do—I like to perform."

One of the six children of Lou Sedaris, who worked for IBM, and Sharon (Leonard) Sedaris, a homemaker, Amy Sedaris was born in about 1961 in New York City. She grew up in Raleigh, North Carolina, with her two brothers and three sisters. Her parents and all the children enjoyed making jokes and cooking together as well as writing and performing their own plays for their own amusement. Sedaris recalled to Rex Doane for *Salon* (May 5, 2000, on-line), "For a long time I had an imaginary classroom. I'd come home from school, put on my mom's high heels and go right to the back bedroom where I had a wall that was one big chalkboard and I would teach my imaginary students. This went on for years and years. Then I realized I was too old to do this, so then I just kind of did it to myself in my head. I still do that—like if I'm making an omelet I pretend it's a cooking show and I'm teaching someone." As a youngster Sedaris joined the Girl Scouts. At Sanderson High School, in Raleigh, she earned good grades. Among other activities, she was a member of the school track team and Junior Achievement, an organization that promotes free enterprise. Out of boredom, by her own account, she attended summer school. After she graduated from high school, she worked at odd jobs at such places as a Winn-Dixie store, a Red Lobster restaurant, and a Steak & Ale tavern. She never acted on any of several career ideas that she entertained during that period, among them becoming a social worker. In an interview with Michael Gartland for *Paper Magazine* (2001, on-line), Sedaris recalled, "I always got along with all types of people—popular people as well as drug addicts"; she also said that she enjoys having friends and acquaintances tell her their problems and then giving them advice.

After some years, at the prodding of her brother David, she moved to Chicago, with the aim of becoming an actress. "If I had stayed in North Carolina," she told Doane, "I'd be wearing ruffles or a uniform. You know, waitressing and taking care of a stroke victim. . . . I probably would have been dating him, too, by now." In the early 1990s Sedaris joined the famed Chicago comedy troupe Second City (whose many successful alumni include Joan Rivers, Dan Aykroyd, Gilda Radner, Bill Murray, and Jim Belushi). While there she met Paul Dinello, whom she dated for eight years, and Stephen Colbert. With Dinello and Colbert, who appeared in skits with her, Sedaris created a bevy of offbeat and outrageous comedic characters.

In 1993 Sedaris moved to New York City, where she and her brother David, dubbing themselves the Talent Family, began writing irreverent comedies. In one of their first efforts, *Stitches* (1994), an attractive and popular high-school girl whose face has been disfigured in a boating accident goes on to star in her own television sitcom. A satire that skewers the Manhattan art scene, Method acting, television, and a host of other targets, *Stitches* was produced at La MaMa Experimental Theater Club, in New York, in 1994 and received generally good reviews. Critiquing the play for the *New York Times* (January 11, 1994, on-line), Ben Brantley described it as "corrosively funny, if overextended." "The play itself feels like the product of minds shaped by an unceasing stream of disjunctive images—from old movie melodramas, perky sitcoms, hypnotic commercials and gritty tabloid news shows—given bizarrely equal weight by the small screen that disseminates them," Brantley wrote.

The Sedarises' next effort, *One Women Shoe* (1995), which was mounted at La Mama, is another far-ranging satire. This play is about four female welfare recipients who learn that because of new government regulations, they must perform one-woman shows in order to receive their welfare checks. Amy Sedaris played Barbara Sheriden, a 58-year-old former golf champion, who has purposefully gone on welfare in an effort to "discover herself." The welfare department tells her and the three other women that with their new vocation, they could become stars. "What results is a skewed world view that reflects the naive, tenacious optimism that this country has never been able to forsake," Ben Brantley wrote for the *New York Times* (January 26, 1995). "It's really only one ironic degree removed from tabloids like *The Star* and *The National Enquirer*, with their combination of gritty prurience and miracle cures for cancer." Although

Brantley enjoyed the play, he thought that it was "not without dead spots. Some of the foul-mouthed insult debates go flat, and much of performance art is so ludicrous to begin with that it is almost impossible to parody." Amy and David Sedaris won special citations from the Obie Award committee for *One Woman Shoe*.

The Sedarises' brazenly bawdy play *Incident at Cobbler's Knob* premiered in 1997 at the LaGuardia Theater, at Lincoln Center, in New York City. Set in a forest, it focuses on animals whose lives are disturbed when a group of polyester-clad witches settle in the woods. Amy Sedaris played a donkey whose disgusting smell repels everyone who comes near him. During much of the play, the donkey uses highly vulgar language in an unsuccessful attempt to lure a doe into bed with him. "Vulgarity just shouldn't be this funny," Anita Gates wrote for the *New York Times* (July 10, 1997), "but it's being ridiculed, not reveled in."

The year 1997 also saw the staging of another Amy and David Sedaris comedy, *The Little Frieda Mysteries*. The miserly Aunt Frieda, played by Amy, is obsessed with dollhouse furniture. She is taking care of her niece, little Frieda, a onetime hand model whose hands are now in casts because of an accident. The two grow to resent each other; when Aunt Frieda falls in love, little Frieda, ostensibly in an effort to help her aunt get her man, assists her in outrageous ways. In a review of a 1999 production of *The Little Frieda Mysteries*, John Longenbauh wrote for the *Seattle Weekly* (July 1–7, 1999, on-line), "It's funny, but also more than a little disturbing, as if the Sedarises can't manage to stifle their darker obsessions under what is, essentially, a slight and quirky comedy about the ridiculous things people will do when in love."

Amy Sedaris has appeared in several Off-Broadway productions written by others, among them Paul Rudnick's *The Most Fabulous Story Ever Told* (1998), a spoof of biblical stories, and Douglas Carter Beane's *The Country Club* (1999), in which she played Froggy, a dissatisfied suburban woman who spends her time planning for social events. Her performance in *The Country Club* earned her a Drama Desk Award nomination for best featured actress.

Sedaris helped to create, and appeared in, the experimental sketch-comedy TV show *Exit 57*, which debuted on the Comedy Central cable network in 1995 and aired for two seasons. At around this time she declined an offer to join the cast of *Saturday Night Live*, because she feared that doing so would interfere with her work as a playwright and actress. In 1999 *Strangers with Candy*, which Sedaris co-wrote with Dinello and starred in, premiered on Comedy Central. The character she portrayed, Jerri Blank, is a onetime teen runaway and reformed drug addict and prostitute who, at age 46, goes to live with her catatonic father and abusive stepmother and returns to high school as a freshman. Most of her efforts to befriend her classmates at Flatpoint High end disastrously. While many of the problems depicted in *Strangers with Candy* resemble those portrayed in typical 1970s after-school specials, Jerri chooses highly unorthodox, immoral, and unethical ways of dealing with them. Sedaris based Blank's appearance on that of Flurrie, a girl from a 1960s antidrug documentary who, in Sedaris's view, bore a striking resemblance to former governor Michael S. Dukakis of Massachusetts. The show became a cult hit but was discontinued after three seasons. Sedaris blames the cancellation on the unwillingness of the people newly placed in charge of Comedy Central programming to air any show that they themselves had not developed. "I think we could have done more, and with each season it was getting better and better," Sedaris told an interviewer for the *Underground* (online). "And I think if we had done another season it would have been really great. We come from sketch comedy not 22 minute comedy, so we were still trying to figure it out."

With David Sedaris, Amy Sedaris co-wrote the play *The Book of Liz*, which premiered in 2001 at the Greenwich House Theater, in New York City. *The Book of Liz* follows Sister Elizabeth Donderstock (portrayed by Amy), who belongs to a religious order known as the Squeamish, whose members wear Pilgrim-style outfits. Liz is responsible for producing the order's famous cheese balls. After a crisis, feeling that she would like to know more about herself and life, she flees the insular community and comes face-to-face with the modern world. In the *New York Times* (March 28, 2001), Ben Brantley wrote that *The Book of Liz* is a "delightfully off-key, off-color hymn to cliches we all live by, whether we know it or not." Assessing Sedaris's performance, he wrote that she "expertly employs her natural overbite and slumped shoulders to suggest both passive dejection and spunky defiance. Even disguised as a top-hatted peanut, her posture is eloquent with Liz's ambivalence."

For a while in the late 1990s, Sedaris waitressed at a New York City diner. She has appeared in small roles in several films, among them *Commandments* (1997), *Six Days, Seven Nights* (1998), and *Jump Tomorrow* (2001). In the short film *Bad Bosses Go to Hell* (1997), which Erin Cramer wrote and directed, Sedaris played a very trendy supervisor who answered questions with a "magic eight-ball" and was far more interested in her interviewee's jacket than in the woman's credentials. In 2001 she appeared as Betsy Frayne on two episodes of the television show *Just Shoot Me*. In the fall of that year, she acted in David Lindsay-Abaire's comedic play *Wonder of the World*, about a homemaker who leaves her cheating husband in an attempt to experience a fuller life. Cast in several roles—all of them eccentrics—Sedaris played three waitresses, a helicopter pilot, and a woman who, as a marriage counselor, wears the costume in which she dresses for her second job, that of clown. Sedaris has bought the rights to Robert Plunket's book *Love Junkie* and, in collaboration with Paul Dinello and Steve Colbert, is adapting it for the silver screen. In 2002 she appeared in three episodes of the television series *Sex and the City*.

According to Michael Gartland, Amy Sedaris "has the lithe frame of a gymnast." Ty Wenzel wrote, "She's beautiful in the *Seventeen Magazine* sense, intelligent and one of the most polite people I've ever known." Sedaris lives with her pet rabbit, Tattletale, in the Greenwich Village section of New York City. She often makes cupcakes and cheese balls to sell during intermissions of her plays.—G.O.

Suggested Reading: *Interview* p96+ May 2001, with photo; *New York* p52+ June 12, 1995, with photo; *Salon* (on-line) May 5, 2000; *Underground* (on-line)

Selected Plays: as actress—*The Most Fabulous Story Ever Told*, 1998; *The Country Club*, 1999; as co-author and actress—*Stitches*, 1994; *One Woman Shoe*, 1995; *Incident at Cobbler's Knob, 1997*; *The Little Frieda Mysteries*, 1997; *The Book of Liz*, 2001

Selected Television Shows: *Exit 57*, 1995; *Strangers with Candy*, 1999–2000

---

Arnaldo Magnani/Liaison/Getty Images

## Seymour, Stephanie

*July 23, 1968– Fashion model*

*Address: c/o Ford Models, 142 Greene St., New York, NY 10012*

The supermodel Stephanie Seymour is perhaps best known from her work during the 1990s as the principal model and spokesperson for Victoria's Secret, a retail and mail-order women's-fashions company that specializes in sexy lingerie. Her image has also appeared in high-profile ads for such upscale clothing/accessory/fragrance firms as Versace, Ralph Lauren, Yves Saint Laurent, and Chanel as well as on dozens of magazine covers, for such publications as *Cosmopolitan*, *Vogue*, *Self*, *GQ*, *W*, and *Allure*. Since she first signed with a modeling agency, in 1985, she has appeared in prestigious fashion shows in New York, London, Paris, and other haute-couture capitals of the world. The renowned photographer Richard Avedon, whose images of Seymour appeared in a series of Versace ads, characterized her as "combin[ing] a perfect body with a dynamite brain and a heart that's always in the right place," as *People* (May 9, 1994) quoted him as saying. *Allure* magazine described Seymour as the epitome of physical perfection for the 1990s; speaking of her at about the time she turned 32, Max Pinnell, a New York City hairstylist who has worked with her for many years, told a writer for *People* (July 31, 2000) that Seymour "can still stand in a lineup of models who are 17 years old and blow them out of the water." In 1994 *People* listed her among the "50 Most Beautiful People in the World," and *Paris Match* named her the world's most beautiful model. Her how-to guide, *Stephanie Seymour's Beauty Secrets for Dummies*, was published in 1998. Regarding the future of fashion, Seymour told Charles Gibson for the ABC News program *Good Morning America* (September 13, 1999), "There are no more rules in fashion. . . . Just anything goes and designers are taking from all periods of fashion. . . . I think that will be the beauty of this new century."

The second of three children, Stephanie Seymour was born on July 23, 1968 (some sources say 1969) in San Diego, California. Her father was a real-estate developer; her mother worked as a hairstylist. At the age of 14, she began to model for San Diego department stores and ads for local newspapers. The next year, as a "skinny and gawky" teenager, in her words, she competed unsuccessfully in the "Elite Look of the Year" contest, held by the Elite modeling agency (now called Elite Model Management).That disappointing outcome notwithstanding, the experience gave her the confidence to move, within a year or two, to New York City, where she further developed her modeling career. In 1985 she signed with Elite, one of the world's biggest modeling agencies. At 16 she became romantically involved with Elite's founder and head, John Casablancas, who was then about 40. During the next few years, she continued to model but received little attention. In 1989 she married Tommy Andrews, a rock musician, with whom she had a son, Dylan. The couple broke up in 1990.

Also in 1990 Seymour signed a contract with Victoria's Secret to model lingerie for the company's catalog and ads. In time she became known as "the face and the figure" of Victoria's Secret. Seymour attracted a great deal of notice in 1991, when she appeared nude in a *Playboy* photo spread. "For me the feeling in [nude] pictures is freedom and strength," Hilary Rowland quoted her as saying on *SupermodelGuide.com* (2000, on-line). "Put clothes on me and I wouldn't look pretty anymore." Soon after her *Playboy* shoot, she appeared on the cover of the British edition of *Vogue*, and before long she was regularly winning assignments on modeling catwalks and in department-store ready-to-wear presentations in Europe and the United States.

In 1991 Seymour began dating Axl Rose, the lead singer of the hard-rock band Guns N' Roses. With Rose and the other members of the group, she appeared in the videos for the Guns N' Roses' songs "Don't Cry" and "November Rain." Accounts of Seymour and Rose's allegedly frequent and immoderate partying were a tabloid stable until the couple split up, in early 1993. Later that year Rose sued Seymour for assault and battery and also sought the return of jewelry reportedly worth over $100,000. He eventually dropped the suit, and Seymour sold the jewelry, giving the proceeds to charity.

Seymour's visibility got another big boost in 1994, thanks to her featured roles in popular ad campaigns for Versace jeans and Chanel's Egoiste cologne for men. That same year she gave birth to her second son. In mid-1995 she married the father of the child, Peter Brant, the publisher of the magazines *Interview* and *Art in America*. Her how-to book, *Stephanie Seymour's Beauty Secrets for Dummies*, was published in 1998. The book is written in down-to-earth language and contains a foreword by Sarah Ferguson, the Duchess of York. It offers Seymour's advice and a description of her "home spa" beauty regimen and includes tips from well-known beauty artists in sections on skin, hair and makeup. The book also includes information about beauty products and a list of useful Web sites and toll-free phone numbers.

Seymour did not renew her Victoria's Secret contract when it expired, in 2000, because she wanted to avoid embarrassing her son Dylan, who was then 10 years old. "His friends at school used to tease him," she told the writer for *People*. "It was only going to get worse. What would his friends say when he's 14?" In 2001, in a $10 million campaign launched by the clothing designer Ellen Tracy, Seymour appeared in several ads along with the supermodel Cindy Crawford. Images of the two women appeared on a 4,500-square-foot, three-panel billboard in New York City's Times Square.

Still considered one of the top models in the world, Seymour continues to represent such firms as Chanel, Versace and L'Oreal. Having given birth to three children (the third, a boy, in about 1996), Seymour told the writer for *People*, "I prefer my body after I've had kids to before. I like a womanly, shapely figure." She added, "I'm more secure as a woman. I know who I am." Seymour currently lives with Brant, who is 22 years her senior, and her three sons—Dylan, Peter Jr., and Harry—in Greenwich, Connecticut, and New York City; the family, which also includes Brant's children from an earlier marriage, spends a great deal of time in the summer in the Hamptons on Long Island, New York. As quoted by *SupermodelGuide.com* (online), Seymour identifies herself as "a model, a mother, but mainly just a normal girl." She has appeared in small roles in the films *Sunny Side Up* (1994) and *Pollock* (2000), and she lent her image and voice to the video game *Hell: A Cyberpunk Thriller*. In her spare time Seymour enjoys playing polo, riding horses, and collecting art. She also likes to take long walks and works out by swimming and doing yoga. According to *People* (May 9, 1994), she owns a collection of dresses from the 1950s, which she regards as a time "when women were really women." — G.O.

Suggested Reading: *People* p54+ May 9, 1994, with photos, p54 July 31, 2000, with photos; *SupermodelGuide.com*

---

## Shalhoub, Tony

(shal-OOB)

*Oct. 9, 1953– Actor; director; producer*

*Address: c/o USA Network, 525 Washington Blvd. #402, Jersey City, NJ 07310-1609*

Ranked among the finest of contemporary character actors, the classically trained Tony Shalhoub has endeared himself to fans and critics alike while building a successful career in theater, film, and television. As a member of the American Repertory Theater in the 1980s, he acted in such thespian staples as *The School for Scandal* and *Waiting for Godot*; in the 1990s he appeared on stage in Wendy Wasserstein's Pulitzer Prize–winning play *The Heidi Chronicles* and gave an extravagantly praised performance in Herb Gardner's Tony Award–winning *Conversations with My Father*. On the small screen he has brought to life such varied characters as the lovable, Italian-immigrant taxi driver in the sitcom *Wings* and the cripplingly neurotic but brilliant detective in the new series *Monk*. In his more than two dozen motion pictures, too, he has played highly diverse characters, ranging from the alien whose head regenerates, in the hit film *Men in Black*, to the stubborn, demanding chef in *Big Night*, in a performance that raised his visibility considerably. According to Jason Buchanan in the *All Movie Guide* (on-line), Shalhoub is "a uniquely gifted and versatile actor possessing the distinct ability to immerse himself in a role so convincingly that he becomes almost unrecognizable. . . . One can always count on Tony Shal-

Bill Davila/Retna Ltd.

*Tony Shalhoub*

houb to deliver a memorable performance no matter how small his role may be."

The ninth of 10 children, Tony Shalhoub was born in Green Bay, Wisconsin, on October 9, 1953. His father, Joe, who came to the United States from Lebanon as an orphan at the age of 10, was a grocery-store owner and food distributor; his mother, Helen, was a second-generation Lebanese-American. According to an interviewer for the *Café Arabica* Web site, the actor "does not remember any Arab-Americans in Green Bay that he was not related to." In the crowded Shalhoub home, young Tony shared a bed with one of his brothers until the age of 11. His first theater experience came when he was six years old: at the request of an older sister, he served as an extra in a production of the musical *The King and I* at her high school. After studying at the University of Southern Maine, in Portland, Shalhoub attended the Yale Drama School, in New Haven, Connecticut, which offers what is widely considered one of the finest acting programs in the U.S. He graduated from Yale in 1980. He then joined the American Repertory Theater (ART), in Cambridge, Massachusetts. He intended to work there for only a year but "ended up staying for four," as he recalled to Joseph Hurley for *New York Newsday* (January 8, 1989). Plays in which he performed at ART include Shakespeare's *Measure for Measure*; Richard Brinsley Sheridan's *School for Scandal*; Diderot's *Rameau's Nephew*, which he also performed Off-Broadway, in 1988; Beckett's *Waiting for Godot*; and Chekhov's *Three Sisters*.

In 1984 Shalhoub moved to New York City. The next year he made his Broadway debut, in Neil Simon's revised version of his comedy *The Odd Couple*, in which the playwright made the two main characters—hilariously mismatched roommates originally named Felix and Oscar—women rather than men. Shalhoub played one of the Costazuela brothers (the Pigeon sisters in the original *Odd Couple*), neighbors of the roommates. Unlike Simon's first version (starring Walter Matthau and Art Carney in the acclaimed Broadway production of 1965, and Walter Matthau and Jack Lemmon in the hugely successful 1968 movie), the new one was roundly panned. In 1989 Shalhoub performed in *The Heidi Chronicles*, which focuses on the effects of the feminist movement on women coming of age in the U.S. during the second half of the 20th century.

Shalhoub earned a Tony Award nomination for his role in Herb Gardner's acclaimed Broadway play *Conversations with My Father* (1992). The actor was cast as Charlie, a successful novelist whose father, the cold, abusive Eddie (Judd Hirsch), owned and managed a bar in the 1930s and '40s (an unusual profession for a Jewish immigrant from Europe, as Eddie was). Charlie, who has returned to the bar to sell it after his parents' deaths, reminisces about his difficult relationship with his father and Eddie's struggle to assimilate into American society. "Mr. Shalhoub, who is on stage continuously, either narrating or participating in every flashback, conveys wisdom, warmth and humor whether he is looking back with embarrassment at his awkward, horny adolescence or trying as an adult to have one conversation with his father that is not one-sided," Frank Rich wrote for the *New York Times* (March 30, 1992). "It is hard to imagine how Mr. Gardner, or any other playwright, could be blessed with a better stand-in than this actor, who keeps you trusting, admiring and enjoying the storyteller even when you spot the holes in his tale." Shalhoub's theater work also includes performances in *Zero Positive* and *For Dear Life* at the Joseph Papp Public Theater, in New York City, and New York Shakespeare Festival productions of *Richard III* and *Henry IV, Part I*.

In 1990 Shalhoub moved to Los Angeles, where he made his feature-film debut as a doctor in the AIDS drama *Longtime Companion*, which Norman Rene directed from a script by Craig Lucas. That same year Shalhoub appeared in a small role as a taxi driver with an intriguing, unidentifiable accent in the engaging caper comedy *Quick Change*, which starred and was co-directed by Bill Murray. In 1991 he won the part of the endearing, self-deprecating, Italian-immigrant cab driver Antonio Scarpacci on the popular TV sitcom *Wings*. That show, which strongly resembled the long-running series *Cheers* (three former *Cheers* producers created it), centered on two brothers (Tim Daly and Steve Webber) who run a small airline; their childhood friend (Crystal Bernard) manages the airport lunch counter. "I got spoiled on *Wings*," Shalhoub told Sabrina Rojas Weiss for an article posted on the *TV Guide* Web site. "I had just landed in L.A., this opportunity opened up to me, and I was on that show for six years. Every year we would come to the end of the season, and they would tell us we'd been picked up for another year. I just thought, 'Oh, that's the norm.'"

Meanwhile, Shalhoub continued to land small parts in movies, among them *Barton Fink* (1991), *Honeymoon in Vegas* (1992), *Searching for Bobby Fischer* (1993), *Addams Family Values* (1993), and *I.Q.* (1994). In the award-winning *Big Night* (1996), he co-starred as Primo, a dedicated and temperamental chef who is struggling to save the failing restaurant he owns with his brother, Secondo (Stanley Tucci, who also co-wrote the script with Joseph Tropiano and co-directed the film with Campbell Scott). Shalhoub assiduously prepared for the role by working for a while alongside the head chef of the trendy Los Angeles restaurant Chianti Cucina. While *Big Night*, set in a late-1950s New Jersey seaside town, made only a modest profit at the box office, it was a critical success. In a review for *Rolling Stone* (October 3, 1996), Peter Travers wrote, "Shalhoub . . . joins Tucci in an unforgettable acting duet that is as richly authentic as the food. . . . In the final scene, done in silence, the brothers make and share a simple omelet in a moment of reconciliation that subtly pierces the heart. You're in for a rare treat." Shalhoub's performance earned him a National Society of Film Critics Award for best supporting actor and an Independent Spirit Award nomination for best male lead, both in 1997.

Shalhoub played Jack Jeebs, an alien whose head reappears after being blown off, in Barry Sonnenfeld's smash hit *Men in Black* (1997), starring Will Smith and Tommy Lee Jones as special agents battling creatures that threaten Earth. He reprised the role in the sequel to that film, *Men in Black II* (2002). Also in 1997 Shalhoub appeared in the futuristic *Gattaca* and the romantic comedy *A Life Less Ordinary*. Among his credits for the following year were the films *Primary Colors*, *Paulie*, *The Impostors*, and *The Tic Code*. He played Kevin Conway, a lawyer, in the legal docudrama *A Civil Action* (1998), in which relatives of cancer victims sue a corporation suspected of polluting the city water supply, and Frank Haddad, a counterintelligence agent, in *The Siege* (1998), a thriller about terrorist attacks on New York City. In the NBC-TV sitcom *Stark Raving Mad* (1999), which was canceled after one season, Shalhoub starred as Ian Stark, a writer of horror novels who likes to play morbid practical jokes.

Shalhoub again proved his knack for comedy in the role of Fred Kwan, in the lighthearted feature-film *Galaxy Quest* (1999), a science fiction/fantasy sendup of the popular television show *Star Trek* that co-starred Tim Allen, Sigourney Weaver, and Alan Rickman. "Tony Shalhoub, always a delight, makes a great deadpan tech guy. ('The ship is breaking apart. Just F.Y.I.')," Stephanie Zarachek wrote in her review of *Galaxy Quest* for *Salon* (January 7, 2000, on-line). In the film noir *The Man Who Wasn't There* (2001), written and directed by Joel and Ethan Coen and photographed in moody black and white by the cinematographer Roger Deakins, Shalhoub depicted a fast-talking lawyer named Freddy Riedenschneider. In that movie, a chain-smoking, cuckolded barber (Billy Bob Thornton) tries to escape his sad, humdrum existence by blackmailing the boss (James Gandolfini) and lover of his wife (Frances McDormand). "Halfway through, Tony Shalhoub shows up as a high-priced, self-intoxicated defense attorney and almost walks off with the film," David Edelstein wrote for *Slate* (November 2, 2001, on-line). Though *The Man Who Wasn't There* grossed less than $10 million at the box office, it received much critical praise. For his turn in the film, Shalhoub was nominated as featured male actor of the year by the American Film Institute and as best supporting actor by the Chicago Film Critics Association.

With *Made-Up* (2001), an independent film that the actress Lynn Adams based on her own one-woman play of that title, Shalhoub made his directorial debut. Co-produced by Adams and her sister, Brooke Adams (Shalhoub's wife), *Made-Up* is a comedy about aging, the cultural obsession with good looks, and relationships between sisters. "Everyone was so patient with me," Shalhoub told Betty Jo Tucker in an interview that appears on the Web site *koaa.com*. "After I found out what I was supposed to do, I learned to delegate responsibility and focus on what I know about—such as staging, acting, and so forth. I'd love to direct again." Lynn Adams, Brooke Adams, and Shalhoub also acted in the film, which won an Audience Award at the 2002 South by Southwest Film Festival and a nomination for a Taos Land Grant Award at the 2002 Taos Talking Picture Festival.

Shalhoub ventured into the horror genre with a major role in the film *Thirteen Ghosts* (2001). He played the criminal mastermind Alexander Minion in Robert Rodriguez's hit family comedy *Spy Kids* (2001) and its sequel, *Spy Kids 2: The Island of Lost Dreams* (2002). He appeared briefly in *Impostor* (2002), about an engineer (Gary Sinise) who designs a powerful weapon to defeat besieging aliens, only to be accused of being an alien himself. In the lightweight comedy *Life or Something Like It* (2002), starring Angelina Jolie and Edward Burns, Shalhoub portrayed a homeless man with psychic powers.

Since its premiere, on the USA Networks cable channel in July 2002, Shalhoub has starred as the title character on the series *Monk*, directed by Dean Parisot (Shalhoub's director for *Galaxy Quest*). Adrian Monk, an uncommonly gifted detective, has suffered from obsessive-compulsive disorder and various phobias since the unsolved murder of his wife four years earlier. His condition led to his suspension from the San Francisco Police Department, which now hires him as a consultant because he has acquired an extraordinary ability to detect clues unnoticed by others. Shalhoub researched obsessive-compulsive disorder to ensure the realism of his portrayal. "I spend so many more of my waking hours as Monk than I do as myself that I'm afraid a little of him is starting to rub off on me," Shalhoub told Sabrina Rojas Weiss. "I am a little bit of a germaphobe. I also have issues about the way people stack the dishwasher. No one but me seems to know how to do it. I sometimes have to re-stack it. . . . And I'm afraid of thong underwear!" In a review of *Monk* for *flakmag.com*, Andy Ross wrote, "Shalhoub manages to hold everything together. Rather than relying on tics and compulsions to create the character, he bookends them with subtle comedy." "Woody Allen has all but spoiled neuroticism as an endearing character trait," Carina Chocano wrote for *Salon* (July 11, 2002, on-line), "but the preternaturally lovable Shalhoub—a veteran of numerous Hollywood character roles—revives and redeems the tired archetype. Intelligent, intense and (hyper)sensitive, Shalhoub is quietly winning as a guy trying to do the job he was born to do in a world that seems dead set on driving him bonkers." In an unprecedented move, ABC-TV bought the rights to four episodes of *Monk* and has rebroadcast them on network television. The show earned good ratings when it aired on ABC; in September 2002 ABC decided to schedule eight additional *Monk* episodes that had been broadcast earlier on the USA Networks.

In other television work, Shalhoub had roles in the made-for-TV movies *Alone in the Neon Jungle* (1988); *Day One* (1989), in which he played the Nobel Prize–winning Italian physicist Enrico Fermi, who participated in the U.S.-led Manhattan Project, which resulted in the world's first atomic bomb; *Money, Power, Murder* (1989); a remake of *Gypsy* (1993); *That Championship Season* (1999); and *The Heart Department* (2001). He has also appeared in installments of *The Equalizer, Spenser: For Hire, The X Files, Frasier*, and *Ally McBeal*, among other series.

Shalhoub will appear in two films scheduled to be released in 2003: *Against the Ropes*, the actor Charles S. Dutton's directorial debut, which will star Meg Ryan in a fictionalized portrayal of the real-life female boxing promoter Jackie Kallen, and the director Robert Altman's ensemble piece *Voltage*, a comedy about the corporate world in the U.S.

"People are consumed by [the entertainment] business and their careers so that rejections can be devastating . . . ," Shalhoub has said, according to *Biography Magazine* (January 1999). "I was like that for years. [But] I was lucky—I met the right woman." Shalhoub and his wife, Brooke Adams, have two daughters: Josie, born in 1989, whom Adams adopted before the couple's marriage, in 1992, and Sophie, born in 1993. — C.F.T.

Suggested Reading: *hollywood.com*; *Internet Movie Database*; *New York Newsday* II p13 Jan. 8, 1989; *New York Times* C p11 Mar. 30, 1992; *Salon* (on-line) July 11, 2002; *TV Guide* (on-line)

Selected Films: *Longtime Companion*, 1990; *Barton Fink*, 1991; *Searching for Bobby Fischer*, 1993; *Big Night*, 1996; *Men in Black*, 1997; *A Civil Action*, 1998; *Primary Colors*, 1998; *Galaxy Quest*, 1999; *Spy Kids*, 2001; *The Man Who Wasn't There*, 2001; *Made-Up*, 2001; *Life or Something Like It*, 2002

Selected Television Shows: *Monk*, 2002–

---

Armando Gallo/Retna Ltd.

## Smith, Maggie

*Dec. 28, 1934– Actress*

*Address: c/o Paul Lyne-Maris, ICM, Oxford House, 76 Oxford St., London W1N 0AX, England*

NOTE: An earlier article about Maggie Smith appeared in *Current Biography* in 1970.

"The boundary between laughter and tears is where Maggie is poised always," the playwright Alan Bennett told Steve Vineberg for *Salon* (June 6, 2000, on-line). Over the course of almost half a century of performing on stage and screen, Dame Maggie Smith has brought an amazing range of expression to both comedic and dramatic roles. Her portrayals of such characters as the scheming, socially ambitious wife in the film *A Private Function* (1985) and the stodgy but charismatic Constance, Countess of Trentham, in the movie *Gosford Park* (2001), among dozens of others, have earned Smith high acclaim from actors, directors, award committees, and the public. Since her first role for the silver screen, in 1958, she has won two

U.S. Academy Awards, five British Academy Awards, and two Golden Globe Awards. "Maggie always plays . . . a three-dimensional person. She isn't just a cipher," the director Robert Altman told Eugenia Zukerman for *CBS News* (January 20, 2002, on-line). "That's the measure of a great actor, of course," Altman added. By all accounts, Smith has never approached a role lightly. "She genuinely agonizes over a very large talent," the theater director Peter Shaffer told Matt Wolf for the *New York Times Magazine* (March 18, 1990). "Maggie's not relaxed at all, ever. She stands all the time and walks up and down, and will keep this up from 10 to 5. Other people are eating sandwiches, and there's this lone figure at the back of the stage, pacing like a caged creature. There is no such thing as a coffee break with Miss Smith."

Margaret Smith was born in Ilford, Essex, England, on December 28, 1934, one of the three children of Nathaniel Smith, an Oxford public-health pathologist, and Margaret Little (Hutton) Smith. From an early age Smith was known as Maggie. She attended the Oxford School for Girls until she was 16, when she began her theatrical studies at the Oxford Playhouse School. Beginning in 1952 Smith played in Oxford University productions, mostly revues, and in 1955 she moved with a revue company into a small theater in London, where she was seen by the American producer Leonard Sillman. Impressed, Sillman signed her to play in *New Faces of 1956*, a revue that opened on Broadway in June of that year. Among the host of unknowns in the Sillman revue, she was one of those who stood out, attracting the eyes of critics as a mock Follies girl, draped in hundreds of oranges and descending a staircase. Smith also attracted the attention of other producers, and after her return to London she was the leading comedienne for six months in the zany revue *Share My Lettuce* (1957–58), opposite Kenneth Williams.

Smith made her cinematic debut starring as a bohemian girl who shelters an escaped convict in *Nowhere to Go*. When the shooting of that film was finished, she returned to the West End of London, in November 1958, to play Vere Dane in *The Stepmother*, which had a short run. With the Old Vic Company in London in 1959 and 1960, she appeared in several classic plays by Congreve, Shakespeare, and J. M. Barrie. In 1960 she portrayed Daisy in *Rhinoceros* at the Strand Theatre and toured as Kathy in *Strip the Willow*, a seriocomic drama about nuclear warfare. In addition, she brought vitality to the role of Lucille, the innocent governess who is the object of an elaborate seduction by a decadent aristocrat, in Jean Anouilh's *The Rehearsal*, which ran at a succession of London theaters for a year beginning in April 1961.

At the Mermaid Theatre in September 1962, Smith participated in readings of *Pictures in the Hallway*, the volume of Sean O'Casey's fictionalized autobiography covering the adolescence and young manhood of the character Sean Cassidy. Later, when the book was adapted to the screen as *Young Cassidy* (1965), she portrayed Nora, the woman Cassidy almost marries. Writing for *Newsday* (March 23, 1965), Richard Gelmis noted that "Smith, with her exquisite bony face, freckles, white thin lips, and gauche straw hat, is radiant with an inner beauty." Starring opposite Kenneth Williams in Peter Shaffer's linked one-act comedies *The Private Ear* and *The Public Eye* in the West End from May to October 1962, Smith won the *London Evening Standard* Drama Award for best actress of the year. During the 1962–63 season, when she played the lead in the hit London production of Jean Kerr's *Mary, Mary*, the reviewer for the *London Times* (February 28, 1963) spoke for many in observing that she was the salvation of that "fluffy Broadway comedy." The critic also noted that, with "eyes signaling panic whenever the backs of others are turned," Smith performed "wonders in making dead lines appear to come to life." For her performance as Mary, the Variety Club of Great Britain named her the best actress of the year.

Richard Burton and Elizabeth Taylor were the marquee magnets in the film *The V.I.P.s* (1963), but Smith, as secretary to one of the title characters, nearly stole the show in a crucial scene with Burton, who good-naturedly referred to her upstaging of him as "grand larceny." "Maggie and Elizabeth never appear together, which is too bad," a critic noted in *Time* (November 22, 1963). "For when Maggie Smith is on the screen, the picture moves." In December 1963 Sir Laurence Olivier, then artistic director of the newly formed British National Theatre Company—which was performing winters at the Old Vic Theatre and summers at the Chichester (England) Festival Theatre—invited Maggie Smith to join the company. Playing Desdemona to Sir Laurence's title characterization in a National Theatre production of Shakespeare's *Othello* in 1964, Smith gave a new dimension to the role, making the usually meek, wooden victim of Iago's treachery a passionate lover bewildered by the fury of Othello's unfounded jealousy. "Her pitiful tragedy becomes all the more moving and terrible," Richard Watts wrote for the *New York Post* (August 16, 1964), "because she is so real and filled with human warmth." The production, with the original cast, was made into a film, released in 1965, and for her screen interpretation of Desdemona, Smith was nominated for an Academy Award. Among several other National Theatre productions between 1964 and 1967, Smith played Silvia in *The Recruiting Officer*, Hilde Wangel in Ibsen's *The Master Builder*, Myra in Noel Coward's *Hay Fever*, the title role in Strindberg's *Miss Julie*, and Clea in Peter Shaffer's farce *Black Comedy*.

On the screen, Smith played the nurse who discovers that a playboy (Rex Harrison) is feigning fatal illness in order to lure his avaricious former lovers to his deathbed in *The Honey Pot* (1967), and in the comedy *Hot Millions* (1968) she portrayed the dizzy accomplice of an embezzler (Peter Ustinov) who programs the computer in the London office of an American industrial conglomerate to send regular large checks to three nonexistent companies—fronts for himself. Smith's next major role was as a militantly nonconformist teacher in a Scots girls school in *The Prime of Miss Jean Brodie* (1969). A complex autocrat, the teacher imposes on the impressionable minds of her students her own frustrated romantic hopes and her guilelessly fascistic prejudices, thereby inspiring them but at the same time maiming both them and herself. "It is certainly the finest single screen performance ever given by Miss Smith," Harold Stern wrote in *After Dark* (April 1969). In the *New York Times* (March 3, 1969), Vincent Canby described the actress's Oscar-winning performance as "a staggering amalgam of counterpointed moods, switches in voice levels and obliquely stated emotions, all of which are precisely right." Smith's co-star in the film, Robert Stephens, had performed with her in several National Theatre productions, and the two married secretly in May 1969.

At the Ahmanson Theatre in Los Angeles in January 1970, the National Theatre presented Farquhar's *The Beaux' Stratagem*, with Smith in the role of Mrs. Sullen. After viewing her performance, Clive Barnes of the *New York Times* (February 10, 1970) wrote: "Maggie Smith is one of those actresses born to play Restoration comedy. Her hands and wrists gesticulate with a pungent eloquence, she can make one solitary monosyllable dropped cryptically into a conversation express a libraryful of emotion, and her eyes, bright and shrewd, tell stories few nice girls are lucky enough to know." On January 1, 1970 Queen Elizabeth II named Smith a Commander of the British Empire in acknowledgment of the service she had rendered the British theater.

Despite her success at the National, Smith left that prestigious theater in 1971 due to the large amount of infighting that went on there. The following year she appeared on British television in Shakespeare's *Merchant of Venice* and George Bernard Shaw's *The Millionairess*. In the George Cukor–directed film *Travels with My Aunt* (1972), based on a novel by Graham Greene, Smith starred as the eccentric and outgoing Aunt Augusta, who travels across Europe with her nephew, Henry Pulling. A stodgy bank clerk, Henry learns from his aunt to be more adventurous. For her role, Smith was nominated for an Academy Award for best actress and for a Golden Globe for best motion-picture actress—musical/comedy. Smith's next film was Alan J. Pakula's *Love and Pain and the Whole Damn Thing* (1972). In that drama, Smith played Lila Fisher, who meets and falls in love with a much younger man (Timothy Bottoms) while traveling in Spain.

Smith's personal life went through a period of upheaval in the early 1970s. With their marriage in a state of turmoil, Smith and Robert Stephens embarked on a U.S. tour of Noel Coward's play *Private Lives*, directed by Sir John Gielgud. During the show's run the couple separated, and Stephens abandoned the cast, leaving a rattled Smith to perform "a nightclub comic's Maggie Smith impression—all tics and nervous affectations"—for the rest of the tour, in the words of the Canadian critic Martin Knelman, according to Steve Vineberg. In 1975 Smith married the playwright and screenwriter Beverly Cross—"the man I should have married in the first place," as she told Chris Chase for the *New York Times* (March 12, 1982). Smith returned to the screen in 1976 in the murder mystery/comedy *Murder by Death*, written by Neil Simon. As Dora Charleston, she portrayed a detective based on Nora Charles from the famous *Thin Man* film series of the 1930s and 1940s.

The actress moved to Ontario, Canada, in 1976 to work in the repertory company at the Stratford Festival. Over the next four years, she performed there primarily alongside the actor Brian Bedford and under the direction of Robin Phillips. Perhaps to dispel the impression that she had become a caricature of herself, she took on weightier roles, appearing to high acclaim in such plays as Shakespeare's *Macbeth* and *Richard III*, Anton Chekhov's *Three Sisters* and *The Seagull*, and a new production of *Private Lives*. As Smith told Chris Chase, playing repertory is "my idea of heaven. And my idea of hell is doing eight performances a week of the same thing. Perhaps it's that I'm getting old, but I hate doing anything for a long time. I want to work in the theater, but I feel you can only really do a play for three months. After that, you just cheat everybody, especially the audience." In her performance as Irinia Arkadina in *The Seagull*, Steve Vineberg noted that she was "imperious . . . treating her sensitive son with superficial concern and dismissing him with chilly impatience." As for her interpretation of Lady Macbeth, Mel Gussow wrote for the *New York Times*, as quoted by Vineberg, that her performance was "an act of intuition and of acting alchemy. She has merged her own vivid personality with that of her charismatic subject." Her performance as Amanda in *Private Lives*, according to Vineberg, was "all tinkling ice cubes and devastating one-liners on the surface" while getting "at the heartbreak beneath, at what Alan Strachan called 'the underlying sadness of these glib and over-articulate people who twist their lives into distorted shapes because they cannot help themselves.'"

During her time in Ontario, Smith continued to work in film. In 1978 she appeared as Miss Bowers, opposite Peter Ustinov, in an adaptation of an Agatha Christie novel, *Death on the Nile*, which also featured David Niven, Bette Davis, and Mia Farrow. That same year she appeared in the Neil Simon–penned *California Suite*, about four groups of guests at the Beverly Hills Hotel. Playing alongside Michael Caine, Smith played Diana Barrie, an actress who has been nominated for an Academy Award. In his review for *All Movie Guide* (on-line), Brendon Hanley noted that Smith and Caine "steal the show." The film, also starring Bill Cosby, Jane Fonda, Walter Matthau, Richard Pryor, and Alan

Alda, received good reviews, and an interesting twist of fate found Smith herself winning an Academy Award for best supporting actress for her part in the movie. In 1980 Smith left Ontario for England, mainly for the sake of her two sons from her marriage to Stephens. "There came a time to decide whether they were going to play ice hockey or cricket," she told Matt Wolf, "so they ended up going back to school [in England]." In 1981 Smith starred as Lois Heidler in the film *Quartet*, based on the novel by Jean Rhys. In the film, set in 1920s Paris, a young woman is left destitute after her husband is jailed. She is then taken in by the Heidler family, only to find herself the object of sexual attention from the husband. That year Smith also appeared as Thetis in the cooly received *Clash of the Titans*, an adaptation of the myth of Perseus and his quest to save Andromeda.

Appearing in another movie version of an Agatha Christie mystery, Smith portrayed the character Daphne Castle in *Evil Under the Sun* (1982), which is set on an island in the Mediterranean. As Smith told Jerry Parker for *Newsday* (March 7, 1982), that assignment felt "like a holiday," as she had just spent several grueling weeks performing as Virginia Woolf in Edna O'Brien's *Virginia*, in London's West End. When the play had premiered, in 1980 at the Stratford Festival in Canada, O'Brien had stated that Smith was the only actress she could imagine playing the role of Woolf. Smith's next film was *The Missionary* (1982), in which she took the role of Lady Ames, a wealthy woman whom the Reverend Charles Fortescue (Michael Palin) meets on his way to London—where he has been called to minister to prostitutes. Ames agrees to fund the married Fortescue's work, but only if he begins an affair with her. After a supporting role in *Better Late Than Never* (1982), Smith appeared as Joyce Chilvers in *A Private Function* (1985). Set in 1947 Britain, the satire depicts the efforts of a couple to get around food-rationing regulations; Chilvers persuades her husband to steal a huge pig that has been illegally raised by a local farmer in order to sell the meat for profit. Smith's performance won her an award for best actress from the British Academy of Film & Television Arts (BAFTA). Smith followed with a performance as Lily Wynn in the 1985 comedy *Lily in Love*.

In one of Smith's best-known roles, she portrayed the spinster Charlotte Bartlett in *A Room with a View* (1986), based on the novel by E. M. Forster. Traveling through Europe as a chaperon for her cousin, Lucy Honeychurch, Bartlett orders the younger woman to return to England when Honeychurch meets a young, attractive bohemian in Italy. The film received excellent reviews, and Smith's acting garnered her an Oscar nomination for best actress in a supporting role, a BAFTA Award for best actress, and a Golden Globe Award for best performance by an actress in a supporting role in a motion picture. In a less successful role, she appeared in 1986 as Jocasta in Jean Cocteau's play *Integral Machine*. Martin Hoyle wrote in the *Financial Times*, as quoted by Matt Wolf, "One charitably assumes Miss Smith resorts to inappropriate clowning in moments of uncertainty, or possibly mutiny. At any rate, she tilts the play's balance precariously towards the over-arch." Smith followed with a highly lauded performance as Judith Hearne, an aging alcoholic who falls in love with a dishonest hotel owner, in the 1987 film *The Lonely Passion of Judith Hearne*, based on the novel by Brian Moore. "Maggie Smith's measured performance fills Jack Clayton's film with a sweet tragedy," Desson Howe wrote for the *Washington Post* (January 22, 1988, on-line). "Her eyes glisten with exhilaration. They're drenched with heartbreak here, cloudy with drunkenness there. Her frailty and desperation are fetching." For her work in that movie, Smith won a BAFTA Award for best actress. In the television miniseries *Talking Heads*, she played Susan, the unhappy alcoholic wife of a vicar in the segment "Bed Among the Lentils," a 50-minute solo performance. "[Smith's] emotional commitment to Judith's collapse as she finds her final romantic hopes dashed, her neighbors mean-spirited and her church unyielding can only be called extreme," Steve Vineberg noted. "She does the kind of acting that first puts you in the character's shoes and then begins to strip away layers of her skin." Her performance garnered her a nomination for a BAFTA TV Award for best actress, and a best-actress award from the Royal Televison Society.

In 1987 Smith appeared in a staging of *Lettice and Lovage* at London's Globe Theater. In 1990 the well-received production was brought to the Ethel Barrymore Theatre, on Broadway, where Smith had made her U.S. debut 34 years earlier. Smith portrayed Lettice, a tour guide who tries to forget the drab present by embellishing her stories of the distant past. "Lettice wants to brighten the whole world, but, yes, I suppose she is in a way sad," Smith told Matt Wolf, "though she wouldn't admit to it; I don't think she ever thinks she's sad. Her ebullience is there all the time, but I mean it is sad. It's very hard for people like that to find employment." Smith gave that performance at a difficult period in her own life. She had recently fallen off a bicycle in the British Virgin Islands, fracturing her shoulder and upper arm, which delayed the opening of the show; during her recovery, she was told that a condition with which she had been diagnosed earlier—Graves' disease, a hyperthyroid condition requiring surgery around her eyes—had worsened. The actress went into near-seclusion for about a year while undergoing radiotherapy and eye surgery. Eventually she was able to resume work on *Lettice and Lovage*, for which she won a Tony Award. "It's been kind of like a fog of despair, really," she told Wolf. "It was ghastly having a broken arm; ghastly with the play, letting everybody down; and on top of that, I looked absolutely frightening, and didn't know which way to turn." In a bright spot, Smith was named a Dame Commander of the Order of the British Empire (the equivalent of knighthood) in 1990 for her accomplishments in theater and film; she thus became the only British actress of her generation, other than her friend Judi Dench, to have been made a dame.

Smith returned from seclusion in 1991 to appear as an aging Wendy in *Hook*, the *Peter Pan* sequel directed by Steven Spielberg. The following year Smith was cast in a supporting role as Mother Superior in the comedy *Sister Act*, starring Whoopi Goldberg. A popular movie, *Sister Act* nonetheless received poor reviews, although Hal Hinson noted for the *Washington Post* (May 29, 1992, on-line), "Only Smith, whose character has seen the convent as a foxhole from the turmoil of the world, is able to give any dimension to her cliched role." Smith would later appear in the film's sequel. She gave a series of lauded performances in 1993, appearing in the television mystery *Memento Mori* as Mrs. Mabel Pettigrew, then as Violet Venable in a television adaptation of Tennessee Williams's *Suddenly Last Summer*, which garnered her an Emmy Award nomination for outstanding lead actress in a miniseries or special. Remarking on her performance, Steve Vineberg wrote, "You think you're listening to a ghost, a desiccated figure smothered in gardenias, and the odor of poison oozes out from behind her white face, waved hair and cool silk. Smith has never looked so diminutive, so the amazing death's-head power of her Mrs. Venable is all that more remarkable." In that year's *The Secret Garden*, an adaptation of the novel by Frances Hodgson Burnett, Smith played Mrs. Medlock, who manages the estate in which the story is set. The movie tells the story of a young British girl who leaves India for England after the deaths of her parents. Settling in at her uncle's estate, she begins to restore a garden that had been neglected for years—and to discover several secrets about the manor. For her role, Smith was nominated for a BAFTA Award for best supporting actress.

After supporting roles as the Duchess of York in a film adaptation of Shakespeare's *Richard III* (1995) and as Gunilla Garson Goldberg in *First Wives Club* (1996), Smith received rave reviews for her portrayal of Lavinia Penniman in the movie *Washington Square* (1997), an adaptation of the Henry James novel. Penniman is the aunt of Catherine Sloper, who is in love with a man of whom her father disapproves. Excited by the illicit affair, Penniman does everything she can to facilitate her niece's romance. "Looking like a newly groomed cocker spaniel with sausage curls dripping on her face," Edward Guthman wrote for the *San Francisco Chronicle* (October 10, 1997, on-line), "Smith seems to be doing a send-up of Aunt Pittypat from *Gone With the Wind*. It's a hoot of a character: When she isn't wagging her tail with vicarious delight over Catherine's romance, she's speaking in lines that sound as if she'd read too many Victorian romances." In *Tea with Mussolini* (1999), directed by Franco Zeffirelli, Smith starred as Lady Hester Random, a leader of an English exile community in Florence, Italy, who live a sheltered existence that they believe is made possible by Smith's teas with the Italian dictator of the title. "Craning her long neck, her saucer eyes bulging with indignation, Ms. Smith suggests a rare, high-strung shore bird crankily peering down its beak at the more common species on the beach," Stephen Holden wrote for the *New York Times* (May 14, 1999, on-line). At the British Academy Awards, Smith won the honor for best performance by an actress in a supporting role for *Tea with Mussolini*. She followed with roles in the drama *The Last September*, based on an Elizabeth Bowen novel, and the comedy *Curtain Call*, in which she appeared with Michael Caine as one half of a ghostly duo.

In 2000 Smith played Betsey Trotwood in an acclaimed television production of Charles Dickens's *David Copperfield*. Her role won her a best-actress award for a television performance from BAFTA and an Emmy nomination for outstanding supporting actress in a miniseries or movie. In a role that made the prolific actress known among movie fans of all ages, Smith appeared in the supporting role of Professor Minerva McGonagall in *Harry Potter and the Sorcerer's Stone* (2001), based on the hugely successful children's novel by J. K. Rowling. She was reportedly the only performer Rowling specifically wanted to act in the film. Smith next appeared as the financially strapped Constance, Countess of Trentham, in *Gosford Park* (2001), a period-piece murder mystery directed by Robert Altman. As the snooty and opinionated but nonetheless charming Constance, Smith was nominated for an Academy Award for best actress in a supporting role, a BAFTA Award, and a Golden Globe. Writing for the *Washington Post* (January 4, 2002, on-line), Stephen Hunter noted that Constance was "holding the crown for malicious malignancy crossed with snobbish grotesqueness. To watch Constance dice her nephew and host Sir William . . . or poor pretty Mr. Novello for the failure of his film 'The Lodger' is probably worth the price of admission." "Maggie Smith is nicely nasty, with a naughty smile that suggests she's fully aware of just how much scenery she is stealing and chewing," Joe Leyden noted for the *San Francisco Examiner* (January 4, 2002, on-line). "I thought she was absolutely horrid," Smith told Eugenia Zukerman about her character in *Gosford Park*. "But it's always quite fun to play those sort of aggressive people, if you know what I mean." In 2002 Smith turned up in *Divine Secrets of the Ya-Ya Sisterhood*, as Caro, and reprised her role as Minerva McGonagall in *Harry Potter and the Chamber of Secrets*. She also acted in the television film *The Roman Spring of Mrs. Stone*. In 2003 she will star in the film *My House in Umbria*.

In his 2000 article for *Salon*, Steve Vineberg wrote, "The etchings of style in a Maggie Smith performance are unmistakable. First observe the face, with its sharp, art-deco angles, which she tends to stretch into a long rectangle to chart psychic damage, the lines creased as if with a palette knife, the lips pressed taut, elongating the skin between her lips and her nose and lending it a moneyed air. She can alter the shape of her luminous nut-brown eyes to italicize a word or a phrase. Her string-bean figure is Modigliani-like in some settings, meager and scarecrowlike in others. . . . But Smith's chief glory is her vocal prowess. She turns nasality into a virtue, whipping it up into a kind of mock-aristocratic fog, and her buzzing sibilance leaves a silvery trail through her lines—sometimes suggesting a man in expert drag working a sly parody on femininity. Her voice can be plush or glassy, or break up into little glittering pebbles; she can pull hard on the syllables as if they were taffy or fold her voice into paper-thin layers or fly into a startlingly high, catfight shriek or an abandoned whine."

Smith's second husband, Beverly Cross, died on March 20, 1998, after a series of aneurysms. Her two sons from her first marriage—Toby Stephens and Chris Larkin—are both actors. Asked by Jeff Gordinier for *Entertainment Weekly* (March 15, 2002) what sort of advice she had given her children with respect to acting, she replied, "None. They've been with me long enough to know that it's *hell.*" Smith's most recent theater performance, as Miss Shepherd in Alan Bennett's *The Lady in the Van*, was a smashing success in London. "[Smith is] funny in that she regards her whole life as a succession of disasters," Alan Bennett told Matt Wolf. "She once defined the appeal of acting: 'You've created a person, and I don't think you can ever create yourself; it's kind of a mess isn't it? I am, anyway.'" Smith enjoys reading, walking, and relaxing at the 15th-century Sussex farmhouse she and her second husband bought in 1981. She also has a flat in the Chelsea neighborhood of London. Along with Ben Kingsley, John Hurt, and Julie Waters, Smith formed United British Artists, a film and theater production company. Smith is notoriously shy and gives few interviews. "I probably am [reclusive]," she told Gordinier. "But that's all right. I mean, the opposite is what? Whirling around and going to all these [celebrity] things?" She also dislikes talking about acting. Smith received the Shakespeare Prize in 1991 and in 1994 was elected to the Theatre Hall of Fame. — G.O.

Suggested Reading: *Christian Science Monitor* p17 Mar. 23, 1970, with photo; *Entertainment Weekly* p32+ Mar. 15, 2002, with photos; *New York Post* p19 Apr. 11, 1970, with photo; *New York Times* II p17 July 21, 1968, with photo, II p1 Aug. 3, 1969, Mar. 12, 1982, with photo; *New York Times Magazine* p37+ Mar. 18, 1990, with photos; *Newsday* II p3 Mar. 7, 1982, with photo; *Salon* (on-line) June 6, 2000, with photo; *Washington Post* F p11 Sep. 28, 1969, with photo

Selected Films: *Nowhere to Go*, 1958; *The V.I.P.s*, 1963; *The Pumpkin Eater*, 1964; *Young Cassidy*, 1965; *Othello*, 1965; *The Honey Pot*, 1967; *Hot Millions*, 1968; *The Prime of Miss Jean Brodie*, 1969; *Travels with My Aunt*, 1972; *Love and Pain and the Whole Damn Thing*, 1972; *Murder by Death*, 1976; *Death on the Nile*, 1978; *California Suite*, 1978; *Quartet*, 1981; *Evil Under the Sun*, 1982; *The Missionary*, 1982; *A Private Function*, 1985; *A Room with a View*, 1986; *The Lonely Passion of Judith Hearne*, 1987; *Sister Act*, 1992; *Suddenly, Last Summer*, 1993; *The Secret Garden*, 1993; *Richard III*, 1995; *Washington Square*, 1997; *Tea with Mussolini*, 1999; *David Copperfield*, 1999; *Harry Potter and the Sorcerer's Stone*, 2001; *Gosford Park*, 2001; *Divine Secrets of the Ya-Ya Sisterhood*, 2002; *Harry Potter and the Chamber of Secrets*, 2002

Selected Plays: *The Stepmother*, 1958; *Rhinoceros*, 1960; *Strip the Willow*, 1960; *The Rehearsal*, 1961; *The Private Ear*, 1962; *The Public Eye*, 1962; *Mary, Mary*, 1963; *Othello*, 1964; *The Country Wife*, 1969; *The Beaux' Stratagem*, 1970; *Virginia*, 1980; *Integral Machine*, 1986; *Lettice and Lovage*, 1987; *The Lady in the Van*, 1999

---

Courtesy of Bill Wiegand/University of Illinois

## Soffer, Olga

(SOH-fer)

*Sep. 9, 1942– Anthropologist; archaeologist*

*Address: University of Illinois at Urbana-Champaign, Dept. of Anthropology, 109 Davenport Hall, 607 S. Mathews, Urbana, IL 61801*

In a typical museum of natural history, the diorama depicting what is labeled a moment in the Upper

Paleolithic era—the last part of the Old Stone Age—shows people clothed in animal furs gazing intently at a woolly mammoth looming dangerously nearby; the men are poised to launch their spears at the gigantic beast, while the women, with babies in their arms and older children by their sides, huddle further away. According to the anthropologist and archaeologist Olga Soffer, such tableaus give the public a misleading conception of life in the Upper Paleolithic, which stretched from about 40,000 B.C. to about 10,000 B.C. Through her research at sites in the Czech Republic and the Central Russian Plain, Soffer has found evidence that *Homo sapiens* discovered the art of weaving in or before 27,000 B.C.—at least twice as early in prehistory as was previously supposed; therefore, the wardrobes of humans contained not only clothing made from animal hides but also woven apparel, some of it indicating an extraordinary degree of skill in weaving. Soffer has also discovered that Paleolithic humans made mesh, such as that used in netting. From that finding, and in light of the abundance of bones of rabbits and other small animals along with those of big game at her study sites, she has also theorized that Paleolithic women hunted small prey with nets. This finding, Soffer has explained, shows that prehistoric women as well as men provided food for their families, and thus they played a far larger role in their societies than was previously believed. Referring to this broadened conception of women's roles in Paleolithic times, Soffer declared to Lisa Parks for *Archaeology Today* (January/February 2000, on-line), "If the public should understand one thing about prehistory, it is that the past was peopled not only by prehistoric men, but also by prehistoric women."

Olga Soffer was born on September 9, 1942 in Belgrade, in the former Yugoslavia (known also at that time as the Kingdom of Serbs, Croats, and Slovenes). The families of her mother and father had fled Russia, their homeland, after that country's civil war (1918–20), in which they had supported the losing, anti-Bolshevik side. Her parents settled in Yugoslavia, only to be banished in 1951, during the regime of the Communist dictator Josip Broz Tito. After some time in a refugee camp in Italy, the Soffers immigrated to New York City. "Life was so fluid and changeable that you did not think, 'What am I going to be 20 years from now?'" Soffer recalled to Lisa Parks. "You didn't know where you were going to live next year." In an interview with Chris Bury for *ABC News* (June 15, 2001, on-line), Soffer said that she grew up primarily in the New York City borough of Brooklyn, where she attended high school. She next enrolled at Hunter College, a division of the City University of New York (CUNY) in Manhattan, and earned a bachelor's degree in political science. She then completed an executive training program with Federated Department Stores in New York City. For the following 10 years, she worked in the field of retail-fashion promotion in New York City, at such venues as the Abraham & Straus (A&S) department store. "This 'real world' experience was invaluable," she wrote for her University of Illinois Web site, "because it taught me organizational as well as leadership and team playing skills."

As the excitement and stimulation of her work began to fade, "I started playing hooky," as Soffer admitted to Kate Wong for *Scientific American* (November 2000). "I'd go to fashion shows and actually sneak off to the library." "To feed her mind," as Wong put it, Soffer began taking classes in art at night. Her studies in modern art piqued her interest in Cubism, which in turn led her to discover African art and then other forms of so-called primitive art. "And from primitive art, I went into prehistoric art," she told Parks, "and from prehistoric art into prehistoric lifeways, and here we are." Soffer returned to Hunter College and received a master's degree in archaeology. During that period she also took a summer off from her job to participate in an archaeological dig in France.

Soffer next enrolled in the Ph.D. program in anthropology at the Graduate Center of the City University of New York. For two years, from fall to spring, she continued to work in the fashion industry, attending classes at night. In the summer of 1977, accompanied by her husband (they later divorced) and young daughter, Soffer conducted research on the Central Russian Plain, where there are remnants of Upper Paleolithic dwellings constructed with the bones of woolly mammoths. (Relatives of the Indian elephant, woolly mammoths became extinct about 10,000 years ago. Adult males stood about nine-and-a-half feet tall at the shoulder and weighed about three tons.) During subsequent summers Soffer did research at Avdeevo, Mezhirich, and other sites on the plain. She was attracted to that area in part because of her ability to speak and read Russian and her familiarity with Russian culture. The region also appealed to her because of the virtual absence of archaeological researchers in what was then the Soviet Union. "It was a natural opening: a vacant niche," she explained to Lisa Parks.

In 1984 Soffer earned a Ph.D. in anthropology from the CUNY Graduate Center. She began her academic career as an adjunct instructor at three colleges: Hunter and Lehman, in New York City, and the University of Wisconsin at Milwaukee. In 1985 she joined the faculty of the University of Illinois at Urbana-Champaign as an assistant professor of anthropology. She was promoted to associate professor in 1988 and to full professor in 1992. Thanks to her fluency in Russian, Serbo-Croatian, and Czech, in some years she has also taught in the university's Department of Slavic Languages and Literatures, which she headed from 1993 to 1998. (She is also fluent in Italian, as well as English, and can read seven other languages.)

In addition to digging at archaeological sites herself, Soffer examined objects discovered by others and then stored in museum collections. At one such museum in 1991, while sifting through hundreds of clay fragments unearthed in the vicinities of Pavlov and Dolní Vestonice, in southern Moravia, in what is now the Czech Republic, she noticed that a few pieces had series of parallel lines indented on their surfaces. She took photos of the fragments but did nothing with the slides until one night in 1995, during a visit to her home by James M. Adovasio; an expert on ancient fiber technology, Adovasio is the chairman of the Department of Anthropology/Archaeology at Mercyhurst College, in Erie, Pennsylvania, and the director of the school's archaeological institute. That night, lacking a movie screen, Soffer projected the slides onto the front of her refrigerator. Adovasio immediately recognized the lines on the images of the clay as impressions of plant fibers. The patterns of the lines on a few of the fragments even appeared to have resulted from the pressure of interlacing fibers.

Soon afterward Soffer and Adovasio returned to the Czech Republic, where Adovasio made positive casts of 90 clay fragments. (These casts showed the lines as raised rather than indented.) When Adovasio and his Mercyhurst colleague David C. Hyland examined the casts under a zoom stereomicroscope, they found that 43 of the 90 pieces showed the impressions of basketry and textiles, including some textiles that appeared to have been as finely woven as a modern-day linen tablecloth. Perhaps even more impressive, Hyland found that four of the samples showed impressions of mesh—cordage with knots. The findings of Soffer, Adovasio, and Hyland were announced at a 1995 meeting of the Society for American Archaeology. In 1997 Adovasio identified imprints of mesh on a series of new casts Soffer had made in the Moravian Museum, in Brno, Czech Republic. The team noted that the impressions of the fiber might have been made accidentally—for example, when a basket was placed on a freshly laid (and therefore still-soft) clay floor. They also could have been made through such deliberate actions as lining a basket with clay to make it watertight.

What made these discoveries extraordinarily exciting—and surprising—was that, as revealed by radiocarbon dating, the imprinted fragments were between 25,000 and 27,000 years old—far older than the oldest-known remains of a basket (thought to be about 9,000 years old) or woven fabric (about 13,000 years old). Moreover, the existence of a remnant of mesh indicated, first, that prehistoric people secured meat not only by killing animals by means of spears, arrows, or stone hammers but also by capturing them with nets; second, as Soffer pointed out to Kate Wong, since "you don't need to be a strong, brawny, skilled hunter" to capture game with nets, "you can participate and help with this kind of communal hunt if you're a kid with no experience, if you're a nursing mother, et cetera."

The realization that Paleolithic humans were able to make nets provided answers to questions that had puzzled Soffer for some time. Scientists had long assumed that during the Paleolithic era, humans had subsisted on meat from woolly mammoths and other large game, and that, in view of the dangerousness of such animals, only men had hunted them; women had remained in their dwellings, caring for their children, according to this theory. What had puzzled Soffer was that nearly 50 percent of the bones discovered near Pavlov and Dolní Vestonice were those of small animals, such as Ice Age rabbits and foxes. Also perplexing was that the skeletal remains of the mammoths included their skulls; since a skull could weigh as much as 220 pounds, Soffer reasoned that the hunters would probably have left the head of a slaughtered mammoth at the site of the killing rather than drag it home. She also found unlikely the long-held idea that Paleolithic humans had relied on mammoths for food, because no known group of hunter-gatherers has made elephant meat a major part of their diet.

Soffer has theorized that Paleolithic humans at her study sites chose to settle at locations where a plentiful supply of mammoth bones already existed; after all, such "cemeteries," containing elephant bones, have been found near water holes in Africa. (As Peter F. Thorbahn pointed out in *Natural History* [April 1984], "Elephant carcasses tend to occur near permanent sources of water, perhaps because sick or aged elephants do not have the strength to keep up with their herd in the search for forage and water.") The mammoth bones, and their tusks, were used as housing material and perhaps as fuel as well.

Soffer and her colleagues further amended theories about prehistorical humans after reexamining several of the so-called Venus figurines from the Paleolithic era. These small sculptures of extremely buxom women are thought to have been made for use in fertility rites. In *Current Anthropology* (Spring 2000), Soffer, Adovasio, and Hyland wrote that carvings on some of the figurines were almost undoubtedly meant to depict articles of woven or mesh clothing. "This was one of my favorite moments of my career," Soffer told Lisa Parks. "Looking at those lines and realizing: 'Aha! They had clothes in the Paleolithic!'" One of the figurines, the 25,000-year-old Venus of Willendorf, is wearing a woven cap (the carvings were previously thought to represent a fancy hairdo); the Venus of Lespugue is adorned with a highly detailed string skirt, which apparently no one had noticed before but which seemed obvious once Soffer had pointed it out. The ability to weave would also have enabled humans to make lightweight containers for transporting food and slings for carrying babies. Paleolithic people might even have used their knowledge of weaving to lash logs together to make rafts.

In addition to Venus figurines, Soffer's current research focuses on Upper Paleolithic technology in Moravia and storage economies (in which seasonally abundant food is stored for use in leaner periods) on the Central East European Plain. She is also trying to identify implements that Paleolithic peoples might have used to produce textiles, a task that entails reexamining items in museum collections and elsewhere that at present are thought to be tools for hunting or other activities unrelated to the making of fabrics.

Soffer, who lives in Urbana, serves on the editorial boards of the journals *Soviet Anthropology and Archaeology* and the *Journal of World Prehistory*. In 1999 the Russian Academy of Sciences awarded her an honorary doctorate. "It's nice when the circle closes—from losing the civil war in [Russia], to returning as an American scholar, to an honorary doctorate from the Russian Academy of Sciences," Soffer told Lisa Parks. "Yes, you can go home again." She also said to Parks, "Some people discover what they want to do for the rest of their lives at age 14. Others, like me, are into serial careers. Who knows what I'll do next?" — G.O.

Suggested Reading: *ABC News* (on-line) June 15, 2001; *Archaeology Today* (on-line) Jan./Feb. 2000; *BBC News* (on-line) June 14, 2000; *Discover* p62+ Apr. 1998; *New York Times* C p1 May 9, 1995, with photo; *Scientific American* p32+ Nov. 2000, with photo; University of Illinois at Urbana-Champaign Web site

---

## Stroman, Susan

*Oct. 17, 1954– Theatrical choreographer; director*

*Address: c/o Flora Roberts Agency, Penthouse A, 157 W. 57th St., New York, NY 10019*

Carol Rosegg/Courtesy of Lincoln Center Theater

"I feel like I'm a painter almost, except my paintings move," the theatrical choreographer and director Susan Stroman told Alona Wartofsky for the *Washington Post* (February 17, 2002). "I know that people are moved by art when they see it, and to think that the movement of this painting could actually reach out . . . is thrilling to me." Stroman, known in New York's theater circles as Stro, has experienced a meteoric rise since she created the Tony Award–winning dances for *Crazy for You*, which ran on Broadway from 1992 to 1996. For years before her name reached national prominence, Stroman worked as a dancer, then slowly ascended through the ranks of assistant choreographers, assistant directors, and choreographers in Off-Broadway and regional productions. The work of the extraordinarily versatile Stroman has ranged from musical revivals (*Showboat*, *The Music Man*, and *Oklahoma!*), to movies-turned-musicals (*The Producers*, *Big*), to an all-dance show (*Contact*). Since 1992 she has won five Tony Awards, one for direction and four for choreography; on three occasions, three productions in which she had a hand ran concurrently in the same season. Stroman won the 2001 *Dance Magazine* Award for her myriad contributions to musical theater.

The second of the three children of Charles and Frances Stroman, Susan Stroman was born on October 17, 1954 in Wilmington, Delaware. Music was a vital part of her family life. Her father, who sold appliances and musical instruments for a living, is an accomplished pianist and guitarist, and he passed on his love of musical theater to his children. "My family didn't have a lot of money, so when those old [movie musicals] came on television they sat me down to watch," Susan Stroman told Jennifer Dunning for the *New York Times* (February 16, 1992). Inspired by the dancer and choreographer Fred Astaire and, indirectly, by his collaborator Hermes Pan, a dancer and choreographer who helped both Astaire and Astaire's frequent movie partner Ginger Rogers, Stroman began to put her ideas to work at age five, when she enrolled in dance lessons. While growing up she studied tap, jazz, and ballet and also had lessons in guitar and piano. "Ever since I was a little girl I would imagine music, and I'd see hordes of people dancing in my head and I'd imagine these huge scenarios," she told Jack Kroll for *Newsweek* (April 17, 2000). "I'd watch Fred Astaire and Ginger Rogers movies and I understood how music supported the dance, how their dances were dramatic situations. Music makes my brain dance." To prepare for her career, Stroman also took baton-twirling lessons. (Her skill in baton twirling is reflected in her dances that make use of flying props, such as dinner rolls in one segment of *Contact*.) She performed with the Candlelight Community Theater and choreographed her first numbers as a teenager, for halftime shows at her high school's sports events. After she completed high school, she studied at the Delaware Center for Tap and Jazz while simultaneously attending the University of Delaware, from which she earned a bachelor's degree in theater in 1976. She vividly remembers becoming entranced with musical theater a few years earlier, after seeing a touring performance of *Seesaw*, starring Tommy Tune, at the Wilmington Playhouse.

After her college graduation Stroman found jobs as a dancer and, in addition, choreography assignments in the Philadelphia area. But she had set her sights on New York, as she explained to Jennifer Dunning: "I got to be sort of a big fish in a little pond. I wanted to come to New York to choreograph. But I knew I couldn't just take over, so I came as a song-and-dance girl." In the late 1970s she danced in touring productions of *Chicago* and *Sugar Babies*. In 1979 she landed a part in a Broadway tap-dance show, *Whoopee!* For the 1980 Off-Broadway production of *Musical Chairs*, which ran for just two weeks, Stroman served as the dance captain, assistant choreographer, and assistant director. In 1983 she and Jeff Veazey, a dancer and choreographer, pitched an idea for a new musical called *Trading Places* to the Equity Library Theater (ELT), in Manhattan. Using old songs and re-created dance routines, they fashioned a story "about two people obsessed with old movies," as Stroman told Hilary Ostlere for *Dance Magazine* (May 1992). "The project was great but never went further than ELT—mainly because of the difficulties in clearing all those song rights."

In the mid-1980s Stroman gave up dancing and promoted herself solely as a choreographer. She worked on the Off-Broadway shows *Broadway Babylon* and *Sayonara* before choreographing the 1987 revival of *Flora, The Red Menace*, by the songwriting duo John Kander and Fred Ebb. The show, mounted in a tiny venue in the Greenwich Village section of Manhattan, attracted the attention of the theatrical director and producer Harold "Hal" Prince and the actress and dancer Liza Minnelli, who had starred in the original, Broadway production. Prince asked Stroman to choreograph his 1989 New York City Opera presentation of *Don Giovanni*; Minnelli, who needed a choreographer who could also tap dance, asked Stroman to help her develop her show *Liza—Stepping Out at Radio City Music Hall*, which ran in 1991. "We worked out in front of a mirror together for a week," Stroman recalled to Ostlere. "I loved working with her." (Stroman received an Emmy nomination for the HBO broadcast of the show.) Speaking of her successful career path, Stroman said during an "Ask a Star" forum on *Broadway.com* (August 10, 2000), "The more experience you can get the better. Create your own work. Create your piece. Create your own presence in the theater community. Don't wait around for someone to hire you. I stirred up most every job that pushed me up the ladder. I was lucky those jobs caught the eyes of the right people."

Stroman's breakthrough came with the assignment to choreograph *Crazy for You*, a musical with well-known and newly rediscovered George Gershwin tunes; the story was loosely based on Ira and George Gershwin's 1930 musical, *Girl Crazy*. *Crazy for You* was an enormous undertaking, with 19 dance numbers; in addition, Stroman helped to rewrite the second act shortly before the Broadway previews. Following the original plot, about an easterner who moves West, *Crazy for You* is set in a 1930s Nevada mining town. To gather ideas for the dances, Stroman researched dance steps popular in the Old West, read about mining towns, and traveled in Nevada. She then planned the dances and demonstrated them to the cast. "If you go in with everything mapped out and thought through, you can feed off the actor's talent," she explained to Jennifer Dunning. "If he spins better to the right or kicks better to the left, I can change my idea according to what they do best." While mounting *Crazy for You*, she was also part of the team that developed *And the World Goes 'Round*, a showcase for the music of Kander and Ebb. "There was a morning at the beginning of February [1992] when I woke up knowing I had three shows running in New York City—Liza's *Stepping Out at Radio City*, *And the World Goes 'Round*, and *Crazy for You* in preview—all within a five-block radius of Broadway. I sobbed for half a day because it was 'dreams realized,'" she told Hilary Ostlere.

The 1991–92 theater season brought Stroman critical applause. *And the World Goes 'Round*, mounted Off-Broadway, earned her a 1991 Outer Critics' Circle Award for best choreography, and *Crazy for You* earned fine reviews. "Around the slender boy-meets-girl plot, director Mike Ockrent, choreographer Susan Stroman and set designer Robin Wagner have spun their confection of high spirits, wit and talent," Lloyd Rose wrote for the *Washington Post* (December 27, 1991). "After so many musicals that are about their sets, their directors or (sometimes) their stars, it's pretty wonderful to see one that's about its music." In his review for the *New York Times* (February 20, 1992), Frank Rich wrote, "Ms. Stroman's dances do not comment on such apparent influences as Fred Astaire, Hermes Pan and Busby Berkeley so much as reinvent them. Rather than piling on exhausting tap routines to steamroll the audience into enjoying itself, the choreographer uses the old forms in human proportion, to bring out specific feelings in the music and lyrics." Stroman won Broadway's top honor, a Tony Award, in 1992 for her *Crazy for You* choreography. Additional prizes followed, including a 1992 Drama Desk Award, a 1992 Outer Critics' Circle Award, and the 1993 Laurence Olivier Award, presented by the Society of London Theatre.

Continuing her hectic pace, Stroman choreographed Tom Jones and Harvey Schmidt's *110 in the Shade* (the musical version of *The Rainmaker)* for the New York City Opera in the summer of 1992. She had "already done the research for it," as she pointed out to Hilary Ostlere. "It's another flat, hot place in the West." Also that year Harold Prince handpicked Stroman to choreograph his Broadway revival of Jerome Kern and Oscar Hammerstein's *Show Boat*. The revival debuted in Toronto, Canada, in 1993; in 1994 it moved to New York, where it ran for over two years. Stroman's work on *Show Boat* won her a second Tony Award for best choreography and an Astaire Award from the Theatre Development Fund, in 1996.

Not all of Stroman's projects have been successful. The 1993 Broadway mounting of a musical version of William Inge's 1953 drama *Picnic*, for which she created the choreography and musical interludes, lasted only six weeks. The theatrical version of the popular 1988 movie *Big*, choreographed by Stroman, received a critical drubbing and survived on Broadway for less than six months. *Steel Pier*, a 1997 musical that Stroman developed and choreographed as a showcase for the music of Kander and Ebb, also suffered from poor reviews and soon closed, although Stroman's dances were generally seen as a bright spot in the production. (Both *Big* and *Steel Pier* earned Tony nominations for best choreography.)

Stroman's distinctive vision for musical theater led her to directing. Her first major directorial effort was a revival of *The Music Man*, the 1957 Meredith Willson classic about a con artist who transforms a staid Iowa town through the power of music and imagination. Stroman put her own spin on the show's romantic ending, in which the con artist wins the love of the town's prim librarian. "That's a proper ending, because it's about an adult relationship," Stroman said to Martin F. Kohn for the *Detroit Free Press* (November 26, 2001). "But then I put the script down and thought: What's everyone in the town doing four months from now. . . . And then I thought to myself, well, maybe they've all taken some sort of lessons. And then I thought, wouldn't it be wonderful if the entire company could play the trombone?" "I ended up sending [all the actors] to trombone class every day at 4 o'clock during rehearsals," Stroman told Kohn. After the last-act curtain fell on Stroman's *Music Man*, it rose again to reveal the 38 members of the cast in band uniforms, playing—with the enthusiasm and unpolished skills of beginners—the trademark song "76 Trombones." The reviews for *The Music Man* were generally positive; Stroman received stellar notices for her choreography but less enthusiastic assessments of her direction. "Ms. Stroman's *Music Man* is not the dream show you might have hoped for. It makes you feel ridiculously happy one instant and seriously sleepy the next," Ben Brantley wrote for the *New York Times* (April 28, 2000). "Here, her transforming imagination stops when the music stops. . . . When the show is singing or especially dancing, it often seems to have winged feet; when it's just talking or clowning around, those feet are decidedly flat." He added, "This *Music Man* . . . still has more helium than any of the other self-described family entertainments on Broadway." Stroman received two 2000 Tony Award nominations for her work, for best director of a musical and best choreographer. (The use of nonunion performers in the touring company of the show ruffled many feathers in the theater community.)

*Contact*, Stroman's second offering in the spring of 2000, premiered at Lincoln Center, in Manhattan; after receiving rave reviews, it moved to Broadway. Conceived, directed, and choreographed by Stroman, *Contact* consists of three acts, each of which presents a different story illustrating the complexity of love and sex; the stories are acted out through dance to the accompaniment of recorded music, with little dialogue and no singing. Stroman rejected the contention by some in the theater community that *Contact* is not a true musical. "The elements that make up musical theater are music, dance and dialogue," she told Alona Wartofsky. "You wouldn't say that [*Les Misérables*] isn't a musical because it has no dance. And you wouldn't say *Fosse* wasn't a musical because it has no book. [*Contact*] has more dance than it does dialogue, but it certainly has music. . . . I think, in the end, people admire it. It's not a new way to do a musical, but it's certainly a musical in a unique form."

The first act of *Contact*, called "The Swing," is based on a painting by Jean-Honoré Fragonard; this segment depicts games of seduction involving a young woman, a nobleman, and a servant. The second act, "Did You Move?," focuses on a woman who attempts to find the courage to leave her oppressive husband. The third act, "Contact," which Stroman conceived before the others, is about a suicidal advertising executive whose life is transformed by a woman in a yellow dress. "I wanted to create a piece that would appeal to all of us who live in [New York City]," Stroman told Chris Jones for the *Chicago Tribune* (April 7, 2002). "We live in a teeming metropolis, yet we don't seem to make contact with anyone. We all know people who have achieved success but who also wake up one morning and feel completely alone." Stroman has traced her idea for the woman in the yellow dress to a mysterious figure she saw one night at an after-hours swing-dancing club in New York. In the midst of a sea of black clothes, she recalled to Martin Kohn, appeared "this beautiful girl in a yellow dress. . . . She would just step forward when she wanted to dance with someone, and I thought to myself that this girl would change somebody's life tonight." Stroman developed *Contact* with the playwright John Weidman and the artistic director of the Lincoln Center Theater, Andre Bishop. Since it relied so heavily on dance to tell the stories, *Contact* required dancers with strong acting skills, as Stroman explained to Michael Kuchwara of the Associated Press, according to the *Naples [Florida] Daily News* (March 18, 2000). "In every show I do, I always ask the dancers to be more than dancers. They have to be actors. At auditions, I will often give them a dance combination, but then I'll call out different emotions for them to do, too—having them do the same dance combination aggressively, romantically, flirtatiously or shyly. That helps me to know if they have the creative mind to be in the show." *Contact* earned Tony Awards for best musical, best choreography, and best featured actress in a musical (for Karen Ziemba, who portrayed the wife in "Did You Move?").

In the spring of 2001 Stroman's name again appeared in lights on Broadway, when she directed and choreographed the musical comedy *The Producers*. A farce about an absurd Broadway scam that backfires, *The Producers* is based on the 1968 movie of the same name, which Mel Brooks both wrote and directed. Brooks co-wrote the book for the musical, along with Thomas Meehan, and wrote both the words and music of 17 new songs for it. Starring Nathan Lane and Matthew Broderick as the characters portrayed in the movie by Zero Mostel and Gene Wilder, *The Producers* opened with multi-million-dollar advance ticket sales and has attracted sellout audiences ever since. "How do you single out highlights in a bonfire?" Ben Brantley asked rhetorically in a glowing review for the *New York Times* (April 20, 2001). "Everybody who sees *The Producers*—and that should be as close to everybody as the St. James Theater allows—is going to be hard pressed to choose one favorite bit from the sublimely ridiculous spectacle. . . . [The show] is much more than the sum of its gorgeously silly parts." Others critics were less enthusiastic. In the *New York Review of Books* (June 21, 2001), for example, Daniel Mendelsohn complained, "If the new *Producers* is a hit, it isn't . . . because it challenges social norms about taste or propriety in any significant way, as the film tried so strenuously to do." Rather, he continued, unlike the movie, "the musical of *The Producers* risks absolutely nothing. . . . Brooks's new musical has smoothly processed his movie, whose greatest virtue was its anarchic, grotesque energy, into a wholly safe evening." Nevertheless, he admitted that the musical is "every bit as sleek and cleverly choreographed, lighted, designed, and costumed—and as splendidly performed—as the delirious critics have unanimously declared it to be, and it deserves its fifteen Tony nominations." *The Producers* won a record 12 Tony Awards. (The previous record holder in Tony Awards was *Hello, Dolly!*, in 1964, with 10; in Tony nominations, *Company*, 1971, with 14.) Stroman herself won Tonys for direction and choreography. "Each show has helped me get to the next show," she explained to Alona Wartofsky. "It's not been one of those things all of a sudden I had this big hit. It took all those 12 shows to allow me to do *The Producers*."

Stroman's next project was a dramatic musical titled *Thou Shalt Not*, an updated version of Émile Zola's 1867 psychological thriller *Thérèse Raquin*, about the costs of adultery. Directed and choreographed by Stroman, with book by David Thompson and music and lyrics by Harry Connick Jr., *Thou Shalt Not* focuses on a young married woman who has an affair with a jazz musician who had served in World War II. "Stroman is a whiz at dreamy dance scenes," Nelson Pressley wrote for the *Washington Post* (October 26, 2001). "But despite the evident seriousness and artful touches, nothing shocks or grabs; for a musical delving into a few deadly sins, it's surprisingly uninvolving." *Thou Shalt Not*, which opened on Broadway on October 25, 2001, suffered from both negative reviews and the slump in ticket sales that followed the September 11 terrorist attacks on New York City. It closed on January 6, 2002.

Meanwhile, in the late 1990s the British director Trevor Nunn had hired Stroman to choreograph a new version of the classic Richard Rodgers and Oscar Hammerstein musical *Oklahoma!* The Rodgers and Hammerstein estate, which had long insisted that all productions of *Oklahoma!* use Agnes de Mille's choreography for the original, 1943 production, gave Stroman permission to create new dances. "I don't think we've reinvented *Oklahoma!* but I do think we've rediscovered it," Stroman explained to Cathleen McGuigan for *Newsweek* (March 25, 2002). "Doing research about the West, about the fights between the farmers and the cowmen—fencing land, against land being open—led me to do choreography that had the theme of fighting and masculinity." She told Celia McGee for the New York *Daily News* (March 12, 2002) that the new choreography, which earned her another Tony nomination, is "more realistic" than de Mille's, an approach that, she said, "normally hasn't been welcomed in musical theater. Maybe it's too raw for people to be entertained, but for me as an artist it's completely fulfilling." On March 21, 2002, after a highly successful run in London, Stroman's version of *Oklahoma!* opened on Broadway, where it was greeted with bravos from audiences and most critics.

Stroman was married to Mike Ockrent, a British theater director, from 1996 until his death, from leukemia, in 1999. The couple met on the set of *Crazy for You*, which Ockrent directed; they later collaborated on *Big*, *Steel Pier*, and *The Producers*. Stroman has credited Ockrent as her inspiration for *Contact*; as she explained to Alona Wartofsky, "He just showed me what it meant to make contact, and how it enriches your life." Before Ockrent died, he and Stroman had been developing a musical based on William Friedkin's 1968 film comedy, *The Night They Raided Minsky's*, about a young Amish woman who flees her tyrannical father and joins a burlesque show in the big city. "The project was so much Mike's that every page of it is difficult for me," Stroman told Michael Kuchwara. "It needs to settle for a while." — K.S.

Suggested Reading: *Dance Magazine* p36+ May 1992, with photos; *Detroit Free Press* E p1 Nov. 26, 2001, with photo; *New York Times* II p5 Feb. 16, 1992, with photo; *Newsweek* p66+ Apr. 17, 2000, with photo; *Washington Post* G p1 Feb. 17, 2002, with photo

Selected Productions: as choreographer—*Don Giovanni*, 1989; *Liza—Stepping Out at Radio City Music Hall*, 1991; *Crazy for You*, 1992; *110 in the Shade*, 1992; *Show Boat*, 1993; *Big*, 1996; *Steel Pier*, 1997; *Oklahoma!*, 1998; as choreographer and director—*Contact*, 2000; *The Music Man*, 2000; *The Producers*, 2001

Courtesy of Bert Randolph Sugar

## Sugar, Bert Randolph

*June 7, 1936– Sportswriter*

*Address: c/o* Sports Business Journal, *120 W. Morehead St., Suite 310, Charlotte, NC 28202*

"Boxing is the one sport every great writer has been interested in. Why? Because it's the purest sport out there. It's the single most one-on-one sport in the world," Bert Randolph Sugar, a veteran sportswriter, editor, and trivia guru whose specialty is boxing, told Dean Bender for *Business Magazine* (August 12, 1979). Over the years Sugar has produced a daunting quantity of sports literature whose trademark is its straightforward, easy-to-understand style. Sugar's colorful personality and his abilities as a raconteur are nearly as celebrated as his writing; in the *New York Times* (March 29, 1995), Frank J. Prial described Sugar as an "old time, hard-drinking, wisecracking newsman." Referred to sometimes simply as "The Hat," Sugar is often found in various New York City bars, wearing a 1920s-style fedora and smoking a large cigar; he told Jack Cavanaugh, writing for the *New York Times* (June 23, 1996), that "some of [his] best, and worst, writing has been done at Manhattan bars. . . ." Sugar, who worked briefly as a lawyer and for a decade as an advertising man, has edited and published several sports magazines and written more than 80 books on sports and other subjects. He remarked to Cavanaugh, "People don't seem to realize that I've written far more books about baseball, about 25 in all, and also books on golf, football, handicapping and even a book about Harry Houdini." Sugar revealed to Prial that he has focused largely on boxing because at the start of his career "there was room" for writers covering that sport; he also explained his attraction to the ring: "Boxing is endlessly fascinating. It plays with death. It's different from other sports—there is no 'us' in boxing. The boxer is never part of a team." Currently, Sugar is the editor of *Fight Game*, a magazine widely considered to be the finest of the boxing publications. (As of mid-November 2002, he was on a leave of absence from the magazine.)

Bert Randolph Sugar was born in Washington, D.C., on June 7, 1937 to Harold Randolph Sugar and Anne Edith Sugar. Sugar has claimed that he is a descendent of one of the first families of Virginia and that his "ancestors"—in the literary sense—include the writer Damon Runyon. As a boy he enjoyed spectator sports, including wrestling. He attended the University of Maryland, where he was a member of the Zeta Beta Tau fraternity and where he boxed and founded a rubgy team, of which he was captain. (He also attended Harvard College, in Cambridge, Massachusetts, for a semester in 1956.) As a competitor in a sport he would later write about—boxing—Sugar was, he told Prial, "the great white hopeless." Upon his graduation from Maryland, in 1957, Sugar enrolled at the University of Michigan, where he studied law, earning LL.B. and J.D. degrees as well as an M.B.A. degree. In 1960 and 1961 he attended American University, in Washington, D.C., where he began—but never finished—work on a doctoral degree. He later passed the bar exam in the District of Columbia ("the only bar I ever passed," he joked to Prial). He practiced law for only a short time, realizing that what he really wanted was to be a sportswriter. He also longed to live and work in New York City. Unable to find work in sportswriting when he first moved there, Sugar took a job in advertising with the McCann-Erickson agency.

After 10 years in the field of advertising, Sugar purchased and became editor of the magazine *Boxing Illustrated*, Champion Publishing's merger of the periodicals *Ringside News* and *Boxing Illustrated/Wrestling News*. In a conversation with Howard Sirota for *Boxingranks.com* (April 27, 2000), Sugar explained that he became a boxing writer for "probably the same reason Roy Campanella once told me he became a catcher." At Overbrook High School, Sugar continued, the coach told Campanella and the other baseball hopefuls to take whichever positions they wanted. "All the kids run out to the outfield. [Campanella] said there were 70 in left, 80 in center, 90 in right. He said nobody was behind home plate. When I decided I wanted to be a sportswriter, there were 70 basketball writers in left, 80 football writers in center, and 90 baseball writers in right. And guess what? There was no boxing writer behind home plate. I ran as fast as I could . . . "

After the sale of *Boxing Illustrated*, in 1973, Sugar left that position to become editor in chief of *Argosy*, an adventure/fiction/fantasy magazine. A short time later he returned to advertising, with the title senior vice president at Baron, Costello & Fine. In 1977 he turned his back on the ad business permanently to devote himself to sports journalism, this time as the editor in chief of *Ring*, into which *Boxing Illustrated* had been consolidated.

Sugar co-wrote *Sting Like a Bee—The Muhammad Ali Story* (1971) with the former light-heavyweight boxing champion Jose Torres; the book is still ranked among the finest biographies of the boxing legend Ali. Jerold LeBlanc commented in the *Edmonton Sun* (March 16, 2002) that "Ali's moxie, bravado and charisma leap from the pages of the book." Sugar's next book was *Inside Boxing* (1972), which he co-authored with the former heavyweight boxing champion Floyd Patterson. He followed with *The Sports Collectors' Bible* (1975). In 1976 he began to earn his reputation as a trivia buff, with the publication of *Who Was Harry Steinfeldt? and Other Baseball Trivia Questions.* Eventually, Sugar's reputation as a veritable bank of trivia knowledge would grow to such proportions that Prial called him a "living, breathing storehouse of sports history, sports trivia and sports memorabilia." Sugar wrote *The Thrill of Victory: The Inside Story of ABC Sports* (1978), which a writer for *Library Journal* (April 1, 1978) described as "informative television history and enjoyable sports reading." The review also credited Sugar with being objective in his analysis of such outsize characters as Howard Cosell and Frank Gifford, both sports commentators for the network.

In 1979 Sugar, in partnership with Dave DeBusschere, a former New York Knicks basketball star, and Nick Kladis, a Chicago White Sox baseball team executive, bought *Ring*. (The magazine, which had been looked upon as a trusted source of objective analyses of boxers' skills, lost credibility—and readers—after it grossly inflated ratings of several boxers during the Don King–promoted Boxing Tournament of Champions, televised on ABC.) A benefit of the purchase for Sugar, as he revealed to Prial, was that when he acquired the magazine's archives he also "got 35 file cabinets of irreplaceable boxing history." Sugar was forced out by his partners five years later because the magazine had not become profitable. Sugar, in return, sued his former partners for over $3 million, accusing them of breach of contract; he settled out of court for an undisclosed sum, plus the ownership of two wrestling magazines and the publication *Boxing Illustrated* (which had been part of *Ring*). In the early 1990s he abandoned *Boxing Illustrated* to take over the dormant magazine *Fight Game.*

Meanwhile, in 1978 Sugar published *Hit the Sign and Win a Free Suit of Clothes from Harry Finklestein*, a book about the effects of commercialism on professional sports. *Hit the Sign* received a favorable review from F. T. De Andrea, who wrote in *Best Sellers* (April 1979), "To his credit, the author escaped the temptation of writing a book that does nothing more then rehash old, worn out sports stories. . . . This is a wonderful book complete with events, anecdotes and an unforgettable cast of professional front-men called promoters. It's a must for any sports library." Sugar followed with *The SEC: A Pictorial History of Southeastern Conference Football* (1979); *Collectibles: The Nostalgia Collectors Bible* (1980), a guide to antique collecting; and *The Baseball Trivia Book* (1982). For his next several books, Sugar returned to his acknowledged field of expertise, writing *Boxing's Greatest Fights* (1981), *505 Boxing Questions* (1982), *Boxing's One Hundred Years* (1982), and *The 100 Greatest Boxers of All Time* (1984). During those years Sugar also wrote several books on wrestling, including *The Pictorial History of Wrestling: the Good, the Bad, and the Ugly* (1984) and *Wrestling's Great Grudge Matches: "Battles and Feuds"* (1985). He contributed to a video titled *Golf's Most Memorable Moments, 100 Years of American Golf* (1989).

The year 1990 saw the appearance of Sugar's *Baseballistics*, which was described in *Booklist* (May 15, 1990) as a "compendium of statistics ranging from the mundane to the esoteric." The reviewer noted, "Although there are nothing but statistics in this volume, they are very interesting." Sugar followed *The Caesars Palace Sports Book of Betting Strategies* (1992) with possibly his most controversial work, *The 100 Greatest Athletes of All Time: A Sports Editor's Personal Ranking* (1995). Seemingly designed to incite barroom arguments, Sugar's book included some hotly debated rankings; his placements low on the list of such athletes as Michael Jordan, Earvin "Magic" Johnson, and Joe DiMaggio, for example, were heavily criticized. As for the criteria he used in compiling the list, Sugar wrote in the book's introduction, quoted by Cavanaugh, "It was a combination of things, an equation that included dominance, perceived greatness, consistent performance, accomplishments transcending time and overall excellence that illumined an athlete's greatness, almost as smoke defined light in the movie houses of my youth." In 1997 Sugar edited three books: *The Great Baseball Players from McGraw to Mantle: with 248 Historic Photographs from the Archives of Photo File, Inc.*; *I Hate the Dallas Cowboys: and Who Elected Them America's Team Anyway?*; and *The Sports 100: A Ranking of the Greatest Athletes of All Time.* Other books he has written include *1978, When Baseball Was Still Baseball* (1999), and *The Complete Idiot's Guide to Pro Wrestling* (2000), with Lou Albano. He also contributed to *Earnie Shavers: Welcome to the Big Time* (2002).

As a fixture at major boxing matches since the 1970s, Sugar has covered the fights of champions from Muhammad Ali, Joe Frazier, George Foreman, and Larry Holmes to Mike Tyson, Evander Holyfield and Lennox Lewis. One example of his fight commentary is his recap of the September 14, 2002 World Super Welterweight Championship bout between Oscar De La Hoya and Fernando Vargas, for the HBO Pay-Per-View Web site: "In the very first round . . . Vargas outmuscled De La Hoya, forcing him into the ropes and falling on him like a heated Banshee as Oscar got entangled in the ropes and simultaneously tried to extricate himself and evade

Vargas' incoming punches. Many of Vargas' body shots landed before De La Hoya could take the fight back to center ring where he began working his jab. It was to go that way for the first five rounds: Vargas winning the fight on the ropes, De La Hoya in center ring with Vargas having the upper hand early, outstrengthening De La Hoya. Even as Vargas was carrying the early rounds it appeared as if like a pyromaniac who had sneezed on his last match, he was blowing his last chance. By this time, De La Hoya had taken the fight to mid-ring and was working his jab like a light switch, finding Vargas' right eye—evidence of an injury that would later be diagnosed as a fractured occipital bone—and landing with his long absent right hand."

Sugar is an outspoken critic of what he sees as boxing's rampant corruption; for example, he told Howard Sirota that one of boxing's regulatory bodies, the International Boxing Federation (IBF), "gives bribery a bad name." Sugar boycotted the 2002 Mike Tyson/Lennox Lewis heavyweight championship fight, held in Memphis, Tennessee, on June 8, 2002, explaining his reasons to Steve Kim for *maxboxing.com*: "Because I'm a fan of boxing, I defend boxing. I cannot defend boxing and Mike Tyson at the same time. He has become the poster-boy for boxing and he's as much the poster-boy for that as Count Dracula is for the Red Cross blood drive. If you look at boxing, bottom line—it's legalized assault, if the two guys were doing the same thing in the back alley, they'd be arrested. The only thing that elevates it, the level of the sport, are the rules and regulations. Similarly, Nascar, if they don't have rules and regulations, they'd be arrested for speeding. You have to have rules and regulations and Mike Tyson admits to none of them. He bites, he tries to break elbows, he hits after the bell, he does all manner of things, including knocking referees down—that's not my sport." Asked by Sirota to identify "the best heavyweight [boxer] today," Sugar responded, "Lennox Lewis and it's in a very shallow class." Pressed to name the best heavyweight of all time, he said, "Jack Dempsey, number one. Joe Louis, number two. Muhammad Ali, number three."

Describing his encounter with the sportswriter, Prial noted that Sugar's "signature fedora, with a wide 1920's brim, framed a high forehead, a long, animated face and a mouth that, it soon became evident, rarely closed." Bert Sugar commutes to New York City from his home in Chappaqua, New York, where he has lived with his wife, Suzanne, for nearly 40 years. The couple have two children, Jennifer Anne and John-Brooks Randolph. Sugar dedicated *Baseball's 50 Greatest Games* (1986) to his wife with an inscription that reads, "To my wife, Suzy, without whose help this book would have been finished four months earlier." Sugar has appeared in several movies about boxing, including Irwin Winkler's *Night and the City* (1992) and Reggie Hudlin's *The Great White Hype* (1996). —L.A.S.

Suggested Reading: *Business Magazine* VI p 75+ Aug.12, 1979; *New York Times* III p 1+ Mar. 29, 1995, XIII p15 June 23, 1996

Selected Books: *Sting Like a Bee*, 1971; *Inside Boxing*; 1972; *The Sports Collectors' Bible*, 1975; *Who Was Harry Steinfeldt? and other Baseball Trivia Questions*, 1976; *Houdini: His Life and Art*, 1976; *Classic Baseball Cards*, 1977; *The Thrill of Victory*, 1978; *Hit the Sign and Win a Free Suit of Clothes from Harry Finklestein*, 1978; *The SEC*, 1978; *Boxing's Greatest Fights*, 1981; *The Baseball Trivia Book to End All Baseball Trivia Books. Promise!*, 1986; *Baseballistics*, 1990; *Great Baseball Players of the Past*, 1992; *The 100 Greatest Athletes of All Time: A Sports Editor's Personal Ranking*, 1995; as editor—*I Hate the Dallas Cowboys: And Who Elected Them America's Team Anyway?*, 1997

---

Courtesy of Harvard University

## Summers, Lawrence H.

*Nov. 30, 1954– President of Harvard University; former U.S. government official*

*Address: Harvard University, Massachusetts Hall, Cambridge, MA 02138*

On July 1, 2001 Lawrence H. Summers, one of the world's leading economists, became the 27th president of Harvard University, in Cambridge, Massachusetts, the oldest school of higher education in the United States. In choosing Summers for the position, Robert G. Stone Jr., a senior fellow of the Harvard Corporation and chairman of the Harvard presidential search committee, told Thomas B.

Edsall for the *Washington Post* (March 12, 2001), "Larry Summers embodies a rare combination as one of the most respected scholars and one of the most influential public servants of his generation." The self-described "market-oriented progressive" and lifelong Democrat has held some of the highest positions attainable in his field, including chief economist of the World Bank and secretary of the U.S. Treasury, a post he filled from 1999 to 2001, during President Bill Clinton's second term.

Lawrence H. Summers was born in New Haven, Connecticut, on November 30, 1954. His parents, Robert and Anita Summers, are respected economists who are retired from the University of Pennsylvania, and two of his uncles—his father's brother Paul Samuelson and his mother's brother Kenneth Arrow—won Nobel Prizes in Economics, in 1970 and 1972, respectively. Summers grew up in Penn Valley, Pennsylvania, a suburb of Philadelphia. In addition to his family's influence, he was inspired to study economics in part by the work of the renowned British economist John Maynard Keynes (1883–1946), who is credited with revolutionizing the discipline and showing how it can be used as a tool for social good.

In 1975 Summers received his bachelor's degree in economics from the Massachusetts Institute of Technology (MIT), in Cambridge, where he was a national champion in debate. After he graduated, he joined the school's economics faculty, remaining there for three years. He was promoted to assistant professor in 1979 and to associate professor in 1982. Concurrently, Summers worked toward his doctorate at Harvard, where he tutored other students and was a teaching fellow for a popular undergraduate economics survey course. His dissertation was titled "An Asset-Price Approach to Capital Income Taxation." He received his Ph.D. in 1982.

Summers served as a domestic policy economist on President Ronald Reagan's council of economic advisers for a year before he returned to Harvard, in 1983. At 28 years of age, he became one of the youngest tenured professors in the history of Harvard, which was then three years short of its 350th anniversary. (Tenure is a mark of respect and status and gives a professor a guarantee that he or she cannot be summarily dismissed.) Summers was a professor of economics at Harvard from 1983 to 1993, holding the title Nathaniel Ropes Professor of Political Economy for the last half-dozen of those years.

In 1991 Summers joined the World Bank, which, as one of the world's largest sources of development assistance, seeks to help the poorest countries by providing loans and credit. From 1991 to 1993, while keeping his professorship at Harvard, he served as the World Bank's vice president for development economics and chief economist. He sat on the World Bank's loan committee; was a major designer of the strategies for assisting countries in need; and was responsible for the bank's research, statistics, and training programs. During this period he became known for being straightforward and even brusque. He also became the target of criticism because of an internal World Bank memo in which he argued that—for reasons that were economically logical and defensible—pollution and waste might be transported from wealthier countries to poorer, developing ones. He later apologized for what he had written, explaining that he had meant the ideas expressed in the memo to be ironic and that he had merely been trying to provoke his colleagues into a different way of thinking.

In 1993 Summers, who had advised Bill Clinton on economic issues during his 1992 presidential campaign, left both Harvard and the World Bank to become the undersecretary of the treasury for international affairs in Clinton's first administration. (Earlier, in 1988, he had served as the chief economic adviser to Michael S. Dukakis during the former Massachusetts governor's unsuccessful presidential campaign.) In 1995 he was promoted to deputy secretary under Secretary of the Treasury Robert E. Rubin. His tasks as deputy, a post he held until 1999, were to help formulate the U.S. government's economic and budget strategies, handle such Treasury Department matters as debt management and tax policies, and work on international issues. He also served as the American deputy in the G-7 international economic cooperation process. (The G-7 is composed of seven of the world's major industrial democracies—France, the United States, Italy, Germany, Japan, Britain, and Canada; the group meets regularly to discuss economic matters affecting them and the rest of the world.)

During this time Summers worked closely with Rubin and Alan Greenspan, the chairman of the Federal Reserve Board, in crafting policies for dealing with financial crises in developing countries and in setting up a new financial system for the rapidly changing world. He was a key player in the successful bailout of Mexico after that country's economy came to the brink of collapse in 1995. Many Republicans in Congress opposed the economic rescue of Mexico and were troubled by what they saw as Summers's overbearing personality and tendency to lecture. Some even sought his resignation from the Department of the Treasury. Ultimately, Summers and Rubin circumvented Congress and aided Mexico through the International Monetary Fund (IMF). (The IMF, whose member states currently number 183, monitors world financial situations, fosters monetary cooperation between countries, and provides temporary financial assistance.) The multi-billion-dollar rescue plan proved successful: further trouble was averted, and Mexico recovered and repaid the loans. Another, briefer controversy was ignited when Summers accused congressional Republicans of "selfishness" in 1997 for wanting to cut estate taxes. He later apologized for his remarks.

During his time as deputy treasury secretary, Summers was a major contributor to the U.S. response to the Asian financial crisis of the late

1990s, when many of the major Asian currencies suddenly lost much of their value and their stock markets tumbled. Summers traveled to many Asian capitals to participate in meetings, conferences, and strategy sessions. Lim Chang Yuel, a former deputy prime minister of South Korea who worked closely with Summers at the end of 1997, recalled to Karl Taro Greenfeld for *Time* (May 24, 1999), "I was surprised to see how energetic and hardworking he was. He was like a fireman putting out fires not only in Korea but throughout Asia." As with the situation in Mexico, the Treasury Department, acting through the IMF, was a pivotal force in pulling Indonesia, South Korea, and other affected countries out of the crisis by offering billion-dollar loans and pressing for reforms that would lead to greater fiscal discipline in those countries. Many observers believe that the episode marked a new era of increased American involvement and leadership on the world's financial front.

In July 1999 Summers succeeded Robert Rubin to become the 71st secretary of the treasury; he held the post until January 2001, when George W. Bush became president. Rubin, considered by many to have been one of the best treasury secretaries of the 20th century, is credited for much of the country's economic well-being during Bill Clinton's time in office. Rubin's influence on Summers extended to aspects of personality: Summers began, to some degree, to emulate Rubin's self-effacing manner. Stanley Fischer, a former IMF deputy managing director and longtime friend of Summers's, told William C. Symonds and Rich Miller for *Business Week* (February 18, 2002), "[Summers] was a very different man after working with Rubin—more diplomatic and more effective."

As treasury secretary Summers directed a federal department with some two dozen bureaus and offices and a workforce of nearly 150,000 employees. He oversaw the implementation of an historic plan—one that as undersecretary he had helped formulate in 1993—to reduce the federal budget deficit; the result was the first budget surplus in the U.S. in 29 years. He bolstered the health of Social Security and Medicare by infusing those programs with fresh funds, and he spearheaded efforts to enact the most wide-ranging deregulation of financial institutions in 60 years. In addition, Summers worked to reform the IMF, secure debt relief for the world's poorest countries, and fight against international money laundering. During his term the Treasury Department continued to expand its role in the formulation of the U.S. government's foreign policies; that involvement, which became firmly established while Rubin was in office, reflected the increase in globalization and the growing economic interdependence of nations. When Summers ended his term as treasury secretary, the U.S. Treasury Department recognized his achievements with its highest honor, the Alexander Hamilton Medal. (Many observers have speculated that had Al Gore won the 2000 presidential election, Summers—one of Gore's closest advisers during the 2000 election campaign—would have retained his position as secretary of the treasury.)

Earlier, during the 1980s, Summers had contributed articles to the *Brookings Papers on Economic Activity*, an important journal in the field of economics. The subjects of the articles included macroeconomic policy issues, unemployment, and market dynamics. After leaving the Treasury Department, Summers joined the Brookings Institution, the Washington, D.C.–based publisher of the journal and an establishment that aims to serve as a bridge between scholarship and the making of public policy at the national level. He was named the institution's Arthur Okun Distinguished Fellow in Economics, Globalization, and Governance.

On July 1, 2001 Summers succeeded Neil L. Rudenstein to become the 27th president of Harvard University. He set an ambitious agenda for the university; among his priorities were reviewing the undergraduate curriculum and taking other steps to improve undergraduate education; making the grading system stricter and fairer; changing the tenure system; encouraging undergraduate study overseas; and ensuring that professors spend more time with students. Summers also sought to restore Harvard's traditional role as a leader in national education reform.

Summers's pursuit of those goals led to a conflict that made front-page news and sparked heated debate both within Harvard and among the general public as 2001 was drawing to a close. The dispute arose between Summers and Cornel West, a prominent, charismatic Afro-American-studies professor at Harvard and a popular public intellectual; it stemmed from Summers's statements at a meeting that he had called, in which he allegedly questioned West about his recent scholarly output. West had written or edited more than 20 books; more recently he had devoted a lot of his time to making a rap-inspired CD, *Sketches of My Culture* (2001), and advising the controversial black leader the Reverend Al Sharpton on a possible campaign for the U.S. presidency. Summers allegedly suggested that West should be working on a project more befitting one of Harvard's tenured professors, such as a scholarly book. He also urged West to help reduce the inflation of grades at Harvard by setting stricter standards in his popular course "Introduction to Afro-American Studies." (In 2001, according to news reports, more than half the grades awarded in all of Harvard's undergraduate classes were A's or A-minuses.) Even before the meeting, West and others in the Afro-American Studies Department had felt unsure of Summers's commitment to them and to Harvard's affirmative-action programs, aimed at both prospective teachers and prospective students. West felt that Summers's remarks at the meeting displayed blatant disrespect for him as a popular and dedicated teacher and an established scholar. Waldo Martin, writing for *Tikkun* (March/April 2002), quoted West as having said during a National Public Radio interview, "In my twenty-six years of teaching this is unprecedented for me. . . . I have never been attacked or insulted in that particular way." The issue grew into a heated public debate about racism, diversity, the roles of university presidents and high-profile scholars, the legitimacy of crossing between academia and popular culture, and the place of ethnic studies at institutions of higher learning. Several members of the Afro-American Studies Department, among them West and the department chairman, Henry Louis Gates Jr., threatened to leave Harvard for Princeton University, while such black leaders as Sharpton and Jesse Jackson sought to meet with Summers. In an attempt to diffuse the situation, Summers issued a statement in which he called the dispute a "misunderstanding." "With regard to the Afro-American studies program at Harvard, we are proud of this program collectively and of each of its individual members," he said, as quoted by *Jet* (January 21, 2002, on-line). "We would very much like to see the current faculty stay at Harvard and will compete vigorously to make this an attractive environment." That statement notwithstanding, in April 2002 West announced that he was leaving Harvard for Princeton. (Another highly regarded member of the department, the philosophy professor Kwame Anthony Appiah, had left Harvard in January 2002, during the height of the dispute, but he said that the reasons for his departure did not include the dispute with Summers.)

In the fall of 2002, Summers publicly condemned what he termed growing anti-Semitism at Harvard and other institutions of higher learning. He did so in response to a petition in which hundreds of Harvard students and professors demanded that the university remove all investments in Israeli companies from the school's stock portfolio, on the grounds that Israel, with U.S. assistance, had been violating the human rights of the Palestinian people. Summers's stand on the issue brought him praise, from those who agreed with his views and applauded his willingness to express them bluntly and publicly, and criticism, from those who felt that his association of the demands of the petitioners with anti-Semitism was a ploy to limit what should have been an open political debate.

Summers has written more than 100 articles for professional economic journals, among them the *American Economic Review*, *Journal of Human Resources*, *European Economic Review*, and *Journal of Finance*. His published books include *Understanding Unemployment* (1990) and *Reform in Eastern Europe* (1991), which he co-authored with Paul Krugman and three others. He edited the series *Tax Policy and the Economy* and also served, from 1984 to 1990, as the editor of the *Quarterly Journal of Economics*, the oldest professional journal of economics in the English language. Many of Summers's publications are on the reading lists of graduate economics programs around the country.

Among other honors, in 1987 Summers became the first social scientist to receive the National Science Foundation's Alan T. Waterman Award, given annually to an outstanding young researcher in any field of science or engineering. In 2000 he presented the American Economic Association's prestigious Ely Lecture. He is a fellow of the Econometric Society, which is described on its Web site as "an international society for the advancement of economic theory in its relation to statistics and mathematics," and of the American Academy of Arts and Sciences, an international society of leading scientists, scholars, artists, businesspeople, and civic leaders. In early 2002 Summers joined the Institute for International Economics, a private, nonprofit research institution in Washington, D.C., whose members include Stanley Fischer, the vice chairman of Citigroup, and William J. McDonough, the president and CEO of the Federal Reserve Bank of New York. Also in 2002 Summers was elected to the National Academy of Sciences, a private organization of scientists and engineers who advocate the use of science for the general welfare of society.

In 1983 Summers was diagnosed with Hodgkin's disease; since he underwent a year of chemotherapy, the disease has been in remission. He married Victoria Perry, a tax attorney, in 1985. They have twin daughters, Pam and Ruth, and a son, Harry. In addition to his almost universally acknowledged intellectual prowess, some sources have noted Summers's absentmindedness and disregard for more mundane matters, such as where he left his passport or whether his socks are matched. He is an avid tennis player. — C.F.T.

Suggested Reading: Harvard University Web site; *Nation* p6+ June 25, 2001; *New Republic* p24+ June 7, 1999; *New York Times* C p4 June 18, 1999; *Newsweek* (on-line) May 24, 1999, with photos, Jan. 14, 2002; *Tikkun* March/April 2002, with photos; *Time* p56+ May 24, 1999; *U.S. News & World Report* p53 Jan. 21, 2002, with photo; *Washington Post* A p8 Mar. 12, 2001

Selected Books: *Understanding Unemployment*, 1990; *Reform in Eastern Europe*, 1991

---

## Sutherland, Kiefer

*Dec. 21, 1966– Actor; director*

*Address: c/o International Creative Management, 8942 Wilshire Blvd., Beverly Hills, CA 90211-1934*

The 36-year-old actor Kiefer Sutherland has long given the impression of being an old Hollywood veteran. "I've chalked up a lot of experience with film, so in that area I feel much older than my age," he told Nancy Mills for the *Chicago Tribune* (August 17, 1993), when he was 26. "In other areas I feel about 8." Since his debut on the silver screen,

Frederick M. Brown/Getty Images

*Kiefer Sutherland*

in 1983, with a small role in *Max Dugan Returns*, Sutherland has appeared in more than 50 films. The familiarity of his face is attributable in part to his close resemblance to his father, the actor Donald Sutherland, who starred in the films *M*A*S*H*, *Klute*, *Invasion of the Body Snatchers*, *Ordinary People*, *A Dry White Season*, and *Six Degrees of Separation*, among many others. The younger Sutherland is best known for his roles as a bully in *Stand by Me*, the leader of a gang of young vampires in *The Lost Boys*, and a renegade in *Young Guns*. While his performances have not always earned him critical praise, he has pursued his career steadfastly. "I don't think I ever will get over just the sheer joy and exhilaration of, 'Oh, my God! I'm making a movie'—and this is what I've been allowed to do for my life," he told Jane Wollman Rusoff for *Mr. Showbiz.com*. Sutherland currently stars in the hit television series *24*, which premiered in November 2001. Less than three months later, his work in *24* brought Sutherland a Golden Globe Award for best performance by an actor in a dramatic television series.

Kiefer Sutherland was born in London, England, on December 21, 1966 to Donald Sutherland, who is a native of Canada, and the Canadian actress Shirley Douglas. He was named for Warren Kiefer, the pen name of Lorenzo Sabatini, who co-wrote and directed *Castle of the Living Dead* (1964), the first movie in which Donald Sutherland appeared. According to various sources, his full given name is Kiefer William Frederick Dempsey George Rufus. Sutherland's maternal grandfather, Tommy Douglas, headed the first Socialist government in North America, as premier of the Canadian province of Saskatchewan from 1944 to 1961; he then became the first leader of Canada's New Democratic Party. As the implementer of a universal healthcare system in Saskatchewan, Tommy Douglas is considered the father of Canada's national health system.

Kiefer Sutherland and his twin sister, Rachel, spent their early childhood in Los Angeles. When they were about four years old, their parents divorced. At age nine Kiefer appeared on stage in a Los Angeles production of Hal Lieberman's *Throne of Straw*, a story about the ghetto in Warsaw, Poland, in which the Nazis forced the city's Jews to live during World War II. The next year he moved with his mother and sister to Toronto, Canada, where he appeared in theatrical productions at his school.

A pivotal moment in his life came when the 13-year-old Sutherland watched his mother perform in a production of Edward Albee's *Who's Afraid of Virginia Woolf?* at the National Arts Centre in Ottawa, the Canadian capital. "I sat in the theater for a good 20 to 30 minutes after everybody had gone," he recalled to E. Kaye Fulton for *Maclean's* (March 17, 1997). "I just kept staring at that stage. I slowly figured out that this void that I knew nothing about—this gap between my mother and the character she played—was what was really cool about being an actor. And I wanted to learn about it." According to Fulton, it was then that he also realized for the first time what good acting was.

Sutherland has said that his parents did not push him toward acting. "For a long time I would be quite smug and defensive when asked about my parents' influence and effect," he told Martin Kasindorf for *New York Newsday* (August 2, 1990). "In all fairness, it's obvious that they've helped me an incredible amount. They created an environment for me by virtue of what they did for a living, and made acting more accessible for me than it was for others." In a conversation with a writer for the magazine *Saturday Night* (December 1990), Shirley Douglas said, "One of the interesting things about Kiefer is that if he sets his mind to something he'll follow it through to the end, just stick it through like a train. It wasn't just acting; he did it with hockey, baseball. He was a wonderful hockey player."

Sutherland dropped out of high school to pursue acting. Thanks to his father, who had been cast in *Max Dugan Returns* (1983), which Herbert Ross directed from a screenplay by Neil Simon, Kiefer, too, got a part in that film. At 16 he was cast as the lead in the director Dan Petrie's film *The Bay Boy* (1984), a coming-of-age story set in Glace Bay, Nova Scotia, during the Great Depression of the 1930s. At around the time of the movie's release in Canada, the actress Liv Ullmann, who played the mother in the film, told Michael Harris for the Toronto *Globe and Mail* (December 16, 1983), "I think Kiefer has a real future. At first, I thought I would take care of him. . . . But here is this really grown-up boy with fantastic integrity." *The Bay Boy* did not garner much attention, but Sutherland's acting earned compliments. In the *New Republic* (March 25, 1985), for example, Stanley Kauffmann singled him out for special praise, writing, "His resemblance to his father is incredible, yet his own personality and talent shine through." Sutherland won a Genie Award from the Academy of Canadian Cinema and Television for his work in *The Bay Boy*. In 1985 he appeared in an episode of Steven Spielberg's successful television series *Amazing Stories*. He next secured a role in the film *At Close Range* (1986), with Sean Penn, and another as a mute in the television movie *Trapped in Silence* (1986).

The part of Ace Merrill, a bully who leads a gang of hoodlums, in the director Rob Reiner's movie *Stand by Me* (1986) is considered Sutherland's breakthrough role. Based on Stephen King's novella *The Body*, *Stand by Me* was lauded by some as a charming evocation of boyhood friendships and criticized by others as cloyingly sentimental, but the acting, Sutherland's included, earned widespread plaudits. *The Brotherhood of Justice*, with Keanu Reeves, and the quirky love story *Crazy Moon* are lesser-known movies in which Sutherland appeared in 1986.

In 1987, in a performance especially memorable for many fans of his, Sutherland played David, the menacing leader of a band of young vampires, in the lightweight film *The Lost Boys* (1987), directed by Joel Schumacher. In a 1989 interview for *Young Americans* (on-line), Sutherland said, "What I liked about David is that . . . he has some kind of style and strength and a manipulative quality that I found very attractive." In *Films and Filming* (January 1988), Colin Houlson wrote that Sutherland came across as "moody and seductively scary" as David.

During the filming of *The Killing Time* (1987), in which he played a murderer, Sutherland met Camelia Kath, another member of the cast. He and Kath, who is a dozen years his senior, married in 1988. They had a daughter together before their divorce, in 1990. Sutherland acted in several films that came out in 1988, among them *Bright Lights, Big City*, with Michael J. Fox, *Promised Land*, with Meg Ryan, and the popular *Young Guns*, which features an ensemble of then–up-and-coming young actors, including Emilio Estevez (who portrayed William H. Bonney, also known as Billy the Kid), Charlie Sheen, and Lou Diamond Phillips. The story of Billy the Kid and his band of likable renegades continued *in Young Guns II: Blaze of Glory* (1990), with Sutherland again cast as the sensitive gunslinger Josiah Gordon "Doc" Scurlock. He also appeared in two other movies in 1990: Joel Schumacher's *Flatliners* and the British wartime drama *Chicago Joe and the Showgirl*, directed by Bernard Rose. Commenting on his drive to keep going at such a pace, he told Martin Kasindorf, "The object is to keep yourself out there."

His work in *Flatliners*, in which he played a medical student experimenting with life after death, proved to be especially satisfying for Sutherland, both professionally and personally. As he said to Kasindorf, "We all share birth and death, and our experiences with them will all be relatively similar, I believe. The story also deals with atonement and forgiveness, particularly with the need to forgive ourselves. It's the first film where what I wanted to say went in at one end and came out the same way at the other end."

On the set of *Flatliners*, Sutherland met the actress Julia Roberts, who portrayed another medical student in the picture. Their off-screen romance was widely publicized; indeed, for a while they were one of the most talked-about couples in Hollywood. When their planned marriage fell through at what was reportedly the last moment, the story became the stuff of Hollywood tabloids. In his interview with Jane Wollman Rusoff, Sutherland recalled, "Certainly at one time we really loved each other very much. The hell period came after we had broken up and I watched the press have a go at me and have a go at her."

In the early 1990s Sutherland set up his own film-development company, called Still Water. The actor told Lawrence Van Gelder for the *New York Times* (March 20, 1992) that he took that step "so I can be very specific about the films I want to do." (Readily available sources do not identify any films made by Still Water Productions.) Of note in 1992 was his brief but effective performance as Marine lieutenant Jonathan James "John" Kendrick in Rob Reiner's hit film *A Few Good Men* (1992), a court-martial drama that features Tom Cruise, Jack Nicholson, and Demi Moore. In 1993 he played a man obsessively searching for his missing girlfriend in a poorly received remake of the Dutch thriller *The Vanishing*, directed, like the original, by George Sluizer. Several critics found Sutherland unconvincing in the role.

Also in 1993, at age 26, Sutherland directed his first film, *Last Light*, a hard-hitting, made-for-cable drama about a death-row inmate. In addition to directing, Sutherland took on the role of the condemned man and earned praise for his work both in front of and behind the camera. Other movies in which Sutherland appeared in the early 1990s include *Article 99* (1992), *The Three Musketeers* (1993), and *The Cowboy Way* (1994). In 1996 he played a Ku Klux Klan boss in the cinematic adaptation of John Grisham's first novel, *A Time to Kill*; a murderous rapist opposite Sally Field in *Eye for an Eye*; and a killer in *Freeway*. In yet another bad-guy role, he took the part of a psychotic killer in *Truth or Consequences, N.M.* (1997), which also marked his debut as a director for the big screen. Described by some critics as a pale imitation of Arthur Penn's groundbreaking 1967 crime film, *Bonnie and Clyde*, *Truth or Consequences, N.M.* fared poorly at the box office. Concerning the many violent roles he has played, Sutherland told Rusoff, "As an actor . . . I like doing a scene and having someone go, Ooh, that scared me! That gave me the creeps." Martin Kasindorf quoted the actor as saying, "I find that evil characters are the most tragic and the most sympathetic. It's the extremes that have always been exciting."

In 1996 Sutherland returned to the stage, acting alongside his mother, Shirley Douglas, in a Canadian production of Tennessee Williams's *The Glass Menagerie*, which opened at the National Arts Centre in Ottawa and then moved to the Royal Alexandra Theatre in Toronto. It was the first time that Douglas, who played Amanda Wingfield, the mother in the play, and Sutherland, who was cast as Tom Wingfield, Amanda's son, appeared on stage together. "I didn't know what to expect," Sutherland told John Coulbourn in an interview for *Fortunecity.com*. "It was amazing, once we started working—it was business. For a long time I thought we'd utilize stuff from our own lives—and you do, but on your own." "Coming back to the theater was a great reminder of a process I was letting go of," he told Coulbourn. "I just loved it." He explained to E. Kaye Fulton, "You make films at a breakneck pace and after 30 of them you start to develop shortcuts. In that craft you are honing your skills but you are also whittling away at the beautiful art of developing a character." When asked about the possibility of his co-starring with his father in a film someday, Sutherland has said that both would love to do so—but only once; therefore everything connected with the project would have to be just right.

Sutherland has worked steadily during the last few years, appearing in more than a dozen films, among them *Dark City* (1998); *A Soldier's Sweetheart* (1998); *The Royal Way* (2000); *Beat* (2000); *Ring of Fire* (2000); *Desert Saints* (2000); *To End All Wars* (2001); *Paradise Found* (2002); and *Behind the Red Door* (2001). He both directed and co-starred in *Woman Wanted* (1999); based on a novel by Joanna McClelland Glass, who also wrote the screenplay, *Woman Wanted* examines the relationships among a housekeeper (Holly Hunter) and the widowed father (Michael Moriarty) and son (Sutherland) for whom she works. The movie, in which Shirley Douglas appeared in a supporting role, failed to attract a distributor and aired on cable television.

In the Fox television series *24*, which premiered in November 2001 and began its second season in 2002, Sutherland stars as special agent Jack Bauer, a man struggling to hold his family together as he tries to prevent the assassination of a presidential candidate. The show unfolds in real time, with each of the hour-long episodes representing a successive hour in one day of Jack's life. "Maintaining the energy level is a challenge," Sutherland explained to Frazier Moore for the Associated Press (December 11, 2001), as posted on *azcentral.com*. "If you were in a fight in the last scene, which is supposed to be just two minutes ago, when they come back to you, you've got to still be breathing hard." *24* has been widely praised; in 2002 it earned a number of awards, including several Emmys, a Television Critics Association Award for program of the year, and a Golden Satellite Award for best dramatic television series. In 2002, in addition to winning a Golden Globe Award for his performance on *24*, Sutherland was nominated for an Emmy for outstanding lead actor in a dramatic series.

In 1996 Sutherland married Kelly Winn, a model. The marriage ended in divorce in 2000. —C.F.T.

Suggested Reading: *Mr.Showbiz.com*; *Moviestarpages.com*; *Maclean's* p66+ Mar. 17, 1997; *Rolling Stone* p25+ Feb. 25, 1988, with photo; *Seventeen* p90+ Oct. 1986, with photo

Selected Films: as actor—*The Bay Boy*, 1984; *Stand by Me*, 1986; *The Lost Boys*, 1987; *Bright Lights, Big City*, 1988; *Young Guns*, 1988; *Flatliners*, 1990; *A Few Good Men*, 1992; *A Time to Kill*, 1996; *Dark City*, 1998; *A Soldier's Sweetheart*, 1998; *Desert Saints*, 2000; *The Royal Way*, 2000; *Beat*, 2000; *Ring of Fire*, 2000; *To End All Wars*, 2001; *Behind the Red Door*, 2001; *Paradise Found*, 2002; as actor and director—*Last Light*, 1993; *Woman Wanted*, 1999

Selected Television Shows: *Fallen Angels*, 1993; *24*, 2001–

---

## Suzuki, Ichiro

(suh-zoo-kee, ee-chi-roh)

*Oct. 22, 1973– Baseball player*

*Address: Seattle Mariners, P.O. Box 4100, Seattle, WA 98104*

When Ichiro Suzuki signed his contract with the Seattle Mariners, on November 18, 2000, he became the first position player (non-pitcher) from Japan to join an American baseball team. (Japanese pitchers, among them Hideo Nomo, Kazuhiro Sasaki, and Shigetoshi Hasegawa, had been signed to U.S. ball clubs in the preceding few years.) In his native country, where he had superstar status, with a following comparable to that of the American sports legend Michael Jordan in the U.S., Suzuki had been heralded for his outstanding offensive production; in seven seasons with the Orix Blue Waves, in Kobe, Japan, his batting average regularly topped .350. Indeed, in Japan, his career has sparked cottage industries: his father founded the Ichiro Museum, in Nagoya, his hometown, and round-trip, $2,000 travel packages from Japan to Seattle, Washington, have been in great demand. A plethora of souvenir merchandise, including posters, action figures, and jerseys, is available in both Japan and the U.S.; Ichi rolls, a variation of sushi (a traditional Japanese dish made with spicy fish, vegetables, and rice) are sold along with hotdogs at Safeco Field, the Mariners' stadium. Widely known in Japan as simply "Ichiro," Suzuki persuaded Major League Baseball officials to make an exception to the rules and permit him to have the

Courtesy of the Seattle Mariners

*Ichiro Suzuki*

letters of his first name rather than those of his surname stitched to the back of his uniform. Speaking about his decision to play for an American team, Suzuki said (through a translator) to Michael Farber for *Sports Illustrated* (December 4, 2000), "Sometimes I am nervous, sometimes anxious, but I want to challenge a new world."

Ichiro Suzuki was born on October 22, 1973 in Kasugai, Japan, and grew up in Nagoya, a nearby city about 120 miles southwest of Tokyo. He first picked up a baseball bat at the age of three. At eight he was playing in the Nagoya youth leagues. He was encouraged by his father, Nobuyuki Suzuki, who regularly played with him and chauffeured him to the local batting cages almost daily. To build arm strength and increase his batting speed, Suzuki practiced swinging a heavy coal shovel; in time, the pitching machines he faced failed to challenge him. "I moved closer to the machine, first a meter, then more," he recalled to Bob Finnigan for the *Seattle Times* (July 10, 2001), explaining how he attempted to hit the ball at its maximum velocity. At his father's urging, he learned to bat from the left side, so he would be a few steps closer to first base. He performed outstandingly on the baseball team at Aiko-dai Meiden High School, in Nagoya, and he was twice selected to participate in Japan's National High School Baseball Tournament.

After he graduated from high school, in 1991, Suzuki immediately entered the Japanese baseball draft. He felt he had no other choices; as he told Bob Finnigan, "If I wasn't going to be a ballplayer, I [couldn't] think of anything else." He was picked in the fourth round of the draft by the Orix Blue Waves, who play in Kobe, a port city, and are in the Pacific League. (Japan has two baseball leagues, the Central and the Pacific. The perennial favorite, the Yomiuri Giants, are in the Central League, whose teams are considered superior, overall, to those in the Pacific League.) Suzuki began his professional career in 1992 with the Blue Waves' minor-league affiliate. In the 58 games in which he played with the affiliate, he compiled a batting average of .366, and he was called up to finish the season with the major-league Blue Waves, in Kobe, where he hit .253 over 40 games. Although he was a successful hitter with great potential, the manager of the Blue Waves, Shozo Doi, disapproved of Suzuki's extremely untraditional batting stance, in which he kept his forward foot off the ground for much of the swing. "Doi told Ichiro that the pendulum-leg swing would never cut it in the majors," T. R. Reid reported in the *Washington Post* (October 12, 1994). "He ordered major changes. Suzuki responded in a very non-Japanese way: he said 'No' to the boss." Doi shipped Suzuki off to the Hilo Stars, a team in the Hawaiian Winter League (a short-lived minor league whose teams consisted of less experienced professionals from Japan and the U.S.). While in Hawaii Suzuki met such future stars as Jason Giambi, the Most Valuable Player (MVP) in the American League in 2000. He enjoyed his stint with the Hilo Stars, but his batting stance remained unchanged. "It was part of my image," he told Michael Knisley for the *Sporting News* (March 19, 2001). "If you think Ichiro, you think of the leg kick." (He has since discovered that he does not need the leg kick for extra power and has dropped it.) In 1993 he again divided his time between the minor-league and major-league Blue Waves, hitting .371 and .188, respectively.

In 1994, Suzuki's rookie year and first full year in the majors, the Blue Waves management decided to refer to their budding star by his first name, which means "Number One Son" in Japanese. ("Suzuki" is an extremely common surname in Japan.) In addition to good defensive playing in right field, he was indisputably dazzling at the plate, finishing the season with a .385 average (the best-ever by a Japanese player), 13 home runs, and 54 runs batted in (RBIs). He was named the MVP of the Pacific League and won a Gold Glove for his defense. (Awarded in Japan since 1971, the Gold Glove honors fielding excellence.) Suzuki was also named to the Best Nine, the Japanese equivalent of Major League Baseball's All-Star squad. He set a Japanese baseball record with 210 hits over a 130-game season.

In the Land of the Rising Sun, tracking Suzuki's career quickly became a national obsession. The NHK television network clocked his swing at .18 seconds, twice as fast as an average batter's. With his impressive speed as a runner, he could beat throws to first base and steal second with little trouble; in 1995, his sophomore season, he stole 49 bases, the Pacific League record that year. That season he led the league in other categories as well, including batting average (.358), RBIs (80), and hits (179). He hit a career-high 25 home runs, and once again earned every possible honor: a batting title, a Gold Glove, Best Nine placement, and the league MVP award. Suzuki's 1996 season was equally fruitful, ending with his third straight batting title—his .356 average and 193 hits led the Pacific League—a third Gold Glove, and a third MVP award. With his help the 1996 Orix Blue Waves won the Pacific League pennant and then defeated the Yomiuri Giants in the Japanese national-championship series. Heavy media coverage of his performances increased Suzuki's stature even further. The press often compared him to Michael Jordan, the Brazilian soccer star Pelé, and even Elvis Presley. A style of yellow Nike sneakers he wore "touched off a minor wave of Air Jordanesque shoe-jackings . . . by roving gangs in nearby Osaka," Michael Farber wrote. Fans hounded him for autographs in restaurants, on the street, and even in public toilets. "This may be rude," Suzuki told Michael Knisley, "but there are some very strange Japanese fans, in that aspect."

Suzuki has suggested that he briefly let the accolades go to his head. "My first two or three years in Japan, people were in high praise of me, they flowered me more than I should have been," he told Bob Finnigan. "I was flattered and I wanted to see what they were saying about me, to read it every day. But I realized I should not have those kinds of feelings. It showed there was something wrong inside me." After gaining that insight Suzuki began focusing on his hitting and fielding, which remained the best in the Pacific League. In 1997 he set a Japanese record by making 216 successive appearances at the plate without striking out. He had 185 hits and a batting average of .345, leading the league for the fourth time in as many seasons. He won another Gold Glove and was named to his fourth Best Nine, and then did so again in 1998, when his batting average hit .358. That year the Blue Waves won another Pacific League pennant. By that time the right-side bleachers, closest to Suzuki's field position, had become the most coveted seats in the Orix Blue Waves park.

Suzuki experienced his first season-ending injury in August 1999, when a pitch broke a bone in his hand. Although he missed the last 32 games of the season, his .343 batting average led the Pacific League again, and he was recognized for the sixth time with a Gold Glove and a Best Nine post. That year he also reached two career milestones: on April 20 he made his 1,000th career hit, and on July 6 he hit his 100th career home run. Suzuki's 2000 season, too, was cut short, because of strained muscles on his rib cage, but over the 105 games he played before the injury, he compiled a league-leading batting average of .387, eclipsing the mark he had set as a rookie. The usual distinctions followed, including a Gold Glove and a Best Nine designation.

Despite the adulation and honors, Suzuki had been seeking a new challenge since competing against U.S. players who had visited Japan in the fall of 1996, and he had asked Orix to release him to free agency. (In Japan players are not eligible to become free agents until they have served for nine full seasons.) "I wanted a change in circumstances in my life," he told Michael Farber. "I saw these good American players, and I wanted to play against them. Every time I would ask, Orix would say, 'No chance.'" In 1999 Suzuki got a second taste of American major-league baseball, when the Blue Waves visited the Arizona-based spring training camp of the Seattle Mariners. He told the Blue Waves management that he would not stay with the team after the 2001 season, when free agency would make him available to either the more prestigious Central League or to major-league U.S. clubs. "I didn't lose my desire to play in Japan, but it wasn't interesting to me anymore," he explained to Ross Newhan for the *Los Angeles Times* (March 9, 2001). "I couldn't make my fans happy if I continued to play there. I felt there was a need for something else." Orix agreed to "post" Suzuki after the 2000 season, opening a four-day window for American teams to bid for the right to negotiate with him. The Seattle Mariners won the negotiation, agreeing to pay Orix more than $13 million; Suzuki then accepted a three-year, $14 million contract to play in Seattle, thus becoming the first position player from Japan to join an American major-league team. Some observers thought that Suzuki's move would inspire all talented Japanese players to defect to the U.S.; others hoped that it would help Japanese baseball by encouraging Japanese teams to sign lucrative, long-term contracts with their star players, who were usually restricted to one-year deals.

"Looking back where I've [played] nine years in Japan, I was a little embarrassed to be called a rookie in the United States," Suzuki told Jack Curry for the *New York Times* (November 13, 2001). "But I have not played in the United States . . . except the time I played winter ball in Hawaii. Maybe I was a rookie this year." Suzuki arrived at the Mariners' spring 2001 training facilities accompanied by a translator on loan from the Blue Waves. "Of course I will have some pressure here," he told Chris Barron for the Scripps Howard News Services, as posted on *Sportserver* (January 24, 2001, on-line), referring to his awareness that American pitchers rely more on fastballs than their Japanese counterparts and that most American ballparks are larger than the ones in his native country. He added, though, that "compared to the pressures I had in the past, this pressure is nothing. When I play in Japan, people expect me to be the leading hitter every year." To Suzuki's dismay, the Japanese press followed him in droves to the United States, straining to record every detail of his life, ranging from his performance at each at-bat to the type of rice balls packed for his lunch by his wife, the former Yumiko Fukushima. (The Japanese press had hounded Suzuki and Fukushima, a TV news reporter, during their courtship, and the two were forced to sneak out on dates. They wed in a secret location in December 1999, in Los Angeles.) The Mariners issued 160 press passes to the Japanese media, and the Japanese television network NHK spent $250,000 to wire Safeco Field, the Mariners' stadium, to have every Seattle home game digitally broadcast to Japan. Paparazzi constantly trailed Suzuki, and rumors sprang up that a Japanese magazine was willing to pay upwards of $1 million for nude pictures of him. (Instead of changing in the locker room, Suzuki began to dress in a private room.) Overwhelmed by the attention, Suzuki arranged to speak only to one reporter, who asked questions on behalf of the scores of other reporters. "There are so many of them," he told Rick Reilly for *Sports Illustrated* (September 17, 2001), "and only one of me." Neither members of the American press corps nor the American public pursued him so relentlessly. "What I like about America is the individual freedom of being able to move around without people following me," Suzuki told Mac Engel for the *Washington Post* (April 15, 2001). "In America, people respect your space."

The mania generated by the Japanese press intensified when the season officially began. The Mariners scouts and coaches, who had seen their new player hit .308 in spring training, had kept their predictions about Suzuki modest, claiming that he would need time to adjust to his new club. Still, he immediately distinguished himself as a player. In the first weeks of the season, his batting average hovered near the .350 mark; it spiked to over .400 after an especially productive game, and he had a 15-game hitting streak in the first month. His speed on the base paths was clocked at 3.8 seconds from home plate to first base (the average for batting from the left is 4.1–4.2 seconds, and for batting from the right, 4.3 seconds), and with his strong throws from right field, he helped his teammates in making outs. In the balloting for the All-Star Game, Suzuki finished first, with 3,373,035 votes (1,538,974 more than the runner-up, Manny Ramirez of the Red Sox), aided by more than a half-million Internet votes from Japan; he was the first rookie to be elected as a starter since 1990. The applause for Suzuki increased during the second half of the season, as the Mariners worked their way to a Major League Baseball record 116 regular-season victories, the best record in the major leagues. (After defeating the Cleveland Indians in the American League Division Series, the Mariners lost to the New York Yankees in the American League Championship Series.) Suzuki ended the season with a .350 average and an American League–high 56 stolen bases. He won the batting title by accumulating 242 hits, the most-ever by a rookie—the previous record of 233 had been set by the Cleveland Indians' "Shoeless" Joe Jackson in 1911. Suzuki was also the first player since 1930 to make more than 240 hits in a season The baseball community was quick to reward him for his achievements: he won the American League titles of Rookie of the Year and MVP, the first player to earn both simultaneously since 1975. Suzuki also won a Gold Glove for his defense plays; in 152 games, he made only one error in the field. (The Gold Gloves have been awarded in the U.S. by the Rawlings sports-equipment company since 1957.)

In the 157 games in which he played during the 2002 season, Suzuki had 208 hits, with eight home runs and 51 RBIs. The latter half of the season found him in something of a slump. In September he went eight for 47, for an average of .170, a career low. Nevertheless, he finished the season with a .321 average. His team came in second in the American League in on-base percentage but landed in sixth place in terms of runs scored.

Suzuki currently lives in Seattle with his wife, Yumiko. During the off-season he enjoys playing golf. The Ichiro Museum, in Nagoya, according to Janie McCauley for the Associated Press (November 21, 2001, on-line), displays baseball memorabilia and such personal keepsakes as Suzuki's baby shoes, childhood toys, and copies of school exams showing his high marks. — K.S.

Suggested Reading: *Far Eastern Economic Review* p66+ July 26, 2001; *Los Angeles Times* D p13 Mar. 9, 2001, with photo; *New York Times* D p4 Apr. 24, 2001, with photo, S p1 Nov. 21, 2001; *New York Times Magazine* p50+ Sep. 16, 2001, with photos; Seattle Mariners Web site; *Sporting News* p12+ Mar. 19, 2001, with photo; *Sports Illustrated* p68+ Dec. 4, 2000, with photos, p36+ Apr. 23, 2001, with photo, p34+ May 28, 2001, with photo, 1994, D p1 Apr. 15, 2001

---

## Taylor, Koko

*Sep. 28, 1935– Blues singer; songwriter*

*Address: c/o Alligator Records and Artist Management Inc., P.O. Box 60234, Chicago, IL 60660*

"Blues is my life. It's a true feeling that comes from the heart, not something that just comes out of my mouth. Blues is what I love, and blues is what I always do." Koko Taylor, who made that declaration, according to the Web site of Alligator Records, her label since 1975, is considered by many to be the "Queen of the Blues." "Possibly the last great tough, brassy blues woman alive," as the music critic Jeremy Hart wrote for *Pop Matters* (2000, on-line), Taylor has made her name "synonymous with Chicago blues," as an on-line *Rolling Stone* biography of her put it. Taylor began singing in public in the 1950s in Chicago clubs, just for the fun of it. Her career took off in 1965, when, thanks to her earlier, serendipitous encounter with the great traditional bluesman Willie Dixon, she recorded the single "Wang Dang Doodle," which sold a million copies and became her signature song. When Taylor was 61 and still singing at some 200 gigs a year, John Roos wrote for the *Los Angeles Times*

Courtesy of Alligator Records

*Koko Taylor*

(January 18, 1997), "This seemingly ageless wonder pours her heart out in one powerful song after another. . . . She's lost little of the fire and emotion she had [four decades ago]. . . . Her raw voice growls and grunts, often building in intensity until it explodes with a killer line." Distinguished by her powerful, evocative voice and trademark growl, Taylor displays "searing power and a steely emotional tautness . . . ," as David Whiteis wrote for the *Chicago Reader* (September 26, 1997) after attending one of her concerts, "and she radiates a warmth that borders on the spiritual: few performers in any genre are as capable as she is of generating genuine intimacy out of fervid house-rocking moments."

A sharecropper's daughter, Taylor has sung in shows all over the world, appeared on television and in movies, and entertained at inaugural galas of two U.S. presidents. Among the most honored female blues singers of all time, she has won one Grammy Award and earned Grammy nominations for nearly every one of her last 10 albums. The mayor of Chicago, Richard Daley, presented Taylor with the city's Legend of the Year Award on March 3, 1993, which he proclaimed "Koko Taylor Day." In 1999 she received a Lifetime Achievement Award from the Memphis, Tennessee–based Blues Foundation, which has inducted her into its Blues Hall of Fame and recognized her achievements with more than 20 W. C. Handy Awards (considered equivalent to the Grammy Awards for the blues community). "A lot of people wonder what keeps me going," Taylor told an interviewer in 1992, as quoted on the African American Publications Web site. "It's for the love that I have for my music. This is my first priority: just to stay out here and sing the blues, make people happy with my music all over the world."

The youngest child of Annie Mae and William Walton, Taylor was born Cora Walton on September 28, 1935 just outside Memphis, Tennessee. According to most sources, she had two sisters and three brothers; in one interview, with Darlene Gavron Stevens for the *Chicago Tribune* (February 24, 1991), Taylor said she had three sisters and three brothers. Recalling to David S. Rotenstein for the *Charlotte Observer* (March 10, 1995) how she acquired the name Koko, she said, "When I was growing up I was a chocolate lover. I loved to eat chocolate candy, cake, cookies, whatever. And everybody started calling me a pet name, . . . 'Little Cocoa'." Taylor's mother died when she was about four, and her father died before she reached her teens; for the next half-dozen years, her siblings took care of her. Beginning when she was old enough to do so—between six and eight years of age, as she has recalled—she picked cotton along with her brothers and sisters on the farm where the family lived as sharecroppers. "[My father] would make everybody in the household work," she told Darlene Gavron Stevens. "When we weren't in the fields working, we would cut wood for our cooking stove and we'd pick up kindling. I got used to working, and eventually I looked forward to it. This has stuck with me. It made a good, hard-working woman out of me. It made me strong, independent and honest." Taylor sang in the fields while picking cotton and in a local Baptist church choir. Her father encouraged his children to sing gospel music and warned them against listening to the blues, which he referred to as "devil's music." She and her brothers and sisters would sneak behind the house to sing and play music together. One brother made his own version of a guitar out of hay-bailing wire tied around nails; another brother made a kind of wind instrument by punching holes into a corncob. Making sure that their father did not know what they were up to, Taylor and her siblings would listen to the blues on a battery-operated radio (their home had no electricity), tuning in to B.B. King, who was then a disc jockey in West Memphis, Arkansas, and to the disc jockey Rufus Thomas, on WDIA in Memphis. One day when she was about 12, one of her brothers brought home a record by Memphis Minnie called "Me and My Chauffeur Blues." "Black Rat Blues," the song on the flip side, had a powerful effect on the young Taylor; as she told Michael Buffalo Smith in 2000 for *Gritz, the Online Southern Music Magazine*, "That was the first song that just stuck to my ribs, when it comes to the blues." Regarding that Memphis Minnie recording, Taylor told Ariel Swartley for the *New York Times Magazine* (June 29, 1980), "We had this—what we called graphonolia—that we wound up with our hands. That's how we played our music. I can remember the whole family listening to that record, playing it over and over. I learned it so well, I knew every word by [heart]."

Taylor attended school only sporadically; the highest grade she attended was the sixth. In 1953, at age 18, Taylor left Memphis with her boyfriend, Robert "Pops" Taylor, a cotton-truck driver 12 years her senior. Owning little more than "35 cents and a box of Ritz crackers," as she recalled to John Floyd for the *Miami New Times* (October 21, 1999), they traveled to Chicago in search of work. The two were married later that year. Her husband found a job in a meat-packing plant, and Taylor earned $5 a day cleaning house and babysitting for families in the wealthy northern suburbs of Chicago. In their home, on the city's South Side, the hotbed of rough-edged Chicago electric blues, Pops would play guitar and Taylor would sing after work. Almost every weekend they would go to the so-called juke joints—the Queen Bee, Pepper's Lounge, and other gritty blues clubs in their part of town as well as on Chicago's West Side. "These were just little neighborhood tavern clubs where the black people went and drank and had a good time," Taylor recalled to Michael Buffalo Smith. "And they would have their band up there playing, and when I'd go in there, I'd just be going in there to have a good time too." With Pops's encouragement, Taylor began to join the musicians and sing on stage, performing with some of the leading Chicago musicians of the time—Muddy Waters, Howlin' Wolf, Elmore James, and Magic Sam. "They got to know me, and they started calling me Little Koko on their own," Taylor told Smith. "'We got Little Koko in the house, and we're going to get her up here to do a few tunes.' And that's what I did. . . . I'd just go up there and sing anything, just to be singing." Among the songs she performed in those venues were Brook Benton's "Make Me Feel Good, Kiddio" and Ike and Tina Turner's "I Idolize You."

Taylor's big break came when she met the bass player and composer Willie Dixon, a major contributor to the development of hard Chicago blues (and, later, an acknowledged influence on such groups as the Rolling Stones and the Grateful Dead). Dixon was also an arranger for Chess Records, which recorded many of the classic Chicago blues performers of the post–World War II generation, among them Sonny Boy Williamson, John Lee Hooker, Memphis Slim, and Buddy Guy as well as Muddy Waters and Howlin' Wolf. In a club one night in about 1962, Dixon approached Taylor as she came off the stage, and he exclaimed, as quoted on the Web site of the Richard De La Font Agency, which represents Taylor, "My God, I never heard a woman sing the blues like you sing the blues. There are lots of men singing the blues today, but not enough women. That's what the world needs today, a woman with a voice like yours to sing the blues."

Dixon became Taylor's mentor and producer. In 1963 he produced Taylor's debut single, "Honky Tonky," for the USA label. Later he helped Taylor secure a contract with Chess Records, where he produced, among her earliest titles, the single "Wang Dang Doodle," which Dixon had written and recorded five years earlier with Howlin' Wolf. ("Wang dang doodle," Taylor told David S. Rotenstein, "means pitching a wang dang doodle on a Saturday night. What I would call a fish-fry, a romp-tromp good time, everybody partying, dancing, getting drunk, fighting, whatever comes first." In some interviews Taylor has said that Dixon wrote "Wang Dang Doodle" for her.) The song urges the listener to tell various people—Razor Totin' Jim, Fast Talking Fanny, Abyssinian Ned, Boxcar Joe—about plans for the evening: "We gonna romp and tromp till midnight / We gonna fuss and fight till daylight / We gonna pitch a wang dang doodle all night long." Taylor's rendition of Dixon's party song was a smash hit; it aired often on the radio, sold a million copies, and in 1966 climbed to number four on *Billboard*'s rhythm-and-blues charts. "When I first heard 'Wang Dang Doodle' I thought it was the silliest song I had ever heard, but people just love that story," Taylor has said, as quoted on the House of Blues Web site. "I can't do a show without that song, because the people won't let me off the stage without playing it." "Wang Dang Doodle" is included on half of the dozen Taylor albums still available.

Dixon, with whom Taylor formed a close friendship, encouraged Taylor to write her own songs, advising her to find inspiration for them in her everyday life. She began doing so in about 1964, when she wrote "What Kind of Man Is This?," which she has described as a tribute to her husband, who became her manager. "It seems like I got the right man for a husband—one that's in my corner all the way when it comes to my career," she told Ariel Swartley. In the same vein, she told Michael Buffalo Smith, "There's plenty of women in their kitchen cooking applepies that can sing as good as I can. Sing good as Aretha Franklin or Whitney Houston, but they can't get out there and do what they do, and why? Because, 'I got a husband,' first of all. And there ain't too many men that are gonna want their wife out there on the road. I traveled, and I had a husband, but my husband was right there with me. That makes a difference."

In the latter half of the 1960s, Taylor worked steadily in Chicago and toured widely in the South as well. She also made additional recordings with Chess Records and Dixon, including the albums *Koko Taylor* (1969) and *Basic Soul* (1972). Late in the 1960s, as a participant in the American Folk Blues Festival, she toured Europe and gained an enthusiastic following of blues fans there. In the largely male-dominated world of blues, Taylor had joined a number of outstanding women, among them Ma Rainey, Bessie Smith, Alberta Hunter, Dinah Washington, and Big Mama Thornton. "I'm showing the men that they're not the only ones . . . ," Taylor told Swartley. "I can do just as good a job as they can at expressing the blues and singing the blues and holding an audience with the blues."

In the early 1970s Taylor became one of the first South Side blues artists to perform regularly at Kingston Mines and other clubs on Chicago's wealthier North Side. The steady change in the composition of her audiences from black to mostly white reflected the shrinking popularity of blues among African-Americans, who were gravitating toward jazz, soul, and rock and roll. In a conversation with Marty Racine for the *Houston Chronicle* (November 5, 1998), Taylor offered one explanation for the shift: "Blues is a reminder of hard times, slavery and just bein' black. Automatically, the black people don't need to be reminded of the way it was. We been there, we lived that."

In 1972 Taylor formed her own band, called the Blues Machine. (Its members have included, at various times, Vince Chappelle on drums, Cornelius Boyson on bass, Mervyn "Harmonica" Hinds on harmonica, Sammy Lawhorn and Mighty Joe Young on guitar, and Abb Locke on saxophone.) Taylor's fiery performance at the Ann Arbor Blues and Jazz Festival, in Michigan, recorded on the live album *Ann Arbor Blues and Jazz Festival 1972*, attracted the attention of Bruce Iglauer. Three years later, when Iglauer founded Alligator Records (now one of the biggest blues labels in the U.S.), Taylor was the first female artist he signed on. (The Chess Records label had come to an end that year, six years after its sale to GRT Records.) In 1999, for an article about Taylor's winning the Blues Foundation Lifetime Achievement Award, Iglauer told Niles Frantz, according to the foundation's Web site, "There is only one Queen of the Blues. [Taylor] is the blueswoman. I consider her music firmly in the tradition of the first generation of Chicago blues artists. She never wanted to sing anything but the blues, and she likes to leave the raw edges showing. In fact, she injects that rawness into all the music she sings. Koko is as tough as they come, and very proudly a country person in the best sense of what that means. She is the essence of what a blues musician should be."

In 1975 Alligator released Taylor's album *I Got What It Takes*, which features the standards "Big Boss Man," written by Luther Dixon and A. Smith, and "Voodoo Woman," which Taylor wrote. *I Got What It Takes* earned a Grammy Award nomination for best traditional blues album. Since then, the majority of Taylor's albums for Alligator have earned Grammy nominations. Earlier, on the Evidence label, Taylor made *South Side Lady* (1973), some cuts on which were recorded in a French studio and others live in the Netherlands during the 1973 American Folk Blues Festival tour of Europe. *The Earthshaker* (1978)—the title refers to Taylor herself—contains, among other songs, Taylor's "Please Don't Dog Me" and "I'm a Woman," Dorothy La Bostrie's "You Can Have My Husband (But Please Don't Mess with My Man)," and Willie Dixon's "Spoonful." Further cementing Taylor's reputation as a blues singer were her albums *From the Heart of a Woman* (1981), which includes swing, R&B, and soul as well as blues and is more tender than most of her other work; *Queen of the Blues* (1985), with contributions by the singer and guitarist Lonnie Brooks, the jazz guitarist Albert Collins, and the harmonica player James Cotton, among others; and *Live from Chicago—An Audience with The Queen* (1987), whose cuts include "Come to Mama," "Let the Good Times Roll," and Taylor's "The Devil's Gonna Have a Field Day." Taylor contributed to *Coast to Coast* (1989), an album by Paul Shaffer, the longtime bandleader for the CBS-TV program *Late Show with David Letterman*.

In February 1988 Taylor, her husband, and several members of her band were badly injured when their tour bus, with Pops at the wheel, tumbled off a cliff after a tire blew out. Neither Taylor nor the others, Dan Kening reported in the *Chicago Tribune* (May 4, 1990), had medical coverage; a benefit concert held by the Fabulous Thunderbirds, a blues, rock, and soul group, raised most of the money to pay the bills. Taylor, who had suffered a broken collarbone and several broken ribs, recovered after about six months and resumed her busy tour schedule. Then, in early 1990, her husband died, from maladies that she believes were related to the accident. "My work was the best thing happening for me—it gave me something to go on," she recalled to Don Snowden for the *Los Angeles Times* (September 6, 1990). "I just stay on the road—that's my life, and if I stay home too long, I get bored." She told Judy Hevrdejs for the *Chicago Tribune* (January 12, 1990), "Something magic happens when I get to a club or get on stage. [It's] the crowd, the musicians. Up on that stage, my personality changes. I put everything behind me when I perform. . . . I don't put a burden on my audience. I give them 100 percent of my energy." Taylor dedicated her next release, *Jump for Joy* (1990), to Pops. The disk includes four songs that Taylor wrote: the title track, "Can't Let Go," "Stop Watching Your Enemies," and "Tired of That." In a review of *Jump for Joy* for *People* (June 25, 1990), Roger Wolmuth wrote, "Taylor's energy and the mileage she has seen in 25 years of performing muscle her music beyond the merely raucous to believable reality. . . . For Taylor fans, this effort should serve as a reminder of just how good she still is."

*Force of Nature* (1993) earned Taylor another Grammy Award nomination, as did her next recording, *Royal Blue* (2000), both for best contemporary blues album. *Royal Blue* features several new songs written by Taylor, covers of songs by Ray Charles and Melissa Etheridge, and contributions by such guest artists as B.B. King, the blues and rock pianist Johnnie Johnson, the blues singer/songwriter Keb' Mo', and the blues-rocker Kenny Wayne Shepard. In a review of *Royal Blue* for *Amazon.com*, Matthew Cooke wrote, "Koko Taylor is the undisputed queen of Chicago blues vocals. . . . This record is . . . a characteristically well-informed tour of contemporary and electric blues, showcasing that gravelly, saucy growl that just gets more satisfying with age. . . . Investing each song with her time-tested, raspy wisdom, Taylor shows that her pipes are still, indisputably, in perfect working order." In 2002 Alligator Records released *Koko Taylor: Deluxe Edition*, a collection of some of her greatest hits.

Among the albums that feature Taylor are *Montreux Festival: Blues Avalanche*, recorded in Switzerland in 1972 and reissued in 1986; *Blues Deluxe*, recorded at the Chicago Blues Festival in 1980; *Willie Dixon: The Chess Box* (1990); *What It Takes: The Chess Years* (1991); *The Alligator Records 20th Anniversary Collection* (1992); and *B.B. King's Blues Summit* (1993).

In 1990 Taylor made her movie debut, as a lounge singer in the director David Lynch's *Wild at Heart*. She also recorded two songs for the soundtrack, both composed by Lynch himself. She appeared as herself in the movie *Mercury Rising* (1998) and as a member of the so-called Louisiana Gator Boys in *The Blues Brothers 2000* (1998). Along with other world-famous artists, Taylor performed at galas celebrating the inaugurations of President George Herbert Walker Bush, in 1989, and President Bill Clinton in 1993. She has appeared on the NBC television programs *Late Night with David Letterman* and *Late Night with Conan O'Brien*; FOX-TV's *New York Undercover*; CBS's *This Morning, Nightwatch*, and *Early Edition*; and the National Public Radio programs *All Things Considered* and *Crossroads*. The singer has also been featured in such national publications as *People, Entertainment Weekly, Rolling Stone*, and *Life*. Taylor was named Chicagoan of the Year by *Chicago* magazine in 1998. Most of the more than 20 W. C. Handy Awards Taylor has won between 1980 and 2002 were in the category contemporary female blues artist of the year. (Some have credited W. C. Handy, a Memphis composer and bandleader, with coining the term "the blues" in 1912, when he published his song "The Memphis Blues.")

Taylor has one daughter, called Cookie, and two grandchildren. In 1996 Taylor married Hays Harris, a tavern owner. The couple maintain a home on Chicago's South Side. Each of the two music clubs that Taylor herself opened in Chicago in the 1990s have closed. Speaking of her stature as a blueswoman, Taylor told Niles Frantz, "It makes me proud to be a role model for young people coming up that wants to sing and play the blues. I'm reaching for the sky, but if I fall somewhere in the clouds, I'll still be happy. I'm gonna keep on doin' what I'm doin', and hanging in there for the best." — C.F.T.

Suggested Reading: African American Publications (on-line); Alligator Records Web site; Blues Foundation Web site; *Charlotte Observer* (on-line) Mar. 10, 1995; *Chicago Tribune* XIII p4 June 5, 1988, with photos, VII p2 Jan. 12, 1990, with photos; *Gritz: The Online Southern Music Magazine* Nov. 27, 2001; *New York Times Magazine* p22+ June 29, 1980, with photos; *Rolling Stone* p56 Feb. 24, 1994, pSupp4 May 28, 1998; *Rolling Stone* (on-line)

Selected Recordings: *Koko Taylor*, 1969; *South Side Lady*, 1973; *I Got What it Takes*, 1975; *The Earthshaker*, 1978; *Queen of the Blues*, 1985; *Live from Chicago—An Audience with The Queen*, 1987; *Jump for Joy*, 1990; *Force of Nature*, 1993; *Royal Blue*, 2000; *Koko Taylor: Deluxe Edition*, 2002

---

Courtesy of Universal Press Syndicate

## Toles, Tom

*Oct. 22, 1951– Editorial cartoonist*

*Address: c/o United Media, 200 Madison Ave, New York, NY 10016*

"I primarily use the cartoon as a vehicle of opinion rather than humor," the editorial cartoonist Tom Toles told Howard Kurtz for the *Washington Post* (April 10, 2002). "Humor is a crucial part of cartooning, but I've always felt the opinion needed to come first." A self-described liberal, Toles practiced his craft for two decades at the *Buffalo News*, a regional newspaper in Buffalo, New York. In 2002, after a six-month search, the *Washington Post* hired him to succeed its longtime editorial cartoonist Herbert Block (who signed his work "Herblock"). Toles thus took over a position widely regarded as the most prestigious in his field. His visual commentaries are syndicated in more than 200 newspapers and have appeared in such national magazines as *U.S. News & World Report*, the *New Republic*, and the *Amicus Journal*; they have been published in six collections and have earned Toles more than 20 awards, most notably the 1990 Pulitzer Prize for editorial cartooning. Toles believes that editorial cartoons can do much more than merely comment on political and social issues; at their best, they can help shape the way readers think about those issues. As he told Clint O'Connor in an interview for the *Washington Journalism Review* (December 1988), "An editorial cartoonist can not only contribute peripherally to the public debate, but under the right circumstances, can help to mold it. . . . If you get good enough and consistent enough and read widely enough, you [can] actually be in a position to make a difference."

Toles's drawings, which include his trademark "cartoonist-in-the-corner"—a tiny image of the artist at his worktable, making an observation or remark related to that day's cartoon—are highly distinctive. They are distinguished also by their sparse details, somewhat childlike style, and simplicity, all of which belie a rapier-sharp intelligence. "I think [Toles] is one of the small handful of cartoonists doing legitimate, original political commentary, as opposed to gag-a-day stuff," the cartoonist Jules Feiffer told Clint O'Connor. "He's got real politics and, more importantly, real intelligence. There's a thoughtfulness that he applies to his work that you don't get a lot of in this business."

The second of the two sons of George Edward Toles and Rose Elizabeth (Riehle) Toles, the cartoonist was born Thomas Gregory Toles on October 22, 1951 in Buffalo, New York. He and his brother, George, grew up in nearby Hamburg. After graduating from high school, in 1969, Toles attended the State University of New York at Buffalo, where he majored in English. As an undergraduate he made illustrations for the campus newspaper, the *Spectrum.* Although Toles was interested in politics at the time, he considered himself more of an observer than an activist. "I wasn't an active activist because I didn't fit the political model," he told O'Connor. "In high school I was like the only liberal in a conservative high school, and in college I was the only liberal among radical students." Toles's drawings caught the attention of several local newspaper editors, among them Douglas Turner of the *Buffalo Courier-Express*, who offered him a position as a staff artist. Toles accepted, and shortly after he earned a B.A. degree, in 1973, he reported for work. "That was pretty much the end of my ambitions," he told O'Connor. "I got a job. My preference would have been not to have a job at all." From time to time, in addition to doing illustrations for the paper, he produced political cartoons. His talents quickly became apparent, and in 1980 he was promoted to editorial cartoonist.

The transition from illustrator to cartoonist was not easy for Toles, who had never taken an art lesson. "I had an illustration style that I had to turn into a cartoon style, and that's been very difficult and awkward for me . . . I've sort of institutionalized awkwardness right into my drawing style," he told O'Connor. Jeffrey Frank, who was the *Courier-Express* editorial-page editor at that time, told O'Connor, "You could really see Tom coming into his own that year [1981 to 1982], when he had to do four or five sketches a week, as opposed to being a staff artist and doing an occasional cartoon. He became a full-fledged editorial cartoonist that year."

In 1982 the *Courier-Express* folded, primarily because of improvements in its competitor, the *Buffalo News*, during the half-dozen years since the financier Warren Buffett had bought the latter paper. From among the several job offers he received, Toles accepted a position with the *Buffalo News*, thus enabling him to remain in his hometown. That same year he signed a contract with United Press Syndicate, and soon his cartoons were appearing in more than 125 newspapers across the nation. Toles now reached a far larger audience than he had through the *Courier-Express* or the *Buffalo News* alone. Perhaps for that reason *Buffalo News* decision makers gave Toles the freedom to express his own opinions, even when they conflicted with those expressed in *Buffalo News* editorials. "I alienated a tremendous number of readers in Buffalo because there had never been a cartoonist as pointed as I was," Toles told Robert H. Boyle in an interview for *Audubon* (September–October 2001). "And they let me know in no uncertain terms." Nevertheless, Toles refused to blunt his opinions.

In one example of his cartoons, published in 1982, Toles showed President Ronald Reagan at what is identified as the Richard M. Nixon Amusement Theme Park. Reagan is roller skating at breakneck speed down a giant replica of Nixon's nose (whose shape writers at the time often compared to that of a ski jump). As Reagan descends, he passes over sections labeled "I didn't know," "I didn't do it," "I didn't break any law," "The law didn't apply to me," "I am not a crook," and lastly, "I will finish my term"—statements that Nixon made during the investigation into the Watergate scandal. In the lower right-hand corner of the cartoon, Toles drew a tiny Reagan saying, "Last time I come here for advice." In another Toles cartoon, this one from 2002, a little man wearing an Uncle Sam top hat (which makes him a stand-in for the U.S.) writes on a piece of paper, "New Policy: The U.S. has the right to do whatever we want . . . whenever we want . . . wherever we want . . . to whomever we want . . . regardless of what anyone else in the world thinks." A second man reads what the first has written and asks, "With rights, don't there also come responsibilities?" In response, the man in the top hat writes on the paper, "It is the responsibility of the rest of the world to help pay for it."

Between 1992 and 1994, while continuing to work for the *Buffalo News*, Toles created cartoons for the *New Republic.* For about five years beginning in 1994, he drew cartoons for *U.S. News & World Report.* To date he has published six collections of his work: *The Taxpayer's New Clothes* (1985), *Mr. Gazoo: A Cartoon History of the Reagan Era* (1987), *At Least Our Bombs Are Getting Smarter: A Cartoon Preview of the 1990s* (1991),

*Curious Avenue* (1993), *My Elected Representatives Went to Washington* (1993), and *Duh: And Other Observations* (1996). His 71-page fantasy *My School Is Worse Than Yours* (1997), written for youngsters from about seven to nine years of age, follows a girl named Raven Royce as she points out the horrendous deficiencies of her school. "Sly social commentary infiltrates this brief but funny look at an absurdly broken-down school victimized by technological innovation," a reviewer for *Horn Book* wrote (as quoted on *Amazon.com*). "Raven's teacher is a defective robot too expensive to trash, and students wear boots to navigate the puddles the architects didn't anticipate when they built the school underground to guard against bombs." According to a critic for *Kirkus Reviews* (also quoted on *Amazon.com*), *My School Is Worse Than Yours* is "a hilarious book that is ideal for classroom read-alouds." By contrast, John Sigwald, writing for the *School Library Journal* (September 1997), complained, "The text jumps around enough to disappoint even diehard readers sucked in by the appealing title and potential goofiness," and he described Raven as an unsympathetic, two-dimensional character.

Toles has also created two comic strips: *Curious Avenue*, which ran from 1992 to 1994 in the *Buffalo News* and other newspapers and focused on the antics of a group of precocious kids, and *Randolph Itch, 2 a.m.*, which ran from 2000 to 2002 in more than 65 papers and revealed the dreams, nightmares, and semiconscious thoughts of the title character.

On October 7, 2001 the political cartoonist Herbert Block died, 55 years after he had joined the staff of the *Washington Post*. As Fred Hiatt, the *Post*'s editorial-page editor, recalled to Kurtz, Donald Graham, chairman of the Washington Post Co., told him to pick the best possible replacement for Block. In April 2002 the *Post* invited Toles to become the paper's new editorial cartoonist. In his conversation with Kurtz, Hiatt described Toles as "very funny, very smart, a very talented artist and a great journalist, which not all funny cartoonists are. He reports, he thinks about issues . . . He's got a very sophisticated sense of politics and how this town works, even though he's never lived here." Although Toles did not want to leave Buffalo—"I've got a vested and ongoing interest in local issues that I've been cartooning," he had told O'Connor a dozen years earlier—he felt he could not turn down the *Post*'s offer. As he told Kurtz, the job was "the premier editorial cartooning position in the country. I figure what I do will have a larger impact there than any other place I could be doing it." In the summer of 2002, Toles began working in Washington, D.C., where he now lives with his wife, Gretchen, whom he married in 1973, and their two teenage children, Amanda and Seth. As part of Toles's agreement with the newspaper, the family will spend part of every year in the Buffalo area. (Their home in Hamburg is just a few doors down from the house in which Toles grew up.)

The bearded Toles is six feet, three inches tall and very thin. Clint O'Connor described him as "very laid-back, very soft-spoken," and "charming, witty, [and] clever." During the period when O'Connor interviewed him, Toles worked from before 6:00 a.m. until about 2:30 p.m., with some of that time devoted to tasks that might be described as clerical, such as having the cartoon of the day reproduced at a commercial copying establishment, for mailing to the publications receiving it through syndication. "My whole life is organized to gather all of the energy that I have available for the three hours every weekday morning that I'm working behind this desk," he told O'Connor while sitting in his *Buffalo News* office. "Usually, even after that, I just barely have enough energy left over to ink it."

Margaret Sullivan, who is now the editor of the *Buffalo News*, recalled to Kurtz that when Toles learned that he had won the Pulitzer Prize, "he rode a unicycle around the perimeter of the newsroom, displaying the award for all to see." Toles's honors also include the John Fischetti Editorial Cartoon Award, from Columbia College, in Chicago, the Free Press Association's H. L. Mencken Award, and the Global Media Award, from the Population Institute, for cartoons that promote environmental conservation. — H.T.

Suggested Reading: *American Journalism Review* p8 May 2002; *Audubon* p32+ Sep.–Oct 2001, with photo; *Buffalo News* B p1 Apr. 10, 2002; *Washington Journalism Review* p24+ Dec. 1988; *Washington Post* A p12+ Apr. 10, 2002

Selected Books: *The Taxpayer's New Clothes*, 1985; *Mr. Gazoo: A Cartoon History of the Reagan Era*, 1987; *At Least Our Bombs Are Getting Smarter: A Cartoon Preview of the 1990s*, 1991; *Curious Avenue*, 1993; *My Elected Representatives Went to Washington*, 1993; *Duh: And Other Observations*, 1996; *My School Is Worse Than Yours*, 1999

---

## Turner, Mark

*Nov. 10, 1965– Saxophonist*

*Address: c/o Susan Higginbotham Artist Management, P.O. Box 62, Valley Cottage, NY 10989*

The tenor saxophonist and composer Mark Turner has impressed critics and won respect among young jazz musicians for his understated, lyrical, sometimes experimental style, which is influenced by the works of the German classical composer Johann Sebastian Bach as well as the music of the jazz saxophonists John Coltrane and Warne Marsh. Writing for the *New York Times* (June 16, 2002), Ben Ratliff called Turner's music "intellectual and rigorously composed, defined by long, flowing, chromatically complex lines that keep their stamina and intensity as they stay dynamically even. He

Guy Aroch/Courtesy of B. H. Hopper Management
*Mark Turner*

has learned how to play the highest reaches of his instrument . . . with a serene strength, never shouting for the effect that audiences love. The overwhelming sense about Mr. Turner is that he wants to get on with his work." In addition to his own material, Turner has played, on his four albums as a bandleader, music from a wide range of composers—including Broadway, pop, and even rock numbers. Although highly acclaimed, Turner has not become a commercial success; indeed, his record label dropped him in 2001. Nevertheless, he is one of the most influential musicians in jazz today. At a recent Thelonious Monk Institute saxophone competition, Ben Ratliff noted, it was evident that Turner's influence on the young musicians was second only to Coltrane's. "His music is the freshest thing around . . . ," the composer and vocalist Luciana Souza told Ratliff, adding: "It's 'out' music that still sounds very musical and consonant."

Mark Turner was born on November 10, 1965 in Ohio. At the age of four, he moved with his family to California, where he lived in the towns of Cerritos and Palos Verdes, near Los Angeles. In high school Turner played saxophone and was also an enthusiastic break-dancer; he once broke his front teeth in an attempt at a back flip. Talented in the visual arts as well, Turner studied design and illustration at Long Beach State University. Deciding to focus on the tenor saxophone instead, he transferred to the prestigious Berklee College of Music, in Boston, Massachusetts, in the late 1980s. "Obviously the mediums are different, in that music happens in the moment and art doesn't in the same way," he said for the official Web site of B. H. Hopper Management, in Munich, Germany, "but I see a lot of similarities in the creative processes. The connection is not that literal, though. You could be a great bricklayer, or a great chef; if you derive the same feeling from doing something completely different, it's bound to shed light and new meaning." At Berklee, Turner focused intensely on the work of the late John Coltrane. "I was fairly methodical," he told Ben Ratliff. "I almost always wrote out Coltrane's solos, and I'd have a lot of notes on the side." Although when a musician studies another musician so intensely there is the danger of mimicry, Turner was not worried. "I knew I would eventually not be interested in [studying Coltrane] anymore," he told Ratliff. "Also, I noticed that if you looked at someone else who was into [Coltrane], and if you could listen through that person's ear and mind, it would be a slightly different version." In 1990 Turner moved to New York City, where he worked for several years as a sideman with a wide variety of jazz artists. "I've played in bands that did only standards," he told Bradley Bambarger for *Billboard* (April 11, 1998), "or only 1960s Coltrane-type stuff. . . . I'd put myself into a situation that was very free, or by contrast, very structured. Sometimes it would be a situation that would be very uncomfortable for me, musically. Even though I didn't think I could pull it off, I'd find a way to make it work." Turner grew tired of the sound of many contemporary tenor saxophonists, who, he told Ratliff, played with "more of an aggressive sound, with a vocabulary that's come to be a bit programmed." By contrast, he was attracted by the sound of the late saxophonist Warne Marsh, "a linear, melodic improviser who managed to merge spontaneity and research, playing nearly Bach-like melodic lines," as Ratliff noted.

Turner released his first album, *Yam Yam* (1994), on the Criss-Cross label. The album featured six original compositions and marked his first recording session with the guitarist Kurt Rosenwinkel, another former Berklee student, and the pianist Brad Mehldau. Writing for *All Music Guide* (on-line), David R. Adler remarked that the album "reveals much about the evolution of all these players, and is therefore well worth the attention of serious fans." Three years passed before Turner released his next album. Signing with Warner Bros., he was featured on *Warner Jams Vol. 2: The Two Tenors* (1997), along with the noted tenor saxophonist James Moody. "I like to interact with another similar voice," Turner told Bambarger about his collaborations. "It adds more energy, more elements. A little sparring doesn't hurt." In his article for the *Village Voice* (April 14, 1998), Gary Giddins noted that on *The Two Tenors*, "Turner holds his own fairly well, but he is clearly unnerved at times, and there is no disgrace in that: Moody is imperial throughout." In a change of pace from his first solo release, only one of the songs on Turner's second solo album, *Mark Turner* (1998), was penned by him. Several tracks featured collaborations between Turner and the acclaimed young tenor saxophonist Joshua Redman. Writing about the record for *All Music Guide* (on-line), Ken Dryden noted that Turner's tune "Mr. Brown" is "a pulsating blues vehicle for the two inspired reedmen," while "Lennie Tristano's slippery bop anthem '327 East 22nd Street' is also an excellent showcase for their talent." His only complaint was about a version of Ornette Coleman's "Kathelin Gray," which he found to be "ponderous, dissonant and overlong." Gary Giddins wrote that Turner "has a sound of his own, anomalously cool, and is in the process of working out a style that favors a sober midrange, sinuous phrases, and a penchant for prettily sustained ballads." Later in 1998 Turner released *In This World*, which features Brian Blade on drums and Mehldau on piano. In his review for *All Music Guide* (on-line), Tim Sheridan noted, "'Mesa,' the album's opening track, meanders from a relaxed melodic path to a switch-back road of surprises," and wrote that Turner's cover of the Beatles' "She Said, She Said" is "a deceptively breezy journey into the unknown." In his review for *All About Jazz* (on-line), David R. Adler characterized the record as "thoughtful" and concluded, "While casual jazz fans might find *In This World* a difficult listen, anybody who's into Coltrane, Tristano or Marsh should really dig it."

Turner's next album was *Two Tenor Ballads* (2000), which comprises collaborations between Turner and the tenor saxophonist Tad Shull on ballad standards. (The tracks were recorded in December 1994.) Later in 2000 Turner released *Ballad Session*, consisting of his versions of other ballad standards, culled from pop, Broadway, and jazz sources. In his review for *All Music Guide* (on-line), William Ruhlman wrote that the record "doesn't break any new ground for Turner, but it demonstrates his grasp of jazz history and repertoire." The album was something of a disappointment for Turner, as his record label had ruled against his preference, a selection of slow material from a wider variety of composers, ranging from himself to the classical composer Olivier Messaien to the experimental electronica artist Aphex Twin. Following *Ballad Session*, Turner toured with Kurt Rosenwinkel, whose album *The Enemies of Energy* (2000) features Turner. The saxophonist was also heard on Rosenwinkel's *The Next Step* (2001), and when Turner recorded *Dharma Days* (2001), he asked Rosenwinkel to be his guitarist for the sessions. Featuring nine Turner originals, *Dharma Days* alternates between post-bop and more experimental pieces. In a review for the *Philadelphia City Paper* (on-line), Nate Chinen wrote that Turner "improvises with the same alluringly elusive quality that distinguishes his compositions." "Sleek but never slick, his compositions are often laced with hip unison passages and intricately designed interludes that trade off between his soulful tenor sax and guitarist Kurt Rosenwinkel's similarly understated guitar lines," Mike Joyce wrote for the *Washington Post* (June 1, 2001). In a dissenting view, Art Lange commented in his review for *Pulse!* (on-line), "Though his themes are sometimes quirky, Turner's tunes just aren't memorable, despite the internal alterations [and] tempo shift here, a change of texture there." In December 2001 Warner Bros. dropped Turner from its roster of artists, noting that his albums were not selling sufficiently. "It's fine," Turner told Ben Ratliff. "I was considering trying to get out of it myself. Nothing against Warner, but I feel relieved and open and free."

Turner currently lives in New Haven, Connecticut, and commutes to play in New York City. He is married to Helena Hansen, a doctoral candidate in anthropology at Yale University. The couple have two children. Remarking on the New York jazz scene to Bradley Bambarger, Turner noted that it is "vibrant, definitely vibrant. It's easy to find a lot of diverse playing experiences in New York. It's not difficult to get in with the other musicians and start playing; it just takes persistence." Turner is known as being quiet, self-assured, and noncompetitive. He practices Buddhism. He has said that he is no longer interested in fronting a group but would like to form a band whose members would share composing and publishing credits. — G.O.

Suggested Reading: *Billboard* Apr. 11, 1998; *New York Times* II p1 June 16, 2002; *Village Voice* p119 Apr. 14, 1998

Selected Recordings: *Yam Yam*, 1994; *Mark Turner*, 1998; *In This World*, 1998; *Ballad Session*, 2000; *Dharma Days*, 2001; with James Moody—*Warner Jams Vol. 2: The Two Tenors*, 1997; with Tad Shull—*Two Tenor Ballads*, 2000

---

## Tweet

*Jan. 21, 1971– Singer; songwriter*

*Address: c/o Elektra Records, 75 Rockefeller Plaza, 16th Fl., New York, NY 10009*

In 2002, after battling deep depression and struggling in vain for years to achieve success in the music world as a member of the group Sugah, the singer/songwriter Tweet fulfilled her long-held dream: with the release of her debut album, *Southern Hummingbird*, she earned both critical and popular acclaim. The songs on the album, among them the risqué number-one hit "Oops (Oh My)," range in style from hip-hop to R&B to gospel and showcase Tweet's passionate and heartfelt songwriting and her skills on acoustic guitar. "A lot of my songs come from the bad situations I've been in," the singer said to Dimitri Ehrlich for *Interview* (March 1, 2001). "The best medicine for a broken heart is to write songs. It's better than seeing a psychiatrist; it's like a healing process for me." Tweet has been compared to the folk-influenced singer, songwriter, and acoustic-guitar player Tracy Chapman and the singer Minnie Riperton. Immediately after its release, in April of this year, *Southern Hummingbird* hit number two on the *Billboard* R&B album charts.

Frederick M. Brown/Getty Images

*Tweet*

The youngest of Tom and Shirley Keys's five children, Tweet was born Charlene Keys on January 21, 1971 in Rochester, New York. According to *People* (August 19, 2002), her father was the foreman of a labor union, her mother a missionary minister. Tweet has said that she cannot remember why she was given her nickname. Referring to a Warner Bros. cartoon character, she joked to Shaheem Reid for the MTV Web site, "Maybe I had a big head like the Tweety bird character. I've been Tweet since I was a little girl. It's been a nickname that everybody in my family wants to get credit for. 'I named her that.' 'No, I named her that.'" Beginning virtually from her birth, Tweet told Kelly L. Carter for the *Detroit Free Press* (July 3, 2002, online), her parents exposed her to music. "I watched my mom and dad sing in gospel groups all my life. That influenced me to want to do music some kind of way. . . . I've always watched my cousins, my brothers, my uncle play. I just jumped to the drums one day in church. I started playing the guitar because I got tired of waiting for people's music. And I never took lessons." Her siblings were also musically inclined and played various instruments. "I think coming from a musical family centered me," the singer wrote in an article posted on *tweet.330.ca*, a Canadian fan site. "I inherited a real passion for music, and a respect for those who dedicate their lives to it as a career." As a teenager, Tweet attended the School of the Arts in Rochester. There, for the first time, she recalled on *tweet.330.ca*, "I was surrounded by so many creative people who were determined to follow their heart. I allowed myself to dream when I was there."

After her graduation from high school, in 1988, Tweet set out to succeed in the music world. She spent six years with the all-female trio Sugah, which disbanded in 2000 without ever releasing an album. "I guess I gave a lot of my life over to this producer and to people that I thought would [bring me success]. I was moving around to a lot of different cities but in the end it wasn't right," she told Chris Lamb for the *Teenmusic* Web site. Adding to her unhappiness was the failure of an eight-year intimate relationship. "For so many years I was stuck," the singer told Gil Kaufman for the MTV Web site. "I couldn't breathe, I was depressed and miserable." After Sugah broke up, Tweet moved to Panama City, Florida, where her parents had taken up residence. There she turned to alcohol and contemplated suicide. She was on the brink of carrying out her plan to kill herself when the hugely successful hip-hop star and music producer Missy "Misdemeanor" Elliott contacted her. Elliott, who had met Tweet in the mid-1990s, before becoming a star herself, asked Tweet to sing background vocals on songs such as "Take Away," a duet by Elliott and Ginuwine, for Elliott's third album, released as *Miss E . . . So Addictive*, in 2001. (Tweet later contributed vocals to three tracks on Elliott's album *Under Construction*, which was scheduled for release in November 2002.) Elliott then signed Tweet to her label, Gold Mind Records, and since then has served as the young singer's mentor. "I call [Elliott] my guardian angel because she truly rescued me from ending my life," Tweet told *Jet* (April 22, 2002). She said to Dimitri Ehrlich for *Interview* (March 1, 2001), "If it wasn't for Missy I don't know what I would have done. I was going through a lot after I left Sugah. . . . I was on the road to self-destruction. I wasn't feeling life at all. If it wasn't for her being concerned and remembering me, I don't know where I would be."

Tweet's album, *Southern Hummingbird*, released in April 2002, debuted at number two on the *Billboard* R&B album chart. Regarding the inspiration for its title, Tweet said to Reid, "I'm the only person in my family that was born in New York. Everybody else is from the South but me. Every summer I go to the South. Everybody thinks I'm Southern because I talk kind of country." Several songs on *Southern Hummingbird* feature Tweet playing acoustic guitar—her instruments also include bass guitar, piano, and drums—creating a sound bridging hip-hop and folk music that has been called alternative soul, or in Tweet's words, "gumbo soul," a stew of gospel, R&B, soul, and country. Tweet wrote most of the songs on *Southern Hummingbird* herself, and most are about love, heartbreak, and redemption. "The album has three seduction songs, two being-seduced songs, three about being in love, one about regret of lost love, one about not regretting lost love, one about betrayal, one about friendship, and one about self-love," Sterling Clover reported in a review of *Southern Hummingbird* for the British Web site *freakytriggerco.uk*. "Oops (Oh My)," the first single from the album, spent six weeks at number one on *Billboard's* chart for R&B/hip-hop singles and tracks in the first half of 2002. The song has polished, seductive beats supplied by Timbaland (whose real name is Timothy Mosley), lyrics full of double entendres, and a rap interlude by Elliott, who, along with Timbaland and Tweet herself, produced the songs on *Southern Hummingbird.* (Tweet also contributed vocals to Timbaland's 2001 album, *Indecent Proposal.*) The lyrics to "Oops (Oh My)" include the lines, "Oops there goes my shirt up over my head, oh my. / Oops there goes my skirt dropping to my feet, oh my." When asked by Chris Lamb if, as the lyrics might suggest, the song is about masturbation, Tweet answered, "No, it's not, although everybody thinks it is. But I want people to take my songs and have it mean whatever it means to you. To me it means a woman coming into tune with herself, self-appreciation." "Oops (Oh My)," which enjoyed frequent airplay on the radio, has been nominated by the *Soul Train* Lady of Soul Awards for best R&B/soul or rap new-artist solo. According to the Web site *tweet.330.ca,* Tweet described another song on the record, "Always Will," as one she had written to the man she had dated for eight years. "I know he won't be able to love another like he loved me and I have no problem putting that into a song." *Southern Hummingbird* also includes, among other songs, "Best Friend," a duet with the R&B star Bilal (Bilal Sayeed Oliver), and "Boogie 2nite," a hip-hop dance track.

The overall critical response to *Southern Hummingbird* has been positive, with many reviewers praising Tweet's smooth voice and her songwriting. "Tweet's a talented singer, with a warm rich voice that's stuck in the melismatic territory of high octaves," Sterling Clover wrote. "She can't do cold or aloof; even her kiss-off songs sound like come-ons. More than anything else she's got the voice of a woman who's got to stop kissing you and catch her train, and tells you this as she keeps kissing you. Sometimes the voice of a woman who's doing more than kissing." In a review of *Southern Hummingbird* for *amazon.com,* Rebecca Levine wrote, "Tweet is the classic show-biz story: an overnight sensation 10 years in the making. The sultry singer/songwriter traveled a long and twisted path to success. . . . Fans of intelligent soul music will be glad Tweet stuck it out. *Hummingbird* is the work of an introspective and talented woman." A fair number of industry insiders, however, while not criticizing Tweet's performance, have credited Elliott and Timbaland with a considerable part of her success.

Black Entertainment Television (BET) nominated Tweet as best new artist in 2002. She sang part of the chorus for "Paradise," a song on L.L. Cool J's 2002 album, *Ten.* The soul singer is due to appear on an episode of the UPN television sitcom *The Parkers* in November 2002. In her leisure time Tweet enjoys going to the movies, playing billiards, and bowling. From a brief marriage that ended in divorce, she has a daughter, Tashawna, who was 12 years old in mid-2002. She and her daughter live in Atlanta, Georgia. — C.F.T.

Suggested Reading: *askmen.com*; *Ebony* p83+ Aug. 2002, with photo; *Interview* p134+ Mar. 1, 2001; *Jet* p57 Apr. 22, 2002, with photo; *mtv.com*; *Rolling Stone* p30 May 9, 2002, with photo; *tweet.330.ca* (on-line)

Selected Recordings: *Southern Hummingbird,* 2002

---

Courtesy of the Denver Nuggets

## Van Exel, Nick

*Nov. 27, 1971– Basketball player*

*Address: Dallas Mavericks, 777 Sports St., Dallas, TX 75207*

Since he entered the National Basketball Association (NBA), in 1993, the left-handed point guard Nick Van Exel has proven himself to be a talented and exciting player—while adding to a reputation for being a troublesome and difficult one. At the same time, off the court, he has devoted time and energy to helping others. While playing with the Denver Nuggets, he was honored with the Chopper Travaglini Award for his generosity to the Denver community; he also hosted Nick Van Exel's Golden Nuggets, a program that brought underprivileged children and their sponsors to basketball games held in Denver, and he is involved with the National Benevolent Association, an arm of the Christian Church (Disciples of Christ). Often described as highly competitive, tough, and hot-headed, Van Exel, with his sure dribbling, crisp passing, and exciting three-point shooting, was a star player for the University of Cincinnati, helped the Los Angeles Lakers recapture some of their former dazzle during the mid-1990s, made the NBA All-Star team in 1998, and found himself the discontented leader of the struggling Nuggets. During the 2001–02 season he was traded to the Dallas Mavericks.

Nickey Maxwell Van Exel was born on November 27, 1971 in Kenosha, Wisconsin. His father left the family before Van Exel was 10, and for undisclosed reasons his mother could not take care of the boy; Jack McCallum and Don Yaeger quoted Van Exel's mother in *Sports Illustrated* (April 29, 1996) as saying only that she "got into some trouble." Van Exel went to live with his aunt Jacqueline Huntley and her family. As a youngster Van Exel admired such NBA stars as Reggie Theus and Marques Johnson, both dynamic scorers who played from the late 1970s to the early 1990s. (Descriptions of Theus as a player are remarkably similar to those currently used for Van Exel: "spectacular"; "explosive"; "sometimes out-of-control"; "a player who drives the fans wild and coaches crazy.") Van Exel attended St. Joseph's preparatory high school in Kenosha, where he was a star player on the basketball team. As a senior he was the top prep-school scorer in Wisconsin, averaging 29.8 points per game. He did not do well academically, however, failing to achieve the minimum 2.0 grade-point average required to play Division 1 college basketball, and he did not even take the college entrance exam. Despite being talented enough to play in Division 1, the highest level of college athletics, Van Exel went to the little-known Trinity Valley Community College (TVCC) in Athens, Texas.

At TVCC Van Exel, a relatively short guard at six-foot-one but fast and skilled, continued to excel on the court. He also ran into some personal trouble, raising doubts about his attitude and personality. In 1991 Van Exel got into a fight with his six-foot eight-inch teammate James Roberts. Witnesses and former team members told McCallum and Yaeger that after Roberts was knocked down by another player on the TVCC team, Van Exel kicked the unconscious man in the face and then repeatedly knocked his head into the floor. (Roberts, who was hospitalized, was unable to press charges, since he could not specify who had done what to him.) Van Exel's ex-girlfriend and former teammates also recalled to McCallum and Yaeger that Van Exel was sometimes physically abusive toward her.

Van Exel eventually left TVCC and entered the University of Cincinnati, where he was a sociology major and a star of the basketball team. As a junior the fiery guard led the Cincinnati Bearcats to the National Collegiate Athletic Association's (NCAA) Final Four. As a senior he averaged 18.3 points per game, led the team in scoring, assists, and steals, and brought the Bearcats as far as the Elite Eight in the tournament. He was a Third Team All-American selection and a finalist for the Wooden Award. (Named after the legendary University of California at Los Angeles [UCLA] basketball coach John Wooden, the award is given every year to the nation's best player.)

Despite those successes, Van Exel's transition to the NBA was a rocky one. After missing two appointments with the Charlotte Hornets, he went for an interview and workout with the Seattle Supersonics, but again failed to acquit himself well. The Sonics' coach, George Karl, was quoted by McCallum and Yaeger as saying, "It was the worst interview we've ever had with a player, bar none." Apparently, Van Exel refused to run hard in the physical drills in which prospective players participate for the coaches' evaluation, even after Karl confronted him directly. At the same time, something in Van Exel's arrogance attracted Karl. As McCallum and Yaeger related, however, that quality did not impress the veteran agent Ron Grinker, who refused to represent Van Exel mainly because of what he called his "punk attitude." Due to questions about Van Exel's attitude and concerns about his height, NBA scouts were not convinced that he was a legitimate prospect. He was not selected until the second round of the 1993 draft, when the Los Angeles Lakers' executive vice president and former star, Jerry West, decided to take a chance on him, making Van Exel the 37th pick overall.

As the Lakers' starting point guard in the 1993–94 season, Van Exel quickly showed his talent: he scored 24 points in his first professional game, set a team record with 123 three-pointers for the season (which just missed the league rookie record of 125, set by former Laker Dennis Scott in 1989–90), and for the year averaged 13.6 points (sixth among first-year players) and 5.6 assists (second among first-year players) per game. He was named to the All-Rookie Second Team for his strong first year, becoming the only second-round draft pick to be so recognized. Of note in particular was that Van Exel had scored more points than any Laker rookie since the legendary Magic Johnson in 1979–80.

During the next season Van Exel established himself as one of the better point guards in the league. Again, he had a big opening day, scoring 35 points against the Detroit Pistons. He hit 183 three-pointers for the year, which was fifth-best in the league and broke his own team record. For the season he averaged 16.9 points and 8.3 assists per game, which was sixth-best in the league; that year, only Van Exel and New Jersey's Kenny Anderson averaged more than 16 points and eight assists per game. In that season's play-offs, Van Exel led the Lakers in points, assists, steals, and minutes played. The team lost in the second round to the San Antonio Spurs, but not before Van Exel won Game 5, sinking a three-pointer just before the end of regulation play and another just before the end of the overtime period. While his play during the series was spectacular, Van Exel angered the Lakers' coach, Del Harris, by refusing to join the team huddles during timeouts.

Van Exel had another solid season in 1995–96. He averaged 14.9 points and 6.9 assists per game and became the first Laker ever to record more than 100 three-pointers in three consecutive seasons. Also, his assist-to-turnover ratio—a revealing statistic for point guards, who handle the ball much of the time and direct the action of the offense—was 3.26:1, ninth-best in the NBA. But once again, other factors marred Van Exel's accomplishments: the league suspended him from the final seven games of the season and fined him a record $25,000 for shoving referee Ron Garretson on top of the scorers' table during the fourth quarter of an April game in Denver, in a dispute over a call Garretson had made. Some observers called what had happened an isolated incident, one that had been blown out of proportion, while others saw it as yet another example of Van Exel's volatility. His agent, James Bryant, told Jackie MacMullan for *Sports Illustrated* (May 26, 1997), "Nick wants to win with such passion that sometimes that passion causes him to do things that get him into trouble." (In his first four years in the league, Van Exel collected 40 technical fouls.) Jerry West was quoted by Frank Litsky in the *New York Times* (April 11, 1996) as saying, "I think it is imperative that the NBA address the incredible number of incidents that are undermining the professionalism of this league. Personally, I am embarrassed and apologize to our fans." Lost salary from the seven games in which Van Exel could not play brought his total losses to almost $190,000.

Although Van Exel experienced pain in his left knee during the 1996–97 season, he nonetheless had another strong year, averaging 15.3 points and 8.5 assists per game, coming in eighth-best in the league in the latter category. His assist-to-turnover ratio was again excellent at 3.17:1, seventh-best in the league. In a game in January 1997, Van Exel recorded 23 assists, the most by any player in a single game that season, and only one shy of Magic Johnson's team record. After a one-point loss to the Miami Heat in March 1997, Van Exel, furious over a foul called against his team in the closing seconds of the game, said to the press that the officials must have been betting on the game's outcome; the league fined him $10,000 for that comment. During a play-off game against the Utah Jazz in May of that same year, the tension between Van Exel and Del Harris boiled over when Van Exel refused to come to the sideline to receive instructions from the coach. Harris promptly pulled Van Exel from the game, and the two got into a shouting match near the bench. The Lakers lost that game, and two nights later the Jazz eliminated the Lakers from the play-offs. As quoted by Jackie MacMullan, Harris stated, "Nick's problem is he has a deep-seated mistrust of authority. He's a high-maintenance kid. West has to meet with him once a month just so he can keep him straightened out."

Van Exel missed several weeks of play during the next season after undergoing arthroscopic surgery on his left knee. He played in a career-low 64 games (a full NBA season consists of 82), but still played well; he averaged a very respectable 6.9 assists per game and led the NBA with an assist-to-turnover ratio of 4.25:1. In 1998 coaches of the Western Conference selected Van Exel to appear for the first time in the NBA All-Star Game. He was the only All-Star who had not been drafted into the league in the first round.

Also in 1998 the Lakers traded Van Exel to the Denver Nuggets. Michael BeDan wrote for the *Rocky Mountain News* (December 11, 2001, online) that what prompted the trade was "Van Exel's stormy relationship with former Lakers coach Del Harris—and numerous teammates complaining to Lakers management." Unfortunately for Van Exel, Denver was, and remains, a struggling team, in contrast to the Lakers, who went on to become champions in 2000, 2001, and 2002. Though Dan Issel, then the Nuggets' coach, signed Van Exel to a seven-year, $77 million contract before the 1999–2000 season and gave him a great deal of freedom on the court, the guard publicly expressed his desire to be traded. A writer for the Associated Press, as cited on *stacks.msnbc.com* (December 10, 2001), quoted the player as saying, "Four years, and we haven't brought anybody in here. Steady losing—it's very tough, very frustrating. It's not about betraying anybody. I love playing basketball. I'm not happy with all this money and losing." Kiki Vandeweghe, a former NBA player and now the general manager of the Nuggets, told the same writer, "My first inclination is not to trade him. Nick is a great player. Nick really wants to win. He's very competitive. If you look back over the history of the NBA, all great players at one point want to be traded. They have a drive to win, and they get frustrated."

In the meantime, Van Exel continued to put up strong numbers for the Nuggets, as he had done over the previous four seasons. In the 1999–2000 season, he averaged a career-high nine assists per game, second-best in the NBA; and in 2000–01 he averaged an impressive 17.7 points and 8.5 assists per contest, which was third-best in the league in the latter category. In January 2002 Van Exel's points-per-game average hovered at about 24—a career high, and one that reflected his efforts to carry the last-place Nuggets. He was also averaging eight assists per game. In February 2002, in a multiplayer deal, Van Exel was traded to the Dallas Mavericks. He played the final 27 games of the 2001–02 season with the Mavericks, averaging 28 minutes and 13.2 points per game, thus helping his new squad to its first 50-win season in 13 years and into the play-offs. There, the San Antonio Spurs eliminated Dallas in the second round, with four games to one.

Van Exel has a large scar under his bottom lip (visible when he appears on televised games or in team photos). The scar resulted from a cut he suffered one night when he was 15; while driving a borrowed car, he fell asleep at the wheel and crashed into a tree. His charitable activities in Denver, for which he earned the Chopper Travaglini Award, included delivering Thanksgiving turkeys to poor families in 2000, accompanied by his Nugget teammate Antonio McDyess. Also in 2000 he launched an annual event called the Nick Van Exel Charity Weekend; activities held on those weekends raise money to support those of the Assets from Nick Charitable Fund, which helps single mothers and children in need. In his leisure time Van Exel enjoys music, video games, and tennis.—C.F.T.

Suggested Reading: *nba.com*; *Sport* p16+ Feb. 1996, with photos; *Sports Illustrated* p38+ Apr. 29, 1996, with photos, p88+ May 26, 1997, with photos; *stacks.msnbc.com* Dec. 10, 2001

---

Walter McBride/Retna Ltd.

## Vieira, Meredith

(vee-EHR-uh)

*Dec. 30, 1953– Television news journalist; co-host of* The View

*Address:* The View, *320 W. 66th St., New York, NY 10023*

The television journalist Meredith Vieira reached the top of her profession in 1989, when she was offered the prestigious position of correspondent on the CBS news program *60 Minutes*, the most popular prime-time show in the history of television. On *60 Minutes* she won praise for her skills as a reporter and writer and for her compassionate, unpretentious persona. But even as she enjoyed success on the show, the Emmy Award–winning Vieira found that her goals were shifting. After spending two years on *60 Minutes*, during which she gave birth to her first child, she realized that her family life had become a greater priority for her than her television career. Following her departure from the series, she continued to do award-winning investigative reports, most of them for the ABC television news magazine *Turning Point*, and she is currently one of the co-hosts of the popular daytime talk show *The View*. Still, her decision to give up the more demanding job at *60 Minutes* marked a pivotal point in her life. "I always wanted kids. I never really thought in terms of a career. I just sort of fell into mine and then I liked it and I did well but it never really drove me—it never was the thing that moved me deep inside, but the thought of family always did," Vieira told Diane Clehane for the *Westchester WAG* (June 1999, on-line). *The View* is a perennial Emmy Award nominee.

Of Portuguese descent, Meredith Vieira was born on December 30, 1953 in Providence, Rhode Island. Her father, Edwin, was a country doctor, and her mother, Mary Elsie, was a homemaker. Vieira attended Tufts University, in Medford, Massachusetts, graduating in 1975 with a bachelor's degree in English. In the same year she took a job as a news announcer for WORC-Radio in Worcester, Massachusetts. One day, while working at the station, Vieira answered a phone call from a recruiter who had not called to speak to Vieira but who, liking the sound of her voice, gave her a job at the radio station WJAR in Providence. Soon afterward she was promoted to the position of reporter and anchor for WJAR-TV. A CBS talent scout saw one of Vieira's reports and asked her to come to New York City to work for WCBS-TV. For three years beginning in 1979, she covered high-profile stories for the station, including the 1980 Republican National Convention, in Detroit, and the well-publicized murder trial of Jean Harris. Vieira also distinguished herself with her series on child molestation, which won a Front Page award from the Newswoman's Club of New York. In addition to reporting, Vieira sometimes served as an anchor on the station's news broadcasts. Stephen Cohen, a former news director at WCBS-TV, told Verne Gay for *New York Newsday* (February 2, 1990) that Vieira had "a warmth and caring of persona that was not in vogue among TV reporters at that time. Most were very tough, hard-hitting. She was the first of a new generation of reporters that were more natural in their approach."

Vieira left New York in 1982 to work as a reporter in CBS's Chicago Bureau, eventually becoming CBS Midwest Bureau chief. She told Gay that in Chicago she got "a tremendous amount of air-time" as well as support from the preeminent TV newsman Dan Rather. In Chicago Vieira also met her future husband, Richard Cohen, a former senior political producer of CBS News. CBS named Vieira a correspondent in 1984; in that capacity she covered the presidential candidacy of U.S. senator Alan Cranston, the 1984 Democratic National Convention, in San Francisco, and the events of election night in the same year.

In 1985, when CBS launched the TV news magazine *West 57th*, Vieira was asked to become the program's principal correspondent. Howard Stringer, the CBS Broadcast Group president, who was largely responsible for the creation of the show, had taken notice of Vieira's talent during her time at WCBS-TV in New York; Stringer was quoted by Elizabeth Sporkin and Maria Speidel for *People* (March 18, 1991) as stating that Vieira was "a wonderful role model for every modern woman you could think of." Though Vieira was reluctant to take the job, Dan Rather persuaded her to do so. The show, designed as a faster-paced version of CBS's long-running *60 Minutes*, with celebrity interviews and investigative reports aimed at a younger audience, achieved only mediocre reviews in the press. Some felt that the program focused more on entertainment than on serious news reporting. Vieira, however, continued to impress viewers and colleagues. Tom Yellin, the senior producer of *West 57th*, said to Dan Yakir for *USA Weekend* (June 20–22, 1986), "There isn't an executive or a senior producer who wouldn't kill to have her on his staff." The telegenic Vieira had to adjust to the larger spotlight, telling Yakir, "I have a problem with the whole star thing. We're supposed to be watchdogs, not celebrities. I want to be judged by the way I write the script, not whether my hair is out of place or not." In 1989, the year the program was taken off the air, Vieira won four Emmy Awards for stories she had done on *West 57th* during the 1987–88 season.

In 1988 Vieira's husband, Richard Cohen, was fired by CBS after publicly criticizing the network and arguing with Dan Rather. While some industry observers predicted that this development would reflect badly on Vieira and possibly damage her standing at the network, Vieira remained popular. That popularity inspired *Esquire* magazine to publish provocative photos of her in its March 1988 issue; the pictures created a minor controversy, with some feminists praising Vieira's decision to pose for them (because of her sexual autonomy and her openness in celebrating her beauty) and others criticizing it. Her career did not suffer as a result.

Indeed, in 1989 Vieira was offered the rare chance to join the on-air staff of *60 Minutes*. (Since it first aired, in 1968, the program had had only six correspondents.) The show's producers were looking for someone to replace Diane Sawyer, one of the most prominent women in network television news, who had left to join ABC. Despite the prestige connected with the position and the fact that the veteran *60 Minutes* correspondents Mike Wallace and Morley Safer were lobbying for her, Vieira was reluctant to accept the job. After having suffered several miscarriages, she was about to give birth to her first child, and she knew that the demands of such a high-profile job, including a substantial amount of travel, would take her away from her family. She explained to Verne Gay, "I was so upset when they offered me *60 Minutes* because I had left CBS the week before I had Ben [her son], and part of the relief I felt was that I could finally get away from this *place*, and really think about what I wanted in life." In the end, however, she couldn't turn the offer down. In a demonstration of how much the show's executives wanted Vieira, she was able to negotiate a deal that let her work part-time for two years—doing about 10 stories a year instead of a full-time correspondent's 20 to 22—for a salary close to half a million dollars per year.

Vieira's first story was about zoos' practice of selling animals to dealers. Other segments of Vieira's included a story on I. King Jordan, the controversial president of Gallaudet University, the Washington, D.C., school for the deaf; "Ward A," about the first AIDS ward in San Francisco, a story for which Vieira won praise; and "Thy Brother's Keeper," a piece about Christians who saved Jews during the Holocaust, for which Vieira won her fifth Emmy Award. Even while working part-time Vieira felt the conflict between her work and her desire to raise a family. She had a nursery in her office for a time, came in late, left early, wore blue jeans, was quite a bit younger than the other correspondents, and was not obsessively devoted to her work—all of which led some of the other *60 Minutes* correspondents and some industry insiders to think that Vieira did not belong at *60 Minutes*.

At the end of 1990, Vieira learned that she was pregnant again and asked Don Hewitt, the show's executive producer, for an extension of her part-time schedule. Hewitt said no, leading to Vieira's departure from *60 Minutes* and sparking a great deal of debate in the press concerning sexism in the industry, the plight of working mothers, and the idea of a woman's "having it all." Hewitt explained to J. Max Robins for *Variety* (March 4, 1991), "[Vieira] was good enough for me to wait two years for her to come aboard full time. But you have to pull your weight around here. This show depends on a small coterie of people. You just can't do it half time. . . . We couldn't keep making a special arrangement for her and expect the other correspondents, who are already overworked, to keep picking up the slack." Vieira recalled to Diane Clehane, "Some of the aftermath was very painful. For a while they were criticizing my work in the press and I thought that was unfair. They sort of stabbed at my professional integrity and I thought that was wrong. It just made it very clear—I always felt my head was more with family than it is with my job but that just crystallized it for me—that's really who I am." Vieira stayed at the network to anchor *CBS Morning News*, a job that allowed her more time with her children, and served as a national correspondent on the *CBS Evening News with Dan Rather*. She also served as a contributing correspondent for the CBS prime-time show *Verdict*, reporting on actual courtroom trials.

In 1993 Vieira left CBS to work for ABC as the chief correspondent on the hour-long news magazine *Turning Point*. In 1995 she won her sixth Emmy Award, for "Inside the Hate Conspiracy:

America's Terrorists," a *Turning Point* investigative report on a group of white supremacists who became the country's most wanted criminals. Also in the mid-1990s, Vieira's story about the city of Baltimore's program for mainstreaming disabled students into public schools won her a Robert F. Kennedy journalism award, and an interview with the "Framingham Eight," eight women who murdered their allegedly abusive partners, earned the journalist an award from the foundation of American Women in Radio and Television.

Next, Vieira was handpicked by Barbara Walters, one of television's best-known personalities, to co-host *The View*, which premiered in 1997. The daytime talk show, which Walters created and produces and on which she sometimes appears, features five women—besides Vieira and Walters, they are Joy Behar, Star Jones, and Lisa Ling—of different ages and social backgrounds who conduct celebrity interviews and candid, unscripted discussions of news events and other topics. The show, lighter in tone than others on which Vieira has worked, has been a surprise hit, emerging as ABC's highest-rated show in the 11 a.m.–noon time slot in the past eight years and earning Emmy Award nominations each year for outstanding daytime talk show and outstanding talk-show host, an honor Vieira shares with the other women. Vieira told Michael Logan for *TV Guide* (July 25, 1998), "There were those who thought I was selling out by doing *The View*, and I bought into that myself. I went to the audition reluctantly. When I got home, I was embarrassed to admit, 'I *really* want this job.'" Referring to *The View*, Vieira said to Diane Clehane, "One of the major advantages of my job is it allows me to have a life." Because the job does not require travel, Vieira is able to spend more time with her family, which now includes three children. Clehane quoted the show's executive producer, Bill Geddes, as saying, "Of all the women on the show I think Meredith is the one our viewers can relate to most . . . because of her background as a journalist and her real-life experience as a working mother."

On most days Vieira wakes at 5:00 a.m., works out in a gym, then readies her children for school and drops them off there. At about 8:00 a chauffeured car (supplied by the network) takes her and her husband into Manhattan for the 11:00 taping of *The View*, in front of a live audience. Vieira discusses with Walters and the show's writer the portion of the program known as "Hot Topics," which takes place in the first 15 minutes. For many fans, "Hot Topics," during which the women sit around a kitchen table and engage in informal, unrehearsed banter about the morning's headlines, is what makes the show special. As Nancy Hass wrote for the *New York Times* (November 8, 1998), "Despite the layered-on glitter of daytime television, it's easy to imagine the women of *The View* as co-workers at, say, a Long Island insurance firm, who after work go out to talk frankly over margaritas." Garth Ancier, the WB network's president for entertainment, told Hass, "It works because these are women whom the viewers wish they could hang out with. They're just a little funnier and a little more glamorous. But not too much more." "The friendships are real," Vieira revealed to Linda Spear for the *New York Times* (November 29, 1998). "You can't fake it on TV because to the public that watches us on a regular basis they see nuances that can't be hidden." She also told Spear, "I get to be myself, state my opinions, laugh with the other women. . . . It's a truly liberating experience." Somewhat reserved during her first few installments, Vieira soon became, as she phrased it to Michael Logan, "the loosest cannon in the group." Barbara Walters said to Diane Clehane, "Meredith is wonderful. I don't know what we would do without her." *The View* was the only television talk show that premiered in the 1997 season to survive its first year.

In 2002 Vieira signed a new contract with the Walt Disney Co., which owns the ABC network, to remain on *The View* for another five years and to become the host of the syndicated, half-hour-long version of the television game show *Who Wants to Be a Millionaire*. Vieira succeeded the host of the original series, Regis Philbin. That syndicated program began airing in the fall of 2002.

Vieira hosted the Miss America Pageant in 1998. In 1999 she was chosen to be the official host of *Intimate Portrait*, a critically acclaimed series on the Lifetime cable channel. Vieira also narrates and hosts television specials for ABC; those include *The Beatles Revolution* and *Open Sesame: The Making of Arabian Nights*, both of which aired in the year 2000. Over the course of her career, Vieira has appeared on the daytime drama *All My Children* and as herself on the sitcoms *Spin City* and *Sports Night*, the talk shows *Larry King Live* and *Charlie Rose*, and *The Late Show with David Letterman*. Vieira has been honored by the Anti-Defamation League and was given the Spirit of Life Award in 2001 by City of Hope, one of the world's leading research and treatment centers for cancer and HIV/AIDS, for her devotion to community service and the field of journalism. In 1999 Vieira co-founded the national organization ClubMom, which is dedicated to celebrating and recognizing the work of mothers.

Vieira lives with her husband, Richard Cohen, and their three children—Ben, Gabe, and Lily—in Westchester County, New York. When asked by Peggy Orenstein for *Mother Jones* (June 1989) to name one of the stories she was proudest of, Vieira responded, "My favorite was about a kid. . . . A little boy named Anthony in Chicago, who'd spoken of poverty as only someone who lives it can. And I have a buddy for life . . . we talk every week. So that's something that I'm going to take with me." — C.F.T.

Suggested Reading: *abc.go.com/theview*; *Mother Jones* p28+ June 1989, with photos; *New York Times* XIV p23 Nov. 29, 1998, with photo; *Westchester WAG* (on-line) June 1999, with photos; Walsh, Elsa. *Divided Lives: The Public and Private Struggles of Three Accomplished Women*, 1995

Selected Television Shows: *West 57th*, 1985–89; *60 Minutes*, 1989–90; *The View*, 1997– ; *Who Wants to Be a Millionaire*, 2002–

---

Courtesy of King Features Syndicate

## Walker, Mort

*Sep. 3, 1923– Cartoonist; creator of* Beetle Bailey

*Address: c/o King Features Syndicate, 2d Fl., 888 7th Ave., New York, NY 10019*

"I feel like I create friends for the people," the cartoonist Mort Walker, creator of the comic strip *Beetle Bailey*, told Jo Sandin for the *Milwaukee Journal Sentinel* (June 22, 2001). "They can spend a minute every morning at breakfast with Beetle and start the day with a little laugh." Walker is one of the country's most successful cartoonists, with a career in newspaper strips that dates back to 1950, when the army-themed *Beetle Bailey* debuted in 12 papers. The creator of nine separate strips, four of which are still running, Walker is known for his remarkable output, witty ideas, and devotion to the art of cartooning. In 1974 he founded the International Museum of Cartoon Art, which has grown to include a collection of more than 175,000 drawings and a wealth of other material. Walker takes special pride in the fact that he still writes and draws *Beetle Bailey*; he sketches the panels in pencil, and then his sons Greg and Brian and collaborator Jerry Dumas ink and produce the final strips. According to King Features Syndicate, which has distributed the strip since it originated, *Beetle Bailey* currently appears internationally, in more than 1,800 newspapers. Referring to Beetle and his army-base cohorts, Walker told an Associated Press reporter, as posted on *CNN.com* (September 4, 2000), "I love them all. I feel like they live. I feel like they're my real children. I don't know what I'd do without them."

Addison Morton Walker was born on September 3, 1923 in El Dorado, Kansas, a small oil town 30 miles from Wichita. Both of his parents were artists, but his father worked in construction, following the oil boom. As a youngster Walker lived in Amarillo, Texas, and Bartlesville, Ohio, before the family settled in Kansas City, Missouri. "My father figured that oil attracted people, people have children and children need schools," he recalled to Daryl Cagle, the president of the National Cartoonists Society (NCS), in a 1999 interview that was posted on the NSC Web site. "So he'd follow the oil and build schools, or churches. . . . My father was a good man but he wasn't as good to himself as he was to others. He never charged enough and so we never had enough." Despite early privations, Walker had ambition, and he set goals for himself at a very young age. "I knew I wanted to be a cartoonist when I was three," he told Bill Ryan for the *New York Times* (September 20, 1992). He elaborated to the Associated Press interviewer: "When I was 2 or 3, my father used to read me the comics, and he'd laugh so hard, tears would come down his cheeks. . . . So I started drawing." At age 11, his first magazine cartoon was published; he pocketed one dollar for his efforts. In his early teens Walker sold scores of cartoons to such magazines as *Child Life*, *Inside Detective*, and *Flying Aces*. At 15 he sold a newspaper comic strip, *The Lime Juicers*, to the *Kansas City Journal*.

Walker borrowed $25 to pay a year's tuition at Kansas City Junior College. In addition to attending classes there, he worked at night in the shipping department of the greeting-card company Hall Brothers (called Hallmark Cards since 1954). He answered a newspaper ad for an artist that turned out to be from Hall Brothers, and he soon found himself working in the firm's art department. "[World War II] had just started and they hoped to get the soldiers to buy cards," he explained to Daryl Cagle. "They sensed a new market for cards and they needed a male point of view." He added, "My cartoon style was an innovation in the greeting card business. . . . Today almost all cards are humorous. I feel I started that trend." Paid a dollar per drawing, Walker earned about $75 per week from Hall Brothers, even after enrolling at the University of Missouri at Columbia, more than 100 miles east of Kansas City.

Walker spent only one semester at the University of Missouri before he was drafted into the Army Air Corps, in 1943, and sent to Europe. "I . . . had never been on an airplane before," he told Joe Burlas for *ArmyLINK News* (May 25, 2000). "They sent me to the Signal Corps but I had no mechanical ability. They sent me to the Engineers but I had no high school math. I was then sent to the Infantry and made a scout, but I was nearsighted." While stationed in Italy and Switzerland, Walker visited museums and scenic spots, where he sketched and took photographs. He eventually became a commissioned officer and was commanding a prisoner-of-war camp in Naples, Italy, when his military service ended.

Walker returned to the University of Missouri in 1946 and received a bachelor's degree in arts and sciences in 1948. While at college he was a member of the Kappa Sigma fraternity, a staffer for the yearbook, and an editor and writer for a campus magazine called *ShowMe*. After graduation Walker moved to New York with dreams of becoming a full-time cartoonist. To support himself, he became a magazine editor, while also attempting to sell his cartoons to newspapers and magazines. Walker has claimed that his first 200 magazine cartoons were rejected. By 1950, however, he had become well known and was regularly selling single-panel cartoons to such magazines as the *Saturday Evening Post*. In spite of this success, Walker felt discouraged, because payment for a single-panel cartoon was less than that for a strip. "A cartoonist publication declared that I was the top selling cartoonist of the year," he told Cagle. "I made about $8,000 that year and I decided I'd get into a better business."

In 1950 Walker pitched his idea for *Beetle Bailey*—originally called *Spider*—to King Features. The strip debuted on September 4, 1950 in 12 newspapers. A lazy but likable student at the fictional Rockview University, Beetle (his name was changed at the request of King Features) didn't make much of a splash with readers at first. That began to change when, on March 13, 1951, he metamorphosed into an army private stationed at Camp Swampy, under the command of General Amos Halftrack. "All the original characters (except Beetle) were discarded and new ones created," Walker explained to Daryl Cagle. "I've always subscribed to the philosophy, 'When something doesn't work, try something else.' Going down with the ship is for dead heroes. Over the years, characters have been introduced, found boring and given the gate." Americans, who were now reading about the Korean War in their daily newspapers, seemed to enjoy Beetle's quiet upending of the army's strict hierarchy, and the strip became a hit. "I don't care whether he's in the Army, or whether he's at the police force or a forest ranger or whatever," Walker told Sandin. "It's the pecking order that people don't like. It's bureaucracy that people don't like. They admire a guy that stands up to the big forces trying to put him down. Beetle is the smartest guy in the Army because he's figured out how to get out of the work nobody wants to do."

The U.S. Army disapproved of Beetle's attitude and, in the early 1950s, on the grounds that Walker was encouraging a lack of respect for officers through his strip, dropped *Beetle Bailey* from the military newspaper *Stars & Stripes*. The army's action drew a larger audience to the cartoon, not least because it led 100 newspapers to add the strip. More controversy erupted in 1970, when Walker racially integrated his *Beetle Bailey* cast with Lieutenant Jack Flap, an African-American who sometimes had run-ins with the whites at Camp Swampy. *Stars & Stripes*, which had reinstated the strip in the 1950s, dropped it again for a time, on the grounds that it stirred up racial tensions. Several newspapers in the southern United States followed suit, while 100 other papers signed on to run the comic. Walker told *CNN.com* that he has tried to avoid controversy; nevertheless, he told Sandin, "You've got to be a little offensive, you know, because cartoonists make fun of people. I get letters all the time saying, 'Don't make fun of bald people.' 'Don't make fun of fat people.' 'Don't use violence.' But you've got to make fun of somebody. That's what cartoons are all about." Walker's most recent skirmish with the army and the American public occurred in about 1997, when objections were raised over General Halftrack's sexist views and ogling of his sultry secretary, Miss Buxley. After six papers, including the *Los Angeles Times*, dropped the strip, Walker had the general attend classes in sensitivity training. On July 4, 2002 a new character, Chip Gizmo, appeared at Camp Swampy. Earlier, Walker had decided to add an information-technology specialist to the strip, and he had solicited input from fans in creating the character. The presence of Gizmo, he explained, would create more opportunities for jokes involving technology. Before that, the most recent new character was the Asian-American corporal Yo, introduced in 1997. *Beetle Bailey* is now international, with characters of Greek, Italian, French, or Asian descent appearing in the barracks. In 1992 the University of Missouri at Columbia installed on its campus a life-size sculpture of Beetle Bailey.

According to Walker, *Beetle Bailey*'s cast provides him with unlimited material for gags; thus, he has never suffered from writer's block. As he told the Associated Press, "I write myself into a corner until I have to come up with a punch line." Speaking of the success of *Beetle Bailey*, Daryl Cagle told the Associated Press, "It has a formula that works. [Walker]'s got an endless basis for gags because of the different characters. He's got the stupid one, the lazy one, the angry one, the lecherous one. Any character you need, he's got it on his palette." Beetle and his pals have spawned comic books, animated specials, and even a short-lived animated series, *Beetle Bailey and His Friends*, which aired on television in 1963.

In 1954 Walker created the strip *Hi and Lois*, a spin-off of *Beetle Bailey*, by having Beetle go on furlough to visit his sister, Lois, and brother-in-law, Hi Flagston. On October 18, 1954 the strip debuted in 32 newspapers, introducing readers to the adventures of the Flagston family, which includes the teenage Chip, the twins, Ditto and Dot, the baby, Trixie, and the dog, Dawg. The strip was written by Walker and illustrated by Dik Browne, who later created *Hagar the Horrible*. Their collaboration extended into the late 1980s, when Browne retired. Since then *Hi and Lois*, which is distributed by King Features to some 1,100 newspapers in 37 countries, has been written by Brian and Greg Walker and drawn by Dik Browne's son, Robert "Chance" Browne.

In 1974 Walker founded the International Museum of Cartoon Art, which, as he wrote in a description of himself for the museum's Web site (*www.cartoon.org*), he considers his greatest achievement. The museum offers a history of cartooning and archives valuable drawings, many of which had been at risk of getting lost or destroyed. Located first in Greenwich, Connecticut, the museum moved to Rye Brook, New York, and then, in 1996, to Boca Raton, Florida.

In addition to *Beetle Bailey* and *Hi and Lois*, Walker's current strips include *Boner's Ark*, which has appeared with the byline Addison since 1968, and *Sam and Silo*, which he created with Jerry Dumas in 1977. Walker won a Reuben Award from the National Cartoonists Society in 1953 (the award is named for the NCS's first president, the legendary cartoonist Rube Goldberg), and in 1966 and 1969 he won the award for best humor strip from the same organization. In 1999, for 50 years of service to the industry, he was awarded the NCS Golden T-Square. In May 2000 Walker received the Army Decoration for Distinguished Civilian Service, the U.S. Army's highest civilian award. Walker has also been recognized internationally: he was twice awarded the Adamson Award, a Swedish honor, for best international cartoonist, and he was named a Chevalier in the French Order of the Legion of Honor in 1999.

The previously married Walker married his second wife, Cathy, in 1985. Between them, they have 10 children, six of whom help to produce Walker's cartoons. At 79, Walker has no plans to retire. ("I'm utterly devoted to this business," he told Bill Ryan in 1992.) A resident of both Stamford, Connecticut, and Boca Raton, he spends approximately three days a week writing and drawing *Beetle Bailey* and his other strips and divides his remaining time among the museum, his family, and golf. — K.S.

Suggested Reading: *CNN.com Book News* (online) Sep. 4, 2000, with photo; *New York Times* (Connecticut edition) XIII p1 Sep. 20, 1992, with photo, XIV p10 Sep. 3, 2000, with photo; *Mort Walker's Private Scrapbook: A Celebration of 50 Years of Comic Excellence*, 2001

Selected Books: *Beetle Bailey: The Rough Riders*, 1987; *Hi and Lois: Say "Cheese,"* 1991; *Still Lazy After All These Years*, 1999; *50 Years of Beetle Bailey*, 2000; *Mort Walker's Private Scrapbook: A Celebration of 50 Years of Comic Excellence*, 2001

---

## Wesley, Valerie Wilson

*Nov. 22, 1947– Mystery writer; novelist; editor*

*Address: c/o Putnam Berkley Publishing Group, 200 Madison Ave., New York, NY 10016*

The writer Valerie Wilson Wesley has given the mystery genre a female African-American hero, and attracted a large and loyal following, with her fictional private investigator Tamara Hayle—a sexy, tough-talking single mother from urban New Jersey. Known collectively as the Tamara Hayle Mystery Series, Wesley's six books have made their way onto best-seller lists in the United States and have been translated and published in Germany, France, Great Britain, and Poland. Wesley, a former executive editor of *Essence* magazine, has also written award-winning books for children and young adults, and her stories and articles have appeared in *Essence, Ms., Creative Classroom, Scholastic News, Family Circle, TV Guide*, and the *New York Times*.

Valerie Wilson Wesley was born in Connecticut on November 22, 1947. As a child, she enjoyed reading and writing poetry and stories. Because her father was in the U.S. Air Force, the family moved frequently; Wesley graduated from high school in Madrid, Spain, then returned to the U.S. and attended Howard University, in Washington, D.C., graduating with a bachelor's degree in philosophy in 1970. She then earned a master's degree in early childhood education from Bank Street College, in New York City. The writing of her thesis proved to be a revelation for Wesley; she told Carol Horner for Knight-Ridder newspapers, as quoted on the Web site *Africanpubs.com*, "It was like something that had been asleep a long time kind of woke up. That's when I started to think of myself as a writer."

Wesley started writing short stories and articles as part of the workshops she attended at the Harlem Writers' Guild. She then earned a second master's degree, this one from the graduate school of journalism at Columbia University, in New York. After working as an assistant editor with the educational publication *Scholastic News*, Wesley began publishing mostly fictional stories for youngsters in that magazine and in a similar publication, *Creative Classroom*. In the late 1980s she joined the staff of *Essence* magazine, where she became a senior editor for the travel section in 1989, senior editor for features in 1990, and executive editor of the magazine in mid-1992. She held that post for two years, until the time that her first Tamara Hayle mystery appeared. (Wesley remains a contributing editor for *Essence*.)

Dwight Carter/Courtesy of HarperCollins

*Valerie Wilson Wesley*

When she was young, Wesley's favorite writers included Edgar Allan Poe, whom many consider the first mystery writer, though he is better known for his stories of the macabre and grotesque, and Agatha Christie, whose mystery novel *And Then There Were None* Wesley names as her favorite in the genre. Inspired by these writers and by Walter Mosley, the African-American novelist who created the fictional detective Easy Rawlins, Wesley developed the character Tamara Hayle. Her intention was to present a hero who would appeal to the same readers she had sought to address at *Essence*—namely, African-American women. The writer told Horner, "We've been a forgotten audience. There's a real boom now in books by black writers, and I think it's good, because the more folks you get reading, the better off everybody is." Wesley set her stories in working-class Newark, New Jersey, and made Tamara a single mother. In this way she was able to make Hayle, as described by a writer on the Web site *Africanpubs.com*, "the literary character representing the millions of smart, tough, single African American mothers who live in big cities all over America." Using Newark as the setting gave Wesley a way to address social and cultural issues of importance to inner-city blacks.

Wesley's first Tamara Hayle mystery, *When Death Comes Stealing*, was published in 1994 (after first being excerpted in *Essence* in August of that year) and found Hayle investigating the murders of several of her ex-husband's sons from another marriage. As quoted in *Contemporary Authors*, a critic for *Publishers Weekly* wrote that the book's strength was "its portrayal of black family life in dangerous times." Wesley has followed that successful mystery debut with a new Tamara Hayle adventure roughly every year. In 1995 came *Devil's Gonna Get Him*, in which Hayle's newest client, the wealthy Lincoln Storey, dies just hours after hiring her, setting up a mystery in which many characters have a motive for the murder. Some reviewers found the plot to be thin, but a critic for *Kirkus Reviews*, as quoted in *Contemporary Authors*, stated that "[Hayle's] unapologetically plainspoken voice . . . makes this tale as memorable as her debut." *Where Evil Sleeps* (1996) finds Hayle embroiled in murder and mystery on the island of Jamaica. In 1997 came *No Hiding Place*, in which Hayle is hired to solve the killing of a Newark gangster. The story looks at the conflicts arising between a new black middle class and poorer blacks of the inner city. While some critics again faulted Wesley's plot, a reviewer for *Publishers Weekly*, as quoted in *Contemporary Authors*, found Hayle to possess a "consistently sharp, honest voice" that is equal to the complex social issues underlying the story. *No Hiding Place* was made an alternate selection by both the Mystery Guild and the Literary Guild and was selected as a Books-on-Tape audio cassette.

In *Easier to Kill* (1998), the fifth mystery in the series, Hayle comes to the aid of one Mandy Magic, a popular radio personality with a shady past. As quoted on the Web site *mysterynet.com*, a writer for the *San Francisco Examiner* opined, "There's richness of language in Wesley's writing. . . . She makes the mean streets of Newark come alive." The sixth book in the series, and the last one to date, *The Devil Riding* (2000), has Tamara Hayle undercover in the casinos of Atlantic City, New Jersey.

Meanwhile, concurrently with her career at *Essence* and with the writing and publishing of her Tamara Hayle books, Wesley was busy with other projects. She collaborated with Wade Hudson on the book *Afro-Bets Book of Black Heroes from A to Z: An Introduction to Important Black Achievers for Young Readers*, which was published in 1988. The book is an example of the social consciousness—in this case, the idea of introducing positive role models to children—that Wesley tries to bring to her writing. Wesley's next work was the young-adult novel *Where Do I Go from Here?*, which told the story of a young black girl who encounters racial tension as a student at a mostly white boarding school. In 1993 the book earned Wesley a Griot Award (which recognizes outstanding individual contributions to African-American heritage) from the New York Chapter of the National Association of Black Journalists. The American Library Association gave the novel a citation as the best book for reluctant readers. In 1995 Wesley contributed an essay titled "Understanding Black Anger" as part of a joint survey on racism conducted by *Essence* and *Family Circle* magazines. As quoted on the Web site *Africanpubs.com*, she wrote in the essay about the black experience: "We make our anger work for us, but we also understand that there are those among us whom anger has conquered, those for whom it has festered into self-destruction and self-hatred and the surrender of a dream not only deferred but never imagined." In 1997 Wesley again presented complex social issues to a young audience. *Freedom's Gifts: A Juneteenth Story* is an illustrated book about two young girls in Texas, whose families celebrate the anniversary of the day in 1865 when slaves in Texas finally learned of their freedom, granted two years earlier by the Emancipation Proclamation. Christopher Paul wrote for the *New York Times Book Review* (June 22, 1997), "Wesley beautifully charts the girls' growing friendship. . . . Anyone who has seen two sassy little girls going at each other with hands on hips and lips stuck out will recognize the dead-on accuracy of the postures. The muted colors of [Sharon] Wilson's illustrations combine perfectly with Wesley's gentle text."

Wesley's mainstream novel for adults, *Ain't Nobody's Business if I Do* (1999), about the trials, tribulations, and joys of a black family, received the 2000 Award for Excellence from the Black Caucus of the American Library Association. Rhonda Stewart wrote in the *Washington Post* (November 16, 1999), "*Ain't Nobody's Business if I Do* is carefully written and sometimes funny. The characters are believable, and Wesley has a keen ear for dialogue. And yet it's not an entirely satisfying read. For one thing, it doesn't offer especially insightful truths about marriage, friendship or family ties. It goes down easily but there's little to savor." Reviewing *Willimena and the Cookie Money* (2001), a novel by Wesley for children, a writer for *Publishers Weekly* (June 18, 2001) stated, "This first-person narrative, composed of brief sentences and clipped dialogue, moves at a brisk pace, ideal for beginning and reluctant readers. Wesley's latest book is the novel *Always True to You in My Fashion*, which follows three independent women who are all romantically involved with the same charismatic man; the book was scheduled to be published in late 2002.

Wesley sits on the board of directors of several art institutions and on the board of Sisters in Crime, an international organization dedicated to raising awareness of women's contributions to the mystery genre and to preventing discrimination against female mystery writers. She lives in Montclair, New Jersey, with her husband, the screenwriter and playwright Richard Wesley. The couple have two grown daughters, Thembi and Nandi. —C.F.T.

Suggested Reading: African American Book Club Web site; *Africanpubs.com* ; *mysterynet.com*; *TamaraHayle.com*; *Voices from the Gaps* Web site; *Washington Post* C p2 Nov. 16, 1999; *Contemporary Authors* vol. 167, 1999

Selected Books: *When Death Comes Stealing*, 1994; *Devil's Gonna Get Him*, 1995; *Where Evil Sleeps*, 1996; *Freedom's Gifts: A Juneteenth Story*, 1997; *No Hiding Place*, 1997; *Easier To Kill*, 1998; *Ain't Nobody's Business if I Do*, 1999; *The Devil Riding*, 2000; *Willimena and the Cookie Money*, 2001

---

## Wilber, Ken

*Jan. 31, 1949– Writer; philosopher*

*Address: c/o Shambhala Publications, Horticultural Hall, 300 Massachusetts Ave., Boston, MA 02115*

"No one . . . has done as much as [Ken] Wilber to open Western psychology to the durable insights of the world's wisdom traditions. Slowly, surely, book by book, Ken Wilber is laying the foundations for a genuine East/West integration." So wrote Huston Smith, a renowned scholar of religion, in a blurb for Wilber's book *The Marriage of Sense and Soul: Integrating Science and Religion*. Dubbed the "Einstein of consciousness," Ken Wilber has written, co-written, or edited 18 books that discuss his beliefs about consciousness, spirituality, and transpersonal psychology, which integrates emotional and spiritual aspects of human development. Highly controversial, his work has often been regarded skeptically by mainstream critics, but it has also received accolades from such well-known figures as former vice president Al Gore and the physician and writer Deepak Chopra, a proponent of holistic healing. Wilber's books have been published in more than 20 languages, among them Chinese, Japanese, Turkish, Czech, German, Portuguese, and Dutch; indeed, he is currently reputed to be the most translated academic author in the United States. Moving beyond a relatively simple merger of Eastern spirituality and Western psychology, his thinking has expanded to embrace a unified theory of consciousness, which attempts to incorporate a wider spectrum of spiritual, psychological, and philosophical beliefs. In an undated interview posted on the Web site of his publisher, Shambhala Publications, which noted that the search engine Excite had 363,000 entries about him, Wilber said, "I'm not nearly the saint some of my fans imagine and I'm nowhere near the devil my detractors wish. . . . I don't want the readers' love, and I certainly don't need their hate. My only hope is that you take [my] books and use those ideas that make sense to you and reject those that don't."

Ken Wilber was born on January 31, 1949 in Oklahoma City, Oklahoma. His father made his career in the U.S. Air Force. After Ken completed high school, in Lincoln, Nebraska, he enrolled at Duke University, in Durham, North Carolina, with the intention of becoming a physician. As an

Courtesy of Shambhala Publications
*Ken Wilber*

undergraduate he became fascinated with psychology and mysticism. On his own, he did research on spirituality and alternative approaches to psychology. "Science gives you all sorts of facts and data, but little or no meaning," he told Debra Hiers, as reported on the Web site of New Leaf Distributing. "Yet I wanted to address all those silly questions, like Why am I here? What does it all mean? What's the purpose of life? How can we get science and religion, truth and meaning, together?" Far more intrigued by such age-old philosophical concerns than by what he was learning in his classes, he dropped out of college, so as to concentrate on his own investigations. Later, he took graduate classes in chemistry and biology at the University of Nebraska.

In the winter of 1972–73, Wilber started composing a book in his head; the following year he began writing it, in longhand. By 1974 the manuscript was finished, and Wilber launched what proved to be a three-year-long search for a publisher. In the meantime, in 1973, Wilber had married Amy Wagner and had begun to practice Zen Buddhism; he has continued to do so ever since. To pay his half of the rent, he took a job as a dishwasher at a Lincoln restaurant. Wilber's first published paper, "The Spectrum of Consciousness," appeared in the November 1974 issue of *Main Currents in Modern Thought*. In 1977 his first book, also called *Spectrum of Consciousness*, was published by Quest Books/Theosophical Publishing House. In that work, which marked his maiden attempt to integrate Eastern spirituality and Western psychology, Wilber argued that spiritual and psychological explorations of the self are not contradictory; rather, the various spiritual and psychological approaches appeal to different "wavelengths" of consciousness. Wilber has called this stage of his intellectual development phase-1, or his "romantic period"; in his introduction to the first volume of his *Collected Works*, he wrote (as reprinted on the "Ken Wilber Online" section of the Shambhala Publications Web site) that his work from this period "represent[s], in my opinion, about the best you can do with the fundamentally flawed notions of Romanticism. These works were extremely important for me, because in trying to make the Romantic ideas work, I found out precisely why they would not." The "romantic" viewpoint postulates that humans begin their lives "merged" with the "oneness" of the world but that, as they get older, that wholeness is lost. It can be regained later, however, in a more mature form, according to this view.

In 1977 Wilber became editor in chief of *ReVision: A Journal of Consciousness and Transformation*, a position he held until 1982. He also started to teach courses based on the material in *The Spectrum of Consciousness*, but stopped when he realized that he would rather write than teach. For his second book, *No Boundary: Eastern and Western Approaches to Personal Growth* (1979), he mostly rephrased what he had written in his first book in language that he felt would be more accessible to lay readers.

At this point Wilber reassessed his beliefs regarding "romanticism"—an endeavor that was "one of the most difficult intellectual episodes of my life," as he wrote in the introduction to volume one of his *Collected Works*. Concurrently, he began an in-depth study of infant development, thus ushering in what he calls his phase-2. In the course of that investigation, he rejected his "romantic" notions, because although he recognized that infants do not clearly differentiate subject and object, "they certainly are not one with the world of language, logic, poetry, art, commerce, economics, or even the Oedipal complex—for none of these have yet emerged," as he stated in the introduction to volume one of his *Collected Works*. He came up with a new theory, in which he hypothesized that infants' development proceeded in a "ladder-like" fashion. Although the infant sense of wholeness did not disappear, he concluded, only the evolutionary progress of a person could lead to enlightenment.

In 1980 Wilber published his first phase-2 book, *The Atman Project: A Transpersonal View of Human Development*. According to *www.theatmanproject.com*, Wilber has said that "the entire structure of the manifest universe is driven by the Atman Project, a project that continues until we . . . awaken to the Spirit whose substitutes we seek in the world of space and time and grasping and despair." In the introduction to the second volume of his *Collected Works*, Wilber wrote, as transcribed on "Ken Wilber Online", that he offered in *The Atman Project* "the first major psychological system to suggest a coherent and detailed map of human consciousness that included most of the major schools of Western psychology and Eastern mysticism." Wilber posited 17 stages of consciousness development in humans, with the first level being present at birth and the highest level exemplified in the Buddha. These stages, or holons, according to Wilber, comprise the basic structure of the evolution of consciousness. Among the book's theses is that all stages of the developing self except the last are simply unsuccessful attempts to obtain ultimate unity.

Wilber's fourth book, *Up from Eden: A Transpersonal View of Human Evolution* (1981), began as a proposed opening chapter to *The Atman Project.* In *Up from Eden* Wilber traced human cultural development from hunting-and-gathering to modern-day societies, while also discussing political and spiritual movements. He next edited *The Holographic Paradigm and Other Paradoxes: Exploring the Leading Edge of Science* (1982), which contains essays from *ReVision* and concentrates primarily on the theories of the physicist David Bohm, an expert on quantum mechanics whose philosophical concerns centered on the nature of reality and consciousness.

During this time Wilber entered his phase-3 period, in which he placed his phase-2 views in a larger context. He no longer described development in terms of a ladder but rather as separate cognitive, emotional, social, and spiritual lines of growth. He also rejected transpersonal psychology as a field of endeavor, because he felt unhappy about its failure to grow and the failure of transpersonal psychologists to agree on fundamental tenets.

In 1983 Wilber published *A Sociable God: A Brief Introduction to a Transcendental Sociology,* which, he has maintained, he completed in a single weekend. In that book he tried to show how a developmental model of consciousness can be used to help distinguish a given religion's "horizontal" qualities—that is, how well it provides meaning in and value to life—from its "vertical" authenticity, or how well it encourages spiritual transformation. In differentiating between the two, Wilber saw the present-day widespread disbelief in God as a step in spiritual development in which people rejected the pre-rational and moved toward the trans-rational. In a review for *Commonweal* (March 9, 1984) quoted in *Contemporary Authors,* John A. Coleman noted that he was "deeply suspicious of the main theoretical premises of this work," but also stated that it "includes perceptive insights, analytic acuity, and genuine wisdom in places." The year 1983 also saw the appearance of *Eye to Eye: The Quest for the New Paradigm,* a collection of essays in which Wilber proposed a fusion of science and mysticism.

In the same year—by which time his marriage to Amy Wagner had come to an amicable end—Wilber married Terry "Treya" Killam. Ten days after their wedding, she was diagnosed with breast cancer. In 1989, after undergoing traditional treatments as well as such alternative therapies as meditation and psychotherapy, Treya Killam Wilber died. "I am immeasurably more, and immeasurably less, because of her presence. Immeasurably more, for having known her; immeasurably less, for having lost her," Wilber wrote in his introduction to volume five of his *Collected Works.* In *Grace and Grit: Spirituality and Healing in the Life and Death of Treya Killam Wilber* (1991), which he wrote at her request, he described both the ordeal he and his wife endured and their spiritual awakenings during her battle with cancer. *Grace and Grit,* the title of which comes from Treya's last diary entry, written 24 hours before her death, includes several long entries from her journal. The book attracted a large readership.

During his wife's illness Wilber edited the book *Quantum Questions: Mystical Writings of the World's Great Physicists* (1984), a compilation of essays in which physicists including Einstein and Werner Heisenberg discussed why physical principles can neither prove nor disprove mystical views of the world and the universe. He also co-edited (with Jack Engler and Daniel P. Brown, who both taught at Harvard University) *Transformations of Consciousness: Conventional and Contemplative Perspectives on Development* (1986), which urges the development of a comprehensive psychology that incorporates findings about the evolution and structure of consciousness. With Dick Anthony and Bruce Ecker, he co-edited *Spiritual Choices: The Problem of Recognizing Authentic Paths to Inner Transformation* (1987), which discusses empirical ways of examining aspects of spirituality. A two-volume work that he wrote during this period was later condensed as *Integral Psychology: Consciousness, Spirit, Psychology, Therapy* (2000); another work, which he titled "The Great Chain of Being: A Modern Introduction to the Perennial Philosophy and World's Great Mystical Traditions," has not been published.

In 1991 a woman wrote a critical letter in response to an article Wilber had written on gender differences. He began writing a letter in reply but soon set it aside to devote himself to a massive new project, which entailed, over the next three years, his reading more than 300 books on feminism, some 300 on ecology, and more than 400 on anthropology, evolution, philosophy, and other subjects. During this time he lived in almost complete seclusion at his house in Boulder, Colorado; by his own account, he saw only four other people. The result of his research was *Sex, Ecology, Spirituality: The Spirit of Evolution* (1995), an 800-page book that attempts to integrate science, morals, and Eastern and Western philosophies within the teaching of the great religions. The book was the first to emerge during Wilber's phase-4, in which he extended his model of individual development to include a sociocultural dimension while also focusing more extensively on neurological processes involved in consciousness.

Among Wilber's most important contributions to the field of psychology is a theoretical construct that he calls the "pre/trans fallacy." As he wrote in the introduction to the third volume of his *Collected Works*, "In any recognized developmental sequence, where development proceeds from pre-x to x to trans-x, the pre states and the trans states, because they are both non-x states, tend to be confused and equated, simply because they appear, at first glance, to be so similar." According to Wilber, when many theorists look at the development of consciousness in humans, they treat the "prerational" stage as if it were the same or similar to enlightenment, the "trans-rational" stage. In another prominent facet of his philosophy, Wilber stresses the importance of the "great nest of being," as he has labeled it, which encompasses the core mystical and philosophical concepts of the world's belief systems. "The idea is simply that reality consists of various levels or dimensions of being, reaching from matter to body to mind to soul to spirit, by whatever names," Wilber told Debra Hiers. "Since each senior dimension transcends but includes its juniors, each higher dimension enfolds, embraces, and envelops the latter. So this is really the Great Nest of Being." Among his models of human consciousness development, Wilber has created a system of four quadrants that represent different aspects of consciousness. Each quadrant consists of nine levels, and Wilber encourages people to engage in various practices for each level. "For the physical level," he told an interviewer for *Pathways* as printed on "Ken Wilber Online," "you might want to include physical yoga, weight lifting, vitamins, nutrition, jogging, etc. For the emotional/body level, you might try tantric sexuality, therapy that helps you contact the feeling side of being, bioenergetics, etc. For the mental level, cognitive therapy, narrative therapy, talking therapy, psychodynamic therapy etc. For the soul level, contemplative meditation, deity yoga, subtle contemplation, centering prayer, and so on. And for the spirit level, the more nondual practices such as Zen, Dzogchen, Advatia Vedanta, Kashmir Shaivism, formless Christian mysticism and so on."

With eight printings in eight months, *Sex, Ecology, Spirituality* became the best-selling academic book of 1995. The first in a planned trilogy, the work met with both fervent praise and harsh criticism. In a review for *Booklist*, as printed on *Amazon.com*, Steve Schroeder expressed the view that the work "suffers from a tendency to make unsubstantiated or inadequately referenced claims." However, he concluded, "Given a widespread hunger for spirituality and a widespread misunderstanding of materialist readings of development, even a flawed attempt to deepen developmental perspectives with developmental insights from mysticism is a step in the right direction."

Wilber next wrote *A Brief History of Everything* (1996); presented in the form of an interview, it summarizes much of the material in his previous books. It was followed by *The Eye of Spirit: An Integral Vision for a World Gone Slightly Mad* (1997), largely a collection of essays, some of them written in response to a 1996 series of articles in *ReVision* about Wilber's work. In 1998 he published *The Marriage of Sense and Soul: Integrating Science and Religion.* Written in more down-to-earth language than many of his other works, the book strives to show commonalities in scientific and religious views of the world; Wilber concluded that while science can uncover truths about the physical world, an understanding of meaning in life can come only through religion. He suggested that those who favor a scientific view and those who prefer religious interpretations consider the possibility of adopting a broad, integral philosophy, while keeping their respective essential qualities. *The Marriage of Sense and Soul* received enthusiastic assessments from people who hold views similar to Wilber's and thumbs-down critiques from others. The latter group included a critic for *Kirkus Reviews*, who complained, as quoted on *Amazon.com*, "Wilber's lack of specificity makes this book an exercise in theoretical, purely academic navel-gazing. This fusion of science and religion fails to take either discipline seriously as multifaceted, complex sets of meaning."

*One Taste: The Journals of Ken Wilber*, published in 1999, is a nearly day-by-day account recorded in 1999. The book shifts back and forth between descriptions of his personal experiences and his views on art, movies, literature, and spirituality. "I really did feel it was appropriate for me to share my own interior life," he said in an interview for the Shambhala Web site. "I often write academic or scholarly works, and you are simply not supposed to include anything 'subjective' or 'personal,' because that is being 'nonobjective.' A diary, on the other hand, is exactly where you would put these things, so it seemed a logical choice." In 2000 Wilber published *A Theory of Everything: Body, Mind, Soul, and Spirit in Self, Culture, and Nature*; aimed at a general audience, the book offers a brief introduction to Wilber's attempted integration of various aspects of the human experience.

Ken Wilber lives in his chalet in Boulder, Colorado. He does not teach or attend conferences or seminars organized by others. For the past decade he has served on the board of directors of Naropa University, in Boulder; his invitation to all students and faculty to attend three-to-four-hour seminars in his home twice a month has been in force for some time. In 2001 Wilber married his longtime partner, Marci; the following year, they separated amicably. (Marci could not reconcile herself to Wilber's refusal to have a child.)

In his new book, the novel *Boomeritis: A Novel That Will Set You Free* (2002), Wilber attempted for the first time to integrate many of his ideas in a fictional format. The protagonist, also named Ken Wilber, is an MIT student; a substantial portion of the book describes in detail a seminar about integral psychology that he attends. The story reflects the author's belief that the generations commonly referred to as "X" and "Y"—the offspring of baby-boomers—may be the first to enter a new tier of communal consciousness. Baby-boomers themselves might have done so, according to the real Wilber, but they became mired in self-obsession. Nevertheless, their stage of development might prove to be extremely important as humanity's consciousness evolves. In a review of *Boomeritis* for *Publishers Weekly* (May 13, 2002), Jeff Zaleski wrote that the real Wilber "has some interesting ideas but, philosophical issues aside, this isn't much of a novel, and Wilber's failure to develop a coherent narrative, some semblance of a plot or interesting characters will deter many readers." Another thumbs-down assessment came from a critic for *Kirkus Reviews* (May 1, 2002), who complained that the author had "deliver[ed] a talky and tedious so-called novel of ideas to explain a cloying system of categorization, the need for which is never made clear. . . . The story provides excuses for professors to say things like 'But in order to move into second tier, the fixation to pluralism and the green meme in general needs to be relaxed' and for Chloe [a 'faceless nympho vixen'] to say things like 'If we live 200,000 years, you and I will be able to make love at least a billion times.'" Debbie Bogenshutz, who reviewed the book for *Library Journal* (June 15, 2002), by contrast, thought that *Boomeritis* was "a perfect introduction to Wilber's theories" and "destined to be a cult classic." In an interview for *Ken Wilber Online*, Wilber said that he had purposefully made the novel flawed, even though he knew that most readers would not realize that the defects were intentional. "Postmodernism is basically a critical stance—you deconstruct what others have said," he explained. "And therefore any truly postmodern novel would have to deconstruct itself, to be critical of itself, and that means that the novel itself has to be everything that it criticizes."

Currently, Wilber is finishing the third volume in his "Kosmos Trilogy," the first being *Sex, Ecology, and Spirituality*. (The planned second volume will be published last.) In the same interview for *Ken Wilber Online*, he described the work-in-progress as being "about the post-postmodern, post-Kantian, post-metaphysical, post-green, post-ontological approach to the Kosmos."

Wilber is the general editor of the New Science Library Series of Shambhala, the publishing house of Vajradhatu, a Tibetan Buddhist organization. He is a co-founder of the recently established Integral Institute, which he has described as "a nonprofit organization dedicated to the integration of body, mind, soul, and spirit in self, culture, and nature."

The complexity of his ideas and writings notwithstanding, Wilber has insisted that simple meditation is the key to opening up one's world. "The practice, the paradigm, the exemplar of transpersonal studies is: meditation or contemplation, by whatever name," he told an interviewer for the Shambhala Web site. "And so, please practice! Please let that be your guide. And I believe that you will find, if your practice matures, that Spirit will reach down and bless your every word and deed, and you will be taken quite beyond yourself, and . . . glories upon glories will be given unto you and you will in every way be home. And then . . . you will find the obligation to communicate your vision. And precisely because of that, you and I will find each other. And that will be the real return of Spirit to itself." — G.O.

Suggested Reading: *Ken Wilber Online*; Shambhala Publications Web site; *Utne Reader* p50+ July/Aug. 1998, with photos; *World of Ken Wilber* Web site; *Contemporary Authors* vol. 184, 1999

Selected Books: as writer—*The Spectrum of Consciousness*, 1977; *No Boundary*, 1979; *The Atman Project*, 1980; *Up From Eden*, 1981; *A Sociable God*, 1983; *Eye to Eye*, 1983; *Grace and Grit*, 1991; *Sex, Ecology, Spirituality*, 1995; *A Brief History of Everything*, 1996; *The Eye of Spirit*, 1997; *The Marriage of Sense and Soul*, 1998; *The Essential Ken Wilber*, 1998; *One Taste*, 1999; *Integral Psychology*, 2000; *A Theory of Everything*, 2000; *Boomeritis: A Novel That Will Set You Free*, 2002; as co-editor—*Spiritual Choices*, 1987; as editor—*The Holographic Paradigm*, 1982; *Quantum Questions*, 1984

---

## Willingham, Tyrone

*Dec. 30, 1953– Football coach*

*Address: Varsity Athletics, University of Notre Dame, Notre Dame, IN 46556*

After 17 years of coaching special teams, running backs, secondary teams, and receivers for a variety of college football and National Football League (NFL) squads, Tyrone Willingham brought the Stanford University Cardinals to back-to-back bowl appearances in his first two seasons as head coach, in 1995 and 1996. Overcoming early recruiting problems and other difficulties, he led Stanford to a total of four bowl appearances in seven seasons while helping to maintain some of the most stringent academic standards among competitive Division I-A football programs in the country. Following a remarkable 2001 season, in which he led the Cardinals to one of their best seasons in half a century, Willingham was hired as head coach of the historic Notre Dame University Fighting Irish, becoming the first African-American to hold that position. "He doesn't get as much credit for being innovative as he deserves," Tampa Bay Buccaneers coach Tony Dungy told an interviewer for *Sports Illustrated* (August 21, 2000), "because he understands that X's and O's go only so far. His attitude is, Let's not overwhelm them or outsmart them; let's just outplay them." Willingham's enthusiasm for hard work and discipline and his ability to listen have earned him a large degree of respect and

Shannon Stapleton/Getty Images/Reuters

*Tyrone Willingham*

loyalty from his players. "It is impossible to discuss the value of hard work and commitment without bringing into play the component of mental toughness," Willingham told Mike Cervantes for the *Daily Trojan* (September 26, 2001). "It is mental toughness that allows one to persevere through physical, mental and emotional difficulty to achieve success. When in possession of mental toughness the value of hard work and commitment become the foundation of success." Willingham also told Cervantes, "The very best leadership is by example. It is critical that I set the tone for how the entire program should flow by the example I provide. I believe that my style to lead is one of example (vocal and visual) and expectation that change the dimensions of the student athlete's mind on what he can accomplish in any arena that he chooses battle."

Tyrone Willingham was born on December 30, 1953 in Jacksonville, North Carolina, the eldest of the four children of Nathaniel Willingham, who managed rental properties, and Lillian Willingham, an elementary-school teacher, school-board member, and city councilwoman. When Willingham was in elementary school, his parents moved out of the first floor of their two-story house so that it could serve as the neighborhood recreation center. From a young age Willingham was forced to deal with racism. He recalled to the interviewer for *Sports Illustrated* (August 21, 2000) that his Little League baseball team, of which he was the only black member, once went to play a game in Smithfield, North Carolina; upon entering the town Willingham noticed a large billboard, which showed a picture of a hooded man on a rearing horse, along with the words "Welcome to the Home of the United Klan." Willingham attended Jacksonville Junior High, walking through all-white neighborhoods to get to the school instead of taking the long way. He planned to attend Georgetown High School, but before he could, the school, which was scheduled to be integrated, was badly damaged by fire. "The origins [of the fire] have never been explained," he told the interviewer for *Sports Illustrated*, "but most of the people who lived in my community believe the school was destroyed by a bomb. Integration came the next fall, so what would you think?"

Willingham attended Jacksonville High School, where he was known as a strong quarterback for the football team. As a senior he wrote letters to 150 colleges, promoting his achievements on the field. As he stood a mere five feet, six inches tall and weighed just 139 pounds, however, he received only two replies. One was from Michigan State University, in East Lansing, Michigan, which Willingham decided to attend. All of his siblings later attended college and received graduate degrees. "We were blessed that we had parents who thought education was important," Willingham told Daniel Sneider for the *Christian Science Monitor* (December 29, 1995), "that made the sacrifices to send their kids to college, believing that that in itself gives you an opportunity to have a better life." Willingham won a spot on Michigan State's football team, the Spartans, as a freshman and eventually worked his way into the second string of players. In addition, he played for the school's baseball team. As a senior he started five games at quarterback after the team's regular starting quarterback was injured. It was also in his senior year that he met his future wife, Kim Normand. He received a B.S. degree in physical education from Michigan State in 1977.

In the fall of 1978, Willingham signed on as a graduate assistant under coach Darryl Rodgers of the Michigan State football team. The following year he was named the secondary coach of Central Michigan University's football team, the Chippewas. In 1980 he returned to Michigan State as a secondary and special-teams coach under head coach Frank "Muddy" Waters. "I had hoped that my path would some day lead to being a head coach," he told Sneider, "but those are things you can't control yourself. What I can control is the job that I do day to day. So when I was at Michigan State, I worked as hard as I could to be the best I could. And at every university or pro team, I have used the same work ethic, the same mentality." After three seasons at Michigan, Willingham was hired by North Carolina State's Wolfpack football team as their secondary and special-teams coach. From 1986 to 1988 he worked in Houston, Texas, as receivers and special-teams coach for the Rice University football team, the Owls. Meanwhile, in 1987, Bill Walsh, the head coach of the San Francisco 49ers of the NFL, initiated a program to promote the hiring of minority coaches in the league. Through this program Willingham met Dennis

Green, an African-American assistant coach for the 49ers. When Green was named head coach of the Stanford Cardinals, in 1989, he asked Willingham to join him as running-backs coach. During his first tenure at Stanford, Willingham coached two of the top running backs in Stanford football history—Glyn Milburn and Tommy Vardell. In 1991 the team played in the Aloha Bowl, its first postseason appearance in five years.

In 1992 Green was named head coach of the Minnesota Vikings NFL team, and took Willingham along with him as his running-backs coach. Despite making the play-offs all three years that Willingham coached in Minnesota, the Vikings were defeated in the first round of postseason play each year. In 1995 Willingham was named head coach of the Stanford University Cardinals, succeeding Bill Walsh, who had moved over from the 49ers. The decision to hire Willingham was a controversial one, with some complaining that Willingham had no experience as a head coach or even as an offensive or defensive coordinator. At the time of his hiring, Willingham was one of only six African-American coaches among the 108 National Collegiate Athletic Association (NCAA) top-division schools. In the previous season the Cardinals had compiled a record of three wins, seven losses, and one tie; under Willingham, the team improved so dramatically that it had its best start in 44 years, not losing until the sixth game of the 1995 season. Stanford finished the year with seven wins, four losses, and one tie. In Pac-10 conference play, the Cardinals won five games and lost three, finishing fourth, and they played in the Liberty Bowl at the end of the season. (They lost.) Willingham was named both National Coach of the Year, by the Black Coaches Association, and Pac-10 Coach of the Year.

After starting off the 1996 season with a record of two wins and five losses, Stanford rallied to win their last four games of the regular season and played in the Sun Bowl, where the team defeated Michigan State, 38–0. "[Willingham] exuded confidence," the former Cardinals tight end Greg Clark told the interviewer for *Sports Illustrated*, "and he has this knack for weathering the ups and downs and transferring that confidence to the players. When the horses are going in a zillion directions, he can harness them and get everyone going to the same place." After the season ended, Willingham was again named National Coach of the Year by the Black Coaches Association. Though many predicted that the Cardinals would have an astounding season in 1997 and play in that year's Rose Bowl, the team finished with a record of five wins and six losses. Some commentators cited the Cardinals' unimaginative offensive strategy and behind-the-scenes tension as causes of the disappointing performance. To correct these problems, Willingham fired his offensive coach and hired Bill Diedrick to replace him. His choice of Diedrick led to one of the few bright spots of the 1998 Stanford team, for although the Cardinals finished with a record of three wins and eight losses, they led their league in passing. That achievement notwithstanding, Willingham was now under intense pressure; his team, the first that was made up mainly of his own recruits, had a defense so ineffective as to be a laughingstock. After the season Willingham fired his defensive coordinator and replaced him with Kent Baer.

The team turned around in 1999, as Willingham led the Cardinals to a record of eight wins and four losses (seven wins and one loss in their conference) and was named Coach of the Year by the American Football Coaches Association. The team won the Pac-10 title and appeared in the Rose Bowl for the first time since 1971; they lost to Wisconsin, 17–9. That season, the quarterback Todd Husak and the wide receiver Troy Walters—recruits of Willingham's—became the most feared pair in college football. The team led their conference in passing and were fifth in the nation in offense. The team's defense was still below par, however, ranking 110th out of 114 for Division I-A teams. After the season Willingham turned down offers to coach for Michigan State and agreed to a contract extension with Stanford through 2004. Although the team felt prepared to dominate the 2000 season, the Cardinals won only five games while losing six. In conference play they won four games and lost four, tying for fourth place. In the off-season, Willingham replaced his two offensive line coaches; the following year the Cardinals won nine games and lost only two, becoming only the second Cardinals team in 50 years to win nine games in a season. In conference play they won six games and lost two, tying for second. The team featured three first-team All Americans and led the league in passing, scoring, total offense, rushing offense, and rushing defense. The Cardinals played against Georgia Tech in the inaugural Seattle Bowl but lost by a score of 24 to 14.

At the end of the 2001 season, Willingham announced his decision to leave Stanford to become head coach of the University of Notre Dame's Fighting Irish football team, signing a six-year contract with the Indiana school. In accepting the position, Willingham became the first African-American to coach any sport at Notre Dame. Willingham, who had grown up watching Notre Dame football games, was quoted on the official Web site of the Stanford Cardinals as saying, "To say it is a dream come true is true." In the previous season the Fighting Irish had won five games and lost six. Most commentators hailed the choice of Willingham and hoped that he would prove to be a stabilizing influence on the team, whose previous head coach had resigned after admitting that he had falsified his academic and athletic records. Further, many noted that Willingham had worked well at Stanford, where, as with Notre Dame, athletes were held to a high standard in the classroom as well as on the field. "I think the decision to hire Tyrone Willingham as Notre Dame's football coach was a smart move because Willingham is an innovative guy and a proven winner," the sports commentator Pat Haden noted for *MSNBC.com*. "He should be able to inject his offensive expertise into an Irish attack that struggled mightily to score points last season." Willingham signed a contract with a base salary of about $1.5 million per year, with another half million dollars or so in bonuses, making him only the third college football coach to earn that much annually. Among his first priorities were filling out his staff, contacting recruits, and getting to know returning players. Stanford's offensive coordinator, Bill Diedrick, moved to Notre Dame, where he works with the team that had the second-worst passing offense in the country in 2001. "We want to be an offense that has the flexibility to throw it, run it or whatever we need to do," Willingham told a reporter for the official Web site of Notre Dame football. "If it means pass it 70 times to win, we're going to pass it 70 times. If it means run it 70 times to win, we want to run it 70 times. That's what we're looking to gain. We want to have complete control of the field." As of November 6, 2002, Notre Dame's record for the year stood at 8–1, although the team continued to rank low in passing offense. For the week of November 5–11, the *USA Today*/ESPN Coaches' Top 25, a poll of college-football coaches, ranked Notre Dame 10th overall in NCAA Division I-A.

Willingham, nicknamed "The Sheriff," has three children with his wife, Kim. Despite his comparatively diminutive stature, he is known as an imposing figure. "Just watching him work out is intimidating," the fullback Jon Ritchie, a former Stanford player, told the interviewer for *Sports Illustrated*. "You get frightened when you talk to him—your palms are sweaty, and you fumble with your words. But once the conversation is over, you want to go back and talk to him some more, because he has interesting things to say." Willingham is known for having a dry, biting sense of humor. He is currently one of only four black football head coaches in the Division I-A schools—less than 3 percent of the total—at a time when more than half of the players are black; his goals include helping to pave the road for African-Americans in his profession. "That's what the people in the previous generation did for me," he told the reporter for *Sports Illustrated*. "That's what my parents and high school coaches did. A lot of the younger African-American coaches have allowed themselves to become frustrated by the lack of opportunities, and that bothers me, because frustration means you can't change a situation. There are a ton of qualified black coaches who aren't getting opportunities. That, to me, is very sad. It's no different than corporate America. If you have someone who can make your organization better and you don't hire that person, we all suffer. In some cases the guys who get the jobs may be good, but maybe there are people of color who can do even better." Willingham has appeared at a number of informal coaching events held to raise money for charity. He was honored with the 2000 Eddie Robinson Coach of Distinction Award, presented each year to a college football coach in recognition of career achievement and outstanding service as a role model. At Stanford he was a board member for OICW (Opportunities Industrialization Center West) and is a former national advisory board member for the Haas Center for Public Service at Stanford. — G.O.

Suggested Reading: *Christian Science Monitor* p3 Dec. 29, 1995, with photo; *ESPN.com* Jan. 1, 2002; *MSNBC.com*; (Notre Dame) *Daily Trojan* (on-line) Sep. 26, 2001; *Sports Illustrated* Aug. 21, 2000

---

Courtesy of James Q. Wilson

## Wilson, James Q.

*May 27, 1931–Political scientist; writer*

*Address: Anderson School of Management, University of California, Los Angeles, CA 90095*

In 1982, a year when many major American cities were experiencing high crime rates, the political scientist James Q. Wilson, along with George L. Kelling, wrote an article for the *Atlantic Monthly* magazine entitled "Broken Windows: The Police and Neighborhood Safety." Challenging theories of law enforcement that were then popular with many policymakers, criminologists, and police chiefs, Wilson and Kelling contended that a campaign against lesser, "nuisance" crimes, such as prostitution, vandalism, public drinking, and panhandling, would make urban residents feel safer and ensure that their neighborhoods were less susceptible to more serious crimes. The ideas expressed in "Broken Windows" were hardly new; in fact, they reflected a desire to return to the days when police officers fought crime by walking beats in local neighborhoods. Determined to reduce crime, many city officials across the nation began experimenting during the 1990s with "community policing," which stressed some of the same solutions advocated by Wilson and Kelling in their article. In New York City under Mayor Rudolph Giuliani, who served from 1994 to 2002, "Broken Windows" became the police department's blueprint for reducing crime by aggressively targeting so-called "quality-of-life" infractions, among them defacing property with graffiti, making excessive noise, prostitution, and fare-beating. By the end of 1995, the rate of violent crime in New York City had dropped by an unprecedented rate. Residents reclaimed many inner-city neighborhoods that had earlier been written off as permanently captive to crime. Other major cities reported similar reductions in crime. Many elected officials, police chiefs, and commentators were quick to acknowledge the contribution of Wilson and Kelling, whose landmark article helped redefine the role of law enforcement.

In more than 40 years as an academic, Wilson has published many articles and books on topics including urban affairs, government, and morality. Among his best-known books are *Thinking About Crime* (1975), *Crime and Human Nature* (1985), co-written with Richard J. Herrnstein, *On Character* (1991), *The Moral Sense* (1993), and *The Ethics of Human Cloning* (1998), co-written with Leon R. Kass. His most recent book is *The Marriage Problem: How Our Culture Has Weakened Families* (2002). Wilson's findings are grounded in empirical research; his work is accessible to the lay reader.

The son of an automobile-parts dealer, James Quinn Wilson was born on May 27, 1931 in Denver, Colorado. A short time after his birth, Wilson and his family moved to Long Beach, California. As a child, he enjoyed reading. The first member of his family to attend college, Wilson enrolled at the University of Redlands, in Redlands, California. Impressed by one of his political-science professors, he decided to major in that subject. He graduated in 1952 with an A.B. degree. During the Korean War he enlisted in the navy, earning a commission as an officer. He served first at the Pentagon, in Washington, D.C., and then aboard an aircraft carrier.

After completing his military service, in 1955, Wilson resumed his education, as a doctoral student in political science at the University of Chicago, in Illinois, where he studied urban politics and policing. He found a mentor in Edward C. Banfield, one of his professors. "Professor Banfield had been a journalist, converted from being a journalist to being a professor," Wilson recalled to Jim Newton for the *Los Angeles Times* (November 27, 1996). "Not only was he one of the smartest people I have ever known, but he still wrote like a journalist, and he insisted his students learn to write reasonably clear[ly]. . . . There was to be no jargon, no passive voice." For his doctoral dissertation Wilson explored the role of African-Americans in Chicago politics during the 1950s. In an interview with Ben Wattenberg for the PBS documentary *The First Measured Century*, which aired in December 2000, Wilson said, "I wanted to know whether black politicians were advancing the interests of their race or simply catering to the white dominant political power structure in Chicago. And I concluded that, by and large, they were doing the latter." Wilson received his doctorate in 1959 and in the following year published his dissertation, titled *Negro Politics: The Search for Leadership*.

After completing his education, Wilson embarked on an academic career. In 1961 he was appointed the Henry Lee Shattuck Professor of Government at Harvard University, in Cambridge, Massachusetts, pursuing scholarly research on urban issues. During this period he wrote two books: *The Amateur Democrat: Club Politics in Three Cities* (1962), about political reform organizations; and, with Edward C. Banfield, *City Politics* (1963), which discusses political pressures on municipal governments. He also began writing articles for such publications as *Commentary* and the *New York Times Magazine*.

Wilson's study of crime began as an outgrowth of his study of cities. "At Harvard in the early 1960s I was studying police departments and trying to understand how the police influence government administration," he told Wattenberg. "I was thinking of police officers as urban bureaucrats." During the same decade violent crime in the United States began to increase by significant rates. Liberals blamed social factors such as poverty and racism for the increase; conservatives, by contrast, argued that a series of decisions by the U.S. Supreme Court, during Earl Warren's tenure as chief justice (1953–69), had undermined the ability of the police to fight crime. For his part, Wilson theorized that shifts in people's attitudes during the 1960s had contributed to the increase in crime. In an interview with a writer for the *American Enterprise* (June 1, 2001), Wilson asserted that during that era, fewer criminals were sent to prison or given long sentences, because many people in positions of authority believed that criminals could be successfully rehabilitated. Additionally, Wilson observed to Wattenberg that in the same decade, a growing "attitude of radical self-indulgence" had "affected a significant fraction of the population, and this weakened the ordinary social constraints that were operating on people," thus making them more willing to break the law.

After learning that Wilson was studying the police, James Vorenberg, a colleague of his at Harvard and the executive director of the federal Commission on Law Enforcement and Administration of Justice, recruited him to serve on President Lyndon B. Johnson's White House Task Force on Crime in 1966. As part of his work for the task force, which he chaired, Wilson began studying the existing literature on crime, concluding that much of it was poor and limited in scope. He explained to Wattenberg that most of the literature focused on gangs, "small groups of boys growing up," and teenagers living in cities. Wilson and his colleagues on the task force began collecting data on crime from different states to see if states that were more likely to send criminals to prison had lower crime rates. "We learned that the answer seemed to be yes," he said to Wattenberg. Wilson was eventually appointed chairman of the task force. During this period he also edited three books—*Urban Renewal: The Record and the Controversy* (1966), *Metropolitan Enigma: Inquiries into the Nature and Dimension of America's Urban Crisis* (1967), and *City Politics and Public Policy* (1968)—and wrote a book about law enforcement, *Varieties of Police Behavior: The Management of Law and Order in Eight Communities* (1968). During the 1968 presidential campaign, Wilson advised Vice President Hubert H. Humphrey, the Democratic nominee, on law-enforcement issues. In 1972 and 1973 he served as chairman of the National Advisory Commission on Drug Abuse Prevention.

In 1975 Wilson published *Thinking About Crime*, a collection of his articles. In it, he argued that society's continued reliance on the ideas of many sociologists and criminologists—who held that identifying and curing the "root causes" of crime would lead to its reduction—was, though well-intentioned, actually contributing to the crime epidemic in the United States by keeping repeat offenders out of prison. Wilson advocated an emphasis on punishment and deterrence, calling specifically for policies that would send convicted criminals to prison, impose longer prison sentences, and lock up repeat offenders.

Wilson's influential article "Broken Windows: The Police and Neighborhood Safety," which he co-wrote with George L. Kelling, appeared in the *Atlantic Monthly* (March 1982). A former student of Wilson's, Kelling was then a research fellow at the John F. Kennedy School of Government at Harvard and the former director of the evaluation field staff of the Police Foundation, a law-enforcement think tank in Washington, D.C. (Currently, he is a fellow in the Program of Criminal Justice Policy and Management at the Kennedy School of Government at Harvard.) The article began by discussing the effect of police foot patrols in Newark, New Jersey. In the mid-1970s, as part of its Safe and Clean Neighborhoods Program, the state of New Jersey allocated funding to 28 cities to have police officers who had been riding in patrol cars walk beats in local neighborhoods instead. Wilson and Kelling wrote that while state officials believed that foot patrols would reduce crime, many police chiefs opposed them, on the assumption that they had no effect on crime rates and that they made it more difficult for the police to respond to 911 calls. Five years after the program was launched, the Police Foundation, on whose board of directors Wilson served, published a study on the effects of foot patrols in Newark neighborhoods. "Based on its analysis of a carefully controlled experiment carried out chiefly in Newark, the foundation concluded, to the surprise of hardly anyone, that foot patrol had not reduced crime rates," Wilson and Kelling wrote. "But residents of the foot-patrolled neighborhoods seemed to feel more secure than persons in other areas, tended to believe that crime had been reduced, and seemed to take fewer steps to protect themselves from crime (staying at home with the doors locked, for example). Moreover, citizens in the foot-patrol areas had a more favorable opinion of the police than did those living elsewhere. And officers walking beats had a higher morale, greater job satisfaction, and a more favorable attitude toward citizens in their neighborhoods than did officers assigned to patrol cars." Intrigued by these findings, Wilson and Kelling decided to explore public order and its relationship to lawbreaking. The authors explained that during the 1960s the role of the police in major cities shifted from keeping public order to fighting crime. The days of the officer walking the beat with his nightstick and keeping an eye out for trouble had passed. By the 1970s the police had come to see themselves primarily as crime fighters, meaning that they solved crimes and made more arrests, which would supposedly lead to reductions in lawbreaking and to a greater feeling of safety among citizens. The police's historical function as keepers of the public order, Wilson and Kelling noted, had gradually been forgotten.

Wilson and Kelling stated that maintaining public order was necessary to control crime, observing that the toleration of disorder invited violent offenses. "Social psychologists and police officers tend to agree that if a window in a building is broken *and is left unrepaired*, all the rest of the windows will soon be broken," they wrote. "Window-breaking does not necessarily occur on a large scale because some areas are inhabited by determined window-breakers whereas others are populated by window-lovers; rather, one unrepaired broken window is a signal that no one cares, and so breaking more windows costs nothing." Wilson and Kelling noted that although many people fear being the victims of violent crime, they also fear being bothered by disorderly individuals such as "panhandlers, drunks, addicts, rowdy teenagers, prostitutes, loiterers, [and] the mentally disturbed." If their neighborhoods are overrun by such individuals, then many residents will conclude that crime has risen—even though that conclusion might not be borne out by the actual crime data—and either move to different neighborhoods or stay off the streets out of fear. "A stable neighborhood of families who care for their homes, mind each other's children, and confidently frown on unwanted intruders can change, in a few years or even a few months, to an inhospitable and frightening jungle," Wilson and Kelling warned. "A piece of property is abandoned, weeds grow up, a window is smashed. Adults stop scolding rowdy children; the children, emboldened, become more rowdy. Families move out, unattached adults move in. Teenagers gather in front of the corner store. The merchant asks them to move; they refuse. Fights occur. Litter accumulates. People start drinking in front of the grocery; in time, an inebriate slumps to the sidewalk and is allowed to sleep it off. Pedestrians are approached by panhandlers." Such a neighborhood, Wilson and Kelling wrote, becomes more susceptible to crime. Drug dealers and car thieves can operate more easily in decaying neighborhoods, where residents have been frightened off the streets and have apparently stopped caring about their surroundings. "Our main argument," Wilson told *Current Biography*, "was that the police and courts ought to take public order seriously, even when the offenses that disrupt it are minor."

To prevent the decay of neighborhoods, Wilson and Kelling called for having the police reclaim their role as guardians of the public order. This would be accomplished by increasing police foot patrols and by improving relations between the police and residents, who would work together to identify problems and keep order. Wilson and Kelling cautioned that this type of policing carried certain risks, including the potential for the police to act as "agents of neighborhood bigotry" against minorities. This problem could be remedied, they wrote, by better selection, training, and supervision of police officers. "Broken Windows," the name given by many to the theory articulated in the article, received mixed reactions. Kelling told Newton that average readers and community groups agreed with its solutions. By contrast, Newton wrote, the "police were perplexed by it and many academics dismissed it as an attempt to rationalize an extension of police power." Nevertheless, by the 1990s many large cities across the nation, including Houston, San Diego, Boston, Jersey City, Milwaukee, Seattle, Los Angeles, and New York, had begun implementing different versions of "community policing," which emphasized strategies similar to those advocated by Wilson and Kelling. Later, many of those cities reported significant decreases in crime. "Page for page, ['Broken Windows'] has had a greater impact than any other article in serious policing," Jeremy Travis, the director of the National Institute of Justice, a research arm of the U.S. Department of Justice, told Newton.

In 1985 Wilson published one of his most controversial works, *Crime and Human Nature*, co-written with Richard J. Herrnstein, a psychologist at Harvard. The authors challenged the assumptions on the part of many social scientists and criminologists that social factors alone, such as poverty, racism, inadequate schools, and broken families, were responsible for crime. Drawing on many crime studies, Wilson and Herrnstein made the controversial assertion that most violent criminals were young men who shared biological and genetic traits—that for the most part they had athletic body types; had IQs lower than those of average people; scored poorly on verbal fluency tests; and had aggressive personalities and an immediate need for gratification. Wilson and Herrnstein stressed that these traits did not "cause" crime but, rather, "predisposed" certain individuals toward lawlessness. Those traits also, the authors theorized, led certain individuals toward careers in professional sports and other lawful professions. The difference in the paths chosen was attributable in part to environment. "All human behavior is a result of some interaction between biology and environment," Wilson explained to Newton. "Crime is no exception. I've always been astonished that people found this assertion controversial. It's hard to think of a piece of human behavior that does not flow out of some interaction between how we were born and how we are raised." Wilson and Herrnstein also sought to determine whether an individual's race predisposed that person to crime. While acknowledging that African-Americans were overrepresented in crime statistics—a fact Wilson and Herrnstein argued was only partially due to racism on the part of the police and the courts—the authors concluded that there "is no reason to believe that the genes determining one's skin pigmentation also affect criminality. At one time in this nation's history, persons of Irish descent were heavily overrepresented among those who committed some crime, but it would have been foolish then to postulate a trait called 'Irishness.'" In an interview with *U.S. News & World Report* (September 30, 1985), Wilson said, "The fact that science can ascertain these predispositions doesn't mean we can now predict criminality. But it's not impossible to conceive that at some point we could make such predictions with some accuracy. Though it would be clearly illegal and immoral to imprison anybody before the fact on that basis, I can see a time when we could provide therapy for such individuals." *Crime and Human Nature* sharply divided reviewers and sparked an intense debate. "The Wilson and Herrnstein work ought not to be judged in isolation," Leon J. Kamin, a psychologist affiliated with Princeton University, in Princeton, New Jersey, wrote for *Scientific American* (February 1986). "Their selective use of poor data to support a muddled ideology of biological determinism is not unrepresentative of American social science in the sixth year of the Reagan presidency." By contrast, in her review for the *Washington Post* (September 22, 1985), Susan Jacoby wrote, "*Crime and Human Nature* is a book that will be useful to anyone who wishes to have access, in one volume, to most of the important criminological studies of the past 50 years. Its main virtues are fairness and common sense. Its main fault is the fact that most of its conclusions will already have occurred to anyone who possesses a modicum of common sense."

During the 1990s Wilson shifted the focus of his writing from crime and government to more philosophical issues. His book *On Character* (1991) is a collection of his essays on personal responsibility and the moral character of societies and individuals. In *The Moral Sense* (1993), Wilson sought to provide a rational basis for morality, arguing that human beings possess innate senses of right and wrong. "Reading this book is a little like talking to a well-intentioned, basically sound, but cranky old dinner partner," Mortimer Sellers observed in his review for the *Washington Post* (August 1, 1993). "Wilson is often convincing. He makes solid arguments. But every once in a while you have to pause and wait while he drones on about kids these days, serotonin, norepinephrine or some other half-relevant project from his youth." Wilson's other books include *Moral Judgment: Does the Abuse Excuse Threaten Our Legal System?* (1997), *The Ethics of Human Cloning* (1998), written with Leon R. Kass, and *Moral Intuitions* (2000). In his most recent book, *The Marriage Problem: How Our Culture Has Weakened Families* (2002), Wilson argued that the weakening of the institution of marriage in the U.S., as evidenced by high divorce rates and an increase in the number of couples opting for cohabitation, has undermined family ties and thus led to greater social instability. Citing various statistics, Wilson argued that children of single mothers are far more likely to drop out of school, abuse drugs, and commit crimes than are children from two-parent households.

Over the decades Wilson has written many articles on a wide range of subjects for such publications as *Commentary*, *National Review*, the *New York Times*, the *New Republic*, and *U.S. News & World Report*, among others. The array of topics Wilson has covered in his books and articles has led to his being described in the media variously as a criminologist, sociologist, social scientist, ethicist, philosopher, and political scientist. Wilson told *Current Biography* that he considers himself a political scientist by profession, since he has a Ph.D. in that subject, and that all "of the other titles, many quite misleading, were invented by third parties."

Wilson served as a member of the Attorney General's Task Force on Violent Crime in 1981 and of the President's Foreign Intelligence Advisory Board from 1985 to 1990. He sits on the boards of directors of the New England Electric System, Protection One, the RAND Corp., and State Farm Mutual Insurance. In 1990 Wilson was honored with the James Madison Award for distinguished scholarship from the American Political Science Association (APSA); he served as the association's president from 1991 to 1992. In 2001 he was appointed to the President's Council on Bioethics, an advisory panel.

Wilson taught at Harvard until 1987. Two years earlier he had joined the staff of the Anderson School of Management at the University of California at Los Angeles (UCLA), with the title James Collins Professor of Management. He also serves as the Ronald Reagan Professor of Public Policy at Pepperdine University, in Malibu, California, where he delivers several guest lectures a year.

James Q. Wilson and his wife, Roberta, live in Malibu; the couple have two children. In 1985 the Wilsons co-wrote the book *Watching Fishes: Life and Behavior on Coral Reefs*. Wilson enjoys scuba diving and horseback riding. — D.C.

Suggested Reading: *American Enterprise* p16+ June 1, 2001; Anderson School of Management Web site; *Atlantic Monthly* p29+ Mar. 1982; *Los Angeles Times* A p+1 Nov. 27, 1996, with photo; *New York Times* B p7 Aug. 22, 1998; *Scientific American* p22+ Feb. 1986; *Time* p54+ Jan. 15, 1996, with photos; *U.S. News & World Report* p54 Sep. 30, 1985, with photo; *Washington Post Book World* p3 Sep. 22, 1985, p2 Aug. 1, 1993

Selected Books: *Negro Politics: The Search for Leadership*, 1960; *The Amateur Democrat: Club Politics in Three Cities*, 1962; *City Politics* (with Edward C. Banfield), 1963; *Varieties of Police Behavior: The Management of Law and Order in Eight Communities*, 1968; *Political Organizations*, 1974; *Thinking About Crime*, 1975; *Investigators: Managing FBI and Narcotics Agents*, 1978; *American Government: Institutions and Policies* (with Richard J. Herrnstein), 1980; *Crime and Human Nature*, 1985; *Watching Fishes: Life and Behavior on Coral Reefs* (with Roberta Wilson), 1985; *Bureaucracy: What Government Agencies Do and Why They Do It*, 1989; *On Character*, 1991; *The Moral Sense*, 1993; *Moral Judgment: Does the Abuse Excuse Threaten Our Legal System?*, 1997; *The Ethics of Human Cloning* (with Leon R. Kass) 1998; *Moral Intuitions*, 2000; *The Marriage Problem: How Our Culture Has Weakened Families*, 2002; as editor—*Metropolitan Enigma: Inquires into the Nature and Dimensions of America's Urban Crisis*, 1967; *City Politics and Public Policy*, 1968; *The Politics of Regulation*, 1980; *Crime and Public Policy*, 1983; *Families, Schools, and Delinquency Prevention* (with Glenn C. Loury), 1987; *Drugs and Crime* (with Michael Tonry), 1990

---

## Winston, Stan

*Apr. 7, 1946– Makeup artist; special-effects designer*

*Address: Stan Winston Studio, 7032 Valjean Ave., Van Nuys, CA 91406*

When asked to name some of the more memorable creatures from recent science-fiction films, many people think of one or more of the creations of the special-effects designer and makeup artist Stan Winston, though they may not have heard of Winston himself. From the 14-foot Alien Queen that dominates the final act of *Aliens* (1986), to the extraterrestrial bounty hunter that pummels Arnold Schwarzenegger in *Predator* (1987), to the slithery liquid-metal assassin from the future in *Termina-*

Ed Geller/Retna Ltd.

*Stan Winston*

*tor 2: Judgment Day* (1991), to the rampaging dinosaurs in *Jurassic Park* (1993), Stan Winston has created a legion of movie monsters that have become nearly as familiar as Dracula, King Kong, or the humanoid stitched together by Dr. Frankenstein. During the last 30 years, Winston has also had a hand in many of the innovations in cinematic special effects. "His incredible talent has contributed a lot to the success of my movies—and my success personally," Schwarzenegger told Paula Parisi for the *Hollywood Reporter* (February 20, 2001). "The actor always gets the credit when a movie does well, but you can't measure what the artistry of someone like Stan brings to the work." Along with the director James Cameron, Winston founded Digital Domain in 1993. Specializing in the creation of computer-driven special effects, Digital Domain has been involved with some of the most lauded films in recent years, including *Interview with the Vampire* (1994), *Apollo 13* (1995), and *Titanic* (1997). The studio has won two Oscars and numerous other awards.

Winston did not initially pursue a career as a makeup artist; rather, he arrived in Hollywood with dreams of becoming an actor. "I'm still searching for that agent for me as an actor," he joked to an interviewer for the *American Movie Classics* Web site (October 16, 2001), "and I'm still pursuing my sideline." According to people who have worked with Winston, what sets him apart from his peers is the humanity he brings to his creations. "When we were working on *Interview with the Vampire*," the director Neil Jordan told Paula Parisi and Jody Duncan in a sidebar to Parisi's *Hollywood Reporter* article, "Stan came over to Ireland, and we went through the whole script, acting out the roles again and again. It was like two guys wrestling in a room. It demonstrates the great thing about Stan: He always comes at it from the dramatic side—the actors and the character. His work is all in support of that. We did some very subtle things in *Vampire*, to the point where it was difficult for the audience to tell where the actor's work ended and Stan's began. He also built some prosthetics and armatures, which he also approached as if they were actors in the film. They had to perform. That's the genius of Stan."

Winston has been honored with four Academy Awards and a slew of other accolades. He is one of the few special-effects designers to earn a star on Hollywood's Walk of Fame. Despite such achievements, Winston has not allowed himself to slow down and bask in his success. He has not lost his creative vision, and he has refused to rely wholly on computers to realize it. "All I'm about is creating memorable characters for motion picture history," he told Elizabeth Snead for *Cigar Aficionado* (January/February 2002). "It's not about technology. It's about writers writing wonderful stories with fantastic characters and me being able to create a visual image that's beyond what you would expect." "I'm a huge fan of the Renaissance artists," he told Parisi. "I firmly believe that if the Renaissance artists were alive today they'd be working in the film industry. In those days, they had churches as patrons. Today, it's the studios. It's important to me to bridge the gap between fine art and commercial art. Movies, now more than ever, are bridging that gap."

Stan Winston was born on April 7, 1946 in Arlington, Virginia. While growing up he was fascinated with puppetry and special effects. "As a kid, I was the nerd, who was inside watching monster movies on TV," he told Elizabeth Snead. "I was always drawing pictures and playing with clay. I had my toys and my puppets. I would do amateur magic shows and create my own little universe, and basically I'm still doing that today. I'm still a huge toy freak, they're just bigger." Winston's interest was fueled further by a trip to Disneyland. "You can put that down as a peak experience," he told Parisi. "I must have been 12 or 13, and I remember seeing Abraham Lincoln, the first audio animatronic character—this robot!—stand up and talk to me. I thought, Oh, that is the most amazing thing. I would love to make robots. What a cool toy!"

Winston earned a bachelor's degree in art, with a minor in drama, from the University of Virginia. "At one point I was going to be a dentist," he told the *American Movie Classics* interviewer. "I was going to do the right thing. Everyone in my family were doctors or lawyers and I couldn't be a doctor, because I couldn't stand the sight of blood—REAL blood. I couldn't be a lawyer because I couldn't read, and still can't, and figured somewhere in there, 'Oh maybe I can be a dentist,' and then I finally realized that well no, I have to pursue the artistic side of me and I'm going to Hollywood."

In Hollywood Winston tried in vain to secure an agent, but he was unwilling to seek any of the usual jobs of would-be actors, such as parking cars or waiting tables. After seeing the film *Planet of the Apes* (1969), he decided to try to get work as a makeup artist as a way to make ends meet. He applied successfully for an apprenticeship position at the Disney studios, where he remained in the makeup department for three years. He was trained by the noted makeup artist Bob Schiffer, who had worked on such films as *The 5,000 Fingers of Dr. T.* (1953) and *Birdman of Alcatraz* (1962).

After ending his apprenticeship Winston found work on the television movie *Gargoyles* (1972). The film, about a colony of gargoyles living in the California desert, attracted a fair-sized audience, and Winston's makeup work won him an Emmy Award. His next project, *The Autobiography of Miss Jane Pittman* (1974), also for television, chronicles the adulthood of an African-American woman (played by Cicely Tyson) who was born into slavery; in the 1960s, as an old woman, she joins the civil rights movement. The story, based on the novel by Ernest J. Gaines, begins when the title character is 19 years old and ends when she is 110. Winston's makeup work, which helped make the aging of Tyson believable, won him his second Emmy. "I'd been out of my makeup apprenticeship for two years and I've won two Emmy Awards," he told the *American Movie Classics* interviewer. "So suddenly I am like extremely successful in my sideline. So my sideline is doing really well and everything sort of snowballed from there, everything just continued to go the way it's been going."

Throughout the remainder of the 1970s, Winston did makeup designs for movies, among them *The Bat People* (1974), *The Man in the Glass Booth* (1975), and *W.C. Fields and Me* (1976). In 1977 he worked on the multi–award-winning TV miniseries *Roots*, based on Alex Haley's book. The following year he created a family of Wookies (a race of hairy bipedal creatures) for George Lucas's *Star Wars Holiday Special*, which aired on CBS. Although, by all accounts, the three-hour sci-fi variety show was a creative disaster, Winston's designs were seen as groundbreaking. In the original *Star Wars* film, the Wookie character, Chewbacca, had limited facial movements. Winston devised a way for the Wookies in the *Holiday Special* to have a wider range of expressions and thus convey subtle emotions. Winston's Wookie design was used in the two *Star Wars* sequels for the big screen, *The Empire Strikes Back* (1980) and *Return of the Jedi* (1983).

Earlier, Winston worked on the 1978 films *The Wiz* and *Dracula's Dog*. In *Heartbeeps* (1981), his makeup turned the actors Andy Kaufman and Bernadette Peters into realistic-looking robots, an accomplishment that earned him his first Oscar nomination. Not long afterward, while he was designing creatures for such films as *Parasite* and *The Thing* (both released in 1982), he met James Cameron, who was developing what would become *The Terminator*, about a robotic hitman from the future. Cameron's concept for the endoskeleton of the Terminator intrigued Winston, and he "loved" the script (co-written by Cameron), as he told an interviewer for the *Sci Fi Magazine* Web site. *The Terminator* (1984), starring Arnold Schwarzenegger, was a smash hit, grossing more than $38 million at the box office and earning high praise for its novel special effects. "*Terminator* was a huge turning point in my career," Winston told Elizabeth Snead. "It really was a movie that set my work aside from every other makeup effects person out there. No one had ever seen anything like it and it was, from an artistic and technical standpoint, a watershed of what we were capable of doing that people hadn't seen before."

Winston and Cameron next embarked on another ambitious project: the sequel to Ridley Scott's acclaimed 1979 sci-fi thriller *Alien*. Cameron envisioned the film's female protagonist, Ripley, returning to the planet where she had discovered the alien creature that had killed her entire crew. Armed with a contingent of marines, she wages war on the aliens, who have built a hive-like colony. Cameron wanted to emphasize the aliens' insectlike characteristics by placing them (like ants and bees) under the control of a giant queen. He created a rough design for the aliens, then tapped Winston to bring it to life. Winston's work on *Aliens* (1986), which also included such monsters as the "face-huggers" and "chest-bursters" as well as legions of alien warriors, won him his first Academy Award for best visual effects.

*Aliens* was one of the biggest blockbusters of 1986. Thanks to its success, Winston found himself even more in demand. In 1987 he helped design the title character for the action film *Predator*. That movie features Schwarzenegger as the leader of a team of commandos; the commandos fall into the clutches of an extraterrestrial hunter who views Earth as the ultimate game preserve. Winston received another Oscar nomination for his contribution to the film. During that period he also worked on such movies as *The Monster Squad* (1987) and *Leviathan* (1989). Winston debuted as a director in 1988, with the horror film *Pumpkinhead*, about a father who summons an ancient demon to avenge the death of his son. Moderately successful at the box office, *Pumpkinhead* became a cult favorite.

In 1990 Winston collaborated with *Batman* director Tim Burton on Burton's cinematic fairy tale *Edward Scissorhands*. Winston helped realize Burton's vision for the title character, a childlike man who has scissors in place of hands. "Tim Burton is less grounded in reality and much more freely imaginative than any director I've ever worked with in the filmmaking process," Winston told the *American Movie Classics* interviewer. "His background is a cartoon artist. He thinks with cartoon images, and as far as *Edward Scissorhands* goes, he had his design of Edward Scissorhands in his head.

It was a sketch—it was a cartoon sketch, it was almost a stick figure. But it was definitely the mind and the essence of Tim Burton."

In 1991 Winston and Cameron reunited to work on *Terminator 2: Judgment Day.* Co-written by Cameron and William Wisher, *Judgment Day* depicts a Terminator (the villain in the film's predecessor) reprogrammed to become a heroic machine that does battle with a seemingly unstoppable enemy. Cameron wanted the enemy to look like liquid metal, a substance that could change into the form of anyone it touched and transform its hands into a myriad of weapons. In designing the liquid, Cameron used a computer technique called "morphing," in which one object or person changes into another. Cameron and Winston pushed the envelope for special effects, having their villain camouflage himself in a tile floor, slither through prison bars, and split in half and then reconstitute himself. *Terminator 2* proved to be the biggest hit of 1991, bringing in $500 million worldwide at the box office and earning Winston a second Oscar for best visual effects. After *Terminator 2* Winston again teamed with Tim Burton, this time to create the character called the Penguin for the blockbuster *Batman Returns* (1992). Also in 1992 Winston directed the feature film *A Gnome Named Gnorm.*

The following year Winston's special effects took a quantum leap forward, in Steven Spielberg's *Jurassic Park.* In that film, an eccentric billionaire finances the breeding of live dinosaurs using preserved DNA. After the dinosaurs are born, they are placed in a theme park on a remote island; they soon break free, placing a group of visitors in jeopardy. Knowing that moviegoers had become exacting critics of special effects, Spielberg wanted to make the dinosaurs as real-looking as possible. To accomplish this, Winston and a team of paleontologists extensively researched what scientists have learned and surmised about dinosaur anatomy and physiology. After making a series of detailed drawings and sculptures, Winston's group fashioned full-scale robotic dinosaurs that could blink, lick their lips, and appear to breathe. "We couldn't make anything up," he told Malcolm W. Browne for the *New York Times* (June 6, 1993). "We just made the dinosaurs as dramatic as we could." Winston enhanced the design of the dinosaurs with the aid of computers, thus achieving uncanny verisimilitude. This cohesion of digital and live-action techniques contributed significantly to *Jurassic Park*'s resounding success. "Steven Spielberg always said, 'If we can do it live, let's do it live. If it can't be done live, *then* we'll do it digitally,'" Winston explained to J. Rentilly for *Audience* (2001, on-line). "That blend keeps an audience off guard. They never know what they're looking at in the movie, in regards to technology. As brilliant as the work was in the Disney movie *Dinosaur* [2000], you were watching an animated film—and you knew it. When you see *Jurassic Park*, you're watching real characters in a real movie, and you never know what's real and what's not." Released on June 11, 1993, *Jurassic Park* ultimately raked in more than $800 million at the box office.

Also in 1993 Winston and Cameron co-founded Digital Domain with Scott Ross, a former general manager at George Lucas's company Industrial Light & Magic. Backed with startup funds from IBM, Digital Domain set out to become a leader in computer-assisted special effects. Its first endeavor was Cameron's film *True Lies* (1994), an action-adventure tale in which an international spy (portrayed by Schwarzenegger) poses as a white-collar salesman. Digital Domain also provided the special effects for *Interview with the Vampire* (1994). Based on a novel by Anne Rice, that film is about the vampire Louis (Brad Pitt), who, along with his mentor, Lestat (Tom Cruise), lives for several centuries. Winston and his team faced the dual challenges of creating vampires that had an air of realism and putting new twists on the hackneyed conventions of horror tales. "There are effects that happened in *Interview with a Vampire* that nobody knows even existed," Winston told the *American Movie Classics* interviewer. "We actually created our most amazing robot, period, that we had ever done. . . . In the scene where Lestat's throat is cut, Lestat goes down on the ground and the scene is written as we watch him shrivel up and die. . . . To accomplish the effect, we had to create the most amazing robot we've ever created. What people don't realize is that when Tom Cruise is on the ground dying, and the camera is moving in on him, it's not Tom Cruise. It's a robot."

In 1995 Winston worked with Spielberg's protégé Frank Marshall on *Congo.* Adapted from a Michael Crichton novel, *Congo* is about a team of explorers who find a city dominated by apes with near-human intelligence. Winston's chief creation for the film was Amy, a gorilla with the ability to communicate with humans through sign language. Amy was portrayed by a costumed gymnast whose facial movements were controlled by a team of puppeteers; she looked so real that an extra once asked Marshall what the cast and crew should do if the gorilla suddenly attacked. Speaking of how far removed Amy and the other gorillas were from previous cinema apes, Winston told Mimi Avins for the *New York Times* (June 4, 1995), "You can't put human eyes in a gorilla face. Eye movement has to be based on gorilla eye movement. We study the anatomy and replicate life as closely as we can. Every gorilla in *Congo* lives and breathes and performs in front of the camera."

For the 1996 film *The Island of Dr. Moreau* (a remake of the 1933 movie *The Island of Lost Souls*), Winston helped design a race of half humans/half beasts who are bred by a mad scientist. Also that year he worked with James Cameron and Arnold Schwarzenegger on *T2 3-D: Battle Across Time*, an interactive film-and-stage show based on the first two *Terminator* films. The show premiered at Florida's Universal Studios theme park, where it remains one of the biggest attractions. The next year

Winston collaborated with Spielberg on *The Lost World: Jurassic Park* (1997), which was as successful as its predecessor. He also directed the 38-minute film *Ghosts*, starring Michael Jackson. In 1999 he worked on another Schwarzenegger vehicle, the end-of-the-world action drama *End of Days*, for which he created Satan as seen in the climactic scene.

In 2001 Winston returned to the *Jurassic Park* series, with *Jurassic Park III*, in which a rescue party is stranded on the island, now overrun with dinosaurs. Winston's team created the Spinosaur, the biggest creature Winston has thus far produced for a movie. "The Spinosaur is 25,000 pounds—twelve *tons* of dinosaur," he told Rentilly. "The T. Rex is 300 horsepower. The Spino is 1,000 horsepower. It's a hot rod. It's a mean machine. . . . Much of what you see in the film is real actors reacting to a real 'jaws of death' machine coming at them." Winston also lent his talents to two other summer 2001 blockbusters. For the first, Michael Bay's *Pearl Harbor*, about the 1941 Japanese attack on that naval base in Hawaii, he created the makeup that transformed the actor Jon Voight into President Franklin Delano Roosevelt; he also fabricated bodies of sailors killed in the attack. "Some of them looked so realistic that there were survivors who walked up and you could see them just welling up," Bay told Parisi and Duncan. The second film was Spielberg's *A.I.: Artificial Intelligence*, a sci-fi tale about David, a robotic child who longs to be human. Stanley Kubrick had planned to make the film; after his death, in 1999, Spielberg took over. Winston created all of the robotic effects for the film, including Teddy, a walking, talking, two-foot teddy bear that serves as David's traveling companion. The visual effects in *A.I.* earned Winston and his team an Academy Award nomination in 2002.

In addition to his work in creature design and digital effects, Winston has stayed busy as a producer. In the fall of 2001, he produced five films as part of a series called *Creature Features*. These films were remakes of such classic 1950s B-movies as *Earth vs. the Spider*, *The Day the World Ended*, and *Teenage Caveman*. "The *Creature Feature* films, by their titles, pay homage to the Sam Arkoff films of the '50s, but are truly present-day in their structure, production and direction," Winston stated during an on-line chat on *cinemax.com*. In tandem with the premiere of *Creature Features*, Winston launched his toy line, Stan Winston Creatures. By his own account, the inspiration for the business came from the toys manufactured by Todd McFarlane, the creator of the comic book and animated series *Spawn*. With the goal of producing "very technically advanced" toys, as he put it, he recruited Bob LoMonaco, who had worked with McFarlane. Winston's first line of toys was based on characters from the *Creature Features* films; the second offers animal figures from a series called "Realm of the Claw."

In 2002 Winston put his signature touches on the latest remake of *The Time Machine*, this one produced by Spielberg and directed by Simon Wells, a grandson of H.G. Wells (whose novel *The Time Machine* was published in 1895). The film is about a time traveler who, 800,000 years from the present, finds the human race enslaved by underground-dwelling creatures called Morlocks. Winston and his studio staff worked closely with Simon Wells to construct the Morlocks, guided by Wells's many sketches. Among Winston's upcoming projects is the designing of robots for the third *Terminator* film, *Rise of the Machines*, which is scheduled for release in 2003.

During the last few years, Digital Domain has assisted the staff of the Digital Life Consortium at the Media Lab of the Massachusetts Institute of Technology, in Cambridge. "They've realized that artificial intelligence requires human interactivity," Winston told Elizabeth Snead. "A robot learns by interacting with a human and there's a better chance for that with an appealing organic character rather than something that looks like a machine. So we're sharing our technology of building robots with organic character and movement."

In talking with Elizabeth Snead, Michael Bay described Winston's meeting room as "the coolest . . . in Hollywood." Decorated with full-size recreations of his most famous creatures, the room is emblematic of Winston's youthful spirit. "I haven't stopped playing," he told Parisi, "and I know I never will." Winston's many interests include collecting cigars. "I love my cigars," he told Snead. "I have more cigars in [my office] than I could smoke the rest of my life." He is also a connoisseur of fine wines; about 4,000 bottles are stored in his wine cellar. Additionally, he owns two Harley Davidson motorcycles and a fleet of sports cars. "I can't help it! I'm just a guy," he told Snead. "I enjoy the best of everything. I mean, it's just toys."

Winston lives in Malibu, California, with his wife, Karen. The couple's son, Matt Winston, is an actor. — J.K.B.

Suggested Reading: *American Movie Classics* Web site; *Cigar Aficionado* p142+ Jan./Feb. 2002, with photos; *Hollywood Reporter* p11+ Feb. 20, 2001; *New York Times* II p17 June 6, 1993, with photos, II p19 June 4, 1995, with photos; Stan Winston Web site

Selected Films: as makeup artist—*The Bat People*, 1974; *The Man in the Glass Booth*, 1975; *W.C. Fields and Me*, 1976; *The Wiz*, 1978; *Dracula's Dog*, 1978; *The Entity*, 1981; *The Thing*, 1982; *The Terminator*, 1984; *Edward Scissorhands*, 1990; *Terminator 2: Judgement Day*, 1991; *Batman Returns*, 1992; *Interview with the Vampire*, 1994; *The Island of Dr. Moreau*, 1996; *Pearl Harbor*, 2001; *A.I.: Artificial Intelligence*, 2001; *The Time Machine*, 2002; *Terminator 3: Rise of the Machines*, 2003; as creature designer—*The Terminator*, 1984; *Starman*, 1984; *Aliens*, 1986; *Predator*, 1987;

*Monster Squad*, 1987; *Leviathan*, 1989; *Predator 2*, 1990; *Terminator 2: Judgement Day*, 1991; *Jurassic Park*, 1993; *Congo*, 1995; *T2 3-D: Battle Across Time*, 1996; *The Relic*, 1997; *The Lost World: Jurassic Park*, 1997; *Mouse Hunt*, 1997; *Small Soldiers*, 1998; *End of Days*, 1999; *Galaxy Quest*, 1999; *Jurassic Park III*, 2001; as director—*Pumpkin Head*, 1988; *A Gnome named Gnorm*, 1992; *T2 3-D: Battle Across Time*, 1996; *Ghosts*, 1997

Selected Television Shows: as makeup artist—*Gargoyles*, 1972; *The Autobiography of Miss Jane Pittman*, 1974; *Roots*, 1977; *Chiller*, 1985; as creature designer—*The Phantom of the Opera*, 1983; *Manimal*, 1983; as producer—*Earth vs. the Spider*, 2001; *How to Make a Monster*, 2001; *Teenage Caveman*, 2001; *The Day the World Ended*, 2001; *Mermaid Chronicles Part 1: She Creature*, 2001

---

Armando Gallo/Retna Ltd.

## Wood, Elijah

*Jan. 28, 1981– Actor*

*Address: c/o William Morris Agency, 151 S. El Camino Dr., Beverly Hills, CA 90212*

"I found something that I love to do at an early age and I'm going to stick with it for a long time," the actor Elijah Wood told an interviewer for *Biography* (December 2001). Only three years after Wood's first performances in elementary-school plays in Iowa, he landed his first professional jobs in Los Angeles—roles in a television commercial and a music video and a bit part in a movie. Since then, Wood, who is widely acknowledged as a talented, natural actor, has grown up in front of millions of viewers. On screen, he has endured child abuse, psychological terror, post-traumatic stress, sexual seduction, and the possession of his teachers by aliens; he has also gone swimming with dolphins, enjoyed magical family Thanksgivings, and embarked on epic adventures, most recently as the hobbit Frodo Baggins in *The Lord of the Rings* (2001). Forgoing a "normal" childhood to make movies, Wood succumbed completely to the spell they cast. "I love film," he told Tom Roston for *Premiere* (September 9, 2001). "I love watching movies and I love everything it takes to make a movie. I am fascinated by the process on every end, from the technician on set to the sound recording to the cinematographer. And I love acting, putting myself into different characters and exploring different people who can learn not only about themselves but about life."

The son of Debbie and Warren Wood, who owned a deli, Elijah Jordan Wood was born on January 28, 1981 in Cedar Rapids, Iowa. He grew up with his older brother, Zack, and younger sister, Hannah. Wood was a mischievous youngster who earned one of his nicknames—Monkey—from his relentless climbing. Hoping to harness his energy, his mother attempted to have him cast in television commercials, as Wood explained to Tom Green for *USA Today* (April 5, 1993): "One day my mom was watching TV and she saw a commercial. . . . I really love life and I like to have fun, so she thought I would like to do that." Instead, at age six, Wood was enrolled in a local modeling school. His mother had reasoned that, as they lived far away from such centers of advertising as New York City and Los Angeles, modeling would be a good alternative path toward show business. She turned out to be correct: a modeling competition brought him to Los Angeles when he was eight, and he was immediately signed by a talent manager. "He asked me, 'Do you want to act?'" Wood recalled to Tom Roston. "At that age, you don't have any fears. Everything was just fun. I was in LA seeing palm trees for the first time. It was a fantasy."

Pinning their hopes on Elijah's potential, the Wood family moved to California in 1989. "[My mom] wanted to move from Iowa," the actor explained to Tom Roston. "She was ready to move. My dad stayed in Iowa to secure everything." While Warren Wood became a salesman in California, Debbie Wood helped to manage her son's burgeoning career. Wood began to get work as soon as he arrived: a spot in a salad-dressing commercial was followed by a part in the video for Paula Abdul's song "Forever Your Girl." Without having taken acting lessons, Wood was hired for small parts in *Back to the Future II* (1989) and *Internal Affairs* (1990). "I had a knack for it," he told Chris Heath for *Rolling Stone* (April 11, 2002). "I felt like I understood people." His first co-starring role was in Barry Levinson's semiautobiographical film *Avalon* (1990). Wood auditioned for Levinson in Baltimore just days before the filming was set to begin. "I called my mom and she freaked out," Wood recalled for Tom Green. "She thought I was going to make a fool of myself. I hadn't been in the business long. She didn't know if I could handle a major audition." After the audition, though, Levinson offered him the part on the spot. *Avalon*'s producer, Mark Johnson, explained to Nancy Griffin for *Premiere* (March 1992) that the casting of Wood "was a gamble, because it was an enormous speaking part." Wood played Michael, the grandson of Sam Krichinsky (portrayed by Armin Mueller-Stahl), an immigrant and the family patriarch; through Michael and Sam, Levinson presented two points of view in this portrait of a large American family. Michael's experience mirrored that of Levinson, who grew up in the 1940s and 1950s. Wood's work was praised on the set and in reviews of the film, and his commitment to movie making solidified.

After three years of spotty school attendance in California, Wood withdrew from the traditional classroom setting and began a course of study that combined classes, tutoring, and home-schooling. "The last time I was in real school was in fifth grade," he told Aljean Harmetz for the *New York Times* (April 24, 1994). "I do miss all the kids, but it's pointless to go to regular school because I'd never be there." The strain of his social isolation, and the infrequency of his interaction with children his own age, caused Wood to consider leaving show business, but he decided against it. "Ultimately I felt like I enjoyed what I was doing much more than what I was missing," he told Chris Heath. Wood had steady work, making the film *Paradise* (1991) with Don Johnson and Melanie Griffith and the science-fiction adventure movie *Forever Young* (1992) with Jamie Lee Curtis and Mel Gibson. His role in each film was that of a linchpin between two adult players: in *Paradise*, his character reunites the estranged and grieving parents played by Johnson and Griffith; in *Forever Young*, he played a boy who finds a cryogenically frozen fighter pilot (Gibson) and brings him home to meet his mother (Curtis).

Wood's first major role was in the 1992 film *Radio Flyer*, in which his character, Mike, tries to save his younger brother, Bobby (Joseph Mazzello), from their abusive stepfather. Wood won a Young Artist Award for his performance, which also drew compliments from critics. "Wood and Mazzello give unforgettable performances," Desson Howe wrote for the *Washington Post* (February 21, 1992). "There's a powerful sibling relationship between them that seems more than merely scripted." In 1993 Wood played the title role in *The Adventures of Huck Finn*, based on the 1884 Mark Twain novel. He explained to Robin Rauzi for the *Los Angeles Times* (April 6, 1993) that Huck was his favorite role up to that time "because I had so much fun doing it, so much adventure. He's so much fun to play." Wood was able to exercise his comic side in the film, after having played completely serious parts in several of his previous movies. The film version of Twain's classic novel—a story about race, among other subjects—received mixed reviews, which included criticism of its script and direction. Wood, however, was almost universally applauded for his acting abilities. "This is a politically sanitized Huck Finn," Jay Carr wrote for the *Boston Globe* (April 2, 1993), "one that puts the gloves on instead of taking them off—as Twain did." He added, "The acting is expert and sometimes more—Elijah Wood's Huck is a shade too cute, yet is believably resourceful."

As he entered his teens, Wood began to take on more mature roles. Playing opposite Macauley Culkin in the 1993 thriller *The Good Son*, Wood portrayed an orphan sent to live with relatives, including a cousin (Culkin) who has dark secrets. Both young actors were praised for their performances. The experience of working with another child star proved to be a positive one for Wood, who was happy to let Culkin's celebrity overshadow his own. "[Culkin] was a good kid," Wood told Tom Roston. "Child acting is a cutthroat world, which is pretty frightening and really silly in retrospect. . . . It's a really difficult world to live in if you don't have a strong sense of yourself. My mom wanted me to maintain a reasonable degree of normalcy and to enjoy my childhood." In 1994 Wood played the main character in *North*, Rob Reiner's film about a young genius who wants to leave his boorish family and join another. The movie, aimed at children but widely deemed too difficult for them to understand, received generally negative reviews, and even Wood's performance got a mixed reception—though not from the film's director. "Elijah is a prodigy," Reiner told Aljean Harmetz. "I've never seen a kid with that kind of facility." Wood received top billing in the 1994 film *The War*, in which he played the 13-year-old son of a struggling Vietnam veteran, portrayed by Kevin Costner. Once again, while the movie itself received mixed reviews, Wood's acting was lauded by many critics. Rod Lurie, writing for *Los Angeles Magazine* (November 1994), referred to "the wonder of Elijah Wood, who manages to bring tremendous restraint—an inner simmering—to a role that, with a lesser actor, could have gone out of control."

Wood attained the status of heartthrob among the preteen set with his appearance in the 1996 movie *Flipper*. Based on the 1960s film and television series, *Flipper* follows the relationship of a boy and a heroic dolphin in Florida. Wood said in a conversation with Serena Kappes for *People.com* (November 16, 2001), "I always chose things that were just interesting and kind of challenged me as an actor. Those are always the things that interest me anyway. . . . I was never really a part of any genre pictures and certainly not any genres that pertained to children specifically or teenagers. I always found myself in more adult-oriented films." Acknowledging that *Flipper* represented an exception to that general rule, he added that he did not regret the decision to make the movie, since he was able to swim and otherwise interact with dolphins during the three months of filming. Another departure for Wood was the 1998 film *The Faculty*, a horror/science-fiction movie about teenagers who come to suspect that their teachers are aliens. (Wood had long professed a fascination with horror movies, even before he was allowed to watch them.)

Wood's role in the 1997 Ang Lee film *The Ice Storm* allowed new themes to enter his repertoire. The film, based on the Rick Moody novel, is set in 1973; Wood played a repressed teenager who is seduced by a 14-year-old neighbor, played by Christina Ricci. *The Ice Storm* represented Wood's first on-screen sexual encounter, an experience made somewhat uncomfortable by the close involvement of his mother, who was still his manager. The film won good critical reviews, and Wood used it as a launching pad for projects that explored more mature themes—such as that of facing mortality, in *Deep Impact* (1998), whose action takes places as an asteroid is about to destroy the earth; and interracial dating and conflict, in *Black and White* (2000). James Toback, who directed *Black and White*, told Tom Roston, "What was bold was to take a shot at something that, in a way, violated all of [Wood's] previous experience as an actor. Elijah was probably experientially the most wide-eyed. He stood out as the one who had explored the issues (sex, deceit, interracial dating) of the film the least, but in terms of acting, he had already gained a lot more of a sense of accomplishment." Although *Deep Impact* received generally good reviews, unlike *Black and White*, neither boosted Wood's career. During this period he also had a part in the 1999 independent film *The Bumblebee Flies Anyway*, in which he played a young amnesiac struggling to reconstruct his life.

In 1999 Wood landed a coveted role: that of Frodo Baggins, a hobbit—an imaginary creature, standing about two-thirds the height of a human, with large ears and furry feet—in the film adaptations of J.R.R. Tolkien's fantasy trilogy *The Lord of the Rings*. He said in an interview with *Time for Kids* (on-line), "I had wanted this role ever since I heard they were going to make the movie." In order to win a meeting with the director, Peter Jackson, Wood prepared an audition videotape of himself reciting dialogue from one of the books while standing in a wooded section of Los Angeles and wearing a hobbit costume. After getting the job, he relocated to New Zealand, where all three of the movies in the trilogy were shot over the course of a year and a half. "The experience really came at a perfect time in my life," Wood told Serena Kappes. "I was 18 when I left for New Zealand and it was really the first time for that length of time that I'd been away from home living on my own. It was kind of accepting my adulthood in the most extreme way that I've ever had to face it before. That was wonderful. I basically propelled myself into a completely different world, made some of the best friends of my life and essentially gained another home in New Zealand." Wood and his fellow actors in the films forged strong bonds that corresponded to those in the story, in which nine inhabitants of Middle-earth (four hobbits, two humans, an elf, a dwarf, and a wizard) aim to rid their world of a powerful, and potentially destructive, ring. As they make the journey to destroy the ring, they are pursued by various evil forces; Frodo, who inherits the ring and safeguards it through the trilogy, is the focus of the story. "Once I had my [costume] ears and feet put on me for the first time, I felt like a Hobbit," Wood told *Time for Kids*. "It all just came alive for me. It sounds bizarre, but I felt like I was playing a historical character, as if Hobbits actually lived once." Many of the actors came to "live" their parts, as Wood recalled to Tom Roston: "Within the first month, we were those characters. We called ourselves the hobbits because we adopted the relationships that were important to those characters." In the final weeks of filming, all nine members of the "fellowship," which included Sir Ian McKellan, Viggo Mortensen, and Sean Astin, got tattooed with an elves' version of the number nine. A tattoo artist in Wellington "opened on a Sunday for us," Wood told Jeff Giles for *MSNBC.com* (December 6, 2001). "And the fellowship entered and we stood by each other as we all got branded." He added, "I have mine just below the waist."

While Wood greatly enjoyed the experience of acting in the film, he also felt the pressure that went along with retelling a world-famous and beloved story. "I think one of my initial fears was trying to live up to other people's interpretations of my character," he told Steve Zahn for *Interview* (December 2001/January 2002). "Every time you read a book it's your own journey, and millions of people have read these books, so I had that pressure on me. 'Is my Frodo going to live up to people's expectations?'" *The Lord of the Rings: The Fellowship of the Ring* was released in December 2001 to excellent reviews, with critics complimenting everything from the acting to the visual effects to the makeup. "The movie works," David Ansen wrote for *Newsweek* (December 10, 2001). "It has real passion, real emotion, real terror, and a tactile sense of evil. . . . Jackson's fierce, headlong movie takes high-flying risks: it wears its earnestness, and its heart, on its muddy, blood-streaked sleeve." Ansen called Wood "an ideal hobbit hero, at once ethereal, determined and funky." "For all its 500,000 words," Rita Kempley wrote for the *Washington Post* (December 19, 2001), "*The Lord of the Rings* is at heart a parable of good vs. evil. . . . The casting is superb and the acting energetic." The next installment of the *Lord of the Rings* trilogy, *The Two Towers*, was scheduled to be released on December 18, 2002; the final film in the trilogy, *The Return of the King*, is scheduled for a December 2003 release.

After his return from New Zealand, Wood filmed *Ash Wednesday*, an Ed Burns movie that premiered in October 2002. *Try Seventeen*, in which Wood portrays a 17-year-old college student pretending to be older than he is, debuted at the Toronto International Film Festival in September 2002. The actor is currently filming *Thumbsucker*, based on Walter Kirn's novel of the same name. In that movie he plays a young man who sucks his thumb until undergoing hypnosis, when the habit is replaced by other destructive behaviors.

Wood, who is single, has been romantically linked with the German actress Franka Potente. He lives in Los Angeles in an apartment adjoining his mother's house. (His parents divorced in the mid-1990s.) In his free time he is a "huge music fan," as he told Serena Kappes, and he sees as many live performances as he can. He would like to write or direct movies someday. "There's so many aspects of films that I'm passionate about and I would love to be involved with those as well," he explained to Kappes, "be it directing or writing or producing." As for future acting assignments, he told Tom Roston, "I want to do something that is completely different from anything I have ever done. Something more mature, more character, more obscure—not your run-of-the-mill person. Something that's a challenge to me and allows me to grow." — K.S.

Suggested Reading: *Entertainment Weekly* p38+ Nov. 25, 1994, with photo; *People* (on-line) Nov. 16, 2001, with photo; *Premiere* p48+ Sep. 9, 2001, with photos; *Rolling Stone* p57+ Apr. 11, 2002, with photos; *USA Today* D p1 Apr. 5, 1993, with photo

Selected Films: *Avalon*, 1990; *Radio Flyer*, 1992; *Forever Young*, 1992; *The Adventures of Huck Finn*, 1993; *The Good Son*, 1993; *The War*, 1994; *North*, 1994; *Flipper*, 1996; *The Ice Storm*, 1997; *The Faculty*, 1998; *Deep Impact*, 1998; *Black and White*, 2000; *The Lord of the Rings: The Fellowship of the Ring*, 2001

---

Armando Gallo/Retna Ltd.

## Wright, Jeffrey

*Dec. 7, 1965– Actor*

*Address: c/o Creative Artists Agency, 9830 Wilshire Blvd., Beverly Hills, CA 90212*

Though he did not begin acting until he was a senior in college, Jeffrey Wright quickly made his presence felt, winning over fans and critics with his work on the Broadway stage and in movies. He is frequently referred to as a top-flight character actor—a performer who can inhabit a variety of roles to such a degree that he seems to *become* each person he portrays. Wright has built his reputation with his turns as a militant gay nurse in Tony Kushner's Broadway play *Angels in America: Perestroika* (1994), for which he won a Tony Award; as the enigmatic, doomed New York artist who served as the subject of Julian Schnabel's film *Basquiat* (1996); as the raffish thug Peoples Hernandez in *Shaft* (2000), a movie inspired by the 1971 film directed by Gordon Parks; and as Martin Luther King Jr. in the HBO movie *Boycott* (2001). Regarding his experience with—and attitude toward—acting, he told Mark Morris for the London *Observer* (July 9, 2000), "The first day, I knew this was going to be it."

Jeffrey Wright was born in Washington, D.C., on December 7, 1965. His father died when Wright was a year old, and he was brought up an only child by his mother, a lawyer who has since retired from the U.S. Customs Department, and his aunt, a former nurse. He attended the private, predominantly white St. Albans School for Boys, in Washington, D.C. Still, as he explained to Kristal Brent Zook in an interview for *USA Weekend* (February 18, 2001), "I grew up knowing the history of [black] leaders, people like [Martin Luther] King, Malcolm X, [Muhammad] Ali, Shirley Chisholm, Angela Davis."

Wright continued his education at Amherst College, in Amherst, Massachusetts, graduating with a degree in political science in 1987. In his senior year, Wright—whose mother wanted him to be a lawyer—turned to acting. "For lack of any clearer idea, I just started acting one day. It had been in the back of my head for a while, but I think in some ways I was afraid to do it, and finally I just stepped up. I think I was afraid of what I might say when I got onto someone's stage or in front of someone's camera," Wright told Martha Frankel for *Interview* (July 2000). His first play was a series of monologues based on the experiences of a black Vietnam War veteran. About his initial experience as an actor, he told Justine Elias for *Interview* (November 1999), "I was drawn in by the sensation of struggling to define some truth for oneself. It was powerful and thrilling."

New York University offered Wright a full scholarship to attend its acting program, but he left the program after just two months, choosing instead to look for paying work as an actor in Washington, D.C., and in New York City. He was quoted in *Entertainment Weekly* (August 16, 1996) as saying, "People in the industry are actively looking for new white actors. But they're not so actively looking for young black actors." He managed to find roles, though, landing a small part as a prosecuting attorney in the popular 1990 film *Presumed Innocent*, which stars Harrison Ford, and appearing in Jeff Stanzler's 1991 movie *Jumpin' at the Boneyard*. In 1992 Wright played the jazz legend Sidney Bechet on an episode of the TV series *The Young Indiana Jones Chronicles* called "The Mystery of the Blues," and in the next year he appeared in two episodes of *Homicide: Life on the Street*—"Blood Ties: Parts 1 and 2."

Wright delighted audiences and critics on Broadway as the militant homosexual nurse Belize in Tony Kushner's play *Angels in America: Perestroika*, the second installment of what was subtitled "A Gay Fantasia on National Themes." The plays, which deal with love, loss, politics, history, and the effects of the disease AIDS, won a slew of awards, including a Pulitzer Prize for drama in 1993 for the first play, subtitled "Millennium Approaches." For his work as Belize, in 1994 Wright received a Tony Award for best featured actor in a play, a Drama Desk Award for outstanding featured actor in a play, and an Outer Critics Circle Award for best supporting actor. When asked by Frankel about his success on the stage, Wright commented, "Movies are easier, and better pay. The great thing about movies is that they're collaborative. And the worst thing is that they're collaborative. When you get on stage, though, all the collaboration is over and you get to control the time and the space. It's satisfying in a way that film is not." But this success did not bring him stardom. He told Frankel that after leaving his agent during the run of *Angels in America*, it took him a year and a half to acquire another one, despite having won a Tony Award.

Wright was on Broadway again in 1996 as the smooth narrator known as Da Voice in the hit show *Bring in Da Noise, Bring in Da Funk*, which starred the young tap-dancing sensation Savion Glover. Wright received attention that same year for his starring performance in the artist Julian Schnabel's movie *Basquiat*. A real-life New York City artist of Haitian and Puerto Rican descent, who began by creating graffiti and lived for a time on the street, Jean-Michel Basquiat was championed by the 1980s art world and became the first black artist to make an impact on that exclusive scene. His rise was a troubled one, and Basquiat died of a drug overdose in 1988, at the age of 27. Playing him, Wright is on-screen for nearly the entire movie. In an interview with Pauline Adamek for the Web site *ozemail.com*, he said, "The biggest pressure I felt was doing justice to Basquiat. I studied pretty much everything I could find, everything ever written on him. I studied video of him for the physicality, I talked to a few friends of his, I painted a lot and then I just took in his work because his spirit is very much alive there." While the film itself did not garner very good reviews, Wright was highly praised for his work in it. James Berardinelli wrote in his assessment for the Web site *colossus.net*, "Jeffrey Wright's amazing portrayal . . . is animated, passionate, and deserving of a better script than he was granted." Steve Rhodes wrote in another review, for the Web site *imdb.com*, "Jeffrey Wright is brilliant in his interpretation of the artist. A nice piece of acting." Julian Schnabel, with whom Wright apparently disagreed over the way Basquiat's life was portrayed, told *Entertainment Weekly* (August 16, 1996), "People who knew Jean-Michel will feel [Wright] touched on his nature." For his work in *Basquiat*, Wright received a 1997 Independent Spirit Award nomination for best debut performance.

During this period Wright also had roles in the films *Faithful* (1996), *Critical Care* (1997), *Too Tired to Die* (1998), *Celebrity* (1998), and *Cement* (1999). In 1999 he played the freed slave Daniel Holt, who fights on the side of the Confederate soldier who once owned him, in Ang Lee's Civil War drama *Ride with the Devil*. The role gave Wright another chance to explore large issues. He told Frankel, "It's about seeking the truth behind the mythology of America. Too often a story is examined through biased eyes, without a sensitivity for everyone who forged it. It's seen from the point of view of the great white savior, and rarely is the perspective of the slave a part." While the film did not get much attention, Wright remains proud of it. The actor told Justine Elias that he dedicated his portrayal of Holt to his grandfather, who, Wright said, was a "great storyteller" who might have succeeded on the stage himself.

In 2000 Wright acted in the films *Hamlet*, with Ethan Hawke; the low-grossing *Crime and Punishment in Suburbia*; *Sin's Kitchen*; and the one for which he got the most attention that year, John Singleton's box-office success *Shaft*. In that movie he played the maniacal Dominican drug lord Peoples Hernandez opposite Samuel L. Jackson's Shaft, a supercool black policeman fighting injustice. Wright found Peoples Hernandez interesting because, as he told Martha Frankel, the character represents the "selfishness" in society: "Peoples strips away all the pseudo morality of America, and goes for the bones of it, which is greed." Wright's role was expanded after his portrayal proved to be so comical. The film's producer, Scott Rudin, told Jess Cagle for *Time Canada* (June 26, 2000) about Wright's acting, "We did a read-through, and I said, 'Cook up some more scenes for this guy.' It's such a witty performance." A number of reviewers found Wright to be a "scene-stealer" and his character to be the most interesting in the movie. For his work in *Shaft*, he won an award for best supporting actor from the Toronto Film Critics Association in 2000.

Wright played Marc Antony in a New York Shakespeare Festival production of *Julius Caesar* in New York City's Central Park in 2000. In the following year he portrayed Martin Luther King Jr. in the HBO movie *Boycott*, which focuses on the civil rights protests of the 1950s. *Boycott's* director, Clark Johnson, informed Zook, "I saw plenty of actors who could get up and do a pretty good impression of Martin. But Jeffrey was the one who actually got the essence of him." Wright himself told Zook, "*Boycott* is about discovering the legacy of King for the post–civil rights generation that has taken advantage of it but has forgotten its importance. We truly live in mediocre times." For his portrayal of the civil rights leader, the American Film Institute named Wright male actor of the year in a TV movie or miniseries, and the National Association for the Advancement of Colored People (NAACP) nominated Wright for an Image Award as outstanding actor in a television movie, miniseries, or dramatic special.

*Entertainment Weekly's* "Best of 2001" issue (December 21–28) mentioned Wright twice: in citing *Boycott* as one of the best television movies of the year, and in praising Suzan-Lori Parks's Pulitzer Prize–winning play *Topdog/Underdog*. In that play, first mounted at the Joseph Papp Public Theater in the summer of 2001, Wright starred alongside Don Cheadle as one of two brothers in a love/hate relationship. For the Web site *blackfilm.com*, Wilson Morales wrote, "The story is somewhat predictable but it's the acting that you will never forget." In March 2002 the play moved to the Ambassador Theater, on Broadway, for a scheduled run of 20 weeks. (For the Broadway run of the play, the hip-hop musician cum actor Mos Def took over Don Cheadle's role opposite Wright.) Wright was nominated for a 2002 Tony Award for best performance by a leading actor, and *Topdog/Underdog* was nominated for best play. In Michael Mann's biopic *Ali* (2001), Wright was cast as Howard Bingham, the great heavyweight champion Muhammad Ali's personal photo-biographer. Critical reaction to *Ali* was mixed. Regarding Wright's contribution to the film, J. Hoberman wrote for the *Village Voice* (December 26, 2001–January 1, 2002, on-line), "The ensemble cast is so showy that even an accomplished scene-stealer like Jeffrey Wright . . . gets lost in the *Ali* shuffle." Wright has a part in Jim Gillespie's action-thriller *D-Tox* (also known as *Eye See You* and starring Sylvester Stallone), which was due to be released in 2002; he is also poised to reprise the role of Belize in a much-anticipated television film of Kushner's *Angels in America*, now in production.

In 2000 Wright married the actress Carmen Ejogo, who played Coretta Scott King in *Boycott*. When asked by *Entertainment Weekly* (June 30–July 7, 2000) whose career he would most like his own to resemble, Wright replied, "Marlon Brando's, but I'd try not to eat as much ice cream." —C.F.T.

Suggested Reading: *Hollywood.com*; *Internet Movie Database*; *Interview* ((on-line) July 26, 2000

Selected Films: *Basquiat*, 1996; *Ride with the Devil*, 1999; *Shaft*, 2000; *Boycott*, 2001

Selected Plays: *Angels in America: Perestroika*; *Julius Caesar*; *Topdog/Underdog*

---

Dana Belcher/Retna Ltd.

## Zahn, Paula

*Feb. 24, 1956– News anchor for CNN*

*Address: CNN Center, P.O. Box 105366, Atlanta, GA 30348*

The broadcaster and journalist Paula Zahn became the subject of headlines herself in early September 2001, when her employer, Fox News, discovered that she had begun tentative negotiations for a new job with the cable news giant (and Fox competitor) CNN. Fox News promptly fired her for breach of contract, claiming that the terms of her contract forbade her to pursue a deal with any other news organization until February 2002. Within hours of her dismissal, Zahn had signed a lucrative contract with CNN to become its regular morning anchor. The CNN post is the most recent in a string of prominent broadcasting jobs for Zahn, who started her television career as a local beat reporter and worked her way up to co-hosting *CBS This Morning* and later to anchoring the Saturday edition of the *CBS Evening News.* In a career in television news that now spans more than two decades, Zahn has won three Emmy Awards for reporting. She hosted her own news show, *The Edge with Paula Zahn*, on Fox News, and now appears for three hours every weekday morning on *American Morning with Paula Zahn* on CNN, the highest-rated cable news network in the United States. She also hosts the show *People in the News*, a CNN–*People* magazine joint venture.

The daughter of an IBM executive and a teacher, Paula Zahn was born on February 24, 1956 in Omaha, Nebraska. She grew up in Naperville, Illinois, a suburb of Chicago. As the third of four siblings, she learned early to speak her mind to keep up with her two older brothers. "I had a choice of playing with them or being left out of everything," she explained to Susan L. Silver in an interview for the *Saturday Evening Post* (January/February 1993). At age five she began studying the cello. She excelled both academically and athletically through high school; she was the captain of the tennis and swimming teams at Naperville Central High School, and she graduated, in 1974, as the valedictorian of her class. Zahn had also dabbled in modeling since the age of 15, and she made the finals of the 1973 Miss Teenage America pageant. But after participating in a few open casting calls in Chicago, she decided against pursuing a career in modeling. "You walk into this room," she recalled to Ann Oldenburg and Charles Salzberg for *Redbook* (February 1995), "and you have someone telling you you're too fat, you're not tall enough, get your teeth fixed, cut your hair. . . . If that didn't convince me I wasn't cut out for that kind of work, I don't know what would."

Zahn enrolled at Stephens College, a women's school in Columbia, Missouri, on a cello scholarship. In addition to her academic work, she participated in workouts of the golf and swim teams and spent hours in cello and orchestra practice. "I've always pushed myself. I like that. I never slept," she recalled to Susan L. Silver. "Music teaches tenacity," she added. Electing to major in journalism rather than music, she focused on television and spent summers interning with WBBM-TV, a CBS affiliate in Chicago. "I can remember when I first got in the TV station as an intern," she told Laura Elizabeth Pohl for *USA Weekend* (May 30, 1999). "I would call my family to let them know when I was passing behind an anchor on TV."

After earning a bachelor's degree, in 1978, Zahn promptly found a job with WFAA-TV in Dallas, Texas, as a field reporter. She was shifted to the Fort Worth bureau and assigned to the city beat, covering events ranging from murders to the machinations of City Hall staffers. "It wasn't an easy place to build a foundation, because I was competing with seasoned reporters," she told Ann Oldenburg and Charles Salzberg. "I was baptized under fire." Ever eager to work in larger markets, in 1979 she moved to San Diego, to anchor at and report for KFMB-TV, a CBS affiliate. While in her mid-20s, she won an Emmy for investigative reporting. Next, in 1981, she was hired as an anchor for KPRC-TV in Houston, Texas—"such an exciting and fun place to live," as she described it to Mike McDaniel for the *Houston Chronicle* (November 11, 1995).

In 1983 Zahn took a position as a late-night anchor and reporter at WNEV-TV (now WHDH-TV), the CBS affiliate in Boston. In 1986 she became a reporter and anchor for KCBS-TV in Los Angeles, the second-largest market in the United States, where she soon earned her second Emmy, for her coverage of a 1986 Aeromexico plane crash. Unhappy about living so far from her fiancé, Richard Cohen, a real-estate developer whom she had met in Boston, Zahn left KCBS, returned to the East Coast, and married Cohen. "I had no choice," she explained to Susan Silver. "You can't tell your heart to quit loving this man." She found work at ABC in New York, where she hosted *The Health Show* and co-anchored the predawn program *World News This Morning.*

In 1990 Zahn gave birth to her first child, a girl. (She now has two sons as well.) Also in 1990 she returned to CBS to serve as a co-host, with Harry Smith, of *CBS This Morning.* "It was an opportunity too good to refuse," she told Katrine Ames and Nina Darnton for *Newsweek* (March 5, 1990). After her arrival, the show, whose ratings had always lagged far behind those of ABC's *Good Morning America* and NBC's *Today*, began attracting many more viewers, although it did not rise from the number-three position. "The ratings are up 18 percent from this time last year," she told Silver less than three years after joining *CBS This Morning.* "Of course I think about [the ratings]—I have to—but I'm not obsessed with them. I think we're putting on a very aggressive, competitive, smart morning show—and I'd like for the audience to be bigger." Although she had to wake up at 4:00 a.m., Zahn appreciated her early hours; as she explained to Ann Oldenburg and Charles Salzberg, "I'm usually home by one or two in the afternoon. No other job in this business would allow you to sit down with President Clinton in the Rose Garden and then go home to your kids. I get to have dinner with them and put them to bed every night."

Not all of Zahn's assignments were within an easy commute of her home. With her family in tow, she co-hosted, with the sports expert Tim McCarver, coverage of the 1992 Winter Olympics in Albertville, France. Susan L. Silver noted that CBS's coverage took advantage of Zahn's athleticism: "She has been showcased in features of her skiing down Aspen Mountain with [the Olympic skier] Andy Mill, . . . and training with gold medal-winning speed skater Bonnie Blair," Silver wrote. Like other aspects of CBS's reporting on the Games, Zahn and McCarver's prime-time anchoring got mixed reviews. "It's been widely commented that the pair lacks chemistry, but the bigger problem is the remarkable degree to which they seem cut off, almost as if they're not even watching, just hearing about the day's doings third-hand," Steve Kettmann wrote for the *San Francisco Chronicle* (February 21, 1992). "Zahn and McCarver do have a tough job, no question. They spend long hours in that widely derided studio, and still need to look enthusiastic and fresh. Zahn does appear both of those things, but we get no sense that she's really following the action. She seems less connected than us at home. She's a fine television talent, but to get closer to sports she needs help." Zahn and Harry Smith's coverage of the 1994 Winter Olympics, held in Lillehammer, Norway, also got a mixed critical reception. One favorable comment came from Hal Boedeker, who wrote for Knight Ridder newspapers, as published in the *Buffalo* [New York] *News* (February 20, 1994), "The chemistry between laid-back Smith and radiant Zahn is apparent, unforced." Zahn's report for *48 Hours* in 1994 on the mainstreaming of mentally handicapped people earned her a third Emmy Award, this one for outstanding coverage of a continuing news story.

In June 1996 Zahn and Smith lost their slot on *CBS This Morning*, thanks to CBS's decision to revamp the show by spotlighting local news, which would rely more on CBS affiliates than on the central New York studio. With two years remaining on her CBS contract, Zahn became the Saturday anchor for the *CBS Evening News*, and on occasion she filled in for Dan Rather as the weekday *CBS Evening News* anchor. She also contributed regularly to the CBS news program *48 Hours* and hosted her own news show on CBS's cable station, Eye on People. (CBS sold Eye on People to the Discovery Channel in 1997.)

In March 1999 Zahn began a new chapter of her broadcasting career, by moving to Fox News, a 24-hour cable news affiliate of Fox Broadcasting. She hosted *The Edge with Paula Zahn*, an hour-long evening newscast that often included in-depth interviews with world leaders and other people in the news. "I really wanted to get back to being part of a daily broadcast," she told Laura Elizabeth Pohl. "This was the perfect mix of duties for me. In addition to hosting, fronting the broadcast was what was critical to me. All the action is in cable news today. . . . I think I am the only woman in the country who's solo anchoring an evening newscast. I have a tremendous responsibility. It hasn't happened at the broadcast networks yet." Zahn also enjoyed her new working hours. "This has been one of the best schedules I've ever had," she told Pohl. "This is the first time in my working life I've had a Monday-through-Friday, come-in-late-morning-and-leave-by-8:30 schedule. I think my kids are even more thrilled than I am. We go to the movies on Saturday afternoons, which we haven't done in three years."

Within the media and broadcasting industry, Fox News was regarded as a politically conservative second fiddle to CNN, the well-established leader of cable news that had become the property of Time Warner in 1996. In early September 2001 Zahn was abruptly fired from Fox News for talking, through her agent, with CNN representatives about obtaining a position with CNN when her contract at Fox News expired, in February 2002. Those discussions, Fox contended, constituted a breach of contract. Within a day of her firing, Zahn had signed a $2 million deal with CNN, according to which she would anchor a three-hour morning news broadcast. "I am delighted," she said at a news conference at which the agreement was announced, as transcribed by *CNN.com* (September 6, 2001). She also said that she was "deeply disappointed" by the actions of Fox management, which included a threat of legal action and a remark to the *New York Times* in which Roger Ailes, the chairman of Fox News, said that a dead raccoon could have garnered better ratings than Zahn. "I was prepared to stay at Fox through the end of my contract," Zahn said. "Everything I have done has been totally consistent with my contractual obligations to Fox." (Fox brought suit against Zahn's agency, N. S. Bienstock and Co., the day after Zahn was fired. In March 2002 a New York State Supreme Court justice dismissed Fox's lawsuit, on the grounds that Zahn's contract gave Fox a "first refusal" clause, not a "first negotiation" clause. "Thus, Zahn was free to negotiate with rival networks at any time, as long as she gave Fox the opportunity to decide whether or not to match any offers obtained," the judge wrote in his decision, as quoted on the Web site of Bienstock's law firm.)

On September 11, 2001, less than a week after CNN hired Zahn, terrorist attacks destroyed the twin towers of the World Trade Center, in New York, and damaged the Pentagon, outside Washington, D.C. Although Zahn and another new recruit, Aaron Brown (who was hired as the lead anchor for breaking news and special events), were not yet scheduled to make on-air appearances, they immediately began taking alternating shifts to follow the breaking story. Zahn remained at the CNN studios for days, anchoring four to six hours at a stretch. "This is where we [the news media] belong," she told *Entertainment Tonight* (September 12, 2001, on-line). "It's important for the public to know." In the weeks that followed, Zahn segued from continuous coverage of the terrorist attacks to her regularly scheduled 7:00 a.m. to 10:00 a.m. slot, without the months of show development that she and CNN had planned.

In 1992 Zahn, who still practices the cello diligently, made an appearance as a soloist with the New York Pops, directed by Skitch Henderson, at Carnegie Hall, in New York City. She hosted the National Symphony Orchestra's farewell to its musical director and conductor Mstislav Rostropovich, in 1994, and performed at the 1997 World Cello Congress in St. Petersburg, Russia, to honor Rostropovich's 70th birthday. During her six years on *CBS This Morning*, she played on the air several times, on one occasion using the Guarneri instrument owned by the famed cellist Yo-Yo Ma. "Music brings me peace," she told Melissa Burdick Harmon for *Biography* (October 1997). "I don't have many free moments now, between raising kids and holding down a demanding job. . . . Music is a great escape. I find it nourishing. I find it relaxing. I feel very whole when I play." Zahn also bikes and lifts weights regularly, and she runs at least 20 miles per week. "I'm a 'stream of consciousness runner,'" she told Beth Moxey Eck and Marty Post for *Runner's World* (November 2000). "My mind wanders all over the place while I run. I find the escape liberating and energizing."

Zahn lives in Manhattan with her husband, Richard Cohen, and their three children—Haley, Jared Brandon (known as J.B.), and Austin. For her family's meals, she relies on the abundant variety of take-out cuisine available in New York. "I've tried to be incredibly well organized and I'm lucky enough to have a husband who's very involved in raising the kids," she told Janet Cawley for *Biography* (October 2000). "But that's not to say it's easy. You can't be ambivalent: My family comes first." In 1992 Zahn appeared as herself on the television sitcom *Murphy Brown*, in a segment in which she and other mothers who work in TV news, including Katie Couric and Joan Lunden, attended a baby shower for the fictional title character, a newscaster played by Candice Bergen.

In addition to three Emmy Awards, Zahn's honors include the National Commission of Working Women Broadcasting Award; the American Women in Radio and Television Award for reporting on gender bias in education; the Albert Einstein College of Medicine Spirit Achievement Award; the Second Annual Cancer Awareness Award from the organization Congressional Families Action for Cancer Awareness; and a citation from New York's beth Israel Medical Center for her efforts in the battle against breast cancer. — K.S.

Suggested Reading: *Biography* p20 Oct. 1997, with photo, p42 Oct. 2000, with photo; *Harper's Bazaar* 125+ Jan. 2002, with photo; *Redbook* p48+ Feb. 1995, with photos; *Saturday Evening Post* p38+ Jan./Feb. 1993; *USA Weekend* (on-line) May 30, 1999; *Working Mother* p20+ June/July 2002, with photo

## Zimmer, Hans

*Sep. 12, 1957– Composer; keyboardist*

*Address: Media Ventures, 1547 14th St., Santa Monica, CA 90404-3302 ; c/o Gorfaine/Schwartz Agency, 13245 Riverside Dr., Suite 450, Sherman Oaks, CA 91423*

Ed Geller/Retna Ltd.

"My job is to look for something that doesn't exist yet in the film . . . ," the composer Hans Zimmer told Caroline Westbrook for *Empire* magazine (November 1995), as quoted on the Media Ventures Web site. "With music, you can express things far better [than the filmmakers can], so what you do is express the things they haven't done eloquently." In the course of writing the scores for nearly 100 motion pictures, Zimmer has developed an often-imitated style that fuses the sounds produced by traditional instruments with those created by means of digital synthesizers, electronic keyboards, and state-of-the-art computer technology. His work has earned him seven Oscar nominations and one Academy Award, for his score to the Disney animated film *The Lion King*. With the hugely successful *Lion King* soundtrack recording and other albums, he has helped to increase public awareness and appreciation of music for the cinema.

While he is perhaps best known for scoring such action-packed pictures as *Black Rain*, *Crimson Tide*, *The Thin Red Line*, *Gladiator*, *Mission: Impossible II*, *Pearl Harbor*, and *Black Hawk Down*, Zimmer's credits also include many other types of films, among them *Rain Man*, *Driving Miss Daisy*, *A League of Their Own*, *Muppet Treasure Island*, *The Preacher's Wife*, and *Riding in Cars with Boys*. "I'm this loose cannon—all over the place," he told Edwin Black for *Film Score Monthly* (on-line). "I can do action movies and romantic comedies. And I'm a good collaborator—which means I'm cantankerous and opinionated. I compose from a point of view. Point of view is the most important thing to have, and it doesn't necessarily have to be the director's point of view. . . . The bottom line is I'm trying to serve the film just like the director is trying to serve the film. A film takes on a life of its own, and you just hang on for dear life. Eventually, it starts talking back to you. It's an odd process."

Zimmer is the co-founder and co-owner of Media Ventures Entertainment Group, which has helped to boost the careers of Mark Mancina, Harry Gregson-Williams, Nick Glennie-Smith, and half a dozen others who compose film music in studios at the firm's Santa Monica, California, site. He has also headed the music department of DreamWorks SKG since shortly after that film studio was launched, in 1994. According to Jeffrey Katzenberg, who formed DreamWorks with the director/producer Steven Spielberg and the producer David Geffen, Zimmer is "incredibly versatile." "There are other composers in town who are extremely talented," Katzenberg told James Bates for the *Los Angeles Times* (April 12, 1996), as posted on the Media Ventures Web site, "but their interests tend to be focused at one specific expertise as opposed to Hans, whose interests are spread over many, many areas."

Hans Florian Zimmer was born on September 12, 1957 in Frankfurt, Germany. During his childhood his family lived in various other European countries as well. When he was 14 he and his family settled in London, England. Zimmer began playing the piano at age three, and although, by his own account, he took only a handful of lessons and had no other formal training in music, early on he developed a strong interest in the creation of music; according to some sources, by age six he had decided that he wanted to be a composer. As reported on *cinemusic.net*, Zimmer told the movie-music critic Edwin Black in 1998, "I got thrown out of an awful lot of schools. I was an academic failure basically. I just hated doing anything other than music. . . . You know, [teachers] do want you to learn something else and be good at other things, and they don't want you to sit at your desk and daydream music all day long."

In one of his first jobs after leaving school, Zimmer wrote commercial jingles for the London branch of Air-Edel Associates, a firm that handles a wide spectrum of music-related business for theater and the television, film, and advertising industries. Soon afterward he joined the vocalist Trevor Horn and the keyboardist Geoff Downes to form the electro-pop group the Buggles. "Video Killed the Radio Star," a song from the Buggles' popular first album, *The Age of Plastic* (1980), became a worldwide hit; it was made into a video that became the first to be shown on the MTV network. After leaving the Buggles, and after a brief stint playing keyboards with the new-wave band Ultravox, Zimmer performed in Europe with the avant-garde rock act Krisma, which released one album, *Cathode Mama* (1981).

In the early 1980s Zimmer wrote music for several British television shows. He made his debut as a composer for the silver screen with the music for one scene in Nicolas Roeg's *Eureka*, about an unhappy millionaire (played by Gene Hackman); the veteran film composer Stanley Myers wrote the rest of the score for *Eureka*, which was released in 1983. Zimmer learned a great deal from Myers, and in about 1982 the two men, forming a partnership, set up the recording studio Lillie Yard, in London. Zimmer and Myers composed the scores for the films *Moonlighting* (1982) and *Success Is the Best Revenge* (1984), both directed by Jerzy Skolimowski, and Nicolas Roeg's *Insignificance* (1985). In the music they wrote for Stephen Frears's *My Beautiful Laundrette* (1985), they took the novel approach of mixing traditional symphonic instrumentation with synthesizers and other electronic equipment. In 1986 Zimmer worked as score producer for Bernardo Bertolucci's *The Last Emperor*; co-written by David Byrne, Ryuichi Sakamoto, and Cong Su, the music won an Academy Award in the category of best original score. Zimmer also co-produced the *Last Emperor* soundtrack album.

The music for the antiapartheid drama *A World Apart* (1988), directed by Chris Menges, was the first film score that Zimmer wrote on his own. According to Edwin Black, the director Barry Levinson, after listening to the *World Apart* soundtrack album at the request of his wife, hired Zimmer to compose the music for the film *Rain Man* (1988). Starring Dustin Hoffman as the autistic savant Raymond and Tom Cruise as Raymond's self-serving brother, Charlie, who undergoes a moral and emotional transformation in the course of the story, *Rain Man* won the Oscar for best picture and earned Zimmer his first Academy Award nomination for best score.

In 1989 Zimmer composed the music for another Academy Award–winning film: Bruce Beresford's *Driving Miss Daisy*, an adaptation by Alfred Uhry of Uhry's Pulitzer Prize–winning play of the same name. *Driving Miss Daisy* concerns the relationship of an elderly white southern woman (played by Jessica Tandy) and the black man (Morgan Freeman) whom her son (Dan Aykroyd)—against her will—hires as her chauffeur. As reported by the British Web site *Soundtrack Express*, the major part of the score, which is entirely digital, is built around two themes: a "bluesy descending clarinet motif that neatly encapsulates the Deep South" and a "secondary piano motif" that resembles a "rather slow and slightly melancholy" rag. According to the writer for the British Web site *mfiles*, much of the music conveys "jovial contentment." Critiquing the score years after the film premiered, William Ruhlmann noted for the *All Music Guide* (on-line), "The music from *Driving Miss Daisy* remains attractive and melodic, even if one is reminded that it was noticeably anachronistic in the film itself."

Another of Zimmer's most famous scores, also composed in 1989, accompanies Ridley Scott's violent action flick *Black Rain*, in which Michael Douglas and Andy Garcia play the leads. The composer told Edwin Black that Stanley R. Jaffe, who co-produced *Black Rain*, "hated everything I was doing. And hated it so much that I actually got shouted at after a screening at Paramount, and I fainted. So by the time we got to the dub stage, I was just living in fear. We were battling the system." With its distinctly Asian flavor, the music in *Black Rain*, Zimmer told Black, sounds "original"—"but only by virtue of my own stupidity," he added. "My lack of knowledge made it original." In an assessment for *cinemusic.net*, Helen San expressed the opinion that *Black Rain* contains Zimmer's "darkest, moodiest" score. "This is much, much more than your average action music," San wrote. "It is action music that also cries, hides, loves, and hurts."

His problems with Jaffe notwithstanding, Zimmer's reputation continued to grow. He wrote grand scores for such action films as Tony Scott's *Days of Thunder* (1990), in which Tom Cruise played a racecar driver; Ron Howard's *Backdraft* (1991), which focuses on Chicago firefighters; Tony Scott's *True Romance* (1993), whose screenplay, by Quentin Tarantino, centers on an adventurous couple (Christian Slater and Patricia Arquette); and *Broken Arrow* (2001), John Woo's special-effects-filled thriller about a pilot (John Travolta) who steals two nuclear weapons. Zimmer composed subtler scores for Ridley Scott's *Thelma & Louise* (1991), about two doomed women (Susan Sarandon and Geena Davis) running from the law; Mike Nichols's *Regarding Henry* (1991), in which Harrison Ford portrayed a man who loses his memory after being shot in the head; and Penny Marshall's *A League of Their Own* (1992), based on the experiences of women's professional baseball teams of the 1940s.

Also in 1992 Zimmer composed the music for the 10-hour PBS television documentary series *Millennium: Tribal Wisdom and the Modern World*, which examined existing indigenous cultures and their relationships to contemporary societies. Composed primarily for synthesizer, the music incorporated a synthesized choir and percussion evocative of tribal drums and more exotic instruments. The principal theme, according to a *crosswinds.net* writer, was performed on an electronic wooden flute; African chanting "in different modes and tonalities," in the words of the *crosswinds.net* writer, added a degree of authenticity.

The music he wrote for *Millennium* and for the movie *The Power of One* (1992), a story set in 1930s and 1940s South Africa, foreshadowed Zimmer's score for *The Lion King* (1994). The latter film was the first Disney animated feature in years that did not have a score by the team of Alan Menken and Howard Ashman. The *Lion King* score, which made use of African soloists and choruses and incorporated songs by Tim Rice and Elton John, won an Academy Award, a Golden Globe Award, and the Chicago Film Critics Award for best original score. The soundtrack album, which has sold more than 10 million copies (according to some sources, the number has exceeded 12 million), won the American Music Award for best album of the year and two Grammy Awards, one for best instrumental arrangement with accompanying vocals and the other for best musical album for children. In its later adaptation as a Broadway musical, *The Lion King* earned Zimmer a Tony Award nomination for best original score written for the theater.

"*The Lion King* . . . made me reassess my situation in [Hollywood]," Zimmer told Black. "You can go two ways. I admit that standing on the stage getting an Oscar is the most seductive moment one can have in one's life. It is truly overwhelming. And then you go, wow, if I just carry on writing nice music like this, I can have this moment again. It's a very Faustian sort of thing. That's why I did the exact opposite, scoring for truly offensive projects like *The Fan*. Just to shake myself out of the desire for that Oscar experience. Otherwise I would just stagnate. Nothing new would happen. For me, it's about trying to write decent music." (*The Fan* [1996]—about an emotionally unstable knife salesman who, in an effort to help the underperforming baseball player he has been stalking, resorts to violence—got mixed reviews.)

The album containing Zimmer's score for John Boorman's *Beyond Rangoon* (1995), a story set in Burma, was praised by Stephen Thomas Erlewine in the *All Music Guide* (on-line) as "an atmospheric, mesmerizing recording, featuring ethnic percussion and woodwinds, combined with hypnotic, floating voices." For Tony Scott's testosterone-driven atomic-submarine thriller *Crimson Tide* (1995), which stars Denzel Washington and Gene Hackman, Zimmer produced what, to some aficionados, is the quintessential Zimmer score. Written primarily for electronic equipment, the music includes singing by members (most of them men) of a London choir; their rendition of the so-called U.S. Navy hymn, "Eternal Father, Strong to Save," serves as a recurring theme. While much of the music is stirring and majestic, it "never resorts to simple volume to accomplish its goal," according to a reviewer for *Filmtracks* (on-line). The *Crimson Tide* soundtrack album earned Zimmer a Grammy Award.

The gospel-infused score for Penny Marshall's feel-good film *The Preacher's Wife* (1996), which features vocals by Whitney Huston, who co-starred with Denzel Washington, earned Zimmer another Academy Award nomination. Also in 1996 he received the Richard Kirk Award for lifetime achievement, from BMI, a performers' rights organization. Zimmer earned his fourth Academy Award nomination for his work for the James L. Brooks comedy *As Good as It Gets* (1997), starring Jack Nicholson as a curmudgeonly, obsessive-compulsive writer and Helen Hunt as a single mother who works in the coffee shop the writer frequents. Zimmer recalled to Black that, disregarding the director's instructions to "write a big romantic Americana score," he instead wrote "a small European score," one that relied heavily on piano and strings.

Zimmer captured Academy Award nominations for his music for two 1998 films: Terrence Malick's *The Thin Red Line* (in the category of best music, original dramatic score) and *The Prince of Egypt*, the DreamWorks SKG animated feature film about the biblical Moses (for best music, original musical or comedy score). (The *Prince of Egypt* score was also nominated for a Golden Globe Award.) The somber, comfortless, and meditative *Thin Red Line*, adapted from James Jones's same-titled novel about the battle for the South Pacific island of Guadalcanal during World War II, inspired Zimmer to make heavy use of stringed instruments. The "bleak, moody, brooding score," as a reviewer for *Filmtracks* (on-line) described it, "reflects the darkness of the human soul and the primal quality of combat. Like the film it accompanies, there is no sense of purpose, and the score comes to an end without any real attempt at emotional resolution. The score is very anti-heroic, instilling a sense of dread and fear." One day during the shooting of *The Thin Red Line*, Zimmer told Mike Zwerin for *Culture Kiosque* (March 22, 2000, on-line), he and Malick discussed "how light falls in certain Renaissance paintings." After Malick complained to him that the camera had failed to capture the sort of light he wanted in one scene, Zimmer wrote some music for the footage. The music seemed to "light" the scene, as he recalled to Zwerin. "Then we took out the music, and the light was gone. The music allowed you to see more than there was."

By his own account, in composing the score for Ridley Scott's brutal *Gladiator* (2000), Zimmer, in collaboration with the composer and singer Lisa Gerrard, tried to make the picture appealing to women, who he felt would not favor graphic depictions of violence. In a conversation posted on *spielberg-dreamworks.com* in 2000, Zimmer said, "I wanted to bring poetry to the film." "I took a deeply emotional approach while taking a deeply savage one as well," he explained to Rudy Koppl for *Music from the Movies* (Summer 2000, on-line). Zimmer's efforts earned him a Golden Globe Award and nominations for an Oscar and a Grammy Award. The *Gladiator* score includes vocals by Lisa Gerrard. Klaus Badelt wrote portions of the music and, with Zimmer, co-produced the score.

Zimmer's most recent credits include the scores for such prominent action films as John Woo's *Mission: Impossible II* (2000), Ridley Scott's *Hannibal* (2001) and *Black Hawk Down* (2001), and Michael Bay's *Pearl Harbor* (2001). In 2002 he provided the music for the successful horror film *The Ring* (based on the 1998 Japanese movie *Ringu*). Excerpts of Zimmer's scores for 10 films, performed by the VRO Flemish Radio Orchestra at the 2000 Flanders Film Festival, in Belgium, were recorded for the CD *Wings of Film: The Music of Hans Zimmer Live* (2001). The composer has said that he feels satisfied with only a handful of his scores, among them those for *A World Apart*; *Driving Miss Daisy*; parts of *Crimson Tide*; *Black Rain;* John Badham's *Drop Zone* (1994), an action-adventure film about professional sky diving; and Nicolas Roeg's *Two Deaths* (1995), a political allegory about the collapse of communism, which aired on BBC television.

Zimmer has often collaborated with the music producer and engineer Jay Rifkin, whom he met in England in the early 1970s. (Both were studying guitar with the same teacher.) In the late 1980s the pair established the Media Ventures Entertainment Group, partly as a way to gain opportunities for composer friends of theirs who were having difficulty finding work in Hollywood. In an interview with Erik Philbrook for *Playback* (March/April 1997, on-line), Zimmer described the company as "the '90s version of the hippie commune. It's a lonely job being a composer, so we all sort of club together. When I get stuck, it's nice wandering down the hall and seeing someone else being stuck. You feel you're not the only idiot." Now located on a 40,000-square-foot site, Media Ventures maintains the record label Mojo Records, which has released albums by such groups as Cherry Poppin' Daddies, Goldfinger, and Reel Big Fish. It also operates Media Revolution, which handles multimedia projects, designs Web sites, and produces music for commercials. Media Revolution's several dozen clients include Fox Television, Paramount Pictures, Mirage Resorts, and Nissan Motors. The Media Cutters division of Media Ventures provides music editorial services.

Mike Zwerin described Zimmer as "boyish [and] bashful" and as having a "ready smile." In his talk with the *spielberg-dreamworks.com* interviewer, Zimmer said, "I am a big procrastinator and never do my research." When the same interviewer asked him how he creates a musical theme for a movie, he answered, "I just sit there until I come up with something. It's hard work and takes forever, but eventually a breakthrough does come. For example, the music for the first battle [in *Gladiator*] took me two weeks. I created ten different versions until I got it right."

Zimmer and his wife, Suzanne, have a daughter, Zoe, and a son, Jake. They own a beachfront home in Malibu, California. — G.O.

Suggesting Reading: *Cinemusic* (on-line); *Culture Kiosque* (on-line) mar. 22, 2000; *Film Score* (on-line); *Filmtracks* (on-line); *German-way.com*; Media Ventures Web site; *Music from the Movies* (on-line) Summer 2000; *Playback* (on-line) Mar./Apr. 1997

Selected Films: *A World Apart*, 1988; *Rain Man*, 1988; *Black Rain*, 1989; *Driving Miss Daisy*, 1989; *Days of Thunder*, 1990; *Green Card*, 1990; *Thelma & Louise*, 1991; *Backdraft*, 1991; *Regarding Henry*, 1991; *A League of Their Own*, 1992; *Toys*, 1992; *True Romance*, 1993; *The Lion King*, 1994; *Crimson Tide*, 1995; *Beyond Rangoon*, 1995; *Nine Months*, 1995; *Broken Arrow*, 1996; *Muppet Treasure Island*, 1996; *The Fan*, 1996; *The Preacher's Wife*, 1996; *The Peacemaker*, 1997; *As Good As It Gets*, 1997; *Prince of Egypt*, 1998; *Gladiator*, 2000; *Mission Impossible II*, 2000; *Hannibal*, 2001; *Pearl Harbor*, 2001; *Black Hawk Down*, 2001; *Spirit: Stallion of the Cimarron*, 2002; *The Ring*, 2002

Courtesy of U.S. Embassy in Tel Aviv

## Zinni, Anthony C.

*Sep. 17, 1943– Retired Marine Corps general; U.S. special envoy to the Middle East*

*Address: c/o USMC CINC US Central Command, Macdill AFB, FL 33621-5101*

Since November 2001 Anthony C. Zinni has been serving as the United States special envoy in the Middle East, charged with trying to end the recent spate of violence between Israelis and Palestinians and to find a long-lasting, peaceful solution to a conflict that has periodically caused , much bloodshed in that part of the world for more than half a century. Zinni became known for his skill in defusing tension in international trouble spots during his 35-year career in the U.S. Marine Corps (USMC). In 1999, midway through his four-year stint as commander in chief of the U.S. Central Command (Centcom), to cite one such instance, Zinni helped to end the tense standoff that ensued after Pakistan placed troops inside India's area of control in the disputed territory of Kashmir. For 20 years before he retired from the Marine Corps, with the rank of four-star general, in 2000, Zinni led not only military campaigns but also humanitarian operations, most notably in Somalia, as well as counterterrorism activities. He also taught at several Marine Corps schools and was a fellow of the Chief of Naval Operations Strategic Studies Group, which, according to its Web site, "generates revolutionary naval warfare concepts." Highly respected and widely admired in the Arab world, Zinni has been described as "outspoken" and "colorful" in the Western press.

Zinni has also been prominent in calling for improvements in military readiness and the adoption of a new set of priorities by both the uniformed services and the U.S. government in the area of foreign relations. He has stressed that while the U.S. military must be made stronger, through better equipment, increased numbers of troops, and other improvements, the U.S. must also address much more forcefully the roots of the world's problems as well as their symptoms. The armed services, as he envisions them, would prepare not only for offensive and defensive actions but for humanitarian missions that would help to secure peace and stability both at home and abroad. "The threats are different [today]," he told Harry Kreisler for the University of California, Berkeley's "Conversations with History" program (March 6, 2001), as quoted on the Web site of the school's Institute of International Studies. "They're nontraditional, they're ones we haven't experienced before. The application of the military isn't as direct as we would like, and our theory and doctrine prevent dealing with the reality, which is overlaid and mixed with politics and economics, and humanitarian and cultural issues. It's a very different world out there. And our interest and conflict and instability—all are defined differently."

A son of Antonio Zinni and Lilla Zinni, Anthony C. Zinni was born on September 17, 1943 in Conshohocken, Pennsylvania, and raised in the same town. Both of his parents immigrated to the United States from Italy as children. "We had a very warm and close family," he told Kreisler. "My parents taught me a lot about the values that carried me through life, and that close family relationship and their sense of values, the importance of integrity in your word and all of that, I carried with me." As a young adult Zinni felt an urge to leave small-town life for something drastically different. "I wanted to not do what normally was done in my small hometown—get a job in the local mill and hang out at the local firehouse and everything else. I wanted to seek adventure and get out," he recalled to Kreisler. "And the military, because I saw a number of movies, especially the World War II vintage movies, seemed like a place to strike out, seek adventure, and define yourself." A number of Zinni's relatives had served in the military: one of his grandfathers, in the Italian army; his father, in the U.S. Army during World War I; his older brother, in Korea; and various cousins and uncles. "The stories I would hear . . . , especially [from] those that had served in combat, always fascinated me and influenced me," Zinni told Kreisler.

In 1961 Zinni entered Villanova University, in Villanova, Pennsylvania, where he majored in economics. The first day he was on campus, he recalled to Kreisler, "I wandered around and found these Marines standing in their dress blues in our local coffee shop there, and with a recruiting poster, and I joined something called the platoon leader's course. We went away in the summers for training at Quantico, [Virginia,] and really had no program on campus. It was really summer training. You were a reservist. . . . But upon the graduation, you were commissioned to Second Lieutenant, and went off to officer training." In 1965 Zinni graduated from Villanova with a bachelor's degree and, at the same time, was commissioned as an infantry second lieutenant in the U.S. Marines. He served two tours of duty in Vietnam during the Vietnam War. Suffering from malaria, hepatitis, and mononucleosis, he was evacuated from that country shortly before the end of his first tour. During his second tour he was wounded and earned two Bronze Star Medals, for "heroic or meritorious achievement or service." His experiences in Vietnam, Zinni told Kreisler, "taught me to question the training we received. I think we did not do a good job in trying to understand the nature of the conflict and translate that into preparing our people in training. It taught me a lot about the causes that we were fighting for or what we believe in, and the political objectives, understanding those and translating those into military objectives. It taught me a lot about making sure that the people are going to fight the war and understand why they're fighting it. . . . And it taught me not to accept things on face value, and not to accept political objectives as a given, and to question those."

Zinni served as commanding officer of the 2d Battalion of the 8th Marine Regiment at Camp Lejeune, in North Carolina, from 1980 to 1981. From 1981 to 1983 he served as an instructor at the Commandant Staff College in Quantico. The following year he was appointed to staff operations at USMC Officer Headquarters in Washington, D.C. He served in that capacity until 1986, when he was named a fellow at the Chief of Naval Operations Strategic Studies Group in Newport, Rhode Island. In 1987 he was appointed commanding officer of the 9th Marine Regiment in Okinawa, Japan. Two years later he became chief of staff of the training and education center at the Combat Development Command in Quantico. In 1990 he was named a brigadier general. That same year he was named deputy operations officer of the U.S. European Command, whose area of responsibility covers more than 13 million square miles and includes 91 countries and territories. In 1991 he was named chief of staff, deputy commanding general of Task Force Provide Comfort, a relief effort aimed at Kurds in Turkey and Iraq. He also served as the military coordinator of Operation Provide Hope, the relief effort for the former Soviet Union. Also in 1991, during the Persian Gulf War, he helped plan and execute Operation Proven Force, the goal of which was to prevent the Iraqi army from finding a safe haven in northern Iraq, and Operation Patriot Defender.

In 1992 Zinni was named director of operations of the multinational, U.S.–led Unified Task Force during Operation Restore Hope, the December 1992 military action to ensure delivery of relief supplies in Somalia, where a civil war was raging. In 1993 he served as the assistant to the U.S. special envoy to Somalia during Operation Continue Hope, which provided support for U.N. efforts to establish a safe environment for humanitarian relief operations. The United Nations operation in Somalia aroused controversy after 18 U.S. rangers were killed in a clash with armed Somalis in Mogadishu, the capital city. Continued internal strife in Somalia, coupled with the hostility of the Somali National Alliance toward the United Nations, led to a total U.N. withdrawal of peacekeepers from the nation in 1995. In the withdrawal, known as Operation United Shield, a combined U.S.–U.N. mission to retrieve all U.N. peacekeeping forces, Zinni served as director of operations. Speaking of the sequence of events in Somalia, Zinni said that during Operation Restore Hope, the U.S. "did extremely well. We saved a lot of lives. We brought a degree of stability to Somalia. And then we became tempted to take the next step, to nation-build, and to reestablish the country as a viable nation state. That was a big bite to take on, and that one became more iffy, more difficult for us, something we don't do well traditionally and was going to cost us. There was risk involved, and I don't think our approaches were necessarily right." From 1994 to 1996 Zinni served as commanding general of the 1st Marine Expeditionary Force.

In 1996 Zinni was named deputy commander in chief of the U.S. Central Command, which coordinates U.S. military operations in Central Asia and part of the Middle East. (Its area of responsibility includes, among other nations, Afghanistan, Egypt, Iran, Iraq, Jordan, Kazakhstan, Kuwait, Oman, Saudi Arabia, Somalia, the Sudan, Tajikistan, Turkmenistan, Uzbekistan, the United Arab Emirates, and Yemen.) The following year he succeeded General J. H. Binford Peay III as commander in chief of Centcom, the position General H. Norman Schwarzkopf held during the Persian Gulf War. At Centcom Zinni established close relationships with many of the military and political leaders of Middle Eastern and Central Asian nations. "In our part of the world," he told Stephen F. Hayes for the *Weekly Standard* (October 22, 2001), referring to the 25 countries in his domain, "everything is done by personal relationship." He was known to be particularly close to the Pakistani leader General Pervez Musharraf and would talk with the general on the phone almost daily. Zinni's relationship with Musharraf helped the U.S. to apprehend Pakistani leaders of a foiled plot to attack Los Angeles International Airport, in California, on the eve of the new millennium. During this period Zinni also collaborated in Operations Resolute Response and Noble Response in Kenya; Desert Spring, Southern Watch, and the Maritime Intercept Operations in the Persian Gulf; and Operation Infinite Reach against terrorist targets in Afghanistan and the Sudan.

In 1998 Zinni was placed in charge of Operation Desert Fox. That four-day air campaign, waged by the U.S. and the United Kingdom against Iraq, was meant to force Iraqi compliance with U.N. inspectors charged with making sure that Iraq did not develop biological, nuclear, or chemical weapons. In January 1999, testifying before the U.S. Senate Armed Forces Committee, Zinni declared that 80 percent of the designated targets had been destroyed or damaged during Operation Desert Fox. Zinni also reported that no U.S. forces had suffered casualties and that the operation had achieved a number of its objectives: reduction of Iraq's capability to produce weapons of mass destruction; damage to the nation's strategic and tactical command-and-control facilities; damage to its industrial infrastructure used for smuggling gas and oil; and the decreased possibility of an Iraqi attack against one of its neighbors.

Zinni has steadfastly opposed suggestions that the United States take military action to try to remove from power the Iraqi dictator Saddam Hussein. The power vacuum in the region that would result from his ouster or death, the general believes, would create an even greater danger for Iraq's neighbors and the West. In 1998 Zinni's fierce objections reportedly led U.S. president Bill Clinton and Congress to abandon their plan to send $97 million to support insurgent groups in Iraq. Regarding Hussein, Zinni told Daniel Pipes and Patrick Clawson for *Middle East Quarterly* (September 1998, on-line), "Obviously he's not as much of a threat as he was during Desert Storm [the U.S. military action against Iraq during the Persian Gulf War]. . . . But he poses a danger in that he probably feels cornered, as if time's running out. He's been unable to modernize and perhaps sees a degradation of his military capabilities. If that continues, he must see he will not possess the power that will allow him to be a regional power or fulfill his hegemonic designs. So he becomes a threat in that he might commit a rash act to turn that around."

In September 2000 Zinni retired as commander in chief of Centcom. In his retirement speech at the U.S. Naval Institute, he offered his personal view of the world and of the future role of the United States military. "In a sense," he said, as quoted by Dave Eberhart on *NewsMax.com* (November 21, 2001), "we're going back to the future, because today's international landscape has some strong similarities to the Caribbean region of the 1920s and 1930s: unstable countries, being driven by uncaring dictators to the point of collapse and total failure. We're going to see more crippled states and failed states that look just like Somalia and Afghanistan, and are just as dangerous." In the same speech he speculated about what kind of operations the Marines would pursue in the new century. "We're going to be doing things like humanitarian operations, peacekeeping, and peace enforcement. We'll have to respond to some kind of environmental disaster or put a U.S. Marine or Army battalion in a place on the Golan Heights, embedded in a weird, screwed-up chain of command." Zinni maintained that the U.S. military was not in the proper state of readiness to carry out its objectives. "You either need to change the structure of the military and the size and the manning, or you need to change the strategy," he said, as quoted by Jamie McIntyre on *CNN.com* (August 10, 2000). "I don't see the strategy changing significantly. We are the world's leader. We fill a void. There is no one out there that even comes close to filling the leadership role that we have, and some of the moral responsibilities that we have." Zinni declared that the army needed two more divisions and that all the branches of the military needed more funding and more personnel. Upon leaving the armed forces, Zinni was named a distinguished senior adviser at the Center for Strategic and International Studies, a Washington, D.C.–based think tank that provides world leaders with insights into current and emerging global issues.

In the month that followed Zinni's retirement, the naval destroyer U.S.S. *Cole* was attacked by terrorists in Yemeni waters, leaving 17 sailors dead. Zinni had been the architect of the plan to send U.S. Navy ships to Yemen as a way of fostering better relations between that country and the U.S. Toward that end the general had also begun joint training exercises with the Yemeni military and U.S. Special Forces; set up a de-mining school in Yemen; and arranged for the U.S. Navy to help remove sunken ships and mines that remained from Yemen's 1994 civil war. "It's important to not have in the gulf region places like Afghanistan that become rats' nests of terrorists and extremists," Zinni told Elizabeth Becker for the *New York Times* (October 15, 2000). "We were helping Yemen help itself, and everyone in the region was interested in having us help them change."

September 11, 2001 saw terrorist attacks on New York City and Washington, D.C.—actions linked to the exiled Saudi millionaire Osama bin Laden and the Al Qaeda terrorist network that he set up. In an interview with Dana Priest for the *Washington Post* (September 14, 2001), Zinni advised that any military action against nations harboring terrorists be accompanied by the closing of bank accounts, businesses, and organizations that the United States government knew were linked to terrorists; he also suggested that the U.S. increase economic aid to countries trying to rid themselves of terrorists and, at the same time, increase military and intelligence contacts with those nations. "You can't just go in and devastate a country," Zinni told Dana Priest. "A military approach that strikes and leaves will only perpetuate the problem." "You have to go back to the root cause," Zinni told Harry Kreisler regarding terrorism. "I don't believe that the vast majority of terrorists do what they do out of some fanatical motivation, religious or political belief. It's usually because we have a part of the world that's traumatized; that through humanitarian or political conditions that are very, very poor, we have a number of young people, usually young men, who are disenfranchised, who are radicalized, dissatisfied, who want to strike out at something. . . . It isn't a religious thing. It isn't an ethnic thing. I really think it traces back to a root cause that we ought to learn to deal with. We don't deal with these well. We don't invest in regions. We don't invest in the stability of regions. The way we go about foreign assistance, foreign aid, in helping others help themselves deal with these problems is woefully inadequate."

On November 21, 2001 Secretary of State Colin L. Powell, a longtime friend of Zinni's, named the general his personal adviser in the attempt to arrange a cease-fire in the Israeli-Palestinian conflict, where violence had once again escalated. A flurry of violent confrontations led Zinni, in December 2001, to cut short his first trip to Israel in his new capacity. He returned on January 4, 2002. After four days there Zinni was optimistic that a peace deal could be brokered, but continuing violence in the following weeks thwarted such efforts. U.S. president George W. Bush sent Zinni to the region again in mid-March 2002, but daily hostilities again prevented Zinni from bringing the two sides together for discussions.

Zinni has publicly criticized President Bush's advocacy of "regime change" in Iraq and the commander-in-chief's threats to order a military attack on that nation. In a remark that was widely quoted (with slightly different wording in various sources), Zinni said, during a question-and-answer session that followed his speech at the Economic Club of Florida on August 23, 2002 about the Israeli-Palestinian conflict, "It might be interesting to wonder why all the generals see it the same way, and all those that never fired a shot in anger and are really hell bent to go to war see it a different way. That's usually the way it is in history." Zinni warned that a preemptive strike on Iraq would lead Saddam Hussein to "drag Israel into the war" and thus worsen the conflict between Israel and the Palestinians.

Zinni was awarded the Distinguished Sea Service Award in 2001. Among his other honors are the Defense Distinguished Service Medal with oakleaf cluster; the Distinguished Service Medal; the Defense Superior Service Medal with two oakleaf clusters; the Bronze Star with Combat "V" and gold star; the Combat Action Ribbon; and decorations from South Vietnam, France, Italy, Egypt, Kuwait, Yemen, and Bahrain. In addition to his mission to Somalia and the Middle East, Zinni has participated in presidential diplomatic missions to Pakistan and Ethiopia-Eritrea. He was also involved in noncombatant evacuation operations in Liberia, Zaire, Sierra Leone, and Eritrea.

Zinni and his wife, the former Dale Elaine Bathke, married on November 19, 1966. The couple have three children—Lisa, Maria, and Anthony, the last of whom is currently serving in the military. — G.O.

Suggested Reading: *CNN.com* (on-line); Institute of International Studies (on-line); *Middle East Quarterly* (on-line) Sep. 1998; *New York Times* I p18 Oct. 15, 2000; *NewsMax.com* (on-line); *Washington Post* A p5 Sep. 14, 2001; *Weekly Standard* p22+ Oct. 22, 2001

John Spellman/Retna

## Zucker, Jeff

*Apr. 9, 1965– Producer; television executive*

*Address: NBC Viewer Relations, 30 Rockefeller Plaza, New York, NY 10112*

One of the most powerful men in television today, Jeff Zucker became the head of NBC's entertainment division in late 2000, after working for nearly a decade as executive producer of the network's morning news show, *Today*. By revamping that show's news and entertainment segments and changing the overall look of the program, Zucker steered *Today* from its early-1990s slump to its current position at the top of its time slot. Thanks to his work, *Today* earns around $500 million a year for the network, claiming almost half of the morning television audience and 70 to 80 percent of the funds spent by advertisers to reach those viewers. In addition to his work with *Today*, Zucker has produced NBC's coverage of several major events, including the elections of 1996 and 2000, celebrations of the start of the new millennium, and the 1996 bombing at Centennial Olympic Park, in Atlanta. Zucker was chosen for his new position largely because of his ability to think "outside the box," and the choice appears to have been a wise one: in little more than a year in the job, Zucker has made NBC competitive in the recent drive to create "reality" programming, while enabling the network to hold its own against its major competitors in other areas as well. "I have worked really hard; several times I have been in the right place at the right time and I've trusted myself," Zucker told Joe Schlosser for *Broadcast and Cable* (January 22, 2001), "and had enough confidence in my gut to make decisions that maybe others would have been scared of that turned out well for me."

Jeff Zucker was born on April 9, 1965 in Miami, Florida. His father was a cardiologist and his mother a high-school teacher. Even as a boy, he was interested in the workings of television; he remembers the resignation of President Richard Nixon, in 1974, as the first major news story that made an impression on him. Zucker attended Harvard College, in Cambridge, Massachusetts, where he pursued his interest in journalism, served as president of the *Harvard Crimson* newspaper from 1985 to 1986, and received his B.A. degree in American history in the latter year. Deciding during his senior year on a career in law, he applied to Harvard Law School, but was not accepted.

Zucker was contemplating attending the University of Virginia when he was recruited by NBC as a researcher for the network's coverage of the 1988 Olympic Games, in Seoul, South Korea. From 1986 to 1988 he traveled worldwide, compiling and writing thousands of pages of background information on athletes to be used by NBC television commentators and producers in their Olympics coverage. Jane Pauley, then the co-host of *Today* and an NBC correspondent for whom Zucker wrote Olympics materials, helped him to land a position as a field producer for *Today* in 1989. In the following year Zucker became Katie Couric's producer when she was named *Today's* national correspondent. He traveled twice with Couric to Saudi Arabia in 1990 to report on the military buildup that preceded the Persian Gulf War. In January 1991 Zucker was appointed to the position of supervising producer of *Today*. In that role he oversaw the daily production of the show and coordinated its coverage of such major news events as the Persian Gulf War and the attempted Soviet coup of 1991. In addition, he served as senior producer of NBC News's coverage of the controversial confirmation hearings for the U.S. Supreme Court nominee Clarence Thomas. In December 1991 Zucker was named *Today*'s executive producer, becoming, at 26, the youngest person ever to take on that position.

At the time of his promotion, *Today* was in the middle of a difficult period, caused by several factors that were not kept behind the scenes: a memo in which the show's co-host Bryant Gumbel had criticized fellow staff members; the clumsy handling of Jane Pauley's departure; and her unsuccessful replacement by Deborah Norville. As a result, the long-favored morning program dropped far behind its chief rival, ABC's *Good Morning America*, in popularity. Zucker instituted major changes almost immediately. Among other things, he was credited with giving the show a harder news edge. He called for longer, more in-depth interviews and decided, for example, to devote a half-hour of the show to the reunion of former hostages after Terry Anderson was released from Lebanon after seven years in captivity. He also extended the interview with the former Klansman turned politician David Duke as it grew increasingly heated. "I like things live, live, live," Zucker told Bill Carter for the *New York Times* (December 9, 1991). "I do want us to get more into issues. But 75 percent of what we do is never going to be very revolutionary. I may be young, but I'm not stupid." During the 1992 presidential race, Zucker set a *Today* precedent by airing call-in questions addressed by viewers to candidates. He also instituted major cosmetic changes—such as moving the set outdoors—while offering viewers travelogues of such countries as Cuba and several nations in Africa. Before long the show had retaken its former position as the number-one morning news show. "I had a lot of success at an early age," Zucker told Lynn Hirschberg for the *New York Times Magazine* (September 16, 2001). "I hate talking about this because it sounds so cocky and arrogant, but I never doubted that I could do those jobs."

In February 1993, in addition to his work on *Today*, Zucker was named executive producer of *NBC Nightly News with Tom Brokaw*. After about a month, however, during which his workdays stretched to 15 hours or more, he decided to leave the post to focus on *Today*. In May 1993 he briefly left his spot on *Today* to become the executive producer of a new NBC news magazine, *Now with Tom Brokaw & Katie Couric*. In addition, he produced several successful prime-time NBC News programs that year, among them *Hillary: America's First Lady*, the first nationally broadcast in-depth television interview with Hilllary Rodham Clinton after she became First Lady. Zucker was also the executive producer of *The Clinton Inaugural*, which was among the highest-rated NBC News specials of the season.

When *Now* was canceled after one season, Zucker returned as *Today*'s executive producer. Over the next five years, he presided over the show's shift in focus to live entertainment events and stunts designed to capture audiences' attention. Going against conventional wisdom, he even showed highlights from rival network CBS's hit show *Survivor*. Ratings for *Today* continued to improve, and in 2000 the show had its best season ever. In the same year Zucker took charge of NBC's election coverage.

Meanwhile, in 1996, in the midst of all his success and around the time of his marriage, Zucker was diagnosed with colon cancer. "I scheduled my chemotherapy so I could continue to work," he told Hirschberg. "It was very important to me that it not interfere with my job. My sense of self was very tied up in working. So I had chemo every Friday afternoon, and then I wouldn't wake up until midday Sunday. I'd go back to work on Monday." Before he got sick, he had been offered the top job at CNN, but his illness led him to view the offer as inconsequential. "I think [getting cancer] did help put everything into perspective," Zucker told Joe Schlosser. "No matter what happens here and whether we have hits or misses, it's only television. At the end of the day, I have my family and my health, and that's what really matters." In 1999 Zucker was again diagnosed with colon cancer; 90

percent of his colon was removed, but he did not require more chemotherapy.

Zucker was named president of NBC's entertainment division in December 2000, after his predecessor, Garth Ancier, was fired for his failure to develop hit sitcoms or capitalize on the popularity of the "reality" shows, such as *Survivor*, that were thriving on other networks. Many in the media were surprised by the decision, since Zucker had never been involved with such processes as script development. Nonetheless, he proved attractive to executives at the network. "If you think about Jeff, he made hundreds of decisions about popular culture every day. And we hope it's going to provide us with new alternatives and opportunities," NBC West Coast president Scott Sassa said, as quoted by Mark Armstrong on *E* (December 14, 2001, online). "I come as an outsider from the inside," Zucker told Joe Schlosser. "I think that can benefit all of us. I know what's important to the success of a prime-time schedule and I can provide a fresh set of eyes to look for that. I think that what I have done in producing and programming translates exactly to what we need to do. These are the same kinds of decisions we make everyday [on *Today*] in terms of what people like and don't like."

Zucker's first major move was to bolster NBC's Thursday-night lineup against competition from CBS's *Survivor* by extending the hit sitcom *Friends* for an extra 10 minutes for four weeks during a key ratings period. "The easiest thing for us to have done would have been to put some repeats in the 8:30 p.m. time slot," he told Joe Schlosser. "But, you know what, we just don't want to take the easy way out. And I think that's what it's all about. We try to take a look at things a little differently." With negotiations between NBC and *Frasier*'s production company, Paramount Television, deadlocked, Zucker helped to secure a new three-year deal for *Frasier*, one of the highest-rated and critically praised NBC shows. In May he unveiled six new series—three dramas and three comedies—to join the fall 2001 lineup. Zucker also revamped the entire NBC Sunday-night lineup, filling the slot with high-quality drama shows to help solve the rating troubles the network faced early in the week. Among the new shows developed by Zucker were *Inside Schwartz*, about a sports-loving man whose life is the subject of a running commentary by famous sports announcers; *Scrubs*, a program shot with a single camera and focusing on a medical resident and his fellow doctors; *Emeril*, with the famous chef Emeril Lagasse; *UC: Undercover*, a detective drama; *Watching Ellie*, a sitcom starring the former *Seinfeld* cast member Julia Louis-Dreyfus; and *Crossing Jordan*, a forensic-science drama. Among all those shows, none except *Scrubs* and *Crossing Jordan* survived the season.

Among Zucker's most controversial moves so far in his short tenure as president of entertainment at NBC has been the launch of several "reality-based" television shows, which premiered in the summer of 2001: *Spy TV*, *Fear Factor*, and *The Weakest Link*. While these shows were for the most part popular with viewers, critics panned them and wondered aloud if NBC, long known for quality programming, was appealing to the lowest common denominator for the sake of good ratings. Zucker, for his part, admitted as much. "We have to appeal to the widest audience possible," he told Rob Owen for the Pittsburgh *Post-Gazette* (July 20, 2001). "Last summer there was a lot of heat for not developing in this genre. You wanted to know why we had not come to the party and now we've come to the party and you don't like the gifts we've brought. That's fine. We'd still like to stay at the party, if you'll have us." Zucker pointed out that the network continued to focus on quality and that the new, reality-based shows had not replaced any of NBC's more critically acclaimed programs. A fourth NBC reality show, *Lost*, premiered in September. New challenges awaited Zucker, however. The successful, long-running *Friends* was rumored to be in its last season, and the hit NBC drama *E.R.* once again faced the possible departure of its most important cast members. "I like the battle," Zucker told Lynn Hirschberg. "This war is big and it's public, but it's fun."

The 2001–02 season was a strong one for NBC; in a May 2002 press release widely quoted on-line, Scott Sasser, the president of NBC, West Coast, declared that in every "daypart," NBC had been "number one in key advertising demographics." For the fall 2002 season, Zucker unveiled several new programs. Among them were the drama *American Dreams*, about a Philadelphia family in 1963; *Boomtown*, which depicts the intertwined experiences of various fictional police officers, paramedics, reporters, and government officials in Los Angeles; the reality game-show *Dog Eat Dog*; the romantic comedy *Good Morning Miami*; the sitcom *Hidden Hills*, set in suburbia; and *In-Laws*, a sitcom in which a newlywed woman's father and husband vie for her attention.

Infamous for his bad temper, aggressive behavior, impatience, and supposed egotism, Zucker has also inspired loyalty in his colleagues. "I've always been this way," he told Hirschberg. "So, if you don't like me or you don't want to like me, then there's nothing I can do about it. And I'm not going to worry about that. I know some people think I'm cocky, but to me, it's just confidence. And confidence makes it easy for me to be myself." He currently spends time on both coasts with his wife, Caryn Nathanson, a former associate producer at *Saturday Night Live*, and their two children, Andrew and Elizabeth. In the spring of 2000, along with the NBC News anchor Tom Brokaw, he taught a weekly seminar on world events at the East Harlem School at Exodus House, in New York City. Zucker has expressed an interest in running for political office someday. "I have made sacrifices along the way, no question," he told Joe Schlosser. "But you know, I have a great wife and two beautiful children, and so I feel my life is really complete, and I don't regret any of those sacrifices that I made long ago." —G.O.

Suggested Reading: *Broadcast & Cable* p8 Dec. 18, 2000, p22+ Jan. 22, 2001, with photos; *E! Online* (on-line) Dec. 14, 2000; *Electronic Media* p26 May 14, 2001; *New York Times* C p11 Dec. 9, 1991, with photo; *New York Times Magazine* p45+ Sep. 16, 2001, with photos; (Pittsburgh) *Post-Gazette* (on-line) July 20, 2001

# OBITUARIES

Written by Kieran Dugan

**ARMITAGE, KENNETH** July 18, 1916–Jan. 22, 2002 British artist; a sculptor most famed for his tall bronze slabs, abstract or semiabstract studies of human figures (often with twig-like protrusions) suggesting a range of moods, from lighthearted and humorous to brooding and thunderous; was inspired by Cycladic and Egyptian sculpture in the British Museum and by his expeditions to the limestone crags of the Burren in County Clare, Ireland, and the ancient standing stone monuments at Newgrange, in Ireland, Orkney, in Scotland, and Carnac, in France; was also inspired by a visit to the dense jungles of Venezuela; at the beginning of his career, devoted himself chiefly to wood carving; after military service in World War II, turned from carving to sculpting; at first, welded thin, string-like lines into flattened and simplified human forms; later, modeled in plaster or terra cotta and then cast in bronze; in 1950, created *People in the Wind*, a bronze plane depicting three figures apparently straining against wind; achieved international recognition when that sculpture was exhibited at the Venice Biennale in 1952; also in the early 1950s, sculpted the screen-like bronzes *Seated Group Listening to Music*, *Friends Walking*, and *Children Playing*; subsequently, created more bulky works, described by Emily Genauer as "strange, pot-bellied figures standing on stick legs and topped by pin heads, their ropy extremities pushing out from a round core instead of shooting, lariat fashion, through space"; in the 1960s, experimented with such embellishments as plastic and spray paint; during the same decade, made his "Pandaru" series of tall bronze standing slabs with projecting funnels, shelves, and arms; in the 1970s, produced many small white or bronze human studies; in the late 1970s and early and mid-1980s, was inspired by the giant old oak trees in London's Richmond Park to create a series of bronzes, including an 18-foot sculpture that stands in the garden of the British Embassy in Brazil; in the late 1980s, executed his series of "Chair" sculptures, ecclesiastical or royal thrones from which human faces and limbs emerge; returned to the flattened forms of his early, best-known work in some of the pieces he executed in the 1990s, including *People Walking*; during the last years of his life, with the help of a sculptor friend, enlarged many of his maquettes that had not yet been cast in monumental size; died in London, England. See *Curremt Biography* (April) 1957.

Obituary *New York Times* B p7 Feb. 18, 2002

**ASH, MARY KAY** May 12, 1918–Nov. 22, 2001 Founder and chairwoman emeritus of Mary Kay Inc., the second-largest direct-sales skin-care and cosmetics company in the U.S.; motivated hundreds of thousands of women, typically homemakers, to become home-based entrepreneurs; did her first direct selling in the 1930s, peddling door to door a set of books titled the *Child Psychology Bookshelf*; later, conducted demonstrations of Stanley Home Products at get-togethers in private homes (1939–52), which would be the modus operandi of Mary Kay Inc.; still later, was training director of the World Gift Co., a Dallas-based direct-sales firm (1952–63); when a male assistant was promoted over her, quit her job with the World Book Co. and set about pursuing her vision of founding a company "where being a woman wasn't a liability"; had been introduced to what would become her stock in trade by a Stanley Home party hostess, Ova Heath Spoonemore, who had developed several skin-care creams and lotions based on solutions used by her father, J. W. Heath, an Arkansas leather tanner, to keep the skin of his hands in good condition; purchased the rights to the formulas for $500; in 1963, founded her own company (originally named Beauty by Mary Kay) in Dallas, Texas, offering a basic five-product skin-care set; over the years would expand her inventory to include some 200 items for men as well as women in skin, hair, and nail care as well as sun protection; sold her inventory through freelance entrepreneurs who demonstrated the products at gatherings in their own homes; by the year 2000, realized annual sales of $1.2 billion through some 850,000 "independent beauty consultants" in some 40 countries; had a predilection for a pale shade of pink, the dominant color in her wardrobe and the packaging of her products; drove a pink Cadillac and lived for many years in a pink mansion in Dallas; wrote of her life, work, and quasi-religious business philosophy in three books, including the best-seller *Mary Kay: You Can Have It All* (1995); was married three times, divorced once, and widowed twice; had three children, 16 grandchildren, and 24 great-grandchildren; died at her home in Dallas. See *Current Biography* (May) 1995.

Obituary *New York Times* D p9 Nov. 23, 2001

**BALAGUER, JOAQUÍN** Sep. 1, 1907–July 14, 2002 Former president of the Dominican Republic; lawyer; founder of the right-of-center Social Christian Reform Party; a relatively moderate protégé of the dictator General Rafael L. Trujillo, who ruled the Dominican Republic overtly or covertly from 1930 until his assassination, in 1961; during the 1930s and 1940s, served in various high diplomatic posts, including several ambassadorships; in the Trujillo cabinet between 1949 and 1957, was successively secretary of education and culture, secretary of foreign affairs, and secretary of state; from 1957 to 1960, was vice president to Hector B. Trujillo, Rafael's brother, then the ceremonial president; in August 1960, when Hector resigned, citing reasons of health, succeeded to the presidency nominally, while General Trujillo, with the title "Benefactor," continued to wield power; in January 1962, seven and a half months after General Trujillo's assassination, resigned the presidency under the pressure of street rioting instigated by leaders of the Unión Cívica Nacional, an extreme right-wing party; for four years, lived in exile in the U.S., where he founded by proxy his political party, originally called the Pardido Reformista; in June 1965, with the permission of the ruling right-wing junta, returned to the Dominican Republic; in the presidential election held on June 1, 1966, with U.S. support, defeated his leftist-liberal opponent Juan Bosch by a landslide; in his first four-year term as president, was credited with launching economic stimulus and public-works programs that spurred the growth of the country's first substantial middle class; on the other hand, severely repressed and punished his enemies, chiefly left-wing politicians and journalists; later, improved his human rights record while maintaining his reputation as a "strongman"; was elected to a second term in 1970 and a third term in 1974; in 1978, was defeated by the candidate of the moderately leftist Pardido Revolucionario Dominicano; in the elections of 1986, was returned to the presidency, where he remained for 10 years; died in Santo Domingo, Dominican Republic. See *Current Biography* (November) 1966.

Obituary *New York Times* B p7 July 15, 2002

**BÁNZER SÁUREZ, HUGO** May 10, 1926–May 5, 2002 Two-time president of Bolivia; army general; a former dictator (1971–78) who led Bolivia to democracy in the late 1990s; even in his term as popularly elected president (1997–2001), did not leave behind his authoritarian temperament; was appreciated in Washington, D.C., for curbing Bolivia's coca production; like other members of Bolivia's ruling elite, was of European descent; received much of his military training under American auspices, in the U.S. and at the School of the Americas in the Panama Canal Zone; in the dictatorship of René Barrientos Ortuño, was minister of education (1964–67) and military attaché at the Bolivian Embassy in Washington, D.C. (1967–69); subsequently, directed the Military Academy of Ejército; on October 6, 1970, played a key role in the overthrow of the leftist/nationalist government of General Alfredo Ovando Candia and the installation in the presidency of the right-wing army chief of staff General Bogelio Miranda; was therefore on the losing side when, in a counter-coup, General Juan José Torres González, a left-wing radical, seized power on October 7, 1970; in January 1971, tried, unsuccessfully, to instigate a coup against the socialistic Torres regime, which courted Cuba and the Soviet Union while expropriating American-owned mines and industries; went into exile in Argentina; over the following months, plotted a coup in clandestine communication with anti-Torres elements in Bolivia, including army officers, businessmen, and some peasant leaders; won the support of a united front of centrist and right-wing political parties; made several secret visits to Bolivia; with his arrest in Santa Cruz, Bolivia, on August 18, 1971, signaled the beginning of the coup, in which his supporters were aided by an elite American-trained 800-man ranger unit; after four days of street fighting and pitched battles, seized power on August 22, 1971; during his eight years of military rule, a period known as the *banzerato*, dispensed with his civilian supporters, prohibited all political activity, and imposed censorship of the news media; headed a regime under which scores of people were killed for political reasons, thousands were arrested, and thousands more fled to other countries, but in which the level of terror never approached that in neighboring Chile and Argentina; was blamed with leaving Bolivia with a heavy burden of debt; was credited with a growth of the economy (at an average rate of 5 percent) that nurtured the expansion of the urban middle class and thus helped create a constituency for Nationalist Democratic Action, the party he founded in 1979; won the highest share (almost 29 percent) of the vote in the presidential election of 1985, but less than a majority, and lost to Victor Paz Estenssoro when the election was decided by a vote of the Congress; in 1989, when the popular vote was again indecisive, finished second at the polls, and then threw his support behind Jaime Paz Zamora; wielded considerable power behind the scenes in the Paz presidency; in the early 1990s, became broken in spirit and even in physical health after his two sons were killed in separate accidents; retired from politics after his defeat in the presidential election of 1993; persuaded by supporters to run again in 1997, finally won a majority of the popular vote; in his second term as president, was plagued by corruption scandals in his government and three general strikes; was unsuccessful in pursuing neoliberal policies in an effort to spur economic growth and raise Bolivia from its status as South America's poorest country; resigned in August 2001 after being diagnosed with lung cancer; died in Santa Cruz, Bolivia. See *Current Biography* (September) 1973.

Obituary *New York Times* B p7 May 6, 2002

**BELAÚNDE TERRY, FERNANDO** Oct. 7, 1912–June 4, 2002 Former president of Peru; architect; a scion of wealth and privilege who brought to politics an understated attitude of noblesse oblige and a progressive democratic vision; came from a long line of statesmen and diplomats in an aristocratic family, part of Peru's ruling minority; studied architecture in Paris before earning a B.S. degree in architecture at the University of Texas in the early 1930s; in his subsequent architectural practice in Lima, Peru, designed private homes; founded the magazine *Arquitecto Peruano*; co-founded an urban-planning institute, the Instituto del Urbanismo; as a member (1945–48) of the national Chamber of Deputies, the lower house of the national Congress, introduced bills for social and economic reform, including legislation leading to the establishment of the National Housing Corp.; drew up plans for and supervised the construction of several major low-cost housing projects; when Congress was suspended in a military coup in 1948, returned to his architectural practice; became dean of the school of architecture at the National University of Engineering, a position he held until 1960; when General Manuel A. Odria, the military dictator, announced a return to popular elections in 1956, formed the Acción Popular Party and ran for president, unsuccessfully; six years later, ran again, with the byword *adelantee* ("forward"); appealed to Indian peasants and urban slum dwellers with his call for a "peaceful revolution" and the "conquest of Peru by the Peruvians"; finished a close second in the 1962 election, which was annulled because none of the candidates received the necessary one-third of the votes cast; in 1963, won the rescheduled election; as president, launched the building of a highway through the Andean jungle, with a view to opening Peru's rich interior to settlement and development; began the establishment of a self-help program for Peru's indigenous majority, but was blocked by an opposition Congress from implementing many if not most of his plans, including agrarian reform targeted at absentee landowners; was undone by an inflationary spiral in the economy, and by his amicable dealings with the U.S.-controlled International Petroleum Co., which antagonized those who favored expropriation of foreign assets; in a military coup in 1968, was deposed and sent into exile; spent most of his exile in the U.S., lecturing on architecture at Harvard, Columbia, and Johns Hopkins universities; returned to Peru following a general amnesty granted by the military in 1975; was elected to his second term as president in 1980; served out his full five years as president, a term beset with economic difficulties, a burgeoning drug trade, and the reign of terror perpetrated by the Maoist insurgents known as the Shining Path; left office in a peaceful transition in 1985; was a senator in Peru's Congress until 1992; in 1959 published an autobiography that was translated as *Peru's Own Conquest* (1965); died in Lima. See *Current Biography* (July) 1965.

Obituary *New York Times* C p12 June 6, 2002

**BERLE, MILTON** July 12, 1908–Mar. 27, 2002 Comedian; a brash, cigar-wielding comic of the old school, rooted in vaudeville; alternated between slick rote delivery of a vast repertoire of one-liners and clownish knockabout antics; over the course of more than 80 years in show business, earned the sobriquets "Thief of Bad Gags," "Uncle Miltie," "Mr. Television," and "Mr. Tuesday Night"; honed his comic skills in relative obscurity in vaudeville, movies, stage revues, nightclubs, and radio before becoming television's first superstar as the galvanic host of the live, hour-long comedy/variety program *Texaco Star Theater* (1948–53), a prime-time Tuesday night program on which Americans with access to TV sets focused en masse at the dawn of the medium's popularity; sparked the sale of television sets more than any advertising campaign could have; was born Mendel Berlinger, in Manhattan; under his mother's management, began performing in amateur shows when he was five years old and acting in silent movies (then being filmed in New York City and Fort Lee, New Jersey) when he was six; joined a children's vaudeville act at 10; ventured into his first solo vaudeville routines in 1924; when he was in his early 20s, became the youngest master of ceremonies on the national vaudeville circuit; as emcee, habitually upstaged the acts he introduced, a practice that he would later carry into the hosting of his television shows; was also notorious for adding the material of other comedians to his own repertoire; ultimately amassed a library comprising tens of thousands of jokes; as vaudeville faded away, turned increasingly to stage musicals and revues, motion pictures, and radio; on Broadway, had featured or star billing in such productions as *Earl Carroll's Vanities* (1932), *Saluta* (1934), the *Ziegfeld Follies* (1938), and *Same Time Next Week*, the 1943 edition of the *Ziegfeld Follies*; co-wrote the lyrics for the popular novelty song "Sam, You Made the Pants Too Long" (1932); collaborated on lyrics for *Saluta*; made his talking-picture debut in *New Faces of 1937*; subsequently had roles in *Radio City Revels* (1938), *Rise and Shine* (1941), *Sun Valley Serenade* (1941), and *Tall, Dark, and Handsome* (1941), among other films; was a guest performer on a number of programs on radio, where he was less effective, because the physicality of his comedy as "a visual performer" (his term) could not be appreciated in that medium; by the mid-1940s, was hosting his own radio programs; became an alternate host of *Texaco Star Theater* when that weekly revue-style show was inaugurated on the NBC television network, in June 1948; emerged as the show's permanent emcee the following September; typically, would greet the audience with the salutation "Good evening, ladies and germs," and go on to introduce and interact with some half-dozen guests, including singers, comedians, acrobats, and ventriloquists; also engaged in comedic counterpoint with regular performers on the show; in slapstick skits, often appeared in fright wigs and outlandish costumes and makeup, including "drag"; remained in the prime-time Tuesday night slot on NBC as host of the one-hour *Buick Berle Show* (1953–55), the one-hour *Milton Berle Show* (1955–56), and the half-hour *Milton Berle Starring in the Kraft Music Hall* (1958–58); moved to the ABC network as host of another one-hour *Milton Berle Show* (1966–67); meanwhile, had begun performing regularly in Las Vegas; returned to Hollywood as a member of the star-studded cast of the madcap comedy *It's a Mad Mad Mad Mad World* (1963) and in a supporting role in *The Loved One* (1965), among other films; made a serious cameo appearance in the movie *Lepke* (1975); as he grew older, was often cast against type in dramatic roles on television; hosted countless benefit shows for a range of charities, including cancer research; was master of ceremonies at numerous celebrity roasts at Manhattan's Friars Club; in 1974, published the autobiography *Milton Berle*, written with Haskell Frankel; also with the help of others, assembled the humor collections *Laughingly Yours* (1939) and *B.S. I Love You: Sixty Funny Years with the Famous and the Infamous* (1988), which includes Friars Club anecdotes; had a number of legendary romantic affairs, including one with Aimee Semple McPherson, before he entered into his four marriages, the first two with the same woman, Joyce Matthews, and the last with Lorna Adams, who survives him; died at his home in Los Angeles, California. See *Current Biography* (June) 1949.

Obituary *New York Times* p1+ Mar. 28, 2002

**BILANDIC, MICHAEL A.** Feb. 13, 1923–Jan. 15, 2002 Democratic mayor of Chicago (1976–79); jurist; for 29 years, beginning in 1949, was a corporate lawyer with the Chicago firm of Anixter, Delaney, Bilandic & Piggott; grew up and lived in Chicago's working-class Bridgeport district (popularly known as Back of the Yards), the heart of the city's 11th Ward, the power base of the Cook County Democratic politicians who controlled Chicago's City Hall from the early 1930s through the 1970s; in 1955, canvassed the 11th Ward for his Bridgeport neighbor Richard J. Daley, then running for the first of his six terms as mayor; with Daley's support, was elected to Chicago's City Council in 1969; ultimately chaired the council's powerful finance and environmental control committees; following Daley's death, in December 1976, served as interim mayor until the following June, when he was elected mayor in his own right; subsequently suffered several public-relations reverses, including blame for inept handling of snow removal during an historic Chicago blizzard; in the Democratic primary election in February 1979, lost to Jane Byrne, who went on to win the mayoralty in the general election in April 1979; returned to the private practice of law; was elected to the First District Appellate Court in 1984 and to the Illinois Supreme Court in 1990; was chief justice of the Supreme Court during the last three years of his 10-year term; died in Chicago, Illinois. See *Current Biography* (February) 1979.

Obituary *New York Times* B p9 Jan. 17, 2002

**BLASS, BILL** June 22, 1922–June 12, 2002 Couturier; an influential designer of elegant but practical and comfortable no-frills women's wear, from exclusive gowns for a socially prominent clientele (including Nancy Reagan, Brooke Astor, and Gloria Vanderbilt) to chic sportswear for the general market; was credited by Ellin Saltzman, a former fashion director with the Saks Fifth Avenue and Bergdorf Goodman stores, with taking "American sportswear to its highest level" and combining it "with sexy menswear touches, giving it new, clean, modern, impeccable style"; also applied his sense of line and color and minimalist style to the creation of furs, children's wear, swimwear, accessories, and, briefly, a line of men's suits having what one observer described as "the Scarsdale Mafia look"; began his career on Seventh Avenue, Manhattan's garment district, as a sketch artist for David Crystal, a mass manufacturer of moderately priced sportswear; during World War II, served as an army camouflage worker and combat engineer; in the process, acquired a slight pseudo-British accent; shortly after his return to Seventh Avenue, became a designer with Anna Miller and Co., which merged into her brother's women's fashion house, Maurice Rentner Ltd., when Miller retired, in 1959; two years later, was named vice president of the Rentner firm and gained name recognition on the tags of the clothing he designed; bought the company in 1970; changed its name to Bill Blass Ltd.; licensed the Bill Blass name to a score of manufacturers of dresses, women's evening clothes, men's clothes, ties, belts, jeans, eyewear, hosiery, shoes, perfumes, bed linens, and even chocolates and the interiors of Lincoln Continental automobiles; presented his last collection in September 1999; sold Bill Blass Ltd. for a reported $50 million; contributed $10 million to the New York Public Library; was deeply involved in AIDS charities; died at his home in New Preston, Connecticut. See *Current Biography* (September) 1966.

Obituary *New York Times* A p1+ June 13, 2002

**BLOCK, HERBERT L.** Oct. 13, 1909–Oct. 7, 2001 Editorial cartoonist; author; one of the most powerful political commentators of his time; wielded pen, pencil, and accompanying language with deft craftsmanship and incisive and biting wit; adopted the pen name Herblock soon after joining the staff of the Chicago *Daily News* in 1929; four years later, moved to Cleveland, Ohio, to the offices of the Newspaper Enterprise Association, which syndicated his daily cartoons nationally until 1943; won his first Pulitzer Prize in 1942, for his work in 1941, especially for a cartoon titled "British Plane," which showed a German soldier in occupied France scanning the sky for an RAF bomber while Parisians in the background look on; joined the U.S. Army in 1943; drew cartoons for the army's Information and Education Division; joined the staff of the *Washington Post* in 1946; created a gallery of standard characters, including an animated and malignant-faced, torpedo-shaped atomic bomb, seen in a 1947 cartoon (captioned "Don't Mind Me—Just Go Right on Talking") towering over and tape-measuring the girth of a globe representing the planet Earth, atop which tiny diplomats haggle while seated at a round table; from 1948, when Richard Nixon was a Republican congressman regarded by his critics as a Red-baiting practitioner of smear tactics, through Nixon's presidency, to his resignation in 1974, caricatured Nixon as a political thug, typically seen emerging from a sewer; similarly caricatured Senator Joseph R. McCarthy, whose vigilante mode of operation inspired him to coin the term "McCarthyism" in 1950; in his caricatures of both men, shaded their faces so as to symbolize a "moral 5 o'clock shadow"; during the presidential election campaign of 1952, sometimes took aim at Dwight D. Eisenhower, the Republican candidate, who at that time showed some support for McCarthy; for a while during the campaign, was banished from the editorial page by the *Post*, which supported Eisenhower; won his second Pulitzer Prize in 1954, for his work in 1953, especially for a cartoon published at the time of Stalin's death, in which the Grim Reaper escorts the Soviet dictator off this mortal coil with the caption, "You Were Always a Great Friend of Mine, Joseph"; shared a Pulitzer Prize with the *Washington Post* for its coverage of the Watergate scandal that culminated in President Nixon's resignation; in 1957, delivered the Joseph Pulitzer Memorial Lecture, in which he declared that the responsibility of the press is to "use its freedom to protect the rights and liberties of all individuals"; in 1979, received a Pulitzer Prize for the entire body of his work; in April 1982, attacked the "supply side" economic policy of the administration of President Ronald Reagan in a cartoon showing the Easter bunny carrying a basket of eggs marked "Breaks for the Well-to-do" while disadvantaged children look on, saying, "He runs out of supplies before he gets to our side"; during most of his career, drew black-and-white cartoons six days a week (in his last years, five); was syndicated in newspapers across the U.S. and in several foreign countries; published his last cartoon on August 26, 2001; published 22 books (with varying ratios of text to black-and-white drawings), including *The Herblock Book* (1952), *The Herblock Gallery* (1968), the autobiography *Herblock: A Cartoonist's Life* (1993), and *Herblock's History: Political Car-*

*toons from the Crash to the Millenium* (2000); died in Washington, D.C. See *Current Biography* (July) 1954.

Obituary *New York Times* D p6 Oct. 9, 2001

**BOLAND, EDWARD P.** Oct. 1, 1911–Nov. 4, 2001 Democratic U.S. representative from Massachusetts (1953–89); a shy legislator who did not seek and did not enjoy the visibility that came to him in the early 1980s, when he authored the "Boland amendments" curtailing and finally ending U.S. funding of aid to the Contras, the rebel military force challenging the rule of the Marxist Sandinistas in Nicaragua at that time; before going to Washington, was a Massachusetts state representative, Hamden (Massachusetts) County register of deeds, and military aide to Governor Paul A. Dever of Massachusetts; in Congress, became the second-ranking Democrat on the powerful Appropriations Committee; as chairman of the Appropriations subcommittee on housing and urban development, promoted President Lyndon B. Johnson's Great Society programs; voted for increased spending for public housing, NASA, and the National Science Foundation; chaired the House Select Committee on Intelligence from July 1977 to December 1984; in the first "Boland amendment," which was attached to the Defense Appropriations Act of 1983, signed into law in December 1982, ensured continuation of aid to the Nicaraguan Contras on condition that the funds were not used "for the purpose of overthrowing the government of Nicaragua"; with the mounting of evidence that the administration of President Ronald Reagan, chiefly through the CIA, was violating that proviso, lowered the ceiling for aid to the Contras to $24 million with the "Boland cap" the following year; flatly banned aid to the Contras with the "Boland cutoff," attached to the Defense Appropriations Act of 1985; in 1987, was seen on national television as a member of the House Select Committee investigating the Iran-Contra scandal, involving the Reagan administration's covert sale of weapons to Iran and the secret diversion of some of the profits from that sale to the Contras; retired from politics without ever having lost an election; died in Springfield, Massachusetts. See *Current Biography* (October) 1987.

Obituary *New York Times* A p19 Nov. 7, 2001

**BORST, LYLE B.** Nov. 24, 1912–July 30, 2002 Nuclear physicist; contributed to the development of both the military and civilian uses of atomic energy; in 1941, earned his Ph.D. degree in physical chemistry at the University of Chicago with a thesis titled "The Angular Distribution of Recoil Nuclei, with Notes on the Deuteron Hydrogen-Three Reaction"; that same year, became a research associate in the metallurgical laboratory set up at the University of Chicago for the purpose of producing plutonium for the Manhattan Project, the U.S. government's top-secret program for developing the first atomic bomb; from 1943 to 1946, was a senior physicist at the Manhattan Project's Clinton Laboratories, in Oak Ridge, Tennessee; during that period, helped to organize the Federation of Atomic Scientists for the purpose of creating, as he said, "a realization of the dangers that this nation and all civilization will face if the tremendous destructive potential of nuclear energy is misused"; at the Atomic Energy Commission's Brookhaven National Laboratory, in Upton, New York, from 1946 and 1951, directed the construction and initial operation of a graphite research reactor, larger and more powerful than any previous nuclear reactor and the first to be dedicated to peaceful applications, including the production of a radioactive iodine for the treatment of thyroid cancer; in 1951, became professor of physics at the University of Utah; at the university, was chief designer of a nuclear reactor (similar to the Los Alamos model) for teaching and research purposes; applying his knowledge of nuclear science to an explanation of supernovae, theorized, in an article published in 1952, that the spectacular stellar explosions are triggered by beryllium 7 (a radioactive isotope that occurs on Earth only when created in a nuclear reactor), formed by a fusion of two lightweight (helium) nuclei after a giant star has exhausted its hydrogen supply; led a team of researchers at the University of Utah in designing a nuclear-powered railroad locomotive that would be "technically feasible to construct"; in 1954, made public that design, along with a 55-page feasibility study; also taught at New York University and the State University of New York at Buffalo; died in Williamsville, New York. See *Current Biography* (July) 1954.

Obituary *New York Times* A p13 Aug. 12, 2002

**BOSCH, JUAN** June 30, 1909–Nov. 1, 2001 Former president of the Dominican Republic; author; a politically engaged non-Communist progressive intellectual; founder of the Pardido Revolucionario Dominicano (in 1939) and the Pardido de la Liberacion Dominicana (in 1975); running on a ticket that appealed to farm and factory workers in December 1962, was elected president in his country's first free elections in 38 years; was inaugurated in February 1963 and ousted in a right-wing coup seven months later; as a young man, studied literature at college in Santo Domingo; in 1933, published his first book, *Camino Real* (1933), a collection of short stories; subsequently published *Indios* (1935), an anthology of Indian legends, and *La Mañosa*; appalled by the massacre of some 15,000 Haitian squatters by order of General Rafael Leónidas Trujillo, dictator of the Dominican Republic since 1930, left the country in 1937; in exile, traveled widely throughout Latin America while making Cuba his base; for a time, taught at the Institute of Political Science in Costa Rica; fled Cuba when the right-wing dictator Fulgencio Batista seized power there, in 1952; returned when Fidel Castro overthrew Batista, in 1959; left again a year later when it seemed to him that Castro was embracing international communism; while in exile, published two more collections of short stories, books on Simón Bolivar and the Dominican man of letters Eugenio Maria de Hostos y Bonilla, and *Trujillo* (1959), an exposé of the tyranny in the Dominican Republic; returned to the Dominican Republic following the assassination of Trujillo, in 1961; in his presidential campaign, promised economic diversification, jobs for the unemployed, land (formerly owned by the Trujillo family) for the landless campesinos, worker ownership of some businesses, improved housing, new schools, hospitals, homes for the aged, better housing, and higher living standards; following his overthrow, went into exile in Puerto Rico; in April 1965, when military followers of his staged an uprising in Santo Domingo and invited him to return to the Dominican Republic and the presidency, was warned not to do so at that time by U.S. president Lyndon B. Johnson, who sent 22,000 Marines to occupy Santo Domingo while a provisional government was formed and new elections were planned; returned to the Dominican Republic to contest the elections held in June 1966; lost to Joaquin Balaguer, as he would time after time over the following years; allied with Balaguer to make it possible for Leonel Fernández, the Pardido de la Liberacion Dominicana candidate, to succeed Balaguer in the presidency in 1996; in his middle and later years published, among other books, the one translated as *Pentagonism, A Substitute for Imperialism* (1968), *Breve Historia de la Oligarquia* (1971), and two collections of his writings in exile; died in Santo Domingo. See *Current Biography* (June) 1963.

Obituary *New York Times* D p9 Nov. 2, 2001

**BROWN, CLAUDE** Feb. 23, 1937–Feb. 2, 2002 Author of the American classic *Manchild in the Promised Land* (1965), a compelling quasi-memoir, narrated with an authentic voice in frank street language, based on his own coming of age as the son of former southern sharecroppers in the black ghetto of New York City's Harlem; there, found himself engulfed in an ethos dictating that a "manchild" must fight to survive; after expulsion from elementary school, at age eight, joined a street gang and went on to spend time in reformatories; encouraged by Ernest Papanek, a psychologist who directed the Wiltwyck School for deprived and emotionally disturbed boys, returned to school, earned a high-school diploma, in 1957, and received a B.A. degree in government and business at Howard University, in 1965; meanwhile, again with Papanek's support, had written and published *Manchild*, an instant sensation, controversial in some middle-class black circles, that became required reading in many secondary schools and colleges; during his lifetime, saw the book realize sales of more than four million copies in 14 languages; after the publication of the book, studied law at Stanford and Rutgers universities and essayed an abortive career in politics; settled in Newark, New Jersey, but continued to spend much time in Harlem; was concerned with the drug epidemics among black youth, including that of heroin in the 1970s, the subject of his second book, *The Children of Ham* (1976), and later that of crack cocaine, the subject of magazine articles he published; died in Manhattan. See *Current Biography* (November) 1967.

Obituary *New York Times* B p8 Feb. 6, 2002

**BROWN, J. CARTER** Oct. 8, 1934–June 18, 2002 Art impresario: director of the National Gallery of Art in Washington, D.C. (1969–92); chairman of the U.S. Commission of Fine Arts (1971–2002); "the pope of public art"; America's "unofficial minister of culture"; "probably the defining museum director of his generation"; was the scion of the wealthy, blue-blooded Rhode Island family that gave Brown University its name; after receiving his B.A. degree at Harvard University, earned graduate degrees at the Harvard Graduate School of Business Administration and New York University's Institute of Fine Arts and studied at several European universities; in his study of art history, specialized in Dutch 17th-century landscapes; joined the staff of the National Gallery as assistant to the director in 1961; as director, transformed the gallery from a respectable repository of old-master paintings into a world-class art museum rivaling the Metropolitan Museum of Art, in New York City, as a grand national showcase of comprehensive and well-balanced collections; persuaded Congress to increase the annual federal funding of the gallery from $3.2 million to $52.3 million; was instrumental in raising the gallery's endowment from $34 million to $186 million; oversaw construction of the gallery's vast East Building, a milestone in museum architecture designed (by I. M. Pei) for the most part to accommodate blockbuster loan shows and the consequent increased attendance by the public; helped launch the era of such shows with such opulent exhibitions as *Treasures of Tutankhamen*, *Art in the Age of Exploration*, and *Treasure Houses of Britain*; as chair of the U.S. Commission of Fine Arts, "had a profound influence on the way the city [of Washington] looks," as Richard Moe, president of the National Trust for Historic Preservation, observed; oversaw the development of numerous monuments and architectural attractions, including the Vietnam Veterans Memorial (the construction of which he pursued undaunted by the opposition of many in the House of Representatives, the Senate, and the White House); after leaving the National Gallery, helped found Ovation, the arts cable-television network; died in Boston, Massachusetts. See *Current Biography* (April) 1976.

Obituary *New York Times* p1+ June 19, 2002

**BROWN, JESSE** Mar. 27, 1944–Aug. 15, 2002 U.S. Secretary of Veterans Affairs (1993–97); one of four blacks in the original Cabinet of President Bill Clinton; in 1963, enlisted in the U.S. Marine Corps; in combat in Vietnam in 1965, suffered a wound that shattered his right arm and left it partially paralyzed; in 1967, joined the Chicago staff of Disabled American Veterans (DAV); in 1973, was promoted to supervisor of national service in the DAV's headquarters in Washington, D.C.; in 1976, was named head of the DAV's National Appeals Office; served as executive director of the DAV from 1988 until he joined President Clinton's Cabinet five years later; as secretary of veterans affairs, effectively worked for an increase in the Veterans Administration's share of federal expenditures and for expansion of benefits for Vietnam veterans who had been prisoners of war, exposed to Agent Orange, radiation, or mustard gas, or were suffering post-traumatic stress syndrome; pushed progress in Veterans Administration (V.A.) research into the causes of puzzling diseases among Gulf War veterans; focused more V.A. attention on the medical problems of female veterans and veterans' children with ailments related to parental military service; after resigning his Cabinet post, in July 1997, formed Brown & Associates, a planning and marketing firm; at that time, was in rapidly declining health, suffering from amyotropic lateral sclerosis, or Lou Gehrig's disease, and lower motor syndrome, which attacks nerve cells in the brain and the spinal cord; died in Warrenton. See *Current Biography* (November) 1993.

Obituary *New York Times* A p12 Aug. 17, 2002

**BRYANT, C. FARRIS** July 26, 1914–Mar. 1, 2002 Democratic governor of Florida (1961–65) during that state's difficult transition from a Jim Crow society to one embracing civil rights; lawyer; began practicing law in Ocala, Florida, in 1938; was a navy gunnery officer in several Pacific combat areas during World War II; before his election as governor, served five consecutive two-year terms in the Florida House of Representatives; was speaker of the Florida House during the 1953–54 session; was elected governor in 1960 on a pro-segregation platform calling for "states rights," at least for the time being; said, "The less said about segregation, the better"; as governor, presided rather quietly as the state of Florida swiftly desegregated its public schools and public accommodations; was credited with promoting the quintupling of the size of Cape Canaveral, with vastly expanding the state's highway system (abetting tourism) and higher-education system (including high-tech programs to prepare workers for jobs with NASA), with establishing increases in state water-control programs and acreage for conservation and recreation, and with persuading the Walt Disney Co. to consider a Florida location for what would become Disney World and other Disney enterprises; was limited by state law to one term as governor; after leaving office, joined the administration of President Lyndon B. Johnson as the director of the federal Office of Emergency Planning and a member of the National Security Council, in 1966; from 1967 to 1969, chaired the U.S. Commission on Intergovernmental Relations; practiced law and ran an insurance company in Jacksonville until his retirement, in 1986; to the end, believed that racial equality should be pursued "by changing the minds of white people, not by forcing them to do something by taking their property away from them"; died in Jacksonville, Florida. See *Current Biography* (September) 1961.

Obituary *New York Times* B p8 Mar. 6, 2002

**BURGESS, CARTER L.** Dec. 31, 1916–Aug. 18, 2002 Business executive; U.S. government official; as an army officer in Europe during World War II, was aide-de-camp to General Walter Bedell Smith and secretary of the general staff of Supreme Headquarters, Allied Expeditionary Forces; as a U.S. State Department aide, participated in the founding conference of the United Nations, in San Francisco in 1945; over the following nine years, held a succession of positions in the private sector, including director of administration of the General Aniline and Film Corp., assistant to the president of the University of South Carolina, and executive vice president of the Citadel Insurance Co.; meanwhile, intermittently, was a consultant on personnel and staff organization to the federal government; served as assistant secretary of defense for manpower and personnel from September 1954 to December 1956; was president of Trans World Airlines from January 1957 to January 1958; later, was president of American Machine and Foundry; briefly (1968–69), was U.S. ambassador to Argentina; subsequently, chaired the National Corp. for Housing Partnerships; was chairman of the Foreign Policy Association from 1971 through 1981 and president for part of that time; died in Roanoke, Virginia. See *Current Biography* (April) 1957.

Obituary *New York Times* C p17 Aug. 21, 2002

**CANNON, HOWARD W.** Jan. 26, 1912–Mar. 6, 2002 Democratic U.S. senator from Nevada (1959–83); following service as a transport-plane pilot with the U.S. Army Air Forces in World War II, practiced law in Las Vegas and served four terms as Las Vegas city attorney; in the U.S. Senate, became a ranking member of the armed services and rules committees and chairman of the commerce, science, and transportation committee; voted to end a filibuster by southern Democrats attempting to block passage of the Civil Rights Act of 1964, a move that set him apart from traditional senators from Nevada, who wished to keep the filibuster option open for themselves, for use in the eventuality of legislation proposing federal regulation of gaming, a major industry in Nevada; sponsored legislation authorizing the expenditure of hundreds of millions of federal dollars for airport construction projects; was a chief sponsor of the Airline Deregulation Act of 1978; also helped to draft legislation deregulating the trucking industry; lost his campaign for election to a fifth Senate term in 1982, under the cloud of a scandal in which Roy L. Williams, president of the Teamsters Union, and several of his associates were accused, and ultimately convicted, of offering Cannon a bribe to use his influence to block a trucking deregulation bill; was not himself indicted; remained in Washington, D.C., as a consultant for Northrup Grumman and other aircraft manufacturers until 1995. See *Current Biography* (February) 1960.

Obituary *New York Times* A p29 Mar. 7, 2002

**CASTLE, BARBARA** Oct. 6, 1911–May 3, 2002 British Socialist; the second most influential woman in politics in the United Kingdom in the 20th century, after Margaret Thatcher; was elected a member of Parliament for Blackburn in Lancashire in 1945, in the landslide victory of the Labour Party in the first election following the end of World War II; held numerous portfolios in the Labour governments of Prime Minister Harold Wilson in the 1960s and the mid-1970s; acquired her last name through her marriage to Ted Castle, a political journalist; joined the Labour Party in 1927; after earning a B.A. degree at Oxford University in the early 1930s, became involved in journalism and left-wing politics in London; with the journalist and Socialist leader Michael Foot, wrote a column on trade unionism for *Tribune*, a Socialist League weekly financed largely by Sir Stafford Cripps, a radical Socialist member of Parliament who was expelled from the Labour Party in 1939 for advocating an alliance with the Communists and who was readmitted to the party in 1945; as a Member of Parliament (M.P.) during Clement Atlee's Labour government (1945–51), contributed to her party's implementation of its agenda, including the establishment of a National Health Service and a comprehensive welfare system, the nationalization of gas and electric utilities, ports, railways, and such industries as coal and steel, and the beginning of the dismantling of the British empire; in addition to her work as an M.P., served as parliamentary private secretary to the president of the board of trade under Atlee, a position filled successively by Stafford Cripps (1945–47) and Harold Wilson (1947–51); in 1950, was elected to the Labour Party's national executive committee, a position she would hold for 19 years; retained her seat in Parliament during 13 years of Labour eclipse (1951–64), when the Conservative Party triumphed in three successive elections and the Labour Party was torn between its moderates and its radical wing, headed by Aneurin Bevan, of whom Castle was a close disciple; after Labour returned to power in 1964, served in Harold Wilson's first two cabinets (1964–70) as, successively, minister of overseas development, minister of transport, and secretary of state for employment and productivity; in the last-named post, first promoted legislation calling for equal pay for women; next, sought to end "indecision and anarchy" in industrial relations; in 1969, issued a white paper, "In Place of Strife," in which she proposed a conciliation pause before the calling of a strike, better negotiating procedures, and the possible invocation of "penal powers"; with that document, drew the wrath of Britain's trade unions and lost her chances for higher office; earlier, as minister of transport, had introduced Breathalyzer testing for suspected drunk drivers; following four years of Tory rule, became secretary of state for social services in Wilson's third government (1974–76); tied pensions to the rate of inflation; ruled that new child allowances could be paid directly to the mother and not necessarily through the paycheck of the father; although an opponent of European federalism, served as an elected member of the European Parliament from 1979 until her retirement, in 1989; wrote the autobiography *Fighting All the Way* (1993), the dual biography of two pioneer feminists, *Sylvia and Christabel Pankhurst* (1987), and a slim Fabian Society tract on the National Health Service, *NHS Revisited* (1976); published two thick volumes of *The Castle Diaries* (1980 and 1984), covering her eight years as a cabinet minister; in 1990, was ennobled as Baroness Castle of Blackburn; died at her home in Buckinghamshire. See *Current Biography* (January) 1967.

Obituary *New York Times* A p11 May 4, 2002

**CELA, CAMILO JOSÉ** May 11, 1916–Jan. 17, 2002 Spanish novelist; the literary leader of the post–civil war generation in Spain; was especially acclaimed for his powerful first novel, *La familia de Pascual Duarte* (1942, translated as *The Family of Pascual Duarte*), probably the most widely read and translated Spanish work of fiction after Cervantes' *Don Quixote*; was awarded the 1989 Nobel Prize in literature with a citation calling attention to his "rich and intense prose, which with restrained compassion forms a challenging vision of man's vulnerability"; with stunning, often grotesque realism (*tremendismo*), innovative use of language, and experimental techniques, combined with poetic lyricism, presented a dark view of human nature and society, focused on corruption, brutality, and hypocrisy; although understandably regarded in left-leaning Spanish literary circles as a Franco sympathizer, was not so regarded by the Franco dictatorship, at least in the beginning, when his descriptions of the material and spiritual privations suffered by ordinary Spaniards were seen by authorities, correctly, as implicit accusations against the violence of the civil war and the repressive policies of the Franco government; prevented from publishing *La familia de Pascual Duarte* in Spain, found a publisher in Argentina; in the antihero Pascual Duarte (an ignorant peasant in a squalid village in the Extremadura region of Spain, who compulsively perpetrates gratuitous murders), presented an example of a pathology produced by familial and wider social forces; subsequently, published *Pabellon de reposo* (1943, *Rest Home)*, in which the characters are agonized consumptives in a tuberculosis sanatorium; later wrote such novels as *La colmena* (1951, *The Hive*), about the prostitutes, petty crooks, and other habitués of a sordid Madrid café, *Mrs. Caldwell habla con su hijo* (1953, *Mrs. Caldwell Speaks to Her Son*), a surrealistic study in incestuous desire, *San Camilo, 1936* (1968), an erotic and scatological work that opens with a list of Madrid brothels in 1936, and *Mazurca para dos muertos* (1983; *Mazurka for Two Dead Men*, 1992), set in Cela's native Galicia at the time of the civil war; in addition to 14 novels, published 60 other volumes, including collections of short stories, essays, and poetry and quasi-fictional travel books in which he explored and described Spain region by region; died in Madrid, Spain. See *Current Biography* (June) 1990.

Obituary *New York Times* C p15 Jan. 18, 2002

**CHILLIDA, EDUARDO** Jan. 10, 1924–Aug. 19, 2002 Spanish artist; a Basque sculptor of monumental cubist-like abstract "meditations in space," many of which were constructed in or designed for installation in public places or natural landscapes, including hilltops in the Basque countryside; viewed his sculptures as a kind of architecture that has been freed of practical considerations; attempted to "sculpt empty space, provoking the vacuum and embracing the horizon"; said that his work had to do with gravity, that it embodied "the great battle that goes on in the vertical plane, between the forces that push up and those that press down"; after graduating from the Colegio Marianistas in his native San Sebastian in the Basque province of Guipúzcoa, studied architecture at the University of Madrid for several years (1942–46) before turning to art, beginning with drawing; in 1948, moved to Paris, where he began sculpting the human figure in clay and plaster; after returning to the Basque country in 1950, turned from the figurative to an abstract style and from clay and plaster to iron; learned the craft of the forge from a local blacksmith; in 1951, hammered out at his forge the relatively small geometrical shape *Ilarik*, inspired by Basque grave slabs; between 1952 and 1956, executed larger works in forged iron generally characterized by jagged shafts that forcefully curve or angle out into space to form a kind of hollow-centered cage; in 1952 and 1953, created *Wind Comb*, the first in a series of giant "comb" sculptures with prongs designed to interact with the wind; in

1954, made the iron doors of the new Franciscan basilica in the Basque town of Aranzazu; in *Resounding Spaces I* (1954), *Music of the Constellations* (1954), the *Tremor of Iron* series (1955–57),and *Place of Silences* (1958), related sculptural volume to musical sound; between 1954 and 1966, worked on a series of 17 pieces titled *Anvil of Dreams*, in which he used wood as a base from which metal forms rise up in explosive, rhythmic curves; used wood as a medium in itself in his *Abesti Gogora* series (1960–64); added steel to his repertoire of materials in some of the pieces in his *Rumor of Limits* series (1956–59); eventually worked primarily in steel, with occasional ventures into clay, porcelain, alabaster, marble, concrete, terra cotta, and granite; in 1966, completed *Abesti Gogora V*, a 50-ton sculpture hewn from granite that stands in the garden of the Houston Museum of Fine Arts; in 1969, executed the steel sculpture *About Emptiness* for the World Bank building in Washington, D.C.; during the 1970s, created the three steel Wind Combs that are attached to rocks overlooking the sea near his home in San Sebastian; in 1992, created the Monument to Tolerance in Seville, Spain; over the years, constructed monuments in Paris, Frankfurt, Barcelona, Seville, and Basle, among other cities; for the German chancellory in Berlin in 2000, created *Berlin*, a metal structure suggesting two giant meshed hands commemorating German reunification; in September 2000, participated in the inauguration of the Chillida da-Leku open-air museum in Hernani, near San Sebastian; was represented in major art galleries and museums in Europe and the U.S.; installed some of his finest work in the Guggenheim Museum in Bilbao, Spain; in addition to sculpture, did abstract graphic work resembling Japanese calligraphy in etchings, lithographs, woodcuts, and brush and black ink; while espousing the cause of Basque political and linguistic autonomy, opposed the terrorist tactics of the Basque separatist organization Euzkadi Ta Askatasuna (ETA, Basque Fatherland and Liberty), and promoted the search for peace; died in San Sebastian. See *Current Biography* (September) 1985.

Obituary *New York Times* A p21 Aug. 22, 2002

**CLOONEY, ROSEMARY** May 23, 1928–June 29, 2002 Vocalist; actress; a versatile pop singer who broke into stardom with her recordings of novelty songs but who was more at home with pensive ballads; rendered the range of pop standards with sureness, simplicity, and faithfulness to their composers (including George and Ira Gershwin, Cole Porter, Richard Rodgers and Lorenz Hart, and Johnny Mercer) ; sang "from the heart," as Billie Holiday observed; was credited by Frank Sinatra with "that great talent which exudes warmth and feeling in every song she sings"; as a teenager, sang with her sister Betty on a Cincinnati radio station; toured the U.S. with Tony Pastor's orchestra from 1945 to 1949; in 1946, made her first solo recording, "I'm Sorry I Didn't Say I'm Sorry When I Made You Cry Last Night"; came to the attention of Mitch Miller, the A&R (artists and repertory) manager at Columbia Records, when she performed on the television show *Songs for Sale* in 1950; recorded a number of children's songs; first registered on the charts with the folk song "Beautiful Brown Eyes"; in 1951, hit the top of the charts and remained there for six weeks with the novelty song "Come On-a My House," which sold more than a million records; subsequently, recorded the novelties "Botch-a-Me," "This Old House," and "Mambo Italiano" and such gentler hits as "Half as Much," "Tenderly," and "Hey There"; in 1956, recorded "Memories of You" with the Benny Goodman Trio and the album *Blue Rose* with Duke Ellington and his orchestra; subsequently, recorded the albums *Ring Around Rosie* (1957), *Clap Hands! Here Comes Rosie* (1960), *Rosie Solves the Swingin' Riddle!* (1961), and, with Bing Crosby, *Fancy Meeting You Here* (1958) and *That Travelin' Two Beat* (1964); as her 14-year marriage (1953–67) to José Ferrer deteriorated, sought escape in an ill-starred affair with Nelson Riddle, the orchestra leader and arranger, and in sleeping pills and alcohol; suffered a nervous breakdown on the day in 1968 when she witnessed firsthand the assassination of her friend Robert F. Kennedy by Sirhan Sirhan; after hospitalization and therapy, returned slowly to her career, doing weekend gigs in lounges in Holiday Inns; in the mid-1970s, toured with Bing Crosby, and also with Margaret Whiting, Helen O'Connell, and Rose Marie in a musical production called *4 Girls 4*: in 1977, released what she called "the debut album of my new career," *Everything's Coming Up Rosie*, and an album of songs by Paul Simon and James Taylor, *Nice to Be Around*; between 1977 and 1989, recorded some half-dozen albums that were tributes to the composers Harold Arlen, Irving Berlin, and Jimmy Van Heusen, among others; recorded duets with Keith Carridine, k.d. lang, and Linda Ronstadt; in 1990, toured in a Christmas show with the Minnesota Symphony Orchestra and many members of her family, including Debby Boone, her daughter-in-law; performed in several motion pictures, most prominently as one of the stars of the musical *White Christmas* (1954); on television, hosted the musical variety program *The Lux Show Starring Rosemary Clooney* (1957–58), was a guest on numerous TV shows, and during the 1990s was nominated for an Emmy Award for her performance in a role in the TV dramatic series *ER*, in which George Clooney, her nephew, was a featured player; in recent years, recorded on the Concord Jazz label; was booked regularly with small pop-jazz groups on concert stages and in upscale cabarets; toured internationally with the pianist/singer Michael Feinstein in 2001; early in 2002, was nominated for a Grammy Award for her album *Sentimental Journey* and was honored with a lifetime-achievement Grammy; wrote the autobiography *This For Remembrance* (1977), which was made into the television movie *Escape from Madness* (1982); published a sequel memoir, *Girl Singer*, in 1999; died at her home in Beverly Hills, California; was survived by her second husband, Dante DiPaolo, five children (all by José Ferrer), 10 grandchildren, and one of her two sisters, Gail Clooney Darley. See *Current Biography* (February) 1957.

Obituary *New York Times* B p7 July 1, 2002

**COLBERT, EDWIN H.** Sep. 28, 1905–Nov. 15, 2001 Paleontologist; the scientist largely responsible for arousing the interest of his peers and the public in the study of the dinosaurs and their relatives; at Columbia University in 1930, received his M.A. degree and began his five years of work for his Ph.D. degree in vertebrate paleontology; during that year, began his long association with the American Museum of Natural History in New York City, as research assistant to the great paleontologist Henry Fairfield Osborn; became assistant curator of fossil reptiles and amphibians at the museum in 1933; over the following dozen years, rose to the positions of curator and chairman of the Department of Vertebrate Paleontology, which he held until 1970; concurrently, was professor of vertebrate paleontology at Columbia University, beginning in 1945; at the American Museum of Natural History, installed the Brontosaur Hall and mounted exhibitions introducing visitors to early fossil reptiles and amphibians; did field work on all seven continents, but preferred doing digs in the American West and Southwest; in New Mexico in 1947, discovered a number of complete skeletons of the Coelophysis dinosaur, a predecessor of the Brontosaurus; in Arizona in 1955, took part in the excavation of fossils of the Tritylodont, a creature considered a significant link in the evolution of reptiles to amphibians; in 1969 in Antarctica, participated in the discovery and identification of a fossil of Lystrosaurus, a nonswimming mammal, an event that helped strengthen the theory of continental drift; after his retirement from the American Museum of Natural History, was honorary curator of vertebrate paleontology at the Museum of Northern Arizona for 30 years; wrote 17 books, including *The Dinosaur Book* (1945) and the classic textbook *Colbert's Evolution of the Vertebrates: A History of the Backboned Animals Through Time* (fifth edition, 2001); died at his home in Flagstaff, Arizona. See *Current Biography* (September) 1965.

Obituary *New York Times* A p47 Nov. 25, 2001

**DAVIS, BENJAMIN O. JR.** Dec. 18, 1912–July 4, 2002 The first African-American general in the history of the U.S. Air Force; was the son of the U.S. Army's first black general, Benjamin O. Davis Sr.; majored in mathematics at the University of Chicago for two years before entering the U.S. Military Academy at West Point; after graduating from West Point, in 1936, attended the army's infantry school at Fort Benning, Georgia; in 1938, became an instructor in military science and tactics at the Tuskegee Institute, in Alabama; in March 1942, three months after the U.S. entered World War II, won his wings as the first of the "Tuskegee Airmen," trained at the Tuskegee Army Air Field; in the spring and summer of 1943, was commanding officer of the 99th Pursuit Squadron in the North African, Sicilian, and Italian campaigns; in 1944 and 1945, commanded the 332d fighter group, which escorted bombers on 200 combat missions over Europe; lost not a single bomber; after the war, commanded army air force groups in the U.S.; after the air force was made a separate military service, in 1947, became a planning officer in the Pentagon; in 1948, when President Harry S. Truman signed an executive order desegregating the armed forces, helped to draft the blueprint for the racial integration of the air force that went into effect the following year; later, was successively director of the Far East Air Forces, with headquarters in Tokyo, vice commander of the Thirteenth Air Force, based in the Philippines, commander of the Air Task Force based in Taipei, and deputy commander in chief of the U.S. Strike Command; after retiring from the military, in 1970, briefly served as director of public safety in Cleveland, Ohio; subsequently, spent five years with the U.S. Department of Transportation, directing federal efforts to bolster security at airports, counter air-cargo theft, and combat airliner hijacking; supervised the sky-marshal program; died at Walter Reed Army Medical Center in Washington, D.C. See *Current Biography* (September) 1955.

Obituary *New York Times* p25 July 7, 2002

**DeCARLO, DAN** Dec. 12, 1919–Dec. 18, 2001 Cartoonist; known for his work at Archie Comics for more than four decades; with the U.S. Army during World War II, did drafting and art work with the 8th Air Force, including the painting of pin-ups on fighter planes, a useful preparation for his later, more modest "good girl" art; after the war, worked for several years as an artist on the staff of Timely Comics; there, created such cartoon characters as Millie the Model and Sherry the Showgirl; subsequently, did freelance assignments for D.C. Comics and other companies, including Archie Comics, where he contributed to the comic strip that Bob Montana had originated in 1941, depicting the adventures and misadventures of the amiable teenager Archie Andrews, his pals Jughead, Reggie, and Moose, and his girlfriends Betty and Veronica; brought his own, modernizing style to the strip, increasingly after he became a full-time member of the Archie Comics staff, in 1957; was principally responsible for the comic book *Betty & Veronica*; during the 1960s, created a new teenage-themed Archie Comics comic book, *Josie and the Pussycats*, about three female musicians, which was spun off into two animated television series in the early 1970s; co-created the comic-book series *Sabrina, the Teenage Witch*; became chief artist at Archie Comics when Bob Montana died, in 1975; was fired by Archie Comics in May 2000, after he sued the company, unsuccessfully, for a share in the motion-picture rights to *Josie*; ended his career working for Matt Groening, creator of the animated television situation comedy *The Simpsons*; died in New Rochelle, New York. See *Current Biography* (August) 2001.

Obituary *New York Times* A p40 Dec. 23, 2001

**DONOVAN, CARRIE** Mar. 22, 1928–Nov. 12, 2001 Fashion journalist; began her career working in the hat department at Saks Fifth Avenue in New York City; after studying dressmaking at Parsons School of Design, worked as a designer on Seventh Avenue, Manhattan's garment district; in 1955, joined the *New York Times* as a fashion reporter; was promoted to associate fashion editor; in 1963, left the *Times* to became an editor at *Vogue* magazine, where she profited from the mentorship of Diana Vreeland; moved on to *Harper's Bazaar* as senior fashion editor and then to a vice presidency at Bloomingdale's department store before returning to the *Times* in 1977 as the style editor of the newspaper's Sunday magazine; after retiring as the style editor of the *New York*

*Times Magazine*, in 1993, remained with the newspaper two more years as editor of the women's edition of *Fashions of the Times*, a Sunday supplement appearing several times a year; in 1997 became spokeswoman for the retail clothing chain Old Navy, an offshoot of the higher-priced chain the Gap; lent her quirky image, a combination of elegance and flamboyance (captured in an Al Hirschfeld caricature of her wearing her outsized glasses) to newspaper and taxicab ads touting T-shirts, cargo pants, and other fashion basics at affordable prices; also appeared in 42 television commercials, accompanied by a dog named Magic; died in Manhattan. See *Current Biography* (September) 1999.

Obituary *New York Times* C p18 Nov. 13, 2001

**ELIZABETH, QUEEN MOTHER OF GREAT BRITAIN** Aug. 4, 1900–Mar. 30, 2002 Queen Consort of the late King George VI; mother of Queen Elizabeth II; was Lady Elizabeth Angela Marguerite Bowes-Lyon before her marriage in 1923 to Prince Albert, Duke of York, the future king; as the Duchess of York, gave birth to Elizabeth, the future queen, in 1926 and a second daughter, Margaret Rose, in 1930; became Queen Consort when her husband became King George VI in 1936, following the abdication of his older brother, King Edward VIII; was a source of great strength to her husband, a naturally timid man with a severe stammer, in his assumption of royal responsibilities; similarly, helped bolster the courage of Londoners by her decision to remain in the city in solidarity with them during the Blitz, the intense wartime bombing of the city by the German Luftwaffe between August 1940 and June 1941; remained Queen Consort until 1952, when George VI died and was succeeded on the throne by Elizabeth II; died in the Royal Lodge at Windsor Palace, Berkshire, England; was predeceased (by seven weeks) by her daughter Princess Margaret Rose. See *Current Biography* (August) 1981.

Obituary *New York Times* p1+ Mar. 31, 2002

**FARRELL, EILEEN** Feb. 13, 1920–Mar. 23, 2002 Singer; a leading dramatic soprano with a vibrant voice as large as her pretensions were small; was one of three children of vaudeville performers billed as "The Singing O'Farrells"; never approached pop and jazz with less love and respect than classical song; saw herself first as "an ordinary person," a Staten Island homemaker (married to a New York City policeman) and mother; began her career as a popular singer on radio; when she arrived, rather belatedly, on the opera stage, created a sensation, along with exasperation among some at her rejection of prima-donna posturings; received vocal training in New York under Merle Alcock and Eleanor McLellon; joined CBS radio as a member of choruses and ensembles in 1940; the following year, began filling solo singing assignments on CBS broadcasts; on the CBS half-hour show *Eileen Farrell Sings* in the mid-1940s, had the opportunity to sing operatic arias and art songs as well as popular favorites; in 1947 and 1948, made her first concert tour of the U.S.; in 1949, toured South America; made her television debut on the *Milton Berle Show* in 1950; in later years, appeared often on the variety shows of Garry Moore and Carol Burnett, among others, as a chat guest, singer, and sketch performer; initiated a long association with the New York Philharmonic Symphony Orchestra with 61 appearances during the 1950–51 season; in opera excerpts performed by the Philharmonic, sang a passionate Isolde and a majestic Brünnhilde, roles she was never to perform on the operatic stage, to the disappointment of Wagner buffs; provided the voice for Eleanor Parker in the role of the Australian opera singer Marjorie Lawrence in the feature-film biography *Interrupted Melody* (1955); during the 1950s, appeared regularly with the Bach Aria Group; sang her first Italian opera role, Medea, in a concert staged by the American Opera Society at Town Hall in 1955; made her debut in a fully staged opera production as Santuzza in *Cavalleria Rusticana* in Tampa, Florida, in 1956; later in the same year, made her debut with the San Francisco Opera in *Il Trovatore*; with éclat, opened the 1959–60 San Francisco season in the title role in the first American production of *Medea*; performed at the Spoletto Festival in Italy in 1959; recorded the crossover album *I've Got a Right to Sing the Blues* (1960); made her Metropolitan Opera debut in the title role in Gluck's *Alceste* in 1960; over the next five seasons at the Met, sang Gioconda, Leonora in *La forza del destino*, Maddalena in *Andrea Chenier*, and Rezia in Weber's *Oberon*; with the tenor Jess Thomas in 1970, gave a celebrated performance of excerpts from *Tristan und Isolde* that has been issued on compact disc; from 1971 to 1980, taught at Indiana University while continuing to give concerts; announced her retirement after the death of her husband, in 1986; continued to make recordings for several more years; with Brian Kellow, wrote the autobiography *Can't Help Singing* (1999); died at a nursing home in Park Ridge, New Jersey. See *Current Biography* (February) 1961.

Obituary *New York Times* B p7 Mar. 25, 2002

**FLANAGAN, TOMMY** Mar. 16, 1930–Nov. 16, 2001 Jazz pianist; an inventive and elegant stylist; was perhaps the premier exponent of the single-note, gracefully improvised line, a style rooted in bebop; over his long career, and especially in his maturity, developed arrangements of increasing authority and fire from his immense repertoire of standards, jazz classics, and his own compositions, including "Beyond the Bluebird"—creations of almost classical balance, alive with melodic thrusts, unexpected accents, and spontaneous associations; said that he "tried to give a song a reading from my soul"; when growing up in one of Detroit's oldest African-American neighborhoods, taught himself to play the clarinet before studying piano, formally in the classical tradition and informally by listening to the recordings of the likes of Nat "King" Cole and Art Tatum; was especially influenced by the fluid and witty bebop pianism of Bud Powell; by his mid-teens, was jamming at the Bluebird Inn on Detroit's west side with such local talent as the instrumentalists Elvin, Hank, and Thad Jones and the singer Betty Carter and such celebrated visitors as Charlie Parker and Miles Davis; in 1953, joined the guitarist Kenny Burrell's combo in Detroit; with Burrell, moved to New York City in February 1956; within weeks, was participating in gigs at Town Hall and Birdland and doing his first recording sessions, as sideman with Burrell, Thad Jones, Oscar Pettiford, Billy Mitchell, Sonny Rollins, and others; in 1957, made his recording debut as leader of his first trio, with the LP *Tommy Flanagan Overseas*; in 1958, led his trio in an engagement at the Manhattan jazz club the Composer; for two decades, however, would be best known as an accompanist with the singer Tony Bennett, as a sideman with J. J. Johnson, Coleman Hawkins, John Coltrane, Freddie Hubbard, Dexter Gordon, and others, and above all as pianist and musical director with the singer Ella Fitzgerald and her band; signaled the beginning of his emergence from the shadow of others with the album *The Tommy Flanagan Tokyo Recital* (1975), featuring the music of Duke Ellington and Billy Strayhorn; subsequently, recorded the solo LP *Alone Too Long* (1977) and the trio recording *Eclypso* (1977); struck out fully on his own as a concert and recording soloist, duo player, and trio leader in 1978; during the 1980s, recorded such albums as *The Magnificent Tommy Flanagan*, *Thelonica* (a tribute to Thelonious Monk), *Nights at the Vanguard*, and *Jazz Poet*; during the 1990s, recorded *Sunset and the Mockingbird*, *Flanagan's Shenanigans*, *Let's Play the Music of Thad Jones*, and *Lady Be Good . . . for Ella*, among other albums; as soloist, duo player, or leader of his trio (including Peter Washington on bass and Lewis Nash on drums), performed before huge audiences at such events as the Newport and Montreux jazz festivals and before small audiences in such intimate settings as Bradley's, the popular Manhattan duo room; played four weeks a year at the Village Vanguard; died in Manhattan. See *Current Biography* (April) 1975.

Obituary *New York Times* F p7 Nov. 20, 2001

**FRANKENHEIMER, JOHN** Feb. 19, 1930–July 6, 2002 Film and television director; after helping to create television's golden age of live drama, took his inventive techniques, including a fluid camera and rapid cutting, to the making of motion pictures, most memorably political thrillers with a satiric edge, including his masterpiece, *The Manchurian Candidate* (1962), a nightmarish adaptation of Richard Condon's novel about a Communist-inspired plot to subvert the U.S. government through a Korean War hero programmed (when he was a prisoner of war) to become an assassin; in his own words, "always seemed attracted to material that deals with characters who aren't what they seem to be"; joined the Williams Theater Group as an English major at Williams College; while earning his B.A. degree, began acting and directing as a member of the summer stock company at Highland Playhouse in Falmouth, Massachusetts; gained experience in the making of documentary films while serving with a photographic unit of the U.S. Air Force in Burbank, California, from 1951 to 1953; upon his military discharge, joined CBS-TV, the flagship station of the CBS television network in New York City; became increasingly interested in reality-based material as assistant director of the CBS network shows *Person to Person* and *You Are There*; at CBS, found a mentor in the producer Martin Manulis; when Manulis moved to Hollywood to produce high-quality television dramas in 1954, moved with him; between 1954 and 1960, directed (sometimes back in New York) at least 127 television plays (presented live on CBS's *Playhouse 90* and *DuPont Show of the Month* and NBC's *Sunday Showcase*), including *The Comedians* (which won an Emmy Award), *The Days of Wine and Roses*, *The Browning Version*, *The Turn of the Screw*, and *For Whom the Bell Tolls*; was displeased with the recutting of his first motion picture, *The Young Stranger* (1957), a sensitive study of the lack of understanding between an adolescent boy and his father; shot his second motion picture, the detective thriller and courtroom melodrama *The Young Savages* (1961), on location in Spanish Harlem; scored a commercial success with *Birdman of Alcatraz* (1962), an adaptation of Thomas E. Gaddis's biography of Robert F. Stroud, the convicted murderer who became an expert on the diseases of birds while incarcerated in solitary confinement for 43 years, and a critical success with *All Fall Down* (1962), an adaptation of James Leo Herlihy's novel of conflict in a middle-class family; followed up *The Manchurian Candidate* with another gripping film of political intrigue, *Seven Days in May* (1964), about a Pentagon junta plotting a coup; subsequently, directed *The Train* (1964), *Seconds* (1966), *Grand Prix* (1966), and *The Fixer* (1968); meanwhile, was grappling with personal problems, including alcoholism (which he eventually overcame); was overwhelmed by the assassination of his friend Robert F. Kennedy in 1968; had driven Kennedy to the Ambassador Hotel in Los Angeles on the day that Kennedy was shot to death there; worked in semi-eclipse in Europe for several years; regained critical favor when he returned to the U.S. and directed *The Iceman Cometh* (1973); had a box-office hit with *Black Sunday* (1977), about a plot by international terrorists to blow up the Super Bowl by crashing a television airship into the stadium; following a string of disappointing formula action movies, found a new lease on career in cable television, beginning with the Home Box Office production *Against the Wall* (1994), a dramatization of the 1971 Attica (New York) prison riot; won an Emmy for that production and for the subsequent cable docudramas *The Burning Season* (HBO, 1994), *Andersonville* (TNT, 1996), and *George Wallace* (TNT, 1997); in his last cable-television project, directed *Path to War* (HBO, 2002), about President Lyndon B. Johnson's decision to escalate the war in Vietnam; was not proud of having been the replacement director of the egregiously grotesque motion picture *The Island of Dr. Moreau* (1996); died in Los Angeles, California. See *Current Biography* (October) 1964.

Obituary *New York Times* A p1+ July 8, 2002

**GARDNER, JOHN W.** Oct. 8, 1912–Feb. 16. 2002 Psychologist; nonpartisan political activist; professor of public service at Stanford University since 1989; author; a progressive Republican who headed the Carnegie Foundation, served as secretary of Health, Education, and Welfare in the Cabinet of Democratic president Lyndon B. Johnson, and founded the citizen-action organization Common Cause, a Washington, D.C.–based public-interest lobby concerned with "systemic" reform—making government accessible, accountable, and responsive—as well as "substantive" issues; led Common Cause in vanguard efforts in the contemporary movements for consumer protection, political campaign-finance reform, public financing of presidential elections, suffrage for 18-year-olds, and congressional reforms, including a renovation of the House seniority system and legislation affecting ethics, conflict of interest, financial disclosures, open hearings on bills, and restrictions on lobbyists; after earning his B.A. and M.A. degrees in psychology at Stanford University, took his Ph.D. at the University of California at Berkeley, in 1938, with a dissertation titled "Levels of Aspiration"; taught briefly at two women's colleges; during World War II, served in two intelligence posts; with the FCC, analyzed Axis radio propaganda beamed to South America; as a Marine Corps officer with the OSS (predecessor of the CIA), was involved in the assessing, processing, and assigning of recruits; in 1946, joined the Carnegie Corp.; as acting president of the corporation (in the early 1950s) and as president of that corporation as well as the Carnegie Foundation for the Advancement of Teaching (1955–65), dispensed millions of dollars each year in grants for seminal projects in educational reform nationally and internationally; as a member of President Johnson's Cabinet (1965–68), set up the White House Fellows program and played a major role in the founding of Medicare, among other "Great Society" programs; also in 1968, became chairman of the National Urban Coalition, an organization financed by businesses in an effort to address the problems contributing to the deterioration of urban America; soon realized that "the instruments you have to use to solve these problems, the instruments of self-government, were themselves in need of repair"; in 1970, launched Common Cause with a mammoth direct mail and advertising campaign aimed at the "middle 80 percent" of the American people who simply want to do something effective for their country at a time when "their parties are in decay, their states aren't working right, and their men in Washington aren't doing their job"; attracted a long-term dues-paying membership of some 200,000; led Common Cause until 1977, when he founded Independent Sector, a coalition of educational, religious, and other institutions; wrote *Excellence; Can We Be Equal and Excellent Too?* (1961), *Self-Renewal: The Individual and Innovative Society* (1963), *The Recovery of Confidence* (1970), *In Common Cause* (1972), *Toward a Pluralistic but Coherent Society* (1980), and *On Leadership* (1990), among other books; died at his home on the Stanford campus in Palo Alto, California. See *Current Biography* (March) 1976.

Obituary *New York Times* B p6 Feb. 18, 2002

**GORTON, JOHN GREY** Sep. 8, 1911–May 19, 2002 Prime minister of Australia (1968–71); a rugged individualist; the first Australian prime minister to vote himself out of office; in the misleadingly named Liberal Party, was much more liberal than the party's conservative mainstream was at that time, not only on social issues but also in political philosophy; promoted a nationalistic Australia, distinct from a British identity and not dependent on foreign capital; thus helped launch what would become, largely under Labor Party leadership, a strong republican movement; as a fighter pilot with the Royal Australian Air Force during World War II, crashed near Singapore in 1942, suffering severe wounds, some of which left his face mangled, even after plastic surgery; running on the Liberal ticket from the state of Victoria, was elected to the federal senate, the upper house of the Australian legislature, in 1949, effective 1950; in 1958, was appointed to the first of a succession of cabinet posts; in 1966, became a member of the policy-making inner cabinet when Prime Minister Harold E. Holt appointed him minister of education and science; in 1967, became government leader of the senate; following the death of Holt, in December 1967, and the interim prime ministership of John McEwen, was elected leader of the majority Liberal Party and, ipso facto, prime minister; with some ambivalence, maintained Australia's association with the U.S. military expedition in Vietnam; encouraged a distinctively Australian cultural expression with a generous program of subsidies for the arts, including filmmaking; was responsible for raises in pensions and easing of the means test; as a protectionist, opposed the free-trade preferences of the treasury; supported such governmental intervention in the private sector as the Australian Investment Development Corp.; alienated a large number of his conservative colleagues not only with his Labor-like policies (including central government trumping of states' rights), but also with his "dangerous reluctance" to consult the cabinet and his "obstinate determination to get his own way," as Malcolm Fraser told Parliament after resigning as defense minister; requested from his party in Parliament a vote of confidence, which took place on March 10, 1971; with the vote tied at 33–33, cast his own vote in favor of "no confidence"; became deputy Liberal leader and defense minister under Prime Minister William McMahon despite a visceral antipathy to McMahon; was dismissed five months later, following the publication of a series of controversial newspaper articles by him; was knighted in 1977; in his later years, enjoyed belated respect from a Liberal Party that had come to appreciate his early anticipation of changing public sentiment; died in Sydney, Australia. See *Current Biography* (July) 1968.

Obituary *New York Times* B p7 May 22, 2002

**GOULD, STEPHEN JAY** Sep. 10, 1941–May 20, 2002 Paleontologist; university professor; writer; a macro-evolutionary reinterpreter of Darwin; reinvigorated the Darwinian debate with his lively and engaging presentation of the concept that evolution is not a gradual and unswerving one-lane process of natural selection but, in the paraphrase of his colleague Richard Lewontin, "a multiform process" in which "different things are happening"; was on a par with the astronomer Carl Sagan as one of modern science's most stimulating and accessible lecturers and writers; as a monthly columnist for *Natural History* magazine from 1974 to 2001, wrote 300 essays, sparkling with puckish wit and analogical insights relating to his other fields of interest (chiefly choir music, church architecture, and baseball), in which he made paleontology understandable to the lay reader without condescension or intellectual compromise;

dreamed "of becoming a scientist, in general, and a paleontologist, in particular, ever since the Tyrannosaurus skeleton awed and scared" him when, as a child, he first visited the American Museum of Natural History, in New York City; after receiving his B.A. degree in geology, at Antioch College, earned his Ph.D. degree at Columbia University with a dissertation on the fossil land snails of Bermuda; following a year as a teacher of geology at Antioch College, joined the faculty of Harvard University as assistant professor of geology, in 1967; became full professor in 1973; taught courses in biology and the history of science as well as geology; was curator of invertebrate paleontology at Harvard's Museum of Comparative Zoology; became Alexander Agassiz Professor of Zoology in 1981; for many years, devoted most of his fieldwork to fossil land snails in the West Indies, regularly contributing studies on their evolution and speciation to scientific journals; with the biologist David F. Woodruff, visited the Bahamas periodically throughout the 1970s, studying and reclassifying the genus Cerion, drastically reducing its number of species; later did broader studies of animal form and function and the relationship between ontogeny and phylogeny; with fellow paleontologist Niles Eldredge, sought to explain the discontinuities ("missing links") in the fossil record; became a center of controversy among evolutionists when, in 1972, he and Eldredge published the seminal paper "Punctuated Equilibria: an Alternative to Phyletic Gradualism," proposing the theory that species differentiation may occur not in a gradual, steady process of evolution but in a separate process, in relatively sudden (albeit in prolonged geological time) fits and starts; amplified that theory in a second paper, "Punctuated Equilibra: the Tempo and Mode of Evolution Reconsidered," in 1977; that same year, published the essay "The Episodic Nature of Evolutionary Change," in which he explained that he did "not assert the general 'truth' of this philosophy of punctuational change" but was making "a simple plea for pluralism in guiding philosophies"; sought to mollify his Darwinian antagonists (chiefly microevolutionists) for the sake of a common front against the promotion of creation science in public-school curricula, which he fiercely fought; believed human evolution to be "a fortuitous cosmic afterthought"; in *Ontogeny and Phylogeny* (1977), addressed to a scientific readership his detailed analysis of, and concerns about, the theory of recapitulation—the hypothesis that the stages of embryonic development of an individual organism repeat in order those that had occurred in the history of its lineage—a theory that flourished in the 19th century, when some evolutionary biologists used it to argue for their racial and ethnic prejudices; concerned about the resurgence of biological determinism, concentrated in his book *The Mismeasurement of Man* (1981) on what he perceived to be the prejudiced misuse of the Binet intelligence tests; published the collections of essays *Ever Since Darwin: Reflections on Natural History* (1977), *Panda's Thumb* (1980), *Hen's Teeth and Horse's Toes* (1983), *The Flamingo's Smile* (1985), *An Urchin in the Storm: Essays about Books and Ideas* (1987), *Bully for Brontosaurus* (1991), *Eight Little Piggies* (1993), *Dinosaur in a Haystack* (1995), *Leonardo's Mountain of Clams and the Diet of Worms* (1998), *The Living Stones of Marrakech: Penultimate Reflections on Natural History* (2000), and *I Have Landed: The End of a Beginning in Natural History* (2002); also wrote *Time's Arrow, Time's Cycle: Myth and Metaphor in the Discovery of Geological Times* (1987), *Wonderful Life: The Burgess Shale and the Nature of History* (1989), *Rocks of Ages: Science and Religion in the Fullness of Life* (1999), and *Questioning the Millennium: A Rationalist's Guide to a Precisely Arbitrary Countdown* (1999); in March 2002 published his magnum opus, *The Structure of Evolutionary Theory*, a 1,484-page book in which he comprehensively explained his attempt to modify and synthesize Darwinian theory; died at his home in the SoHo section of Manhattan. See *Current Biography* (September) 1982.

Obituary *New York Times* p1+ May 21, 2002

**GRIGG, JOHN** Apr. 15, 1924–Dec. 31, 2001 British journalist; author; was a son of Ned Grigg, the first Lord Altrincham (a title John inherited in 1955 and renounced in 1963), who was private secretary to Prime Minister David Lloyd George and, later, colonial governor of Kenya; in 1948, became associate editor of the *National and English Review*, a Conservative journal of opinion that had been bought by his father; succeeding his father, was editor and publisher of the magazine from 1954 until it ceased publication in 1960; converted it from a voice of unreconstructed imperialism and upper-class consciousness to the organ of an enlightened new kind of Toryism in line with contemporary realities and his own "radical temperament"; urged Britain to reject the primacy of "national interests" and set an example of prudence and decency in its international conduct; in home affairs, attacked class distinctions and sought the reform of elite prep schools based on such distinctions; as a loyal monarchist, offered the Crown what he felt was constructive criticism; pointed out that the queen was shut off from the great mass of her subjects, partly because of a royal court unrepresentative of British society; created a national uproar when he described Queen Elizabeth's speaking style as "a pain in the neck" and compared her public personality to "that of a priggish schoolgirl"; subsequently, became a regular columnist for the *Guardian* newspaper; later wrote for the London *Times* newspaper and the *Spectator* magazine; switched from the Conservative to the Social Democratic Party in 1982; wrote, among other books, a biography of Nancy Astor (his godmother) and a volume critical of Winston Churchill's D-Day strategy in World War II; to the series *The History of the Times*, contributed volume six, *The Thomson Years, 1966–1981* (1993); left as his greatest literary legacy a monumental biography of David Lloyd George, three volumes of which were published between 1973 and 1985; was completing the fourth and final volume when he was taken ill in November 2001; died in London. See *Current Biography* (October) 1964.

Obituary *New York Times* p37 Jan. 20, 2002, (London) *Independent* p6 Jan. 8, 2002

**HALASZ, LASZLO** June 6, 1905–Oct. 26, 2001 Hungarian-born music director; first director of the New York City Opera; studied piano and conducting at the Royal Academy of Music in Budapest; made his debut as a piano soloist with the Budapest Philharmonic Society in 1928; concertized in Hungary, Czechoslovakia, and Romania until 1931, when he decided to concentrate solely on conducting; was assistant conductor of the Royal Hungarian Opera from 1928 to 1930 and conductor of the Prague Opera from 1930 to 1932; toured Europe as music director of the Sakharoff Ballet in 1932; conducted the Vienna Volksoper from 1933 to 1936; during that same period, fulfilled conducting engagements with the Budapest Opera, at the Salzburg Festival, and elsewhere; in 1936, at the invitation of Arturo Toscanini, came to the U.S. to assist Toscanini in conducting the NBC Symphony Orchestra; through Toscanini, obtained a job as chorus master of the St. Louis Opera Company; when that company was reorganized as the St. Louis Grand Opera, in 1939, was appointed its artistic and music director; arrived at the New York City Opera in 1943, in time to plan the season that opened in February 1944; given a shoestring budget, assembled his troupe not on a star system but, rather, a repertory system, in which all leading singers were paid alike; cast singers who fit their roles visually as well as vocally; offered a launching platform for the careers of such singers as Jennie Tourel, Martha Lipton, Regina Resnik, Dorothy Kirsten, Hugh Thompson, Francis Bible, Mark Harrell, Todd Duncan, and Robert McFerrin, who later became the first black singer to join the roster of the Metropolitan Opera; offered a varied and often adventurous repertoire, ranging from the likes of *Tosca*, *Carmen*, *La Bohème*, *Rigoletto*, *The Barber of Seville*, and *Ariadne auf Naxos* (in its American premiere) to *The Flying Dutchman*, *Martha*, *The Gypsy Baron*, and the world premiere of William Grant Still's *Troubled Island* (with libretto by Langston Hughes); strove for at least one production in English every season; with his scheduling of the world premiere of David Tamkin's *The Dybbuk*, ignited a dispute over choice of repertoire with the City Opera's board; also became involved in a union dispute; was fired by the board in 1951; subsequently was a pioneering producer of opera, symphony, and other stereo recordings for Remington Records; conducted opera at various houses in Europe and South America; taught at the Peabody Conservatory, in Baltimore, Maryland, and the Eastman School of Music, in Rochester, New York; developed a music curriculum for the State University of New York at Old Westbury, Long Island; died at his home in Port Washington, New York. See *Current Biography* (January) 1949.

Obituary *New York Times* C p19 Oct. 31, 2001

**HAMPTON, LIONEL** Apr. 20, 1908–Aug. 31, 2002 Musician; band leader; the last of the giants of the big band era; "Vibes President of the United States"; with his ebullient mastery of the vibraphone (which he called the vibraharp), established the legitimacy of that instrument in jazz and swing music; acquired what he called "the beat in me" as a child attending a Holiness church while temporarily living with his grandmother in Birmingham, Alabama; learned to play the drums, xylophone, and piano while attending Roman Catholic parochial schools in Chicago, Illinois, and Kenosha, Wisconsin, and a music school for boys sponsored by the *Chicago Defender*, a black newspaper; in 1927, moved to Los Angeles to play drums with the band of Les Hite, a friend of his grandmother's; in a recording studio in Culver City, California, one day in 1930, came across his first vibraphone, a xylophone with an electric resonator that gives it a distinctive vibrato and a bell-like tone; later that day, played the instrument for the first time on a now famous recording of "Memories of You" by the Hite band, with Louis Armstrong "fronting"; also recorded with Paul Howard's Quality Serenaders, in 1929; from 1936 to 1940, was a member of the Benny Goodman Quartet (the first racially mixed ensemble to work regularly in public), alongside Goodman, Gene Krupa, and Teddy Wilson; directed the quartet's recording sessions, out of which came such memorable performances as "Dinah," "Exactly Like You," "Moonglow," and "My Last Affair"; also in the late 1930s, recorded with some pickup bands he organized, which included the likes of Benny Carter, Dizzy Gillespie, and Coleman Hawkins; in 1940, formed the first Lionel Hampton orchestra, a 30-member aggregation that, over the years, boasted the presence of such luminaries as Charles Mingus, Quincy Jones, Illinois Jacquet, Charlie Parker, Dexter Gordon, and Dinah Washington; with that talent, and his swinging showmanship and dervish-like energy, generated excitement in audiences and pandemonium on dance floors from Harlem to Back Bay Boston society gatherings; propelled his orchestra to the top of the crowded list of big bands, where it remained for years after most of the other bands dissolved; with his orchestra, registered such hits as "Down Home Jump," "Hamp's Boogie Woogie," "Hey! Ba-Ba-Re-Bop," "Central Avenue Breakdown," and "Glad Hamp"; in 1942, cut one of the 20th century's most influential recordings, a precursor of rock and roll: the single "Flying Home," on which Illinois Jacquet's tenor sax solo pulsates over a shrill brass section and a hard rhythm backbeat; subsequently, recorded such albums as *Steppin' Out* (1944), *The Original Stardust* (1947), *The Blues Ain't News to Me* (1955), and *You Better Know It* (1964); beginning in the 1950s, made numerous goodwill tours of foreign countries under the sponsorship of the U.S. Department of State; in 1965, pared down his orchestra to a combo-sized group called the Inner Circle, which included, at various times, six to eight men; recorded *Reunion at Newport* in 1967; with James Haskins, wrote the autobiography *Hamp* (1975); in 1978, recorded live performances at Carnegie Hall and in Emmen, Holland; in 1991, recorded two albums of live performances at the Blue Note in Manhattan; during the 1990s, led the Golden Men of Jazz (including Clark Terry, James Moody, Al Grey, and Harry "Sweets" Edison) in recording sessions; on stage, often moved from vibes to drums to piano; dazzled audiences with his raw bluesy riffs; in private life, was conservative and frugal; owned a record company and several blocks of real estate in Harlem, where he developed the Gladys Hampton Houses, a low-income complex named for his wife of 34 years, who died in 1971; while favoring the Republican Party (which, in his view, approached the black community "without ballyhoo"), was honored and welcomed to the White House by Democratic presidents; played at a succession of presidential inaugurations, beginning with that of Harry S. Truman; promoted the teaching of the black musical heritage in colleges and universities; set up music scholarships; died in Manhattan. See *Current Biography* (October)1971.

Obituary *New York Times* p1+ Sep. 1, 2002

**HARRISON, GEORGE** Feb. 25, 1943–Nov. 29, 2001 Musician; singer; songwriter; the youngest member and the lead guitarist of the Beatles, the mop-haired British foursome (including the guitarists John Lennon and Paul McCartney and the drummer Ringo Starr) who took the world of rock music by storm in the 1960s; was "the quiet Beatle," a spiritual searcher known for the meditative serenity and beauty of such of his songs as "Something" and "While My Guitar Gently Weeps"; was also capable of creating such upbeat anthems as "Here Comes the Sun" and the incisive political wit of his composition "Taxman"; in the early 1970s, following the breakup of the Beatles, recorded solo albums on his own label, Dark Horse; in his native Liverpool, England, in 1956, met McCartney, a slightly older teenager, with whom he shared an interest in the guitar and the recordings of such American rhythm-and-blues and rock-and-roll musicians as Carl Perkins, Duane Eddy, Chet Atkins, Eddie Cochran, and Buddy Holly; in 1958, was introduced by McCartney to the older Lennon, founder of the local rock group the Quarry Men, of which McCartney was a member; the following year, was inducted by Lennon into the Quarry Men, the name of which was changed to the Beatles in 1960; sang lead on the Lennon-McCartney composition "Do You Want to Know a Secret?" on the Beatles' debut album, *Please Please Me*; made his songwriting debut with "Don't Bother Me," on the group's second LP, *With the Beatles* (1963), and was featured in the Beatles' first motion picture, *A Hard Day's Night* (1964); on subsequent Beatles' albums, was represented as a composer with "I Need You," "You Like Me Too Much," and "If I Needed Someone"; in the mid-1960s, immersed himself in Eastern music and spirituality; in India, studied the sitar, a lute-like Hindustani instrument, under Ravi Shankar; became a devotee of the Maharishi Mahesh Yogi, a leading exponent of transcendental meditation and the founder of the Spiritual Regeneration Movement; introduced the sitar to Western rock music in a recording of the John Lennon song "Norwegian Wood" late in 1965; subsequently composed for the sitar the songs "Love You To," "Within You, Without You," "Blue Jay Way," and "The Inner Light"; returned to the guitar in 1968; in November 1970, released his solo magnum opus, the triple album *All Things Must Pass*, which generated the hit singles "My Sweet Lord" and "What Is Life"; among subsequent releases, struck gold with his album *Living in the Material World* (1973) and had hit singles in "Give Me Love (Give Me Peace on Earth)" (1973), "You" (1976), "All Those Years Ago" (1981), and his cover of Rudy Clark's "Got My Mind Set on You" (1987); on *Best of Dark Horse 1976–1989*, included the hit singles "Crackerbox Palace" and "Blow Away"; collaborated on musical projects with Eric Clapton and others; with Bob Dylan and others, recorded two *Traveling Wilburys* albums (1988 and 1990); organized two widely acclaimed benefit concerts to raise money to help feed starving people in Bangladesh; under the aegis of his company Homemade Films, produced such motion pictures as *Life of Brian* (1979) and *Privates on Parade* (1984); wrote the autobiography *I Me Mine* (1980); was married twice; died in Los Angeles. See *Current Biography* (January) 1989.

Obituary *New York Times* p1+ Dec. 1, 2001

**HASKINS, CARYL P.** Aug. 12, 1908–Oct. 8, 2001 Research scientist; administrator; an interdisciplinary authority, in areas ranging from entomology to art; from 1956 to 1971, was president of the private, nonprofit Carnegie Institution in Washington, D.C., dedicated to free-ranging investigations in the physical and biological sciences (including plant biology, genetics, and embryology), astronomy, and archaeology; earned a bachelor's degree in chemistry at Yale University, in 1930, and a doctorate in physiology at Harvard University, in 1935; between 1933 and 1944, was a research associate in physics, biology, and public health at the Massachusetts Institute of Technology; from 1937 to 1955, was a research professor in biophysics at Union College, in Schenectady, New York; founded and headed (1935–55) Haskins Laboratories Inc., a nonprofit educational institution for training and research in speech and hearing, cancer biology, nutrition, and genetics, among other fields; at Haskins Labs during World War II, worked on the rehabilitation of men who had been blinded in combat; from 1939 to 1955, headed an acquisition of Haskins Labs, the National Photocolor Corp.; as president of the Carnegie Institution, oversaw the facility's work at the Mount Wilson and Palomar observatories and its acquisition of 100 square miles in the Andes Mountains and its building there of another astronomical observatory; published the books *Of Ants and Men* (1939), *The Amazon: The Life History of a Mighty River* (1943), *Of Societies and Men* (1951), *The Scientific Revolution and World Politics* (1964), and the collection of essays *This Our Golden Age* (1994); died in Westport, Connecticut. See *Current Biography* (February) 1958.

Obituary *New York Times* A p11 Oct. 13, 2001

**HECKART, EILEEN** Mar. 29, 1919–Dec. 31, 2001 Actress; a tall woman with a distinctive gravelly voice and pearly smile who skillfully played a variety of character roles in comedy and drama on stage, screen, and television; won Emmy Awards for her roles in the 1966 PBS television productions *Save Me a Place at Forest Lawn* and *The Effect of Gamma Rays on Man-in-the-Moon Marigolds*; received the Academy Award for best supporting actress for her performance as the domineering mother of the blind young man in the motion picture *Butterflies Are Free* (1972), a role she had created on stage in 1969; in the year 2000, was awarded a special Tony Award for her lifetime work in the theater; began acting Off-Broadway in 1942; toured with *Janie* in 1944 and

*Windy Hill* in 1945; was subsequently cast in pre-Broadway productions of *Burlesque* and *The Stars Weep*; created her first Broadway role as Nell Bromley in *Hilda Crane* in January 1950; achieved prominence on Broadway three seasons later, as the despondent spinster schoolteacher Rosemary Sidney in *Picnic*; during the 1954–55 Broadway season, won the Donaldson Award (for best actress in a straight play) for her performance as Mrs. Daigle, the grief-stricken mother of the murdered boy in *The Bad Seed* (a role she would reprise in the 1956 motion picture); subsequently had roles in two plays by Arthur Miller, Beatrice in *A View from the Bridge* and Agnes in *A Memory of Two Mondays*; in 1957–58, again impressed Broadway audiences and critics with her portrayal of Aunt Lottie Lacey in *The Dark at the Top of the Stairs*; created the role of the disapproving mother of one of the newlyweds in *Barefoot in the Park* on Broadway in 1965; toured as Eleanor Roosevelt in the one-woman show *Eleanor* in 1976; during television's "golden age" of live drama, was cast in numerous productions on the *Philco Television Playhouse*, the *Kraft Television Theatre*, the *Alcoa Hour*, *Studio One*, the *Goodyear Playhouse*, *Playhouse 90*, and *Suspense*; later on television, played Mary Richards's Aunt Flo in the long-running situation comedy *The Mary Tyler Moore Show*, Eleanor Roosevelt in the miniseries *Backstairs at the White House* (1979), and the mother of the Mary Tyler Moore character in the abortive series *Annie McGuire* (1988); made her motion-picture debut in a supporting role in *Miracle in the Rain* (1956); subsequently, was seen on screen as the prizefighter's mother in *Somebody Up There Likes Me* (1956) and the waitress friend of the Marilyn Monroe character in *Bus Stop* (1956); returned to the stage in *Eleemosynary* (1989); in her last stage appearance, in 2000, played the leading role of Gladys Green, a woman with Alzheimer's disease, in *The Waverly Gallery*; died at her home in Norwalk, Connecticut. See *Current Biography* (June) 1958.

Obituary *New York Times* B p10 Jan. 2, 2002

**HEYERDAHL, THOR** Oct. 6, 1914–Apr. 18, 2002 Norwegian ethnologist; anthropologist; archaeologist; explorer; challenged, as he said, "a lot of old dogmas," including the scientific establishment's view of the ocean as "a barrrier" to cultural diffusion in antiquity; "proved," in his words, "that all the ancient pre-European civilizations could have intercommunicated across oceans with the primitive vessels they had at their disposal"; did so, to his satisfaction, through a combination of archaeological evidence and dramatic seafaring demonstrations, the most famous of which was his voyage across the Pacific aboard the raft *Kon-Tiki*; was a highly readable writer of books chronicling his voyages, including the international best-seller *Kon-Tiki* (1948; American translation, 1950); won an Academy Award for the documentary feature film *Kon Tiki* (1951); after studying zoology and geography at the University of Oslo, lived on the island of Fatu Hiva in the Marqueses for a year (1936–37); surmised that the earliest settlers of Polynesia could have come, not necessarily from Southeast Asia, as the accepted theory had it, but possibly from the Americas; became firm in that conviction two years later, when he did fieldwork in British Columbia, where he excavated rock carvings similar to Polynesian artifacts, and Peru, where he traced a legend related to that of the Polynesian mythological hero Tiki: the story of Viracocha, originally known as Kon-Tiki Viracocha, the leader of a race of tall, fair-skinned, fair-haired people who dominated the aboriginal Indian tribes of pre-Inca Peru until abut 500 A.D., when most of them were massacred at Lake Titicaca; learned that, according to Peruvian Indian legends, at the time of the massacre Kon-Tiki and some of his followers escaped by sea, apparently propelled southwestward across the Pacific by prevailing winds and currents; after serving with the Free Norwegian armed forces in World War II, returned to Peru to supervise the construction of a replica of the most seaworthy of the water craft known to have been used by pre-Inca South American Indians, a 45-foot balsa-log raft with sails that he named the *Kon-Tiki*; with five companions, was set adrift at Callao, Peru, on April 28, 1947; propelled southwestward by sea currents and the southeast trade wind, traveled 4,300 miles , arriving at Raroia, a coral reef near Tahiti in the Tuamotu Archipelago, in French Polynesia, after 101 days at sea; bolstered proof of his hypothesis with pre-Spanish archaeological data and ethnographic art and botanical findings garnered in an expedition to the Galápagos Islands in 1953; did field research on Easter Island in 1955–56; in one direction, saw a connection between the giant statues on Easter Island and stone carvings in Peru; in another, saw a connection between pharaonic Egypt and the Inca stepped pyramids, illustrations on pottery shards, and other pre-Columbian artifacts in Peru, as well as the reed boats still in use on Lake Titicaca (in Peru and Bolivia); set out to demonstrate the possibility of ancient intercontinental migration from Egypt to the Americas; in Egypt in 1969, oversaw the construction of a primitive-style boat made of bundles of papyrus reeds, the *Ra*; transported the *Ra* to Safi, Morocco, whence he sailed for Barbados; terminated that voyage when the vessel became waterlogged 600 miles short of its destination; successfully made the entire 3,263 voyage to Barbados in *Ra II* in 1970; in 1977, sailed the Indian Ocean in another reed vessel, the *Tigris*; later researched the art and archaeology of pre-Columbian Cuba; in addition to the accounts of his first year in Polynesia and his voyages and reports on his archaeological digs, published *American Indians in the Pacific* (1952), a comprehensive tome, and *Early Man and the Ocean* (1978); in addition to documentary films of the *Kon Tiki* and *Ra* expeditions, narrated the biographical film/video *Thor Heyerdahl: Explorer and Scientist* (1977), which includes footage of his adventures; fiercely campaigned against pollution of the world's oceans, especially by petroleum waste; championed world federalism; married his third wife, Jacqueline Beer, in 1996; lived with her chiefly in the Canary Islands; died at a residence she owned in the Mediterranean village of Alassio, Italy. See *Current Biography* (September) 1972.

Obituary *New York Times* A p25 Apr. 19, 2002

**HEYM, STEFAN** Apr. 10, 1913–Dec. 17, 2001 Bilingual German novelist; political observer; an idealistic Marxist-Leninist who was never fully at home on either side of the Iron Curtain during the Cold War; wrote more than a dozen novels, including *Ahasver* (1981, translated into English as *The Wandering Jew*, 1984), in which "the eternal Jew" Ahasver and the fallen archangel Lucifer conduct a survey of German history and conclude that the devil has rightful claim to the German Democratic Republic, or Communist East Germany, of which Heym was a citizen at the time; was the son of a Jewish textile manufacturer in Chemnitz, Germany; when Hitler assumed power, in 1933, fled to Czechoslovakia; there, became a regular contributor to Communist periodicals published in Prague and Moscow; in 1935, through the instrumentality of a Jewish fraternity at the University of Chicago, obtained a scholarship to that school; after earning an M.A. degree in Chicago, moved to New York City, where he became editor of the left-wing German-language weekly *Deutsches Volksecho*, in which he wrote exposés of the infiltration of Nazi agents in the U.S. and supported the Hitler-Stalin pact of 1939; was a member of the Communist Party U.S.A. for three years (1936–39); in New York in 1942, published his first novel, *Hostages*, a thriller about the underground opposition to the Nazi occupation of Czechoslovakia that was made into a motion picture in 1943; during the final years of World War II, served with a psychological-warfare unit of the U.S. Army in Europe; in Munich following the defeat of Germany, was one of the founding editors of *Neue Zeitung*, the first American Occupation Zone newspaper; after returning to the U.S., published *The Crusaders* (1948), a World War II novel; presented a sympathetic view of the 1948 Soviet takeover of Czechoslovakia in his third novel, *The Eyes of Reason*, published in London in 1951; to avert a possible confrontation with the Communist-hunting Un-American Affairs Committee of the U.S. House of Representatives, left the U.S. in 1951; with his first wife, settled in East Germany; renounced his American citizenship (which he had acquired in 1943); as a columnist for *Berliner Zeitung* in the 1950s, was a propagandist for the German Democratic Republic and for international Stalinism; wrote apologias justifying the brutal crushing by Soviet armored columns of a demonstration by construction workers in East Germany in 1953 and the popular uprising against the Communist regime in Hungary in 1956; however, because he increasingly insisted on holding communism to its utopian promises, was never entirely in accord with party orthodoxy and fell totally from grace with the East German regime in the early 1960s; while continuing to live in East Germany, was more respected in West Germany, where he appeared regularly on television and published his novels; attacked Stalinist-style socialism in *Die Architekten* (The Architects, 1968) and *Collin* (1979); in the guise of a biblical story, dealt with the censorship of truth and the rewriting of history under a dictatorship in *The King David Report* (1972; *Der Koenig David Bericht*, 1979); later published *Radek* (1995) and *Goldsborough* (1998), among other novels; in addition to his novels, published an autobiography, *Nachruf* (Obituary, 1988), collections of essays and short stories, and a book of fairy tales for children; used one of his short stories, "Auf Sand gebaut" (1990), as the vehicle of an argument against German reunification; wanted "a new, better socialism" in East Germany; in 1994, four years after the unification of Germany, was elected to the German Parliament as a representative of the Democratic Socialist Party, a regrouping of ex-Communists; died while on a lecture tour in Israel. See *Current Biography* (March) 1943.

Obituary *New York Times* C p15 Dec. 18, 2001

**HAILSHAM OF MARYLEBONE, QUINTIN HOGG** Oct. 9, 1907–Oct. 12, 2001 British Conservative politician and statesman; barrister; at the pinnacle of his career, was Lord Chancellor, chief of the British judiciary, in the Tory cabinets of prime ministers Edward Heath (1970–74) and Margaret Thatcher (1979–87); was a son of Douglas McGarel Hogg, 1st Viscount Hailsham; after reading law at Oxford University and taking a first at his final bar examination, was called to the bar in 1932; as a barrister, at first specialized in accident law; was elected to the House of Commons from the Oxford riding in 1938; during World War II, was a lieutenant in the British Army until his discharge, on medical grounds, in 1942; returned to his seat as an M.P.; was appointed undersecretary of state for air in 1945; was reelected to Commons in July 1945 and February 1950; became ineligible to sit in Commons in August 1950, when his father died, making him the 2nd Viscount Hailsham; sought legislation to nullify his succession to the peerage, at that time to no avail; took his seat in the House of Lords in September 1950; was first lord of the Admiralty from September 1956 to January 1957; over the following several years, served first as minister of education and then as Conservative Party chairman; under legislation passed in 1963, was able to relinquish his hereditary peerage; in 1964, was elected to the House of Commons from London's St. Marylebone electoral district; held that seat until he was named a life peer (with the title of Lord Hailsham of St. Marylebone) when appointed Lord Chancellor by Edward Heath; wrote a number of books, including *The Time We Live In* (1944), *The Left Was Never Right* (1946), *Making Peace* (1945), *The Purpose of Parliament* (1946), *The Case for Conservatism* (1947), *Science and Government* (1961), *Hamlyn Revisited: The British Legal System Today* (1983), and books on British arbitration and monopoly law and European Community law; contributed to and edited the 37-volume *Halsbury's Laws of England* (1931–49); wrote a book of memoirs, *A Sparrow's Flight* (1990); died at his home in London. See *Current Biography* (July) 1954.

Obituary *New York Times* D p6 Oct. 16, 2001

**HOYLE, FRED** June 24, 1915–Aug. 20, 2001 British astronomer; cosmologist; author of both science fact and science fiction; ignored the borders between the disciplines, from chemistry and biology to nuclear physics, in his bold explorations outside the beaten astronomical path; led a revolution in astrophysical research that all but ended an uncritical acceptance of cosmological orthodoxy; perhaps more than any of his scientific peers in the pre–Stephen Hawking era, contributed to a profound change in the way we think about the origin and nature of the universe, the chemical formation of its stars, and the age of its galaxies; with his paradigm of an eternal "steady-state" cosmos, without beginning or end, continually contracting and expanding as a "fully self-operating system," challenged the fashionable hypothesis of the "Big Bang" (a term, derisively coined by him, that ironically became standard); in collaboration with N. Chandra Wickramasinghe, began to challenge another hallowed hypothesis, the "primordial soup" theory, when he proposed the carbon (graphite) grain paradigm—now generally accepted—for organic interstellar dust particles; completed that challenge with his and Wickramasinghe's later "panspermia" theories, which hold that interstellar molecules seed life (as well as pathogenic bacteria and viruses) on planets, including Earth; was elected a fellow of St. John's College, Cambridge University, in 1939; following service with the British Admiralty in World War II, became a lecturer in mathematics at Cambridge in 1945; later became a professor of astronomy and experimental philosophy and founder and director of the Institute of Theoretical Astronomy at the university; between 1945 and 1972, pursued his researches at Cambridge in collaboration with, among others, Hermann Rondi, Thomas Gold, and Wickramasinghe; after leaving Cambridge, continued to collaborate with Rondi, Gold, and, especially, Wickramasinghe; also collaborated with Jayant Naeliker, the astrophysicists Geoffrey Burbidge and Virginia Trimble, and the nuclear physicist Willy Fowler; on leave from Cambridge, was appointed to the staff of the Mount Wilson and Palomar observatories in California in 1956; was an honorary research professor at Manchester University (1972–2001) and University College, Cardiff (1975–2001); was equally gifted at communicating with both his scientific colleagues and lay audiences and readers; achieved a popular *succès fou* in 1950 with a series of BBC radio broadcasts that were published that year under the title *The Nature of the Universe*; wrote or co-wrote dozens of books on astronomy, cosmology, and the philosophy of science, including *Nucleosynthesis in Massive Stars and Supernovae* (1964), *Galaxies, Nuclei, and Quasars* (1965), *Man in the Universe* (1966), *From Stonehenge to Modern Cosmology* (1972) and several textbooks; revised his steady-state theory in *A Different Approach to Cosmology* (1999); wrote an autobiography, *Home Is Where the Wind Blows* (1994); published 15 of the strangest science-fiction novels ever written, including *The Black Cloud* (1957), *Fifth Planet* (1959), *Ossian's Ride* (1959), *In Deepest Space* (1974), and the most popular, written with John Eliot, *A for Andromeda* (1962); was knighted in 1972; died in Bournemouth, England. See *Current Biography* (April) 1960.

Obituary *New York Times* C p15 Aug. 22, 2001

**HUNTER, KIM** Nov. 12, 1922–Sep. 11, 2002 Actress; a talented stage, screen, and television performer who, in her words, eschewed "jazzy stardom" in her dedication to "the work itself"; was most closely identified with the role of Stella, the long-suffering wife of brutish Stanley Kowalski (Marlon Brando) in *A Streetcar Named Desire*, which she created on Broadway in 1947 and reprised for the motion-picture screen four years later; won the Academy Award for best supporting actress for her performance in that film; began acting as a student at Miami Beach (Florida) High School; when she was 17, joined a little theater group in Miami; subsequently, acted with stock companies in Hendersonville, North Carolina, and Baltimore, Maryland; was performing in *Arsenic and Old Lace* at the Pasadena (California) Playhouse when she was discovered by a Hollywood talent scout; made her screen debut in the supporting role of a guileless young woman who becomes involved in a New York City Satanic cult in the horror flick *The Seventh Victim* (1943), one of the producer Val Lewton's highly esteemed low-budget pictures; in *Tender Comrade* (1943), written by Dalton Trumbo and directed by Edward Dmytryk, played a member of a group of female World War II defense workers who rent a house and live communally while their husbands are at the war front, a role for which she (along with Dmytryk and Trumbo) would later pay dearly at the hands of some who viewed the movie as Communist propaganda; in *When Strangers Marry* (1944), a superior grade-B movie, played a newlywed who suspects that her husband may be a murderer; co-starred with David Niven in the British film *A Matter of Life and Death* (1946; titled *Stairway to Heaven* in the U.S.), a well-wrought combination of reality and fantasy about an American Wac (Women's Army Corps) wireless operator in communication with an RAF (Royal Air Force) pilot who is in touch with the supernatural; in 1949, helped to sponsor an international peace conference regarded by some as pro-Soviet; on Broadway, followed up her triumph in *A Streetcar Named Desire* with the female leads in *Darkness at Noon* (1951) and *The Chase* (1952); among later stage roles, played Karen in *The Children's Hour*, Sylvia in *The Tender Trap*, and Madame Ranevskaya in *The Cherry Orchard*; back in Hollywood, co-starred with Humphrey Bogart in the newspaper drama *Deadline U.S.A.* (1952) and played Helen in *Anything Can Happen* (1952), an adaptation (described by Leonard Maltin as an "intriguingly awful comedy/propaganda piece") of George and Helen Papashvily's autobiographical 1945 best-seller; by that time, realized that she had been "blacklisted" as a subversive, an alleged Communist fellow traveler, in the right-wing pamphlet *Red Channels*, which then wielded deadly influence in Hollywood; was unable to find any work in motion pictures during a four-year period that ended with a leading role alongside Bette Davis in *Storm Center* (1956); thereafter, worked intermittently in film for 12 years, in roles in *The Young Stranger* (1957), *Lillith* (1964), and *The Swimmer* (1968), among others; interpreted several roles at the Shakespeare Festival Theater in Stratford, Connecticut, in 1961; experienced rejuvenation in her movie career in the role of Dr. Zira, the chimpanzee psychiatrist in *The Planet of the Apes* (1968) and its sequels *Beneath the Planet of the Apes* (1970) and *Escape from the Planet of the Apes* (1971); on television, had hundreds of credits beginning with performances in *Playhouse 90* dramas in the 1950s and including roles in *Rawhide*, *Naked City*, *Dr. Kildare*, *Gunsmoke*, and *Murder, She Wrote*, among other series; had a long-term role on the ABC network soap opera *The Edge of Night* in 1979 and 1980; wrote *Loose in the Kitchen* (1975), an autobiographical cookbook; died in her apartment above the Cherry Lane Theater in Greenwich Village, New York City. See *Current Biography* (May) 1952.

Obituary *New York Times* C p11 Sep. 12, 2002

**JARRING, GUNNAR4** Oct. 12, 1907–May 29, 2002 Swedish diplomat; a multilingual transglobal envoy; United Nations mediator; studied foreign languages at the University of Lund; after receiving his master's degree, was called up for military service; because of his knowledge of Turkish, was assigned to duty as an attaché in Ankara, Turkey; after his discharge from military service, spent about a year traveling in Turkestan and Sinkiang, learning local dialects; back in Sweden, earned a doctorate with a dissertation on East Turkestan phonetics; subsequently, traveled in Kashmir, western China, and Central Asia; was an assistant professor of Turkish at the University of Lund from 1933 until the outbreak of World War II, when Sweden, as a neutral power, had to expand its foreign service to provide so-called intersections for relations between belligerent governments in dozens of world capitals; in his first diplomatic assignment, returned to Ankara as an attaché in 1940; from 1941 to 1945, was chief of the intersection in Tehran; after the war, was chargé d'affaires in both Tehran and Baghdad (1945) and in Addis Ababa (1946–48); in 1948, was sent to New Delhi as envoy to India; served as envoy to Ceylon as well in 1950 and 1951; in the latter year, was shifted to Karachi as envoy to Iran, Iraq, and Pakistan; in Stockholm from 1952 to 1955, was chief of the political section in the foreign ministry; at the U.N., was an adviser to the Swedish delegation (1955–56) and Swedish ambassador and permanent representative (1956–58); in 1957, traveled to Karachi and New Delhi to mediate the dispute between India and Pakistan over Kashmir; was ambassador to the U.S. from 1958 to 1964 and to the Soviet Union from 1964 to 1973; held extensive talks with Arab and Israeli leaders as special envoy to the U.N. secretary general on the Middle East from 1961 to 1967; died in Helsingburg, Sweden. See *Current Biography* (October) 1957.

Obituary *New York Times* p43 June 2, 2002

**JENNINGS, WAYLON** June 15, 1937–Feb. 13, 2002 Singer; songwriter; musician; leader of the band the Waylors; an ornery-looking self-described Texas "hillbilly" who was at the center of the "outlaw" movement in country music and in the vanguard of an alternative country-rock crossover in popular music; proclaimed, "My music ain't no Nashville Sound. It's my kind of country. It's not Western. It's Waylon"; sang in a grittily textured, resonant voice; played his Telecaster guitar in a stuttering fashion, picking at its lower strings; recorded 60 albums, including *Honky Tonk Heroes* (1973), which comprised barroom ballads by Billy Joe Shaver, *Dreaming My Dreams* (1975), which reflected the rowdy, carousing side of Jennings's life, with its accompanying sadness, *Wanted! The Outlaws* (1976), a collaboration with Jessi Colter (the last of his four wives), Willie Nelson, and Tompall Glaser that became the first Nashville-produced album to go platinum, *I've Always Been Crazy* (1978), and *Greatest Hits* (1979), which sold four million copies; had 16 Top10 singles, including "Ladies Love Outlaws," "You Ask Me To," co-written with Billy Joe Shaver, "Good Hearted Woman," co-written with Willie Nelson, and "Mama, Don't Let Your Babies Grow Up to Be Cowboys," a duet with Nelson; received two Grammy Awards and four Country Music Association Awards; began his career in 1958 as bassist with Buddy Holly's seminal rock band, the Crickets; was on tour with the Crickets in the Midwest in February 1959 when Holly and others died in the crash of a small private airplane; escaped being on that plane only by a fluke of fortune (displacement by J. P. "the Big Bopper" Richardson, a musician more prominent than he at the time); was a radio disc jockey in Lubbock, Texas, for two years; played with the hard-beat Waylors in southwestern honky-tonks for several years; entered into a brief, not very successful recording arrangement with A&M Records (owned by Herb Alpert, who, as Jennings unhappily surmised, wanted "to make a pop star" out of him); in 1965, was signed to a recording contract by Chet Atkins, then RCA Records' chief in Nashville, Tennessee, the country-music capital; moved to Nashville in 1966; during that year, recorded the albums *Folk Country*, which included the Jennings original "That's the Chance I'll Have to Take," and *Leavin' Town*, which included "Anita, You're Dreamin'"; starred as the title character in the motion picture *Nashville Rebel* (1966), the soundtrack of which became the album *Nashville Rebel* (1966); interpreted the compositions of Harlan Howard in *Ol' Harlan* (1967); subsequently, recorded, among other albums, *Only the Greatest* (1968), including his first country hit, the catchy, up-tempo "Only Daddy That'll Walk the Line," and *Jewels* (1968), including "Yours Love," which dented even the pop charts; subsequently, turned increasingly away from the standardized, sanitized "Nashville Sound," with its lush strings, to what is called "modern country" by some and "progressive country" by others; sought for his repertoire the compositions or collaboration of such new-breed Nashville songwriters as Billy Joe Shaver, Kris Kristofferson, and Steve Young—as became clear in the LP *Singer of Sad Songs* (1970); had Top 10 country hits in the title songs of *The Taker* (subtitled *Tulsa*, 1971) and *Cedartown, Georgia* (1971); presented RCA Records with a declaration of his independence in 1972; had a controlling hand in the artistic control of his recordings and their promotion beginning with *Lonesome, On'ry and Mean* (1973); began recording with the Waylors rather than studio musicians; was credited as full producer for the first time on *Ramblin' Man* (1974); recorded four duet albums with Willie Nelson, including the long-term country and pop smash hit *Waylon & Willie* (1979); recorded duet singles with Jessi Colter and Johnny Cash; with Cash, Nelson, and Kristofferson, formed the Highwaymen, a quartet with which he recorded and toured during the 1980s; for the network television situation comedy *The Dukes of Hazard* (1979–85), wrote and sang the theme song, "Good Ol' Boys," and did the off-screen narration; confessed to a 21-year amphetamine and cocaine addiction, which ended in 1984; moved to MCA Records in 1985; had his last hit, "Rose of Paradise," in

1987; continued to tour constantly with the Waylors even as his health declined; in 1999, released *Waylon Live*, an expanded version of a 1976 recording by him and the band; in 1997, published *Waylon: An Autobiography*; in 2001, was inducted into the Country Music Hall of Fame; died in Chandler, Arizona, where he and his wife had been living since 1999. See *Current Biography* (April) 1982.

Obituary *New York Times* C p17 Feb. 14, 2002

**JOBERT, MICHEL** Sep. 11, 1921–May 26, 2002 French foreign minister (1973–74) and minister of trade (1981–83); as a technocrat in France's civil service elite in the two decades following World War II, held numerous top-level staff posts in the offices of ranking government officials before moving into political power under President Georges Pompidou; received his early education in his native Morocco; after receiving a diploma at the École Libre des Sciences Politiques in Paris in 1940, returned to Morroco; during World War II, was an officer in a Free French regiment that fought in Italy in 1943 and 1944 and took part in the invasion of southern France in August 1944 and the subsequent northward drive up the Rhône Valley; in the fighting around Belfort, suffered a wound that left his right arm permanently atrophied; after graduating from the École Nationale d'Administration in 1948, was an auditor in the Cours des Comptes, the French government's general accounting office, until 1952; over the following dozen years, served as a chargé de mission, technical adviser, or staff director in several ministries, including that concerned with overseas territories; was deputy director of Prime Minister Georges Pompidou's personal staff from 1963 to 1965, when he became director; when Pompidou was elected president in 1969, was named secretary general of the office of the president; as secretary general, was the Elysée Palace's point man in such matters as arranging the secret Vietnam peace talks in Paris and selling more than 100 Mirage fighter-bombers to Libya; oversaw relations with the U.S. and the Soviet Union; was regarded as an adversary by American secretary of state Henry Kissinger; served as foreign minister under Pompidou for a little more than one year, until just after Pompidou's death, in April 1974; up to that point, was associated with center-right politics; subsequently, became an independent; was appointed minister of trade under the presidency of François Mitterrand, a Socialist; published a number of novels, memoirs, and collections of political essays; died in Paris. See *Current Biography* (February) 1975.

Obituary *New York Times* C p13 May 31, 2002

**JONES, CHUCK** Sep. 21, 1912–Feb. 22, 2002 Cartoon animator and director; during a career that began at the dawn of the golden age of cinematic animation, participated in the making of some thousand cartoons and was director/animator of more than 300, including those featuring such creations of his as Road Runner, Wile E. Coyote, and Marvin Martian as well as other characters, such as Bugs Bunny and Daffy Duck, that became familiar to successive generations of Americans through television syndication; growing up in Hollywood, was, like his three siblings (all of whom became visual artists), encouraged by his parents to draw; at the age of 15, enrolled at the Chouinard Art Institute, then in Valencia, California, where he learned, he said, to "live by the single line. . . . No shading, no multiple lines, no cross-hatching, no subterfuge"; after graduating from Chouinard, began his career at Ub Iwerks's Celebrity Productions, where he was soon promoted, in the early 1930s, from relatively menial tasks to assistant to the veteran animator Grim Natwick, the creator of Betty Boop; in 1933, joined Leon Schlesinger Productions (purchased by Warner Bros. in 1944), where he became an animator, working for several years under the direction of Fred "Tex" Avery and Isadore "Friz" Freleng, among others; learned to draw movements of the whole body of a character, not simply eyes, head, and limbs, as would become customary with television-bred animators; made his debut as a director, in charge of the entire animation, with "The Night Watchman" (1938), about a cat standing guard against hungry mice; in 1939, set the pace of 10 six-minute cartoons that he would maintain annually thereafter for nearly a quarter-century; proceeded to bring his personal touch to characters developed under Avery and others, including Porky Pig, the sly, hip Bugs Bunny, Bugs's inept nemesis, the hunter Elmer Fudd, and manic Daffy Duck; during World War II, along with others, created Private Snafu cartoons for the armed forces; in "Odor Able Kitty" (1945), introduced his creation Pepe le Pew, an amorous skunk with a suave French accent who seems to have a sexual attraction to cats; in "Fast and Furry-ous" (1949), introduced two of the characters he created in collaboration with the writer Michael Maltese: Road Runner, a southwestern bird whose single pastime is to move endlessly through the desert at blinding speed, and the swift creature's hapless pursuer, the carnivorous Wile E. Coyote; directed Academy Award–winners in "For Scent-imental Reasons" (1949), a Pepe le Pew vehicle, and "So Much for So Little" (1950); in 1955, introduced his creation Michigan J. Frog, a top-hatted, song-belting amphibian vaudevillian, in "One Froggy Evening," which was later inducted into the National Film Registry; in 1957, directed the highly praised Bugs Bunny short "What's Opera, Doc?," a spoof of Wagner's Ring Cycle; after Warner Bros. shut its cartoon studio, in 1962, contracted with Metro-Goldwyn-Mayer to make the Academy Award–winning "The Dot and the Line" (1965), to supervise the production of some new MGM Tom and Jerry cartoons, and to direct his first feature film, *The Phantom Tollbooth* (1969), a fantasy combining animation with live action; meanwhile, had begun making half-hour animated television specials, the first of which was *How the Grinch Stole Christmas* (1966), an adaptation of the Dr. Seuss book, which became a TV classic, presented annually; over the next 12 years, made other animated half-hour specials for TV, including three based on short stories by Rudyard Kipling; helped to develop the PBS head-start show *Sesame Street*; during a year as vice president of children's programming at the ABC network, devised and produced the series *The Curiosity Shop*; directed *The Bugs Bunny/Road Runner Movie* (1979), in which 25 of his best Warner shorts were woven together in a wrapping of new footage; spurred by the success of that feature film, mixed old and new material in several made-for-TV features; in 1986, directed an outstanding special celebrating the 50th anniversary of Looney Tunes, one of the Warner logos; at the age of 84, created for television the Saturday morning half-hour series *Dropsy, Master Detective* (1993–94), starring an animated private-eye hound dog, and contracted to make five new cartoons with Warner characters; won four Oscars, including a lifetime achievement award in 1996; published two profusely illustrated books of autobiography, *Chuck Amuck* (1989) and *Chuck Reducks* (1996); died at his home in Corona del Mar, California. See *Current Biography* (May) 1996.

Obituary *New York Times* p34 Feb. 24, 2002

**KANE, JOSEPH NATHAN** Jan. 23, 1899–Sep. 22, 2002 Research historian; journalist; during a career spanning three-quarters of a century, tracked down elusive and obscure items in American history, including persons cheated of due credit for their achievements, such as Gustave Whitehead, the first to pilot an airplane a significant distance (a mile and a half, in 1901), Walter Hunt, who invented the sewing machine, the safety pin, the fountain pen, and the radiating stove, and Thomas McKean, the forgotten first president of the U.S. (under the Articles of Confederation); presented his findings in magazines and newspapers, over the airwaves, on the lecture circuit, and above all in books, the most popular of which are the standard reference compendiums *Famous First Facts: A Record of First Happenings, Discoveries, and Inventions* and *Facts About the Presidents: A Compilation of Biographical and Historical Data*, both published by the H. W. Wilson Co.; in 1922, founded the one-man Kane Feature News Service, under the aegis of which he practiced freelance journalism for 10 years; during the 1920s, began his hunt for "firsts," traveling the country tirelessly, interviewing the descendants of achievers and frequenting museums, historical societies, and libraries ranging from special collections and rural libraries to the Library of Congress; pored over public documents and records, including patents, sales records, and newspaper files; in 1933, published the first edition of *Famous First Facts*, a 757-page book cataloging some 3,000 facts including such diverse items as the first imported camels (1856), the first African-American army major (Martin Robinson Delany, 1865), and the first subway (the Beach Pneumatic Underground Railway in New York City, 1870); in 1938 and 1939, hosted the weekly half-hour radio program *Famous First Facts* on the Mutual network; during the 1940s and 1950s, was the foremost authority for the questions asked on radio and television quiz shows; supplied all the questions for the long-running show *Break the Bank* (1945–57); in 1959, published the first edition of *Facts About the Presidents*, in which he provided the fundamental curriculum vitae of each of the occupants of the Oval Office and such trivia as the shortest president (James Monroe, five feet, four inches) and Grover Cleveland's 20 nicknames; updated that work in successive editions, the most recent in 2001; in 1993, published the sixth edition of *Famous First Facts*, containing approximately 10,000 items, more than three times the number in the original edition; under imprints other than H. W. Wilson, published, among other books, *What Dog Is That?* (1944), containing descriptions of 122 canine purebreds, *How to Win on Quiz Shows* (1956), *Perma Quiz Book* (1956), books on the history of American cities and counties, and a history of King Solomon Lodge No. 279, the Masonic lodge to which he belonged; in 1997, published *Necessity's Child: The Story of Walter Hunt, America's Forgotten Inventor*; did so with trepidation, according to his nephew David N. Kane, because of a Faustian pact in which he had agreed that he would "be ready to go [to die] two days after I finish my last project"; lived in his native Manhattan most of his life; died in West Palm Beach, Florida. See *Current Biography* (November) 1985.

Obituary *New York Times* A p29 Sep. 17, 2002

**KARSH, YOUSUF** Dec. 23, 1908–July 14, 2002 Armenian-born Canadian photographic portraitist; a preeminent photographer of world leaders in all fields of endeavor, known to millions for the solemnity of his theatrically posed, carefully lighted, uncannily telling portraits; achieved "visual idealization . . . as well as an expressive interpretation of the subject's character," as the photography historian Peter Pollack observed, and "transform[ed] the human face into legend"; apprenticed in the studio of his uncle George Nakash in Sherbrooke, Quebec, and that of John H. Garo in Boston, Massachusetts; became assistant to the photographer John Powis in Ottawa in 1931, shortly before Powis's retirement—after which Karsh made Powis's studio his own; in 1941, took his most famous photograph, a portrait of Winston Churchill, whose defiant posture and bulldog expression personified the indomitable spirit of Great Britain during World War II; subsequently, captured the status of the Supreme Commander of the Allied Expeditionary Force in his photograph of General Dwight D. Eisenhower, the personality of the grizzled, turtleneck-wearing novelist in that of Ernest Hemingway, and the serenely confident spirit of the youthful president-elect in that of John F. Kennedy; in a career spanning more than half a century, brought his distinctive, artful touch to an international who's who of portraiture, ranging from royals and prime ministers to giants of business and industry to notables in entertainment, the arts, the sciences, and religion; did many of his portraits on commission from major magazines; collected them, with commentaries, in the books *Faces of Destiny* (1947), *Portraits of Greatness* (1959), *Faces of Our Time* (1971), and *Karsh Portraits* (1976) and the publications accompanying the exhibitions *Men Who Make Our World* (1967), which toured internationally for many years, and *Karsh: A Fifty-Year Retrospective* (1983); was represented in major art museum collections in Canada, the U.S., Great Britain, and Japan; wrote *In Search of Greatness: Reflections of Yousuf Karsh* (1966); with Bishop Fulton J. Sheen and others, collaborated on a series of books about the Roman Catholic faith; died in Boston, Massachusetts. See *Current Biography* (February) 1980.

Obituary *New York Times* B p7 July 15, 2002

**KEPES, GYÖRGY** Oct. 4, 1906–Dec. 29, 2001 Hungarian-born artist; painter; designer; sculptor; typographer; aesthetic theorist; an avant-garde structuralist with a holistic vision; applied a wealth and diversity of skills to his efforts to resolve the dichotomy between art and science/technology and arrive at a "humanism in design" and recognition both of the individual and of "our world as an interconnected whole"; was best known as the founder and director (1967–72) of the Center for Advanced Visual Studies at the Massachusetts Institute of Technology, which was formally dedicated in 1968, jointly with the institute's Center for Theoretical Physics; created interactive sculpture and other art forms utilizing technological innovations, such as neon lights, strobe lights, ignited gas, and various metals, and contributing to the development of an organic architecture; concentrated on painting as a student at the Royal Academy of Fine Arts in Budapest, Hungary; in Berlin, Germany, beginning in 1930 and later in London (1935–37), worked in film, stage set design, and graphic design with the older Hungarian artist Lásló Moholy-Nagy, a founder of Constructivism (a movement known for its use of abstract geometric shapes inspired by modern machine technology) and an erstwhile teacher at the Bauhaus, a school that championed the union of aesthetics with utilitarian function in art and architecture; experimented in photography without camera, exposing photographic paper directly to light and shadow; in the late 1930s, emigrated to the U.S. to head the light and color department at the Chicago Institute of Design (originally called the "New Bauhaus"), founded by Moholy-Nagy; after leaving the institute, taught briefly at small colleges in Texas and Brooklyn, New York; in 1946, became professor of visual design in the School of Architecture and Planning at the Massachusetts Institute of Technology; envisioned his Center for Advanced Visual Studies at MIT as "a closely knit work community" of "promising young artists and designers" where new ideas would be generated through contact with each other and with "the academic community of architects, city planners, scientists, and engineers"; over the years, created designs ranging from graphics for *Fortune* magazine and the Container Corp. of America and fountains for housing projects to stained-glass windows for churches (including St. Mary's Cathedral in San Francisco), a light-and-water monument for Boston Harbor, a 40-foot series of kinetically lighted screens fronting Manhattan's Pan-Am Building, and such architectural murals as those gracing the Time-Life Building and a number of Sheraton hotels; in his heavily layered and textured abstract and semiabstract paintings, such as *Serene Image, Sky Mirror, Whispering Winter Whites,* and *Inviting Mistscape,* found "a new meaning for landscape" and a "coherence and completeness so lacking in our urban industrialized society"; elucidated his aesthetic and educational theories and methods in *The Language of Vision* (1944); was the chief contributor to *The Arts as Related to the Book* (1949); compiled and edited the landmark "Vision + Value" series (1965–72) of seven volumes (including *Structure in Art and Science, The Nature and Art of Motion,* and *Arts of the Environment*), a collection of essays by 84 contributors representing a kaleidoscope of disciplines pushing at the frontiers of the "language of vision"; died at his home in Cambridge, Massachusetts. See *Current Biography* (March) 1973.

Obituary *New York Times* B p9 Jan. 10, 2002

**KESEY, KEN** Sep. 17, 1935–Nov. 10, 2001 Novelist; free-spirited antiauthoritarian activist; as a Pied Piper of the psychedelic-drug-fueled counterculture of the 1960s, was a leader in the transition from the poetry-focused Beat generation to the flower-powered Hippie revolution; wielded his most enduring influence through the black humor of his writings, especially that of his first novel, *One Flew Over the Cuckoo's Nest* (1962), a perennially republished American classic that has been translated into numerous foreign languages and was adapted for the Broadway stage (1963–64) and the silver screen (1975); was extremely unhappy with the film version, which deviated from the book in its narrative voice; as an undergraduate in speech at the University of Oregon in the mid-1950s, participated in wrestling and drama; in the late 1950s, had bit parts in several motion pictures, spent a year in the graduate writing program at Stanford University, and volunteered as a paid subject for experiments on the effects of hallucinogenic (or psychomimetric) drugs, chiefly LSD and IT-1290, at the Veterans Hospital in Menlo Park, California; stayed on at the hospital as a night attendant in the mental ward, where he was inspired (with some help from peyote) to write *One Flew Over the Cuckoo's Nest*; projected his own personality in that book's protagonist, Randle Patrick McMurphy, a blithe, mirth-making misfit who feigns insanity to beat a jail sentence and is committed to a mental institution, where he is lobotomized after he begins to incite the inmates to challenge the rules by asserting their individualities; in 1964, published his mammoth second novel, the more ambitious and elaborately structured *Sometimes a Great Notion*, a saga about the fictional Stamper family, a ruggedly independent Oregon logging dynasty that refuses to bow to the demands of a labor union; saw that work adapted into the film *Sometimes a Great Notion* (1971), the title of which was changed to *Never Give an Inch* (the Stamper family motto) when it was released for television; during 1964, bought a 1939 International Harvester school bus and, with the help of some dozen acolytes, fellow "Merry Pranksters," converted it into "Furthur," a Day-Glo-painted mobile home/studio; in Furthur (driven by Neal Cassady, the model for the character Dean Moriarty in the Beat novelist Jack Kerouac's book *On the Road*), traveled across the U.S. for two months, creating absurdist "happenings" along the way—a tour chronicled by Tom Wolfe in his book *The Electric Kool-Aid Acid Test* (1968); when Furthur began to deteriorate, replaced it with another converted 1939 International Harvester bus; in the Haight Ashbury in San Francisco, "dropped acid" with such hippies as the members of the rock group the Grateful Dead; to evade incarceration for possession of marijuana, lived in exile in Mexico during most of 1966; served five months in prison in California in 1967 for possession of an unlawful substance; the following year, assumed ownership of his father's dairy farm in Oregon and settled down there permanently with his wife, Faye, and their four children; published his third major novel, *Sailor Song*—about the encroachment of civilization on nature in Alaska—in 1992; with research assistance from Ken Babbs, wrote a fourth novel, *Last Go Round: A Dime Western* (1994), about a celebrated Oregon rodeo; in *Kesey's Garage Sale* (1973), brought together short autobiographical pieces by himself and contributions from Paul Krassner and others; in 1986, published *Demon Box*, a collection of essays and short stories; in *The Further Inquiry* (1990), recalled the 1964 bus tour and evoked the spirit of Neal Cassady (who had died) in transcriptions of conversations and photographs; also wrote two children's books; with Paul Krassner, edited the *The Last Supplement to The Whole Earth Catalogue*; in 1987, became an instructor in the Master of Fine Arts creative-writing program at the University of Oregon; with 13 of his graduate students, wrote the novel *Caverns* (1989), published under the pseudonym O. U. Levon; died in Eugene, Oregon. See *Current Biography* (May) 1976.

Obituary *New York Times* A p47 Nov. 11, 2001

**KOCH, KENNETH** Feb. 27, 1925–July 6, 2002 Poet; playwright; educator; an alumnus of the New York School of poetry of the 1950s, which consisted essentially of the triumvirate of Koch, John Ashbery, and Frank O'Hara, who tried to apply the principles of abstract expressionist painting to verbal constructs; came away from that "apprenticeship," as Hayden Carruth once observed, with a poetic "felicity" that occasionally descended to "surrealistic gibberish" but at its best was "remarkably inventive"; built a reputation that rested as firmly on his innovative experiments in teaching the writing of verse to children and old people as on his own witty, ebullient poetry, which, like his teaching techniques, pressed for the free play of feeling and imagination; at Columbia University, became an associate professor in 1966 and a full professor of English and comparative literature five years later; began teaching elementary-school children to write verse in 1968 at Public School 61 on Manhattan's Lower East Side; reported on that experiment in *Wishes, Lies and Dreams* (1970); subsequently, taught great poetry to the children; reported on that in *Rose, Where Did You Get That Red?* (1973); in 1976, carried his experiment in the teaching of verse-writing into the American Nursing Home on the Lower East Side; reported on that in *I Never Told Anybody* (1977); taught and lectured at Columbia University for nearly 40 years; collected his early poetry in such volumes as *Thank You* (1962), *The Pleasures of Peace* (1969), *The Art of Love* (1975), and the antic epics *Ko* (1960) and *The Duplications* (1977), zany, free-wheeling multi-plotted narratives exuding, like all of his work, the joy of creation; collected his short dramatic works, mostly dada-like burlesques of academic or patriotic pageantry, in *Bertha and Other Plays* (1966), *A Change of Hearts* (1973), and *The Red Robin* (1975); later published the book of plays *The Gold Standard* (1996) and the poetry collections *On the Edge* (1986), *One Train* (1994), *Straits* (1998), and *New Addresses* (2000); wrote *Making Your Own Days: The Pleasures of Reading and Writing Poetry* (1996); suppressed writing about his harrowing combat experiences as an infantryman in the Philippines during World War II until the very end of his life; when he died (at his home in Manhattan), had two new books nearing publication. See *Current Biography* (February) 1978.

Obituary *New York Times* A p16 July 8, 2002

**KOLAR, JIRI** Sep. 24, 1914–Aug. 11, 2002 Czech poet; artist; wrote futurist verse and made collages that he regarded as a "poetry of objects"; at 16, read a Czech translation of *Parole in libertá* by Filippo Tommaso Marinetti, the Italian poet who founded futurism; was profoundly affected by Marinetti's advocacy of a poetry not bound by formal rules of syntax but dedicated to using words freely so as to portray the modern world in all its multiplicity and simultaneity of effect; later came under the influence of Surrealism and Dadaism; in 1941, published his first collection of verse (entitled *Birth Certificate* in the English translation); the following year, in Prague, in what was then Czechoslovakia (now the Czech Republic), became a founding member of Group 42, a circle of artists and scholars devoted to upholding modernism in art and literature in the face of Nazi oppression; remained active in the group until the 1948 Communist coup d'état, which ushered in a government inimical to Western cultural influences; was twice officially barred from publishing his "subversive" writings, for several years beginning in 1953 and again following the Warsaw Pact invasion of Czechoslovakia in 1968; meanwhile, having long experimented with collages, easily made the transition to a visual form of communication in the 1950s; devoted himself to what Sanford Schwartz called "visual puzzles of a literary sensibility," works that compel the eye with their ingenuity and beauty of form and at the same time stimulate the mind with questions about their meaning; in one of his best-known collages, *Smile of Memory* (1971), cut a reproduction of Leonardo da Vinci's *Mona Lisa* into vertical strips, which he pasted down, alternating them with strips of the same width bearing bits of reproductions of other pictures; made three-dimensional collages by pasting paper fragments onto small sculptures, household objects, and the like; wrote two plays and wrote and illustrated a number of children's books; went into exile in France in 1980, after signing the Charter 77 human rights manifesto; returned to Czechoslovakia when the Communist dictatorship there ended, in 1989, five years before the country was divided into the Czech Republic and Slovakia; died at his home in Prague, the capital of the Czech Republic. See *Current Biography* (April) 1986.

Obituary *New York Times* C p11 Aug. 23, 2002

**KOTT, JAN** Oct. 27, 1914–Dec. 22, 2001 Polish-born scholar; literary critic; dramaturge; professor emeritus of comparative literature, State University of New York at Stony Brook; the most influential Shakespeare interpreter of his time; to his essays on Shakespeare, collected in *Szkice o Szekspirze* (1961; translated as *Shakespeare, Our Contemporary*, 1964) and *Szekspir Współczesny* (1965), brought a pessimistic 20th-century Central European vision of history as a "grand mechanism" in which mankind is "caught in the wheels"; as the scholar Richard Wilson has observed, "for a generation . . . taught students that [Shakespeare's] plays were set in a concentration camp," that the work of the Bard "was as pitiless as Poland"; with that perspective, influenced productions by Britain's Royal Shakespeare Company and National Theatre, the director Giorgio Strehler, and others; with his essay "*King Lear* or *Endgame*," for example, inspired the British director Peter Brook in 1962 to treat *Lear* as a vehicle of Elizabethan despair mirroring the psychopathy of the Theater of the Absurd; similarly, inspired Ariane Mnouchkin in Paris in 1968 to stage *A Midsummer Night's Dream* as a cruel and violent erotic fantasy; was raised a Catholic by his parents, who were assimilated Jews; joined the Communist Party during World War II; earned a master's degree in law at the University of Warsaw in 1936 and a Ph.D. degree in literature at the University of Lodz in 1947; taught Romance languages at the University of Wroclaw for three years before joining the faculty of the University of Warsaw as professor of the history of Polish literature, in 1952; was literary director of the Jaracz Theatre in Lodz (1958–60); translated plays by Molière, Montherlant, Ionesco, and Sartre; edited the comedies of F. Bohomolec; produced and/or directed plays by Slawomir Mrozek, Stanislaw Ignacy Witkiewicz, and Euripides; beginning in 1960, on vacation or leave from the University of Warsaw, lectured at universities in France, England, and the U.S.; was visiting professor at Yale University in 1966–67 and again in 1968–69; meanwhile, having become an opponent of the Stalin cult, resigned from the Communist Party in 1957; seven years later, joined 33 other Polish intellectuals in signing a letter to Premier Wladyslaw Gomulka protesting literary censorship; following his dismissal from the University of Warsaw for political reasons in 1969, was granted asylum in the U.S.; taught at the State University of New York at Stony Brook from 1969 until his retirement, in 1983; published, among other books, *Theatre Notebook: 1947–1967* (1968), *The Eating of the Gods: An Interpretation of Greek Tragedy* (1973), *The Theater of Essence* (1984), *The Bottom Translation: Marlowe and Shakespeare and the Carnival Tradition* (1987), *The Memory of the Body: Essays on Theater and Death* (1992), the autobiography *Still Alive* (1994), an anthology of Polish poetry, and editions of the works and letters of the poet S. Trembecki; died in Santa Monica, California, which he had first visited as a Getty Foundation visiting scholar in 1986. See *Current Biography* (April) 1969.

Obituary *New York Times* C p10 Jan. 4, 2002

**KYPRIANOU, SPYROS** Oct. 28, 1932–Mar. 12, 2002 Second president of post-independence Cyprus; founder of the moderate right-of-center Democratic Party; protégé of the first president of the Republic of Cyprus, Archbishop Makarios III, the father of Cypriot independence and the former leader of the enosis movement, for union of Cyprus with Greece; was attracted to the Greek Cypriot national cause when he was a young man, a time when Cyprus, once a possession of Turkey, was a British crown colony in which long-term hostility between the Greek majority and the Turkish minority was brewing; as a law student in London in 1952, founded the National Union of Cypriot Students in England; after becoming a barrister-in-law, in 1954, remained in England as the liaison of Archbishop Makarios and as the London secretary of the Cypriot Ethnarchy, a position in which he was charged with representing that community's views and interests in Britain; was forced to leave England in 1956, after enosist insurgents began a guerrilla war against British forces on Cyprus; with Makarios, participated in negotiations in London and Zurich in which representatives of Great Britain, Greece, Turkey, and the two Cypriot factions came to an agreement, signed in February 1959, on a plan for an independent republic, with constitutional guarantees for the Turkish minority and allowance for a British military enclave; in April 1959, helped to found the moderately right-of-center National Democratic Front, with the backing of which Makarios was elected president, effective August 1960; as foreign minister in Makarios's cabinet, engaged in a busy itinerary of shuttle diplomacy, establishing or strengthening relations with the Council of Europe, the Soviet Union, the Arab states, and the emerging African nations; increasingly, however, had to turn his attention to the turbulent domestic scene, where fighting between Greek and Turkish Cypriots broke out in 1963 and was kept in check only with the help of international intervention, including the presence of a U.N. peacekeeping force; because he resisted undue Greek mainland influence on Cyprus, in 1972 was forced to resign as foreign minister, under pressure from the ruling military junta in Greece; following a turbulent sequence of events in 1974—a coup by the Cypriot National Guard led by army officers from mainland Greece that temporarily ousted Makarios, and the occupation by Turkish troops of the northeastern 35 percent of the island—returned to government service as a close adviser to Makarios and a member of the Cypriot delegation to the U.N.; in the parliamentary election of 1976, became president of the Cypriot House of Representatives; following Makarios's death, in the autumn of 1977, assumed caretakership of the presidency of Cyprus for the remainer of Makarios's term; when enosist extremists kidnapped his son Achilleas in December 1977, refused to meet the demands of the kidnappers, who released Achilleas unharmed; facing no opposition in the presidential balloting of 1978, became president for a five-year term; was reelected in 1983, the year in which the Turkish Cypriots proclaimed the Turkish Republic of Northern Cyprus, a breakaway state recognized only by Turkey; to compensate for the loss of tourism in the Turkish-occupied northeast and the U.N.-occupied buffer zone, promoted the development of holiday resorts on the island's south coast, which resulted in a sustained economic boom; tried in vain to negotiate a federal alternative to the partition of Cyprus; after his failure to win reelection in 1988, remained an influential figure in his party and a strong voice against concessions to opponents of Cypriot unification; died in Nicosia, Cyprus. See *Current Biography* (May) 1979.

Obituary *New York Times* C p13 Mar. 14, 2002

**LANDERS, ANN** July 4, 1918–June 22, 2002 Syndicated newspaper columnist; invented the modern straight-talking, wisecracking advice column, as distinct from the earlier straight-laced "lovelorn" variety; was, as Rupert Cornwell wrote in his obituary in the British newspaper the *Independent*, "just possibly . . . the most influential American woman of the 20th century," a claim based "not on political achievement or pioneering social reform but on her unchallenged status as the agony aunt of her age"; reached 95 million readers in recent years with her judicious, common-sense responses to people (like "Baffled in L.A." and "Distressed in Dubuque") seeking guidance on everything from acne to zoophobia; was born Esther Pauline Friedman, the identical twin of her sister Pauline Esther Friedman Phillips, who uses the pseudonym Abigail Van Buren in writing her own advice column, "Dear Abby," syndicated by the *San Francisco Chronicle* Syndicate; in 1939, married Jules William Lederer, the founder of the Budget Rent-a-Car Corp.; by Lederer (from whom she was divorced in 1975), had a daughter, Margo; in 1955, learned that the Chicago *Sun-Times* was holding a competition to find a successor to Ruth Crowley, the original "Ann Landers," who died in July of that year; with her answers to a sample stack of letters from readers, won the competition; published her first column in the *Sun-Times* and 25 newspapers subscribing to the *Sun-Times* Syndicate on October 16, 1955; in less than two years, was appearing in well over 100 newspapers, and ultimately passed the 1,200 mark; moved from the *Sun-Times* to the *Chicago Tribune* in 1985; was finally distributed by the Creators Syndicate; while progressive in her political and social perspective, was not a moral relativist and could be devastating in some of her moral judgments; by her advocacy of gun control and abortion rights and her approval of the use of animals in medical research, earned the enmity of the National Rifle Association, the "pro-life" movement, and People for the Ethical Treatment of Animals, respectively; said, "Those three groups really despise me, and I'm proud of it"; died at her home in Chicago. See *Current Biography* (November) 1957.

Obituary *New York Times* B p7 June 24, 2002

**LEE, PEGGY** May 26, 1920–Jan. 21, 2002 Singer; songwriter; "one of the most sensitive and jazz-oriented singers in the pop field," as the music critic and composer Leonard Feather observed; was, in the words of her daughter, Nikki Lee Foster, "a perfectionist" with "an incredible ear" who "saw her performance as a total, complete musical picture from start to finish"; delivered readings of plaintive torch songs, blues, swing tunes, cabaret songs, and pop ballads in a sultry voice, pianissimo, gracefully, and with conviction; compensated for her limited vocal range (one and a half octaves at best) with masterly phrasing, supple timing, and an uncanny instinct for cutting to the heart of a lyric's meaning; in 1938, left Jamestown, North Dakota, to seek her fortune as a club and radio singer; three years later, was discovered in Chicago by Benny Goodman, the leader of the most popular swing band of the time, when he heard her singing "These Foolish Things"; toured as the featured female vocalist with Goodman for almost two years; during that time, recorded, among other songs, the minor hit "I Got It Bad (and That Ain't Good)" and her first smash hit, "Why Don't You Do Right?"; left the Goodman orchestra when she married the guitarist Dave Barbour, with the intention of devoting herself to family life; began collaborating in songwriting with Barbour; beginning in 1944, recorded a long string of hits, including the Lee/Barbour songs "It's a Good Day," "Manana (Is Soon Enough for Me)," and "I Don't Know Enough About You"; also recorded such successes as "Golden Earrings," "You Was Right, Baby," and "What Can a Woman Do?"; continued to collaborate on music and lyrics with Barbour after they divorced, in 1951 (at his self-sacrificing request, because of his alcoholism); in the long term, cherished Barbour alone among her four husbands; confirmed her reputation for vocal flexibility and rhythmic inventiveness with her interpretations of such songs as "Lover" (1952); subsequently, recorded the major LP *Black Coffee* and the songs "When the World Was Young," "If I Should Lose You," and her own favorite recording, "The Folks Who Live on the Hill"; became closely identified with her playful rendition of John Davenport and Eddie Cooley's steamy "Fever" (1958); during the 1950s, was cast in movies, most memorably as the alcoholic chanteuse in *Pete Kelly's Blues* (1955), for which role she earned an Academy Award nomination; wrote the theme music for several movies, including *Johnny Guitar* (1954) and The *Heart Is a Lonely Hunter* (1968); with Sonny Burke, wrote the songs for the animated film *Lady and the Tramp* (1955), for which she also supplied female voice-overs; 36 years later, sued for a share in the profits of the videocassette release of the cartoon and won a court award of $2.3 million; still later, was the lead plaintiff in a class-action suit (apparently nearing success at the time of her death) launched against the Universal Music Group in behalf of several hundred black musicians and other recording artists, for past royalties; as lyricist, collaborated with Duke Ellington in writing "I'm Gonna Go Fishin'" for the film *Anatomy of a Murder* (1950); also collaborated with Harold Arlen ("Happy with the Blues") and Cy Coleman ("Then Was Then and Now Is Now"); recorded the albums *The Man I Love* (1957) with Frank Sinatra conducting the orchestra, *If You Go* (1961) with Quincy Jones conducting, and *Mink Jazz* (1961) with Benny Carter conducting; recorded many songs by Mike Leiber and Jerry Stoller, including "I'm a Woman" (1953), "Is That All There Is?" (1969), her last major hit, and "Some Cats Know," on her 1975 LP *Mirrors*; was a fixture on jukeboxes, radio, and television from the late 1940s until the ascendency of rock music in the 1960s; was best appreciated in concert performances, especially in intimate venues, such as the Manhattan supper clubs Basin Street East and the Ballroom, where she drew full houses that included such musical luminaries as Count Basie, one of her inspirations; as in all her work, was attentive to every detail contributing to her star persona and regal stage presence, from artful lighting to platinum-blond coiffure, impeccable makeup, and glamorous wardrobe; often ended her performances with one of her signature songs, Irving Kahal and Sammy Fain's "I'll Be Seeing You"; on Broadway in 1983, had a brief run starring in the autobiographical musical *Peg*; recorded well over 50 albums, including *Peggy Lee Sings the Blues* (1988) and *The Peggy Lee Songbook: There'll Be Another Spring* (1991), her last; wrote an autobiography, *Miss Peggy Lee* (1989); died at her home in the Bel Air section of Los Angeles. See *Current Biography* (March) 1963.

Obituary *New York Times* A p17 Jan. 23, 2002

**LEONE, GIOVANNI** Nov. 3, 1908–Nov. 9, 2001 Former president of Italy; a moderate who played a conciliatory role in Italy's dominant but badly splintered Christian Democratic Party; after earning degrees in law and political and social science, taught criminal law and penal procedure at a succession of Italian universities; was elected to the Chamber of Deputies, the lower house of the Italian Parliament, in 1948; was vice president of the chamber from 1950 to 1955 and president of the chamber, or speaker, from 1955 to 1963; served as transitional prime minister of Italy twice, in 1963 and 1968; played his most memorable role as a legislative mediator in 1970, when a controversial divorce bill opposed by his own Catholic Church–affiliated party was deadlocked in Parliament; on that occasion, adroitly gained support for ameliorating amendments that opened the way for passage of the legislation, which ended the ban on divorce in Italy; was elected to a seven-year term as president of Italy by parliamentary vote in December 1971; resigned in June 1978, six months before the end of his term, amid allegations in the left-wing press of a payoff scandal involving the Lockheed aircraft corporation; in 1985, was gratified by the revelation by the Communist Party member assigned to organize his impeachment that "we never really had any proof against him"; in 1998, accepted the public apologies of the Radical Party for its attacks on him; during the two decades following his resignation, limited his public appearances to visits to the presidential palace as an adviser on forming new governments and important votes in the Parliament, where he was a senator for life; died at his home on the outskirts of Rome. See *Current Biography* (May) 1972.

Obituary *New York Times* A p12 Nov. 10, 2001

**LEWIS, FLORA** July 29, 1922–June 1, 2002 Print journalist; foreign correspondent; world-affairs columnist; a nonideological, tough-minded, incisive observer of the international scene for six decades; was eulogized by the editors of the *International Herald Tribune* (published jointly by the *New York Times* and the *Washington Post*)—to which she contributed for 37 years—for the combination of the "nimbleness and ferocity of her intelligence" and her ability to "write like a dream"; had a "hard edge" that "allowed her to cut through the bland nonsense of the diplomatic world she often covered"; earned degrees in journalism from the University of California–Los Angeles, and Columbia University; began her career as a cub reporter with the *Los Angeles Times*; in 1942, joined the New York bureau of the Associated Press; was soon transferred to Washington, D.C., where she covered the navy and state department for the Associated Press; in London in 1945, married Sydney Gruson, a *New York Times* foreign correspondent; left the Associated Press so as to be free to travel with her husband from one world capital or hot spot to another; as she traveled, did freelance writing and contract reporting for a number of American, British, and French newspapers and magazines, including the London *Observer*, *Financial Times*, the *Economist*, *France-soir*, *Time*, and the *New York Times Magazine*; could not work for the *New York Times* itself because of the *Times*'s policy at that time against employing a husband and wife simultaneously; in 1956, joined the *Washington Post* as that newspaper's first female correspondent; at first covered Eastern Europe, including Poland, for the *Post*; later headed the paper's bureaus in Bonn, West Germany, and London; in 1965, became the first chief of the *Post*'s newly established New York City bureau; in January 1967, left the *Post* to begin writing a syndicated column called "Today Abroad"; as a columnist, traveled to Vietnam and the Middle East; returned to daily journalism as chief of the *New York Times*'s Paris bureau in 1972, the year in which she and her husband (the parents of three children) separated; from her base in Paris, traveled as far afield as Tokyo, Havana, and Cape Town; beginning in 1976, doubled as the *Times*'s European diplomatic correspondent; relinquished both posts to write the *Times*'s twice-weekly foreign-affairs column for 10 years, from 1980 to 1990; was a *Times* senior columnist from 1990 to 1994; subsequently, until April 2002, wrote a column for the New York Times Syndicate and the *International Herald Tribune*; published five books: *Case History of Hope: The Story of Poland's Peaceful Revolution* (1958), *Red Pawn* (1965), the puzzling story of American-Soviet double agent Noel Field, *One of Our H-Bombs Is Missing* (1967), *Europe: A Tapestry of Nations* (1987), and *Europe: Road to Unity* (1992); died at her home in Paris, France. See *Current Biography* (January) 1989.

Obituary *New York Times* p43 June 2, 2002

**LILLY, JOHN C.** Jan. 6, 1915–Sep. 30, 2001 Biophysicist; neurophysiologist; author; a New Age visionary medical scientist who boldly ventured into the frontiers of animal intelligence and human consciousness, including interspecies communication with dolphins, the large-brained, playful, aquatic mammals that are smaller members of the whale family; earned a B.S. degree at the California Institute of Technology in 1938 and an M.D. degree at the University of Pennsylvania in 1942; remained at the university for 14 more years, as a research fellow, assistant professor of biophysics, and associate professor of experimental neurology; did wartime research in the physiology of high-altitude flying for the U.S. military; invented electronic instruments for measuring gas pressure, blood pressure, and the amount of nitrogen in air that is being inhaled and expired and an apparatus for recording the electrical activity of the cerebral cortex of the brain in terms of visible light and shade on a monitor; on leave from the University of Pennsylvania, joined the U.S. Public Health Service as a commissioned officer/surgeon in 1953; with the service, was chief of the section on cortical integration research in the neurophysiology laboratory at the National Institute of Mental Health;

in his experiments with animals, stimulated different cortical sections with electrical current and noted the movements of body parts thus provoked; also used electrical stimulation to investigate motivational circuits in animals' brains; was able to induce feelings of pleasure or pain and to make an animal feel hungry, thirsty, satiated, hot, or cold, regardless of actual physical conditions; devised a technique using harmless diphasic current rather than direct electrical current, which damages brain cells—a development that opened new vistas for treating the mentally ill; investigated the effects of sense deprivation on the brain by making himself the subject of isolation-tank experiments, an experience intensified by the ingestion of psychedelic drugs; floating face down in the lukewarm water of the tank, wearing only a breathing mask, began wondering about the consciousness of creatures who live in water all day, every day, such as dolphins; working with monkeys, devised a method of inserting electrodes into the brain without the use of anesthesia—a necessity for working safely with dolphins; studied dolphins at Marine Studios in St. Augustine, Florida, in October 1957 and January 1958; later in 1958, bought and began clearing land on St. Thomas in the Virgin Islands, where he built a pool for dolphins and a laboratory and opened his Communication Research Institute, in 1959; discovered that dolphins learned the electrical "reward and punishment" program immediately, on the first trial (as contrasted with several hundred trials with monkeys), and that reward was better than punishment as an inducement to learning in dolphins; induced dolphins to vocalize in the human sound range; realized that dolphins are, in their own way, at least as intelligent as human beings, that they have a complex language, enabling them to transmit species memory, and that to some extent human beings may learn how to communicate with them; during a 10-year hiatus from dolphin research, concentrated on experimentation with psychedelics and altered states of consciousness; for two years, conducted group sessions on expanded consciousness at the Eselen Institute in Big Sur, California; in 1978, briefly returned to his research with dolphins; wrote a score of books, including *Man and Dolphins* (1961), *The Mind of the Dolphin: A Nonhuman Intelligence* (1967), *The Center of the Cyclone: An Autobiography of Inner Space* (1972), *Programming and Metaprogramming in the Human Biocomputer* (1972), *Simulations of God: The Science of Belief* (1975), *Lilly on Dolphins: Humans of the Sea* (1975), *The Deep Self: Profound Relaxation and the Tank Isolation Technique* (1977), *Communication Between Man and Dolphin* (1978), and *The Scientist: A Novel Autobiography* (1978); with his third wife, Antonietta, wrote *The Dyadic Cyclone: The Autobiography of a Couple* (1976); with his work and the ideas expressed in his books, inspired the motion pictures *The Day of the Dolphin* (1973) and *Altered States* (1980); in his last years, lived in Maui, Hawaii; died in Los Angeles, California. See *Current Biography* (November) 1962.

Obituary *New York Times* A p44 Oct. 7, 2001

**LINDGREN, ASTRID** Nov. 14, 1907–Jan. 28, 2002 Swedish author; her country's best-known and most honored contemporary writer; had a subversive, transformative influence in juvenile literature, bringing to her fiction for children a sense of humor reminiscent of that of Heinrich Hoffmann's *Struwelpeter* and Wilhelm Busch's *Max and Moritz* and a child's scorn for bourgeois respectability; in a field where juvenile rebel characters had been exclusively male, from Huck Finn onwards, created tough, supremely independent heroines, most famously the totally self-powered, self-sufficient nine-year-old enfant terrible Pippi Longstocking, who lives alone, outside of adult control, in a ramshackle house with a monkey and a horse—a rambunctious marvel in the admiring eyes of her conventional neighborhood peers Tommy and Annika; grew up in a family of storytellers on a farm in Vimmerby, Sweden, on which there were no modern amenities, such as electricity, and where transportation was by horse, a setting similar to those often presented in her fiction; began creating stories about the escapades of Pippi Longstocking orally, for the entertainment of her seven-year-old daughter, Karin, in 1941; three years later, started transcribing the stories; in 1945, published *Pippi Långstrump*, which was issued in translation in the U.S. with the title *Pippi Longstocking* in 1950; later wrote sequels translated as *Pippi Goes on Board*, *Pippi on the Run*, and *Pippi in the South Seas*; saw her Pippi stories adapted into four motion pictures in Sweden and one in the U.S.; created such other juvenile characters as Mischievous Meg, Ronja Rovardotter (Ronja the robber's daughter), a male counterpart of Pippi named Karlsson, another boy, named Anders, an unloved foster child who is rescued by a genie he has released from a bottle and is transported to a new existence as the son of the King of Farawayland, and several more-realistic runaways, including five-year-old Lotta, who, following an argument with her parents, hides out in a neighbor's attic until her father finds her and they reconcile; in her series of Bill Bergson detective stories (which originated as very popular radio programs), followed in the tradition of Erich Kastner's *Emil and the Detectives*, by depicting children as capable of solving mysteries by themselves; provided the text for several books of photographs by others; published a total of at least 115 books, including volumes of fairy tales and an account of an extraordinary adult love affair, that of her parents; was translated into 60 languages; enjoyed sales of more than 40 million copies worldwide; for many years, headed the children's book division of the Stockholm publishing company Rabén and Stögren; successfully lobbied for reform of Sweden's punitive income-tax laws (under which she had been assessed at a rate of 102 percent of her income); died at her home in Stockholm. See *Current Biography* (October) 1996.

Obituary *New York Times* B p9 Jan. 29, 2002

**LIPPOLD, RICHARD** May 3, 1915–Aug. 22, 2002 Sculptor; chiefly by forging and welding, created large-scale metal abstractions, many of which are suspended by wires and radiate light and/or appear to be hovering or moving through space; after graduating from the Art Institute of Chicago, in 1937, did industrial designing, most of it for the Chicago Corp.; in 1940, began teaching art; in 1942, inspired by the Constructivists Naum Gabo and Antoine Pevsner, began to work, at first on a small scale, with iron, stainless steel, brass, and copper; in 1947, held his first one-man show, at the Willard Gallery in New York City, where he continued to exhibit periodically for a quarter century; in his third one-man show, in 1950, included *Variation within a Sphere No. 7: Full Moon*, a wire construction suggesting the radiation of moonlight; that same year, was commissioned to construct *World Tree*, a 27-foot stainless-steel outdoor structure of straight and circular tubes resembling a radio antenna for the Graduate Law School Center campus at Harvard University; subsequently, constructed the metal-and-wood *Dead Bird*, intended to describe not death but the mood of the observer of death; at the historic show "Fifteen Americans" mounted at the Museum of Modern Art, in New York City, in 1952, was represented with *Juggler in the Sun* and *Ganymede*, among other sculptures; in an international competition in 1953, won third prize with a proposal later realized in the public monument *The Unknown Political Prisoner*, a cage-like wire memorial to all 20th-century martyrs in the cause of human freedom versus inhuman tyrannies; worked with two miles of gold wire, held together by 14,000 hand-welded joints, in constructing the 22-foot- by-11-foot-by-five-and-a-half-foot *Variation within a Sphere No. 10: The Sun*, which went on permanent display in the Metropolitan Museum of Art in 1956; for the lobby of Avery Fisher Hall at Lincoln Center in Manhattan, constructed *Orpheus and Apollo* (commissioned in 1961), a five-foot-by-100-foot hanging constellation of polished brass connected by wires; for the lobby of the Pan Am Building (now the MetLife Building) in Manhattan, created *Flight* (1963), a hanging construction of gilded wires; for the façade of the National Air and Space Museum in Washington, D.C., constructed *Ad Astra* (1976), two 115-foot-tall spires filled with starlike wire clusters; at the Haggerty Museum of Art at Marquette University in 1990, was given a retrospective, accomplished by a definitive catalog of his work; taught art at several schools, including Hunter College, in New York City (1952–67); settling with his family in Lattingtown, on Long Island, New York, in 1955; died in nearby Roslyn, New York. See *Current Biography* (November) 1956.

Obituary *New York Times* C p11 Aug. 30, 2002

**LOMAX, ALAN** Jan. 15, 1915–July 19, 2002 Musicologist; preeminent chronicler and collector of American traditional music; played a key role in the preservation of America's musical heritage; with a missionary's zeal, dedicated his life to "giving a voice to the voiceless" and "putting neglected cultures and silenced people into the communications chain"; during a career spanning seven decades, traveled the country's highways and back roads, from the Mississippi Delta and the Georgia Sea Islands to Appalachian Mountain communities, western cattle ranches, and southern prison farms, seeking out grassroots musicians of diverse traditions and recording their music; made thousands of field recordings of folk, blues, and jazz musicians, including black gospel singers and Cajun choirs; contributed to the folk-music revival of the 1950s, which in turn contributed to the folk rock of the mid-1960s (a development that he regarded as inauthentic and therefore deplorable); related American music and dance traditions to recurring styles and patterns he found in traditions in other countries; was the son of John A. Lomax, the pioneering folklorist who published the collections *Cowboy Songs and Other Frontier Ballads* (1910) and *Songs of the Cattle Trail and Cow Camp* (1918) and served as first curator of the Archive of American Folk Song, established at the Library of Congress in 1928; made his first field expedition in 1933, accompanying his father across the South and West, collecting and recording the music of cowboys, plantation workers, sharecroppers, and prisoners; with his father, published *American Ballads and Folk Songs* (1934), *Negro Folk Songs as Sung by Leadbelly* (1936), *Cowboy Songs* (1937), *Our Singing Country* (1938), and *Folk Songs: USA* (1946); after earning a degree in philosophy at the University of Texas, in 1936, made his first solo field trip, to eastern Kentucky, including the town of Harlan; in 1938, interviewed and recorded at length the New Orleans jazz musician Jelly Roll Morton; published the book *Mister Jelly Roll: The Fortunes of Jelly Roll Morton, New Orleans Creole and "Inventor of Jazz"* (1950); in 1941, recorded three record sides by the blues singer McKinley Morganfield, who went on to win popularity and commercial success as Muddy Waters; during the 1940s, hosted two network radio shows; during the presidential election campaign of 1948, sang alongside Pete Seeger and Paul Robeson in support of Henry A. Wallace, the Progressive Citizens of America candidate; with the advent of McCarthyism in the U.S., went into exile; from 1950 to 1957, lived in Britain, where, with a Guggenheim Fellowship, he compiled an archive of British folk songs; on British radio and television, presented programs of American folk and hillbilly music that helped inspire the development of skiffle among such young English musicians as John Lennon; also during his exile, compiled archives of Spanish and Italian folk songs that became the basis of two 10-part series on BBC radio; published *The Folk Songs of North America* in 1960; after his return to the U.S., revisited many of the sites of his early monaural recordings to make stereo recordings, beginning in the South; provided recordings for 19 albums released on the Atlantic and Prestige labels; had earlier provided the recordings for the five-album set *Folk Songs of North America*; made several field trips to the Caribbean; compiled an archive of Caribbean music, housed at the University of the West Indies; from 1962 to 1989, was a research associate in the Department of Anthropology and the Center for the Social Sciences at Columbia University; at Hunter College in 1969, established the Association for Cultural Equity to handle his Global Jukebox, a database cross-referencing thousands of songs and dances with anthropological information; won the National Book Critics Circle Award for nonfiction with his book *The Land Where the Blues Began* (1993); was involved in the making of several films, including the documentary *The Land Where the Blues Began* (1985), which he wrote, produced, and directed and which won the blue ribbon at the 1985

American Film Festival; for public television in the early 1990s, created, narrated, and produced the five-hour series *American Patchwork*; died in Florida. See *Current Biography* (September) 1941.

Obituary *New York Times* A p1+ July 20, 2002

**LORD, WALTER** Oct. 8, 1917–May 19, 2002 Best-selling author of what he called "living history"; beginning with his spectacularly successful *A Night to Remember*, was a pioneer in the now commonplace application of the narrative techniques of contemporary journalism—in conjunction with scrupulous research, in his case—to the creation of pseudo-eyewitness historical accounts; by using that personal, "You are there" perspective, turned the dull inevitability of actual past events into the stuff of suspenseful fiction; interrupted his study of law at Yale University to work as a code clerk and intelligence analyst with the Office of Strategic Services during World War II; received his law degree at Yale in 1946; during the late 1940s and early 1950s, wrote and edited business newsletters on legal subjects for the Research Institute of America, was editor-in-chief with Business Reports, another information service, collaborated with J. K. Lasser, the tax expert, in the writing of the book *Payroll Almanac*, and wrote copy for the J. Walter Thompson advertising agency in New York City; meanwhile, was working in his spare time on his first two historical books; edited and annotated the Civil War diary of Sir Arthur James Lyon Freemantle, a British military officer and Confederate sympathizer who toured the South in 1863; published *The Freemantle Diary* in 1954; spent years of concentrated research on the story of the "unsinkable" British ocean liner *Titanic*, which struck an iceberg and sank in the North Atlantic on its maiden voyage, from Southampton, England, to New York in 1912, with an attendant loss of 1,500 lives; tracked down and interviewed some 60 *Titanic* survivors; weaved together the research and interviews to produce a minute-by-minute account of the disaster in *A Night to Remember* (1955), a Book of the Month Club selection (like many of his subsequent books) that has, long term, sold in the millions of copies and inspired a television adaptation (1956) and several motion pictures, the most accurate of which was the 1958 British version; again created the illusion of a live news story in *Day of Infamy* (1957), about the Japanese attack on Pearl Harbor in 1941; in a departure from pointillistic technique, turned to broad strokes of panoramic history to cover the first 15 years of the 20th century in the U.S. in *The Good Years* (1960); returned to pointillism in his reconstruction of the two-week siege of the Alamo and the final slaughter of 180 Texans there in *A Time to Stand* (1961); for junior and senior high-school students, wrote *Peary to the Pole* (1963); drew mixed reactions with *The Past That Would Not Die* (1952), a history of race relations in Mississippi back to the Civil War; traveled thousands of miles gathering facts and conducting interviews for *Incredible Victory* (1967), about the critical American naval victory over the Japanese at Midway in 1942; spent three years researching and writing *The Dawn's Early Light* (1972), in which he dealt with the War of 1812 from its point of climax, the American repulse of the British in the battle of Baltimore in 1914; traveled to the jungles of Guadalcanal in the South Pacific in the course of researching *Lonely Vigil* (1977), a tribute to the civilian coast watchers in the Solomon Islands who spotted Japanese aircraft and spied on Japanese ships for the U.S. during World War II; recounted the evacuation of British and French troops from France in a motley flotilla in 1940 in *The Miracle of Dunkirk* (1977); wrote a second book on the *Titanic, The Night Continues* (1986), containing new information garnered from correspondence with survivors, their families, and students of the disaster over a period of three decades; died in his bachelor apartment in Manhattan. See *Current Biography* (October) 1972.

Obituary *New York Times* B p7 May 21, 2002

**LOVE, JOHN A.** Nov. 29, 1916–Jan. 21, 2002 "Citizen governor" of Colorado (1963–73); former federal official; lawyer; was a moderate, virtually nominal, Republican, in disagreement on many issues with the party establishment; as governor, signed the Colorado Air and Water Pollution Act and legislation legalizing abortion and reducing picayune possession of marijuana from a felony to a misdemeanor; attracted high-tech businesses to the state; oversaw the expansion of state aid to public schools; was remembered as "the last political innocent elected governor of Colorado . . . untouched by scandal and personally liked even by his political enemies" in a eulogy in the Denver *Rocky Mountain News* titled "Colorado Prospered During His Administration"; served as a member of President Richard M. Nixon's Fact Finding Commission on Vietnam in 1970; during his third term as governor, in 1973, resigned to accept Nixon's invitation that he come to Washington, D.C., as director of the Office of Energy Policy; served in that post only six months; subsequently, taught history at the University of Northern Colorado; later, was chief executive officer and chairman of the board of Ideal Basic Industries Inc., a concrete and potash company; died in Aurora, Colorado. See *Current Biography* (November) 1963.

Obituary *New York Times* B p8 Jan. 24, 2002

**LUNS, JOSEPH M. A. H.** Aug. 28, 1911–July 17, 2002 Dutch politician and diplomat; former foreign minister; secretary general of the North Atlantic Treaty Organization (NATO, 1971–84); an early and avid promoter of the European Economic Community; held a degree in jurisprudence from the University of Amsterdam; in September 1938, joined his country's foreign service as an attaché at the ministry of foreign affairs in the Hague; in January 1940, was transferred to a similar post at the Netherlands' legation in Berne, Switzerland; later that year, when German forces occupied his homeland, was sent by the Dutch government-in-exile in London to the legation in Lisbon, Portugal, where he became second secretary; was first secretary of the embassy in London from 1944 to 1948; completed his career in the foreign service as a member of the Netherlands' permanent delegation to the United Nations in New York City, from 1948 to 1952; during the following two decades, was elected to four terms (as a Catholic People's Party candidate) in the Estates General, the Dutch Parliament, and served as foreign minister in a series of governments; following his retirement as head of NATO, chose to remain in Brussels, Belgium, rather than return to the Netherlands, which, he explained, had become too "permissive" an environment for a cultural conservative such as he. See *Current Biography* (April) 1982.

Obituary *New York Times* A p19 July 18, 2002

**MANSFIELD, MIKE** Mar. 16, 1903–Oct. 5, 2001 Democratic U.S. representative from Montana (1943–53); U.S. senator (1953–77); ambassador to Japan (1977–87); before entering politics, was a professor of Far Eastern and Latin American history and political science at the University of Montana; maintained a centrist liberal voting record throughout his years in Washington; during his tenure in the House of Representatives, was sent on a confidential mission to China (1944–45) and served as a delegate to the ninth Inter-American Conference in Bogotá and the sixth session of the U.N. General Assembly (1951); was first elected to the Senate by a 5,800-vote margin (in 260,400 ballots cast) in 1952; in the Senate, became assistant to majority leader Lyndon B. Johnson, or "majority whip," in 1957; four years later, when Johnson became vice president of the U.S., succeeded him as majority leader in the Senate; brought to that post a low-keyed, accommodating style, in sharp contrast to that of Johnson, a swaggering browbeater; following President John F. Kennedy's assassination and Johnson's succession to the presidency, guided Johnson's historic Great Society program—a mass of civil rights, antipoverty, health, and education legislation—through the Senate, toward passage by the Congress; was proudest of his key role in passage of legislation leading to ratification of the 26th amendment to the Constitution, which lowered the minimum voting age from 21 to 18; was an early opponent of the war in Vietnam; cosponsored the War Powers Act (1973), limiting the president's authority to commit American troops to combat abroad without a congressional declaration of war; despite his firm advocacy of gun control (not a popular position in Montana), was reelected to the Senate three times with more than 60 percent of the votes cast each time; following his service as ambassador to Japan, was a senior adviser in the Washington office of Goldman Sachs, the investment-banking firm, actively so until a week before his death; died at Walter Reed Army Medical Center. See *Current Biography* (June) 1973.

Obituary *New York Times* p1+ Oct. 6, 2001

**MARCUS, STANLEY** Apr. 20, 1905–Jan. 22, 2002 Retail entrepreneur; the eldest scion of the German-American Jewish family that founded the Neiman Marcus Co., the upscale Dallas, Texas, department-store business that now comprises 30 emporiums appealing to well-to-do conspicuous consumers in 17 states and the District of Columbia, all of which are components (along with the Bergdorf Goodman and DM Direct stores) of the Neiman Marcus Group; upon receipt of his master's degree in business administration at Harvard University, in 1936, began his career as a floor man in the apparel department of the original Neiman Marcus store, in Dallas; during his first year, introduced the fashion shows for which the store was to become famous; two years later, became merchandise manager of the store's sportswear shop; at the same time, became secretary and treasurer of the Neiman Marcus Co. and a member of its board of directors; in 1929, was promoted to merchandise manager of all apparel divisions; expanded the store's fur sales; personally sold more than $10 million worth of furs to customers; in 1935, took on the duties of executive vice president of the company; in 1938, originated the Neiman Marcus awards, regarded as the "Oscars" of the fashion world; in 1950, became president of the Neiman Marcus Co.; over the following two decades, expanded operations from one store to four, three in and around Dallas and one in Houston; presided over an increase in the company's annual sales from $20.6 million to more than $62 million and profits from $880,000 to more than $2 million; became an international jet-set celebrity with entrée to White House social events and royal garden parties in London; in 1969, sold the Neiman Marcus Co. to the merchandising conglomerate Carter Hawley Hale Stores in return for conglomerate stock then valued at $40 million and with the understanding that he would retain independent control of the company; remained president until 1972, when he was succeeded by his son, Richard; was, successively, chairman of the company's board for four years and chairman of its executive committee for three years; was a corporate vice president and member of the board of Carter Hawley Hale; died in Dallas, Texas. See *Current Biography* (June) 1949.

Obituary *New York Times* A p16 Jan. 23, 2002

**MARGARET, PRINCESS OF GREAT BRITAIN** Aug. 21, 1930–Feb. 9, 2002 The younger sister of Queen Elizabeth II; a free spirit who chafed at the shackles of royal convention; the tragic heroine in a public drama of renounced love; was described in the British press as "the party princess," "the Diana of her day," a "tearaway princess ahead of her time"; "was born into a fairy tale and lived to see it become a soap opera"; in the years immediately following World War II, was the namesake of British high society's "Margaret set" and the epitome of the beautiful, vivacious, and stylishly dressed socialite, a persona that would be damaged at a relatively early age by hard drinking and chain smoking; in the mid-1950s (when convention regarding the marriage of royals was stricter than today), was induced by pressure from the court, the British cabinet, the Church of England, and the London *Times* to renounce her proposed marriage to the love of her life, the dashing Royal Air Force group captain Peter Townsend, a divorced commoner twice her age who had been an aide to her father, the late King George VI; thereafter, threw herself into flamboyant partying in Mayfair and the West End and a series of romantic affairs extending over some 25 years; in 1960, married the society photographer Antony Armstrong-Jones (later ennobled as Lord Snowdon); by that marriage, had two children, David (Lord Linley) and Sarah (Lady Chatto); was divorced from Lord Snowdon in 1978, 12 years after the marriage's de facto end; annually retreated to her villa, Les Jolies Eaux, built on property (given to her by her friend Lord Glenconner) on the West Indian island of Mustique; there, entertained a virtual who's who of aristocracy, music, film, and fashion; was the royal patron of numerous charities; assiduously supported the arts, especially the Royal Ballet and the Scottish Ballet; died in London. See *Current Biography* (November) 1953.

Obituary *New York Times* p38 Feb. 10, 2002

**MARTIN, ARCHER** Mar. 1, 1910–July 28, 2002 British biochemist; with Richard Lawrence Millington Synge, shared the 1952 Nobel Prize for chemistry for their advancement of the science of chromatography, with positive repercussions in all branches of chemistry; began working with Synge as a graduate student at Cambridge University in the mid-1930s; beginning in 1938, continued his work with Synge at the Wool Industries Research Association laboratories in Leeds, where they investigated the amino-acid compounds in wool-fiber proteins; to better study the subtly differing compounds, developed a technique known variously as paper chromatography and liquid-liquid partition chromatography, reported by them in a paper published in 1941; from 1946 to 1948, worked at the Boots Pure Drug Co. in Nottingham; was on the staff of the Medical Research Council from 1948 to 1952; headed the National Institute of Medical Research from 1952 to 1956; was director of Abbotsbury Laboratories from 1959 to 1970; was a professorial fellow at Sussex University from 1973 to 1978; in the U.S., was a professor at the University of Houston from 1974 to 1979; died in Llangarron, Herefordshire, England. See *Current Biography* (November) 1953.

Obituary *New York Times* B p8 Aug. 6, 2002

**MARTIN, JAMES S. JR.** June 21, 1920–Apr. 14, 2002 Aeronautical engineer; with the National Aeronautics and Space Administration (NASA), was assistant manager of the unmanned Lunar Orbiter Project in the mid-1960s; subsequently, directed NASA's Viking unmanned space missions, which provided the space agency with the first maps and close-up photographs of Mars; held a B.S. degree from the University of Michigan; did graduate work in middle management at the Harvard University School of Business; during World War II, helped to design fighter planes as an engineer at Republic Aircraft Corp.; in his two-decade tenure with Republic, was successively chief research engineer, assistant director of administration, and, finally, manager of space systems requirements; joined NASA's Langley Research Center in 1964; as assistant manager of the Lunar Orbiter Project, was chiefly responsible for contract administration and technical management of the project, comprising five unmanned lunar orbital missions, which sent back from the moon photographs and information essential for the success of the subsequent manned Apollo lunar flights; as Viking project manager, beginning in 1969, led the massive scientific, engineering, and logistical effort culminating in the launch from Cape Canaveral in April and May 1975 of Viking I and Viking II, robot-controlled spacecraft that reached Mars the following year and continued orbiting and landing on the red planet and transmitting data for more than five years; resigned from NASA at the end of 1976 to become vice president for advanced programs and planning with Martin Marietta Aerospace in Bethesda, Maryland; later served as a consultant to NASA on the Mars Pathfinder, Explorer, and Odyssey missions; died in Crofton, Maryland. See *Current Biography* (March) 1977.

Obituary *New York Times* A p18 Apr. 20, 2002

**McINTIRE, CARL** May 17, 1906–Mar. 19, 2002 Protestant clergyman; schismatic Presbyterian preacher; a firebrand radio evangelist who combined a fundamentalist Christian message with hawkish patriotism and right-wing politics in his crusade against the evils of "modernism and socialism"; in Collingswood, New Jersey, in 1936, founded the Bible Presbyterian Church, a splinter group that would grow into a denomination comprising some 55 congregations; in 1948, founded the International Council of Christian Churches (ICCC) to counter the "liberalism and apostasy" of that "ecumenical monster," the World Council of Churches; in 1957, launched his daily 30-minute radio program, the *Twentieth Century Reformation Hour*; during the 1960s, was heard on more than 600 radio stations in the Bible Belt of the South, the Midwest, and the Southwest; alerted his listeners to the dangers of loose interpretation of scripture, the "social Gospel" of mainstream Protestantism, the "fascist" Roman Catholic Church's alleged drive for power, the government-imposed socialization of life in the U.S., any and every form of friendly coexistence with communism, and the infiltration of Communist influences that he perceived happening in American government, religion, education, and family life; at his Twentieth Century Reformation Center in Collingswood, taped broadcasts for distribution to Bible Belt radio stations; did live broadcasting from the radio station owned by his seminary in Elkins Park, Pennsylvania, across the state line from Collingswood; pursuant to complaints filed by the Greater Philadelphia Council of Churches, was denied renewal of his broadcasting license by the Federal Communications Commission in the early 1970s, on the ground that, by refusing to allow competing opinion on his station, he was in violation of the then operative "Fairness Doctrine"; subsequently, broadcast from a "pirate" station offshore, from a ship in Delaware Bay, until the Coast Guard shut him down; at his Twentieth Century Reformation Center in Collingswood, operated a library, a bookstore, a plant for printing his tracts, the headquarters for the ICCC's missionary charities, and a small high school; in Cape May, New Jersey, operated a Bible conference center, a Christian resort, and Shelton College; also owned a large hotel and conference center in Cape Canaveral, Florida, and a Bible college in El Cajun, California; during the Vietnam War, led several pro-war rallies in Washington, D.C.; retired as Bible Presbyterian Church pastor in 1999; died in Voorhees, New Jersey. See *Current Biography* (October) 1971.

Obituary *New York Times* B p9 Mar. 22, 2002

**McNALLY, ANDREW 3d** Aug. 17, 1909–Nov. 15, 2001 Publisher; great-grandson of the Andrew McNally who in the mid-1800s co-founded Rand

McNally & Co., which thereafter developed from a midwestern printer of railroad tickets into the world's largest publisher of maps (while continuing to print about half the railroad and bus tickets in the U.S., most of the airline tickets, and about five million railroad timetables); joined the company in 1931; became president in 1948; set about modernizing the company's map production; in 1949, added to its several printing plants that of W. B. Conkey Co. in Hammond, Indiana, a facility capable of printing large books; within that year, published the outsized *Cosmopolitan World Atlas*, which had been eight years in preparation; between 1948 and 1954, oversaw an increase in annual sales from $8.3 million to $18.5 million; served as president of Rand McNally until 1974 and thereafter as chairman, until 1993; died at his home in Chicago, Illinois. See *Current Biography* (November) 1956.

Obituary *New York Times* D p9 Nov. 22, 2001

**MILLER, NEAL E.** Aug. 3, 1909–Mar. 23, 2002 Experimental psychologist; behavioral scientist; pioneered in the therapeutic use of biofeedback in the course of his groundbreaking studies establishing the ability of the brain to modify autonomic bodily functions; after earning his Ph.D. degree in psychology, at Yale University in 1935, studied psychoanalysis (which in those days was done by undergoing psychoanalysis) in Vienna, Austria, for eight months under Heinz Hartmann, a student of Freud's; in 1936, returned to Yale, where he joined the faculty of the Institute of Human Relations as an instructor and research associate in psychology; in collaboration with the Yale sociologist John Dollard, set about combining "the three great traditions" of psychoanalysis, experimental psychology, and sociology "to aid in the creation of a psychological base for a general science of human behavior"; began his research into emotional behavior by inserting tiny electrical probes into the hypothalamuses of cats and rats, thus locating the exact centers of pain, pleasure, hunger, and fear; modified the behavior of the animals by electrically rewarding and punishing them; in 1961, announced his conclusion that the brain is not a passive cerebral switchboard but an active organ capable of considerable control over its sensory input and of learning to affect not only the "voluntary" nervous system but such "involuntary" functions of the autonomic nervous system as blood pressure, heart rate, bowel contractions, and kidney function—a conviction at that time regarded as heretical by the psychology establishment; in 1966, cofounded the Laboratory of Physiological Psychology at Rockefeller University, where he developed more sophisticated, less intrusive operant-conditioning techniques; in 1969, began applying those techniques to human beings; taught tachycardia patients at Cornell University Medical Center to slow their heart rates to a more normal level; in a series of tests at Rockefeller University, proved that both healthy and hypertensive individuals could be trained to raise or lower their diastolic pressure; wrote *Fact and Fancy about Biofeedback and Its Clinical Implications* (1976) and *The Scientists' Responsibility for Public Information: A Guide to Effective Communication with the Media* (1985); co-wrote *Frustration and Aggression* (1939), *Social Learning and Imitation* (1941), *Personality and Psychotherapy: An Analysis in Terms of Learning, Thinking, and Culture* (1950), and *Graphic Communication and the Crisis in Education* (1957); co-edited *Biofeedback—Basic Problems and Clinical Applications* (1982). See *Current Biography* (July) 1974.

Obituary *New York Times* A p21 Apr. 2, 2002

**MONTRESOR, BENI** Mar. 31, 1926(?)–Oct. 11, 2001 Italian-born artist; stage designer; illustrator of children's books, some written by him; won the Caldecott Medal for his fun-spirited pictures for Beatrice Schenk de Regniers's *May I Bring a Friend?* (1964), about a little boy who invites his animal friends from the zoo to accompany him to daily royal tea parties; had a banner year in 1966, with a New York City Opera production at Lincoln Center of Mozart's *The Magic Flute* with his scenery (which reminded the critic Alan Rich of "an autumn landscape . . . sprinkled with gold") and the publication of Stephen Spender's retelling for children of the story of *The Magic Flute*, illustrated by Montresor; for a 1985 production of *The Magic Flute*, revived his original sets, which that time around suggested to one critic "a happy mixture of J.R.R. Tolkien and Maxfield Parrish"; studied art (chiefly painting) at the Liceo Artistico in Verona (1942–45) and the Académia di Belle Arti in Venice (1945–49) and cinematic set and costume design at the Centro Sperimentale di Cinematografia in Rome (1950–52); as a set designer at the Cinecittà Studios in Rome during the 1950s, collaborated with such film directors as Federico Fellini, Vittorio de Sica, and Roberto Rossellini; designed the decor for a score of motion pictures, including *Siegfried* (1958); also designed costumes and sets for several European stage productions, including *Beatrice Cenci* and *La Folle de Chaillot*; in 1960, left Italy for what he intended to be a short visit to the U.S.; in New York City, became friends with the Italian-born Gian Carlo Menotti, who had become the foremost composer/librettist of popular American opera and who had recently founded the Festival of Two Worlds in Spoletto, Italy; was commissioned by Menotti to do the sets and costumes for a production of Samuel Barber's opera *Vanessa*, with libretto by Menotti, at Spoletto in the summer of 1961; the following year, executed the stage designs for *Pelléas et Mélisande* at the Glyndebourne Festival in England; in 1964, did the stage designs for the New York premiere of Menotti's *The Last Savage* at the Metropolitan Opera and the costume designs for a production of the play *Marco Millions* at the Repertory Theater of Lincoln Center as well as a revival of the ballet *Dim Lustre* by the New York City Ballet; at Spoletto in 1964, was the stage designer for a British Royal Ballet revival of *Raymonda*; created the sets and costumes for the Richard Rodgers and Stephen Sondheim musical *Do I Hear a Waltz?*, which opened on Broadway in March 1965; on that occasion, according to the critic John McLain, gave the audience "an atmospheric tour and a simple lesson in stage artistry" with his set changes—"absolutely magnificent beige and pastel etchings . . . which fall magically into place" without a lowering of the curtain or a halt in the action; according to Alan Rich, "sprayed the stage with every happy color you could imagine" in his designs for a production of *La Cenerentola* by the Metropolitan Opera's national company later in 1965; was director (for the first time) as well as stage designer of the memorable 1966 production of *The Magic Flute* at Lincoln Center; following his work as stage designer for a 1995 Metropolitan Opera production of *L'Elisir d'Amore* in 1995, did some more directing at small opera houses around the world; illustrated, among children's books by others, *On Christmas Eve* (1951), *Belling the Tiger* (1961), and *The Princesses: Sixteen Stories About Princesses* (1962); was the author as well as the illustrator of *House of Flowers, House of Stars* (1962), *The Witches of Venice* (1963), *Cinderella* (1965), and *I Saw a Ship A-Sailing* (1967); lived alternately in the U.S. and Italy; died in Verona, Italy. See *Current Biography* (December) 1967.

Obituary *New York Times* A p11 Oct. 13, 2001

**MOORE, DUDLEY** Apr. 19, 1935–Mar. 27, 2002 British actor; comedian; pianist; composer; a diminutive performer, five feet, two and one-half inches tall, who was known affectionately to British audiences as "Cuddly Dudley"; in stage productions (including the seminal satirical revue *Beyond the Fringe*) and motion pictures (including *Arthur*), demonstrated a gift for comic timing and a droll sense of humor ranging from subtle to clownish; growing up in Dagenham, Essex, England, was the butt of other children's jokes because of his short stature and a club foot; on a music scholarship, attended Magdalen College, Oxford University; received his B.S. degree in music in 1957 and his B.Mus. degree in composition in 1958; meanwhile, had begun writing incidental music for theater and television, acting, and performing in cabarets; after leaving Oxford, toured as a jazz pianist with bands in Britain and the U.S.; at the Edinburgh Festival in 1960, joined with Peter Cook, Alan Bennett, and Jonathan Miller in creating the satirical revue *Beyond the Fringe*, a zany, politically savvy lampoon of serious and not-so-serious public issues; with Cook, Bennett, and Miller, proceeded to present the revue with great success in London's West End for two years and on Broadway for another two years and for a brief revival (1965); with Cook, collaborated on writing and performing the popular BBC-TV series *Not Only. . . But Also* (1964–70), a comic dialogue between two working-class blokes, Dud and Pete; co-starred with Cook in the motion picture *The Wrong Box* (1966), a farce about two villainous nephews greedy for an inheritance; was more successful with the farcical film *Bedazzled* (1967), a campy updating of the Faust legend in which the Moore character ultimately succeeds in wresting his soul back from the grasp of the Prince of Darkness (Cook); composed the score and co-wrote the screenplay for *30 Is a Dangerous Age, Cynthia* (1968), a comedy in which he was cast as a pianist and composer, Rupert Street, a mama's boy tardily cutting the apron strings; starred in the London stage version of *Play It Again, Sam* (1969); while touring Australia with his jazz trio in 1971, again teamed up with Cook, to create the revue *Behind the Fringe*; after touring Australia and New Zealand, presented the revue in London in 1972; the following year, took the show, retitled *Good Evening*, to New York, where it became the smash hit of the 1973–74 Broadway season and won Moore and Cook a special Tony Award; beginning in the early 1970s, recorded with Cook a series of three *Derek and Clive* comedy albums in which, Moore admitted, they "went just about as far as [they] could go with filth"; became a resident of Southern California in the mid-1970s; began to establish himself in Hollywood in the relatively small role of a sex-obsessed swinger in the comedy *Four Play* (1976); made his breakthrough to stardom in American film as George Webber, the composer infatuated with the Bo Derek character in the immense hit *10* (1979); headed the cast of the film *Wholly Moses!* (1980), a lackluster biblical spoof; won a Golden Globe Award and was nominated for an Academy Award for his performance in the title role of the movie *Arthur* (1981), about a drunken New York playboy whose inheritance depends on his moderating his layabout lifestyle and renouncing his love for a common waitress in favor of a planned wedding; as Arthur, was described by the critic Vincent Canby as "a satyr, a sprite, an over-age waif and a consistently endearing showoff"; continued in that role in the less successful *Arthur 2: On the Rocks* (1988); was charming in his first straight dramatic film role, opposite Mary Tyler Moore in the tearjerker *Six Weeks* (1982); again won a Golden Globe Award for his portrayal in *Micki and Maude* (1984) of a television reporter whose wife and mistress become pregnant at the same time; as a pianist, played with the Los Angeles Philharmonic Orchestra in Hollywood Bowl in 1981 and with a classical chamber-music ensemble at the Metropolitan Museum of Art in 1982; in 1991, collaborated with the conductor Sir Georg Solti on the *Orchestra!* series on Channel 4 television in Britain; on American television, appeared in the short-lived series *Dudley* (1993) and *Daddy's Girls* (1994); was married and divorced four times, to the actresses Suzy Kendall and Tuesday Weld, the model Brogan Lane, and lastly, Nicole Rothschild; lived with the singer Susan Anton for several years; died at his home in Plainfield, New Jersey. See *Current Biography* (June) 1982.

Obituary *New York Times* A p28 Mar. 28, 2002

**MOORE, ELISABETH LUCE** Apr. 4, 1903–Feb. 9, 2002 Philanthropist; public-service volunteer; organization official; sister of the late publisher Henry R. Luce; was born in China, the daughter of a Presbyterian missionary/educator who was instrumental in developing the United Board of China Christian Colleges; during World War II, chaired the national council of the USO; over the following half-century, served terms as a member of the advisory committee to the Marshall Plan, chair of the board of the foreign division of the Young Women's Christian Association of America, chair of the board of trustees of the Institute of International Education, vice chair of the Aid to Refugee Chinese Intellectuals, and a trustee of the Asia Foundation, the United Board of Christian Higher Education in Asia, and Wellesley College, her alma mater; served on the board of the Henry R. Luce Foundation for 63 years, until 1999; died at her home in Manhattan. See *Current Biography* (February) 1960.

Obituary *New York Times* B p9 Feb. 27, 2002

**MYDANS, SHELLEY SMITH** May 20, 1915–Mar. 7, 2002 Journalist; author; in 1938 married Carl M. Mydans, whom she had met the previous year in the offices of *Life* magazine, where he was a photographer and reporter and she a researcher; became a *Life* correspondent in 1939, when she and her husband were sent overseas to cover, first, the war in Europe and then war in China; in September 1941 flew to the Philippines with her husband; with him, was interned by the Japanese (first at the San Tomás camp in Manila and later in the Shanghai International Settlement) for 21 months in 1942 and 1943; after World War II, wrote for *Time* magazine as well as *Life* and did commentary on a New York radio station owned by *Time*; reported from Japan when her husband was chief of the *Time/Life* bureau in Tokyo; gave a fictionalized account of life in the San Tomás prisoner-of-war camp in her novel *The Open City* (1945); wrote two historical novels, *Thomas; A Novel of the Life, Passion, and Miracles of Becket* (1965) and *The Vermilion Bridge* (1980), set in the Nara period (eighth century A.D.) in Japan; with her husband, wrote *The Violent Peace* (1968), a survey of the outbreaks of terrorism, guerrilla insurgency, civil war, and other forms of armed conflict throughout the world in the two decades after World War II; died in New Rochelle, New York. See *Current Biography* (May) 1945.

Obituary *New York Times* A p16 Mar. 9, 2002

**NASON, JOHN W.** Feb. 9, 1905–Nov. 17, 2001 Educator; after graduating from Phillips Exeter Academy in New Hampshire and Carleton College in Northfield, Minnesota, studied at Yale Divinity School, earned an M.A. degree at Harvard University, and spent three years at Oriel College, Oxford University as a Rhodes scholar; was president of Swarthmore College, a Quaker institution in Pennsylvania, from 1940 to 1953; as chairman of the National Japanese-American Student Relocation Council, an interdenominational organization, from 1942 to 1945, was instrumental in effecting the release of more than 3,000 American students of Japanese descent from federal wartime detention camps and their enrollment in American colleges and universities; as president of the Foreign Policy Association, beginning in 1953, oversaw the establishment in many cities across the country of World Affairs Councils as forums for public debate on international issues; was president of Carleton College from 1962 to 1970; died in Kennett Square, Pennsylvania. See *Current Biography* (July) 1953.

Obituary *New York Times* D p9 Nov. 22, 2001

**NEHRU, B. K.** Sep. 4, 1909–Oct. 31, 2001 Indian diplomat; a cousin of the late prime minister Jawaharlal Nehru and his daughter, the late prime minister Indira Gandhi; was educated at the University of Allahabad, the London School of Economics, and Balliol College, Oxford University; read law at the Inner Temple in London; entered the Indian civil service in 1934; rose in the Indian Ministry of Finance to joint secretary (1947–49); between 1949 and 1954, was assigned to India's United Nations delegation; during that period in the U.S., held an executive position with the International Bank for Reconstruction and Development; after returning to his homeland, was commissioner general for economic affairs, a post in which he was, essentially, India's international fund-raiser; co-founded the Aid India Club, a consortium of donor nations that committed $2 billion to development in India, beginning in 1961, and promised another $2 billion later; in 1961, became India's ambassador to the U.S.; was highly favored to succeed Dag Hammarskjold as secretary-general of the U.N., but rejected that opportunity after Hammarskjold died in a plane crash, in 1961; did so on the advice of the Indian foreign minister, V. K. Krishna Menon; later realized, as he wrote in his memoirs, *Nice Guys Finish Second* (1997), that he had made "an idiotic decision" and that Menon had deliberately misadvised him, resentful of a height of international success that had been denied Menon himself; in 1968, returned to India to become governor of India's northeastern states, including Assam and Nagaland; was Indian high commissioner in London from 1973 to 1977; back in India in the 1980s, was governor of Jammu, Kashmir, and Gujarat; later chaired the U.N. Investment Committee; died in Kasauli, India. See *Current Biography* (February) 1963.

Obituary *New York Times* C p13 Nov. 9, 2001

**NOZICK, ROBERT** Nov. 16, 1938–Jan. 23, 2002 Philosopher; author; professor of philosophy at Harvard University; a leading political thinker of his time, and one with an accessibility to the lay reader rare among academics; achieved fame, and stirred controversy, with his first book, *Anarchy, State, and Utopia* (1974), a wittily argued libertarian/laissez-faire response to the liberal rationale for the redistributive welfare state presented by his Harvard colleague John Rawls in *A Theory of Justice* (1971); was born in Brooklyn, New York, "just one generation from the *shtetl*," in his words; as an undergraduate in philosophy at Columbia University, joined the Socialist Party and founded the Columbia branch of the Student League for Industrial Democracy; underwent the radical change in his philosophical perspective when he was earning his doctorate at Princeton University; taught at Princeton for two years and studied at Oxford University for one year before joining the Harvard faculty, in 1965; became a full professor four years later; for *Anarchy, State, and Utopia*, won the National Book Award in philosophy; with the book, attracted a large following among Reaganites, Thatcherites, and other conservatives, many of whom fell away when they realized that the support Nozick provided for the concerns of economic conservatism (private-property rights and the free market) was rooted in a philosophy of absolute individual rights and freedom from coercive government that extended to behaviors (such as homosexuality, prostitution, and recreational use of drugs) to which social conservatism is inimical; subsequently wrote *Philosophical Explanations* (1981), in which he sharply differentiated his approach to epistemology (as a sort of art form) from that of the logical positivists, who view science as the only sure way to true knowledge; as the Socratic title of the book suggested, addressed himself to ethics, or the conduct of life, in *The Examined Life: Philosophical*

*Meditations* (1981); was concerned with reasoning in *The Nature of Rationality* (1993), with methodology in *Socratic Puzzles* (1997), and with truth and relativity in *Invariances: The Structure of the Objective World* (1991); chaired the Philosophy Department at Harvard from 1981 to 1984; was elevated to Harvard's prestigious Joseph Pellegrino chair in philosophy in 1998; died in Cambridge, Massachusetts. See *Current Biography* (June) 1982.

Obituary *New York Times* B p8 Jan. 24, 2002

**PÉREZ JIMÉNEZ, MARCOS** Apr. 25, 1914–Sep. 20, 2001 Venezuelan army general; last military dictator of Venezuela (1952–58); headed what was reputed to be the most corrupt and repressive regime in Venezuelan history, supported by a brutal security force that silenced opponents by incarceration and torture; on the other hand, was lavish in his expenditure of money on tourist attractions in Caracas and grand public works, including a highway burrowed through mountains to connect Caracas to Venezuela's Caribbean coast; in 1945, participated in the military coup that overthrew the government of General Isáias Medina Angaritar and installed in the presidency Rómulo Betancourt, who lost to Rómulo Gallegos Freire in Venezuela's first democratic election, in 1947; was a member of the three-man military junta that ousted Gallegos Freire in 1948; was minister of defense in a government headed by Carlos Delago Chalbaud; following the assassination of Delago Chalbaud, in 1950, became the power behind the ostensibly civilian presidency of Germán Duárez Flamerich; founded a new political party, the Frente Electoral Independiente; called for a popular election, in which he ran for the presidency as the FEI candidate in 1952; when the balloting appeared to be going in favor of a minority party, the Union Republicana Democrática, blacked out news coverage of the election, forced the URD leaders into exile, and had himself declared president by a constituent assembly, pending reestablishment of a "constitutional government"; in 1957, replaced a scheduled popular election with an apparently rigged plebiscite favoring his continuance in power; in 1958, was driven from office by a popular rebellion (abetted by air force and navy revolts) that ushered in 43 years of continuous democratic rule in Venezuela; with his family, fled to the Dominican Republic, where he lived under the protection of the dictator Rafael Leonidas Trujillo until Trujillo's assassination, in 1961; subsequently, lived in Miami, Florida; in 1963, was extradited by American authorities to Venezuela, where he was tried and sentenced to prison for embezzling $250 million from the Venezuelan national treasury; on his release from prison, in 1968, moved to Spain, where he lived out the rest of his life; died in Madrid, Spain. See *Current Biography* (November) 1954.

Obituary *New York Times* A p12 Sep. 23, 2001

**PERUTZ, MAX** May 19, 1914–Feb. 6, 2002 Austrian-born British biochemist; a rightful claimant to the title of father of molecular biology; co-winner of the 1962 Nobel Prize in chemistry for his elucidation of the structure of the hemoglobin molecule; shared the prize with his associate John Kendrew, who had determined the structure of myoglobin; as an undergraduate in chemistry at the University of Vienna, became interested in biochemistry; was particularly fascinated by reports from Cavendish Laboratory at Cambridge University, where scientists were succeeding in determining the type and distribution of atoms in simple inorganic molecules through the use of X-ray crystallography; at Cambridge in 1936, became a candidate for the Ph.D. degree (received in 1940); in the Cavendish Laboratory, under Professor J. D. Bernal and with the assistance of the physicist Isidore Fankuchin, addressed himself to the application of X-ray diffraction to proteins, relatively large and complex molecules that are the most important constituents of living matter; in 1938, began subjecting crystals of horse hemoglobin (grown for him by Gilbert S. Adair, a Cambridge physiologist) to the technique; suspended those experiments during World War II, when he worked for the British Navy on plans to use glacial ice floes as aircraft carriers, a project that never reached fruition; at Cambridge after the war, overcame a major obstacle to progress in his experiments with horse hemoglobin early in 1953, when he discovered the "heavy atom" method of labeling the hemoglobin crystals with mercury, which made isomorphous replacement (as in Fournier's synthesis) possible; over the following six years, through the instrumentality of Cambridge University's high-speed computer bank (state of the art for the time), analyzed hundreds of X-ray pictures; in 1960, published his findings on the structure of the hemoglobin molecule, showing 574 amino-acid units in four folded chains twisted in three dimensions, as Linus Pauling had predicted a decade earlier; later, studied the transportation of oxygen in the molecular structure and the effect of the protein globulin on the iron-containing haem group and its relation to the effect of protein on the catalytic properties of metals and co-enzymes; published two collections of essays on science, scientists, and medicine: *Is Science Necessary?* (1989) and *I Wish I'd Made You Angry Earlier* (1998); died at his home in Cambridge, England. See *Current Biography* (November) 1963.

Obituary *New York Times* A p21 Feb. 8, 2002

**PHILLIPS, WILLIAM** Nov. 14, 1907–Sep. 13, 2002 Editor; writer; co-founder (in the 1930s) of the quarterly *Partisan Review*, perhaps the most influential political/literary journal of the mid-20th century, when it served both as a forum for the great ideological debates then taking place among American Marxist intellectuals and as a showcase for such avant-garde writers of fiction, poetry, and criticism (literary, art, and social) as Delmore Schwartz, Lionel Trilling, Clement Greenberg, Edmund Wilson, Elizabeth Hardwick, Bernard Malamud, Saul Bellow, Irving Howe, Meyer Shapiro, Allen Tate, Robert Penn Warren, and Susan Sontag; co-edited the review until 1965; was editor in chief from 1965 until 2002; was born in New York City, into a family originally called Litvinsky; absorbed modernist aesthetics when earning a degree in English at the City college of New York and taking graduate courses at New York University; was politicized by the great economic depression that followed the Wall Street crash of 1929; in Manhattan's Greenwich Village in the early 1930s, joined the John Reed club, a group of writers and artists that was a creature of the Communist Party; there, met Philip Rahv, a young Jewish immigrant from Eastern Europe who, like he, was drawn to radical leftist politics and, at the same time, was open to avant-garde culture; with Rahv, decided to "launch a new literary movement, combining . . . the best of the new radicalism with the innovative energy of modernism"; founded the *Partisan Review* as the organ of the John Reed Club; published the first issue in February 1934, the beginning of what he called the publication's "Stalinist phase," which lasted through eight more issues, until the fall of 1936; during that phase, became disillusioned with Communism in all its forms and increasingly resented and rebelled against the constant pressure to subordinate literary standards to the expediencies of the soviet-dominated party line; assembled a new editorial board that included such independent spirits as Dwight Macdonald and Mary McCarthy; in December1937, published the first issue of a revamped, independent *Partisan Review*; was subjected to a torrent of abuse from the American Communist press, which described him and Rahv, in his paraphrase, as "Trotskyites, counterrevolutionaries, literary snakes, [and] agents of imperialism"; on the other hand, as the social historian Christopher Leach observed, "earned from American intellectuals a lasting debt of gratitude by exposing the totalitarian character of Soviet Communism . . . at a time when not only radicals but many liberals still looked to [the Stalinist Soviet Union] as the hope of the world"; during the 1960s and 1970s, steered a middle course between the New Left and the neoconservatism of such former Marxist cohorts as Norman Podhoretz and William Barrett; from 1963 to 1978, published *Partisan Review* under the auspices of Rutgers University, which provided him with editorial office space and a professorship; beginning in 1978, published under the auspices of Boston University; wrote the memoir Partisan View: Five Decades of a Literary Life (1983); edited the anthology *Sixty Years of Great Fiction from the Partisan Review* (1997); was succeeded in the editorship of the review by his second wife, Edith Kurzwell; died in Manhattan. See *Current Biography* (October) 1984.

Obituary *New York Times* A p26 Sep. 14, 2002

**PIERCE, JOHN ROBINSON** Mar. 27, 1910–Apr. 2, 2002 Electrical engineer; satellite-communications pioneer; acoustics expert; science-fiction writer; synthetic music composer; author; in one of the least of his accomplishments, gave the transistor its name; after earning a Ph.D. degree at the California Institute of Technology in 1936, joined the staff of the Bell Telephone Laboratories in New York, where he worked on high-frequency electron tubes and, during World War II, radar and other electronic devices for the U.S. military; after the war, joined with researchers at the Massachusetts Institute of Technology in developing a radio navigation system known as "loran," for launching guided missiles; when approached by colleagues who needed help in naming a solid-state device they had invented for amplifying electrical signals in 1948, coined the term "transistor"; at the Bell Laboratories division in Murray Hill, New Jersey, was director of electronic research (1952–55), director of research in electrical communications (1955–58), and executive director of research in communications (1958-71); in 1954, began promoting an idea that had been conceived by Arthur C. Clarke nine years earlier: that a relay satellite could greatly increase the capacity for global telephone communications and might ultimately make intercontinental cables obsolete; in collaboration with others, including the National Aeronautics and Space Administration, developed Echo I, a giant aluminum-coated plastic balloon, launched into orbit in 1960, that bounced phone calls across the U.S. via the Bell Labs facility in Crawford Hills, New Jersey, and made possible the first direct transcontinental television transmissions; in 1962, played a key role in the development and launch of Telstar, the first active communications satellite, which not only carried international phone traffic but relayed the first live television images between the U.S. and Europe; in 1971, left Bell to become a professor of engineering at the California Institute of Technology and a researcher in the institute's jet-propulsion laboratory; was also a professor of music at Stanford University for 12 years; composed music by computer, selections of which are on the recording *The Historical CD of Digital Sound Synthesis*; flew gliders; held some 90 patents, including one for a reflex klystron, a vacuum tube used in radar; wrote a score of books, including *Theory and Design of Electron Beams* (1949), *Electrons, Waves, and Messages* (1956), *Symbols, Signals, and Noise* (1961), *Quantum Electronics* (1966), *An Introduction to Information Theory* (1980), and *The Science of Musical Sound* (1983); retired from his teaching positions in 1983; died in Sunnyvale, California. See *Current Biography* (February) 1961.

Obituary *New York Times* C p11 Apr. 5, 2002

**POLETTI, CHARLES** July 2, 1903–Aug. 8, 2002 Democratic politician; attorney; judge; interim governor of New York (1942–43); was the son of Italian immigrants; after earning a B.A. degree in political economy at Harvard University, in 1924, did postgraduate work at the University of Rome for a year; took his LL.B. degree at Harvard in 1928; practiced law in New York City and elsewhere in New York State from 1928 to 1937; became counsel to Governor Herbert H. Lehman in 1933; was appointed by Lehman to fill a vacancy in the New York State Supreme Court in 1937; six months later, was elected to a full term on the court; in 1938, stepped down from the court to run successfully for lieutenant governor; moved up to the governorship on December 3, 1942, when Lehman (then a lame duck) resigned to become director of U.S. war relief in Europe; served as governor for less than a full month, until Thomas E. Dewey, who had been elected governor in November 1942, took office at the beginning of January 1943; on January 4, 1943, became special assistant to Secretary of War Henry L. Stimson; three months later, was commissioned a lieutenant colonel in the U.S. Army; was later promoted to full colonel; in July 1943, landed in Sicily with troops of the Seventh Army; as a senior officer in the Allied military government for territories liberated from Nazi and Fascist control, directed the reconstruction of infrastructure, the restoration of public services, and the equitable distribution of food in Italy in the wake of the British/American drive northward through the country; later directed civil affairs operations in Naples, Milan, and Rome; after the war, became senior partner in a New York law firm; in 1946 and 1947, arbitrated labor disputes in the garment industry; later, worked under Robert Moses at the New York State Power Authority and in overseeing foreign pavilions at the 1964–65 New York World's Fair; is memorialized by the Power Authority's plant in Astoria, Queens, named in his honor; in retirement, lived on Marco Island, Florida; died there. See *Current Biography* (September) 1943.

Obituary *New York Times* A p11 Aug. 10, 2002

**POTOK, CHAIM** Feb. 17, 1929–July 23, 2002 Author; the first American novelist to present to a wide audience an insider's view of conflicted human beings in the insular world of orthodox Judaism (including its ultra-orthodox branch, Hasidism), which he summed up as "tremendous piety, tremendous intelligence, and a frozen creed"; as he has explained, began his first novel, *The Chosen* (1967), a classic best-seller (with a million paperback copies in print in 2002) "mostly out of a desire to write about the confrontation of the twentieth century," especially Freudianism, "with those Jews who were not hung up with their Jewishness"; in that novel, set in Williamsburg, Brooklyn, told the story of two yeshiva students: Danny Saunders, the son of Reb Saunders, a stern *tzaddik* ("righteous one," as the Hassids' traditional rabbis are called), who rejects his role as the "chosen" heir to an Hasidic dynasty, and Reuven Malter, the son of a "merely" Orthodox, progressive Talmudic scholar regarded as an *apikoros* (atheist) by Reb Saunders; published *The Promise*, a sequel to *The Chosen*, in 1969; continued to explore the tension between faith and modernity in subsequent novels, including *My Name Is Asher Lev* (1972), *In the Beginning* (1975), and *Davita's Harp* (1985); in *The Book of Lights* (1981), his darkest and most enigmatic novel, was concerned with the age-old problem of good and evil (especially the involvement of Jewish scientists in the development of the atomic bomb) as seen through the magical prisms of the Kabbalah; later published the novels *The Gift of Asher Lev* (1990), *I Am the Clay* (1992), and *Old Men at Midnight* (2001); described his own upbringing in the Bronx, New York, as "very Orthodox . . . Hasidic without the beard and earlocks"; after graduating from a yeshiva (parochial school) in the Bronx and the Talmudical Academy High School of Yeshiva University in Manhattan, became an English major at Yeshiva University; by the time he received his B.A. degree, in 1950, had completely broken from Orthodox tradition, at great personal cost, as he later observed ("I had to rebuild my world literally from zero, and to this day there are people from the old world who won't speak to me"); embraced Conservative Judaism, a Westernized approach to the Torah and Talmud that permits an intellectual and artistic breadth and maneuverability forbidden under Orthodoxy; for his rabbinical studies (which he wanted to pursue for the good of his writing, without the intention of becoming a pulpit rabbi), transferred to the Jewish Theological Seminary of America, a Conservative institution in Manhattan; received his rabbinical ordination and an M.A. degree in Hebrew literature in 1954; later earned a doctorate in philosophy at the University of Pennsylvania, served as a U.S. Army chaplain in Korea, and taught at the University of Judaism in Los Angeles and the Jewish Theological Seminary of America; was editor in chief at the Jewish Publication Society in Philadelphia from 1965 to 1974; saw *The Chosen* made into a feature film in 1981; in addition to his novels, wrote *Wanderings: Chaim Potok's History of the Jews* (1978) and *The Gates of November* (1996), the multigenerational chronicle of a Soviet Jewish family; died in Merion, Pennsylvania. See *Current Biography* (May) 1983.

Obituary *New York Times* A p17 July 24, 2002

**PUSEY, NATHAN M.** Apr. 4, 1907–Nov. 14, 2001 Former university president; former teacher of classics; as president of Harvard University (1953–71), was the author of a grand plan for university growth, liberalization, and what he called a richer "environment of undergraduate life"; implemented that plan until Vietnam War–era political activists targeted him as an enemy and ended his effectiveness; was a tutor in Greek classics at Harvard while earning his Ph.D. degree there in the mid-1930s; subsequently taught at Scripps College in Claremont, California, and Wesleyan University in Middleton, Connecticut; was president of Lawrence College in Appleton, Wisconsin, from 1944 to 1953; as president of Harvard, launched a fund-raising program that made possible a doubling of the number of buildings on campus; created an interdisciplinary research center, a visual-arts center, and better housing for faculty and administrators; through an outreach program to the less advantaged, created greater diversity in the student population; at the same time, defended the ideal of the free, self-governing university against "outside pressure" from right-wing entities—notably U.S. senator Joseph R. McCarthy, who in the mid-1950s demanded that Pusey dismiss four faculty members McCarthy regarded as "Fifth Amendment Communists"—as well as the leftist radicals who infiltrated and intensified the campus protests of the late 1960s; after his retirement as president of Harvard, served as president of the Andrew W. Mellon Foundation until 1975; was a member of the board of Fountain House, a mental-health organization, until shortly before his death; published two books, *The Age of the Scholar* (1962), a collection of speeches, and *American Higher Education, 1945–70* (1978); died in Manhattan. See *Current Biography* (December) 1953.

Obituary *New York Times* D p11 Nov. 15, 2001

**REUSS, HENRY S.** Feb. 22, 1912–Jan. 12, 2002 Democratic U.S. representative from Milwaukee, Wisconsin (1955–83); lawyer; in 1936, began practicing law in Milwaukee; in 1940, voted for Wendell Willkie, the liberal Republican candidate for president; was assistant general counsel with the Office of Price Administration in Washington, D.C., in 1941 and

1942; as an infantryman in World War II, won a Bronze Star; from June to December 1945, headed the price-control division of the U.S. military government in Germany; later, was deputy general counsel for the Marshall Plan; in 1948, ran unsuccessfully for mayor of Milwaukee as an independent; began running as a Democrat in 1948, when he lost a race for attorney general of Wisconsin; in 1951, with others, organized "Operation Truth," a campaign against Wisconsin's Communist-baiting right-wing Republican U.S. senator Joseph R. McCarthy; in Congress, was an early proponent of civil rights and congressional reform legislation; in 1959, made the first proposal for the creation of what would become the Peace Corps; was attentive to living conditions in the District of Columbia; became a proponent of home rule for the district; voiced opposition to the Vietnam War; as a champion of environmental conservation, in 1964 wrote the legislation for the establishment of the 1,200-mile Ice Age National and State Trail in Wisconsin; in 1970, discovered and began personally to implement the Refuse Act, an 1899 statute permitting individuals to initiate action against corporate polluters and share in the punitive fines extracted from them; subsequently, chaired a special congressional committee devoted to studying the decline of major American cities; as chairman of the House Banking Committee, beginning in 1976, crusaded for more financial regulation and disclosure of financial activity; pushed for landmark legislation increasing federal insurance on savings-and-loan accounts; in 1981, relinquished the banking chair in order to assume the chairmanship of the House–Senate Joint Economic Committee, where he might more effectively oppose high interest rates and the economic policies of the administration of President Ronald Reagan, which he viewed as favoring the rich and corporations; decided not to seek reelection in 1982; after leaving Congress, practiced law with the Washington firm of Rose, Schmidt, Chapman, Duff & Halsey; was active with the Enterprise Institute, a nonprofit affordable-housing organization; in 1995, moved with his wife to California; died in San Rafael, California. See *Current Biography* (October) 1959.

Obituary *New York Times* A p19 Jan. 15, 2002

**REYNOLDS, JOHN W. JR.** Apr. 4, 1921–Jan. 10, 2002 Former Democratic governor of Wisconsin (1963–65); federal judge; had degrees in both economics and law; was a district director in Wisconsin with the federal Office of Price Administration in 1951 and 1952 and U.S. commissioner for the eastern judicial district of Wisconsin from 1955 to 1958; was elected to a two-year term as state attorney general in 1958 and to a second term in 1960; as governor, established an arts council and a woman's commission; generally, had limited success in pushing his liberal agenda in civil rights, health, education, and welfare; was named to the federal bench by President Lyndon B. Johnson in 1965; became chief judge of the federal district court in Milwaukee, Wisconsin, in 1971; presided over the judicial initiative to bring about the racial integration of the Milwaukee public school system, a case that was settled out of court in 1979, when the city school board agreed to initiate a comprehensive student busing program; after resigning as chief judge, retained a senior seat on the court; died in Milwaukee, Wisconsin. See *Current Biography* (April) 1964.

Obituary *New York Times* C p18 Jan. 12, 2002

**RICKEY, GEORGE W.** June 6, 1907–July 17, 2002 Sculptor; constructed (or, in his view, choreographed) delicately balanced kinetic works, including giant stainless-steel outdoor mobiles that interact with the wind; acknowledged that Alexander Calder was "the obvious example" for him in his early, relatively small-scale efforts to make "things of metal which move like machines"; was also influenced by the work of Naum Gabo and Antoine Pevsner, constructivist pioneers who held that time and space were fundamental elements in visual art; was the grandson of a clockmaker and the son of a mechanical engineer employed by the Singer Sewing Machine Co., first in the U.S. and then in Scotland; grew up in both countries; torn between academe and art, earned B.A. and M.A. degrees in history at Oxford University and studied art in Paris and elsewhere; after teaching history at the Groton (Massachusetts) School in the early 1930s, turned to painting and drawing full time; in his painting, was influenced by cubism, the post-impressionism of Cézanne, and social realism; between 1937 and 1941, was artist in residence or art teacher at several small colleges, including Muhlenberg College, in Pennsylvania; working on ballistics problems involving computers alongside engineers in a U.S. Army Air Corps machine shop during World War II, experienced a rekindling of his childhood interest in mechanics; after the war, returned to the teaching of art in small colleges; studied Bauhaus teaching methods at the Chicago Institute of Design in 1948–49; in addition to teaching techniques, absorbed Bauhaus constructivist concerns for geometry of form and for designs that take into consideration the nature of materials; became associate professor of fine arts at Indiana University in 1949; during that year, assembled his first mobiles, using window glass; soon turned to more durable materials—plastic, brass, copper, and steel; contributed *Square and Catenary* to a group show at the Metropolitan Museum of Art in 1951; used silver and lead solder to join the parts of his early sculptures; in 1954, began to weld with oxyacetylene, making it possible for him to construct ever larger and more complicated sculptures in stainless steel; applied paint to some of his early sculptures, including *Cocktail Party* (1954), *Ship I* (1954), and *Diptych—The Seasons* (1956); beginning in the early 1960s, simplified and streamlined those sculptures, excluding details not related to "movement itself"; thus, created his "line" series, constructions of hollow steel needles or blades, tapered to accommodate a counterweight and fulcrum, that are dependent for the sweep of their wide arc upon their mounting on knife-edge bearings; thought of those sculptures as drawings in space; assured his international recognition with the spare and elegant 36-foot-tall scissors-like construction *Two Lines Temporal I*, first displayed at Documenta III in Kassel, West Germany, in 1964 and acquired by the Museum of Modern Art in New York the following year; commissioned by the

Hirshhorn Collection, constructed his steel *Three Red Lines* for permanent display at the Hirshhorn Museum and Sculpture Garden, in Washington, D.C.; moved from lines to geometric planes in a series including his highly burnished *Four Squares in a Square* (1969), installed in the terrace of the Neue Nationalgalerie in Berlin, and *Two Rectangles Vertical Gyratory* (1969), installed in a shopping mall in Rotterdam, the Netherlands; with those sculptures and others, such as *Unstable Cube* (1968) and his series of space churns of the late 1960s and early 1970s, explored variously shaped illusionary volumes; in such sculptures as *Two Open Rectangles Excentric* (1974), achieved paths of movement describing a conical shape; published the authoritative study *Constructivism: Origins and Evolution* (1967); died in St. Paul, Minnesota. See *Current Biography* (February) 1980.

Obituary *New York Times* p25 July 21, 2002

**RIESMAN, DAVID** Sep. 22, 1909–May 10, 2002 Sociologist; professor emeritus, Harvard University; "a seminal figure in the study of the American psyche, which was his lifelong work," as his son, Michael Riesman, observed; co-wrote *The Lonely Crowd* (1950), probably the most popular work of scholarly sociology in American literary history, a perennial international best-seller that is required reading in many college and university classrooms; after earning degrees in the biochemical sciences and law at Harvard University and passing the bar, clerked for Justice Louis Brandeis at the U.S. Supreme Court, practiced law, served as deputy assistant district attorney in Manhattan, and was World War II contract-termination director with the Sperry Gyroscope Co.; at the University of Chicago, became a visiting professor of social sciences in 1945 and a full professor the following year; in 1948, was granted a leave of absence from the university to conduct a research project on mass communications for the Yale University Committee on National Policy in collaboration with Reuel Denney and Nathan Glazer; with Denney and Glazer, wrote *The Lonely Crowd: A Study of the Changing American Character*; in that work, argued that character types tend to change as human groups from a primitive era, where ancient rules and taboos hold sway, through an adventurer stage, to a corporate-dominated consumerist society with low individual productivity; from another angle, introduced the population factor in relating typical character types or modes to socioeconomic contexts;: thus, connected the "tradition-directed" to periods or societies of high population growth, such as the Middle Ages and today's nonindustrialized countries, "inner-directed" to those of transitional population growth, such as the Renaissance, and "other-directed" to those in which incipient population decline appears, as in today's highly industrialized countries; went on to differentiate between "adjusted," "anomic," and "autonomous" character types; collaborated with Glazer on the companion volume *Faces in the Crowd; Individual Studies in Character and Politics* (1952), containing interviews/profiles of 21 varied American individuals, which, he hoped, might "indicate the possible usefulness of [his] typology in the understanding of individual character in its social setting"; in 1953, published his third major work, *Thorstein Veblen*, a critical study of another scholarly sociologist who had struck a popular chord; in one of his essays collected in *Individualism Reconsidered* (1954), wrote, "What is feared as failure in American society is, above all, aloneness. . . . Even success . . . often becomes impossible to bear when it is not socially approved"; as a solution, proposed "the nerve to be oneself when that self is not approved of by the dominant ethic of a society"; later published, among other books, *Constraint and Variety in American Education* (1956) and *On Higher Education: The Academic Enterprise in an Era of Rising Student Consumerism* (1980); was Henry Ford II professor of social sciences at Harvard University from 1958 to 1980; while generally identified with liberal causes, opposed the radical campus demonstrations of the 1960s; died in Binghamton, New York. See *Current Biography* (January) 1955 .

Obituary *New York Times* A p18 May 11, 2002

**RIOPELLE, JEAN-PAUL** Oct. 7, 1923–Mar. 12, 2002 Artist; the most internationally celebrated Canadian painter of his time; was generally regarded as an abstract-expressionist action painter influenced by the Symbolists and their "automatic" artistic technique; objected to such labeling, declaring that his paintings were "landscapes," a description in accord with the judgment of those sophisticated viewers who saw in many of his canvases aspects of the Canadian landscape, rendered abstractly through the juxtaposition of colors and conveying a sense of light and energy; insisted that even in the least figurative work, "the mind always has its concrete references"; until his last years (when osteoporosis required him to work seated, with spray paints, markers, and stencils), worked with extreme physicality, at a frenzied pace, for hours at a time; originally aspired to a career in engineering, which he studied at the École Polytechnique in Montreal; subsequently, studied art at the Académie des Beaux Arts in Montreal and painting under Paul-Émile Borduas at the École Meuble, also in Montreal; became one of Borduas' "automatistes," anarchist painters who issued the manifesto *Refus global*; in 1946 moved to France with his wife, Françoise l'Espérance, by whom he had two daughters; the following year, in Paris, was included by André Breton and Marcel Duchamp in the last major group show of the Surrealist movement; soon abandoned brushes, squeezing pigment directly from the tube; had his first one-man show in Paris in 1949; according to J. Russell Harper in his introduction to a Riopelle catalogue of 1963, progressed through five stages: tachist brushwork (1947–48), "controlled drip" (1950–51), mosaiclike surfaces impastoed with a palette knife (1953), such as the triptych *Pavanne*, larger canvasses crisscrossed by wandering lines (mid-1950s), and a trend toward figuration (1959–60); in his work in the 1960s, in the view of some critics, created canvases devoid of form, exhibiting "energy" and "richness," but in an "unharnessed" way; in the 1970s, reverted, as Réné Pavant observed, "to the method and style which originally earned him his laurels: the colors applied with the palette knife in broken fragmented touches

that produce a mosaiclike effect on the canvas"; in Paris in 1977, mounted a retrospective titled "Grand Formats" comprising twelve large oils completed between 1952 and 1975, including *Lac du Nord-Est* and *Vert-de-Gris*; according to Marci McDonald, writing in *Maclean's* in 1981, "from the dense eruptions of color dating from his rebellious student days . . . to the stark, simmering tension of his uncharacteristic black and white iceberg series [1977] . . . if there is one constant, it is the artist's sense of the land . . . [forging a link] between Cézanne's reduction of the mountains of Provence . . . and the ultimate distillation of an horizon by the abstractionists"; in addition to painting in oil and other mediums, created watercolors, pastels, sculptures, ceramics, lithographs, and engravings; cultivated the public profile of the archetypical bohemian and libertine, living as fast and furiously as he worked, drinking and smoking hard and collecting vintage cars and trophy girlfriends; in the mid-1950s, left his wife and began a tumultuous 24-year relationship with Joan Mitchell, the late American abstract-expressionist painter; from the late 1980s on, lived with Huguette Vachon; during the last three decades of his life, spent more and more time back in Canada; in 1993, settled on the Ile-aux-Grues (in the St. Lawrence River, near Quebec); died there. See *Current Biography* (October) 1989.

Obituary *New York Times* p49 Mar. 24, 2002

**RIVERS, LARRY** Aug. 17, 1923–Aug. 14, 2002 Artist; painter; collagist; sculptor; jazz musician; a New York bohemian hipster with a mischievous if not perverse sense of humor who delighted in shocking and relished his own notoriety; burst into an art world dominated by abstract expressionism when he was in his mid-20s and proceeded to subvert it; learned the trappings of abstract expressionism—its expansive spatial forms and spontaneous, random look—and used them as camouflage under which he referenced back (with tongue in cheek) to the grand figurative tradition on the one hand and, on the other, anticipated the quotidian iconography of pop art, both of which were in violation of abstract expressionism's strict prohibition against representation—the telling of stories and depicting of objects; was born Yitzrock Loiza Grossberg in the Bronx, New York; began playing the soprano saxophone profes- onally when he was 17; after he turned to drawing which he was the envy of most abstract expres- ists) and painting, in 1945, continued playing bands in and around New York (including his ast Thirteenth Street Band) on and off through- life; early on, drew and painted clinically de- de studies of his aging mother-in-law, Ber- r; in 1952, completed the five-by-eight-foot *e Burial*, his version of Gustave Courbet's *Ornans*, embellished with details of his other's funeral; in perhaps his greatest *hington Crossing the Delaware* (1953), anuel Gottlieb Leutze's salon classic, of showing the absurdity of painting in general and of "a painting dedi- l cliché" in particular; in 1963, steemed project, his *Dutch Mas-* by the reproduction of Rembrandt's *Syndics of the Clothmakers' Guild* in an vertisement for Dutch Masters cigars; in 1965, c structured *History of the Russian Revolution: Fr Marx to Mayakovsky*, a 13-by-33-foot tableau cor prising paintings, photographs, drawings, and thre dimensional objects, including found art; subse quently painted *The Greatest Homosexual*, his fop pish take on Jacques-Louis David's hand-in-vest portrait of Napoleon, *Olympia*, in which he changed Manet's reclining female nude from white to black and the nude's maid from black to white, *Girls on Bicycles*, inspired by Fernand Léger's cubist style, his *Homages to Hollywood* series, his paintings relating to the Holocaust in Nazi Germany and slavery in the American South, and his version of Marcel Duchamps's *Nude Descending a Staircase*; in 1984, created the sprawling three-part panorama *History of the Matzo: The Story of the Jews*; also worked in film and video, dabbled in theatrical set design, taught art briefly, wrote poetry, and did some acting; in his shockingly honest autobiography, *What Did I Do?* (1992), written with Arnold Weinstein, described a life as outrageously unorthodox as his art, one marked by a wide-ranging intellectual curiosity and a ravenous pursuit of the sensual that took him into the worlds of drugs and bisexuality; died at his home in Southampton, New York. See *Current Biography* (April) 1969.

Obituary *New York Times* p1+ Aug. 16, 2002

**ROSS, HERBERT** May 13, 1927–Oct. 9, 2001 Motion-picture director; a former choreographer who, beginning in 1969, directed more than a score of feature films with unobtrusive camera work, deft editing, a choreographer's rhythmic sense, a focus on the humanity of the characters more than the plot, and a sure hand with actors; gained an unmannered, three-dimensional performance from the normally shtick-driven comedian Woody Allen in *Play It Again, Sam* (1972); came of age as a film director with *The Seven-Per-Cent Solution* (1976), an elegant and meticulously detailed adventure about Sherlock Holmes and Sigmund Freud; collaborated with his first wife, the celebrated prima ballerina Nora Kaye, on a number of projects, including the ballet-oriented films *The Turning Point* (1977) and *Nijinsky* (1980), and with the playwright Neil Simon on the translation of several of Simon's comedies to the screen; at the beginning of his career, danced as a chorus boy in several Broadway musicals; was inspired by Goya's paintings and etchings in creating his first ballet, *Caprichos*, first performed at Hunter College's Choreographers Workshop in 1950 and subsequently selected by the American Ballet Theatre for inclusion in its 10th anniversary season; over the next few years, created a number of short ballets for the American Ballet Theatre, generally dark works, many focusing on death or morbid eroticism, the most successful of which, perhaps, was his balletic version of Jean Genet's *The Maids*; during the same period, choreographed for Broadway *A Tree Grows in Brooklyn* and *House of Flowers*, supervised the City Center Light Opera Company's revival of *Wonderful Town*, and created supper-club acts for Marlene Dietrich, Imogene Coca, and others; in 1959, married Nora Kaye; with her, formed the short-lived

troupe Ballet of Two Worlds, which, with Kaye as prima ballerina, toured Europe in 1960, performing such Ross ballets as *The Dybbuk* and *Within the Grave*; in the early 1960s, staged the musical numbers for several Broadway shows, including *Anyone Can Whistle, I Can Get It for You Wholesale*, and *On a Clear Day You Can See Forever*; in 1965, directed the Broadway musical *Kelly*; did his first Hollywood choreography for *Carmen Jones* (1954); choreographed the musical sequences for *Inside Daisy Clover* (1965), *Dr. Dolittle* (1968), and *Funny Girl* (1968); made his debut as a motion-picture director with the musical version of *Goodbye, Mr. Chips* (1969); went on to direct *The Owl and the Pussycat* (1970), *T. R. Baskin* (1971), and *Funny Lady* (1975); treated his first Neil Simon screenplay, *The Sunshine Boys* (1975), not as a comedy about two aging, feuding vaudevillians but as, in his words, "a drama about relationships and the refusal to give in"; filmed Simon's theatrical love story *The Goodbye Girl* (1977) in continuity so that, again in his words, "the actors could really develop their relationship"; subsequently, collaborated with Simon on the New York stage production of *Chapter Two* and the films *California Suite* (1978), *I Ought to Be in Pictures* (1982), and *Max Dugan Returns* (1983); directed Steve Martin in the film *Pennies from Heaven* (1981) and Kevin Bacon as a dancer in a puritanical town in *Footloose* (1984); following the death of Nora Kaye, in 1987, was married to and divorced from Lee Radziwill; died in Manhattan. See *Current Biography* (August) 1980.

Obituary *New York Times* A p23 Oct. 11, 2001

**ROTE, KYLE** Oct. 27. 1928(?)–Aug. 15, 2002 Football player; a triple-threat halfback who, when hobbled by knee injuries, became a record-setting receiver with the New York Giants of the National Football League; was born in 1927, according to some sources (including his son, Kyle Rote Jr., a former soccer player), in 1928 according to others; as a halfback at Southern Methodist University (SMU), did yeoman service in the shadow of tailback Doak Walker during his first two varsity seasons (1948 and most of 1949); burst out of Walker's shadow and into national prominence on November 3, 1949, when he replaced an injured Walker at tailback and turned in the most dazzling one-man performance in Texas college-football history; on that occasion, ran for 115 yards, passed for 146, punted for an average of 48, and scored all three SMU touchdowns in a 27–20 loss to national champion Notre Dame; after the 1949 season, with Walker in professional ranks, became SMU's unrivaled star; in 1950, was a unanimous All-American choice and runner-up to Vic Janowicz of Ohio State University in the balloting for the Heisman Trophy; finished his college career with a total of 2,049 yards rushing, ranking eighth on the SMU all-time list; as the National Football League's first draft choice after his last season at SMU, signed with the New York Giants; before joining the Giants, played professional baseball for two months with the Corpus Christi club in the Class B Gulf Coast League, early in 1951; that same year, finished second to Cary Middlecoff in the Celebrity Golf Tournament; played with the New York Giants for 11 years (1951 through 1961); was benched with a left knee injury during much of the 1951 season; after suffering a right knee injury in 1953, was moved from halfback to flanker back and finally to end; as a pass receiver, made up for his loss of speed with crafty zigzagging and feinting; established three team records (two of which are tallied with slight differences in sources): most pass receptions (301), most yards gained in pass receptions (at least 4,797), and most touchdowns on passes (at least 48); was named to the All-Pro team four times; was captain of the Giants' offensive squad from 1953 to 1960; following his retirement as a player, coached the Giants' offensive backfield for two seasons; resigned as coach after the 1963 season in order to concentrate on his second career, as a broadcaster of sports news and commentaries with radio station WNEW in New York City; with the NBC television network, was an analyst in broadcasts of professional football games in the late 1960s and early 1970s; was inducted into the National Football Foundation's Hall of Fame in 1964; served as first president of the National Football League Players Association; died in Baltimore, Maryland. See *Current Biography* (May) 1961.

Obituary *New York Times* B p10 Aug. 16, 2002

**RUSSELL, HAROLD** Jan. 14, 1914–Jan. 29, 2002 Canadian-born disabled U.S. military veteran; an advocate for veterans and the handicapped; international peace advocate; enlisted in the U.S. Army in February 1942, two months after the U.S. entered World War II; on June 6, 1944, was instructing a parachute infantry demolition squad at Camp Mackall, North Carolina, when a defective fuse exploded a charge of TNT he was holding; lost both his hands, which were replaced by prosthetic metal claws; was the principal subject of the 20-minute Army Signal Corps documentary film *Diary of a Sergeant*, widely used in rehabilitation work with amputees in military hospitals; in Hollywood, was cast as the handless sailor Homer Parrish in *The Best Years of Our Lives* (1946), a motion picture dealing with the problems experienced by World War II veterans in readjusting to peacetime life; for his poignant interpretation of that role, received two Academy Awards, one for best supporting actor and the other for "bringir aid and comfort to disabled veterans through the dium of motion pictures"; served as comma the Amvets (American Veterans of Worl from 1949 into the 1960s; helped four Veterans Federation (WVF); as a W tive, traveled worldwide in beha war and persecution; also co and energy to the President's ment of the Handicappe *Victory in My Hands* ( sachusetts. See *Cur*

Obituary *Nev*

**SAVIMBI**
lan poli
of th
g
wa
tutes
mately

scholarship, studied at universities in Portugal and Switzerland from 1958 to 1965; while studying abroad, joined the nationalist movement that Holden Roberto was forming in exile; helped to develop that movement into the National Front for the Liberation of Angola (ENLA); subsequently, fell into disagreement with Roberto; after taking his licence in political science at the University of Lausanne in 1965, returned to Angola; in a remote village in the province of Moxico in 1966, founded UNITA; after Angola won its independence from Portugal, in 1975, waged a power struggle with the ENLA, based in Zaire, and Agostinho Neto's Soviet-backed Popular Movement for the Liberation of Angola (MPLA), which quickly won control of most of the country with the help of Cuban military intervention; led a guerrilla war against the MPLA government with American and South African support for 16 years, until the end of the Cold War, in 1991; following two internationally brokered peaceful hiatuses, resumed hostilities in 1978; was killed in combat in eastern Angola. See *Current Biography* (August) 1986.

Obituary *New York Times* p1+ Feb. 23, 2002

**SENGHOR, LÉOPOLD SÉDAR** Oct. 9, 1906–Dec. 20, 2001 Senegalese statesman; poet; essayist; as the father and first president of independent Senegal, a former French colony, was widely regarded as "the conscience of Africa," a towering exemplar of rectitude among post-colonial leaders there; as an intellectual, was a principal theoretician of *négritude*, which he defined as "the totality of the cultural values of the black world," rooted not in "soulless" rationalism (the Hellenic legacy) but in an African tradition in touch with ancient and natural rhythms, a spiritual/emotional heritage capable of reviving "the world that has died of machines and cannons"; at the same time, was a fervent and authoritative Francophone, even a member of the Académie Française; envisioned the African and European traditions as, ideally, mutually enriching each other and contributing to a "civilization of the universal"; was the son of a prosperous peanut merchant and exporter and a member of the Mandingo tribe of the Serer ethnic group, a Christian minority in largely Muslim Senegal; in Senegal, was educated at Catholic schools and a French lycée; as a student at the University of Paris, in 1934 joined with the poet Aimé Césaire, of Martinique, and others in publishing the journal *L'Étudiant noir*, in which they first articulated their philosophy of *négritude*; also helped found the Association of West African Students, whose goal was to absorb French culture without being assimilated by it; after receiving his *agrégé* degree in French language in 1936, became a teacher in the French school system; returned to teaching after serving in an all-African French army unit at the beginning of World War II and spending two years in a German prisoner-of-war camp; in 1945, published his first book of poems, *Chants d'ombre* (Shadow Songs); during the same year, was elected to represent Senegal in the French Constituent Assembly; represented Senegal in the French National Assembly from 1946 to 1958; was a Socialist before forming his own party (the first of three), the Bloc Démocratique Sénégalais; when Senegal joined with the Sudanese Republic to form the Federation of Mali, in 1959, became president of the federation's federal assembly; was elected president of Senegal in August 1959, when the country separated from the Federation of Mali and declared its full independence; was reelected in every election over the following 18 years; survived several attempted coups and an attempted assassination; at one point, made his Union Progressiste Sénégalaise the only legal political party, but in the long run promoted democratic debate, nurtured a responsible opposition, and permitted a free press; became the first of the new African leaders voluntarily to relinquish office when, in 1980, he resigned to make way for the democratic election of his successor, Abdou Diouf; as a poet, wrote, often exuberantly, on themes of cultural tension, negritude, nostalgia, and love; mythologized his years growing up in Senegal (in a magical "Kingdom of Childhood"), his wartime and other experiences, and his views of world affairs and world leaders; between 1945 and 1961 published six volumes of poetry, including *Hosties noires* (Black Sacrifices), *Chants pour Naeett* (Songs for Naeett), *Ethiopiques*, and *Nocturnes*; during the 1980s, revised the poems, which were published in a definitive French-English bilingual edition in 1990; also published anthologies of poetry, including new black verse, and books of nonfiction on various philosophical, political, linguistic, and cultural subjects, ranging from African socialism to the thought of Pierre Teilhard de Chardin; lived out his last years in Verson, Normandy, France, with his second wife, Colette, a native of Normandy; died at his home in Normandy; was buried in Dakar, Senegal. See *Current Biography* (July) 1994.

Obituary *New York Times* C p15 Dec. 21, 2001

**SMITH, HOWARD K.** May 12, 1914–Feb. 15, 2002 Broadcast journalist; a pioneer radio and television news reporter, anchorman, and analyst whose dignified mien belied a passionate editorial stance on current events and issues; as an undergraduate at Tulane University, studied journalism and German; subsequently, studied economics as a Rhodes scholar at Oxford University; at the outbreak of World War II, in September 1939, began reporting on the war with United Press from London; in January 1940, was sent by UP to Berlin, Germany; in Berlin, moved from UP to CBS radio in 1941; crossed from Germany into Switzerland in December 1941; related the conditions he had experienced and witnessed in Nazi Germany in *Last Train from Berlin* (1942); was based in Berne, Switzerland, for the next several years; in 1944 and 1945, did on-the-spot coverage of the Allied advance across Europe into a defeated Germany; replaced Edward R. Murrow as CBS's chief European correspondent in 1949; for the next 11 years, reported on Europe and the Middle East from his base in London, with occasional trips to trouble spots, such as Suez in 1956; after returning to the U.S. in 1957, did 90-second commentaries on the CBS television network's nightly news broadcasts and 15-minute news analyses on CBS radio; moderated the first televised presidential debate, between John F. Kennedy and Richard M. Nixon, in 1960; won an Emmy Award for his writing and narration of the television documentary *The Population Explosion* (1960); in 1961, was named chief correspondent and general manager of CBS's Washington, D.C., bureau; when several trenchant editorializing remarks were censored from his script for *Who Speaks for Birmingham* (1961), a CBS special report on racial conflict in the South, had a showdown with CBS executives, which he lost; joined the ABC television network, where he launched the weekly half-hour program *Howard K. Smith—News and Comment* in February 1962; in one of that program's installments, "The Political Obituary of Richard M. Nixon," included a sympathetic interview with Alger Hiss, the former State Department employee charged with spying and convicted of perjury in 1950 in a case in which Nixon, then a Communist-hunting congressman, was a prime mover; with that interview, touched off a torrent of 80,000 angry letters and telegrams; hosted the program until June 1963, when it was canceled due to the loss of its sponsor; in 1969, conducted the first one-on-one televised interview with a sitting president of the U.S., Richard M. Nixon; as anchor of the weekly ABC investigative series *ABC Scope* from 1964 to 1968, focused on the war in Vietnam; said he "hated" that war, but was nevertheless hawkish, seeing no alternative to escalation "on an overwhelming scale"; co-anchored *ABC Evening News* from 1969 to 1975; remained at ABC as a commentator until his retirement, in 1979; in his book *The State of Europe* (1949), an historical and political survey, argued that a modified socialism—the welfare state and a planned economy, within democratic limits—might be more suited to modern industrialized nations than a laissez-faire system; wrote the autobiography *Events Leading Up to My Death: The Life of a Twentieth-Century Reporter* (1996); died in Bethesda, Maryland. See *Current Biography* (July) 1976.

Obituary *New York Times* C p9 Feb. 19, 2002

**SNEAD, SAM** May 27, 1912–May 23, 2002 Golfer; "Slammin' Sam"; a dominant figure in professional golf from the late 1930s into the 1950s; the only player ever to win sanctioned tournaments in six decades, into the 1980s; growing up on his family's farm in Ashwood, Virginia, began developing his accurate eye by squirrel hunting and his fluid, powerful swing by hitting stones with tree limbs in a cow pasture; became a caddy on a golf course near his home when he was 15 and assistant pro at White Sulphur Springs, West Virginia, when he was 23, in 1935; won one Professional Golf Association (PGA) tournament in 1936 and eight tournaments in 1937, his first full year on the PGA tour; between 1936 and 1965, won a record 81 events, including seven major titles: two PGA Opens (1943, 1949, 1951), one British Open (1946), and three Masters (1949, 1952, 1954); was the leading money-winner on the tour three times; was a member of seven Ryder Cup teams and captain of three; in 1965, won the Greater Greensboro Open for the eighth time; thus became the oldest golfer to win a PGA event and set a record for most victories in a single event; joined the senior tour in 1980; on the links, was appreciated not only for his talent and the natural grace of his swing but also for his homespun, unpretentious manner, his constant good humor, and his friendly rapport with the gallery; was an honorary starter at the Masters for 19 years (1984–April 2002); died at his home in Hot Springs, Virginia. See *Current Biography* (June) 1949.

Obituary *New York Times* C p11 May 24, 2002

**STANLEY, KIM** Feb. 11, 1925–Aug. 20, 2001 Actress; an intense "method" performer; on the Broadway stage, was most memorable in her glowing creation of Cherie, the failed night-club singer (a self-described "chantoosie") stranded with other bus passengers in a Kansas diner in the original Broadway production of the comedy/drama *Bus Stop* (1955); made her motion-picture debut in *The Goddess* (1958), with her powerful portrayal of Rita Shawn, a Marilyn Monroe–like screen sex idol whose real life is tormented and tragic; received Academy Award nominations for her roles as the sinister medium in *Séance on a Wet Afternoon* (1964) and the ambition-crazed and spiteful mother of the ill-starred 1930s movie actress Frances Farmer in the film biography *Frances* (1982); after receiving a degree in psychology at the University of New Mexico, in 1946, took a general arts course at the University of Texas, where her father was a professor; was persuaded to pursue a career in acting by a director from the Pasadena (California) Playhouse who had seen her perform in a college dramatic production; following stints at the Pasadena Playhouse and in stock in Kentucky and New Jersey, studied under Lee Strasberg and Elia Kazan at the Actors Studio in Manhattan; played the title role of *St. Joan* Off-Broadway in 1949; moved to Broadway as Barbara Harris's replacement in the cast of *Montserrat* during the 1949–50 theatrical season; in subsequent Broadway performances, was one of the daughters in *The House of Bernarda Alba* (1951), the wife of the hunted Texas killer in *The Chase* (1952), the gauche tomboy sister in *Picnic* (1953), and the title protagonist in *The Traveling Lady* (1954); left the cast of a 1958 Broadway production of *A Touch of the Poet* because of conflicts with other cast members (Helen Hayes and Eric Portman); in subsequent New York stage appearances, was seen opposite Horst Buchholz in *Cherie* (1959) and as the hysterical Freudian patient in *A Far Country* (1961), directed by her third (and last) husband, Alfred Ryder; suffered a nervous breakdown and quit the stage following her participation (as Masha) in a disastrous (both on Broadway and in London's West End) 1964 Actors Studio revival of *The Three Sisters* (a taped version of which was released as a motion picture in 1966); in a final return to the silver screen, was cast in the minor role of a barn-storming pilot in *The Right Stuff* (1983); was seen in scores of dramatic roles on television; received Emmy Awards for her performance in an episode of *Ben Casey* in 1983 and her portrayal of Big Mama in a PBS production of *Cat on a Hot Tin Roof* in 1984; died in Santa Fe, New Mexico. See *Current Biography* (May) 1955.

Obituary *New York Times* C p14 Aug. 21, 2001

**STEIGER, ROD** Apr. 14, 1925–July 9, 2002 Character actor; first made his mark on television, during that medium's golden age of live drama, most memorably as the lonely Bronx butcher who finds love in Paddy Chayefsky's play *Marty* (1953); made his motion-picture debut as Frank in *Teresa* (1951); brought an intensity just short of over-acting to a wide variety of screen roles, including historical figures ranging from Napoleon, Mussolini, and Pope John XXIII to W. C. Fields, Al Capone, and Lucky Luciano; was nominated for an Academy Award for his portrayal of Sol Nazerman, a Harlem pawnbroker haunted by memories of Nazi concentration camps, in *The Pawnbroker* (1965); received the Academy Award for his characterization of Bill Gillespie, a stereotypical small-town southern segregationist sheriff who grudgingly accepts the aid of a black northern detective (Sidney Poitier) in solving a murder case, in *In the Heat of the Night* (1967); on Broadway, starred as Captain Ahab in Orson Welles's blank-verse adaptation of *Moby Dick* (1962); following combat service with the U.S. Navy in the Pacific during World War II, studied acting in Manhattan at the New School for Social Research, the American Theatre Wing, the Drama Workshop, and the Actors Studio, the principal American school promoting the Stanislavski method of acting; to him, "the method" meant simply total immersion in a part, "so that you can communicate in human terms with an audience"; after receiving his Equity union card, in 1947, made his professional stage debut as a bit player in a road company production of *The Trial of Mary Dugan*; in 1951, made his Broadway debut in the role of a 55-year-old detective in a revival of Clifford Odets's *Night Music*; between 1948 and 1953, appeared in some 250 live television productions, rising from minor roles to major ones in plays and docu-dramas; on *Goodyear TV Playhouse* on May 24, 1953, created the title role in *Marty*, which would be played by Ernest Borgnine in the motion-picture version released in 1955; on the strength of his performance as Marty, won the role of the lawyer Charley Malloy, the corrupt and crafty older brother of the Marlon Brando character who has a change of heart in the movie *On the Waterfront* (1954); continuing his Hollywood career, was cast as a ruthless movie producer in *The Big Knife* (1955), the prosecutor in *The Court-Martial of Billy Mitchell* (1955), the sinister Jud Fry in the film version of the musical *Oklahoma!* (1955), the greedy boxing promoter Nick Benko in *The Harder They Fall* (1956), an idealistic South American assassin in *Back from Eternity* (1956), the villain in the adult Western *Jubal* (1956), the laconic villain in *Cry Terror* (1958), a prison psychiatrist in *The Mark* (1961), Mr. Joyboy, the asexual undertaker, in the gross comedy *The Loved One* (1965), Komarovsky in *Dr. Zhivago* (1965), and the repressed homosexual Sergeant Callan in *The Sergeant* (1968); exploited his bravura style to fullest advantage as Christopher Gill, a chamelion-like actor with an unresolved Oedipus complex who sheds one persona after another in his serial killing of women, in the black farce/melodrama *No Way to Treat a Lady* (1968); later, was cast as Carl in *The Illustrated Man* (1969), Father Delaney in *The Amityville Horror* (1979), and Reb Saunders in *The Chosen* (1982), among other screen roles; was married five times and divorced four; sought relief from chronic depression through extensive psychoanalysis; died in Los Angeles, California. See *Current Biography* (June) 1965.

Obituary *New York Times* A p19 July 10, 2002

**STERN, ISAAC** July 21, 1920–Sept. 22, 2001 Violinist; the first American-trained violin virtuoso to achieve world-class status; was drawn to violin music of all periods, from Baroque through Romantic and early 20th century to contemporary (including works by Ernest Chausson, Krzysztof Penderecki, and Joseph Wieniawski); as the violinist Yehudi Menuhin observed, played without self-consciousness, with "warmth, musicality, good taste, discipline, and spontaniety"; was an activist in high-arts causes, including the preservation of Carnegie Hall and the funding of the National Endowment for the Arts; emigrated to the U.S. with his parents, Ukrainian Jews, when he was an infant; at six, began playing the piano under the tutelage of his mother; first showed an interest in the violin at eight; at the San Francisco Conservatory, studied under Naoum Blinder, who encouraged instinctive musicianship over rote exercises; made his recital debut in San Francisco in 1935; the following year, made his first guest appearance with the San Francisco Symphony Orchestra; made his New York City debut at Town Hall in 1937; under the management of the noted impresario Sol Hurok (from 1939 to Hurok's death, in 1974), became one of the busiest musicians of his time; in 1940, began collaborating with Alexander Zakin, who remained his piano accompanist for 34 years; gave his first concert in Carnegie Hall in 1943; made the first of some 100 guest appearances with the New York Philharmonic in 1944; during World War II, performed for Allied troops in Iceland, Greenland, and the South Pacific; in 1947, made a 10-week tour of Australia; in the summer of 1948, performed in nine European countries; in seven months in 1949, gave 120 concerts in the U.S., Western Europe, and South America; later performed in the Soviet Union; never performed in Germany; played on the soundtracks of the motion pictures *Humoresque* (1946) and *Fiddler on the Roof* (1970); was cast as the violinist Eugène Ysaÿe in the motion picture *Tonight We Sing* (1953), based on the life of Sol Hurok; when Carnegie Hall was threatened with demolition in 1960, organized the Citizens' Committee to Save Carnegie Hall; subsequently served as lifetime president of the Carnegie Hall Corp.; in 1961, formed his first chamber ensemble, with pianist Eugene Istomin and cellist Leonard Rose; by the 1970s, was playing as many as 200 concerts a year and was reputed to be the world's highest-paid classical musician; in the 1970s and 1980s, performed on television in such series as *Live from Carnegie Hall* and *Live from Lincoln Center*; in 1979, visited China, performing and giving master classes in a tour chronicled in the motion picture *From Mao to Mozart*, which won the Academy Award for best full-length documentary of 1980; reduced his performing schedule during the 1990s; spent much of his time in Israel, performing with the Israel Philharmonic, giving master classes, and nurturing such protégés as the violinists Itzhak Perlman and Pinchas Zukerman and the pianist Yefim Bronfman; chaired the America-Israel Cultural Foundation; founded the Jerusalem Music Center; published an autobiography, *My First Seventy-five Years* (1999), written with the novelist Chaim Potok; left a vast discography, including a 44-CD collection titled *Isaac Stern: A Life in Music* (1995); died in Manhattan. See *Current Biography* (February) 1989.

Obituary *New York Times* A p28 Sep. 24, 2001

**STEWART, ALICE** Oct. 4, 1906–June 23, 2002 British physician; pioneering research epidemiologist; alerted the world to the carcinogenic hazard posed by radiation even at low levels; did so over the fierce opposition of such formidable entities as the National Radiation Protection Board of Great Britain, American government agencies, nuclear-industry lobbies, and much of the old-guard medical establishment; was denied government funding by Britain's Coordinating Committee on Cancer Research, chaired by a rival epidemiologist, Sir Richard Doll, her nemesis; as first assistant researcher in the Nuffield Department of Clinical Medicine at Oxford University during World War II, correlated the suppression of munitions workers' ability to form blood cells with their exposure to the explosive TNT, a discovery that led to changes in munitions manufacturing procedures; after the war, became first assistant researcher in the Department of Social Medicine at Oxford; there, conducted a national survey on children who died of cancer between 1953 and 1955; aided by statisticians, demonstrated that there was a correlation between the incidence of juvenile cancer and the prenatal exposure of the fetuses to X-rays; made a preliminary announcement of her findings in 1956; two years later, published the full report of her conclusions, which gained general acceptance gradually over the next dozen years; was long ignored by the International Commission for Radiation Inspection (ICRI), whose standards for safe levels of exposure to radiation were based on flawed readings of long-term Hiroshima and Nagasaki fatalities; in 1974, became senior research fellow in the Department of Social Medicine at Birmingham University; that same year, traveled to the U.S. with her statistician colleague George Kneale to assist Thomas A. Mancuso, an occupational epidemiologist who, on a grant from the U.S. Atomic Energy Commission (AEC), was studying the health of workers at the Hanford Nuclear Reservation, a weapons-grade plutonium-producing complex in the state of Washington, which was required by law to work within the standards set by the ICRI; working with Mancuso and Kneale, found that Hanford workers exposed to half the federal safety limit had more cases than expected of pancreatic cancer, lung cancer, and myeloma; although their official data had been confiscated by the AEC, was able, with Mancuso and Kneale, to publish a mortality study of Hanford workers—a 1977 report that was rejected by the U.S. Department of Energy (DOE, successor to the AEC), which fired Mancuso; subsequently, with Kneale, examined data on Japanese atom-bomb survivors who had died in the years 1950 to 1982 and discerned effects of low-dose radiation that had been missed by others; in U.S. Senate and House committee hearings in 1988 and 1989, testified that the DOE program for assessing radiation hazards was badly flawed and that its regulations hindered the free exchange of information; conducted studies for the Three Mile Island Public Health Fund, which successfully sued for access to the Hanford documents through the Freedom of Information Act; was named an honorary professor at Birmingham University in 1996; retired in 1997; was the subject of Gayle Greene's biography *The Woman Who Knew Too Much: Alice Stewart and the Secrets of Radiation* (1999); died in Oxford, England. See *Current Biography* (July) 2000.

Obituary *New York Times* B p6 July 4, 2002

**STOLTENBERG, GERHARD** Sep. 29, 1928–Nov. 23, 2001 Former German government official; headed the ministries of scientific research, finance, and defense in Christian Democratic governments; after receiving his Ph.D. degree in history at Kiel University, remained at the university as a research assistant (1954–60) and lecturer (1960–65); meanwhile, had begun his political career; after joining the Christian Democratic Union (CDU) in the state of Schleswig-Holstein in 1947, became chairman of the state CDU youth group, the Junge Union, and deputy chairman (and ultimately chairman) of the state CDU; was first elected to the Schleswig-Holstein Parliament when he was 27 and to the West German Parliament, the Bundestag, two years later (three years, according to the *New York Times*); was minister of scientific research in the West German CDU Cabinet of Chancellor Ludwig Erhard in 1965–66; retained that portfolio in the coalition government of Kurt Georg Kiesinger (1966–69); in that post, presided over the rapid expansion of West Germany's computer, nuclear, and space industries; in 1971, was elected prime minister of Schleswig-Holstein; retained that post through two subsequent elections, until 1982; returned to national office as finance minister in the government formed by Helmut Kohl in 1982; in his early years as finance minister, pursued a policy of fiscal austerity, slashing federal spending and executing a series of rigorous tax cuts; by 1985, had reduced the West German government's new borrowing to 33 billion marks, or $88 billion, annually, the lowest since the 1970s, and the national rate of inflation to zero, the lowest since the 1950s; during 1987, unsettled world financial markets when he introduced an unpopular withholding tax on interest income; shortly thereafter, was requested by James Baker, the U.S. secretary of the treasury, to lower West German interest rates; when he balked, was threatened by Baker with a devaluation of the dollar at the expense of German exports; thus contributed, along with Baker, to an international contretemps that precipitated the stock-market crash of October 19, 1987; in a reshuffling of the Kohl Cabinet in April 1989, was assigned the defense portfolio; after Germany's reunification, in 1990, oversaw the integration of the former East German armed forces into the Bundeswehr (the West German armed forces); during 1992, was embarrassed when a shipment marked "agricultural machinery" was seized by Hamburg police and revealed to be a secret shipment of arms by Germany's intelligence service, destined for Israel; resigned later in the same year, when he took responsibility for the failure of defense-ministry bureaucrats to stop the shipment of 15 tanks to Turkey after Parliament had banned their sale; after leaving government, served as deputy director of the Konrad Adenauer Stiftung, the CDU's political foundation; died in Bad Godesberg, Germany. See *Current Biography* (September) 1989.

Obituary *New York Times* A p33 Dec. 6, 2001

**STONE, W. CLEMENT** May 4, 1902–Sep. 3, 2002 Insurance-company executive; self-made multimillionaire; philanthropist; civic leader; attributed his success to a combination of merchandising know-how, a knack for using "O.P.M." (other people's money), and a philosophy of "P.M.A." (positive mental attitude) that he promoted in lectures, books, and a magazine, *Success Unlimited*; began his career as an insurance salesman helping his mother in an insurance agency she opened in Detroit when he was 16; when he was 20, invested his savings of $100 in his own insurance agency in Chicago; by 1930, had some thousand agents selling insurance for him throughout the U.S.; specialized in low-cost life and accident policies; in 1939, acquired the management contract of the American Casualty Co. of Dallas, Texas, of which he became president; also in 1939, organized the Combined Mutual Casualty Co. in Chicago; the following year, became president and general manager of the Combined Casualty Co. of Des Moines, Iowa; in 1946, bought the Pennsylvania Casualty Co. with money borrowed from the Commercial Credit Co. of Baltimore, which owned the Pennsylvania Casualty Co.; changed the company's name to the Combined Insurance Co. of America, into which he merged his Combined Mutual Casualty Co. of Chicago in 1947; subsequently, acquired subsidiary insurance companies in Massachusetts, Wisconsin, and New York; by 1969, was presiding over an insurance empire with assets of $150 million and a personal fortune of some $400 million; in 1982, merged the Combined Insurance Co. of America into the Ryan Insurance Group, the name of which was changed to the Aon Corp. in 1987; wrote the book *The Success System That Never Fails* (1962); co-wrote (with Napoleon Hill) *Success Through a Positive Mental Attitude* (1960) and (with Norma Lee Browning) *The Other Side of the Mind* (1964); in 1964, bought a majority interest in Hawthorn Books, for the purpose of publishing what he described as "inspirational self-help action books"; contributed to the campaign funds of numerous political candidates, mostly Republicans; made his largest contributions (totaling several million dollars) to his friend Richard M. Nixon's successful presidential campaigns in 1968 and 1972; through the W. Clement and Jessie V. Stone Foundation, contributed more than $50 million to scores of charitable and cultural causes; was survived by Jessie Verna Stone, his wife of 79 years, by one of their three children, by 12 grandchildren, and by 13 great-grandchildren; died in Evanston, Illinois. See *Current Biography* (February) 1972.

Obituary *New York Times* A p21 Sep. 6, 2002

**TALMADGE, HERMAN E.** Aug. 9, 1913–Mar. 21, 2002 Former Democratic governor of Georgia (1948–55); U.S. senator (1957–81); lawyer; a populist powerhouse in the old-fashioned Dixie tradition who outlived his early notoriety as a defiant segregationist; in a public recantation in 1985, explained that "it takes time" to change entrenched mores, habits, and views; served as a navy officer in combat in the Pacific during World War II; in 1946, managed the successful gubernatorial campaign of his father, who had previously served two nonconsecutive terms as Georgia governor (Georgia law forbade consecutive terms); after his father's death, on December 21, 1946, 21 days before the date set for his inauguration, was named governor by a vote of the state House of Representatives—an action soon reversed by the state Supreme Court; won a special gubernatorial election in 1948; was elected to a full four-year term as governor in 1950; as governor, established a record that was in many ways progressive; instituted competitive bidding and a merit system for engineers that facilitated the paving of 12,800 miles of road; was the first Georgia governor to use federal funds to build rural hospitals; oversaw a state agriculture department that planted millions of pine seedlings and placed more than 20 million acres under fire protection; in 1951, succeeded in winning from the state legislature a 3 percent sales tax, targeted for education; created a veterinary school at the University of Georgia; launched the first major spending program for public schools in Georgia history, a program under which some 1,000 schools were built; raised the salaries of black schoolteachers to parity with those of whites (but allocated twice as much funding for white as for black schools); in 1954, emerged as a leader of southern resistance to the U.S. Supreme Court decision outlawing racial segregation in public schools; was elected to the first of his four terms in the U.S. Senate in 1956; chaired the Senate agriculture committee and was a ranking member of the finance committee; was instrumental in the passage of the Rural Development Act of 1972 and legislation for the funding of food stamps, school lunches, job training, Medicare, and Medicaid; sponsored some anti–school-busing amendments; with North Carolina senator Sam J. Ervin, brought a down-home southern presence to the nationally televised 1972 Senate committee hearings regarding the Watergate scandal; was among the last of the Senate's conspicuous tobacco-chewing spittoon users; in an investigation spurred in part by allegations made by his first wife, Betty, in divorce proceedings in 1977, and bolstered by testimony of a former member of his staff, was found guilty of financial malfeasance by the Senate ethics committee and formally "denounced" by the full Senate in 1979; lost his race for a fifth Senate term in 1980; subsequently, practiced law with an Atlanta firm and retired, with his second wife to his 2,500-acre tree farm in Henry Country, Georgia; wrote the autobiography *Talmadge: A Political Legacy, A Politician's Life* (1987); died at his home in Hampton, Georgia. See *Current Biography* (March) 1947.

Obituary *New York Times* B p9 Mar. 22, 2002

**TAYLOR, JOHN W.** Sep. 26, 1906–Dec. 11, 2001 Educator; former deputy director general of the United Nations Educational, Scientific and Cultural Organization (UNESCO); on his way to a Ph.D. degree at Columbia University during the 1930s, did intensive study in Germany; during World War II, was a high-ranking officer with the U.S. Army in Europe; headed the educational and religious division of the military government in Germany under General Lucius D. Clay from 1945 to 1947; helped to de-Nazify the German school system; was president of the University of Louisville from 1947 to 1951, when he became deputy director general of UNESCO; later served as acting director general; died in Denver, Colorado. See *Current Biography* (January) 1954.

Obituary *New York Times* F p19 Dec. 31, 2001

**THIEU, NGUYEN VAN** Apr. 5, 1923–Sep. 29, 2001 South Vietnamese army general; politician; the last popularly elected president (1967–75) of South Vietnam, which comprised the 19 southern provinces of what is now (since 1975) the unified Socialist Republic of Vietnam; in 1949, was a member of the first class to graduate from the French-run Vietnamese National Military Academy at Dalat; after the division of Vietnam at the 17th parallel, into the Communist North and the non-Communist South, in 1954, became an infantry division commander in the South Vietnamese army; played a key role in the military coup that overthrew the South Vietnamese government of President Ngo Dinh Diem in November 1963; in an effort to end the political and social turmoil triggered by the assassination of President Diem, in December 1964 participated in a coup headed by Air Vice Marshall Nguyen Cao Ky; served as deputy prime minister in a government installed by the military junta in February 1965; four months later, when the junta formed a new government, was named chief of state while Ky was named prime minister; in September 1967, in the first national popular election in South Vietnam since 1961, was elected president on a ticket that included Ky as vice president; without Ky on the ticket, was reelected to the presidency in 1971; was pressured by the U.S. to agree to the Paris peace accords of 1973, which allowed the North Vietnamese (known as the Viet Minh) to keep their military footholds in the south (and which secretly promised withdrawal of American troops), with no guarantees that the North would refrain from further offensive operations; as the North Vietnamese troops were closing in on Saigon (the South Vietnamese capital, now called Ho Chi Minh City) on April 21, 1975, resigned the presidency; was succeeded by General Duong Van ("Big") Minh, who formally surrendered to the North Vietnamese nine days later; on April 25, 1975, flew to Taiwan; lived quietly in exile, first in England and later in the U.S., in the Boston suburb of Foxboro; died in Boston, Massachusetts. See *Current Biography* (June) 1968.

Obituary *New York Times* p1+ Oct. 1, 2001

**THOMAS, R. DAVID** July 2, 1932–Jan. 8, 2002 Restaurateur; founder of Wendy's International Inc., the world's third-ranking chain of fast-food restaurants; began life as an orphan, adopted when he was six weeks old; aspired from childhood to running his own affordable restaurant or restaurants; after finishing the 10th grade, dropped out of school to work full-time in the Hobby House restaurant in Fort Wayne, Indiana; rose from bus boy to short-order grill man to manager; found a mentor in the restaurant's owner, Phil Clauss; in the 1960s, in return for a 40 percent share in ownership, successfully managed several troubled Kentucky Fried Chicken (KFC) franchises for Clauss in Columbus, Ohio; had a mutually beneficial business relationship with Harland "Colonel" Sanders, the founder of the KFC chain; meanwhile, was planning his own kind of restaurant, which would specialize in hamburgers made with fresh ground meat (not the standard frozen patty), a choice of various toppings, and potato and green salad options; found a company name and logo in the person of one of his five children, his freckled, red-haired eight-year-old daughter Melinda Lou, nicknamed Wendy; opened the first Wendy's Old Fashioned Hamburgers in Columbus in 1969; in the early 1970s, launched the strategy of expansion that over a period of three decades grew his enterprise into an empire of more than 6,000 restaurants with total annual sales exceeding $4 billion; known familiarly as Dave Thomas, contributed mightily to Wendy's marketing success by acquainting viewers with his grandfatherly persona in 800 television commercials, a record documented as such in the *Guinness Book of Records*; to promote and facilitate the adoption of children, founded the Dave Thomas Foundation for Adoption, in 1992; wrote the autobiography *Dave's Way: A New Approach to Old-Fashioned Success* (1991); died at his home in Fort Lauderdale, Florida. See *Current Biography* (March) 1995.

Obituary *New York Times* B p9 Jan. 9, 2002

**THYSSEN-BORNEMISZA, BARON HANS HEINRICH** Apr. 13, 1921–Apr. 27, 2002 Dutch-born Swiss multi-billionaire industrialist; art collector; jet-set cosmopolite; was a grandson of August Thyssen, whose sprawling industrial empire in Germany, based in steel, armaments, and shipbuilding, earned him the epithet "the Andrew Carnegie of Europe"; in 1947, inherited from his father, Heinrich, remnants of the family's financial and other holdings; on the strength of those remnants, built a diversified conglomerate with interests in shipyards, shipping, stevedoring, electric-power stations, natural-gas distribution, storage and container leasing, information systems, Heineken breweries, and the manufacture of farm machinery, glass, and plastics; invested in new technologies in the U.S.; sat on the boards of 30 companies in Europe and U.S.; at his professional height, was regarded as Europe's foremost business leader; as he aged, turned the administration of his conglomerate increasingly over to his eldest son, Georg, in order to concentrate on his art collecting; before the death of his father (the first baron), had been placed in charge of Heinrich's 500-item art collection, consisting chiefly of paintings by the old masters of northern Europe, especially Germany; inherited part of that collection, and bought the rest back from his three siblings; first, added to the collection works by French, Spanish, and Italian old masters; went on to acquire 19th-century American paintings and more recent art, including that of German Expressionists, French Impressionists and Cubists, the Russian avant garde, Italian Futurists, and American Abstract Expressionists and Pop artists; amassed a collection that ultimately totaled more than 1,500 items, including sculpture and tapestries, the greatest private art collection in the world after that of Queen Elizabeth II of England; in addition, subsidized the art collecting of his fifth wife and widow, Carmen Cervera, a former Miss Madrid and Miss Barcelona, who acquired some 600 works; in 1988, began the process of selling most of the best of his collection for a fraction of its worth to the Spanish government; in the early 1990s, moved 787 paintings into the Thyssen-Bornemisza Museum in Madrid, Spain, and 75 religious paintings into Pedrables, a former medieval monastery building in Barcelona; kept some of the rest of his collection in the museum at "La Favorita," his estate in Lugano, Switzerland, while the remainder was on international loan or on tour; in the mid-1990s, sued his son Georg for holding back funds meant for distribution to the other Thyssen-Bornemisza children; settled out of court; shuttled between "La Favorita" and his six other residences, including a mansion on the outskirts of Madrid and another mansion in Sant Feliu de Guixois, Spain, near Barcelona on the Mediterranean coast; died at home in Sant Felin de Guixois. See *Current Biography* (February) 1989.

Obituary *New York Times* p50 Apr. 28, 2002

**TOBIN, JAMES** Mar. 5, 1918–Mar. 11, 2002 Economist; professor emeritus of economics, Yale University; received the 1981 Nobel Prize in economics "for his analysis of financial markets and their relations to expenditure decisions, employment, production, and prices"; was a Keynesian, with qualifications; accepted Keynes's doctrine that government intervention is necessary for the achievement of national goals, but thought that the Keynesian model was too sweeping, because Keynes had been "too Depression-oriented"; saw a role for both monetary policy (affecting economic fluctuation through the supply of money) as well as fiscal policy (changing the direction of the economy through changes in government spending or taxation); as a member of President John F. Kennedy's Council of Economic Advisers, was credited with initiating the tax cut that energized the American economy during the 1960s; in his macroeconomic research, benefitted from his work in microeconomics, including his investment-under-uncertainty and equilibrium theories; was the author of the "portfolio selection" theory, based on the observation that investors do not necessarily choose stocks with the highest rate of return, but are more likely to balance the rate-of-return factor with that of security; when pressed to explain that theory in lay language, said, "Don't put all your eggs in one basket"; as a partial explanation for the state of financial markets, offered what is known as Tobin's Q, which draws a ratio between the market value of a company and the cost of replacement of the company's plant and equipment; explained, for example, that if the latter side of the ratio is higher than the former, the company is likely to expand by acquisition or merger rather than by plant construction or the purchase of more equipment; after earning his B.A. degree at Harvard University, served during World War II in the U.S. Navy, where he underwent officers' training alongside the future novelist Herman Wouk; later, was represented in Wouk's novel *The Caine Mutiny* as midshipman Tobit, a name that became the appellation of the Tobit regression, a statistical technique Tobin developed for analyzing spending decisions; in 1946, received a Ph.D. degree at Harvard, with the dissertation "The Theoretical and Statistical Study of Consumption Function"; was a junior fellow at Harvard from 1947 to 1950, when he joined the Yale faculty; wrote *Essays in Economics*, comprising the volumes *Macroecomics* (1975), *Consumption and Econometrics* (1975), *Theory and Policy* (1982), and *The New Economics, One Decade Older* (1982); in 1971, proposed a small levy on international financial transactions that became known as the Tobin tax; was dismayed when, in recent years, radical opponents of "globalism" co-opted his proposal and attempted to turn it against the ultimate aim Tobin had intended, which was to give poorer nations a share in the benefits of free international trade; died in New Haven, Connecticut. See *Current Biography* (October) 1984.

Obituary *New York Times* B p10 Mar. 13, 2002

**TRIGÈRE, PAULINE** Nov. 4, 1908–Feb. 13, 2002 Fashion designer; a trendsetter in women's wear for half a century; recognized in the industry as both "an intellectual designer" and an imaginative one; created not from sketches but extemporaneously, draping the fabric on the model and cutting it freehand; designed clothes that, by virtue of their couture-type structure and apparently seamless tailoring, in the words of the fashion journalist Bettijane Levine, "make even average-height women look statuesque"; as Valerie Steele, acting director of the Fashion Institute of Technology's museum, observed, turned out coat and dress designs "with a kind of deceptive simplicity that belied the kind of intelligence that went into making them"; was born in Paris, France, to a tailor father and a seamstress mother; mastered the subtleties of bias cut and fabric fit in the salon of Martial et Armand at Place Vendôme in Paris; immigrated to the U.S. in 1937; founded Trigère Inc. in a humble Manhattan loft in 1942; sold her first collection of 12 ready-to-wear outfits (the masters of which her brother, Robert, carried by bus from city to city) to department stores across the U.S.; soon attracted buyers to her loft, from which she later moved to a prestigious suite of workrooms and showrooms on Seventh Avenue, in Manhattan's garment district; between 1949 and 1959 (when she was grossing more than $2 million a year) won three Coty Awards and a Nieman Marcus Award; annually designed four collections of some 80 outfits each, priced from $150 to $1,500; introduced pioneering or distinctive designs in reversible coats, cotton and wool evening dresses, sheer-topped black dresses, sleeveless coats, coats with cape collars, inverted trumpet silhouettes, and spiral jackets; in the 1960s, introduced the jumpsuit; also created scarves, jewelry, and men's ties; attracted many famous clients but was her own most chic model; admitted to being a "prima donna"; in 1994, quit her ready-to-wear business and Seventh Avenue address and moved into more modest quarters in the garment district; under a new corporate name, P. T. Concepts, marketed her scarves and jewelry; retired in 2000; died in her apartment on Manhattan's Upper East Side. See *Current Biography* (February) 1960.

Obituary *New York Times* C p14 Feb. 15, 2002

**UNITAS, JOHNNY** May 7, 1933–Sep. 11, 2002 Professional football player; legendary Baltimore Colts quarterback; one of the few pro quarterbacks to call his own plays; a pure dropback passer who, with receiver Raymond Berry, constituted one of the most prolific passing combinations in National Football League history; was the first NFL quarterback to throw for 40,000 yards; what distinguished him, in Berry's words, was his "uncanny ability to call the right play at the right time, his icy composure under fire, his fierce competitiveness, and his utter disregard for his own safety"; as quarterback with St. Justin's High School team in Pittsburgh, Pennsylvania, was named to the city's All Catholic team; during four seasons at the University of Louisville, completed 245 of 502 passes and tossed for 27 touchdowns; in the summer of 1955, was drafted by the Pittsburgh Steelers of the National Football League, but was sent home from training camp; played semi-pro ball in the 1955 season; in February 1956, was signed by the Baltimore Colts as backup for quarterback George Shaw; took over as quarterback when Shaw was sidelined by a leg injury during the fourth game of the 1956 season; in 1957, paced the previous lowly Colts to a 7–5 record; in 1958, led them in a series of victories culminating in the defeat of the New York Giants in the NFL championship game in Yankee Stadium, an historic overtime thriller; again led them to the NFL championship in 1959, when he set a league record by throwing 32 passes for 264 yards; on the occasion of the NFL's 50th anniversary, in 1969, was voted greatest quarterback of all time; in 1970, led the Colts to the Super Bowl, where they lost to the New York Jets; played with the Colts through 1972 and with the San Diego Chargers in 1973; retired after the 1973 season with career totals of 2,830 passes completed in 5,186 attempts for 40,239 yards and 290 touchdowns; set 22 NFL records, most of which were later surpassed; in the NFL record book, remains unchallenged in first place for most consecutive games with at least one touchdown pass (47, from 1956 through 1960); is tied in first place for most seasons leading the league in touchdown passes (four) and most consecutive seasons leading in passing attempts (three: 1959–61), in second place for most seasons leading the league in attempts (four: 1957, 1959–61), and in third place for most seasons leading the league in passing yardage (four); played in 10 Pro Bowl games and was voted most valuable player three times; in 1979, was inducted into the Pro Football Hall of Fame, in Canton, Ohio; in the selections for the NFL's 75th anniversary team, in 1984, shared the quarterback choice with Sammy Baugh, Otto Graham, and Joe Montana; in 2000, was selected at quarterback for the NFL's All-Time Team by the 36 Hall of Fame voters; died in the Baltimore suburb of Timonium, Maryland. See *Current Biography* (February) 1962.

*New York Times* C p11 Sep. 12, 2002

**VAN DEN HAAG, ERNEST** Sep. 15, 1914–Mar. 21, 2002 Dutch-born psychoanalyst; writer; educator; a New York intellectual who made major contributions to the development of conservative political and social thought in the U.S.; was described by William F. Buckley Jr. as a "tuning fork of reason in the cacophonous world of social science"; expressed controversial views on such subjects as the Vietnam War, racial relations, civil disorder, and crime and punishment; contended that avowed Communists, bound to a party line, were ipso facto out of place on the faculty of any university professing to support free academic inquiry; lamented the "de-individualization" of the modern city; criticized popular culture as "entertainment bereft of meaning"; favored restriction of pornography; advocated a tax on advertising to reduce the public's exposure to it; endorsed the thesis of Richard J. Herrnstein and Charles Murray's book *The Bell Curve*; attended universities in Italy and France before arriving in the U.S. in 1940; worked as a propaganda analyst for the Office of War Information during World War II; earned an M.A. degree from the State University of Iowa in 1942 and a Ph.D. in economics from New York University in 1952; began his teaching career in 1946 at the New School for Social Research (now the New School University); later taught at the City College of New York, the School of Criminal Justice at the State University of New York in Albany, and Queens College, among other schools; was John M. Olin professor of jurisprudence and public policy at Fordham University (1982–88); practiced psychoanalysis privately from 1955 to 1982; in the revised appendix to his first book, *Education as an Industry* (1956), read into the U.S. Supreme Court's 1954 *Brown v. Board of Education* decision an "intolerant and passionate desire to compel people to congregate"; with Ralph Gilbert Ross, co-wrote *The Fabric of Society: An Introduction to the Social Sciences* (1957); in *Passion and Social Constraint* (1963), made clear his rejection of the possibility of a "value-free" social science; in *The Jewish Mystique* (1969), examined from psychoanalytical and sociological viewpoints such subjects as anti-Semitism; advocated a law-and-order approach to ghetto unrest, as reflected in his book *Political Violence and Civil Disobedience* (1972); with others, wrote *The Balancing Act* (1974), in which he criticized the concept of "black studies" and urged a greater concern with vocational relevance in education; published *Punishing Criminals: Concerning a Very Old and Painful Question* in 1975; opposite John P. Conrad, argued in favor of capital punishment in *The Death Penalty: A Debate* (1983); argued for "out" in *The U.N., In or Out?* (1987), in which Conrad was again his liberal opponent; contributed to such periodicals as the *American Journal of Psychoanalysis* and the journals of opinion *Commentary* and *National Review*; was a contributing editor of the latter and a distinguished scholar with the Heritage Foundation, a conservative think tank; died in Mendham, New Jersey. See *Current Biography* (October) 1983.

Obituary *New York Times* A p21 Mar. 27, 2002

**VANCE, CYRUS R.** Mar. 27, 1917–Jan. 12, 2002 U.S. secretary of state during the administration of President Jimmy Carter; specialized in civil litigation as a member of the Wall Street law firm of Simpson, Thacher & Martlett, beginning in 1947; became a partner in the firm in 1959; between 1957 and 1960 served as counsel with several U.S. Senate committees concerned with issues of national defense and space and astronautics; entered full-time government service in 1961, as general counsel for the Department of Defense in the administration of President John F. Kennedy; was secretary of the army from 1962 to 1964, when President Lyndon B. Johnson named him deputy secretary of defense, a post he held until 1967; during his years in the Pentagon, was regarded as hawkish regarding the war in Vietnam; subsequently, was deputy chief delegate at the Vietnam peace talks in Paris; as President Carter's secretary of state (1977–80), played key roles in normalizing relations with China, winning Senate approval of the Panama Canal treaty, and negotiating the peace treaty between Egypt and Israel; on the negative side, saw, on his watch, an expansion of Soviet influence in some parts of the world and the overthrow of the pro-American government of the shah in Iran; chafed at President Carter's increasing rejection of his advice in favor of that of Zbigniew Brzezinski, the president's national security adviser; with uncanny prescience, resigned on a matter of principle—his disagreement with Carter's ill-starred decision to attempt a military rescue of American hostages in Iran; in the 1990s, served as a peace negotiator in the Balkans; was on the boards of directors of the New York Times Co., the Manufacturers Hanover Trust Co., U.S. Steel, and several other corporations; died in New York City. See *Current Biography* (November) 1977.

Obituary *New York Times* B p6 Jan. 14, 2002

**VOULKOS, PETER** Jan. 29, 1924–Feb. 16, 2002 Abstract-expressionist ceramist; sculptor; painter; printmaker; the person most credited with elevating pottery from a functional and/or decorative craft into a fine art; a spontaneous artist who was influenced by Zen Buddhism philosophy and the Japanese tradition in ceramics as well as mid-20th-century American avant-garde painting; aspired to be a painter until he discovered clay during his senior year (1950–51) at Montana State College in Bozeman, Montana, his native city; in the beginning, made utilitarian tableware; soon was experimenting with the improvisation of large forms, based to some extent on the shapes of everyday plates, cups, bowls, and cylindrical vessels, but constituting anarchic flights into another reality; created ceramic pieces increasingly larger in scale; during the 1960s, turned to casting in bronze such works as a spectacularly tall sculpture commissioned for the Hall of Justice in San Francisco, "Miss Nitro," a sculpture on view in Highland Park, Illinois, and "Barking Sands," which stands in front of the Federal Building in Honolulu, Hawaii; later returned his full attention to ceramics; during the 1980s, created, among other ceramic works, a series called "stacks," in which clay forms, many resembling oversized bottles, were thrown together, and a series of tublike forms, called "ice buckets"; was as inventive in his tools as in his techniques; worked with a variety of kilns, including the traditional Japanese wood-burning kiln (introduced into the U.S. by Peter Callas); with his student Paul Soldner, built several prototypes of wheels, including an electric wheel; applied his talents at paint and graphics to the glazing and embellishment of his ceramic creations; in much of his later work, joined clay with collage and monotypes; during the summer following his earning of a degree in applied art at Montana State College, worked at Archie Bray's brick factory in Helena, Montana; after taking his master of fine arts degree at the California College of Arts and Crafts, in 1952, set up his first studio at Bray's factory, which was then in the process of becoming the Bray Foundation, with Voulkos as its most important ceramist and teacher; established the ceramics departments at the Los Angeles County Art Institute (later renamed the Otis College of Art and Design), where he joined the faculty in 1954, and the University of California at Berkeley, where he began teaching in 1959; was a visiting professor at the University of Montana and other universities and colleges; had his work exhibited in group and solo shows in galleries across the U.S. and Japan; was represented in museums around the world; lived in Oakland, California; died of a heart attack he suffered on the campus of Bowling Green State University in Ohio, where he was participating in an event titled "Peter Voulkos and Friends: A BGSU Interdisciplinary Art Symposium." See *Current Biography* (November) 1997.

Obituary *New York Times* B p9 Feb. 21, 2002

**WALL, ART** Nov. 25, 1923–Oct. 31, 2001 Golfer; during his career on the Professional Golf Association tour, won 14 championships and was named to the U.S. Ryder Cup team three times; in 1959, was the Masters champion, winner of the Vardon Trophy (for lowest score of the year), and the leading moneymaker on the tour; in the annual poll of sportswriters and broadcasters, was voted the PGA golfer of the year 1959; had 40 holes-in-one during his career; garnered eight victories on the Caribbean circuit; as a 19-year-old amateur, won the Pan-American Open in 1943; studied business at Duke University, where he was on the golf team that finished second in a national championship in 1947; was captain of the Duke team when it won Southern Conference titles in 1948 and 1949; turned professional after winning the Pennsylvania amateur title in 1949; over the following several years, usually finished high on the list of tournament winners; in his first major professional victory, in 1954, won the Tournament of Champions in Las Vegas by six strokes over his nearest rival; captured the Fort Wayne Open in 1956, the Pensacola Open in 1957, and the Akron Rubber City Tournament in 1958; early in 1959, won the Bing Crosby Invitation and the Azalea Tournament in Wilmington, Delaware; at the Masters Tournament in Augusta, Georgia, in April 1959, came from behind to birdie five of his last six holes and close with a 66 to beat Cary Middlecoff by one stroke and the defending champion, Arnold Palmer, by two; with the $15,000 Masters prize, had accumulated winnings of $33,000, the largest amount ever won in one year by a professional golfer up to that point; followed his Masters win with second-place finishes in the Tournament of Champions, the Canadian Open, and the Insurance City Tournament; in July 1959 captured first place and $9,000 in the Buick Open at Grand Blanc, Michigan; in 1975, became the second-to-oldest winner in PGA history; on the Senior PGA Tour in 1980, teamed with Tommy Bolt to win the Legends of Golf, his last PGA victory; played for the last time in 1988; died in Scranton, Pennsylvania. See *Current Biography* (December) 1959.

Obituary *New York Times* A p26 Nov. 1, 2001

**WALTERS, VERNON A.** Jan. 3, 1917–Feb. 10, 2002 Former U.S. diplomat; former deputy director, Central Intelligence Agency; lieutenant general, U.S. Army, retired; a multilingual cosmopolite who served five U.S. presidents as a confidant, translator, facilitator, international troubleshooter, and personal envoy; spoke at least seven languages, five fluently; was born in New York City to a British-born insurance executive; received his schooling in Paris, France, and at Stonyhurst College, England; as a U.S. Army intelligence officer during World War II, fulfilled liaison assignments that laid the foundation for his international network of contacts; after the war, accompanied General George C. Marshall to Europe as an interpreter in the Marshall Plan negotiations; similarly served President Harry S. Truman in several postwar summits; was at Truman's side in the president's confrontation with General Douglas MacArthur in 1951; in the early 1950s, accompanied Ambassador W. Averell Harriman on international diplomatic missions; was a staff assistant to and interpreter for President Dwight D. Eisenhower from 1956 to 1961; endured the fury of a Venezuelan mob with Vice President Richard Nixon during a "goodwill" tour of Latin America in 1958; subsequently, served as a military attaché in Brazil and France; as deputy director of the CIA (1972–76), repulsed President Nixon's attempt to involve the agency in the Watergate coverup; retired from the army in 1978; returned to government service in 1981, when President Ronald Reagan appointed him a roving ambassador at large; served as ambassador to the U.N. (1985–88) and ambassador to West Germany (1989-91); wrote an autobiography, *Silent Missions* (1978); died in West Palm Beach, Florida. See *Current Biography* (February) 1958.

Obituary *New York Times* C p15 Feb. 15, 2002

**WARD, BENJAMIN** Aug. 10, 1926–June 10, 2002 The first black commissioner of the New York City police department (1984–89); while coping with record-breaking crime, gun violence, and drugs in the streets, promoted preventive community policing and diversity in police recruitment; declared himself to be "very, very liberal" regarding race relations but "very, very conservative" regarding law enforcement; after graduating from the Brooklyn High School of Automotive Trades, served in the U.S. Army as a military police officer in Europe (1944–46); back in New York City following his military discharge, was employed for several years at such trades as auto mechanic and truck driver and for one year as a worker with the city's Department of Sanitation, his first civil service job; in the New York City police examination in June 1951, ranked third among some 78,000 applicants; during his early years as a New York Police Department (NYPD) foot patrolman, studied at Brooklyn College, receiving an associate degree in police science in 1958 and a B.A. in sociology in 1960; later earned a law degree at Brooklyn Law School; advanced in rapid succession from patrolman to juvenile-aid specialist, detective, trial counsel in charge of departmental prosecutions, legal adviser to Commissionaer Howard Leary, executive director of the Civilian Complaint Review Board, deputy commissioner in charge of trials, and deputy commissioner for community affairs; in the last-named post, found himself in the middle of a cause célèbre when, in April 1972, one of the police officers responding to a false alarm at a Black Muslim mosque in Harlem headed by Minister Louis Farrakhan was fatally shot; by apologizing to Farrakhan for the armed entry of police into the mosque, sparked anger among police rank and file, a sentiment exacerbated by the mistaken impression that it was he who had ordered the release of the suspects in the shooting; left the NYPD to serve as New York City traffic commissioner (1973–75), New York State commissioner of correctional services (1975–78), head of the New York City Housing Authority police force (1978–79), and commissioner of the New York City Department of Corrections, from 1979 through 1983; was appointed police commissioner by Mayor Edward I. Koch; took charge of the NYPD aggressively, with the slogan, "Give the streets back to the people"; launched Operation Pressure Point and Operation Closedown, aimed at crimes that affected the immediate "quality of life" in the city's neighborhoods—rampant drug dealing, especially in crack cocaine, gambling, prostitution, and vandalism; also introduced what he called the "Total Patrol Concept," which stressed the cop on the neighborhood beat over the centralized 911 emergency-call response system: in his farewell address, said: "Most importantly to me, we've changed this police department—without a lot of noise, without a lot of legislated or judicially imposed affirmative action programs—by increasing the number of black officers by 17 percent, Hispanic officers by 60 percent, and females by an astonishing 85 percent"; died at his home in the borough of Queens, New York City. See *Current Biography* (August) 1988.

Obituary *New York Times* A p27 June 11, 2002

**WARNKE, PAUL C.** Jan. 31, 1920–Oct. 31, 2001 Former U.S. government official; lawyer; a Pentagon Cold War dove; regarding the Vietnam War as "a tragic mistake," tried, with some success, to help brake President Lydon B. Johnson's pursuit of that war when he, Warnke, was assistant secretary of defense for international security affairs from July 1966 to January 1969; under President Jimmy Carter, from March 1977 through November 1978, was director of the U.S. Arms Control and Disarmament Agency and chief American negotiator at the Strategic Arms Limitations Talks (SALT) with the Soviet Union; in 1948, after receiving his LL.B. degree at Columbia University, joined the Washington, D.C., law firm of Covington & Burling, where he specialized in trade regulations and antitrust law; was made a partner of the firm in 1957; early in 1966, was named general counsel of the Department of Defense by President Johnson; subsequently, as assistant secretary of defense, often did policy briefing work for the defense secretary (first Robert McNamara, then Clark Clifford); according to Clifford, helped to persuade the Johnson administration to open peace talks with the Vietnamese; when Richard M. Nixon succeeded Johnson in the White House, joined Clifford in the Washington law firm of Clifford, Warnke, Glass, McIlwain, & Finney; later in 1966, was named chairman of the arms control and defense policy section of the Democratic National Committee's policy council; in 1972, was the major foreign policy adviser to Senator George McGovern when McGovern ran for president, unsuccessfully, on a Democratic peace platform; in 1978, resigned his position as the Carter administration's chief arms negotiator under attack from conservative hawks who accused him of making too many concessions to the Soviets; practiced law with Clark Clifford until 1991, when he joined the law firm of Howrey Simon Arnold & White; died at his home in Washington, D.C. See *Current Biography* (August) 1977.

Obituary *New York Times* A p26 Nov. 1, 2001

**WASSERMAN, LEW R.** Mar. 15, 1913–June 3, 2002 Entertainment-industry executive; the last of the great Hollywood moguls; former chairman of the Music Corporation of America (MCA), now known as Universal Studios; was a protégé of Jules Stein, who founded MCA to represent bands and vaudeville acts in the 1920s; in 1938, began building MCA into Hollywood's dominant talent agency; later, as president, moved MCA into theater and, especially, motion-picture and television production and shaped it into a huge entertainment conglomerate; at the beginning of his career, when he was in his early 20s, handled publicity for a Cleveland nightclub, the Mayfair Casino, which did most of its bookings of bands through MCA; was hired by Jules Stein in 1936; at first, was MCA's national director of advertising and publicity; became vice president in 1940, president in 1946, and chairman in 1973; redefined the previously glitzy image of talent agents by insisting that all MCA agents, like he, wear dark suits and white shirts; also insisted that they, like he, work 16-hour days if necessary, so as always to be available to their clients; in 1950, successfully challenged the seven-year contract policy then in force in Hollywood studios; in the same year, in behalf of his client Henry Fonda, initiated the practice of actors' sharing in the profits of their movies; went on to show his clients how to incorporate themselves for the dual purpose of protecting themselves against high taxes and empowering their independence from studio control; forced movie studios and radio networks to accept "packaging" projects profitable to both MCA and its clients; in the early 1950s, unlike Hollywood studio heads, saw television not as a threat but an opportunity; in negotiations with the Screen Actors Guild in 1952, was granted an exception from the guild's prohibition against talent agencies acting as producers; thus, opened the way for MCA's television arm, Revue Productions, to capitalize on the growing popularity of the new medium; in the mid-1950s, oversaw the production of such popular TV series as *Alfred Hitchcock Presents* and *General Electric Theater*; in 1958, bought Paramount Studio's entire pre-1948 film library; later in the same year, purchased Universal Pictures' name and back-lot facilities; in 1962, acquired controlling interest in Universal Studios by buying Decca Records; in 1962, was threatened with an antitrust lawsuit by the U.S. Justice Department under Attorney General Robert F. Kennedy; under that pressure, agreed to opt out of the talent-agency business while keeping ownership of Universal, Revue, and Decca; emerged from that experience with a newfound awareness of the importance of having influence in Washington; therefore, co-founded the President's Club, a fund-raising organization opening political access to campaign contributors; was responsible for the installation of President Lyndon B. Johnson's close aide Jack Valenti as president of the Motion Picture Association of America; in 1966, was elected to the first of six terms as chairman of the Association of Motion Picture and Television Producers; proceeding to enlarge and diversify MCA, bought such properties as ABC Records and the publishing house G. P. Putnam's Sons; on television, pioneered production of the made-for-TV movie, one-hour police dramas, and the miniseries; presided over the production of such television shows as *Columbo*, *The Rockford Files*, *Murder, She Wrote*, and *Miami Vice* and such hit motion pictures as *The Sting*, *American Graffiti*, *Jaws*, *E.T.*, and *Back to the Future*; after MCA was purchased by the Matsushita Corp. of Japan, in 1990, remained as a manager until 1995, when Matsushita sold 80 percent of MCA stock to the Seagram Co.; under the chairmanship of Edgar Bronfman Jr. (who changed MCA's name to Universal Studios), was a highly paid consultant; after Vivendi of France bought out Seagram in 2001, continued to make a ceremonial appearance every day in his office in the building named for him at Universal Studios; died in Beverly Hills, California. See *Current Biography* (May) 1991.

Obituary *New York Times* p1+ June 4, 2002

**WEAVER, PAT** Dec. 21, 1908–Mar. 15, 2002 Former National Broadcasting Co. executive; a marketing and programming genius who, as NBC's vice president in charge of television (1949–53) and president (1953–55), displayed innovative daring in helping to shape and give direction to a medium then in its formative stage; against the common wisdom of the time, for example, came up with the insight that breakfast-time and late-night TV offerings could succeed in luring audiences away from their radios, a "folly" that resulted in *Today* and *Tonight*, the two most profitable among all of network television's enduring series; was the younger brother of the comedian Winstead "Doodles" Weaver and the father of the actress Sigourney Weaver; originally aspired to fiction writing, but became discouraged when his short stories brought rejection slips; in 1932, began working at radio stations in Los Angeles in a range of jobs, from writer and announcer to station manager; after three years, moved to New York City, where he worked for NBC on a weekly radio musical show (1935) and for the Young & Rubicam advertising agency (1935–38), for which he planned and produced the comedian Fred Allen's radio show before becoming supervisor of all the programs for the agency's radio division, in 1937; the following year, joined the American Tobacco Co. as advertising manager; took a leave of absence from the tobacco company to become associate director of communications with the office of the U.S. Coordinator of Inter-American Affairs in 1941; during World War II, served in the U.S. Navy; during the last nine months of the war, produced the radio show *Command Performance* for the armed forces overseas; after the war, returned to the American Tobacco Co. until

1947, when he went back to Young & Rubicam as vice president in charge of radio and television; on his first day in charge of television at NBC in 1949 (when NBC was well behind CBS in its share of the limited television audience), rescinded the cancellation of *Meet the Press*, NBC's pioneering current-affairs panel interview show, among the most durable programs in television history and still in NBC's weekly schedule in 2002; in his most radical innovation, shifted creative control of programs away from the sponsors (a tradition carried over from radio) to the network; in 1950, asked Max Liebman, a producer of theatrical revues, to put together a 90-minute weekly comedy/variety TV program, which became *Your Show of Shows*, the fledgling TV medium's big Saturday-night attraction for four years (1950–54); conceived network television's first daily late-night show, *Broadway Open House* (1950–51), the prototype of *Tonight*, which began its run in 1954 and was never seriously challenged in its time slot by any rival offering until 1993; launched the equally successful *Today* in 1952; was also responsible for the creation of such programs as *The Colgate Comedy Hour*, *Home*, and *Wide, Wide World*; was the first television programing executive to introduce network specials, exceptional offerings preempting regular prime-time programming; commissioned such live specials as a production of *Peter Pan* starring Mary Martin and a production of *Amahl and the Night Visitors*, the first opera to be performed live on network television; on radio, introduced *Monitor*, a 48-hour weekend program of news and special events; was kicked upstairs, to the chairmanship of the board of NBC, in 1944, when Robert Sarnoff, son of David Sarnoff, the head of RCA, then NBC's parent corporation, replaced him as president; resigned as chairman in 1956; in the 1960s, headed Subscription Television Inc., an abortive California pay-cable company that was crushed by the weight of a negative campaign waged by commercial broadcasters and theater owners; was honored with a special Emmy Award in 1967; in his later years, expressed disappointment and dismay over network television's dearth of arts programming; co-wrote an autobiography, *The Best Seat in the House: The Golden Years of Radio and Television* (1994); died at his home in Santa Barbara, California. See *Current Biography* (January) 1955.

Obituary *New York Times* A p23 Mar. 18, 2002

**WEISS, PAUL** May 19, 1901–July 5, 2002 Philosopher; a metaphysician in the tradition of Aristotle, Aquinas, Kant, Spinoza, and other builders of grand ontological systems that attempt, in his words, "to understand, clarify, and explain every aspect of being and knowledge"; carried forward that tradition against the prevailing current of positivism, in an era when most of his peers were specializing in analyses of language, logic, or scientific principles; was one of four sons of an immigrant Jewish tinsmith on Manhattan's Lower East Side; after earning a B.A. degree in philosophy at the City College of New York, studied under Alfred North Whitehead at Harvard University; at first, was more interested in logic than in metaphysics; in 1929, took his Ph.D. degree at Harvard with a dissertation offering a general theory descriptive of all symbolic systems of logic and mathematics and their interrelations; after further study abroad, at the universities of Freiburg and Paris, taught philosophy at Harvard (1931–32) and Bryn Mawr College (1932–45); co-edited *The Collected Papers of Charles Sanders Peirce* (1931); in 1938, published his own first book, *Reality*, a study of finite beings, which he called "actualities"; in *Nature and Man* (1947), focused on the nature of one finite being, the human being, and a dimension or mode behind "actuality" that he later named "ideality"; in 1947, founded the Metaphysical Society of America and its journal *Review of Metaphysics*; began teaching at Yale University as a visiting professor in 1945; became a permanent member of the Yale faculty the following year; explained his system of ethics in *Man's Freedom* (1950); in his magnum opus, *Modes of Being* (1958), presented his fourfold ontology of actuality, ideality, existence, and God; in subsequent books, systematically speculated on politics and law, the arts (including "cinematics"), history, sport, and religion; in keeping with Yale University policy, was forced to retire as Sterling Professor of Philosophy when he turned 68; in 1969; supported by numerous colleagues and former students, protested the policy, to no avail; in 1969, became Heffer visiting professor of philosophy at the Catholic University of America, with a contract subject to annual renewal; in 1970, was offered a chair by Fordham University, which soon withdrew the offer because of Weiss's age; in 1971, lost an age-discrimination suit against Fordham; continued teaching at Catholic University of America, in Washington, D.C.; when that university refused to renew his contract in 1992, challenged the firing with the help of his son, Jonathan, the director of Legal Services for the Elderly in New York; won from the U.S. Equal Employment Opportunity Commission the judgment that Catholic University was guilty of age discrimination and from the university an apology and reinstatement; retired after two additional years at Catholic University; was elected to the Library of Living Philosophers, which published *The Philosophy of Paul Weiss* (1995), edited by Lewis Edwin Hahn, volume 23 in its series The Library of Living Philosophers; in 2000, published his book *Emphatics*, about language; at the time of his death, was readying for publication his last book, *Surrogates*; died at his home in Washington, D.C. See *Current Biography* (May) 1969.

Obituary *New York Times* A p16 July 8, 2002

**WEISSKOPF, VICTOR F.** Sep. 19, 1908–Apr. 22, 2002 Austrian-born nuclear physicist; professor emeritus, Massachusetts Institute of Technology (MIT); "was the first person to make significant progress in taming the infinities of field theory," according to Robert L. Jaffe, director of the Center for Theoretical Physics at MIT; helped to develop the first atomic bomb during World War II; thereafter, for the rest of his life, was an almost obsessive campaigner for arms control, warning against use of the weapon, which he described as "a shadow over [his] life"; took his doctorate in philosophy at the University of Gottingen, Germany, in 1931; as a postdoctoral research associate during the following half-dozen years, concentrated on work in quantum electrodynamics with Eugene P. Wigner at the University of Berlin, with Wolfgang Pauli at the Zurich Institute of Technology, with Neils Bohr at the University of Copenhagen, and with A. M. Dirac at Cambridge University; with Pauli, in 1934 published a paper presenting the first consistent quantum theory of "spinless" charged particles; during those years, also had occasion to work with Werner Heisenberg and Erwin Schrodinger; fled to the U.S. as a Jewish refugee from Nazi oppression in 1937; at the University of Rochester, was an instructor in physics from 1937 to 1940 and an assistant professor from 1940 to 1943; began his work in nuclear physics in the U.S. by applying the principles of thermodynamics (specifically, temperature and evaporation) to nuclear phenomena; at Rochester in 1939, joined with Leo Szilard in calling for voluntary secrecy about new findings involving nuclear fission, to prevent the Axis powers from obtaining that information; in 1943, became a research administrator with the Manhattan project, as America's top-secret effort to develop the atomic bomb was known; at the project's scientific laboratories at Los Alamos, New Mexico, was deputy head of the theoretical division, under Hans Bethe; when the test bomb was detonated at the desert site called Trinity on July 16, 1945, was assigned to calculate the effects of the blast; regarded the second bomb dropped on Japan, on Nagasaki (the first having dropped on Hiroshima), in August 1945 as "a crime"; joined the MIT faculty in 1946; on leave of absence from MIT, was director-general of the Geneva-based Centre Européene pour la Récherche Nucleare for several years in the early 1960s; chaired the Department of Physics at MIT from 1967 to 1974; was a founder of the *Bulletin of Atomic Scientists*; wrote *The Privilege of Being a Physicist* (1989) and the memoir *The Joy of Insight: Passions of a Physicist* (1991); also published the collection of lectures *Knowledge and Wonder: The Natural World as Man Knows It* (1962) and the collection of essays *Physics in the Twentieth Century* (1972); co-wrote the standard textbook *Theoretical Nuclear Physics* (1952); died at his home in Newton, Massachusetts. See *Current Biography* (November) 1976.

Obituary *New York Times* B p8 Apr. 25, 2002

**WHITE, BYRON R.** June 8, 1917–Apr. 15, 2002 Associate justice of the U.S. Supreme Court (1962–93); a constitutional strict constructionist who was consistently, albeit independently, conservative; acquired the nickname "Whizzer" as an All-American halfback with the University of Colorado football team; after graduating from college, played professional football with the Pittsburgh Pirates (later renamed the Steelers) during the 1938 season, when he led the National Football League in rushing; two years later, duplicated that achievement playing with the Detroit Lions; meanwhile, read law as a Rhodes scholar at Oxford University (where he met John F. Kennedy) and began working for a law degree at Yale University; received the degree in 1946, following wartime service in the U.S. Navy; during the 1946–47 term of the U.S. Supreme Court, served as clerk to Fred M. Vinson, then the chief justice; practiced corporate law in Denver, Colorado, from 1947 to 1961; headed the Citizens for Kennedy organization during John F. Kennedy's successful campaign for the U. S. presidency in 1960; in January 1961, joined the Kennedy administration as deputy attorney general under Robert F. Kennedy at the Department of Justice; for the department, monitored civil rights developments in the South; in May 1961, supervised a contingent of 600 U.S. marshals dealing with violent civil rights resistance in Alabama; was named to the Supreme Court by President Kennedy effective April 1962; two months later, filed his first dissenting opinion, in the case of *Robinson v. California*, in which the court for the first time used the Eighth Amendment to overturn a state criminal conviction, for drug addiction; set the tone for his entire tenure when he wrote on that occasion, "I fail to see why the court deems it more important to write into the Constitution its own abstract notions of how best to handle the narcotics problem, for it obviously cannot match either the States or Congress in expert understanding"; wrote majority opinions giving federal courts extensive powers to implement the racial integration of northern school districts, including taxation mandates to upgrade some schools; later opposed decisions expanding the use of affirmative action; dissented from the majority in *Miranda v. Arizona* (1966), which affirmed rights of criminal suspects, and *Roe v. Wade* (1973), protective of abortion on grounds of "privacy"; voted with the majority in invalidating existing death penalty laws across the U.S. in 1972; in 1976, again voted with the majority in authorizing the resumption of capital punishment under state laws that had been revised to the court's satisfaction; wrote the majority opinion in *Coker v. George* (1977), declaring unconstitutional capital punishment for rape; wrote the majority opinion in the racially charged *Washington v. Davis* case (1976), declaring that a District of Columbia police-department employment and promotion examination did not violate the Constitution's guarantee of equal protection; was probably best known for writing the *Bowers v. Hardwick* (1986) decision, in which the court refused to read into the Constitution's due-process clause a "privacy" protection for homosexual sodomy; in his majority opinion in that case, commented, "The court is most vulnerable and comes closest to illegitimacy when it deals with judge-made constitutional law having little or no recognizable roots in the language or design of the Constitution"; similarly, in his dissent from a 1986 decision reaffirming the right to abortion, deplored the court's "unrestrained imposition of its own extraconstitutional value preferences"; on First Amendment grounds, dissented from the majority decision in *Barnes v. Glen Theatre* (1991), which upheld an Indiana law banning nude dancing; said he regretted having voted with the majority on First Amendment grounds in *New York Times Co. v. Sullivan*, which provided the press a shield from libel suits by public officials unless the injured party could prove malice; tended to take a hard line on law and order; wrote several court decisions enhancing police authority; in retirement, sat on occasion as a visiting judge in federal appeals courts; moved back to Colorado in 2001; died in Denver, Colorado. See *Current Biography* (December) 1962.

Obituary *New York Times* p1+ Apr. 16, 2002

**WILDER, BILLY** June 22, 1906–Mar. 27, 2002 Galician-born film director; writer; producer; regarded himself as a protégé of Ernst Lubitsch; with mischievous sardonic wit, focused on the unethical side of human nature; was "a lover of Old World farce conventions and practitioner of New World *verismo* [realism]," as one critic observed; brought to the making of his powerful screen melodramas and mordant comedies what some studio heads considered "vulgar energy" and what a co-screenwriter (I. A. L. Diamond) described as "a Middle-European attitude," a cynicism that was "sort of a disappointed romanticism at heart—[like] whipped cream that's gotten curdled"; in the view of the critic Andrew Sarris, was "too cynical to believe even his own cynicism"; created what is widely admired as the definitive film noir in *Double Indemnity* (1944); won two Academy Awards (as co-screenwriter and director) for *The Lost Weekend* (1945), an unrelenting expressionistic depiction of two days of agony in the life of an alcoholic at the bottom of the bottle, regarded as a landmark of maturity in Hollywood filmmaking; contributed to the Oscar-winning script for his black comedy/drama *Sunset Boulevard* (1950), a corrosive statement on the Hollywood mystique, in which he directed Gloria Swanson in the role of a faded silent-screen star; won three Oscars (as co-writer, director, and producer of best picture) for *The Apartment* (1960), a comedy/drama about an insurance-company clerk (Jack Lemmon) who seeks to curry favor by loaning his apartment to his bosses for extramarital trysts; hit box-office and critical gold with his legendary hilarious cross-dressing farce *Some Like It Hot* (1959); grew up in Sucha, Galicia, and Vienna, Austria; began his career as a journalist, first in Vienna and then in Berlin, Germany; was a promising apprentice film scenarist in Berlin when he was in his mid-20s; as a Jew with left-wing sympathies, fled Germany in March 1933; in Paris, France, co-directed the film *Mauvaise Graine* (1933; Bad Seed); emigrated to the U.S. in 1934, with no functional knowledge of English; while learning English in Hollywood, contributed ideas and story lines for several screenplays; as a scenarist, in the late 1930s teamed up with the veteran writer Charles Brackett, in a partnership in which the two soon became director (Wilder) and producer (Brackett) as well; over the course of 12 years, worked on 13 films with Brackett; co-wrote *Ninotchka* (1939), *Hold Back the Dawn* (1941), and *Ball of Fire* (1942); made *The Major and the Minor* (1942), his first American directorial effort; on military leave, in the rank of colonel, spent six months in Germany with the U.S. Army's Psychological Warfare Division in 1945, overseeing the denazification of the German motion-picture and radio industries; back in Hollywood with Brackett, made, among other pictures, *The Emperor Waltz* (1948) and *A Foreign Affair* (1948), a daring political farce about a holier-than-thou junketing U.S. congresswoman in a love triangle in postwar Berlin's sleazy demimonde; in addition to directing and co-writing, began producing his own films with *Ace in the Hole* (1951), about a newsman exploiting the plight of a man trapped in a cave; became an independent producer/director with the erotic farce *The Seven Year Itch* (1955); with the May-December romance *Love in the Afternoon* (1957), began a new long-term scenario-writing partnership, with I. A. L. Diamond; subsequently, made *Irma La Douce* (1963), an adaptation of the hit French musical about a Parisian prostitute, *Kiss Me, Stupid* (1964), a spouse-swapping farce that was condemned by the Catholic Legion of Decency, a remake of *The Front Page* (1974), and *Fedora* (1978), his most personal disquisition on the dark side of Hollywood stardom and mythmaking; over a period of 39 years, made a total of 25 films, including *Five Graves to Cairo* (1943), *Stalag 17* (1953), *Sabrina* (1954), *The Spirit of St. Louis* (1957), *One, Two,Three* (1961), *The Fortune Cookie* (1966), *Avanti!* (1972), and *Buddy, Buddy* (1981); died at his home in Beverly Hills, California. See *Current Biography* (October) 1984.

Obituary *New York Times* p1+ Mar. 29, 2002

**WILHELM, HOYT** July 26, 1923–Aug. 23, 2002 Baseball player, the first major-league relief pitcher elected to the Baseball Hall of Fame; a career-long master of the knuckleball, a fluttering, unpredictable pitch, bewildering to opposing batters and even to some of his own catchers (while easy on his own arm), which earned him extraordinary longevity on the mound; taught himself the knuckleball when he was a 12-year-old growing up in North Carolina; as a starting pitcher with Mooresville in the North Carolina League in 1942, won 10 games and lost three; drafted into the U.S. Army for service in World War II, won a Purple Heart for wounds received in the battle of the Bulge; after the war, returned to the minor leagues and labored there as a starting pitcher for six more years, winning a total of 97 games and losing 31 with a succession of teams; became a relief hurler—one sent to the mound in crises—when he was called up to the major leagues in 1952; in the majors, pitched in succession for the New York Giants and St. Louis Cardinals in the National League, the Cleveland Indians, Baltimore Orioles, Chicago White Sox, and California Angels in the American League, and again in the National League for the Atlanta Braves, Chicago Cubs, and Los Angeles Dodgers; was the only pitcher to lead both the National (1952) and American (1959) leagues in earned-run average; in one of his relatively few performances as a starter, pitched a no-hit game against the New York Yankees in 1958; when he retired, in 1972, held a major-league record for games pitched, with 1,070, a mark later surpassed by Jesse Orosco and Dennis Eckersley; had a career win–loss record of 143–122, with 227 saves and a 2.52 earned-run average; struck out 1,670 batters (all but 19 in relief); died in Sarasota, Florida. See *Current Biography* (July) 1971.

Obituary *New York Times* B p7 Aug. 26, 2002

**WILLIAMS, HARRISON A. JR.** Dec. 10, 1919–Nov. 17, 2001 Liberal Democratic U.S. senator from New Jersey (1959–82); lawyer; was a U.S. representative from New Jersey's Sixth Congressional District from 1953 to 1957; in the Senate, became prominent as a stalwart of liberal causes, including civil rights, Social Security and other social programs, foreign aid, education, public housing, urban renewal, environmental conservation, and a pro-labor agenda including migrant-workers' rights; chaired the Committee on Labor and Human Resources, a banking and securities subcommittee, and the Senate Select Committee on Aging; was instrumental in the passage of the Employee Retirement Income Security Act and the Coal Mine Health and Safety Act; helped pass the legislation that created the Occupational Health and Safety Administration; played a major role in the passage of the Urban Mass Transit Act of 1964, the first federal law providing mass-transit assistance to states and cities; in an FBI sting operation known as Abscam (short for Arab scam), begun in 1978, was approached (as were five U.S. representatives) by agents posing as Arab sheiks or their representatives, who offered him a secret 18 percent share in a Virginia titanium mine in return for his help in obtaining government contracts; was caught on camera accepting the offer; in 1981, was convicted in a federal court on nine counts of bribery and conspiracy; was fined $50,000 and sentenced to three years in prison; under threat of expulsion, resigned his Senate seat; died in Denville, New Jersey. See *Current Biography* (October) 1960.

Obituary *New York Times* A p17 Nov. 20, 2001

**WILLIAMS, TED** Aug. 30, 1918–July 5, 2002 Baseball player; Boston Red Sox outfielder; arguably, the purest power hitter in the history of the major leagues; certainly, the dominant New England athlete of his time; with a batting average of .406 in 1941, was the only major-league batter to break the .400 barrier since 1930, when Bill Terry hit .401; was nicknamed "the Splendid Splinter," a reference to his lanky, six-foot-three frame; while naturally right-handed, batted left from boyhood on; played with the Red Sox from 1939 through 1960, with the exception of two periods of military service; while training as a Marine pilot and working as a Marine flying instructor during World War II, missed the 1943, 1944, and 1945 seasons; as a Marine fighter pilot during the Korean conflict, missed most of the 1952 and 1953 seasons; as a quick-tempered young player, had a stormy relationship with Boston fans and sportswriters; typically, refused to acknowledge the cheers of the crowd with the traditional tip of the cap when completing a home run; led the American League in batting average six times, slugging eight times, runs batted in four times, runs scored six times and walks eight times; won the triple crown (for home runs, RBIs, and batting average) twice; was voted the American League's Most Valuable Player twice; contributed crucially to the league's victories in the 1941 and 1946 All-Star games; in his last time at bat, on September 28, 1960, hit a home run, bringing his career total to 541 homers (12th highest in major-league history); had a career batting average of .344 (the sixth highest since 1900), slugging percentage of .634 (second only to Babe Ruth's), on-base percentage of .483 (highest ever in the majors), 1,839 runs batted in (12th highest), and 2,019 walks (third highest); in 1966, was elected to the Baseball Hall of Fame; in 1969, became manager of the Washington Senators, who had finished in last place among the 10 teams in the American League in 1968; for managing the Senators to an 86–76 record and fourth place in the expanded American League's new East Division, was voted 1969 American League manager of the year; managed the team for two subsequent seasons in Washington; moved with the team to Texas when it became the Texas Rangers, in 1972; retired after the 1972 season with a career managerial win–loss record of 273–354, for a .429 average; in retirement, pursued fishing as intensely as he had baseball; with John Underwood, wrote three books: the autobiography *My Turn at Bat* (1969), *The Science of Hitting* (1970), and *Fishing the Big Three* (1982); in 1994, presided at the opening of the Ted Williams Museum and Hitters Hall of Fame in Hernando, Florida; in 1995, was present at the dedication of the Ted Williams Tunnel under Boston Harbor; at the All-Star Game in Fenway Park, Boston, in 1999, was inducted into the All-Century team; was married and divorced three times; died in Inverness, Florida; in death, became a subject of dispute between Barbara Joyce Ferrell, his daughter from his first marriage, who said that her father had wanted to be cremated, and John Henry Williams, his son from his third marriage, who had the corpse flown to Alcor Life Extension Foundation in Arizona, where it was deep-frozen in liquid nitrogen. See *Current Biography* (April) 1947.

Obituary *New York Times* A p1+ July 6, 2002

**WOJCIECHOWSKA, MAIA** Aug. 7, 1927–June 13, 2002 Polish-born author; a prodigious, multilingual autodidact; wrote 19 published books, most of them works of juvenile fiction, including rites-of-passage stories with courageous adolescent protagonists; was the daughter of a Polish air-force officer; before the age of 11, parachuted from an airplane three times; after the Germans invaded Poland at the beginning of World War II, fled with her mother and two brothers through southern France and Spain—spending prolonged periods in each of those countries—on their way to England, where her father, having preceded them, was serving as chief of staff of the Polish air force in exile; with her family, arrived in the U.S. in 1942; dropped out of Immaculate Heart College in the Hollywood section of Los Angeles after one year; as a young woman, worked as an undercover detective, restaurant hostess, masseuse, ghost writer, translator for Radio Free Europe, and copy assistant with *Newsweek* magazine; also raced motorcycles, studied bullfighting, and did a stint as a matador in Mexico; visited with Ernest Hemingway, another bullfighting aficionado, in Cuba; played professional tennis and was a tennis instructor; in 1952, published her first book, *Market Day for Ti André*, a children's story set in Haiti; was assistant editor of the trade publication *American Hairdresser* from 1958 to 1960; created the protagonist Manolo, a Spanish boy who realizes his own identity (that of an aspiring physician) after his matador father is killed in the ring in *Shadow of a Bull* (1964), which won the Newbery Medal in the U.S. and the Deutscher Jugenbuch prize in Germany (one of the many foreign countries in which the novel was published in translation); returned to the theme of bullfighting in *Life and Death of a Brave Bull* (1972); combined historical fact with lively imaginary dialogue in the children's book *Odyssey of Courage* (1965), a fictionalized biography of the Spanish conquistador Cabeza de Vaca; told the story of a boy and his horse in *A Kingdom for a Horse*

(1965); chose the milieu of her own adolescence as the setting for the juvenile novel *The Hollywood Kid* (1966). about a boy who rejects tinseltown values, and her beloved Andalusia for *A Single Light* (1968), a about a 15-year-old Spanish girl who discovers a treasure; also in 1968, published the controversial adolescent self-realization novels *Tuned Out*, about a 16-year-old boy in New York City who is deeply worried about his older brother's experimentation with drugs; for younger readers, wrote the lighthearted and sentimental *Hey, What's Wrong with This One?* (1969), about a boy's efforts to find a new wife for his father; created the perceptive, compassionate adolescent protagonist Byron in *Don't Play Dead Until You Have To* (1970); wrote *The Rotten Years* (1971) as "a textbook of survival for 12-to-15-year-olds"; returned to the theme of bullfighting in *Life and Death of a Brave Bull* (1972); wrote the autobiographical *Till the Break of Day: Memories, 1939-42* (1972); in 1980, published her first novel for adults, the critically acclaimed *The People in His Life*, inspired by the life of Ernest Hemingway; in 1984, published the children's story *How God Got Christian into Trouble* (1984); translated a number of stories and plays from the Polish; was married to the author Selden Rodman from 1950 until their divorce, in 1957; married Richard Larkin, a poet and antiques dealer, in 1972 and was divorced from him in 1973; wrote some of her books under the name Maia Rodman; died in Long Beach, New Jersey. See *Current Biography* (September) 1976.

Obituary *New York Times* C p13 June 21, 2002

**WOLFF, MARITTA M.** Dec. 25, 1918–July 1, 2002 Popular novelist; received a B.A. degree in English at the University of Michigan in 1940; created a sensation on the American literary scene with the publication of her first novel, *Whistle Stop* (1941), a seamy story, told with raw language, about a bottom-of-the gene-pool family in a small town near Detroit in which a brother and sister have a subtly depicted incestuous relationship; saw that book adapted into a 1946 motion picture starring George Raft and Ava Gardner; in 1942, published her second novel, *Night Shift*, of which the *New York Times* reviewer Orville Prescott wrote: "One feels certain this is a scientifically exact record of the speech of factory workers in an automobile bumper plant, of taxi drivers, waitresses in cheap restaurants, beautiful dumb women and beautiful smart ones who haunt small-time night clubs"; saw that novel, toned down and retitled *The Man I Love*, become a motion picture starring Ida Lupino in 1946; later published the novels *About Lyddy Thomas* (1947), *Back of Town* (1952), *The Big Nickelodeon* (1956), and *Buttonwood* (1962); wrote another novel that was not published; died at her home in Los Angeles, California. See *Current Biography* (July) 1941.

Obituary *New York Times* July 14, 2002 p33

**WORTH, IRENE** June 23, 1916(?)–Mar. 10, 2002 Actress; an actor's actor; brought to an ambitious range of challenging classical and contemporary stage roles a penetrating intelligence, a distinctive voice vibrant and rich in its variety, and a remarkable physical presence that, while versatile, was at base elegantly patrician; was born Harriet Abrams in Lincoln, Nebraska (in 1915, according to her sister, Carol); after earning a degree in education, was a schoolteacher for several years; in New York City in 1942, successfully auditioned with Elisabeth Bergner, the celebrated Viennese actress in exile; made her professional acting debut as Fenella in the road company of *Forget Me Never!*, starring Bergner, in 1942; the following year, made her Broadway debut as Cecily Harden in *The Two Mrs. Carrolls*, again starring Bergner; moved to England in 1944; at the Central School in London, learned to speak impeccable "stage English" under the great voice teacher Elsie Fogerty; made her London stage debut in *The Time of Your Life* in 1946; first displayed her talent for high comedy as Ilona Szabo in *The Play's the Thing*, on tour in 1946 and in London in 1947; in the late 1940s also played, in London or on tours of the British provinces, Donna Pascuala in *Drake's Drums*, Olivia Brown in *Love in Idleness*, Mary Dalton in *Native Son*, Lady Fortrose in *Home Is Tomorrow*, Olivia Raines in *Champagne for Delilah*, and the title role in *Lucrece*; playing opposite Alec Guinness, made her breakthrough to celebrity with her perceptive and passionate creation of the profoundly lonely, doomed Celia Coplestone in the premiere of T. S. Eliot's *The Cocktail Party* at the Edinburgh Festival in 1949; reprised that role on Broadway and in London's West End in 1950; with the Old Vic Repertory Company, was cast as Helena in *A Midsummer Night's Dream* (1951), Desdemona in *Othello* (1951), Catherine in *The Other Heart* (1951), Portia in *The Merchant of Venice* (1952), and Lady Macbeth in *Macbeth* (1953); in 1953, was a member of the inaugural company of the Shakespeare Festival Theatre in Stratford, Ontario, Canada, starring opposite Alec Guinness as Helena in *All's Well That Ends Well* and Queen Margaret in *Richard III*; over the following three decades, returned to Stratford in other roles, including Hedda Gabler, and in three one-woman shows, including *Ulysses and Mrs. Dalloway* (1983); hit another high point in her comedic career as the redoubtable wife of the timidly adulterous Guinness character in the farce *Hotel Paradiso* at London's Winter Garden in 1956; Off-Broadway in New York in 1957, played the title role in *Mary Stuart*, opposite Eva Le Gallienne as Queen Elizabeth; began her association with the Royal Shakespeare Company in 1962, playing the Marquise in *The Art of Seduction* and Goneril in Peter Brooks's innovative production of *King Lear* in 1962; away from repertory during the 1960s, was seen on the London stage as Dr. Mathilde von Zahnd in *The Physicists*, Clodia Pulcher (opposite John Gielgud) in *The Ides of March*, and Jocasta (again opposite Gielgud) in *Oedipus*, among other roles; co-starred with Noel Coward and Lilli Palmer in Coward's trilogy *Suite in Three Keys* in 1966 and with John Gielgud in Peter Brooks's production of *Oedipus* in 1968; on Broadway, won her first Tony Award, for best actress, for her 1964 performance as Miss Alice in *Tiny Alice*, her second, for best actress, for her 1975 portrayal (opposite Christopher Walken) of the superannuated screen idol Alexandra del Lago in a revival of *Sweet Bird of Youth*, and her third, for featured actress, for her 1990 performance as Grandma Kurnitz in Neil Simon's comedy-drama *Lost in Yonkers*; Off-Broadway, played Winnie in

Samuel Beckett's *Happy Days* (1979), Miss Madrigal in *The Chalk Garden* (1982), and Volumnia in *Coriolanus* (1988); in London in 2001, played Olga Knipper, the wife of Anton Chekhov (Paul Scofield), in *I Take Your Hand in Mine*; reprised many of her theatrical performances in radio and television productions; in motion pictures, was cast as Leonie in *Orders to Kill* (1958), as Françoise in *The Scapegoat* (1959), and Queen Elizabeth I in *Seven Seas to Calais* (1962); later accrued credits in the films *Nicholas and Alexandra* (1971), *Eyewitness* (1981), and *Deathtrap* (1982); reprised her stage performances in the film versions of *King Lear* (1971) and *Lost in Yonkers* (1993); was made an honorary Commander of the British Empire in 1975; died in New York City. See *Current Biography* (May) 1968.

Obituary *New York Times* A p25 Mar. 12, 2002

**YOKICH, STEPHEN P.** Aug. 20, 1935–Aug. 16, 2002 Labor leader; as president of the United Automobile, Aerospace, and Africultural Implement workers of America (better known as the United Auto Workers, or UAW) from 1995 to 2002, capped a career of more than 40 years in union activism; grew up in a household steeped in union tradition; after serving in the U.S. Air Force (1952–56), began a skilled-trades apprenticeship at the Heidrich Tool and Die Co. in Oak Park, Michigan, where his father worked; promptly joined UAW Local 155; soon became head of the local's political action committee; in 1966, joined the staff of the union's Region 1, a division with a membership of 83,000 at that time; was elected director of the Region 1 staff in 1977; as UAW vice president, directed the union's department of skilled trades from 1980 to 1995; during shorter intervals within that period, handled the union's relations with the Ford Motor Co., General Motors (G.M.), International Harvester, Mack Trucks, and the John Deere and Caterpillar companies; earned a reputation as a tough contract negotiator; in 1994 alone, authorized five strikes against G.M., the largest of the "big three" automakers (the other two being Ford and Chrysler); balanced his toughness with an understanding of the precarious position of the American companies vis-à-vis foreign competition and the dwindling membership of the UAW, which decreased from 1.5 million in the late 1970s to approximately 740,000 in 2000; as president, oversaw efforts to organize nonunion auto plants in the South and to consolidate the UAW with machinist and steelworker unions; died in Detroit, Michigan. See *Current Biography* (November) 1998.

Obituary *New York Times* A p12 Aug. 17, 2002

# CLASSIFICATION BY PROFESSION—2002

ANTHROPOLOGY
Ortner, Sherry B.
Soffer, Olga

ARCHAEOLOGY
Soffer, Olga

ARCHITECTURE
Herzog, Jacques, and de Meuron, Pierre

ART
Clowes, Daniel
Eggleston, William
Marlette, Doug
Mitchell, Dean
Rall, Ted
Richter, Gerhard
Toles, Tom
Walker, Mort

ASTRONAUTICS
Currie, Nancy

ASTRONOMY
Marcy, Geoffrey W., and Butler, R. Paul
Queloz, Didier

BUSINESS
Aigner-Clark, Julie
Beckman, Arnold O.
Bible, Geoffrey C.
Bloomberg, Michael R.
Cheney, Richard B.
Collier, Sophia
Frist, Bill
Garza, Ed
Grasso, Richard
Harrison, William B. Jr.
Jackson, Hal
Kamen, Dean
Letterman, David
Lucas, George
Matsui, Connie L.
McQueen, Alexander
Messier, Jean-Marie
Mickelson, Phil
Moore, Gordon E.
Mulcahy, Anne M.
Nelly
Ollila, Jorma
Paulson, Henry M. Jr.
Pitt, Harvey
Rimsza, Skip
Ross, Robert
Rumsfeld, Donald H.

COMPUTERS
Moore, Gordon E.

CONSERVATION
Paulson, Henry M. Jr.

DANCE
Brown, Ronald K.
Stroman, Susan

ECONOMICS
Hewlett, Sylvia Ann
Summers, Lawrence H.

EDUCATION
Adams, Yolanda
Anderson, Don L.
Appiah, Kwame Anthony
Beckman, Arnold O.
Brier, Bob
Brown, Lee P.
Brown, Ronald K.
Clinton, Hillary Rodham
Eustis, Oskar
Faber, Sandra
Frist, Bill
Gonzales, Alberto R.
Hewlett, Sylvia Ann
Hopkins, Nancy
Hull, Jane Dee
Johnson, Elizabeth A.
Jones, Bobby
Kennedy, Randall
Krause, David W.
Lucas, George
Marcy, Geoffrey W., and Butler, R. Paul
Meyer, Edgar
Millman, Dan
Mirabal, Robert
Monk, T. S.
Morial, Marc
Moses, Robert P.
Novacek, Michael J.
Ortner, Sherry B.
Reynoso, Cruz
Rimm, Sylvia B.
Ross, Robert
Summers, Lawrence H.
Wilson, James Q.
Zinni, Anthony C.

FASHION
McQueen, Alexander
Nelly
Seymour, Stephanie
Soffer, Olga

FILM
Anderson, Wes
Bakula, Scott
Barnett, Etta Moten
Black, Jack
Clowes, Daniel
Cohen, Rob
Connelly, Jennifer
Forrest, Vernon
Grubin, David
Holm, Ian
Jackson, Peter
Keener, Catherine
Letterman, David
Levy, Eugene
Lincoln, Abbey
Lucas, George
Mac, Bernie
Maguire, Tobey
Mendes, Sam
Messing, Debra
Meyers, Nancy
Najimy, Kathy
Pascal, Amy
Pau, Peter
Plimpton, Martha
Raimi, Sam

Rampling, Charlotte
Shalhoub, Tony
Smith, Maggie
Sutherland, Kiefer
Winston, Stan
Wood, Elijah
Wright, Jeffrey
Zimmer, Hans

GOVERNMENT AND POLITICS, FOREIGN
Eyadéma, Etienne Gnassingbé
Karzai, Hamid
Koizumi, Junichiro
Messier, Jean-Marie
Meta, Ilir

GOVERNMENT AND POLITICS, U.S.
Bloomberg, Michael R.
Brown, Lee P.
Cheney, Richard B.
Clinton, Hillary Rodham
Cochran, Thad
Dean, Howard
Franklin, Shirley C.
Frist, Bill
Garza, Ed
Gerson, Michael
Gonzales, Alberto R.
Henderson, Donald A.
Hull, Jane Dee
Kass, Leon R.
Lincoln, Blanche Lambert
Morial, Marc
Myers, Richard B.
Paulson, Henry M. Jr.
Pitt, Harvey
Reynoso, Cruz
Rimsza, Skip
Rumsfeld, Donald H.
Summers, Lawrence H.
Wilson, James Q.
Zinni, Anthony C.

JOURNALISM
Arrarás, María Celeste
Banfield, Ashleigh
Bowden, Mark
Bragg, Rick
Broeg, Bob
Brokaw, Tom
Buckley, Priscilla L.
Clinton, Hillary Rodham
Cohn, Linda
Egan, Jennifer
Gibson, Charles
Hax, Carolyn
Higgins, Chester Jr.
Judd, Jackie
Marlette, Doug
Rall, Ted
Rimm, Sylvia B.
Rimsza, Skip
Sandford, John
Saramago, José
Sugar, Bert Randolph
Toles, Tom
Vieira, Meredith
Wesley, Valerie Wilson
Zahn, Paula

LAW
Brown, Lee P.
Clinton, Hillary Rodham
Cochran, Thad
Gonzales, Alberto R.
Kennedy, Randall
Morial, Marc
Pitt, Harvey
Ressler, Robert K.
Reynoso, Cruz
Romero, Anthony
Sugar, Bert Randolph

LITERATURE
Appiah, Kwame Anthony
Clowes, Daniel
DeMille, Nelson
Egan, Jennifer
Foer, Jonathan Safran
Kushner, Tony
Lucas, George
Marlette, Doug
Millman, Dan
Mirabal, Robert
Park, Linda Sue
Pollitt, Katha
Rall, Ted
Sandford, John
Saramago, José
Sedaris, Amy
Toles, Tom
Wesley, Valerie Wilson

MEDICINE
Alibek, Ken
Beckman, Arnold O.
Dean, Howard
Frist, Bill
Gayle, Helene
Henderson, Donald A.

MILITARY
Alibek, Ken
Cochran, Thad
Currie, Nancy
Eyadéma, Etienne Gnassingbé
Franks, Tommy R.
Myers, Richard B.
Zinni, Anthony C.

MUSIC
Adams, Yolanda
Barnett, Etta Moten
Black, Jack
blink-182
Bocelli, Andrea
Borodina, Olga
Creed
Eddins, William
Emerson String Quartet
Flaming Lips
Fugazi
Grohl, Dave
Hahn, Hilary
India.Arie
Ja Rule
Jay-Z
Jones, Bobby
La India
Levy, Eugene
Lincoln, Abbey
Linkin Park
Lloyd, Charles
McGraw, Tim
Meyer, Edgar
Mirabal, Robert
Monk, T. S.
Nelly
Riley, Terry
Scott, Jill
Taylor, Koko
Turner, Mark
Tweet
Zahn, Paula
Zimmer, Hans

NONFICTION
Anderson, Don L.
Arrarás, María Celeste
Bowden, Mark
Bragg, Rick
Brier, Bob
Broeg, Bob
Brokaw, Tom
Brown, Lee P.
Buckley, Priscilla L.
Cheney, Richard B.
Clinton, Hillary Rodham
Collier, Sophia
Graham, Franklin
Hax, Carolyn
Hewlett, Sylvia Ann
Higgins, Chester Jr.
Jackson, Hal
Johnson, Elizabeth A.
Kass, Leon R.
Kennedy, Randall
McGraw, Phillip
Millman, Dan
Moses, Robert P.
Ortner, Sherry B.
Pelzer, Dave
Pollitt, Katha
Rall, Ted
Ressler, Robert K.
Rimm, Sylvia B.
Saramago, José
Seymour, Stephanie
Sugar, Bert Randolph
Summers, Lawrence H.
Wilber, Ken
Wilson, James Q.

ORGANIZATIONS
Barnett, Etta Moten
Clinton, Hillary Rodham
Gayle, Helene
Gonzales, Alberto R.
Graham, Franklin
Grasso, Richard
Gregory, Wilton D.
Hewlett, Sylvia Ann
Joyner, Tom
Kamen, Dean
Krause, David W.
Leiter, Al
Matsui, Connie L.
Monk, T. S.
Moses, Robert P.
Paulson, Henry M. Jr.
Pelzer, Dave
Reynoso, Cruz
Romero, Anthony
Van Exel, Nick

PALEONTOLOGY
Krause, David W.
Leakey, Meave

PHILANTHROPY
Beckman, Arnold O.
Bloomberg, Michael R.
Harrison, William B. Jr.
Joyner, Tom
Van Exel, Nick

PHILOSOPHY
Brier, Bob
Kass, Leon R.
Wilber, Ken

PHOTOGRAPHY
Higgins, Chester Jr.
Rall, Ted

PSYCHOLOGY
McGraw, Phillip
Rimm, Sylvia B.

RADIO
Broeg, Bob
Cohn, Linda
Gibson, Charles
Jackson, Hal
Jones, Bobby
Joyner, Tom
Judd, Jackie
Letterman, David
Rimm, Sylvia B.

RELIGION
Graham, Franklin
Gregory, Wilton D.
Johnson, Elizabeth A.

SCIENCE
Alibek, Ken
Anderson, Don L.
Beckman, Arnold O.
Brier, Bob
Currie, Nancy
Faber, Sandra
Gayle, Helene
Henderson, Donald A.
Hopkins, Nancy
Kass, Leon R.
Leakey, Meave
Marcy, Geoffrey W., and Butler, R. Paul
Novacek, Michael J.
Soffer, Olga

SOCIAL ACTIVISM
Clinton, Hillary Rodham
Ensler, Eve
Graham, Franklin
Hewlett, Sylvia Ann
Hopkins, Nancy
Joyner, Tom
Moses, Robert P.
Najimy, Kathy
Pelzer, Dave
Pollitt, Katha
Reynoso, Cruz
Romero, Anthony

SOCIAL SCIENCE
Ortner, Sherry B.
Ressler, Robert K.
Rimm, Sylvia B.
Wilson, James Q.

SPORTS
Belichick, Bill
Brenly, Bob
Brodeur, Martin
Broeg, Bob
Brown, Kwame
Carter, Vince
Counsell, Craig
Forrest, Vernon
Hewitt, Lleyton
Hill, Grant
Hopkins, Bernard
Inkster, Juli
James, Edgerrin
Kidd, Jason
Kournikova, Anna
Law, Ty
Lee, Jeanette
Leiter, Al
Mickelson, Phil
Millman, Dan
Murray, Ty
Nowitzki, Dirk
Pierce, Paul
Ramirez, Manny
Suzuki, Ichiro

Van Exel, Nick
Willingham, Tyrone

TECHNOLOGY
Kamen, Dean

TELEVISION
Arrarás, María Celeste
Bakula, Scott
Banfield, Ashleigh
Brier, Bob
Brokaw, Tom
Bunim, Mary-Ellis, and Murray, Jonathan
Cohn, Linda
Fallon, Jimmy
Fey, Tina
Gibson, Charles
Hall, Deidre
Holm, Ian
Jackson, Hal
Jones, Bobby
Judd, Jackie
Letterman, David
Levy, Eugene
Lucas, George
Mac, Bernie
Maguire, Tobey
Mann, Emily
McGraw, Phillip
Messing, Debra
Najimy, Kathy
Plimpton, Martha
Raimi, Sam
Sedaris, Amy
Shalhoub, Tony
Sutherland, Kiefer
Vieira, Meredith
Winston, Stan
Zahn, Paula
Zucker, Jeff

THEATER
Bakula, Scott
Barnett, Etta Moten
Black, Jack
Ensler, Eve
Eustis, Oskar
Holm, Ian
Kushner, Tony
Levy, Eugene
Maguire, Tobey
Mann, Emily
Mendes, Sam
Messing, Debra
Najimy, Kathy
Plimpton, Martha
Sedaris, Amy
Shalhoub, Tony
Smith, Maggie
Stroman, Susan
Sutherland, Kiefer
Wright, Jeffrey

# 2001–2002 INDEX

This is the index to the January 2001–November 2002 issues. For the index to the 1940–2000 biographies, see *Current Biography: Cumulated Index 1940–2000.*


Abakanowicz, Magdalena Jan 2001
Abraham, Spencer May 2001
Adams, Douglas obit Sep 2001
Adams, Yolanda Mar 2002
Adler, Larry obit Oct 2001
Adler, Mortimer J. obit Sep 2001
Aigner-Clark, Julie Jan 2002
Ailes, Stephen obit Oct 2001
Alibek, Ken Jun 2002
Alibekov, Kanatjan *see* Alibek, Ken
Allen, Betsy *see* Cavanna, Betty
Allen, Steve obit Jan 2001
Amado, Jorge obit Oct 2001
Amichai, Yehuda obit Jan 2001
Ammons, A. R. obit Jul 2001
Anderson, Constance obit Apr 2001
Anderson, Don L. Oct 2002
Anderson, Wes May 2002
Appiah, Kwame Anthony Jun 2002
Archer, Michael D'Angelo *see* D'Angelo
Armitage, Kenneth obit May 2002
Armstrong, J. Sinclair obit Mar 2001
Arnesen, Liv Jun 2001
Arrarás, María Celeste Aug 2002
Ash, Mary Kay obit Feb 2002
Atashin, Faegheh *see* Googoosh
Atkins, Chet obit Sep 2001
Atkins, Jeffrey *see* Ja Rule
Austin, "Stone Cold" Steve Nov 2001

Bailey, Glenda Oct 2001
Baker, Dusty Apr 2001
Bakula, Scott Feb 2002
Balaguer, Joaquín obit Yrbk 2002
Balthus obit May 2001
Bandaranaike, Sirimavo obit Jan 2001
Banfield, Ashleigh Jul 2002
Bánzer Suárez, Hugo obit Yrbk 2002
Barker, Travis *see* blink-182
Barnard, Christiaan N. obit Nov 2001
Barnett, Etta Moten Feb 2002
Barnouw, Erik obit Oct 2001
Beame, Abraham D. obit Apr 2001
Bebey, Francis obit Sep 2001
Beckinsale, Kate Aug 2001
Beckman, Arnold O. Jan 2002
Belaúnde Terry, Fernando obit Yrbk 2002
Belichick, Bill Sep 2002
Bennett, Lerone Jan 2001
Bennington, Chester *see* Linkin Park
Benzer, Seymour May 2001
Berle, Milton obit Yrbk 2002
Bethune, Gordon M. Jun 2001
Bible, Geoffrey C. Feb 2002
Bilandic, Michael A. obit Apr 2002
Birendra Bir Bikram Shah Dev, King of Nepal obit Sep 2001
Björk Jul 2001
Black, Jack Feb 2002
Blackburn, Elizabeth H. Jul 2001
Blaine, David Apr 2001
Blakemore, Michael May 2001
Blass, Bill obit Nov 2002
Blind Boys of Alabama Oct 2001
blink-182 Aug 2002
Block, Herbert L. obit Jan 2002
Bloomberg, Michael R. Mar 2002
Bocelli, Andrea Jan 2002
Boland, Edward P. obit Feb 2002
Bond, Julian Jul 2001
Borge, Victor obit Mar 2001
Borodina, Olga Feb 2002
Borst, Lyle B. obit Yrbk 2002
Bosch, Juan obit Feb 2002
Boudreau, Lou obit Oct 2001
Bourdon, Rob *see* Linkin Park
Bowden, Mark Jan 2002
Boyd, John W. Feb 2001
Bragg, Rick Apr 2002
Brenly, Bob Apr 2002
Brier, Bob Sep 2002
Brier, Robert *see* Brier, Bob
Brin, Sergey and Page, Larry Oct 2001
Brodeur, Martin Nov 2002
Broeg, Bob May 2002
Brokaw, Tom Nov 2002
Brooks, Gwendolyn obit Feb 2001
Brower, David obit Feb 2001
Brown, Claude obit Apr 2002
Brown, J. Carter obit Yrbk 2002
Brown, Jesse obit Yrbk 2002
Brown, Kwame Feb 2002
Brown, Lee P. Sep 2002
Brown, Robert McAfee obit Nov 2001
Brown, Ronald K. May 2002
Brueggemann, Ingar Nov 2001
Bryant, C. Farris obit Yrbk 2002
Buckley, Priscilla L. Apr 2002
Bundy, William P. obit Feb 2001
Bunim, Mary-Ellis *see* Bunim, Mary-Ellis, and Murray, Jonathan
Bunim, Mary-Ellis, and Murray, Jonathan May 2002
Burgess, Carter L. obit Yrbk 2002
Burnett, Mark May 2001
Bush, George W. Aug 2001
Bush, Laura Jun 2001
Butler, R. Paul *see* Marcy, Geoffrey W., and Butler, R. Paul

Caballero, Linda *see* La India
Cactus Jack *see* Foley, Mick
Calderón, Sila M. Nov 2001
Calle, Sophie May 2001
Camp, John *see* Sandford, John
Canin, Ethan Aug 2001
Cannon, Howard W. obit Yrbk 2002
Canty, Brendan *see* Fugazi
Capriati, Jennifer Nov 2001
Caras, Roger A. obit Jul 2001

Carroll-Abbing, J. Patrick obit Nov 2001
Carter, Jimmy *see* Blind Boys of Alabama
Carter, Shawn *see* Jay-Z
Carter, Vince Apr 2002
Castle, Barbara obit Yrbk 2002
Castro, Fidel Jun 2001
Cavanna, Betty obit Oct 2001
Cela, Camilo José obit Apr 2002
Chaban-Delmas, Jacques obit Feb 2001
Chandrasekhar, Sripati obit Sep 2001
Chao, Elaine L. May 2001
Chase, David Mar 2001
Cheney, Richard B. Jan 2002
Chillida, Eduardo obit Yrbk 2002
Clinton, Hillary Rodham Jan 2002
Clooney, Rosemary obit Nov 2002
Clowes, Daniel Jan 2002
Clyburn, James E. Oct 2001
Coca, Imogene obit Sep 2001
Cochran, Thad Apr 2002
Cohen, Rob Nov 2002
Cohn, Linda Aug 2002
Colbert, Edwin H. obit Feb 2002
Collier, Sophia Jul 2002
Columbus, Chris Nov 2001
Como, Perry obit Jul 2001
Connelly, Jennifer Jun 2002
Connor, John T. obit Feb 2001
Counsell, Craig Sep 2002
Coyne, Wayne *see* Flaming Lips
Cranston, Alan obit Mar 2001
Creed May 2002
Cruz, Penelope Jul 2001
Cuban, Mark Mar 2001
Currie, Nancy June 2002

Daft, Douglas N. May 2001
D'Angelo May 2001
Davis, Benjamin O. Jr. obit Yrbk 2002
de la Rúa, Fernando Apr 2001
de Meuron, Pierre *see* Herzog, Jacques, and de Meuron, Pierre
De Valois, Ninette obit Aug 2001
Deakins, Roger May 2001
Dean, Howard Oct 2002
DeCarlo, Dan Aug 2001 obit Mar 2002
Del Toro, Benicio Sep 2001
DeLonge, Tom *see* blink-182
Delson, Brad *see* Linkin Park
DeMille, Nelson Oct 2002
Destiny's Child Aug 2001
Djerassi, Carl Oct 2001
Djukanovic, Milo Aug 2001
Donovan, Carrie obit Feb 2002
Douglas, John E. Jul 2001
Drozd, Steven *see* Flaming Lips
Drucker, Eugene *see* Emerson String Quartet
Dude Love *see* Foley, Mick
Dunst, Kirsten Oct 2001
Dutton, Lawrence *see* Emerson String Quartet

Eddins, William Feb 2002
Edwards, Bob Sep 2001
Egan, Edward M. Jul 2001
Egan, Jennifer Mar 2002
Eggleston, William Feb 2002
Elizabeth, Queen Mother of Great Britain obit Jun 2002
Elliott, Sean Apr 2001
Emerson String Quartet Jul 2002
Eminem Jan 2001
Ensler, Eve Aug 2002
Epstein, Samuel S. Aug 2001
Ericsson-Jackson, Aprille J. Mar 2001
Estenssoro, Victor Paz *see* Paz Estenssoro, Victor
Etherington, Edwin D. obit Apr 2001
Eustis, Oskar Oct 2002
Eustis, Paul Jefferson *see* Eustis, Oskar
Evanovich, Janet Apr 2001
Evans, Dale obit Apr 2001
Evans, Donald L. Nov 2001
Eyadéma, Etienne Gnassingbé Apr 2002
Eytan, Walter obit Oct 2001

Faber, Sandra Apr 2002
Fallon, Jimmy Jul 2002
Farhi, Nicole Nov 2001
Farrell, Dave *see* Linkin Park
Farrell, Eileen obit Jun 2002
Farrelly, Bobby *see* Farrelly, Peter and Bobby
Farrelly, Peter and Bobby Sep 2001
Fay, J. Michael Sep 2001
Ferrer, Rafael Jul 2001
Ferris, Timothy Jan 2001
Fey, Tina Apr 2002
Finckel, David *see* Emerson String Quartet
Flaming Lips Oct 2002
Flanagan, Tommy obit Mar 2002
Foer, Jonathan Safran Sep 2002
Foley, Mick Sep 2001
Fong-Torres, Ben Aug 2001
Forrest, Vernon Jul 2002
Fountain, Clarence *see* Blind Boys of Alabama
Fox Quesada, Vicente May 2001
Francis, Arlene obit Sep 2001
Francisco, Don Feb 2001
Frankenheimer, John obit Oct 2002
Franklin, Shirley C. Aug 2002
Franks, Tommy R. Jan 2002
Fraser, Brendan Feb 2001
Fredericks, Henry St. Clair *see* Mahal, Taj
Friedman, Jane Mar 2001
Frist, Bill Nov 2002
Fugazi Mar 2002
Fukuyama, Francis Jun 2001

Gandy, Kim Oct 2001
Garcia, Sergio Mar 2001
Gardner, John W. obit May 2002
Garfield, Henry *see* Rollins, Henry
Garrison, Deborah Jan 2001
Gary, Willie E. Apr 2001
Garza, Ed Jun 2002
Garzón, Baltasar Mar 2001
Gaskin, Ina May May 2001
Gaubatz, Lynn Feb 2001
Gayle, Helene Jan 2002
Gebel-Williams, Gunther obit Oct 2001
Geis, Bernard obit Mar 2001
Gennaro, Peter obit Feb 2001
Gerson, Michael Feb 2002
Gibson, Charles Sep 2002
Gierek, Edward obit Oct 2001
Gilbreth, Frank B. Jr. obit Jul 2001
Gilmore, James S. III Jun 2001
Goff, M. Lee Jun 2001
Goldberg, Bill Apr 2001
Golden, Thelma Sep 2001
Goldovsky, Boris obit Aug 2001
Goldsmith, Jerry May 2001
Gonzales, Alberto R. Apr 2002
Gonzalez, Henry obit Feb 2001
Good, Mary L. Sep 2001
Googoosh May 2001
Gordon, Cyrus H. obit Aug 2001
Gorman, R. C. Jan 2001

Gorton, John Grey obit Yrbk 2002
Gottlieb, Melvin B. obit Mar 2001
Gould, Stephen Jay obit Aug 2002
Gowers, Timothy Jan 2001
Gowers, William Timothy *see* Gowers, Timothy
Graham, Franklin May 2002
Graham, Katharine obit Oct 2001
Grasso, Richard Oct 2002
Graves, Morris obit Sep 2001
Greco, José obit Mar 2001
Green, Darrell Jan 2001
Greenberg, Jack M. Nov 2001
Greenwood, Colin *see* Radiohead
Greenwood, Jonny *see* Radiohead
Gregory, Wilton D. Mar 2002
Grigg, John obit Apr 2002
Grohl, Dave May 2002
Gruber, Ruth Jun 2001
Grubin, David Aug 2002
Gudmundsdottir, Björk *see* Björk
Guerard, Albert J. obit Mar 2001
Gursky, Andreas Jul 2001

Hahn, Hilary Sep 2002
Hahn, Joseph *see* Linkin Park
Hailsham of St. Marylebone, Quintin Hogg obit Feb 2002
Halasz, Laszlo obit Feb 2002
Hall, Deidre Nov 2002
Hall, Gus obit Jan 2001
Hall, Richard Melville *see* Moby
Hall, Steffie *see* Evanovich, Janet
Hampton, Lionel obit Yrbk 2002
Hanna, William obit Sep 2001
Harden, Marcia Gay Sep 2001
Harjo, Joy Aug 2001
Harrison, George obit Mar 2002
Harrison, Marvin Aug 2001
Harrison, William B. Jr. Mar 2002
Haskins, Caryl P. obit Feb 2002
Hass, Robert Feb 2001
Hax, Carolyn Nov 2002
Haynes, Cornell Jr. *see* Nelly
Headley, Elizabeth *see* Cavanna, Betty
Heckart, Eileen obit Mar 2002
Henderson, Donald A. Mar 2002
Henderson, Joe obit Oct 2001
Hendrickson, Sue Oct 2001
Herblock *see* Block, Herbert L.
Herzog, Jacques *see* Herzog, Jacques, and de Meuron, Pierre
Herzog, Jacques, and de Meuron, Pierre Jun 2002
Hewitt, Lleyton Oct 2002
Hewlett, Sylvia Ann Sep 2002
Heyerdahl, Thor obit Yrbk 2002
Heym, Stefan obit Mar 2002
Higgins, Chester Jr. Jun 2002
Hill, Faith Mar 2001
Hill, Grant Jan 2002
Hinojosa, Maria Feb 2001
Hoffman, Philip Seymour May 2001
Hogg, Quintin *see* Hailsham of St. Marylebone, Quintin Hogg
Holm, Ian Mar 2002
Hooker, John Lee obit Sep 2001
Hopkins, Bernard Apr 2002
Hopkins, Nancy May 2002
Hoppus, Mark *see* blink-182
Horwich, Frances obit Oct 2001
Hoyle, Fred obit Jan 2002
Hughes, Karen Oct 2001
Hull, Jane Dee Feb 2002
Hunter, Kermit obit Sep 2001
Hunter, Kim obit Yrbk 2002

India.Arie Feb 2002
Inkster, Juli Sep 2002
Ivins, Michael *see* Flaming Lips

Ja Rule Jul 2002
Jackson, Hal Oct 2002
Jackson, Peter Jan 2002
Jackson, Thomas Penfield Jun 2001
Jakes, T.D. Jun 2001
James, Edgerrin Jan 2002
Jarring, Gunnar obit Yrbk 2002
Jay-Z Aug 2002
Jeffords, James Sep 2001
Jennings, Waylon obit Apr 2002
Jet *see* Urquidez, Benny
Jimenez, Marcos Perez *see* Pérez Jiménez, Marcos
Jobert, Michel obit Yrbk 2002
Johnson, Eddie Bernice Jul 2001
Johnson, Elizabeth A. Nov 2002
Jones, Bobby Jun 2002
Jones, Chipper May 2001
Jones, Chuck obit May 2002
Jones, Larry Wayne Jr. *see* Jones, Chipper
Joyner, Tom Sep 2002
Judd, Jackie Sep 2002
Judd, Jacqueline Dee *see* Judd, Jackie

Kabila, Joseph Sep 2001
Kael, Pauline obit Nov 2001
Kainen, Jacob obit Aug 2001
Kamen, Dean Nov 2002
Kane, Joseph Nathan obit Nov 2002
Kani, John Jun 2001
Karbo, Karen May 2001
Karsh, Yousuf obit Nov 2002
Karzai, Hamid May 2002
Kass, Leon R. Aug 2002
Katsav, Moshe Feb 2001
Kcho Aug 2001
Keener, Catherine Oct 2002
Kelleher, Herb Jan 2001
Kennedy, Randall Aug 2002
Kentridge, William Oct 2001
Kepes, György obit Mar 2002
Kesey, Ken obit Feb 2002
Ketcham, Hank obit Sep 2001
Keys, Charlene *see* Tweet
Kid Rock Oct 2001
Kidd, Jason May 2002
Klaus, Josef obit Oct 2001
Knowles, Beyoncé *see* Destiny's Child
Koch, Kenneth obit Yrbk 2002
Koizumi, Junichiro Jan 2002
Kolar, Jiri obit Yrbk 2002
Konaré, Alpha Oumar Oct 2001
Koner, Pauline obit Apr 2001
Kostunica, Vojislav Jan 2001
Kott, Jan obit Mar 2002
Kournikova, Anna Jan 2002
Kramer, Stanley obit May 2001
Krause, David W. Feb 2002
Kreutzberger, Mario *see* Francisco, Don
Krugman, Paul Aug 2001
Kushner, Tony Jul 2002
Kyprianou, Spyros obit May 2002

La India May 2002
Lacy, Dan obit Nov 2001
Lally, Joe *see* Fugazi
Landers, Ann obit Nov 2002

Lapidus, Morris obit Apr 2001
Lara, Brian Feb 2001
Lardner, Ring Jr. obit Feb 2001
Law, Ty Oct 2002
Le Clercq, Tanaquil obit Mar 2001
Leakey, Meave Jun 2002
Lederer, Esther Pauline *see* Landers, Ann
Lee, Geddy *see* Rush
Lee, Jeanette Oct 2002
Lee, Peggy obit May 2002
Leiter, Al Aug 2002
Lemmon, Jack obit Oct 2001
Leone, Giovanni obit Feb 2002
Letterman, David Oct 2002
Levy, Eugene Jan 2002
Lewis, David Levering May 2001
Lewis, Flora obit Yrbk 2002
Lewis, John obit Jun 2001
Li, Jet Jun 2001
Li Lian Jie *see* Li, Jet
Lifeson, Alex *see* Rush
Lilly, John C. obit Feb 2002
Lima do Amor, Sisleide *see* Sissi
Lincoln, Abbey Sep 2002
Lincoln, Blanche Lambert Mar 2002
Lindbergh, Anne Morrow obit Apr 2001
Lindgren, Astrid obit Apr 2002
Lindo, Delroy Mar 2001
Lindsay, John V. obit Mar 2001
Link, O. Winston obit Apr 2001
Linkin Park Mar 2002
Lippold, Richard obit Yrbk 2002
Lloyd, Charles Apr 2002
Lomax, Alan obit Oct 2002
London, Julie obit Feb 2001
Lord, Walter obit Yrbk 2002
Love, John A. obit Apr 2002
Lucas, George May 2002
Ludlum, Robert obit Jul 2001
Luns, Joseph M. A. H. obit Yrbk 2002
Lupica, Mike Mar 2001
Lynne, Shelby Jul 2001

Mac, Bernie Jun 2002
Machado, Alexis Leyva *see* Kcho
MacKaye, Ian *see* Fugazi
Magloire, Paul E. obit Nov 2001
Maguire, Tobey Sep 2002
Mahal, Taj Nov 2001
Maki, Fumihiko Jul 2001
Maloney, Carolyn B. Apr 2001
Mankind *see* Foley, Mick
Mann, Emily Jun 2002
Mansfield, Michael J. *see* Mansfield, Mike
Mansfield, Mike obit Jan 2002
Marcinko, Richard Mar 2001
Marcus, Stanley obit Apr 2002
Marcy, Geoffrey W. *see* Marcy, Geoffrey W., and Butler, R. Paul
Marcy, Geoffrey W., and Butler, R. Paul Nov 2002
Margaret, Princess of Great Britain obit May 2002
Marlette, Doug Jul 2002
Martin, A. J. P. *see* Martin, Archer
Martin, Archer obit Yrbk 2002
Martin, James S. Jr. obit Yrbk 2002
Martin, Mark Mar 2001
Martinez, Pedro Jun 2001
Mary Kay *see* Ash, Mary Kay
Masters, William H. obit May 2001
Mathers, Marshall *see* Eminem
Matsui, Connie L. Aug 2002
McCaw, Craig Sep 2001
McDonald, Gabrielle Kirk Oct 2001
McGraw, Eloise Jarvis obit Mar 2001
McGraw, Phillip Jun 2002
McGraw, Tim Sep 2002
McGreal, Elizabeth *see* Yates, Elizabeth
McGruder, Aaron Sep 2001
McGuire, Dorothy obit Nov 2001
McIntire, Carl obit Jun 2002
McIntosh, Millicent Carey obit Mar 2001
McKinney, Robert obit Yrbk 2001
McLean, Jackie Mar 2001
McLean, John Lenwood *see* McLean, Jackie
McNally, Andrew 3d obit Feb 2002
McQueen, Alexander Feb 2002
Mendes, Sam Oct 2002
Menken, Alan Jan 2001
Messier, Jean-Marie May 2002
Messing, Debra Aug 2002
Meta, Ilir Feb 2002
Meyer, Cord Jr. obit Aug 2001
Meyer, Edgar Jun 2002
Meyers, Nancy Feb 2002
Mickelson, Phil Mar 2002
Middelhoff, Thomas Feb 2001
Miller, Jason obit Yrbk 2001
Miller, Neal obit Jun 2002
Millman, Dan Aug 2002
Minner, Ruth Ann Aug 2001
Mirabal, Robert Aug 2002
Mitchell, Dean Aug 2002
Miyazaki, Hayao Apr 2001
Moby Apr 2001
Monk, T. S. Feb 2002
Montresor, Beni obit Feb 2002
Moore, Dudley obit Yrbk 2002
Moore, Elisabeth Luce obit Yrbk 2002
Moore, Gordon E. Apr 2002
Morella, Constance A. Feb 2001
Morial, Marc Jan 2002
Morris, Errol Feb 2001
Moseka, Aminata *see* Lincoln, Abbey
Moses, Bob *see* Moses, Robert P.
Moses, Robert P. Apr 2002
Mosley, Sugar Shane Jan 2001
Moten, Etta *see* Barnett, Etta Moten
Mulcahy, Anne M. Nov 2002
Murray, Jonathan *see* Bunim, Mary-Ellis, and Murray, Jonathan
Murray, Jonathan *see* Bunim, Mary-Ellis, and Murray, Jonathan
Murray, Ty May 2002
Musharraf, Pervaiz *see* Musharraf, Pervez
Musharraf, Pervez Mar 2001
Mydans, Shelley Symith obit Aug 2002
Myers, Richard B. Apr 2002

Najimy, Kathy Oct 2002
Narayan, R. K. obit Jul 2001
Nason, John W. obit Feb 2002
Nasser, Jacques Apr 2001
Nathan, Robert R. obit Nov 2001
Nehru, B. K. obit Feb 2002
Nelly Oct 2002
Nguyen Van Thieu *see* Thieu, Nguyen Van
Nixon, Agnes Apr 2001
Norton, Gale A. Jun 2001
Novacek, Michael J. Sep 2002
Nowitzki, Dirk Jun 2002

Nozick, Robert obit Apr 2002

O'Brien, Ed *see* Radiohead
O'Connor, Carroll obit Sep 2001
O'Hair, Madalyn Murray obit Jun 2001
Ollila, Jorma Aug 2002
O'Neill, Paul H. Jul 2001
Ortner, Sherry B. Nov 2002
Osawa, Sandra Sunrising Jan 2001
Osbourne, Sharon Jan 2001

Page, Larry *see* Brin, Sergey, and Page, Larry
Paige, Roderick R. Jul 2001
Palmeiro, Rafael Aug 2001
Park, Linda Sue Jun 2002
Pascal, Amy Mar 2002
Pau, Peter Feb 2002
Paulson, Henry M. Jr. Sep 2002
Paz Estenssoro, Victor obit Sep 2001
Peart, Neil *see* Rush
Pelzer, Dave Mar 2002
Pérez Jiménez, Marcos obit Feb 2002
Perkins, Charles obit Feb 2001
Perutz, Max obit Apr 2002
Petersen, Wolfgang Jul 2001
Phillips, Sam Apr 2001
Phillips, Scott *see* Creed
Phillips, William obit Yrbk 2002
Phoenix *see* Linkin Park
Piano, Renzo Apr 2001
Picciotto, Guy *see* Fugazi
Pierce, David Hyde Apr 2001
Pierce, John Robinson obit Jun 2002
Pierce, Paul Nov 2002
Pierce, Samuel R. Jr. obit Feb 2001
Pincay, Laffit Sep 2001
Pitt, Harvey Nov 2002
Plimpton, Martha Apr 2002
Poletti, Charles obit Yrbk 2002
Pollitt, Katha Oct 2002
Pomeroy, Wardell B. obit Yrbk 2001
Popeil, Ron Mar 2001
Potok, Chaim obit Yrbk 2002
Powell, Colin L. Nov 2001
Pusey, Nathan M. obit Feb 2002

Queloz, Didier Feb 2002
Quine, W. V. obit Mar 2001
Quine, Willard Van Orman *see* Quine, W. V.
Quinn, Anthony obit Sep 2001

Radiohead Jun 2001
Raimi, Sam Jul 2002
Rall, Ted May 2002
Ralston, Joseph W. Jan 2001
Ramirez, Manny Jun 2002
Rampling, Charlotte Jun 2002
Rania Feb 2001
Reeves, Dan Oct 2001
Reid, Antonio *see* Reid, L. A.
Reid, L. A. Aug 2001
Reitman, Ivan Mar 2001
Ressler, Robert K. Feb 2002
Reuss, Henry S. obit Mar 2002
Reynolds, John W. Jr. obit Mar 2002
Reynoso, Cruz Mar 2002
Rhodes, James A. obit Jul 2001
Rice, Condoleezza Apr 2001
Richler, Mordecai obit Oct 2001
Richter, Gerhard Jun 2002
Rickey, George W. obit Yrbk 2002
Ridge, Tom Feb 2001
Riesman, David obit Yrbk 2002
Riley, Terry Apr 2002
Rimm, Sylvia B. Feb 2002
Rimsza, Skip Jul 2002
Riopelle, Jean-Paul obit Yrbk 2002
Ripley, S. Dillon obit Aug 2001
Ritchie, Robert James *see* Kid Rock
Rivers, Larry obit Nov 2002
Robards, Jason Jr. obit Mar 2001
Robb, J. D. *see* Roberts, Nora
Robbins, Anthony *see* Robbins, Tony
Robbins, Tony Jul 2001
Roberts, Nora Sep 2001
Rodriguez, Arturo Mar 2001
Rogers, William P. obit Mar 2001
Rollins, Edward J. Mar 2001
Rollins, Henry Sep 2001
Romero, Anthony Jul 2002
Ross, Herbert obit Feb 2002
Ross, Robert Oct 2002
Rote, Kyle obit Yrbk 2002
Rowan, Carl T. obit Jan 2001
Rowland, Kelly *see* Destiny's Child
Rowley, Janet D. Mar 2001
Rule, Ja *see* Ja Rule
Rumsfeld, Donald H. Mar 2002
Rush Feb 2001
Russell, Harold obit Apr 2002
Ryan, George H. Sep 2001
Ryder, Jonathan *see* Ludlum, Robert
Ryer, Jonathan *see* Ludlum, Robert

Sánchez, David Nov 2001
Sandford, John Mar 2002
Saramago, José Jun 2002
Savimbi, Jonas obit Jun 2002
Sayles Belton, Sharon Jan 2001
Scammon, Richard M. obit Sep 2001
Schaap, Phil Sep 2001
Schilling, Curt Oct 2001
Schindler, Alexander M. obit Feb 2001
Schultes, Richard Evans obit Sep 2001
Scott, George *see* Blind Boys of Alabama
Scott, Jill Jan 2002
Scottoline, Lisa Jul 2001
Scully, Vin Oct 2001
Sears, Martha *see* Sears, William and Martha
Sears, William and Martha Aug 2001
Seau, Junior Sep 2001
Sedaris, Amy Apr 2002
Selway, Phil *see* Radiohead
Senghor, Léopold Sédar obit Mar 2002
Setzer, Philip *see* Emerson String Quartet
Seymour, Lesley Jane Nov 2001
Seymour, Stephanie Oct 2002
Shaheen, Jeanne Jan 2001
Shalhoub, Tony Nov 2002
Shapiro, Irving S. obit Nov 2001
Shearer, Harry Jun 2001
Shepherd, Michael *see* Ludlum, Robert
Shinoda, Mike *see* Linkin Park
Simon, Herbert A. obit May 2001
Sinopoli, Giuseppe obit Sep 2001
Sissi Jun 2001
Slater, Kelly Jul 2001
Smith, Elinor Mar 2001
Smith, Howard K. obit Aug 2002
Smith, Maggie Jul 2002

Snead, Sam obit Yrbk 2002
Soffer, Olga Jul 2002
Sothern, Ann obit Aug 2001
Sparks, Nicholas Feb 2001
Spence, Hartzell obit Yrbk 2001
Spencer, John Jan 2001
Sprewell, Latrell Feb 2001
Stackhouse, Jerry Nov 2001
Stanley, Kim obit Jan 2002
Stanton, Bill May 2001
Stapp, Scott *see* Creed
Stargell, Willie obit Sep 2001
Stassen, Harold E. obit May 2001
Steele, Claude M. Feb 2001
Steiger, Rod obit Yrbk 2002
Stein, Benjamin J. Sep 2001
Stern, Isaac obit Jan 2002
Stevens, Ted Oct 2001
Stewart, Alice obit Yrbk 2002
Stoltenberg, Gerhard obit Mar 2002
Stone, W. Clement obit Yrbk 2002
Storr, Anthony obit Sep 2001
Stratton, William G. obit Aug 2001
Stroman, Susan Jul 2002
Sucksdorff, Arne obit Sep 2001
Sugar, Bert Randolph Nov 2002
Sullivan, Leon H. obit Sep 2001
Summers, Lawrence H. Jul 2002
Sun Wen Apr 2001
Sutherland, Kiefer Mar 2002
Suzuki, Ichiro Jul 2002
Swinton, Tilda Nov 2001
Syal, Meera Feb 2001

Tajiri, Satoshi Nov 2001
Talmadge, Herman E. obit Jun 2002
Tarter, Jill Cornell Feb 2001
Tauscher, Ellen O. Mar 2001
Taylor, John W. obit Apr 2002
Taylor, Koko Jul 2002
Thieu, Nguyen Van obit Jan 2002
Thomas, Dave *see* Thomas, R. David
Thomas, R. David obit Apr 2002
Thomson, James A. Nov 2001
Thomson, Meldrim Jr. obit Sep 2001
Thyssen-Bornemisza de Kaszan, Baron Hans Heinrich obit Yrbk 2002
Tigerman, Stanley Feb 2001
Titov, Gherman obit Jan 2001
Tobin, James obit May 2002
Toledo, Alejandro Nov 2001
Toles, Thomas G. *see* Toles, Tom
Toles, Tom Nov 2002
Tremonti, Mark *see* Creed
Trenet, Charles obit Sep 2001
Trenkler, Freddie obit Yrbk 2001
Trigère, Pauline obit Jul 2002
Trout, Robert obit Jan 2001
Trudeau, Pierre Elliott obit Jan 2001
Tsui Hark Oct 2001
Turner, Mark Nov 2002
Turre, Steve Apr 2001
Tweet Nov 2002
Tyson, John H. Aug 2001

Unitas, Johnny obit Yrbk 2002
Urquidez, Benny Nov 2001

Valentine, Bobby Jul 2001
Van den Haag, Ernest obit Jul 2002
Van Exel, Nick Mar 2002
Van Gundy, Jeff May 2001
Vance, Cyrus R. obit Apr 2002
Verdon, Gwen obit Jan 2001
Vieira, Meredith Apr 2002
Voulkos, Peter obit Aug 2002

Walker, Mort Feb 2002
Wall, Art obit Feb 2002
Walsh, John Jul 2001
Walters, Vernon A. obit Jul 2002
Ward, Benjamin obit Yrbk 2002
Warnke, Paul C. obit Feb 2002
Wasserman, Lew R. obit Yrbk 2002
Waugh, Auberon obit May 2001
Wayans, Marlon *see* Wayans, Shawn and Marlon
Wayans, Shawn and Marlon May 2001
Weaver, Pat obit Yrbk 2002
Weaver, Sylvester *see* Weaver, Pat
Weinrig, Gary Lee *see* Rush
Weiss, Paul obit Yrbk 2002
Weisskopf, Victor F. obit Yrbk 2002
Wek, Alek Jun 2001
Welty, Eudora obit Nov 2001
Wesley, Valerie Wilson Jun 2002
Wexler, Jerry Jan 2001
White, Byron Raymond obit Jul 2002
Whitehead, Colson Nov 2001
Wiggins, James Russell obit Mar 2001
Wilber, Ken Apr 2002
Wilder, Billy obit Yrbk 2002
Wilhelm, Hoyt obit Yrbk 2002
Williams, Harrison A. Jr. obit Mar 2002
Williams, Michelle *see* Destiny's Child
Williams, Ted obit Oct 2002
Willingham, Tyrone Nov 2002
Wilson, James Q. Aug 2002
Winston, Stan Jul 2002
Wojciechowska, Maia obit Yrbk 2002
Wolff, Maritta M. obit Yrbk 2002
Wong-Staal, Flossie Apr 2001
Wood, Elijah Aug 2002
Woodcock, Leonard obit Apr 2001
Woods, Donald obit Nov 2001
Woodward, Robert F. obit Yrbk 2001
Wooldridge, Anna Marie *see* Lincoln, Abbey
Worth, Irene obit Aug 2002
Wright, Jeffrey May 2002

Xenakis, Iannis obit Jul 2001

Yates, Elizabeth obit Nov 2001
Yates, Sidney R. obit Jan 2001
Yokich, Stephen P. obit Yrbk 2002
Yorke, Thom *see* Radiohead

Zahn, Paula Feb 2002
Zaillian, Steven Oct 2001
Zatopek, Emil obit Feb 2001
Zhu Rongji Jul 2001
Zimmer, Hans Mar 2002
Zinni, Anthony C. May 2002
Zivojinovich, Alex *see* Rush
Zucker, Jeff Jan 2002